Lecture Notes in Computer Science 3177

Commenced Publication in 1973
Founding and Former Series Editors:
Gerhard Goos, Juris Hartmanis, and Jan van Leeuwen

Editorial Board

David Hutchison
  Lancaster University, UK
Takeo Kanade
  Carnegie Mellon University, Pittsburgh, PA, USA
Josef Kittler
  University of Surrey, Guildford, UK
Jon M. Kleinberg
  Cornell University, Ithaca, NY, USA
Friedemann Mattern
  ETH Zurich, Switzerland
John C. Mitchell
  Stanford University, CA, USA
Moni Naor
  Weizmann Institute of Science, Rehovot, Israel
Oscar Nierstrasz
  University of Bern, Switzerland
C. Pandu Rangan
  Indian Institute of Technology, Madras, India
Bernhard Steffen
  University of Dortmund, Germany
Madhu Sudan
  Massachusetts Institute of Technology, MA, USA
Demetri Terzopoulos
  New York University, NY, USA
Doug Tygar
  University of California, Berkeley, CA, USA
Moshe Y. Vardi
  Rice University, Houston, TX, USA
Gerhard Weikum
  Max-Planck Institute of Computer Science, Saarbruecken, Germany

Zheng Rong Yang   Richard Everson   Hujun Yin (Eds.)

Intelligent Data Engineering and Automated Learning – IDEAL 2004

5th International Conference
Exeter, UK, August 25 - 27, 2004
Proceedings

Springer

Volume Editors

Zheng Rong Yang
Richard Everson
University of Exeter, Department of Computer Science
Exeter EX4 4QF, UK
E-mail: {z.r.yang, r.m.everson}@exeter.ac.uk

Hujun Yin
University of Manchester, Institute of Science and Technology (UMIST)
Department of Electrical and Electronic Engineering
Manchester M60 1QD, UK
E-mail: h.yin@man.ac.uk

Library of Congress Control Number: 2004095626

CR Subject Classification (1998): H.2.8, F.2.2, I.2, F.4, K.4.4, H.3, H.4

ISSN 0302-9743
ISBN 3-540-22881-0 Springer Berlin Heidelberg New York

This work is subject to copyright. All rights are reserved, whether the whole or part of the material is concerned, specifically the rights of translation, reprinting, re-use of illustrations, recitation, broadcasting, reproduction on microfilms or in any other way, and storage in data banks. Duplication of this publication or parts thereof is permitted only under the provisions of the German Copyright Law of September 9, 1965, in its current version, and permission for use must always be obtained from Springer. Violations are liable to prosecution under the German Copyright Law.

Springer is a part of Springer Science+Business Media

springeronline.com

© Springer-Verlag Berlin Heidelberg 2004
Printed in Germany

Typesetting: Camera-ready by author, data conversion by Olgun Computergrafik
Printed on acid-free paper   SPIN: 11314066   06/3142   5 4 3 2 1 0

Preface

The Intelligent Data Engineering and Automated Learning (IDEAL) conference series began in 1998 in Hong Kong, when the world started to experience information and data explosion and to demand for better, intelligent methodologies and techniques. It has since developed, enjoyed success in recent years, and become a unique annual international forum dedicated to emerging topics and technologies in intelligent data analysis and mining, knowledge discovery, automated learning and agent technology, as well as interdisciplinary applications, especially bioinformatics. These techniques are common and applicable to many fields. The multidisciplinary nature of research nowadays is pushing the boundaries and one of the principal aims of the IDEAL conference is to promote interactions and collaborations between disciplines, which are beneficial and bringing fruitful solutions.

This volume of Lecture Notes in Computer Science contains accepted papers presented at IDEAL 2004, held in Exeter, UK, August 25–27, 2004. The conference received 272 submissions from all over the world, which were subsequently refereed by the Program Committee. Among them 124 high-quality papers were accepted and included in the proceedings. IDEAL 2004 enjoyed outstanding keynote talks by distinguished guest speakers, *Jim Austin, Mark Girolami, Ross King, Lei Xu* and *Robert Esnouf*.

This year IDEAL also teamed up with three international journals, namely the *International Journal of Neural Systems*, the *Journal of Mathematical Modelling and Algorithms*, and *Neural Computing & Applications*. Three special issues on *Bioinformatics, Learning Algorithms*, and *Neural Networks & Data Mining*, respectively, have been scheduled for selected papers from IDEAL 2004. The extended papers, together with contributed articles received in response to subsequent open calls, will go through further rounds of peer refereeing in the remits of these three journals.

We would like to thank the International Advisory Committee and the Steering Committee for their guidance and advice. We also greatly appreciate the Program Committee members for their rigorous and efficient reviewing of the submitted papers, and the Organizing Committee for their enormous effort and excellent work. In addition, we are especially grateful to the Exeter University Computer Science Department, the IEEE Neural Networks Society, and Springer-Verlag for their support and continued collaborations. We look forward to further, closer collaboration with the IEEE in the future.

Hujun Yin
University of Manchester Institute of Science and Technology, UK

Zheng Rong Yang and Richard Everson
University of Exeter, UK

Organization

General Co-chairs

Derek Partridge — University of Exeter, UK
Nigel Allinson — University of Sheffield, UK
Ross King — University of Wales, Aberystwyth, UK

International Advisory Committee

Lei Xu — Chinese University of Hong Kong (Chair)
Yaser Abu-Mostafa — CALTECH, USA
Shun-ichi Amari — RIKEN, Japan
Michael Dempster — University of Cambridge, UK
Nick Jennings — University of Southampton, UK
Erkki Oja — Helsinki University of Technology, Finland
Latit M. Patnaik — Indian Institute of Science, India
Burkhard Rost — Columbia University, USA

IDEAL Steering Committee

Hujun Yin — UMIST, UK (Co-chair)
Laiwan Chan — Chinese University of Hong Kong (Co-chair)
Nigel Allinson — University of Sheffield, UK
Yiu-ming Cheung — Hong Kong Baptist University, China
Marc van Hulle — K.U. Leuven, Belgium
John Keane — UMIST, UK
Jimmy Lee — Chinese University of Hong Kong, China
Malik Magdon-Ismail — Rensselaer Polytechnic Institute, USA
Ning Zhong — Maebashi Institute of Technology, Japan

Organizing Committee

Zheng Rong Yang — University of Exeter, UK (Co-chair)
Richard Everson — University of Exeter, UK (Co-chair)
Hujun Yin — UMIST, UK
Andy Dalby — University of Exeter, UK
Emily Berry — University of Exeter, UK
James Hood — University of Exeter, UK
Richard Freeman — UMIST, UK
Natasha A. Young — University of Exeter, UK

Program Committee

Ajit Narayanan (Co-chair) (UK) Hujun Yin (Co-chair) (UK)

Nigel Allinson (UK) Martyn Amos (UK)
Jim Austin (UK) Emily Berry (UK)
Max Bramer (UK) David Brown (UK)
Matthew Casey (UK) Laiwan Chan (China)
Ke Chen (UK) Sheng Chen (UK)
Songcan Chen (China) Yiu-ming Cheung (China)
Sungzoon Cho (Korea) Kuo Chen Chou (USA)
Emilio Corchado (Spain) David Corne (UK)
Andy Dalby (UK) Tom Downs (Australia)
Robert Esnouf (UK) Richard Everson (UK)
Martyn Ford (UK) Colin Fyfe (UK)
Marcus Gallagher (Australia) Antony Galton (UK)
John Qiang Gan (UK) Joydeep Ghosh (USA)
David Holye (UK) Tony Holden (UK)
De-Shuang Huang (China) Simon Hubbard (UK)
Christopher J. James (UK) David Jones (UK)
Gareth Jones (Ireland) Ata Kaban (UK)
Samuel Kaski (Finland) John Keane (UK)
Martin Kersten (Netherlands) Irwin King (China)
Ross King (UK) Jimmy Lee (China)
Kwong S. Leung (China) Brian Lings (UK)
Paulo Lisboa (UK) Jiming Liu (China)
Malik Magdon-Ismail (USA) Luc Moreau (UK)
Jose Principe (USA) Omer Rana (UK)
Magnus Rattray (UK) Andreas Rauber (Austria)
Vic Rayward-Smith (UK) Jennie Si (USA)
Michael Small (China) Nick Smirnoff (UK)
Sameer Singh (UK) Ben Stapley (UK)
Amos Storkey (UK) David Taniar (Australia)
Christos Tjortjis (UK) Rebecca Thomson (UK)
Peter Tino (UK) Marc van Hulle (Belgium)
Lipo Wang (Singapore) Dong-Qing Wei (China)
David Whitly (UK) Olaf Wolkenhauer (Germany)
Kevin Wong (China) Andy Wright (UK)
Zheng Rong Yang (UK) Xin Yao (UK)
Xinfeng Ye (New Zealand) Liming Zhang (China)
Georg Zimmermann (Germany) Du Zhang (USA)
Chun-Ting Zhang (China) Ning Zhong (Japan)
Guo-Ping Zhou (USA)

Table of Contents

Bioinformatics

Modelling and Clustering of Gene Expressions
Using RBFs and a Shape Similarity Metric 1
  Carla S. Möller-Levet and Hujun Yin

A Novel Hybrid GA/SVM System for Protein Sequences Classification ... 11
  *Xing-Ming Zhao, De-Shuang Huang, Yiu-ming Cheung,
  Hong-qiang Wang, and Xin Huang*

Building Genetic Networks for Gene Expression Patterns 17
  Wai-Ki Ching, Eric S. Fung, and Michael K. Ng

SVM-Based Classification of Distant Proteins Using Hierarchical Motifs .. 25
  Jérôme Mikolajczack, Gérard Ramstein, and Yannick Jacques

Knowledge Discovery in Lymphoma Cancer from Gene–Expression 31
  Jesús S. Aguilar-Ruiz and Francisco Azuaje

A Method of Filtering Protein Surface Motifs
Based on Similarity Among Local Surfaces 39
  *Nripendra Lal Shrestha, Youhei Kawaguchi, Tadasuke Nakagawa,
  and Takenao Ohkawa*

Qualified Predictions for Proteomics Pattern Diagnostics
with Confidence Machines 46
  Zhiyuan Luo, Tony Bellotti, and Alex Gammerman

An Assessment of Feature Relevance in Predicting Protein Function
from Sequence 52
  *Ali Al-Shahib, Chao He, Aik Choon Tan, Mark Girolami,
  and David Gilbert*

A New Artificial Immune System Algorithm for Clustering 58
  Reda Younsi and Wenjia Wang

The Categorisation of Similar Non-rigid Biological Objects
by Clustering Local Appearance Patches 65
  Hongbin Wang and Phil F. Culverhouse

Unsupervised Dense Regions Discovery in DNA Microarray Data 71
  Andy M. Yip, Edmond H. Wu, Michael K. Ng, and Tony F. Chan

Visualisation of Distributions and Clusters Using ViSOMs
on Gene Expression Data 78
   Swapna Sarvesvaran and Hujun Yin

Prediction of Implicit Protein-Protein Interaction
by Optimal Associative Feature Mining 85
   Jae-Hong Eom, Jeong-Ho Chang, and Byoung-Tak Zhang

Exploring Dependencies Between Yeast Stress Genes
and Their Regulators 92
   Janne Nikkilä, Christophe Roos, and Samuel Kaski

Poly-transformation 99
   Ross D. King and Mohammed Ouali

Prediction of Natively Disordered Regions in Proteins
Using a Bio-basis Function Neural Network 108
   Rebecca Thomson and Robert Esnouf

The Effect of Image Compression on Classification
and Storage Requirements in a High-Throughput Crystallization System . 117
   Ian Berry, Julie Wilson, Chris Mayo, Jon Diprose, and Robert Esnouf

PromSearch: A Hybrid Approach to Human Core-Promoter Prediction .. 125
   Byoung-Hee Kim, Seong-Bae Park, and Byoung-Tak Zhang

Data Mining and Knowledge Engineering

Synergy of Logistic Regression and Support Vector Machine
in Multiple-Class Classification 132
   Yuan-chin Ivar Chang and Sung-Chiang Lin

Deterministic Propagation of Blood Pressure Waveform
from Human Wrists to Fingertips 142
   Yi Zhao and Michael Small

Pre-pruning Decision Trees by Local Association Rules 148
   Tomoya Takamitsu, Takao Miura, and Isamu Shioya

A New Approach for Selecting Attributes Based on Rough Set Theory ... 152
   Jiang Yun, Li Zhanhuai, Zhang Yang, and Zhang Qiang

A Framework for Mining Association Rules in Data Warehouses 159
   Haorianto Cokrowijoyo Tjioe and David Taniar

Intelligent Web Service Discovery in Large Distributed System 166
   Shoujian Yu, Jianwei Liu, and Jiajin Le

The Application of K-Medoids and PAM to the Clustering of Rules 173
   Alan P. Reynolds, Graeme Richards, and Vic J. Rayward-Smith

A Comparison of Texture Teatures for the Classification
of Rock Images 179
   Maneesha Singh, Akbar Javadi, and Sameer Singh

A Mixture of Experts Image Enhancement Scheme for CCTV Images.... 185
   Maneesha Singh, Sameer Singh, and Matthew Porter

Integration of Projected Clusters and Principal Axis Trees
for High-Dimensional Data Indexing and Query 191
   Ben Wang and John Q. Gan

Unsupervised Segmentation on Image with JSEG Using Soft Class Map.. 197
   Yuanjie Zheng, Jie Yang, and Yue Zhou

DESCRY: A Density Based Clustering Algorithm
for Very Large Data Sets... 203
   Fabrizio Angiulli, Clara Pizzuti, and Massimo Ruffolo

A Fuzzy Set Based Trust and Reputation Model in P2P Networks....... 211
   Zhang Shuqin, Lu Dongxin, and Yang Yongtian

Video Based Human Behavior Identification
Using Frequency Domain Analysis 218
   Jessica JunLin Wang and Sameer Singh

Mobile Data Mining by Location Dependencies 225
   Jen Ye Goh and David Taniar

An Algorithm for Artificial Intelligence-Based Model Adaptation
to Dynamic Data Distribution 232
   Vincent C.S. Lee and Alex T.H. Sim

On a Detection of Korean Prosody Phrases Boundaries 241
   Jong Kuk Kim, Ki Young Lee, and Myung Jin Bae

A Collision Avoidance System for Autonomous Ship Using Fuzzy
Relational Products and COLREGs 247
   Young-il Lee and Yong-Gi Kim

Engineering Knowledge Discovery in Network Intrusion Detection 253
   Andrea Bosin, Nicoletta Dessì, and Barbara Pes

False Alarm Classification Model for Network-Based Intrusion
Detection System 259
   Moon Sun Shin, Eun Hee Kim, and Keun Ho Ryu

Exploiting Safety Constraints in Fuzzy Self-organising Maps
for Safety Critical Applications 266
   Zeshan Kurd, Tim P. Kelly, and Jim Austin

Surface Spatial Index Structure of High-Dimensional Space 272
  Jiyuan An, Yi-Ping Phoebe Chen, and Qinying Xu

Generating and Applying Rules for Interval Valued Fuzzy Observations .. 279
  Andre de Korvin, Chenyi Hu, and Ping Chen

Automatic Video Shot Boundary Detection Using Machine Learning 285
  Wei Ren and Sameer Singh

On Building XML Data Warehouses 293
  Laura Irina Rusu, Wenny Rahayu, and David Taniar

A Novel Method for Mining Frequent Subtrees from XML Data 300
  Wan-Song Zhang, Da-Xin Liu, and Jian-Pei Zhang

Mining Association Rules Using Relative Confidence 306
  Tien Dung Do, Siu Cheung Hui, and Alvis C.M. Fong

Multiple Classifiers Fusion System Based
on the Radial Basis Probabilistic Neural Networks 314
  *Wen-Bo Zhao, Ming-Yi Zhang, Li-Ming Wang, Ji-Yan Du,
  and De-Shuang Huang*

An Effective Distributed Privacy-Preserving Data Mining Algorithm 320
  *Takuya Fukasawa, Jiahong Wang, Toyoo Takata,
  and Masatoshi Miyazaki*

Dimensionality Reduction with Image Data 326
  Mónica Benito and Daniel Peña

Implicit Fitness Sharing Speciation and Emergent Diversity
in Tree Classifier Ensembles 333
  Karl J. Brazier, Graeme Richards, and Wenjia Wang

Improving Decision Tree Performance
Through Induction- and Cluster-Based Stratified Sampling 339
  Abdul A. Gill, George D. Smith, and Anthony J. Bagnall

Learning to Classify Biomedical Terms Through Literature Mining
and Genetic Algorithms 345
  Irena Spasić, Goran Nenadić, and Sophia Ananiadou

PRICES: An Efficient Algorithm for Mining Association Rules 352
  Chuan Wang and Christos Tjortjis

Combination of SVM Knowledge for Microcalcification Detection
in Digital Mammograms 359
  Ying Li and Jianmin Jiang

Char: An Automatic Way to Describe Characteristics of Data 366
    Yu-Chin Liu and Ping-Yu Hsu

Two Methods for Automatic 3D Reconstruction
from Long Un-calibrated Sequences 377
    Yoon-Yong Jeong, Bo-Ra Seok, Yong-Ho Hwang, and Hyun-Ki Hong

Wrapper for Ranking Feature Selection 384
    Roberto Ruiz, Jesús S. Aguilar-Ruiz, and José C. Riquelme

Simultaneous Feature Selection and Weighting for Nearest Neighbor
Using Tabu Search 390
    Muhammad Atif Tahir, Ahmed Bouridane, and Fatih Kurugollu

Fast Filtering of Structural Similarity Search
Using Discovery of Topological Patterns 396
    Sung-Hee Park and Keun Ho Ryu

Detecting Worm Propagation Using Traffic Concentration Analysis
and Inductive Learning 402
    Sanguk Noh, Cheolho Lee, Keywon Ryu, Kyunghee Choi,
    and Gihyun Jung

Comparing Study for Detecting Microcalcifications
in Digital Mammogram Using Wavelets 409
    Ju Cheng Yang, Jin Wook Shin, and Dong Sun Park

A Hybrid Multi-layered Speaker Independent Arabic Phoneme
Identification System 416
    Mian M. Awais, Shahid Masud, Shafay Shamail, and J. Akhtar

Feature Selection for Natural Disaster Texts Classification
Using Testors 424
    Jesús A. Carrasco-Ochoa and José Fco. Martínez-Trinidad

Mining Large Engineering Data Sets on the Grid Using AURA 430
    Bojian Liang and Jim Austin

Self-tuning Based Fuzzy PID Controllers:
Application to Control of Nonlinear HVAC Systems 437
    Behzad Moshiri and Farzan Rashidi

Ontology-Based Web Navigation Assistant 443
    Hyunsub Jung, Jaeyoung Yang, and Joongmin Choi

A Hybrid Fuzzy-Neuro Model for Preference-Based Decision Analysis 449
    Vincent C.S. Lee and Alex T.H. Sim

Combining Rules for Text Categorization
Using Dempster's Rule of Combination 457
    Yaxin Bi, Terry Anderson, and Sally McClean

Genetic Program Based Data Mining for Fuzzy Decision Trees 464
    James F. Smith III

Automating Co-evolutionary Data Mining............................. 471
    James F. Smith III

Topological Tree for Web Organisation, Discovery and Exploration 478
    Richard T. Freeman and Hujun Yin

New Medical Diagnostic Method for Oriental Medicine
Using BYY Harmony Learning 485
    JeongYon Shim

An Intelligent Topic-Specific Crawler Using Degree of Relevance 491
    Sanguk Noh, Youngsoo Choi, Haesung Seo, Kyunghee Choi,
    and Gihyun Jung

Development of a Global and Integral Model of Business Management
Using an Unsupervised Model 499
    Emilio Corchado, Colin Fyfe, Lourdes Sáiz, and Ana Lara

Spam Mail Detection Using Artificial Neural Network
and Bayesian Filter 505
    Levent Özgür, Tunga Güngör, and Fikret Gürgen

An Integrated Approach to Automatic Indoor Outdoor Scene
Classification in Digital Images 511
    Matthew Traherne and Sameer Singh

Using Fuzzy Sets in Contextual Word Similarity 517
    Masrah Azmi-Murad and Trevor P. Martin

Summarizing Time Series: Learning Patterns
in 'Volatile' Series.. 523
    Saif Ahmad, Tugba Taskaya-Temizel, and Khurshid Ahmad

Cosine Transform Priors for Enhanced Decoding of Compressed Images .. 533
    Amos Storkey and Michael Allan

Partial Discharge Classification Through Wavelet Packets
of Their Modulated Ultrasonic Emission 540
    Mazen Abdel-Salam, Yassin M.Y. Hasan, Mohammed Sayed,
    and Salah Abdel-Sattar

A Hybrid Optimization Method of Multi-objective Genetic Algorithm
(MOGA) and K-Nearest Neighbor (KNN) Classifier
for Hydrological Model Calibration 546
   Yang Liu, Soon-Thiam Khu, and Dragon Savic

Cluster-Based Visualisation of Marketing Data 552
   Paulo J.G. Lisboa and Shail Patel

Dynamic Symbolization of Streaming Time Series 559
   Xiaoming Jin, Jianmin Wang, and Jiaguang Sun

A Clustering Model for Mining Evolving Web User Patterns
in Data Stream Environment 565
   Edmond H. Wu, Michael K. Ng, Andy M. Yip, and Tony F. Chan

An Improved Constructive Neural Network Ensemble Approach
to Medical Diagnoses 572
   Zhenyu Wang, Xin Yao, and Yong Xu

Spam Classification Using Nearest Neighbour Techniques 578
   Dave C. Trudgian

Learning Algorithms and Systems

Kernel Density Construction Using Orthogonal Forward Regression 586
   Sheng Chen, Xia Hong, and Chris J. Harris

Orthogonal Least Square with Boosting for Regression 593
   Sheng Chen, Xunxian Wang, and David J. Brown

New Applications for Object Recognition and Affine Motion Estimation
by Independent Component Analysis 600
   Liming Zhang and Xuming Huang

Personalized News Reading via Hybrid Learning 607
   Ke Chen and Sunny Yeung

Mercer Kernel, Fuzzy C-Means Algorithm, and Prototypes of Clusters .. 613
   Shangming Zhou and John Q. Gan

DIVACE: Diverse and Accurate Ensemble Learning Algorithm 619
   Arjun Chandra and Xin Yao

Parallel Processing for Movement Detection in Neural Networks
with Nonlinear Functions 626
   Naohiro Ishii, Toshinori Deguchi, and Hiroshi Sasaki

Combining Multiple k-Nearest Neighbor Classifiers
Using Different Distance Functions 634
   Yongguang Bao, Naohiro Ishii, and Xiaoyong Du

Finding Minimal Addition Chains Using Ant Colony 642
  Nadia Nedjah and Luiza de Macedo Mourelle

Combining Local and Global Models
to Capture Fast and Slow Dynamics in Time Series Data 648
  Michael Small

A Variable Metric Probabilistic k-Nearest-Neighbours Classifier 654
  Richard M. Everson and Jonathan E. Fieldsend

Feature Word Tracking in Time Series Documents..................... 660
  Atsuhiro Takasu and Katsuaki Tanaka

Combining Gaussian Mixture Models 666
  Hyoung-joo Lee and Sungzoon Cho

Global Convergence of Steepest Descent for Quadratic Functions 672
  Zhigang Zeng, De-Shuang Huang, and Zengfu Wang

Boosting Orthogonal Least Squares Regression....................... 678
  Xunxian Wang and David J. Brown

Local Separation Property of the Two-Source ICA Problem
with the One-Bit-Matching Condition 684
  Jinwen Ma, Zhiyong Liu, and Lei Xu

Two Further Gradient BYY Learning Rules for Gaussian Mixture
with Automated Model Selection..................................... 690
  Jinwen Ma, Bin Gao, Yang Wang, and Qiansheng Cheng

Improving Support Vector Solutions by Selecting a Sequence
of Training Subsets... 696
  Tom Downs and Jianxiong Wang

Machine Learning for Matching Astronomy Catalogues 702
  David Rohde, Michael Drinkwater, Marcus Gallagher, Tom Downs, and Marianne Doyle

Boosting the Tree Augmented Naïve Bayes Classifier 708
  Tom Downs and Adelina Tang

Clustering Model Selection for Reduced Support Vector Machines 714
  Lih-Ren Jen and Yuh-Jye Lee

Generating the Reduced Set by Systematic Sampling 720
  Chien-Chung Chang and Yuh-Jye Lee

Experimental Comparison of Classification Uncertainty for Randomised
and Bayesian Decision Tree Ensembles 726
    Vitaly Schetinin, Derek Partridge, Wojtek J. Krzanowski,
    Richard M. Everson, Jonathan E. Fieldsend, Trevor C. Bailey,
    and Adolfo Hernandez

Policy Gradient Method for Team Markov Games 733
    Ville Könönen

An Information Theoretic Optimal Classifier
for Semi-supervised Learning 740
    Ke Yin and Ian Davidson

Improving Evolutionary Algorithms by a New Smoothing Technique 746
    Yuping Wang

In-Situ Learning in Multi-net Systems 752
    Matthew Casey and Khurshid Ahmad

Multi-objective Genetic Algorithm Based Method
for Mining Optimized Fuzzy Association Rules 758
    Mehmet Kaya and Reda Alhajj

Co-training from an Incremental EM Perspective 765
    Minoo Aminian

Locally Tuned General Regression for Learning Mixture Models
Using Small Incomplete Data Sets
with Outliers and Overlapping Classes 774
    Ahmed Rafat

Financial Engineering

Credit Risks of Interest Rate Swaps:
A Comparative Study of CIR and Monte Carlo Simulation Approach 780
    Victor Fang and Vincent C.S. Lee

Cardinality Constrained Portfolio Optimisation 788
    Jonathan E. Fieldsend, John Matatko, and Ming Peng

Stock Trading by Modelling Price Trend
with Dynamic Bayesian Networks 794
    Jangmin O, Jae Won Lee, Sung-Bae Park, and Byoung-Tak Zhang

Detecting Credit Card Fraud by Using Questionnaire-Responded
Transaction Model Based on Support Vector Machines 800
    Rong-Chang Chen, Ming-Li Chiu, Ya-Li Huang, and Lin-Ti Chen

Volatility Forecasts in Financial Time Series
with HMM-GARCH Models 807
　　Xiong-Fei Zhuang and Lai-Wan Chan

Agent Technologies

User Adaptive Answers Generation for Conversational Agent
Using Genetic Programming 813
　　Kyoung-Min Kim, Sung-Soo Lim, and Sung-Bae Cho

Comparing Measures of Agreement for Agent Attitudes 820
　　Mark McCartney and David H. Glass

Hierarchical Agglomerative Clustering for Agent-Based Dynamic
Collaborative Filtering 827
　　Gulden Uchyigit and Keith Clark

Learning Users' Interests in a Market-Based Recommender System 833
　　Yan Zheng Wei, Luc Moreau, and Nicholas R. Jennings

Visualisation of Multi-agent System Organisations
Using a Self-organising Map of Pareto Solutions 841
　　Johnathan M.E. Gabbai, W. Andy Wright, and Nigel M. Allinson

Author Index 849

Modelling and Clustering of Gene Expressions Using RBFs and a Shape Similarity Metric

Carla S. Möller-Levet and Hujun Yin

Electrical Engineering and Electronics, University of Manchester
Institute of Science and Technology, Manchester M60 1QD, UK
c.moller-levet@postgrad.umist.ac.uk
h.yin@umist.ac.uk

Abstract. This paper introduces a novel approach for gene expression time-series modelling and clustering using neural networks and a shape similarity metric. The modelling of gene expressions by the Radial Basis Function (RBF) neural networks is proposed to produce a more general and smooth characterisation of the series. Furthermore, we identified that the use of the correlation coefficient of the derivative of the modelled profiles allows the comparison of profiles based on their shapes and the distributions of time points. The series are grouped into similarly shaped profiles using a correlation based fuzzy clustering algorithm. A well known dataset is used to demonstrate the proposed approach and a set of known genes are used as a benchmark to evaluate its performance. The results show the biological relevance and indicate that the proposed method is a useful technique for gene expression time-series analysis.

1 Introduction

With microarray experiments it is possible to measure simultaneously the activity levels of thousands of genes [1]. An appropriate clustering of gene expression data can lead to meaningful classification of diseases, identification of functionally related genes, logical descriptions of gene regulation, etc. Various statistical and clustering methods have been applied successfully to microarray data [2–5].

Gene expression time-series are generally noisy, short and usually unevenly sampled. To overcome these undesirable characteristics, we propose to model gene expression profiles, using the RBF neural networks [6]. Most existing methods used to compare expression profiles directly operate on the time points. While modelling the profiles can lead to more generalised, smooth characterisation of gene expressions. Standard time-series models are limited by the underlying assumptions of the model, such as stationarity or length of the time-series. In contrast, the use of artificial neural networks for modelling time-series is not restricted by model assumptions and linearity, as well as the noise, irregular sampling and shortness of the time-series. Other modelling techniques have been proposed recently, e.g., in [7, 8], gene expression time-series are modelled using mixed-effect models within a mixture model based clustering. Equally spaced cubic spline[1] are used for both mean and random effects, that is, sum of the smooth population mean spline function dependent on time and gene cluster, and a spline function with random coefficients for individual gene effects and Gaussian measurement noise. One of the advantages of the proposed modelling over the mixed-effects modelling is that each gene can be modelled independently, which make the models useful for different types of analysis, not just for clustering.

In microarray experiments, the absolute intensity of gene expression is not relevant, instead, the relative change of intensity characterised by the shape of the expression profile is regarded as characteristic and informative. In addition, biological processes are often sampled at short or long intervals of time when intense or moderate biological activity is taking place, leading to unevenly distributed sampling points. We identified that the use of the correlation coefficient of the derivative of the modelled profiles allows the comparison of profiles based on their shape and the distribution of their time points. This measure is further used in a correlation based fuzzy clustering algorithm.

2 Modelling with Radial Basis Function Neural Networks

Radial basis networks have a single hidden layer, where the nodes are Gaussian kernels, and a linear output layer. The radial basis function has the form:

$$f(x) = \sum_{i=1}^{n_r} w_i \phi(\|c_i - x\|) + b \qquad (1)$$

where x is the input vector, $\phi(\cdot)$ is a Gaussian function kernel, $\|\cdot\|$ denotes the Euclidean norm, w_i are the weights of the second layer, c_i is the vector of the centre of the i-th kernel, and n_r is the total number of kernels.

The problem of RBF approximation is to find appropriate centres and widths of the hidden nodes, and weights of the linear layer. The network is linear in the parameters when all RBF centres and widths of the hidden layer are fixed. Then, the output layer linearly combines the output of the hidden layer and the only adjustable parameters are the weights. We chose the Orthogonal Least Squares (OLS) learning algorithm proposed in [9] for training the RBF neural networks. The algorithm allows the selection of the centres one by one in a rational procedure. Each selected centre maximises the increment to the explained variance of the desired output and it is not necessary to use all the time points as the centres. However, this method considers all kernels with an equal width, which is inadequate when the sampling points are not evenly distributed. In order to improve the approximation, we complemented the OLS learning algorithm with a heuristic search for the optimal width for each of the candidate centres, which implies the recalculation of the regression matrix before a new centre is selected. The optimal width minimises the mean square error of a piecewise linear fit of a segment of the series and the RBF model of the segment [10].

---

[1] Spline functions are piecewise polynomials of degree n that are connected together (at point called knots) so as to have $n-1$ continuous derivations.

3 Correlation-Based Similarity Metric and Fuzzy Clustering

The Pearson correlation coefficient is a popular similarity measure to compare time-series. Yet, the correlation is not necessarily coherent with the shape and it does not consider the order of the time points and uneven sampling intervals. If the correlation, however, is performed on the derivatives of the modelled profiles[2], these drawbacks can be solved. The differentiation refers to the rates of change or shape of the profile.

The objective function that measures the desirability of partitions in fuzzy c-means clustering (FCM) [11] is described by,

$$J(x,v,u) = \sum_{i=1}^{n_c} \sum_{j=1}^{n_g} u_{ij}^m \, d^2(x_j, v_i) \quad (2)$$

where n_c is the number of clusters, n_g is the number of vectors to cluster, u_{ij} is the value of the membership degree of the vector x_j to the cluster i, $d^2(x_j, v_i)$ is the squared distance between vector x_j and prototype v_i, and m is the parameter that determines the degree of overlap of fuzzy clusters. The FCM optimisation process is operated on the inner product induced norms, the use of a different metric will require the recalculation of v and u to minimise the objective function. In [12], a correlation-based fuzzy clustering is presented by defining d as $d_2^2(x_j, v_i) = f(\rho(x_j, v_i))$, where f is a continuously decreasing function and ρ is the Pearson's correlation coefficient between x_j and v_i. If the time-series are normalised with mean values set to cero and norm set to one, every time point is localised at the perimeter of an hypersphere of radius one and the value of $\rho(x_j, v_i)$ is the cosine of the angle θ, between x_j and v_i. The chord d_2, formed by x_j and v_i, is $d_2^2(x_j, v_i) = 2(1 - \rho(x_j, v_i))$, which is the Euclidean distance in this particular space.

There are two user-defined parameters in the FCM algorithm, i.e., the number of clusters n_c and the fuzziness parameter m. In this paper, we have chosen the PBM-index, proposed in [13], to validate the number of clusters. In addition, to avoid the random initialisation of the partition matrix, the mountain clustering initialisation was implemented [14]. The selection of m for an optimal performance of fuzzy clustering for microarray data is addressed in [3], and can be aided by validity measures and membership plots (plot of membership degrees into grayscales in a hierarchical fashion).

4 Yeast Cell Cycle Dataset

In Spellman *et al* [2], cell-cycle-regulated genes of the Yeast *Saccharomayces cerevisiae* were identified by microarray hybridisation. Yeast cultures were synchronised by three independent methods: α factor arrest, elutriation and arrest

---

[2] The modelled profiles are further smoothed to reduce noise impact of the derivatives.

of a cdc15 temperature sensitive mutant. We utilised the temporal expression of the yeast culture synchronised by α factor arrest to illustrate the proposed method.

In the analysis of Spellman et al [2], 800 cell-cycle-regulated genes were identified using Fourier analysis of combined data of all three experiments. Among the 800 genes, 511 with no missing values for the α experiment are available from their web site[3]. Recently, Luan and Li [15] re-analysed the data using a shape-invariant model together with a false discovery rate procedure to identify periodically expressed genes. They identified 297 cell-cycle-regulated genes in the α experiment. Out of these 297 genes, 208 have no missing values. In addition, there are 104 genes determined to be cell-cycle-regulated by traditional methods. Out of these 104 genes, 71 with no missing values are available from the Spellman et al [2] dataset. In [2], 95 of the 104 genes were identified as cell-cycle-regulated, while in [15] 47 were identified. We utilised the 511, 208 and 71 genes corresponding to the cell-cycle-regulated genes identified by Spellman et al [2], Luan and Li [15], and traditional methods, respectively, to form three test datasets.

4.1 Modelling

The first step for the proposed approach is the modelling of the series with the RBF neural networks. The moving average smoothing technique was used to further smooth the modelled series. Figure 1 presents three example model profiles from the Spellman et al dataset and their corresponding smoothed expressions.

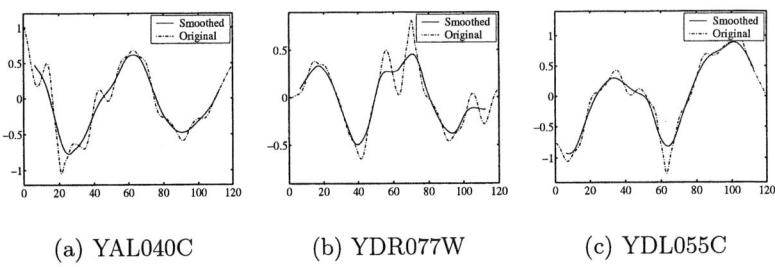

(a) YAL040C (b) YDR077W (c) YDL055C

Fig. 1. Example genes and their corresponding smoothed expression. In every figure the horizontal axis denotes time [mins] and the vertical axis denotes the expression level (log_2(ratio)).

The cell cycle period for the α dataset has been identified with different methods, producing different results. In [16], a time-frequency analysis using wavelet transforms is used to identify the period. The authors conclude that the dominant period is not that of the cell cycle but, the higher frequency 30-40

---

[3] Dataset available from http://cellcycle-www.stanford.edu

min submultiples of the cycle period. In [4], the authors analyse the similarity of a time-series curve with itself and deduce that the period is 70 minutes. As in [16], the authors in [4] observe that there are very strong indications of underlying oscillatory phenomena with periods smaller that the observed cell cycles, around 20 and 40 minutes. Later, in [8], five clusters are identified and the times between peaks for four clusters are estimated to be 67, 63.4, 54.2, and 61.4 minutes. The modelling and smoothing of the profiles proposed in this paper allow the estimation of times between peaks. The estimated times are comparable to the previous period identification results, having higher occurrences at periods between 55 and 65 minutes. Table 1 presents the summery of the estimated times between two peaks for the three datasets, and Figure 2 presents the corresponding histograms.

Table 1. Summary of the estimated times (in minutes) between two peaks, for the 71, 208 and 511 genes datasets.

Dataset	Mean	Median	Std. Dev.
71 genes	60.2289	59.2500	10.1421
208 genes	59.1010	58.7500	5.7688
511 genes	57.0186	57.7500	13.6742

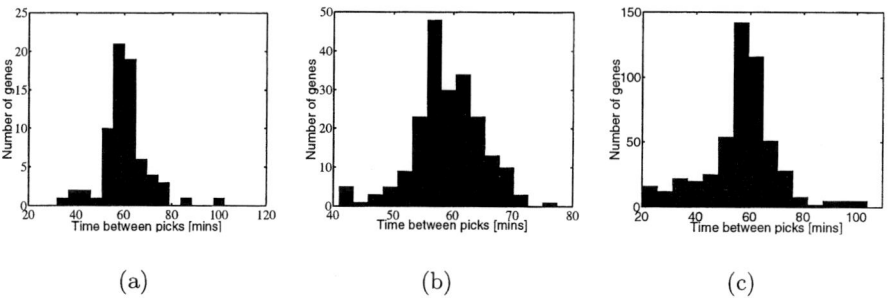

(a)   (b)   (c)

Fig. 2. Histograms of estimated times between peaks of genes of the three datasets used. (a) 71 genes, (b) 208 genes and (c) 511 genes.

4.2 Clustering

The PBM-index validates 4 clusters for all three datasets. Figure 3 plots the PBM-index as a function of the number of clusters for the three datasets. The genes were assigned to the clusters according to their highest membership degree. A hierarchical clustering of the partition matrix was performed to order the genes and obtain a complete visualisation of the results. In this way, the membership plot can be utilised to identify genes with similar distribution of membership degree across all the clusters. The clustering results are shown in Figure 4. We classified the clusters according to the different cell cycle phases used in [2]. The genes were classified based on the minimum error, comparing their peak times

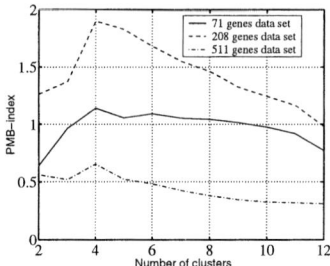

Fig. 3. The maximum value of the PBM-index indicates the formation of the smallest number of compact clusters with large separation.

to the peak times described in [2] for each phase. Tables 2 and 3 present the distributions of the genes in each cluster among the cell cycle phases. In the 71 and 208 genes datasets, the genes in each cluster belong mainly to one phase or the two adjacent phases. In the 511 genes dataset, the genes are more spread mainly due to the inclusion of genes which are not cell-cycle-regulated and have a low membership degree to all the clusters, for example genes in Figure 4(f), cluster II.

In the 71 genes identified by traditional methods, the phase of the genes with the highest membership degree to each cluster coincide with the phase represented by the cluster. The clustering results of these previously known genes, indeed show biological relevance, indicating that the proposed method is a useful technique for gene expression time-series analysis. In Figure 4 (a), a region of genes with an extremely high membership to cluster II can be observed. All those genes correspond to the Histons identified by traditional biological methods and their profiles are illustrated in Figure 5.

Table 2. Distribution of the 71 genes dataset, among the five different cell-cycle phases over the four clusters obtained using the proposed method. The column "Gene" corresponds to the gene with the highest membership to the cluster, and "Phase", corresponds to the phase of the gene identified by traditional methods.

Cluster	M/G1	G1	S	G2	M	Gene	Phase
I(14)	0	29	0	0	0	YKL113C	G1
II(7)	0	1	13	0	0	YNL030W	S
III(8)	7	6	0	0	3	YNL192W	M/G1
IV(12)	3	3	0	2	7	YMR001C	G2/M

In the case of the dataset formed by the 208 genes identified as cell-cycle-regulated by [15], the gene with the highest membership degree to the first cluster, YPR174C, has not been characterized. Table 4, presents the genes with high similarity to YPR174C according to their membership distribution. YPR019W, essential for initiation of DNA replication, presents the highest membership de-

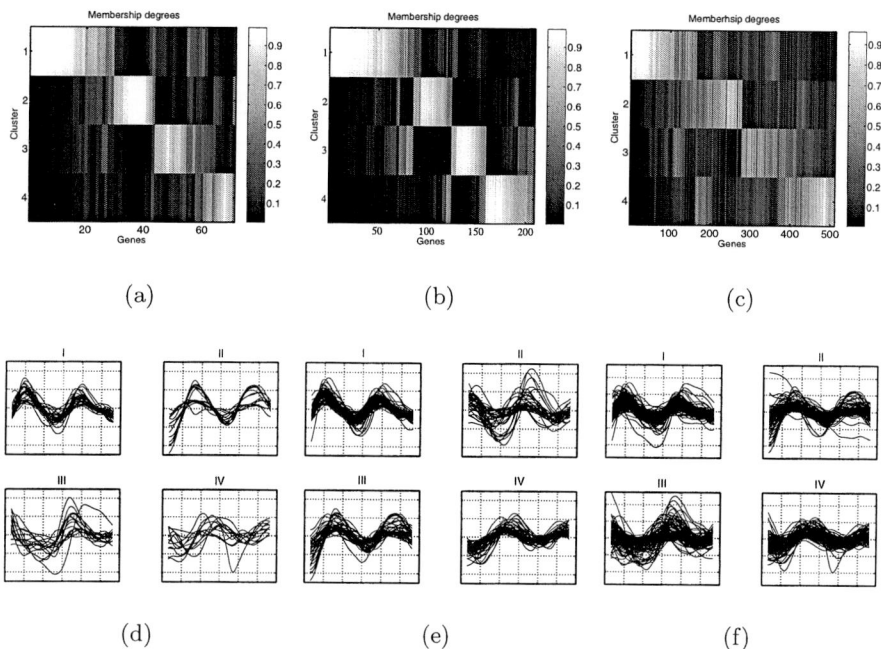

Fig. 4. Clustering results (membership plots and time-series plots) for the 71 genes dataset (figures (a) and (d)), 208 genes dataset (figures (b) and (e)) and 511 genes dataset (figures (c) and (f)). In figures d, e, and f, the horizontal axis denotes time [0, 20, 40, 60, 80, 100, and 120 mins] and the vertical axis denotes the expression level (log_2(ratio)).

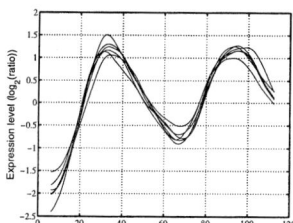

Fig. 5. Genes with high membership to cluster II, illustrated in Figure 4 (a).

gree to the second cluster. YNL030W, core histone required for chromatin assembly and chromosome function, presents the highest membership degree to the third cluster which mainly represents genes of the S phase. Figure 4(b) shows a sharp boundary between clusters II and III. The corresponding time-series plots, Figure 4(e), show that these clusters are shifted almost half cell cycle, thus, presenting opposite shapes. Finally, YGL021W, presents the highest membership degree to the fourth cluster.

In the dataset formed by the 511 genes identified as cell-cycle-regulated by [2], cluster I mainly contains genes belonging to phase G1, and the gene with the

Table 3. Distribution of the 208 and 511 genes datasets, among the five different cell cycle phases over the four clusters obtained using the proposed method.

208 genes dataset						511 genes dataset					
Cluster	M/G1	G1	S	G2	M	Cluster	M/G1	G1	S	G2	M
I(78)	0	78	0	0	0	I(158)	5	148	1	2	2
II(37)	28	2	0	0	7	II(107)	4	33	39	31	0
III(42)	0	10	24	8	0	III(113)	49	20	4	10	30
IV(51)	0	0	0	33	18	IV(133)	27	4	5	53	44

Table 4. Genes with high similarity to YPR174C according to their membership distribution. "Phase" corresponds to the phase identified by traditional methods, "U" stands for uncharacterised gene.

Membership	Gene	Phase
0.9803	YAR007C	G1
0.9837	YLR103C	G1
0.9794	YDL156W	U
0.9882	YDL163W	U
0.9896	**YPR174C**	U
0.9773	YDL164C	G1
0.9812	YBR088C	G1
0.9739	YPL153C	G1
0.9739	YDL003W	G1

highest membership degree to cluster I, YLR103C, was identified to peak in the G1 phase by traditional methods. YOR248W, uncharacterised, has the highest membership degree to cluster II, which has genes associated to the G1, S and G2 phases. YHR005C, presents the highest membership degree to cluster III. Cluster IV is mainly formed by genes belonging to phases G2 and M. YGL021W, has the highest membership degree to this cluster. This gene, is also the highest member of cluster IV (formed by G2 and M phase genes) in the 208 genes dataset.

The membership and time-series plots indicate that the correlation based fuzzy clustering of the derivatives allow the grouping of profiles based on their shape. The distribution of the genes from the three datasets among the cell cycle phases indicates that the proposed method is able to extract meaningful groups with biological relevance.

5 Conclusions

In this paper, the modelling of gene expression profiles using the RBF neural networks is proposed, leading to a more generalised, smooth characterisation of gene expressions. An extended ORS method is proposed to optimise the network parameters. The models obtained are smoothed to reduce noise and differentiated to characterise the shapes of the expression profiles. Then, the use of the correlation coefficient of the derivatives of the modelled profiles as a similarity measure, allows the comparison of profiles based on their shapes and the distributions of their time points. Finally, considering the advantages of fuzzy membership, a correlation based fuzzy clustering algorithm to group profiles according to the proposed similarity metric has been used. The well known dataset in [2] has been used to demonstrate the advantages of the proposed approach. The set of genes identified by traditional methods was used as a benchmark to evaluate the performance of the proposed approach with coherent biological meanings.

Acknowledgments

This research was supported by grants from ABB Ltd. U.K., an Overseas Research Studentship (ORS) award by Universities U.K. and Consejo Nacional de Ciencia y Tecnologia (CONACYT).

References

1. Brown, P., Botstein, D.: Exploring the new world of the genome with DNA microarrays. Nature Genetics supplement **21** (1999) 33–37
2. Spellman, P.T., Sherlock, G., Zhang, M.Q., Iyer, V.R., Anders, K., Eisen, M.B., Brown, P.O., Botstein, D., Futcher, B.: Comprehensive identification of cell cycle-regulated genes of yeast *Saccharamyces cerevisiae* by microarray hybridization. Mol. Biol. Cell **9** (1998) 3273–3297
3. Dembélé, D., Kastner, P.: Fuzzy C-means method for clustering micoarray data. Bioinformatics **19** (2003) 973–980
4. Filkov, V., Skiena, S., Zhi, J.: Analysis techniques for microarray time-series data. Journal of Computational Biology **9** (2002) 317–330
5. Möller-Levet, C.S., Cho, K.H., Wolkenhauer, O.: Microarray data clustering based on temporal variation: FCV with TSD preclustering. Applied Bioinformatics **2** (2003) 35–45
6. Park, J., Sandberg, I.: Approximation and radial basis function networks. Neural Computing **5** (1993) 305–316
7. Bar-Joseph, Z., Gerber, G., Gifford, D.K., Jaakkola, T.S., Simon, I.: A new approach to analyzing gene expression time series data. In: Proceedings of RECOMB, Washington DC, USA (2002) 39–48
8. Luan, Y., Li, H.: Clustering of time-course gene expression data using a mixed-effects model with B-splines. Bioinformatics **19** (2003) 474–482
9. Chen, S., Cowan, C.F.N., Grant, P.M.: Orthogonal least squares learning algorithm for radial basis function networks. IEEE Transactions on Neural Networks **2** (1991) 302–309
10. Möller-Levet, C.S., Yin, H., Cho, K.H., Wolkenhauer, O.: Modelling gene expression time-series with radial basis function neural networks. In: Proceeding of the International Joint Conference on Neural Networks (IJCNN'2004). (to appear)
11. Bezdek, J.: Pattern Recognition with Fuzzy Objective Function Algorithms. Plenum Press, New York (1981)
12. Golay, X., Kollias, S., Stoll, G., Meier, D., Valavanis, A., Boesiger, P.: A new correlation-based fuzzy logic clustering algorithm for fMRI. Magnetic Resounance Medicine **40** (1998) 249–260

13. Pakhira, M.K., Bandyopedhyay, S., Maulik, U.: Validity index for crisp and fuzzy clusters. Pattern recognition **37** (2003) 487–501
14. Yager, R.R., Filev, D.P.: Approximate Clustering Via the Mountain Method. IEE Transactions on systems, man, and cybernetics **24** (1994) 1279–1284
15. Luan, H., Li, H.: Model-based methods for identifying periodically expressed genes based on time course microrray gene expression data. Bioinformatics **20** (2004) 332–339
16. Klevecz, R.R., Dowse, H.B.: Tuning in the transcriptome: basins of attraction in th yeast cell cycle. Cell Prolif **33** (2000) 209–218

A Novel Hybrid GA/SVM System for Protein Sequences Classification

Xing-Ming Zhao[1,2], De-Shuang Huang[2], Yiu-ming Cheung[3], Hong-qiang Wang[1,2], and Xin Huang[2]

[1] Department of Automation, University of Science and Technology of China
P.O.Box.1130, Hefei, Anhui, 230027, China
{x_mzhao,hqwang}@iim.ac.cn

[2] Intelligent Computing Lab, Hefei Institute of Intelligent Machines, CAS
P.O.Box.1130, Hefei, Anhui, 230031, China
{x_mzhao,dshuang,hqwang,xhuang}@iim.ac.cn

[3] Department of Computer Science, Hong Kong Baptist University
Kowloon, Hong Kong, P.R. China
ymc@comp.hkbu.edu.hk

Abstract. A novel hybrid genetic algorithm(GA)/Support Vector Machine (SVM) system, which selects features from the protein sequences and trains the SVM classifier simultaneously using a multi-objective genetic algorithm, is proposed in this paper. The system is then applied to classify protein sequences obtained from the Protein Information Resource (PIR) protein database. Finally, experimental results over six protein superfamilies are reported, where it is shown that the proposed hybrid GA/SVM system outperforms BLAST and HMMer.

1 Introduction

A core problem in computational biology is the annotation of new protein sequences with structural and functional features. The newly discovered sequences can be classified into known protein family so that the structural and functional features of the sequences can be easily induced. So far there have been many generative approaches developed for protein sequences classification. These include BLAST [1], profiles [2], and Hidden Markov Models (HMMS) [3], etc. And there are also some discriminative methods that have been developed to classify protein sequences, such as Radial Basis Function (RBF) neural network [4] and Multilayer Perceptrons (MLP) neural networks [5], etc. Support Vector Machine (SVM) [6] is a new generation of machine learning algorithm that has been successfully applied to the analysis of biological problems. So the SVM is also used here to classify the protein sequences.

A key issue in constructing the discriminative classifiers for protein sequences classification is the selection of the best discriminative features. The selection of these features can have a considerable impact on the effectiveness of the resulting classification algorithm. Generally, irrelevant or noisy features can increase the complexity of the classification problem. Consequently, feature selection have become one important part of the protein sequences classification. The main purpose of feature selection is to select those features containing most discriminative information and discard the less discriminatory features, which can be seen as an optimization problem. Genetic algorithm has been used to solve optimization problems based on Darwinian evolution and natural selection, which is comprise of the application of selection, mutation and crossover to a population of competing problem solutions [7]. Recently, genetic algorithm has been applied to the problem of feature selection by Siedlecki [8] and Oliveira [9], etc.

In this paper, we proposed a novel hybrid GA/SVM system, which can select features from protein sequences and train the SVM classifier simultaneously. Experimental and comparative results show that our proposed GA/SVM hybrid system outperforms BLAST and HMMer as for the classification of protein sequences obtained from the Protein Information Resource (PIR) protein database[10].

2 Hybrid GA/SVM System

A protein sequence S, of length n, is defined as a linear succession of n symbols from the 20-letter amino acid alphabet {A, C, D, E, F, G, H, I, K, L, M, N, P, Q, R, S, T, V, W, Y }. The 2-gram encoding method [5] and the 6-letter exchange group encoding method [5] are adopted here. For each protein sequence, both encoding methods are employed, respectively, so we can get $20^2 + 6^2 = 436$ possible features in total.

Generally, for any classification tasks there always exist the problems that the number of the significant features is far less than the number of possible features.

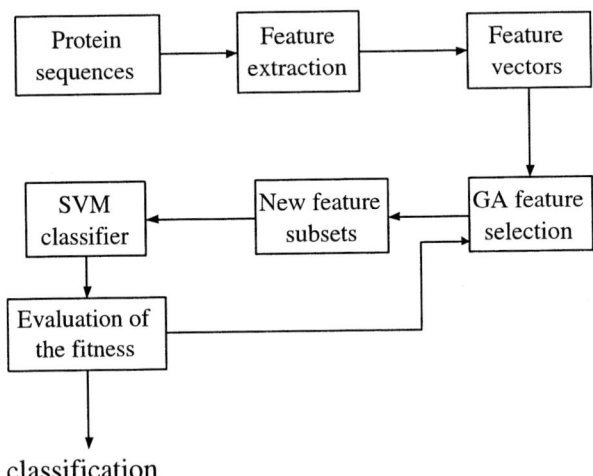

Fig. 1. Model for the hybrid GA/SVM system to classify protein sequences. The feedback from the evaluation of the fitness value allows for the GA to iteratively find a feature vector that provides optimal fitness value.

In this paper, we proposed a hybrid GA/SVM system that selects features from protein sequences and trains the SVM classifier simultaneously. Fig.1. shows the model for the hybrid GA/SVM system, where the feedback from the evaluation of the fitness function allows the GA to iteratively search for a feature vector that optimizes the fitness function value. The key issues in the hybrid GA/SVM system are how to encode a solution as a chromosome and how to define a fitness function. The similar genetic encoding method introduced by Siedlecki and Sklansky [8] is adopted here to encode each candidate solutions. Assume that m be the total number of the features available to choose from ($m = 436$ in our case). The chromosome is represented by a binary vector of dimension m (Fig.2.). As shown in Fig.2., if the ith bit of the vector equals 1, the corresponding ith feature is selected; Otherwise, the corresponding ith feature will not be selected. As for feature selection, our aim is to optimize the two objectives: minimization of the feature numbers and maximization of the classification accuracy, which is a multi-objective optimization problem. The fitness function can be defined as:

$$f(x) = w1 * f1(x) + w2 * f2(x) \qquad (1)$$

where $w1$ and $w2$ are weight coefficients; $f1(x)$ is the recognition rate and $f2(x)$ the number of the features removed from the original feature sets. However, there exit trad-offs between $f1(x)$ and $f2(x)$. The similar settings used for $w1$ and $w2$ in [9] are adopted here. Consequently, the feature selection problem becomes one single-objective optimization problem, i.e., maximization of $f(x)$.

The parameter settings adopted by the system for the experiments in this paper are: Population size 50; Generation 1000; Crossover rate 0.8; Mutation rate 0.01; $w1$ 10000 and $w2$ 0.4, respectively.

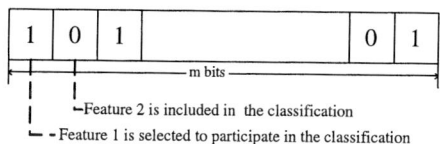

Fig. 2. m-dimensional binary string, comprising an individual of the GA population, which is a potential solution to the feature selection problem.

3 Experimental Results

In this section, six protein superfamilies data, which are used as positive datasets, are used to test the SVM classifier. Both the six positive protein superfamilies and the negative dataset were obtained from the PIR Non-Redundant Reference Sequence Database (PIR-NREF), Release 1.35. The six superfamilies to be trained/classified are: Globin(560/280), Ribitol dehydrogenase(552/276), Lectin(106/54), Triose-phosphate isomerase(132/62), Ferredoxin(208/104), and Ligas(452/226), respectively. The negative dataset containing 506 sequences is used as training set and the one including the remaining 253 sequences as test sets. The negative dataset doesn't belong to any of the above six superfamilies.

Assume that the recognition rate used to evaluate the relative performance of the classifiers is defined as:

$$Rr = \frac{NumCorrect}{NumTotal} \times 100\% \qquad (2)$$

where $NumCorrect$ is the number of the testing sequences classified correctly and $NumTotal$ is the total number of the testing sequences.

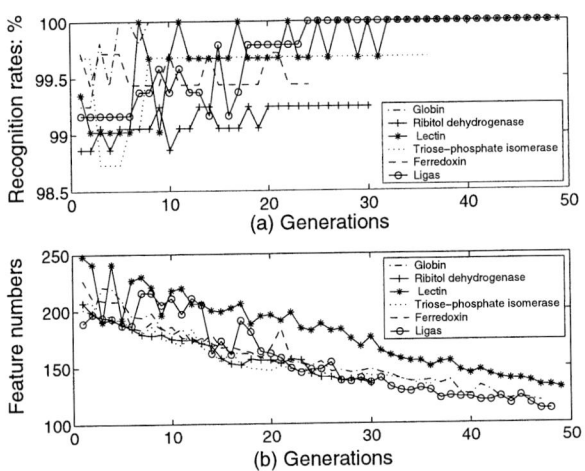

Fig. 3. Evolution of the feature numbers and the recognition rates.

Fig.3. shows the evolution process of the feature numbers and the evolution process of the recognition rates, respectively. Fig.4. shows Performance of the hybrid GA/SVM system, where (a) shows the evolution of the fitness function; (b) shows the comparison of recognition rates for the SVM over the six superfamilies before and after dimensionality reduction, where the black bars are recognition rates using 436 features as inputs for the SVM and the white ones are recognition rates using our proposed hybrid GA/SVM system. It can be seen that using the hybrid GA/SVM system, the classification accuracy can be indeed improved. Table 1. summarizes the comparison of the recognition rates and the feature numbers before and after the dimensionality reduction for the SVM classifier over six superfamilies.

In addition, Table 2. summarizes the results of the classification performance for the three classifiers over six protein superfamilies, where the BLAST version number is 2.0.10, and the HMMer version number is 2.2g. From Table 2., it can be readily found that our proposed hybrid GA/SVM system outperforms the BLAST and the HMMer, which greatly supports our claims.

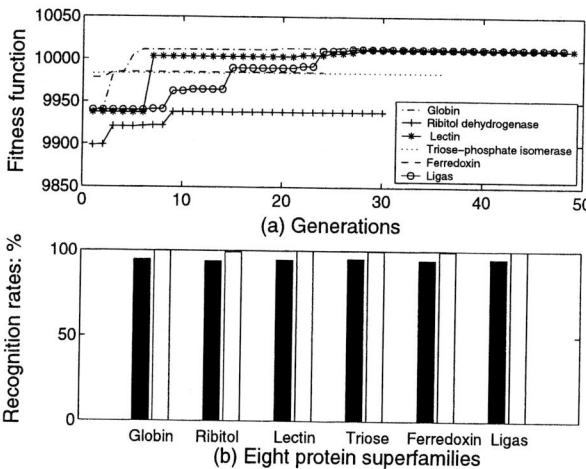

Fig. 4. Performance of the hybrid GA/SVM system. (a)Evolution of the fitness function; (b)Comparison between recognition rates of the six superfamilies before and after dimensionality reduction using SVM.

Table 1. Comparison of the recognition rates and the feature numbers before and after the dimensionality reduction for the SVM classifier over six superfamilies.

Protein datasets	original feature set		feature subset for the hybrid system	
	features	classification accuracy	features	classification accuracy
Globin	436	94.49%	119	100.00%
Ribitol dehydrogenase	436	93.67%	135	99.244%
Lectin	436	94.36%	131	100.00%
Triose-phosphate isomerase	436	95.04%	134	99.68%
Ferredoxin	436	94.31%	150	99.44%
Ligas	436	95.16%	112	100.00%

Table 2. Comparison of the recognition rates for the three classifiers over six superfamilies.

	Globin	Ribitol	Lectin	Triose	Ferredoxin	Ligas
SVM	100.00%	99.24%	100.00%	99.68%	99.45%	100.00%
BLAST	99.25%	99.81%	99.35%	99.68%	100%	98.96%
HMMer	97.56%	98.11%	95.44%	98.41%	96.08%	84.55%

4 Conclusions

Finding the most informative features and reducing the dimensionality of the feature vectors are important steps to protein sequences classification. A novel hybrid GA/SVM system has been proposed in this paper, which can select features containing accurate and enough discriminative information for classification and train the SVM classifier simultaneously. Experimental results for protein sequences classification over six protein superfamilies obtained from the Protein Information Resource (PIR) database show that the hybrid GA/SVM system outperforms BLAST and HMMer.

References

1. S. F. Altschul, T. L. Madden, A. A. Schafer, J. Zhang, Z. Zhang, W.Miller, and D. J. Lipman, "Gapped Blast and PSI-Blast: A new generation of protein data", *Nucleic Acids Research*, vol. 25, no. 17, pp3389-3402, 1997.
2. Michael Gribskov, Andrew D. McLachlan, and David Eisenberg, "Profile analysis: Detection of distantly related proteins", *Proceedings of the National Academy of Sciences of the USA*, vol. 84, pp4355-4358, July 1987.
3. A. Krogh, M. Brown, I. S. Mian, K. Sjölander, and D.Haussler, "Hidden Markov Models in Computational Biology: Applications to Protein Modeling", *Journal of Molecular Biology*, vol.235, pp1501-1531, February 1994.
4. D. H. Wang, N. K. Lee, and T. S. Dillon, "Data mining for building neural protein sequence classification systems with improved performance", *Proceedings of 2003 International Joint Conference on Neural Networks (IJCNN'03)*, pp1746-1751, July 20-24, 2003, Portland, Oregon, USA.
5. C. H. Wu, Y. S. Fung, and J. McLarty, "Neural networks for full-scale protein sequence classification: Sequence encoding with singular value decomposition", *Machine Learning*, vol. 21, pp177-193, 1995.
6. V. N. Vapnik, "The Nature of Statistical Learning Theory", New York: Springer-Verlag, 1999.
7. J.H.Holland, "Adaptation in Natural and Artificial Systems", *Ann Arbor, MI:Univ.Michigan Press*, 1975.
8. W. Siedlecki and J. Sklansky, "A Note on Genetic Algorithms for Large-Scale Feature Selection", *Pattern Recognition Letters*, vol. 10, pp.335-347, 1989.
9. L. S. Oliveira, N. Benahmed, R. Sabourin and F. Bortolozzi, "Feature Subset Selection Using Genetic Algorithms for Handwritten Digit Recognition", *Proceedings of the 14th Brazilian Symposium on Computer Graphics and Image Processing*, pp.362-369, 2001.
10. Winona C. Barker, John S. Garavelli, Hongzhan Huang, Peter B. McGarvey, Bruce C. Orcutt, Geetha Y. Srinivasarao, Chunlin Xiao, Lai-Su L. Yeh, Robert S. Ledley, Joseph F. Janda, Friedhelm Pfeiffer, Hans-Werner Mewes, Akira Tsugita, and Cathy Wu, "The Protein Information Resource (PIR)", *Nucleic Acids Research* vol.28, no.1, pp41-44, 2000.

Building Genetic Networks for Gene Expression Patterns

Wai-Ki Ching[1], Eric S. Fung[2], and Michael K. Ng[3]

The University of Hong Kong, Pokfulam Road, Hong Kong

Abstract. Building genetic regulatory networks from time series data of gene expression patterns is an important topic in bioinformatics. Probabilistic Boolean networks (PBNs) have been developed as a model of gene regulatory networks. PBNs are able to cope with uncertainty, corporate rule-based dependencies between genes and uncover the relative sensitivity of genes in their interactions with other genes. However, PBNs are unlikely used in practice because of huge number of possible predictors and their computed probabilities. In this paper, we propose a multivariate Markov chain model to govern the dynamics of a genetic network for gene expression patterns. The model preserves the strength of PBNs and reduce the complexity of the networks. Parameters of the model are quadratic with respect to the number of genes. We also develop an efficient estimation method for the model parameters. Simulation results on yeast data are given to illustrate the effectiveness of the model.

1 Introduction

An important focus of genomic research concerns understanding the mechanism in which cells execute and control the huge number of operations for normal functions, and also the way in which the cellular systems fail in disease. One of the possible reasons is the cell cycle. Cells in the body alternately divide in mitosis and interphase, and this sequence of activities exhibited by cells is called the cell cycle. Since all eukaryotic cells have important physical changes during the cell cycle, if we have better understanding of when and where the cell cycle occur, a higher prediction accuracy for cell activities can be obtained. Models based on methods such as neural network, non-linear ordinary differential equations, Petri nets have been proposed for such problem, see for instance Smolden et. al (2000), DeJong (2002) and Bower (2001).

Boolean network is commonly used for modeling genetic regulatory system because it can help discovering underlying gene regulatory mechanisms. The Boolean network is a deterministic network and it was first introduced by Kauffman (1969). In this network, each gene is regarded as a vertex of the network and is quantized into two levels only (over-express (1) or under-express (0)). However, the deterministic assumption is not practical in both biological and empirical aspect. In the biological aspect, an inherent determinism assumes an environment without uncertainty. In the empirical aspect, sample noise and relatively small amount of samples may cause incorrect results in logical rules. Later,

Shmulevich et al. (2002) proposed Probabilistic Boolean Networks (PBNs) that can share the appealing rule-based properties of Boolean networks and it is robust in the face of uncertainty. The dynamics of their PBNs can be studied in the context of standard Markov chain. However, the number of parameters in a PBN grows exponentially with respect to the number of genes n, and therefore heuristic methods are needed for model training, see for instance Akutsu et al. (2000).

The main contribution of this paper is to propose a multivariate Markov chain model (a stochastic model) which can capture both the intra- and inter-transition probabilities among the gene expression sequences. Moreover, the number of parameters in the model is only $O(n^2)$. We develop efficient model parameters estimation methods based on linear programming. We also propose a method for recovering the structure and rules for a given Boolean network.

The rest of the paper is organized as follows. In Section 2, we give a review on PBNs. In Section 3, we propose the multivariate Markov chain model. We then present estimation methods for model parameters. An example is given to illustrate the actual parameters estimation procedure in Section 4. In Section 5, we apply the proposed model and method to gene expression data of yeast, and illustrate the effectiveness of the new model. Finally, concluding remarks are given to address further research issues in Section 6.

2 Probabilistic Boolean Networks

In Shmulevich et al. (2000), PBNs are proposed and the model can be written as follows:

$$\mathbf{F}_i = \{f_j^{(i)}\}_{j=1,\ldots,l(i)}, \quad 1 \leq i \leq n$$

where n is the number of genes, the predictor $f_j^{(i)}$ is a possible function determining the expression level (0 or 1) of the i-th gene, and $l(i)$ is the number of possible functions for the i-th gene. Let $c_j^{(i)}$ be the probability that the jth predictor $f_j^{(i)}$ is chosen to predict the i-th gene. This probability can be estimated by using the Coefficient of Determination (COD), see Dougherty et al. (2000).

For any given time point, the expression level of the i-th gene is determined by one of the possible predictors $f_j^{(i)}$ for $1 \leq j \leq l(i)$. The probability of a transition from $\mathbf{v}(t)$ to $\mathbf{v}(t+1)$ can be obtained as:

$$\prod_{i=1}^{n} \left[\sum_{k=1}^{l(i)} \left\{ c_k^{(i)} : f_k^{(i)}(\mathbf{v}(t)) = v_i(t+1) \right\} \right]$$

where $\mathbf{v}(t) = (v_1(t), \ldots, v_n(t))$ and $v_l(t) = 0$ or 1. The degree of influence of the j-th gene to the i-th gene can be estimated by:

$$l_j(v_i) = \sum_{k=1}^{l(i)} \text{Prob}\{f_k^{(i)}(v_1, \ldots, v_{j-1}, 0, v_{j+1}, \ldots, v_n) \neq$$
$$f_k^{(i)}(v_1, \ldots, v_{j-1}, 1, v_{j+1}, \ldots, v_n)\} \times c_k^{(i)},$$

see Shmulevich et al. (2000). We remark that for each set of $f^{(i)} = \{f_j^{(i)}\}$ with $1 \leq i \leq n$, the maximum number of predictors is equal to 2^{2^n} as $1 \leq l(i) \leq 2^{2^n}$, it is also true for its corresponding set of prediction probabilities $\{c_k^{(i)}\}$. It is almost not practical for using this model due to its complexity and the imprecision of parameters based on limited sample size.

3   The Multivariate Markov Chain Model

In this paper, the gene sequence in PBNs $\{v(1), \ldots, v(T)\}$ is logically represented as a sequence of vectors $V_1, \ldots, V_T$, where T is the length of the sequence, and $V_j = E_{k+1}$ (E_{k+1} is the unit column vector with the $(k+1)$-th entry being one) if $v(j) = k$ (i.e., it is in the expression level k, $k = 0$ or 1). A first-order discrete-time Markov chain satisfies the following relationship:

$$\text{Prob}\,(V_{t+1} = E_{v(t+1)} \mid V_0 = E_{v(0)}, \ldots, V_t = E_{v(t)})$$
$$= \text{Prob}\,(V_{t+1} = E_{v(t+1)} \mid V_t = E_{v(t)}).$$

These probabilities are assumed to be independent of t and can be written as

$$p_{ij} = \text{Prob}\,(V_{t+1} = E_{i+1} \mid V_t = E_{j+1}), \quad \forall\, i, j \in \{0, 1\}.$$

The matrix P, formed by placing p_{ij} in row i and column j is called the transition probability matrix.

In our proposed multivariate Markov chain model with a network of n genes, we assume the following relationship among the genes:

$$\mathbf{V}_{t+1}^{(j)} = \sum_{k=1}^{n} \lambda_{jk} P^{(jk)} \mathbf{V}_t^{(k)}, \quad j = 1, 2, \ldots, n \qquad (1)$$

where $\lambda_{jk} \geq 0$ for $1 \leq j, k \leq n$ and $\sum_{k=1}^{n} \lambda_{jk} = 1$, and $\mathbf{V}_t^{(i)}$ is the expression level probability distribution of the i-th gene at the time t. The expression level probability distribution of the j-th gene at the time $t+1$ depends on the weighted average of $P^{(jk)}\mathbf{V}_t^{(k)}$. Here $P^{(jk)}$ is a transition probability matrix from the expression level of the k-th gene to the expression level of the j-th gene. In matrix form, we write

$$\mathbf{V}_{t+1} \equiv \begin{pmatrix} \mathbf{V}_{t+1}^{(1)} \\ \mathbf{V}_{t+1}^{(2)} \\ \vdots \\ \mathbf{V}_{t+1}^{(n)} \end{pmatrix} = \begin{pmatrix} \lambda_{11} P^{(11)} & \lambda_{12} P^{(12)} & \cdots & \lambda_{1n} P^{(1n)} \\ \lambda_{21} P^{(21)} & \lambda_{22} P^{(22)} & \cdots & \lambda_{2n} P^{(2n)} \\ \vdots & \vdots & \vdots & \vdots \\ \lambda_{n1} P^{(n1)} & \lambda_{n2} P^{(n2)} & \cdots & \lambda_{nn} P^{(nn)} \end{pmatrix} \begin{pmatrix} \mathbf{V}_t^{(1)} \\ \mathbf{V}_t^{(2)} \\ \vdots \\ \mathbf{V}_t^{(n)} \end{pmatrix} \equiv Q\mathbf{V}_t.$$

Although each column sum of Q is not equal to one, we still have the following two propositions, Ching et al. (2002).

Proposition 1. *If $\lambda_{jk} > 0$ for $1 \leq j, k \leq n$, then the matrix Q has an eigenvalue equal to 1 and the eigenvalues of Q have modulus less than or equal to 1.*

Proposition 2. *Suppose that $P^{(jk)}$ $(1 \le j,k \le n)$ are irreducible and $\lambda_{jk} > 0$ for $1 \le j,k \le n$. Then there is a vector $\bar{\mathbf{V}} = [\bar{\mathbf{V}}^{(1)}, \bar{\mathbf{V}}^{(2)}, \ldots, \bar{\mathbf{V}}^{(n)}]^T$ such that $\bar{\mathbf{V}} = Q\bar{\mathbf{V}}$ and $\sum_{i=1}^{m}[\bar{\mathbf{V}}^{(j)}]_i = 1$, $1 \le j \le n$.*

4 Model Parameters Estimation

In this section, we propose numerical methods to estimate $P^{(jk)}$ and λ_{jk}. For the j-th and the k-th genes, we estimate the transition probability matrix $P^{(jk)}$ by the following method by counting the transition frequency from the expression level i_k of the k-th gene at time t to the expression level i_j of the j-th gene at time $t+1$. After the usual normalization, we obtain an estimate of the transition probability matrix $\hat{P}^{(jk)}$. In the model, we require to estimate n^2 of 2-by-2 transition probability matrices in the multivariate Markov chain model. After all $P^{(jk)}$ are estimated, we can estimate the parameters λ_{jk} based on $P^{(jk)}$.

The stationary vector $\bar{\mathbf{V}}$ can be estimated from the sequences of gene expression levels by computing the proportion of the occurrence of each expression level of the gene. Let us denote it by $\hat{\mathbf{V}} = (\hat{\mathbf{V}}^{(1)}, \hat{\mathbf{V}}^{(2)}, \ldots, \hat{\mathbf{V}}^{(n)})^T$. In view of Proposition 2, we therefore expect $\hat{Q}\hat{\mathbf{V}} \approx \hat{\mathbf{V}}$. From this approximation, it suggests one possible way to estimate the parameters $\lambda = \{\lambda_{jk}\}$ as follows. For each j, we solve the following optimization problem:

$$\min_{\lambda} \max_{i} \left| \left[\sum_{k=1}^{n} \lambda_{jk} \hat{P}^{(jk)} \hat{\mathbf{V}}^{(k)} - \hat{\mathbf{V}}^{(j)} \right]_i \right|$$

subject to $\sum_{k=1}^{n} \lambda_{jk} = 1$ and $\lambda_{jk} \ge 0$ for $1 \le j,k \le n$. Here $[\cdot]_i$ denotes the ith entry of the vector. This minimization problem can be formulated as a linear programming problem for each j, Ching et al. (2002). Since there are n independent linear programming (LP) problems of each being n constraints and n variables, the expected total computational complexity of solving such LPs is of $O(n^4)$, see for instance Fang and Puthenpura (1993).

4.1 An Example

Consider the following two binary sequences:

$$s_1 = \{0,0,1,0,0,0,0,0,1,1,0,0\} \quad \text{and} \quad s_2 = \{1,1,0,0,1,0,0,0,0,1,0,1\}.$$

We obtain the transition frequency matrix and probability matrix:

$$F^{(21)} = \begin{pmatrix} 5 & 2 \\ 3 & 1 \end{pmatrix} \quad \text{and} \quad \hat{P}^{(21)} = \begin{pmatrix} \frac{5}{8} & \frac{2}{3} \\ \frac{3}{8} & \frac{1}{3} \end{pmatrix}, \quad \text{(after normalization)}$$

Similarly, the others can be computed and are given as follows:

$$\hat{P}^{(11)} = \begin{pmatrix} \frac{3}{4} & \frac{2}{3} \\ \frac{1}{4} & \frac{1}{3} \end{pmatrix}, \quad \hat{P}^{(12)} = \begin{pmatrix} \frac{5}{7} & \frac{3}{4} \\ \frac{3}{7} & \frac{1}{4} \end{pmatrix} \quad \text{and} \quad \hat{P}^{(22)} = \begin{pmatrix} \frac{4}{7} & \frac{3}{4} \\ \frac{3}{7} & \frac{1}{4} \end{pmatrix},$$

Moreover, we get $\hat{\mathbf{V}}_1 = (\frac{3}{4}, \frac{1}{4})^T$ and $\hat{\mathbf{V}}_2 = (\frac{7}{12}, \frac{5}{12})^T$. After solving the LPs, the multivariate Markov chain model of the two binary sequences are given by

$$\begin{cases} \mathbf{V}^{(1)}_{t+1} = 0.5\hat{P}^{(11)}\mathbf{V}^{(1)}_t + 0.5\hat{P}^{(12)}\mathbf{V}^{(2)}_t \\ \mathbf{V}^{(2)}_{t+1} = 1.0\hat{P}^{(21)}\mathbf{V}^{(1)}_t + 0.0\hat{P}^{(22)}\mathbf{V}^{(2)}_t. \end{cases} \quad (2)$$

Based on the above models, we can estimate the probability $c_j^{(i)}$ of the predictor $f_j^{(i)}$ and the degree of influence of the j-th gene to the i-th gene. Let $X_{i_1,\ldots,i_n}^{(d)}$ be the conditional probability vector of the dth gene when the previous expression level of the genes are $i_1, i_2, \ldots, i_n$ respectively. From (2), we obtain

$$X^{(1)}_{0,0} = (\frac{41}{56}, \frac{15}{56})^T, \quad X^{(1)}_{0,1} = (\frac{3}{4}, \frac{1}{4})^T, \quad X^{(1)}_{1,0} = (\frac{29}{42}, \frac{13}{42})^T, \quad X^{(1)}_{1,1} = (\frac{17}{24}, \frac{7}{24})^T.$$

and

$$X^{(2)}_{0,0} = X^{(2)}_{0,1} = (\frac{5}{8}, \frac{3}{8})^T, \quad X^{(2)}_{1,0} = X^{(2)}_{1,1} = (\frac{2}{3}, \frac{1}{3})^T$$

for the above two sequences. For example,

$$X^{(2)}_{1,0} = \sum_{k=1}^{2} \lambda_{2k}\hat{P}^{(2k)}E_{i_k} = 1.0 \times \hat{P}^{(21)}E_{i_1} + 0.0 \times \hat{P}^{(22)}E_{i_2} = \hat{P}^{(21)}(0,1)^T = (\frac{2}{3}, \frac{1}{3})^T.$$

With these probabilities, we obtain the probabilities $c_j^{(i)}$ as in the following table:

v_1 v_2	$f_1^{(1)}$	$f_2^{(1)}$	$f_3^{(1)}$	$f_4^{(1)}$	$f_5^{(1)}$	$f_6^{(1)}$	$f_7^{(1)}$	$f_8^{(1)}$	$f_9^{(1)}$	$f_{10}^{(1)}$	$f_{11}^{(1)}$	$f_{12}^{(1)}$	$f_{13}^{(1)}$	$f_{14}^{(1)}$	$f_{15}^{(1)}$	$f_{16}^{(1)}$
0 0	0	0	0	0	0	0	0	0	1	1	1	1	1	1	1	1
0 1	0	0	0	0	1	1	1	1	0	0	0	0	1	1	1	1
1 0	0	0	1	1	0	0	1	1	0	0	1	1	0	0	1	1
1 1	0	1	0	1	0	1	0	1	0	1	0	1	0	1	0	1
$c_j^{(1)}$	0.27	0.11	0.12	0.05	0.08	0.04	0.04	0.02	0.1	0.04	0.04	0.02	0.03	0.01	0.02	0.01

For instance,

$$c_6^{(1)} = [X^{(1)}_{0,0}]_1 \times [X^{(1)}_{0,1}]_2 \times [X^{(1)}_{1,0}]_1 \times [X^{(1)}_{1,1}]_2 \approx 0.04.$$

Since $\lambda_{22} = 0$, the set of predictors for the second sequence can be reduced and their corresponding probabilities are given in the following table:

v_1 v_2	$f_1^{(2)}$	$f_2^{(2)}$	$f_3^{(2)}$	$f_4^{(2)}$
0 —	0	0	1	1
1 —	0	1	0	1
$c_j^{(2)}$	0.42	0.2	0.25	0.13

From the above two tables, the best predictors are $f_1^{(1)}$ and $f_1^{(2)}$ for the first and the second sequences respectively. We can also obtain the degree of influence of the ith sequence to the jth sequence $(i,j = 1,2)$ as follows:

$$l_1(v_1) = 0.4, \quad l_1(v_2) = 0.45, \quad l_2(v_1) = 0.4, \quad l_2(v_2) = 0.$$

For instance,

$$l_1(v_1) = \sum_{k=1}^{l(1)} \text{Prob}\{f_k^{(1)}(0, v_2) \neq f_k^{(1)}(1, v_2)\} \cdot c_k^{(1)}$$
$$= 0(0.27) + \frac{1}{2}(0.11) + \frac{1}{2}(0.12) + 0.05 + \frac{1}{2} = 0.4.$$

According to the calculated values $l_i(v_j)$, we know that the first sequence somehow determine the second sequence. However, this phenomena is already illustrated by the fact that $\lambda_{22} = 0 (\lambda_{21} = 1)$ in the multivariate Markov chain model.

4.2 Fitness of the Model

We note that the multivariate Markov chain model presented here is a stochastic model. Given all the state vectors $\mathbf{V}_t^{(k)}$ with $k = 1, \ldots, n$, the state probability distribution $\mathbf{V}_{t+1}^{(k)}$ can be estimated by using (1). According to this state probability distribution, one of the prediction methods for the j-th sequence at time $t+1$ can be taken as the state with the maximum probability, i.e., $\hat{\mathbf{V}}(t+1) = j$ if $[\hat{\mathbf{V}}(t+1)]_i \leq [\hat{\mathbf{V}}(t+1)]_j$ for all $1 \leq i \leq 2$. By making use of this procedure, our multivariate Markov chain model can be used to uncover the rules (build a true table) for a PBNs. To evaluate the performance and effectiveness, the prediction accuracy of all individual sequences r

$$r = \frac{1}{nT} \times \sum_{i=1}^{n} \sum_{t=1}^{T} \delta_t^{(i)} \times 100\%, \quad \text{where} \quad \delta_t^{(i)} = \begin{cases} 1, & \text{if } \hat{\mathbf{v}}_i(t) = \mathbf{v}_i(t) \\ 0, & \text{otherwise.} \end{cases}$$

5 Gene Expression Data of Yeast

Genome transcriptional analysis is an important analysis in medicine and bioinformatics. One of the applications of genome transcriptional analysis is used for eukaryotic cell cycle in yeast. If we have better understanding of when and where the cell cycle occurs, a higher prediction accuracy for cell activity can be obtained. Several biological changes associated with the cell cycle activities, discovering this process gives important information for internal standard comparison of gene activity over time. Hartwell and Kastan (1994) showed that without appropriate cell cycle regulation leads to genomic instability, especially in etiology of both hereditary and spontaneous cancers, instances in Wang et al. (1994); Hall and Peters (1996). Raymond et al. (1998) examined the present of cell cycle-dependent periodicity in 6220 transcripts and found that cell cycle appears in about 7% of transcripts. Those transcripts are then extracted for further investigation. When the time course was divided into early G1, late G1, S, G2 and M phase based on the size of the bugs and the cellular position of the nucleus, the result showed that more than 24% of transcripts are directly adjacent to other transcripts in the same cell cycle phase. The data set used in our study is the selected set from Yeung and Ruzzo (2001). In the discretization, if an expression level is above (below) a certain standard deviation from the average expression of the gene, it is over-expressed (under-expressed) and the corresponding state is 1 (0).

There are two problems of using PBN for such data set. The first is that the number of genes is too large and the PBN complexity is too high. The second is that the length of transcript (17 samples) is too short and therefore almost all values of $c_j^{(i)}$ are equal to 0 by using the method of COD.

The construction of the multivariate Markov chain models for such date set only requires about 0.1 second with CPU=AMD 1800+ and RAM=512Mb. This demonstrate the proposed method is quite efficient. In our study, we assume that there is not any prior knowledge about the genes. Therefore, in the construction of the multivariate Markov chain models, we consider each target gene can be related to other genes. Based on the values of λ_{ij} in our model, we can determine the occurrence of cell cycle in transcript j, i.e., the presence of inter-relationship between transcript j and the other transcripts in different phases. And we find that such cell cycle appears in 93% of the target genes in the multivariate Markov chain models. Some of the results are illustrated in the following table:

Name of target transcript	Cell cycle phase	Length of cell cycle	Related transcripts (its phase, λ_{ij}, level of influence)
YDL101c	late G1	1	YMR031c(early G1,1.00,1.00)
YPL127c	late G1	2	YDL101c (late G1,0.33,0.38)
			YML027w (late G1,0.33,0.39)
			YJL079c (M,0.33,0.38)
YLR121c	late G1	3	YPL158c (early G1,0.33,0.42)
			YDL101c (late G1,0.33,0.43)
			YKL069W (G2,0.33,0.43)
YLR015w	early G1	4	YKL113c (late G1,1.00,0.88)

In the above table, the last column displays the name of required transcripts for predicting the target transcript, the corresponding phase of required transcripts, their corresponding weightings λ_{ij} in the model, as well as an estimated value of the level of influence from related transcript to the target transcript. Although the level of influence can be estimated based on our model parameters, the computational cost increases exponentially respect to the value of n. We find in the table that the weighting λ_{ij} provides a reasonable measure for the level of influence. Finally, we present the prediction result of different lengths of cell cycle for the whole data set in the following table and the results show that the performance of the model is quite good.

Length of cell cycle phases required	No. of occurrence in this type of cell cycle (in %)	Average prediction accuracy (in %)
1	5	86
2	9	87
3	9	83
4	70	86

6 Concluding Remarks

In this paper, we proposed a multivariate Markov chain model. Efficient parameters estimation methods are presented. Experimental results on gene expression data of yeast are given to demonstrate the effectiveness of our proposed model. The model can be easily extended to the case when the gene expression data has more than two levels. The estimation method and prediction method can still be applied. Another direction for further research is to consider higher-order multivariate models, and develop estimation method for the model parameters and prediction method.

References

1. Akutsu, T., Miyano, S. and Kuhara, S. (2000). Inferring Qualitative Relations in Genetic Networks and Metabolic Pathways. *Bioinformatics*, **16**, 727-734.
2. Bower, J. (2001). Computational Modeling of Genetic and Biochemical Networks. MIT Press, Cambridge, M.A.
3. Ching, W., Fung, E. and Ng, M. (2002). A Multivariate Markov Chain Model for Categorical Data Sequences and Its Applications in Demand Predictions. *IMA Journal of Management Mathematics*, **13**, 187-199.
4. de Jong, H. (2002). Modeling and Simulation of Genetic Regulatory Systems: A Literature Review. *J. Comput. Biol.*, **9**, 69-103.
5. Dougherty, E.R., Kim, S. and Chen, Y. (2000). Coefficient of Determination in Nonlinear Signal Processing. *Signal Process*, **80**, 2219-2235.
6. Fang, S and Puthenpura, S. (1993). *Linear Optimization and Extensions.* Prentice-Hall, Englewood Cliffs, NJ.
7. Hall, M. and Peters, G. (1996). Genetic alterations of cyclins, cyclin-dependent kinases, and Cdk inhibitors in human cancer. *Adv. Cancer Res.*, **68**, 67-108.
8. Hartwell, L.H., and Kastan, M.B. (1994). Cell cycle control and cancer. *Science*, **266**, 1821-1828.
9. Kauffman, S. (1969). Metabolic Stability and Epigenesis in Randomly Constructed Gene Nets. *J. Theoret. Biol.*, **22**, 437-467.
10. Raymond J., Michael J., Elizabeth A., Lars S. (1998), A Genome-Wide Transcriptional Analysis of the Mitotic Cell Cycle. *Molecular Cell*, **2**, 65-73.
11. Shmulevich, I., Dougherty, E., Kim S. and Zhang W. (2002). From Boolean to Probabilistic Boolean Networks as Models of Genetic Regulatory Networks. *Proceedings of the IEEE*, **90**, No.11, 1778-1792.
12. Smolen P., Baxter D. and Byrne J. (2000) Mathematical Modeling of Gene Network. *Neuron*, **26**, 567-580.
13. Wang, T.C., Cardiff, R.D., Zukerberg, L., Lees, E., Amold, A., and Schmidt, E.V. (1994). Mammary hyerplasia and carcinoma in MMTV-cyclin D1 transgenic mice. *Nature*, **369**, 669-671.
14. Yeung, K. and Ruzzo, W. (2001). An Empirical Study on Principal Component Analysis for Clustering Gene Expression Data. *Bioinformatics*, **17**, 763-774.

SVM-Based Classification of Distant Proteins Using Hierarchical Motifs

Jérôme Mikolajczack[1], Gérard Ramstein[2], and Yannick Jacques[1]

[1] Département de Cancérologie, Institut de Biologie
9 Quai Moncousu, F-44035 Nantes Cedex
[2] LINA Ecole polytechnique de l'Université de Nantes
rue Christian Pauc, BP 50609 F-44306 Nantes Cedex 3

Abstract. This article presents a discriminative approach to the protein classification in the particular case of remote homology. The protein family is modelled by a set M of motifs related to the physicochemical properties of the residues. We propose an algorithm for discovering motifs based on the ascending hierarchical classification paradigm. The set M defines a feature space of the sequences: each sequence is transformed into a vector that indicates the possible presence of the motifs belonging to M. We then use the SVM learning method to discriminate the target family. Our hierarchical motif set specifically modelises interleukins among all the structural families of the SCOP database. Our method yields a significantly better remote protein classification compared to spectrum kernel techniques.

1 Introduction

Considering that our purpose is to discover new members of a protein family, we need an efficient and fast classifier compatible with genome mining. Support vector machines (SVM) are one of the most powerful supervised learning algorithm. An SVM [1], [2] is a binary classifier that builds a decision boundary by mapping training data from the original input space into a high dimensional feature space. The SVM selects the hyperplan which maximises the separation between two data classes. Due to the high dimensionality of the feature space, the SVM algorithm uses a function called a kernel to compute dot products directly into the input space. SVMs have been successfully applied to different problems in bioinformatics, such as protein fold class prediction and microarray data analysis [3]. SVM-based methods for protein classification transform input protein sequences into fixed-length feature vectors. This vectorisation step is crucial for the future performances of the classifier. The SVM-Fisher method [4] uses a hidden Markov model (HMM) trained on a protein family to compute the gradient vector of input sequences. The drawback of this technique is the computation cost due to the scoring of the sequences. The SVM-pairwise method [5] applies a pairwise sequence similarity algorithm using the Smith-Waterman algorithm. The computational expense of this method remains too high for our purpose. A very efficient algorithm is the spectrum kernel method

[6]. The features are the set of all possible susbsequences of amino acids of fixed length k. The same author also proposes the mismatch kernel technique [7], an extension of the previous method that authorizes a certain proportion of wildcards into the subsequences of length k. As these two last techniques have a linear time complexity and perform remarkably well, they will serve as reference methods. This paper is organised as follows. Section 2 introduces the concept of hierarchical motif. Section 3 describes the algorithm for discovering motifs. Section 4 presents the SVM classifier and section 5 presents the results of our experiments on the classification of interleukins.

2 Hierarchical Motifs

The primary structure of a protein is represented by a sequence $s = \langle s_1 s_2 \ldots s_n \rangle$ where each s_i belongs to Ω, the amino acid set:

$$\Omega = \{A, C, D, E, F, G, H, I, K, L, M, N, P, Q, R, S, T, V, W, Y\}$$

Let $P(\Omega)$ be the set of the subsets of Ω. Some elements of $P(\Omega)$ comprises amino acids sharing particular physicochemical properties of the amino acids. Several classes have been proposed: we have chosen the Taylor code (table 1). The relevance of this classification is verified by the study of conserved regions. For instance, sequence similarities show that mutations often take place inside the same physicochemical class (e.g. the residues I, L, V belonging to the aliphatic class are frequently exchanged). Let $C(\Omega)$ be the union of the physicochemical classes, the singleton set of Ω and Ω:

$$C(\Omega) = \{\{A\}, \{C\}, \ldots, \{Y\}\} \cup \{\alpha, \beta, \gamma, \delta, \varepsilon, \zeta, \eta, \theta\} \cup \Omega$$

We will consider the ordered set $(C(\Omega), \subseteq)$ that forms a semi-lattice: every pair (x, y) of $C(\Omega) \times C(\Omega)$ has a least upper bound denoted $sup(x, y)$.

A motif $m = \langle m_1 m_2 \ldots m_k \rangle$ is a k-sequence of sets $m_i \in C(\Omega)$. For the sake of concision, we denote by R the singleton $\{R\}$ (e.g. the motif $K\alpha$ comprises the class $\{K\}$ followed by the class $\{I, L, V\}$). An *occurrence* of a motif m is a subsequence $\langle s_{i+1} s_{i+2} \ldots s_{i+k} \rangle$ of s such as $s_{i+j} \in m_j \ \forall j, \ 1 \leq j \leq k$. A sequence

Table 1. Amino acid classes based on physicochemical properties

Symbol	Class	Members
α	aliphatic	ILV
β	aromatic	$FHWY$
γ	non-polar	$ACFGHIKLMVWY$
δ	charged	$DEHKR$
ε	polar	$CDEHKNQRSTWY$
ζ	positive	HKR
η	small	$ACDGNPSTV$
θ	tiny	$ACGST$

that contains at least one occurrence of m is said to *verify* m. The *support* of a motif m in a sequence set $\mathcal{S}$ is the number of sequences of $\mathcal{S}$ that verify m. The sequence MH verifies 21 motifs of size $k=2$, including MH, $M\beta$, $\gamma\delta$, and $\Omega\Omega$.

Only one subsequence verifies the motif MH, whereas any sequence of length greater than or equal to 2 verifies the motif $\Omega\Omega$. We therefore have to consider the specificity of a motif which is the probability of its occurrence in a sequence. As the estimation of the probability is time consuming, we instead propose the cost function $c(m) = \prod_{i=1}^{k} f(m_i)$ where $f(m_i)$ is the frequency of the m_i class in SCOP database [8]. This database includes a large panel of different protein families. In practice, we observe a good correlation between $c(m)$ and the effective support of m in the training database. The specificity of a motif m will be defined by $\phi(m) = -\log(f(m))$. Our experiments reveal that this specifity estimator of a given motif is well correlated with the effective frequence of this motif in a wide panel of proteins belonging to different families.

It is important to note that support and specificity are opposed concepts: the more a motif presents a high support, the less it is specific, and conversely. Motifs can be hierarchised according a relation of generalisation. Let m^1 and m^2 be two k-motifs. We note $\preceq$ the following relation: $m^1 \preceq m^2$ if for all $i \in [1, k]$ $m_i^1 \subseteq m_i^2$.

The definition of the estimator $\phi(m)$ implies that $\phi(m^1) \geq \phi(m^2)$ for all pairs of motifs that verify $m^1 \preceq m^2$.

We call least upper bound of motifs m^1 and m^2 (denoted $sup(m^1, m^2)$) the motif $m^{1,2}$ verifying: $m_i^{1,2} = sup(m_i^1, m_i^2)$ for all $i \in [1, k]$. The motif $m^{1,2}$ represents the most specific motif that generalises m^1 and m^2: every subsequence verifying m^1 or m^2 will verify $m^{1,2}$. Table 2 gives some examples of least upper bounds.

3 Hierarchical Motif Discovery

The discovery algorithm proceeds in two steps:

1. the extraction of seed motifs,
2. the generation of hierarchical motifs.

The first step consists in the extraction of seed motifs from the sequence set $\mathcal{S}$. A seed motif is a motif having no minoring elements. More pratically, a seed motif only contains singleton classes. To define the seed motif set, we use a filter that only considers the putative interesting k-subsequences of $\mathcal{S}$. This step consists in the computation of the least upper bound of every pair of k-subsequences. If the least upper bound presents a minimal support, the k-subsequences that verify this motif are kept. With a minimal support of 3, we reduce the size of k-subsequences by a factor of 8.

The second step is inspired by the ascending hierarchical classification technique. A dendrogram of motifs is generated from the seed motifs of the previous step. This phase proceeds as follows:

algorithm motifDiscovery
   inputs
      M, the seed motif set obtained at step 1
      $supMin$, the minimal support threshold
      $speMin$, the minimal specificity threshold
   output
      E, the set of hierarchical motifs

   $E = \{m \in M \mid support(m) \geq supMin \text{ et } \phi(m) \geq speMin\}$;
   Repeat
      Let m^1 and m^2 be the pair of motifs of M such as:
         1. $m^{1,2} = sup(m^1, m^2)$
         2. $\phi(m^{1,2}) \geq \phi(m^{i,j})$ for all m^i and m^j in M
      $M \leftarrow M - \{m^1, m^2\}$;
      $M \leftarrow M \cup \{m^{1,2}\}$;
      if $support(m^{1,2}) \geq supMin$ and $\phi(m^{1,2}) \geq speMin$
         then $E \leftarrow E \cup \{m^{1,2}\}$;
   until $cardinal(M) = 1$ or $\phi(m^{1,2}) < speMin$;

Table 2 presents hierarchical motifs of size $k = 4$ obtained from the sequences: HIWY, HIDY, KLTY, HVSG and DARG. Motifs m^1 to m^5 are the seed motifs extracted from the previous sequences. Fig. 1 shows the dendrogram tree built by our algorithm.

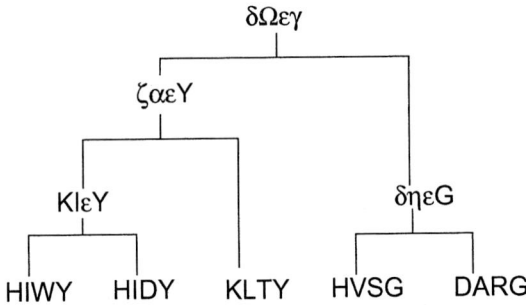

Fig. 1. Dendrogram of motifs

4   Application and Discussion

The members of the cytokine superfamily are soluble glycoproteins acting in the regulation of immunity responses. The set of positive examples that we use consists in 45 primary sequences of interleukins belonging to the human family of cytokines. We set the size k of our motifs to 8 because of the typical helix secondary structure of this family. The negative examples are extracted from

Table 2. Motifs extracted by motifDiscovery algorithm

motif	content	support	specificity
m^1	HIWY	1	14.25
m^2	HIDY	1	12.83
m^3	KLTY	1	11.44
m^4	HVSG	1	11.79
m^5	DARG	1	10.96
$m^6 = m^{1,2}$	KIεY	2	10.64
$m^7 = m^{3,6}$	$\zeta\alpha\varepsilon$Y	3	7.55
$m^8 = m^{4,5}$	$\delta\eta\varepsilon$G	2	5.26
$m^9 = m^{7,8}$	$\delta\Omega\varepsilon\gamma$	5	2.56

Table 3. Classification results. VP, FN, VN, FP are the percentage of true positives, false negatives, true negatives and false positives

classifier	error rate	TP	FN	TN	FP
KNN	18.9	88.9	11.1	73.3	26.7
SKSVM	13.3	84.4	15.6	88.9	11.1
MKSVM	12.0	82.7	17.3	93.3	16.7
SVMotifs 13	2.2	95.6	4.4	100	0
SVMotifs 14	0	100	0	100	0
SVMotifs 15	5.5	88.9	11.1	100	0

the SCOP database (6615 sequences). As inputs of the SVM are fixed-length vectors, we associate to a sequence s a boolean vector $v(s)$: the ith element of $v(s)$ is set to true iff the sequence s verifies the ith element of the set of hierarchical motifs. This vectorisation step has a linear time complexity. Table 3 compares the results obtained with different classifiers according to the leave-one-out validation technique. The validation set comprises all the 45 positive examples as well as 45 negative examples selected from all the structural superfamilies of SCOP. All SVM classifiers use the radial basis function as kernel. Line KNN corresponds to K-nearest neighbour method based on the similarity measure corresponding to the dot product of the normalised vectors. The better performance of the spectrum kernel method confirms the superiority of the SVM algorithm (line SKSVM). We also give the results obtained with the mismatch kernel technique (line MKSVM). Our method (line SVMotifs) surpasses the spectrum and mismatch kernel techniques (100% of good classification), provided that the specificity threshold is optimised. A value of 14 seems to be the best compromise: beyond this threshold the number of discovered motifs is too low for some interleukins, and below motifs are not specific to the interleukin family.

Applied to the SCOP data set, the SKSVM method presents an error rate of 4% while our method only gives 0.12% (8 false positives among 6615 sequences).

The experiments have shown the relevance of hierarchical motifs for the discrimination of protein families. The last ones form a signature in the sense that they are specific to the family studied. We have proposed an algorithm that extracts motifs having a desired degree of specificity. The capacity of SVM to handle high dimensional spaces yields excellent results on the interleukin family: error-free recognition of positives and a very low rate of false negatives on the SCOP database (0.12%). In the future, we intend to work on improving the motif discovery module in order to reduce the cardinal of the motif set.

References

1. V. N. Vapnik, The nature of statistical learning theory, Springer-Verlag, 1995.
2. V. N. Vapnik, Statistical Learning Theory, Springer-Verlag, 1998.
3. B. Scholköpf and I. Guyon and J. Weston, Statistical learning and kernel methods in bioinformatics, in Artificial Intelligence and Heuristic Methods in Bioinformatics, pp 1-21 IOS Press, ed. P. Frasconi and R. Shamir, 2003.
4. T. Jaakola and M. Diekhans and D. Haussler, A discriminative framework for detecting remote protein homologies, Journal of Computationnal Biology, 7(1-2): 95-114, 2000.
5. L. Li and W. S. Noble, Combining pairwise sequence similarity and support vector machines for detecting remote protein evolutionnary and structural relationships, Journal of Computationnal Biology, 10(6): 857-868, 2003.
6. C. Leslie and E. Eskin and W. S. Noble, The spectrum kernel: a string kernel for SVM protein classification, in Proceedings of the Pacific Biocomputing Symposium, pp 564-575, 2002.
7. C. Leslie and E. Eskin and D. Zhou and W. S. Noble, Mismatch String Kernel for SVM protein classification, Bioinformatics, 20(4):467-476, 2004.
8. Murzin A.G. and Brenner S.E. and Hubbard T. and Chothia C. (1995), SCOP: a structural classification of proteins database for the investigation of sequences and structures, Journal of Molecular Biology, 247 pp. 536-540. ISBN 3-540-41066-X, PP. 581-586.

Knowledge Discovery in Lymphoma Cancer from Gene–Expression

Jesús S. Aguilar-Ruiz[1] and Francisco Azuaje[2]

[1] Department of Computer Science, University of Seville, Spain
aguilar@lsi.us.es
[2] School of Computing and Mathematics, University of Ulster
fj.azuaje@ulster.ac.uk

Abstract. A comprehensive study of the database used in Alizadeh et al. [7], about the identification of lymphoma cancer subtypes within *Diffuse Large B–Cell Lymphoma* (DLBCL), is presented in this paper, focused on both the feature selection and classification tasks. Firstly, we tackle with the identification of relevant genes in the prediction of lymphoma cancer types, and lately the discovering of most relevant genes in the *Activated B–Like Lymphoma* and *Germinal Centre B–Like Lymphoma* subtypes within DLBCL. Afterwards, decision trees provide knowledge models to predict both types of lymphoma and subtypes within DLBCL. The main conclusion of our work is that the data may be insufficient to exactly predict lymphoma or even extract functionally relevant genes.

1 Introduction

In the last two decades, a better understanding of the immune system and the genetic abnormalities asociated with non–Hodgin's lymphoma (NHL) have led to the identification of several previously unrecognized types or subtypes of lymphoma.

Advances in technology are allowing to screen large numbers of genes, what fosters a considerable increase of research in favour of desease diagnosis. The gene–expression profiling might became, to a certain extent, a promoter of the prognosis advance, as the activity of a group of genes can define premises about the behaviour of specific tumours. These techniques, based on micro–array analysis, provide a great amount of numeric information, which should be processed with sofisticated algorithms that are capable of extracting useful knowledge for the domain expert, in this case, the physician or biologist. In fact, gene–expression profiling is thought to be a revolutionary technique for the cancer diagnosis [1].

A first approach to the study of genetic information consists in applying some statistical techniques, although in many cases these cannot extract valid knowledge from data. Thus, the Knowledge Discovery in Databases (KDD) [2] appears like a useful framework for many researchers from different fields. In particular, the identification of relevant genes, so–called *feature selection* [3], for the prediction of disease types (or subtypes) states great interest in this field. Other theoretical variant within KDD is the searching of behaviour patterns within information, and it is called *clustering* [4]. Without any doubt, the most encouraging technique, due to its repercussion, is the *classification* [5], by using generally *decision trees* [6], as they will help to predict types or subtypes of diseases. From the point of view of the patients, these techniques will avoid that some of them must undergo aggressive treatments, as we would know whether their genetic profiles match one or another subtype of desease.

In this paper, we carry out an exhaustive study of a database well–known in the scientific community: the one used by Alizadeh et al. [7], about the identification of lymphoma cancer subtypes within *Diffuse Large B–Cell Lymphoma* (DLBCL), with 4026 genes and 96 patients. DLBCL is the most common subtype of non–Hodgkin's lymphoma, and there are no reliable indicators -morphological, clinical, immunohistochemical or genetic- that can be used to recognize subtypes of DLBCL and point to a different therapeutic approach to patients [8].

Firstly, we tackle with feature selection techniques, for the identification of relevant genes in the prediction of lymphoma cancer types, as for the identificacion of most relevant genes in the *Activated B–Like Lymphoma* and *Germinal Centre B–Like Lymphoma* subtypes within DLBCL. Among them, the information gain criterion, based on the entropy measure, the Relief method and $\chi 2$ ranking and filtering, have been selected. Afterwards, decision trees provide knowledge for the classification task..

Our study revealed that not only the genes identified by Alizadeh et al. are relevant for the prediction of the two subtypes of DLBCL, but many others can have the same consideration. In fact, many decision trees can be built by using non–identified as relevant genes, producing similar error rate for the classification task. In general, KDD techniques demonstrate to be efficient for extracting valid and very useful knowledge from biomedical data.

2 Feature Selection in Gene–Expression

Attribute or feature subset selection is the process of identifying and removing as much of the irrelevant and redundant information as possible. Decreasing the dimensionality of the data reduces the size of the hypothesis space and allows learning algorithms to operate faster and more effectively, leading to smaller and easily–to–understand knowledge models of the target concept. Feature selection techniques produce ranked lists of attributes, providing the data analyst with insight into their data by clearly demonstrating the relative merit of individual attributes.

In this study, we used three feature selection techniques, both belonging to the *filter* category [9], *Information Gain Attribute Ranking*, ReliefF [10, 11] and χ^2 [12]. The information gain attribute ranking is often used where the sheer dimensionality of the data precludes more sophisticated attribute selection techniques, as the case being investigated here on lymphoma cancer, with 4026 attributes. ReliefF works by randomly sampling an instance from the data and

Table 1. Most relevant genes provided by Relief, InfoGain and χ^2, ordered by ranking.

ReliefF	Freq.	InfoGain	Freq.	χ^2	Freq.	ReliefF	Freq.	InfoGain	Freq.	χ^2	Freq.
G1610X	•••	G707X	••	G2400X	•••	G717X	••	G467X	••	G2202X	•
G1636X	•	G655X	•••	G788X	••	G2403X	•••	G646X	••	G2199X	••
G1648X	•	G694X	•••	G3639X	••	G2270X	•	G3639X	••	G844X	••
G1622X	•••	G1622X	•••	G707X	••	G784X	•	G2395X	••	G777X	••
G1702X	•	G844X	••	G655X	•••	G2486X	•	G2668X	••	G654X	••
G653X	•	G1635X	••	G1992X	•	G1603X	•	G788X	••	G1990X	•
G1637X	•	G2400X	•••	G1675X	••	G2489X	•	G1672X	•	G2424X	••
G712X	••	G1610X	•••	G694X	•••	G703X	•	G2379X	•	G276X	•
G1607X	•	G717X	••	G3767X	•	G692X	•	G770X	••	G2862X	•
G611X	•	G711X	•	G769X	•	G2271X	•	G648X	•	G794X	•
G1647X	•	G639X	••	G2387X	••	G2401X	•	G642X	•	G770X	••
G708X	••	G2402X	••	G1622X	•••	G1653X	•	G593X	•	G768X	•
G1651X	•	G769X	••	G1610X	•••	G1646X	•	G1606X	•	G2778X	•
G2402X	••	G641X	•	G2032X	•	G2244X	•	G734X	•	G3764X	•
G537X	•	G628X	•	G467X	••	G694X	•••	G604X	•	G2395X	••
G1658X	•	G669X	•	G3685X	•	G655X	•••	G777X	••	G2374X	••
G654X	••	G2403X	•••	G2403X	•••	G538X	•	G1673X	•	G1324X	•
G1608X	•	G647X	•	G1371X	•	G731X	•	G2374X	••	G1343X	•
G2393X	•	G712X	••	G2033X	•	G2668X	••	G2199X	•	G2795X	•
G1641X	•	G783X	••	G646X	••	G584X	•	G649X	•	G653X	•••
G721X	•	G653X	•••	G753X	•••	G1776X	•	G708X	••	G1320X	•
G651X	•	G691X	•	G783X	••	G713X	•	G1675X	••	G3334X	•
G1644X	•	G753X	•••	G764X	•	G2400X	•••	G2387X	••	G2000X	•
G1635X	••	G2495X	•	G639X	••	G710X	•	G2424X	••	G473X	•
G753X	•••	G651X	••	G2428X	•	G714X	•	G706X	•	G1323X	•

then locating its nearest neighbour (or k nearest neighbours when there is noise in data and weighting their contributions by the prior probability of each class when data contains multiple classes) from the same and a different class. The values of the attributes of the nearest neighbours are compared to the sampled instance and used to update relevance scores for each attribute. The rationale is that a useful attribute should differentiate between instances from different classes and have the same value for instances from the same class. χ^2 statistic conducts a significance test on the relationship between the values of an attribute and the classes.

In our study, we present results for the original set of genes (4026) and for 50 genes selected from the 4026 genes, as in the paper from Alizadeh et al. [7].

2.1 Lymphoid Malignancies

The three methods provided different results and they were compared to find coincidences. Table 1 shows the genes selected by each method, and ordered by their relevance from top to bottom. We found 8 common genes for the three methods, 25 common pairs of genes and 76 without pair or trio. Note that there are 105 different genes in Table 1, from 150 possible choices.

In Figure 1 appear the genes which have been selected by three feature selection methods (*very high relevance*) and by any two of them (*high relevance*). In total, we have 8 very high relevant genes and 25 high relevant genes. We would like to know whether these 8 very high relevant genes or, in the worst case, the 33 genes including the high relevant ones, can predict any type of cancer by using a decision trees, as we will shown later, in section 3. Alizadeh et al. discovered 50

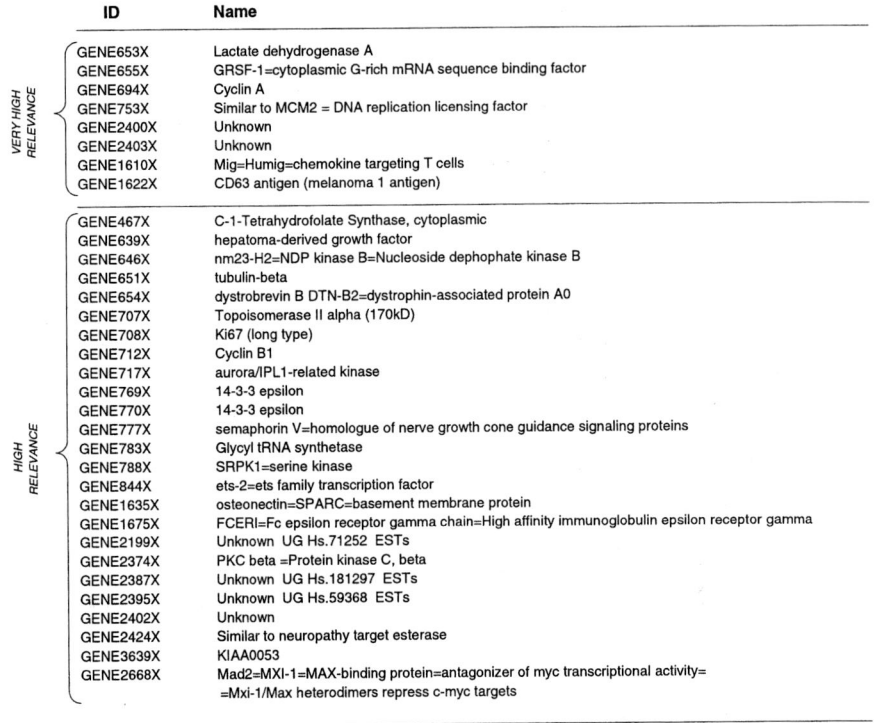

Fig. 1. Relevant genes to differentiate the types of lymphoma cancer from the complete dataset (96 patients and 4026 attributes). Firstly, the 50 most relevant genes for each feature selection method were selected. So, *very high relevant* means that the gen was relevant for the three methods; *high relevant* means that it was relevant for any two methods. There is no order of relevance in the list.

relevant genes to differentiate the GC B–Like from Activated B–Like subtypes of DLBCL (supplemental Figure 3 in their work, not published in the paper but in the webpage), and only one of them, GENE2395X, also appeared in our list.

It is important to note that several attributes are strongly correlated with others (correlation coefficient greater than 0.90), even among these selected as very high or high relevant in Figure 1. This fact shows that, firstly, most methods for feature selection does not taken into account the correlation among extracted features; and secondly, therefore, this information needs to be post–processed, removing genes of similar functionality.

2.2 DLBCL Subtypes

There exist 45 patients with DLBCL, so we are now interested in the two subtypes of DLBCL: Activated B–like DLBCL (ACL) and Germinal Centre B–like

ID	Name
GENE1296X	MCL1=myeloid cell differentiation protein
GENE1719X	TTG-2=Rhombotin-2=translocated in t(11;14)(p13;q11) T cell acute lymphocytic leukemia=cysteine rich protein with LIM motif
GENE1720X	TTG-2=Rhombotin-2=translocated in t(11;14)(p13;q11) T cell acute lymphocytic leukemia=cysteine rich protein with LIM motif
GENE3228X	JNK3=Stress-activated protein kinase
GENE3254X	Unknown UG Hs.145058 ESTs
GENE3255X	Unknown
GENE3256X	JAW1=lymphoid-restricted membrane protein
GENE3258X	JAW1=lymphoid-restricted membrane protein
GENE3259X	Unknown UG Hs.124922 ESTs
GENE3261X	Unknown
GENE3314X	Unknown
GENE3315X	FMR2=Fragile X mental retardation 2=putative transcription factor=LAF-4 and AF-4 homologue
GENE3318X	CD10=CALLA=Neprilysin=enkepalinase
GENE3325X	Unknown UG Hs.120245 Homo sapiens mRNA for KIAA1039 protein, partial cds
GENE3326X	Unknown UG Hs.105261 EST
GENE3327X	Unknown UG Hs.169565 ESTs, Moderately similar to !!!! ALU SUBFAMILY SB WARNING ENTRY !!!! [H.sapiens]
GENE3328X	Unknown UG Hs.136345 ESTs
GENE3329X	Unknown UG Hs.224323 ESTs, Moderately similar to alternatively spliced product using exon 13A [H.sapiens]
GENE3330X	Unknown
GENE3331X	Unknown UG Hs.208410 EST, Moderately similar to !!!! ALU SUBFAMILY SB WARNING ENTRY !!!! [H.sapiens]
GENE3332X	Unknown UG Hs.120716 ESTs
GENE3335X	myb-related gene A=A-myb
GENE3355X	Unknown
GENE3939X	Unknown UG Hs.169081 ets variant gene 6 (TEL oncogene)
GENE3968X	Deoxycytidylate deaminase

(VERY HIGH RELEVANCE)

Fig. 2. Relevant genes to differentiate Activated B–like DLBCL from Germinal Centre B–like DLBCL (45 patients and 4026 attributes). Firstly, the 50 most relevant genes for each feature selection method were selected. There is no order of relevance in the list.

DLBCL (GCL). Among these 45 examples, we find 22 belonging to class GCL and 23 to class ACL.

We have done experiments by using the Relief algorithm, InfoGain and χ^2 methods to select the most relevant attributes. The three methods provided 25 common attributes, which will be considered as very high relevant, and they are enumerated in Figure 2.

Figures 1 and 2 do not have genes in common. It seems like differentiating among types of lymphoma cancer involves different genes as between subtypes of lymphoma within DLBCL. Nevertheless, several genes which experts had identified as having some functionality associated with lymphoma, are present in the subset, among them, TTG–2 and CD10. In addition, others like MCL1, JNK3 or FMR2, are so far not related with DLBCL.

3 Decision Trees

Decision trees are a particularly useful technique in the context of supervised learning because they perform classification by a sequence of tests whose semantics are intuitively clear and easy to understand. Some tools, like J48, construct decision trees selecting the best attribute by using a statistical test to determine how well it alone classifies the training examples. Our experiments were carried out by using the WEKA library for machine learning [13].

To avoid statistical problem of over-estimating prediction accuracy that occurs when a model is trained and evaluated with the same samples, we used the "leave-one-out" testing method, i.e. a 45–fold cross–validation when the interest resides in differentiating subtypes of DLBCL.

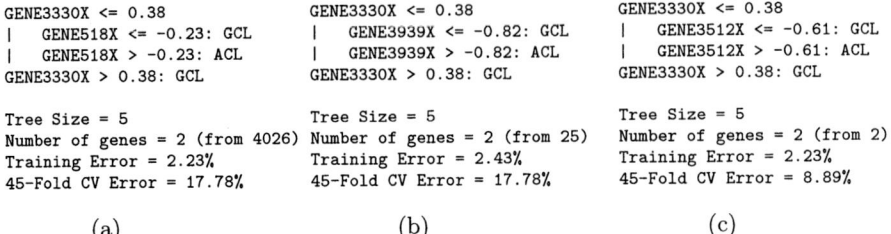

Fig. 3. All of the decision trees were generated using 45 patients. However, in (a) 4026 genes were used (the whole set); in (b) 25 genes (very high relevant); and in (c) only 2 genes (randomly chosen from sampling).

3.1 Prediction in DLBCL Subtypes

Based on medical research about the significance of specific genes to differentiate subtypes of DLBCL, we have selected 5 genes which seem to play an important role. They are those which are related to CD10 (GENE3317X, GENE3318X and GENE3319X), BCL–6 (GENE3340X and GENE3341X), TTG–2 (GENE-1719X and GENE1720X), IRF–4 (GENE1212X and GENE1213X) and BCL–2 (GENE2514X, GENE2536X, GENE2537X, GENE2538X), and also some genes belonging to the BCL–2 family (GENE385X, GENE386X, GENE387X, GENE3619X and GENE3620X). The importance of these genes has already been proven by Azuaje by means of simplified fuzzy ARTMAP, a neural network–based model [14].

To differentiate among subtypes within DLBCL, ACL and GCL, we also produced three decision trees. Two genes were sufficient to build the trees, which share the gen GENE3330X, what seems to be interesting as it might play an important role for this task. However, this gene can be combined with many others without considerably increasing the error rate. In fact, we randomly select an a priori non–relevant gene, the gene GENE3512X, and the error rate was even lower than before, about 8.8% (leave–one–out). Therefore, we can state that the difference in relevance among the more important genes -about three hundreds- is very slight.

Results provided by the decision tree used only four genes (GENE1719X, GEN3318X, GENE3340X and GENE385X) and the error rate was 0% (training) and 26.67% (leave–one–out). The overfitting was very high, and therefore, these genes are not appropriate to predict accurately the subtype of DLBCL.

4 Discussion

A more complex analysis consisted of using a neigbourhood–based feature selection method, as ReliefF, to extract 100 genes. Afterwards, another feature selection method based on correlation of gene subset with respect to the class, as CSF [9], was applied and it selected 34 genes. From these genes, we selected only four genes, those with correlation near zero among them (GENE3355X,

GENE2116X, GENE404X, GENE3821X). Finally, an principal component analysis transformed this four genes into one expression, which was evaluated with J48 by using leave–one–out testing. The result, shown in Figure 4, was 2.22% of error rate, predicting accurately all the cases of GCL and just one error for ACL. It is worthy to note that all of the selected genes are labelled as "unknown" in the database. This gives an idea of the non–lineal inter–relationship among genes to predict lymphoma subtypes.

```
NewAttribute = 0.459 GENE3355X +
               0.514 GENE2116X +
               0.459 GENE404X  +
               0.561 GENE3821X

NewAttribute <= 1.000338: ACL (23.0)
NewAttribute >  1.000338: GCL (22.0)

45-Fold CV Error = 2.22%
```

Fig. 4. Decision tree generated by J48 after two feature selection methods (Relief+CSF) and transformations of attributes by means of principal components.

5 Conclusions

A complete study of the database used in Alizadeh et al. [7] is presented in this paper, focused on both the feature selection and classification tasks.

From the biomedical point of view, we can state that the known relevance of specific genes is not present in our conclusions, perhaps because other genes play a more important role than those previously known as relevant. However, this conclusion cannot be strongly based in results, as these have been obtained from a small amount of patients, in comparison to the large number of genes.

Analysing the data, as experts on data mining, we have appreciate that data are insufficient to properly state many observations. Many subsets of genes can achieve a good prediction, although most of them would provide an overfitted decision tree. Some genes are very important indeed, but we would need more data to guarantee this fact. Alizadeh et al. stated that a subset of genes could differentiate among two subtypes of DLBCL, even though not only one subset of genes can do that, as we have proven.

The study reveals the importance of non–linear inter–dependencies among genes in order to find functional relationships or to build prediction models as an interesting future research direction.

Acknowledgements

The research was supported by the Spanish Research Agency CICYT under grant TIC2001–1143–C03–02.

References

1. A. A. Alizadeh, M. Eisen, D. Botstain, P. O. Brown, and L. M. Staudt, "Probing lymphocyte biology by genomic-scale gene expression analysis," *Journal of Clinical Immunology*, , no. 18, pp. 373–379, 1998.
2. Jiawei Han and Micheline Kamber, *Data Mining – Concepts and Techniques*, Morgan Kaufmann, 2001.
3. Huan Liu and Hiroshi Motoda, *Feature Selection for Knowledge discovery and Data Mining*, Kluwer Academic Publishers, 1998.
4. K. C. Gowda and G. Krishna, "Agglomerative clustering using the concept of mutual nearest neighborhood," *Pattern Recognition*, vol. 10, pp. 105–112, 1977.
5. A. D. Gordon, *Classification*, Chapman & Hall/CRC, 1999.
6. L. Breiman, J. H. Friedman, R. A. Olshen, and C. J. Stone, *Classification and regression trees*, Wadsworth International Group, Belmont, CA, 1984.
7. Ash A. Alizadeh et al., "Distinct types of diffuse large b-cell lymphoma identified by gene expression profiling," *Nature*, vol. 403, pp. 503–511, 2000.
8. N. L. Harris, E. S. Jaffe, J. Diebold, G. Flandrin, H. K. Muller-Hermelink, J. Vardiman, T. A. Lister, and C. D. Bloomfield, "World health organization classification of neoplastic diseases of the hematopoietic and lymphoid tissues: Report of the clinical advisory committee meeting–airlie house, virginia, november 1997," *Journal of Clinical Oncology*, vol. 17, pp. 3835–3849, 1999.
9. M. A. Hall, *Correlation–based feature selection for machine learning*, Ph.d., Department of Computer Science, University of Waikato, New Zealand, 1998.
10. K. Kira and L. Rendell, "A practical approach to feature selection," in *Proceedings of the Ninth International Conference on Machine Learning*, 1992, pp. 249–256.
11. I. Kononenko, "Estimating attributes: analysis and extensions of relief," in *Proceedings of European Conference on Machine Learning*. 1994, Springer-Verlag.
12. H. Liu and R. Setiono, "Chi2: Feature selection and discretization of numeric attributes," in *Proceedings of the Seventh IEEE International Conference on Tools with Artificial Intelligence*, 1995.
13. I. H. Witten and E. Frank, *Data Mining: Practical Machine Learning Tools and Techniques with Java Implementations*, Morgan Kaufmann, 2000.
14. Francisco Azuaje, "A computational neural approach to support discovery of gene function and classes of cancer," *IEEE Transactions on Biomedical Engineering*, vol. 48, no. 3, pp. 332–339, 2001.
15. R. C. Holte, "Very simple classification rules perform well on most commonly used datasets," *Machine learning*, vol. 11, pp. 63–91, 1993.

A Method of Filtering Protein Surface Motifs Based on Similarity Among Local Surfaces

Nripendra Lal Shrestha[1], Youhei Kawaguchi[1],
Tadasuke Nakagawa[2], and Takenao Ohkawa[1]

[1] Graduate School of Information Science and Technology, Osaka University
{nripen_s,kawaguch,ohkawa}@ist.osaka-u.ac.jp
[2] Hitachi, Ltd., System Development Laboratory
tadasuke@sdl.hitachi.co.jp

Abstract. We have developed a system for extracting surface motifs from protein molecular surface database called SUrface MOtif mining MOdule (SUMOMO). However, SUMOMO tends to extract a large amount of surface motifs making it difficult to distinguish whether they are true active sites. Since active sites, from proteins having a particular function, have similar shape and physical properties, proteins can be classified based on similarity among local surfaces. Thus, motifs extracted from proteins from the same group can be considered significant, and rest can be filtered out. The proposed method is applied to 3,183 surface motifs extracted from 15 proteins belonging to each of four function groups. As a result, the number of motifs is reduced to 14.1% without elimination of important motifs that correspond to the four functional sites.

1 Introduction

The functions of a protein are expressed through localized functional structures called active sites. Protein surface motifs can be defined as commonly appearing patterns of shape and physical properties in protein molecular surfaces, and can be considered as "possible active sites".We have developed a system for extracting surface motifs from protein molecular surface database called SUrface MOtif mining MOdule (SUMOMO) [1].

Before extracting surface motifs, each protein molecular surface data from eF-site[1] is converted into normal vectors with attributes[2] such that the surfaces can be compared as projections and depressions. A normal vector with attributes (shown in Fig.1) is a normal vector at the apex of an irregular surface of high curvatures, with attributes of curvature and physical properties, viz., electrostatic potential, hydrophobicity, etc., of the surface attached to it [2].

In SUMOMO, a given set of protein molecular surfaces is divided into several small surfaces consisting of a pair of normal vectors, as shown in Fig. 2, called *unit surfaces*. Then, using multi-dimensional buckets, unit surfaces are sorted

---
[1] http://ef-site.protein.osaka-u.ac.jp/eF-site/

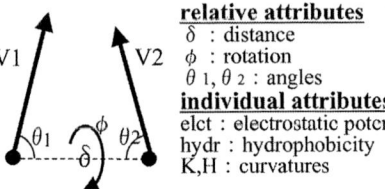

Fig. 1. Normal vectors with attributes.   **Fig. 2.** Vector pairs.

and extracted according to their relative as well as individual attributes. Each of the vector pairs in a sets of similar vector pairs, which have relatively larger number of vector pairs in them, are potential surface surface motifs, and collectively called *candidate motifs*. Candidate motifs are repeatatively merged and output as surface motifs.

SUMOMO extracts surface motifs only focusing on similarity of local structures from different combination of proteins. As all of the similar localized structures cannot be functional structures, all of the extracted surface motifs cannot be related to function. As a result, even the insignificant structures get extracted. For example, 3183 surface motifs are extracted from 15 proteins, and motifs corresponding to all four types of active sites are recognized. However, the task of confirming whether 3183 surface motifs correspond to the active sites of 15 proteins involves an immense amount of time and effort.

In this paper, we shall address to the issue of filtering significant surface motifs out of a large quantity of motifs extracted using SUMOMO.

2 Filtering Surface Motifs

2.1 Approach to Filtering

An approach to filter surface motifs is to extract surface motifs from proteins having the identical functions. However, the primary goal of motif extraction is to discover functional structures from proteins whose functions are not yet known.

In order to filter surface motifs, it is important to perceive the characteristics of active sites and associate them with surface motifs. As local molecular surface structures of active sites are highly conserved, they can be seen occurring commonly in some proteins. Nevertheless, active sites require specific structures to express functions, and instead of occurring as merely abundant ones, active sites occur in proteins with similar functions as structures with common shapes and properties. Therefore, as shown in Fig. 3, by grouping proteins based upon the similarity of local structures, surface motifs which occur frequently within the same group of proteins are filtered as significant motifs.

Considering surface motifs as a kind of local structures occurring in a number of proteins, the proteins from which particular surface motifs are extracted have similar local structures. Hence, similarity among the proteins can be determined

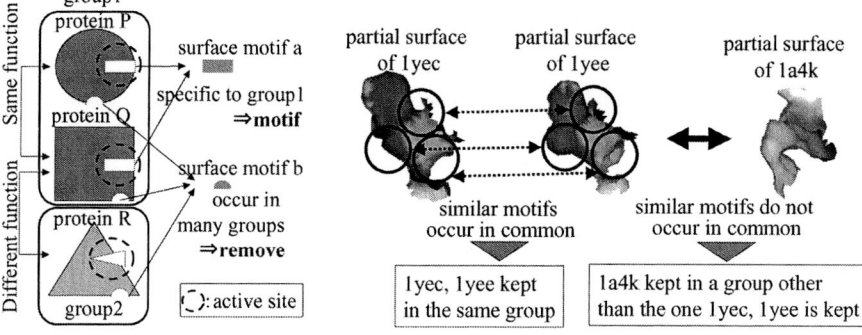

Fig. 3. Difference in significance of motifs.

Fig. 4. Grouping based on surface motifs.

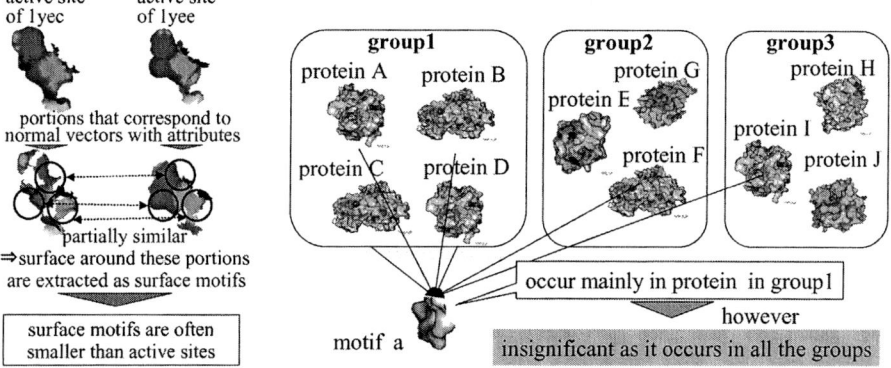

Fig. 5. Same active site composed of different motifs.

Fig. 6. Exclusion of a characteristic surface motif.

by focusing on surface motifs common to the both. In example shown in Fig. 4 the portions common in both (marked by circles) 1yec and 1yee are extracted as surface motifs. So these proteins can be said to have high degree of similarity, and classified into the same group.

Moreover, the structures corresponding to active sites tend to be composed of several surface motifs. As shown in Fig. 5 active sites are often composed of several discontinuous surface motifs. Therefore, proteins can be grouped focusing on the similarity among *adjacent motif sets*, which can be defined as the sets of surface motifs close to each other around the same area on the molecular surface. Thereby, using adjacent motifs sets, proteins can be compared more precisely at local structures comparable to active sites.

Finally, for each classified group, the degree of significance of the shapes which characterizes each classified group must be evaluated. As the primary criterion, only those surface motifs which are extracted from the same group of proteins are distinguished as potential active sites. However, as shown in Fig. 6 some surface motifs found frequently within a group can also found within other groups. To prevent exclusion of such surface motifs, it is necessary to apply flexible metrics to discriminate characteristics of surface motifs.

The problem of discriminating surface motifs is similar to the problem of determining significance of terms in documents. As such, by considering protein groups as documents, proteins as sentences, and surface motifs as terms, and applying the concept of significance of terms to surface motifs, unnecessary surface motifs can be removed.

2.2 Expression of Proteins Based on Extracted Motifs

Similarity of proteins is determined based upon the common occurance of surface motifs. A simple method is to express a protein in terms of vector (hereinafter, protein vector) with dimension equal to the number of surface motifs extracted, with values 1 to represent presence, and 0 otherwise.

However, without considering the size of surface motifs, mere information about presence or absence is insufficient to figure out similarity of proteins. Thus, for each element in a protein vector is assigned the value of number of normal vectors composing the respective surface motif. Each protein can be expressed as protein vector defined as:

$$P = (p_1, p_2, ..., p_i, ..., p_n),$$

where n is the total number of motifs extracted and $p_i (1 \leq i \leq n)$ is the number of composing normal vectors for each surface motif.

2.3 Similarity of Proteins Focused on Adjacent Motif Sets

Since surface motifs can be found concentrated around active sites, motifs belonging to adjacent motif sets can be discriminated as significant. While evaluating similarity between two proteins, a surface motif can exist as a member of adjacent motif set in a protein, but can have an isolated existence in another. Therefore, such surface motifs cannot be taken into consideration for evaluating the similarity between two proteins. As shown in Fig. 7, in protein P motifs a, b, c are members of adjacent motif sets. While comparing proteins P and Q, both have a, b, c as adjacently located motifs, but in case of P and R, motif b is isolated from motifs a and b. Hence, P and R, as well as Q and R, have to be compared focusing on motifs a and c, unlike P and Q, which can be compared focusing on all of the motifs a, b and c.

Proteins are expressed as protein vectors, and their similarity is calculated using cosine of the vectors. Similarity $S(P,Q)$ between any two proteins P,Q is defined as:

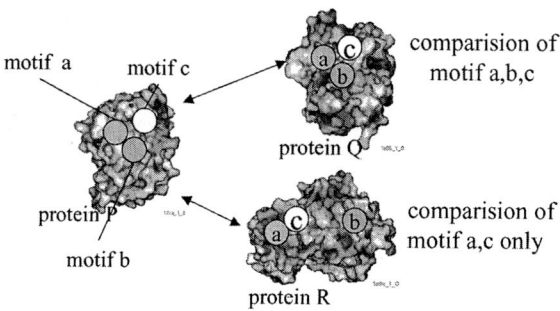

Fig. 7. Protein similarity and adjacent motif sets.

$$S(P,Q) = \frac{P' \cdot Q'}{||P|| \cdot ||Q'||} = \frac{\sum_i p'_i q'_i}{\sqrt{\sum_i p'^2_i}\sqrt{\sum_i q'^2_i}},$$

where $P'(p'_1, p'_2, ..., p'_n)$, $Q'(q'_1, q'_2, ..., q'_n)$, are protein vectors with values of elements which do not exist in common adjacent motif sets set as 0, and n is the number of input surface motifs for the system. Furthermore, for clustering, the distance $D(P,Q)$ between proteins P,Q is defined as:

$$D(P,Q) = 1 - S(P,Q).$$

2.4 Clustering of Proteins

Since the types of targeted functions is variable, the number for clusters to be formed cannot be determined uniquely. During clustering, the minute differences among the partial surfaces have to be neglected. Thereby, agglomerative clustering is applied.

In order to evaluate clusters for agglomeration, it is necessary to calculate the threshold value T_{cl} for the distance between a newly formed cluster and pre-existent clusters. Surface motifs extracted from as set of 39 proteins having 10 known functions were clustered by nearest neighbor method, furthest neighbour method, Ward method, and flexible-beta method. As the result, flexible-beta method yielded the clustering optimum for the need of classification.

2.5 Significance of Surface Motif

Significance of the surface motif can be evaluated on the analogy of term weighting in the field of document analysis. A number methods of term weighting have already been proposed [3]. TF (Term Frequency) is a measure of how often a term is found in a collection of documents. IDF (Inverse Document Frequency) is a measure of how rare a term is in a collection, calculated by total collection size divided by the number of documents containing the term.

As active sites with similar shapes are unevenly distributed across a certain groups of proteins, to discriminate whether shape of a surface motif characterizes a group, we have to consider both, the common occurrence in proteins within the same group, as well as exclusive occurrence across different groups. Coupling the concepts of TF and IDF, the degree of significance E_i of a surface motif i can be defined as:

$$E_i = \max_j(TF_{ij} \times (\log \frac{N}{DF_i} + 1)),$$

where N is number of groups of proteins, TF_{ij} is the frequency of surface motif i in protein group j, and DF_i is the number of groups in which surface motif i occurs.

By removing the motifs with significance less than a threshold value T_e, filtering of surface motifs is achieved.

3 Evaluations and Results

Tuning of Thresholds. As the results of tuning, the threshold for distance between proteins to discriminate the cluster each protein belongs to (T_{cl}) was found to be 0.95 and the threshold for significance of surface motifs such that each cluster represents a function (T_e) was found to be 1.6.

Evaluation of Filtering Methods. 3183 surface motifs extracted from 15 proteins having four known functions were extracted by SUMOMO and subjected to filtering by three different methods, viz., filtering by clustering only, filtering by focusing on adjacent motif sets only, and filtering by the proposed method. Table 1 shows the list of interacting ligands (functions) and respective proteins.

Table 1. Input protein data set.

ligands	proteins
SGA	1brr, 1fwu, 1fwv
MET	1inn, 1j6w, 1j6x, 1qq9
TYD	1e2g, 1gtv, 1h5t, 1ket, 1kew
PNB	1yec, 1yee, 1yeh

Table 2. Result of Filtering.

method	no. of motifs	percent. of motifs left	no. of func.
clustering only	764	24%	4
adjacent motif sets only	1,194	37.5%	3
proposed method	448	14.1%	4

From Table 2, we can confirm that the proposed method can filter more surface motifs than the other methods without eliminating important motifs that correspond to all of the known functional sites.

4 Conclusion

In this paper, we proposed a method of filtering protein surface motifs extracted from SUMOMO. In this method, proteins are expressed in terms of surface motifs extracted, the concept of finding similarity among protein using adjacent motif set is introduced, and also the significance of surface motifs is defined. Then, using the proposed method insignificant surface motifs were filtered reducing the number of surface motifs upto 14.1% without any loss in the number of functions.

Presently, surface motifs extracted by SUMOMO is expressed by a collection of normal vectors of source proteins, unlike sequence motifs which use regular expressions to generalize into single expression. Generalized expression of surface motif will not only help in query of functions and proteins for a given surface motif, but also adjacent motif sets can be expressed as a single, larger surface motif. This may help in reducing the number of surface motifs actually extracted by SUMOMO. To generalize the expression of surface motifs can be regarded as a future issue.

The authors thank Prof. Norihisa Komoda and Prof. Haruki Nakamura who offered useful discussion related to this research. A part of this research was supported by BIRD of Japan Science and Technology Corporation and Grant-in-Aid for Scientific Research of the Ministry of Education, Culture, Sports, Science and Technology.

References

1. N. L. Shrestha, Y. Kawaguchi and T. Ohkawa: "A method for extraction of surface motifs from protein molecular surface database using normal vectors with attributes," *Proc. 5th Int. Conf. on Computational Biology and Genome Informatics*, pp.911-914, (2003).
2. Y. Kaneta, N. Shoji, T. Ohkawa, and H. Nakamura: "A Method of Comparing Protein Molecular Surface Based on Normal Vectors with Attributes and Its Application to Function Identification," *Information Sciences*, Vol.146, Issue.1-4, pp.41-54 (2002).
3. Y. Yang: "An evaluation of statistical approaches to text categorization," *J. Information Retrieval*, Vol.1, No.1/2, pp.67–88 (1999).

Qualified Predictions for Proteomics Pattern Diagnostics with Confidence Machines

Zhiyuan Luo, Tony Bellotti, and Alex Gammerman

Computer Learning Research Centre, Royal Holloway, University of London
Egham, Surrey TW20 0EX, UK
{zhiyuan,tony,alex}@cs.rhul.ac.uk

Abstract. In this paper, we focus on the problem of prediction with confidence and describe the recently developed transductive confidence machines (TCM). TCM allows us to make predictions within predefined confidence levels, thus providing a controlled and calibrated classification environment. We apply the TCM to the problem of proteomics pattern diagnostics. We demonstrate that the TCM performs well, yielding accurate, well-calibrated and informative predictions in both online and offline learning settings.

1 Introduction

Recent advances in biotechnology and the human genome project have presented a new horizon for early detection and diagnosis of human diseases. One such advancement is the development of protein mass spectrometry (MS) and the ability to analyse biologically complex samples using this technique. MS technology produces a graph (profile) of the relative abundance of ionized protein/peptides (y-axis) versus their mass-to-charge (m/z) ratios (x-axis) for each biological sample. These MS data are typically characterised by a large number of attributes and relatively few samples. In addition, these data often contain technical noise which can be introduced at a number of different stages in the experiment process and biological noise which can come from non-uniform genetic backgrounds of the samples being compared. All these present new challenges to data analysis and pattern recognition.

There has been much interest in proteomics pattern diagnostics recently, that is, using patterns in proteomic mass spectra derived from serum to differentiate samples from patients both with and without diseases [3,7,8]. Due to the noisy nature and high dimensionality of the MS data, pre-processing and feature selection methods are applied to the raw data to find out the feature sets which can then be used for classification. Different classification approaches, including conventional statistical methods, machine learning approaches and modern classification algorithms, have been tried to deal with the MS data. Despite the success of these proteomics pattern diagnostics [3,7,8], the learning techniques used can only provide bare predictions, i.e. algorithms predicting labels for new examples without saying how reliable these predictions are.

In this paper, we focus on the problem of prediction with confidence and describe the recently developed transductive confidence machines (TCM) which can provide valid and well-calibrated confidence measures [2, 6]. This allows us to make predictions within predefined confidence levels, thus providing a controlled and calibrated classification environment. We implement TCM on two representative classification methods, and apply these TCM implementations with proteomic datasets in both online and offline learning settings. Experimental results show that TCM can provide accurate classifications and most importantly the prediction results are well-calibrated.

2   Transductive Confidence Machines

Transductive confidence machines (TCM) are supervised machine learning algorithms that make a prediction regarding a new object based on a training sequence, without the explicit use of a generalization rule. In proteomics pattern diagnostics, a sequence of training examples of objects x_i with labels y_i, where x_i are multi-dimensional peak vectors and y_i are diagnostics taking only finite number of values such as {normal, cancer, benign}, for $i = 1$ to $n - 1$, is given, then a prediction for a new unlabelled object x_n is made.

In confidence machines, the problem of prediction with confidence is formalised as that of computing "predictive regions" (sets of labels) rather than bare predictions. Prior to classification we set a confidence level $1 - \delta$ for $0 \leq \delta \leq 1$. For each new example, we predict the set of labels,

$$R = \{y : p_y > \delta\} \cup \{\arg\max_y(p_y)\} \tag{1}$$

which includes all labels with a p-value greater than δ, but also ensures that at least one label is always predicted by including the label with the highest p-value. If $|R| = 1$, i.e. only one label is predicted, it is called a **certain prediction**. Otherwise, if $|R| > 1$, it is an **uncertain prediction**. A prediction is correct if the true label for the example is a member of the predicted region. Otherwise it is an error.

In the TCM algorithm, p-values are calculated for each possible label prediction $y_n = y$, based on "strangeness values" α_i that are calculated for each example and indicate how "strange", or how typical, each example is with respect to the entire sequence. Intuitively an object is considered strange if it is in the middle of objects labelled in a different way and is far from the objects labelled in the same way. The p-value for each (x_n, y) is then calculated as,

$$p_y = \frac{\#\{i : \alpha_i \geq \alpha_n\}}{n}.$$

Clearly, $0 < p_y \leq 1$. Intuitively, the greater the value of p_y, the more typical the new example (x_n, y) is of the training sequence. The use of p-values in this context is related to the Martin-Löf test for randomness [2]. Indeed, the p-values generated by TCM form a valid randomness test, under the the iid (independently and identically distributed) assumption.

TCM can be applied in different learning settings: online and offline. In online setting, examples are presented one by one. The classifier takes x_i, predicts $\hat{y}_i$, and then gets a feedback y_i. The new example (x_i, y_i) is then included in the training set for the next trial. In the offline setting, the classifier is given a training set $(x_1, y_1), (x_2, y_2), ..., (x_n, y_n)$ to predict on $x_{n+1}, x_{n+2}, ..., x_{n+k}$. It has been proved that TCM is well-calibrated for online learning, in the sense that in the long run the predictions are wrong with relative frequency at most δ [1]. This is done by showing that the sequence of prediction outcomes (i.e. whether correct or an error) is bounded by a Bernoulli sequence [6]. This is always true regardless of which strangeness measure is used so long as it has the exchangeability property.

Construction of a TCM relies on the definition of a strangeness measure. Once the strangeness measures are calculated, TCM makes a transition from strangeness measure to a region predictor. In the next section, we will describe how to define strangeness measures for the support vector machines and nearest centroid algorithms.

3 Experiments

3.1 Dataset

The proteomic dataset used in this paper, "Ovarian Dataset 8-7-02", is publicly available from the web (http://ncifdaproteomics.com/download-ovar.php). The ovarian dataset has 91 normal cases and 162 cancer cases. Each case is presented in a text file with two columns: the first column is a list of 15154 m/z values and the second column shows the corresponding intensities. Note that the m/z values reported are common across all the files.

Based on the data pre-processing and feature selection methods described in [1], 9 significant peak regions are identified, with m/z values equal to: 64, 245, 434, 618, 886, 1531, 3010, 3200 and 8033. Only the intensity values at these regions are input to the TCM for experiments.

3.2 Methods

The implementations of TCM on support vector machines and nearest centroid algorithms are presented.

Support vector machines (SVM) are effective learning systems based on statistical learning theory and have been applied successfully to many real problems [5]. For pattern recognition, SVM finds the hyperplane that separates the data set $(x_1, y_1), ..., (x_l, y_l), x_i \in \mathbf{R}^d, y_i \in \{-1, +1\}$ with maximal margin. If the data are not linearly separable one can introduce slack variables (ζ_i) in the optimization,

---

[1] The formula (1) for region predictions R is an adaptation of the formula actually given by [6]. It behaves in the same way except that it makes no empty predictions, and so it may give less errors, but never more. Therefore the formulation given here is also well-calibrated.

$$min \frac{1}{2} \| \mathbf{w} \| + C \sum_{i=1}^{l} \zeta_i$$

under the constraints $y_i[(\mathbf{w} \cdot \mathbf{x}_i) + b] \geq 1 - \zeta_i$ and $\zeta_i \geq 0$, where C is a constant chosen a priori. This optimization problem can then be translated into its corresponding dual problem

$$max \sum_{i=1}^{l} \alpha_i - \frac{1}{2} \sum_{i,j=1}^{l} \alpha_i \alpha_j y_i y_j (\mathbf{x}_i \cdot \mathbf{x}_j),$$

under the constraints,

$$0 \leq \alpha_i \leq C, \sum_{i=1}^{l} \alpha_i y_i = 0.$$

The Lagrangians α_i obtained in the dual setting of SVM can be used as strangeness values [2].

The nearest centroid algorithm (NC) is a nonparametric approach to classification where the prediction for a new example is the label whose centroid (i.e. mean value), calculated from a training set, is nearest the new example [4]. We compute the strangeness value of an object x_i with label y_i as the distance of x_i from the centroid for y_i, relative to the minimum distance across all other possible class labels,

$$\alpha(x_i, y_i) = \alpha_i = \frac{d(\mu_{y_i}, x_i)}{\min_{y \neq y_i} d(\mu_y, x_i)}$$

where μ_{y_i} is the centroid for each label y_i and d is the Euclidean distance measure, weighted to ensure that the distances across each feature are standardized and thus contribute proportionately to the distance measure.

The exchangeability condition demands that this strangeness measure must be independent of the order that examples are presented to the algorithm. For this reason, it is important that the centroids are computed using all examples, including the new example x_n.

The implemented systems, namely TCM-SVM and TCM-NC, are evaluated in both online and offline learning settings. For offline learning, we specifically use m-fold cross validation. Online learning is especially good for testing error calibration, since it is within that setting that TCM is theoretically well-calibrated. Offline learning is good for deriving certain predictions since it is possible to use a larger training set to better inform the learning process. However, both frameworks can be used for either tests.

3.3 Results

TCM-SVM and TCM-NC were applied to the ovarian dataset in both online and offline learning settings. We used 10-fold cross validation with the dataset in the offline settings. To ensure our results were independent of the ordering

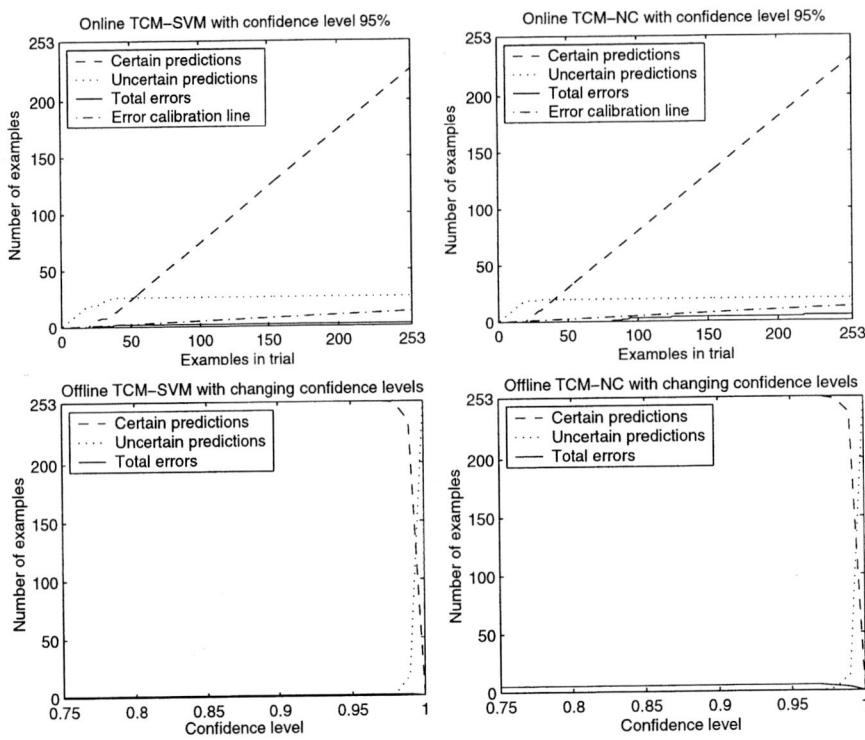

Fig. 1. Ovarian data: learning results

of the training sequences, the experiments were conducted over several random permutations. The graphs shown in figure 1 are typical results of the online and offline learning.

In the online learning experiments, the error calibration lines show the maximum error rate we expect if the TCM is well-calibrated. This expectation is met for both implementations, since the number of actual errors is always below this line. For example, at 95% confidence level, we would expect no more than 13 errors, and the actual number of errors made by TCM-SVM is 2. These results also show the region predictions become narrower as we include more examples, with a decreasing number of uncertain predictions. This indicates the learning process has stabilized.

Table 1 shows the performance of TCM implementations (at 95% confidence level) and comparison with their conventional counterparts in the offline experiments. It is clear that the TCM implementation can provide confidence measures without detriment to the performance of the underlying classification algorithms.

4 Conclusions

We have described the recently developed transductive confidence machines. Our experiments demonstrate that the TCM algorithm is successful at performing

Table 1. Performance of offline learning experiments

Algorithm	Accuracy	Sensitivity	Specificity
SVM	98.9%	98.9%	97.8%
TCM-SVM (at 95% confidence level)	99.6%	100%	98.9%
NC	97.6%	98.1%	96.7%
TCM-NC (at 95% confidence level)	98.0%	98.1%	97.8%

proteomics pattern diagnostics with confidence. In particular, predictions using this algorithm are not only accurate but also, unlike many conventional algorithms, well-calibrated. These empirical results also corroborate the theoretical claim that TCM is well-calibrated in the online setting.

References

1. Keith A. Baggerly, Jeffrey S. Morris, and Kevin R. Coombes. Reproducibility of seldi-tof protein patterns in serum: Comparing data sets from different experiments. *Bioinformatics*, 20(5):777–785, January 2004.
2. Alex Gammerman and Volodya Vovk. Prediction algorithms and confidence measures based on algorithmic randomness theory. *Theoretical Computer Science*, 287:209–217, 2002.
3. Emanuel F III Petricoin, Ali M Ardekani, Ben A Hitt, Peter J Levine, Vincent A Fusaro, Seth M Steinberg, Gordon B Mills, Charles Simone, David A Fishman, Elise C Kohn, and Lance A Liotta. Use of proteomic patterns in serum yo identify ovarian cancer. *Lancet*, 359(9306):572–577, Feburary 2002.
4. Robert Tibshirani, Trevor Hastie, Balasubramanian Narasimhan, and Gilbert Chu. Diagnosis of multiple cancer types by shrunken centroids of gene expression. *Proceedings of the National Association of Science (USA)*, 99(10):6567–6572, May 2002.
5. V. Vapnik. *Statistical Learning Theory*. New York: Wiley, 1998.
6. Vladimir Vovk. On-line confidence machines are well-calibrated. In *Proceedings of the 43rd Annual Symposium on Foundations of Computer Science*, pages 187–196. IEEE Computing, 2002.
7. Baolin Wu, Tom Abbott, David Fishman, Walter McMurray, Gil Mor, Kathryn Stone, David Ward, Kenneth Williams, and Hongyu Zhao. Comparison of statistical methods for classification of ovarian cancer using mass spectrometry data. *Bioinformatics*, 19(13):1636–1643, 2003.
8. Wei Zhu, Xuena Wang, Yeming Ma, Manlong Rao, James Glimm, and John S. Kovach. Detection of cancer-specific markers amid massive mass spectral data. *Proceedings of the National Academy of Sciences of the USA*, 100(25):14666–14671, December 2003.

An Assessment of Feature Relevance in Predicting Protein Function from Sequence

Ali Al-Shahib, Chao He, Aik Choon Tan, Mark Girolami, and David Gilbert

Bioinformatics Research Centre, Department of Computing Science
University of Glasgow, Glasgow G12 8QQ, UK
{alshahib,chaohe,actan,girolami,drg}@dcs.gla.ac.uk

Abstract. Improving the performance of protein function prediction is the ultimate goal for a bioinformatician working in functional genomics. The classical prediction approach is to employ pairwise sequence alignments. However this method often faces difficulties when no statistically significant homologous sequences are identified. An alternative way is to predict protein function from sequence-derived features using machine learning. In this case the choice of possible features which can be derived from the sequence is of vital importance to ensure adequate discrimination to predict function. In this paper we have shown that carefully assessing the discriminative value of derived features by performing feature selection improves the performance of the prediction classifiers by eliminating irrelevant and redundant features. The subset selected from available features has also shown to be biologically meaningful as they correspond to features that have commonly been employed to assess biological function.

1 Introduction

Performing protein sequence comparison to achieve homology generally indicates similarity in function and structure. The standard way of predicting the function of a newly sequenced protein is to use sequence comparison tools, such as BLAST [1] that can identify the most similar proteins and use their function to infer that of the new sequence. However this method often fails for low sequence similarity proteins. Thus, other alternative techniques such as predicting protein function from microarray expression analysis [3], protein secondary structure [4] and protein sequence features [5, 8] have been proposed. King et al. [5] show that using physical and chemical properties directly derived from protein sequence provides a novel way of predicting protein function with reasonable accuracy. Different from direct sequence comparisons, this method allows an appropriate classification algorithm, which is learned from appropriate discriminative features, to be used as a discrimination function which maps the protein sequence to a biological function. However, the question is how to obtain those most appropriate and discriminative features from all available features for higher performance of the prediction system.

The elimination of irrelevant and redundant features in the data results in many advantages. First, it enables the classification system to achieve good or even better performance with a selected feature subset, thus reducing the computational costs and avoiding the dimensional curse generally faced by machine learning [2, 10]. Secondly, it helps the human expert to focus on a relevant subset of features, hence providing useful biological knowledge [10]. The most obvious way of performing feature selection is to manually select the biologically most relevant features in the dataset. However, this is not always practical, as many bioinformatics data sets could be associated with large numbers of features and it would be time consuming to manually perform feature selection. Also, there could be some hidden features that one could not possibly recognize the importance by just visualising the dataset. Thus we need an effective, fast and biologically reliable automatic method.

In this study, we employed the theoretically sound and practically feasible *filter* and *wrapper* feature subset selection methods [2] to eliminate irrelevant and redundant features in our feature set, and utilised naive Bayes and decision tree classifiers to asses the accuracy of the prediction as a result of the feature selection. We have shown that performing automatic feature selection when predicting protein function from sequence improves the performance of the predictive classifier compared with considering a full set of derived features. In addition, we have found that as a result of the feature selection, biologically relevant features were chosen that indicates the importance of feature selection in this task.

2 Methodology

2.1 Data Collection and Pre-processing

We have populated a database containing protein sequence information for seven sexually transmitted disease (STD) causing bacteria. These bacteria were chosen because the long term goal of this research is to predict large numbers of novel proteins in these bacteria, in order to further understand the pathogenicity of these organisms. The proteins and their functional annotation were obtained from the Los Alamos Laboratory[1]. By utilising a variety of bioinformatics tools, diverse sequence related features were obtained, which include those derived from the distribution of amino acids (e.g. amino acid composition, length of protein, molecular weight) and those derived from the properties associated with the molecular composition of the protein (e.g. pI, Hydropathicity, aliphatic index). More features such as structural and phylogenetic predictions/hypotheses could have been extracted, but first we want to focus our attention on sequence data alone in order to understand the possible limits of prediction accuracy when forced to rely on the information available within sequence alone. Further work considering additional biologically useful features will be carried out in the future. The entire data set contains 5,149 proteins represented as 33-dimensional feature vectors from 13 different functional classes. The description and sample size of each class are shown in Tab. 1. We have performed a linear normalisation (standardisation) on the data to rescale each feature to mean of 0 and standard deviation of 1.

---

[1] http://www.stdgen.lanl.gov/

Table 1. Functional classification of proteins according to the classification in [7].

Class ID	Class Name	Sample Size
1	Amino acid biosynthesis	231
2	Biosynthesis of cofactors, prosthetic groups, and carriers	264
3	Cell envelope	577
4	Cellular processes	409
5	Central intermediary metabolism	146
6	DNA metabolism	456
7	Energy metabolism	513
8	Fatty acid and phospholipid metabolism	155
9	Purines, pyrimidines, nucleosides, and nucleotides	261
10	Regulatory functions	250
11	Transcription	210
12	Translation	906
13	Transport and binding proteins	771

2.2 Feature Selection Methods

There are two common approaches for feature selection [2]: a *filter* evaluates features according to measures based general statistical characteristics of the data, while a *wrapper* uses the intended prediction algorithm itself to evaluate the usefulness of features. In this study, a variety of both filter and wrapper methods were examined. Experiments were carried out using the WEKA[2] environment [6].

Within the filter, four different search algorithms (forward, backward, genetic and ranker) along with two evaluation criteria (correlation based feature subset evaluation and relief attribute evaluation) were investigated. The selected feature subsets were further employed to devise a multi-class Gaussian naive Bayes classifier to predict protein function. Its performance was compared with that obtained using the full feature set.

For the wrapper feature selection approach, a genetic search algorithm was employed to generate feature subsets which were then evaluated by a decision tree using 5-fold cross-validation. To analyse the discriminatory power of the features that the wrapper selected, we induced decision tree classifiers from the full feature set and the selected feature subset respectively, and their performance was evaluated using 10-fold cross validation.

3 Experimental Results

Filter and wrapper methods have consistently selected common features[3], which illustrates the high discriminatory power. Experimental results on the full feature set as well as the selected subsets by the filter and the wrapper are shown in Fig. 1 and Fig. 2 respectively, which display the boxplots of coverage measurements (percentage of true positives over the sum of true positives and false

---

[2] http://www.cs.waikato.ac.nz/ml/weka/
[3] Please refer to http://www.brc.dcs.gla.ac.uk/~alshahib/fs.htm for the entire list of selected features.

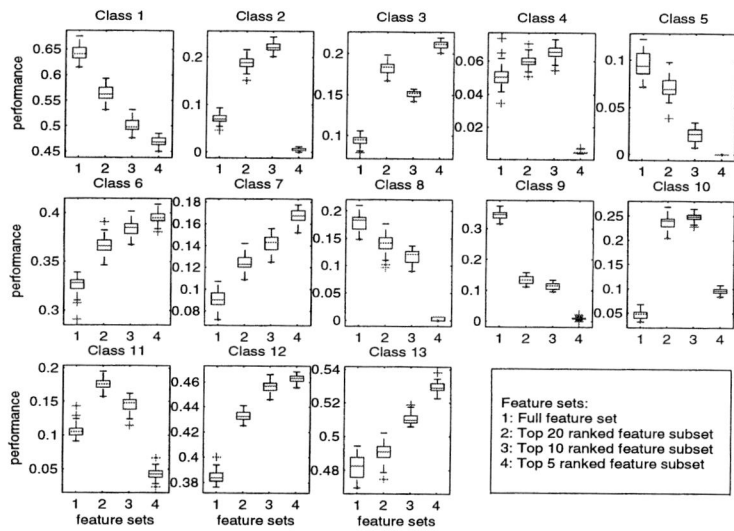

Fig. 1. Boxplot of prediction performance using feature sets selected by filter.

negatives) of 13 classes using 10-fold cross-validation. The performance of 9 out of 13 classes for the filter (using the top 20 and top 10 ranked feature subsets) and 7 out of 13 classes for the wrapper has been improved. Even when using just the top 5 filter-ranked feature subset, the performance of 6 out of 13 classes has been improved. It indicates that original features for most of the protein functional classes are redundant and irrelevant, thus using selected subsets improves performance. All of the 7 classes improved by the wrapper approach were also improved by the filter approach. The performance of four functional classes decreases using both feature selection approaches. They are class 1 (amino acid biosynthesis), 5 (central intermediary metabolism), 8 (fatty acid and phospholipids metabolism) and 9 (purines pyrimidines nucleosides and nucleotides). We argue that for those classes the discriminative information is provided by all features. This indicates that the importance of features differs when predicting different protein functions, which will be further discussed in the following section. Although feature selection improves the performance, the overall performance is still not optimal because it is difficult to predict protein function from amino acid sequence alone [5, 8] which consists of insufficient information for defining protein functions. Adopting additional features such as structural, gene expression or phylogenetic profile may improve the performance. Imbalanced data suffered by the classifier may be another reason (Further investigation addressing this problem is presently being undertaken).

4 Discussion

Having shown in our experiments that employing selected feature subsets improved the prediction performance, we have further noticed that some impor-

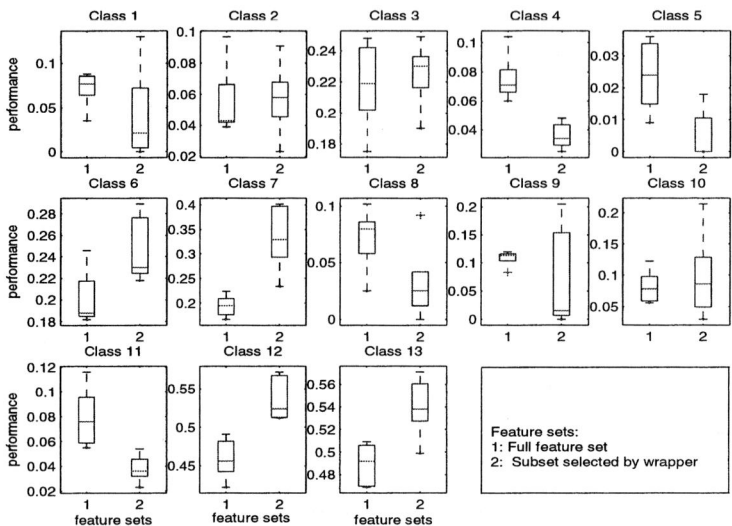

Fig. 2. Boxplot of prediction performance using feature sets selected by Wrapper.

tant features such as Isoelectric point (pI) and Grand Average of Hydropathicity (GRAVY) were commonly selected by both filter and wrapper methods. The filter consistently ranks them as the top 2 discriminative features. In the wrapper, the pI and GRAVY were constantly chosen as the root nodes of decision tree classifiers which indicates the importance of these features in predicting protein function. These selected features are indeed biologically meaningful.

The pI of a protein is the pH of a solution in which the protein has a net electrical charge of zero. The reason why the pI is a biologically relevant discriminatory feature in predicting particular functional classes is because it determines the functionally important charge status of a protein in a given environment, and certain functions critically depend on the net charge of the particular protein. Prominent examples are DNA replication (DNA metabolism), transcriptional and translational functional classes. All of these functions require an interaction with highly acidic nucleotide sequences (DNA or RNA), thus positively charged proteins (i.e. protein with a high pI) are needed. Moreover, certain pI values could be discriminatory for transport and binding proteins especially in pathogenic bacteria (such as the ones in our database). This is because bacterial pathogenic cells tend to acidify the environment by metabolic processes, thus their secreted proteins should have a low pI to function properly in acidic environment compared to intracellular proteins (about neutral environment).

The GRAVY value for a protein is calculated as the sum of hydropathy values of all the amino acids, divided by the number of residues in the sequence [9]. The hydrophobicity of the cell membrane is a major factor in the transport of the metabolites to and out of the cell. It makes biological sense to associate discriminatory GRAVY values with predicting proteins with transport and binding functions. In addition, certain GRAVY values can also be discriminatory in predicting other classes that are hydrophobicity dependent: such as cell envelope, fatty acid and phospholipid metabolism and energy metabolism.

We believe that the reason why other features, such as molecular weight, protein length and atomic composition were not chosen as top features is because of the redundancy between these features, thus making it less possible for a classifier to discriminate between these features in predicting function. We have also understood from this feature selection process that in many cases more abstract features that have been combined at a high level such as pI and GRAVY are the most discriminatory features compared to low-level features such as composition of a single amino acid in a protein. In future work, we intend to combine similar but not redundant features for example the amino acids' glutamate and aspartate composition as one feature in predicting protein function.

5 Conclusion

In this paper we have reported the employment of theoretically sound and practically feasible filter and wrapper feature selection methods to investigate the feature relevance in predicting protein function from sequence. Our experimental results have shown that performing feature selection on protein chemical and physical sequence data improves the performance of the predictive classifier compared with considering a full set of derived features. We have also shown that the selected features are biologically meaningful to provide high discriminatory power of determining protein functions. We plan further work taking into account additional features such as structural, phylogenetic and expression information in selecting the biologically most relevant features. Other well-established machine learning algorithms such as Support Vector Machines will also be investigated.

References

1. Altschul, S.F., et al.: Basic local alignment search tool. J Mol Biol. **215** (1990) 403-10
2. Guyon, I., Elissee, A.: An introduction to variable and feature selection. JMLR, **3** (2003) 1157-1182
3. Pavlidis, P., et al.: Learning gene functional classifications from multiple data types. J Comp Biol, **9** (2002) 401-11
4. Rost, B.: Protein secondary structure prediction continues to rise, J Struc Biol, **134** (2001) 204-18
5. King, R.D., et al.: The utility of different representations of protein sequence for predicting functional class. Bioinformatics, **17** (2001) 445-54
6. Witten, I.H., Frank, E.: Data Mining: Practical Machine Learning Tools and Techniques with Java Implementations. Morgan Kaufmann (2000)
7. Riley, M.:. Functions of the gene products of Escherichia coli. Microbiol Rev, **57:** (1993) 862-952
8. Jensen, R., et al.: Prediction of human protein function according to Gene Ontology categories. Bioinformatics, **19** (2003) 635-42
9. Kyte, J., Doolittle, R.F.: A simple method for displaying the hydropathic character of a protein. J Mol Biol, **157** (1982) 105-32
10. Saeys Y, et al.: Fast feature Selection using a simple estimation of distribution algorithm: a case study on splice site prediction. Bioinformatics, **19** (2003) 179-88

A New Artificial Immune System Algorithm for Clustering

Reda Younsi and Wenjia Wang

School of computing sciences, University of East Anglia, Norwich NR4 7TJ, UK
r.younsi@uea.ac.uk, wjw@cmp.uea.ac.uk

Abstract. This paper describes a new artificial immune system algorithm for data clustering. The proposed algorithm resembles the CLONALG, widely used AIS algorithm but much simpler as it uses one shot learning and omits cloning. The algorithm is tested using four simulated and two benchmark data sets for data clustering. Experimental results indicate it produced the correct clusters for the data sets.

1 Introduction

Natural immune system has several important abilities that can be very useful to computational scientists. The immune system is a complex but self organizing and highly distributed system. It has a decentralised information processing capability and uses adaptive memory for solving problems. These capabilities are used to develop models which automatically discover similar patterns or clusters in data and for data compression.

In this paper we describe a novel idea for data clustering using techniques based on the CLONALG algorithm [1]. We disregard the clonal process as proposed by [1]. As an alternative we introduce a fixed population of B cells generated randomly if no antigen is recognised by B cells. Furthermore we introduce a new technique called the elimination process that is used to eliminate the procedure of matching similar cells repeatedly and is used as a stopping criterion.

2 Related Work

The computational interest shown in the natural immune system is essentially based on the interaction between different cells, such as B cells, T cells and antigens, the decentralised flow of information, the generalisation capability for unseen antigens and the adaptive nature of the natural immune system. The clonal selection and the immune network theory, as proposed by Jern [5], are two models used for data clustering. In Immune system the shape space [7] is used to model the recognition between the immune cells and the antigens. Cells are represented by a string of features, such as the length, height, charge distribution, etc. String $s=\{s_1,s_2,...,s_L\}$ can represent an immune cell in L-dimensional shape-space S where $(s \in S^L)$. In natural immune system B cell recognises the antigen if its affinity is greater than a certain threshold.

Cell that encounters an antigen and recognises it proliferates and differentiates into memory cells and blast cells. This process is called clonal selection. Blast cells produce antibodies that bind to the antigen. Next time an individual encounters that same antigen the immune system is primed to destroy the same antigen using memory cells.

The CLONALG algorithm, as the name suggests, is inspired by the clonal principle of the immune system and first implemented by [1]. The CLONALG basically generates a set of memory cells by repeatedly exposing randomly created antibodies to the set of antigens. The memory cells are a generalisation of the data being learned.

Cloning in AIS is principally generating a number of duplicate cells. Diversity is introduced by applying a random mutation to the duplicated cells (clones) [8] and [9]. The mutation in [2] is used to direct learning in the clones, the better the match is, the smaller the mutation variation the child clone will have.

Determining the affinity of the antibodies, selecting and re-selecting the n highest affinity antibodies and the hyper mutation make CLONALG a computationally expensive algorithm [4] to an order $O(M(N + N_c L))$. Where M = Memory cells; N = the size of the total population; N_c = The size of clone population; L = Length of the antibody vector (or bit string).

Two distinct works that have been extensively mentioned in the literature for data clustering are RLAIS [8] a resource limited artificial immune system for data analysis, and aiNET [2] an artificial immune network for data analysis. [9] Have combined the two above concepts while [6] proposed fuzzy AIS for clustering. There are essentially three models that use metaphors from the immune system that are used in data analysis, negative and positive clonal selection and the immune network theory. These models are described in [3].

3 Proposed Algorithm

The proposed algorithm does not use the cloning process because it introduces intensive matching computation between antibodies and antigens. We have introduced the elimination process, first as a stopping criterion and second, to eliminate the process of matching similar cells for the same antigens repeatedly.

B cell is represented by an m-dimensional real vector that has the same dimension (length) than the antigen in the data set.

$b_i = \{f_1, f_2, ..., f_n\}, i = 1,.., N (b_i \in B)$ and

$Ag_i = \{f_1, f_2, ..., f_n\}, i = 1,..., N (Ag_i \in Ag)$ f_i is the input feature.

B cell is said to recognise an antigen if the Euclidean distance is less than a threshold value called the network affinity threshold (NAT). The proposed algorithm is given below.

Phase One: Recognition and Elimination
1. *Generate randomly* a population of B cells of size N
2. *Read* the set of antigens Ag from the data set
3. *Calculate* the NAT value using the whole Ag data set

Do
For (every member of the set Ag)
4. *Select* an antigen *Agi* from the set *Ag*
5. *For* every member of B cell calculate its Euclidean distance to the antigen
5.1 *if* the antigen is recognised by a single B cell than store the B cell in memory
5.2 *if* the antigen is recognised by more then one B cell then choose the closest and store in memory

End for
6. *Introduce* a new population of B cells of size *N if* no B cell has recognised an antigen and go to step 4
7. *Eliminate* that antigen from the sample (hide it from the next generations) Once all the B cells have been presented to that antigen and is been recognised.
8. *Select* B cells that have recognised the antigens in this generation
9. *Mutate* B cells and go to step 4 using the mutated cells only (population = mutated B cells)

While (all the antigens have been eliminated or after a number of generations)
Step 4 to 9 represents one generation

Phase Two: Clustering

A. *Select* memory B cells
B. *Re-calculate* the NAT value using memory B cells
C. *if* the Euclidean distance between two B cells is less then NAT value *link* those B cells
D. *Show* the network using a visualisation tool

This algorithm has two distinct phases. The first phase is made of the recognition and the elimination processes. The second phase is to do clustering. A random population of B cells is generated representing a data vector of L-dimensions. The antigen set *Ag* is read from an external file to the working memory of the algorithm. The Network Affinity Threshold (NAT) value is computed using the set Ag. The NAT value is calculated as $<\delta>\cdot \alpha$, where $<\delta>$ is the average distance between each item in *Ag*. α is a constant between 0 and 1 (NAT scalar) [8].

$$D = \{d(Ag_i, Ag_j): i = 1,\ldots, k-1, j = 2,\ldots, k, j > i\} \quad \text{Then}$$

$$\delta = (\sum d) \div n \quad \text{Where} \quad n = \text{number of distances d.} \tag{1}$$

$NAT = (\delta) \times \alpha \quad \alpha = \text{constant value between 1 and 0}$

The NAT value is very important parameter. If the value is too large then memory cells will not represent the training data set and different numbers of clusters are represented in the final network.

The Euclidean distance is calculated by matching each B cell (data vector) from the population to the antigens from the training data set.

Each antigen is presented to the population of B cells. The Euclidean distance is calculated between each B cell and the antigen, if this distance is less or equal to the NAT value the B cell is selected and stored in long term memory. If more than one B cell recognises the antigen then the B cell that is the closest is selected. Once all B cells have been presented to the antigen, the B cell that is selected will eliminate the antigen (the antigen is hidden from the next generations of B cells).

One B cells can recognise more than one antigen. The resulting cells are the representation of the data being compressed. Finally, B cells that have recognised antigens are selected for mutation. The mutation value is calculated using the formula below [10].

$$m_i = m_i + r \times \Delta, i = 1,......,n$$
(2)

m represents B cells from 1 to m
r = random number from the unit interval [0, 1],
Δ=the mutation rate between 0 and 1

The mutation value is calculated using a user defined value multiply by a random number between 0 and 1. This value is added to each instance of the vector. Separate mutation value is calculated for each instance. The mutated cells are shown to the set of antigens and again the same matching procedure is used, however if the mutated cells fail to recognise the antigens, a new randomly number of generated B cells, of the same size as the initial population, is introduced. The new B cells are matched against each antigen and the ones that have been recognised are selected to the memory set.

The second phase of the algorithm is used for clustering and data visualisation. All B cells that have been stored in the memory are then matched to each other to form clusters. The NAT value is re-calculated using the memory cells and a new randomly chosen scalar value. The cells that are close to each other are linked if the Euclidean distance value is less or equal to the NAT value. This can be seen as simplification of the immune network where cells that have high similarity to each other are connected to form clusters.

The illustration below explains the generalisation (and data compression) of the algorithm. In fig 1, each antigen point is a representation of a data sample in two-dimensional surface. Cell B1 has eliminated two Antigens, while cell B2 found antigens in set C2. However cell B1 has first eliminated antigens in set C1 thus the antigens in C1 are hidden to C2. Cell B4 represents all the antigens in set C3 which results in data compression.

Fig 2 represents B cells in the memory set which are linked to form a network. Memory cells are a generalisation of the set of antigens (data set). When presented with unseen antigen, memory cells are capable of recognising and eliminating the intruders. Experiments, not shown in this paper, demonstrate the algorithm succefully detect unseen antigens when presented to the memory set.

4 Experimentations and Results

The proposed algorithm is tested with a number of data sets with different number of clusters (not shown in this paper). Four data sets are used, all with two dimensional features. The First data set with two clusters, the second data set with four clusters, all with 50 samples. The main purpose of the stimulated data sets is to test that the algorithm is performing the task of finding clusters. We have presented the algorithm with two well known benchmark data sets, the two spirals problem SPIR [11] and

CHAINLINK [12], fig 3 and 5. The data set in fig 7 has two dimensional features with 245 samples. Clusters formations are shown using a 3-D plot (fig 4 and 6) and the network formation in fig 8.

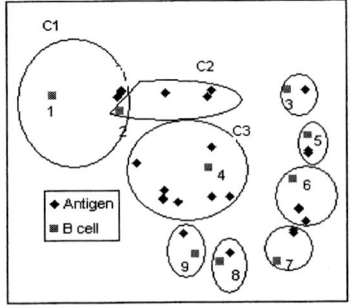

Fig. 1. Data generalisation   Fig. 2. Network formation

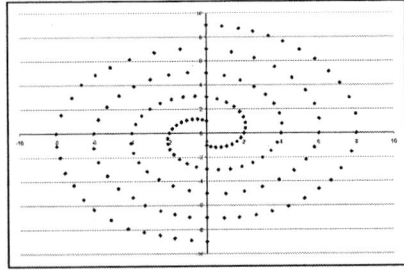 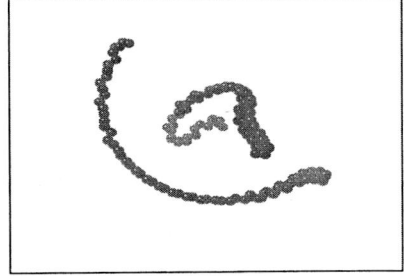

Fig. 3. Two Spirals original data set   Fig. 4. 3D plot of the network

The two spiral problem is composed of two non-linearly separable clusters. The distance between data points of one cluster is closer than the distance between points of different clusters. This makes the algorithm capable of distinguishing between antigens of different clusters by simply using the Euclidean distance and the NAT value. The memory cells representing the two clusters are plotted using a 3-D package. The algorithm managed to find the two clusters by identifying antigens that are close to each other. If presented with data sets with data points that have different distances and belong to different clusters then the algorithm may need a different recognition system that is not based solely on the Euclidean distance and the NAT value.

The chainlink problem is also a two non-linearly separable clusters in 3-D space. The data set is made of 1000 data points that form the shape of two intertwined 3-D rings. Each ring consists of 500 data points. The algorithm has succefully found two clusters with a good data reduction and without loss of generality using the Euclidean distance and the NAT value to distinguish between data points of each cluster. Memory cells are plotted using a 3-D package.

The data set in Fig.7 contain two clusters. Again the algorithm did find two clusters. The memory cells are a reduction and a generalisation of the data set learned.

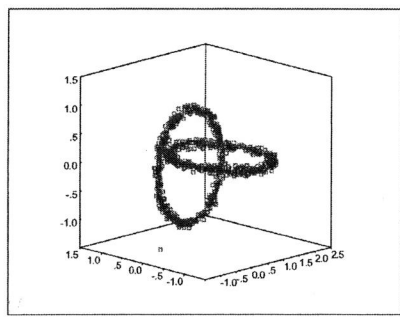

Fig. 5. Chainlink   **Fig. 6.** 3D plot of the network

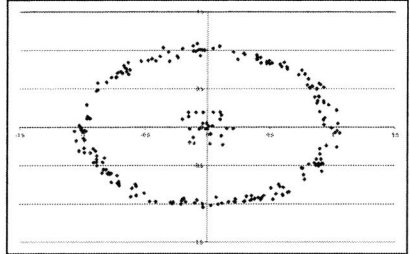 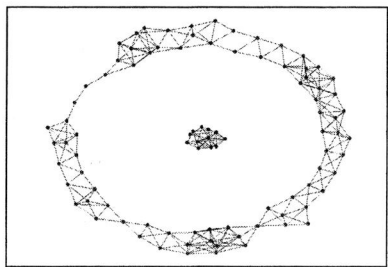

Fig. 7. Original data set   **Fig. 8.** Network plot

5 Conclusion and Future Work

We have developed and used a new artificial immune system algorithm for data clustering. The algorithm presented in this paper uses the interaction between B cells and antigens. The cloning process is omitted. Instead a random number generator is used to introduce new B cells. These new B cells are introduced only if the mutated B cells have failed to recognise the antigens. The recognition system employed is the Euclidean distance, used as a distance measure between the antigen and the B cell, if the Euclidean distance is less then the NAT value then that B cell is selected to became a memory cell. We introduced the elimination process. Antigens are kept away from further matching once there is recognition between B cell and the antigen. The elimination of antigen reduces the time complexity of matching similar cells repeatedly and is used as stopping criteria. Memory cells are used for clustering.

Further analysis is needed to explain the importance of cloning process in AIS for data clustering. The algorithm presented has important data compression capability. Antigens that are similar are represented by smaller number of B cells. Memory cells are a generalisation of the data set learned. The generalisation capability of the proposed algorithm is being investigated by the authors for data classification with very encouraging results.

References

1. de Castro, L. N. & Von Zuben, F. J. The Clonal Selection Algorithm with Engineering Applications, (full version, pre-print), In Proceedings of GECCO'00, Workshop on Artificial Immune Systems and Their Applications, pp. 36-37, 2000.
2. de Castro, L. N. & Von Zuben, F. J. aiNet: An Artificial Immune Network for Data Analysis. (Full version, pre-print). Book Chapter in Data Mining: A Heuristic Approach, Hussein A. Abbass, Ruhul A. Sarker, and Charles S. Newton (Eds.), Idea Group Publishing, USA, 2001.
3. de Castro, L. N. & J. Timmis, Artificial Immune Systems: A Novel Paradigm to Pattern Recognition,(pre-print), In Artificial Neural Networks in Pattern Recognition , J. M. Corchado, L. Alonso, and C. Fyfe (eds.), SOCO-2002, University of Paisley, UK, pp. 67-84, 2002.
4. de Castro, L. N. & Von Zuben, F. J. Learning and Optimization Using the Clonal Selection Principle, IEEE Transactions on Evolutionary Computation, Special Issue on Artificial Immune Systems, 6(3), pp. 239-251, 2002.
5. Jerne, N. K. Towards a network theory of the immune system, Ann, Immunol. (Inst. Pasteur), 125C:373 389, 1974.
6. Nasaroui, O., Gonzales, F., and Dasgupta, D. The fuzzy artificial immune system: Motivations, basic concepts, and application to clustering and Web profiling. In Proc. of the IEEE International Conf. On Fuzzy Systems at WCCI, pp. 711-716, Hawaii, May 12-17, 2002.
7. Perelson, A. Immune network theory, immunological review, 110, 5-36, 1989.
8. Timmis, J. Artificial immune systems: A novel data analysis technique inspired by the immune network theory, Ph. D thesis, Department of Computer Science, University of Wales, Aberystwyth, Ceredigion, Wales, 2000.
9. Wierzchon, S., Kuzelewska, U. Stable Clusters Formation in an Artificial Immune System. In Timmis, J., Bentley, P.J., eds.: Proceedings of the 1st International Conference on Artificial Immune Systems (ICARIS), University of Kent at Canterbury, University of Kent at Canterbury Printing Unit (2002) 68–75, 2002.
10. Fahman, S, E. & lebiere, C. The Cascade-Correlation Learning Architecture, In: Advances in Neural Information Processing Systems, 2, D. S. Touretzky (ed.), Morgan Kauf-mann, San Mateo, pp. 524-532, 1990.
11. Ultsch, A. Self-Organizing Neural Networks Perform Different from Statistical k-means, Gesellschaft für Klassifica-tion, 1995.

The Categorisation of Similar Non-rigid Biological Objects by Clustering Local Appearance Patches

Hongbin Wang and Phil F. Culverhouse

Centre for Interactive Intelligent Systems
School of Computing, Communications and Electronics
University of Plymouth, Plymouth, PL4 8AA, UK
{hongbin.wang,phil.culverhouse}@plymouth.ac.uk

Abstract. A novel approach is presented to the categorisation of non-rigid biological objects from unsegmented scenes in an unsupervised manner. The biological objects investigated are five phytoplankton species from the coastal waters of the European Union. The high morphological variability within each species and the high similarity between species make the categorisation task a challenge for both marine ecologists and machine vision systems. The framework developed takes a local appearance approach to learn the object model, which is done using a novel-clustering algorithm with minimal supervised information. Test objects are classified based on matches with local patches of high occurrence. Experiments show that the method achieves good results, given the difficulty of the task.

1 Introduction

Recognition of visual objects is a fundamental task in computer vision. Currently, there are generally two approaches to the object recognition problem. The global approach [1] uses a whole image of the object as representation. It requires pre-segmentation and no occlusion, which is very restrictive in practice. Hence the local approach [2,3,4 and 5] has gained more attention recently. Typically, objects to be recognised are represented by local features or local parts. Test images are processed by extraction of local features and then matched with the object's model. The local representation has been shown to be more robust to clutter and partial occlusion and less restrictive than a global approach. In this work the local approach is taken to meet the requirement of our difficult data.

The data used are images of five closely related phytoplankton species found in the coastal waters of the European Union: *Dinophysis acuminata, D. caudata, D. fortii, D. rotundata* and *D. tripos*. Typical images of these five species are shown in Fig.1, they are in the 20-70μm size range. These plankton species show high variability. The specimens are non-rigid, sometimes partially overlapped and cluttered. They can be translucent (ie. some background can be seen through the specimen) and undergo translation, some scale changes, and some rotation in the image plane. The images are

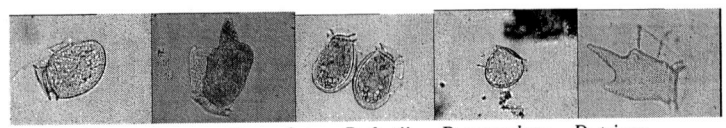

D. acuminata　　D. caudata　　D. fortii　　D. rotundata　　D. tripos

Fig. 1. Example plankton images [source: B. Reguera, IEO, Spain]

low-resolution, low-contrast and can have appearance change due to illumination. All these characteristics challenge the previous recognition approaches. Automatic segmentation of such images before recognition is difficult due to cluttered background and unclear or missing contours. The species are all microplankton from the dinoflagellate genus. Previous work has established that natural variation of shape in this genus causes difficulty for identification. Trained personnel range in their ability to discriminate these species returning an average of 72% in one study [6]. Family and class-level categorisation may be likened to telling apples and oranges from bananas. Species-level discriminations, as studied here, require the software to make expert judgements as the species in question are closely related.

Earlier work by the authors for a plankton recognition system DiCANN [7,8] utilised multiple coarse channels based on multi-scale local feature detection. The six channels include global and local descriptors: area measurement, local contrast moments, texture information, texture density, junction information and scale-space representation. DiCANN is limited by a requirement of segmentation before recognition and is therefore not robust to occlusion. DiCANN achieved 72% accuracy on this present data set, using all six channels of analysis and simple pre-segmentation [6].

In this paper, the goal is to develop a system, which can categorise the plankton without pre-segmentation and is robust to clutter and partial occlusion. It is also required that object model can be learned with minimal supervised information. A balance between the high variability of the plankton images and the high similarity between plankton species needs to be struck to optimise recognition across species and genera. To achieve that goal, a local appearance based plankton recognition system has been developed. The approach consists of two steps, outlined below.

Step 1: Learning Object Model

The object model is learnt using local appearance patches, as shown in Fig.2. The local patches are extracted around the multi-scale local interest points. The appearance of the local patch is represented using spin image [9]. By using a novel-clustering algorithm developed by the authors, the local patches are clustered within one image and across the unsegmented training images for each species. A subset of patches is selected based on its high occurrence in the species. The patches in the final species model are obtained by clustering across all species and being selected by occurrence statistics.

Step 2: Object Categorisation

When test images are processed, the local patches are extracted and matched with patches in the species model database, which is a patches-species matrix. The test images are classified based on the voting from matched patches.

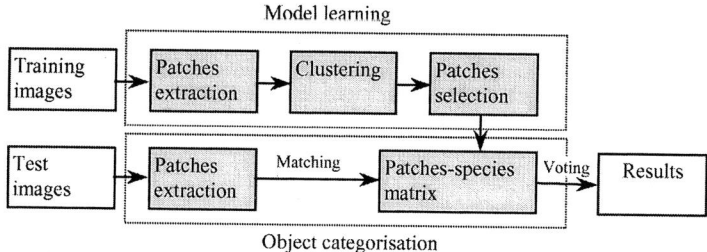

Fig. 2. The scheme of our approach

Each step of the approach is described in detail in Section 2 and Section 3. Section 4 presents the experimental results. Section 5 gives conclusion and future directions.

2 Learning Object Model

The section describes several stages in object model learning.

2.1 Selection of Local Appearance Patches

The local appearance patches are small circular image areas around the interest points since salient information is contained in the neighbourhood of interest point. Previous work selected the local patches based on transformation invariant interest points [10] or at fixed scale [4, 5], which limited the repeatability and coverage of the patches. Here four types of interest points select the local patches (A Trous wavelet maxima [8], Harris corner detector [11], DOG detector [2] and Laplace detector [11]) at multi-scale. The scale in which the interest points are detected determines the patch size.

Since the plankton undertakes rotation in the image plane, a rotation invariant descriptor is needed to represent the raw image patch. Local descriptors like SIFT [2] and steerable filters [11] are rotation invariant but not suitable for large patches (in our case 97x97 maximum). So the spin image descriptor [9] is used here. A spin image is a two-dimensional intensity histogram. One dimension is the distance from the centre of the patch; the other is the intensity histogram at that distance. This descriptor is rotation invariant and achieves similar results to steerable filters [11]. To compensate for any illumination change, the patches are normalised by the mean and the standard deviation of pixel intensity in the patches [11].

2.2 Clustering

The most common clustering methods are agglomerative hierarchical clustering and K-means [12]. Agglomerative hierarchical clustering can produce hierarchical clusters without the pre-requisite of cluster number, but the time complexity is $o(n^2)$. K-means produce flat clusters with linear time complexity, but requires definition of the desired number of clusters. In this work, there are more than two thousand patches in one image needing to be clustered, with an unknown numbers of clusters. To solve this problem, a simple clustering algorithm is presented, which combines the virtue of agglomerative hierarchical clustering and K-means, called T-Cluster. The algorithm produce flat clusters and has no need for prior estimates of cluster number. Its time complexity is the same as agglomerative hierarchical clustering in the worst case and is same as K-means in the best case. Conceptually, a new cluster is defined if the distances between any data and existing clusters exceed a set threshold. The algorithm is as follows.

Given n data samples $\{x_1, \cdots x_n\}$,
1. Initialize the cluster $c_1 = x_1$.
2. If the distance (x_2, c_1)<threshold, merge x_2, c_1 and recompute new centre of cluster. Otherwise, add a new cluster $c_2 = x_2$.
3. Continue this process and go through all the data. result is k clusters $\{c_1, \cdots c_k\}$.
4. Merge the k clusters $\{c_1, \cdots c_k\}$ using the same procedure above.
5. Iterate the steps 1-4 until the cluster centres and cluster number not change.

The distance measure used is the normalised correlation value between two matrices (the 2D spin image). In practice, the algorithm normally converges in 3-4 iterations.

2.3 Patches Selection Based on Occurrence

After clustering across the training images in the species, the patches are selected by the occurrence information, which defined as:

$$\text{The occurrence of the patch} = \frac{\text{the number of images contained the patch}}{\text{the total number of images for the specie}}$$

It measures the correlation between a patch and species. High occurrence of a patch results in a strong possibility it belongs to this species. However, this is a not sufficient criterion; patches are also selected across the species. The characteristic patches of species are the patches that appear with high frequency in that species and low frequency in other species.

3 Object Categorisation

The final species model consists of the characteristic patches. A matrix is used to describe the patches-species relations based on Bayesian statistics. The row is patch and the column is species. The item (i,j) is the possibility of the patch i belongs to the species j. When the test images are processed, the local patches are extracted and matched with the patches in the patches-species matrix. The possibilities are accumulated and vote for the final classification.

4 Experiments

The training data set has a total of 139 plankton images, which consists of 18 *D. acuminata*, 32 *D. caudata*, 47 *D. fortii*, 20 *D. rotundata* and 22 *D. tripos*. The image size is 256x192 with monochrome pixels. At the patch extraction stage, the local interest points are detected in 4 scales: 2, 4, 8 and 16 pixels. The correspondent patch radius is $3 \times scale$. The histogram bin in the spin image descriptor is set to 8. The typical number of patches extracted in one image is about 2,000 and is reduced by clustering and patch selection. The distance threshold in the clustering algorithm is 0.85. For example, image 499cum01.bmp of species *D. acuminata* contains 1878 patches. After clustering the patches in one image, the number is reduced to 645. After clustering across the 18 images in this species, the number is 7213. The patches that appear in over one third of images in the species are selected. Then the number is reduced to 77. After patch selection across the species, the number of patches in species *D. acuminata* is only 51. Table 1 shows the final number of patches in five species.

Table 1. The number of patches per species. The second row is the number after selection in the species, third row is the number after selection across species

D. acuminata	D. caudata	D. fortii	D. rotundata	D. tripos
77	59	56	43	57
51	37	33	21	37

The test set has 53 images, which consists of 7 *D. acuminata*, 8 *D. caudata*, 14 *D. fortii*, 18 *D. rotundata* and 6 *D. tripos*. The patches extracted in the test images are matched with the patches in the patches-species matrix. Table 2 shows the classification accuracy of 5 species. The *D. rotundata* species is classified incorrectly, which lowers the overall accuracy. The reason is *D. rotundata* lacks characteristic patches; of the 21 patches, 20 are shared with other species. It is also the smallest of the plankton and the sampling resolution probably needs increasing to provide more texture information. Categorisation performance over four species, excluding *D. rotundata* increases to 88%.

Table 2. Classification accuracy of the system by species

D. acuminata	D. caudata	D. fortii	D. rotundata	D. tripos	Total
7/7	8/8	11/14	0/18	5/6	31/53 (58%)

5 Conclusion

This paper presents a plankton recognition system that learns an object model by clustering local appearance patches and categorises test images by matching local patches extracted with patches in a species model. 58% categorisation accuracy was achieved with such difficult data. Possible improvements are increasing the histogram bin in the spin image descriptor and using other classifiers such as support vector machine to find the boundaries between similar species.

A categorisation method has been described that performs well above chance, yet requires no shape information from the object set. It is envisioned that such a technique could be employed to assist segmentation, which provides the top-down object information to resolve the ambiguity from bottom-up cues.

Acknowledgement

This work has been partially supported by European Union grant Q5CR-2002-71699.

References

1. M. Turk and A. Pentland. Eigenfaces for recognition. Cognitive Neuroscience, 3 (1990) 71-86.
2. D.G. Lowe. Object recognition from local scale-invariant features. In Proc. ICCV, pages 1150-1157, 1999.
3. B. Schiele and J.L. Crowley, Recognition without Correspondence using Multidimensional Receptive Field Histograms. In Int. J. Computer Vision 36 (1), p 31-50, January 2000.
4. M. Weber, M. Welling, and P. Perona. Unsupervised learning of object models for recognition. In ECCV00, 18-32,2000.
5. S. Agarwal and D. Roth. Learning a sparse representation for object detection. In ECCV'02, 2002.
6. Culverhouse PF, Williams R, Reguera B, Herry V, González-Gil S (2003) Do Experts Make Mistakes? Mar-Ecol-Prog-Ser. 247. 17-25.
7. P.F. Culverhouse, R. Williams, B. Reguera, R. Ellis and T. Parisini, Automatic Categorisation of 23 species of Dinoflagellate by Artificial Neural Network. Mar. Ecol. Prog. Ser. 139 (1996) 281-287.
8. L. Toth and P.F. Culverhouse, 3D object recognition from static 2D views using multiple coarse data channels. Image and Vision computing, 17 pp. 845-858, 1999.
9. S. Lazebnik, C. Schmid, and J. Ponce. Sparse texture representation using affine-invariant neighborhoods. In CVPR03, 2003.
10. K. Mikolajczyk and C. Schmid. An affine invariant interest point detector. In Proc. ECCV, vol. I, pages 128-142, 2002.
11. K. Mikolajczyk, C. Schmid, A performance evaluation of local descriptors. in IEEE Comp. Vis. and Patt. Rec., vol II, pp.257-263, 2003.
12. R.O. Duda, P.E. Hart, and D.G. Stork. Pattern Classification. John Wiley & Sons, NewYork, 2001.

Unsupervised Dense Regions Discovery in DNA Microarray Data

Andy M. Yip[1,*], Edmond H. Wu[2,**], Michael K. Ng[2,**], and Tony F. Chan[1,*]

[1] Department of Mathematics, University of California,
405 Hilgard Avenue, Los Angeles, CA 90095-1555, USA
{mhyip,chan}@math.ucla.edu
[2] Department of Mathematics, The University of Hong Kong
Pokfulam Road, Hong Kong
hcwu@hkusua.hku.hk, mng@maths.hku.hk

Abstract. In this paper, we introduce the notion of dense regions in DNA microarray data and present algorithms for discovering them. We demonstrate that dense regions are of statistical and biological significance through experiments. A dataset containing gene expression levels of 23 primate brain samples is employed to test our algorithms. Subsets of potential genes distinguishing between species and a subset of samples with potential abnormalities are identified.

1 Introduction

In the analysis of massive microarray data, one typically employ techniques such as clustering, classification, association rule mining, correspondence analysis and/or multi-dimensional scaling plots to understand the structure of the datasets, identify abnormalities and generate a list of interesting genes for further analysis [4]. Besides the patterns discovered by aforementioned methods, we realize that *dense regions*, which are two-dimensional regions defined by subsets of genes and samples whose corresponding values are mostly constant, are another type of patterns that are of practical use and are significant. For example, one may want to find a subset of genes and samples that are co-regulated or are results of errors during preparation of the data.

To the best of the authors' knowledge, dense region patterns have not been previously studied. A similar but not identical notion is error-tolerant frequent itemset introduced by Yang et al in [6] which focuses on mining association rules. In fact, one may expect that the most natural way is to use clustering techniques with the results displayed as a heat map [3] and look for patches of similar color (dense regions). While such a method does allow identification of some of

---

[*] The research of this author is partially supported by grants from NSF under contracts DMS-9973341 and ACI-0072112, ONR under contract N00014-02-1-0015 and NIH under contract P20 MH65166.

[**] The research of this author is supported in part by Hong Kong Research Grants Council Grant Nos. HKU 7130/02P and HKU 7046/03P.

these regions, we find that there are many other significant "patches" that are hidden and are observable only after a suitable permutation of the genes and the samples, whereas cluster analysis only produces a single reordering of the genes and the samples. More importantly, cluster analysis generally uses information from all genes (when clustering samples) and all samples (when clustering genes) whereas dense regions allow a subset of identified genes to behave differently in some samples. The use of subspace clustering is also prohibited because each region depends on a different subspace and it will be computationally intensive to identify all these subspaces. Techniques such as multi-dimensional scaling and correspondence analysis do not emphasize the existence of dense regions as these techniques are not specifically designed for such purposes.

Given the usefulness of dense region patterns in the analysis of microarray data, it is essential to derive effective and efficient algorithms to discover such patterns, which is our goal in this paper. From the computational point of view, our algorithms are also very suitable for microarray data ($\sim$10000 genes and $\sim$100 samples) because the computational cost mostly depends on the smaller dimension of the data matrix which is around $\sim$100 in most studies. Due to the lack of space, we refer the readers to [7] for a thorough treatment on the basic theory of dense regions and justification of the correctness of the algorithms.

2 Definition of Dense Regions

Let X be a given n-by-p data matrix where n, p are the numbers of genes and samples respectively. Denote by $X(R, C)$, or simply $R \times C$, the submatrix of X defined by a subset of rows R and a subset of columns C.

Definition 1 (Dense regions (DRs)). *A submatrix $X(R, C)$ is called a maximal dense region with respect to v, or simply a dense region with respect to v, if $X(R, C)$ is a constant matrix whose entries are v (density), and, any proper superset of $X(R, C)$ is a non-constant matrix (maximality).*

Example 1. Let X be a data matrix given by the first matrix below. The DRs of X with value 1 are given by the four matrices in the brace.

$$\begin{pmatrix} 1 & 0 & 0 & 1 \\ 1 & 1 & 0 & 1 \\ 1 & 1 & 0 & 1 \\ 1 & 1 & 2 & 0 \end{pmatrix} ; \left\{ \begin{pmatrix} 1 & * & * & * \\ 1 & * & * & * \\ 1 & * & * & * \\ 1 & * & * & * \end{pmatrix}, \begin{pmatrix} 1 & * & * & 1 \\ 1 & * & * & 1 \\ 1 & * & * & 1 \\ * & * & * & * \end{pmatrix}, \begin{pmatrix} * & * & * & * \\ 1 & 1 & * & 1 \\ 1 & 1 & * & 1 \\ * & * & * & * \end{pmatrix}, \begin{pmatrix} * & * & * & * \\ 1 & 1 & * & * \\ 1 & 1 & * & * \\ 1 & 1 & * & * \end{pmatrix} \right\}.$$

Definition 2 (μ-Dense regions (μ-DRs)). *A submatrix $X(R, C)$ is called a μ-dense region with respect to v if at least μ percent of the entries of $X(R, C)$ have value v, and, any proper superset of $X(R, C)$ has less than μ percent of entries with value v.*

3 The DRIFT Algorithm

The BasicDRIFT Algorithm. This starts from a given point (s, t) containing the target value v and returns two regions containing (s, t) where the first one is obtained by a vertical-first-search; the other is by a horizontal-first-search. It is proven in [7, Theorem 1] that the two returned regions are in fact DRs.

Algorithm: BasicDRIFT(X, s, t)
$R_v \leftarrow \{1 \leq i \leq n | X_{it} = X_{st}\}$, $C_v \leftarrow \{1 \leq j \leq p | X_{ij} = X_{it} \forall i \in R_v\}$
$C_h \leftarrow \{1 \leq j \leq p | X_{sj} = X_{st}\}$, $R_h \leftarrow \{1 \leq i \leq n | X_{ij} = X_{sj} \forall j \in C_h\}$
Return $\{R_v \times C_v, R_h \times C_h\}$

To determine the time complexity, we suppose the two resulting DRs have dimensions n_v-by-p_v and n_h-by-p_h respectively. The number of computations required by the algorithm is $n + n_v p + p + p_h n$. Moreover, in practice, $n_v, n_h \ll n$ and $p_v, p_h \ll p$. In this case, the complexity is of $O(n + p)$ essentially.

The ExtendedBasicDRIFT Algorithm. The BasicDRIFT algorithm is very fast but it may miss some DRs. To remedy such a deficiency, we introduce the ExtendedBasicDRIFT algorithm which first obtains the set C_h as in the BasicDRIFT starting at (s, t), and then performs vertical searches over all possible subsets of $C_h \setminus \{t\}$. Non-redundant DRs are returned.

This algorithm returns all DRs containing (s, t). However, since it requires more computations than the BasicDRIFT does, we only invoke it to find DRs that the BasicDRIFT misses. The question now becomes how to combine the two algorithms in an effective way which is the purpose of our next algorithm.

The DRIFT Algorithm. We begin by introducing a key concept, called *isolated point*, which allows us to fully utilize the fast BasicDRIFT algorithm to find as many regions as possible while minimizes the use of the more expensive ExtendedBasicDRIFT algorithm.

Definition 3 (Isolated points). *A point (i, j) in a dense region D is isolated if it is not contained in any other dense region.*

By Theorem 3 in [7], (s, t) is an isolated point iff the two DRs obtained from the BasicDRIFT are identical. Moreover, each isolated point belongs only to one DR, hence, after we record this region, the removal of such a point does not delete any legitimate DR but enhances the search for other DRs by the BasicDRIFT. After we remove all the isolated points recursively, the ExtendedBasicDRIFT is run on the reduced data matrix to find all remaining DRs.

Algorithm: DRIFT(X, v)
Repeat
    Start the BasicDRIFT at every point having value v
    Record all the regions found that are legitimate DRs
    Set the entries in X corresponding to the identified isolated points to be ∞
Until no further isolated point is found
Start the ExtendedBasicDRIFT at every point in the updated X having value v
Record all the regions found that are legitimate DRs

We remark that, a DR is "legitimate" if it is not a subset of any previously found DR. Moreover, one might want to discard DRs with small size. To do so, one may define a DR to be "illegitimate" if its size is below a user-specified threshold and thus it is not inserted into the output sequence.

The μDRIFT Algorithm. This algorithm takes the data matrix and the DRs found by DRIFT as inputs. For each of the input region, this algorithm greedily appends rows and columns to the region while maintains the percentage of the target value to be at least μ. Different starting 100%-DRs may result in the same region, such redundancies are removed from the final output list of μ-DRs.

4 Experimental Results

We employ the dataset consisting of gene expression measurements of 23 primate brain samples (7 human, 8 chimpanzees, 8 Rhesus macaques) studied by Cáceres et al in [1]. Oligonucleotide microarrays were used to measure expression levels of ~10000 genes simultaneously. The purpose of the study was to explain phenotypic differences between human and chimpanzees at level of gene regulation using macaques are an outgroup, despite the fact that the two species have ~99% of their DNA sequences in common.

For illustration purposes, a subset of 376 genes is selected based on the coefficient of variation and percentage of present calls generated by the dChip 1.3 software [5]. Next, model-based expression indices are calculated and all replicates are pooled resulting in a dataset with 13 samples and 376 genes. Each gene is then normalized to have mean 0 and standard deviation 1 across the samples. Finally, the values are rounded off to integers.

Example 1. We apply our algorithms to find DRs in the dataset. The results are shown in Fig. 1(a–d). The heat map of the dataset is shown in (a) where the genes and the samples are ordered according to the results of average linkage hierarchical clustering. Three sample DRs identified by μDRIFT are illustrated in (b–d). Moreover, we apply the annotation tool DAVID [2] to find the functional categories of genes in each DR. The region in (b) suggests that most of the genes under the study are down-regulated in the macaque brain samples (Mm1–Mm4). Among the 326 genes in this region, 130 (39.9%) of them are involved metabolism and 96 (29.4%) in cellular physiological process. The region in (c) mostly consists of genes that are down-regulated in the two human samples (Hs1–Hs2) but not other human samples (Hs3–Hs5). The samples Hs1 and Hs2 differ from the other three human samples by (i) they had longer postmortem intervals (~13 hrs) so that the degradation of the RNA samples may have been more pronounced; (ii) they were collected from a different region (the frontal pole) which may show a different pattern of gene expression than samples collected from other regions. If case (i) is the major reason that causes the deviation of Hs1 and Hs2 from Hs3–Hs5, then one may want to discard Hs1 and Hs2 before any further analysis. Thus, it will be helpful to look at the functional categories of the genes in this region. Indeed, 15 genes (31.9%) are involved metabolism while 14 genes (29.8%) in cellular physiological process. The region in (d) consists of genes that are consistently up-regulated in the human samples (Hs3–Hs5) but not in other samples. This gives a list of candidate genes to analyze the difference between human and chimpanzees while reducing the effects (i) and (ii) in Hs1 and Hs2 mentioned above. In this region, out of the 59 genes, 30 (50.8%) of them are involved in metabolism and 17 (28.8%) in cellular physiological process.

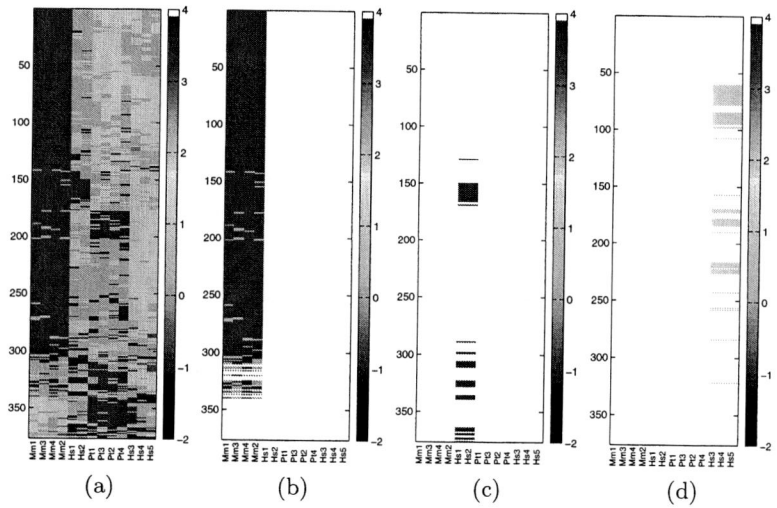

Fig. 1. (a) Heat map (ordered according the results of average linkage hierarchical clustering) of the expression level of 376 genes and 13 samples. (b) A 90%-DR with value -1 (326 genes, 4 samples). (c) A 90%-DR with value -1 (47 genes, 2 samples). (d) A 90%-DR with value 1 (59 genes, 3 samples).

Example 2. This example utilizes permutation tests to estimate statistical significance of DRs. We randomly permute the entries of the original data matrix, apply the μDRIFT with $v = -1, \mu = 90\%$ and record the size of each identified DR. The same procedure is repeated 40 times each with different permutations. The cumulated counts of the size of the DRs are visualized in Fig. 2(a). It can be seen that all of the DRs have very small sizes and that none of the regions have size equal to the ones in Fig. 1(b–c) found from the real dataset. Although we only use a small number of permutations, it is reasonable to expect that the probability of observing 90%-DRs having sizes equal to that in Fig. 1(b–c) from a randomly permuted matrix is extremely low.

Example 3. We evaluate the performance of our algorithms. In Fig. 2(b), the numbers of DRs found by the three algorithms using the dataset in Example 2 are shown as boxplots. We observe that the number of DRs found by BasicDRIFT is around 1/4 of that by the ExtendedBasicDRIFT. Moreover, the μDRIFT does

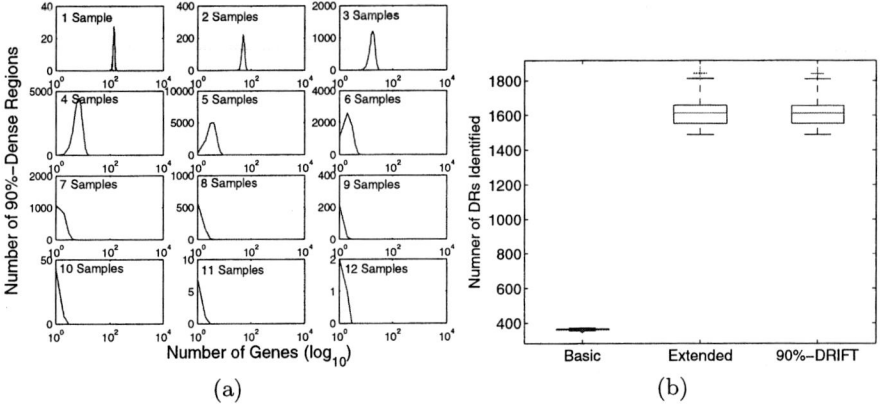

Fig. 2. (a) Frequency counts of the number of genes in the DRs. Each curve represents the regions with a fixed number of samples. (b) Boxplots of the number of DRs identified by the three algorithms. The data is generated by pooling 40 different permutations of the original data matrix.

Table 1. Number of dense regions found by the BasicDRIFT, the ExtendedBasic-DRIFT, and the μDRIFT with various values of μ.

v	Basic	Extended	10%	20%	30%	40%	50%	60%	70%	80%	90%
-1	119	433	1	1	18	40	46	70	110	163	305
1	170	316	3	14	18	27	43	89	153	208	312

not reduce the number of DRs found by the ExtendedBasicDRIFT at all indicating that most regions are of very small sizes. In contrast, the numbers of DRs found by the three algorithms in Example 1 are 119, 433 and 305 respectively. Thus, the μDRIFT is useful when the data matrix contains DRs of relatively large sizes.

Example 4. This example studies the effect of the choice of μ. The data matrix used is the original non-permuted one. In Table 1, we show the number of μ-dense regions found for various values of μ and $v = \pm 1$. The number of dense regions decreases as μ decreases. This is because many regions of small sizes are merged to form large regions. We empirically found that it is the most effective to use $\mu = 90\%$ followed by a filtering (at least 30 genes and 2 samples) to obtain a small list of most significant dense regions from which meaningful regions can be identified.

5 Conclusion and Future Work

In this paper, we introduce the notion of dense regions in microarray data and present effective and efficient algorithms for discovering them. Such patterns are very natural that microarray users may want to look at in the beginning of high-level analysis. Moreover, traditional unsupervised or statistical methods fail to identify these patterns. We demonstrate the usefulness of our algorithms on a dataset with 23 primate brain tissue samples where several biologically interesting dense regions are discovered. We also employ permutation tests to assess statistical significance of dense regions where the particular three regions illustrated are very significant. Empirical studies of the behavior of the algorithms and the choice of the parameter μ are also given. We remark that although we use the matrix of expression values as input to our algorithms in our examples, it is equally-well to apply transformed data as input. For example, one may transform the matrix to a 0/1 matrix depending whether the corresponding gene is up or down-regulated in the sample. Thus, our method can be applied to answer a wider range of queries. We conclude that dense regions are very useful patterns in microarray data that many insights on the dataset can be gained by examining them. As a future work, we would like to incorporate genes' functional categories to enrich the information of the dense regions.

References

1. M. Cáceres et al, *Elevated gene expression levels distinguish human from non-human primate brains*, PNAS, 100, pp.13030–13035, 2003.
2. G. Dennis et al, *DAVID: database for annotation, visualization, and integrated discovery*, Genome Biology, 4(5):P3, 2003.
3. M. B. Eisen, P. T. Spellman, P. O Brown, and D. Botstein, *Cluster analysis and display of genome-wide expression patterns*, PNAS, 85, pp.14863–14868, 1998.
4. M. T. Lee, *Analysis of microarray gene expression data*, Kluwer Academic Publishers, 2004.
5. C. Li and W. H. Wong, *Model-based analysis of oligonecleotide arrays: expression index computation and outlier detection*, PNAS, 98, pp.31–pp.36, 2001.
6. C. Yang, U. Fayyad, and P. S. Bradley, *Efficient discovery of error-tolerant frequent itemsets in high dimensions*, Proc. of ACM SIGKDD Intl. Conf. on Knowledge Discovery and Data Mining: San Francisco, California, pp. 194–203, 2001.
7. A. M. Yip, E. H. Wu, M. K. Ng, and T. F. Chan, *An efficient algorithm for dense regions discovery from large-scale data streams*, Proc. of 8th Pacific-Asia Conf. on on Knowledge Discovery and Data Mining: Sydney, Australia, pp.116–120, 2004; an extended version availiable at: UCLA CAM Reports 03-76, Math. Dept., University of California, Los Angeles, CA, 2003.

Visualisation of Distributions and Clusters Using ViSOMs on Gene Expression Data

Swapna Sarvesvaran and Hujun Yin

University of Manchester Institute of Science and Technology (UMIST)
Department of Electrical Engineering and Electronics
Manchester, M60 1QD, UK

Abstract. Microarray datasets are often too large to visualise due to the high dimensionality. The self-organising map has been found useful to analyse massive complex datasets. It can be used for clustering, visualisation, and dimensionality reduction. However for visualisation purposes the SOM uses colouring schemes as a means of marking cluster boundaries on the map. The distribution of the data and the cluster structures are not faithfully portrayed. In this paper we applied the recently proposed visualisation induced Self-Organising Map (ViSOM), which directly preserves the inter-point distances of the input data on the map as well as the topology. The ViSOM algorithm regularizes the neurons so that the distances between them are proportional in both the data space and the map space. The results are similar to the Sammon mappings but with improved details on gene distributions and the flexibility to nonlinearity. The method is more suitable for larger datasets.

1 Introduction

Microarray technologies make it straightforward to monitor simultaneously the expression patterns of thousands of genes during cellular differentiation and response [1, 2]. Tens of thousands of data points are generated from every experiment. DNA arrays provide a snapshot of all the genes expressed in a cell at a certain time. One of the ultimate goals of biological research is to determine the proteins involved in specific physiological pathways. Hence DNA arrays play a major role in understanding biological processes and systems ranging from gene regulation, to development and to disease from simple to complex. The information obtained can be studied and analysed, to identify the underlying genetic causes of many human diseases, drug discovery and clinical research. One way of discovering pathways and families of similarly acting proteins is to monitor the expression levels of messenger RNA (mRNA), which encodes for the corresponding proteins. The state of a particular cell and its functions is reflected in the levels of mRNA. So subjecting a cell to environmental stimuli and measuring the mRNA levels of genes of interest over time provides expression patterns for the genes.

The concept of microarrays is as follows: mRNAs are extracted from genes that are under study, converted into corresponding complimentary DNAs (cDNA), and tagged with a florescent dye. This is then washed over a glass slide (DNA chip) bearing a grid spotted with DNA sequences of known genes. Tagged cDNAs hybridise (bind) with corresponding DNA sequences on the microarrayer. Analysing the location and intensity of the florescent signals we can determine the levels of activity for each gene. The DNA chip allows scientists to study the entire genome of an organism. This presents a problem, in a statistical aspect, as the data produced from microarray experiments are enormous and trying to visualise datasets of high dimensionality proves very difficult. Since there is no single "best method" available to analysis and visualise microarray data, various methods have been proposed. Numerous dimensionality reduction methods exist that have been used on expression level datasets [7, 9, 12].

Section 2 briefly describes various projection methods. Section 3 describes the related work, ViSOM and potential applications. Section 4 gives a brief explanation about the datasets used and details about the proposed work and the results, together with discussions, are presented in Section 5. Finally Section 6 concludes.

2 Projection Methods

Dimensionality reduction methods map the original data typically into two dimensions, in order to display them onto a screen. The mapping, in order to be useful, needs to serve a human observer by preserving important structures of the original data. The best projection method is not self-evident, but depends on the distribution and nature of the original data and the usage of the resulting configuration. Two popular methods are the principal component analysis (PCA) and multidimensional scaling (MDS). SOMs have also been used as a dimensionality reducing technique, and in conjunction with other clustering methods such as the k-means and hierarchical clustering [14].

2.1 Principal Component Analysis

PCA allows data to be displayed in two dimensions with as much of the variation in the data as possible. It helps to filter noise and reduce the dimensionality of the data without a significant loss of information, making the data more accessible for visualisation and analysis. For a more in depth view on PCA, its application to microarray data and its extensions to nonlinear forms see [4, 6, 7, 10]. One of the disadvantages of PCA is its inability to capture nonlinear relationships in a dataset and if the input dimensionality is much higher than two, the projection onto a linear plane will provide limited visualisation power [16].

2.2 Multidimensional Scaling

MDS, well described in [3], searches for a low dimensional space, which is usually Euclidean, where each point in the mapping space represents one object/variable (genes in the microarray aspect) and such that the distances between the points in the map space, match as well as possible the distances of these points in the input space. That is, it tries to preserve the pairwise distances between data points, so that they are proportional in both the mapping space and the input data space. MDS is generally nonlinear and can reveal the overall structure of the data, but cannot provide the underlying mapping function [16]. Sammon [8, 9] mapping is a popular MDS method; its algorithm is based upon the Newton optimisation techniques. Since Sammon mapping is a point-to-point mapping, like other MDS methods, every time a new point is introduced, the projection has to be recalculated from scratch based on all data points, making it computationally intensive especially when dealing with large datasets (like microarray data). Therefore it requires large amounts of computer memory. Torkkola, et al. [12] suggest, combining Sammon with the SOM algorithm to over come these problems. The Sammon mapping is applied to the results of the SOM algorithm, which has already achieved a substantial data reduction by replacing the original data with fewer representative prototypes.

2.3 Self-organising Maps

Kohonen's SOM is one of the most popular artificial neural networks [5]. The SOM is both a projection method, which maps high-dimensional data into low-dimensional space, and a clustering method so that similar data samples tend to be mapped to nearby neurons (topology preservation). The SOM has been used in data mining and visualization for complex datasets. The network consists of a number of neurons or nodes, usually arranged on a rectangular or hexagonal grid. The SOM is used to reduce the amount of data by clustering and constructing a nonlinear projection of the data onto a lower-dimensional display. For visualisation purposes the SOM uses a colouring scheme such as U-matrix [14], to visualise the relative distances between data points in the input space on the map. But this does not faithfully portray the distribution of the data and its structure.

3 Related Work

The ViSOM, proposed in [17, 18], is a nonlinear projection method for data visualisation but of simple computational structure compared to Sammon mapping that requires the first and second order derivative for every data point in every iteration. ViSOM projects high dimensional data in an unsupervised manner, similar to the SOM, but constrains the lateral contraction force between the neurons and hence regularises the inter-neuron distances with respect to a scalable parameter that define and controls the resolution of the map. The ViSOM preserves the inter-point distances as well as the topology as faithfully as possible therefore providing direct visualisation of the structure and distribution of the data. This paper used a smoothed version of the ViSOM. The algorithm is described as follows [17]:

1. Initialise the weights with principal components or to small random values.
2. At time step t, an input $x(t)$ is drawn randomly from the dataset or data space. A winning neuron, say v, can be found according to its distance to the input,
$$v = \arg\min_{c \in \Omega} \|x(t) - w_c\|$$
3. Update the winner according to equation $\Delta w_v(t+1) = \alpha(t)[x(t) - w_k(t)]$

4. Update the weights of the neighbouring neurons using

$$\Delta w_k(t+1) = \alpha(t)\eta(v,k,t)\left([x(t)-w_v(t)]+[\xi+(1-\xi)(\frac{d_{vk}}{\Delta_{vk}\lambda}-1)][w_v(t)-w_k(t)]\right)$$

Here d_{vk} and Δ_{vk} are the distances between nodes v and k in the data space on the map respectively, ξ is the smooth variable varying from 1 to 0 gradually with time during the training period, λ the resolution parameter depending on the size of the map and the variance or breadth of the data. The smaller the value of λ, the higher resolution the map can provide.

5. Refresh the map by randomly choosing a neuron and using its weight vector as the input for a small percentage of updating times (say for 20% of the iterations). Then the process is repeated until the map converges.

The constraint is introduced gradually for a smooth convergence. More details on this aspect and also the relation to principal curves/surfaces can be found in [17, 18]. This algorithm has already been applied to visualise high dimensional datasets [17, 18], but not microarray datasets.

4 Experiments

Several experiments have been conducted and their results are presented in section 5. The experiments are to demonstrate the usefulness of the ViSOM in visualising multivariate data and its advantages over other methods. The ViSOM has not been previously applied to gene expression datasets.

In the first example, the publicly available dataset of Saccharomyces cerevisiae bakers yeast is used[1]. A sample of size 232x17 (232 rows and 17 columns) was chosen as these 232 genes have been fully identified [1]. Four methods: PCA, Sammon mapping, SOM and ViSOM, were applied to this dataset. The second example uses the rat dataset[2], 112x9 was used same as [16].

5 Results and Discussion

The results shown in Fig. 1 are the results of various projection methods applied to the first dataset. In [1], 6220 (Saccharomyces cerevisiae, bakers yeast) trancripts were monitored. To obtain synchronous yeast culture, cdc28-13 cells were arrested in late G1 at START by raising the temperature to 37°C, and the cell cycle was reinitiated by shifting cells to 25°C. Cells were collected at 17 time points taken at 10 min intervals, covering nearly two full cell cycles. Out of which 416 showed cell cycle-dependent periodicity. 232 biologically characterized genes that showed transcriptional periodicity is listed in [1]. These are the genes used in this paper and referred to as the mitotic dataset.

In the plots seen in Fig. 1, the crosses (x) indicate all the 232 genes listed in [1]. The different shapes, i.e., triangles, circles, squares, diamonds and plus signs indicate genes that were previously identified to be cell cycle regulated by traditional

---

[1] Dataset available at http://genomics.stanford.edu
[2] Dataset available at http://rsb.info.nih.gov/mol-physiol/PNAS/GEMtable.html

methods[3]. Triangles indicate functionally characterized genes in the G2/M phase, diamonds the S/G2 phase, squares are from the M/G1 Boundary, circles represent Late G1, and plus signs are known genes in the S phase, the onces marked are the histones (proteins that are required for normal transcription at several loci) [11]. Not all the genes from the "known regulated genes" list have been marked, not all of them are in the list given in [1] showed transcriptional periodicity. Various shapes and colours are used to specifiy the five phases of the cell cycle.

In Fig. 2 the rat dataset is used [16]. The dataset consists of 112 genes over 9 conditions. This study was conducted so that relationships between members of important gene families during different phases of rat cervical spinal cord development, assayed over nine time points before (E=embryonic) and after birth (P=postnatal) could be discovered.

A rectangular ViSOM was applied to both the datasets and the projected data on the map is shown in Fig.1(d) and Fig.2(b). For comparison, a SOM of the same size and structure has been applied to map the mitotic data and the result is shown in Fig.1(a). The Sammon output for the rat dataset is shown in Fig.2 (a). The intial states of the Sammon mapping, SOM and ViSOM were all placed on a plane spanned by the first two principal components of the data. As can be seen, the ViSOM result closely resembles that of the Sammon mapping except that the data point are more seperated in the ViSOM (i.e. it has captured more details of intra-cluster and inter-point distribution) so each individial cross can be seen more clearley , instead of a lot of overlapping as seen in the Sammon output. The Sammon method is better than the linear PCA in revealling nonlinear structural details, and in the SOM it is impossible to see the inter-cluster and intra-cluster distribution. It can be asssumed that, points plotted near genes with known functions have similar functions to the genes surrounding it or are involved in similar biological pathways.

The advantage of applying the ViSOM to biological data is that the algorithm can be generalised so that no matter how big the data size , the ViSOM algorithm can be adapted accordingly. It is not computationally intensive like Sammon mapping, which requires storing all interpoint distances and second order optimisation processes. Both Sammon mapping and ViSOM can preserve the inter-cluster and intra-cluster details as well as the inter-point distribution of the data, this enable biologists to view each point or gene in the projected space more clearly compared to the other three methods mentioned.

6 Conclusion

In this paper, the ViSOM has been applied on gene expression datasets. The use of ViSOM intends to uncover the structure and patterns from the datasets, and to provide graphical representations that can support understanding and knowledge construction. The ViSOM has been compared to the SOM and Sammon mapping. It is similar in structure to that of the SOM and has similar capabilities as the Sammon mapping; preserving the inter-point distribution of the data. It allows for new points to be added to be projected on to the lower dimensional map without the need for re calculation from scratch based on all data points. The ViSOM constrains the lateral contraction force within the updating neighborhood; without this the ViSOM is the same as the SOM.

---

[3] List available at http://genome-www.stanford.edu/cellcycle/data/rawdata/

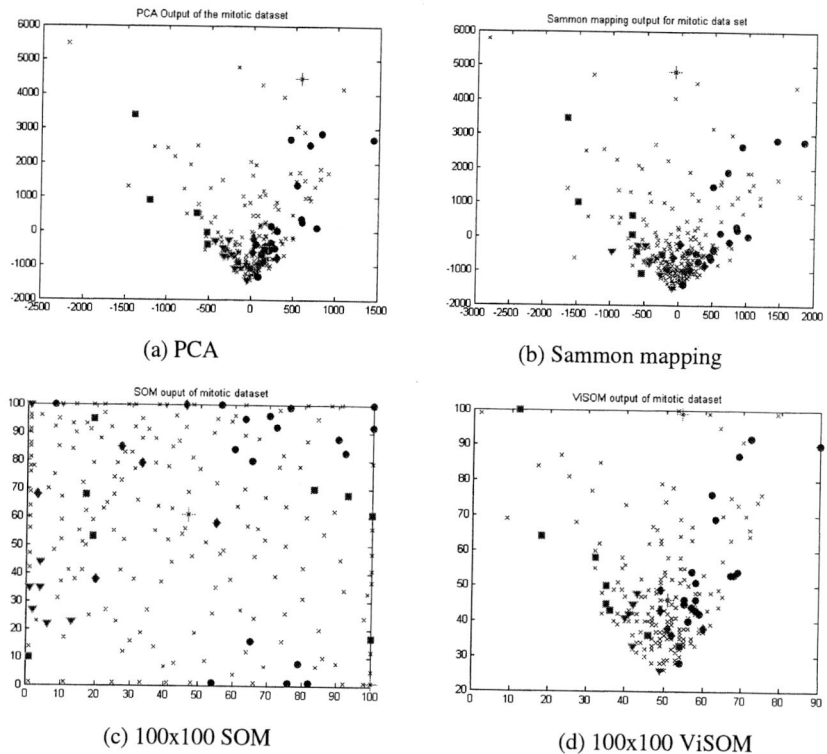

Fig. 1. Projections of mitotic dataset. Each projection shows genes whose functions have been identified within the mitotic cell cycle. The different shapes show characterized genes in different phases of the cell cycle: circles – Late G1, squares – M/G1 boundary, diamonds – S/G2, triangles – G2/M, and crosses – S. The application of the ViSOM algorithm to this dataset resulted in a better visualisation of the genes compared to the PCA, Sammon mapping and SOM. The inter-point distances as well as the neighbouring genes from the original data space are preserved in the lower 2-D space.

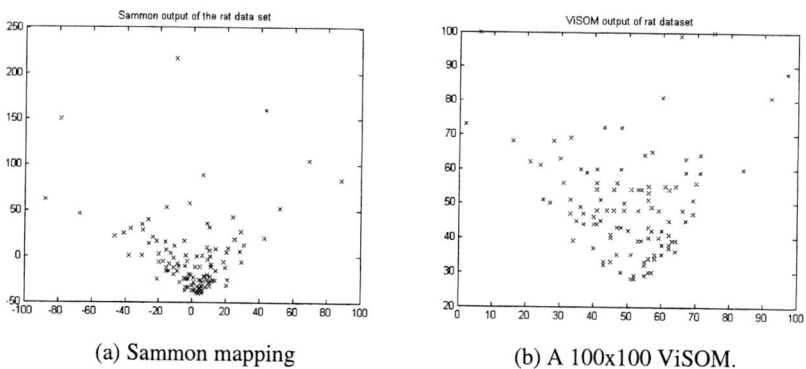

Fig. 2. Projections of rat dataset. It can be clearly seen that the projections of the rat dataset onto a ViSOM map are more discernable compared to the Sammon mapping of the same dataset.

The ultimate goal for researchers in the area of microarray data visualization, is to design tools for visual representations that will allow biologists to view appropriate underlying distributions, patterns, and therefore contribute to enhance their understanding of microarray analysis results. So they can then predict various genomic pathways and protein functions.

References

1. Cho, R. et al.: A Genome-Wide Transcriptional Analysis of the Mitotic Cell Cycle, *Molecular Cell*, Vol.2, 65-73, July1998.
2. Chu, S. et al.: The transcriptional program of sporulation in budding yeast, *Science* 282, 699-705, 1998.
3. Cox, T. F., Cox, M. A. A.: *Multidimensional scaling*, London: Chapman and Hall, 1994.
4. Karhunen, J., Joutsensalo, J.: Generalisation of principal component analysis, optimisation problems, and neural networks, *Neural Networks* 8, 549-562, 1995.
5. Kohonen, T.: *Self-Organizing Maps*, 2nd edition, Springer. 1995.
6. Kramer, M.A.: Nonlinear principal component analysis using autoassociative neural networks, *AICHE Journal*, 37, 233-243, 1991.
7. Raychaudhuri, S.et al.: Principal Components Analysis to Summarize Microarray Experiments- Application to Sporulation Time Series, *Pac Symp Biocomput*: 455-66, 2000.
8. Ripley B. D.: *Pattern recognition and neural network*, Cambridge, UK: Cambridge University Press, 1996.
9. Sammon, J.W.: A nonlinear mapping for data structure, *IEEE Transactions on Computer*, 18, 401-409, 1969.
10. Schölkopf,B., Smola, A., Müller, K.R.: Nonlinear component analysis as a kernal eigenvalue problem, *Neural Computation*, 10, 1299-1319, 1998.
11. Spellman P.T. et al.: Comprehensive Identification of Cell Cycle-regulated genes of the yeast saccharomyces cerevisiae by microarray hybridisation, *Molecular Biology of the Cell* 9, 3273-3297, 1998.
12. Torkkola, K. et al.: Self-organizing maps in mining gene expression data, Information Sciences 139: 79-96, 2001.
13. Törönen, P. et al.: Analysis of gene expression data using self-organising maps, *FEBS Letters*, 451, 142-146, 1999.
14. Ultsch, A.: *Self-organizing neural networks for visualization and classification*. In O.Opitz, B. Lausen, & R. Klar (Eds.), Information and classification (pp. 864-867), 1993.
15. Wang et al.: Clustering of the SOM easily reveals distinct gene expression patterns: results of a reanalysis of lymphoma study, *Bioinformatics* 3:36, 24 Nov 2002.
16. Wen, X. et al.: Large-Scale Temporal Gene Expression Mapping of CNS Development, *Proc Natl Acad Sci USA*, 95:334-339, 1998.
17. Yin, H.: *Visualisation induced SOM (ViSOM)*, In N. Allinson, H. Yin. L. Allinson, &J. Slack (Eds.), Advances is self-organising maps, (pp. 81-88), Proceedings WSOM'01, London: Springer, 2001.
18. Yin, H.: Data visualisation and manifold mapping using the ViSOM, *Neural Networks* 15: 1005-1016, 2002.

Prediction of Implicit Protein–Protein Interaction by Optimal Associative Feature Mining

Jae-Hong Eom, Jeong-Ho Chang, and Byoung-Tak Zhang

Biointelligence Lab., School of Computer Science and Engineering
Seoul National University
Seoul 151-744, South Korea
{jheom,jhchang,btzhang}@bi.snu.ac.kr

Abstract. Proteins are known to perform a biological function by interacting with other proteins or compounds. Since protein–protein interaction is intrinsic to most cellular processes, protein interaction prediction is an important issue in post–genomic biology where abundant interaction data has been produced by many research groups. In this paper, we present an associative feature mining method to predict implicit protein–protein interactions of *S.cerevisiae* from public protein–protein interaction data. To overcome the dimensionality problem of conventional data mining approach, we employ feature dimension reduction filter (FDRF) method based on the information theory to select optimal informative features and to speed up the overall mining procedure. As a mining method to predict interaction, we use association rule discovery algorithm for associative feature and rule mining. Using the discovered associative feature we predict implicit protein interactions which have not been observed in training data. According to the experimental results, the proposed method accomplishes about 94.8% prediction accuracy with reduced computation time which is 32.5% faster than conventional method that has no feature filter.

1 Introduction

With the advancement of genomic technology and genome–wide analysis of organisms, one of the great challenges to post-genomic biology is to understand how genetic information of proteins results in the predetermined action of gene products, both temporally and spatially, to accomplish biological function and how they act together with each other to build an organism. Also, it is known that protein–protein interactions are fundamental biochemical reactions in the organisms and play an important role since they determine the biological processes [1]. Therefore comprehensive description and detailed analysis of protein–protein interactions would significantly contribute to the understanding of biological phenomena and problems.

After the completion of the genome sequence of *S.cerevisiae*, budding yeast (bakers yeast), many researchers have undertaken the task of functionally analyzing the yeast genome comprising more than 6,300 proteins (YPD) [2] and abundant interaction data have been produced by many research groups. Subsequently, several promising methods have been successfully applied to this field.

The technique to uncover useful information or facts underlying huge data, which called 'data mining', attracts a lot of attention, and much research applying data mining to bioinformatics have already been conducted. One of the most popular data mining methods is 'association rule discovery' developed by Agrawal *et al.* [3]. Satou *et al.* [4] and Oyama *et al.* [5] applied this method to find rules describing the association among heterogeneous genome data. But, nearly all data mining approaches to bioinformatics suffer from high dimensional property of data which have more than thousand features. In data mining, features describing each data represent the dimensionality of each data item. Oyama *et al.* [5], for example, predicted protein–protein interaction using the data which have more than 5,240 feature dimensions.

In this paper, we propose an efficient protein–protein interaction mining technique which performs efficiently with feature dimension reduction. Here we combine the feature selection approach which was originally introduced by Yu *et al.* [6] and the protein interaction mining based on association rule discovery which was originally introduced by Oyama *et al.* [5]. We formulate the problem of protein-protein interaction prediction as the problem of mining feature-to-feature association of each interacting protein. To predict protein–protein interactions with the association information, we use as many features as possible from several major databases such as MIPS, DIP and SGD [7, 8, 9]. And feature dimension reduction filter (FDRF) method based on the information theory is used to select the most informative features and to speed up the overall mining procedures. After the feature filtering, we apply the association rule discovery method to find optimal associative feature sets and predict additional interactions (i.e., implicit interactions) between unknown proteins using discovered associative features.

The paper is organized as follows. In Section 2, the concept of FDRF and its procedure are described. In Section 3, the concept of association mining and the approach for protein–protein interaction analysis with feature association are described. In Section 4, we show experimental results in comparison with conventional mining method. Finally, Section 5 presents concluding remarks and future direction.

2 Feature Dimension Reduction

In many applications such as genome projects, the data size is becoming increasingly large in both rows (i.e., number of instances) and in columns (i.e., number of features). Therefore, feature selection is necessary in machine learning tasks when dealing with such high dimensional data [6].

Feature selection is the process of choosing a subset of original feature so that the feature space is optimally reduced according to a certain evaluation criterion. Generally, a feature is regarded as s good feature if it is relevant to the class concept but is not redundant to any other relevant features and the correlation between two variables can be regarded as a goodness measure.

The correlation between two random variables can be measured by two broad approaches, based on classical linear correlation and based on information theory. Linear correlation approaches (e.g., *linear correlation coefficient, least square regression error*, and *maximal information compression index*) have several benefits. These approaches can remove features with near zero linear correlation to the class and reduce redundancy among selected features. But, linear correlation measures may not be able to capture correlations that are not linear in nature and the calculation requires all features contain numerical values [6]. In this paper, we use an information theory-based correlation measure to overcome these drawbacks.

Each feature of data can be considered as a random variable. And the uncertainty of a random variable can be measured by *entropy*. The entropy of a variable X is defined as

$$H(X) = -\sum_i P(x_i) \log_2(P(x_i)), \tag{1}$$

And the entropy of X after observing values of another variable Y is defined as

$$H(X|Y) = -\sum_j P(y_j) \sum_i P(x_i|y_j) \log_2(P(x_i|y_j)), \tag{2}$$

where $P(y_j)$ is the prior probability of the value y_j of Y, and $P(x_i|y_j)$ is the posterior probability of X being x_i given the values of Y. The amount by which the entropy of X decreases reflects additional information about X provided by Y and is called *information gain* [10], which is given by

$$IG(X|Y) = H(X) - H(X|Y) \tag{3}$$

According to this measure, a feature Y is considered to be more correlated to feature X than feature Z, if $IG(X|Y) > IG(Z|Y)$. Symmetry is a desired property for a measure of correlation between features and information gain. However, information gain is biased in favor of features with more values and the values have to be normalized to ensure they are comparable and have the same affect. Therefore, here we use the *symmetrical uncertainty* as a measure of feature correlation [11], defined as

$$SU(X,Y) = 2\left[\frac{IG(X|Y)}{H(X)+H(Y)}\right], \ 0 \leq SU(X,Y) \leq 1 \tag{4}$$

Figure 1 shows the overall procedure of the correlation-based feature dimension reduction filter which was earlier introduced by Yu *et al.* [6], named fast correlation-based filter (FCBF). In this paper, we call this FCBC procedure as feature dimension reduction filter (FDRF) for our application. The algorithm finds a set of principal features S_{best} for the class concept. The procedures in Figure 1 are divided into two major parts. In the first part (Step 1 and Step 2), it calculates the symmetrical uncertainty (*SU*) values for each feature, selects relevant feature into S'_{list} based on the predefined threshold δ, and constructs an ordered list of them in descending order according to their *SU* values. In the second part (Step 3 and Step 4), it further processes the ordered list to remove redundant features and only keeps principal ones among all the selected relevant features.

With symmetrical uncertainty as a feature association measure, we reduce the feature dimension through the feature selection procedure. In Figure 1, the class C is divided into two classes, conditional protein class (C_C) and result protein class (C_R) of interaction. The relevance of a feature to the protein interaction (interaction class) is decided by the value of c–correlation and f–correlation, where an SU value δ is used as a threshold value.

Given training dataset $S = (f_1,\ldots,f_N,C)$, where $C = C_C \cup C_R$ and User-decided threshold δ, do following procedure for each class C_C and C_R.

1. **Repeat** Step 1.1 to 1.2, for all i, $i = 1$ to N.
   1.1 **Calculate** $SU_{i,c}$ for f_i.
   1.2. **Append** f_i to S'_{list} when $SU_{i,c} \geq \delta$.
2. **Sort** S'_{list} in descending order with $SU_{i,c}$ value.
3. **Set** f_p with the first element of S'_{list}.
4. **Repeat** Step 4.1 to 4.3, for all $f_p \neq NULL$.
   4.1 **Set** f_q with the next element of f_p in S'_{list}.
   4.2 **Repeat** Step 4.2.1 to 4.2.3, for all $f_q \neq NULL$.
      4.2.1 **Set** $f'_q = f_q$.
      4.2.2 if $SU_{p,q} \geq SU_{q,c}$,
         Remove f_q from S'_{list} and **Set** f_q with the next element of f'_q in S'_{list}.
         else **Set** f_q with the next element of f_q in S'_{list}.
      4.2.3 **Set** f_q with the next element of f_q in S'_{list}
   4.3 **Set** f_p with next the element of f_p in S'_{list}.
5. **Set** $S_{best} = S'_{list}$
Output the most informative optimal feature subset: S_{best}

Fig. 1. The procedures of feature dimension reduction filter (FDRF).

Definition 1 (c–correlation $SU_{i,c}$, f–correlation $SU_{j,i}$). Assume that dataset S contains N ($f_1,\ldots,f_N$) features and a class C (C_C or C_R). Let $SU_{i,c}$ denote the SU value that measures the correlation between a feature f_i and the class C (called c–correlation), then a subset S' of relevant features can be decided by a threshold SU value δ, such that $f_i \cdot S'$, $1 \leq i \leq N$, $SU_{i,c} \geq \delta$. And the pairwise correlation between all features (called f–correlation) can be defined in same manner of c–correlation with a threshold value δ. The value of f–correlation is used to decide whether relevant feature is redundant or not when considering it with other relevant features.

3 Mining Associative Feature

Association Mining
To predict protein–protein interaction with feature association, we adopt the association rule discovery algorithm (so-called Apriori algorithm) proposed by Agrawal et

al. [3]. Generally, an association rule $R\ (A \Rightarrow B)$ has two values, *support* and *confidence*, representing the characteristics of the association rule. Support (*SP*) represents the frequency of co-occurrence of all the items appearing in the rule. And confidence (*CF*) is the accuracy of the rule, which is calculated by dividing the *SP* value by the frequency of the item in conditional part of the rule.

$$SP(A \Rightarrow B) = P(A \cup B),\ CF(A \Rightarrow B) = P(B\,|\,A) \tag{5}$$

where $A \Rightarrow B$ represents association rule for two items (set of features) A and B in that order. Association rule can be discovered by detecting all the possible rules whose supports and confidences are larger than the user-defined threshold value called minimal support (SP_{min}) and minimal confidence (CF_{min}) respectively. Rules that satisfy both minimum support and minimum confidence threshold are taken as to be *strong*. Here we consider these strong association rules as interesting ones.

In this work, we use the same association rule mining and the scoring approach of Oyama *et al.* [5] for performance comparison.

Protein Interaction with Feature Association

An interaction is represented as a pair of two proteins that directly bind to each other. To analyze protein–protein interactions with feature association, we consider each interacting protein pair as a transaction of data mining. These transactions with binary vector representation are described in Figure 2. Using association rule mining, then, we extract association of features which generalize the interactions.

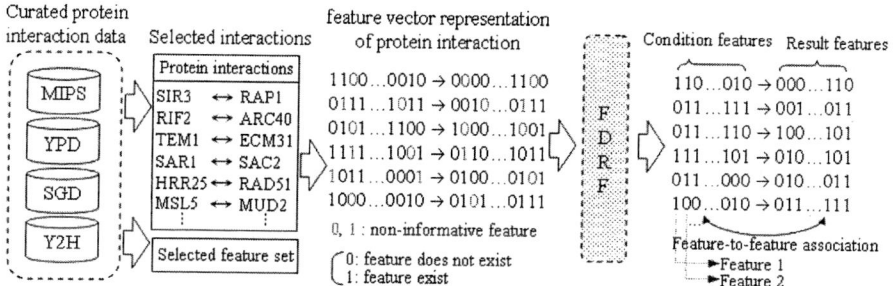

Fig. 2. Representation of protein interaction by feature vectors. Each interaction is represented with binary feature vector (whether the feature exists or not) and their associations. The FDRF sets those features as 'don't care' which have *SU* value less than given *SU* threshold δ. This is intended to consider in association mining only those features that have greater *SU* value than a given threshold. The features marked 'don't care' are regarded as 'don't care' also in association rule mining (i.e., these features are not counted in the calculation of support and confidence). These features are not shown in the vector representation of right side of Figure 2.

4 Experimental Results

Data Sets

Major protein pairs of the interactions are obtained from the same data source of Oyama *et al.* [5]. It includes MIPS [7], YPD [12] and two Y2H data by Ito *et al.* [13]

and Uetz et al. [14]. Additionally, we use SGD to collect additional feature set [8]. Table 1 shows the statistics of each interaction data source and the number of features before and after the application of FDRF.

Table 1. The statistics for the dataset.

Data Source	# of interactions	# of initial features	# of filtered features
MIPS	10,641		
YPD	2,952	6,232	1,293
SGD	1,482	(total)	(total)
Y2H (Ito et al.)	957		
Y2H (Uetz et al.)	5,086		

Results

First, we selected more informative features using the filtering procedure of Figure 1 (δ=0.73). Then, we performed association rule mining under the condition of minimal support 9 and minimal confidence 75% on the protein interaction data, resulting in 1,293 features from 6,232 features in total. With the mined feature association, we predicted new protein–protein interaction which were not used in association training step. We run 10-fold cross-validation and predictions were validated with comparison to the collected dataset.

Table 2 shows advantageous effects obtained by the filtering of non-informative (redundant) features. By the application of FDRF, the accuracy increased about 3.4% and the computation time decreased by the fraction of 32.5%, even including the FDRF processing time, compared with the conventional method which perform association rule mining without feature filtering. To summarize, we can see that our proposed method which combines feature filtering and association mining not only prevents wrong associations by eliminating a set of misleding or redundnt features of interaction data but also contribute to the reduction of computational complexity accompanying rule mining procedure.

Table 2. Accuracy of the proposed method and the effect of the FDRF-based feature selection in terms of computation time. The elapsed time was measured on Pentium IV 2.4GHz and 1GB RAM system running Windows.

Prediction method	# of interactions			Accuracy ($|P|/|T|$)	Elapsed Time
	Training set	Test set (T)	Correctly predicted (P)		
Without FDRF	4,628	463	423	91.4 %	212.34 sec
With FDRF	4,628	463	439	94.8 %	143.27 sec
Improvement	–	–	–	3.4 %	32.5 %

5 Conclusions

In this paper, we presented a novel method for predicting protein–protein interaction by combining information theory based feature dimension reduction filter with feature association mining. The proposed method achieved the improvement in both the prediction accuracy and the processing time. In Table 2, it is also suggested that further detailed investigation of the protein–protein interaction can be made with smaller granularity of interaction (i.e., not protein, but a set of features of proteins). As a result, we can conclude that the proposed method is suitable for efficient prediction of the interactive protein pair with many features from the experimentally produced protein–protein interaction data which have moderate amount of false positive ratios. But, the current public interaction data produced by such as high-throughput methods (e.g., Y2H) have many false positives. And several interactions of these false positives are corrected by recent researches through the reinvestigation with new experimental approaches. Thus, studies on new methods for resolving these problems remain as a future work.

Acknowledgements

This research was supported by the Korean Ministry of Science and Technology under the NRL Program and the Systems Biology Program.

References

1. Deng, M., *et al.*: Inferring domain–domain interactions from protein–protein interactions. *Genome Res.* 12, 1540–1548, 2002.
2. Goffeau, A., *et al.*: Life with 6000 genes. *Science* 274, 546–567, 1996.
3. Agrawal, R., *et al.*: Mining association rules between sets of items in large databases. In *Proc. of ACM SIGMOD-93* 207–216, 1993.
4. Satou, K., *et al.*: Extraction of substructures of proteins essential to their biological functions by a data mining technique. In *Proc. of ISMB-97* 5, 254–257, 1997.
5. Oyama, T., *et al.*: Extraction of knowledge on protein–protein interaction by association rule discovery. *Bioinformatics* 18, 705–714, 2002.
6. Yu, L. and Liu, H.: Feature selection for high dimensional data: a fast correlation-based filter solution. In *Proc. of ICML-03* 856–863, 2003.
7. Mewes, H.W., *et al.*: MIPS: a database for genomes and protein sequences. *Nucleic Acids Res.* 30, 31–34, 2002.
8. Xenarios, I., *et al.*: DIP: The Database of Interacting Proteins. A research tool for studying cellular networks of protein interactions. *Nucleic Acids Res.* 30, 303–305, 2002.
9. Christie, K.R., *et al.*: Saccharomyces Genome Database (SGD) provides tools to identify and analyze sequences from Saccharomyces cerevisiae and related sequences from other organisms. *Nucleic Acids Res.* 32, D311–D314, 2004.
10. Quinlan, J.: C4.5: Programs for machine learning. Morgan Kaufmann, 1993.
11. Press, W.H., *et al.*: Numerical recipes in C. *Cambridge University Press.*, 1988.
12. Csank, C., *et al.*: Three yeast proteome databases: YPD, PombePD, and CalPD (MycoPathPD). *Methods Enzymol.* 350, 347–373, 2002.
13. Ito, T., *et al.*: A comprehensive two-hybrid analysis to explore the yeast protein interactome. *Proc. Natl Acad. Sci. USA* 98, 4569–4574, 2001.
14. Uetz, P., *et al.*: A comprehensive analysis of protein-protein interactions in Saccharomyces cerevisiae. *Nature* 403, 623–627, 2000.

Exploring Dependencies Between Yeast Stress Genes and Their Regulators*

Janne Nikkilä[1], Christophe Roos[2], and Samuel Kaski[3,1]

[1] Neural Networks Research Centre, Helsinki University of Technology
P.O. Box 5400, FIN-02015 HUT, Finland
[2] Medicel Oy, Huopalahdentie 24, FIN-00350 Helsinki, Finland
[3] Dept. of Computer Science, P.O. Box 26, FIN-00014 University of Helsinki, Finland

Abstract. An environmental stress response gene should, by definition, have common properties in its behavior across different stress treatments. We search for such common properties by models that maximize common variation, and explore potential regulators of the stress response by further maximizing mutual information with transcription factor binding data. A computationally tractable combination of generalized canonical correlations and clustering that searches for dependencies is proposed and shown to find promising sets of genes and their potential regulators.

1 Introduction

Yeast stress response has been studied intensively during recent years [2,4]. A group of genes appears to be always affected in various stress treatments, and this set has been called *common environmental response (CER)* or *environmental stress response (ESR)* genes. Such stress response is practically the only way for the simple yeast to respond to various adverse environmental conditions, and because it is so easy to elicit, it has been used as a paradigm to study gene regulatory networks. Even this response is far from being completely understood, however; different studies do not even agree on the sets of stress genes.

In practice we have available a set of gene expression profiles, a time series of expression for each gene, for each stress treatment. The common environmental response should be visible as some properties that are unknown but common to all treatments. We will search for such properties among all the other variation in the gene expression profiles by maximizing the variation that is common to the stress treatment data sets.

To explore regulation of the stress response, we further search for commonalities with data about how likely different transcription factors (TF), regulators of gene expression, are to bind to the promoter regions of the genes. If a set of genes has commonalities in their expression patterns across stress treatments, and furthermore commonalities in the binding patters, they are likely to be stress response genes regulated in the same way.

---

* This work was supported by the Academy of Finland, decisions 79017 and 207467. We wish to thank Eerika Savia for insights about gCCA.

This kind of dependency exploration can be done by maximizing the mutual information, or preferably its finite-data variant, between the data sets. We will use so-called *associative clustering* [10] which maximizes dependency between data sets and hence should suit the task perfectly. In practice, a linear projection method scales better to multiple data sets, and we use a generalization of *canonical correlations* as a preprocessing to reduce the number of data sets.

Clusterings that maximize mutual information have been formalized also in the information bottleneck [11] framework. Our clusterings can be viewed as extensions of the current information bottleneck algorithms, suitable for finite sets of continuous-valued data.

Graphical models of dependencies between variables are another related popular formalism. They have been applied to modeling regulation of gene expression [3]. The main practical difference from our clustering approach, which makes the models complementary, is that our clusterings are intended to be used as general-purpose, data-driven but not data-specific, exploratory tools. Associative clustering is a multivariate data analysis tool that can be used in the same way as standard clusterings to explore regularities in data. The findings can then be dressed as prior beliefs or first guesses in the more structured probabilistic models.

The technical difference from standard clusterings, as well as from standard graphical models, is that our objective function is maximization of dependency between the data sets. Instead of modeling all variability in the data the models focus on those aspects that are common in the different data sets. This fits perfectly the present application.

2 Methods

2.1 Generalized Canonical Correlation Analysis

Canonical correlation analysis (CCA) is a classical method for finding (linear) dependencies between two data sets. It searches for a component from each set, such that the correlation between the components is maximized. The next pair of components maximizes the correlation subject to the constraint of being uncorrelated with the first components. For normally distributed data CCA maximizes mutual information.

There exist several generalizations of CCA to multiple data sets. We selected the generalization (abbreviated gCCA here) that preserves the connection of CCA to mutual information [1]. The gCCA for M multivariate, normally distributed variables $V_1, ..., V_M$ can be formulated as a generalized eigenvalue problem $C\xi = \lambda D\xi$, where $\lambda = 1 + \rho$ (ρ being the canonical correlation), C is the covariance matrix of the concatenated original variables $V = [V_1^T \ ... \ V_M^T]^T$, $\xi = [\xi_1^T \ ... \ \xi_M^T]^T$ are the eigenvectors, and $D = diag(C_{11}, ..., C_{MM})$ is the block diagonal matrix consisting of the covariance matrices of the original variables.

For more details see [1] and [8] where the closest method is SUMCOR.

We use gCCA in a possibly novel way for dimensionality reduction. Standardizing the data, i.e. making $C_{mm} = I$, does not affect the eigenvalues, but reduces the eigenvalue equation (for the standardized data) to a standard eigenvalue problem $C\xi = \lambda\xi$ that produces an orthogonal set of ξ. The whole concatenated, standardized data set is then projected onto the reduced-dimensional space formed of these eigenvectors. It can be shown that the first p eigenvectors $\xi^{(1)}, ..., \xi^{(p)}$ (corresponding to the p largest eigenvalues) then preserve maximally the mutual information between the original variables V_m. As a result we obtain a new, low-dimensional representation Y that preserves the mutual dependency between the original variables: $Y = \Xi^T V$, where $\Xi = [\xi^{(1)}, ..., \xi^{(p)}]$.

2.2 Associative Clustering

Given a set of paired observations $\{(\mathbf{x}_k, \mathbf{y}_k)\}_k$ from two continuous, vector-valued random variables X and Y, associative clustering (AC) [10] produces two sets of partitions, one for X and the other for Y. The aim is to make the cross-partition contingency table represent as much of the dependencies between X and Y as possible. The Bayesian criterion is detailed below.

Because the partitions for **x** and **y** define the margins of the contingency table, they are called *margin partitions*, and they split the data into *margin clusters*. The cells of the contingency table correspond to pairs of margin clusters, and they split data pairs $(\mathbf{x}, \mathbf{y})$ into clusters. Denote the count of data within the contingency table cell on row i and column j by n_{ij}, and sums with dots: $n_{i\cdot} = \sum_j n_{ij}$.

The AC optimizes the margin partitions to maximize dependency between them, measured by the *Bayes factor* between two hypotheses: the margins are independent (H) vs. dependent ($\bar{H}$). The Bayes factor is (derivation omitted)

$$\frac{P(\{n_{ij}\}|\bar{H})}{P(\{n_{ij}\}|H)} \propto \frac{\prod_{ij} \Gamma(n_{ij} + \alpha_{ij})}{\prod_i \Gamma(n_{i\cdot} + \alpha_i) \prod_j \Gamma(n_{\cdot j} + \alpha_j)}, \quad (1)$$

where the α come from priors, set equal to 1 in this work. The cell frequencies are computed from the training samples $\{(\mathbf{x}_k, \mathbf{y}_k)\}_k$ by mapping them to the closest margin cluster in each space, parameterized by a respective prototype vector **m**. In the optimization the partitions are smoothed to facilitate the application of gradient-based methods. More details in [10].

Note that our use of Bayes factors is different from their traditional use in hypothesis testing, cf. [5]. In AC we do not test any hypotheses but the Bayes factor is maximized to explicitly hunt for dependencies. It may also be worth pointing out that we do not expect to find dependencies between the margins for the *whole data*. Instead, a reproducible dependency between the margin clusters will be regarded as evidence for dependency for some *subsets of the data*. Reproducibility is in this work evaluated by comparing, with cross-validation, contingency tables produced by AC and independent K-means clusterings computed for both spaces separately. Should AC not find a non-random dependency, Bayes factors from AC and K-means should be about equal for test data.

Uncertainty in the AC clusters, stemming from the finiteness of the data sets, is accounted for by a bootstrap analysis [7]. We wish to find clusters (contingency table cells) that signify dependencies between the data sets, and that are reproducible. The AC produces an estimate of how unlikely a cell is given the margins are independent (details in [10]), and the reproducibility is evaluated by the bootstrap. These two criteria will be combined by evaluating, for every gene pair, how likely they are to occur within the same significant cluster. This similarity matrix will finally be summarized by hierarchical clustering.

2.3 GCCA as Preprocessing for AC

Having observed for one set of objects (genes) several multivariate variables $V_1, ..., V_M, X$ (stress treatments and TF-binding) forming several data sets, our aim is to find clusters of genes that maximize the mutual information $\text{MI}(V_1, ..., V_M, X)$, or its finite-data version, that is, the Bayes factor. In principle, AC could be extended to search for a multiway contingency table between the multiple data sets, but this would lead to severe estimation problems with a finite data set.

Noting that $\text{MI}(V_1, ..., V_M, X) = \text{MI}(V_1, ..., V_M) + \text{MI}((V_1, ..., V_M), X)$ we propose a sequential approximation: first approximate $\text{MI}(V_1, ..., V_M)$ by forming the optimal representation $Y(V_1, ..., V_M)$ with gCCA, then maximize $\text{MI}(Y, X)$ with AC. In this way we can reduce our problem to the AC of two variables and, in a sense, preserve dependencies between all the data sets in a computationally tractable way. Additionally, note that we are here specifically interested in *clusters* of genes, which justifies the use of AC instead of using only gCCA which only produces a projection of the data.

3 Data

We used data from several experiments to analyze the dependencies between yeast stress genes and their regulators. Common stress response was sought from expression data of altogether 16 stress treatments [2,4]. A short time series had been measured from each, and in total we had 104 dimensions. For these genes we picked up the TF-binding profiles of 113 transcription factors [9], to search for dependencies with expression patterns. In total we ended up in 5998 yeast genes. All the values were normalized with respect to the zero point of each time series (or other control) and then the natural logarithm of these ratios was taken. Missing values were imputed by genewise averages in each data set.

4 Results

Dependencies between the 16 different stress treatment time series were first extracted with gCCA. The number of gCCA components was chosen to maximize the mutual information in left-out data, in 20-fold crossvalidation. This resulted in 12 components. gCCA was validated by testing the association of the 12 first gCCA components to genes known to be affected by stress, namely the environmental stress genes (ESR) found in [4]. Most of the components showed significant association to ESR genes (Wilcoxon rank sum test; $p < 0.01$), thus validating the use of gCCA.

This 12-dimensional expression data and the TF-binding data were then clustered with AC (with 30x20 cells in contingency table).

To verify that there are dependencies the AC is able to detect, the contingency table produced by AC was compared to the contingency table obtained with independent K-means clusterings in both data spaces, in a 10-fold crossvalidation run. AC found statistically significantly higher dependency between the data sets than K-means (p< 0.01; paired t-test). This confirmed that some subset of the genes has a non-random dependency between TF-binding and expression (discernible from these data sets).

After these preliminary checks we used the AC to search for salient dependencies between the stress expression data and the TF binding data. A similarity matrix was produced by bootstrap analysis with 100 samples as described in Section 2.2, and summarized by hierarchical clustering. Figure 1 shows a few clear clusters interspersed within a background that shows no apparent dependencies. We cut the dendrogram at the height of 80. This defines a threshold on reliability: if genes occur together, within significant clusters, on average more than in 20 of the 100 bootstrap AC:s, their association is reliable.

Fig. 1. Hierarchical clustering that summarizes reliable dependencies between stress genes and binding patterns of regulators. The y-axis represents the average distance of the genes in clusters, and each vertical line represents one gene or cluster. The similarity matrix is computed from bootstrap samples of AC. The mass of clusters has an average within-cluster distance between 80 and 100, showing no obvious dependency. The groups of lines protruding downwards from the non-dependent mass are potential reliable gene groups with non-random dependency between their TF-binding and stress-related expression.

We validated the clusters extracted from Figure 1 by investigating the distribution of earlier-found ESR genes within them. Since we had designed the models to hunt for regulation patterns of ESR genes, we expected some of our clusters to consist of ESR genes. Indeed, upregulated ESR genes were enriched statistically significantly in 14 out of the 51 clusters (hypergeometric distribution; p-value < 0.001), and downregulated ESR genes in 12 of them. This confirms that our method has succeeded in capturing stress related genes in clusters.

Finally the clusters were analyzed with EASE [6] to find significant enrichments of gene ontology classes. In total we found 14 statistically significant enriched (Bonferroni corrected p-value < 0.05) GO slim classes[1] in our 51 clusters. The most common (7 out of 14) was the biological process "ribosome biogenesis

---

[1] go_slim_mapping.tab at ftp://genome-ftp.stanford.edu/pub/yeast/data_download/literature_curation/

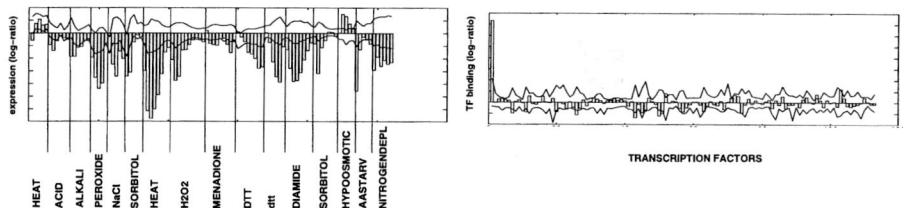

Fig. 2. An example cluster revealing an interesting dependency between gene expression in stress and TF-binding. Left: the average expression profile of the genes in the cluster. Right: the average TF-binding profile of the same genes. Continuous lines depict the 0.999 confidence intervals (computed from 10000 random clusters). The cluster profiles suggest that this set of genes is nearly always downregulated under stress, and that this behaviour might be due to transcription factors with the highest peaks in TF-profile. The specific TFs are currently under analysis.

and assembly" and its subclasses that were found in clusters where genes were strongly downregulated. This is a clear indication of yeast's response to stress by driving down the different components of protein synthesis machinery. The TFs in these clusters will be analyzed further; an example is shown in Figure 2.

5 Discussion

We explored dependencies between yeast gene expression under stress and putative gene regulators by dependency maximization methods.

We applied generalized canonical correlations (gCCA) in a novel way to multiple stress expression sets to produce one representation for the sets, which preserves mutual information between the sets. This preprocessed data was then clustered with AC to maximize the dependency to binding profiles of a set of regulators.

Biological relevance of the clusters was confirmed with several tests and database searches. We can conclude that our approach succeeded notably well both in confirming some known facts, and in generating new hypotheses.

References

1. F. R. Bach and M. I. Jordan. Kernel independent component analysis. *JMLR*, 3:1–48, 2002.
2. H. C. Causton et al. Remodeling of yeast genome expression in response to environmental changes. *Molecular Biology of Cell*, 12:323–337, February 2001.
3. N. Friedman. Inferring cellular networks using probabilistic graphical models. *Science*, 303:799–805, 2004.
4. A. P. Gasch et al. Genomic expression programs in the response of yeast cells to environmental changes. *Molecular Biology of the Cell*, 11:4241–4257, 2000.
5. I. J. Good. On the application of symmetric Dirichlet distributions and their mixtures to contingency tables. *Annals of Statistics*, 4(6):1159–1189, 1976.

6. D. A. Hosack et al. Identifying biological themes within lists of genes with ease. *Genome Biology*, 4(R70), 2003.
7. M. K. Kerr and G. A. Churchill. Bootstrapping cluster analysis: Assessing the reliability of conclusions from microarray experiments. *PNAS*, 98:8961–8965, 2001.
8. J. R. Kettenring. Canonical analysis of several sets of variables. *Biometrika*, 58(3):433–451, 1971.
9. T. I. Lee et al. Transcriptional regulatory networks in *Saccharomyces cerevisiae*. *Science*, 298:799–804, 2002.
10. J. Sinkkonen, J. Nikkilä, L. Lahti, and S. Kaski. Associative clustering by maximizing a Bayes factor. Technical Report A68, Helsinki University of Technology, Laboratory of Computer and Information Science, Espoo, Finland, 2003.
11. N. Tishby, F C. Pereira, and W. Bialek. The information bottleneck method. In *37th Annual Allerton Conference on Communication, Control, and Computing*, pages 368–377. Urbana, Illinois, 1999.

Poly-transformation

Ross D. King and Mohammed Ouali

Department of Computer Science, University of Wales, Aberystwyth
Aberystwyth, SY23 3DB, Wales, UK
Tel: +44 (0)1970-622432, Fax: +44 (0)1970-622455
rdk@aber.ac.uk

Abstract. Poly-transformation is the extension of the idea of ensemble learning to the transformation step of Knowledge Discovery in Databases (KDD). In poly-transformation multiple transformations of the data are made before learning (data mining) is applied. The theoretical basis for poly-transformation is the same as that for other combining methods – using different predictors to remove uncorrelated errors. It is not possible to demonstrate the utility of poly-transformation using standard datasets, because no pre-transformed data exists for such datasets. We therefore demonstrate its utility by applying it to a single well-known hard problem for which we have expertise - the problem of predicting protein secondary structure from primary structure. We applied four different transformations of the data, each of which was justifiable by biological background knowledge. We then applied four different learning methods (linear discrimination, back-propagation, C5.0, and learning vector quantization) both to the four transformations, and to combining predictions from the different transformations to form the poly-transformation predictions. Each of the learning methods produced significantly higher accuracy with poly-transformation than with only a single transformation. Poly-transformation is the basis of the secondary structure prediction method Prof, which is one of the most accurate existing methods for this problem.

1 Introduction

One of the main characteristics which distinguishes Knowledge Discovery in Databases (KDD) from traditional statistics and machine learning, is its emphasis on discovery as a *process* which transforms raw data into knowledge [1]. This emphasis on transformation contrasts with the more static approach of traditional statistics and machine learning, where data is generally assumed to have been already pre-processed and transformed into a suitable form for analysis, and where interpretation of the results is a matter for "domain experts". To use KDD terminology, traditional statistics and machine learning have focused only on the "data mining step" of the process. The broader KDD view opens up research directions not traditionally considered.

Over the last few decade perhaps the most important advance in data analysis has been the development of new ways of combining classification predictions [2]. These methods have been very successful at improving the accuracy of classifiers over that possible for a single model. The starting point for all of these methods for combining predictions is that the input dataset is *fixed*, and the objective of these methods is to improve classification accuracy by combining predictions on that input dataset. *In this paper we extend the idea of combing multiple predictions to the KDD transformation step.* We call this new approach *poly-transformation*. We show that combining predictions from multiple ways of transforming data can produce higher prediction accuracy than use of the best single method of transforming the data. The theoretical basis for poly-transformation is the same as for that for other combing methods: uncorrelated errors from different predictions are removed by combining them [2]. This basis can be justified in Bayesian terms.

The standard way of demonstrating the utility of a new machine learning method is to demonstrate that it performs well on a large number of standard datasets - normally taken from the UCI repository. *This approach is not possible for poly-transformation because the raw data before transformation is not available for the standard datasets.* We therefore demonstrate the utility of poly-transformation by applying it to a single well-known hard problem for which we have expertise in the transformation step - the problem of predicting protein secondary structure from primary structure. On this problem we show that for each learning method tried, poly-transformation produces a significantly higher accuracy than is possible while using a single transformation.

1.1 KDD and Poly-transformation

The KDD process, as described in [1], identifies five steps for transforming raw data to knowledge: selection (creating a target dataset), pre-processing (removing noise, handling missing variables, etc.), transformation (finding useful features to represent the data, data reduction and projection), data mining (selection of method, searching for patterns), and interpretation/evaluation (consolidating learned knowledge). In the transformation step of KDD, data is transformed from an initial state into a form suitable for application of a data mining algorithm. In KDD it is common to experiment with different transformations (although this is rarely documented). It has long been recognised within machine learning that finding a good representation of the data is crucial for success, and this is closely related to finding a good transformation of the data. Surprisingly little research has been done on transformation, and most of this has focused on dealing with "high dimensional" datasets with very large numbers of attributes. Such datasets cause problems because the data mining search space is greatly increased, and subsequently there is an increased chance of finding a spurious model with high accuracy. The problem is greater if many of the attributes are irrelevant. Many learning algorithms scale badly on such datasets, and a transformation of the attributes to a lower dimensional form is necessary for successful data mining. Within inductive logic programming (ILP) the use of background knowledge can be considered as a form of transformation of the data. It has been shown that use of appropriate background knowledge is essential for learning success [3].

The idea of learning multiple classifiers and then combining them into a single superior predictor has in recent years received a great deal of research interest. There is now a large body of empirical evidence showing that ensemble learners are generally more accurate than single model learners e.g. [4]. Many different approaches to learning different classifiers have been used. The one that is closest to poly-transformation is to generate multiple classifiers by manipulating the input features available to the learning algorithm. For example: in the work of Cherkauer [5] different neural networks were trained, both with different subsets of attributes, and with different numbers of hidden units, to produce a better classifier than any single net; and in the Stochastic Attribute Selection (SASC) method of [6], different classifiers are generated by stochastically modifying the set of attributes considered, but keeping the distribution of training examples constant.

1.2 Protein Secondary Structure Prediction

The problem of predicting protein secondary structure from primary structure is a well known hard one, and many different types of classifiers have been applied: linear statistics e.g. [7], nearest-neighbour methods e.g. [8], symbolic machine learning e.g [9], neural networks e.g. [10]. The best published methods have an accuracy of ~80% (see http://PredictionCenter.llnl.gov/).

The key to predicting protein secondary structure, as in most data analysis problems, is to find a good representation. In abstract terms, the prediction of protein secondary structure can be considered as a string prediction problem: given one string, predict another. The problem is difficult because positions (amino acids) that are linearly distant along the sequence fold up in 3-dimensional space and interact with each other. This means that it is in general impossible to fully predict secondary structure by only looking at fixed length strings (less than the full length of the protein). The problem is analogous to that of understanding natural language sentences, where words linearly distant interact to give meaning. Despite this, almost all approaches to predicting secondary structure have been based on using a fixed window of amino-acids to predict the secondary structure type of the central amino-acid in the window. The advantage of this approach is that it is the most natural way of representing it for propositional learning systems. The disadvantage is that it ignores the "context" problem. An exception to the use of a fixed window is the use of the ILP system Golem [9].

The representation of the problem of predicting protein secondary structure is further complicated by the existence of homologous proteins. These are proteins with similar primary structure (the term homology refers to them having a common evolutionary ancestor) and near identical secondary structure (secondary structure evolves more slowly than primary structure does). Use of homologous proteins is now considered essential for high accuracy. When learning it is customary to assume that all the homologous primary structures have identical secondary structure. This gives the problem an interesting structure: each example consists of a set of related primary structures with the same secondary structure, and the size of the set varies from example to example. This structure is similar to the "multiple instance" problem [11]. The difference is that in the multiple instance problem you know that there exists at least one feature vector in the set describing the example that has the observed class ($\exists v \in \{feature\ vectors\ describing\ example\}. observed\_class(v)$): in the secondary structure prediction problem, an example of what we term the "all instance" problem, you know that all the feature vectors in the set describing the example have the observed class ($\forall v \in \{feature\ vectors\ describing\ example\} . observed\_class(v)$. In secondary structure prediction, the first-order nature of the all instance problem is usually simplistically dealt with by either averaging predictions, or by forming an averaged primary structure to use in learning. A related aspect of the problem that is important is that the classes of neighbouring residues are auto-correlated. This means that example positions from the same protein are not independent and should not be treated as such. This needs to be considered when resampling, and standard error estimates should not be based on the total number of examples. A final important feature to note about the structure of the secondary structure prediction problem is that the problem is notorious for having a large amount of class noise. This is caused by both experimental errors in obtaining the structures, and to a larger extent by ambiguity in the definition of secondary structure. The problem of ambiguity is caused by borderline cases, which cannot confidently be placed in a single class (due to thresholding effects); these examples occur particularly at the edges of secondary structures. This problem could perhaps be best dealt with by giving each amino acid a probability of each class, or by a fuzzy logic approach; as the secondary structure classes seem to be fuzzy in the formal sense. The standard method of measuring prediction success is accuracy. This has the disadvantage of treating all errors equally, which is incorrect, as certain types of error are worse in predicting tertiary structure.

2 Methodology

The basic experimental methodology was as follows:
1. Four different transformations of the basic data were made (GOR, Rost-Sander 1, Rost Sander 2, and PSI-BLAST)
2. Four different learning algorithms were applied to each of the transformations (back-propagation, linear discrimination, C5.0, learning vector quantization) to predict secondary structure.
3. The four learning algorithms were used to combine together (using stacking) their predictions from the four different transformation (the poly-transformation predictions).
4. The poly-transformation predictions were compared with non combined predictions.

2.1 Data

We used a set of 496 non-homologous protein domains especially designed for the problem of secondary structure prediction (The database can be freely obtained by academics upon request from Geoffrey J. Barton of the University of Dundee, Scotland). The database contains 82,847 residues (examples): 28,678 are classed as α-helix, 17,741 as β-strand, and 36,428 as coil. Secondary structure was determined using the DSSP program. We formed sequence alignments and database searches as used by the Prof program [12].

2.2 Transformation

The input to the transformation step is a set of protein alignments: *such alignments cannot directly be used for learning by propositional learners*. There are variable numbers of proteins in the different alignments, and within each alignment there are variable numbers of proteins aligned at different positions on the sequence. The raw data must therefore be transformed in some way into a fixed length feature vector form suitable for learning.

The first of the four transformations was based on the standard GOR approach [13]. This transformation treats each protein independently and transforms the sequence of amino acids (20 possible types at each position) into a sequence of Bayes like estimates of class probabilities. Each estimate is made using a window of 17 amino acids, and five different levels of approximation of the GOR algorithm. For each position in the alignment the mean of the probabilities from the different sequences are averaged to give the final sequence of probabilities. Full details of this procedure are described in [12]. This form of representation was previously used by the successful DSC prediction method [7].

The second transformation used was based on standard Rost-Sander profiles [7]. A Rost-Sander profile is a transformation of the input multiple alignment into the sequence of estimated probabilities of occurrence of the 20 different types of amino-acids at each position. This representation explicitly takes into account more information about variation in sequence in the alignment than the GOR method does. Rost-Sander profiles are the basis of the successful PHD prediction method.

The third transformation was a modification of standard Rost-Sander profiles. It differs by including a dummy residue position to represent gaps in the alignment. Each position in sequence therefore consists of 21 real numbers (the probabilities of the different types of amino-acid and of a gap). The position of gaps is known to be important in prediction [7].

The final transformation was based on PSI-BLAST profiles [14]. This type of profile uses a more sophisticated statistical technique to estimate the profile than the Rost-Sander approach. Prior knowledge of amino-acid mutation probabilities embodied in the substitution matrix (BLOSUM62) is used to estimate the probabilities, and the different sequences in the alignment are weighted according to the amount of information they carry. PSI-BLAST profiles are the basis of the successful prediction method PSI-PRED [15].

2.3 Classifiers

We compared using poly-transformation against single transformations using four separate classification algorithms: neural networks, C5.0, and Learning Vector Quantization (LVQ). These algorithms test the utility of poly-transformation over a wide variety of different learning approaches. Linear discrimination [16] is a standard robust statistical method. We wrote our own code for this algorithm. For back-propagation neural networks we used a standard three-layered fully connected feed-forward network with momentum learning to avoid oscillation problems. The width of the gradient steps was set to 0.05 and the momentum term was 0.2. The initial weights of the neural nets were chosen randomly in the range of [-0.01, 0.01]. To generate the neural network architecture and for the learning process, we make use of the SNNS program version 4.2, which is freely available from the ftp site: ftp.informatik.uni-stuttgart.de. To include a standard symbolic propositional learner we used C5.0 (http://www.cse.unsw.edu.au/~quinlan/). We ran C5.0 with its standard settings. For LVQ [17] we used the Learning Vector Quantization Program Package (version, 3.1). In the LVQ algorithms, vector quantization is not used to approximate to density functions of the class samples, but to directly define the class borders according to a nearest neighbour rule. We used 500 codebook vectors for each class and a neighbourhood of 5 codebooks.

Poly-transformation involves combining predictions from different transformations. As described in the introduction, there are many different ways to combine predictions: voting, stacking, etc. We used a stacking scheme based on the underlying classifier: to combine the four linear discrimination predictions from the different transformations we used linear discrimination, to combine the back-propagation predictions we used back-propagation, etc. This scheme has the advantage of being more sophisticated than simple voting, and allowing only one learning algorithm to be used in each experiment.

3 Results

We used the four different classification algorithms (linear discrimination, back-propagation neural networks, C5.0, and LVQ) to learn on the four different transformations using a 10 fold cross-validation procedure. We then compared the results of each of the standard four transformations with that of combining the predictions from the different transformations - poly-transformation. The results (Table 1) show that poly-transformation produces more accurate results than any single transformation with all four classification algorithms. These results are significant at the 99% level based on using a binomial sign test (Table 2). Poly-transformation is therefore demonstrated to be effective across a wide variety of classification algorithm.

Back-propagation is the most accurate classification algorithm. It produces an estimated accuracy of 75.8%, which is 2% greater than the best single transformation (PSI-BLAST), and state-of-the-art for this problem [15]. The greatest increase in accuracy through use of poly-transformation is that of 2.7% for linear discrimination, and the lowest is 1.2% for C5.0. It is interesting that the profile transformations (Rost-Sander 1, Rost-Sander 2, and PSI-BLAST) appear to be best suit back-propagation, the learning method for which they were originally used [10,15]. The GOR transformation is surprisingly effective, despite its failure to represent important information in alignments (see above). The DSC prediction method [7] was based on use of linear discrimination and a GOR type representation, this choice of representation seems to have been correct for the algorithm. The performance of C5.0 on the three profile transformations is very poor (~55%), almost 20% worse than back-propagation. We believe this was because successful prediction using this representation involves the combination of a large number of attributes, and this conflicts with C5.0's learning bias. To avoid this problem it might have been possible to use a PCA decomposition and making the learning process on the extracted principal components. Note that if we had used a voting combination method instead of stacking we would have produced a very poor C5.0 classifier.

4 Discussion and Conclusion

In applying KDD to scientific domains there is an important distinction between two types of problem: those where it is essential that a single comprehensible theory is output, and those where predictive performance is the most important criterion. If a

Table 1. Comparative average accuracy of classification algorithm on the different transformations. The numbers in parentheses are the estimated standard errors. The combined accuracy of using poly-transformation is shown in the final column.

Methods	Accuracy GOR	Accuracy Rost-Sander 1	Accuracy Rost-Sander 2	Accuracy PSI-BLAST	Combined
BackProp.	71.7 (0.41)	70.7 (0.39)	70.8 (0.39)	73.7 (0.37)	75.8 (0.38)
Lin-Discr.	71.0 (0.39)	68.3 (0.43)	68.3 (0.43)	70.0 (0.44)	73.7 (0.40)
C5.0	68.7 (0.38)	54.5 (0.54)	54.8 (0.54)	55.4 (0.31)	69.7 (0.39)
LVQ	69.0 (0.41)	65.6 (0.47)	66.4 (0.43)	68.4 (0.43)	70.8 (0.41)

Table 2. Binomial sign test of significance of improved accuracy of poly-transformation over the four standard transformations at 99% level on the test set of 496 proteins. + means that poly-transformation is significantly better. (i/j) means that poly-transformation is more accurate than the standard transformation i times out of j considered examples. We do not count when the two methods produce equal accuracies.

Standard Transforms	Poly-transform NN	Poly-transform LD	Poly-transform C5.0	Poly-Transform LVQ
GOR	+ (374/470)	+ (355/460)	+ (316/434)	+ (332/466)
Rost-Sander 1	+ (407/473)	+ (414/476)	+ (446/491)	+ (391/470)
Rost-Sander 2	+ (411/476)	+ (410/474)	+ (443/490)	+ (387/469)
PSI-BLAST	+ (364/461)	+ (366/463)	+ (475/491)	+ (316/462)

single comprehensible theory is required then Ockham's razor is the guiding principle: if predictive performance is essential, then there is an important role for ensemble methods. When predicting secondary structure it is predictive performance that is important, and for the last ten years the most popular methods for the problem with molecular biologists have been black-box predictors. This emphasis on performance is probably justified by the low probability that a simple theory (other than quantum mechanics) can predict protein secondary structure. A more practical bias in favour of performance is that it is very difficult to publish on the problem in the molecular biology literature without making accurate predictions, and difficult to publish if a method has not been successfully tested at the biannual CASP competition.

We consider poly-transformation to be an appropriate and promising KDD technique when the data does not provide sufficient information to choose a single best transformation, or when the optimal transformation is unsuitable for the classifier available and so approximations are needed. The theoretical justification for poly-transformation is the same as for other ensemble based learning methods. We have demonstrated the practical utility of poly-transformation on the problem of predicting protein secondary structure. For this problem poly-transformation was shown to improve the performance of linear discrimination, back-propagation, C5.0, and LVQ learning algorithms.

Poly-transformation was used as the basis of the Prof secondary structure prediction method [12]. This classifier has an estimated accuracy of 76%. Prof is one of the most accurate existing prediction methods (http://cubic.bioc.columbia.edu/eva). Prof can also produce an accuracy of 78% for β-strands, this is very important for prediction of higher-level protein structure. A trial server is available at http://www.aber.ac.uk/~phiwww/prof/index.html.

Acknowledgements

Ross D. King and Mohammed Ouali were funded by the BBSRC/EPSRC Bioinformatics initiative grant BIF08765. Thanks are due to Geoffrey Barton and James Cuff for kindly providing us with the database of non-homologous sequences.

References

1. Fayyad, U., Pietetsky-Shapiro, G., Smyth, P. Advances in Knowledge Discovery and Data Mining. MIT Press, 1996.
2. Dietterich, T. G., Lathrop, R. H., Lozano-Perez, T. Solving the multiple-instance problem with axis-parallel rectangles. Artificial Intelligence, 89(1-2), 31-71, 1997.
3. King, R.D., Srinivasan, A., Sternberg, M.J.E. Relating chemical activity to structure: an examination of ILP successes. New Gen. Computing. 13, 411-433, 1995.
4. Bauer, E., Kohavi, R. An empirical comparison of voting classification algorithms: bagging, boosting, and variants. Machine Learning, 36 105-139, 1999.
5. Cherkauer, K.J. Human expert-level performance on a scientific image analysis by a system using combined artificial neural network. In Chan, P. (Eds.), Working Notes of AAAI Workshop on Integrating Multiple Learned Models, 15-21, 1996.
6. Zheng, Z., Webb, G.I. Stochastic attribute selection committees. Proceedings of the Eleventh Australian Joint Conference on Artificial Intelligence (AI'98), Berlin: Springer-Verlag, 321-332, 1998.
7. King, R.D., Sternberg, J.E. Identification and application of the concepts important for accurate and reliable protein secondary structure prediction. Protein Science 5, 2298-2310, 1996.
8. Salamov, A.A., Solovyev, V.V. Prediction of protein secondary structure by combining nearest-neighbor algorithms and multiple sequence alignments. J. Mol. Biol. 247, 11-15, 1995.
9. Muggleton, S. King, R.D. Sternberg M.J.E. Protein secondary structure prediction using logic. Protein Eng. 5, 647-657, 1992.
10. Rost, B., Sander, C. Prediction of protein secondary structure at better than 70% accuracy. J. Mol. Biol. 232, 584-599, 1993.
11. Dietterich T.G. Machine Learning Research: Four Current Directions. AI Magazine. 18, 97-136, 1997.
12. Ouali, M., King, R.D. Cascaded multiple classifiers for secondary structure prediction. Protein Sci. 9, 1162-1176, 2000.
13. Garnier, J. Gibrat, J.F., Robson, B. GOR Method for Predicting Protein Secondary Structure from Amino Acid Sequence. Methods in Enzymology 266: 541-553, 1996.

14. Altschul, S.F. Madden, T.L., Schäffer, A.A., Zhang, J., Zhang, Z., Miller, W., Lipman D.J. Gapped BLAST and PSI-BLAST: a new generation of protein database search programs. Nucleic Acids Research 25, 3389-3402, 1997.
15. Jones, D. Protein secondary structure prediction based on position-specific scoring matrices. J. Mol. Biol. 292, 195-202, 1999.
16. Hastie, T., Tibshirani, R., Friedman, J. The elements of statistical learning. Springer Verlag, 2001.
17. Kohonen, T., Kangas J., Laaksonen J., Torkkola. K. LVQ_PAK: A program package for the correct application of Learning Vector Quantization algorithms. In: Proceedings of the International Joint Conference on Neural Networks, 725-730, 1992.

Prediction of Natively Disordered Regions in Proteins Using a Bio-basis Function Neural Network

Rebecca Thomson and Robert Esnouf

Division of Structural Biology and Oxford Protein Production Facility
University of Oxford, The Henry Wellcome Building for Genomic Medicine
Roosevelt Drive, Oxford OX3 7BN, UK
{rebecca,robert}@strubi.ox.ac.uk

Abstract. Recent studies have found that many proteins contain regions that do not form well defined three-dimensional structures in their native states. The study and detection of such disordered regions is very important both for facilitating structural analysis and to aid understanding of protein function. A newly developed pattern recognition algorithm termed a "Bio-basis Function Neural Network" has been applied to the detection of disordered regions in proteins. Different models were trained studying the effect of changing the size of the window used for residue classification. Ten-fold cross validation showed that the estimated prediction accuracy was 95.2% for a window size of 21 residues and an overlap threshold of 30%. Blind tests using the trained models on a data set unrelated to the training set gave a regional prediction accuracy of 81.4% (±0.9%).

1 Introduction

Recent studies have begun focusing attention on sequences which show no propensity to form specific three-dimensional structures, yet may still be functionally significant. Many proteins, contain local regions of disorder, and some are totally unfolded in their native states [1]. These studies have found that many natively unfolded proteins or regions are involved in molecular recognition, often depending on disorder-to-order transitions to enable the natively unfolded proteins to form complexes with their cognate partners [2, 3].

Accurate recognition of disordered regions in proteins is therefore important to molecular biology for enzyme specificity studies, function recognition and drug design. The detection of such regions is also crucial to structural biology since structure determination by x-ray crystallography and NMR relies on a specific three-dimensional structure. At best disordered regions are invisible to these techniques; at worst they can disrupt the whole experiment by affecting solubility and/or crystallizability.

Garner *et al.* [4] have shown that disordered regions comprise a sequence-dependent category distinct from that of ordered protein structure. This means that certain amino acids will have a higher frequency of occurrence in disordered regions than in ordered regions, and vice versa. For instance, Trp, Tyr and Phe are found to be less common in long disordered regions [5], the biological interpretation being that aromatic amino acids have a strong interaction capability. Cys and His are also less common in disordered regions, whereas Glu, Asp and Lys are more likely to appear in disordered regions since charge imbalance tends to favour disorder. Ser is also associated with disorder since it increases both solubility flexibility, two properties inherent to disordered regions.

Several pattern recognition algorithms have been combined with well-established biological knowledge to define a set of features for the recognition of disordered regions in proteins [4, 6-12]. The first report of prediction of disordered regions was based on the frequency measurements of eight amino acids (His, Glu, Lys, Ser, Asp, Cys, Trp and Tyr) and two average attributes (hydropathy and flexibility) [6]. A feed-forward neural network model with six hidden units was constructed leading to prediction accuracies from 59% to 67%. A comparison was also given for neural networks trained using disorder data derived from x-ray crystallographic and NMR methods [4], and the prediction accuracies were 73% and 75%, respectively. Various pattern recognition models have been compared using different compositions of features selected from 51 possible features. Disorder has been predicted for N-terminal regions, internal regions and C-terminal regions with 5-cross validation prediction accuracies of 78.8%, 72.5% and 75.3% respectively [9].

We are developing a novel method for the detection of disordered regions based on an extension of a sequence alignment technique developed for the detection of protease cleavage sites, termed the Bio-basis Function Neural Network (BBFNN) [13, 14]. If two sequences are similar then they are usually expected to have a similar or related function. We apply this expectation to the detection of disordered regions: sequences are compared to a series of prototype regions of known folding states and the sequence alignment scores against these prototypes are used to classify the sequence as ordered or disordered using a suitably trained neural network. Since the lengths of ordered and disordered regions in proteins vary, we have revised the original BBFNN technique by using the concept of non-gapped homology alignment to maximise the alignment score between a pair of sequences.

2 Methods

Figure 1 demonstrates demonstrates schematically application of the BBFNN to the prediction of disorder. Five prototypes, each corresponding to either an ordered or disordered region in a protein, requiring five parameters weighting the five homology alignment scores, are used to classify the central residue of a sliding window covering the query sequence. The weighted scores are then combined to give a prediction of disorder probability for the central residue of the window.

2.1 Data

Our main data set comprised a total of 1100 ordered and 253 disordered regions. The ordered set was collected from the PONDR® website (www.pondr.com). Of the

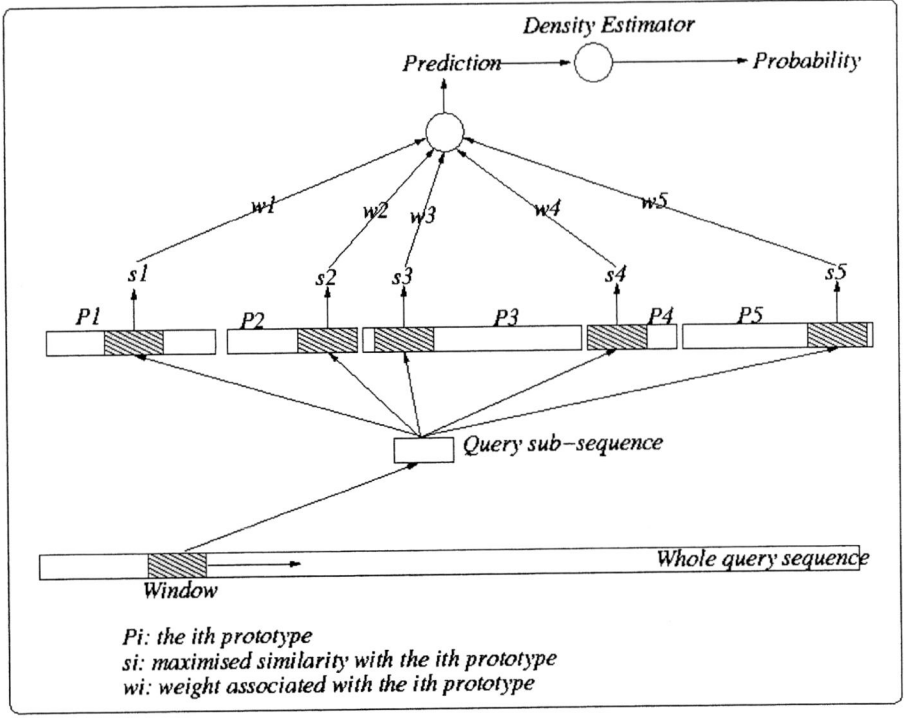

Fig. 1. Diagrammatic representation of the application of the bio-basis function neural networks technique to the prediction of disordered regions in proteins

disordered regions, 69 were collected from [15], 35 were collected from [16], and the rest were collected from the PONDR® website.

As we have limited data, prototypes were randomly selected from the training data set. A more rigorous procedure of determining a set of prototypes having maximum sequence dissimilarity could follow a statistical pattern recognition method [17]. The remaining sequences were divided into training, validation and testing sets. These three sets are composed of sub-sequences having the same length, produced using a sliding window of predetermined size to scan the remaining sequences residue by residue.

2.2 Training of the BBFNN Model

Each training sub-sequence is aligned with each prototype in turn to maximise the non-gapped homology alignment scores. The bio-basis function is then used to transform the homology alignment scores to normalised similarity measurements. We consider each prototype to be an independent variable and assume that the relationship between these independent variables and their corresponding prototype class labels is simple, allowing a linear classifier to be constructed. Parameters that weight the similarity measurements are determined using a pseudo inverse method [13, 14].

2.3 Optimization of the Discrimination Threshold

After inputting all the validation sub-sequences to the model constructed in Step 3, we assume that the probability density functions of the outputs follow two Gaussian distributions. A parametric method is used to estimate the density functions. Based on the estimated probability density functions, a threshold for discrimination can be determined using Bayes' rule [17].

2.4 Testing the Model

The testing data are used with the trained and validated model. The results are expressed as a regional prediction accuracy defined as follows: (i) for windows of a given width centered on each residue in the test set in turn, the trained network is used to make a prediction as a posterior probability of disorder, (ii) if the probability of disorder is greater than the 0.5 then the central residue is classified as disordered, (iii) we use regional prediction accuracy to assess the model performance. If the overlap between predicted residues and observed residues is larger than an overlap threshold value, a region is correctly identified. The accuracy of disorder prediction is the fraction of the correctly identified disordered regions over total number of the disordered regions. The accuracy of order prediction is the fraction of the correctly identified ordered regions over total number of the ordered regions. The total accuracy is the fraction of the correctly identified regions over total number of the regions. We used 10-fold cross validation (no-replacement) to give a more realistic estimate of model performance.

2.5 Blind Testing

We downloaded further data sets from two independent resources for blind testing. One is a set of 17 protein sequences selected from proteins in the PDB having residues annotated as missing in the structure, and the second set was provided by Center for Informatics and Technology, Temple University and contains sequences for 154 proteins. For these data, windows centered on each residue in turn were evaluated with the trained model and the residues were classified as above. These predictions were again converted to regional prediction accuracies.

3 Discussion

Six window sizes were initially evaluated (11, 21, 31, 41, 51 and 61 residues) for training and validation. Since prototype sequences must be longer than the window, all regions shorter than the window size used were removed. Table 1(a) shows the

Table 1. Cross-validation simulation accuracies for different threshold values and window sizes. Results are quoted as percentage accuracies for ordered regions (OR), disordered regions (DR) and overall weighted accuracy as defined in the main text

Threshold	Window size (residues)	OR prediction accuracy (%)	DR prediction accuracy (%)	Overall accuracy (%)
(a): Cross-validation accuracy using different overlap threshold values.				
20%	21	99.3	87.3	96.6
30%	21	98.2	84.5	95.2
40%	21	96.2	74.9	91.7
50%	21	90.4	61.0	84.4
60%	21	73.9	47.8	68.6
70%	21	46.4	39.4	44.9
80%	21	19.7	29.8	21.6
90%	21	7.5	21.9	10.3
(b): Cross-validation accuracy using different window sizes.				
30%	11	85.6	97.2	87.3
30%	21	98.2	84.5	95.2
30%	31	97.0	78.9	93.6
30%	41	98.5	75.9	94.1
30%	51	98.7	74.7	94.9
30%	61	98.6	74.5	94.3

results of cross-validation simulation using different threshold values and a window size of 21. A threshold of 30%, where the Disordered Region (DR) prediction accuracy was 84.5% and the Ordered Region (OR) prediction accuracy was 98.2% was chosen to be used for all subsequent simulations. The accuracies obtained by varying the window size from 11 to 61 residues are summarized in Table 1(b) as regional prediction accuracies for 10-fold cross validation simulations. These simulations showed that as the window size increases, the DR prediction accuracy decreases while the OR prediction accuracy increases. The overall prediction accuracy was maximal for a window size of 21 residues.

The simulations were repeated as blind tests for the Blind data set (Table 2). In blind testing, no knowledge about the classifications in the data sets was used at any stage of model construction and sequences of high similarity to the unified set were excluded. The sequences were analysed individually and the OR and DR prediction accuracies were calculated as above. Ten models were constructed for each window size, allowing ten predictions to be made for each sequence in the test set to produce the error estimates in Table 2. The Blind set contains 643 regions (356 ordered and 287 disordered) and the average lengths are 73 residues and 86 residues for OR and DR, respectively. The simulations confirmed that trained models with a window size of 21 residues performed best, with accuracies of 75.3% and 89.1% for OR and DR prediction accuracies, respectively. Simulations showed that as the window size increased, the DR prediction accuracy decreased dramatically while the OR prediction accuracy was less sensitive.

Table 2. Blind simulations against models constructed with a threshold of 30%. Results are quoted as percentage accuracies for ordered regions (OR), disordered regions (DR) and overall weighted accuracy as defined in the main text. In each case, 10 models were trained using different prototype sequences to give an estimate for the standard deviation in accuracy. The quality of the predictions is also assessed using the Matthews correlation coefficient [18]

Window size (residues)	OR prediction accuracy (Specificity) (%)	DR prediction accuracy (Sensitivity) (%)	Overall accuracy (%)	Matthews Coefficient
11	56.1 ± 10.9	99.4 ± 0.5	75.5 ± 5.8	0.60 ± 0.08
21	75.3 ± 4.1	89.1 ± 5.3	81.4 ± 0.9	0.64 ± 0.02
31	76.4 ± 4.4	82.5 ± 5.0	79.1 ± 1.7	0.59 ± 0.04
41	77.0 ± 4.6	80.6 ± 4.8	78.6 ± 1.8	0.57 ± 0.04
51	76.3 ± 5.2	80.3 ± 4.1	78.1 ± 1.5	0.57 ± 0.03
61	77.4 ± 6.2	80.0 ± 5.7	78.5 ± 2.2	0.57 ± 0.39

Investigations with window sizes between 11 and 21 residues (Table 3) showed that the overall accuracy of the method was not overly sensitive to window size over this range. However, the trend was that the DR prediction accuracy generally decreased while the OR prediction accuracy generally increased with increasing window size. Further blind simulations where the threshold value was varied for window sizes of between 11 and 21 residues (data not shown) supported the selection of 30% as the threshold. However, again the method was not overly sensitive to the precise value selected.

We have revised the Bio-basis Function Neural Network technique to make it applicable to the prediction of natively disordered regions in proteins. Tests suggest that this method, in its current stage of development, is able to detect the presence of regions of disorder with an accuracy comparable to other techniques. Work is under way to improve the accuracy further. One problem we are facing is the quality and size of available training data sets. Annotation of disorder is often unreliable, for example regions of structures may appear to be disordered because they are attached to flexible linkers or even absent altogether due to proteolysis. A trial version of the program is available for evaluation at http://www.strubi.ox.ac.uk, which gives as output a graph similar to those of other prediction techniques of probability of disorder against residue number. Figure 2 compares the predictions of PONDR® (www.pondr.com) and our method for Deoxyuridine 5'-triphosphate nucleotidohydrolase (dUTPase) from M. tuberculosis (PDB code 1MQ7). This protein was one of the CASP 5 (Critical Assessment of Techniques for Protein Structure Prediction 2002) targets and was not in our training data set. Residues 136-154 were not observed in the structure so are assumed to be disordered. Our program predicts residues 135-154 to be disordered. It also predicts some small regions of disorder near the N-terminus of the protein which were observed in the structure, but the majority of the protein is predicted to be ordered. PONDR® predicts residues 119-154 to be disordered, as well as regions 24-33 (also predicted by our program) and 69-86.

Table 3. Prediction accuracies for window sizes between 11 and 21 residues with a threshold of 30%. Results are quoted as percentage accuracies for ordered regions (OR), disordered regions (DR) and overall weighted accuracy as defined in the main text. For the blind simulations, 10 models were trained using different prototype sequences to give an estimate for the standard deviation in accuracy

Window size (residues)	OR prediction accuracy (Specificity) (%)	DR prediction accuracy (Sensitivity) (%)	Overall accuracy (%)	Matthews Coefficient
(a): Cross-validation accuracy				
11	85.6	97.2	87.3	0.71
13	90.0	94.8	90.4	0.76
15	92.0	92.8	91.6	0.78
17	98.1	87.2	95.4	0.87
19	98.1	87.0	95.3	0.78
21	98.2	84.5	95.2	0.85
(c): Blind simulations				
11	56.1 ± 11.0	99.4 ± 0.6	75.5 ± 5.9	0.60 ± 0.08
13	64.4 ± 11.2	98.1 ± 2.7	79.5 ± 5.3	0.65 ± 0.07
15	69.9 ± 6.1	95.9 ± 4.5	81.5 ± 2.1	0.67 ± 0.03
17	73.5 ± 4.8	94.5 ± 4.5	82.9 ± 1.8	0.68 ± 0.03
19	74.6 ± 4.5	91.2 ± 3.8	82.0 ± 1.7	0.66 ± 0.03
21	75.3 ± 4.1	89.1 ± 5.3	81.4 ± 0.9	0.64 ± 0.02

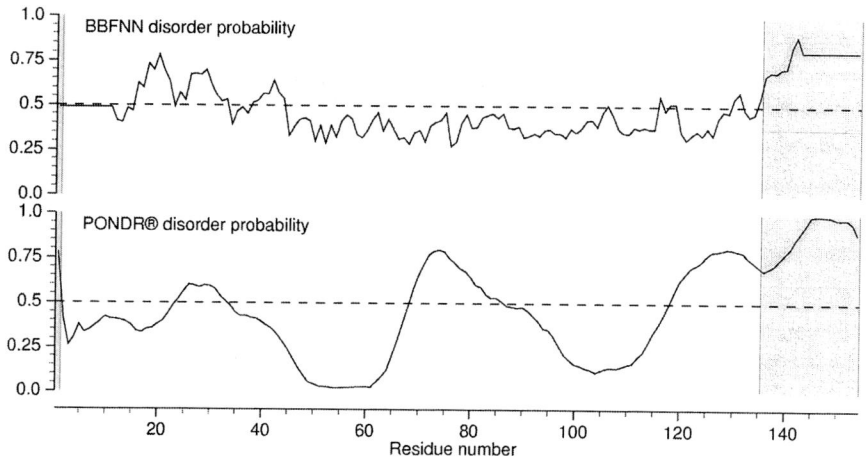

Fig. 2. Comparison of the output of our disorder prediction with that of PONDR® for the protein Deoxyuridine 5'-triphosphate nucleotidohydrolase (dUTPase) from M. tuberculosis (PDB code 1MQ7). The region not observed in the crystal structure is shaded in grey

Acknowledgements

The OPPF is funded by the UK Medical Research Council. We thank Dr Ron Yang for the use of the bio-basis function neural network.

References

1. Dunker, A.K., et al.: Intrinsic protein disorder in complete genomes. Genome Inform Ser Workshop Genome Inform. **11** (2000) 161-71.
2. Alber, T., et al.: The role of mobility in the substrate binding and catalytic machinery of enzymes. Ciba Found Symp. **93** (1983) 4-24.
3. Weinreb, P.H., et al.: NACP, a protein implicated in Alzheimer's disease and learning, is natively unfolded. Biochemistry. **35**, 43 (1996) 13709-15.
4. Garner, E., et al.: Predicting Disordered Regions from Amino Acid Sequence: Common Themes Despite Differing Structural Characterization. Genome Inform Ser Workshop Genome Inform. **9** (1998) 201-213.
5. Kissinger, C.R., et al.: Crystal structures of human calcineurin and the human FKBP12-FK506-calcineurin complex. Nature. **378**, 6557 (1995) 641-4.
6. Romero, P., et al. Identifying disordered regions in proteins from amino acid sequence. in Proc. IEEE Int. Conf. On Neural Networks. 1997. Huston: TX.
7. Xie, Q., et al.: The Sequence Attribute Method for Determining Relationships Between Sequence and Protein Disorder. Genome Inform Ser Workshop Genome Inform. **9** (1998) 193-200.

8. Garner, E., et al.: Predicting Binding Regions within Disordered Proteins. Genome Inform Ser Workshop Genome Inform. **10** (1999) 41-50
9. Li, X., et al.: Predicting Protein Disorder for N-, C-, and Internal Regions. Genome Inform Ser Workshop Genome Inform. **10** (1999) 30-40
10. Li, X., et al.: Comparing predictors of disordered protein. Genome Inform Ser Workshop Genome Inform. **11** (2000) 172-84
11. Romero, P., Z. Obradovic, and A.K. Dunker: Intelligent data analysis for protein disorder prediction. Artificial Intelligence Reviews. **14** (2000) 447-484
12. Radivojac, P., et al.: Protein flexibility and intrinsic disorder. Protein Sci. In Press (2004)
13. Thomson, R., et al.: Characterizing proteolytic cleavage site activity using bio-basis function neural networks. Bioinformatics. **19**, 14 (2003) 1741-7
14. Yang, Z.R. and R. Thomson: novel neural network method in mining molecular sequence data. IEEE Trans. on Neural Networks. In Press (2005)
15. Uversky, V.N., J.R. Gillespie, and A.L. Fink: Why are "natively unfolded" proteins unstructured under physiologic conditions? Proteins. **41**, 3 (2000) 415-27
16. Dunker, A.K., et al.: Intrinsic disorder and protein function. Biochemistry. **41**, 21 (2002) 6573-82
17. Duda, R.O., P.E. Hart, and D.G. Stork, Pattern Classification and Scene Analysis Wiley New York. (2002)
18. Matthews, B.W.: Comparison of the predicted and observed secondary structure of T4 phage lysozyme. Biochim Biophys Acta. **405**, 2 (1975) 442-51

The Effect of Image Compression on Classification and Storage Requirements in a High-Throughput Crystallization System

Ian Berry[1], Julie Wilson[2], Chris Mayo[1], Jon Diprose[1], and Robert Esnouf[1]

[1] Division of Structural Biology and the Oxford Protein Production Facility
University of Oxford, The Henry Wellcome Building for Genomic Medicine
Roosevelt Drive, Oxford, OX3 7BN, UK
{ian,mayo,jon,robert}@strubi.ox.ac.uk
http://www.strubi.ox.ac.uk

[2] York Structural Biology Laboratory, Department of Chemistry, University of York
Heslington, York, YO10 5DD, UK
julie@ysbl.york.ac.uk

Abstract. High-throughput crystallization and imaging facilities can require a huge amount of disk space to keep images on-line. Although compressed images can look very similar to the human eye, the effect on the performance of crystal detection software needs to be analysed. This paper tests the use of common lossy and lossless compression algorithms on image file size and on the performance of the York University image analysis software by comparison of compressed Oxford images with their native, uncompressed bitmap images. This study shows that significant (approximately 4-fold) space savings can be gained with only a moderate effect on classification capability.

1 Introduction

The Oxford Protein Production Facility (OPPF) is a facility within the Division of Structural Biology at the University of Oxford that is funded by the MRC to develop technologies for the high-throughput production and crystallization of proteins. It is seeking to develop a protein production pipeline by automating, parallelizing and miniaturizing all stages of the process. Target proteins are human proteins and those of human pathogens, selected for their direct biomedical relevance. The OPPF is the first stage in a structural genomics programme for the UK and represents an essential stepping stone toward the practical exploitation of the wealth of information coming from the human genome sequencing projects.

The key stages in the OPPF pipeline are target selection, cloning, expression, purification and crystallization. It is the crystallization phase that is relevant to this paper. Crystallization experiments are performed in 96-well Greiner crystallization plates using the sitting drop vapour diffusion method and a Cartesian Technologies Microsys MIC400 (Genomic Solutions, Huntingdon, UK) to dispense 100nL drops [1-2].

Once the plates are created, they are sealed and placed in a temperature-controlled storage vault (The Automation Partnership, Royston, UK) that has a capacity for 10000 crystallization plates. An automated Oasis 1700 imaging system (Veeco, Cambridge, UK) has been integrated with the storage vault and images of the crystallization droplets are taken automatically at regular intervals. Images are classified automatically using York University image analysis software and presented in a web interface for manual inspection.

At this time, this system has taken over nine million images and is now generating up to seventy-five thousand images per day. Native images are 1 megabyte bitmap (BMP) images and after cropping by Veeco software, they are reduced to 520 kilobytes. This causes a distinct storage problem and while it is necessary to keep all the images taken on-line, ready for access through a web interface by the crystallographers, there is also a need to minimise storage required.

In order to make all images available on-line for browsing, the file size was reduced as much as possible without affecting the visual state of the image. This led to the choice of jpeg with a quality setting of 60% as the image file type for the permanent on-line storage. The original bitmap images are currently stored online for about a month before being migrated to tape.

As improvements are made to the crystal classification software and as new techniques such as time-course analysis are introduced, more and more uncompressed images are needed on-line. As a result, there is a need to determine the best trade off between image file size and the ability to repeat the original classification.

2 Image Classification

The crystal image classification software [3-7], used to detect the presence of crystals in drops, is still under development and its accuracy is still such that manual classification is also required. The software, described elsewhere [3-4], currently makes classifications based on single images, as they are generated, to determine a simple numerical classification score (Table 1).

Table 1. Classification output categories from the image classifier provide the simple score output from the classifier

Class Number	Class Description
-1	Unable to classify drop
0	Empty Well / Drop
1	Rubbish
2	Precipitate
3	Interesting or granular precipitate
4	Small crystals or something else interesting
5	Some Crystals
6	Good Crystals

3 Jpeg Compression

Jpeg compression [8-9] is a four stage process. The first stage separates the image into 8×8 pixel tiles and converts the image colour space from red-green-blue (RGB) into a luminance / chrominance colour space such as YUV (where Y is luminance [brightness] and UV is the chrominance [colour]).

For the second stage, each block is then passed through a Discrete Cosine Transform (DCT) which calculates and stores the value of the pixel relative to the average for the block.

The third stage is the where the compression occurs – according to the quality setting chosen when encoding the file. It determines the number of quantisation levels that are applied to the array of DCTs. This is achieved by generating two tables, one each for luminance and chrominance, of quantisation levels between the minimum and maximum DCT values and split according to the quality value. The DCT coefficients are then quantised using these tables.

The final stage involves encoding the reduced DCT coefficients using a Huffman encoding scheme which compresses the data (but adds no extra compression to the image information itself).

The final jpeg image will also have header information (including details of the encoding process) added to it to complete the file.

4 Method

In order to ascertain the properties of the different image encoding, a selection of around 1100 images was chosen that showed most of the different types of features that can occur in crystallization experiments. The original bitmap images were converted using ImageMagick [10] into the various different formats on test. Code was also added to the classifier to allow it to parse the different image types. For this study, the image formats chosen were limited to jpeg (with various quality factors – Fig. 1), Graphic Interchange Format (GIF) and Run Length Encoded Bitmap (RLE BMP).

The purpose of this study is not to evaluate the accuracy of the image classification software; rather it is to compare the consistency of classification of reduced-size images with those obtained using the original bitmap images. This allows two useful simplifications: First, the classification program does not need to be trained individually for each image type. Second, it gives an obvious metric for assessing consistency as the fraction of images classified the same way for the reduced-size and native images.

Image classification was performed using a C version of the image classifier running under Red Hat Linux 9.0 on a PC containing two 2.66GHz Intel Pentium 4 Processors. Average classification time per image on this system was 2 – 4 seconds depending on the complexity of the image and the level of compression.

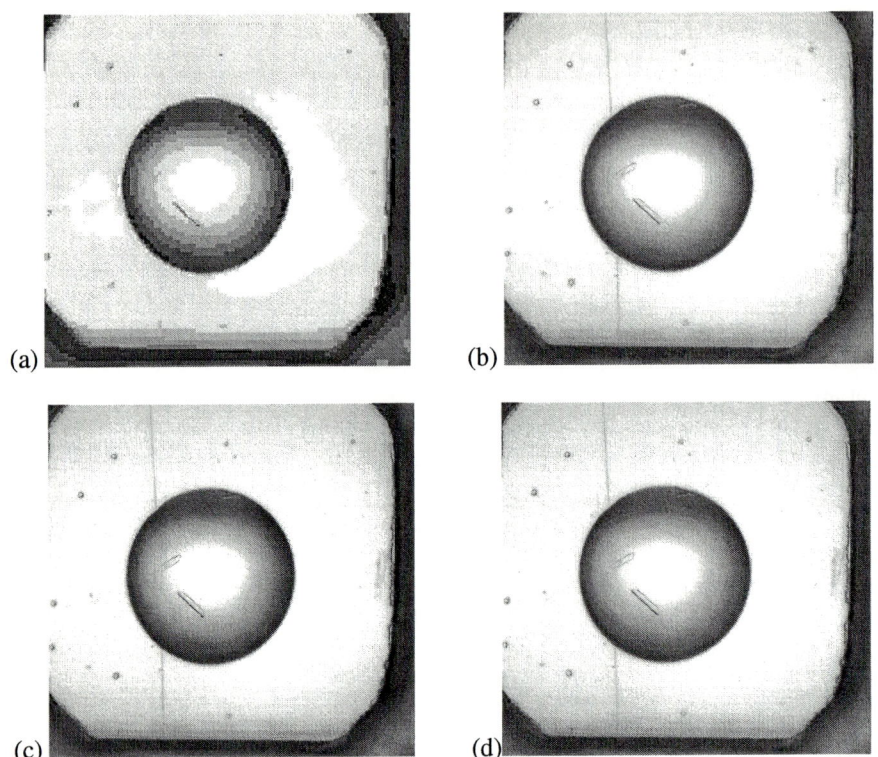

Fig. 1. A sample image compressed with various jpeg quality settings (a) 1%, (b) 30%, (c) 60% and (d) 100%

5 Results

The bitmap drop images typically cover the full 8-bit range of the grey scale and there is significant variation in background intensity over both the background and drop (e.g. Fig. 1(d)). Unsurprisingly, therefore, the two lossless 'compression' algorithms failed to reduce the image size (Table 2) and so were not tested further against the classifier. GIF images use an indexed colour palette and so the use of the full dynamic range in the images renders this ineffective. In the case of the RLE bitmap, the bloated size is due to the noisiness of the images – in a low noise image, RLE can provide significant file size savings as it compresses lines of pixels of the same value together (first pixel is the number of pixels, next pixel is the colour) so where there a few pixels that are the same, each pixel is replaced by two pixels, hence expanding the file size.

For the jpeg images, the resulting file size is critically dependent on the quality setting (Fig. 2), but as a guide 90% quality setting reduces the file size by approximately 90%.

Table 2. Overall file size information for various image formats

File Type	Average File Size (bytes)
BMP	526078
RLE BMP	1576454
GIF	596089
Jpeg	Min: 2903
	Max: 190863

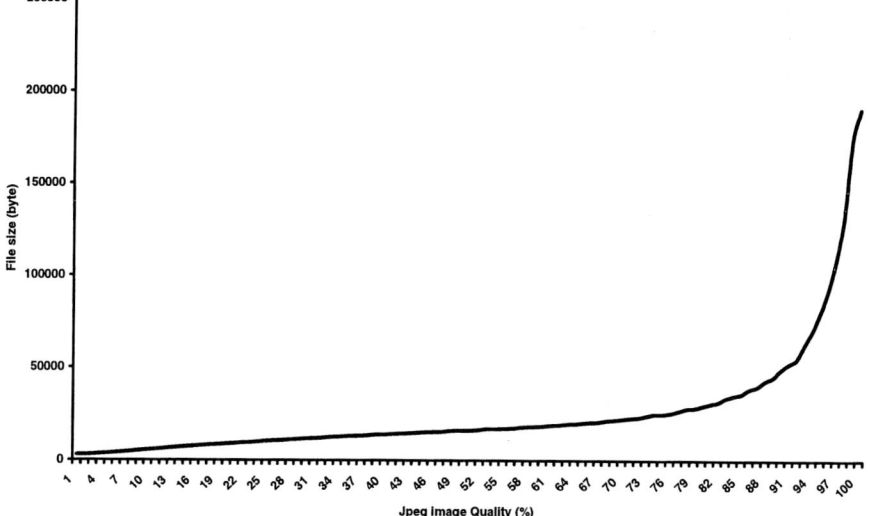

Fig. 2. The variation of image size against image quality

The ensemble of images were converted to jpegs with quality settings ranging from 1% to 100%. These were tested using the classifier and the results compared with those obtained from the original bitmaps. As a control, the results were also compared to a "dumb classifier" that made all the images equal to one class only (the sum of the percentage accuracies for these dumb classifiers being 100%). The results can be seen in Fig. 3 as percentage agreement with classifications for the original bitmap images.

The results show a striking dependence of classification quality on jpeg quality setting. Even with a quality setting of 95%, less than 50% matched those with the uncompressed bitmap. For a jpeg image quality of 100%, the agreement is still only 80%. This demonstrates the approximations inherent in the jpeg algorithm (which could be attributed the colour space transform and DCT calculations) and the sensitivity of the classification algorithm to the fine details of the image. For low quality jpeg images (< 90% quality), the classifications are little better than random, and indeed a fixed classification of "All Class 6" (all drops contain a crystal) would give a comparable classification consistency with this ensemble! It should be noted that 'interesting' drops are heavily over-represented in this test set – for our complete

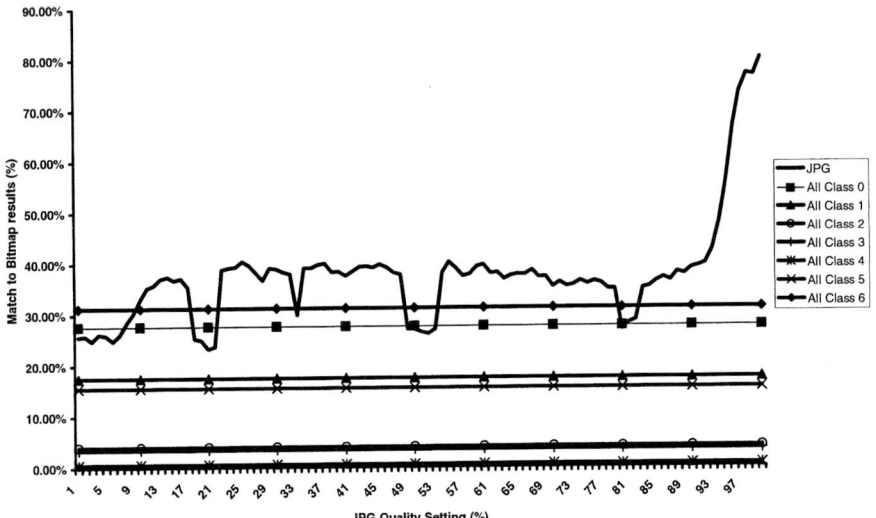

Fig. 3. Comparison of different image types and classifier outputs for different jpeg image quality settings

'interesting' drops are heavily over-represented in this test set – for our complete database, only 1-2% of drops contain crystals, whereas 50% are empty drops.

In the low quality region, there are several places where the consistency drops significantly further (e.g. 20%, 50% and 80% quality). It appears that these may be explained by a combination of the artifacts caused by the compression algorithm, particularly the tiling, and the techniques used in the classification.

At the low quality limit, the losses in the image are so severe that even the drop detection algorithm begins to fail and the consistency tends to the "All Class 0" classification (i.e. no drop detected).

The main purpose of this study is to relate image storage requirements to image classification. Fig. 4 summarizes this as the correlation between classification matches and file size. For a reasonable (> 75%) consistency with bitmap classifications, the smallest file size is around 120 kilobytes. This is a good reduction from the 512kb that is required for the uncompressed bitmap files, but would result in a significant misclassification of images. At this compression level and with the current image acquisition rate, our database would grow by approximately 8 gigabytes per day.

6 Conclusion

As crystallization storage and imaging systems become more affordable and widespread, many labs will be faced with the twin problems of image classification and

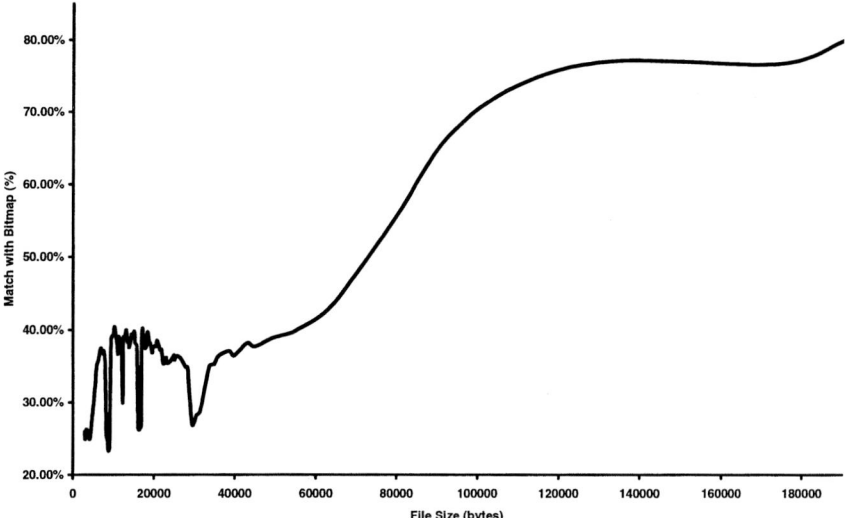

Fig. 4. Comparison of file size against similarity to bitmap results for different bitmap quality settings

image storage. Software developments have focussed on the analysis of bitmap images, but these can pose data storage problems – even at its current rate, the OPPF is acquiring about 3 terabytes annually. If disk and data redundancy are included to ensure data integrity, then the problem is even bigger. Whilst a development facility such as the OPPF may be able to provide sufficient resources, the cost of keeping image libraries may become prohibitive for some sites and ways to reduce this requirement need to be investigated.

Lossless compression algorithms may provide some saving with no cost to classification accuracy, but savings are likely to be modest – and in some cases even increase the file size.

We have investigated lossy jpeg compression as giving a potential for far greater savings that have to be offset against loss of image analysis accuracy. For our test data set (heavily biased in favour of 'interesting' images compared to our full database) a compression ratio of approximately 4:1 (95% image quality) yielded a classification consistency of 75% that may still be sufficient.

As the image classification software develops, two trends can be foreseen. First the method becomes more robust and therefore becomes less affected by image compression. Second, increasingly subtle characteristics of the image may be used to improve classification accuracy and therefore the method may become increasingly sensitive to loss of image detail. More radical changes may also be foreseen such as the use of multiple imaging or time course data, both of which will require substantially more images to be analysed and stored.

Acknowledgements

The OPPF is funded by the UK Medical Research Council, Ian Berry is supported by the Wellcome Trust and Julie Wilson is supported by a Royal Society University Research Fellowship.

References

1. Walter, T, et al: A procedure for setting up high-throughput, nanolitre crystallization experiments. I: Protocol design and validation. J Appl Cryst 36 (2003) 308-314
2. Brown, J., Walter, T., et al: A procedure for setting up high-throughput, nanolitre crystallization experiments. II: Crystallization results. J Appl Cryst 36 (2003) 315-318
3. Wilson, J.: Towards the automated evaluation of crystallization trials. Acta Cryst. D58 part 11 (2002) 1907-1914
4. Wilson, J.: Automated evaluation of crystallisation experiments. Cryst. Rev., Vol. 10, No.1 (2004) 73-84
5. Spraggon, G., Lesley, S.A., Kreusch, A. and Priestle, J.P.: Computational analysis of crystallization trials. Acta Crystallographica, D58 part 11 (2002) 1915-1923
6. Cumbaa, C.A., Lauricella, A., Fehrman, N., Veatch, et al: Automatic classification of sub-microlitre protein-crystallization trials in 1536-well plates. Acta Cryst. D59 (2003) 1619-1627
7. Bern, M., Goldberg, D., Stevens, R.C. and Kuhn, P.: Automatic classification of protein crystallization images using a curve-tracking algorithm. J. Appl. Cryst., 37 (2004) 279-287
8. Joint Photographic Experts Group (JPEG): http://www.jpeg.org
9. JPEG Image Compression FAQ: http://www.faqs.org/faqs/jpeg-faq/
10. ImageMagick: http://www.imagemagick.org

PromSearch: A Hybrid Approach to Human Core-Promoter Prediction

Byoung-Hee Kim, Seong-Bae Park, and Byoung-Tak Zhang

Biointelligence Laboratory, School of Computer Science and Engineering
Seoul National University, Seoul 151-744, Korea
{bhkim,sbpark,btzhang}@bi.snu.ac.kr

Abstract. This paper presents an effective core-promoter prediction system on human DNA sequence. The system, named PromSearch, employs a hybrid approach which combines search-by-content method and search-by-signal method. Global statistics of promoter-specific contents are included to represent new significant information underlying the proximal and downstream region around transcription start site (TSS) of DNA sequence. Local signal features such as TATA box and CAAT box are encoded by the position weight matrix (PWM) method. In the experiment for the sequence set from the review by J.W.Fickett, PromSeach shows 47% positive predictive value which surpasses most of previously systems. On large genomic sequences, it shows reduced false positive rate while preserving true positive rate.

1 Introduction

A promoter is a part of DNA sequence that regulates gene expression, i.e. initiates and regulates the transcription of a gene. Gene regulation is one of the most important research topics in molecular biology and is closely related with several hot issues like regulatory network construction and target gene finding. It is therefore very important to identify regulatory regions exactly in DNA sequences, in that it makes it possible for one to examine the characteristics of the regions in more detail and to understand mechanism that control the expression of genes. Since huge amount of data out of DNA sequencing is being generated rapidly and requirement for gene/protein research emerges constantly, a reliable computational prediction of promoter regions becomes more indispensable to cellular and molecular biology fields than ever before.

There have been many algorithms and systems to predict promoter region computationally, especially promoter of higher eukaryotes, but few of them are applicable to real DNA sequence mainly owing to high false positive rates [4].

The approach to computational promoter prediction can be categorized roughly into three: search-by-signal approach, search-by-content approach and combination of the two [5]. Search-by-content algorithms identify regulatory regions by using measures based on the sequence composition of promoter and non-promoter regions. Search-by-signal algorithms make predictions based on the detection of core promoter elements such as the TATA box, the initiator, and/or transcription factor binding sites outside the core.

PromSearch takes a hybrid approach. From the search-by-signal point of view, we utilize well-known position weight matrices (PWMs) of four core-promoter elements [3]. As a search-by-content approach, we introduce new features extracted from wide range around core-promoter region. Searcy-by-content approach has a tendency to lose positional information. These shortcomings are supplemented by features from core element signal in our system and PromSearch includes a two-step criterion to determine transcription start site (TSS) position on DNA sequences of human more reasonably.

2 Methods and Materials

Fig. 1 shows the outline of the PromSearch system. PromSearch takes four steps to predict TSS position on the fragment within a window which slides every 10 base pairs (bp) from 5' to 3' direction on the input DNA sequence.

The first step is applying our model on the main target region of PromSearch, which leads from 250bp upstream from TSS to 50bp downstream including TSS, total 300bp region. We represent this region as [-250, 49][1]. Fig. 2 shows the model on this region. We take two sorts of features into account: locally over-represented signals and globally distinguishable content information.

There are four well-known core promoter elements; INR (initiator or cap signal), TATA-box, GC-box and CAAT-box [3]. These can be regarded as good local signals.

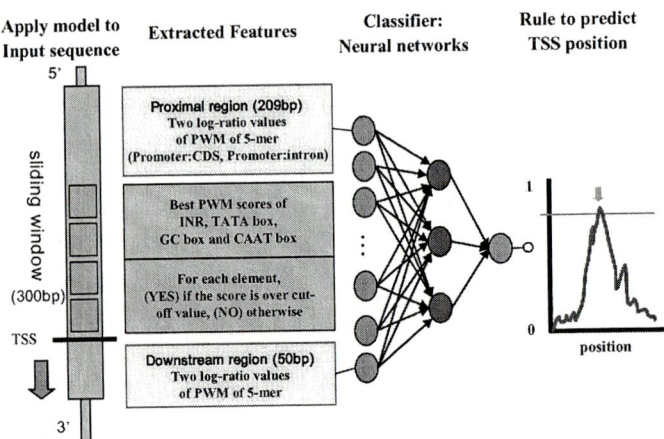

Fig. 1. Outline of the PromSearch system.

---

[1] Usually, the TSS position is marked by +1, where there is no 0 point and the coordinate immediately 1bp up from TSS is -1. In this paper, for the description purpose, we denote TSS position by 0, or the origin.

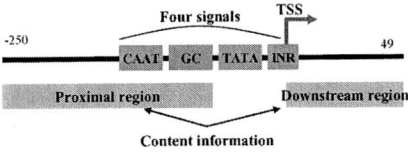
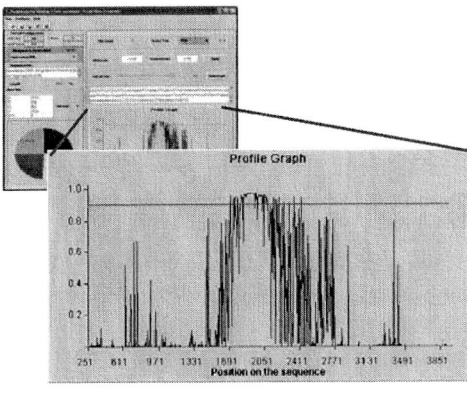

Fig. 2. Model on the 300bp region around TSS applied to PromSearch. The model combines locally overrepresented signals with globally distinguishable content information around TSS.

Fig. 3. (right) Software implemented by Java. Profile graph shows a 'plateau' around TSS.

But the combination and constitution of them are not well conserved among promoters and there are many fakes on non-promoter region that resemble these elements. So, these local signals are not sufficient to locate promoter accurately. Hence, we extract more global features out of proximal region and downstream region by search-by content approach.

Feature Extraction and Classification

We utilize position weight matrix (PWM) scores of core promoter elements as features to catch local signals. PWMs for each core element included in TRANSFAC [10] 6.0 are out-dated and built from only 502 eukaryotic RNA polymerase II promoter sequence. So, we have constructed new PWMs out of 2,538 vertebrate promoter sequences of eukaryotic promoter database (EPD) [8] release 76 with the aid of the pattern optimization (PatOp) algorithm of Bucher [3], which is served at the SSA web site [1]. Bucher's algorithm produces another two output values other than matrix: applying range of the matrix and cut-off value. We apply each PWM on its own applying range and searched the position where the score has maximum value and checked if the score is over cut-off value. These maximum score within given range and a binary value which represents if the score is over cut-off value, are used as representative features of corresponding promoter element. So, there are two features for each element, total 8 features.

We apply 5-mer pseudo-PWM score, as a measure for promoter and non-promoter. We introduce the definition that was used in dragon promoter finder (DPF) [2]. Two 5-mer PWMs are constructed from proximal region, [-250, -42], and downstream region, [1, 50], respectively. As non-promoter examples, we construct additional 5-mer PWMs from coding sequence (CDS) and intron sequences. Two are from 209 bp sequences of CDS and intron respectively as comparison examples of proximal PWM. Also for downstream PWM, two 5-mer matrices are built out of 50bp sequences of CDS and intron, respectively. So, there are three 5-mer PWMs for proximal and downstream region, respectively. Now, we construct two new features for each region. On the 209bp-long sequence of input window that corresponds to the proximal region of the model in fig 2, we produce three scores (v_p, v_c, v_i) from each PWM and calculate log ratio values (F_1, F_2) as following: $F_1 = \ln(v_p / v_c)$, $F_2 = \ln(v_p / v_i)$. Same process goes on a 50bp long sequence. This results in four content features.

As described above, PromSearch extracts total 12 features from input window of which size is 300bp. The next step is to judge if the window contains core-promoter region using these features. This process results in a binary classification.

We use neural networks as a classifier. Training set is made up of positive samples composed of 1871 human promoter sequence from EPD release 76 and negative samples constituted with 890 CDS and 4345 intron sequences of human from 1998 GENIE set, which was extracted from GenBank version 105. On the input layer of the neural network, we apply 'standardization' to all input features, i.e., extract mean value and divide by standard deviation. Trained network was built with the aid of Weka 3.4 S/W. On the output node of the neural networks, we omit the final classification step and take the output value of sigmoid function as a profile for given sequence within a window. The final step is replaced by a step to decide a TSS position.

Deciding TSS Position and Evaluation

If current window is classified as containing core-promoter, we reflect signal information to determine TSS position. First, if INR PWM score is larger than cut-off value, we take the origin of INR PWM as TSS position. If INR_cut value is 0 and TATA_cut value is 1, 30bp downstream from the origin of TATA PWM is predicted as a TSS. Otherwise, 50bp upstream from the 3' end of the input window is selected. We define a 'core range' as the region from 5' end of TATA region to 3' end of INR region. In case of 300bp window size, the core range is 61bp. If several TSS' predicted within a core range, they are regarded as one. With this criterion, unreasonable duplicative check, or overlapping of several core ranges, is prevented.

Applying previous criterion, there are two problems to be solved. First, there is a trend that the profile score jumps up before TSS and forms a plateau (see fig. 3). We decide a series of TSS as a plateau if any adjacent two are within 250bp. On the basis of analysis on DBTSS [9], we select a point 152bp down from jump-up point of any plateau as a TSS. Second, we need to adjust the cut-off value on the final decision step of the classifier. On the usual output node of neural networks, the class is determined as positive if the probability is over 0.5 and negative if less than 0.5. But, the value 0.5 produces many meaningless false positives and we need to apply more strict condition to reflect the tendency of jumping-up near TSS. All the results on the following section are from the system with 0.9 as new cut-off value.

Fig. 3 shows the software implemented in Java. With this software, we analyzed the sequence set from the review by J.W.Fickett [4], long sequence set that was used to evaluate PromoterInspector [6] and human chromosome 22 release 3.1b. Fickett's data consist of 24 promoters covering a total of 18 sequences and 33,120 bp. Long sequence data from the paper of (Scherf et al.) [6] consist of 35 promoters covering a total 6 sequences and about 1.38 million bp. We follow the criterion of Fickett in his paper [4]: we consider our prediction is correct if predicted TSS is within 200 bp upstream, or 100 bp downstream of any experimentally mapped TSS.

3 Results

Results on the Fickett's data set are presented in table 1. PromSearch shows better positive predictive value (PPV), which represents the reliability of positive predictions of the induced classifier, except PromoterInspector. But, considering that PromoterInspector predicts promoter 'regions', PromSearch has an advantage as a TSS predictor submitting to slightly more false positive rate. It also shows better PPV than DPF.

Table 2 shows results from several systems on several long sequences. Result of DPF1.4 was not available because the service on WWW supports only the analysis of maximum 10,000 bp sequence. Results except PromSearch are from [6]. L44140 shows very different pattern. PromSearch shows 98 FPs on L44140 and PromoterInspector also shows 14 FPs on this sequence, resulting in 3 times more FPs. Excluding L44140, PromSearch shows 17.8% PPV and one false positive in every 25kbp. It is far better than TSSG which shows 3.9% of PPV in this case.

Table 3 shows the result of the analysis of human chromosome 22 release 3.1b, applying the same conditions and criteria with [7]. One out of about ten predictions are supported by current gene annotation and the total number of predictions (3,517) is far less than that of other programs (11,890 or more) [7], which means reduced FP rate.

Table 1. Results for the Fickett data set. It is based on the assumption of [6] : the gene orientation is known, i.e. if the experimental TSS is found on the sense strand of the sequence, only TSS predictions on the sense strand were considered. The result of PromoterInspector is from [6]. We set the sensitivity of DPF1.4 as 65% for the data below. TP: true positive, FP: false positive, PPV (positive predictive value) = TP/(TP+FP), Sensitivity = TP/(TP+FN).

Method	TP	FP	PPV	Sensitivity	Specificity(FP rate)
PromFind	11	24	0.31	0.46	1/1,380
TSSG	10	17	0.37	0.42	1/1,948
TSSW	14	33	0.30	0.58	1/1,004
PromoterInspector	7	3	0.7	0.29	1/11,040
DPF1.4 (65% Se)	10	19	0.34	0.42	1/1,743
PromSearch	8	9	0.47	0.33	1/3,680

Table 2. Results for the dataset consisting of long promoter sequence from [6]: AC002397, D87675, AF017257, AF146793, AC002368. We exclude L44140 which shows exceptional pattern. Total length is about 1.16million bp and the number of TSS is 24.

Method	TP	FP	PPV (%)	Sensitivity	Specificity(FP rate)
TSSG	11	274	3.9	0.46	1/4,234
TSSW	11	317	3.4	0.46	1/3,660
NNPP2.1	15	2,979	0.5	0.63	1/389
Promoter2.0	6	1,408	0.4	0.25	1/824
PromoterInspector	10	5	66.7	0.42	1/232,048
PromSearch	10	46	17.9	0.42	1/25,223

Table 3. The results on the analysis of human chromosome 22 release 3.1b.

	Number of annotated genes	Annotation-supported prediction	Sensitivity
All genes	936	300	0.32
Coding genes	393	143	0.36
Additional predictions	3,217	PPV = 8.53%	

4 Discussion

PromSearch is a hybrid system of search-by-signal and search-by-content approach. It combines features of four core-promoter elements with that of proximal and downstream region. Newly introduced features are from proximal and downstream regions and they help to discriminate promoter from non-promoter. We have set some rules to locate TSS more reasonably and precisely. We utilize the information that can be extracted from PWM of TATA box and INR. The profile graph built with the values from neural networks output node shows notable 'plateaus' around TSS in the middle of low and flat region on non-core-promoter part. Reflecting an analysis on all human sequences in DBTSS, we determine a position on a plateau as a TSS.

Experiments demonstrated that PromSearch predicts TSS position with much lower false positive rates than most of previous systems. One out of about five predictions can be expected to be true positives. PromoterInspector, which shows superior performance, focuses on the genetic context of promoters and predicts some promoter region, rather than their exact location [6]. Experiments show that PromSearch can be a good alternative for those who want exact TSS location submitting to the increase of FP. DPF [2] takes multiple model approach on vertebrate promoters and it predicts TSS position based on search-by-content approach only. We applied its 5-mer PWM concept but processed the score in different view and we tried to locate TSS position more robustly by search-by-signal approach as well as a two-step prediction rule.

The main advantage of PromSearch comes from the fact that it produces profile that constitute notable plateau around TSS with reduced FPs and it predicts a TSS more precisely based on the signal information and the result of analysis on DBTSS.

References

1. Ambrosini, G., Praz, V., Jagannathan, V., Bucher, P.: Signal search analysis server, *Nucleic Acids Res.*, 31, 3618-3620, 2003.
2. Bajic, V.B., Chong, A., Seah, S.H., Krishnan, S.P.T., Koh, J.L.Y., Brusic, V.: Computer model for recognition of functional transcription start sites in polymerase II promoters of vertebrates, *Journal of Molecular Graphics & Modeling*, 21, 323-332, 2003.
3. Bucher, P.: Weight matrix description of four eukaryotic RNA polymerase II promoter elements derived from 502 unrelated promotor sequences. *J Mol Biol.*, 212, 563-578, 1990.

4. Fickett, J. W., Hatzigeorgiou, A.G.: Eukaryotic Promoter Recognition. *Genome Research*, 7, 861-878, 1997.
5. Ohler, U.: Computational promoter recognition in eukaryotic genomic DNA, PhD thesis, Technische Fakultät Erlangen-Nürnbeg, 2001.
6. Scherf, M., Klingenhoff, A., Werner, T.: Highly specific localization of promoter regions in large genomic sequences by PromoterInspector: a novel context analysis approach. *J Mol Biol.*, 297, 599-606, 2000.
7. Schef, M., et al.: First Pass Annotation of Promoters on Human Chromosome 22. *Genome Research*, 11, 333-340, 2001.
8. Schmid, C.D., Praz, V., Delorenzi, M., Périer, R., Bucher, P.: The Eukaryotic Promoter Database EPD: the impact of in silico primer extension. *Nucleic Acids Res.* 32, D82-5, 2004.
9. Suzuki, Y., Yamashita, R., Nakai, K., and Sugano, S.: DBTSS: DataBase of human Transcriptional Start Sites and full-length cDNAs. *Nucleic Acids Res.*, 30, 328-331, 2002.
10. Wingender, E., et al.: The TRANSFAC system on gene expression regulation. *Nucleic Acids Res.*, 29, 281-283, 2001.

Synergy of Logistic Regression and Support Vector Machine in Multiple-Class Classification

Yuan-chin Ivar Chang and Sung-Chiang Lin

Institute of Statistical Science, Academia Sinica
128, Section 2, Academia Road, Taipei, Taiwan 11529
ycchang@sinica.edu.tw

Abstract. In this paper, we focus on multiple-class classification problems. By using polytomous logistic regression and support vector machine together, we come out a hybrid multi-class classifier with very promising results in terms of classification accuracy. Usually, the multiple-class classifier can be built by using many binary classifiers as its construction bases. Those binary classifiers might be trained by either one-versus-one or one-versus-others manners, and the final classifier is constructed by some kinds of "leveraging" methods; such as majority vote, weighted vote, regression, etc. Here, we propose a new way for constructing binary classifiers, which might take the relationship of classes into consideration. For example, the level of severity of a disease in medial diagnostic. Depending on the methods used for constructing binary classifiers, the final classifier will be constructed/assembled by nominal, ordinal or even more sophisticated polytomous logistic regression techniques. This hybrid method has been apply to many real world bench mark data sets and the results shows that this new hybrid method is very promising and out-performs the classifiers using the technique of the support vector machine alone.

1 Introduction

The multiple-class classification problems are very common in many applications; such as pattern recognition, medical diagnostic, bio-informatics, etc. Usually, the multiple-class classifier can be built by using binary classifiers as its construction bricks. Those binary classifiers might be trained by either "one-versus-one" or "one-versus-others" manners, and the final classifier is constructed/assembled by some kinds of "leveraging" methods; such as majority vote, weighted vote, regression, etc. For more detail discussion about the "one-versus-one" and "one-versus-others", we refer to Allwein et al.(2000), Rifkin and Klautau (2004).

In multiple-class classification problems, there may be some relationship among classes; i.e. the labels might be not just categorical/nominal. For example, in medical diagnostics, we want to classify patients by the level of severity of a disease; and in placement tests, we would like to classify the students according to their ability levels. In this paper, we propose a new scheme for constructing binary classifiers, which allows us to take the information of the relationship among classes into consideration. According to the scheme used for constructing binary classifiers, we might use different polytomous logistic regression techniques to assemble them into a final multiple-class classifier.

Due to the advantage of polytomous logistic regression, the total number of binary classifiers we need for constructing the final multi-classifier is no greater than the number of classes. Thus, it is definitely more efficient than the "one-versus-one" method. Moreover, it is as efficient as the "one-versus-other" method, but with extra information from the relationship among labels. If labels are categorical then a nominal polytomous logistic regression will be used. If labels are used to indicate the ordinal relationship among classes, then to construct the binary classifiers in an ordinal way might be a reasonable choice in order to preserve their ordinal information. In this case, we should use the ordinal logistic regression to assemble the results of binary classifiers instead of nominal logistic regression. For some multi-class classification problems, the relationship among classes might be very complicated, as well as the construction scheme of binary classifiers. Depending on the relationship among classes and the scheme for constructing binary classifiers, a more sophisticated logistic regression model could be used. For simplicity, we only consider nominal and ordinal polytomous logistic regression here.

The support vector machine(SVM) is now a very popular tools in machine learning, which explores the kernel techniques and has good geometric explanation. Usually, it performs very well in many classification applications. For the details and recent development of the support vector machine, we refer readers to Cristianini and Shawe-Taylor (2000) and Vapnik (1995). The hybrid method we proposed here is to use (nominal/ordinal) polytomous logistic regression to combine the binary classifiers obtained by SVM. We compare the performance of the hybrid method proposed here with that of classifiers using SVM alone. The empirical results show that the proposed hybrid method is very promising in terms of classification accuracy as well as very efficient in terms of total number of binary classifiers needed for constructing the final multiple-class classifiers.

2 Nominal and Ordinal Logistic Regression

Before describing our hybrid classification procedure, we briefly introduce the nominal and the ordinal polytomous logistic regression methods. For detail discussions of logistic regression, please see McCullagh (1989).

2.1 Logistic Regression

The logistic regression methods are common statistical tools for modeling the discrete response variables; such as binary, categorical and ordinal responses. Suppose $Y \in \{0, 1, \cdots, k\}$, for some integer $k \geq 1$, be a categorical response variable, and $X \in R^p$ denotes the corresponding vector of covaraites. We say that the data (X, Y) satisfies a nominal logistic regression model, if for each $i = 1, \cdots, k$, (X, Y) satisfies that

$$\log\left(\frac{P(Y=i|X)}{P(Y=0|X)}\right) = f_i(X,\beta) = \beta_{0,i} + X^t\beta_i. \tag{1}$$

Depending on the number of classes k, the model (1) is called a dichotomous ($k = 1$) or a (nominal) polytomous ($k > 1$) logistic regression models.

If we believe that the response variable Y is ordinal, then instead of (1), we might use the following ordinal logistic regression model: For $i = 1, \cdots, k$,

$$\log\left(\frac{P(Y=i|X)}{P(Y<i|X)}\right) = f_i(X,\beta) = \beta_{0,i} + X^t\beta_i. \tag{2}$$

Due to the nonlinearity of the model, the estimate of coefficients must be calculated by some iteration algorithms.

Remark 1. It is known that when the data are completely separated, the maximum likelihood estimate for the logistic regression models will not converge. In this case, we can apply the method of Firth (1993) to fit the logistic regression by maximum penalized likelihood with a Jeffrey's invariant prior such that the iteration algorithm will always converge (see also Firth (1992), Heinze and Schemper (2002)).

2.2 Nominal Case

Suppose we have a multi-class classification problems with $k+1$ classes. Let C_i, $i = 0, \cdots, k$ denote these $k+1$ sub-classes of training examples. Let $(x, z) \in C_i$ denote the example, where $\mathbf{x} \in R^p$, for some integer p, be the feature vector of data, and $z \in \{0, 1, \ldots, k\}$ be its corresponding label.

Nominal Procedure:

Step 1. (Construct SVM binary classifiers)
Use C_0 as a baseline. Let Δ_j denote the SVM classifier trained with C_0, and C_j for $j = 1, \ldots, k$ and let H_j denote the hyperplane defined by the SVM classifier Δ_j.
Step 2. (Data transformation/DimensionReduction)
Compute the "signed" distances for each example to the separating hyperplanes obtained by the SVM classifiers in **Step** 1. Let $d_j = d_j(\mathbf{x})$ be the "signed" distance of example $\mathbf{x}$ to the hyperplane H_j, $j = 1, \ldots k$. Then the feature vector $\mathbf{x}$ of each example in the training set can be represented as a k-dimension vector $\mathbf{d} = \mathbf{d}(\mathbf{x}) = (d_1, \ldots, d_k)$. That is each data $(\mathbf{x}, z)$ is transformed/re-coded to $(\mathbf{d}, z)$.
Step 3. (Fit A Logistic Regression Model)
Fit a polytomous logistic regressions using (d, z); that is to use d as the vectors of independent variables and z as the response variables. If it is necessary, we can also apply model selection techniques to select the best subset of independent variables.
Step 4. (Predict Probability of Testing Example)
Repeat **Step** 2 and 3 for all testing data. Then compute the predicted probability $\mathbf{p} = (p_0, \ldots, p_k)$ for all testing examples using the logistic regression model obtained from **Step** 3, where $p_j = prob(z = j|\mathbf{d})$, $j = 0, \ldots, k$.

Step 5. (Assign Label For Each Example)
Assign the testing data x to Class j, if $p_i = max\{p_0, \cdots, p_k\}$.
Step 6. (Training Error) Compute the fitted probability for each training example. Assign the data x to Class j, if $p_i = max\{p_0, \cdots, p_k\}$. Let $\hat{z}(x)$ denote the predicted label of data x, then the Training error is

$$\frac{\sum I(z \neq \hat{z}(x))}{\text{(Total Number of Training Data)}}. \tag{3}$$

(In our empirical studies below, the testing errors are calculated in the same way as in (3).)

Remark 2. Step 2 can be viewed as an data transformation. We use the signed-distance to represent the original data. This can also be viewed as an dimension reduction. Further details of using SVM as a tool for dimension reduction will be reported in another paper.

Remark 3. Certainly, it is possible that the maximum probabilities of $\mathbf{p} = (p_0, \ldots, p_k)$ are not unique. In this case, some randomization method could be used to assign label.

2.3 Ordinal Case

Ordinal Procedure:

Step 1. (Construct binary classifiers using "one-against-preceding" scheme.)
Use SVM to produce k binary classifiers $(\Delta_1, \cdots, \Delta_k)$ based "one-against-preceding-classes"; i.e. the classifier Δ_j, $j = 1, \ldots, k$ is constructed using C_j versus $\bigcup_{i=0}^{j-1} C_i$.
Step 2. (Data Transformation)
Compute the "signed-distance" from each subject to the separating hyperplane of each classifiers (same as Step 2 of Nominal Procedure).
Step 3. (Fit An Ordinal Logistic Regression Model)
Fit an ordinal polytomous logistic regressions using the transformed data $(\mathbf{d}, z)$. (Again, the model selection methods can assist us to select the best subset of independent variables.)
Step 4. (Compute Prediction Probability of Testing Example)
Repeat *Step 2*, and calculating the prediction probability p_i, for $i = 0, \cdots, k$ for all testing examples using the final model obtained in *Step 3*.
Step 5. Assign a testing example to Class i, if $p_i = \max\{p_0, \cdots, p_k\}$. (Randomization might be needed if there is a tie in p's.) The training error can be computed as in Step 6 of previous nominal case.

3 Empirical Studies

The data we used for demonstration are obtained from UCI Machine Learning Repository (Blake and Merz (1998)). Detail descriptions for all the data sets

Table 1. Nominal Procedure: Accuracy (Standard Deviation)

Kernel	Linear	Poly	RBF	Linear	Poly	RBF
Data Set	Training Accuracy			Testing Accuracy		
Pen Digits	53.9(0.9)	70.9(2.9)	58.6(0.2)	53.8(1.3)	70.6(2.9)	58.5(1.7)
Ecoli	85.6(1.5)	83.3(2.4)	85.0(2.9)	81.8(3.9)	78.8(4.3)	82.4(5.4)
Letter Recognition	74.9(0.1)	72.0(1.5)	71.7(1.1)	74.9(0.9)	72.5(2.2)	69.5(1.5)

Table 2. Ordinal Procedure: Accuracy (Standard Deviation)

Kernel	Linear	Poly	RBF	Linear	Poly	RBF
Data Set	Training Accuracy			Testing Accuracy		
Pen Digits	85.5(0.2)	99.3(0.1)	99.6(0.1)	85.1(1.2)	98.9(0.4)	99.3(0.3)
Ecoli	85.2(1.7)	92.6(0.7)	88.5(1.2)	81.5(4.0)	82.1(4.9)	85.4(4.6)
Letter Recognition	59.3(0.1)	(Nan)	99.1(0.1)	58.8(1.2)	(Nan)	96.4(0.6)

used here, we refer readers to their website. All the empirical results are based on 10-fold cross-validation. The corresponding standard deviation are also recoded in parentheses. Table 1 and Table 2 summarize the results for multiple-class problems, and Table 7 and 8 state the results of binary classification problems. The "Linear", "Poly" and "RBF", stand for the linear, polynomial and radius based function (gaussian) kernels, respectively. Both training and testing errors are reported. The parameters for all binary classifiers might be different; i.e. all the parameters are individually tuned when the binary classifiers are constructed. So, for simplicity, we do not report the parameters we used in our empirical studies here. All the studies are done by using statistical package – R(URL:www.r-project.org; glm and brlr and e1071(SVM). All the results are based on multi-fold cross-validation (10-fold for Pen Digit and Letter Recognition, and 5-fold for Ecoli) and summarized in percentage. The numbers within parentheses are its corresponding standard deviations. (To prevent the computational difficulty, we also used Begg and Gray (1984) and its modification to estimate the regression coefficients; which allows us to estimate the polytomous regression coefficients from binary logistic regressions models.)

Table 1 and 2 are the results of the nominal and the ordinal procedures, respectively. We have try three different kernels: linear, polynomial and radial basis functions. Both training and testing accuracy are recorded.

Here we also compare our hybrid(ordinal) procedures with two popular ensemble methods: One versus One, and One versus Rest. For comparison purpose, we also use SVM as base-classifiers with either linear or radial basis function(RBF) kernels. (Note that the "one-versus-rest" scheme we used here follows from Schölkopf and Smola(2001).) The results are summarized in Table 3.

Comparing Table 3 with Table 2, we can see that among classifiers with linear kernel, the SVM classifier with "one versus one" voting scheme is the best. Our ordinal procedure is better then the SVM classifier based on "one versus rest" scheme. For those classifiers based on radial basis function, the ordinal procedure method proposed here is slightly better than the other two methods.

Table 3. Compare with Different Ensemble Methods

Method	SVM one vs. one		SVM one vs. rest	
Data Sets	Linear	RBF	Linear	RBF
Pen Digits	98.1(0.6)	98.9(0.4)	82.9(2.1)	96.6(0.9)
Ecoli	84.4(5.6)	85.2(3.4)	71.9(3.1)	84.4(5.4)
Letter Recognition	85.1(1.2)	96.1(0.6)	55.8(1.0)	95.8(0.8)

It is known that to construct a multi-class classifiers based one-versus-one voting scheme, we will need to build C_2^N binary classifiers. If we apply the one-versus-rest scheme, then we must tune the parameter carefully to prevent the effect of the imbalanced training sample. So based on the results above, the ordinal procedure proposed here could be a good alternative for multi-class classification problems.

3.1 Application to Binary Classification

This hybrid method can be applied to binary classification problems, too. Especially, when the sizes of two classes are highly imbalanced. In this case, we can partition the one with larger sample size, then apply the nominal procedure mentioned above to constructed a binary classifier with slight modification. The required modification is highlighted below:

Step 0. (Data Preprocessing/Pseudo Classes)
Suppose the size of negative class outnumber the size of positive class. Divide the negative examples into k partitions by a clustering algorithm. Let C_0 denote the positive class and $\{C_j, j = 1, \cdots, k\}$ be the k sub-classes of the negative examples. (The parameter k is chosen by user.)
Step 1 to **Step 4.** Perform Step 1 to Step 4 of the nominal procedure.
Step 5*. (Assign Label)
Find a probability threshold T by cross-validation. The testing example is said to be positive, when p_0 is larger than a threshold T. (Note the slight modification of Step 5*.)

Before we apply these hybrid method to real data sets, we like to illustrate it by applying it to some synthesized data sets. In this simple simulation study, the data are generated from some two-dimension normal distributions with different mean vectors. The positive example(P) is generated from a bivariate normal distribution with mean vector $(0,0)$ and covariance matrix equals I_2 (a 2×2 identity matrix). There are four groups of negative examples($N_i, i = 1, \cdots, 4$). The examples of each N_i, are also generated from a bivariate normal with covariance I_2, but with different mean vectors: $\mu_1 = (m, m)$, $\mu_2 = (-m, m)$, $\mu_3 = (-m, -m)$ and $\mu_4 = (h \times m, -h \times m)$, where $m = 1.0, 1.5, 2.0$ and 2.5, and $h = 0.5$. Figure 1 shows us the scatter plots of the synthesized data sets with different m's. The red dots in the center of each scatter plot denotes the positive examples and the dots with others colors are negative examples. There are 200 examples of each

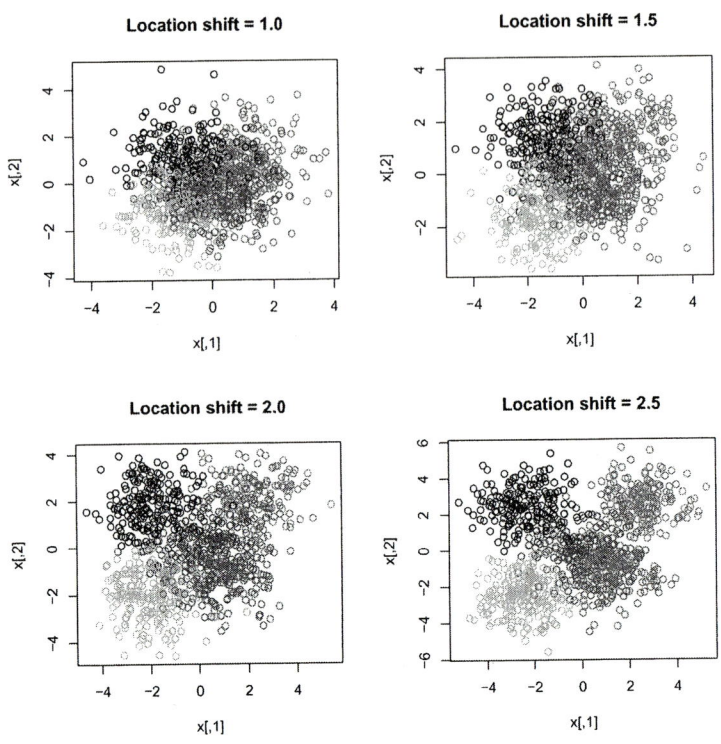

Fig. 1. Scatter Plots of Synthesized Data Sets

groups (P and $N_i, i = 1, \cdots, 4$) and the testing data are generated at the same manner. The simulation results are based 1000 runs for each of them.

We apply the nominal procedure (SVM classifiers with linear kernel function and categorical logistic regression) to these data sets. For comparison purpose, we also apply SVM classifiers with either linear or radial basis kernels to these synthesized data sets. We treat it as a multi-class classification and apply the SVM classifier with one-versus-one scheme to them. Here we are only interested in how good these three classifiers (hybrid, SVM linear and SVM RBF) can separate the positive examples from the negative examples, and we do not care about the classification accuracy for the negative sub-groups. (In other words, we classify the data use multiple classification scheme, but evaluate their performances as binary classification problems. This might provide some hint about the effect of partitioning.) In Table 4, to 6, we summarize not only their accuracy but also the precision and recall.

We found that all three classifiers have similar accuracies, but the hybrid method (nominal procedure based on SVM linear classifiers) has more balanced precision and recall rates. In Figure 2 shows the ROC curve of the hybrid method we used here for different m's.

It is clear that if there is no partitioning of negative examples, then the SVM classifiers with linear kernel will fail in these simulations. So, from these simu-

Table 4. Hybrid Method with Partitioned Negative Examples

Method	Hybrid (Nominal Proc.)			
Shift (m)	1.0	1.5	2.0	2.5
Accuracy	74.1(1.6)	81.3(1.1)	88.3(1.2)	93.3(0.9)
Precision	33.7(6.9)	52.2(8.7)	70.5(5.9)	83.3(3.0)
Recall	34.1(7.1)	52.2(8.8)	70.6(6.0)	83.6(3.2)

Table 5. SVM Linear Kernel with Partitioned Negative Examples

Method	SVM Linear Kernel			
Shift (m)	1.0	1.5	2.0	2.5
Accuracy	77.0(1.1)	81.9(1.0)	87.7(0.9)	92.2(0.8)
Precision	36.8(4.3)	56.8(3.7)	75.0(3.3)	87.5(2.7)
Recall	20.6(3.3)	39.8(3.9)	57.6(4.0)	71.3(3.6)

Table 6. SVM RBF Kernel with Partitioned Negative Examples

Method	SVM RBF Kernel			
Shift (m)	1.0	1.5	2.0	2.5
Accuracy	76.7(1.4)	81.7(1.1)	87.6(1.0)	92.2(0.9)
Precision	35.9(4.6)	56.3(3.9)	74.8(3.4)	87.4(2.7)
Recall	21.0(5.8)	39.7(5.5)	57.3(4.9)	71.2(4.0)

lation results, we can say that to partitioning of negative examples into smaller groups (some clustering algorithms are required) can improve the performance of SVM linear classifier. The hybrid method built on the SVM linear classifier can even improve the performance further by balancing the precision and the recall. Certainly, to apply this method we will need to apply some clustering algorithm first. How to choose the clustering algorithm will be reported elsewhere. In empirical results below, we simply use K-mean algorithm. Of course, this might not be the best choice, and it is mostly for illustration purpose.

The following are some empirical results of binary classification problems. Compare these two tables, we found that the hybrid method with RBF is the best, which also out-performs, in terms of classification accuracy, the classier using SVM alone.

4 Summary and Discussion

From the empirical results, we found that our hybrid method is very promising in both multiple classes and binary classification problems. We are not clear at this moment why the ordinal model outperforms the nominal model even in some non-ordinal cases; such as pen-digit and letter-recognition problems. We think below is one the possible reason. The more similar the two classes are, the more difficult to classify them correctly. By the way we construct the ordinal model, we might effectively avoid the difficult classification problems; that is we

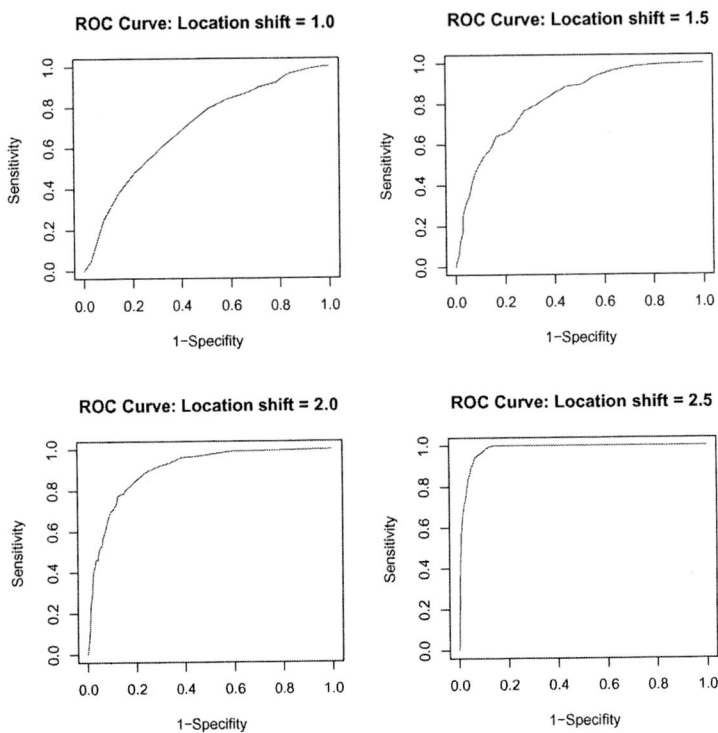

Fig. 2. ROC Curve of Hybrid Method

Table 7. Hybrid Binary Classifier

Kernel	Linear		Poly		RBF	
Data Set	Train	Test	Train	Test	Train	Test
Hepa Domain	90.5(1.4)	79.3(8.1)	1.00(0.0)	82.7(6.1)	87.8(1.4)	81.8(7.8)
ionosphere	90.9(0.8)	84.7(4.2)	98.4(0.4)	88.7(6.7)	99.4(0.1)	93.8(4.1)
liver-disorders	72.7(1.8)	69.3(5.3)	64.4(2.9)	58.9(9.9)	82.9(0.8)	69.3(3.2)
pima-diabetes	78.3(0.5)	77.2(3.7)	83.8(0.8)	75.5(3.4)	77.3(0.5)	77.1(3.7)
tic-tac-toe	67.8(1.4)	65.9(4.6)	98.9(0.4)	97.4(5.3)	1.00(0.0)	78.6(4.2)
wdbc	97.7(0.5)	96.3(1.9)	98.5(0.3)	96.4(2.0)	98.3(0.2)	97.9(2.1)
wpbc	80.6(2.0)	77.5(10.5)	94.4(1.7)	71.3(6.5)	79.9(1.1)	79.1(8.0)

do not need to construct binary classifiers for very difficult cases. For example, in the pen-digit recognition problem, to classify the digit "0" and "6" might be more difficult than to classify "{0, ..., 5}" and "6" . In nominal model, if we use Class "0" as basis, then we must face to this harder problem. But in ordinal model, we do not have to classify "0" and "6", directly. That is depending the order we used for modeling the ordinal model, we might effectively prevent to classify difficult cases, directly. This might be the reason why the ordinal model performs better even in some non-ordinal cases.

Table 8. SVM Classifier

Kernel	Linear		Poly		RBF	
Data Set	Train	Test	Train	Test	Train	Test
Hepa Domain	91.6(1.1)	78.0(7.7)	1.00(0.0)	82.1(7.5)	79.4(0.2)	79.4(1.6)
ionosphere	92.8(0.9)	87.8(4.6)	97.7(0.5)	90.9(6.2)	98.2(0.4)	94.6(4.7)
liver-disorders	70.9(1.1)	68.1(4.1)	91.3(1.0)	70.4(5.1)	78.9(0.8)	67.2(4.4)
pima-diabetes	77.9(0.8)	77.2(3.1)	85.7(0.6)	76.1(5.6)	76.1(0.9)	75.4(3.6)
tic-tac-toe	65.3(0.1)	65.3(0.3)	98.4(0.6)	98.0(5.3)	1.00(0.0)	75.5(4.8)
wdbc	98.8(0.2)	97.6(2.1)	98.8(0.2)	98.1(1.8)	98.1(0.3)	97.7(2.5)
wpbc	80.2(1.8)	71.8(6.7)	1.00(0.0)	71.3(9.3)	76.3(0.2)	76.3(1.9)

It is known that SVM with RBF is more stable than the other two kernels we used here in many applications. In our studies, the hybrid classier with RBF kernel is also the best. That might due to its VC-dimensionality (see Vapnik (1995)). It is obvious that the SVM classifier in our procedures can be replaced by other linear classifiers; such as (Kernel)-FDA. The performances of using polytomous with other linear classifiers will be reported in the future.

References

Allwein, E., Schapire, R. and Singer, Y.:Reducing Multiclass to Binary: A unifying Approach for Margin Classifiers. Journal of Machine Learning Research (2000), 113 – 141.

Begg, C. B. and Gray, R.: Calculation of polychotomous logistic regression parameters using individualized regression. *Biometrika*, (1984), 71:11 – 18.

Blake, C. L. and Merz, C. J.: UCI repository of Machine Learning databases (1998).

Cristianini, N. and Shawe-Taylor, J. (2000). *An Introduction to Support Vector Machines and Other Kernel-based Learning Methods.* Cambridge University Press, Cambridge, United Kingdom.

Firth, D.: Bias reduction, the Jefferys prior and GLIM. In Fahemeir, L. Francis, R. G. and Tutz, G., editors, Advances in GLIM and Statistical Modelling, pages (1992) 91 – 100. Springer-Verlag, New York.

Heinze and Schemper: A solution to the problem of separation in logistic regression. Statist. Med., **21** (2002) 2109 – 2149.

McCullagh, P. (1989). *Generalized Linear Models, 2nd Edition.* Chapman and Hall, New York, 2nd edition.

Rifkin, R. and Klautau, A.: In defence of one-vs-all classification. Journal of Machine Learning Research, (2004), 101 – 141.

Schölkopf, B and Smola, A. J. (2001). *Learning with Kernels:Support Vector machines, Regularization, Optimization, and Beyond.* MIT press.

Vapnik, V. (1995). *The Nature of Statistical Learning Theory.* Springer, NY.

Deterministic Propagation of Blood Pressure Waveform from Human Wrists to Fingertips

Yi Zhao and Michael Small

Hong Kong Polytechnic University, Kowloon, Hong Kong, China
zhao.yi@polyu.edu.hk

Abstract. Feeling the pulse on the wrist is one of the most important diagnostic methods in traditional Chinese medicine (TCM). In this paper we test whether there is any difference between feeling the pulse on the wrist or at any other part of the body, such as at the fingertips? To do this we employ the optimal neural networks estimated by description length to model blood pressure propagation from the wrist to the fingertip, and then apply the method of surrogate data to the residuals of this model. Our result indicates that for healthy subjects measuring pulse waveform at the fingertip is equivalent to feeling pulse on the lateral artery (wrist).

1 Introduction

Traditional Chinese medicine practitioners (TCMP) always feel the pulse on a patient's wrists during diagnosis. This procedure has been routine in TCM for thousands of years. It is both convenient and easy for TCMP to feel the pulse on the wrist. But is there any other significant advantage for feeling the pulse on the wrist? What about feeling the pulse at other locations, such as carotid artery or fingertips, is there any significant difference other than the signal intensity? Similarly, one may ask the same questions for other cardiac data, such as human electroencephalogram (ECG) data. Do ECG data collected from different parts of one person reflect the same result? More generally, is there any distinction between measuring ECG and lateral arterial pulse.

In this paper we take the approach of surrogate data to address the first part of this problem. Surrogate data provides a rigorous way to apply statistical hypothesis testing to experimental time series. One may apply it to determine whether an observed time series has a statistically significant deterministic component. But surrogates alone cannot separate the noise and deterministic components. We need to model and identify the deterministic component of blood propagation from wrists to fingertips.

To achieve this, we adopt backpropagation neural networks to model the nonlinear transformation from wrists to fingertips. From a large number of potential modeling regimes, a nearest neighbor technique and a neural network model were found to perform best [1]. Rather than early stopping and regularization techniques [2], we take an alternative approach, description length [3], to determine how many parameters (i.e. neurons) of the neural network are enough to provide adequate fit and yet avoid overfitting. In [4], we prove that the information criterion of description length can estimate the optimal neural networks for four kinds of nonlinear time series: the Ikeda map, the Rössler system, chaotic laser data, and ECG data. Consequently we employed the optimal neural networks decided by MDL to model and identify the deterministic component of blood propagation from wrists to fingertips.

2 Surrogate Data and Description Length

2.1 Linear Surrogate Data

The rationale of surrogate data hypothesis testing is to generate an ensemble of artificial surrogate data sets that are both "like" the original data and consistent with some null hypothesis. The addressed null hypothesis that we used is NH1: The data is independent and identically distributed (i.i.d.) noise of unspecified mean μ and variance σ^2 [5]. And one then applies some test statistic (or indeed a battery of test statistics) to both the surrogates and the original data.

If the test statistic value for the data is different from the ensemble of values estimated for the surrogates, then one can reject the associated null hypothesis as being a likely origin of the data. If the test statistic value for the data is not distinct from that for the surrogates, then one can not reject the null hypothesis.

To test the hypothesis of surrogate data one must select an appropriate statistic tool. As these surrogate methods were originally introduced as a "sanity test" for correlation dimension estimation, correlation dimension is a popular choice [6]. We compute correlation dimension using Gaussian Kernel algorithm (GKA) method [7].

2.2 Computation of Description Length

We adopt backpropagation neural networks, which have multi-layer perceptron models with a single hidden layer, sigmoid activation functions, and linear output. Hence, for inputs $(x_{t-1}, x_{t-2}, ..., x_{t-d})$ the model f is of the form

$$f(x_{t-1}, x_{t-2}, ..., x_{t-d}) = b_0 + \sum_{i=1}^{k} v_i \phi\left(\sum_{j=1}^{d} \omega_{i,j} x_{t-j} + b_i\right) \quad (1)$$

where $v_i, \omega_{i,j}, b_i \in R$, k is the model size and d is the number of inputs [4]. The parameters of the model k are therefore $\{b_0, b_i, v_i, \omega_{i,j} \mid i=1,...,k \; j=1,...,d\}$; Denote by $\wedge_k$ the model parameters.

The description length of the data with respect to the model size k is given by the sum of the cost of describing the model prediction errors, $E(k)$ and the cost of describing the model parameters, $M(k)$. $E(k)$ is the negative log likelihood of the model prediction error. Assuming that the model prediction errors are Gaussian distributed, we can make the approximation

$$E(k) = -\ln \text{Prob}(e \mid \wedge_k) \approx \frac{N}{2} + \ln\left(\frac{2\pi}{N}\right)^{N/2} + \ln\left(\sum e_i^2\right)^{N/2} \quad (2)$$

Assuming the model can be parameterized by $\{v_i \mid i=0,...,k\}$, and no other parameters. Rissanen [3] showed that the description length of parameters v_i (specified to some finite precision δ_i) is

144   Yi Zhao and Michael Small

$$M(k) = \sum_{i=0}^{k} \ln \frac{\gamma}{\delta_i} \qquad (3)$$

where γ is a constant related to the number of bits in the mantissa of the binary representation of v_i. Suppose that the precision of the nonlinear parameters is similar to that of the linear ones, but not all the parameters are significant for a particular neuron [4], we have

$$M(k) = \sum_{i=0}^{k} n_p \ln \frac{\gamma}{\delta_i} \qquad (4)$$

But we often assume $n_p(i)$ to be almost constant, n_p which is somewhat like the effective number of parameters computed by False Nearest Neighbors proposed by Kennel et al. [8]. Because it estimates the number of the degrees of freedom of the system, a parameterized model will require this number of parameters [4].

3 Application and Examples

Our idea is to confirm that deterministic propagation of blood pressure from human wrists to fingertips can be modeled with a nonlinear transfer function.

Referring to this purpose, we utilize neural networks with different numbers of neurons to model blood pressure propagation from the wrist to the fingertip. Note that we collect the pulse data on both the wrist and the fingertip for each subject at the same time. The neural network uses pulse data on the wrist to predict pulse data on the fingertip so as to try to find some relation between them.

We then adopt minimum description length to decide the optimal model size. As discussed in [4], we have found minimum description length can estimate the optimal model in many different applications, including ECG data.

In the following we generate 30 surrogates of the one-step error of testing set of the optimal model and calculate correlation dimension of this error and the distribution of correlation dimension for all surrogates. Typical results of one volunteer for GKA embedding dimension m=5, 6, 7, and 8 are depicted in figure 1.

One can find correlation dimension of the original error stays in the center or close to the center of the distribution of correlation dimension for all surrogates, and therefore the original data cannot be distinguished from the results of the surrogates. The other five cases show similar results. Hence we cannot reject the given hypothesis that the original error is i.i.d noise, i.e. we find no evidence of dynamic noise between the pulse data on the wrist and the fingertip.

However, it may be possible that the optimal models failed to distinguish between data and surrogates even though significant differences exist. As a test of this possibility, we examine the prediction of pulse data on the finger with (deterministic but independent) observational "noise". Figure 2 shows results of this volunteer data with such "noise" for GKA embedding dimension m=5, 6, 7, and 8.

For comparison, we selected the pulse data of the previous volunteer to add x-component of the Rössler dynamics data to pulse data on the fingertip prior to prediction. The standard deviation of the varieties is set at 10% of the standard deviation of the pulse data on the fingertip.

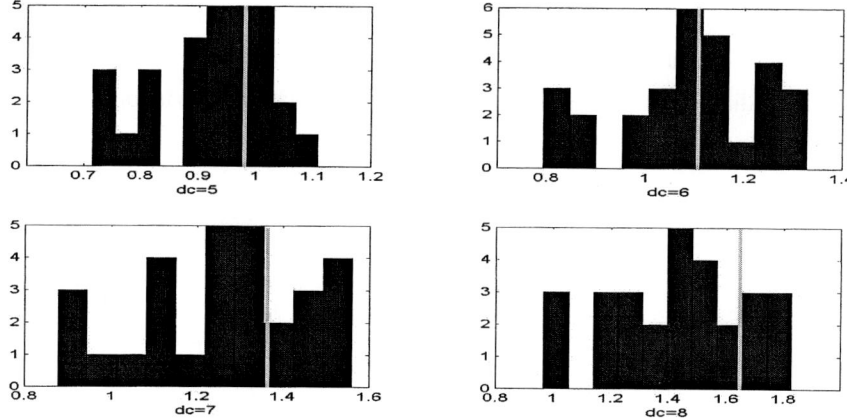

Fig. 1. The histogram shows the distribution of correlation dimension for 30 surrogates from a one-step error of the optimal model decided by MDL. The x-axis of the light line in every sub figure is the correlation dimension of the original one-step error.

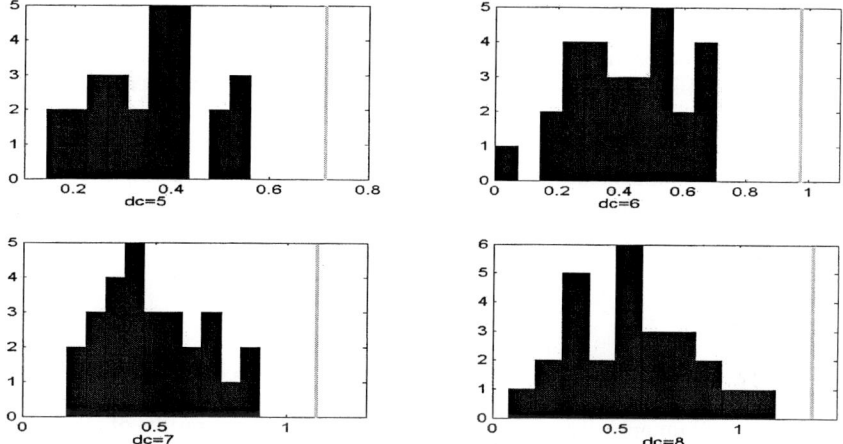

Fig. 2. The histogram shows the distribution of correlation dimension for 30 surrogates from a one-step error of the optimal model with observational noise. The x-axis of the light line in every sub figure is the correlation dimension of the original one-step error.

According to Fig. 2, correlation dimension of the original error is far away from the distribution of surrogates. Consequently we can reject the given hypothesis: the original error is i.i.d noise. This is consistent with our expectation. Because we have artificially added the Rössler dynamics data to the pulse data on the fingertip, and such dynamics should exist in the error.

We therefore conclude that if there is some significant difference, i.e. some dynamic noise between pulse data on the wrist and the fingertip the optimal model can identify them from the pulse data, and then the method of surrogate data can show the existence of this deterministic dynamics in the residuals.

Table 1 illustrate results of all six cases, which are calculated by $|d_c - <d_c>|/\sigma_{d_c}$, in which d_c is correlation dimension of the original error, and $<d_c>$ is the mean of the correlation dimension of all surrogates, and σ_{d_c} is the standard deviation of the correlation dimension of all surrogates.

Table 1. Estimates of the number of standard deviations separating data and surrogates for each of six different subjects and for one further case with deterministic independent dynamics added to case 1[1].

Subject \ d_e	5	6	7	8
Case1	0.5790	0.2932	0.5764	0.9606
Case2	0.5965	0.0929	0.1822	0.2888
Case3	0.4410	0.720	1.0946	1.2607
Case4	0.8707	1.0879	0.9628	1.198
Case5	0.0674	0.1289	0.1488	0.2464
Case6	0.036	0.1939	0.6016	0.307
Case1[1]	3.2535	3.3404	3.3735	2.9802

In the first six cases there is no significant difference between the model prediction errors (i.i.d.) and surrogates of that signal. Consequently, in these cases the model captures all the deterministic structure very well. In the remaining case (case 1[1]) we see that the independent deterministic signal added to the output (but not able to be modeled from the input) leads to the conclusion that the optimal model does not capture all the underlying dynamics, as we expected.

4 Conclusion

We have described the procedure to confirm deterministic propagation of blood pressure from human wrist to fingertip, and demonstrated the application of this method to recordings of human pulse of six subjects. Referring to these results of all cases, we cannot reject the hypothesis that the prediction error is i.i.d noise. We therefore conclude that with the statistics at our disposal, pulse measurements on fingertips and wrist are indistinguishable.

For comparison we repeat the experiments with addition of observational "noise" (x-component Rössler data) to the pulse data of the fingertip of one volunteer under the same hypothesis. This result implies that once deterministic deviation exists in the pulse data on the fingertip (in other words, there is significant difference between the pulse data on the wrist and the finger), surrogate techniques can detect the deterministic signals.

Hence, taking the results of two experiments into consideration, we conclude that measuring pulse pressure at the fingertips (as is done in western medicine) is equivalent to "feeling the pulse" in TCM. This conclusion may appear somewhat straight-

---

[1] We deliberately add observational noise (the *x*-component of the Rössler system) to pulse data on the fingertip of case 1.

forward. In the future work we intend to explain this to study the relationship between ECG and pulse data, and also to understand the correspondence between the various distinct pulses described in TCM.

Acknowledgements

This work was supported by a Hong Kong Polytechnic University Research Grant (A-PE46) and a Hong Kong University Grants Council Competitive Earmarked Research Grant (PolyU 5235/03E).

References

1. E.A. Wan. Time series prediction: Forecasting the future and understanding the past. Vol. XV of studies in the sciences of complexity, MA: Addison-Wesley, pp. 195–217, 1993.
2. Neural Network Toolbox User's Guide, 4th Ver., the Math Works, Inc., 5:52–57, 2000.
3. J. Rassanen. Stochastic complexity in statistical inquiry, Singapore: World Scientific, 1989.
4. Yi Zhao, M. Small. How many neurons? An information theoretic method for selecting model size. IEEE Transactions on Neural Networks, submitted for publication.
5. A. Galka, Topics in Nonlinear Time Series Analysis with Implications for EEG Analysis, Singapore: World Scientific, 2000.
6. M. Small, C. K. Tse. Detecting determinism in time series: the method of surrogate data. IEEE Trans. on Circuits and System-I, vol. 50, pp. 663-672, 2003.
7. Dejin Yu, Michael Small, Robert G. Harrison, and Cees Diks. Efficient implementation of the Gaussian kernel algorithm in estimating invariants and noise level from noisy time series data. Phys. Rev. E, vol. 61, 2000.
8. M. B. Kennel, R. Brown, and H. D. I. Abarbanel. Determining embedding dimension for phase-space reconstruction using a geometrical construction. Phys. Rev. A 45: 3403, 1992.

Pre-pruning Decision Trees by Local Association Rules

Tomoya Takamitsu[1,*], Takao Miura[1], and Isamu Shioya[2]

[1] Dept. of Elect. & Elect. Engr., HOSEI University
3-7-2 KajinoCho, Koganei, Tokyo, 184–8584 Japan
[2] Dept.of Management and Informatics, SANNO University
1573 Kamikasuya, Isehara, Kanagawa 259–1197 Japan

Abstract. This paper proposes a *pre-pruning* method called KLC4 for decision trees, and our method, based on KL divergence, drops candidate attributes irrelevant to classification. We compare our technique to conventional ones, and show usefulness of our technique by experiments.

1 Motivation

In *Data Mining*, one of the typical activities is *decision tree* which is a classification model based on hierarchical structure[8]. Several algorithms have been proposed such as ID3 and C4.5[8, 3]. Decision trees have been evaluated in terms of *size* and *error ratio* of classification. Two techniques have been investigated mainly in two categories: post-pruning and *pre-pruning*[3, 9]. The authors have investigated several quality improvement of decision trees[10, 11].

We propose pre-pruning technique by extracting local property among attribute values and removing attributes which are irrelevant to classification. The technique provides us with distinguished properties suitable for large amount of data: (1) We extract association rules automatically among attribute values from training data. We utilize KL divergence to examine class distribution so that we obtain rules very efficiently. We don't need experimental or probabilistic prerequisites. (2) We can generate the rules quickly to every part of data.

Most activities in decision trees have been focused on quality improvement by post-pruning where we remove redundant parts after we generate big (sometimes overfitting) trees[3, 9].

On the other hand, pre-pruning for decision trees has been considered doubtful for long time[8]. PreC4 is one of the typical approaches of pre-pruning[7], and examine input data by means of cross validation and we obtain global error estimation in advance. Some experiment of PreC4 results to DNA database say that the error ratio is comparable to C4.5 but half size of the tree. Combination of pre-/post-pruning has been proposed but is not specific to decision trees[2]. Some investigation has been reported for the generation of decision trees by using association rules[12]. Another approach shows how to generate classifiers

---

* Takamitsu, T. is currently working at CRC Solutions Co. in Japan.

using association rules[6]. They have examined improved classifiers compared to to C4.5 but not specific to decision trees.

In this paper, section 2 gives the definition and generation of decision trees, review association rules quickly and discuss some relationship with entropy, and develop our theory about attribute removal for pre-pruning. Section 3 shows some experimental results, and we conclude our work in section 4.

2   Pre-pruning Decision Trees Using Association Rules

We discuss how entropy is related to association rules against attribute values, and assume a finite multiset T of objects as below:

$$T = \begin{pmatrix} A_1 \ldots A_k : \mathcal{C} \\ a_1^1 \ldots a_n^1 : c_1 \\ .. \ldots .. : .. \\ a_1^n \ldots a_k^n : c_n \end{pmatrix} = \begin{pmatrix} \mathcal{A} : \mathcal{C} \\ t_1 : c_1 \\ .. \\ t_n : c_n \end{pmatrix}$$

Let us note that each object corresponds to one line which describes several characteristics in a form of $< a_1, a_2, ..., a_k >$ where each a_i is a value in a domain of an attribute $A_i \in \mathcal{A}$, and that the objects belongs to a class $c \in \mathcal{C}$. Thus T is defined over $\mathcal{A} = \{A_1, A_2, ..., A_k\}$ and $\mathcal{C}$.

For the purpose of the attribute selection we introduce a notion of *entropy*. For a class c_j, $\log(1/p_j) = -\log p_j$ is called an amount of information of c_j in T where T contains n lines and the n_j objects belong to the class c_j. An (class) entropy $Ent(T)$ is defined as an expect value of the amount of information as follows:

$$Ent(T) = \Sigma_{j=1}^h p_j \log_2(1/p_j) = -\Sigma_{j=1}^h p_j \log_2 p_j$$

To examine properties of entropy $Ent(T)$, let us define class distribution $dist(T)$

$$dist(T) = < n_1/n, ..., n_h/n >$$

where there are n elements in T, n_j elements of a class c_j in T and $n_1 + .. + n_h = n$. Let a be an element on A and $T_{A(a)}$ be a sub multiset as:

$$T_{A(a)} = \{t \in T \mid t[A] = \text{``}a\text{''}\}$$

where $t[A]$ means a value of t on A. Given two similar distributions with respect to an attribute A, we could remove A from candidates for an intermediate node. In the following, we discuss how entropy is closely related to association rules against attribute values.

This leads us to the idea of pre-pruning. We discuss how to generate simple and reliable decision trees by removing attributes not useful for classification. Our basic idea is that we put our attention on difference between class distributions on a node and on its child node. The information gain for selecting attributes is examined based on change of the class distribution: the larger the change amount is, the more likely the attribute is selected. This idea provides us with a new kind of pre-pruning technique for decision trees. Let α, β be two parameters where $0 \leq \alpha, 0 \leq \beta \leq 1.0$. Intuitively α means a threshold value to specify the similarity of distribution and β means a ratio of the elements under same distribution with which the information gain is negligible. Given $dist(T)$ and $dist(T_{A(a_i)})$, we say the two are similar if the following holds.

$$KL(dist(T)||dist(T_{A(a_i)})) \leq \alpha$$

Given two similar distributions T and $T_{A(a_i)}$, we remove an attribute A as a candidate for selection, if the ration of the number of elements of $T_{A(a_i)}$ to T is greater than or equal to β. This is because A can't be selected since the information gain is negligible. Here is our new procedure KLC4 for attribute selection for given T and α, β.

(0) Generate a root node and start with T
(1) Examine whether a node could be a leaf or not
(2) If it can, we do and return to caller.
(3) Otherwise we generate an intermediate node if there remain attributes
(3-1) Obtain class entropy $Ent(T)$ and a class distribution $dist(T)$
(3-2) For each attribute of T
(3-2-0) Let $s = \phi$
(3-2-1) For each value a on A, obtain KL divergence of $dist(T)$ and $dist(T_{A(a)})$. If the value is less than α, add $T_{A(a)}$ to s
(3-2-2) Remove A if the ratio of the number of elements in s is greater than β. Otherwise obtain the relative entropy $Ent_A(T)$
(3-3) Select the attribute G of the maximum gain.
(3-4) Generate child nodes according to the values on G in T and divide T into $T_1, \ldots$. Repeat the process recursively at each child node with T_i. Then return to caller.
(4) When no attribute remains, the node should be a leaf to which we put the dominant class of T.

Note that in this approach we examine whether attributes should be removed or not *before* developing trees, i.e., this is one of the pre-pruning techniques. However the process works efficiently since we utilize only KL divergence and relative entropy during the calculation, but not cross-validation many times nor global error estimation. Also note that KLC4 is independent of any post-pruning techniques, although we only discuss pre-pruning here for the simplicity.

3 Experimental Results

We compare the results to the conventional C4.5[8]. In this experiment, we assume $\alpha = 0.15, \beta = 0.8$. To avoid zero-divide in class distribution, we replace all 0.0 value by 0.001. Also we assume standard parameters in C4.5, thus the pruning ratio is 25 % (i.e., -c25) and we examine the test only if there exist several data and several arcs (i.e., -m2). We discuss UCL ML data archives for comparison with other results[13]. The following figure illustrates the overall results of KLC4:

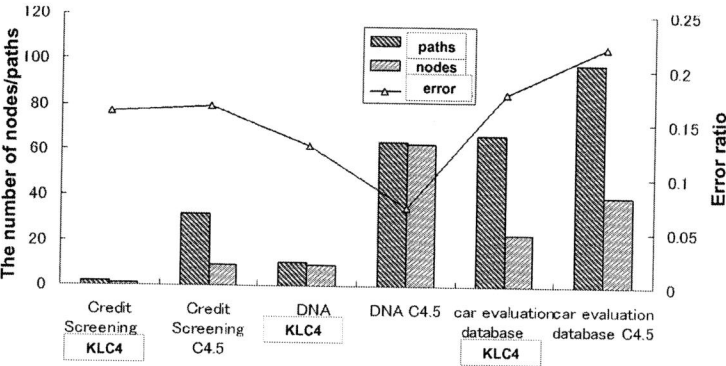

4 Conclusion

We have proposed a new kind of pre-pruning technique KLC4, based on association rules on (local) attribute values and KL divergence for similarity of class distributions, to decision trees, where we remove attributes before developing trees if we see they are not useful to classify. Experiments say this works very well in terms of node size while keeping reliability useful.

We would like to acknowledge the financial support by Grant-in-Aid for Scientific Research (C)(2) (No.14580392) in 2002/2003 from Japanese Government.

References

1. Agrawal, R., Srikant,R.: Fast Algorithms for Mining Association Rules, VLDB 1994
2. Fürnkranz,J.: Pre-Pruning and Post-Pruning, *Machine Learning* 27-2, 1997, pp.139-171
3. Furukawa, K., Ozaki, T. et al: Inductive Logic Programming, *Kyoritsu*, 2001
4. Han, J. and Kamber M.: Data Mining - Concepts and Techniques, Morgan Kauffman, 2000
5. Holte, R.C.: Very Simple Classification Rules Perform Well on Most Commonly Used Datasets, *Machine Learning* 11-1, 1993
6. Liu,B.,Hsu,W., and Ma,Y.: Integrating Classification and Association Rule Mining, proc. *Conference on Knowledge Discovery and Data Mining*, pp.80-86, 1998
7. Pfahringer, B.: Inducing Small and Accurate Decision Trees, *Technical Report* TR-98-09, Oesterreichisches Forschungsinstitut für Artificial Intelligence, Wien, 1998.
8. Quinlan, J.R.: C4.5: Programs for Machine Learning, Morgan Kaufmann, 1993
9. Safavian, S.R. and Landgrebe, D.: A survey of decision tree classifier methodology, IEEE *Transactions on Systems, Man, and Cybernetics* 21(3), pp. 660-674, 1991
10. Takamitsu, T., Miura, T. and Shioya, I.: Testing Structure of Decision Trees, proc.*Info. Syst. and Engr.*(ISE), 2002
11. Takamitsu, T., Miura, T. and Shioya, I.: Decision Trees using Class Hierarchy, proc. *Hybrid Intelligent System* (HIS), 2003
12. Terabe, M., Katai, O., Sawaragi, T., Washio, T., Motoda, H.: Attribute Generation Based on Association Rules, J.of *JSAI* 15-1, 2000
13. UCI Machine Learning Repository, http://www1.ics.uci.edu/~mlearn/, 2004

A New Approach for Selecting Attributes Based on Rough Set Theory*

Jiang Yun[1,2], Li Zhanhuai[1], Zhang Yang[1], and Zhang Qiang[2]

[1] College of Computer Science, Northwestern Polytechnical University
710072, Xi'an, China
jiangyun@mail.nwpu.edu.cn, {lzh,zhangy}@co-think.com
[2] College of Mathematics and Information Science, Northwest Normal University
730070, Lanzhou, China
zhangq@nwnu.edu.cn

Abstract. Decision trees are widely used in data mining and machine learning for classification. In the process of constructing a tree, the criteria of selecting partitional attributes will influence the classification accuracy of the tree. In this paper, we present a new concept, weighted mean roughness, which is based on rough set theory, for choosing attributes. The experimental result shows that compared with the entropy-based approach, our approach is a better way to select nodes for constructing decision trees.

1 Introduction

Classification analysis is a main problem for data mining. Its task is to classify the sample data into some predefined categories. Currently, there are many categorization algorithms, such as Bayesian classifiers, decision tree classifiers [1], decision rule classifiers[2], neural network classifiers[3], SVM classifiers [4], and so on. The classification model for decision tree classifiers is understandable by human experts, which makes decision tree classifiers very widely used for classification.

While constructing a decision tree, the algorithm used to select the suitable attribute as partitional node is very important. ID3[1] and C4.5[1] are classical algorithms to construct decision trees based on information entropy. C4.5, which is an improvement of ID3, uses information gain for selecting attributes. However, the main problem of these algorithms is that a sub-tree may repeat several times in a decision tree, and that an attribute may be used for several times in some certain paths of the tree, which degrades the efficiency of classification.

Rough set theory, which is used for processing uncertainty and imprecise information, is proposed by Z. Pawlak in 1982 [5][6]. It tries to get the inherent characteristic of the given task from its data description, without the detailed information about some attributes, which is more applicable for real life tasks. It is being studied and

---

* This paper is supported by National Science Foundation of China No. 60373108 and Network Computing Key Specialities of Northwest Normal University.

used in AI, information processing and especially in data mining or knowledge discovery in databases. In [7], rough set is used for classification analysis, which is based on the theory of attribute reducts. But the reduct method can lose some important middle results when reducts attributes. In this paper, we propose a new measure for attribute selection, *weighted mean roughness*, and use this measure for building decision trees. Our idea is that, the smaller the *weighted mean roughness* of a condition attribute is, the more certain this attribute is. So, we use this attribute as an inner node of the decision tree, and partition the sample data on that branch of the tree. The experiments on UCI datasets [8] prove that the decision trees constructed by rough set-based method tend to have not only simpler structure but also higher classification accuracy than the trees constructed by entropy-based method.

The rest of this paper is organized as following: Section 2 makes an introduction to rough set; Section 3 proposes weighted mean roughness and algorithm to build decision trees; Section 4 makes a comparison between the trees constructed by rough set-based method and by entropy-based method; Section 5 gives the experimental result; and Section 6 makes our conclusion.

2 Rough Set Theory

In this section, we review basic definitions of rough set theory. For the detailed review on the rough set theory, readers can refer to Z.Pawlak [5][6].

Definition 2.1: *(Information systems)* An *information system* $S=(U, A, V, f)$ consists of : U is a nonempty, finite set named *universe*, which is a set of objects, $U=\{x_1, x_2, \ldots, x_m\}$; A is a nonempty, finite set of *attributes*, $A = C \cup D$, in which C is the set of *condition attributes*, and D is the set of *decision attributes*; $V = \bigcup_{a \in A} Va$ is the domain of a ; f: $U \times A \rightarrow V$ is an *information function*.

Definition 2.2: *(Lower and upper approximation)* Due to imprecision which exists in the real world data, there are always conflicting objects contained in a decision table. Here *conflicting objects* refers to two or more objects that are undistinguishable by employing any set of condition attributes, but they belong to different decision classes. Such objects are called *inconsistent*. Such a decision table is called *inconsistent decision table*. If $S=(U, A, V, f)$ is a decision table, suppose $B \subseteq A$, and $X \subseteq U$, then the *B-lower* and *B-upper approximations* of X are defined as:

$$\underline{B(X)} = \bigcup\{Y \in U / IND(B) : Y \subseteq X\} \text{ and } \overline{B(X)} = \bigcup\{Y \in U / IND(B) : Y \cap X \neq \phi\} \quad (1)$$

Here. *U/IND(B)* denotes the family of all equivalence classes of B; $IND(B) = \{(x,y) \in U \times U \mid \forall a \in B, f(x, a) = f(y, a)\}$ is the *B-indiscernibility relation*;

The set $Bnd_B(X) = \overline{B(X)} - \underline{B(X)}$ is called the *B-boundary* of X. If $Bnd_B(X) \neq \phi$, then we say that X is a *rough set* on B.

3 Rough Set-Based Approach to Select Attribute

When building decision trees for classification, we prefer a simpler tree than a complicated tree, so that the tree could have better classification accuracy. Because of the uncertainties in the training data, the measure for selecting attribute as the inner node of the tree is very important to the classification accuracy of the tree.

Considering the influence made to classification accuracy by the created equivalence classes by each possible attribute value of decision attributes, and the influence to attribute selection made by the approximate precision of each condition attribute, we propose a new measure for attribute selection, *weighted mean roughness*, which takes full consideration of all the possible attribute value of decision attributes. Here we give the definition of *weighted mean roughness*.

Definition 3.1:(*Weighted Mean Roughness*) For a *information system S=(U, A, V, f)*, $X \subset U$, $B \subseteq A$, the *precision* of X in space B could be written as $\mu_B(X) = card(B(X))/card(\overline{B(X)})$, here, $0 \leq \mu_B(X) \leq 1$. The *weighted mean roughness* of X with respect to B is defined as:

$$\beta_B(i) = 1 - (\sum_{j=1}^{m} \omega_j \mu_B(X_j)). \qquad (2)$$

In this definition, we write i for the ith condition attribute; and j for the jth equivalence class of the decision attribute, $j=1...m$ (m is the count of equivalence classes of the decision attribute); X_j represents the jth set of equivalence class of the decision attribute, $X_j \subset U$; ω_j represents the proportions of X_j in the universe U, ω_j = card(X_j)/card(U).

The range of $\beta_B(i)$ is [0, 1]. If $\beta_B(i) = 0$, then the partition on attribute i is a certain partition, which means that there exists no uncertainty; if $\beta_B(i) = 1$, then the partition on attribute i is the most uncertain partition. Therefore, the smaller $\beta_B(i)$ is, the more certain the partition on attribute i is. The weight here is used to take full consideration of the contribution made to classification by each partition of the decision attribute. This idea is used in our attribute selection algorithm, WMR(*Weighted Mean Roughness*), which is illustrated in the following subsection.

In the WMR algorithm, the decision tree is built in the following way. The attribute with the smallest *weighted mean roughness* is selected as the best condition attribute, and the training dataset is partitioned into some data subsets by this attribute, and thus constructing the decision tree to a deeper layer. This step is repeated recursively in each subset, until all sample data in the subset belongs to a same category, and then, this category is made the leaf node of that branch of the tree. The following is the detailed steps of the WMR algorithm.

Algorithm 1. WMR(Q, Att)
Input: Training dataset Q ; Attributes set Att
Output: Decision Tree
1. Calculate Weighted Mean Roughness of each attribute in Q.
   - For each condition attribute, calculate its upper approximation, and lower approximation with respect to each partition set of the decision attribute.
   - For each condition attribute, calculate its weighted mean roughness.
2. Select the attribute with the smallest weighted mean roughness as the partition attribute, T.
3. Take T as the root of the decision tree
   - Root ← T // Root is the root node of the tree.
   - For each possible attribute value Vi of T create a branch from Root, which corresponds to the condition that T.value = Vi. Let XVi be the set of samples whose attribute value on T is Vi.
4. For each subset XVi:
   - If all the sample of this subset belongs to a same category, then make this category as the leaf node of this tree; else call WMR(XVi, Att-{a}).
5. Return.

4 Comparison with Information Entropy-Based Approach

The main difference between our approach and the classical information entropy based approach is the measure for selecting attribute as the inner node of the tree. Here we use a sample dataset to compare the building of decision tree for the two approaches. Please refer to table 1 for the dataset.

Table 1. A information table

Objects U	Condition attributes (C) a1 a2 a3 a4	Decision attribute (D) d
1	1 2 2 1	1
2	1 2 3 2	1
3	1 2 2 2	1
4	2 2 2 1	1
5	2 3 2 3	2
6	1 3 2 1	1
7	1 2 3 1	2
8	2 3 1 2	2
9	1 2 2 2	1
10	1 1 3 2	1
11	2 1 2 3	2
12	1 1 2 2	1

Here, we use the algorithm proposed in section 3 to build the decision tree. The *weighted mean roughness* of the condition attributes are $\beta(a1)=1$, $\beta(a2)=1$, $\beta(a3)=0.972$, $\beta(a4)=0.944$. It is obviously that the *weighted mean roughness* of attribute *a4* is the smallest. So, *a4* is taken as the root of the decision tree, and 3 branches are created by its 3 attribute values, with each branch presenting a sub-table of the original information table. This step is repeated on each of the sub-table, until the situation that all the sample data in a branch belong to a same category is satisfied. Then, this category is made a leaf node in the tree. Figure 1, and figure 2 give the decision tree built by our approach, and the information entropy based approach, respectively.

In figure 1, the complexity of the tree (the count of all the nodes) is 8, which corresponds to 5 decision rules. While in figure 2, the complexity of the decision tree is 12, and has 7 decision rules. It is obviously that the complexity of the former tree is simpler than the latter tree.

Fig. 1. Decision tree based on weighted mean roughness

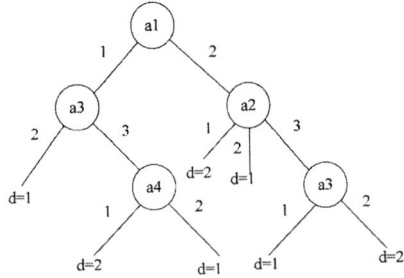

Fig. 2. Decision tree based on information entropy

This sample dataset shows that the *weighted mean roughness* concept proposed in this paper could be used to decrease the complexity of decision trees. In the worst condition, when the equivalence classes of every condition attribute corresponding decision attribute are equal, this approach will build a tree which is the same as the tree built based on the information entropy approach. Such a condition occurs with a very low probability. The decision tree built based on the *weighted mean roughness* approach need less space, and has less decision rules, which means that it is more helpful for making decision.

5 Experiment

To evaluate the classification accuracy and the decision tree complexity of WMR, we ran WMR and C4.5 on some data sets from the UCI machine learning repository [8].

All the numeric attributes are discrete using algorithm DBChi2 [9]. Ten-fold cross-validation is carried out for each data set to evaluate the classification accuracy, and the average leaf nodes number of ten times is calculated for comparing the complexity of the resulted decision tree. Table 2 shows the experimental results.

When we do the experiment, there exists such a situation that the upper approximation of a condition attribute is zero in the corresponding subset. It means that the partition on this condition attribute is already certainty in the corresponding subset. So that this condition attribute should be chosen as partition node, and it is no need to calculate the other condition attributes' weighted mean roughness. The other situation is that the values of the choosing attribute are equal in a subset, but the values of decision attribute are not equal correspondingly. It will result in the endless of the present branch. The decision attribute value, which has the largest proportion in the sub-table, is chosen as the leaf node of the corresponding sub-tree. The last situation is that two attributes have both the same value on weighted mean roughness in the sub-table. The one that appears first in the attribute list will be chosen.

Table 2. The comparison on 6 datasets

Dataset	#Instance	#Concept	#Attribute	C4.5		WMR	
				Accuracy	Leaf	Accuracy	Leaf
Breast	699	2	9	95.0	6	95.6	5.2
Diabetes	768	2	8	74.2	14.4	78.1	11.8
Iris	150	3	4	75.9	5	77.5	4
Lymph	148	4	18	77.0	6.6	75.4	7
Austra	690	2	14	84.7	9	88.2	8.3
Monk1	556	2	6	75.7	8.9	80.1	8
Average				80.4	8.3	82.5	7.4

From the results of the experiment, we can see that WMR achieves a significant improvement on classification accuracy and the complexity of decision tree over C4.5. The experiment is made on a computer with single 996MHz Pentium 3 CPU and 256MB memory, and the WMR program is written in Borland C++ Builder 6. The source program of C4.5 is downloaded from [10].

6 Conclusion

In this paper, we propose a new concept, *weighted mean roughness*, which is based on theory of rough set to select attributes to construct decision tree. For a certain attribute, the smaller the *weighted mean roughness* is, the more crisp embodied in this attribute, and hence it is better to use this attribute as a partitional attribute for building decision trees. Furthermore, *weighted mean roughness* takes full consideration of the influence made by each partition of decision attribute to condition attribute, so, the result is closer to the reality. In our experiment, we compare the classification accuracy of the decision trees based on *weighted mean roughness* and information entropy. The result shows that the decision tree, which is based on *weighted mean roughness*, has a simpler structure, and a better classification accuracy.

References

1. J. Ross Quinlan. C4.5: Program for Machine Learning . Morgan Kaufmann, 1992.
2. B. Liu, W. Hsu, Y. Ma.. Intergrating Classification and Association Rule Mining . In Proc. KDD, 1998.
3. Wray L. Buntine , Andreas S. Weigend. Computing Second Derivatives in Feed-forward Networks: A Review . IEEE Transactions on Neural Networks, 5, 480-488, 1991.
4. N.Cristianini, J. Shawe-Taylor. An Introduction to Support Vector Machines. Cambridge Press, 2000.
5. Pawlak Z.W.. Rough Sets . International Journal of Information and Computer Science, 11, 341-356, 1982.
6. Pawlak Z.W.. Rough Sets and Intelligent Data Analysis . Information sciences, 147, 1-12, 2002.
7. Beynon M.. Reducts within the Variable Precision Rough Set Model: A Further Investigation European Journal of Operational Research, 134, 592-605, 2001.
8. Murphy P., Aha W.. UCI Repository of Machine Learning Databases. http://www.ics.uci.edu/~mlearn/MLRepository.html, 1996.
9. Hu X., and Cercone N.. Data Mining Via Generalization , Discretization and Rough Set Feature Selection . Knowledge and Information System: An International Journal, 1, 1999.
10. Zhi-Hua Zhou. AI Softwares&Codes (Maintained by Zhi-Hua Zhou). http://cs.nju.edu.cn/people/zhouzh/zhouzh.files/ai_resource/software.htm, 2004-02-29.

A Framework for Mining Association Rules in Data Warehouses

Haorianto Cokrowijoyo Tjioe and David Taniar

School of Business Systems, Monash University
Clayton, Victoria 3800, Australia
{Haorianto.Tjioe,David.Taniar}@infotech.monash.edu.au

Abstract. The effort of data mining, especially in relation to association rules in real world business applications, is significantly important. Recently, association rules algorithms have been developed to cope with multidimensional data. In this paper we are concerned with mining association rules in data warehouses by focusing on its measurement of summarized data. We propose two algorithms: *HAvg* and *VAvg*, to provide the initialization data for mining association rules in data warehouses by concentrating on the measurement of aggregate data. These algorithms are capable of providing efficient initialized data extraction from data warehouses and are used for mining association rules in data warehouses.

1 Introduction

A traditional association rule for a transaction database was first introduced by Agrawal [1]. There are two steps to discover association rules: (i) generating large item sets that satisfy user minimum support; and, (ii) rule generation based on user minimum confidence [2]. Association rules for transactional data have been developed to handle hierarchical, quantitative and categorical attributes [9,10]. Moreover, they can also use more than one predicate or dimension [5] for transactional data without any classification or measurement of aggregate data. Unlike others, multidimensional guided association rules use minimum support quantity rather than minimum support count and are also capable of handling classification [4]. However, this approach is inadequate since minimum support quantity itself will misguide the user, preventing him from finding interesting patterns.

Apparently, both concepts in [1,2,9,10] are concerned only with applying association rules in transactional data and concepts in [4,5] miss the most important attribute which is the measurement of aggregate data in a Data Warehouse (DW). The data in the DW contains only summarized data such as quantity sold, amount sold, etc. No transaction data is stored. In this paper, we focus on providing a framework for mining association rules on data warehouses by concentrating on the measurement of aggregate data. We propose two algorithms, namely *HAvg* and *VAvg*, to create an initial table to be used as a framework for mining association rules relating to a DW. After this process, using various association rules techniques [2,7,8] we can mine interesting rules.

2 Background: Data Modelling in Data Warehouses

A data warehouse is typically built using a star schema, where it has more than one dimension and each dimension corresponds to one or more facts [3] (see figure 1a). Dimensions store the description of business dimensions (eg. Product, customer, vendor and store), while fact tables consist of aggregate data of measurements such as quantity sold, amount sold [3]. DW contains aggregate data which are a summary of all the details of and operational database. These data will be kept based on the lowest granularity of data which will be stored in a data warehouse [3]. DW can also be viewed using a multidimensional model [3]. As illustrated in figure 1b, there is a multidimensional model which involves three dimensions: products, customers and time. Discovering Information on enquiry (such as products in number 10 to 100 and customers in numbers 20 to 100 in year 2000) can be done using a multidimensional model. Finally, as we can see, finding association rules for DW is different from transactional data, since in DW measurements of aggregate data are very important.

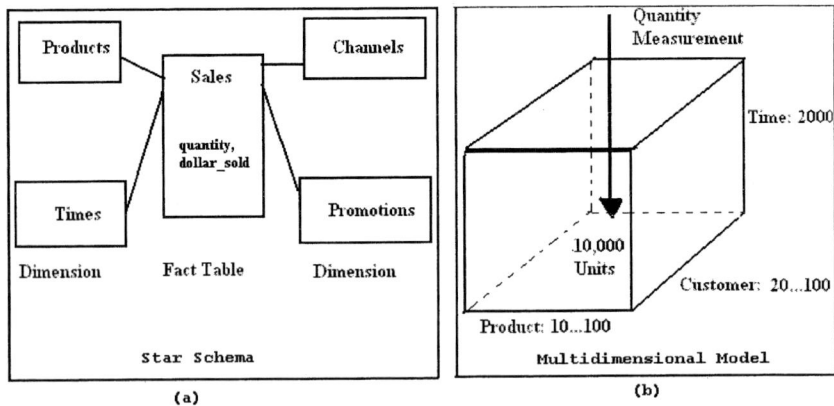

Fig. 1. Sample of a Star Schema and Multidimensional Model

3 Proposed Algorithms for Mining Data Warehouses

We propose *Vavg* and *Havg* algorithm to produce the extracted data from a DW to be used for mining association rules. Both algorithms focus on the quantitative attribute (such as quantity) of the fact table in order to prepare an initialized data for mining association rules in DW. We use the average of quantity in a fact table on m-dimensions. We prune all those rows in a fact table which have less than the average quantity.

```
SELECT <d_{m-1}.key>, <d_m.key>, SUM(quantity)AS Qty FROM Fact Table
WHERE  (d_1 = duser_1) AND (d_2 = duser_2) AND ... AND (d_{m-2} = duser_{m-2})
GROUP BY <d_{m-1}.key>, <d_m.key>;
```

Assume that in a fact table there is m-dimensions and the quantity attribute exists. The structure of the fact table is: $FactTab = (\{d_1.key, d_2.key,..., d_m.key\}, quantity)$. There are user input variables to decide which dimensions will be used. $UserVar = (duser_1, duser_2,..., duser_m)$ where input variables for $(duser_1, duser_2,...,duser_{m-1})$ can be treated as a single value or an interval. An interval on user input dimension variables can be treated as a classification when the interval has already been declared within the classification class. Note that notations on Table 1 are used in our proposed algorithms.

Table 1. Notations

Notation	Description
Db	Fact Table; contains(d_{m-1}.key, d_m.key, qty)
N	Total rows in fact table
VAvgTab	Vertical Avg quantity table; containts(d_m.key,d_m.qty,d_m.count,d_m.avg)
VInitTab	Vertical Initialize Table; contains(d_{m-1}.key,d_m.key,d_m.qty)
HAvgTab	Horizontal Avg quantity table; containts(d_{m-1}.key,d_{m-1}.qty,d_{m-1}.count, d_{m-1}.avg)
HInitTab	Horizontal Initialize Table ; contains (d_{m-1}.key,d_m.key,d_m.qty)

3.1 VAvg Algorithm

Using the *VAvg* algorithm, we find the average quantity of the defined dimensions vertically. As shown in figure 2, we use the *VAvg* algorithm to find the average product dimension quantity vertically from the first row of the fact table until the last row. This example uses *Time_Dim* as d_{m-1} dimension and *Product_Dim* as d_m dimension.

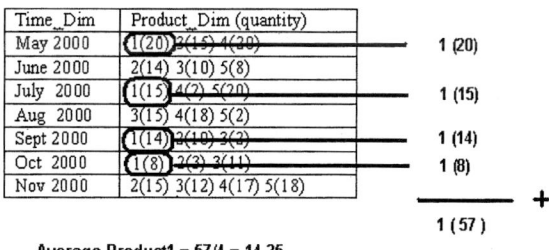

Average Product1 = 57/4 = 14.25

Fig. 2. An example of how the VAvg's algorithm works

We apply Procedure VAvg to create an initialized table (*VInitTab*) for mining association rules in a DW (see figure 3). As shown in figure 4, function Check_Key is used to check whatever the selected row (Db_i) on selected fact table (Db) already exist on *VAvgTab*. If the return value is Found then we update the contents of table *VAvgTab* (Update_VAvgTab). We update its quantity, count and average on the selected *dm.key*. Otherwise, we insert a new record to table *VAvgTab* (Insert_VAvgTab). A function Check_quantityVavg is used to search all rows in the selected fact table (*Db*) which satisfied the minimum quantity based on table *VAvgTab*. If the row has satisfied the minimum quantity, we then insert a new row on table *VInit_Tab*.

After creating table *VInit_Tab*, the next step is mining association rules in DW using one association rule from various association rules algorithms (e.q Apriori) [2,7,8]. After identifying all the large item sets, we generate the interesting rules using a predefined confidence. Here we add an average quantity to show that these rules are satisfied only when they satisfy the average quantity (see figure 4).

```
Procedure VAvg
Begin
  For I = 1 to N loop
    Td = Check_Key(Db_i); IF Td Found then Update_VAvgTab(Db_i);
    Else Insert_VAvgTab(Db_i); End if; End loop;
  For J = 1 to N loop
    Sd = Check_quantityVavg(Db_i);
    IF Sd = True Then Insert_VInitTab(Db_i); End if; End Loop;
End;
```

Fig. 3. The VAvg Algorithm

$d_1, d_2, d_3, ..., d_{m-1}, d_m$ (≥ average quantity) → d_m (≥ average quantity)
d_m have more than one attribute.
$d_1, d_2, d_3, ..., d_{m-1}$ can be a single value or an interval

Fig. 4. Modified Rule Formula

Table 2. An example of how the proposed HAvg algorithm works

Prod	Country_Dim (quantity)	Total	Count	Avg
10	DE(8), IE(2), NL(32), PL(92), UK(131), US(120)	377	6	62.83
20	FR(125), IE(171), NL(69), UK(170), US(160)	570	5	114
30	NL(61), TR(93), US(2)	156	3	52
40	DE(109), ES(93), IE(39), NL(195), UK(25), US(108)	569	6	94.83

3.2 HAvg Algorithm

Using the proposed *HAvg* algorithm we find the average quantity of the defined dimensions horizontally. We use the *HAvg* algorithm to find the average product dimension quantity horizontally from the first row of fact table until the last row (see table 2). This example uses *Prod_Dim* as d_{m-1} dimension and *Country_Dim* as d_m dimension.

```
Procedure HAvg
Begin
  For I = 1 to N loop
    Td = Check_Key(Db_i); IF Td Found then Update_HAvgTab(Db_i);
    Else Insert_HAvgTab(Db_i); End if; End loop;
  For J = 1 to N loop
    Sd = Check_quantityHAvg(Db_i);
    IF Sd = True Then Insert_HInitTab(Db_i); End if;
  End Loop;
End;
```

Fig. 5. Algorithm HAvg

We apply Procedure HAvg to create the initialized table (*HInitTab*) for mining association rules in DW (see figure 5). A function Check_Key is used to check whether the selected row (*Dbi*) in the selected fact table (*Db*) already exists in *HAvgTab*. If the return value is Found then we update the content of table *HAvgTab* (Update_HAvgTab). We update its quantity, count and average on selected *dm*-1.key. Otherwise, we insert new record on table *HAvgTab* (Insert_HAvgTab). A function Check_quantityHAvg is used to search all rows in the selected fact table (*Db*) which satisfied the minimum quantity based on table *HAvgTab*. If the row has satisfied the minimum quantity, then insert a new row in table *HInit_Tab*. After creating table *HInit_Tab*, we start mining association rules in DW. This is the same step as the one used after we discover *VInit_Tab*.

4 Performance Evaluation

In our performance experimentations, we used a sample sales DW [6] which contains five dimensions (e.q products, times, channels, promotions, customers) and one sales fact table with size one million rows. We performed our experiments using a Pentium IV 1,8 Gigahertz CPU with 512MB with Oracle9i Database as the DW repository.

As shown in figure 6a, we compare the number of rows produced by the *VAvg* and *HAvg* approaches when using a single attribute, with the 'no method' approach. As we see, from one to four dimensions, there is a significant reduction of rows when compared with the 'no method'. Both proposed methods have shown a similar trend across dimensions where both have reduced the rows up to 60%. However, on five dimensions, the results are similar. This is because the records involved in these dimensions are few. Moreover, in figure 6b, the results of classification or interval attributes across five dimensions have shown that both proposed methods have been significantly affected by the number of rows produced when compared with the 'no method' approach. Furthermore, as shown in figure 6c, we used a combination of five dimensions with interval and single attribute and compared its effectiveness with our approach. In general, the number of rows reduced on *HAvg* is similar to those for the 'no method' approach. Meanwhile, the *VAvg* approach has a significant gap in the

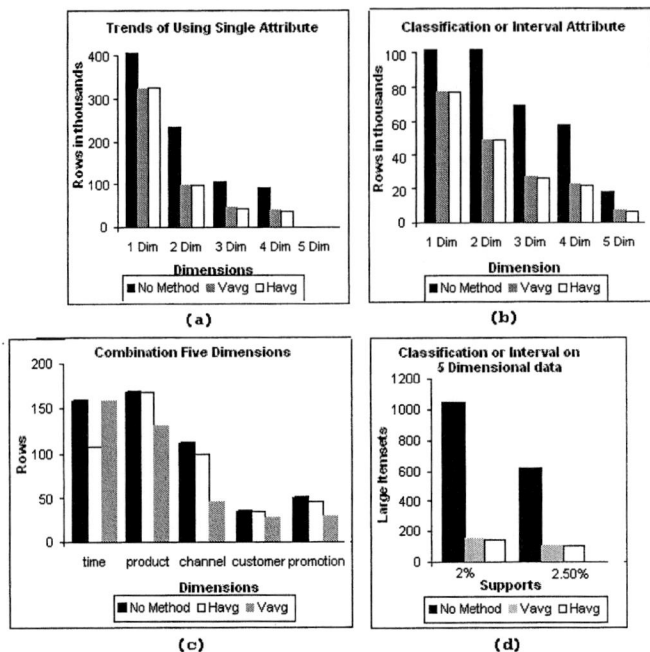

Fig. 6. Comparison HAvg, VAvg and No Method

number of rows when compared with 'no method'. However, an exception is given on the time dimension when the *HAvg* approach has reduced more rows rather than the *VAvg*. This happens each time when the dimension's attribute appears once in the vertical data. Finally, on figure 6d, we apply the Apriori algorithm implemented by Bodon [2] using two supports on interval or classification five dimensional data to discover large item sets. The results are clear with both our proposed algorithms having reductions of up to 86% for support 2% and 83% for support 2.5% compared with the 'no method' approach.

5 Conclusion and Future Work

Our proposed algorithms mainly work by filtering the data taken from data warehouses. The overall studies found that our algorithms significantly reduce the number of rows used as the data initialization for mining association rules in DW and also reduce the number of large item sets discoveries in DW. For future work, we consider developing various algorithms concerned only with mining DW.

References

1. Agrawal, R., Imielinski, T., Swami, A., Mining Association Rules between Sets of Items in Large Databases, *SIGMOD'93*, 207-216, 1993.

2. Bodon, F., A Fast Apriori Implementation, *FIMI'03*, November 2003.
3. Chaudhuri, S., Dayal, U., An Overview of Data Warehousing and OLAP Technology, *ACM SIGMOD Record*, 26, 65-74, 1997.
4. Guenzel, H., Albrecht, J., Lehner, W., Data Mining in a Multidimensional Environment, *ADBIS'99*, 191-204, 1999.
5. Kamber, M., Han, J., Chiang, J.Y., Metarule-Guided Mining of Multi-Dimensional Association Rules Using Data Cubes, *KDD'97*, 207-210, Aug 1997.
6. Oracle, Oracle 9i Data Warehouse Guide, http://www.oracle.com, 2001.
7. Park, J.S., Chen M.S., Yu, P.S., An Effective Hash based Algorithm for Mining Association Rules, *SIGMOD'95*, 175-186, May 1995.
8. Savasere, A., Omiecinski, E., Navathe S., An Efficient Algorithm for Mining Association Rules in Large Databases, *VLDB'95*, 432-444, 1995.
9. Srikant, R., Agrawal, R., Mining Generalized Association Rules, *VLDB'95*, 407-419, 1995.
10. Srikant, R.; Agrawal, R., Mining Quantitative Association Rules in Large Relational Tables, *SIGMOD'96*, 1-12, 1996.

Intelligent Web Service Discovery in Large Distributed System[*]

Shoujian Yu, Jianwei Liu, and Jiajin Le

College of Information Science and Technology, Donghua University
1882 West Yan'an Road, Shanghai, China, 200051
{Jackyysj,Liujw}@mail.dhu.edu.cn
Lejiajin@dhu.edu.cn

Abstract. Web services are the new paradigm for distributed computing. Traditional centralized indexing scheme can't scale well with a large distributed system for a scalable, flexible and robust discovery mechanism. In this paper, we use an ontology-based approach to capture real world knowledge for the finest granularity annotation of Web services. This is the core for intelligent discovery. We use a distributed hash table (DHT) based catalog service in P2P (peer to peer) system to index the ontology information and store the index at peers. We have discussed the DHT based service discovery model and discovery procedure. DHT supports only exact match lookups. We have made improvement to the matching algorithm for intelligent services discovery. The experiments show that the discovery model has good scalability and the semantic annotation can notably improve discovery exactness. The improved algorithms can discover the most potential service against request.

1 Introduction

Web services are emerging as a dominant paradigm for constructing distributed business applications and enabling enterprise-wide interoperability. In order to integrate these services, one must be able to locate and acquire specified services. Existing Universal Description Discovery Integration (UDDI) [1] technology uses a central server to store information about registered Web services. However, in large distributed system, such a centralized approach quickly becomes impractical. WSDL (Web Service Description Language) provides descriptions for Web services [2]. But these descriptions are purely syntactic. The problem with syntactic information is that the semantics implied by the information provider are not explicit, leading to possible misinterpretation by others. Improving Web services discovery requires explicating the semantics of both the service provider and the service requestor.

In this paper, we present a methodology for building dynamic, scalable and decentralized registries with intelligent search capabilities. We focus on a fully distributed

---

[*] This work has been partially supported by The National High Technology Research and Development Program of China (863 Program) under contract 2002AA4Z3430.

architecture motivated by recent advances in P2P computing [3, 4]. This work also uses an ontology-based approach to capture real world knowledge for semantic service annotation. The rest of this paper is structured as follows: Section 2 presents the ontology based Web services annotation method. The detailed explanation for DHT based Web services discovery model is in section 3. In section 4 the services matching exactness and system scalability are evaluated. Section 5 concludes this paper.

2 Intelligent Web Services Annotation Based on Ontology

Research in the Semantic Web area has shown that annotation with metadata can help us solve the problem of inefficient keyword based searches [5]. Adding semantics to Web services descriptions can be achieved by using ontologies which support shared vocabularies and domain models for use in service description [6, 7]. In our approach, we identify two aspects of semantics for Web services description elicited from object-oriented model: the class has attributes and behaviors. From this point, we also model concept into domain ontology from both attributes and behaviors aspects. As shown in Fig. 1, the concept *Itinerary* has attributes as *StartPlace, ArrivalPlace*, etc. It is also associated with behaviors as *Search, Book, Cancel* etc. As a Web service is implemented by several functions, i.e. operations, the behaviors aspect is used to describe operations of Web services. As an operation has inputs and outputs, the attributes aspects can be used to describe the i/o interface of operations.

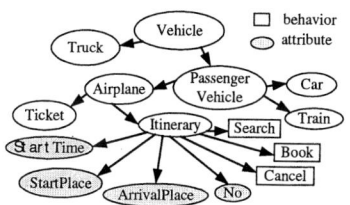
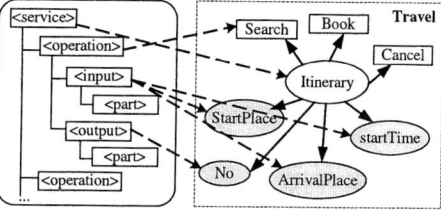

Fig. 1. Organizing concepts into ontology

Fig. 2. Incorporating semantics into WSDL

WSDL is the current standard for the description of Web services. We add semantics to Web services by mapping service, operation, input and output in WSDL document to concepts in the domain specific ontologies. Fig. 2 shows the method of annotating WSDL document. By this method, Web services are semantically annotated in different granularity, which facilitates multi-level services discovery.

3 DHT Based Service Discovery

DHTs are benchmarked to introduce a new generation of large-scale Internet services. Their goal is to provide the efficient location of data items in a very large and dynamic distributed system without relying on any centralized infrastructure. Chord serves as the experimental substrate of our work. Nevertheless, our design does not depend on the specific DHT implementation and can work with any DHT protocols. For a detailed description of Chord and its algorithms refer to [4].

3.1 System Model

Let N_i denote the n providers (a provider is a node in Chord identifier ring), each of which publishes a set C_i of Web services. When a node N_i wants to join the system it creates catalog information, which is the set $C_i = \{(k_j, S_{ij}) \mid S_{ij}$ is a summary of k_j on node $N_i\}$. In Sect. 2, we have discussed the semantic annotation of Web services. Thus the concept should be the key, i.e. k_j, as mapped by Chord protocol and *Behavior(Attributes Set)* should be the corresponding data item associated with the key, i.e. S_{ij}, the summary of k_j. As a Web service consists of several operations, there are sets of data summaries S_{ij}, and not just single data summaries.

An example illustrates how the outlined conceptual catalog model can be put into practice. Consider four service providers which want to publish services as shown in Table 1. Assume that the service providers have chosen appropriate concept in the domain ontology to refer to, i.e. as shown in *Concept in Domain Ontology* column of Table 1. Thus this column acts as the key for mapping. Operations of the service are also semantically annotated by *Mapped Behavior & Attributes* column in Table 2, 3, which act as the summary for the associated key. For example, as provider N_1: *Itinerary* is the key to be mapped. Operation name *SearchItinerary* is referred to *Search*, which is a behavior of concept *Itinerary*, as shown in Fig. 1. *(startPlace, arrivalPlace, startTime)* are attributes of concept *Itinerary* mapped for inputs of operation *SearchItinerary*. According to the conceptual catalog model, $S_{1, \text{Itinerary}}=\{Search (startPlace, arrivalPlace, startTime), Book (No), Cancel (No)\}$ (see Table 2), while $S_{2, \text{Itinerary}}=\{Search (No), Delivery (No)\}$ (see Table 3). Table 4 shows how the DHT assigns the keys to the nodes in the network. The summary sets are stored along with the keys.

Table 1. Nodes with Web services example

Service Provider	Web Services	Concept in Domain Ontology
N_1	Itinerary service	Itinerary
	Insurance service	Insurance
N_2	Itinerary service	Itinerary
	Car Rental service	Car
	Hotel service	Hotel
N_3	Car Rental Service	Car
	Hotel Service	Hotel
N_4	Itinerary service	Itinerary
	Hotel service	Hotel

Table 2. Operations and Mapped Behavior & Attributes for N_1's Itinerary Service

Operation	Mapped Behavior & Attributes
SearchItineary (StartCity, ArrivalCity, time)	Search (startPlace, arrivalPlace, startTime)
Book (ItinearyNo)	Book (No)
Cancel (ItineraryNo)	Cancel (No)

Table 3. Operations and Mapped Behavior & Attributes for N_2's Itinerary Service

Operation	Mapped Behavior & Attributes
SearchItineary (ItinearyNo)	Search (No)
Delivery (Ticket)	Delivery (No)

Table 4. DHT based catalog index in each node

	DHT Index
N_1	Hotel {$(S_2$, Hotel), $(S_3$, Hotel), $(S_4$, Hotel)}
N_2	Itinerary {$(S_1$, Itinerary), $(S_2$, Itinerary), $(S_3$, Itinerary)}
N_3	--
N_4	Car {$(S_2$, Car), $(S_3$, Car)}; Insurance {$(S_1$, Insurance)}

3.2 Web Services Discovery

For Web services discovery, the requestor should first choose appropriate concept to which the preferred service may refer. Then he (or she) decides the interested behaviors and attributes he would like to provide as input for the preferred Web service. As an example, a service requestor wants to inquire about the itinerary information from Shanghai to Beijing on 1 October 2004. The requestor may choose *Itinerary* as the domain concept, *search* as behavior and *startPlace, arrivalPlace, startTime* as attributes. This is the first step for service discovery. We assume that the service request is submitted on N_3. *Itinerary* serves as the DHT lookup key and it returns that summary of *Itinerary* lies in N_2, which stores the portion of the catalog that contains *Itinerary* information. Then the request with domain ontology information is sent to N_2. This is the second step. On N_2, the behaviors and attributes of the query is matched against $S_{i, \text{Itinerary}}$, (1<i<3). N_2 replies to N_3 with the node set {N_1} since only $S_{1, \text{Itinerary}}$ matches the given query and so N_1 is the only node that satisfies the request. This is the third step. Finally, N_3 contacts N_1 for detail information, e.g. WSDL.

3.3 Improvements for Intelligent Discovery

During the service discovery procedure in Sect. 3.2, step 3 executes exact match between behaviors and attributes against summary $S_{i, \text{Itinerary}}$. Sometimes the exact match becomes inefficient because the service provider and service requestor may use approximate but not identical ontology information to express the same meaning. In our approach, we use various name and string matching algorithms like NGram, synonym matching, stemming, tokenization etc. The *NGram* algorithm calculates the similarity by considering the number of qgrams that the names of two concepts have in common [8]. The *CheckSynonym* algorithm uses WordNet to find synonyms [9]. The *TokenMatcher* uses the Porter Stemmer algorithm, tokenization, and substring matching techniques to find the similarity [10]. This linguistic similarity match approach discovers the potential matches between request and summary, which also results in unexpected results in some degree. Therefore we will first try to get the exact match. These algorithms won't be utilized unless no exact match results returns.

4 Implementation and Experiments

We have implemented a prototype to illustrate the discovery model we have proposed. The prototype is based on the Chord protocol implementation found on the Chord project website. WordNet 2.0 is embedded into the system through APIs to further understand the semantics of Web services described. An evaluation of the Web services discovery exactness and the system scalability is presented below.

To test service discovery exactness we first obtain a corpus of Web services from SALCentral.org and XMethods.com. We have limited our testing to two domains, i.e. Weather and Geographical domains. We compare the discovery results in three circumstances: (a) exact word match is used for discovery and Web services are not annotated with ontology information. (b) Web services are manually annotated with domain ontology. (c) The optimization algorithms in Sect. 3.3 are used to achieve versatile discovery.

Table 5. Web services discovery exactness evaluation results

	Domain 1		Domain 2	
	Correct Rate	Error Rate	Correct Rate	Error Rate
(a)	20%	0	17%	0
(b)	70%	0	73%	0
(c)	98%	2%	95%	2%

From the results in Table 5, we can conclude that method (a) has low correct rate and error rate. Comparatively, method (b) gets considerably increase in correct rate, but only about 70% are discovered. Method (c) gets almost all the services satisfying the request. But on the other hand, the error rate is a little high than the other two methods. This can be overcome by using appropriate domain ontology for Web services annotation.

We evaluate system scalability by constantly changing the number of nodes and operations. From Fig. 3 (a), we can see that the discovery time changes steadily with peer nodes increase. This is because the cost mainly results from the matching of query against the summary in the catalog index. Thus it is not obviously irrelevant to

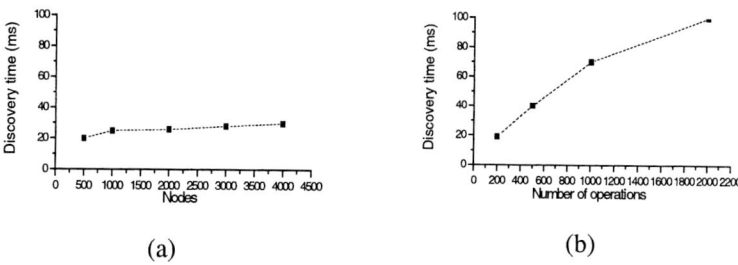

Fig. 3. System scalability evaluation results

the number of nodes. On the other hand, with the increasing of number of operations, the catalog index becomes larger, which results in longer discovery time as show in Fig. 3 (b). But the matching is processed only in one node, the increase ration of discovery time is not obvious. It inclines to stabilization. Thus this is not a critical problem for application in large distributed system. Also this can be overcome by optimizing the matching algorithm.

5 Conclusions and Future Work

This paper presents a flexible Web services discovery model by combining semantic Web services with P2P networks. This system does not need a central registry for Web services discovery. We use an ontology-based approach to capture real world knowledge for semantic service annotation. A DHT based catalog service is used to store the semantic indexes for direct and flexible service discovery. We have discussed the discovery system model and made several improvements for intelligent service discovery. Our experiments have shown that the semantic annotation method can significantly improve Web services discovery exactness and the DHT based discovery model has good scalability in large distribute system. With Web services being as the enabling technology for next generation network, we believe that this service discovery infrastructure will help organizations and businesses in carrying out their business goals in a more scalable environment.

References

1. UDDI. UDDI white papers. http://www.uddi.org/whitepapers.html.
2. E. Christensen, F. Curbera, G. Meredith, and S. Weerawarana: Web Services Description Language (WSDL) 1.1. http://www.w3.org/TR/wsdl, 2001.
3. A. Rowstron, P. Druschel: Pastry: Scalable, distributed object location and routing for large-scale peer-to-peer systems. IFIP/ACM International Conference on Distributed Systems Platforms. Heidelberg Germany, 329–350, 2001.

4. I. Stoica, R. Morris, D. Karger, M.F. Kaashoek, H. Balakrishnan: Chord: A Scalable Peer-to-Peer Lookup Protocol for Internet Applications. IEEE/ACM Transactions on Networking. 11, 17–32, 2003.
5. McIlraith, S., Son, T.C. and Zeng, H.: Semantic Web Services. IEEE Intelligent Systems, Special Issue on the Semantic Web. 16, 46–53, 2001.
6. Rama Akkiraju, Richard Goodwin, Prashant Doshi, Sascha Roeder: A Method for Semantically Enhancing the Service Discovery Capabilities of UDDI. Proceedings of the Workshop on Information Integration on the Web, IIWeb-03. Acapulco Mexico, 2003.
7. DAML-S Coalition: DAML-S: Web Service Description for the Semantic Web. In: Ian Horrocks, James Hendler (eds.): The Semantic Web - ISWC 2002. Lecture Notes in Computer Science, vol. 2342. Springer-Verlag, Berlin Heidelberg New York, 348–363, 2002.
8. R.C. Angell, G.E. Freund, et al: Automatic spelling correction using a trigram similarity measure. Information Processing and Management. 19, 255–261, 1983.
9. G. Miller: Special Issue, WordNet: An on-line lexical database. International Journal of Lexicography. 3, 235–312, 1990.
10. M. Porter: An algorithm for Suffix Stripping. Program – Automated Library and Information Systems. 14, 130–137, 1980.

The Application of K-Medoids and PAM to the Clustering of Rules

Alan P. Reynolds, Graeme Richards, and Vic J. Rayward-Smith

School of Computing Sciences
University of East Anglia, Norwich

Abstract. Earlier research has resulted in the production of an 'all-rules' algorithm for data-mining that produces all conjunctive rules of above given confidence and coverage thresholds. While this is a useful tool, it may produce a large number of rules. This paper describes the application of two clustering algorithms to these rules, in order to identify sets of similar rules and to better understand the data.

1 Introduction

Data mining often involves the production of accurate yet simple rules that describe records of interest within a database. For example, in a motor insurance database, the records of interest may be those motorists who have claimed on their insurance. Often, rules produced are conjunctions of simple clauses, where each clause applies to one field within the database (e.g. [1]). For example,
   `if age < 25 and car_type = sports then claim = yes`
is such a rule.

Although this approach produces useful rules, these rules may describe only small subsets of the records of interest. To describe larger subsets accurately, collections of such rules are required. B. de la Iglesia et al. [2] have researched the application of multi-objective genetic algorithms to data mining, using confidence and coverage as two separate objectives. This approach leads to the production of a collection of Pareto-optimal rules. Richards et al. [3] have created software that produces *all* the rules, above given confidence and coverage thresholds, that apply to the data.

This all-rules algorithm can produce many thousands of rules. For example, on the 'adult' database [4], seeking rules of greater than 15% coverage and greater than 60% confidence results in 4785 rules. Examining these rules by eye immediately reveals that many are very similar. Others, while appearing to be different, may in fact match similar sets of records. In order to determine which rules match similar sets of records, we applied two clustering algorithms to the rules produced by the all-rules algorithm: k-medoids and Partitioning About Medoids (PAM).

2 Rule Dissimilarity

Let D be the database from which rules of the form $\alpha \rightarrow \beta$ are deduced. If ρ is such a rule then the set of support for ρ, $S(\rho)$, is the set of records in D on which the rule holds, i.e.

$$S(\rho) = \{r \in D : \alpha(r) \wedge \beta(r)\}.$$

If ρ_1 and ρ_2 are two arbitrary rules, we can define a dissimilarity measure

$$\begin{aligned} d(\rho_1, \rho_2) &= |S(\rho_1) \cup S(\rho_2)| - |S(\rho_1) \cap S(\rho_2)| \\ &= |S(\rho_1) - S(\rho_2)| + |S(\rho_2) - S(\rho_1)|. \end{aligned}$$

Dividing this measure by the number of records in the database gives the simple matching coefficient [5]. Alternatively, we can use the Jaccard coefficient [6] on the sets of support and define

$$n(\rho_1, \rho_2) = d(\rho_1, \rho_2) / |S(\rho_1) \cup S(\rho_2)|.$$

Both of these dissimilarity measures are pseudometrics [7].

Intuitively, two rules that are mutually supported by a thousand records and differ over only six are more similar than two rules that are mutually supported by no records and differ over five. For this reason, the results described in this paper are those obtained using the Jaccard dissimilarity coefficient.

3 K-Means

The k-means algorithm [8] is a well known technique for performing clustering on objects in $\mathbb{R}^n$. Each cluster is centred about a point called the centroid, where the centroid's coordinates are the mean of the coordinates of the objects in the cluster. K-means can be applied to the clustering of rules but there are two reasons for not doing so. Firstly, although each rule may be represented as a binary string, centroids will not have this structure and will make little sense as rules. More importantly, the k-means algorithm requires that distances to the centroids be calculated for each object at each iteration. Since the original database may have tens of thousands of records, such calculations will be slow.

4 K-Medoids

The k-medoids algorithm, as used to produce the results of this paper, is an adaptation of the k-means algorithm. Rather than calculate the mean of the items in each cluster, a representative item, or medoid, is chosen for each cluster at each iteration. Medoids for each cluster are calculated by finding object i within the cluster that minimizes

$$\sum_{j \in C_i} d(i,j),$$

where C_i is the cluster containing object i and $d(i,j)$ is the distance between objects i and j.

There are two advantages to using existing rules as the centres of the clusters. Firstly, a medoid rule serves to usefully describe the cluster. Secondly, there is no need for repeated calculation of distances at each iteration, since the k-medoids algorithm can simply look up distances from a distance matrix.

The k-medoids algorithm can be summarized as follows:

1. Choose k objects at random to be the initial cluster medoids.
2. Assign each object to the cluster associated with the closest medoid.
3. Recalculate the positions of the k medoids.
4. Repeat Steps 2 and 3 until the medoids become fixed.

Step 3 could be performed by calculating $\sum_{j \in C_i} d(i,j)$ for each object i from scratch at each iteration. However, many objects remain in the same cluster from one iteration of the algorithm to the next. Improvements in speed can be obtained by adjusting the sums whenever an object leaves or enters a cluster.

Step 2 can also be made more efficient in terms of speed, for larger values of k. For each object, an array of the other objects, sorted on distance, is maintained. The closest medoid can be found by scanning through this array until a medoid is found, rather than comparing the distance of every medoid.

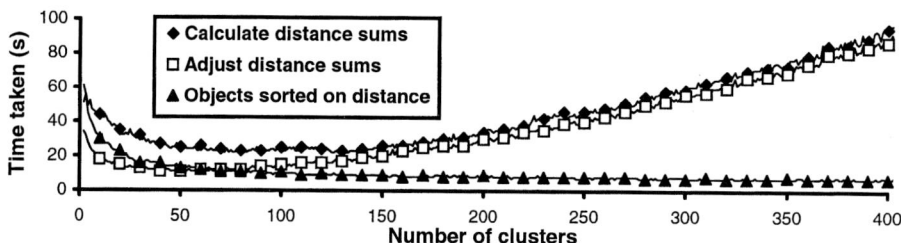

Fig. 1. Time requirements of the k-medoids algorithm.

Figure 1 shows a comparison of the time requirements for each version of the code. The first series shows the requirements of the naive implementation. The second shows the speed improvements obtained by adjusting the sums required in step 3, rather than recalculating them. The third shows the extra improvements obtained by maintaining, for each object, an array of the other objects sorted on distance. Each point in the graph indicates the time required to run the k-medoids algorithm 100 times on 4785 rules extracted from the 'adult' database, using a AMD Athlon XP 1800+ (1.53GHz) with 480Mb of RAM.

5 Partitioning About Medoids (PAM)

Partitioning about medoids (PAM) also clusters objects about k medoids, where k is specified in advance. However, the algorithm takes the form of a steepest ascent hillclimber, using a simple swap neighbourhood operation. In each iteration medoid object i and non-medoid object j are selected that produce the best clustering when their rôles are switched. The objective function used is the sum of the distances from each object to the closest medoid.

As this search phase of the algorithm is slow, the initial set of medoids is constructed in a greedy build phase. Starting with an empty set of medoids, objects are added one at a time until k medoids have been selected. At each step, the new medoid is selected so as to minimize the objective function.

6 Silhouettes

Kaufman and Rousseeuw [5] suggest the use of *silhouettes* both to determine which objects lie well within their clusters and which do not and also to judge the quality of the clustering obtained. For each object i, let $a(i)$ be the average distance of i from all other objects in cluster C_i. For every other cluster $C \neq C_i$, let $d(i,C)$ be the average distance of i from the objects in C. After computing $d(i,C)$ for all clusters $C \neq C_i$, let $b(i)$ be the smallest. The cluster for which this minimum is attained is called the *neighbour* of i.

The number $s(i)$ is given by

$$s(i) = \frac{b(i) - a(i)}{\max(a(i), b(i))}$$

and provides a measure of how well object i fits into cluster C_i rather than the neighbouring cluster. If $s(i)$ is close to one, object i can be said to be 'well classified'. If $s(i)$ is close to zero, it is unclear whether i should belong to cluster C_i or to its neighbour. A negative value suggests that i has been misclassified.

The following summary values are also defined:

- The mean of $s(i)$ for all objects i in a cluster is called the *average silhouette width* of that cluster.
- The mean of $s(i)$ for all the objects is called the *average silhouette width for the entire data set* and is denoted by $\bar{s}(k)$, where k is the number of clusters.

Kaufman and Rousseeuw suggest that $\bar{s}(k)$ can be used for the selection of a best value of k, by choosing that k for which $\bar{s}(k)$ is maximal.

7 Results

We applied these two clustering algorithms, with small values of k, to the 4785 rules derived from the 'adult' database. Figure 2 shows the sum of distances from rules to medoids. Figure 3 shows the silhouette widths for the clusterings. PAM typically outperforms the k-medoids algorithm according to both measures.

The results presented are for small values of k, since we are endeavouring to simplify our understanding of the data. On the basis of silhouette width,

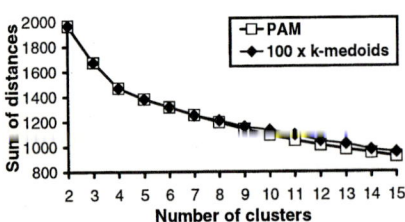

Fig. 2. Sum of the distances of rules to the closest medoids.

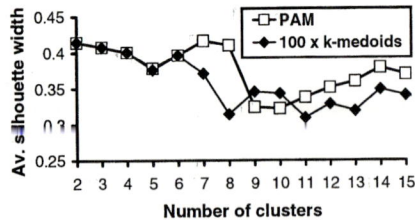

Fig. 3. Silhouette widths of clusterings obtained from PAM and k-medoids.

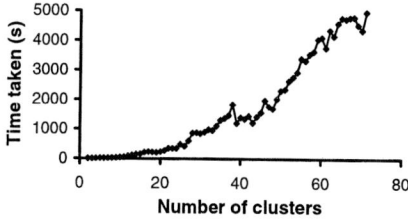 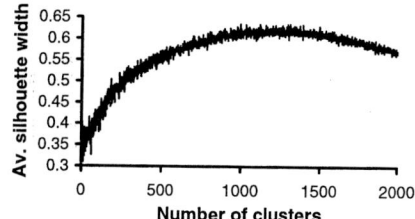

Fig. 4. Time requirements for the PAM algorithm.

Fig. 5. Results of 100 runs of the k-medoids algorithm for k up to 2000.

PAM obtains the best clusterings when k equals two or seven. In both cases, the strongest cluster contains all 1433 rules with a clause of the form 'Cap_gain >= x'. This cluster has an average silhouette width of 0.74 in both cases and has 'IF Age >= 32 AND Cap_gain >= 3103 THEN *Salary = >50K' as its medoid. In the two cluster case, the other 3352 rules appear in the second cluster, which has an average silhouette width of 0.27. In the seven cluster case, these rules are split into six clusters, with average silhouette widths from 0.07 to 0.37.

It is unclear from figures 2 and 3 whether better clusterings might be obtained for larger values of k. The time requirements for PAM increase considerably as the number of clusters increases, as shown in figure 4, but figure 1 shows that the k-medoids algorithm may be used with much larger values of k. Figure 5 shows the silhouette widths of clusterings obtained for values of k up to 2000. These results suggest that the best clusterings are obtained for values of k around 1200. However, such large values of k do not adequately simplify the data.

8 Conclusions and Further Research

The PAM and k-medoids algorithms have been applied to the clustering of rules obtained from the all-rules algorithm. PAM obtains better results according to both the sum of distances to medoids and the overall silhouette width for most values of k. However, it requires considerably more time than k-medoids for larger values of k. The clusters obtained seem to be reasonable, especially the cluster of all rules containing a clause of the form 'Cap_gain $\geq x$', which is the only strong cluster in the two and seven cluster cases.

There are a number of potential areas for further research:

- Experimentation with other medoid based clustering algorithms, such as CLARANS [9], may result in improved clusterings and efficiency. The application of heirarchical clustering algorithms [5] to the clustering of rules might also reveal useful information.
- Better methods for summarizing clusters that give more information than just the cluster medoid are required if we are to improve our understanding of the data via clustering of rules.

- Numeric fields lead to the production of many similar rules differing only in the bounds on these fields. Every rule has the same weight when applying k-medoids or PAM, so if essentially the same rule is produced many times a bias is created towards clusters centred about such rules. More interesting clusters might be found if such rules were given a lesser weight or if the all-rules algorithm were prevented from producing almost identical rules.
- Our difference measures are 'semantic-based', i.e. related to the sets of support. An alternative strategy would be 'syntactic-based', i.e. based on the actual expressions used in the rules. A comparison of the clusters obtained using the two strategies is a matter for further research.

References

1. R. Bayardo, R. Agrawal, and D. Gunopulos. Constraint-Based Rule Mining in Large, Dense Databases. In *Proceedings of the 15th International Conference on Data Engineering*, pages 188–197. IEEE, 1999.
2. B. de la Iglesia, M. S. Philpott, A. J. Bagnall, and V. J. Rayward-Smith. Data Mining Rules Using Multi-Objective Evolutionary Algorithms. In *Proceedings of 2003 IEEE Congress on Evolutionary Computation*, 2003.
3. G. Richards and V. J. Rayward-Smith. Discovery of association rules in tabular data. In *Proceedings of IEEE First International Conference on Data Mining, San Jose, California, USA*, pages 465–473. IEEE Computer Society, 2001.
4. C.L. Blake and C.J. Merz. UCI Repository of machine learning databases, 1998. http://www.ics.uci.edu/~mlearn/MLRepository.html.
5. Leonard Kaufman and Peter J. Rousseeuw. *Finding Groups in Data: An Introduction to Cluster Analysis*. Wiley series in probability and mathematical statistics. John Wiley and Sons Inc., 1990.
6. P. Jaccard. Étude comparative de la distribution florale dans une portion des Alpes et des Jura. *Bulletin de la Société Vaudoise de la Sciences Naturelles*, 37:547–579, 1901.
7. J. C. Gower and P. Legendre. Metric and Euclidean properties of dissimilarity coefficients. *Journal of Classification*, 3:5–48, 1986.
8. J. B. MacQueen. Some Methods for Classification and Analysis of Multivariate Observations. In *Proceedings of the 5th Berkeley Symposium on Mathematical Statistics and Probability*, volume 1, pages 281–297. University of California Press, 1967.
9. Raymond T. Ng and Jiawei Han. CLARANS: A Method for Clustering Objects for Spatial Data Mining. *IEEE Transactions on Knowledge and Data Engineering*, 14(5):1003–1016, 2002.

A Comparison of Texture Teatures for the Classification of Rock Images

Maneesha Singh, Akbar Javadi, and Sameer Singh

ATR Lab, Department of Computer Science
University of Exeter, Exeter EX4 4QF, UK
{M.Singh,A.A.Javadi,S.Singh}@ex.ac.uk

Abstract. Texture analysis plays a vital role in the area of image understanding research. One of the key areas of research is to compare how well these algorithms rate in differentiating between different textures. Traditionally, texture algorithms have been applied mostly on benchmark data and some studies have found certain algorithms are better suited for differentiating between certain types of textures. In this paper we compare 7 well-established image texture analysis algorithms on the task of classifying rocks.

1 Introduction

Rocks are aggregates of one or more minerals. The nature and properties of a rock are determined by the minerals in it and the arrangements of the minerals relative to each other, i.e., the texture of the rock. An individual rock type or specimen is always described in terms of its mineral composition and its texture, and both are used in the classification of rocks. Rocks are classified by means of formation, mineral content and structure. In terms of formation, rocks are classified into three main groups of igneous, sedimentary and metamorphic rocks.

1. Igneous rocks are formed by the solidification of material direct from the mantle. Igneous rocks make up over 90% of the Earth's crust. However, large portions of these rocks go unnoticed because they are covered by sedimentary rocks. Igneous rocks make up most of the mountains. They are produced through cooling of magma, either below the surface of the earth's crust or above it (lava).
2. Sedimentary rocks are formed from rocks of any type, broken down due to mechanical, thermal or chemical processes, and re-deposited. Rock formation involves temperature, pressure and cementing agents. The complication with sedimentary rocks is that they form from such a diversity of processes that their straightforward classification is difficult. Sedimentary rocks are typically characterized by a bedding structure of different layers of deposition.
3. Metamorphic rocks are formed from any of the previous rocks, altered by extremes of pressure and temperature. In the process of metamorphism the rock does not melt but it changes state by the process of mineral changes (growth of minerals that are more stable under conditions of high temperature / pressure),

Fig. 1. Example images of the three rock types; igneous, Sedimentary and Metamorphic (left to right).

textural changes (re-crystallization or alignment of platy minerals, usually as a result of unequal application of pressure) or both. Flow patterns during these changes cause characteristic patterns in the rock, which may lead to complex rock structures.

Each of the above main classes includes a number of subclasses with each subclass covering a large number of different rocks. Example images of each rock type are shown in Figure 1.

In civil engineering, it is often necessary to arrive at engineering judgments in the field with the minimum information on the ground conditions. In particular, the type and physical parameters of rock and soil need to be identified at early stages of site investigation. Therefore, the ability to identify rocks and soils is an important skill for civil engineers to develop. However, the nature of the fieldwork is such that the rock types are unlikely to be perfect examples and the conditions may preclude straight-forward systematic identification systems. In addition, presence of fractures, fissures, folds, faults, weathering and other geological effects makes identification of rocks even more difficult. An automated image analysis approach to classification of geological materials can help engineers in their judgment on rock/soil types and in decision making on ground conditions.

In what follows, a review of different methods of texture analysis is presented. Details of the data sets of rock images used in this study are described. The results of application of 7 different texture analysis methods on the data sets are presented and discussed. Finally conclusions are made from the results presented.

2 Texture Analysis

Texture analysis is fundamental to most studies involving image understanding. Image object texture is a crucial clue as to the identity of the image objects and several methods of texture analysis have been proposed in literature. One of the main motivations of this study is to investigate which method of image texture analysis is best suited for distinguishing rock textures.

In general, there is a consensus that no single texture analysis method is suitable for all types of image data. Weszka et al.[14] compared texture measures including those categorized into four sets as Fourier power spectrum, second order grey level statistics, grey level difference statistics, and grey level run length statistics. They find that the statistical features better capture the essence of texture than Fourier features. Also, grey level statistics gave better results than statistics based on single grey levels. Conners and Harlow[2] compared four different texture algorithms including Co-occurrence matrices, Grey Level Run Length Method, Grey Level Difference Method and Power Spectral Method. The methods are tested on Markov generated textures and random fields of order two. Comparing the merits of the four algorithms, the authors note that co-occurrence matrices is the most powerful of all methods considered. Reed and Buf[12] presented a review of three categories of feature extraction methods namely feature-based, model-based and structural. The authors find that no universally best feature set is found. The best feature set depends on the data to be classified. A general review on texture analysis can be found in [3,5].

Some of the key observations from above studies can be stated as follows. First, there is no consensus on which texture features perform the best. The results are very much application dependent and due to most studies working with small data sets, results are hard to generalize. Second, texture evaluation is based on mostly images that do not necessarily need segmentation prior to texture analysis.

A small number of studies have addressed the issue of rock classification using image processing techniques. Lepisto et al. [8, 9] authors have used texture and spectral features for classifying rock textures on a set of 118 images. Spectral features are computed by converting the image to Hue Saturation Intensity colour space and using H and I values as features. Texture features are obtained by computing mean contrast and mean entropy values from co-occurrence matrices. The authors report the results to be 100% correct (using contrast and hue separately) when they use 54 samples of easy to classify textures and the correct classification of 90.6 % (using entropy) when they use 65 difficult to classify rock texture samples. Similarly, texture analysis has been used by Partio et al. [11] who computed only 4 co-occurrence features namely: energy, entropy, contrast and inverse difference moment for rock texture retrieval. They also compare their results with Gabor filters. The authors report the classification results of 67.5% using the co-occurrence features and 46.95% using the Gabor features. Other approaches based on the use of colour histograms Bruno et al. [1]and LeBrun et al. [7] have been less successful than the use of texture analysis. One of the major weaknesses of these studies is the use of small sample sizes for experiments, and the small and basic features used for classification.

In this paper, we aim to study the suitability of five well-established and popular texture analysis methods for the classification of rock images. These texture analysis methods are detailed as follows.

Autocorrelation [13] - 24 coefficients extracted using the equation

$$C_{ff}(p,q) = \frac{MN}{(M-p)(N-q)} \frac{\sum_{i=1}^{M-p}\sum_{j=1}^{N-q} f(i,j)f(i+p,j+q)}{\sum_{i=1}^{M}\sum_{j=1}^{N} f^2(i,j)}$$

where, $q = 1...10$ is the positional difference in the i, j direction, and M, N are image dimensions.

Co-occurrence Matrices [4,5] - 25 texture features including angular second moment, contrast, variance, inverse different moment, sum average, sum variance, sum entropy, entropy, difference variance, difference entropy, two information measures of correlation, and maximum correlation coefficient and six other measures on statistics of co-occurrence matrices.

Edgefrequency [13] – 25 coefficients extracted using the following equation

$$E(d) = |f(i,j) - f(i+d,j)| + |f(i,j) - f(i-d,j)|$$
$$+ |f(i,j) - f(i,j+d)| + |f(i,j) - f(i,j-d)|$$

for $1 \leq d \leq 50$

Law's Mask Features [13] - A total of 125 features are extracted by applying a total of 25 Law's masks. On the application of each mask, we determine the average mean, standard deviation, skewness, energy and entropy.

Run Length [13] - Let $B(a, r)$ be the number of primitives of all directions having length r and grey level a. Let A be the area of the region in question, let L be the number of grey level within that region and let N_r be the maximum primitive length within the image. The texture description features can then be determined as follows. Let K be the total number of runs: $K = \sum_{a=1}^{L} \sum_{r=1}^{Nr} B(a,r)$, then the features are given by:

$$f_1 = \frac{1}{K} \sum_{a=1}^{L} \sum_{r=1}^{Nr} \frac{B(a,r)}{r^2}, \quad f_2 = \frac{1}{K} \sum_{a=1}^{L} \sum_{r=1}^{Nr} B(a,r)r^2$$

$$f_3 = \frac{1}{K} \sum_{a=1}^{L} [\sum_{r=1}^{Nr} B(a,r)r^2], \quad f_4 = \frac{1}{K} \sum_{a=1}^{L} [\sum_{r=1}^{Nr} B(a,r)]^2$$

$$f_5 = \frac{K}{\sum_{a=1}^{L} \sum_{r=1}^{Nr} rB(a,r)} = \frac{K}{A}$$

Texture Operators - Manian et al. [10] presented a new algorithm for texture classification based on logical operators. These operators are based on order-2 elementary matrices whose building blocks are numbers 0, 1, and −1 and matrices of order 1x1. These matrices are operated on by operators such as row-wise join, column-wise join, etc. A total of six best operators are used and convolved with images to get texture features. Features are computed using zonal-filtering using zonal masks that are applied to the standard deviation matrix. Features obtained include horizontal and vertical slit features, ring feature, circular feature and sector feature.

Texture Spectrum - He and Wang [6] proposed the use of texture spectrum for extracting texture features. If an image can be considered to comprise of small texture units, then the frequency distribution of these texture units is a texture spectrum. The features extracted include black-white symmetry, geometric symmetry, degree of direction, orientation features and central symmetry.

All texture features are computed on grey-scale images.

3 Experimental Details

We have used 110 hand specimens of three different rock types from a collection of rocks in the Geotechnics laboratory at the Engineering Department at Exeter University. The selected specimens cover a wide range of rocks belonging to the three main groups considered in this paper, i.e., igneous (27 samples), sedimentary (61 samples) and metamorphic rocks (22 samples). Digital images were obtained from these specimens. A white background and lighting from three different angles was used to minimize shading in the images. These images are then segmented from the background using Fuzzy-C-means clustering algorithm. All images were segmented into two clusters. Texture features were then extracted using 7 texture extraction methods as explained before. We then use k nearest neighbour classifier for classification using the data obtained from all texture extraction methods.

4 Results

The results are shown in Table 1. The Table shows that the value of k must be optimized for testing on a validation set since different values of k give different results. The overall best result is obtained using co-occurrence matrices that outperform all other methods. Other good results come from edge-frequency, and Law's masks. The worst performance is shown by the run-length method.

Table 1. Comparison of the 7 texture analysis methods using leave-one-out cross validation using k nearest neighbour classifier.

Algorithm	Nearest neighbour classifier					
	K=1	K=3	K=5	K=7	K=9	K=11
Autocorrelation	79.09	72.73	75.45	77.27	76.52	**77.85**
Co-occurrence	80.91	80.91	87.27	**91.82**	90.73	90.52
Edge frequency	89.09	80.00	76.36	80.91	**85.67**	72.74
Laws masks	92.64	89.73	93.65	**94.21**	91.63	92.44
Run length	58.73	52.66	58.92	61.42	63.04	**66.41**
Texture operators	79.09	79.09	80.00	**81.24**	78.62	72.30
Texture spectrum	70.53	**79.62**	67.35	63.62	62.06	69.27

5 Conclusions

The main focus of this work has been to rank a number of texture analysis methods on the basis of their ability to classify the three main categories of rocks. Our results show that Law's masks and co-occurrence matrices are the most powerful scheme for rock classification. Application of image processing in classification of rocks to subgroups of the three main groups is currently under investigation by the authors.

References

1. R. Bruno, S. Persi, P. Laurenge, M.O. Cica and E.O. Serrano, "Image analysis for ornamental stone standards characterization", International symposium on imaging applications in geology, pp. 29-32, May 6-7, 1999.
2. R.W. Conners and C.A. Harlow, A theoretical comparison of texture algorithms, IEEE Transactions on Pattern Analysis and Machine Intelligence, vol. 2, no. 3, pp. 204-222, 1980.
3. L.S. Davis, Image texture analysis techniques - a survey, Digital Image Processing, Simon and R. M. Haralick (eds.), pp. 189-201, 1981.
4. R.M. Haralick, K. Shanmugam and I. Dinstein, Textural features for image classification, IEEE Transactions on Systems, Man and Cybernetics, vol. 3, no. 6, pp 610-621, 1973.
5. R.M. Haralick, Statistical and structural approaches to texture, Proceedings of IEEE, vol. 67, pp. 786-804, 1979.
6. D.C. He and L. Wang, Texture features based on texture spectrum, Pattern Recognition, vol. 25, no. 3, pp. 391-399, 1991.
7. V. Lebrun, C. Toussaint and E. Pirard, "On the use of image analysis for the quantitative monitoring of stone alteration", Weathering 2000 International Conference, Belfast, 2000.
8. L. Lepisto, I. Kunttu, J. Autio, and A. Visa., "Comparison of some content based image retrieval systems with rock texture images", Proceedings of 10th Finnish Artificial Intelligence Conference, Oulu, Finland, pp. 156-163, Dec. 16-17, 2002.
9. L. Lepisto, I. Kunttu J. Autio and A. Visa, "Rock image classification using non-homogeneous textures and spectral imaging", Proceedings of the 11th International conference in central Europe on Computer Graphics, Visualization and Computer Vision, Plzen – Bory, Czech Republic, 3-7 February, 2003.
10. V. Manian, R. Vasquez and P. Katiyar, Texture classification using logical operators, IEEE Transactions on Image Analysis, vol. 9, no. 10, pp. 1693-1703, 2000.
11. M. Partio, B. Cramariuc, M. Gabbouj and A. Visa, "Rock texture retrieval using gray level co-occurrence matrix", 5th Nordic Signal Processing Symposium, On board Hurtigruten M/S Trollfjord, Norway, October 4-7, 2002.
12. T.R. Reed and J.M.H. Buf, A review of recent texture segmentation and feature extraction techniques, Computer Vision Graphics and Image Processing: Image Understanding, vol. 57, no. 3, pp. 359-372, 1993.
13. M. Sonka, V. Hlavac and R. Boyle, Image processing, analysis and machine vision, PWS press, 1998.
14. J.S. Weszka, C. R. Dyer and A. Rosenfeld, A comparative study of texture measures for terrain classification, IEEE Transactions on Systems, Man and Cybernetics, vol. 6, no. 4, pp. 269-285, 1976.

A Mixture of Experts Image Enhancement Scheme for CCTV Images

Maneesha Singh, Sameer Singh, and Matthew Porter

ATR Lab, Department of Computer Science
University of Exeter, Exeter EX4 4QF, UK
{M.Singh,S.Singh,M.Porter}@ex.ac.uk

Abstract. The main aim of this paper is to present a mixture of experts framework for the selection of an optimal image enhancement. This scheme selects the best image enhancement algorithm from a bank of algorithms on a per image basis. The results show that this scheme considerably improves the quality of test images collected from CCTV.

1 Introduction

Over the last ten years the use and impact of Closed-Circuit Television (CCTV) has grown immensely. Their uses are vast, from providing police with photographic evidence of criminal activities, checking the amount of traffic on busy roads, to merely surveying areas of buildings for security purposes. Unfortunately, cameras are prone to produce poor image quality because of high levels of noise apparent in the picture due to a number of reasons including interference during transmission, motion in video, weather and lighting conditions, and occlusion. Some of these problems can be corrected by image enhancement as we attempt in this paper.

In this paper we propose that no single image enhancement algorithm is optimal for all images. Different images are best enhanced by different image enhancement algorithm. The suitability of an image enhancement algorithm for a given image can be based on statistical image features. Hence, a predictive system needs to be based on mapping image features to the suitability of image enhancement algorithms. In this paper we develop such a predictive system based on multiple feature regression. The paper is laid out as follows. In section 2 we briefly detail a number of image enhancement algorithms that form the mixture of experts framework. We also detail the predictive module. In section 3 we detail a number of statistical image viewability measures that are used to capture the quality of images and such measurements are used as independent variables in regression. In section 4 we show the results on a number of CCTV images and discuss the utility of our approach. The paper concludes in section 5.

2 Mixture of Experts Framework

The mixture of experts framework is based on using a collection of image enhancement algorithms $(e_1, e_2, ..., e_m)$. Each of the image enhancement algorithm adopts a different approach to enhancement and works in an independent manner. For developing a machine learning based predictive system, we propose to use a number of training images. For each training image, we apply different enhancement algorithms giving a total of *m* enhanced images. On the basis of human visual inspection, each image can now be ranked which in effect ranks the quality of image enhancement algorithm. The rank of an algorithm is used as the output of the system to be mapped (dependent variable). Also, for each original image we can extract some statistical measures that define its viewability (as defined in the next section). These measures define the statistical properties of the image and are used as input to the system (independent variables). The task of the system is to predict the output if only input is available. Our work uses multiple regression as the mapping system. Such a system, for a given test image, computes its viewability measures and inputs them to the system. The output gives the rank of each enhancement algorithm, and chooses the best algorithm to be applied.

The image enhancement algorithms used in this work include:
1) Lowpass filter [5]; 2) Highpass filter [5]; 3) Highboost filter [5]; 4) Median filter [5]; 5) Adaptive unsharp masking [1,2]; 6) Cubic unsharp masking - separable [9]; 7) Cubic unsharp masking – non-separable [9]; 8) Product of linear operators [8]; 9) Local window based Histogram Equalisation [5]; 10) Adaptive contrast enhancement [10]; 11) Adaptive contrast enhancement based on local entropy [10]; 12) Fuzzy contrast enhancement [12]; 13) Extreme value sharpening [5]; 14) Local Adaptive scaling [6]; and 15) Global Histogram equalisation [5].

3 Image Viewability Measures

In order to compare enhancement techniques, we must have a measure of image viewability before and after enhancement. During the course of our research we have found that no single measurement is sufficient and a range of measurements is needed. We briefly summarise here the viewability measures that can be computed on a single image.

Cumulative Edge Strength - Cumulative edge strength is the average edge strength per pixel of the whole image. Where g_{xx} and g_{yy} are the gradients in x and y directions.

$$\left|\vec{\nabla}C\right| = \sqrt{\lambda_+} = \left[\frac{1}{2}\left\{g_{xx} + g_{yy} + \sqrt{(g_{xx} - g_{yy})^2 + 4g_{xy}^2}\right\}\right]^{\frac{1}{2}} \quad (1)$$

Proportion of Edge Pixels – If the edge strength of a pixel is greater than the cumulative edge strength, it is termed as an edge pixel. All the edge pixels in the image are computed. The proportion of edge pixels is given by:

$$edge\_pixels\_proportion = \frac{no\_of\_edge\_pixels}{Total\_pixels} \quad (2)$$

Histogram Area - This measure can be calculated as the area under the edge-strength and frequency curve.

Edge Contrast - All the edge pixels are first computed using Prewitt edge detection operator. For each pixel we find the non-edge pixels in its 'neighbourhood'. We average the Euclidean distance between the pixel and these neighbours, which gives the contrast value for the pixel. Contrast of the image is computed by averaging the 'contrast matrix'.

Proportion of Very Dark Pixels - Very dark pixels are the pixels that are almost black in the scale image. The proportion of very dark pixels in the image is computed by counting the number of pixels with the RGB values less than 100.

$$V5 = \frac{Number\_of\_dark\_pixels}{Total\_pixels} \quad (3)$$

Mean of Pixel Intensity, Standard Deviation of Pixel Intensity, Skewness of Pixel Intensity, Kurtosis of Pixel Intensity, Uniformity of Texture in the Edge Removed Image - This is computed by taking into account the non-edge pixels and computing the texture variability in a neighbourhood around it. The neighbourhood considered in this case is 3x3.

$$mean = \frac{sum}{(M)*(N)} \quad (4)$$

$$st\_devn = \left(\sqrt{\frac{sum\_r}{M*N-1}} + \sqrt{\frac{sum\_g}{M*N-1}} + \sqrt{\frac{sum\_b}{M*N-1}}\right)/3.0 \quad (5)$$

$$skewness = \frac{sum}{(M*N-1)*st\_devn^3} \quad (6)$$

$$kurtosis = \frac{sum}{(M*N-1)*st\_devn^4} \quad (7)$$

Difference in the Neighbourhood Pixels - The average difference between the neighbourhood edge pixels and non-edge pixels is computed and is used as a viewability measure.

4 Experiments and Evaluation

We collected a total of 41 images from the Internet that come from CCTV. Each image is of poor quality and requires significant amount of enhancement. The images are different to each other in the sense that they are captured using different CCTV equipment at different places. We performed a 4-fold cross validation by dividing our image set into a training set (31 images) and a test set (10 images), we first computed the viewability measures as discussed earlier. In addition, we applied the 15 image enhancement methods and obtained the resulting enhanced images (Figure 1 shows 3 example enhanced images). We also manually rank each image to have a rank between 1 and 5, where 1 represents poor quality and 5 represents the very high quality.

We next use multiple linear regression to map the input features (viewability measures) to output (image rank). A total of 15 regression equations are derived for the 15 image enhancement experts. For test images, we again manually rank them after enhancing them with different experts but use this information only for verifying our results and calculating the error of our system. We refer to this ranking information as the ground-truth for the test data. For test data we first calculate viewability features and input them using the same regression equations we derived from the training data. Each regression scheme outputs a predicted rank corresponding to its enhancement technique, for which we also know the true rank from ground-truth. Table 1 shows the residual error averaged over 4 folds (difference between predicted and true rank) mean and standard deviation values. It is important to note that the results show that the mean error value is considerably low given that the ranks lie between the range [1,5]. Some high values of standard deviation correspond to the fact that some predicted ranks were found to lie outside the range and skewed the output values considerably. For a real system, instead of enhancing an image 15 times with different methods, the viewability measures computed from an image can be used to quickly compute the rank of these enhancement methods on this image and the best ranked enhancement expert is used.

We next determine which enhancement method is predicted to work best on most images. The results for optimal enhancement selection and the ground-truth are shown in Table 2. We find that on training images, Adaptive Contrast Enhancement was found to work the best. On predicted ranks, the methods unsharp masking and median filtering work quite well. The methods that work very poorly include cubic unsharp masking, product of linear operators, extreme value sharpening, and local adaptive scaling.

Table 1. Residual Error (mean and standard deviation) on the application of linear regression on test data.

Enhancement Expert	Residual Error (Mean)	Residual Error (Std. dev)
Low pass Filter (*LP*)	-0.102	0.559
High pass Filter (*HP*)	-0.199	1.088
High Boost Filter (*HB*)	-1.805	2.627
Median Filter (*MF*)	0.249	0.959
Unsharp Masking (*UM*)	-1.449	3.225
Cubic Unsharp Masking (separable) (*CUMS*)	0.522	2.079
Cubic Unsharp Masking (non-separable) (*CUMN*)	-0.261	1.233
Product of Linear Operators (*PLO*)	-0.669	0.408
Histogram Equalisation (*HE*)	2.034	5.325
Adaptive Contrast Enhancement (*ACE*)	-0.999	1.840
Adaptive Contrast Enhancement Local Entropy (*ACELE*)	2.069	6.016
Fuzzy Contrast Enhancement (*FCE*)	0.522	2.115
Extreme Value Sharpening (*EVS*)	0.085	0.393
Local Adaptive Scaling (*LAS*)	0.593	1.100
Global Histogram Equalisation (*GHE*)	-0.752	4.278

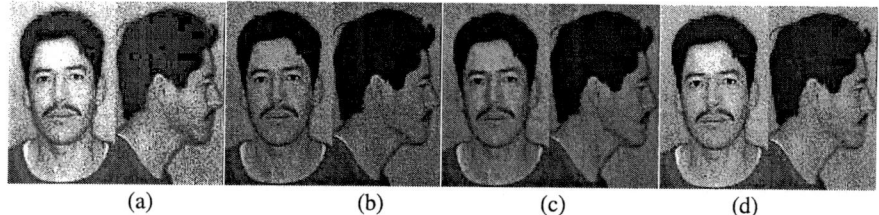

Fig. 1. (a) Original Image , (b) Median Filtered, (c) Histogram Equalised and (d) Adaptive Contrast.

We next perform Principal Components Analysis. In this analysis, we extract the two principal components that explain the two largest variances in data. Each data point is labelled by its rank. We find that almost all plots (one for each enhancement algorithm) follow the similar pattern. Initial observations of the graphs show that there are distinct clusters of images which share similar rankings. These clusters prove that viewability measures of the similarly ranked images are similar and that is why they cluster well.

Table 2. The ground truth and the predict ranks. The first column shows the enhancement technique, and the next five columns show the ranks 1 (poor) to 5 (best). The first value in each row is the number of training images that were ground-truthed to be of that rank. The values within ( ) show the predicted rank using regression.

Enhancement Expert	1s	2s	3s	4s	5s
Low pass Filter (*LP*)	0 (0)	5 (3)	19 (10)	3 (0)	3 (1)
High pass Filter (*HP*)	6 (4)	16(9)	7 (1)	1 (0)	0 (1)
High Boost Filter (*HB*)	0 (0)	5 (3)	12 (7)	5 (3)	8 (4)
Median Filter (*MF*)	0 (0)	3 (2)	14 (11)	9 (5)	4 (3)
Unsharp Masking (*UM*)	0 (0)	7 (5)	14 (7)	7 (3)	2 (0)
Cubic Unsharp Masking - sep	8 (6)	22 (17)	0 (0)	0 (0)	0 (0)
Cubic Unsharp Masking - ns	20 (14)	10 (4)	0 (0)	0 (0)	0 (0)
Product of Linear Operators (*PLO*)	3 (2)	17 (12)	8 (7)	1 (0)	1 (0)
Histogram Equalisation (*HE*)	2 (0)	8 (3)	9 (5)	5 (3)	6 (2)
Adaptive Contrast Enhancement (*ACE*)	0 (1)	5 (5)	7 (1)	8 (2)	10 (2)
ACE Local Entropy (*ACELE*)	1 (0)	19 (14)	3 (1)	6 (2)	1 (0)
Fuzzy Contrast Enhancement (*FCE*)	29 (18)	1 (0)	0 (0)	0 (0)	0 (0)
Extreme Value Sharpening (*EVS*)	27 (11)	3 (0)	0 (0)	0 (0)	0 (0)
Local Adaptive Scaling (*LAS*)	2 (0)	26 (19)	1 (0)	0 (0)	1 (0)
Histogram Equalisation (*GHE*)	0 (0)	4 (2)	16 (7)	8 (4)	2 (0)

5 Conclusions

In this paper we have introduced a knowledge based approach to image enhancement. It is well known that no single image segmentation method is appropriate for all images. In this paper we used a regression approach to map image viewaility features to rank such that for a given image, one best-suited image enhancement method can be selected from a large set of methods. Our results showed that such a mapping scheme using even simple methods such as regression is possible. Obviously, much better mapping is possible using non-linear techniques such as neural networks. We also found that viewability measures adequately capture the quality of image enhancement. We recommend that for further studies that our proposed approach should be used for a much larger data set with a non-linear approach to feature to rank mapping.

References

1. F. A. Cheikh and M. Gabbouj, Directional unsharp masking-based approach for color image enhancement, Proc. of the Noblesse Workshop on non-linear model based image analysis, 173-178, Glasgow, 1998.
2. F. A. Cheikh and M. Gabbouj, Directional-rational approach for color image enhancement, Proceedings of the IEEE International Symposium on Circuits and Systems, Geneva, Switzerland, May 28-31, 2000.
3. B.L. Deekshatulu, A.D. Kulkarni, and K.R. Rao, Quantitative evaluation of enhancement techniques, Signal Processing, 8, 369-375, 1985.
4. R.O. Duda, P.E. Hart and D.G. Stork, *Pattern Classification*, John Wiley, 2000.
5. R.C. Gonzalez and R.E. Woods, Digital Image Processing, Addison-Wesley publishing company, 1993.
6. R. Klette and P. Zamperoni, Handbook of image processing operators, John Wiley, 1996.
7. A. Polesel, G. Ramponi and V.J. Mathews, Image enhancement via adaptive unsharp masking, IEEE Transactions on Image Processing, 9, Issue 3, 2000.
8. G. Ramponi, Contrast enhancement in images via the Product of Linear filters, Signal Processing, 77, Issue 3, 349-353, 1999.
9. G. Ramponi, A cubic unsharp masking technique for contrast enhancement, Signal Processing, 67, Issue 2, 211-222, 1998.
10. M. Singh, D. Partridge, S. Singh, A knowledge based framework for image enhancement in aviation security, IEEE Trans SMC, 2004.
11. D.C.C. Wang, A.H. Vagnucci, and C.C. Li, Digital image enhancement: a survey, CVGIP Journal, 24, 1983.
12. L. A. Zadeh, Fuzzy logic and its applications, 1965.

Integration of Projected Clusters and Principal Axis Trees for High-Dimensional Data Indexing and Query

Ben Wang and John Q. Gan

Department of Computer Science
University of Essex
Colchester CO4 3SQ, UK
{bwangm,jqgan}@essex.ac.uk

Abstract. High-dimensional data indexing and query is a challenging problem due to the inherent sparsity of the data. Fast algorithms are in an urgent need in this field. In this paper, an automatic subspace dimension selection (ASDS) based clustering algorithm is derived from the well-known projection-based clustering algorithm, ORCLUS, and a two-level architecture for high-dimensional data indexing and query is also proposed, which integrates projected clusters and principal axis trees (PAT) to generate efficient high-dimensional data indexes. The query performances of similarity search by ASDS+PAT, ORCLUS+PAT, PAT alone, and Clindex are compared on two high-dimensional data sets. The results show that the integration of ASDS and PAT is an efficient indexing architecture and considerably reduces the query time.

1 Introduction

There is an increasing need to support the indexing and retrieval of multimedia data, such as images, video, audio snippets from large datasets. The feature vectors that characterize multimedia data are often considerably high. As a result, the efficiency in multimedia applications very much depends on high-dimensional data indexing and query algorithms that usually suffer from the curse of dimensionality problem, that is, the performance of indexing methods degrades drastically as the dimensionality increases (dimensionality curse). A survey by Lu [6] has introduced the state-of-the-art high-dimensional data indexing structures in detail. The indexing structures that support k-nearest neighbor (k-NN) query have been widely used for similarity search, although they are computationally expensive. Particularly, in high-dimensional data spaces the computational cost of k-NN imposes practical limits on the data set size. Recently, McNames proposed a principal axis tree (PAT) method that outperforms or matches sixteen leading k-NN algorithms on benchmark data sets [8]. However, using PAT on large data sets would be inefficient if the data is high-dimensional. Clustering-based data indexing has been proved to be efficient for indexing high-dimensional data [3][5]. For instance, Clindex [5] is a clustering-based indexing method for k-NN query in high-dimensional space, in which the high-dimensional data points are firstly clustered and stored in separate files and a Hash table data structure is then utilized to search the cluster where the query point exists. However, clustering high-dimensional data is also a challenging problem [4][7]. As the dimension increases, the number of irrelevant attributes grows, which makes clustering in the original space very difficult.

Subspace clustering is one of the effective solutions to high-dimensional data clustering. Aggarwal et al. [1][2] developed projected clustering algorithms, PROCLUS and ORCLUS, which are able to construct clusters in arbitrarily aligned subspaces with low dimensions, providing a good approach to high-dimensional data clustering. However, it is quite hard to define a proper value for the number of clusters and the dimensions of subspaces extended by the clusters in ORCLUS.

To resolve these problems in indexing high-dimensional data, this paper firstly proposes an automatic subspace dimension selection (ASDS) based clustering algorithm in section 2. Secondly, a two-level efficient indexing architecture that combines ASDS and PAT is suggested in section 3. Experimental results and conclusion are given in section 4 and section 5 respectively.

2 ASDS Clustering Algorithm

The input to the clustering algorithm is a set of high-dimensional data and the output of the algorithm is the number of clusters and the cluster centroids. The ASDS clustering algorithm determines the number of clusters and the dimensions of projection subspaces automatically. It consists of the following steps:

S1. Initialize parameter values for *denseP*, pr_1, pr_2, *ERROR*, *D*, and *N*, where *denseP* is the percentage of points that belong to dense regions, pr_1 is the ratio of the number of finally returned clusters and the number of initial clusters, pr_2 is a ratio to control the merging of clusters, *ERROR* is a factor to control the subspace dimensions, *D* is the dimension of the data, and *N* is the total number of points in the data set.

S2. Generate initial clusters. Firstly, create cells by partitioning each dimension of the data space with one-to-two division. Count the number of data points in each cell, represented by *numP*. If (*numP* < *denseP*×*N*) is true on a cell, consider this cell as a dense region. Set the initial number of clusters, k_0, as the number of dense regions. Set $k_c = k_0$ and $m = k_0 \times pr_1$, where k_c is the current number of clusters and *m* is the number of finally returned clusters. The initial cluster seeds $s = \{s_1, \cdots, s_{k_c}\}$ are obtained by randomly selecting k_c points, one from each dense region.

S3. Generate subspaces described by ε_i, l_i, $(1 \le i \le k_c)$ and l_{min}, where ε_i represents a set of coordinate vectors in the subspace of cluster C_i, $l_i = |\varepsilon_i|$ is the dimension of ε_i, and l_{min} is the minimum dimension of all the subspaces. Firstly, calculate covariance matrix of the data in C_i [3], *Co*, and its *trace*, eigenvectors e_j, eigenvalues λ_j $(1 \le j \le D)$. Set $\varepsilon_i = \{e_1, e_2, \ldots, e_{l_i}\}$ such that the following equation holds:

$$error_{l_i} = \sum_{j=1}^{l_i} \lambda_j \Big/ trace < ERROR \quad (1)$$

Finally, set $l_{min} = \min_{1 \le i \le k_c} \{l_i\}$.

S4. Assign all the data points to their corresponding clusters in terms of the following projected distance:

$$P'dist_i(p, s_i, \varepsilon_i, l_{min}) = \sum_{j=1}^{l_{min}} (p.e_j - s_i.e_j)^2 \quad (2)$$

where "." represents dot product. The data point p is assigned to cluster $l = \arg\min_{1 \le i \le k_c}\{P'dist_i\}$.

S5. Calculate the centroids, si, and the radius (the maximum distance between the centroid and the data points in a cluster), ri, of all the clusters, respectively.

S6. Merge clusters. Set $k=k_c \times pr_2$.

S6.1 Calculate the projected energy for possible merged clusters $C_{ij} = C_i \cup C_j$ ($1 \le i, j \le k_c$ and $i < j$), which is defined as:

$$r_{ij} = R'(C_{ij}, s_{ij}, \varepsilon_{ij}, l_{min}) = \{\sum_{t=0}^{N_{ij}} P'dist(p_t, s_{ij}, \varepsilon_{ij}, l_{min})\} / N_{ij} \quad (3)$$

where s_{ij} and ε_{ij} represent the seed and subspace of C_{ij}, and N_{ij} is the number of points in C_{ij}. Merge C_i and C_j if r_{ij} takes minimum value among all the projected energies. Calculate s_i and ε_i for the newly merged cluster.

S6.2 Set $k_c = k_c-1$. If $(k_c > k)$ is true, go to S6.1.

S6.3 If $(k_c > m)$ is true, go to S3. Otherwise, output si and ε_i of all the finally generated clusters and stop.

3 A Two-Level Indexing Architecture Using Projected Clusters and PAT

A two-level indexing architecture that combines a projected clusters and an indexing structure is developed in this section. Fig. 1 (a) shows that the data set is partitioned into clusters by ASDS, and PAT is then used to create a tree structure for each cluster.

PAT itself is an efficient indexing structure for k-NN query [8]. At first, it creates a root node, and the root is partitioned into child nodes along principal axes, which is generated by singular value decomposition (SVD) [3]. Let n_p be the number of data points in the root node, n_c be the number of child nodes from a parent node, and n_y be the number of points assigned to a node. The partition is repeated for each child node until $n_y < n_c$. This algorithm requires $O(n_p \log n_p)$ indexing time [8].

The query process based on this indexing architecture is carried out as follows:

(i) The Euclidian distance between a query point q and each cluster centroid s_i is calculated, and the clusters are sorted in terms of the distances.
(ii) The cluster nearest to q is searched by PAT. The process starts with the root node, and then recursively searches the child node that contains q until a terminal

node is reached. A list of k-NN distances so far is obtained and the maximum distance is recorded as d_k. Next, the algorithm moves back to the parent node of the terminal node and searches its sibling node if the distance to q is less than d_k.
(iii) Searching continues until the distance to q from a cluster is greater than dk. Return the k-NN query results.

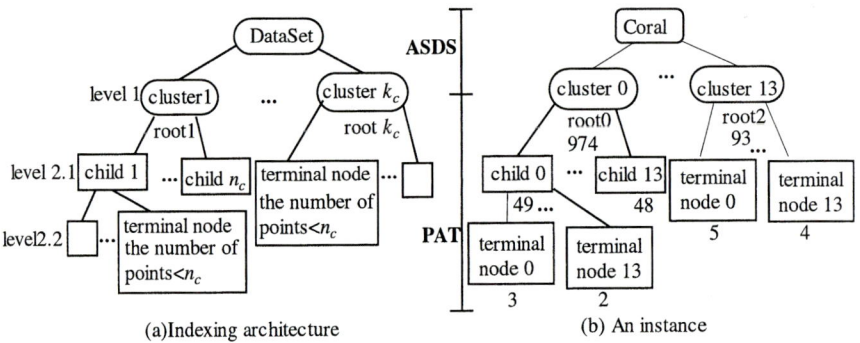

Fig. 1. The indexing architecture and an instance generated by ASDS+PAT

4 Experimental Results

Experiments are conducted on two data sets. The first is the Coral feature vector data set (Coral for short), which contains 68040 points (or vectors) with 32 dimensions. Coral is a commonly used image feature vectors for challenging high-dimensional indexing structures, downloadable from the UCI databases archive, (http://kdd.ics.uci.edu/). The second is a synthetic data set (SYN for short), which contains 12040 points with 40 dimensions. SYN is a data set for challenging high-dimensional clustering and indexing. The process of generating SYN has been described by Aggarwal [2]. We choose these two data sets to test the efficiency of the newly developed indexing structure. Every point in a data set has been chosen as a query, denoted as q, for a k-NN search on the whole data set, e.g., 68040 query points have been tested for Coral. By using trial and error approach, the parameter values are set as follows: pr_1=60%, pr_2=85%, ERROR=0.05, denseP=0.001 for Coral and denseP=0.00002 for SYN because SYN is very sparse. Four performance criteria adopted in the experiments are *ClusteringTime*, the time for clustering, *IndexTime*, the time for generating indexing tree structures, *TotalQueryTime*, the sum of query time for all the query points, and *AveQueryTime*, the average query time over all the query points.

Experiments on indexing and query by ASDS+PAT (method 1), ORCLUS+PAT (method 2), PAT alone (method 3), and Clindex (method 4) [5] are conducted respectively on the same data sets. The first three methods return the same exact k-NN results (all the points returned are real nearest neighbours of the query q), while Clindex is able to return the same results as the first three methods by searching at least two nearest clusters to a query point. Their performances on Coral and SYN data sets are given in Table 1. It is clear that method 1 has achieved the shortest query time among all the methods and outperforms method 2 in terms of all the performance criteria.

Although no clustering time is needed for method 3, its query time, the most important criterion, is about the double of that by method 2, and about 5 times of that by method 1 on Coral. The clustering time of method 4 is less than the one of other clustering methods, but its query time is the longest on Coral, and only a bit shorter than method 3 on SYN.

Table 1. Performances of k-NN (k=20) search on Coral and SYN by four methods

Dataset	Method	Clustering Time	Index Time	TotalQuery Time	AveQuery Time
Coral	1	389.661	37.544	158.318	2.327E-03
	2	605.34	53.817	475.533	6.989E-03
	3	0	47.318	866.426	1.273E-02
	4	25.453	0.016	2832.625	4.160E-02
SYN	1	206.466	3.765	71.983	5.979E-03
	2	299.911	6.409	86.715	7.202E-03
	3	0	11.106	353.108	2.933E-02
	4	7.5	0.01	312.48	2.600E-02

Table 2. The number of points in clusters generated on Corel by three clustering algorithms

Clustering Algorithm	Number of Clusters	Number of Data Points in the Generated Clusters
ASDS	14	974, 15747, 2664, 691, 2826, 401, 16700, 910, 84, 3929, 11709, 8146, 3166, 93
ORCLUS	9	275, 322, 1705, 39999, 507, 430, 12951, 10992, 859
Clindex	42	9, 64595, 524, 436, 356, 319, 184, 173, 153, 134, 134, 87, 87, 78, 65, 61, 60, 58, 57, 56, 51, 48, 35, 33, 32, 30, 28, 24, 24, 23, 14, 13, 12, 8, 7, 6, 6, 5, 4, 4, 4, 3

The two-level indexing structure generated by ASDS+PAT on Coral is illustrated in Fig.1 (b). Working on Coral data set, ASDS generates 14 clusters. The dimensions of subspaces embedded in the clusters are determined automatically as 17, 21, 19, 16, 17, 18, 21, 18, 18, 20, 20, 21, 17, 18, respectively. For ORCLUS, nine clusters with 15 dimensions in every subspace correspond to its best performance on Coral. However, Clindex generates 42 clusters and the data are clustered in the original space with dimension equal to 32 on Coral. Table 2 displays the number of points in each cluster generated by the three methods. It can be seen that the points are distributed more evenly in ASDS than in ORCLUS. Furthermore, Clindex generates a very large cluster with 64595 points plus many small clusters, which is obviously not efficient for indexing and query. Due to the limited space, other indexing structures and clustering information are omitted.

5 Conclusion

The ASDS cluster algorithm and the two-level indexing architecture have been developed for high-dimensional data indexing and query. ASDS improves ORCLUS by automatically choosing the number of clusters and the dimensions of projected subspaces, which also uses new criteria for data point assignment to clusters and for merging clusters. Experimental results have shown that clusters generated by ASDS are more suitable for indexing than by ORCLUS or Clindex on high-dimensional data. Moreover, the two-level indexing architecture that combined ASDS and PAT is proved to be efficient and considerably speeds up the k-NN query process without sacrificing the query precision.

References

1. Aggarwal, C.C., Procopiuc, C., Wolf, J.L., Yu, P.S., and Park, J.S.: Fast algorithms for projected clustering, Proc. of the ACM SIGMOD Conf., Philadelphia, PA, 61-72, 1999.
2. Aggarwal, C.C. and Yu, P.S.: Finding generalized projected clusters in high dimensional spaces, Sigmod Record, 29, 70-92, 2000.
3. Castelli, V., Thomasian, A., and Li, C.-S.: CSVD: clustering and singular value decomposition for approximate similarity searches in high dimensional space, IEEE Trans on Knowledge and Data Engineering, 15, 671-685, 2003.
4. Grabmeier, J., and Rudolph, A.: Techniques of Cluster Algorithms in Data Mining, Data Mining and Knowledge Discovery, 6, 303–360, 2002.
5. Li, C., Chang, E., Garcia-Molina, H., Wang, J., and Wiederhold, G.: Clindex: Clustering for similarity queries in high-dimensional spaces, IEEE Trans. on Knowledge and Engineering, 14, 792-808, 2002.
6. Lu, G.: Techniques and data structures for efficient multimedia retrieval based on similarity, IEEE Trans. on Multimedia, 4, 372-384, 2002.
7. Jain, A. and Dubes, R.: Algorithms for Clustering Data, Prentice Hall, 1998.
8. McNames, J.: A fast nearest neighbor algorithm based on a principal axis search tree, IEEE Trans. on Pattern Analysis and Intelligence, 23, 964-976, 2001.

Unsupervised Segmentation on Image with JSEG Using Soft Class Map

Yuanjie Zheng, Jie Yang, and Yue Zhou

Institute of Image Processing and Pattern Recognition, Shanghai Jiaotong University
Shanghai of China, 200030
yuanjiezheng@yahoo.com.cn, zhengyuanjie@sjtu.edu.cn

Abstract. Soft class map is presented for JSEG. The definitions of J values etc. in JSEG are adjusted correspondingly. The method of constructing soft class map is provided. JSEG with soft class map is a more robust method in unsupervised image segmentation compared with the original JSEG method. Our method can segment correctly image in which there exists color smooth transition in underlying object region.

1 Introduction

Image segmentation is a difficult problem. Unsupervised segmentation seems more like a nettlesome one. However, unsupervised image segmentation is critical to many tasks like content based image retrieval and progress in object recognition etc..

JSEG [1] is a computationally more feasible segmentation method which is to test the homogeneity of a given color-texture pattern. The results produced by JSEG are mainly based on a class-map formed by the color class label of every pixel, which is the production of color quantization. It is certain for any color quantization to lose some information of color spatial distribution. Nevertheless, when too much necessary color spatial distribution information is lost in the process of quantization, it is difficult or even impossible for JSEG to segment the image correctly. In fact, the problem caused by losing color spatial distribution information has also been mentioned in [1] as the major one of the limitations of JSEG.

We argue that if the information can be preserved as much as possible with some mechanisms, and at the same time the quantization isn't be influenced too much, the problem mentioned above may be solved and the behaviours of JSEG may be improved.

In this paper, we construct soft class-map for JSEG. It gives more detailed description in labelling a pixel to representative classes and can preserve well the information of color spatial distribution. We have also adjusted the definitions in JSEG to soft class-map. With the soft class map, JSEG becomes a more robust method especially for images which haven't been heavily blurred near boundaries of underlying regions.

2 JSEG with Soft Class Map

In order to identify the texture homogeneity and color smooth transition, assumptions which are similar to but different from the ones in [1] are made as follows:

- Each image contains a set of approximately homogeneous color-texture regions.
- The color information in each image region can be represented by a set a few quantized colors.
- The colors can vary smoothly in each image region. On the other hand, the ones between two neighbouring regions are distinguishable.

Enlightened by segmentations base on fuzzy theories [5][6], we use soft class-map to preserve the color spatial information.

We use N to denote the number of data points in JSEG. Each data point corresponds to a pixel in an image.

For a pixel $i(1 \leq i \leq N)$, we give a vector $\overline{\mu}_i = [\mu_{i1} \; \mu_{i2} \; \cdots \; \mu_{iM}]^T$ to denote the membership degrees of pixel i belonging to the M reference classes, where $0 \leq \mu_{ij} \leq 1$ for any $1 \leq j \leq M$, and $\sum_{j=1}^{M} \mu_{ij} = 1$. We know μ_{ij} means the degree of pixel i to class j.

The image of vector $\overline{\mu}_i$ is exactly the requisite soft class-map.

For a soft class-map, a pixel can be assigned to several classes simultaneously, and the degree of a pixel to a reference class can be expressed in more details.

2.1 Segmentation Given Soft Class-Map

Here we call the class map adopted in JSEG [1] a hard one, because every pixel is determined to belong to only one reference class with membership degree value 1.

We denote Z as the set of all N data points.

If a soft class-map for an image has been given, to segment the image with JSEG, the definitions of J value and the other related ones must be adjusted according to the soft class map.

The variance of data points in Z, denoted S_T, is defined unchangeably as below

$$S_T = \sum_{\overline{z} \in Z} \|\overline{z} - \overline{m}\|^2, \qquad (1)$$

where

$$\overline{m} = \frac{1}{N} \sum_{\overline{z} \in Z} \overline{z} \qquad (2)$$

The total variance of points belonging to the same class is defined as follows:

$$S_w = \sum_{i=1}^{M} S_{w_i} = \sum_{i=1}^{M} \sum_{\overline{z} \in Z} \|\overline{z} - \overline{m}_i\|^2 \mu_{zi} \qquad (3)$$

where

$$\bar{m}_i = \frac{1}{N_i} \sum_{\bar{z} \in Z} \bar{z} \mu_{\bar{z}i} \tag{4}$$

$$N_i = \sum_{\bar{z} \in Z} \mu_{\bar{z}i} \tag{5}$$

With S_T in equation (1) and S_w in equation (3), the definitions of J and $\tilde{J}$ are as below:

$$J = (S_T - S_w)/S_w \tag{6}$$

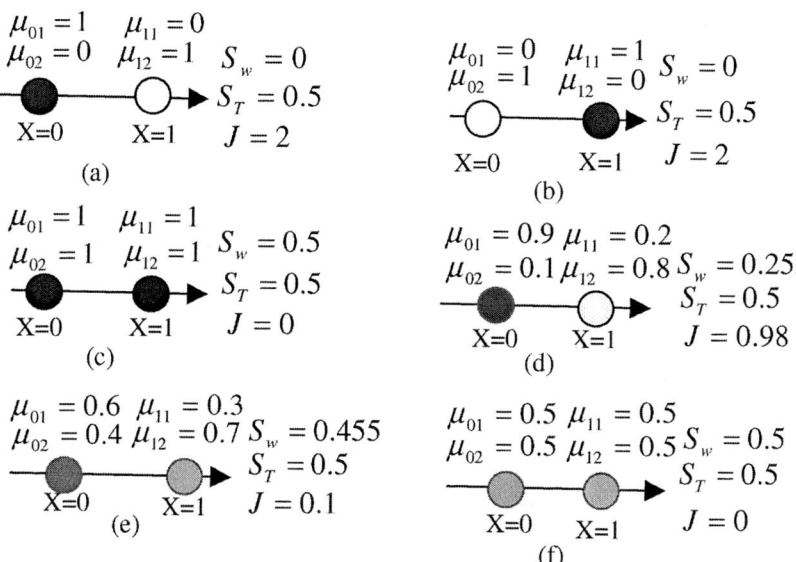

Fig. 1. Several soft class-maps for two point samples on a 1-dimensional line given 2 reference classes, and their corresponding J values. (a), (b) and (c) can also be seen as hard class-maps which are actually specific cases of soft class-maps.

JSEG applies J to a local area of the class-map, and with it judges whether the area is in the region interiors or near region boundaries. An image of J values is constructed after all J values are calculated over small windows centred at every pixel.

Based on the image of J values, region growing is used to do segmentations after automatic seed determination. To overcome over-segmentation, the regions, as the results of region growing, are merged based on their color similarities.

To see how soft class map gives more detailed color spatial distribution information, please see Fig. 1. Fig. 1 shows several quantizations (suppose there are only 2 reference classes) of two point samples on a 1-dimensional line, and their corresponding J values. The only three hard class-maps that can be constructed are shown in

Fig. 1a, 1b and 1c. However, many more other soft class-maps can be constructed, three of which are shown in Fig. 1d, 1e and 1f. The hard class-maps are only specific cases of soft class-maps for an image. From Fig. 1, we can see, with soft class-maps much more detailed J values can be provided for a local area given reference classes.

2.2 Construction of Soft Class-Map

A method to provide soft class-map should consider the factor of color gradual variation and can preserve most of the necessary spatial distribution information of color.

It has been reported that fuzzy connectedness can solve well the problems in image segmentation of shading in image, and a gradation of image intensities in an object [3][4]. So we use fuzzy connectedness to construct soft class-map for an image.

The seeds are provided for computing fuzzy connectedness according to the quantization results by the algorithm in [2] because it has been proven an effective one in JSEG segmentation [1].

Suppose the image has been quantized into M reference classes and the reference feature values are $\overline{v}_j (j = 1, 2, \cdots M)$. Here $\overline{v}_j$ is a t-dimensional vector, and t is the number of features used in JSEG. For example, t is 3 for color image and 1 for grey image. We calculate the variances of feature values of pixels assigned to a same reference class, and denote them by vector $\overline{\sigma}_j$ for any $j (1 \le j \le M)$. $\overline{\sigma}_j$ is also a t-dimensional vector as $\overline{v}_j$. Pixels with their feature values locating in the range from $\overline{v}_j - \alpha \overline{\sigma}_j$ to $\overline{v}_j + \alpha \overline{\sigma}_j$ are considered as seeds for fuzzy connectedness to the reference class j, where α is a constant taking its value in [0,1].

The fuzzy connectedness value of every pixel to each reference class is computed by the method in [3].

Suppose we have got the fuzzy connectedness of a pixel i to reference class j as $f_{ij} (0 \le f_{ij} \le 1)$, then the fuzzy degree of the pixel to the reference class is determined as bellows:

$$\mu_{ij} = (f_{ij})^{\frac{1}{p}} / \sum_{l=1}^{M} (f_{il})^{\frac{1}{p}} \qquad (7)$$

Where $p (0 \le p \le 1)$ is a constant and it controls the fuzzy degree of the soft class map. If $p \to 0$, a hard class map will be constructed, and only the reference class, to which fuzzy connectedness takes the largest value, will own the pixel. As did in all the experiments in section 3, we can generally set $p = 1$.

3 Validation and Experiments

Fig. 2 shows a synthetic color image. It is used mainly for validating the efficiency of JSEG with soft class-map on the segmentation of region with color smooth transition. The synthetic image was created by several steps: At first, a circular disk was gener-

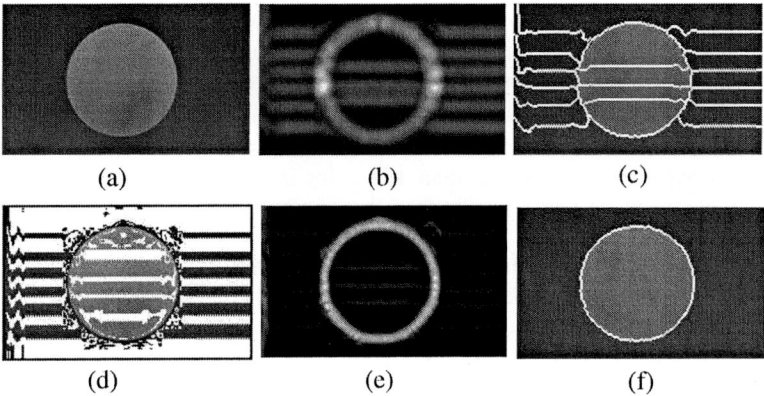

Fig. 2. (a) A synthetic image with ramps of color, but different color component values, in the circular disk and background. (b) J values by JSEG with hard class-map. (c) Segmentaion result of JSEG with hard class-map. (d) Seeds specified for constructing soft class-map with fuzzy connectedness. (e) J values by JSEG with soft class-map. (f) Segmentaion result of JSEG with soft class-map.

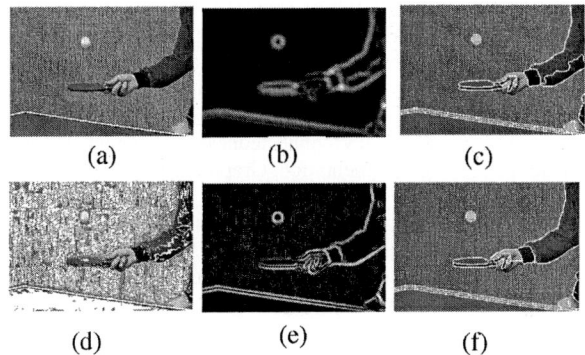

Fig. 3. (a) An original color image. In the region of "arm", there are obviously "light" and "dard" parts of "cloth" colors, and from one part to the other one there exist color smooth transitions. (b) J values got from JSEG with hard class-map. (c) Segmentation result of JSEG with hard class-map. (d) Specified seeds for construction soft class-map. (b) J values got from JSEG with soft class-map. (c) Segmentation result of JSEG with soft class-map.

generated with its spel's color components values varying from up to below as a ramp. Then a similar ramp was also added in background with different color components. Thirdly, the whole image was blurred by a Gaussian kernel. And, at last, a Gaussian noise was added to the whole image. Eleven reference classes were obtained by the color quantization in [2]. We can note JSEG in [1] can't segment correctly the regions in the image. The whole image is partitioned into 16 regions. In contrast, JSEG with soft class map provides much better result. Here we set the constant α for specifying seeds as 0.8, and p for determining the fuzzy degree of soft class-map as 1. We can know that, for soft class-map, the J values are not higher for the pixels near the boundaries of regions got from hard class-map and where there are obvious color smooth variations. For the boundaries where there is not color smooth variation, the J values are kept to be higher. Though much more reference classes have been given than the underlying regions, JSEG offers decent segmented results.

Through experiments on more than 150 color images, we found JSEG with soft class map can produce better results than the original JSEG algorithm for more than 93% of them. For JSEG with soft class map, the worse results are mostly caused by the heavy blurring near boundaries of underlying regions in image. One of the results by the method in this paper and the original JSEG [1] is presented in Fig. 3. Our method can easily segment the region of "arm" with excellent result and at the same time preserve the decent results of other regions.

References

1. Deng, Y., Manjunath, B.S.: Unsupervised segmentation of color-texture regions in images and video. IEEE Transactions on Pattern Analysis and Machine Intelligence. 23, 800-810, 2001.
2. Deng, Y., Kenney, C., Moore, M.S., Manjunath, B.S.: Peer group filtering and perceptual color image quantization. Proc. IEEE Int'l Symp Circuits and Systems. 4, 21-24, 1999.
3. Saha, P.K. Udupa, J.K.: Fuzzy connected object delineation: axiomatic path strength definition and the case of multiple seeds. Computer Vision and Image Understanding. 83, 275-295, 2001.
4. Udupa, J. K., Samarasekera, S.: Fuzzy connectedness and object definition: theory, algorithms, and applications in image segmentation. Graphical Models and Image Processing. 58, 246-261, 1996.
5. Karayiannis, N.B., Pai, P.-I.: Fuzzy vector quantization algorithms and their application in image compression. IEEE Transactions on Image Processing. 4, 1193–1201, 1995.
6. Marques. F., Kuo, C.-C.J.: Classified vector quantization using fuzzy theory. IEEE International Conference on Fuzzy Systems. 237–244, 1992.

DESCRY: A Density Based Clustering Algorithm for Very Large Data Sets

Fabrizio Angiulli, Clara Pizzuti, and Massimo Ruffolo

ICAR-CNR
c/o DEIS, Università della Calabria
87036 Rende (CS), Italy
{angiulli,pizzuti,ruffolo}@icar.cnr.it

Abstract. A novel algorithm, named *DESCRY*, for clustering very large multidimensional data sets with numerical attributes is presented. *DESCRY* discovers clusters having different shape, size, and density and when data contains noise by first finding and clustering a small set of points, called *meta-points*, that well depict the shape of clusters present in the data set. Final clusters are obtained by assigning each point to one of the partial clusters. The computational complexity of DESCRY is linear both in the data set size and in the data set dimensionality. Experiments show the very good qualitative results obtained comparable with those obtained by state of the art clustering algorithms.

1 Introduction

Clustering is a data analysis unsupervised technique that consists in partitioning large sets of data objects into homogenous groups [1,6]. All objects contained in the same group have similar characteristics, where similarity is computed using suitable coefficients. Generally, an object (tuple) is described by a set of d features (attributes) and it can be represented by a d-dimensional vector. Thus, if the data set contains N objects, it can be viewed as an $N \times d$ matrix. Rows of the matrix correspond to the objects and columns to the features. Each object can then be considered as a point in an d-dimensional space, where each of the d attributes is one of the axis of the space.

In this paper we present a novel algorithm, named *DESCRY*, that finds clusters having different shape, size, and density in very large high-dimensional data sets with numerical attributes and when data contains noise. The method combines hierarchical, density-based and grid-based approaches to clustering by exploiting the advantages of each of them. *DESCRY* considers clusters as dense regions of objects in the data space arbitrarily shaped and separated by regions of low density that represent noise. Given a data set D of N objects in the d-dimensional space, the number K of clusters to find, and the minimum number F of points that a region must contain to be considered dense, *DESCRY* finds the K most homogeneous groups of objects in D by first finding a small set of points, called *meta-points*, that well depict the shape of clusters present in the data set. To obtain the *meta-points* the search space is recursively divided into a finite number of non-overlapping rectangular regions. The partitioning process of each region continues until the number of points it contains is below the threshold value F. $DESCRY$ consists of four phases: sampling, partitioning, clustering and labelling. Sampling allows to efficiently manage very large data sets. Partitioning obtains the *meta-points*, well spread in the data space and representative of the clusters really present in the data set. Clustering groups the meta-points by using a hierarchical agglomerative clustering method and builds the partial clusters. Finally, labelling assigns each point to one of the partial clusters and obtains the final clusters. The computational complexity of DESCRY is linear both in the data set size and in the data set dimensionality, and qualitative results obtained are very good and comparable with those of state of the art clustering algorithms, as confirmed by the reported experimental results. The rest of the paper is organized as follows. Section 2 gives a detailed description of the DESCRY algorithm. Section 3 briefly surveys existing clustering methods related to DESCRY and points out the main differences with our approach. Finally, Section 4 shows the effectiveness of the proposed algorithm on some data sets.

2 The DESCRY Algorithm

In this section the $DESCRY$ algorithm is presented. Let D be a data set of N data points (or objects) in $\mathbb{R}^n$, the d-dimensional Euclidean space. We denote by I_D the minimum bounding rectangle (MRB) of D, that is $I_D = [[lb_1, up_1], \times, [lb_d, up_d]]$, where lb_i (ub_i) denotes the minimum (maximum) value of the i-th coordinate among the N points of D. Given the number K of clusters to find and the number F of points that a region of the data set must contain to be considered dense, we formulate the problem of finding K clusters in D as the problem of finding the K most homogeneous regions of I_D, according to a suitable similarity metrics. $DESCRY$ consists of four phases: sampling, partitioning, clustering and labelling. Next, we give a detailed description of the four steps composing the algorithm.

Sampling. A random *sample* S of n points is drawn from D. The Vitter's *Algorithm Z* [8] was used to extract S. The *Algorithm Z* performs the sampling in one pass over the data set, using constant space and time $\mathcal{O}(n(1+\log(\frac{N}{n})))$, where n denotes the size of the sample. This phase allows to efficiently manage very large data sets and performs a preliminary filtering of noise present in the data set.

Partitioning. The random sample S of size n, calculated in the sampling step, constitutes the input to the partitioning step. Partitioning consists in dividing the search space into a finite number of non-overlapping rectangular regions by selecting a dimension a and a value c in this dimension and splitting I_S (the MRB of S) using $(d-1)$-dimensional hyperplanes such that all the data points having a value in the split dimension smaller than the split value c are assigned to the first partition whereas the other data points form the second partition. Hyperplanes are parallel to the axes, and placed so that one finds about the same number of elements on both the sides. In order to efficiently partition the space

I_S, an *adaptive k-d-tree* [7] like data structure was used. The adaptive k-d-tree is a binary tree that represents a recursive subdivision of the space I_S in subspaces. Each node p of the k-d-tree has associated a set of points D_p. Initially, the tree consists of a single root node p, with D_p coinciding with the sample set S. The partitioning step consists in splitting points D_p, associated with a leaf node p of the k-d-tree, into two disjoint subsets D_q and D_r, associated with two new child nodes q and r of p, respectively. The splitting process continues until there exists a set of points D_p, associated with a leaf node p of the tree, such that $|D_p|$ is above the user-provided threshold F. The center of gravity of the points contained in each leaf node, called *meta-points*, are then computed and stored in an appropriate data structure. Meta-points constitute a small set of points well scattered (i.e. uniformly distributed) in the denser regions of the search space representative of the true clusters present in the data set. This phase mitigates the undesirable presence of bridges of outliers. Notice that the leaf nodes of the tree represent regions of I_S containing approximatively the same number F of points, though the distances among points contained in the same node can be very different with respect to those of other leaf nodes. Thus, the density of the data set in these regions can be considered inversely proportional to the volume of each region.

Clustering. The m meta-points $M_1, \ldots, M_m$, calculated in the partitioning step, constitute the input of the clustering step. The goal of the clustering step is to arrange the m meta-points into K homogeneous groups, or *partial clusters*, $C_1, \ldots, C_K$. The final clusters can be obtained from these partial clusters with a final step of labelling that assigns each point of the data set to the closest cluster, at a low cost. To perform clustering we used a *hierarchical agglomerative* clustering algorithm [4]. An agglomerative algorithm receives in input the number K of desired clusters and a set $M_1, \ldots, M_m$ of m points to group. Among the elements of the set $M_1, \ldots, M_m$ it must be defined a *similarity metrics* σ, i.e. a function $\sigma(M_i, M_j)$ returning a real number ($1 \leq i \leq j \leq m$). Each hierarchical agglomerative clustering algorithm is characterized by a different similarity metrics Σ on subsets of $M_1, \ldots, M_n$. Σ is formulated as a function of σ. Hierarchical agglomerative algorithms have all the same basic structure: first, assign each element $M_1, \ldots, M_m$ to its own cluster $C_1, \ldots, C_m$, respectively (call this set of clusters P); next, while the number of clusters is greater than K, choose the pair of clusters C_i, C_j of P scoring the maximum value of similarity $\Sigma(C_i, C_j)$, delete the clusters C_i and C_j from P, and add the new cluster $C_i \cup C_j$ to P. In general, hierarchical agglomerative clustering algorithms can be executed in time $\mathcal{O}(dm^2)$, for suitable choices of the similarity metrics. In the implementation of DESCRY we used the single linkage clustering algorithm [4], and the Euclidean distance between points as similarity metrics. In the single linkage algorithm the similarity $\Sigma(X, Y)$ between two sets of objects X and Y ($X, Y \subseteq M_1, \ldots, M_m$) is defined as follows: $\Sigma(X, Y) = \min\{\sigma(x, y) \mid x \in X, y \in Y\}$. The main advantage of this method is its fast computability (if the number of points is not large), because of its close relationship to the minimum spanning tree (MST) of the objects, ant its versatility, as it is able to extract, for example, concentric clusters. Nevertheless, usually the single linkage algorithm is adversely effected by the presence of "bridges" of outliers connecting two clusters. The partitioning step of the DESCRY algorithm greatly mitigates this undesirable effect, as experimental results confirm.

Labelling. During the labelling procedure each point of the original data set D is assigned to one of the partial K clusters. In particular, let p be a point of D, and let M_i ($1 \leq i \leq m$) be the meta-point closest to p. Then p is assigned with the label l, where C_l is the cluster to which M_i is assigned. This step requires a single scan of the data set, and can be performed in time $\mathcal{O}(N \log m)$, for low dimensional data sets, by storing the m meta-points in an appropriate data structure T, as k-d-tree or an R-tree, and then performing a nearest-neighbor query on T for each point of the data set, or in time $\mathcal{O}(Nmd)$, for high-dimensional data sets, by comparing each point of the data set with each meta-point.

2.1 Time and Space Complexity

Now we state the space and time complexity of the algorithm DESCRY. As for the space complexity, the algorithm needs $\mathcal{O}(nd)$ space to build the k-d-tree representing the partitioning of the sample S of n points. Meta-points require space $\mathcal{O}(md)$. Finally, the hierarchical agglomerative clustering can be performed using $\mathcal{O}(m)$ space. As $m = \frac{n}{F}$, then the space required by the algorithm is $\mathcal{O}(nd)$, i.e. it is linear in the size of the sample. We recall that the size of the input data set is $\mathcal{O}(Nd)$ and that $n \ll N$. The time required by DESCRY is the sum of the times required by the sampling, partitioning, pre-clustering, and labelling steps. The actual implementation of the sampling step requires time $\mathcal{O}(n(1+\log(\frac{N}{n})))$. The partitioning step requires time $\mathcal{O}(dn \log m)$. The pre-clustering step has time complexity $\mathcal{O}(dm^2)$, as we used a hierarchical agglomerative clustering algorithm. Finally, the labelling process has a complexity $O(Nmd)$. Thus, simplifying we obtain an overall time complexity $\mathcal{O}(Nmd)$. Furthermore, if we consider low dimensional data sets, or data sets with fixed dimensionality, the complexity reduces to $\mathcal{O}(N \log m)$, provided that $N \geq n \left(\log \frac{N}{n} / \log \frac{n}{F}\right)$. We point out that, when the size n of the random sample increases, for most data sets, the value of the population threshold F can be simultaneously increased without losing in clustering quality. Thus, the ratio $\frac{n}{F}$, i.e. the number of meta-points m to consider, can be considered a fixed constant. This leads to a final time complexity $\mathcal{O}(Nd)$, for high-dimensional data sets, or $\mathcal{O}(N)$, for low dimensional data sets, linearly related, by the small constant m or $\log m$, to the data set size N and to the data set dimensionality d. We can conclude that DESCRY is very fast, as it scales linearly both w.r.t. the size N and the dimensionality d of the data set, and that it outperforms existing clustering algorithms. We'll see in Section 4 that, despite its low time complexity, DESCRY guarantees a very good clustering quality.

3 Related Works

In the last few years a lot of efforts have been made to realize fast clustering algorithms for large data sets. Many surveys and books have been written on clustering [6, 4]. Clustering methods can be classified into four categories [3]: *partitioning method, hierarchical method, density-based method and grid-based method*. *DESCRY* combines hierarchical, density-based, and grid-based approaches by exploiting the advantages of each of them. Being a density-based method, it can discover clusters of arbitrary shape. *DESCRY* quantizes the space into a finite number of regions, like the grid-based approach, but the grid structure is not fixed in advance, it is dynamically built on the base of the random sample extracted from the data set. Because of the partitioning technique adopted, *DESCRY* can find clusters when the number of dimensions is high. Finally the utilization of a hierarchical agglomerative method on a small number of points, the meta-points, instead of the overall data set provides a very efficient and fast method for very large data sets. Among the widely known clustering algorithms, the most related to DESCRY are BIRCH [9] and CURE [2]. Next, we briefly survey these algorithms and put in evidence the main differences with our approach. BIRCH incrementally and dynamically groups incoming multi-dimensional metric data points to try to produce the best quality clustering with the available resources and with a single scan of the data. The algorithm makes use of a new data structure, the CF tree, whose elements are *Clustering Features*, i.e. short summaries representing a cluster. The radius of the clusters associated with the leaf nodes, representing a partitioning of the data set, has to be less than a threshold T. After the building of the CF tree, the clusters associated with the leaf nodes of the tree are clustered by an agglomerative hierarchical clustering algorithm using a distance metrics. The following main differences between DESCRY and BIRCH can be depicted: BIRCH works on the entire data set, while DESCRY performs sampling; the partitioning of BIRCH is introduced in order to obtain small clusters, i.e. regions of the space of bounded diameter, while DESCRY partitions the space in equally populated regions; BIRCH labels data sets points using the centroid of the clusters obtained, and if the clusters are not spherical in shape then BIRCH does not perform well because it uses the notion of radius to control the boundary of a cluster, while DESCRY uses all the meta-points belonging to the pre-clusters obtained, thus its clusters are arbitrarily shaped. CURE identifies clusters having non-spherical shapes and wide variance in size. It achieves this by representing each cluster with a certain fixed number of points that are generated by selecting well scattered points from the cluster, and then shrinking them toward the center of the cluster by a user-specified fraction. The algorithm (a) obtains a random sample of the data set, (b) partitions the sample into a set of partitions or disjoint samples, (c) performs a preclustering of the samples using the BIRCH algorithm, (d) eliminate outliers, (e) clusters the preclusters, and (e) assigns each data set point to one of the final clusters obtained. The clustering is performed using an agglomerative procedure that works on *representative* points, i.e. each cluster is represented by c points uniformly distributed over the cluster. When two clusters are merged, the representative points of the new cluster are recalculated and then shrunk toward the mean, by a fraction α, to dampen the effects of outliers. CURE partitions the sample in a set of partitions, clusters each partition by using BIRCH and

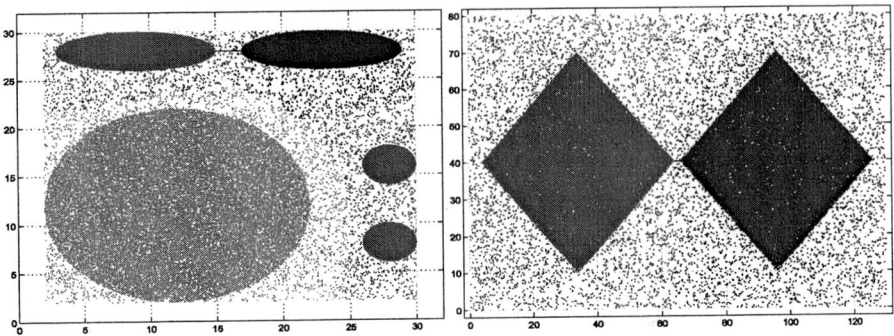

Fig. 1. Data sets DS1 and DS2, and clusters found by DESCRY

obtains the representative points of each partial cluster, $DESCRY$ partitions the sample in a finite number of non-overlapping rectangular regions in order to obtains *meta-points*, but it does not cluster the sample. $CURE$ considers outliers the partial clusters that grows too slowly, removes them and performs again clustering on the partial clusters, $DESCRY$ directly clusters *meta-points* to obtain partial clusters and outliers are automatically removed during the partitioning step. The computational complexity of CURE is quadratic w.r.t. the data set size, while DESCRY depends linearly on the data set size.

4 Experimental Results

In this section we report the results of some experiments performed with DESCRY. In these experiments, we considered the two synthetic data sets shown in Figure 1, that we call DS1 and DS2. DS1 is a data set described in [2], consisting of 100,000 two dimensional points, grouped in 5 clusters of different size, density and shape. DS2 is a data set described in [5], consisting of 100,000 two dimensional points, grouped in 2 non-spherical clusters. Both DS1 and DS2 are characterized by the presence of outliers and of bridges linking two different clusters. Figure 1 shows also the clusters reported by DESCRY when the sample size n has been set to 2500, and the population threshold F has been set to $F_1 = 35$ for DS1 and $F_2 = 20$ for DS2. As the figure show, the clustering quality of DESCRY is very good. In Figure 2 are depicted the meta-points resulting from the partitioning step on these two data sets. We can observe that the meta-points depicts very well the shape of the clusters. We also studied how the clustering quality is affected by the choice of the population threshold F, varying this value in a suitable neighborhood of F_1 and F_2, respectively. These experiments show that DESCRY is little sensitive to suitable variations of the parameter F. We do not report these experiments, due to space limitations.

To show how the algorithm scales w.r.t. the sample size n, we report in Figure 3 the execution times (in milliseconds[1]) of DESCRY on DS1, obtained

---

[1] We implemented the DESCRY algorithm using the Java programming language and we ran the experiments on a machine with an AMD Athlon 4 processor at 1.2MHz and 256MB of main memory.

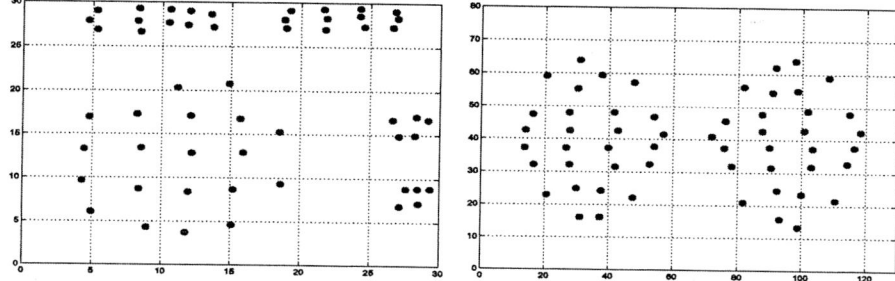

Fig. 2. Meta-Points of DS1 and DS2

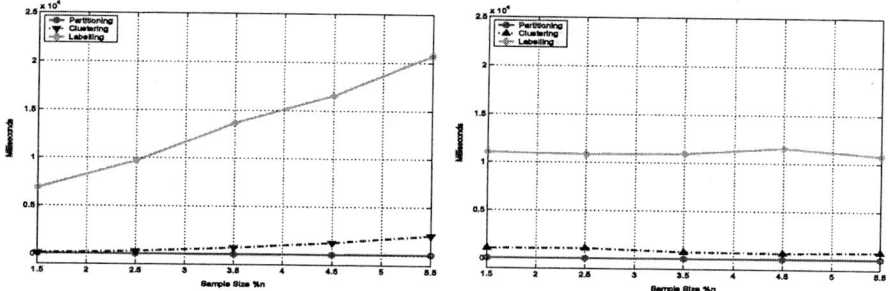

Fig. 3. Execution time of DESCRY on DS1 as a function of the sample size n when F is fixed (on the left) or $\frac{n}{F}$ is fixed (on the right)

varying n from 1500 to 5500, and maintaining F fixed to $F_1 = 35$ (on the left), while in the figure on the right the ratio $\frac{n}{F}$ is fixed to 75. The figure on the left shows that, when F is fixed, the execution time is practically constant for the partitioning step, and that it grows linearly for the pre-clustering and labelling steps. The figure on the right points out that, if the ratio $\frac{n}{F}$ is fixed, increasing the sample does not increase the execution times of the algorithms. Finally we studied the behavior of the algorithm when the number of dimensions increases. Figure 4 shows that also in this case the partitioning and pre-clustering steps the execution time is constant, and for the labelling step it grows linearly.

5 Conclusions

This paper described a new method, named DESCRY, to identify clusters in large high dimensional data set having different size and shape. The algorithm is parametric w.r.t. the agglomerative method used in the pre-clustering step and the similarity metrics σ of interest. DESCRY has a very low computational complexity, indeed it requires $\mathcal{O}(Nmd)$ time, for high-dimensional data sets, and $\mathcal{O}(N \log m)$ time, for low dimensional data sets, where m can be considered a constant characteristic of the data set. Thus DESCRY scales linearly both

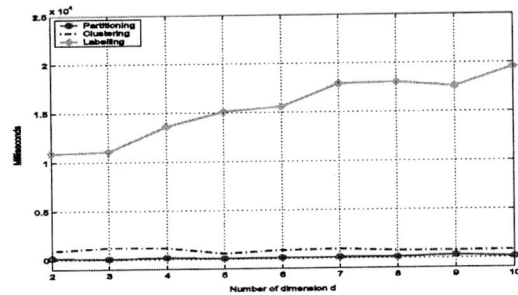

Fig. 4. Execution time of DESCRY on DS1 for increasing dimension

w.r.t. the size and the dimensionality of the data set. Despite its low complexity, qualitative results are very good and comparable with those obtained by state of the art clustering algorithms. Future work includes, among other topics, the investigation of similarity metrics particularly meaningful in high-dimensional spaces, exploiting summaries extracted from the regions associated to metapoints.

References

1. R.C. Dubes A.K. Jain. *Algorithms for Clustering Data*. Prentice Hall, 1988.
2. S. Guha, R. Rastogi, and K. Shim. Cure: An efficient clustering algorithm for large databases. In *Proceedings of the ACM SIGMOD Int. Conf. on Managment of Data*, pages 73–84, New York, May 1998.
3. J. Han and M. Kamber. *Data Mining- Concepts and Techniques*. Morgan Kaufman, 2001.
4. A. K. Jain, M. N. Murty, and P. J. Flynn. Data clustering: a review. *ACM Computing Surveys*, 31(3):264–323, 1999.
5. G. Karypis, S. Han, and V. Kumar. Chameleon: Hierarchical clustering using dynamic modeling. *IEEE Computer*, pages 65–75, 1999.
6. L. Kaufman and P.J. Rousseew. *Finding Groups in Data: an Introduction to Cluster Analysis*. John Wiley & Sons, 1990.
7. H. Samet. The quadtree and related hierarchical data structures. *ACM Computing Surveys*, 16(2):187–260, 1984.
8. J. Vitter. Random sampling with a reservoir. *ACM Transaction on Mathematical Software*, 11(1):37–57, 1985.
9. T. Zhang, R. Ramakrishnan, and M. Livny. Birch: An efficient data clustering method for very large databases. In *Proceedings of the ACM SIGMOD Int. Conf. on Managment of Data*, pages 103–114, june 1996.

A Fuzzy Set Based Trust and Reputation Model in P2P Networks

Zhang Shuqin[1], Lu Dongxin[2], and Yang Yongtian[1]

[1] College of Computer Science and Technology, Harbin Engineering University
Harbin 150001,China
zsqheu@yahoo.com.cn, yangyt8@hotmail.com
[2] Technology Center Chengdu Institute, ZTE corporation, Chengdu 610041, China
lu.dongxin@zte.com.cn

Abstract. Trust plays an important role in making collaborative decisions, so the trust problem in P2P networks has become a focus of research. In this paper, a fuzz set based model is proposed for building trust and reputation in P2P collaborations based on observations and recommendations, and using fuzzy set a peer can present differentiated trust and combine different aspects of trust in collaborations. Depending on fuzzy similarity measure, a good recommenders set can be maintained. The evaluation of the model using simulation experiments shows its effectiveness.

1 Introduction

Peer-to-Peer (P2P) computation architecture facilitates how the network is moving toward many-to-many interactions. However, the open and dynamic nature in P2P networks has brought much more risks. Recently, some literatures propose to model trust mechanisms among people for ensuring the reliable P2P collaborations with good peers and to protect them from offending ones.

Due to lack of sufficient knowledge in P2P collaborations, it is difficult to express trust or distrust in collaborators precisely, what's more, trust evaluation usually depends on principal's subjective judgments, so fuzzy set theory [1] has been attempted to deal with trust. For example, TangW. [2] gives formalized valuation of subjective trust, the definition of trust class, and presents the derivation rules of trust relationships, etc; Ramchurn. S. D. [3] develops a trust model for Multi-Agent Interactions based on confidence and reputation, which uses fuzzy set for evaluating past interactions and establishing new contracts with one another. In this paper, a fuzzy set based trust and reputation model is proposed, which gives peers a robust means of assessing trust in their collaborative partners, and simulation experiments to test the model's performance are developed in the later part.

2 Fuzzy Set-Based Trust Evaluation

Trust in collaborators is the firm belief in the competence and other aspects in collaborations to act as expected, which is subject to the cooperative behaviors of the collaborator and applies only within a specific collaboration context. In general, the approach to estimate the trust in other peers needs to review one's experiences and aggregate the opinions of other peers, which is called reputation that is the trust information propagated among peers, so the total trust value of a target peer in particular collaboration context can be computed as following:

$$T_{total} = \alpha \cdot DT + (1-\alpha) \cdot R \qquad 0 < \alpha < 1 \qquad (1)$$

where T_{total} is the total trust value for a particular collaborator, DT is the direct trust value, and R is the reputation value, and α represents the importance proportion of direct trust to the total trust.

2.1 Direct Trust Evaluation in Collaborations

The linguistic labels which constitute a set represented as $\mathcal{L}=\{L1, L2, L3, \ldots\}$, such as $\{high, average, low\}$, can be used to describe different trust levels, and provide a means of approximate characterization of trust degree, which are too complex or too ill-defined to be amenable to description in conventional quantitative terms. Each linguistic label L is associated with a fuzzy set whose membership function m_L gives the degree of membership to linguistic label L, and the trust value $T(m_{L1}, m_{L2}, m_{L3}, \ldots)$ is a fuzzy vector, each element of which represents the degree of membership to the trust level L.

Statistical methods are used to determine the degree of membership in the fuzzy sets associated with linguistic labels. In each aspect, the degree of membership m_L can be defined as the percentage of collaborations assessed at L, and measured by the number of such collaborations, k, divided by the total number of collaborations, n.

$$m_L = \frac{k}{n} \qquad (2)$$

For example, only considering the three linguistic labels, "high", "average" and "low", the trust value $(p/(p+q+r), q/(p+q+r), r/(p+q+r))$ reflects the evaluation result on these collaborations with a particular collaborator.

As discussed above, trust in collaborators can be examined from different aspects, such as competence, response etc. For each aspect, the trust value can be described by using the same linguistic labels set, so the direct trust combining the trust value for these aspects can be computed as following:

$$DT = W \cdot M = (w_1, w_2, \cdots, w_n) \cdot \begin{bmatrix} m_{11} & m_{12} & \cdots & m_{1l} \\ m_{21} & m_{22} & \cdots & m_{2l} \\ & & & \\ m_{n1} & m_{n2} & \cdots & m_{nl} \end{bmatrix} \quad (3)$$

where W is the weight vector for these aspects, which reflects the importance of each aspect considered in the direct trust, and the sum of these weights is 1; element m_{ij} in the matrix M represents the degree of membership for the aspect $A_i (i=1, 2, ..., n)$ with respect to trust level L_j ($j=1, 2, ..., l$); every row in M is the trust vector for one aspect, so the direct trust value of a collaborator can be represented as a fuzzy vector $DT = w_c \cdot V_c + w_r \cdot V_r + w_s \cdot V_s$, which combines the three trust vectors V_c, V_r, and V_s, for "*competence*", "*response*" and "*stability*", respectively, and corresponding weight vector is $W=(w_c, w_r, w_s)$.

After collaboration a peer assigns a trust level described by linguistic label in every aspect concerned. Through gathering the historical assignments, the degree of membership to every trust level m in each aspect can be computed with the formula (2). Then, together with the predefined weight vector W for these aspects, the direct trust in the collaborator can be computed with formula (3).

3 Computing Comprehensive Reputation

Reputation, another important information source for the total trust in P2P collaborations, is the trust propagated among peers, the computation of which is in a distributed way, so the reputation networks are defined for delivering reputation information.

3.1 Reputation Networks

Reputation network, as seen in Figure 1, is P2P network to deliver reputation information among peers, in which, RMs are the peers responsible for collecting and processing recommendation information from other peers, and publishing reputation of a particular peer. Other peers can get reputation from RMs, also take charge of providing RMs with recommendations based on their experiences or interaction records with other collaborative partners, so RMs can sum up received recommendations to acquire the reputations of target peers.

A peer's recommendation can be represented as <*rv, tp, sp*> which means that peer *sp* gives the recommendation value *rv*; and a comprehensive reputation <*cr, tp*> which is derived from peers' recommendations, denotes that reputation value *cr* of peer *tp*.

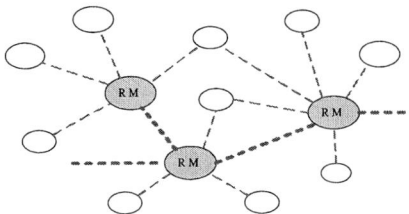

Fig. 1. Reputation Networks. Peers maintained by a RM report recommendations actively, at the same time, a RM can also multicast questionnaires among its members for peers' reputations, or request other RMs for help. According to the recommendations from others a RM can calculate the comprehensive reputation of a specific peer.

3.2 Handling Recommendations

Considering that different peers may provide diverse recommendations about the same peer, a weighted approach is adopted to compute a peer's comprehensive reputation. In computing the comprehensive reputation, the information associated with the peers acting as recommenders is kept in RMs' Recommendation Tables (RTs), which contains recommenders' recommendations of peers, as well as the weights assigned to them. The comprehensive reputation value is computed as following:

$$CR = \sum_{i=1}^{n} \frac{w_i}{S} \cdot RV_i \qquad (4)$$

where CR denotes the comprehensive reputation value of a target peer, RV_i denotes the recommendation value given by peer i; w_i denotes the weight for the recommender i; n denotes the number of peers who give recommendations on the target peer for this time; S is the sum of weights for these recommenders.

3.3 Adjustment of Weight

The weights for recommenders can be tuned up or down through detecting the accuracies of their recommendations: weights assigned to the recommenders who give more accurate recommendations should be increased, and weights assigned to those who give deceptive recommendations should be decreased [4]. In this way, recommenders may have different impacts on the comprehensive reputations.

Here a peer's recommendation accuracy is formally defined as the degree of similarity between the individual recommendation and the comprehensive reputation computed from the current recommendations. Let the comprehensive reputation be $CR\{cr_{L1}, cr_{L2}, cr_{L3}, ...\}$, and recommendation given by peer i be $R_i\{r_{L1}, r_{L2}, r_{L3}, ...\}$, then according to the similarity measure based on Minkowski's distance, the similarity S_i for peer i is computed as following:

$$S_i = Similarity\ (R_i, CR) = 1 - \frac{\sum_{k=1}^{n}|r_{L_k} - cr_{L_k}|}{n} \qquad (5)$$

Due to the accuracy changes of the recommendations from peers, their weights should be updated dynamically to reflect those changes. Furthermore, to prevent a few peers from dominating the overall computation results, an upper limit w_u can be set for weights, so a weight is updated as follows:

$$w_i' = \begin{cases} w_u & (1+\theta(S_i)) \cdot w_i > w_u \\ 0 & (1+\theta(S_i)) \cdot w_i < 0 \\ (1+\theta(S_i)) \cdot w_i & otherwise \end{cases} \qquad (6)$$

where the monotonic increasing function θ should ensure the stabilities of the average weight. With formula (6) RMs can update the weights for corresponding recommenders after each computation of comprehensive reputation.

4 Experiments

To evaluate the trust and reputation model proposed in this paper, the experiment system developed in Java simulates collaborations and reputations networks among with 1000 peers and 10 RMs. For simplicity, one peer randomly selects one RM. Most peers are assigned as collaborators/recommenders, and lesser are the target peers, trust and reputation about whom are examined. In every cycle of collaboration these collaborators randomly collaborate with target peers, and collaborators can give their recommendations on the target peer based on the target peer's collaborative behaviors, so RM can compute the comprehensive reputation about the target peer.

In experiments, two collaborative strategies for target peers are predefined in collaborations: good, bad, which means the cooperativeness that is most probably provided for collaborative partners. As a recommender these collaborators may give two types of recommendations: normal and dishonest. Normal means reporting directly the true estimation, while dishonest means reporting altered dramatically trust evaluation. Here three linguistic labels are used to represent different trust levels: *"high"*, *"average"*, *"low"*, and θ function in formula (6) is defined as following:

$$\theta(S) = \frac{S - C}{10} \qquad (7)$$

where the threshold C is the average similarity of all current recommendations.

4.1 Results

Results of experiments are shown in Figures 2-3. In Fig.2 the reputations of peers with different collaborative strategies are shown, and the experiment result proves that the proposed model runs well in representing peer's behavior. In Fig.3, based on the weight changes for different type of recommenders, the deceptive recommenders can be detected.

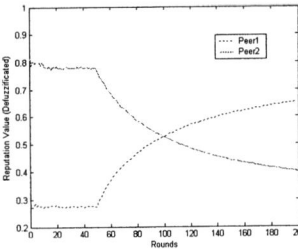
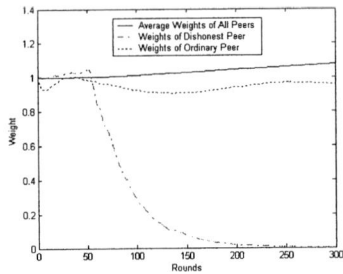

Fig. 2. Simulation result for reputations of peers with different collaborate strategies. The collaborative strategies of the two target peers: peer1 and peer2 are initially good, bad, respectively. At cycle 50, peer1 switches from bad to good, and its reputation curve ascends, but peer2 switches from good to bad, and its reputation curve descends (To obtain a crisp value in the form of coordinates, a de-fuzzification formula $r=m_{high}+0.5*m_{average}+0.2*m_{low}$ is subjectively used for representing the reputation values.).

Fig. 3. Simulation result for weight changes of pees. At the randomly selected RM three weights curves are showed: average weights curve of all recommenders, weights curve of a dishonest recommenders, and weights curve of an ordinary recommender. At cycle 50, the dishonest peer begins to give the deceptive recommendations. The weight curve of ordinary peer fluctuates irregularly, but the weight of dishonest peer has been dropping since cycle 50, so its importance on the comprehensive reputation becomes less.

5 Conclusions

In this paper, a fuzzy set-based trust and reputation model is proposed to build the trust of collaborators in P2P networks. Fuzzy set theory provides an appropriate method to present the fuzzy linguistic descriptors for trust and combine different aspects of trust, but in the model proposed by Wang Y. [5] the probability method is used to represent different aspects of the collaborator's capability. Through the reputation networks, the comprehensive reputations of peers can be formed based on recommendations from recommenders, furthermore, by adjusting weights for recommenders according to the accuracies of them, deceptive recommenders can be easily detected.

The results of the simulation experiments show that the proposed model is able to reflect trust and reputation of collaborators based on their behaviors, and detect dishonest peers who give the deceptive recommendations based on changes of weights.

The model has room for further improvements, for example, the process of indirect recommendations, the adjustments of weights for experienced and non-experienced recommenders are still to be tackled. In future, trust evaluation scheme and the way to computing comprehensive reputation will be improved for better performance.

References

1. Zadeh LA: The Concept of a Linguistic Variable and Its Application to Approximate Reasoning. Beijing: Science Press, (1982) 23~33 (in Chinese)
2. Tang W.,Chen Z.: Research of Subjective Trust Management Model Based on the Fuzzy Set Theory. Chinese Journal of Software, Vol.14 (8) (2003) 1401~1408
3. Ramchurn. S. D., Sierra, C., Godo, L. and Jennings, N. R.: A Computational Trust Model for Multi-Agent Interactions Based on Confidence and Reputation. Proc. of 6th Intl. Workshop of Deception, Fraud and Trust in Agent Societies, (2003) 69-75
4. Bin Yu and Munindar P. Singh: Detecting Deception in Reputation Management. Proc. of 2nd Intl. Joint Conf. on Autonomous Agents and Multi-Agent Systems, (2003) 73-80
5. Wang Y., Vassileva J.: Bayesian Network-Based Trust Model in Peer-to-Peer Networks. Proc. of 6th Intl. Workshop of Deception, Fraud and Trust in Agent Societies, (2003) 372-378

Video Based Human Behavior Identification Using Frequency Domain Analysis

Jessica JunLin Wang and Sameer Singh

ATR Lab, Computer Science Department, School of Engineering
Computer Science and Mathematics, Harrison Building, University of Exeter
{J.Wang,S.Singh}@ex.ac.uk

Abstract. The identification of human activity in video, for example whether a person is walking, clapping, waving, etc. is extremely important for video interpretation. Since different people would perform the same action across different number of frames, matching training and test actions is not a trivial task. In this paper we discuss a new technique for video shot matching where the shots matched are of different sizes. The proposed technique is based on frequency domain analysis of feature data and it is shown to achieve very high recognition accuracy on a number of different human actions with synthetic data and real life data.

1 Introduction

Human activity recognition from video streams has a wide range of applications such as human-machine interaction, security surveillance, choreography, content-based retrieval, sport, biometric applications, etc. In our work, we distinguish between two main categories of actions: *passive action* e.g. sit and do nothing, or thinking, or turning the head to follow someone across the room (watch the world go by); and *active action* e.g. waving, clapping (repetitive actions), or lifting, reading (non-repetitive actions). These actions can be performed with the person sitting or standing. Our aim is to develop a machine learning system that uses training data on different actions (performed by a number of subjects) to automatically classify (identify) actions in test videos.

The main problem with matching training and test video shots (a shot is a sequence of video frames) is that each shot is of a different length and exact matching is impossible. For example, consider two people waving in two different videos. This action in the first video v_1, say, takes L1 frames and this action in the second video v_2 takes L2 frames. In addition, these actions would most likely start at different times in their corresponding shots since there might be some random action in some frames. Hence it is not trivial to solve the problem: "Given: videos v_1 and v_2 that have been pre-processed to have shots: $v_1 = (a_1, a_2, ..., a_n)$ and $v_2 = (b_1, b_2, ..., b_n)$. The video v_1 is training video, with shot a_i ground truthed as "waving" and v_2 is test video.

Problem: Match all shots of v_2 with a_i to confirm if any of them are "waving". This will be based on a measure of similarity. The problem of speed variation is however more difficult. In most real cases the same activity is performed with different speed and acceleration by different people (Fig. 1). The solution to such a problem requires a complex search for the optimum match with various sequence lengths and phase shifts.

In order to understand the matching process, one needs to understand two important concepts: phase shift þ and sequence length L. Consider matching two video shots $a = (x_1, x_2, ..., x_N)$ and $b = (y_1, y_2, ..., y_M)$. The matching process is aimed at matching different sub-strings of a with those of b systematically. If $M<N$, then L can be varied between 1...M. For a chosen value of L, the phase shift þ can be varied between 0 and N-L times. When the string a is phase shifted by þ1 for a given value of L, and the string b is phase shifted by þ2 then the sub-strings matched are $a = (x_{1+þ1}, x_2, ..., x_{þ1+L})$ with $b = (y_{1+þ2}, y_2, ..., y_{þ2+L})$.

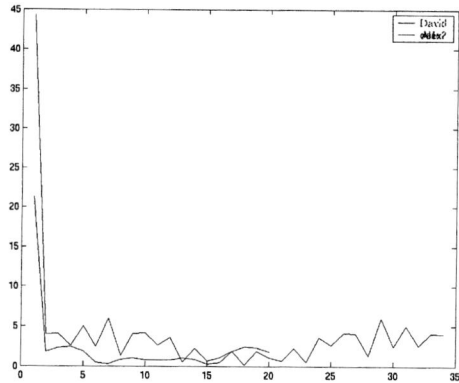

Fig. 1. A plot showing that the same action can be performed by two different people over different lengths of time.

2 Previous Research

The problem of video shot matching has been tackled in the past with a view to video retrieval. For the purposes of video retrieval, only key frames rather than all frames are used for matching. However, there has been limited effort at solving this problem for understanding human dynamics. This problem is slightly different since we need to match all frames within a shot rather than a set of disjoint key frames.

There are three mentionable solutions to the problem of matching two video sequences (either a set of key frames or a continuous set of frames) discussed by Kim and Park [3], Ben-Arie et al. [1], and Duda and Hart [2]. We briefly discuss them here.

In Kim and Park's approach [3] for matching video sequences, they first extract the key frames. Then modified Hausdorff distance is used to evaluate the similarity between two sets of key frames. In Ben-Arie *et al.*'s approach [1], they describe human activity as a temporal sequence of pose vectors that represent sampled poses of body parts. Multi-dimensional indexing is used to represent angles and angular velocities of each body part. For all 9 body parts votes are accumulated and the voting is done only on a few representative frames which are sparsely sampled from the test video sequence. It is also possible to use edit-distances [2] for matching video sequences. A number of statistical features can be extracted from each video frame that are then recoded as discrete alphabets, where each alphabet represents an interval within the overall min-max range of that feature. A single frame is then represented as a multidimensional vector (string) of alphabets, and a video sequence can be represented as a one dimensional vector of multidimensional vectors (string of strings). The process of matching is now based on calculating the cost of transforming one string into another and the best match is based on the least cost. And Finally, correlation and Fourier transform techniques can be used to detect cycles in 2D trajectories created by points on a moving object [5]. The trajectories are represented as two 1D trajectories, namely speed and direction, and are considered as a spatio-temporal curve in (x,y,t) space. The cyclic motions (e.g walking motions) are detected by finding cycles in the curvature of the spatio-temporal curve. The detected cycles are then applied to a method proposed by Rangarajan *et al.* [4] for matching paris of single trajectories. Only one complete cycle of the trajectory is used as model and only one cycle of the input trajectory is used for matching.

Unfortunately, all of the above approaches assume that there is no speed variation, i.e. the strings that are matched will be of the same length in terms of number of frames. In this paper we propose a frequency based analysis solution to this problem. This approach is detailed in the next section.

3 Data for Analysis

We use both synthetic and real data for analysis as described in sections 3.1 and 3.2.

3.1 Video Sequences (Synthetic)

The use of stick figures is common in research involving human dynamics. The use of stick figures allows us to create a range of human actions with variable complexity. In our experiments we generate a number of synthetic video sequences based on stick figures. Each stick figure comprises of the following important features of the human body (face, left arm, right arm, left leg and right leg). Most human actions can be created by varying the positions of these body parts with time in a well-defined manner. The videos so constructed closely resemble the true-life situation. In a real video, preprocessing steps of face detection and hand detection based on skin analysis, coupled with motion analysis (feature based tracking) can be used to identify the coordinates of the centroid of these regions. The advantage of using stick figures is that such information need not be extracted using a tedious procedure and can be easily extracted from a stick figure video. There is no doubt that any successful technique on such data can be easily transferred with on real data.

We generated video data of 8 different human actions based on the real-life actions captured on video: standing, turning head, thinking, clapping, waving, walking (including out of sight completely), lifting and reading. These actions are simulated using stick figures [4]. For each action set, we created between 6-9 training sequences which gives us 51 training sequences and 33936 fourier subsequences for training; between 2-3 testing sequence of different length which gives us 17 testing sequence and 5977 fourier subsequences for testing.

Each sequence in an action set of the training and testing data, will either have different phase shift from each other, or will have speed variation with/without random variation to different body parts. Random variation is introduced by adding small random movements to body parts such that videos of two different people doing the same action do not exactly match.

3.2 Video Sequences (Real Life Data)

The experiments on the real life data are on actions performed sitting down. There are 7 actions performed including *sitting, turning head, thinking, clapping, waving, drinking* and *reading*. There are 174 sequences and we use 4-fold cross-validation on the data set, i.e. select a different 25% of the sequences for testing and 75% for training four times and average the results.

Our real-life sequences are more complicated than the synthetic sequences, each sequence in the same action set is performed slightly different from each other, which could have different phase shift and/or speed variation and/or random variation from each other.

4 Frequency Domain Approach to Matching and Experimental Results

In our proposed approach, we apply Fourier energy-based approach to solve the problem of recognising activities in video sequences. The Fourier transform, in essence, decomposes or separates a waveform or function into sinusoids of different frequency which sum to the original waveform. It identifies or distinguishes the different frequency sinusoids and their respective amplitudes. The main idea is perform classification on Fourier rather than raw features. The computation of the raw and Fourier features is described in the next section.

4.1 Feature Extraction

We extracted 11 raw features $f_1, \ldots, f_{11}$ from each frame in a video sequence, where f_1, f_2 are $\Delta x, \Delta y$, the difference of the x, y coordinates of the head region centroid from the previous frame to the current frame; feature f_3 is $\Delta \theta$ the difference of the movement/angle (measure in radian) of the head region from previous frame to the current frame (for stick figures the angles are calculated in a straightforward manner, however, for videos containing real humans this may be based on the relative change in position of major/minor axis of the best fitting ellipse around the face or arm); feature f_4 is $\Delta\theta$ the difference of the movement/angle of the left-arm region from previous frame to the current frame; feature f_5 is $\Delta\theta$ the difference of the movement/angle of right-arm region from the previous frame to the current frame; f_6, f_7 is w_1, w_2 the window position of the head region in the current frame; features f_8, f_9 are w_3, w_4, the window position of the left-arm region in the current frame; features f_{10}, f_{11} are w_5, w_6, the window position of the right-arm region in the current frame. The window position of each region is calculated by sub-dividing each image into 9 windows (in sequence, left to right, their positions are: (1,1), (2,1), (3,1), (1,2), (2,2), (3,2), (1,3), (2,3) and (3,3).

Hence, for each frame we get a feature vector of size 11. Let us denote this feature vector for frame i as $(f_{1i}, f_{2i}, ..., f_{11i})$. If the size of the sequence is N frames, then for the same feature j, $1 \leq j \leq 11$, the vector of measurements across N frames is given by $f_j = (f_{j1}, f_{j2}, ..., f_{jN})$. We applied WFT (Windowed Fourier Transform) to this vector, which calculates Fourier values on combinations of different number of frames across the sequence, ranging from 5 to the total number of frames in the sequence, represented as vector f_M, where M is the number of combinations across the sequence. This vector f then can be simply plotted as a two-dimensional image F of size $M \times M$ (by keeping all rows the same value). From a given image F, we can extract 5 Fourier features $(\mathfrak{I}1, \mathfrak{I}2, \mathfrak{I}3, \mathfrak{I}4, \mathfrak{I}5)$. If the image is divided into 5 concentric rings then the first feature corresponds to the total energy within the first ring of the Fourier spectrum, and so on. We next describe the sequence matching algorithm.

4.2 Sequence Matching Process Algorithm

Given: test strings $(a_1, a_2, ..., a_n)$ and training strings $(b_1, b_2, ..., b_m)$. All training strings are ground-truthed (they have a class label).
Objective: The aim is to allocate each test string to a class.
  Now the algorithm to do this is as follows:

1. Start with the first test string a_1. We first match its substrings with training substrings of b_1 (of different lengths and phase shifts), Each time we get a similarity score based on Euclidean distance of features (raw or Fourier). The overall distance must be normalised (divided by the size of the string).
2. Plot a graph with the x-axis being the size of the substring matched and y-axis is the normalized Euclidean distance. Find the area under the curve as $\phi(a_1, b_1)$.

3. Similarly determine all $\phi(a_1, b_j)$, for $1 \leq j \leq m$. The class of a_1 is the class of the b_j for which $\phi(a_1, b_j)$ is maximum for $1 \leq j \leq m$. Similarly allocate the class for test strings $(a_2, ..., a_n)$.

5 Experiments and Results

We discuss our results on synthetic data in section 5.1 and real data in section 5.2.

5.1 Synthetic Data

The result of our experiment is shown in Table 1. The actions are labeled as follows: Standing (S), Turning head (Th), Thinking (Ti), Clapping (C), Waving (Wv), Walking (Wk), Lifting (L) and Reading (R). For a total of 17 test sequences, we find the dissimilarity between them and the set of training sequences of each class. As Table 3 shows, the diagonal values in this dissimilarity matrix are the least (compared to other values in the same row), giving us a 100% correct allocation of test strings to their true classes (AC-Allocated Class; TC-True Class).

Table 1. Dissimilarity Matrix (each value represents the measurement ϕ of test sequence (column1) and the training sequences of known classes (row1)). Column2 is the true class of the test string and column11 is the predicted class of the test string.

Test Data	TC	S	Th	Ti	C	Wv	Wk	L	R	AC
S1	1	0.00	37.21	31.86	91.98	93.81	43.44	97.55	99.45	1
S2	1	0.00	37.21	31.86	91.98	93.81	43.44	97.55	99.45	1
Th1	2	384.95	30.02	77.31	157.71	158.26	124.66	160.01	161.20	2
Th2	2	614.89	32.73	614.90	614.89	614.89	614.89	614.90	614.90	2
Ti1	3	139.39	25.47	22.31	55.59	56.03	65.98	57.80	58.53	3
Ti2	3	139.40	25.47	22.31	55.59	56.03	65.98	57.47	58.53	3
C1	4	824.17	104.60	26.89	1.80	9.90	122.36	24.36	31.53	4
C2	4	824.17	104.60	26.87	1.83	9.91	122.36	24.36	31.53	4
Wv1	5	1976.16	239.43	409.57	51.66	11.17	234.65	46.28	61.47	5
Wv2	5	1976.20	239.42	409.52	51.51	11.22	234.67	46.27	61.46	5
Wk1	6	7720.18	1753.76	4443.86	2711.28	1332.22	296.07	1665.67	1514.62	6
Wk2	6	7720.36	1754.49	4444.05	2711.47	1332.11	295.76	1665.76	1514.68	6
Wk3	6	7714.77	1751.78	4430.68	2704.86	1335.16	310.86	1668.24	1519.46	6
L1	7	1357.37	192.33	163.10	37.22	22.82	190.04	3.01	15.32	7
L2	7	1357.36	192.32	163.11	37.21	22.81	190.05	3.01	15.33	7
R1	8	853.37	138.64	67.72	32.10	23.54	144.95	11.14	1.01	8
R2	8	853.37	138.64	67.72	32.10	23.54	144.95	11.14	1.01	8

5.2 Real Life Data

The result of our real life data is shown in Table 2 below. The classes are labeled as follows: Sitting (C1), Turning head (C2), Thinking (C3), Clapping (C4), Waving (C5), Drinking (C6) and Reading (C7). The table shows the result of using different combinations of training and testing sequences (trials or folds) and the result of reducing the number of classes to recognize. We find that if we use all classes for classification, the results are not very good (on average 56.1%). This is because some classes are particularly hard to identify (e.g. confusion between Drinking and Thinking). However, as the classification is done on a reduced set of classes the results rapidly increase as shown in Table 2. For each fold, we successively remove the difficult classes (in Table 2, ¬C denotes the class removed from analysis) and calculate the recognition rate. Different classes are removed from different folds as the quality of training is different depending on which samples are present in that fold.

Table 2. Real life data classification result.

# of Classes Left	Fold 1 ¬C	Fold 1 CR %	Fold 2 ¬C	Fold 2 CR %	Fold 3 ¬C	Fold 3 CR %	Fold 4 ¬C	Fold 4 CR %	Average result %
7		56.10		63.41		56.10		48.78	56.10
6	C5	63.89	C4	66.67	C5	63.89	C3	57.58	63.10
5	C2	70.97	C5	70.97	C6	67.74	C4	64.29	68.49
4	C6	69.23	C6	76.92	C2	69.23	C6	69.57	71.24
3	C7	75.00	C3	83.33	C4	71.43	C1	81.25	77.75
2	C3	75.00	C7	91.67	C3	76.92	C5	90.91	83.63

6 Conclusion

Our Fourier energy-based approach has proven to perform excellent activity recognition on sequences of different length, regardless of whether the sequences are different from each other because of time shift or activity speed variation. On the 17 synthetic video sequences tested we achieved 100% correct recognition and on the 41 real life video sequence tested we achieved different performances depending on which classes were considered in classification (results ranging between 56.1% to 83.6%). These results show that our basic methodology produces good results and there is a need for further investigation on better features and improved similarity algorithm that perform even better on real data.

References

1. J. Ben-Arie, Z. Wang, P. Pandit and s. Rajaram, "Human Activity Recognition Using Multidiensional Indexing", *IEEE Transactions on Pattern Analysis and Machine Intelligence*, Vol. 24, No. 8, August 2002, pp1091-1104.
2. R. Duda, P.E. Hart and D. Stork, Pattern Classification, John Wiley, 2001.
3. S. H. Kim and R-H. Park, "An Efficient Algorithm For Video Sequence Matching Using The Modified Hausdorff Distance and the Directed Diergence", *IEEE Transactions on Circuits and Systems for Video Technology*, Vol. 12, No. 7, July 2002, pp. 592-596.
4. K. Rangarajan, B. Allen and M Shah, "Matching motion Trajectories", Pattern Recognition, Vol.26, No. 4, pp595-610, July, 1993.
5. P-S. Tsai, M. Shah, K. Keiter and T. Kasparis, "Cyclic Motion Detection", Department of Computer Science Technical Report, University of Central Florida, Orlando, 1993.
6. J. Wang and S. Singh, "Video Based Human Dynamics: A Review", Real Time Imaging, 2003.

Mobile Data Mining by Location Dependencies

Jen Ye Goh and David Taniar

Monash University, School of Business Systems, Clayton, Vic 3800, Australia
{Jen.Ye.Goh,David.Taniar}@infotech.monash.edu.au

Abstract. Mobile mining is about finding useful knowledge from the raw data produced by mobile users. The mobile environment consists of a set of static device and mobile device. Previous works in mobile data mining include finding frequency pattern and group pattern. Location dependency was not part of consideration in previous work but it would be meaningful. The proposed method builds a user profile based on past mobile visiting data, filters and to mine association rules. The more frequent the user profiles are updated, the more accurate the rules are. Our performance evaluation shows that as the number of characteristics increases, the number of rules will increase dramatically and therefore, a careful choosing of only the relevant characteristics to ensure acceptable amount of rules.

1 Introduction

Data mining is the process of mining useful knowledge out from a set of raw data. Classical data mining aims to find out knowledge such as association rule [2], sequential pattern [3]. Time series analysis [9-11] can also be applied by using data mining methods so that patterns which are relevant to the decision maker can be found. Mobile data mining [4-7, 12, 13] involves finding out useful knowledge out from mobile users. Outcomes of mobile data mining includes frequency pattern [5], group pattern [13] and parallel pattern [6, 7].

Data mining has now entered a new era of research focusing on analysing the event sequences that is happening in a mobile environment. This is known as *mobile data mining* [5-7]. The essence of mobile data mining consists of a sequence of events happening over a time series, along with the ability of mobile units to be able to move within the coverage area. Processing power and memory capacity of mobile equipment is expensive and could occasionally be down due to poor receptions.

This paper describes the process of location based data mining in the mobile environment by using user profile method. There are different kinds of mobile devices in the mobile environment. These include the mobile phone, Personal Digital Assistant (PDA), laptop and car. Some of these mobile devices have the ability to reply a signal back to the static station and some mobile device either cannot or is too expensive to reply a signal back.

2 Background

The mobile environment described in this paper consists of a set of mobile devices, which can be mobile phone, PDA and many more. The static devices described in this paper are devices such as the wireless access point, which stays static in a particular location over time, which mainly have two purposes. First, it is to provide resources to the mobile devices such as bandwidth. Second, it is to record the user visiting data by identifying a particular mobile device in the mobile environment. The static device will regularly send the list of mobile users to a central location, which contains the user profile, and update the user profile.

The concept of location dependency described in this paper means the relationship of the knowledge about mobile user produced which are closely associated with the particular location. Location dependent knowledge is useful for decision making in relation to a particular location. Often, a decision unit is limited to a particular location and therefore, location dependency will support the decision unit.

A related work in mobile mining is group pattern mining [13]. Group pattern [13] aims to find out a set of group, which are nearby to each other over a distance and time. A frequency pattern is produced from the mining of raw data of mobile user based on their physical distance data, and time series data. A group of mobile users can be qualified as a group pattern when they meet the criteria of both physically close to each other below a certain distance threshold, and being physically close to each other over a certain time threshold [13].

3 Proposed Method

3.1 Initial Requirements

In a mobile environment, it consists of a set of mobile devices and also a set of static devices, which tends to be the access points for the mobile devices providing bandwidth for communication and authentication for mobile network access. Each of the static devices have a set of characteristics, $(c1, c2, ..., c_n)$. These characteristics can be generic characteristics such as entertainment, sports, education, shopping to more detailed characteristics such as *comedy.entertainment, badminton.sports, law.education* arranged by means of hierarchical organisation.

3.2 Raw Mobile Data Collection

As mobile devices moves along these static devices, the mobile devices are configured in such a way that it will transmit a identification signal at regular time interval which can be the hardware address and is unique worldwide, thus the ability to uniquely identify a particular mobile device. At the static device end, these signals are received and recorded. At the end of the process, the raw data collected from the static devices will consist of the following format: (*device_id, static_device_id*).

The *device_id* is the unique identification mark of the mobile device. The *static_device_id* is the unique identifier for the static device. The raw data from each static device can then be gathered and be represented by the following format {*device_id, static_device_id[(c1, c2, ..., c_n)]*}. As the mobile users moves along the static devices, user profiles are generated at the same time.

3.3 User Profile Updating Process

User profile consists of a set of characteristics, which the users enjoy. The set of characteristics are found from the static device, as the characteristics are pre-recorded. The more the mobile users visits a particular static device, the set of characteristics listed in the static device will be updated to the user profile more often.

Each mobile user characteristics have a value of 0 % to 100%. The higher the percentage, the higher the indication of the mobile user has visited the static device recently and frequently. Mobile user identification and the list of characteristics represent a user profile. A list of user profiles that visited a particular location is then extracted, and passed to the data mining system to find out association rules from the list. The result of this process is a list of association rules with *support%* and *confidence%* that if *characteristic1* and *characteristic2* is higher than the *characteristic_threshold* in one of the user profile, *characteristic3* will also be higher than the *characteristic_threshold* in the same user profile. A user profile with a characteristic higher than the *characteristic_threshold* would mean that the particular user visits locations, which contain those characteristics.

3.4 Algorithms for Proposed Method

The algorithm for assigning characteristics is described as below. Each location is equipped with a static device, which can be used to communicate with mobile device. Each static device is assigned to a list of characteristics that represents the overall theme of the location, such as {*trainstation.transport, cinema.entertainment, grocery.shopping*} may represent a train station, with a cinema and grocery shopping center nearby the wireless coverage area.

Figure 1 provides the algorithm and result of user profiling. The *VisitedLocation* contains a list of characteristics that a particular location contains, such as a list of {*badminton.sports, comedy.entertainment*}. The identified characteristics are then added into the mobile user profile, with each characteristics an assigned percentage value, such as {*badminton.sports*=0.5, *comedy.entertainment*=0.3} and if the location contains comedy.entertainment, the list will become {*badminton.sports*=0.5, *comedy.entertainment*=0.33}.

```
Function Train User Profile (MobileUser, VisitedLocation) {
    VisitedLocation = V;
    MobileUser.Update (V.Char1, V.Char2, ..., V.Char3)
    # MobileUser.Char1 = MobileUser.Char1 + (MobileUser.Char1 * V.Char1/ 10)
}
User Profile Database {
    User A = {comedy.entertainment=0.7, badminton.sports=0.8, law.education=0.5}
    User B = {comedy.entertainment=0.4, badminton.sports=0.3, law.education=0.9}
    User C = {trainstation.transport=0.8, grocery.shopping=0.5, drama.entertainment=0.4}
    User D = {comedy.entertainment=0.6, badminton.sports=0.5, infotech.education=0.4}
}
```

Fig. 1. Algorithm to Train User Profile & User Profile.

As the visiting location of the mobile user data are being collected, they are used to train the user profile database to better represent the overall life picture of the mobile user. The static device then starts to collect the identification code of the mobile device over a certain period of time. The result of this data collection would be: *Location1* = {*User A, User C, User D*}. The algorithm to retrieve the user profile record is described as below.

The list of user profile retrieved is then passed to a mining algorithm, such as association rule mining algorithm. In the above example, the user profiles retrieved are as below. The *confidence* value for both *comedy.entertainment* and *badminton.sports* coexist in the same transaction is = 2/3 = 66%. Considering the *threshold* value is 55%, this association rule exists. Therefore, the conclusion for this mining exercise is that, the current location has a *cinema.entertainment* background. Although most mobile users visited this location has a *cinema.entertainment* profile, it is found that mobile users who visited this particular physical location not only likes the location theme but also likes *comedy.entertainment* and *badminton.sports* at the same time.

```
Function Retrieve Profile (UserList) {
    Return UserList.1, UserList.2, UserList.3, ..., UserList.N;
}
User A = {comedy.entertainment=0.7, badminton.sports=0.8, law.education=0.5}
User C = {trainstation.transport=0.8, grocery.shopping=0.5, drama.entertainment=0.4}
User D = {comedy.entertainment=0.6, badminton.sports=0.5, infotech.education=0.4}
```

Fig. 2. Algorithm to Retrieve User Profile & User Profile Structure.

Figure 2 is useful for the decision makers to make a more informed decision by having the knowledge of the association of interests of the mobile users that visited a particular physical location, which was found based on the overall life picture of the mobile user.

4 Performance Evaluation

The performance evaluation was tested on a Pentium IV machine, equipped with 384MB of RAM. The association rule mining [2] process for the performance testing lasts from 1 second to 7 seconds. Three sets of data are generated. The first set is random data, which has been generated from random.org [8]. The random data set is random in terms of the display of random integer of 1 or 0 based on atmospheric noise. The source data consists of 200 records of mobile users visiting a particular location. The association rule mining software is XLMiner Demo Version [1].

The set of random data is labelled as Random. An integer of 1 will represent that the user characteristics has reached greater or equal to the acceptable threshold, say, 60%. Every single piece of data in Random has equal chance of occurring. The other set of data, R2, is produced from Random. R2 aims to show the repetition characteristics of mobile users and aims to produce more repetitions of similar user characteristics in the list. In R2, the first two records are repeated every next eight mobile users.

The dataset R4, which have the concept similar to R4, is obtained from Random with the first four record repeated every six mobile users. This shows a much more repetition of similar user characteristics for mobile users visiting a particular mobile location. There are instances when the number of rules is too high and the system refused to output to prevent crashes.

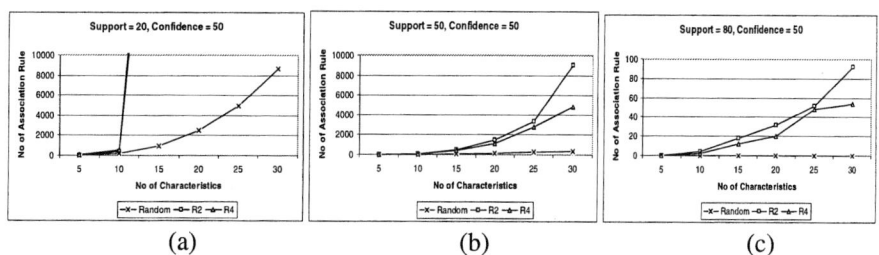

Fig. 3. Performance Chart Using Various Supports.

Figure 3(a) above has shown a gradual steady increase in the number of association rules [2] as the number of user characteristics increases for the Random dataset. However, the number of association rules becomes too many to the extent that the data mining software have rejected the mining process at 15 user characteristics level for dataset R2 and R4. Figure 3(b) have shown that with the *support*=50, *confidence*=50, the number of rules generated from Random, R2 and R4 increases gradually. There are more rules found in R2 than R4, and there are more rules found in R4 than Random. All dataset have a gradual increase over the number of user characteristics. Figure 3(c) have shown that with the *support*=80, *confidence*=50, the number of rules generated from R2 and R4 are non linear. For Random, due to the nature of random data which every single number have equal chance to occur, no rules are generated with stronger support threshold. From the graph, it can be seen that R4 always have lesser rules found than R2. At the point of 25 user characteristics, the magnitude of difference is relatively lesser than other readings. But overall, R2 and R4 increase over the number of user characteristics. Figure 3(c) also have the y-axis range from 0 to 100 because the range of number of rules significantly reduces as the support threshold is increased, thus only rules with very high confidence are presented.

The conclusion is increase of user characteristics leads to significant increase in the number of association rules [2] mined. In Figure 3(c), Random set increased in a steady fashion, but R2 and R4 have generated too much rules by 15 characteristics. This suggests that when mining is performed ensure to choose only the relevant set of characteristics for quicker and more relevant rule generation.

5 Conclusion and Future Work

User profile being represented as a set of characteristics and percentage value represents how much the user is likely to be involved with a particular characteristic, based on past information. The more frequent the user profile is updated, the more meaningful the user profile. It was found that as the number of characteristics increases, the number of rules found increased significantly. Therefore, careful choosing of the set of characteristics of user profile should be done before mining the source data in order to improve performance and economy.

Future work is to find out time dependent knowledge of location based knowledge. Time dependent knowledge involves putting a timestamp for each knowledge found and gives an expiry date for each knowledge.

References

1. XL Miner. Cytel Software Corporation, 2004.
2. R. Agrawal and R. Srikant. Fast Algorithms for Mining Association Rules. In Proc. 20th Int. Conf. Very Large Data Bases, pp. 487-499, 1994.
3. R. Agrawal and R. Srikant. Mining Sequential Patterns. In Proc. 11th Int. Conf. on Data Engineering, pp. 3-14, 1995.
4. J. Goh and D. Taniar. Mining Density Pattern from Mobile Users. 2004. (submitted)
5. J. Goh and D. Taniar. Mining Frequency Pattern from Mobile Users. Knowledge-Based Intelligent Information & Eng. Sys., 2004. (accepted)
6. J. Goh and D. Taniar. Mining Logical Parallel Pattern from Mobile Users. Int. Conf. on Intelligence in Communication Systems, 2004. (submitted)
7. J. Goh and D. Taniar. Mining Parallel Pattern from Mobile Users. Int. Conf. on Embedded and Ubiquitous Computing, 2004. (submitted)
8. M. Haahr. True Random Number Service. Random.org, 1998.
9. J. Han, G. Dong, and Y. Yin. Efficient Mining of Partial Periodic Patterns in Time Series Database. In Proc. of Int. Conf. on Data Engineering, pp. 106-115, 1999.

10. J. Han, W. Gong, and Y. Yin. Mining Segment-Wise Periodic Patterns in Time Related Databases. In Proc. 4th Int. Conf. on Knowledge Discovery and Data Mining, vol. no. pp. 214-218, 1998.
11. J. Han, J. Pei, and Y. Yin. Mining Frequent Patterns without Candidate Generation. In Proc. Int. Conf. SIGMOD, pp. 1-12, 2000.
12. E.-P. Lim, Y. Wang, K.-L. Ong, and et al. In Search of Knowledge About Mobile Users. ERCIM News, vol. 1, no. 54, pp. 10, 2003.
13. Y. Wang, E.-P. Lim, and S.-Y. Hwang. On Mining Group Patterns of Mobile Users. In Proc. of DEXA, pp. 287-296, 2003.

An Algorithm for Artificial Intelligence-Based Model Adaptation to Dynamic Data Distribution

Vincent C.S. Lee* and Alex T.H. Sim

School of Business Systems, Faculty of Information Technology,
Monash University, 63 Wellington Road, Vic 3800, Australia
Telephone: +613-99052360, Fax: +613-99055159
vincent.lee@infotech.monash.edu.au
http://www.bsys.monash.edu.au

Abstract. Changes in data distribution for in-sample training and out-sample validation can be unavoidable due to presence of random dynamic noises created by external uncontrollable environmental factors. To compensate for the variation in data distribution, one approach is to recursively use immediate past prediction error to augment the current data. This paper proposes a simple algorithm that ensures the parameter settings in an ANFIS model are adaptive to its unique data distribution. Such an 'open ended' strategy allows the ANFIS to be more accurate in predicting chaotic time series problems. An application of the proposed a procedure to predict Dow Jones Industrial Average index has yielded better prediction accuracy than using the conventional prediction model.

Keywords: fuzzy systems, neural network, chaotic time series.

1 Introduction

Most time series nonparametric (e.g. neural network) prediction models have implicitly assumed that the training and testing data sets have a same data distribution for short period prediction. This assumption is not valid in noisy time series data sets of real world problems, where the underlying series behavior varies much with time [1, 2]. The consequence of this unrealistic assumption has led to inevitable high prediction errors.

Conventional approaches to the development of prediction systems comprise two sequential stages. The first stage is to analyse the time-series data for an appropriate model. The second stage carries out iterative refinement for a 'best' model that is subsequently used to predict future data series. This process takes a long time. During the training phase, the 'best' model is learned from available actual data based on an initial system settings (i.e. fixed number of input neurons in neural networks, number of membership functions in fuzzy system). This is a typical system that will not adapt sufficiently to the fluid and noisy data of real world problems. Thus the system can

---
* Corresponding author.

only be used for very short period prediction and it cannot be reused in other similar problem domains because of the system's uncertain predictive power.

Analytically, an optimal design of a prediction system can be formulated as a global feasible solution of search problem [3]. It is only with optimal parameters settings, accurate prediction result can be obtained. For other parameter settings will result in high prediction errors.

In general, a unique data distribution is applicable to a specific set of problems. On each data distribution, we propose to use a different set of system parameters settings. Such settings must be adaptive to problem that is non stationary dynamic even for an existing correlated problem. That is, within a same problem (for example, predicting stock index), one should use varying but appropriate sets of system parameters settings.

This paper proposes a simple learning method for compensating variation in the data distribution due to the fluid and noisy data sets.

2 ANFIS Parameter Structure and Its Optimum Settings Under Invariant Data Distribution

2.1 ANFIS

An ANFIS, an innovative design for data-based fuzzy modelling [4], is based on the first-order Sugeno fuzzy model [4, 5]. The aim of an ANFIS is to systematically generate unknown fuzzy rules from a given input-output data set. Also, by using error back propagation (chain rule) with least-squared error criterion, it adjusts the shape and position of input fuzzy membership functions. Based on the learned rules and adjusted membership functions, the ANFIS then implements function-approximation and prediction on similar incoming data pattern. A typical ANFIS is a six-layer feed forward back-propagation neural network. It uses first order Sugeno model and has the rule of the form:

IF Input 1, x_1 is A AND Input 2, x_2 is B
THEN Output $y = aA + bB + c$

where a, b, c are parameters and A and B denote membership functions.

For illustration, considering a problem that can be solved by a two input and two membership function per input (2I: 2MF) ANFIS, all Sugeno fuzzy rules based on first-order polynomial are given as below,

IF x_1 is A_1 AND x_2 is B_1 THEN $f_1 = a_1A_1 + b_1B_1 + c_1$
IF x_1 is A_1 AND x_2 is B_2 THEN $f_2 = a_2A_1 + b_2B_2 + c_2$
IF x_1 is A_2 AND x_2 is B_1 THEN $f_3 = a_3A_2 + b_3B_1 + c_3$
IF x_1 is A_2 AND x_2 is B_2 THEN $f_4 = a_4A_2 + b_4B_2 + c_4$

where x_i is the ith input, A_i & B_i are the membership functions, f_i is the single number output from first-order polynomial calculation and a_i, b_i, c_i are parameters. Such problem can be modelled into ANFIS as shown in Figure 1.

Layer 1 is the input layer, in this case, we have 2-Inputs (x_1, x_2). Layer 2 is the membership function (MF) layer that contains the number of membership functions per input. There are 2MF per input. (i.e. $A1 = \mu_{A_1}(x_1)$, $B1 = \mu_{B_1}(x_2)$). Nodes in layer 3 are used to manipulate incoming signals to output the firing strength, w_i (i.e. $w_1 = \mu_{A_1}(x_1) \times \mu_{B_1}(x_2)$). Every node in layer 4Is is equivalent to a ratio over all rules' firing strength. (i.e. $\overline{w_1} = \dfrac{w_1}{w_1 + \ldots + w_4}$). In layer 5, nodes are adaptive. Each node, $y_i = \overline{w_i} f_i$, where f_i is the input function at i^{th} node. Lastly, layer 6 contains the output node that computes overall output as a summation of all signals from layer 5,

$$y = \sum_i \overline{w_i} = \dfrac{\sum_i w_i f_i}{\sum_i w_i}$$

Through solving optimization problem using error back propagation (chain rule) and least-squared error criterion, ANFIS is able to minimise the output error by adjusting the parameters (i.e. a_i, b_i, c_i), which are associated with bell-shape functions of the fuzzy membership function resided in the layer 2 can be expressed as

$$\mu_{A_i}(x_i) = \dfrac{1}{1+[(\dfrac{x_i - c_i}{a_i})^2]^{b_i}} \qquad (1)$$

Thus, ANFIS is able to learn adaptively.

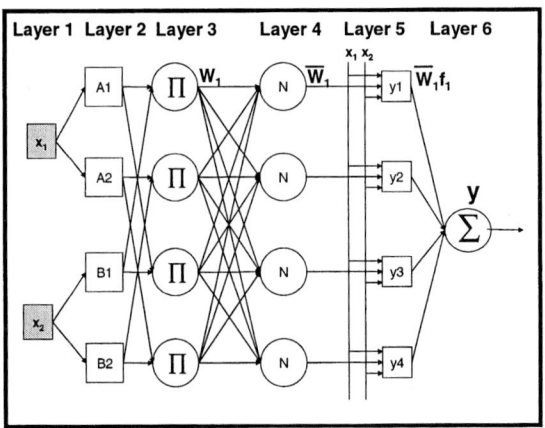

Fig. 1. Adaptive Neuro-Fuzzy Inference System (ANFIS) [6].

2.2 Number of Inputs and Membership Functions

In ANFIS, each input leg has a minimum 2MF. Each MF has predefined linguistic variables (for example, big, medium, small) to a specific input. The MF and the number of input jointly determine the number of linguistic rules

$$= (\text{\# of MF}) \wedge (\text{\# of Input}) \qquad (2)$$

The characteristic of a membership function depends on the number of parameters used. Total number of input membership parameters

$$= [(\text{\# of Inputs}) \times (\text{\# of membership functions})] \times 3 \qquad (3)$$

Whereas, the total number of output parameters

$$= [(\text{\# of membership functions}) \wedge (\text{\# of Inputs})] \times [(\text{\# of Inputs}) + 1] \qquad (4)$$

With reference to (2), (3) & (4), number of rules in ANFIS increases with both increases in the number of input and MF. An increase in number of input, however, generates more rules and more parameter structure (variables) in comparison with the increase in the number of MF.

Combination structure of the product of input and MF is very much dependent on data distribution. Each combination produces its predicted result with a different accuracy. Also, certain combination would require a long time to run but the accuracy is unsatisfactory.

2.3 Simulation of Chaotic Time Series

In determining a right setting for non-linear and chaotic time series, we solve Mackey-Glass time delay series using fourth order Runge-Kutta with an integration step of 0.001 and an initial value of 1.2. 1.2 million sample were generated using time delay, s = 17. Mackey-Glass time delay series becomes chaotic when s >16.8 and is given by

$$dx(t)/dt = a*x(t-s) / (1+x(t-s)^c) - b*x(t) \qquad (5)$$

While, Y = dx(t)/dt, parameter, s = 17, parameter, a = 0.2, parameter, b = 0.1, parameter, c = 10, the chaotic series can be denoted as

$$Y(t) = \frac{0.2x(t-17)}{1+x^{10}(t-17)} - 0.1x(t) \qquad (6)$$

After discarded the first 17 thousand initial values, we collect 1000 sample data through a sampling step of 1000. 500 sample data is used for training and another 500 is used for testing. In order to show that different data distribution required different parameter settings for best prediction results, we compared statistical properties of testing error (i.e. actual (testing data) – predicted result) at a same ratio level. The ratio is derived by comparing a proportion between the size of sample data to a total number of inputs and output parameter structure. The following results were obtained: Yellow colored rows denoted a comparison at a ratio of ~4.8, light green colored rows denoted a comparison at a ratio of ~1.0.

Results from both simulations show that in order to predict non-linear and chaotic problem (i.e. at a same pattern of data distribution), we should always use a high number of input but a minimum number of MF (i.e. 4I: 2MF). This would produce a minimum prediction error within a short time. This has been the common believe in making chaotic nonlinear time-series prediction through ANFIS and its prediction errors are summarized in figure 4. Although, an increase in number of MF can reduce prediction error (i.e. decreases in RMSE & NRMSE%) but the effect is not as strong as an increase in number of input. Besides, it prompts to an increase in number of error 'sparks' (a few high error points), thus increases the overall value of standard deviation and maximum error (i.e. the bubble size).

Ratio	# of Input	# of MF	Time(Sec.)	RMSE	NRMSE	Std Dev.	Max	Min
50.0	1	2	0.1	0.17	0.78%	0.14	0.71	0.00
4.8	1	21	1.9	0.17	0.78%	0.14	0.75	0.00
1.0	1	101	45.5	0.20	0.96%	0.19	1.42	0.00
20.8	2	2	0.3	0.08	0.36%	0.05	0.26	0.00
4.8	2	5	4.0	0.06	0.29%	0.05	0.30	0.00
1.0	2	12	179.9	0.06	0.27%	0.05	0.42	0.00
10.0	3	2	0.9	0.02	0.09%	0.02	0.07	0.00
3.7	3	3	8.4	0.02	0.07%	0.01	0.07	0.00
0.9	3	5	241.8	0.01	0.06%	0.01	0.07	0.00
4.8	4	2	4.5	0.00	0.01%	0.00	0.01	0.00
1.1	4	3	156.3	0.00	0.01%	0.00	0.01	0.00

Fig. 2. Statistical properties on prediction error base on trained ANFIS at different combination of input and MF. Mackey-Glass parameter, $s = 17$, $x(0) = 1.2$.

Ratio	# of Input	# of MF	Time(Sec.)	RMSE	NRMSE	Std Dev.	Max	Min
50.0	1	2	0.1	0.16	0.77%	0.15	0.69	0.00
4.8	1	21	1.0	0.16	0.78%	0.14	0.73	0.00
1.0	1	101	29.2	0.20	0.93%	0.21	1.42	0.00
20.8	2	2	0.2	0.13	0.60%	0.09	0.37	0.00
4.8	2	5	2.1	0.14	0.68%	0.11	0.52	0.00
1.0	2	12	137.0	0.26	1.22%	0.22	1.50	0.00
10.0	3	2	0.5	0.13	0.61%	0.11	0.60	0.00
3.7	3	3	3.9	0.20	0.93%	0.20	1.95	0.00
0.9	3	5	184.9	0.32	1.52%	0.29	1.77	0.00
4.8	4	2	2.4	0.12	0.58%	0.14	1.01	0.00
1.1	4	3	113.3	0.18	0.84%	0.21	1.73	0.00

Fig. 3. Statistical properties of prediction error based on trained ANFIS at different at different combination of input and MF. Mackey-Glass parameter, $s = 30$, $x(0) = 1.1$.

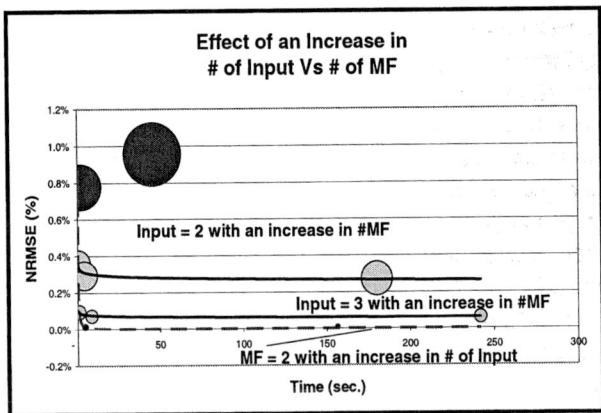

Fig. 4. An increase in number of inputs reduces NRMSE% exponentially (red line). (Bubble size represents the value of maximum error). The biggest bubble (1 I: 101 MF) does not follow a decreasing power trend line. Its prediction result contains unusual high errors ('error sparks') that increased its NRMSE%. Mackey-Glass parameter, $s = 17$, $x(0) = 1.2$.

Next, we increased the complexity of MG series by changing the MG parameter, s to 60 with an initial condition x(0) = 5.6 and we iterated our simulations. The results are shown in Figure 5. This time, the settings of 2I: 2MF is much preferred over 4I: 2MF. Another set of simulation results at s = 110 and x(0) = 5.6 are given in Figure 6. These results show that 3I: 2MF has lower NRMSE% in comparison to both 2I: 2MF (slightly) and 4I: 2MF. All these differences are due to variation in data distribution generated through a same nonlinear chaotic equation (6) but with different parameters.

Ratio	# of Input	# of MF	Time(Sec.)	RMSE	NRMSE	Std Dev.	Max	Min
50.0	1	2	0.1	0.15	0.73%	0.14	0.57	0.00
4.8	1	21	0.9	0.17	0.80%	0.15	0.84	0.00
1.0	1	101	29.3	0.25	1.21%	0.33	4.76	0.00
20.8	2	2	0.1	0.14	0.70%	0.14	0.62	0.00
4.8	2	5	2.0	0.16	0.75%	0.20	1.18	0.00
1.0	2	12	137.3	0.36	1.73%	0.41	4.26	0.00
10.0	3	2	0.5	0.17	0.82%	0.17	0.91	0.00
3.7	3	3	4.0	0.25	1.21%	0.32	1.63	0.00
0.9	3	5	187.8	0.47	2.29%	0.84	6.30	0.00
4.8	4	2	2.2	0.17	0.80%	0.19	1.13	0.00
1.1	4	3	113.9	0.32	1.55%	0.52	3.42	0.00

Fig. 5. Statistical properties of prediction error based on trained ANFIS at different at different combination of input and MF. Mackey-Glass parameter, s =60, x(0) = 5.6.

Ratio	# of Input	# of MF	Time(Sec.)	RMSE	NRMSE	Std Dev.	Max	Min
50.0	1	2	0.1	0.18	0.89%	0.13	0.65	0.00
4.8	1	21	0.9	0.18	0.90%	0.14	0.77	0.00
1.0	1	101	30.8	0.41	1.99%	0.40	3.05	0.00
20.8	2	2	0.1	0.15	0.73%	0.12	0.52	0.00
4.8	2	5	2.0	0.14	0.70%	0.12	0.66	0.00
1.0	2	12	139.8	0.41	1.99%	0.40	4.83	0.00
10.0	3	2	0.5	0.15	0.72%	0.17	1.37	0.00
3.7	3	3	3.9	0.17	0.84%	0.14	0.66	0.00
0.9	3	5	194.3	0.24	1.19%	0.21	1.28	0.00
4.8	4	2	2.2	0.30	1.49%	0.24	1.57	0.00
1.1	4	3	118.5	0.22	1.06%	0.17	1.13	0.00

Fig. 6. Prediction error statistics based on trained ANFIS at different combination of input and MF. Mackey-Glass parameter, s =110, x(0) = 5.6.

It has so far been shown through these experiments that a problem having different data distribution needs a different ANFIS parameter setting in order to make more accurate prediction. This is an important contribution of this paper.

3 The Proposed Learning Algorithm-Simple Steps to Ensure a Right Setting Before Predicting

The aim of the proposed algorithm is to provide a procedure for selecting the best number of parameters combination, which can effectively used to perform function approximation of a chaotic nonlinear with variant data distributing problem. There are five main steps in searching for a right ANFIS configuration for a chaotic and nonlinear series can be described as follows:

1) Perform a search among the possible combinations (in the example used, i.e. 4I: 2MF, 3I: 2MF, 2I: 2MF and 1I: 2MF over a range of data points, D. A further increase from 4 inputs to 5 inputs is not necessary in view of a long time needed to improve over a small percentage of accuracy.
2) Calculate statistical properties on the 4 combinations for its RMSE, NRMSE%, standard deviation, maximum percentage and minimum percentage of the prediction error, i.e. the differences between the actual (testing data) and the prediction.
3) Select the best combination (i.e. lowest NRMSE%, lowest standard deviation). Based on this combination increases its training epoch (e.g. 300 epoch run) for fine-tuning its prediction accuracy.
4) Repeat from step (1) with an increment s, before making a next prediction, which is based on data points D + s.
5) Terminate the search when the desired prediction error is reached.

4 An Example on the Use of the Proposed Simple Algorithm – Dow Jones Industrial Average Index

In this section, we apply the four steps given in Section 3 to predict the Dow Jones Industrial Average stock index from 12th Sep 2000 to 12th Sep 2002. ANFIS is trained with historical data from 13th Aug 1998 to 31st Aug 2000 (~2 years daily opening stock index). The results are summarised in Figure 8 with the details on Figures 9-11.

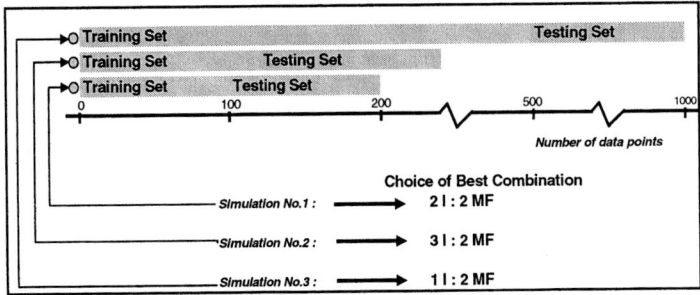

Fig. 7. Shows an increasing number of data sets (both training and testing) used for time series prediction with a change in its best combination. Such changes are due to data variances within each training data set.

Ratio	# of Input	# of MF	Time(Sec.)	RMSE	NRMSE	Std Dev.	Max	Min
50.0	1	2	0.078	1,085.9	1.05%	0.05	0.15	0.00
20.8	2	2	0.094	703.5	0.68%	0.03	0.11	0.00
10.0	3	2	0.219	1,398.5	1.36%	0.09	0.29	0.00
4.8	4	2	1.109	2,744.6	2.66%	0.16	0.47	0.00

Fig. 8. Search result on sample data points of size 100. This small size of sample represents an initial simulation run. We let 'a' to represent this set of data. (Time taken: ~2 seconds).

Ratio	# of Input	# of MF	Time(Sec.)	RMSE	NRMSE	StdDev.	Max	Min
50.0	1	2	0.016	1,120.3	0.96%	0.03	0.14	0.02
20.8	2	2	0.063	1,000.1	0.85%	0.04	0.16	0.00
10.0	3	2	0.125	880.1	0.75%	0.05	0.18	0.00
4.8	4	2	0.516	5,619.7	4.80%	0.24	0.79	0.03

Fig. 9. Search result on sample data points of size 120. This increasing size of sample represents further simulation after the first run. We let 'b' to represent this set of data. (Time taken: ~1 second).

Ratio	# of Input	# of MF	Time(Sec.)	RMSE	NRMSE	StdDev.	Max	Min
50.0	1	2	0.922	341.1	0.15%	0.03	0.22	0.00
20.8	2	2	0.406	382.1	0.17%	0.03	0.23	0.00
10.0	3	2	1.11	1,109.8	0.49%	0.11	1.66	0.00
4.8	4	2	4.89	1,807.3	0.80%	0.19	2.30	0.00

Fig. 10. Search result on sample data points of size 500. This large size of sample represents simulation after much data collection over time. We let 'c' to represent this set of data. (Time taken: ~7 seconds).

Having selected a right parameter, we increased each combination with training epoch up to 300 runs thus produces the following comparisons. (Note that axis-x is the axis for trading day. Axis-y is the opening index of Dow Jones.)

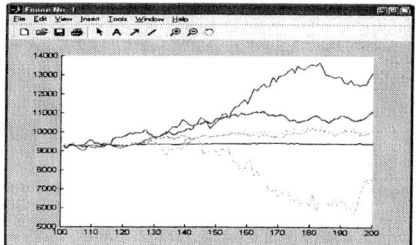 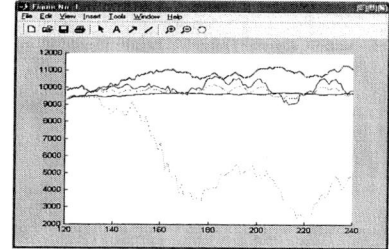

Fig. 11. On 'a' problem, we chose 2I:2MF and increased its training epoch. (Actual (Red), 1I : 2MF (Black), 2I : 2MF (Green, Best in the scenario), 3I : 2MF (Blue), 4I : 2MF(Cyan)).

Fig. 12. On 'b' distribution problem, it is a problem for 3I:2MF. (Actual (Red), 1I : 2MF (Black), 2I : 2MF (Green), 3I : 2MF (Blue, Best in the scenario), 4I : 2MF(Cyan)).

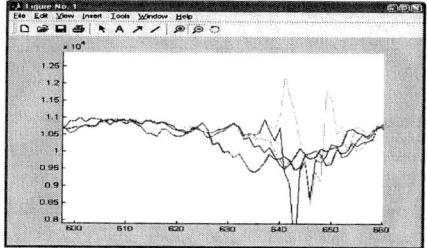

Fig. 13. On 'c' distribution problem, based on RMSE%, we chose 1I : 2MF. (Actual (Red), 1I : 2MF (Black, Best in the scenario), 2I : 2MF (Green), 3I : 2MF (Blue), 4I : 2MF(Cyan)).

Based on Figure 9, it is worth to point out that if we were to fixed a parameter settings in ANFIS, based on high sample data study (i.e. 500 sample data), we would have easily chosen 1I : 2MF to predict all data series, especially on prediction that have sample data less than 500, for example. This greatly sacrifices accuracy for both problem 'a' and 'b'. Total prediction error would have then increased by 0.6% in NRMSE or 622.6 in RMSE. By utilizing the algorithm, we have improved its accuracy by using right ANFIS parameter at the right time. Although, the result is far from perfect, it is not for this paper to rectify them after having it necessary constrained to learn with limited historical data.

5 Conclusions

This paper has proposed a simple algorithm to make parametric settings adaptive to incoming data series. Such strategy is important to guarantee a good level of accuracy in making prediction on chaotic and nonlinear series, such as stock index. We tested our strategy on Dow Jones index (Sep 2000-2002) with limited historical learning (Aug 1998-2000), the algorithm brings significant improvement (i.e. 0.6% in NRMSE) over in prediction error than that if it were to predict based on static parameter settings. Further investigation on the use of type-2 fuzzy logic to model uncertainties in data for further improvement of prediction accuracy is underway.

References

1. Novak, M., Pelikan, E. and Beran, H., Time-Series Prediction by Artificial Neural Networks: Electric Power Consumption, in *Frontier Decision Support Concepts*, G. Visaggio, Editor. 1994, John Wiley & Sons, Inc. pp. 221-239.
2. Mouzouris, G.C. and Mendel, J. M., Nonlinear Time-Series Analysis with Non-Singleton Fuzzy Logic Systems, in *Conference on Computational Intelligence for Financial Engineering (CIFEr)*. 1995. New York City, Crowne Plaza Manhattan: IEEE press.
3. Liu, Y. and Yao, X., Evolving neural networks for Hang Seng stock index forecast, in *Proceedings of the Congress on Evolutionary Computation, 2001*.
4. Jang, J.-S.R., ANFIS: Adaptive-Network-Based Fuzzy Inference System. *IEEE Transactions On Systems, Man, and Cybernetics*, 1993. 23(3): pp. 665-685.
5. Sugeno, M. and Kang, J. T., Fuzzy Modeling and Control of Multilayer Incinerator, *Fuzzy Sets and Systems*, 1986. 18: pp. 329-346.
6. Negnevitsky, M., *Artificial Intelligence: A Guide to Intelligent Systems*. 2002: Pearson Education Limited, England.
7. Boston, J.R., *A Measure of Uncertainty for Stock Performance*, in *proceedings IEEE International Conference on Computational Intelligence for Financial Engineering (CIFEr)*. 1998: IEEE.
8. Wan, E.A., Modeling Nonlinear Dynamics with Neural Networks: Examples in Time Series Prediction, in *proceedings of Fifth Workshop on Neural Networks: Academic/ Industrial/NASA/Defense, WNN93/FNN93*,1993. San Francisco, CA.
9. Kotsakis, E. and Wolski, A., MAPS: A Method for Identifying and Predicting Aberrant Behaviour In Time Series, *Lecture Notes in Computer Science: 14th International Conference on Industrial and Engineering Applications of Artificial Intelligence and Expert Systems*, 2001. 2070: pp. 314-325.
10. Saad, E.W., Prokhorov, D.V., and Wunsch, D. C. II, Comparative study of stock trend prediction using time delay, recurrent and probabilistic neural network, *IEEE Transactions on Neural Networks*, 1998, 9(6): pp. 1456-1470.

On a Detection of Korean Prosody Phrases Boundaries

Jong Kuk Kim[1], Ki Young Lee[2], and Myung Jin Bae[1]

[1] Department of Information Telecommunication Engineering, SoongSil University
Sangdo 5-dong, Dongjak-gu, Seoul, 156-743, Korea
kokjk@hanmail.net, mjbae@ssu.ac.kr
[2] Department of Information Communication Engineering, KwanDong University
7 San Imcheon-ri, Yangyang-eup, Yangyang-gun, Gangwon-do, Korea
kylee@mail.kwandong.ac.kr

Abstract. This paper describes an automatic detection technique of Korean accentual phrase boundaries by using one-stage DP, and the normalized pitch pattern. For making the normalized pitch pattern, we propose a method of modified normalization for Korean spoken language. The results shows that 76.4% of the accentual phrase boundaries are correctly detected while 14.7% are the false detection rate. Also we can know that accentual phrase detection method by pattern matching shows the more superior detection rate than detection method by LH tone from this result.

1 Introduction

In many recent linguistic studies, the relations between prosodic structures and syntactic or phonological structures are examined and the usefulness of prosodic information is proved for understanding semantic, syntactic or discourse structures. But the results of these studies have little been integrated yet into current speech recognition or understanding systems[7]. Especially, into the systems for Korean, they have never been integrated. The main reason for this is that it is difficult to develop the proper method for drawing out these prosodic features, because they are varied according to speakers. Nevertheless, the studies have been continually made in the 1990's on the possibility of integrating prosodic features into speech recognition or understanding systems, and as the result, Ostendorf for English, Verbmobil project for German, Shimodaira for Japanese[1][2], etc. propose the methods of detecting and labelling the boundaries of prosodic units, as a part of the study for recognizing and understanding the spoken language. The purpose of this study is to propose a method of detecting Korean accentual phrase boundaries automatically, as the prearrangement process for recognizing and understanding continuous speech. We observe speech signals with the naked eye at first, and draw out distinctive features proper to the accentual phrase(AP). The distinctive features are marked with pitch contour. To compose the standard patterns of AP, we adopt a method of modified normalization, because the pitch contours of APs show the down-step phenomenon. By using these standard patterns, we segment the input of continuous speech automatically into AP units by using one-stage DP[3].

2 Structure of Korean Prosody Phrases

The intonational phrases(IP) of Sun-Ah Jun is a prosodic unit which corresponds to the intonational phrase of Nespor and Vogel, and is characterized by an intonational contour made up of two tonal levels H(igh) and L(ow)[1-2]. The intonational contour of the IP is derived from two constituents: the pitch accent and the phrase tone. Thus, the phrase accent marks the boundary of intermediate phrase which are smaller units than the IP. The smaller units than the IP are accentual phrase(AP) which are submit of the IP. The AP is marked by F0 contour[6].

Although the F0 contour has various patterns according to pragmatic meaning such as focus, topic, etc. and to dialects in Korean, Seoul dialect has the basic pattern of LH or LHLH according to the number of syllables which are contained in an AP, and if two H tones appear in an AP the second one is higher than the first one. As another characteristics, AP's contours show the down-step or declination phenomenon in an IP. Using these characteristics, we can set up the basic pitch pattern of APs, as follows Figure1.

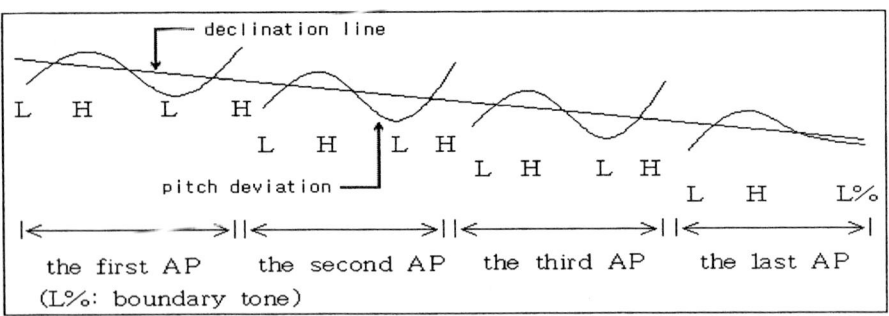

Fig. 1. The basic pitch pattern of Aps.

3 Detection Method of Prosody Phrases Boundaries

The segmentation algorithm of APs is to segment a presegmented IP into APs. We employ the one-stage DP and the standard patterns made by normalization. Figure 2 shows detection system of Korean prosody phrases boundary[5].

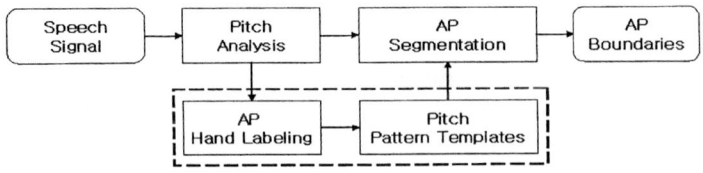

Fig. 2. Detection system of Korean Prosody Phrases Boundary.

3.1 Pitch Analysis

We adopt the center-clipped autocorrelation method for the algorithm of drawing out the pitch contour[4]. For auto segmenting APs, we compose multi-templates with pitch contours of hand-labelled APs, and employ the algorithm of one stage DP. But we must normalize the slant pitch contours because the pitch contour of speech is sloped by the down-step effect, as mentioned in the previous chapter. We propose the modified normalization as the method of pitch normalization. The algorithm is as follows : N is the number of frames of speech, and p(n) is the pitch value of each frame[3].

(1) Average pitch value in the first and last frame of speech, p_{s_avg} , p_{e_avg}

$$p_{s\_avg} = \tfrac{4}{N} \sum_{n=0}^{\frac{N}{4}-1} p(n) \tag{1}$$

$$p_{e\_avg} = \tfrac{4}{N} \sum_{n=0}^{\frac{N}{4}-1} p(N-n) \tag{2}$$

(2) To get the slope, $s_{p\_avg}(n)$, by linear-interpolating between p_{s_avg} , p_{e_avg}

$$s_{p\_avg}(n) = \tfrac{n}{N}\left(p_{e\_avg} - p_{s\_avg}\right) \tag{3}$$

(3) Altered pitch countour , $\overline{p}(n)$,by using slope $s_{p\_avg}(n)$

$$\overline{p}(n) = p(n) - s_{p\_avg}(n) \tag{4}$$

As a result of procedure, Normalize each value of the equation (4) by dividing it by the maximal value. Figure 3 shows the normalized pitch contour extracted from the speech by using the above method.

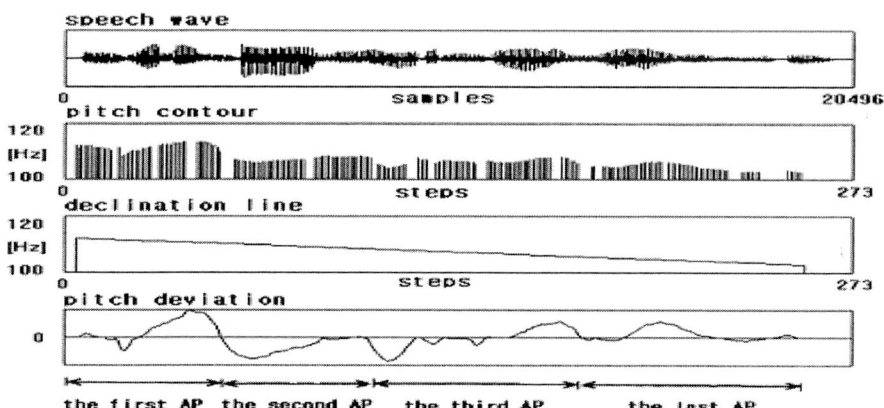

Fig. 3. Pitch model.

3.2 Segmentation of APs by Pattern Matching

There is a strong correlation(but no 100% agreement)between syntactic and prosodic phrases. In Korean, syntactic phrases are divided in orthography by a space, and are in accordance with accentual phrases although there are some exceptions(e.g., defective nouns). Because the pitch contour marks the AP, we segment the speech signal of a sentence into APs by handlabelling, as follows, and then use the pitch contours of the segmented units as the standard patterns[3][5]

[inju-nín]$_{TOPIC}$ / [maím-í]$_{SUBJECT}$ / [arímdaun]$_{ADJECTIVE}$ /[y^ín-ímnída]$_{NOUN\ PREDICATE}$
" Eunju is a woman whose heart is beautiful."

The real speech signal of this example is shown in Figure 3. The pitch contour of the signal appears as the form of LH. The normalized pitch contour extracted by the proposed method in the previous section has the leveled slope of the down-step effect, and its form of LH is more evident. We employ the comparison of pattern in the algorithm of segmenting APs. The method of pattern comparison is one stage DP which is able to compare continuous patterns, and the standard pattern is made of the normalized pitch contour extracted from the real speech signal and marked manually. The equation of the distance measure used in one-stage DP is as follows:

$$d_{AB}(n,m) = (1-\alpha) \cdot \{\overline{p}_A(n) - \overline{p}_B(m)\} + \alpha \cdot \{\Delta\overline{p}_A(n) - \Delta\overline{p}_B(m)\} \quad (5)$$

$$\Delta \overline{p}(n) - \Delta \overline{p}(n-1), \quad 0 \leq \alpha \leq 1 \quad (6)$$

where α (0≤α≤ 1) is a weighting ratio of the distance for the normalized pitch value of the equation (4) to the distance for the difference pitch value of the equation (6) which is the pitch variation .

4 Experimental Results

We use speech signals of 10 kHz sampling rate, and 25.6 msec per frame, 12.8 msec for scanning interval. The script for data collection is composed of 16 sentences(all sentences are declarative), of which 4 sentences consists of 4 APs, 4 sentences of 5 APs, and 8 sentences of 3 APs. The total number of APs is sixty. This experiment employs 192 sentential speech data of 12 men's voice spoken in standard Korean, in which 720 APs are included. In the experiment, two cases are compared : one is the case in which the single-pattern of one sentence pronounced by one speaker is used as the standard pattern, and the other is the case in which the multi-pattern of one sentence(the same sentence of the case one) pronounced by three speakers is used as the standard pattern.

The standard pattern of the single-pattern is made up of the normalized pitch contours of 4 APs which are extracted from a sentence spoken by a speaker, and that of the multi-pattern is made up of the normalized pitch contours of 16 APs which are extracted from the same sentence spoken respectively by three speakers. Also we compared LH tone and pattern matching method. In pattern matching method, If continuous speech is inputed, it analyzes pitch first and use normalized pitch contour and one-stage DP, boundary point of accentual pharse detect automatically. In LH tone method, for automatic detection of accentual pharse, classify of intonational phrase using period pause of continuous speech inputed and using pitch contour of each intonation, accentual phrases is detect.

In pattern matching use one-stage DP and detect accentual boundary, the woman speaker whole average detection rate is 80.8% and the man speaker whole average detection rate is 83.3%. and in searching LH ton and result of detection boundary of accentual phrase by each speaker's, the woman speaker whole average detection rate is 74.2% and the man speaker whole average detection rate is 75.0%. The woman speaker whole average detection rate is 74.2% and the man speaker whole average detection rate is 75.0%.We can know that accentual phrase detection method by pattern matching shows the more superior detection rate than detection method by LH ton from this result. Figure 4 shows the correct detection rates according to weights, α in the equation (5). SP indicates the case of the single pattern, and MP indicates the case of the multi-pattern.

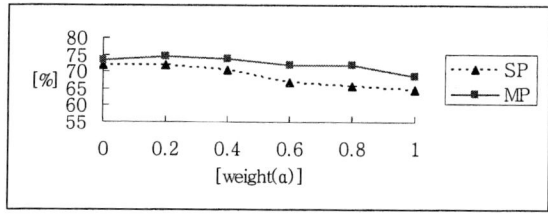

Fig. 4. Correct detection rates according to weights.

We can see the highest correct detection rate,74.1% for the SP and 76.4%for the MP, when the weight, o is 0.2 in both cases. This result reveals that there is a prosodic unit of AP in Korean and that the pitch contour of LH tones plays a significant role in segmenting or marking APs in Seoul dialect of Korean. We can also see the fact that the multi-pattern is superior to the single pattern as the standard pattern. Table 1 shows false detection rates according to weights, which mean boundaries detected the wrong position by automatic segmentation.

The rates are also lower when the multi-pattern is used as the standard pattern, and are lowest when the weight, α is 0.2. We consider that these errors might occur because the LH pattern can appear within the AP, not in the boundary of AP. We expect that the correct detection rate will increase or the false detection rate will decrease if other prosodic parameters such as the duration of AP's final syllable, energy, etc. are used, or if Mark of chain with large amount of data is employed as the segmentation.

Table 1. False detection rates according to weights, α(%).

weights(α)	0.0	0.2	0.4	0.6	0.8	1.0
SP	17.5	16.7	16.3	16.9	17.4	18.5
MP	15.3	14.7	14.0	16.0	14.7	16.5

5 Conclusions

This study proposes a method of segmenting Korean speech signals automatically into accentual phrases(AP).We employ one stage DP as the segmentation algorithm, and single-pattern(SP) and multi-pattern(MP) templates of normalized pitch contour made by hand, For experiment, we use speech data of 12 speakers. The results of the experiment show the correct detection rate of 76.4% and the false detection rate is 14.7%, when the multi-template is used as the standard pattern. Consequently, for recognizing AP boundaries, the normalized normalization is useful and as the standard pattern, the multi-pattern template is superior to the single-pattern template. But the difference pitch value, which is the pitch variation, is helpful for improving segmentation accuracy. Also we can know that accentual phrase detection method by pattern matching shows the more superior detection rate than detection method by LH ton from this result.

Acknowledgement

This work was partially supported by interdisciplinary research grants of the KOSEF (Subject Number:R01-2002-000-00278-0).

References

1. Sun-Ah Jun, The Phonetics and Phonology of Korean Prosody, Doctoral Dissertation, The Ohio State University, 1993.
2. C. W. Wightman and M. Ostendorf, " Automatic labeling of prosodic patterns ", IEEE Trans. Speech, Audio Processing, Vol. 2, No. 4, pp. 469-481, 1994.
3. KiYoung Lee, MyungJin Bae, HoYoung Lee, JongKuk Kim, " Pitch Contour Conversion Using Slanted Gaussian Normalization Based on Accentual Phrases", Korean Journal of Speech Sciences, Vol. 11, No 1, pp. 31-41, 2004.
4. J.K. Kim, M.J Bae, " A study of Pitch Extraction Method by using Harmonics Peak-Fitting in Speech Spectrum ", in Proc. of ICSP2001 Conf. , Vol. 2, pp. 617-621, 2001.
5. K. Lee, " Statistical Approaches to Convert Pitch Contours Based on Korean Prosodic Phrases ", Proc. The Journal of The Acoustic Society of Korea, Vol. 23, No. 1E, 2004.
6. H. Shimodaira and M. Kimura, " Accent phrase segmentation using pitch pattern clustering", in Proc. of IEEE Inf. Conf. ASSP, pp.1-217, 1992.
7. M.J BAE, " The TTS Speech Synthesis Techniques", Proceedings of Korea Inst. Commun. Sciences, Vol.11, No.9, pp.67-78, 1994.

A Collision Avoidance System for Autonomous Ship Using Fuzzy Relational Products and COLREGs

Young-il Lee and Yong-Gi Kim

Department of Computer Science, Gyeongsang National University
Jinju, Kyungnam, Korea, 660-701
ygkim@nongae.gsnu.ac.kr

Abstract. This paper presents a collision avoidance system for autonomous ship. Unlike collision avoidance system of other unmanned vehicles, the collision avoidance system for autonomous ship aims at not only deriving a reasonable and safe path to the goal but also keeping COLREGs (International Regulations for Preventing Collisions at Sea). The heuristic search based on the fuzzy relational products is adopted to achieve the general purpose of collision avoidance system; deriving a reasonable and safe path. The rule of "action to avoid collision" is adopted for the other necessary and sufficient condition; keeping the COLREGs.

1 Introduction

Among the disasters at sea, the rate of collision with another vessel has been gradually increasing [1]. These collisions are not caused by shortage of navigation skill but by human's mistake which comes from low visibility and carelessness. A study for reducing the collision brings about the development of collision avoidance system. There exist two kinds of study for collision avoidance system with respect to the property of design.

One approach to the collision avoidance method is based on a knowledge-based system. The knowledge-based system embodies the collision avoidance technique by using COLREGs as the key to expertise. A representative example of this approach is the study of Koyama and Yan [2]. Also researchers including Hasegawa developed a Ship Auto-navigation Fuzzy Expert System [3]. The other approach to collision avoidance of autonomous ship is based on the heuristic search technique. Various collision avoidance technique based on the heuristic search have been studied for autonomous ship such as Imazu and Koyama [4][5], Lee and Rhee [6], and Xianyi [7].

COLREGs describe the action taken to avoid collision for one-to-one meeting case [8]. Due to this fact, the knowledge-based system cannot take a reasonable action in the case of many-vessels. The heuristic search technique has an advantage that the vessel can consider all approaching obstacles. On the other hand, it has also a disadvantage that the vessel could take unreasonable action breaking COLREGs. Consequently, the best choice is to develop a new type collision avoidance system which takes only advantages of two approaches. In this paper we suggest a collision avoidance system, which integrates the properties of two techniques. The verification of proposed collision avoidance system for autonomous ship is performed with scenarios that represent an encounter situations classified in the COLREGs.

2 Fuzzy Relational Products

With the mathematical implement which analyzes interactions-cognition, decision and action-between the domain experts and the navigation environment, we can develop an intelligent navigation system mimicking those interactions. Fuzzy relational products [9][10][11] are chosen as the mathematical implement. Let $\tilde{R}$ denotes a fuzzy relation from set A to set B, and $\tilde{S}$ from set B to set C. A product of a fuzzy relation $\tilde{R}$ with a fuzzy relation $\tilde{S}$ represents the relation from set A to set C, which has three kinds of products.

$$(\tilde{R} \triangleleft \tilde{S})_{ik} = \frac{1}{|B|} \sum (\tilde{R}_{ij} \rightarrow \tilde{S}_{jk}) \quad (1)$$

$$a \rightarrow_s b = \min(1, 1 - a + b) \quad (2)$$

Here equation (1), $(\tilde{R} \triangleleft \tilde{S})_{ik}$ is intended to be the (mean) degree to which the fuzzy afterset $_{a_i}\tilde{R}$ is contained in the fuzzy foreset Sc_k. Fuzzy implication operators extend the classical material implication for the operation of fuzzy relation. In this paper, we use Lukasiewicz fuzzy implication operator as shown in equation (2) to construct the fuzzy triangle sub-product $(\tilde{R} \triangleleft \tilde{S})_{ik}$.

3 The Collision Avoidance System for Autonomous Ship

When the collision avoidance system recognizes approaching obstacles, it should take into consideration following two aims; deriving a reasonable and safe path, and observing the rule of "action to avoid collision" stipulated in the COLREGs. In order to satisfy the two aims, the collision avoidance system consists of two independent modules such as CSSM (Candidate Sector set Selection Module) and KBSM (Knowledge-Based System Module) as shown in Fig. 1.

3.1 Candidate Sector Set Selection Module

The CSSM aims at selecting a candidate sector guaranteeing optimized collision avoidance out of component sectors of each candidate valley, which has five sub-components.

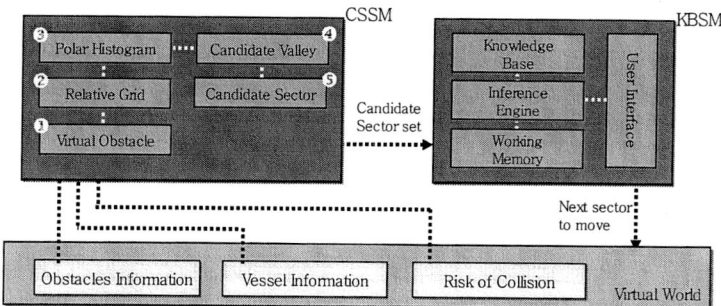

Fig. 1. The structure of collision avoidance system.

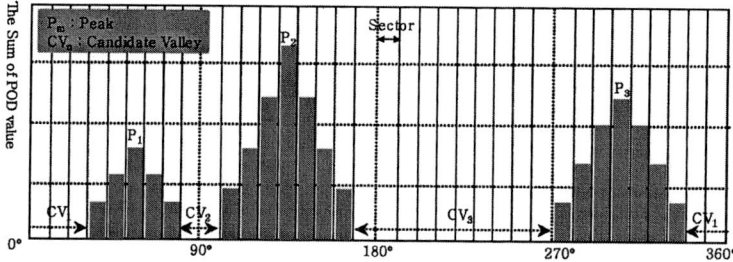

Fig. 2. Polar Histogram consists of n sectors which have a polar obstacle density.

3.1.1 Polar Histogram and Candidate Valley

The polar histogram consists of $n(=360/\alpha)$ sectors as shown in Fig. 2 [12][13]. Each sector in the polar histogram has a polar obstacle density (POD) which is the degree of risk for obstacle included in the sector. Also the polar histogram has peaks which are the set of sectors with high PODs, and valleys which are the set of sectors with low PODs. Any valley comprised of sectors with PODs below a certain threshold is called a *candidate valley*. One sector of each candidate valley is selected as candidate sector guaranteeing optimized collision avoidance.

3.1.2 Candidate Sector

Each candidate valley consists of many sectors. There exist specific relationship between the sectors in valley and the sectors in peak by energy unit in terms of optimality and safety. Any sector satisfying the optimality and safety in each candidate valley is called a *candidate sector*. Evaluation function is adopted to represent a relationship between sectors in valley and sectors in peak, and the fuzzy relational products are adopted to analyze a semantic implication among the sectors.

The Procedure of Selecting Candidate Sector based on Fuzzy Relational Products
In order to select a candidate sector, we present the following procedure based on fuzzy relational products [14].

$$V = \{s_1, s_2, \cdots, s_k\} \quad P = \{o_1, o_2, \cdots, o_i\} \tag{3}$$

$$\tilde{R} = V \times P = \begin{bmatrix} r_{11} & r_{12} & \cdots & r_{1i} \\ r_{21} & r_{22} & \cdots & r_{2i} \\ \vdots & \vdots & \ddots & \vdots \\ r_{k1} & r_{k2} & \cdots & r_{ki} \end{bmatrix} \begin{matrix} s_1 \\ s_2 \\ \vdots \\ s_k \end{matrix} \quad \tilde{T} = \tilde{R} \triangleleft \tilde{R}^T = \begin{bmatrix} f_{11} & f_{12} & \cdots & f_{1k} \\ f_{21} & f_{22} & \cdots & f_{2k} \\ \vdots & \vdots & \ddots & \vdots \\ f_{k1} & f_{k2} & \cdots & f_{kk} \end{bmatrix} \begin{matrix} s_1 \\ s_2 \\ \vdots \\ s_k \end{matrix} \tag{4}$$

$$C_\alpha = \alpha\_cut(\tilde{T}, \alpha) = \begin{bmatrix} b_{11} & b_{12} & \cdots & b_{1k} \\ b_{21} & b_{22} & \cdots & b_{2k} \\ \vdots & \vdots & \ddots & \vdots \\ b_{k1} & b_{k2} & \cdots & b_{kk} \end{bmatrix} \begin{matrix} s_1 \\ s_2 \\ \vdots \\ s_k \end{matrix} \quad H(C_\alpha) \tag{5}$$

3.2 Knowledge-Based System Module

KBSM makes the selection of one element keeping COLREGs out of candidate sector set created in the CSSM. It is possible to apply COLREGs, which every seagoing vessel must keep, to the collision avoidance by adopting a knowledge-based system. In order to apply COLREGs to the collision avoidance, it is necessary to define the encounter situations of vessels. Three different encounter situations of vessels, namely, overtaking, head-on, and crossing are classified in COLREGs and the rule of "action to avoid collision" for each situation are stipulated as shown in table 1.

Table 1. Action to avoid collision stipulated in COLREGs.

Situation	Bearing		Action to avoid collision
Overtaking (Rule 13)	More than 22.5° abaft beam	Overtaking vessel	Keep out of the way of overtaken vessel
		Overtaken vessel	Keep the current course
Head-On (Rule 14)	Less than 6° on the bow	Each vessel	Alter course to starboard
Crossing (Rule 15)	More than 6° & Less than 106.5°	Give-way vessel	Alter course to starboard
		Stand-on vessel	Keep the current course

4 Simulation Results

In order to verify the performance of proposed collision avoidance system, a simulation is conducted with scenarios which take into account an encounter situations classified in COLREGs. Seven different simulation scenarios, s1 through s7, are defined such as head-on situation, overtaking situation, crossing situation, head-on and overtaking situation, head-on and crossing situation, overtaking and crossing situation, and random situation.

The collision avoidance system for autonomous ship should takes into consideration not only deriving a reasonable path to the goal but also keeping COLREGs. The paths generated by proposed collision avoidance system are shown in figures 3 and figure 4. Figure 3 shows the trajectory of head-on situation. At a first computation on the start position, the collision avoidance system selects a sector on the right-hand side numbered as 1 even if the goal position is located on the left-hand side of the vessel. When vessels are faced with head-on situation, each vessel should alter course to starboard as mentioned in the table 1. This is the reason of selecting a sector on the right-hand side. Figure 4 shows the trajectory of overtaking situation. At the start position, the vessel selects a sector of same course. It is reasonable for general collision avoidance system to select a sector on the left-hand side as next sector. Because the goal is located on the left-hand side, and we do not need to consider obstacle1 located on the backside. But seagoing vessels should keep the COLREGs. Therefore, the overtaken vessel in the scenario 1 cannot change the heading of vessel.

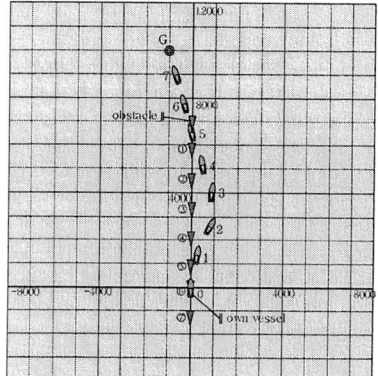 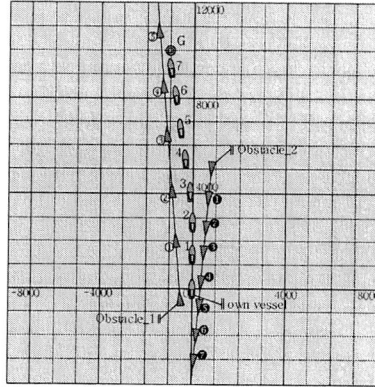

Fig. 3. The trajectory of scenario 1.　　Fig. 4. The trajectory of scenario 2.

5   Conclusion

In this paper we have presented a collision avoidance system for autonomous ship, which satisfies the optimality and safety of derived path and keeps the rule of "action to avoid collision" stipulated in the COLREGs. The simulation results with scenario1 through scenario 7 classified in COLREGs show that the proposed collision avoidance system is a practical and effective candidate for real-time path planning system of autonomous ship.

References

1. Samuelides, E. and Frieze. P.: Experimental and Numerical Simulation of Ship Collisions, Proc. Congress on Marine Technology, Vol. 1, Athens, Greece, 1984.
2. Koyama, T. and Yan, J.: An Expert System Approach to Collision Avoidance, 8th Ship Control System Symposium, Hague, 1987.

3. Hasegawa, K., Kouzuki, A., Muramatsu, T., Komine, H. and Watabe, Y.: Ship Autonavigation Fuzzy Expert System(SAFES), Journal of the Society of Naval Architecture of Japan, 166, 1989.
4. Imazu, H. and Koyama, T.: The Determination of Collision Avoidance Action, Journal of Japan Institute of Navigation, 70, 1984.
5. Imazu, H. and Koyama, T.: The Optimization of the Criterion for Collision Avoidance Action, Journal of Japan Institute of Navigation, 71, 1984.
6. Lee, H., Yoo, W., and Rhee, K.: Development of Collision Avoidance System by Fuzzy Theory, Joint Workshop on Ship & Marine Hydrodynamics, 1993.
7. Xianyi, Y., Mzx M.: A Neural Netwok Approach to Real-Time Collision-Free Navigation of 3-D.O.F. Robots in 2D, ICRA, 1999.
8. Yoon, J. D.: COLREGs, 1972 And Related Domestic Rules in Korea, Se-Jong, 2000.
9. Bandler, W., and Kohout, L. J.: Semantics of Implication Operators and Fuzzy Relational Products, Intl. Journal of Man-Machine Studies, 1980.
10. Bandler, W., and Kohout L. J.: Fuzzy Power Sets and Fuzzy Implication Operator, Fuzzy Set and System, 4, 13–30, 1980.
11. Bandler, W., and Kohout, L. J.: Fuzzy Relational Products as a Tool for Analysis and Synthesis of the Behaviour of Complex natural and Artificial System, in: Wang, S. K, and Chang, P. P. eds., Fuzzy Sets: Theory and Application to Analysis and Information Systems, Plenum Press, New York, 341–367, 1980.
12. Borenstein, J., and Koren, Y.: Real-time Obstacle Avoidance for Fast Mobile Robots, IEEE Transactions on System, Man, and Cybernetics, 19, 1989.
13. Borenstein, J., and Koren, Y.: The Vector Field Histogram - Fast Obstacle Avoidance for Mobile Robots, IEEE Journal of Robotics and Automation, 1991.
14. Lee, Y. I., Kim, Y. G., and Ladislav J. Kohout, An Intelligent Collision Avoidance System for AUVs using Fuzzy Relational Products, Information Sciences, 158, 2004.

Engineering Knowledge Discovery in Network Intrusion Detection

Andrea Bosin, Nicoletta Dessì, and Barbara Pes

Università degli Studi di Cagliari, Dipartimento di Matematica e Informatica
Via Ospedale 72, 09124 Cagliari
andrea.bosin@dsf.unica.it
{dessi,pes}@unica.it

Abstract. The use of data mining techniques for intrusion detection (ID) is one of the ongoing issues in the field of computer security, but little attention has been placed in engineering ID activities. This paper presents a framework that models the ID process as a set of cooperative tasks each supporting a specialized activity. Specifically, the framework organises raw audit data into a set of relational tables and applies data mining algorithms to generate intrusion detection models. Specialized components of a commercial DBMS have been used to validate the proposed approach. Results show that the framework works well in capturing patterns of intrusion while the availability of an integrated software environment allows a high level of modularity in performing each task.

1 Introduction

The rapid growth of the Internet has lead to increased interest in intelligent methods and tools to detect attacks against the network and its resources. Most of ongoing research concentrates on promoting Intrusion Detection Systems (IDS) providing detection capabilities for malicious or otherwise unauthorized activity on a network.

A major issue is the process of knowledge acquisition i.e. the encoding of human expertise, which is the current state of practice, into decision rules that must be incorporated in the systems. This process is considered a bottleneck because a human expert is required to spend many time in analysing a large amount of raw audit data to identify a useful set of rules that capture substantial security expertise. In addition, when decision rules have been determined and employed, it is necessary to update the rules continuously in order to detect new types of attack.

This approach has proved to be insufficient [1] and recent experiences show that data mining techniques can be successfully applied to automate the human time-intensive and error-prone data evaluation. This automation can be characterized as a learning by example where a set of raw data provides decision examples made by a human expert and the knowledge discovered through this process is used to automatically recognize attacks. In addition, both researchers and human experts accept that ID process has specific needs that cannot be properly addressed by current IDS. It has been pointed out [1] that current IDS have too little of extensibility, adaptability as well as built-in mechanisms for customisation of ID processes that include creating a target dataset, focusing on a subset of attack features, cleaning and pre-processing audit data, discovering patterns from data and consolidating discovered. However, while considerable effort has taken place in ID techniques and models, to date there appears to be no study which has focused on the IDS infrastructure in terms of its components and required technology.

Toward this end, this paper abandons the data-centric view point that considers the ID as a mere data analysis process and introduces a functional approach intended to model an IDS as a set of specialized tasks including capabilities to analyse raw audit datasets. The central theme of our approach is to focus on the activities that support ID and to propose a framework for their organization.

The framework is intended to be a reference model for IDS design by providing methodological support for modelling both the data structure and the data mining process in a uniform and modular way. Data is gathered into relational tables and data mining algorithms are used in order to build knowledge-based models providing information to user needs or suggesting new ways to explore the available data. This approach allows to distinguish among the different expertises involved in the ID process, going from pre-processing of raw audit data by an ID expert to the choice and the evaluation of the intrusion model by the researchers.

Even if the actual framework implementation can take many semantically equivalent forms, we tried to validate its effectiveness on top of a commercial tool because the availability of such a framework as an extension of existing information systems is doubly important.

The paper is organized as follows. Section 2 describes the framework. Section 3 reports the framework evaluation using the KDD Cup 1999 datasets. Conclusions are outlined in Section 4. Finally, Section 5 presents some related works addressing ID issues.

2 The Framework

The proposed framework aims to capture the data mining activity within ID, while it provides support for data manipulation and the flow of information. Towards this end, the ID process is organised as a set of cooperative tasks each supporting a specialized activity. Process information is stored into normalized data structures, which guarantee an organized management of raw data. Tasks exchange information among themselves, through flows that carry information items from a producer task to a consumer task, as described in the following.

Table 1 describes the framework emphasizing tasks and their I/O flows. In particular, the first task organizes raw data into a set of relational tables in order to take advantage of DBMS built-in facilities. The resulting environment provides standard data structures (e.g. reusable relational tables) and can be customized to specific applications. Task 2 inherits choices and settings from the previous task and applies data mining algorithms to obtain a set of rules expressing the ID model. Task 3 is a critical step because it evaluates the model effectiveness. Finally task 4 provides model application.

Table 1. The proposed framework.

	Task	Input Flow	Output Flow
1	Data pre-processing	data streams	relational tables
2	Model building	relational tables data mining algorithms	intrusion detection rules
3	Model testing	relational tables intrusion detection rules	parameters for model performance evaluation
4	Model application	relational tables intrusion detection rules	intrusion detection

In order to give the reader a task overview, we shortly detail an exemplificative ID process. First, raw audit data streams are processed and summarized into connection records which in turn are partitioned and stored inside relational tables (task 1). This results in a knowledge warehouse that serves as a repository for original data, test sets as well as for training sets whose instances are labelled as "normal" or "intrusion" by a human expert. A data mining algorithm is then applied to a training set and the corresponding ID model is built. The model can be stated in terms of a set of ID rules (task 2). The performance of the model is evaluated against a test set in order to asses its effectiveness in both classifying well know attacks and detecting new types of intrusions (task 3). If the model works well it is ready to be used in classifying new unknown connections (task 4), otherwise the model can be refined.

The framework explicitly engineers the ID process and promotes good separation among activities. This allows IDS designers to be able to specify the contents of the knowledge warehouse and the task behaviour in an implementation-independent way.

Although framework tasks are *per se* not new, their modular organisation has a profound effect on the extensibility of the framework. For example, we can detail each task in any specific subtask allowing framework to be easily customized.

In addition, the framework does not depend on a specific model because the knowledge warehouse is organised around a relational database and it is therefore very flexible with regard to features for extracting and combining models. This allows models to be used as input to other mining algorithms in order to refine the model building task.

The framework enables several kinds of implementations through different software applications. Specifically, tasks can be mapped to software components that can be combined easily to build custom-tailored IDS.

3 Framework Evaluation

The proposed framework has been evaluated in order to both validate the approach and verify its effectiveness in supporting the ID process. As a running example we refer to the KDD Cup 1999 [9] dataset, which can be processed into about 5 million connection records. Each record encodes 41 connection features including a classification label ("normal" or "type_of_attack"). All connection features are assumed to be conditionally independent. Four main categories of attacks were simulated: DOS, denial of service; R2L, unauthorized access from a remote machine; U2R, unauthorized access to local superuser (root) privileges and PROBING, information gathering. In order to evaluate the performance of the models against unclassified data, we used an additional unlabeled dataset.

The implementation has been performed on top of a commercial DBMS [8] in order to take advantage of its built-in data mining components and to provide a high level of automation and integration while preserving a user-friendly environment. Basic and specialized DBMS modules have been used to implement the following tasks:

Data Pre-processing. We split the labeled dataset into three different sets: training data (60% of original records), evaluation data (10% of original records, to determine which rules were valid) and test data (30% of original records). All sets were organized in relational tables where each row makes up a connection and where features are identified by columns.

Model Building. Data mining for ID has the following peculiarities inspired by the nature of the application:

1) *The training set has a large number of attributes.* Even if previous studies suggested [1] to reduce and select appropriate features, our experiment includes all the extensive set of 41 indicators to provide a more effective evaluation scenario.
2) *It is necessary to provide model transparency*, that is, a set of human-readable rules explaining the model and supporting predictive information.

The above considerations suggest to select the Adaptive Bayes Network (ABN) algorithm [10] to produce the following two intrusion detection models:

- the binary target model whose training set includes only two classification labels (normal/attack)
- the multi-target model whose training set includes 22 types of attack.

Model Testing. Both models have been tested using the same test dataset. Table 2.A, 2.C and 2.E show the performance of the detection models in terms of their detection rates assessed by the % of correct predictions. Table 2.C summarizes global results (normal/attack) while Table 2.E details the predictions of multi-target model grouped by categories (dos, probe, r2l, u2l, normal).

The multi-target model was trained on single attack instances and performs best in predicting attack categories with a large number of training examples.

Model Application. Table 2.B and 2.D show the performance of models against the unlabeled dataset containing new types of attacks that do not have corresponding instances in the training data. Results show a worse detection rate because models are not effective for new attacks that are mostly misclassified as normal (only 12% of new attacks are correctly detected).

Table 2. Actual (Act.) vs predicted (Pred.) connections and detection rate.

A. Test dataset (binary target model)

Pred. / Act.	attack	normal	Rate
attack	118337	867	99.3%
normal	233	28899	99.2%

B. Unlabeled dataset (binary target model)

Pred. / Act.	attack	Normal	rate
attack	228732	21704	91.3%
normal	1320	59273	97.8%

C. Test dataset (multi-target model)

Pred. / Act.	attack	normal	rate
attack	118406	798	99.3%
normal	768	28364	97.4%

D. Unlabeled dataset (multi-target model)

Pred. / Act.	attack	Normal	rate
attack	228014	22392	91.1%
normal	1396	59197	97.7%

E. Test dataset (multi-target model) – attacks grouped by class

Pred. / Act.	dos	probe	r2l	u2l	normal	Rate
dos	116937	2	10	2	681	99.4%
probe	67	1110	4	0	34	91.4%
r2l	1	2	263	0	70	78.3%
u2l	1	0	7	0	13	0%
normal	76	243	447	2	28364	97.4%

Our results show that models compare well with other ad-hoc intrusion detection models proposed in the literature [1,6], i.e. they work well in detecting attacks for which they are trained and poorly for new types of attacks.

4 Conclusions

This paper introduced a framework that models the activities supporting intrusion detection in a uniform and modular way. In order to validate its effectiveness, we developed a reference implementation on top of a commercial integrated environment, taking advantage of its built-in modular components. This strategy allowed us to reach a high level of automation and integration between tasks in a user-friendly environment. While our preliminary results are promising, many important challenges remain. The framework is by no means complete and requires further investigations addressing important problems such as real-time processing, mixed model support and distributed data mining techniques. Important next steps to expand the framework include providing tasks that can dynamically determine what are actions that should be taken against an attack.

5 Related Work

IDS are generally classified as *signature-based systems*, that look for predefined patterns known to be malicious, and *anomaly-based systems*, that look for deviations from the expected behaviour. Signature-based and anomaly-based techniques, having a complementary nature, can be combined in the development of IDS.

A data mining framework for building intrusion detection models is presented in [1]. The key idea is to first analyse audit data by data mining programs which compute frequent patterns and extract relevant features. Then, classification algorithms (such as [2]) are used to inductively learn the detection models, that are intended for off-line analysis but may be also adapted to real-time IDS. Specifically, the proposed framework produces misuse detection models for network and host systems as well as anomaly detection models for users. Some interesting results from the 1998 DARPA ID Evaluation Program are presented. A discussion on usefulness of data mining techniques in intrusion detection can be found in [6].

[3] is an attempt to apply to network intrusion detection a distributed data mining approach that integrates inductive generalization and agent-based computing. [4] presents an intrusion detection system that uses statistical anomaly detection to find remote-to-local attacks targeted at essential network services. The proposed approach utilizes application specific knowledge of the network services that should be protected. A statistical detection method is adopted also in [5]; the paper describes an anomaly-based ID tool and discusses the results obtained both with simulated and real data. Web-based vulnerabilities are specifically addressed in [7], that presents different anomaly based techniques to detect attacks against web servers and web applications.

References

1. Lee W., Stolfo S. J., A Framework for Constructing Features and Models for Intrusion Detections Systems, ACM Transactions on Information and System Security, Vol. 3, No. 4, November 2000, pages 227-261.
2. Cohen W. W., Fast effective rule induction, in Proceedings of the 12th International Conference on Machine Learning (Lake Tahoe, CA, 1995). Morgan Kaufmann, San Mateo.
3. Bala J., Baik S., Hadjarian A., Gogia B.K., Manthorne Chris, Application of a Distributed Data Mining Approach to Network Intrusion Detection, in Proceedings of AAMAS'02, July 15-19, 2002, Bologna, Italy.
4. Krügel C., Toth T., Kirda E., Service Specific Anomaly Detection for Network Intrusion Detection, in Proceedings of SAC 2002, Madrid, Spain.
5. Taylor C., Alves-Foss J., An Empirical Analysis of NATE – Network Analysis of Anomalous Traffic Events, New Security Paradigms Workshop '02, September 23-26, 2002, Virginia Beach, Virginia.
6. Barbará D., Couto J., Jajodia S., Wu N., ADAM: A Testbed for Exploring the Use of Data Mining in Intrusion Detection, SIGMOD Records, Vol. 30, No. 4, December 2001.
7. Kruegel C., Vigna G., Anomaly Detection of Web-based Attacks, in Proceedings of CCS'03, October 27-31, 2003, Washington, DC, USA.
8. Oracle 9i Data Mining Concepts, release 9.2.0.2, October 2002.
9. UCI KDD Archive. http://kdd.ics.uci.edu/databases/kddcup99/kddcup99.html.
10. Yarmus J.S., ABN: A Fast, Greedy Bayesian Network Classifier, 2003.
11. http://otn.oracle.com/products/bi/pdf/adaptive_bayes_net.pdf.

False Alarm Classification Model for Network-Based Intrusion Detection System*

Moon Sun Shin, Eun Hee Kim, and Keun Ho Ryu

Database Laboratory
Chungbuk National University, Korea
{msshin,ehkim,khryu}@dblab.cbu.ac.kr

Abstract. Network-based IDS(Intrusion Detection System) gathers network packet data and analyzes them into attack or normal. But they often output a large amount of low-level or incomplete alert information. Such alerts can be unmanageable and also be mixed with false alerts. In this paper we proposed a false alarm classification model to reduce the false alarm rate using classification analysis of data mining techniques. The model was implemented based on associative classification in the domain of DDOS attack. We evaluated the false alarm classifier deployed in front of Snort with Darpa 1998 dataset and verified the reduction of false alarm rate. Our approach is useful to reduce false alerts and to improve the detection rate of network-based intrusion detection systems.

1 Introduction

As the network-based computer systems play the vital roles increasingly these days, they have become the targets of the intrusions. Because of the large traffic volume, IDS often needs to be extended and be updated frequently and timely. Currently building the effective IDS is an enormous knowledge engineering task. Recent data mining algorithms have been designed for the application domains involved with the several types of objects stored in the relational databases. All IDSs require a component that produces basic alerts as a result of comparing the properties of an input element to the values defined by their rules. Most of systems perform the detection of basic alarms by each input event to all rules sequentially, and IDSs raise the alarm when possible intrusion happens. Consequently, IDSs usually generate a large amount of alerts that can be unmanageable and also be mixed with false alerts. Sometimes the volume of alerts is large and the percentile of the false alarms is very high. So it is necessary to manage alerts for the correct intrusion detection. As a result, nearly all IDSs have the problem of managing alerts, especially false alarms, which cause seriously to impact performance of the IDSs. A general solution to this problem is needed. We describe an approach that decreases the rate of false alarms.

There are standard measures for evaluating IDSs: detection rate, false alarm rate, performance and tolerance. False alarm rate is a ratio between the number of normal

---

* This work was supported by University IT Research Center, KOSEF RRC and ETRI in Korea.

connections that are incorrectly misclassified as attacks and the total number of normal connections. In this paper, we propose a false alarm classification model to reduce the false alarm rate using classification analysis of data mining techniques. The proposed model can classify the alarms generated by intrusion detection systems into false alert or true attack. Our approach is useful to improve the detection rate of network-based intrusion detection systems and to reduce the sheer volume of alerts.

2 Related Works

Some of the recent researches have started to apply the data mining techniques to the IDSs[3]. Because of the sheer volume of audit data, the efficient and intelligent data analysis tools are required to discover the behavior of the system activities. Data mining generally refers to the process of extracting useful information from large stores of data. The aim of our research is to develop mining system for reducing false alarms.

The current intrusion detection systems do not offer grouping the related alerts logically. Also the existing intrusion detection systems are likely to generate false alerts, either false positive or false negative. To solve these critical problems, the intrusion detection community is actively developing standards for the content of the alert messages and some researches are on going about the alert correlation. Specifically, each alert has a number of attributes such as timestamp, source IP, destination IP, ports, user name, process name, attack class, and sensor ID, which are defined in the standard document "Intrusion Detection Message Exchange Format(IDMEF)" drafted by the IETF Intrusion Detection Working Group.

In [8] they introduced probabilistic approach for the coupled sensors to reduce the false alarm. An aggregation and correlation algorithm is presented in [7] for acquiring the alerts and relating them. The algorithm could explain more condensed view of the security issues raised by the intrusion detection systems.

IDSs usually generate a large amount of alerts. Whereas actual alerts can be mixed with false alerts and also the amount of alerts becomes unmanageable. In [10] they propose the intrusion alert correlator based on the prerequisites of intrusions.

This paper presents applying decision tree to reduce false alarms from IDS and improve the performance of intrusion detection system. In our approach, we use associative classification mining to reduce the redundancy of alerts while keeping the important information.

3 Building False Alarm Classification Model

The idea of false alarm classification model is to filter the false alarms from intrusion detection system and minimize the false alarm rate by matching the alarms compared to the false alarm classification rules. Then we can expect the higher detection rate of intrusion detection system at the same time. For that purpose, we applied data mining techniques for the classification. The data mining techniques can be generally used in data reduction and data clustering. Classification is to build a model(called classifier) to predict future data objects for which the class label is unknown. Decision tree, rule learning, naive-Bayes classification and statistical approaches can be used. In general, given a training data set, the task of classification is to build a classifier from the data set such that it can be used to predict class labels of unknown objects with high accuracy. So we extend the basic decision tree algorithm C4.5[4] to the association based classification for the feature construction.

Network-based IDS outputs the sheer volume of alerts that can be mixed with false alerts. The false alarm is the alarm classified as attack while in fact it is not. Table 1 shows the standard metrics.

Table 1. Intrusion Evaluation Confusion Metrics.

Standard metrics		Predicted Connection Label	
		Normal	Intrusions
Actual Connection Label	Normal	True Negative(TN)	False Positive(FP)
	Intrusions	False Negative(FN)	True Positive(TP)

Actually a large volume of false alarms makes it impossible for IDS to respond immediately and prevents IDS from correct detection. So we propose false alarm classifier to improve intrusion detection rate of IDS.

Here is the framework of our approach that has two parts: First is feature construction and second is classification part as shown in figure 1. From the sensor, we preprocess the alert data and store them into database. And then we construct the false alarm classification model by learning false positive alarm pattern from false alarm decision tree using training dataset.

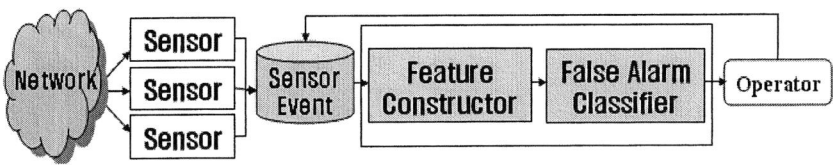

Fig. 1. Framework of False Alarm Classifier.

Building accurate and efficient classifiers for large databases depends on training dataset. We used association rule-based feature construction. We built our false alarm classification model by using decision tree especially C4.5[4] algorithm because this algorithm is very efficient in memory and performance.

The whole process consists of four phases: feature construction, rule generation, rule analysis and classification. In the first phase, feature construction, the preprocessor computes the high correlated attributes based on associative feature construction in order to decide the nodes for decision tree. Association rule mining searches for interesting relationships among the given data set under the assumption in terms of confidence and support. Large itemsets of training dataset were extracted as the feature from the alert_DB and stored in attribute_list table. We sent Darpa Tcpdump data through the Snort and counted all the false positives for the generation of training dataset. The training data set was stored in alert_DB w.r.t. each protocol after preprocessing task because they were raw network data. In the second phase, rule generation, the decision tree builder computed the complete set of rules in the form of R: P->c, where P is the pattern in the training data set, and c is a class label such that $sup(R)$ and $conf(R)$ pass the given support and confidence thresholds, respectively.

Furthermore, following task prunes some rules and only selects a subset of high quality rules for classification. Before the tree construction, information gain of each attribute must be computed. The attribute which had the highest value of information gain can be used as root node. The expression of (1) is the information value for each attributes and (2) is the entropy of each attribute.

$$Information = \log_2 p \qquad (p = number\ of\ attributes) \qquad (1)$$

$$Entropy(S) = p_{FP} \log_2 p_{FP} - p_{TP} \log_2 p_{TP} \qquad (2)$$

Using the values of (1) and (2), we can compute the information gain value of each attributes as shown in (3) where S is the class labels of nodes, S_v is the class labels of branches. Then decision tree builder can make root node and repeat the process of computing (1)-(3) and decide root node of subtree again. The recursive process will be finished when there is no split. Then final rule sets are generated after pruning.

$$Gain(S, A) = Entropy - \sum |S_v|/|S| * Entropy(S_v) \qquad (3)$$

The pruning process was performed to remove outliers. Final rules were generated as the form of <IF><THEN>. These rules were stored in the rule table, too.

In the third phase, rule analysis, the validation task was performed about constructed decision tree using test data. If needed, the tree must be overfitted and pruned.

In the last phase, the classification model classifies new data by pattern matching with rule and gives the class for each new data.

4 Implementation

The prototype of false alarm classifier consists of four components such as Data Preprocessor, Feature Constructor, Decision Tree Builder and Data Classifier. Data Preproceesor transformed binary raw data and stored them into database table. Feature Constructor selects attributes using association rule-based or probabilistic correlation method. Decision Tree Builder constructs classification model based on training data and Data Classifier actually classifies test data.

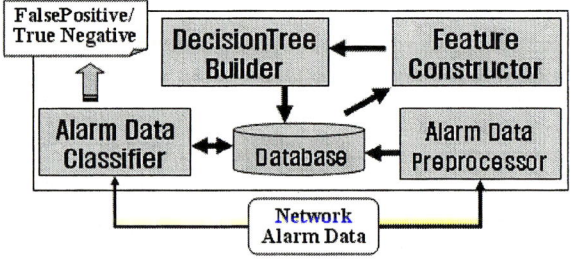

Fig. 2. Architecture of False Alarm Classifier.

Final rules were also stored in the relational database and they were used by security administrator or intrusion detection system. Figure 2 shows the architecture of the false alarm classifier and the relationships among the components. The false alarm classifier was implemented by Java and Oracle 8i as database. For evaluation, we used Snort-1.8.7 as sample IDS. The implemented prototype had three levels such as user interface, data repository and main program that were composed of database connection, decision tree builder and data classifier. Decision tree builder class constructs the decision tree of false positive with the training data set. Data classifier class classifies the test data by using the rules of the decision tree. All the rules and dataset were stored in the relational database. So the database connection class performs the tasks that were related to the database. We implemented C4.5 algorithm as the extension of association rule based-classification for the decision tree of false alarm classification. The C4.5 algorithm has the advantage of memory and performance comparing to other decision tree algorithms.

5 Experiments and Evaluation

This section presents the experimental results of our false alarm classifier. Two experiments were performed. For the experiments, we placed the implemented system in front of Snort-1.8.6[5]. And we sent the Darpa tcpdump data through the Snort that obtained the false alarm classifier. Our performance results are compared to those of only Snort alone. Other experiments were preformed to handle the processing of an input element at nodes of decision tree efficiently. The ability of false classification depended on feature construction. We proposed association rule-based classification. So the features for nodes of decision tree were selected by association rule-based approach. Also we tried to evaluate statistical based correlation analysis for the feature construction. The mixed method of those approaches was evaluated for the best feature construction. Experimental data were Darpa 1998 raw packet data of DOS attack. We could find out the different nodes of the each method for feature construction, the correctness of false alarm classifier and the performance of the detection rate of Snort. The training data set for the classification model was the tcpdump data for 7 weeks. We only chose the DOS attack labeled data among the various types of attack data. The ratio of normal and intrusive was same. We used 1-4 weeks data as training dataset and 5-7 weeks data as test data.

■ *The Node Changes of Decision Tree as the Feature Construction*
For utilizing the decision tree, we had to remove the improper attributes and select appropriate attributes. For the feature construction, we proposed association rule-based feature selection. However, we tried to do statistics approach too.

From the results of statistical correlation analysis, the attributes of strong correlation were FSI(fagment size), ILN(Ip length), IOF(Ip Offset), FOS(fragment Offset), SEQ(sequence Number). So the five attributes were extracted for nodes based on probabilistic correlation analysis.

The maximum lengths of large itemset as the changes of support value were decreased. The minimum support value was changed from 0.5 to 1. From the experiments, the support value was 0.5 and the length of large item set was 8.

So we could decide the minimum support from this experiment as the average of support, 0.75. Therefore the length of large itemset was 4 according to the support 0.75. The 4 attributes such as TTL(Time to Live), ACK(Acknowledgement), TLN(Tcp length) and FLG(Flag) were selected by association rule-based approach.

■ *The Correctness of False Alarm Classification Model*

From the first experiment, the nodes of decision tree were made and two decision trees were constructed. One is the statistical correlation based decision tree. And the other was constructed by the feature construction based on association rule based approach. We evaluated these decision trees correctly.

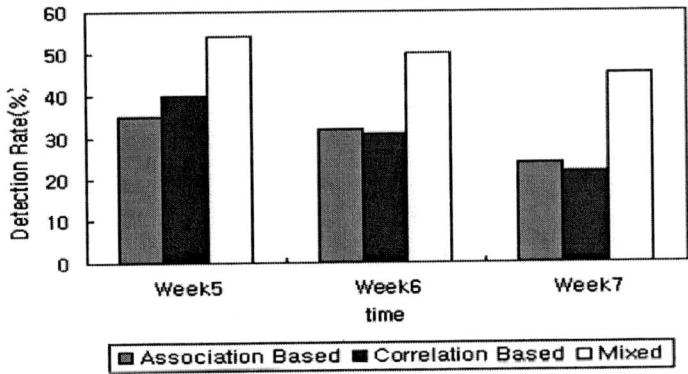

Fig. 3. Detection rate of Normal Packet for Each Decision Tree.

Figure 3 shows the results of detection rate of normal packets. The experiments were performed with three methods like association based, statistical correlation based and the mix of both above methods. Figure 3 shows that association rule-based decision tree marked higher performance than statistical correlation based decision tree. And among the three approaches, the mixed method was the most efficient in detection rate of normal packet.

■ *The Performance of the IDS with False Classifier*

The last experiment was performed for the evaluation of false positive rate of IDS in both cases: with false alarm classifier and without false alarm decision tree. For this experiment, we used Snort-1.8.6 open source[5] and Darpa data that were already used in previous experiments.

As shown in figure 4, the mixed method and association rule based decision tree were more effective. But in the case of week 5 data, it showed especially high value.

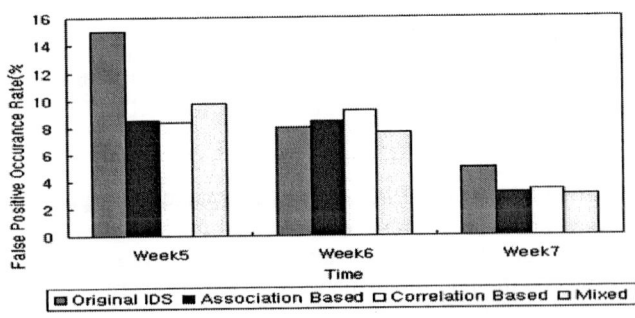

Fig. 4. Results of False Positive Rate of Each Decision Tree.

6 Conclusion

In this paper we presented a false alarm classification model to reduce the false alarm rate of intrusion detection systems using data mining techniques. The proposed model could classify the alarms from the intrusion detection systems into false alert or true attack. We also implemented the false alarm classifier of DDOS attack. We proved that the proposed false alarm classifier worked effectively in reducing false alarm rate.

References

1. D. Schnackenberg, K. Djahandari, and D. Sterne, Infrastructure for Intrusion Detection and Response, Proceedings of the DARPA ISCE, Hilton Head, SC, Jan. 2000.
2. M.J. Lee, M.S. Shin, H. S. Moon, K. H. Ryu Design and Implementation of Alert Analyzer with Data Mining Engine, in Proc. IDEAL'03, HongKong, March. 2003.
3. W. Lee, S. J. Stolfo, K. W. Mok A Data Mining Framework for Building Intrusion Detection Models in Proc. The 2nd International Symposium on Recent Advances in Intrusion Detection, RAID, 1999.
4. J. Ross Quinlan, C4.5: Programs for and Neural Networks, Machine Learning, Morgan Kaufman publishers, 1993.
5. Snort. Open-source Network Intrusion Detection System. http://www.snort.org.
6. E.H. Spafford and D. Zamboni., Intrusion detection using autonomous agents, Computer Networks, 34, 547–570, 2000.
7. H. Debar and A.Wespi, Aggregation and correlation of intrusion-detection alerts, In Recent Advances in Intrusion Detection, in Lecture Notes in Computer Science, 85 – 103, 2001.
8. A.Valdes and K. Skinner, Probabilistic alert correlation, in Proc. The 4th International Symposium on Recent Advances in Intrusion Detection, RAID, 54–68, 2001.
9. Tcpdump/Libpcap, Network Packet Capture Program, http://www.tcpdump.org, 2003.
10. P. Ning and Y. Cui., An intrusion alert correlator based on prerequisites of intrusions, Technical Report TR-2002-01, Department of Computer Science, North Carolina State University, 2002.

Exploiting Safety Constraints in Fuzzy Self-organising Maps for Safety Critical Applications

Zeshan Kurd[1], Tim P. Kelly[1], and Jim Austin[2]

[1] High Integrity Systems Engineering Group
[2] Advanced Computer Architectures Group
Department of Computer Science
University of York, York, YO10 5DD, UK
{zeshan.kurd,tim.kelly,austin}@cs.york.ac.uk

Abstract. This paper defines a constrained Artificial Neural Network (ANN) that can be employed for highly-dependable roles in safety critical applications. The derived model is based upon the Fuzzy Self-Organising Map (FSOM) and enables behaviour to be described qualitatively and quantitatively. By harnessing these desirable features, behaviour is bounded through incorporation of safety constraints – derived from safety requirements and hazard analysis. The constrained FSOM has been termed a 'Safety Critical Artificial Neural Network' (SCANN) and preserves valuable performance characteristics for non-linear function approximation problems. The SCANN enables construction of compelling (product-based) safety arguments for mitigation and control of identified failure modes. Illustrations of potential benefits for real-world applications are also presented.

1 Introduction

Artificial Neural Networks (ANNs) are employed in a wide range of applications such as defence, medical and industrial process control domains [1]. There are a plethora of appealing features associated with ANNs such as adapting to a changing environment and generalisation given novel data. They are efficient tools for finding swift solutions using little input from designers. However, there exist several problems associated with ANNs that commonly restrict operation to advisory roles in safety related applications. Recent work [2] has examined verification and validation of ANNs for critical systems. This work aims to provide guaranteed output (within bounds) for ANN models whose behaviour is represented neither in structured nor organised forms. As a result, the approach treats the ANN as a black-box and uses pedagogical approaches to analyse and control behaviour (using error bounds [2]). This analytical approach is common to the main thrust of existing work for developing ANNs for safety critical contexts as reviewed in [3]. Limitations experienced from black-box analysis clearly highlight the need for improved neural models to allow compelling safety and performance arguments required for certification.

Within the scope of this paper, section 2 defines a potentially suitable ANN model with learning algorithms. Section 3 presents an overview of how key failure modes are tackled by means of safety constraints. Section 4 describes the benefits of the approach using an abstract control system example.

2 Fuzzy Self-organising Maps

Our previous work [4] has identified 'hybrid' neural networks as potential models for allowing white-box style (decompositional) analysis. 'Hybrid' ANNs facilitate potential arguments about specific functional properties. This section describes an existing ANN model known as the Fuzzy Self-Organising Map (FSOM) [5]. The FSOM is a 'neuro-fuzzy' system and is based upon Kohonen's Self-Organising Map. It is endowed with the ability to describe its behaviour using Takagi-Sugeno (TS) fuzzy rules. TS fuzzy rules encapsulate both qualitative and quantitative descriptions of the functional behaviour where rule outputs are linear functions. The FSOM has been used for pattern recognition problems [5] and non-linear function approximation [6]) with fruitful results. The FSOM architecture consists of six stages and is illustrated in figure 1.

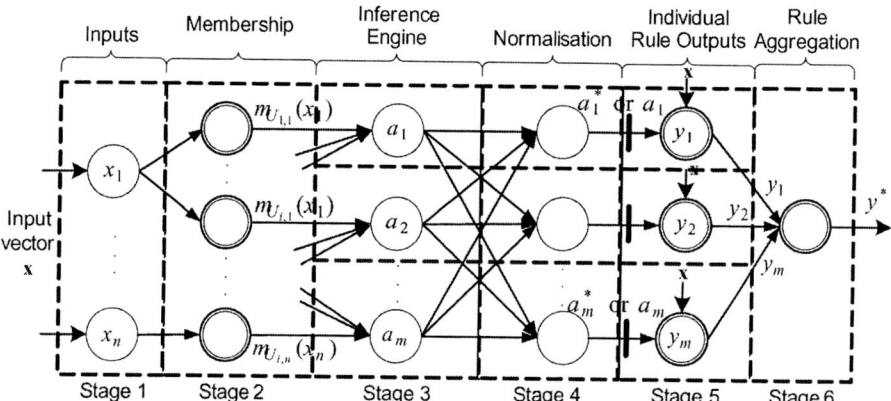

Fig. 1. Fuzzy Self Organising Map with constrained neurons depicted by double circles.

Stage 1 involves no pre-processing and simply propagates inputs x_j where $j = 1,2,...,n$, (n is the total number of input variables) to stage 2. The number of neurons equals the number of input variables (or sensors).

Stage 2 performs the set membership function and contains a neuron for every fuzzy set. The membership is defined by the triangular function [6]. Each fuzzy set is defined as $U_{i,j}$ for the ith rule where $i = 1,2,...,m$, (m is the total number of rules). The adaptable parameters for each fuzzy set are centre, left and right edges of the spread (or support) as defined by (1).

$$\{c_{i,j}, sl_{i,j}, sr_{i,j}\}. \tag{1}$$

Stage 3 performs fuzzy inference, where the firing strength α_i for each rule is determined by the minimum operator. The firing strength is greater than zero only if all rule antecedents are true. **Stage 4** normalises firing strengths and **Stage 5** determines crisp rule outputs for the ith rule using (2).

$$y_i = f_i(x_1,...,x_n) = a_{i,0} + a_{i,1}x_1 + a_{i,2}x_2 +,..., + a_{i,n}x_n. \tag{2}$$

There are $n+1$ adaptable output parameters per rule defined by (3).

$$\{a_{i,0}, a_{i,1}, \ldots, a_{i,n}\}. \tag{3}$$

Stage 6 consists of a single neuron which performs weighted averaging (using rule firing strengths α_i). This determines the final output from multiple firing rules.

The FSOM employs a static learning algorithm for tuning parameters (1) and (3) using training samples or input data. It is performed in two stages as defined in [6]:

- **Phase 1:** Antecedent parameters are frozen and the consequent parameters (3) of the rules are adapted (supervised) using the Least Mean Square algorithm.
- **Phase 2:** Consequent parameters are frozen and the antecedent parameters (1) are tuned using the modified LVQ algorithm [6] (supervised or unsupervised mode).

The FSOM can also self-generate (dynamic learning) as described by Vuorimaa [5]. This automatically acquires novel features described by training data whilst adapting the neural architecture without user intervention. Dynamic learning is an integral feature of the safety lifecycle [4] and further details can be found in [6].

3 Safety Arguments

In previous work [7], the safety criteria were established as a number of high-level goals with a safety argument expressed in GSN (Goal Structuring Notation). These goals were based upon encapsulating different failure modes associated with the generalisation and learning abilities of ANNs. A set of failure modes have been identified for the FSOM that have been derived from HAZOP (Hazard Operability Study) [8] guide words (which originates from the process-control theory domain). The principal failure modes are summarised below:

1. Output is too high or too low for the given input vector.
2. Missing output given valid inputs (output omission).
3. Output increases when it should decrease (and vice versa).
4. Output rate of change is too high or too low (derivatives).

Enabling the FSOM to be used in safety critical systems requires integrating mechanisms to prevent systematic faults from being incorporated during learning. This is achieved through inflexible bounds for flexibility (in behaviour) using constraints on both the generalisation and learning processes. As a result, the modified (or constrained) FSOM is called the SCANN and is used for non-linear function approximation [6]. For ease of explanation, several major arguments will be outlined for SISO (Single-Input-Single-Output) fuzzy rules.

3.1 Safety Argument for Function Mappings

There are several interpretations of Fuzzy Logic Systems (FLS) that do not lend well to critical domains. These include 'likelihood' and 'random' views [9] of set membership which involve probabilistic reasoning. For safety critical domains, the satisfaction of fuzzy rule pre-conditions can lead to safety concerns. For rule firing there must be certainty in set membership for an input (if the rule post-condition is to be considered 'safe'). Our interest is in interpretations such as 'measurement' and 'similarity' views [9]. These interpret degree of membership as relative to other members within the set. The first failure mode to consider is if the output is too high or too low for the current input. Existing approaches neglect the internal behaviour by simply using output error bounds [2]. This is extremely limiting as these 'monitor' technologies result in few or no arguments about the implicit underlying functional properties. During learning, behaviour may digress from the desired function using flawed training samples. Remedial actions for this failure mode include incorporating bounds for each fuzzy rule antecedent and consequent.

Bounds are placed upon (1) to provide assurance that the input fuzzy set always lies within the interval $[\min sl_{i,j}, c_{i,j}]$ for $sl_{i,j}$ and $[c_{i,j}, \max sr_{i,j}]$ for $sr_{i,j}$. The constants $[\min sl_{i,j}, \max sr_{i,j}]$ are the extremes the fuzzy set support can expand to. Moreover, the centre of the input set is constrained to lie within the input set as defined by the interval $[sl_{i,j}, sr_{i,j}]$. This prevents the centre going beyond the spread edges leading to false satisfaction of rules pre-conditions. The rule post-condition (consequent) is also bounded to $[\min y_i, \max y_i]$ although there is no adaptation of the output set (illustrated in figure 2(a)). Attempts to violate input bounds are rejected or used again when the learning rate is smaller. One potential fault is that the rule may output a value that is beyond the output bounds. To avoid over-constraining learning, this problem can be solved by bounding the rule output as described by (4):

$$y_i = \begin{cases} \min y_i, & \text{if } f_i(x_1,...,x_n) < \min y_i, \\ \max y_i, & \text{if } f_i(x_1,...,x_n) > \max y_i. \end{cases} \quad (4)$$

All bounds (constraints) placed upon the semantic interpretations of fuzzy sets are determined from safety analysis [4]. This contributes to providing safe post-conditions (output) for all pre-conditions (inputs) during generalisation and learning.

3.2 Safety Argument for Input Space Coverage

Failure mode 2 is related to faults associated with an incomplete knowledge base or faulty input set tuning. The input space that must be covered (at all times) is defined prior to certification. This is provided through analytical processes during hazard analysis [4]. Once the required input space is defined, the safety argument can be described as forming two main branches. The strategy is to first argue that the rule base completely covers the defined input space during generalisation. Assurance for coverage is provided through Preliminary System Safety Assessment (PSSA) [4]. This evaluates the input space coverage by examining rule input sets to identify "holes". Even if the input space is covered, there may still be omission of output, since the output function may partially cover the input set. The solution to this problem is provided by the rule output bounds defined by (4).

The second branch of the safety argument is concerned with input space coverage during static learning. This argument relies upon the property that no "hole" should be created between input sets of overlapping rules. The solution is to prevent spread updating which may result in exposure of the input space (which can occur in phase 2 of the static learning algorithm). This argument contributes to providing assurance about the functional input-output mappings during generalisation and learning phases.

3.3 Safety Argument for Function Derivatives and Discontinuities

Further safety requirements may be expressed using fuzzy rules of the form (5):

$$\hat{A}i : \text{IF } (x \text{ is } INCREASING \text{)THEN } (y_i \text{ is } DECREASING) \tag{5}$$

The purpose of this rule is to qualitatively express a constraint on the input-output relationship (related to failure mode 3) by constraining the sign of $a_{i,1}$ in (3). Optionally, another constraint can be expressed by quantifying the rule (5). This quantification simply prescribes limits on output derivatives. The maximum output derivative for $a_{i,1}$ is $\pm \max a_{i,1}$ and the minimum is $\pm \min a_{i,1}$ (for SISO rules). These constraints remove potentially hazardous output fluctuations for failure mode 4. The static learning algorithm can adhere to these constraints through enforcement during optimisation of (3). This is achieved by analysing overlapping rule outputs at each input set edge and ensuring the difference is within prescribed limits. This type of product-based argument prevents failure modes that may result in the output changing rapidly, too slowly or in the wrong direction. Incorporating such constraints highlight the potential to control various functional properties according to safety requirements.

4 Example of SCANN Operation

The original FSOM has been used for a wide range of non-linear function approximation problems. The ability of the SCANN can be demonstrated by dynamic and static learning algorithms. Due to space constraints, details of full case study cannot be presented here. However, figure 2(a-b) illustrates the ability to adapt given unrepresentative and representative training data. Figure 2(c) illustrates how unsafe behaviour is constrained within bounds hinting that performance is always limited to keep within safe regions.

A real-world example which has used fuzzy control systems is the gas turbine aero-engine [10]. This approach can potentially help reduce cost by optimising the fuel flow under changing conditions (engine wear). All attempted bound violations can be logged and used to indicate the need for engine maintenance. The SCANN approach can provide efficiency in terms of reduced cost though maximising performance without compromising on safety.

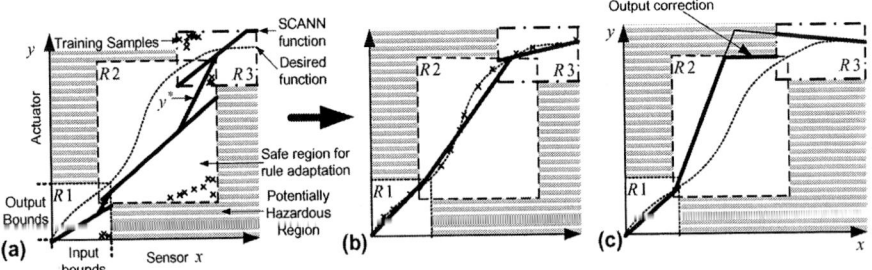

Fig. 2. (a) Bounding boxes used to define extremes for function mappings and converges onto unrepresentative data. (b) Non-linear function using representative data. (c) Constraints force behaviour within safe region (for $R2$) during generalisation.

5 Conclusions

This paper exploits the 'transparency' offered by the FSOM to easily integrate safety constraints over various functional properties. Our approach demonstrates how the behaviour of the SCANN is both predictable and controllable whilst enabling generalisation and learning post-certification. To adhere to safety requirements, constraints are enforced by the SCANN learning algorithms. For ease of explanation, a handful of solutions to safety arguments (extracted from a complete safety case) have been outlined. Compelling analytical certification arguments such as these are required for highly-dependable roles in safety critical systems.

References

1. Lisboa, P., Industrial use of safety-related artificial neural networks. Health & Safety Executive 327, (2001).
2. Hull, J., D. Ward, and R. Zakrzewski, Verification and Validation of Neural Networks for Safety-Critical Applications, Barron Associates, Inc. and Goodrich Aerospace, Fuel and Utility Systems (2002).
3. Kurd, Z., Artificial Neural Networks in Safety-critical Applications, First Year Dissertation, Department of Computer Science, University of York, 2002
4. Kurd, Z. and T.P. Kelly, Safety Lifecycle for Developing Safety-critical Artificial Neural Networks. 22nd International Conference on Computer Safety, Reliability and Security (SAFECOMP'03), 23-26 September, (2003).
5. Vuorimaa, P., Fuzzy self-organising map. Fuzzy Sets and Systems. 66 (1994) 223-231.
6. Ojala, T., Neuro-Fuzzy Systems in Control, Masters Thesis, Department of Electrical Engineering, Tampere University of Technology, Tampere, 1994
7. Kurd, Z. and T.P. Kelly, Establishing Safety Criteria for Artificial Neural Networks. In Seventh International Conference on Knowledge-Based Intelligent Information & Engineering Systems (KES'03), Oxford, UK, (2003).
8. CISHEC, A Guide to Hazard and Operability Studies, The Chemical Industry Safety and Health Council of the Chemical Industries Association Ltd. (1977).
9. Bilgic, T. and I.B. Turksen, *Measurement of membership functions: theoretical and empirical work*, in Handbook of fuzzy sets and systems, In Dubois and Prade (1997).
10. Chipperfield, A.J., B. Bica, and P.J. Fleming, Fuzzy Scheduling Control of a Gas Turbine Aero-Engine: A Multiobjective Approach. IEEE Trans. on Indus. Elec. 49(3) (2002).

Surface Spatial Index Structure of High-Dimensional Space

Jiyuan An[1], Yi-Ping Phoebe Chen[1,2], and Qinying Xu[3]

[1] Faculty of Science and Technology, Deakin University, VIC 3125 Australia
[2] Australian Research Council Centre in Bioinformatics
{jiyuan,phoebe}@deakin.edu.au
[3] Master's Program in Science and Engineering, University of Tsukuba, Japan
qinying@kslab.is.tsukuba.ac.jp

Abstract. This paper proposes a spatial index structure based on a new space-partitioning method. Previous research proposed various high dimensional index structures. However, when dimensionality becomes high, the effectiveness of the spatial index structure disappears. This problem is called the "curse of dimensionality". This paper focuses on the fact that the volume of high dimensional space is mostly occupied by its surface and then proposes a new surface index structure. The utility of this new surface spatial index structure is illustrated through a series of experiments.

1 Introduction

To index high dimensional dataset, R-tree [7] and its varieties [4][2] are well-used index methods. However, when the dimensionality increasing, the tree index structures degrade their performance and their effectiveness are even worse than a linear scan [1].

The size of the spatial index structure is proportional to the dimensionality. It is one of the reasons why R-tree and its varieties are not effective in high dimensional space. To squeeze the index file, a Pyramid-tree [3] technique was proposed [3], where high dimensional data corresponds to linear order sequence, and classical index structure B+-tree is then used, this results a better performance with the X-tree spatial index structure. However, for one pyramid, most data concentrates at the base in high dimensional space. Therefore, much data corresponds to *one* linear order and the selectivity of indexing declines. To modify this drawback, this paper proposes a new index structure by partitioning the pyramid recursively.

2 Motivation

A square (2-dimension) consists of 4 edges and 4 vertexes; a cube(3-dimension) consists of 6 squares, 12 edges and 8 vertexes. In general, the number of $(d-1)$-dimensional hyperplanes in a d-dimensional hypercube is $2d$. Moreover, one hyperplane consists of $(d-2)$-dimensional hyperplanes. Therefore, the relation of all hyperplanes is as follows. Two $(d-1)$-dimensional hyperplanes intersect at a $(d-2)$-dimensional hyperplanes. Three $(d-1)$-dimensional hyperplanes intersect at a $(d-3)$-dimensional hyperplanes. At the end, $d-1$ $(d-1)$-dimensional hyperplanes intersect at a line. The number of hyperplanes which cover a hypercube is given in Lemma 1. For example, in the case of 3-dimensionality, a cube is covered by $2 \times C_3^1 = 6$ planes, $2^2 \times C_3^2 = 12$ lines and $2^3 \times C_3^3 = 8$ vertexes. Table 1 shows the number of hyperplanes covering a 20-dimensional hypercube.

Lemma 1 *A d-dimensional hypercube is covered by $(d-1)$-dimensional hyperplanes, $(d-2)$-dimensional hyperplanes, $\cdots$, and 0-dimensional hyperplanes (vertexes). The number of $(d-i)$-d hyperplanes is $2^i * C_d^i$.*

Table 1. The number of hyperplanes of 20-d hypercube

The number of dimensionality of hyperplanes	Shape of hyperplanes	The number of hyperplanes
19	hyper-plane	40
18	hyper-plane	760
17	hyper-plane	9,120
16	hyper-plane	77,520
15	hyper-plane	496,128
14	hyper-plane	2,480,640
13	hyper-plane	9,922,560
12	hyper-plane	32,248,320
11	hyper-plane	85,995,520
10	hyper-plane	189,190,144
9	hyper-plane	343,982,080
8	hyper-plane	515,973,120
7	hyper-plane	635,043,840
6	hyper-plane	635,043,840
5	hyper-plane	508,035,072
4	hyper-plane	317,521,920
3	Hyper-plane	149,422,080
2	plane	49,807,360
1	line	10,485,760
0	vertex	1,048,576

As dimensionality increases, the number of hyperplanes expands rapidly. This number is beyond the size of most datasets. It is therefore possible that one data point corresponds to one hyperplane of hypercube. The hyperplane becomes the key of the data point. Searching similar data point becomes to examine near hyperplanes. The corresponding method is to partition a hypercube by pyramids whose tops are the centres of hypercube and whose bases are the hyperplanes. Because most data points are in the surface of data space, the data points in the pyramid can be represented with its base (a hyperplane). If the hyperplanes are ordered in a sequence, the data points within pyramids can be indexed with linear index structure B+-tree. That is, a high dimensional data changes to linear data. When an error range of a query point is given, to search for similar data points becomes to find the pyramids overlapping with the query's pyramid. For a d-dimensional hypercube, the method used to pyramids with bases os $(d-1)$ dimension is given by Berchtold [3]. In this paper, the number of dimension of the pyramid is extended to $1, 2, ..., d-1$. A recursive algorithm is subsequently proposed to compute the overlapping pyramids.

3 Surface Spatial Index Structure

Data space is assumed to be normalized into a hypercube having edge 1. The bases of two opposite pyramids are perpendicular to an axis x_i. They can be expressed with $x_i = 0$ and $x_i = 1$. In the pyramid whose base is $x_i = 0$, a data point $(x_0, x_1, ..., x_{d-1})$ satisfies Equation 1. By using this property, the pyramid to which a data point belongs can be determined. The order number of the pyramid becomes the key of the data point. Then B+-tree linear index structure is used to search for similar data.

$$x_i \leq min(x_j, 1 - x_j) \quad \text{where} \quad (j = 0, 1, .., i-1, i+1, ..., d-1) \quad (1)$$

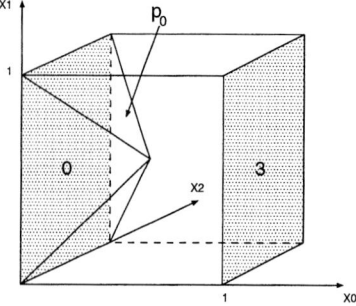

hyperplane	order	order of pyramids
$X_0 = 0$	0	p_0
$X_0 = 1$	d	p_d
$X_1 = 0$	1	p_1
$X_1 = 1$	$d+1$	p_{d+1}
⋮	⋮	⋮
$X_{d-1} = 0$	$d-1$	p_{d-1}
$X_{d-1} = 1$	$2d-1$	p_{2d-1}

Fig. 1. The order of pyramid. A 3-dimensional hypercube. The bases $x_0 = 0$ and $x_0 = 1$ are assigned the order number 0 and 3 respectively. Corresponding pyramids are denoted as p_0 and p_3

Fig. 2. The order of pyramids in d-dimensional hypercube

Order of Pyramid. A d-dimensional hypercube is covered by $(d-1)$-dimensional hyperplanes. We assume its axes are $x_0, x_1, ..., x_{d-1}$. The order number of the pyramids are assigned in Figure 2. The order number of pyramid is determined by its base. Figure 1 shows the 3-dimensional cube. The pyramid with base $x_0 = 0$ has an order number of 0, illustrated as p_0. Its opposite pyramid is denoted as p_3.

Constitution of Data's Key. All data keys are initialized with null. When a hypercube is partitioned, the order number of a pyramid is appended to the data key, the data point is included in the pyramid. The process is done recursively, the size of the keys becomes longer. Figure 3 shows the computing key in a 3-dimensional cube. Firstly, the data key is initialized with null. Secondly, the data point belongs to the pyramid whose base is $x_1 = 0$, so the order number 1 is appended to the data key as shown in subfigure (A). To partition data space recursively, the data point is projected into the pyramid's base as illustrated in the subfigure (B). The base is partitioned into 4 triangles. Since the data point is in No. 3 triangle (described in Figure 2), the data key becomes longer by adding 3 as shown in subfigure (C). Finally, the triangle is divided into 8 slices, 2 is appended into the data key. The total key of the data point consists of $1, 3, 2$ as shown in subfigure (D). It can easily be transformed to an integer, such as $1*6+3*4+2*8 = 35$. In this formula, $6, 4, 8$ are the number of planes, lines and slices shown in the subfigure (A), (C), (D) respectively. In general, the partitioning process can be described with the 2 steps below.

1. A d-dimensional hypercube is partitioned into $2d$ pyramids, their tops are the center points of the hypercube, and their bases are $(d-1)$-dimensional hyperplanes.
2. Within one pyramid, we projected all data into its base. Step 1 is repeated within the base of the pyramid which is also a hypercube. Because the base is a $(d-1)$-dimensional hypercube, it can be split into $2(d-1)$ pyramids having the center points of the hypercube and $(d-2)$-dimensional surfaces as its base.

With every step of the partition, the data key becomes longer by appending the order number of its pyramid. On the last partition, the slice number which the data belongs to is appended to the data's key like the algorithm of the pyramid-tree [3].

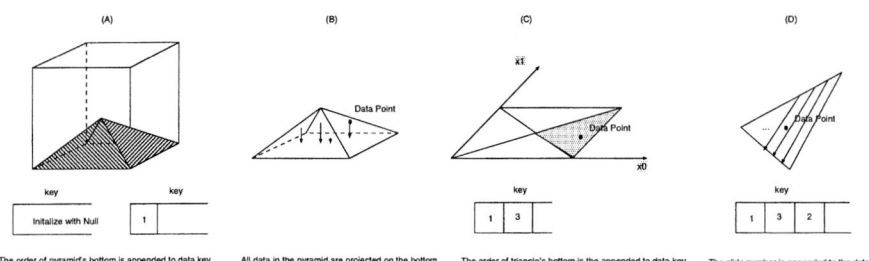

Fig. 3. Construction of key. The data space is partitioned recursively, key of a data is composed the order of bases of the pyramids which the data in

Similarity Search. By using the data key described at the begining of Section 3, a similarity search with B+-tree index structure is available. Given a query range, it is necessary to determine the pyramids overlapping with the query range. The given d-dimensional range is denoted as $[X_{0min}, X_{0max}], [X_{1min}, X_{1max}], \cdots$. The method is proposed below.

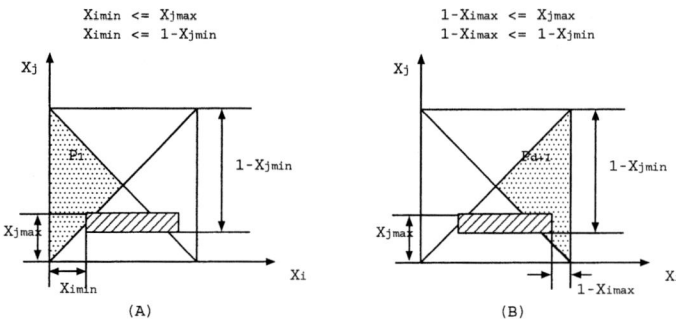

Fig. 4. Similarity search. The pyramids overlapping with search range can be calculated with the formula shown in the right

Figure 4(A) shows the conditions of pyramid P_i ($0 \leq i < d$) which overlap the query range. The following formula describes the conditions: $X_{imin} \leq X_{jmax}, X_{imin} \leq 1-X_{jmin}$ When the two conditions are satisfied, the query range overlaps with pyramid P_i. For the other side of a pyramid P_{d+i} ($0 \leq i < d$), as shown in Figure 4(B). The condition of overlapping with query range can be explained using the following formula:$1-X_{imax} \leq X_{jmax}, 1-X_{imax} \leq 1-X_{jmin}$.

The above computing process should be done recursively just like a computing data key. All pyramids overlapping with query range will be searched by using B+-tree index structure.

4 Experiment

To evaluate the effectiveness of surface index structure, the range search for high dimensional dataset was performed. The surface spatial index structure is implemented based on GiST C++ Package [8] on GNU/Linux (Pentium-II, 500Hz). The node size of B+-tree was set at 8K bytes. A 100,000 high dimensional cluster dataset was used. All data points are generated in a data space with the range of [0 : 1]. The search range is 2% of the data space. 1000 query data points were tested. *Similarity search range* 1000 data points were randomly selected. These data points are the center of the search range which is $\pm 0,02$.

Figure 5 shows the relationship between the number of page accesses and the number of dimensions. Note that the pyramid-tree index is a special case where the hypercube is divided into "1 times", because the number of dimension of its pyramid's base is $d - 1$. The number of page accesses is shown in the surface index structures. Two index structures are listed, one is dividing the pyramid "2 times", another "3 times". When the number of dimension increases, the number of pyramids grows significantly. At the same time, the length of key becomes longer and the fan out therefore decreases. As a result, the number of page accesses increases. As shown in Figure 5, dividing "2 time" is the best solution when the dimension is below 60. Figure 6 shows search time in three spatial index structures. Dividing "2 time" shows its priority.

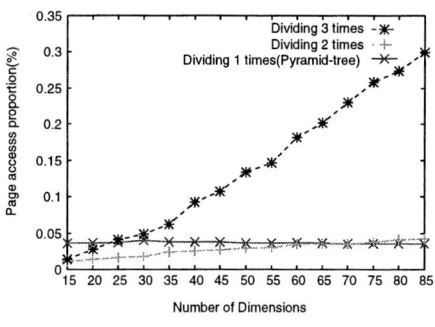 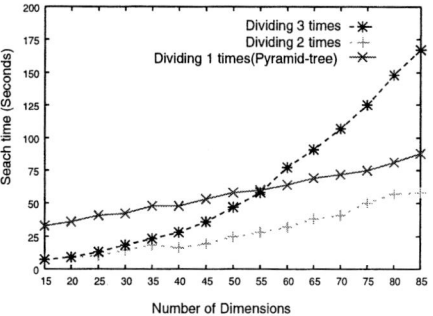

Fig. 5. The number of page access   **Fig. 6.** Similarity search time

5 Summary

This paper proposes a new index structure based on recurive partitioning space. To the best of our knowledge, this paper is the first one to focus on the surface to index high dimensional dataset. To break the curse of dimensionality, high dimensional data points are transformed to 1-dimensional values. Therefore, classical index structure B+-tree can be adapted. By partitioning the space recursively, our approach overcomes the restriction of $2d$ pyramids in the Pyramid-tree. More pyramids are divided and the selection of key is improved. In future work, we will estimate the partitioning times required to construct an index structure from the distribution of dataset.

Acknowledgments

The work in this paper was partially supported by the Australian Research Council's Discovery Grant DP0344488.

References

1. An J., Chen H., Furuse K., Ohbo N.: 'CVA-file: An Index Structure for High-Dimensional Datasets', Knowledge and Information Systems 2004. to appear.
2. Berchtold S., Keim D., Kriegel H.-P.: 'The X-tree: An Index Structure for High-Dimensional Data', 22nd Conf. on Very Large Database, 1996. Bombay, India, pp. 28-39.
3. Berchtold S., Keim D., Kriegel H.-P.: 'The pyramid-Technique: Towards Breaking the Curse of Dimensional Data Spaces', Proc. ACM SIGMOD Int. Conf. Managment of Data, Seattle, 1998, pp. 142-153.
4. Beckmann N., Kriegel H.-P., Schneider R., Seeger B.: 'The R*-tree:An efficient and Robust Access Method for Points and Rectangles', Proc. ACM SIGMOD Int. Conf. Managment of Data, NJ, 1990, pp. 322-331.
5. Beyer K. S., Goldstein J., Ramakrishnan R., Shaft U.: 'When Is "Nearest Neighbor" Meaningful', Proceedings of the 7th Int. Conf. on Database Theory, 1999, pp. 217-235.

6. Ciaccia P., Patella M., Zezula P.: *M-tree:An Efficient Access Method for Similarity Seach in Metric Spaces*, Proc. 23rd Int. Conf.on Very Large Data Bases, Athens, Greece, 1997, pp. 426-435.
7. Guttmann, R.: 'R-tree: A Dynamic Index Structure for Spatial Searching', Proc. ACM SIGMOD Int. Conf. Managment of Data, Boston, MA 1984, pp. 47-57.
8. Hellerstein J. M., Naughton J. F., Pfefer A.: 'Generalized search trees for database systems', Proc. of the 21th VLDB conference, Zurich, Switzerland, Sept. 1995, pp. 562-573.

Generating and Applying Rules for Interval Valued Fuzzy Observations

Andre de Korvin[1], Chenyi Hu[2], and Ping Chen[1]

[1] Department of Computer and Mathematical Sciences
University of Houston-Downtown, Houston, Texas 77002, USA
[2] Department of Computer Science
University of Central Arkansas, Conway, AR 72035, USA

Abstract. One of the objectives of intelligent data engineering and automated learning is to develop algorithms that learn the environment, generate rules, and take possible courses of actions. In this paper, we report our work on how to generate and apply such rules with a rule matrix model. Since the environments can be interval valued and rules often fuzzy, we further study how to obtain and apply rules for interval valued fuzzy observations.

1 Introduction

In artificial intelligence, knowledge-based agents are designed and implemented to observe the environments and to reason about their possible courses of actions. In such automated decision making systems, decisions are usually made through matching input data (relevance of each environment feature) with a certain set of rules. Examples of such systems are widely available in the literatures of fuzzy systems [2, 4, 6, 8, 11] and neuro-fuzzy systems [9].

1.1 The Rule Matrix Model

Assume that an environment e contains m features, and n possible different decisions, $d_1, d_2, \cdots, d_n$, that could be made based on the presences of the environment features. Let $e = (e_1, e_2, \cdots, e_m)^T$ be an observation of the environment, i.e., e denotes the degree to which certain features of an environment are present. Then, a knowledge-based agent may select a specific decision according to the m by n matrix below:

$$P = \begin{bmatrix} p_{11} & p_{12} & \cdots & p_{1n} \\ p_{21} & p_{22} & \cdots & p_{2n} \\ \cdots & \cdots & & \\ p_{m1} & p_{m2} & \cdots & p_{mn} \end{bmatrix} \quad (1)$$

by matching the input e with column vectors of P. If the observation vector e matches P_j, the jth column of P, then the jth decision d_j should be selected. We call P the rule matrix. The decision making process is called the rule matrix model. In this paper, our study is focused on the rule matrix model.

1.2 Problems to Be Addressed in This Paper

In this paper, we mainly address the following two questions: (1) How to establish and adjust a rule matrix P; and (2) How to make a reasonable decision from a general observation that does not match any column of P?

In section 2 and 3, we address the above respectively. Then, we extend the results to interval valued training set, fuzzy rule matrix, and observations in section 4. We conclude our study in section 5.

2 Establishing and Adjusting the Rule Matrix

The main purpose of this section is to sketch a method that estimates the rule matrix P. Without losing of generality, we normalize the environment observation vector e such that $0 \leq e_i \leq 1 \ \forall i \in \{1, 2, \cdots, m\}$ and $\Sigma_{i=1}^{m} e_i = 1$. We also assume that each column vector of P is also normalized which means that $0 \leq p_{ij} \leq 1 \ \forall j \in \{1, 2, \cdots, n\}$ and $\forall i \in \{1, 2, \cdots, m\}$; and $\Sigma_{i=1}^{m} p_{ij} = 1$ for any given $j \in \{1, 2, \cdots, n\}$.

Let E be a known data set that contains N environment-decision pairs. Since we have used a subscript e_k to indicate the kth feature of an environment, we use a superscript e^k to denote the kth observation of the environment. Then, an environment-decision pair, $[e^k, d_{k^*}]$ in E represents the desired decision d_{k^*} under a given environment e^k where, $1 \leq k \leq N$ and $1 \leq k^* \leq n$. A naive way to determine P_j, the jth column of P, is to let $P_j = e^k$ if $j = k^*$. This certainly ensures that the jth decision will be selected if the environment is e^k. However, this simple method will not work appropriately since the same decision d_j may be taken for different environment observations and very likely, in most cases, $n << N$.

Reasonable properties of P_j should include the following: It should be close enough to all of these e^ks such that $k^* = j$ and far away from those e^ks that $k^* \neq j$. Since observation vectors and columns of rule matrices are normalized, to determine P_j, we need to solve the problem below:

To find a P_j that minimizes: $W_j = \sum_{k^*=j} ||e^k - P_j|| + \sum_{k^* \neq j} (1 - ||e^k - P_j||)$ (2)

It is assumed that a feature extraction has been previously performed, thus the feature vectors generating a decision are presumably well separated. An alternate method would be to do a least square fit for each decision k^*. If we use the 2-norm in equation (2), then the problem we need to solve is to find a P_j that

Minimizes: $W_j = \sum_{k^*=j} (\sum_{i=1}^{m}(e_i^k - p_{ij})^2) + \sum_{k^* \neq j} (1 - (\sum_{i=1}^{m}(e_i^k - p_{ij})^2))$ (3)

Since all environment-decision pairs, $[e^k, d_{k^*}]$s, are given, we can solve (3) numerically. Hence, we have an algorithm to establish the rule matrix P:

```
for k = 1 to N
  input environment-decision pairs
  normalize the environment vectors
  for j = 1 to n
    minimize (3) subject to the normalization condition
```

The matrix obtained by the above algorithm is from the training set E. Since new data may be obtained from time to time, we may adjust the matrix P "online" dynamically with newly available data.

3 Making Decision from an Observation

3.1 The Problem

After obtaining the rule matrix P, for a new observation e, one may pick the decision d_{j^*} if $||e - P_{j^*}|| = \min_{j \in \{1,2,\cdots,n\}} ||e - P_j||$. However, there are still questions that need to be answered. For a general observation $e \neq P_j, \forall j \in \{1, 2, \cdots, n\}$, there could be possibly multiple output of the j^*. Multiple j^* may come from calculating j^* with different norms, or from the fact that e almost equally close to several columns of P. In addition, the measurement of e may not be exact due to noise. Therefore, we need to further study decision making with fuzzy systems.

3.2 Decision Making with Fuzzy Logic

Let us first recall a few basic definitions and facts about inference in a fuzzy system.

- If U denotes a set, a fuzzy subset of U is characterized by a function φ from U into $[0,1]$. The function φ is called the membership function of the set.
- If we denote a fuzzy subset of U by A and if φ is its membership function, then for $u \in U$, $\varphi(u)$ denotes the membership of u in A. Of course, if A is a standard subset (i.e., a "crisp subset") of U, $\varphi(u)$ is either 1 (i.e., $u \in A$) or 0 (i.e., $u \notin A$).
- Let p_{ij} and d_j be fuzzy sets for $1 \leq i \leq m$, and $1 \leq j \leq n$. A fuzzy rule R_j for an m-dimensional vector $e = (e_1, e_2, \cdots, e_m)$, is defined as if e_1 is p_{1j}, e_2 is p_{2j}, $\cdots$, e_m is p_{mj}, then d is d_j;
- For an input $e = (e_1, e_2, \cdots, e_m)$, $\varphi_j(e) = \dfrac{\Pi_{k=1}^m \varphi_{kj}(e_k)}{\Sigma_{l=1}^n \Pi_{k=1}^m \varphi_{kl}(e_k)}$ denotes the strength of the rule R_j relative to e. That is to what extent rule R_j should be counted (on a scale of 0 to 1) when input e is applied.

For additional information on fuzzy systems and inference, we refer readers to [2, 4, 8, 11].

We now build the matching process between e and the jth column of P in terms of fuzzy systems. Here after, we replace the entries p_{ij} of P as fuzzy sets whose membership functions are triangular functions, having value 1 at p_{ij} obtained from Algorithm 2.1. More specifically, if we let σ be a positive real number less than 1, we can define the triangular function φ_{ij} as the follow:

$$\varphi_{ij}(x) = \begin{cases} 1 & \text{if } x = p_{ij} \\ \dfrac{x}{\sigma p_{ij}} + 1 - \dfrac{1}{\sigma} & \text{if } (1-\sigma)p_{ij} < x < p_{ij} \\ \dfrac{-x}{\sigma p_{ij}} + 1 + \dfrac{1}{\sigma} & \text{if } p_{ij} < x < (1+\sigma)p_{ij} \\ 0 & \text{otherwise} \end{cases} \quad (4)$$

Then, the strength of the jth rule for given input e can be defined as

$$\varphi_j(e) = \frac{\Pi_{k=1}^m \varphi_{kj}(e_k)}{\sum_{j=1}^n \Pi_{k=1}^m \varphi_{kj}(e_k)} \quad (5)$$

Through using fuzzy rules, the $\varphi_j(e)$ above provides a degree of matching between e and the antecedent of each rule/decision d_j. One could select the d_{j^*} with the strongest strength, which means that $\varphi_{j^*}(e) = \max\limits_{j \in \{1,2,\cdots,n\}} \varphi_j(e)$, as the decision.

4 Interval Valued Observations

4.1 Why Intervals?

In the above discussion, we implicitly assume that training data set are point valued. However, in real world applications, it would be most appropriate to study interval valued observations [1, 10]. This is mainly because of that environment observations usually contain errors. Using intervals to represent them is more appropriate than using points. In this section, we use boldface letters to denote interval variables. For example, we use **x** to denote an interval, and $\underline{x}$ and $\bar{x}$ for its greatest lower bound and least upper bound respectively.

4.2 Using Interval Valued Training Set

We now consider an interval valued training set $(\mathbf{e}^1, j_1), \cdots, (\mathbf{e}^N, j_N)$, where $\mathbf{e}^i$ is a vector with interval valued components and $j_1, ..., j_N$ are integers in $\{1, 2, ..., n\}$. With interval arithmetic [3, 5], one may apply the algorithm in section 2 to obtain an interval valued rule matrix **P** such that $[\underline{p}_{ij}, \bar{p}_{ij}] \subseteq [0, 1]$. To make a decision for an interval valued environment observation **e**, an exact match would be $\forall k \in \{1, 2, \cdots, m\}$, $\mathbf{e}_k \subseteq [\underline{p}_{kj}, \bar{p}_{kj}]$ for a fixed j. This implies that decision d_j is the right one when features are presented as indicated by the interval vector **e**. We now have introduced an uncertainty on the presence of features by specifying the lower and upper bound of that presence.

If for any fixed j the input **e** may not have the property that $\mathbf{e}_k \subseteq [\underline{p}_{kj}, \bar{p}_{kj}]$ for all k. There could be some overlap between intervals $\mathbf{e}_k$ and $[\underline{p}_{kj}, \bar{p}_{kj}]$. We need to extend the concept of strength of a rule defined previously in section 3. In order to define the strength of rule j relative to an interval valued observation vector $\mathbf{e} = [\mathbf{e}_1, \mathbf{e}_2, \cdots, \mathbf{e}_m]^T$, let us first define a trapezoidal function $\varphi_{ij}(x)$ for a real x similar to (4) to fuzzify the rule matrix:

$$\varphi_{ij}(x) = \begin{cases} 1 & \text{if } x \in \mathbf{p}_{ij} \\ \dfrac{x}{\sigma \underline{p}_{ij}} + 1 - \dfrac{1}{\sigma} & \text{if } (1-\sigma)\underline{p}_{ij} < x < \underline{p}_{ij} \\ \dfrac{-x}{\sigma \overline{p}_{ij}} + 1 + \dfrac{1}{\sigma} & \text{if } \overline{p}_{ij} < x < (1+\sigma)\overline{p}_{ij} \\ 0 & \text{otherwise.} \end{cases} \quad (6)$$

To apply (6) for an interval $\mathbf{x}$, we get an interval

$$\phi_{ij}(\mathbf{x}) = [\min\{\varphi_{ij}(\underline{x}), \varphi_{ij}(\overline{x})\}, \max\{\varphi_{ij}(\underline{x}), \varphi_{ij}(\overline{x})\}] \quad (7)$$

For the ith entry of an interval valued environment vector $\mathbf{e}$, denoted as $\mathbf{e}_i$, the largest intersection of $\phi_{i,j}$ and $\mathbf{e}_i$ is defined as the possibility function below

$$\text{Poss}[\phi_{i,j}|\mathbf{e}_i] = \sup\{\phi_{i,j}(v) \wedge \mathbf{e}_i(v)\} \quad (8)$$

where $\mathbf{e}_i(v) = \begin{cases} 1, & \text{if } v \in \mathbf{e}_i \\ 0, & \text{otherwise} \end{cases}$.

We define the strength of a specific rule/decision, say j, with respect to an interval observation $\mathbf{e}$ through the use of possibility functions as

$$\phi_j(\mathbf{e}) = \frac{\Pi_{k=1}^m \text{Poss}[\phi_{k,j}|\mathbf{e}_k]}{\Sigma_{t=1}^n \Pi_{k=1}^m \text{Poss}[\phi_{k,t}|\mathbf{e}_k]} \quad (9)$$

To make a decision for an input $\mathbf{e}$ based on interval valued fuzzy rule matrix, we may pick the strongest rule j^*, where $\phi_{j^*}(\mathbf{e}) > \phi_j(\mathbf{e})$ for $j \in \{1, 2, \cdots, n\}$. Then, d_{j^*} is the decision. We could also take the index approach (6) similarly provided that the decisions are arranged so that the distance between the columns $d_1, d_2, ...d_n$ reflects the distance between the interval vectors $d_1, d_2, ...d_n$.

Another approach for decision making with interval valued fuzzy rule matrix is based on the idea of the necessity function. A necessity function of $\phi_{i,j}$ with $\mathbf{e}_i$ is defined as the follow:

$$\text{Nec}[\phi_{i,j}|\mathbf{e}_i] = \sup_v \{[1 - \mathbf{e}_i(v)] \vee \phi_{i,j}(v)\} \quad (10)$$

We then have

$$\psi_j(\mathbf{e}) = \frac{\Pi_{k=1}^m \text{Nec}[\phi_{k,j}|\mathbf{e}_k]}{\Sigma_{t=1}^n \Pi_{k=1}^m \text{Nec}[\phi_{k,t}|\mathbf{e}_k]} \quad (11)$$

For more properties of possibilities and necessities, readers may refer [7] and [11]. One may select the decision according to the highest necessity as well. The term $|\psi_j(\mathbf{e}) - \phi_j(\mathbf{e})|$ reflects to some extend the uncertainty surrounding the input e, since it represents the difference generalized by taking the possibility versus the necessity function.

Once the strength of rule R_j is defined relative to the interval input e as $\phi_j(\mathbf{e})$ if we use the possibility function, or as $\psi_j(\mathbf{e})$ if we use necessity function, there are many ways to obtain the fuzzy output generalized by e and then obtaining the defuzzification. We refer the reader to [4] to see these different approaches to defuzzification.

5 Summary

In this paper, we have studied the rule matrix model for an intelligent agent. To obtain a rule matrix for an agent, we use a training environment-decision data set. Since the training data set and the input observation may not be exact in real world applications, we have fuzzified the rule matrix and then developed methods of decision selection by calculating strength of a rule.

In addition of using point valued training data to obtain a rule matrix, we have applied interval arithmetic which makes us able to obtain interval rule matrix from interval valued training data set. By doing this, we have allowed uncertainty on the input. Through applying possibility and necessity functions, we yield an interval-valued functions ϕ_j and ψ_j for an input e. Making a decision becomes a defuzzification problem. In case the input is a degenerated interval vector i.e. a point, then $\phi_j(e)$ will be the same as $\psi_j(e)$.

References

1. D. Berleant and et al, *Dependable Handling of Uncertainty*, Reliable Computing, pp. 407-418, Volume 9, 2003.
2. A. de Korvin, C. Hu, and O. Sirisaengtaksin, *On Firing Rules of Fuzzy Sets of Type II*, J. Applied Mathematics, pp. 151-159, Volume 3, No.2, 2000.
3. B. Kearfott, M. Dawande, K. Du, and C. Hu, *Algorithm 737: INTLIB: a Portable Fortran-77 Interval Standard Function Library*, ACM, Trans. on Math. Software, Vol. 20, No.4, pp. 447-459, 1994.
4. J. M. Mendel, *Uncertain Rule-Based Fuzzy Logic Systems: Introduction and New Directions*, Prentice Hall, 2000
5. R. Moore, *Methods and Applications of Interval Analysis*, Society for Industrial and Applied Mathematics, 1979.
6. Z. Pawlak, *Rough Sets and Fuzzy Sets and Systems*, pp. 99-102 1985
7. W. Pedrycz, F. Gomide, *An Introduction To Fuzzy Sets Analysis and Design*, MIT Press, 1998
8. H. Rasiowa, *Towards Fuzzy Logic Infuzzy Logic for the Management of Uncertainty*, Ed L. Zadh and J. Kacprzyk, pp. 121-139, New York. Wiley Interscience.
9. J. S. Roger, *ANFIS: Adaptive Network-based Fuzzy Inference System*, IEEE Trans. on Systems, Man and Cybernetics, 23(03) 665-685, May 1993
10. S. Shary, *A New Technique in Systems Analysis Under Interval Uncertainty and Ambiguity*, Reliable Computing, pp. 321-418, Volume 8, 2002.
11. A. L. Zadeh, *Outline of a new approach to the analysis of complex systems and decision processes*, IEEE Trans. on Systems, Man and Cybernetics 3(1), pp. 28-44, 1973

Automatic Video Shot Boundary Detection Using Machine Learning

Wei Ren and Sameer Singh

ATR Lab, Department of Computer Science, University of Exeter, Exeter EX4 4QF, UK

Abstract. In this paper we present a machine learning system that can accurately predict the transitions between frames in a video sequence. We propose a set of novel features and describe how to use dominant features based on a coarse-to-fine strategy to accurately predict video transitions.

1 Introduction

Video segmentation is a fundamental step in content-based video indexing, editing, retrieval, and object tracking. It also plays an important role in upcoming video database standard MEPG-7. Shot transitions can be classified as of two types: abrupt transitions (cut) and gradual transitions (fade, wipe, dissolve, etc.) A detailed discussion including survey and comparison of the various methods to detect abrupt and gradual changes is available in [5][6][13][9][12][3][17][14]. The modelling of shot transitions and the development of a machine learning system to predict these is very important for: a) improving image region classification; b) improving image retrieval; iii) modelling spatio-temporal relationship between objects in successive frames; and iv) video abstraction.

Several approaches to shot transition modelling have been adopted by other researchers. Approaches related to video segmentation have been proposed to detect transitions. These approaches either make use of some statistical measure [1][8][24][31][32][20][22] that is thresholded to identify whether a transition happens or not, or use some form of machine learning, e.g. use hidden markov models [4]. One of the main problems using some threshold to statistically identify transition is that of optimal threshold selection that maximizes accuracy with the least false alarm rate, e.g. Leinhart [15]. Some attempts have been made on defining adaptive thresholds that adapt to sequence statistics, e.g. Yusoff *et al.* [28], Zhang *et al.* [33], Boccignone *et al.* [2], Yu and Srinath [30]. The limitations with methods such as hidden markov models include setting of priors, small amounts of data for learning, dealing with high dimensional data, choice of Gaussians and over- and under-fitting.

Abrupt transitions are easier to detect compared to gradual transitions. Yeo and Liu [25] propose that a comparison based on successive frames alone is not adequate for the detection of gradual transitions. One alternative is to use every k-th frame instead. Compare the i-th frame to the following $i+k$-th frame. Then a sequence of delayed inter-frame distance can be obtained. If k is chosen greater than the length of the gradual transition measured in frames, then the sequence inter-frames exhibits a plateau of maximal width, which are consistently higher than preceding or successive values.

A number of studies have compared well-established features for detecting and predicting video transitions. Yusoff et al. [29] compare a number of features proposed in other studies for detecting camera breaks including Likelihood Ratio, Average Intensity Measurement, Histogram Comparison, Motion Estimation, Euclidean distance and DCT clustering. They conclude that the choice of shot detection algorithm depends on the type of application in which it is to be used, and for fast computational needs, the global measurement methods are the best. Boreczky and Rowe [3] present a comparison of several shot boundary detection and classification techniques and their variations including histograms, DCT, motion vector, and block matching methods. They conclude that region-based comparison, running differences and motion vector analysis produce good results. Dailianas et al. [6] compare the following methods of video segmentation for detecting fades, dissolves, cuts etc.: absolute frame-difference segmentation, histogram based segmentation, moment invariants, and edge detection. Their main conclusion is that the choice of the best segmentation method is not straightforward. The time requirements, the sensitivity to the threshold parameter, the percentage of correct and false identifications, and type of videos should be taken into account. Kobla et al. [11] compare their Video Trail approach which is based on colour-wise Euclidean distance and colour histogram bin-wise distance with the plateau algorithm (Yeo and Liu [26]), the variance curve algorithm (Meng et al. [16]), the twin comparison algorithm (Song et al. [23]), and the chromatic edit model algorithm (Zhang et al. [33]). They conclude their algorithm will give better accuracy and they are better able to point the starting and ending frames of the special effect edits.

2 Novel Features for Video Transition

In this section we detail a novel set of features used for predicting video transition. These features are used with other well-known features discussed in Section 3. We consider the following transition: *cut, fade and dissolve.*

Algorithm b-Coefficient (Block-Coefficient) (f_5)

Given two successive frames of a video, say A and B, which are colour images $f(x, y)$, of size $M \times M$ pixels. Divide the image into $m \times n$ blocks, where $m, n \geq 2$. Calculate colour moments from each block. The output is an L dimensional vector $(f_1, f_2, ..., f_L)$.

For image A, across all blocks, calculate the standard deviation across feature values as σ_A and for image B as σ_B and the covariance between features of the two image as Σ_{AB}. Calculate a measure of correlation between two images based on these block features as:

$$b\text{-coefficient} = \frac{\Sigma_{AB}}{\sigma_A \cdot \sigma_B}.$$

This measure is sensitive to local neighbourhood information of blocks. It is, however, not sensitive to object location and camera movement even though it uses some spatial information. When two images have a similar structure, b-*coefficient* returns a value close to 1.

In addition to the above measure, we also propose the calculation for another measure of correlation between two frames, called *c*-coefficient. This measure is computed on the grey-scale image equivalent of the colour image.

Algorithm c-Coefficient (Cell-Coefficient) (f_6)

Given two successive frames of a video, say A and B, which are grey-scale images $f(x, y)$, of size $M \times N$.

At each pixel, centre a mask of size $m \times m$, where $m \geq 3$, and m is odd.

In each cell, find the grey-scale median value of the pixels. For the complete image, all median values of pixels can be represented as a one-dimensional vector.

For images A and B, we have therefore two such vectors. Calculate Pearson's correlation coefficient between these two vectors and assign this to *c*-coefficient.

This measure is not sensitive to object location and camera movement or spatial change in a frame.

The two proposed measurements are quite efficient. They can be applied to colour pixel values or frequency domain features such as DCT coefficient or wavelet coefficient. When the two images have similar structure, *c-coefficient* also returns a value near to 1.

Difference of Maximum Luminance Level and Difference of Percentage Maximum Luminance Level. (f_{12} and f_{13})

Since fade-in is a frame intensity increase and fade-out is a frame intensity decrease, we choose luminance change as the main cue to identify the change. We use two measures to extract dominant information.

i) The first is the difference of maximum luminance level in successive frames.
ii) The other is the difference of percentage maximum luminance level. In order to eliminate the effect of noise, we extract the average of a very small amount of higher intensity level in each frame and compare that with the previous frame.

3 Machine Learning System

We use both *k*-nearest neighbour and neural network as classifiers to predict video transitions: cut C, fade-in F_{in}, fade-out F_{out}, and dissolve D.

Data Collection

We collected a total of 20 natural scene video clips. Each video is the combination of several video shots and video transitions including cut, fade-in, fade-out and dissolve between these shots. Ten video clips were used for training and another ten video clips for testing. Each video clip contains between 3000 and 5000 frames.

Features

The features we used are quite different from those used in other studies aimed at video transition detection. A number of features are generated based on colour and structure dissimilarity. In addition to our already described novel features, we also used additional statistical features to boost our prediction performance, and reduce the effect of outliers, noise, and large camera movements. We initially computed a total of 139 features that are reduced to a set of 18 features described below using sequential forward feature selection technique. The reduced set of features is:

1) ADSR (Normalized Absolute Difference to Sum Ratio) (feature f_1): measures normalized pixel based distance in pair-wise frames [20].
2) NDE (Normalized Difference in Energy) (feature f_2): summarizes the normalized difference in energy of corresponding pixel in pair-wise frames [20].
3) B_D (Bhattcharyya Distance) (feature f_3): measures the probabilistic distance between the histograms of two successive frames [7]
4) D (Divergence) (feature f_4): measures the probabilistic distance between the distributions of two successive frames [27].
5) b-coefficient and c-coefficient (feature f_5, f_6): See section 2.
6) D_{mean} (Difference Mean) (features f_7, f_8, f_9): compares two pair-wise frame intensity means.
7) EMD (The Earth Mover's Distance) (feature f_{10}): distance measure between distributions with applications in image retrieval and matching [21]. EMD is used to identify colour change by comparing colour histograms of successive frames and reflects the minimal amount of work that must be performed to transform one distribution into an other by moving the "distribution mass" around.
8) Histogram-comparison (features f_{11}): compares the cumulative bin difference between the current and the previous frame, [22].
9) I_Level (Intensity Level) (features f_{12}, f_{13}): See section 2.
10) JD (Jeffrey-divergence)[19] (feature f_{14}): This feature is based on mutual information and used to detect dissolve.
11) KS statistic (Kolmogorov Smirnov Statistic) (features f_{15}): measures the histogram difference across two distributions [20].
12) OMC (Observer Motion Coherence) (feature f_{16}): measures the difference between consecutive frame pairs using a similarity ratio [20].
13) χ^2 (Chi-square) test (features f_{17}): χ^2 test is based on [20].
14) SNR (Signal over Noise Ratio) (features f_{18}): SNR is non-symmetric method that evaluates the difference between two distributions by the ratio of the amount of differences relative to the amount of variations in one distribution [10].

We next verify the quality of our features. For the ground-truthed training data, we performed principal components analysis and plot the first two principal components in Figure 1. We find that different transitions form a different neat cluster that proves the fact that our features cluster them well together. We also plotted the same graph for the test data that follows exactly the same distribution of different transition data.

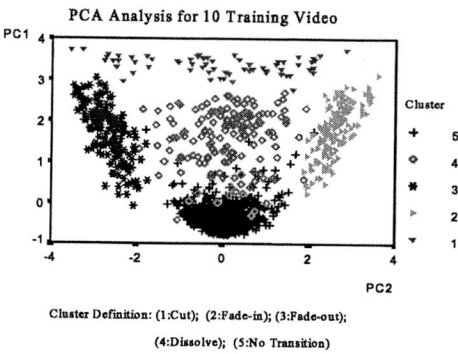

Fig. 1. Principal components plot for the transition data from 10 training videos.

4 Results

We first show the result of using a k- nearest neighbour classifier on test data (Table 1). The value of k is optimised on a validation set. The results are shown when 50% of the data (10 videos) are used for training and the remainder for testing. Next, in Table 2 we show the confusion matrix for the average neural network (NN) results. The neural network is optimised on a validation set for the number of hidden nodes and other parameters.

Table 1. Confusion matrix as the average kNN result from 10 test videos. Average accuracy is 99.3% with K=7.

	C	F_{in}	F_{out}	D	N
C	100	0	0	0	0
F_{in}	0	100	0	0	0
F_{out}	0	0	99.4	0	0.6
D	0	0	0.6	91.0	8.4
N	0	0	0	0.2	99.8

Table 2. Confusion matrix of average neural network result from 10 test videos; Average accuracy is 99.7%.

	C	F_{in}	F_{out}	D	N
C	100	0	0	0	0
F_{in}	0	100	0	0	0
F_{out}	0	0	99.3	0	0.7
D	0	0	0.6	96.1	3.3
N	0	0	0	0.1	99.9

In Table 1 and 2, class symbols are cut C, fade-in F_{in}, fade-out F_{out}, dissolve D, and N denotes no transition. All results are percentage (%).

Our key observations are:

1. Both classifiers achieve very high accuracy of more than 99% correct transition prediction.
2. It was found that dissolve is the hardest to predict with the lowest accuracy of 91% correct. Our analysis shows that the majority of the mistakes were made either at the beginning or at the end of the transition frames. This is because frames that are at the start or the end of a dissolve sequence are highly dominated by one single frame, and the system finds it hard to detect minor changes in content. Also, due to unpredictable illumination changes when panning or tilting the camera, the system makes some mistakes in fade detection.

We next compare our result with two very common approaches for video transition detection based on motion comparison where features are extracted from optical flow and colour histogram comparison. Colour histogram comparison is sensitive to the amount of colour difference between original shots and transition speed. Moreover, two frames from different shots may have similar colour histograms, despite their rather different appearances [18]. Motion comparison approach is sensitive to a fast camera movement. These two approaches are all based on adaptive threshold setting. Our approaches using kNN generated 99.3% (max. Individual false alarm 2.6%) and with Neutral Network generated 99.7% recognition rate (max. Individual false alarm 0.3%). This is much better than the use of colour histogram comparison that gives 87.1% recognition rate (max. Individual false alarm 33.7%) and motion based analysis that gives 67.9% recognition rate (max. Individual false alarm 45.3%).

5 Conclusions

In this paper we proposed a machine learning system that can accurately predict the transition between frames in a video sequence. We introduced a set of novel measures that allow accurate detection of transitions. Our results show that these transitions can be predicted with high accuracy.

References

1. A.M. Alattar, Detecting fade regions in uncompressed video sequences, Proc. IEEE. ICASSP 1997, pp. 3025-3028, 1997.
2. G. Boccignone, M. de Santo and G. Percanella, An algorithm for video cut detection in Mpeg sequences, Proc. SPIE, Storage and Retrieval for Media Databases, San Jose, CA, 2000.
3. S. Boresczky and L.A. Rowe, A comparison of video shot boundary detection techniques, Proc. SPIE 2664, 170-179, 1996.

4. J.S. Boreczky and L.D. Wilcox, A Hidden Markov Model framework for video segmentation using audio and image features, Proceedings of ICASSP'98, 3741-3744, Seattle, May 1998.
5. R. Brunelli, O. Mich and C.M. Modena, A survey on video indexing, IRST-Technical report 9612-06, 1996.
6. A. Dailianas, R.B. Allen and P. England, Comparison of automatic video segmentation algorithms, Proc. SPIE Photonics West, 2615, 2-16, 1995.
7. R.O. Duda, P.E. Hart and D.G. Stork, Pattern classification, Wiley, 2001.
8. W.A.C. Fernando, C.N. Canagarajah and D.R. Bull, Fade and dissolve detection in uncompressed and compressed video sequence, Proc. ICIP Conference, 299-303, 1999.
9. U. Gargi, R. Kasturi and S. Antani, Performance characterization and comparison of video indexing algorithms, Proc. IEEE CVPR, 559-565, 1998.
10. J.M. Jolion, Feature similarity, in *Principles of Visual Information Retrieval*, M.S. Lew (Ed.), Springer, 2001.
11. V. Kobla, D. Dementhon and D. Doermann, Special effect edit detection using VideoTrails: a comparison with existing techniques, Proc. SPIE , 302-310, 1999.
12. Koprinska and S. Carrato, Video segmentation- a survey, Signal Processing: Image Communication, 16, no. 5, 477-500, 2001.
13. R. Lienhart, Comparison of automatic shot boundary detection algorithms, Proceedings of SPIE, 3656-29, 1999.
14. R. Lienhart, Reliable Transition Detection in Videos: A survey and practitioner's guide, International Journal of Image and Graphics. 1, 469-486, 2001.
15. R. Lienhart and A. Zaccarin, A system for reliable dissolve detection in videos, Proc. IEEE ICIP Conference, Thessaloniki, 2001.
16. J. Meng, Y. Juan and S.F. Chang, Scene change detection in a MPEG compressed video sequence, Proc. IS&T/SPIE Symposium, vol. SPIE 2419, 14-25, 1995.
17. A. Nagasaka and Y. Tanaka, Automatic video indexing and full-video search for object appearances, Proc. of IFIP TC2/WG2.6, 113-127, 1991.
18. G. Pass, R. Zabih and J. Miller, Comparing images using colour coherence vectors, Proc. Of the Fourth ACM Multimedia Conference, 65-73, 1996.
19. Jan Puzicha, Yossi Rubner, Carlo Tomasi, Joachim M. Buhmann, Empirical Evaluation of Dissimilarity Measures for Color and Texture, IEEE ICCV, Greece, 1165-1172, 1999.
20. W. Ren, M. Singh and S. Singh, Automated video segmentation, Proc. 3rd International Conference on Information, Communications & Signal Processing, 2001.
21. Y. Rubner, C. Tomasi, L.J. Guibas, The Earth Mover's Distance as a metric for image retrieval, IJCV Journal, 99-121, 2000.
22. I.K. Sethi and N. Patel, A statistical approach to scene change detection, SPIE, 2420, 329-339, 1995.
23. H.S. Song, I.K. Kim and N.I. Cho, Scene change detection by feature extraction from strong edge blocks, Proc. of SPIE,4671, 484-492, 2002.
24. B.T. Truong, C. Dorai and S. Venkatesh, New enhancements to cut, fade, and dissolve detection in video segmentation, ACM Multimedia 2000, 219-227,. 2000.
25. B.L. Yeo and B. Liu, Rapid scene analysis on compressed video, IEEE Transactions on Circuits and Systems for Video Technology, 5, 533-544, 1995.
26. B.L. Yeo and B. Liu, A unified approach to temporal segmentation of motion JPEG and MPEG compressed video, Proc. IEEE ICMCS, pp. 81-88, 199b.
27. A.Webb, Statistical Pattern Recognition, Arnold, 1999.
28. Y. Yusoff, W. Christmas and J. Kittler, Video shot cut detection using adaptive thresholding, Proc. British Machine Vision Conference, 2000.

29. Y. Yusoff, W. Christmas and J. Kittler, A study on automatic shot change detection, Proc. 3rd European Conference on Multimedia Applications, Services and Techniques (ECMAST), 177-189, 1998.
30. J. Yu and M.D. Srinath, An efficient method for scene cut detection, Pattern Recognition Letters, 22, 1379-1391, 2001.
31. R. Zabih, J. Miller and K. Mai, A feature-based algorithm for detecting and classifying scene breaks, Proc. ACM Multimedia, 189-200, 1995.
32. R. Zabih, J. Miller and K. Mai, A feature-based algorithm for detecting and classification production effects, Multimedia Systems, 7, 119-128, 1999.
33. J. Zhang, A. Kankanhalli, and S.W. Smoliar, Automatic partitioning of full-motion video, Multimedia Systems, 1, 10-28, 1993.

On Building XML Data Warehouses

Laura Irina Rusu[1], Wenny Rahayu[1], and David Taniar[2]

[1] LaTrobe University, Department of Computer Science and Computer Engineering
Bundoora, VIC 3086, Australia
{lrusu,wenny}@cs.latrobe.edu.au
[2] Monash University, School of Business Systems, Clayton, VIC 3800, Australia
David.Taniar@infotech.monash.edu.au

Abstract. Developing a data warehouse for XML documents involves two major processes: one of creating it, by processing XML raw documents into a specified data warehouse repository; and the other of querying it, by applying techniques to better answer user's queries. The proposed methodology in our paper on building XML data warehouses covers processes such as data cleaning and integration, summarization, intermediate XML documents, and updating/linking existing documents and creating fact tables.

1 Introduction

In the last few years, building a data warehouse for XML documents has become a very important issue, when considering continual growing of representing different kind of data as XML documents [1]. Many papers have analysed how to design a better data warehouse for XML data, from different points of view (e.g. [1, 2, 5, 6]) and many other papers have focused on querying XML data warehouse or XML documents (e.g. [7, 8]), but almost all of them considered only the design and representations issues of XML data warehouse or how to query them and very few considered optimisation of data quality in their research.

In this paper, we propose a practical methodology for building XML documents data warehouse, by ensuring that the number of occurrences of dirty data, errors, duplications or inconsistencies is minimized as much as possible and a good summarisation exists. The main purpose of this paper is to show systematic steps to build an XML data warehouse and it is important to note that our proposed steps for building an XML data warehouse is generic enough to be applied on different XML data warehouse models.

2 Related Work

Many researchers have studied how to construct a data warehouse, first for relational databases [2, 3, 4] but in the last years, for XML documents [5, 6], considering the spread of use for this kind of documents in a vast range of activities.

A concrete methodology on how to construct an XML data warehouse analysing frequent patterns in user historical queries is provided in [6], starting from determining which data sources are more frequently accessed by the users, transforming those queries in *Query Path Transactions* and calculating the *Frequent Query Paths* which stay at the base of building data warehouse schema. In [5], an XML data warehouse is designed from XML schemas, proposing a semi-automated process. Authors choose facts for data warehouse and, for each fact, follow few steps in order to obtain star-schema: building the dependency graph from schema graph, rearranging the dependency graph, defining dimensions and measures and creating logical schema. [3] considers the aspect of data correctness and propose a solution where data-cleaning application is modelled as a directed acyclic flow of transformations, applied to the source data.

Our proposed method focuses on practical aspects of building XML data warehouses through several practical steps, including data cleaning and integration, summarization, intermediate XML documents, and updating/linking existing documents and creating fact tables. We have developed generic methods whereby the proposed method is able to be applied to any collection of XML documents to be stored in an XML data warehouse.

3 Proposed Method on Building XML Data Warehouses

Our paper proposes a systematic approach on building a data warehouse from initial XML documents, developing necessary fact and dimensions and linking them.

Each of the steps involved is described in the next sections of our paper. Generalisation of the proposed methodology is extremely important; therefore for each of these steps we propose general rules or techniques, with examples on how to apply them.

3.1 Data Cleaning and Integration

Cleaning data is a very important step in our process, so it should be analysed very carefully, as it can save a lot of future workload and time during the following steps. In both cases, whether an XML schema exists or not, applying rules provided below will give positive results. The main difference is that without an XML Schema the rules below will have to be applied iteratively throughout the XML document.

Rule1. If a schema exists, we should verify ***correctness of all schema stipulations***:
- verify if a correct use of *name of elements and attributes* in the entire document;
- observe if *data type & natural logic* is respected;
- verify if all elements and attributes are entered in their *schema-specified hierarchy*;
- verify if *order indicators* are respected ("all", "choice", "sequence" etc);
- verify if number of occurrences of elements/attributed is respected;
- verify any other schema related specification / restriction;

Rule2. Eliminating duplicate records, for example a name can be entered two or more times, in a different manner (surname&firstname, firstname&surname etc).

Rule3. Eliminate inconsistencies from elements & attributes values, for example existence of two different dates of birth for the same person [3]. As they cannot be two, the right one only should be kept.

Rule4. Eliminating errors in data, determined by entering process, for example mistyping.

Some of the data-cleaning processes have to be done manually, because they require user intervention and occasionally domain expert understanding of the area.

3.2 Data Summarisation

Because not the entire volume of existing data in the underlying database will be absorbed into the XML data warehouse, during *data summarisation* we must extract only useful and valuable information, so we will create another XML document(s) which will be, at the end, part of the data warehouse. Depending of how many levels of summarisation we will have for a specific dimension, we will either (i) create or populate new documents that contain *extraction* from initial data, or (ii) create *special-constructed* values (see Figure 1 as example).

a) we do not possess required data for the dimension, so we will need to create and populate the dimension as a new document – *a "constructed" dimension*;
b) we can find this necessary information by querying directly the primary document and searching for distinct values of a specific element– thus *an "extracted" dimension"*.

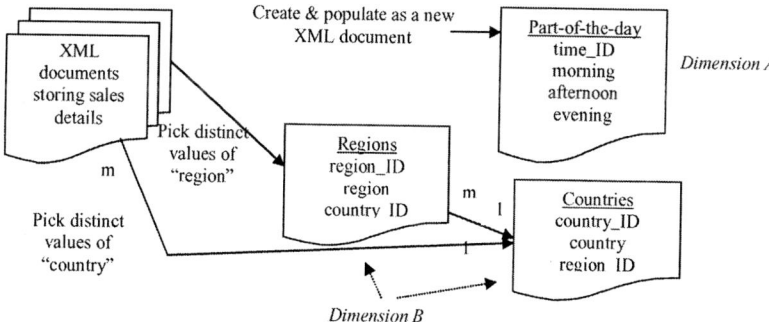

Fig. 1. Dimensions created and populated as new XML documents.

Techniques to Create "Constructed" Dimensions:

If necessary data do not exist in our document, steps are to identify which elements need to be created and which one will be the unique key for linking the dimension with the fact document in the data warehouse. A general way to construct it is:

```
for $a in (1,2,...n)
document {
  <new_element>
        <element_ID>{$a}</element_ID>
        <element_name1>{value}</element_name1>
        <element_name2>{value}</element_name2>
               ............
  </new_element>
        ............
}
```

where <new_element> is a tag representing a new node in the new created dimension, <element_namei>,i=1,2..are names of node's children, taking specific *values*, and <element_ID> will be the unique identifier of <new_element>.

Techniques to Create "Extracted" Dimensions:
If necessary data already exist in the document, we will extract distinct values of elements involved, in a newly created document, creating in the same time keys (e.g. <element_ID>).

```
let $a:=0
document {
for $t in distinct-values(doc("doc_name.xml")//element)
let $a:=$a+1
return
   <new_element>
         <elementID>{$a}</elementID>
         <element_name>{$t}</element_name>
            ............
   </new_element>
}
```

where <new_element> is a tag representing a new created element in the dimension. It contains a key (<elementID>, which takes predetermined values), actual value which is the value of interest (that is <element_name>, e.g. values of "country") and any other elements which can be helpful in the dimension.

There can be situations where the desired data do not exist in the initial document, but they can be extracted from other existing elements, using specific XQuery functions. A general way to construct such a *partial-extracted* dimension is described below:

```
let $a:=0
document {
for $b in distinct-svalues(doc(doc_name.xml")/element)
   let $a:=$a+1
   return
        <new_element>
           <element_ID>{$a}</element_ID>
           <element1>{function1($b)}</element1>
           <element2>{function1($b)}</element2>
           <element3>{function2($b)}</element3>
              ............
        </new_element>
}
```

where elements in are similar with the above example.

3.3 Creating Intermediate XML Documents

In the process of creating a data warehouse from collection of documents, creating intermediate documents is a common way to *extract valuable & necessary information*.

During this step, we are interested only in main activity data (data involved in queries, calculations etc.), from our initial document. At the same time, we will bring in the intermediate document elements from our initial document, which are keys to dimensions, if already exist. Actual fact document in data warehouse will be this intermediate document, but linked to the dimensions.

```
document {
for $t in (doc("doc_name.xml"))
return
        <temp_fact>
            <elem1_name>{$t//elem1_content}</elem1_name>
            <elem2_name>{$t//elem2_content}</elem2_name>
            ..................
        </temp_fact>
}
```

where `<temp_fact>` is a tag representing a new element, containing `<elem1_name>` (name of the element) and `<elem1_content>` (value of element which is valuable for our fact document), etc.

3.4 Updating/Linking Existing Documents and Creating Fact Document

At this step all intermediate XML documents created in the earlier steps should be linked, in such a way that relationships between keys are established (see Fig 2).

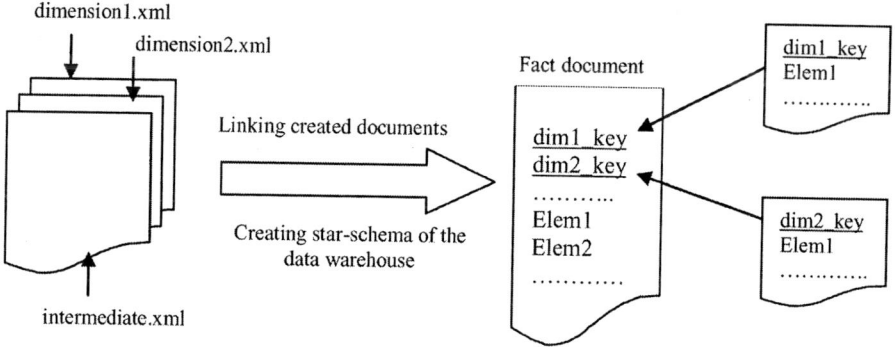

Fig. 2. Linking documents and creating star-schema of data warehouse.

If linking dimensions to intermediate document and obtaining fact are processed all together, the number of iterations through our initial document will be lower, so it subsequently reduces the processing time. A general way to do it can be:

```
let $a:=doc("dimension1.xml")          →e.g. time dimension
let $b:=doc("dimension2.xml")          →e.g. customer dimension
document
{
for $t in (doc("intermediate.xml")/node)
return
    <dim1_key>{for $p in $a where $p//element=$t//element
               return $p//dim1_key}
    </dim1_key>
    <dim2_key>{for $p in $b where $p//element=$t//element
               return $p//dim2_key}
    </dim2_key>
    -------------- ( for all dimensions ) ---------
    <elem1>{$t//elem1_name}</elem1>
    <elem2>{$t//elem2_name}</elem2>
    <elem3>{$t//elem1 * $t//elem2}</elem3>
    --- (for all extracted & calculated elements ) ----
}
```

In the example above, we just obtained the fact, where `<dim1_key>`, `<dim2_key>` etc represent the new created keys elements which will link the fact to dimensions and `<elem1>`, `<elem2>`, `<elem3>` etc are elements of the fact, extracted from intermediate document. A large range of operators can be applied, in order to obtain desired values for analysis (e.g. price * quantity=income).

4 Conclusions

Our paper has presented a systematic approach on how to build a data warehouse for XML documents, in a generic way, so that the rules and techniques can be applied to a wide-range of XML data warehouse models and implementations. After covering all steps involved, we obtain not only an efficient processing of creating a data warehouse, but also high quality data and a low level of redundancy.

Another strong accomplishment is that the steps of work and examples are presented in a very clear and easy manner, so that people who don not have too much knowledge of XQuery can iterate them, with adequate and proper modifications, in order to obtain a data warehouse corresponding to their necessities.

References

1. Widom J., Data Management for XML: Research Directions, *IEEE Data Engineering Bulletin*, 22, 44-52, Sept.1999.
2. Goffarelli, M., Maio, D., Rizzi, S., Conceptual design of data warehouses from E/R schemes Proc. *HICSS-31*, Kona, Hawaii, 1998.
3. Galhardas, H., Florescu, D., Shasha, D., Simon, E., An Extensible framework for data cleaning, Proc. of the *International Conference on Data Engineering*, 2000.

4. Roddick, J.F., Mohania, M.K., Madria, S.K., Methods and Interpretation of Database Summarisation, Database and Expert Systems Application, Florence, Italy, *Lecture Notes in Computer Science*, 1677, 604-615, Springer-Verlag, 1999.
5. Vrdoljak, B., Banek M. and Rizzi S., Designing Web Warehouses from XML Schema, Data Warehousing and Knowledge Discovery, 5th *International Conference DaWak 2003*, Prague, Czech Republic, Sept.3-5, 2003.
6. Zhang J., Ling T.W., Bruckner R.M. and Tjoa A.M., Building XML Data Warehouse Based on Frequent Patterns in User Queries, Data Warehousing and Knowledge Discovery, 5th *International Conference DaWak 2003*, Prague, Czech Republic, 2003.
7. Fernandez M., Simeon J. and Wadler P., XML Query Languages: Experiences and Exemplars, Draft manuscris, September 1999.
http://homepages.inf.ed.ac.uk/wadler/topics/xml.html
8. Deutch A., Fernandez M., Florescu D., Levy A. and Suciu D., A Query Language for XML, Computer Networks, 31,1155-1169, Amsterdam, Netherlands, 1999.

A Novel Method for Mining Frequent Subtrees from XML Data

Wan-Song Zhang, Da-Xin Liu, and Jian-Pei Zhang

Department of Computer Science and Technology, Harbin Engineering University
150001, Harbin, China
zhangwansong@hrbeu.edu.cn

Abstract. In this paper, we focus on the problem of finding frequent subtrees in a large collection of XML data, where both of the patterns and the data are modeled by labeled ordered trees. We present an efficient algorithm RSTMiner that computes all rooted subtrees appearing in a collection of XML data trees with frequent above a user-specified threshold using a special structure Me-tree. In this algorithm, Me-tree is used as a merging tree to supply scheme information for efficient pruning and mining frequent sub-trees. The keys of the algorithm are efficient pruning candidates with Me-Tree structure and incrementally enumerating all rooted sub-trees in canonical form based on a extended right most expansion technique. Experiment results show that RSTMiner algorithm is efficient and scalable.

1 Introduction

As XML (eXtensible Markup Language) prevails over the Internet, XML forms an important data-mining domain, and it is valuable to find methods to discovery the commonly occurring subtrees from XML data trees.

Researches have been done on data mining from semi-structured data [2-12,14]. Akihiro Inokuchi [5] considered mining of collections of paths in ordered trees with Apriori-style technique. Miyahara et al. [14] developed a straightforward generate-test algorithm for discovering ordered trees in a similar setting as ours.

Previous researches on mining tree-like patterns basically adopted a straightforward generate and test strategy [4,7,14,]. In this paper, we adopted Me-tree as data structure to help candidate generation and tree matching test. The key of our method is the extended rightmost-expansion, a technique to grow a tree by attaching new nodes, appeared in the Me-tree, only on the rightmost branch of the tree.

In this paper, we present an efficient algorithm called RSTMiner, to discover frequent RSTs. In order to optimize the algorithm, a document compound structure (Me-tree) is constructed, which can reduce the initial response time of this algorithm by corresponding signature matrix. Experiment results show that RSTMiner is efficient and scalable.

The rest of this paper is organized as follows. In Section 2, we prepare basic notions and definitions. In Section 3, we present our algorithm for solving the frequent pattern discovery problem for labeled ordered trees using the techniques of rightmost-expansion and Me-tree. In Section 4, we run experiments on real datasets to evaluate the proposed mining algorithm. In Section 5, we conclude this paper.

2 Preliminaries

2.1 Problem Statement

In this paper, we model XML data and patterns with labeled ordered trees[15]. A database, which is a collection of XML documents, is a triple $D = (D, \Gamma, \delta)$, where

1. D is ordered tree on Σ, and is called a merging tree (Me-tree). We assume that the root v_0 of D, has a special label that does not belong to Σ.
2. $\Gamma = \{d_1, ..., d_m\}$ is a set of XML document names.
3. $\delta: V_D \to \delta$ is a document name function defined as follows. Let D_i be a sub-tree whose root is the i-th child of v_0. Then, δ is defined as the function that satisfies $\delta(v) = d_i$ for all $v \in V_D$, and v_0 is the root of D.

A finite document collection $D = \{D_1, \cdots, D_n\}$, where each $D_i \in D$ is an ordered tree, called data tree, and $V_{D_i} \cap V_{D_j} = \phi$ for every $1 \leq i, j \leq n$ ($i \neq j$).

Given a data set $D = (D, \Gamma, \delta)$, and a k-edge RST, we define the occurrence as follows: $freq_D(RST) = Occu(RST)/|D|$.

Let $0 < \sigma < 1$ be a positive number. If $freq_D(RST) \geq \sigma$, we say the k-edge RST is σ-frequent. The mining problem can be summarized as follows:

Given a XML database D=(D_1, ..., D_n,) and a positive number, $0 < \sigma \leq 1$, called the minimum support, find F, the set of all σ-frequent rooted sub-trees, that is rooted sub-trees RSTs such that support(RST) $\geq \sigma$, ie., $freq_D(RST) \geq \sigma$.

3 Mining Frequent RSTs

3.1 Overview of the Algorithm

In this section we formulate the RSTMiner algorithm for discovering all frequent rooted sub-tree patterns. RSTMiner uses a global merging tree to store frequent information to pruning the infrequent items. During the tree pattern mining, difficulties arise in enumeration candidates and detection pattern tree matching. We tackle these problems by introduction a extended rightmost branch expansion technique and a document compound structure Me-tree for efficiently enumerating all candidate without duplicates and for incrementally computing the containment test by Me-tree signature.

We use a document compound structure (Me-tree) to collect all the data set into a global information scheme that are further supply the source of candidate generation for rightmost expansion function.

```
RSTMiner(Me – tree, Matrix, D, min Supp)
Input: A constructed Me-tree identified by the prefix-path,
       Me-tree, the database D, minSupp
Output: set of all frequent RST sets
1. F₁ = {all frequent 1-edge rooted subtrees in Me-tree}
2. Given a initial matrix for the Me-tree M₁
3. For(k=1; F_k ≠ ∅; k++)
4. C_{k+1}=CandidateGen(F_k, M_{k+1})
5.    If freq(RST, M_{k+1}) ≥ σ then F_k = F_k ∪ {RST^{k+1}}
6. k = k +1
7. return {F_i|i=1,2,.....,k}
```

Fig. 1. RSTMiner algorithm.

Supplied with Me-tree, we develop an efficient frequent pattern-mining algorithm, named RSTMiner. In the algorithm, a k-edge rooted subtree is denoted by RST^k; and C_k is a set of k-edge candidate RST.

Before RSTMiner works, a Me-tree is initialized w.r.t dataset in D. Then, RSTMiner enumerates all the frequent 1 edge RSTs by scanning the Me-tree, not the database D in order to reduce the scan space.

3.2 Me-Tree Construction

In this section, we define some of the basic concepts used in Me-tree for frequent pattern tree mining.

For the sake of clarity, we introduce a rooted graph-based structural description, called Document Compound Structure (DCS), to portray the structural composition of XML documents. Figure 2 shows the DCS tree of database D.

Definition 1 (Me-tree): A Me-tree is a directed graph such that it contains a node designated as the root, from which there is a path to every other node. Each node in the graph carries its own label, which is a literal of an XML element mark-up. A Me-tree node is also known as an element. A child {parent pair of nodes in the Me-tree preserves the child {parent relationship between two mark-ups in an XML document. Paths are allowed to appear at most once in the graph.

A Me-tree is a 3-tuple, Me-tree=(V_G, E_G, dlist) to be global against database D={D_1,...,D_n}, provided:

1. $V_G \subseteq V_1 \cup \cdots \cup V_n$, where V_i is the node set of D_i, and
2. $E_G \subseteq E_1 \cup \cdots \cup E_n$, where E_i is the tagSet of D_i.

Where dlist denotes that a database list will be record attaching to a root-path when the Me-tree obtained against D by merging the corresponding structures from D_i. Given the parameter dlist of a path, we can get the path or subtree signature w.r.t a list of document data. Just depicted in figure 2, a merged tree M is constructed based on D_1, D_2 and D_3.

A merged Me-tree depicts a extended XML schema which combines two or more XML trees. The introduction of the concept of merger Me-tree aims at limiting the

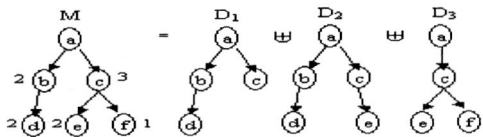

Fig. 2. DCS merging: $M = D_1 \uplus D_2 \uplus D_3$.

initial search space by merging primitive Me-trees into more general ones, which may then be used as matching targets against XML data.

Definition 2 (Me-tree matrix): Given a set of data tree $(T_1, T_2, \ldots T_k)$ and their merged tree M, we can get all the path from the root v_0 to a node d_i, which is appeared in M distinctly, denoted by $P = (p_1, p_2, \cdots, p_j)$. If p_i can be found in T_j, then $(p_i, T_j) = 1$. Consequently, all the pairs can construct a matrix, which is showed the relation between the path in M and all the data trees.

Definition 3 (Path signature): Given a path p_i in M, a set of 1s gotten by pairs from (p_i, T_1) to (p_i, T_k), we say these {1,0}s the signature of the path p_i.

3.3 Enumerating RSTs

Traditional mining algorithms [6,7] enumerate all the frequent 1-pattern sub-trees by scanning all the trees in database D to initiate the frequent set F firstly. And then, use the right-most method to generate the up-level candidate frequent set. By the description motioned above, we can find there is some repeated information, when constructing the candidate frequent set and test the containment. In contrast, we save the information in the M-tree with paths and the occurrence number parameter for the RSTMiner algorithm.

Figure 3 shows the candidate generation algorithm CandidateGen. Firstly, by rightmost expansion technique, the next level candidate set C_{k+1} is generated based on the rooted subtree RST_i in a rooted subtree set RST^k. Next work is how to test this tmpRST is a real subtree in any D_j. if so, the tmpRST can be laid in C_{k+1}.

4 Experimental Results

In this section, we evaluate the performance of RSTMiner. The mining algorithms were ruined on a windows 2000 platform with Petium IV 1.8 G, 256 M RAM. All the algorithms are implemented with Java and Xerces-J 1.4.4. We prepared *Stock-dataset* [13], its size is from 20k to 5M. After collecting pages, datasets were parsed to create DOM tree, and then attribute value pairs in a DOM tree were converted into a set of nodes as follows. We treated the attribute node and element node as the same node in DOM tree. Then Dom trees were generated by lexicographic order. After preprocessing, the data trees for *Stock-dataset* had nodes from 500 to 20000.

```
Algorithm CandidateGen($C_k$, D)
Input: $C_k$ - frequent candidate k-edge root subtrees
Output: $C_{k+1}$
1.  $C_{k+1} = \phi; F_{k+1} = \phi;$
2.  for each $RST_i^k \in F_k$ do
3.      $tmpRST = RightmostGen(RST_i^k)$
4.      for each $RST_i \in C_{k+1}$ do
5.          //for each branch of tmpRST
6.          if $\exists D_n$ in D, $\cup Signature(branch_j) = 1$
7.              $C_{k+1} \leftarrow tmpRST_i$
8.  return
```

Fig. 3. Algorithm CandidateGen.

In the experiments, we implemented the algorithm to detect the expansibility of algorithm RSTMiner. In what follows, the parameters n and σ denote the data size as the number of nodes and the minimum support.

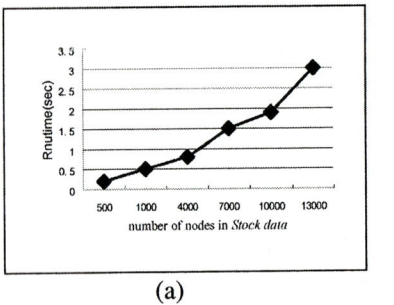
(a)

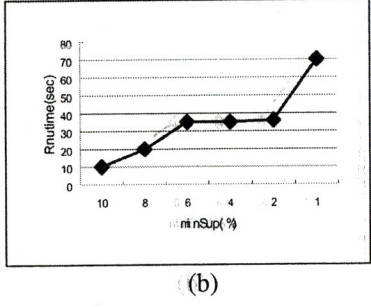
(b)

Fig. 4. Effect of varying data set and effect of varying σ.

In figure 4(a), when the number of nodes varied from 500 to 12000, the running time of RSTMiner with $\sigma = 5\%$. The running time scales almost linearly with size as the data size is increased. Figure 4(b) shows the running time on the Stock data as the minSupp σ is decreased form 10% to 1.5%. For the $\sigma = 10\%$, the running time is Figure 4 shows the running times for *Stock* data by the σ varied from 10% to 2%. We can find that the response time is affected by the size of frequent patterns in the data set.

5 Conclusions

In this paper, we studied a data-mining problem of XML data by modeling XML data as labeled ordered trees. We proposed an efficient algorithm, RSTMiner, to find all frequent rooted subtrees form a collection of XML documents. We run experiments in real data with parameter variable to evaluate the proposed algorithms. Experiments results showed that RSTMiner has good response time and scales well.

References

1. Ke Wang, Huiqing Liu: Discovering Structural Association of Semistructured Data. IEEE Trans. Knowl. Data Eng. 12, 353-371, 2000.
2. Rakesh Agrawal, Heikki Mannila, Ramakrishnan Srikant, Hannu Toivonen,A. Inkeri Verkamo. Fast Discovery of Association Rules. Advances in Knowledge Discovery and Data Mining, 307-328, 1996.
3. S. Nijssen and J.N. Kok . Efficient discovery of frequent unordered trees: Proofs. Technical Report 1, Leiden Institute of Advanced Computer Science, Universiteit Leiden, 2003.
4. X. Yan and J. Han, gSpan: Graph-Based Substructure Pattern Mining, Proceedings of the IEEE International Conference on Data Mining (IEEE ICDM), 2002.
5. Akihiro Inokuchi, Takashi Washio, Hiroshi Motoda: An Apriori-Based Algorithm for Mining Frequent Substructures from Graph Data. PKDD, 13-23, 2000.
6. Liang Huai Yang, Mong-Li Lee, Wynne Hsu, Sumit Acharya: Mining Frequent Quer Patterns from XML Queries. DASFAA, 355-362, 2003.
7. Mohammed Javeed Zaki: Efficiently mining frequent trees in a forest. KDD, 71-80, 2002.
8. S. Nijssen and J.N. Kok . Efficient discovery of frequent unordered trees. In Proceedings of the first International Workshop on Mining Graphs, Trees and Sequences (MGTS'03), 2003.
9. Tatsuya Asai, Kenji Abe, Shinji Kawasoe, Hiroki Arimura, Hiroshi Satamoto, Setsuo Arikawa: Efficient Substructure Discovery from Large Semi-structured Data. SDM 2002.
10. Guimei Liu, Hongjun Lu, Yabo Xu, Jeffrey Xu Yu: Ascending Frequency Ordered Prefixtree: Efficient Mining of Frequent Patterns. DASFAA, 65-72, 2003.
11. Serge Abiteboul, Peter Buneman, Dan Suciu: Data on the Web: From Relations to Semistructured Data and XML. Morgan Kaufmann 1999.
12. Liang Huai Yang, Mong-Li Lee, Wynne Hsu: Efficient Mining of XML Query Patterns for Caching. VLDB , 69-80, 2003.
13. http://www.cs.wics.edu/niagara/data.html.
14. T. Miyahara, T. Shoudai, T. Uchida, K. Takahashi, H. Ueda, Discovery of Frequent Tree Structured Patterns in Semistructured Web Documents, In Proc. PAKDD-2001, 47–52, 2001.
15. Aho, A. V., Hopcroft, J. E., Ullman, J. D. "Data Structures and Algorithms", Addison-Wesley, 1983.

Mining Association Rules Using Relative Confidence

Tien Dung Do, Siu Cheung Hui, and Alvis C.M. Fong

School of Computer Engineering, Nanyang Technological University
Nanyang Avenue, Singapore
{pa0001852a,asschui,ascmfong}@ntu.edu.sg

Abstract. Mining for association rules is one of the fundamental tasks of data mining. Association rule mining searches for interesting relationships amongst items for a given dataset based mainly on the *support* and *confidence* measures. *Support* is used for filtering out infrequent rules, while *confidence* measures the implication relationships from a set of items to one another. However, one of the main drawbacks of the *confidence* measure is that it presents the absolute value of implication that does not reflect truthfully the relationships amongst items. For example, if two items have a very high frequency, then they will probably form a rule with a high *confidence* even if there is no relationship between them at all. In this paper, we propose a new measure known as *relative confidence* for mining association rules, which is able to reflect truthfully the relationships of items. The effectiveness of the *relative confidence* measure is evaluated in comparison with the *confidence* measure in mining interesting relationships between terms from textual documents and in associative classification.

1 Introduction

Association rule mining [1] searches for interesting relationships amongst items in a given dataset. An association rule $X \Rightarrow Y$, where X and Y are sets of items (or *itemsets*), means that whenever a transaction contains X, it will probably contain Y. The probability is called the *confidence* of the rule. The rule $X \Rightarrow Y$ with a high *confidence* represents a high "imply" relationship (or implication) from X to Y. It means that Y will likely be present in transactions that contain X. However, the absolute value of the implication is not very effective to reflect the actual relationship between X and Y. A rule may have a high *confidence*, but it may not be interesting and useful. For example, let Y_1 be a very popular itemset in the dataset, then Y_1 will likely be present in any transactions in the dataset. This can imply, with X_1 as a certain itemset, that Y_1 will likely be present in transactions containing X_1. It means that the *confidence* of the rule $X_1 \Rightarrow Y_1$ is potentially high for any itemset X_1 regardless of how related X_1 to Y_1 is.

This paper proposes a new measure, known as *relative confidence*, for mining association rules. *Relative confidence* is able to represent "relative implication" relationship of a rule with respect to the frequencies of the itemsets instead of the pure absolute value of the implication relationship reflected by the *confidence* measure. In this paper, we will show experimentally that the *relative confidence* measure can be used effectively to find interesting relationships between terms from a set of textual documents in a specific domain. In addition, we will also evaluate the effectiveness of the *relative confidence* measure in comparison with the *confidence* measure based on the accuracy of the mined association rules for associative classification.

The rest of this paper is organized as follows. We first review the concepts on association rules and the associated measures. The proposed *relative confidence* measure is introduced. The evaluation on the effectiveness of the proposed *relative confidence* measure is then presented. Finally, the conclusion is given.

2 Association Rules and Measures

Formally, an association rule R is an implication $X \Rightarrow Y$, where X and Y are sets of items in a given dataset. The *confidence* of the rule $conf(R)$ is the percentage of transactions that contains Y amongst the transactions containing X. The *support* of the rule $supp(R)$ is the percentage of transactions containing X and Y with respect to the number of all transactions.

Let P[S] be the probability of an itemset S present in a certain transaction of the database. Similar to the definition of *support* of a rule, P[S] can be considered as the *support* of the itemset S (it is denoted as $supp(S)$ in some papers). We call P[X] the *antecedence support* and P[Y] the *consequence support* of the rule R. Assume that the database contains N transactions with the numbers of transactions that contain X, Y, and both X and Y are a, b, and c respectively. It can be implied from the definitions of *support* and *confidence* of association rules that $supp(R) = c/N$ and $conf(R) = c/a$; and from the definition of *support* of an itemset that $P[X] = a/N$, $P[Y] = b/N$ and $P[X \wedge Y] = c/N$. Thus, the values of $supp(R)$ and $conf(R)$ can be computed using $P[X \wedge Y]$ and $P[Y]$ as follows:

Support: $$supp(R) = P[X \wedge Y] \qquad (1)$$

Confidence: $$conf(R) = \frac{P[X \wedge Y]}{P[X]} \qquad (2)$$

In addition to the conventional measures of association rules, the following measures [2-4] were also proposed with an intention to fully characterize association rules:

Interest: $$intr(R) = \frac{P[X \wedge Y]}{P[X] \times P[Y]} = \frac{conf(R)}{P[Y]} = \frac{conf(Y \Rightarrow X)}{P[X]} \qquad (3)$$

Conviction: $$conv(R) = \frac{P[X] \times P[\neg Y]}{P[X \wedge \neg Y]} = \frac{1}{intr(X \Rightarrow \neg Y)} \qquad (4)$$

Reliability: $$relb(R) = \frac{P[X \wedge Y]}{P[X]} - P[Y] = conf(R) - P[Y] \qquad (5)$$

In [2], Brin *et al.* proposed *interest* as a measure of correlation between items. The *interest* value of a rule R is the proportion of the *confidence* value of the rule with respect to the value of the consequence support of R. An *interest* value above 1 represents a positive correlation between two items (or itemsets), whereas a value below 1 represents a negative correlation. The *conviction* of a rule was introduced in [3] as an asymmetric version of the *interest* measure. The *conviction* of a rule R, therefore, logically reflects the dis-correlation of X and $\neg Y$. In other words, the *conviction* of R also reflects the correlation of X and Y as the *interest* measure. In [4], the *reliability* of a rule R measures "the effect of the available information about the antecedence on the probability of the consequence". The greater the *reliability* is, the stronger the association "if X then Y". Positive correlation is indicated by a positive value of *reliability*, while negative correlation is indicated otherwise. However, this pure difference in values does not truthfully reflect the implication as well as the correlation amongst the items. If $P[Y]$ is high, then the *reliability* value is low regardless of the values of *confidence* and *interest* (relb(R) = conf(R) – $P[Y] \leq 1 - P[Y]$).

3 Relative Confidence

The *confidence* of a rule R reflects the implication "if a transaction contains X, then it will probably contain Y". The transaction will contain Y because X is related to Y so that once it contains X it will be likely to contain Y, or because Y is contained in some transactions of the database so that it will possibly be contained in the transaction. Therefore, the *confidence* of R is influenced by two factors: (i) the degree on how X is related to Y; and (ii) the density of random distribution of transactions containing Y amongst transactions containing X. The first factor can be considered as the actual value of the relationship from X to Y. We call this as *relative confidence* of the rule R (denoted as $Rconf(R)$). The second factor is the same as the degree of distribution of the transactions containing Y on the whole database of transactions which is represented by the *support* of Y (i.e. $P[Y]$).

Let A be the set of transactions containing X and B be the set of transactions in A that contains Y, then $conf(R) = p(B|A)$ (probability of B on A). According to the two factors on the *confidence* of the rule R, B would be compounded from (i) a set of transactions B_1, which reflects the relationships of X to Y; and (ii) a set of transactions B_2, which reflects the random distribution of the transactions containing Y. We can now imply that $p(B_1|A) = Rconf(R)$, $p(B_2|A) = P[Y]$ and $B = B_1 \cup B_2$. We can then find the relationship of the probabilities of these sets of transactions. In the following equations, the probabilities are considered in the sample space of A. It means that, for example, $p(B)$ denotes $p(B|A)$.

$$p(B) = p(B_1 \cup B_2) \quad (6)$$
$$= p(B_1) + p(B_2) - p(B_1 \cap B_2) \quad (7)$$
$$= p(B_1) + p(B_2) - p(B_1) \times p(B_2) \quad (8)$$
$$p(B) - p(B_2) = p(B_1) - p(B_1) \times p(B_2)$$
$$p(B_1) = \frac{p(B) - p(B_2)}{1 - p(B_2)} \quad (9)$$

Equations (7) and (8) are based on probability theorems of union of arbitrary events and multiplication rule for independent events. Note that the two sets B_1 and B_2 are independent because B_2 is a result from a random distribution. Now, we replace the equations on the probabilities of B, B_1 and B_2 into (9) to derive the formula for the *relative confidence* of R:

$$\text{Rconf}(R) = \frac{\text{conf}(R) - P[Y]}{1 - P[Y]}$$

$$= \frac{\frac{P[X \wedge Y]}{P[X]} - P[Y]}{1 - P[Y]} = \frac{P[X \wedge Y] - P[X] \times P[Y]}{P[X] - P[X] \times P[Y]} \quad (10)$$

Definition 1. The *relative confidence* of a rule R ($X \Rightarrow Y$) is defined as:

$$\text{Rconf}(R) = \frac{P[X \wedge Y] - P[X] \times P[Y]}{P[X] - P[X] \times P[Y]} \quad (11)$$

Figure 1 shows the relationship of the *relative confidence* and *confidence* measures with respect to the consequence support inferred from formula (10). With a small value of P[Y], the two measures are identical. The higher the value of supp(Y), the larger the difference between the two measures. For example, if a rule R (X⇒Y) with conf(R) = 80% and P[Y] = 5%, then Rconf(R) = 79%. If another rule R_1 ($X_1 \Rightarrow Y_1$) has the same value of *confidence* (i.e. 80%) but with P[Y_1] = 50%, then Rconf = 60%. Notice that when the *confidence* value is 100%, the *relative confidence* value will also be 100% regardless of the value of P[Y].

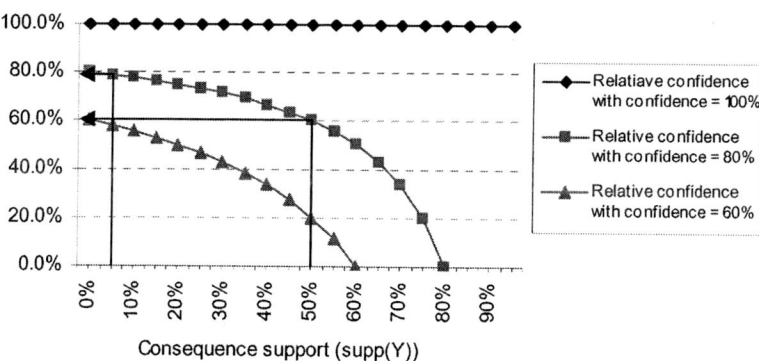

Fig. 1. Relative confidence and confidence measures w.r.t. the consequence support.

4 Experiments

Two experiments had been conducted to evaluate the effectiveness of the proposed *relative confidence* measure for mining association rules. The first experiment aims to compare the *relative confidence* measure with the *confidence* and *interest* measures based on the interestingness of the minded association rules from a set of textual documents. The second experiment aims to compare the *confidence* and *relative confidence* measures based on the effectiveness of the mined association rules for associative classification [5]. The accuracy of the classifiers based on the two measures can then be used to evaluate the effectiveness of the measures.

4.1 Interesting Association Rules from Data Mining Documents

This experiment had been conducted using abstracts of 514 published papers downloaded from the Science Direct web page (http://www. sciencedirect.com) on June 2003 from searching the website using the keyword "data mining" in the title, abstract and keyword fields. The papers were obtained from the data mining domain with the intention that the rules found could be evaluated from the meanings of the terms, which should be familiar to the readers as well as the authors of this paper. For example, we can recognize easily that "neural" $\Rightarrow$ "network" is a good rule, whereas "university" $\Rightarrow$ "data" is not in the data mining domain. The preprocessing tasks including stop-word removal, word stemming and infrequent word removal were performed. The final dataset contains 622 terms with document frequencies from 10 to 416.

During this experiment, we only examined rules in which the antecedence and consequence were single terms. We first mined association rules using the *support* threshold of 1%. Next, the *confidence*, *relative confidence* and *interest* measures were used to search for interesting rules. Table 1 lists the ten highest rules for each measure. The numbers given in the parentheses next to a term are the document frequencies of the terms. Here, we ignore the 62 rules (not shown in the table) in which the *confidence* value is 100% because the *relative confidence* of them will also be 100%. They are, therefore, not meaningful for evaluation purpose.

Table 1. Assocation rules with highest values of confidence, relative confidence and interest.

Confidence	Relative confidence	Interest
technology (32) $\Rightarrow$ data (416)	neural (50) $\Rightarrow$ network (72)	department (10) $\Rightarrow$ university (11)
integrate(28) $\Rightarrow$ data(416)	intelligence (15) $\Rightarrow$ artificial (33)	play (13) $\Rightarrow$ role (22)
deal(26) $\Rightarrow$ data(416)	play (13) $\Rightarrow$ role (22)	care (13) $\Rightarrow$ health (15)
extraction(26) $\Rightarrow$ data(416)	execution (11) $\Rightarrow$ time (78)	text (12) $\Rightarrow$ document (17)
aim(24) $\Rightarrow$ data(416)	cdna (10) $\Rightarrow$ gene (35)	commonly (10) $\Rightarrow$ quantitative (16)
environment(24) $\Rightarrow$ data(416)	lack (12) $\Rightarrow$ analysis (149)	cdna (10) $\Rightarrow$ express (20)
solve (24) $\Rightarrow$ data(416)	apriori (11) $\Rightarrow$ algorithm (157)	bound (10) $\Rightarrow$ low (21)
mine (330) $\Rightarrow$ data(416)	massive (12) $\Rightarrow$ method (189)	intelligence (15) $\Rightarrow$ artificial (33)
event (23) $\Rightarrow$ data(416)	decomposition (10) $\Rightarrow$ model (140)	text (12) $\Rightarrow$ retrieval (18)
handle (22) $\Rightarrow$ data(416)	automatic (20) $\Rightarrow$ mine (330)	cdna (10) $\Rightarrow$ gene (35)

From Table 1, we find that all the ten rules of highest *confidence* are in the form of X $\Rightarrow$ "data" which are not very interesting. As we have discussed earlier that the *confidence* measure of a rule is influenced by two factors, namely the *relative confidence* and the consequence support (P[Y]). In this case, due to the very high value of support of the term "data" (416/514=81%), all the rules in the form $X \Rightarrow$ "data" will potentially have a high value of *confidence*. In fact, amongst the 100 best rules with the *confidence* measure, there are up to 95 rules in which the consequence is "data" or "mine", the two most frequent terms in the dataset. In contrast, the rules mined with the *relative confidence* measure are quite interesting in the data mining domain. The noise on the frequency of items is removed making the terms of the rules with high *relative confidence* strongly related. Finally, the ten rules with the highest *interest* values consist of strongly correlated terms. However, they are not so interesting in the domain of data mining. We can also observe that the term frequencies of the rules are relatively small. The reason is that with a given *confidence* value of a rule $X \Rightarrow Y$ (or $Y \Rightarrow X$), according to formula (3), the *interest* value is inversely proportional to the value of P[Y] (or P[X]).

4.2 Associative Classification

In associative classification [5], association rules are mined from the training dataset in the form of *itemset* $\Rightarrow c$ where *itemset* is a set of items and c is a class. The main idea of associative classification is based on the implication relationships of association rules. An association rule R (*itemset* $\Rightarrow c$) means that if a given transaction contains the *itemset*, then it will probably belong to the class c. Here, the *confidence* measure (say 80%) guarantees the reliability of the classification decision. The transaction is classified into the class c because 80% of the transactions that also contain the *itemset* fall into class c.

In this experiment, we used the dataset on the Census database from UCI Machine Learning Repository [6]. The database consists of a training dataset of 32,561 transactions and a test dataset of 16,281 transactions. A transaction contains the employee's information of 14 attributes (6 continuous and 8 nominal). Each employee belongs to one of the following classes: "<=50K" and ">50K" according to the income. In the training set, 76% of the transactions belong to the class "<=50K", whereas the remaining 24 % belong to the class ">50K". The performance of the classifiers is evaluated using the F measure, $F = \dfrac{2PR}{P+R}$, which is computed using the precision and recall measures P and R.

During this experiment, association rules were first mined with the minimal *support* threshold set to 1%. Next, the association rules were then filtered using the *confidence* and *relative confidence* measures to gather the set of association rules for the classifiers, namely AC_1 and AC_2 respectively. In this step, the minimal *confidence* and *relative confidence* thresholds were set such that the same number of association rules was gathered for AC_1 and AC_2. Finally, the classifiers AC_1 and AC_2 were used to classify the test dataset.

As shown in Table 2, the accuracy of the classifier AC_2 using the *relative confidence* measure has performed much better than that of the classifier AC_1 using *confi-*

dence. As an example, let's examine closer for the case when the *confidence* and *relative confidence* thresholds are set at 70% and 25.3% respectively. In fact, as 76% of the transactions belong to the class "≤50K", the *confidence* of the rule X ⇒ "≤50K" with a random itemset X is about 76%. As such, the *confidence* value of 70% is unable to determine whether the rule X ⇒ "≤50K" is interesting or not. In contrast, the rules in the form of X ⇒ ">50K" with the same 70% *confidence* value is far more interesting because only 24% of the transactions belongs to the class ">50K". Therefore, the association rules that were mined using the *confidence* measure contained many weak rules of the class "≤50K", and too few rules of the class ">50K". Using formula (5), the value of 25.3% of *relative confidence* has the equivalent 82% *confidence* value for rules in the form of X ⇒ "≤50K" and 43% *confidence* value for the rules in the form of X ⇒ ">50K". As the rules of the two classes using the *relative confidence* measure have a more balanced degree of interestingness, the classifier AC_2 has achieved better performance than the classifier AC_1.

Table 2. Accuracy for AC_1 and AC_2.

Conf	Rconf	No of rules	AC_1 (using confidence measure)			AC_2 (using relative confidence measure)		
			F(≤50K)	F(>50K)	F(average)	F(≤50K)	F(>50K)	F(average)
60	3.8	8026	0.89	0.50	**0.70**	0.83	0.63	**0.73**
70	25.3	6766	0.90	0.52	**0.71**	0.84	0.63	**0.74**
80	47.3	5346	0.90	0.46	**0.68**	0.90	0.67	**0.78**
90	66.9	4071	0.92	0.61	**0.77**	0.91	0.70	**0.81**

In addition, to improve accuracy, we have applied additional techniques including using multiple support values [7] and pruning weak and specific association rules [8] to associative classification. This aims to evaluate whether *relative confidence* is efficient for the classification task. Table 3 gives the performance of both classifiers with *confidence* thresholds setting at 75%, 80%, 85% and 90%. As shown in Table 3, the classifier AC_2 has archived good accuracy compared with the classifier AC_1. The error rate (for each transaction) of the classifier is from 12% to 16%, which is also comparable to that of other classifiers such as C4.5, Naive-Bayes or Nearest-neighbor with error rate ranging from 14%-21% documented in the dataset [6].

Table 3. Improved accuracy for AC_1 and AC_2.

Conf	Rconf	AC_1 (using confidence measure)			AC_2 (using relative confidence measure)		
		F(≤50K)	F(>50K)	F(average)	F(≤50K)	F(>50K)	F(average)
75	53.1	0.90	0.60	**0.75**	0.89	0.69	**0.79**
80	62.7	0.89	0.56	**0.72**	0.91	0.73	**0.82**
85	69.3	0.92	0.60	**0.76**	0.92	0.74	**0.83**
90	75.0	0.93	0.66	**0.79**	0.91	0.70	**0.81**

5 Conclusion

One of the main issues in mining association rules is the large number of rules generated, of which many are uninteresting. This paper has proposed a new measure known as *relative confidence* for mining association rules which can reflect truthfully the relationships of items. In the paper, we have shown that the *relative confidence* measure is effective over the *confidence* measure, especially when the database contains items with high frequency. Nevertheless, even for database in which frequencies of items are relatively low, the *relative confidence* measure will behave the same as the *confidence* measure. In other words, the *relative confidence* measure can be used instead of the *confidence* measure in mining association rules more effectively.

References

1. R. Agrawal and R. Srikant, Fast algorithms for mining association rules, Proc. of the 20th Int'l Conf. on Very Large Databases (VLDB '94), Santiago, Chile, 487-499, June 1994.
2. S. Brin, R. Motwani and C. Silverstein, Beyond Market Baskets: Generalizing association rules to correlations, Proc. of the ACM SIGMOD Conference, 265-276, 1997.
3. S. Brin, R. Motwani, J. D. Ullman and S. Tsur, Dynamic itemset counting and implication rules for market basket data, Proc. of the ACM SIGMOD Conference, 255-264, May 1997.
4. K. Ahmed, N. El-Makky and Y. Taha, A note on 'Beyond Market Baskets: Generalizing association rules to correlations', ACM SIGKDD Explorations, 1, Issue 2, 46-48, 2000.
5. B. Liu, W. Hsu and Y. Ma, Integrating classification and association rule mining, In Proc of the Fourth International Conference on Knowledge Discovery and Data Mining, 80-86, New York, NY, 1998.
6. UCI Machine Learning Repository, Available online at <http://www.ics.uci.edu/~mlearn/MLRepository.html> .
7. B. Liu, Y. Ma and C.K. Wong, Classification Using Association Rules: Weaknesses and Enhancements. In Vipin Kumar, et al, (eds), Data mining for scientific applications, 2001.
8. M.L. Antonie and O. R. Zaïane, Text Document Categorization by Term Association, In Proc. of the IEEE International Conference on Data Mining, 2002.

Multiple Classifiers Fusion System Based on the Radial Basis Probabilistic Neural Networks

Wen-Bo Zhao[1], Ming-Yi Zhang[1], Li-Ming Wang[1],
Ji-Yan Du[1], and De-Shuang Huang[2]

[1] Artillery Academy of People Liberation Army
[2] Institute of Intelligent Machines, Chinese Academy of Sciences

Abstract. The fusion system designing of multiple classifiers, which is based on the radial basis probabilistic neural network (RBPNN), is discussed in this paper. By means of the proposed design method, the complex structure optimization can be effectively avoided in the designing procedure of the RBPNN. In addition, D-S fusion algorithm adopted in the system greatly improves the classification performance for the complexity problem of the real-world. The simulation results demonstrate that the designing case of the fusion system based on the RBPNNs is feasible and effective.

1 Introduction

The radial basis probabilistic neural network (RBPNN) model [1] is in substance developed from the radial basis function neural network (RBFNN) [2] and the probabilistic neural network (PNN) [3]. Therefore, the RBPNN possesses the common characteristic of the original two networks, i.e., the signal is concurrently feed-forwarded from the input layer to the output layer without any feedback connections within the three layers network models. On the other hand, the RBPNN, to some extent, decreases the two original models' demerits. In the aspects of pattern recognition and time sequence prediction, the RBPNN has good performance [4]. Similar to the other traditional feed-forward neural networks (FNN), however, in order to gain the best performance, i.e., generalization performance, the initially designed RBPNN need to be optimized. Generally, the seeking procedure of the optimal structure of the RBPNN can lead to produce a great of time and computation requirement. In other words, the FNNs structure optimization, including the RBPNN, is a procedure of complexity and difficulty. To overcome the structure optimization, and improve the performance of the designed networks, the fusion system of multiple networks is an effective solution method. Recently the fusion system of multiple networks has been developed greatly, and widely used in the characteristic recognition, image classification & retrieval, and creature feature recognition, etc. The basic theory of fusion of multiple networks is that, designing multiple non-optimal networks, taking place of the single optimal network for solving the same problem, make use of complementarity and redundancy of these multiple classifiers so as to avoid the complex and time-consuming structure optimization.

The usual fusion algorithms include voting [5,6], Bayes [7,8], D-S [9,10]. D-S fusion algorithm, however, can overcome the disadvantages of Bayes algorithm and voting algorithm. This algorithm do not need large samples set. Even though the training procedure is not too perfect, the testing output performance by D-S method would be very good. In other words, D-S algorithm has good robusticity. Furthermore D-S algorithm takes the error characteristics of each classification units into account. This fusion algorithm will be preferred for designing the multiple classifiers fusion system of RBPNNs.

2 Basic Theory of D-S Fusion Algorithms

Given that the discriminating space was made of exhaustive and mutually exhaustive propositions, denoted by $A_1, A_2, \cdots, A_M$. The truth function Bel and basic probabilistic assignment function (BPA) are used to express believable degrees of the propositions belonging to the discriminating space, i.e., $A \subset \Theta$. BPA, which was generalized from the probabilistic density distribution function, represents effect of the evidence individual for the discriminating space, denoted by m. If two or over two evidences, denoted by $e_1, e_2, \cdots, e_K$, support proposition A, the corresponding BPAs and $Bels$ expressed by $m_1(A), m_2(A), \cdots, m_K(A)$ and $bel_1(A), bel_2(A), \cdots, bel_K(A)$ by means of Dempster combination rule these evidences can be integrated into a new BPA and $Bels$ in the case of mutual independence of those evidences. In mathematics, Dempster rule can be expressed as the following:

$$m(A) = m_1 \oplus m_2 \oplus \cdots \oplus m_K \qquad (1)$$

$$bet(A) = \sum_{B \subseteq A} m(B) \qquad (2)$$

3 The Designing of the Fusion System Based on Multiple RBPNNS

Supposed K RBPNNs constructed in the fusion system of multiple classifiers, M pattern classes existed in the samples space, and input sample $\mathbf{X}$ belonged to the i-th class, denoted by proposition $\{A_i | \mathbf{X} \in C_i\}$, and output decision-making of the k-th RBPNN, denoted by $e_k(\mathbf{X}) = j_k, k = 1, 2, \cdots, K, j_k \in \wedge = \{1, 2, \cdots, M\}$. So $\Theta = \{A_1, A_2, \cdots, A_M\}$ consists of the discrimination space of input samples. For input sample $\mathbf{X}$, K RBPNNs produce K classification results, i.e., $\{e_1(\mathbf{X}), e_2(\mathbf{X}), \cdots, e_K(\mathbf{X})\}$, by which, D-S fusion algorithm is used to form the final classification result of the fusion system.

3.1 The Designing of the RBPNN Classification Units

For the sake of avoiding complexly designing of the single optimal RBPNN each RBPNN unit in the fusion system can not be undergone structure optimization procedure, but persuade as possible as simply designing, besides guaranteeing working independence of each RBPNN. Therefore two kinds of designing methods for the RBPNN units are proposed in this paper, i.e., a feature assignment method and a space separation method.

By means of the feature assignment method, the high dimensions of input samples will be allotted the low dimensions processing RBPNNs. Furthermore the features assigned into each RBPNN unit are not overlapped at each other in the case of making insure of integrality of samples space. The merits of feature assignment method is not only alleviating transacting expense of each RBPNN unit, but also guaranteeing independence of decision-making of each unit. If each dimension of the input samples is not correlated, the feature assignment method does not require the features abstracting procedure, or dimensions compressing procedure, so the classification information of samples will not be loss generally.

The space separation method is mostly applied for the samples set with the large scale of components. By this method the sample space will be separated into many independent sections, which can be combined as the whole space. Samples in each separated subspace are trained only by one RBPNN unit.

Although each RBPNN unit of the fusion system does not require optimal in structure, by complementing and collaborating of each unit the whole classification performance will be better than all of RBPNNs units. So the selection of hidden center vectors of each RBPNN unit can adopt simple methods, such as random selecting, in order to simplifying the designing procedure.

3.2 The Fusion Procedure of D-S Fusion Algorithm

Although D-S theory was proposed by Dempster and Shafer firstly, Xu [11] had greatly developed it and firstly used it solve the problem of pattern classification. According to reference [11], D-S fusion algorithm used for pattern classification can be summarized as the three following steps.

Firstly for the given input sample, there are possibly several RBPNNs with the same decision-making, for convenience, we combine those RBPNNs into one new classification unit. Given $e_{k1}, e_{k2}, \cdots, e_{kn}$ with the same output decision-making, the BPA of new combined classification unit can be computed by the following:

$$m_{E_k} = m_{k1} \oplus m_{k2} \oplus \cdots \oplus m_{kp} \quad (3)$$

Secondly change different output decision-makings of the new classification units into decision-takings of the fusion system.

Lastly form the final decision-making according to the truth function values of decision-takings of the fusion system. Given the truth function values of decision-makings of the fusion system denoted by $bel(A_{jk})$, the final decision-making $E(\mathbf{X})$ can be obtained as the following:

$$E(\mathbf{X}) = \begin{cases} j_k^* & if \quad bet(A_{jk}*) = max_{j_k' \in \wedge} bel(j_k') \\ M+1 & other \end{cases} \quad (4)$$

Table 1. Comparison of recognition performance of 4 RBPNNs units for the training set solving for breast-cancer classification

Index of RBFNN units	Correct recognition rate	Wrong recognition rate	Refused recognition rate
I	76%	22%	2%
II	74%	24%	2%
III	82%	16%	2%
IV	82%	16%	2%
The best (IV)	82%	16%	2%

4 Simulations and Discussions

In order to validate the above analyses, two examples, (1) breast-cancer classification (2) flare-solar classification were used in this paper.

Breast-cancer standard data [12] includes 100 pairs of training & testing. There are 200 training samples and 77 testing samples in each pair. We use the above discussed space separation method divide 200 training samples into 4 groups, each of which consists of 50 samples and training a RBPNN independently. All samples of both the training set and testing set belong to two classes. The four RBPNNs are used to training each group of training samples. Then 77 testing samples are checked by the 4 trained RBPNNs. We can see that for each of 77 testing samples, 4 RBPNNs will give respective classification result. Lastly D-S fusion decision-making will give the final classification result.

In order to describe the work mechanism of the fusion system based on four RBPNNs, we select experimental result of one pair of training & testing set to discuss the fusion procedure. For the training set, training results of 4 RBPNNs are listed as Table 1. Using D-S algorithm training results of the fusion system is 99.52% correct recognition rate, 0.48% wrong recognition rate respectively. For the testing set, final classification results fused by D-S algorithm is respectively 80.52% correct recognition rate, 19.48% wrong recognition rate. The partially detail results can be shown as Table 2. Obviously D-S algorithm is different from the voting algorithm as D-S algorithm fully considers the error characteristics of each RBPNN unit in the fusion system. Those RBPNNs with high correct recognition rates and low wrong recognition rates will take the key role in the fusion system.

For the 100 pairs of training & testing sets, average correct recognition and its scope of variety is 0.7409 ± 0.0428. And the system output and the best output of 4 RBPNNs are plotted as Fig.1. From this figure, we can see that performance of the system based on 4 RBPNNs is better than anyone of the single RBPNN. For the flare-solar classification, designing of the fusion system is as following. In each pair of training & testing, 666 samples and 400 samples are included in training set and testing set, respectively. So 3 RBPNNs are constructed in the fusion system, i.e., each RBPNN transacting 222 training samples. For 100 pairs of training & testing, average rate of correct recognition and its scope of variety is 0.6307 ± 0.0264. The detail information of transacting is described as Fig.2.

Table 2. Comparison of recognition performance of 4 RBPNNs units for the testing set solving breast-cancer classification problem

Index of RBFNN units	Correct recognition rate	Wrong recognition rate	Refused recognition rate
I	72.73%	6.49%	20.78%
II	62.34%	0%	37.66%
III	74.03%	0%	25.97%
IV	66.23%	0%	23.77%
The best (I)	72.73%	6.49%	20.78%

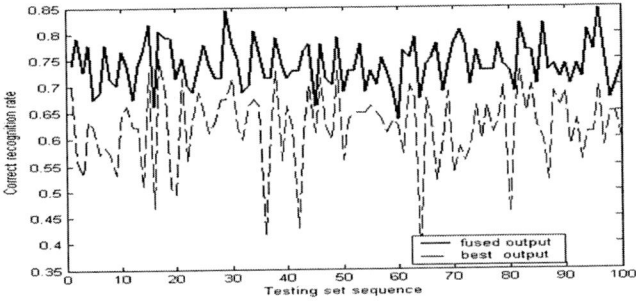

Fig. 1. Compare between the system output and best output of 4 RBPNNs for breast-cancer classification

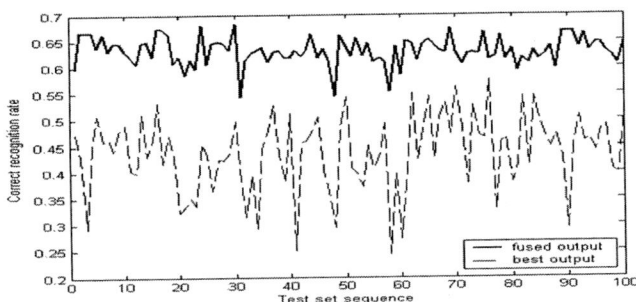

Fig. 2. Compare between the system output and best output of 3 RBPNNs for flare-solar classification

From it, it can be seen that the fusion system based on 3 RBPNNs is better than anyone of 3 RBPNNs in generalization ability. As the limit of paper length, the detail fusion procedure is not discussed in this paper. Future work is focused on the application of real-world problem using the fusion system based on the multiple RBPNNs.

5 Conclusions

Designing of D-S fusion system based on multiple RBPNNs is discussed in this paper. The multiple RBPNNs case overcomes the demerit of the single RBPNN in the structure optimization, i.e. avoiding complex computation of searching for the optimal RBPNN. The adopted effective fusion algorithm, D-S algorithm, greatly improves recognition precision for the complexity pattern recognition problem.

References

1. D.S. Huang, "Radial basis probabilistic neural networks: Model and application" International Journal of Pattern Recognition and Artificial Intelligence, 13(7), 1083-1101, 1999.
2. D. Lowe, "daptive radial basis function nonlinearities and the problem of generalization" First ICANN, London, 171-175, Oct., 1989.
3. D.F.Specht, "Probabilistic neural networks" Neural Networks, Vol.3, 109-118, 1990.
4. Wenbo Zhao and D.S.Huang, "Comparative study between radial basis probabilistic neural networks and radial basis function neural networks," Lecture Notes in Computer Science 2690: 389-396, 2003.
5. Y.Lu, P.F.Shi,Y.M.Zhao. "The voting rule of muliti-classifiers combination", Journal of Shang Hai Jiaotong University, 34(5), pp.680-683, 2000.
6. C. Y. Suen, C. Nadal, T. A. Mai, R. Legault, and L. Lam, "Recognition of totally unconstrained handwritten numerals based on the concept of multiple experts," Frowiers in Handwriting Recognition, C. Y. Suen, Ed., in Proc. Int. Workshop on Frontiers in Handwriting Recognition, Montreal, Canada, Apr. 2-3, 1990, pp. 131-143.
7. H.Han, J.Y.Yang. "Application of multi-classifiers combination," Computer Science, 27(1), pp.58-61, 2000.
8. J. Pearl, Probabilistic Reasoning in Intelligent System: Networks of Plausible Inference. San Mateo, CA: Morgan Kaufmann Publishers, 1988.
9. H.J.Sun, Z.S.Hu, J.Y.Yang. "Study of fusion algorithms based on evidence theory," Computer Journal, 24(3), pp.1 5, 2000.
10. G. A Shafer. mathematic Theory of Evidence, Princeton: Princeton University Press, 1976.
11. Lei Xu, Ching Y Suen. "Methods of combining multiple classifiers and their applications to handwriting recognition," IEEE Trans. Systems. Man. And Cybernetics, 22(5), pp.418 435, 1992
12. G. Rätsch, T. Onoda, K. R. Müller. Soft margins for AdaBoost. Machine Learning, 42(3), pp. 287-320, 2001

An Effective Distributed Privacy-Preserving Data Mining Algorithm

Takuya Fukasawa[1], Jiahong Wang[1],
Toyoo Takata[1], and Masatoshi Miyazaki[2]

[1] Faculty of Software and Information Science, Iwate Prefectural University
152-52 Sugo, Takizawa, Iwate 020-0193, Japan
[2] Digitally Advanced Integrated Solutions Labs, Ltd., Japan

Abstract. Data mining is useful means for discovering valuable patterns, associations, trends, and dependencies in data. Data mining is often required to be performed among a group of sites, where the precondition is that no privacy of any site should be leaked out to other sites. In this paper a distributed privacy-preserving data mining algorithm is proposed. The proposed algorithm is characterized with (1) its ability to preserve the privacy without any coordinator site, and specially its ability to resist the collusion; and (2) its lightweight since only the random number is used for preserving the privacy. Performance analysis and experimental results are provided for demonstrating the effectiveness of the proposed algorithm.

1 Introduction

Nowadays our everyday lives are closely related to the database, and the database should be "mined" for upgrading our everyday lives. Association mining is a useful data mining approach for analyzing relationship among data items of a database. Its applications can be found, e.g., in supermarkets where *transactions*, i.e., sets of *items* that customers purchase at a time in the form of, e.g., {milk, cheese, bread, meal}, are dealt in and transaction data are stored in a *transaction database*. By mining the transaction database managers of a supermarket may find that customers who purchased the milk frequently purchased the bread. Such a relationship is called an *association rule*, denoted as $milk \rightarrow bread$. Frequently occurred association rules will help managers to purchase items, arrange their locations in a supermarket, and schedule advertisements.

An influential association mining algorithm is the *apriori* algorithm [1], which consists of two steps: the step1 for discovering all frequent occurred groups of items called *frequent itemsets*, and the step2 for using the set of frequent itemsets to generate the association rules $X \rightarrow Y$ that have high enough confidence. Here the *support* of an itemset is defined as the number of transactions that contain the itemset, the *frequent itemset* as the itemset that its support is not less than a specified minimum support, and the *confidence* C as $C\%$ of transactions in transaction database that contain X also contain Y.

An influential distributed association mining algorithm based on the *apriori* is the FDM [2]. As other distributed ones, FDM also suffers from the problem that the privacy of a site that participates in data mining may be leaked out, since candidate itemsets and their supports have to be sent to other sites. This problem limits the usage of existing distributed data mining algorithms. For example, (1) several credit card agencies would cooperate to detect patterns matching credit card frauds; and (2) hospitals, insurance companies, and public health agencies would cooperate to discover the relationship between diseases and people' life styles. For both cases it is required that we can accomplish the desired results while still preserving privacy of individual entities.

In fact, for distributed data mining it is often required that "no site should be able to learn contents of a transaction at any other site, what rules are supported by any other site, or the specific value of support/confidence for any rule at any other site, unless that information is revealed by knowledge of one's own data and the final result" [3]. In this paper, we propose a Secure Distributed Data Mining ($SDDM$) algorithm that obeys the above privacy requirements. The $SDDM$ approach is characterized with (1) its ability for preserving the privacy; (2) its ability to resist the collusion; (3) its lightweight since only the random number is used for preserving the privacy; and (4) no coordinator site is required. Performance analysis and experimental results are reported for demonstrating the effectiveness of the proposed algorithm.

2 System Model

Let $I = \{i_1, i_2, ..., i_m\}$ be a set of items, and $DB = \{T_1, T_2, ..., T_n\}$ be a set of transactions where each transaction T is a set of items such that $T \subseteq I$. We assume a distributed system with M sites $S_1, S_2, ..., S_M$. The transaction database DB is partitioned over the M sites into $\{DB_1, DB_2, ..., DB_M\}$ with DB_i being located at S_i for $i = 1, 2, ..., M$.

An association rule is an implication of the form $X \to Y$, where $X \subset I$, $Y \subset I$ and $X \cap Y = \phi$. The rule $X \to Y$ holds in DB with support S if $S\%$ of the transactions in DB contains $X \cup Y$, and confidence C if $C\%$ of transactions in DB that contain X also contain Y. Then given the transaction database DB, our aim is to discover all association rules that have support and confidence greater than the user-specified minimum support and minimum confidence.

Let $X.sup$ (global support) and $X.sup_i$ (local support at S_i) be the number of transactions containing itemset X in DB and DB_i respectively. Given a minimum support threshold s, X is said locally frequent at S_i if $X.sup_i \geq s \times DB_i$, and globally frequent if $X.sup \geq s \times DB$. let $L_{(k)}$ and $LL_{i(k)}$ be the set of all globally frequent k-itemsets (i.e., itemsets contains k items) and the set of all locally frequent k-itemsets at site S_i respectively. Then formally our aim is to (1) discover $L_{(k)}$ (including their supports) for all $k \geq 1$, and (2) from these compute association rules with the specified minimum support and confidence, where the global confidence of rule $X \to Y$ is given as $\{X \cup Y\}.sup / X.sup$. In this paper, only the (1) is considered since given the results of (1), (2) can be performed easily and safely.

The data mining is assumed to be conducted under a semi-honest computing environment [4], in which a site is assumed to use its input correctly, but is free to later use what it sees during the process of data mining to compromise security. This is somewhat realistic in the real world because parties who want to mine data for their mutual benefit will follow the protocol to get correct results. Also, a protocol that is buried in large, complex software can not be easily altered.

3   Privacy-Preserving Distributed Data Mining Algorithm

The privacy-preserving distributed data mining algorithm $SDDM$ is given in *Algorithm 1*. For each *k-itemsets*, the task of data mining is done in two phases. In PHASE 1, two messages are circulated through all sites: the message for collecting frequent itemset candidates, which are masked by random numbers; and the message for collecting the random numbers.

Algorithm 1: $SDDM$ – Secure Distributed Data Mining
---

input   : (1) $M(M \geq 5)$: Total number of sites participating in data mining
        (2) N: Total number of items in transaction database DB
        (3) DB_i: Database located at site i, $1 \leq i \leq M$
        (4) Min_{sup}: Minimum support threshold
output : A set of itemsets with support not less than Min_{sup}

$SDDM(M, N, \{DB_i\}_{1 \leq i \leq M}, Min_{sup})$ **begin**
  initialization:
    $ItemsetLen \longleftarrow 1$;
    for *each site* S_i **do** $GL_{i(0)} \longleftarrow$ {1-itemsets};
  repeat
    PHASE1 :
    for *each site* S_i **do**
      generate candidate set $CG_{i(ItemsetLen)}$ by using $GL_{i(ItemsetLen-1)}$ (note that for $ItemsetLen = 1$, $CG_{i(ItemsetLen)} = GL_{i(0)}$; and for $ItemsetLen > 1$, $GL_{i(ItemsetLen)} = L_{(ItemsetLen)}$);
      $ItemsetNum \longleftarrow |CG_{i(ItemsetLen)}|$;
      create an array $A_i[1..ItemsetNum]$;
      every element of A_i corresponding to a frequent itemset is set to 1;
    calculate $B = \sum_{i=1}^{M}(A_i + Y_i)$ along the route $S_M \rightarrow S_{M-1} \rightarrow ... \rightarrow S_1 \rightarrow S_M$, where Y_i is an array of random numbers generated at S_i;
    calculate $X = \sum_{i=1}^{M} Y_i + X_M$ along a different route starting also from S_M, where X_M is an array of random numbers generated at S_M;
    for *site* S_M **do**
      $B \longleftarrow B - (X - X_M)$;
      for *each* $B[j] \neq 0$ **do** $CG_{(ItemsetLen)} \longleftarrow$ the jth itemset;
      $ItemsetNum \longleftarrow |CG_{(ItemsetLen)}|$;
      broadcast $CG_{(ItemsetLen)}$ and $ItemsetNum$ to all sites;

    PHASE2 :
    for *every site* S_i **do**
      create an array $A_i[1..ItemsetNum]$;
      every element of A_i is set to the support of the corresponding itemset in $CG_{(ItemsetLen)}$;
    calculate $B = \sum_{i=1}^{M}(A_i + Y_i)$ along the route $S_M \rightarrow S_{M-1} \rightarrow ... \rightarrow S_1 \rightarrow S_M$, where Y_i is an array of random numbers generated at S_i;
    calculate $X = \sum_{i=1}^{M} Y_i + X_M$ along a different route starting also from S_M, where X_M is an array of random numbers generated at S_M;
    for *site* S_M **do**
      $B \longleftarrow B - (X - X_M)$;
      for *each* $I \in CG_{ItemsetLen}$ **do**
        $I_{sup} \longleftarrow$ the value of B's corresponding element ;
        if I *is a globally frequent according to* I_{sup} **then** $L_{(ItemsetLen)} \longleftarrow I$
      $ItemsetNum \longleftarrow |L_{(ItemsetLen)}|$;
      broadcast $L_{(ItemsetLen)}$ to all sites;
      $ItemsetLen \longleftarrow ItemsetLen + 1$;
  until *no new frequent itemsets can be generated*;
end

Similarly, in PHASE 2, there are also two rounds of messages, the round for collecting supports of frequent itemset candidates, which are also masked by random numbers; and the message for collecting the random numbers. Assume the number of sites is M, then the communication cost of $SDDM$ can be estimated to be $4M$.

In either phase, secret entities (*frequent itemsets or supports*) are transferred among sites with two kinds of random numbers to protect them, X and Y. Y is used to mask secret entities so that they cannot be known by others while they are transferred. X is used to collect the sum of Ys safely so that pure secret entities can be extracted from masked ones. Unless both the secret entity masked by Ys and the corresponding Ys protected by X are known, no information leakage occurs. If two sites, the site $i-1$ and $i+1$ collude, a secret entity of site i masked by Y_i can be known, and if two other specified sites, site $j-1$ and $j+1$ collude the Y_i can be known. As a result, if more than three sites collude information leakage would occur, and the *degree of collusion resistance* is 3.

Note that the number of sites is required to be not less than 5. For a system with site number less than 5 and greater than 2, approaches such as that of [3] can be used, and the degree of collusion resistance becomes 1.

4 Performance Study

In this section performance analysis results based on the degree of collusion resistance and the communication cost are reported firstly, and then experimental results are reported.

(1) Performance Analysis Results

A very recent implementation of the privacy-preserving data mining algorithm can be found in [3], which we called the $SFDM$. In addition to $SFDM$, two other approaches can also be used for privacy-preserving data mining, which are the *Crowds*-based approach [5] and the MIX-based approach [6][7]. In the following we give a comparison of *Crowds*, $SFDM$, and our $SDDM$. We here do not take MIX-based approaches into our comparison since for them special hardware supports are required, and therefore they are not the suitable one for our assumed application environment.

Figure 1 gives the degree of collusion resistance of *Crowds*, $SFDM$, and our $SDDM$. For $SDDM$, its degree of collusion resistance is 3 as stated in the previous section. For $SFDM$, its degree of collusion resistance is 1 since if sites $i-1$ and $i+1$ collude, supports of site i would be leant. For *Crowds*-based algorithms, its degree of collusion resistance is variable, and for very fair parameter settings $SDDM$ has a higher degree of collusion resistance than *Crowds*-based approaches until the number of sites becomes larger than about 95.

Figure 2 gives the communication cost, which is defined as the amount of messages occurred while data mining is performed. For $SFDM$, its communication cost is estimated to be $3M$ (M is the number of sites participating in data mining) [3], and for $SDDM$ to be $4M$. $SDDM$ has slightly higher communication cost than $SFDM$. Consider that, however, only the random number rather

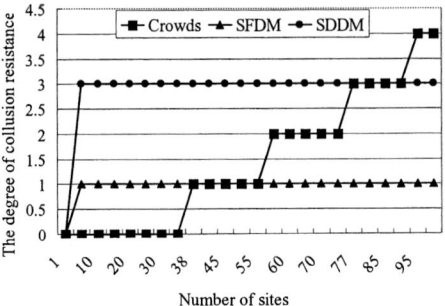

Fig. 1. The degree of collusion resistance

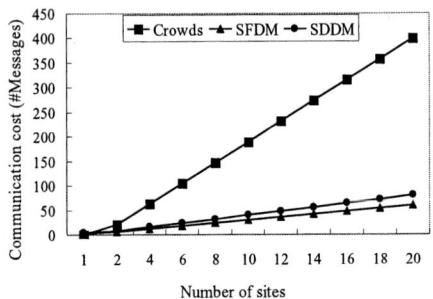

Fig. 2. Communication cost in the number of messages

than the RSA-like algorithm is used for preserving privacy, we think that the total computation cost would be expected to be far lower than that of $SFDM$. Figure 2 shows that $Crowds$-based algorithms have far higher communication cost than both $SDDM$ and $SFDM$.

(2) Experimental Results
We have implemented $SDDM$ and FDM and compared them by two experiments. The aim is to take the performance of the FDM as a basis, and to see how $SDDM$ is different from the FDM due to the extra communication cost incurred by preserving the privacy.

The one experiment is to test the time requirement for completing a data mining when the database at every site is of the same size. The results are given in Fig.3. This figure shows that the privacy-preserving ability of $SDDM$ is achieved only with slightly higher communication cost than that of FDM.

The other experiment is conducted with the skewed distribution of data. Due to the space limitation we do not give the experimental results here. From the experimental results we also find that $SDDM$ is effective even under a data-skew environment.

5 Conclusion

In this paper we proposed a secure data mining algorithm. With the proposed algorithm data mining can be performed among a group of sites with privacy of

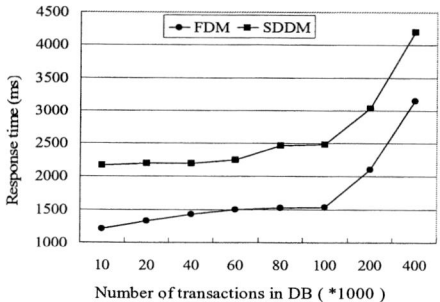

Fig. 3. Time requirements of data mining in the case that the data are evenly distributed across the five sites

every site being preserved. More concisely, during data mining no site would be able to learn contents of a transaction at any other site, what rules are supported by any other site, or the specific value of support/confidence for any rule at any other site, unless the number of colluding sites is not less than four against one site. Unlike other alternatives the proposed algorithm is also very light since only random numbers are used to protect the privacy instead of the commutative encryption method such as the RSA. Considering the high computation cost of the data mining, we think this lightness would be very helpful in speeding up data mining. Our performance analysis and experiments based on a prototype system have demonstrated the effectiveness of the proposed algorithm. We are now working toward improving the scalability of the proposed algorithm $SDDM$ by dividing sites into groups of five sites and applying $SDDM$ to each group.

References

1. R. Agrawal and R. Srikant, Fast algorithms for mining association rules, in *Proc. the 20th International Conference on Very Large Data Bases*, (Santiago, Chile, 1994), pp.487-499.
2. D.W. Cheung, J. Han, V.T. Ng, A.W. Fu, and Y. Fu, Fast Distributed Algorithm for Mining Association Rules, in: *Proc. the 1996 International Conference on Parallel and Distributed Information Systems*, (Florida, USA, 1996), pp.31-42.
3. M. Kantarcioglu and C. Clifton, Privacy-preserving Distributed Mining of Association Rules on Horizontally Partitioned Data, *IEEE Transactions on Knowledge and Data Engineering*, To Appear.
4. O. Goldreich, Secure multi-party computation, Sept. 1998, (working draft). [Online]. Available: http://www.wisdom.weizmann.ac.il/~oded/pp.html.
5. M.K. Reiter and A.D. Rubin, Crowds: Anonymity for Web Transactions, *ACM Transactions on Information System Security*, Vol.1, No.1, pp.66-92.
6. D. Chaum, Untraceable Electronic Mail, Return Addresses, and Digital Pseudonyms, *Comm. of the ACM*, Vol.24, No.2, pp.84-88.
7. D. Goldschlag, M. Reed, and P. Syverson, Onion Routing for Anonymous and Private Internet Connections, *Comm. of the ACM*, Vol.42, No.2, pp.39-41.

Dimensionality Reduction with Image Data

Mónica Benito and Daniel Peña

Universidad Carlos III de Madrid, Spain

Abstract. A common objective in image analysis is dimensionality reduction. The most often used data-exploratory technique with this objective is principal component analysis. We propose a new method based on the projection of the images as matrices after a Procrustes rotation and show that it leads to a better reconstruction of images.

Keywords: Eigenfaces; Multivariate linear regression; Singular value decomposition; Principal component analysis; Generalized proscrustes analysis.

1 Introduction

Exploratory image studies are generally aimed at data inspection and dimensionality reduction. One of the most popular approaches to reduce dimensionality and derive useful compact representations for image data is Principal Component Analysis (PCA). Kirby & Sirovich (1990) proposed using PCA to reduce the dimensionality when representing human faces. Alternative approaches using Independent Component Analysis (ICA) for face representation have been proposed by Barlett and Sejnowski (1997). In the last two decades, PCA has been especially popular in the object recognition community, where it has succesfully been employed by Turk & Pentland (1991)and Valentin et. al (1996). The problem we are interested in is as follows. We have a set of images which represent similar objects, for instance, human faces, temporal images of the same scene, objects in a process of quality control, and so on. Any particular image (say the $n-th$ image) is represented by a matrix X_n of I rows and J columns. We assume that the sample contains the set of N images, $X_1, X_2, ..., X_N$. Each matrix consists of elements x_{ij}, with $i = 1, ..., I$ and $j = 1, ..., J$, that represent the pixel intensities extracted from digitized images. All the elements x_{ij} are in the range between 0 and 255, where the value 0 represents black color, and the value 255 white. Suppose that each matrix is transformed into a vector $\mathbf{x}_n$ by row (or column) concatenation. Therefore, we have a set of N vectors in a high dimensional space, specifically, $\mathbf{x}_n \in \Re^d$ where $d = I \times J$, $n = 1, ..., N$. For convenience, the vectors are assumed to be normalized, so that $\mathbf{x}_n^T \mathbf{x}_n = 1$. Note that this set of vectors can be represented by an $N \times d$ matrix X in which the $n-th$ row is equal to $\mathbf{x}_n$. When dealing with high-dimensional observations, linear mappings are often used to reduce dimensionality of the data by extracting a small (compared to the original dimensionality of the data) number of linear features. Among all linear, orthonormal transformations, principal component analysis is optimal in the sense that it minimizes, in mean square sense, the errors in the reconstruction of the original signal $\mathbf{x}_n$ from its low-dimensional representation, $\widehat{\mathbf{x}}_n$. As is well known, PCA is based on finding directions of maximal variability. In this paper we propose an alternative way of projecting the original data on a subspace of lower dimension. Instead of concatenating rows or columns, we keep the structure of the matrix in the projection. The rest of the paper is organized as follows. In the next section, we propose a new approach which keeps the internal structure of the image and we show that this procedure has important advantages compared to classical PCA. In section 3 we discuss the problems of aligning and scaling images before the dimension reduction is carried out, and introduce a generalized proscrustes rotation to solve this problem. Finally, we present the experimental results of the procedure when applied to a human face data base.

2   An Alternative Approach Based on Matrix Projections

We are interested in a projection method which keep the matrix structure of the image. Yang & Yang (2002) proposed the projection of the rows of the matrix in the context of feature extraction. Here we follow a similar approach. Assume without loss of generality that $I > J$. Then, given a **a** unit norm $J \times 1$ vector, we can project the rows of X_n on the **a** direction by,

$$\mathbf{w}_n = X_n \mathbf{a} \qquad (1)$$

We will call this I-dimensional projected vector $\mathbf{w}_n$ the projected feature vector of X_n. Suppose that we project all the images in this way and obtain a set of vectors, $\mathbf{w}_n$, $n = 1, ..., N$. In order to find a good projection direction, let us call S_r the $I \times I$ covariance matrix for these vectors representing the rows, (the subindex r is due to the projection of the rows). This matrix is given by

$$S_r = \frac{1}{N} \sum_{n=1}^{N} (\mathbf{w}_n - \overline{\mathbf{w}})(\mathbf{w}_n - \overline{\mathbf{w}})^T, \qquad (2)$$

where $\overline{\mathbf{w}}$ is the mean of the projected vectors. The two most often used measures to describe scatter about the mean in multivariate data are the total variation, given by the trace of the covariance matrix, and the generalized variance, given by the determinant of this matrix. For simplicity let us find the direction **a** which maximizes the total variation given by the trace of S_r. It follows that vector **a** is the eigenvector linked to the largest eigenvalue of the matrix

$$\Sigma_c = \frac{1}{N} \sum_{n=1}^{N} (X_n - \overline{X})^T (X_n - \overline{X}) \quad ; \quad \Sigma_c \in \Re^{J \times J} \qquad (3)$$

As we need more than one direction of projection to characterize the sample, we compute the set of eigenvectors $\mathbf{a}_1, \mathbf{a}_2, ..., \mathbf{a}_p$, which constitute a basis for

$\Re^p$ from which the data can be estimated using a subspace of lower dimension, $p \leq \min\{I, J\}$. It is easy to prove that the same criterion is obtained if we start projecting the columns instead of the rows. Let $W_n = [X_n \mathbf{a}_1, ..., X_n \mathbf{a}_p] = X_n A_p$, be the feature vectors obtained. We can use these data to predict the matrix X_n by the multivariate regression model

$$X_n = W_n \beta_n + \varepsilon_n \qquad (4)$$

where the matrix X_n is predicted from its feature vectors W_n using some parameters $\beta_n = [\beta_n^1, ..., \beta_n^J] \in \Re^{p \times J}$, which depend on the image. The least squares estimate is given by $\widehat{\beta}_n = (W_n^T W_n)^{-1} W_n^T X_n$ and the prediction of the matrix X_n with this model is

$$\widehat{X}_n = H_n X_n \qquad (5)$$

where $H_n = W_n (W_n^T W_n)^{-1} W_n^T$ is the perpendicular projection operator onto the column space of W_n.

3 Image Registration

When dealing with a set of homogeneous objects, as in the case of the human face database, the different ilumination and facial expressions greatly increase the difficulty of the reconstruction task. The sample can be seen as a set of shapes with respect to a local 2D coordinates system. We can combine these different local coordinate systems into a common system in order to have a normalized sample of objects before they are analyzed by subspace techniques. This geometric transformation process is known as registration. Depending of the complexity of the object, it may require two or more viewpoints, also called landmarks, to register it appropiately. The most often used procedure in which the landmark points are selected so that these landmarks have the same coordinates in all the images is called Affine transformation. This can be solved easily by,

$$\mathbf{b}_i = D\mathbf{a}_i + \mathbf{s} \quad , \quad i = 1, ..., d \qquad (6)$$

where d is the number of pixels, $d = I \times J$ and the vectors $\mathbf{a}_i$ and $\mathbf{b}_i$ belong to $\Re^2$, due the pixel's spatial coordinates. Thus, for any pixel in the image, say the $i-th$, this transformation maps the vector $\mathbf{a}_i$ to $\mathbf{b}_i$. This approach has two main limitations. The first one is that we can select only three points to fix the object normalization. The second is that we are not keeping the relative distances among the landmarks in the transformation. As an alternative, we propose a new procedure to estimate the similarity transformation that avoids these two liminations.

3.1 Procrustes Analysis

Procrustes analysis theory is a set of mathematical tools to directly estimate and perform simulteneous similarity transformations among the objects landmarks up to their maximal agreement. Based on this idea, we can focus on a goodness of fit measure used to compare N configurations of points. The basic procedure is as follows. Let A_n be the $r \times 2$ matrix of coordinates of r landmarks in the $n-th$ image, $n = 1, ..., N$. We wish to find simultaneous translations, rotations, and scale factors of these N sets of points into positions of best fit with respect to each other. The functional model of the transformation is stated as follows,

$$\widehat{A}_n = c_n A_n T_n + \mathbf{1} t_n^T \quad , \quad n = 1, ..., N \tag{7}$$

where c_n is the scale factor, T_n is 2×2 orthogonal rotation matrix, t_n is a 2×1 traslation vector, and $\mathbf{1}$ is a 2×1 unit vector. According to Goodall (1991), there is a matrix B, also called consensus matrix, which contains the true coordinates of the r points defined in a mean and common coordinate system. The N matched configurations are measured by means of the residual sum of squares between each point of each configuration and the corresponding point of the average configuration or common coordinate system. For this task, Generalized Orthogonal Procrustes Analysis (Gower, 1975) provides least-squares correspondence of more than two point matrices. To obtain the initial centroid C, we should define one of the coordinates matrices A_n as fixed, and sequently link the others by means of the Extended Orthogonal Procrustes (EOP) algorithm (Beinat and Crosilla, 2001). Defining $C = \frac{1}{N} \sum_{n=1}^{N} \widehat{A}_n$, as the geometrical centroid of the transformed matrices, the solution of the registration problem is achieved by using the following minimum condition

$$\sum_{n=1}^{N} tr \left\{ \left[\widehat{A}_n - C \right]^T \left[\widehat{A}_n - C \right] \right\} \tag{8}$$

in an iterative computation scheme of centroid C until global convergence. Hence, the final solution of the centroid corresponds to the least squares estimation $\widehat{B}$ and shows the final coordinates of r points in the maximal agreement with respect to least squares objective function. Finally, the unknown similarity transformation parameters (T_n, t_n, c_n), $n = 1, ..., N$, are then determined using the procrustes algorithm procedure for fitting two given sets of points, A_n and $\widehat{B}$ (Schoenemann and Carroll, 1970).

4 Experiments

In the first example the method proposed in (5) for dimension reduction is compared to the standard eigenface technique on a gray-level database. We compare the dimensionality reduction performance when a frontal view face database is used, showing that the new technique leads to a better result for the data analyzed. In the second example we show that the proposed Procrustes analysis works well for the image registration problem.

4.1 Example 1

We use a gray-level frontal view face database that comprises 114 full-face pictures, 56 males and 58 females ($N = 114$). Each image is digitized in a gray-scale, with a resolution of 248×186, i.e. 248 rows and 186 columns ($I = 248$, $J = 186$). We compare the reconstruction performance of the traditional method with the new one when the number of singular values used (i.e. dimension of the subspace) increase gradually. The quality of the reconstruction, as the efficiency of representing the data by the subspace, is measured by the mean square error (MSE). In Figure 1 we plot the average reconstruction error ($AMSE$) for the training sample when the number of estimated parameters k increase as a function of the number of singular values used, p, in the reconstruction by the standard method and the new one. For simplicity, we only consider $p = 1, ..., 40$. Figure 1 is a 3D graph, in which each point has three coordinates, $(x, y, z) = (k, AMSE, p)$. Thus, when the number of singular values are fixed, the x-axis represents the amount of parameters needed to reconstruct the image, and the average mean square error (AMSE) in the reconstruction is computed (y-axis). The upper plotted points correspond to the singular values used by the standard method, and the lower points are the ones used by the proposed method. This graph demostrates that the quality of the reconstruction by the new procedure is better than the traditional one. To visualize in more detail the performance of the reconstruction by both methods, Figure 2 gradually shows the reconstruction of one individual of the sample when the number of singular values is $p = 5, 10, 20$ and 50. Its reconstruction accuracy is measured by the MSE.

These figures clearly demostrate that when the dimensionality of the subspace is the same, the new method always perform better than the standard eigenface technique.

4.2 Example 2

In this example, we will show that the proposed image registration procedure is more effective than the affine transformation. For this purpose, we will register

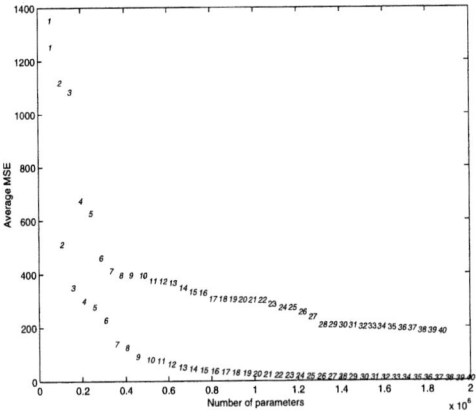

Fig. 1. Comparision of the average mean square error between eigenface method (upper points) and the proposed method (lower points) when the number of singular values used increases from 1 to 40

Fig. 2. Image Reconstruction by means of the standard method (left panels) and by the new method (right panels) using $p = 5, 10, 20$ and 50 singular values

Fig. 3. Image Registration of one individual in the sample

the face database used in example 1 in order to work with normalized objects. We choose as control points (landmarks) the coordinates associated to the left and right eyes and the end point of the chin. As an illustration, Figure 3 shows the solution of the registration problem for the $10 - th$ image in the sample. The left panel in Figure 3 shows the original image. The middle panel shows the image registration by means of the affine transformation and the right panel by means of the procrustes analysis. Notice that while in the middle panel the classical affine transformation procedure deforms the original image, in the left image the procrustes algorithm perfectly reproduces the image.

References

[Barlett and Sejnowski (1997)] Barlett, M.S. and Sejnowski, T.J. (1997). Independent components of face images: a representation for face recognition. *Proceedings of the Fourth Annual Joint Symposium on Neural Computation, CA.*

[Beinat and Crosilla (2001)] Beinat, A. and Crosilla, F. (2001). Generalized Procrustes analysis for size and shape 3-D object reconstruction. *Optical 3-D Measurements Techniques V, Viena*, pp. 345-353.

[Christensen (1991)] Christensen, R. (1991). *Linear Models for Multivariate, Time Series and Spatial Data.* New York: Springer-Verlag.

[Goodall (1991)] Goodall, C. (1991). Procrustes methods in the statistical analysis of shape. *Journal Royal Statistical Society Series B*, **53**, pp.285-339

[Gower (1975)] Gower, J.C. (1975). Generalized Procrustes analysis. *Psychometrika*, **40**, pp.33-51

[Kirby and Sirovich (1990)] Kirby, M. and Sirovich, L. (1990). Application of the Karhunen-Loeve procedure for the characterization of human faces. *IEEE Trans. Pattern Anal. Machine Intell.*, **12**, pp.103-108

[Krzanowski and Marriot (1994).] Krzanowski, W.J. and Marriot, F.H.C. (1994). *Multivariate Analysis: Distributions, ordination and inference.* UK: Edward Arnold.

[Mardia, Kent and Bibby (1992).] Mardia, K.V., Kent, J.T. and Bibby, J.M. (1992). *Multivariate Analysis.* CA: Academic Press.

[Schoenemann and Carroll (1970)] Schoenemann, P.H. and Carroll, R. (1970). Fitting one matrix to another under choice of a central dilation and a rigid motion. *Psychometrika*, **35**, pp.245-255

[Turk and Pentland (1999)] Turk,M. and Pentland, A. (1999). Face recognition using Eigenfaces. *Proceedings of the IEEE Conference in Computer Vision and Pattern Recognition*, pp.586-591.

[Valentin, Abdi and O'Toole (1996)] Valentin, D., Abdi, H. and O'Toole, A. (1996). Principal Component and Neural Network Analysis of face images. *Progress in Mathematical Psycology.*

[Yang and Yang (2002)] Yang, J. and Yang, J. (2002). From Image vector to matrix: a straightforward image projection technique. *Pattern Recognition*, **35**, pp.1997-1999

Implicit Fitness Sharing Speciation and Emergent Diversity in Tree Classifier Ensembles

Karl J. Brazier, Graeme Richards, and Wenjia Wang

School of Computing Sciences, University of East Anglia, Norwich, UK, NR4 7TJ
{kb,gr,wjw}@uea.ac.uk

Abstract. Implicit fitness sharing is an approach to the stimulation of speciation in evolutionary computation for problems where the fitness of an individual is determined as its success rate over a number trials against a collection of succeed/fail tests. By fixing the reward available for each test, individuals succeeding in a particular test are caused to depress the size of one another's fitness gain and hence implicitly co-operate with those succeeding in other tests. An important class of problems of this form is that of attribute-value learning of classifiers. Here, it is recognised that the combination of diverse classifiers has the potential to enhance performance in comparison with the use of the best obtainable individual classifiers. However, proposed prescriptive measures of the diversity required have inherent limitations from which we would expect the diversity emergent from the self-organisation of speciating evolutionary simulation to be free. The approach was tested on a number of the popularly used real-world data sets and produced encouraging results in terms of accuracy and stability.

1 Introduction

Speciation, also known as niching, in evolutionary computation refers to the inclusion of a mechanism that penalises similarity between the individuals of a population and thus creates a resistance to convergence to a single optimum. Of particular interest in this application is the method of implicit fitness sharing, originating in the immune system model [1] and successfully applied as an inhibition to premature convergence [2], [3].

Sharing methods operate by causing the reward available to an individual for its performance to be shared among other members of a population according to some decreasing function of the proximity of those other members. The fitnesses of individuals are then equated with this modified value of the reward, rather than the unmodified value of a conventional scheme for fitness determination.

In practice, this approach has been vulnerable to the criticism that the optima in the fitness landscape need to be evenly spaced to achieve effective speciation. This problem has been associated with the requirement for a radially decreasing sharing function and a distance metric on which it is based. A key contribution of immune system modelling is that it obviates the need for an explicit distance metric and effectively makes the sharing function adaptive to the distribution of optima [1]. This implicit fitness sharing is achieved by rewarding performances of individuals over a number of succeed/fail trials.

This formulation makes implicit fitness sharing particularly amenable to classifier induction problems, in which an individual must be evaluated according to its success in predicting a categorical outcome on the basis of a number of observations of multiple attribute values. Furthermore, a prominent topic for current investigations in such work is the creation of ensembles of classifiers of appropriate diversity to improve on the performance of individual classifiers through an aggregation of their results. There is a profusion of proposals for measures of diversity [4], [5], [6] and these have been shown to contribute to the analysis of constructed ensembles, eg. [7]. However, we cannot expect such summary metrics to contain sufficient information about diversity requirements to allow them to be used prescriptively to drive induction. Thus processes in which diversity is an emergent property of the interactions between classifiers and data demand attention. The application of implicit fitness sharing to induction of classifiers in the form of production rule sets for this problem has been addressed by McKay [3]. This paper describes experimentation to investigate extension of implicit fitness sharing to the evolution of tree classifiers, widely employed in data mining applications.

2 Description of Approach

The evolutionary method adopted was based on a gene expression programming representation of tree structures as linear genes, as described by Ferreira [8]. This allows a flexible representation of tree structured information while maintaining the simplicity of crossover operations associated with linear string representations. Each chromosome consisted of a single gene encoding a binary splitting decision tree in terms of attribute threshold (function) and categorical outcome (terminal) literals.

Implicit fitness sharing was implemented, following the formulation of McKay, as

$$F_i = \sum_{n=1}^{N} \frac{R_{i,n}}{\sum_{i': C_{mod}(i',n) = C_{mod}(i,n)} R_{i',n}} \quad (1)$$

Where $R_{i,n} = 1$ iff $C_{mod}(i,n) = C_{obs}(n)$; $R_{i,n} = 0$ otherwise.

Here, F_i is the fitness of classifier i, N is the number of observations, $R_{i,n}$ is the raw reward for classifier i from observation n (ie. the reward before sharing), and $C_{mod}(i,n)$ and $C_{obs}(n)$ are the modelled and observed classes of observation n, respectively. It is necessary also to define 0/0=0 in eqn. (1) to give the correct result of a zero contribution to a classifier's fitness when its classification does not match the outcome class of the observation.

In each experiment, ten fold cross validation was applied, the sets of observations being randomly partitioned into ten disjoint groups and each group in turn being selected as the test data set, the remainder being the training set. An aggregated classification result for a population was formed by the use of a simple majority vote. A mean was calculated of the results over each of the ten data configurations of the cross validation, and a standard deviation across the configurations computed to give an indication of the stability of the results.

The algorithm applied to each data configuration was as follows:

```
For each attribute, a
{Sort data on column a
Record values of a where outcome class changes in vector
F}
Record outcome class labels in T
Randomly fill gene head sections with splitting criteria
F_i and classes, T_i, tails with T_i
For each generation
{Decode genes as trees and evaluate fitness on training
data (eqn. 1)
Evaluate performance on test data for output
Replicate (elitism), recombine and mutate}
```

Selection for recombination was by stochastic universal sampling.

The reported results were obtained using populations of 100 classifiers allowed to evolve for 100 generations, which inspection of preliminary trials suggested was sufficient to reach long term stability on training data. A maximum of eight decision nodes (attribute thresholds) was permitted in each classifier. Specification of this figure is a requirement of the gene expression programming formulation, determining the fixed length of each gene. A modest figure was chosen so that the hypothesis space to be searched would not demand an excessive population size. Allele mutation probability was set at 0.05 and deterministic elitism (retention of the fittest members of a population) was applied to the fittest 10% of each generation.

The trials used data sets taken from the UCI Machine Learning Databases Repository [9]. These were the Cleveland Heart (with dichotomised outcome class), Thyroid, Pima Indian Diabetes and E. Coli data (Table 1).

Table 1. Summary figures for trial databases.

Data set	Observations	Numerical attributes	Categorical attributes	Classes
Heart	303	7	6	2
Thyroid	215	5	0	3
Pima	768	8	0	2
Ecoli	336	5	2	8

3 Results and Discussion

The evolutionary development of classification accuracies for each dataset is shown in Fig. 1 as the mean of the values obtained for each of the ten test sets of the cross validation. The accuracies obtained by aggregating the classifications for the entire population of classifiers under the implicit sharing regime are contrasted with those obtained from the best individual in the population when the same experiments were carried out using the raw accuracy of each classifier as its fitness function. In each case it can be seen that the accuracy of the classifier results aggregated across the population evolves under the implicit fitness sharing regime to exceed that of the best individual classifier obtained under the raw fitness regime. Although the values obtained under implicit sharing are not quite as stable, they all show the shared fitness population eventually consistently outperforming the best raw fitness individual. Similar effects were observable with respect to training set accuracies.

Some reduction in inter-generational stability is an unsurprising price to pay for the use of a speciating mechanism, the competing pressures to convergence and diversity having the capacity to cause a phase change in the nonlinear dynamics of an evolutionary algorithm. McKay, for example, notes an oscillatory behaviour [2], the explanation for which indicates a limit cycle of period 2. Investigation of such nonlinear phenomena in genetic algorithms, and the potential to control them, are ongoing topics of research. In the meantime, however, we are satisfied to note that once longer term stability is established, the means and lower accuracy limits of the classifiers subject to sharing improve on the best individual under raw fitness.

Mean test set accuracies of the fused classifications at the 100th generation were Heart: 75.9%, Thyroid: 93.0%, Pima: 75.5% and E. coli: 73.8%. For comparison the C5.0 classifier as implemented in SPSS Clementine software gives accuracies of Heart: 78.8%, Thyroid: 92.1%, Pima: 74.2% and E. coli: 81.8%. It is notable that the latter substantially higher figure is obtained only with a tree having twice as many decision nodes as were permitted in our experiments. None of the 100th generation

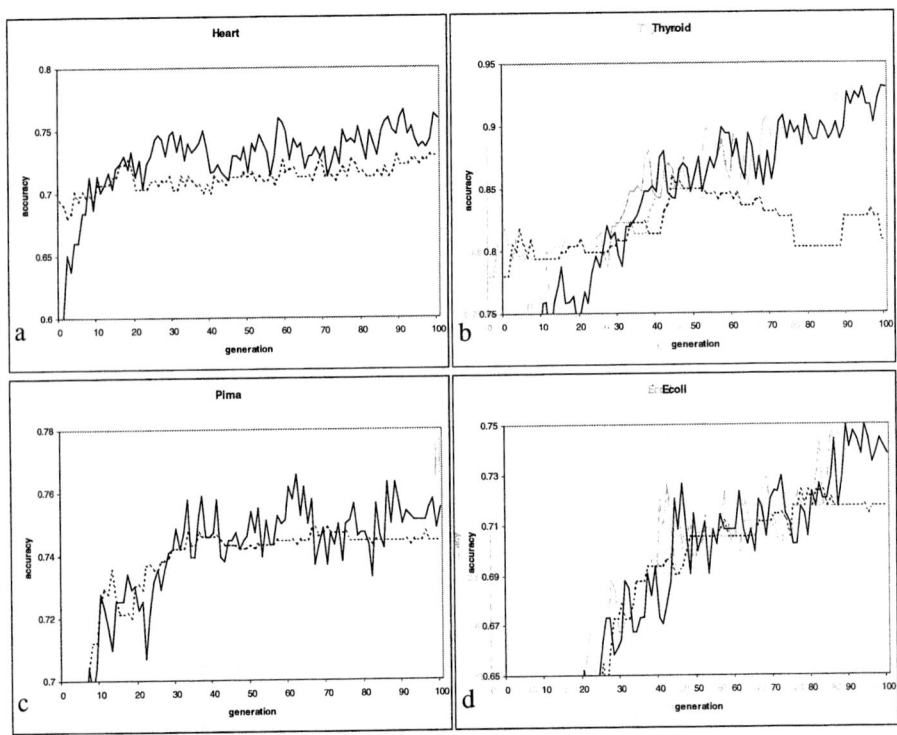

Fig. 1. Evolution of accuracies as mean of cross validation test sets
a) Cleveland heart data   b) Thyroid data
c) Pima Indians diabetes data d) E. coli data
(*Dashed lines: Best individual, raw fitness*
Solid lines: Fused classifications, shared fitness).

accuracies reached those of 10-stage boosted [10] C5.0 at Heart: 82.2%, Thyroid: 94.4%, Pima: 75.7% and E. coli: 84.3%.

While the implicit sharing regime results in a small sacrifice in stability of performance from generation to generation of the evolutionary algorithm, stability across the folds of the cross validation appears to be little affected (Table 2).

Table 2. Standard deviations in accuracy at the 100th generation.

	Heart	Thyroid	Pima	Ecoli
Raw fitness	0.089	0.081	0.057	0.102
Shared fitness	0.080	0.067	0.080	0.085

For three of the four data sets there is a marginal improvement to stability for the fused shared fitness classifiers and for one a slight deterioration. The figures are sufficiently similar to suggest no significant general effect of the difference in regime.

4 Conclusions

The pressure to speciation produced by implicit fitness sharing has been demonstrated to be able to enhance the applicability of evolutionary computation to the task of developing tree classifiers of a diversity suited to a given real-world data environment. The accuracy of classifications aggregated across the population improves over that of a best classifier from a population in which the evolutionary pressure is toward simple optimality of individuals. Thus diversity of the required character appears to be emerging.

The assessment of stability across the cross validation folds at the 100th generation revealed no substantive effect of the difference in method. This indicates that the two regimes perform with a similar level of consistency with respect to the selection of the training and test partitions. Thus the accuracy improvement is made without significant effect on stability with respect to data sampling.

The performance obtainable from this approach has yet to rival that obtainable from boosting, however we believe that this is attributable primarily to the use of a simple aggregation method that does not fully exploit the character of the diversity of the ensemble (see next section).

5 Further Investigations

There are several parameters of the algorithm that may merit further attention, in particular the limit on the number of decision nodes in a classifier and the size of the population which were kept small in comparison with most applications of evolutionary programming owing to constraints on computational resources.

Regarding the population's stability, the conjecture that it is affected by the algorithm's nonlinear dynamics is amenable to investigation through computational Lyapunov exponent estimation and the construction of time-delay phase plots.

Related to the issue of the tree size constraint is the desirability to introduce a pruning pressure, ie. a modification to the shared fitness that favours more compact trees.

The use of such a pressure would allow the restriction on tree size to be relaxed (ie. a considerably larger maximum tree size could be used). Investigation has begun into whether an approach based on minimum description length can be applied in this role.

We believe that a key area that would benefit from attention is the form of the aggregation. Having limited the work to the use of the simplest approach (majority voting) to focus on the development of a diverse ensemble through speciation we now feel it is expedient to seek an approach more appropriate to the exploitation of the character of this diversity. Trials on an unpublished database of a confidence-based voting method have suggested that it may have a substantial contribution to make and we now aim to test it with benchmark data and develop it to take support into account.

Preliminary investigations have also taken place into an alternative to summary statistics to elucidate the form of the diversity that emerges in the population. These have looked into graphical visualisation of the development of emergent diversity through the dendrograms resulting from the hierarchical clustering of the population.

Acknowledgement

The authors gratefully acknowledge the collaboration of Dr. John Etherington of the Defence Service Medical Rehabilitation Centre, Professor Derek Partridge of University of Exeter, and the financial support of the UK EPSRC (GR/R85914/01) for this work.

References

1. Smith, R.E., Forrest, S., Perelson, A.S.: Searching for Diverse, Cooperative Populations with Genetic Algorithms. Evolutionary Computation 1, 127-149, 1993.
2. McKay, R.I.: An Investigation of Fitness Sharing in Genetic Programming. Australian J. Intelligent Processing Systems 7, 46-54, 2001.
3. McKay, R.I.: Variants of Genetic Programming for Species Distribution Modelling – Fitness Sharing, Partial Functions, Population Evaluation. Ecological Modelling 146, 231-241, 2001.
4. Partridge, D. and Yates, W.B.: Data-Defined Problems and Multiversion Neural-Net Systems. J. Intelligent Systems 7, 19-32, 1996.
5. Partridge, D. and Krzanowski, W.: Distinct Failure Diversity in Multiversion Software. Research report 348, Neural Computing Laboratory, University of Exeter, UK http://www.dcs.ex.ac.uk/research/neural/pub/paper14.ps, 1997.
6. Kuncheva, L.I., Whitaker, C.J.: Measures of Diversity in Classifier Ensembles and their Relationship with Ensemble Accuracy. Machine Learning 51, 181-207, 2002.
7. Wang, W., Jones, P., Partridge, D.: Diversity Between Neural Nets and Decision Trees for Building Multiple Classifier Systems. In: Kitter, J. and Roli, F. (eds.): Multiple Classifier Systems. Lecture Notes on Computer Science, 1857, Springer-Verlag, Berlin Heidelberg New York, 240-249, 2000.
8. Ferreira, C.: Gene Expression Programming: A New Adaptive Algorithm for Solving Problems. Complex Systems 13, 87-129, 2001.
9. Hettich, S., Bay, S.D.: The UCI KDD Archive. Department of Information and Computer Science, University of California, Irvine, CA, USA http://kdd.ics.uci.edu, 1999.
10. Freund, Y., Schapire, R.E.: A Decision-Theoretic Generalization of On-Line Learning and an Application to Boosting. J. Computer and System Sciences 55, 119-139, 1997.

Improving Decision Tree Performance Through Induction- and Cluster-Based Stratified Sampling

Abdul A. Gill, George D. Smith, and Anthony J. Bagnall

School of Computing Sciences
UEA Norwich, Norwich, England
Aziz.Gill@uea.ac.uk, {gds,ajb}@cmp.uea.ac.uk

Abstract. It is generally recognised that recursive partitioning, as used in the construction of classification trees, is inherently unstable, particularly for small data sets. Classification accuracy and, by implication, tree structure, are sensitive to changes in the training data. Successful approaches to counteract this effect include multiple classifiers, e.g. boosting, bagging or windowing. The downside of these multiple classification models, however, is the plethora of trees that result, often making it difficult to extract the classifier in a meaningful manner. We show that, by using some very weak knowledge in the sampling stage, when the data set is partitioned into the training and test sets, a more consistent and improved performance is achieved by a single decision tree classifier.

1 Introduction

It is generally recognised that recursive partitioning, such as used in the construction of classification trees, is inherently unstable, particularly for small data sets. Classification accuracy and, by implication, tree structure, are sensitive to changes in the training data [1, 2].

Approaches to counteract this effect include the use of multiple classifiers, for example bagging [3], boosting [4], or windowing [5], each of which has been shown to generally improve the overall classification accuracy of decision tree induction. In bagging, replicate training sets are produced by sampling *with replacement* from the training instances and each is used to construct a (decision tree) model. In boosting, all training cases are used but each has an associated weight. These weights are adjusted after the initial learning iteration, in order to give higher priority to cases that were incorrectly classified. This and subsequent iterations each produce a classifier model. In windowing [5], a classifier is constructed from an initial sample of the training set. Subsequently, training cases on which this initial classifier performed poorly are added to this sample and the process repeated, each iteration yielding a different classifier model.

One of the disadvantages of these multiple classification models, however, is the plethora of trees that result, often making it difficult, though not impossible, to extract the actual classifier in a meaningful manner. Shannon [6] presents a method of combining the trees based on a maximum likelihood estimate of a central tree, used to represent the set. Quinlan [7] shows how to combine decision trees equivalent to the combined voting classifier, but while this may be manageable and interpretable for a small number of first-order classifiers, such as prescribed in *Miniboosting*, it is not so for the numbers of first-order classifiers typically used in practice.

The question is, can a single classifier be 'boosted' in any way by ensuring that key variables are properly represented in both the training and test sets? We show that, by using some very weak knowledge in the sampling stage, when the data set is partitioned into the training and test sets, a more consistent and improved performance is achieved by a single decision tree classifier. The weak knowledge referred to is achieved through one of two forms of stratified sampling, one based on identifying the key predicting variable by applying a pre-processing *information gain* analysis on each predicting variable, the other based on a pre-processing *clustering* of the entire data set. Details of these are presented in the following section.

2 Sampling Techniques

In sampling data sets to generate training and test sets for the construction of and subsequent testing of classifiers, there are a few standard techniques that are used in practice.

One of the most widely used is the simple random partitioning of the data set into two subsets, one for training the classifier, the other for testing. These can be equal-sized, viz. a 50/50 split, or some other combination, such as 70/30. In such cases, the sampling and subsequent induction process are normally repeated and the results presented are an average over the multiple runs.

Another approach is to use n-fold cross-validation, in which the data set is initially partitioned into n equal-sized subsets. In turn, each subset is used as a test set, whilst the remaining $n-1$ subsets are combined to form the training set, with the results presented as averages over the n fold experiments.

Stratified sampling is a method of sampling in which it is desirable to maintain certain characteristics of the data set in any subset sampled. It is achieved by firstly partitioning the data set into a number of mutually exclusive subsets of cases, each of which is representative of some aspect of the real-world process involved. Sampling from the population is then achieved by *randomly* sampling from the various subsets so as to achieve representative proportions - see Figure 1. We present two forms of stratified sampling on which our experiments are based, namely *Induction-based stratified sampling* (IBSS), which uses knowledge from a pre-processing *Information Gain* analysis of the predicting variables to form the partition, and *Cluster-based stratified sampling* (CBSS), which uses a k-means clustering algorithm to construct the partition.

3 Experiments and Methodology

We perform analysis of each sampling technique on a number of standard public domain data sets available from the UCI Machine Learning Repository. These are

Table 1. Data Sets used in experimental work.

Data Set	No. of Cases	No. of Classes	Attributes Cont.	Disc.
Boston Housing	506	2	13	1
Credit-A	690	2	6	9
Credit-G	1,000	2	7	13
Heart-C	303	2	8	5
Hepatitis	155	2	6	13
Ionosphere	351	2	34	-
Iris	150	3	4	-
LD-BUPA	345	2	6	-
PID	768	2	8	-
Sonar	208	2	60	-
WBC	699	2	9	-

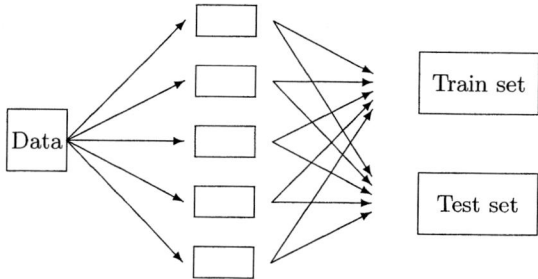

Fig. 1. Stratified sampling methodology.

shown in Table 1. Note that the Boston Housing class attribute is the discretised version from [8], and note also that LD-Bupa is the Liver Disorder data, PID is the Pima Indian Diabetes data and WBC is the Wisconsin Breast Cancer data.

Approximately equal-sized training and test sets are generated using one of three sampling processes.

For simple random sampling (*SRS*), the training and test sets are produced using a normal pseudo-random process. For both the stratified sampling sets of experiments, the data set is firstly partitioned into a number of smaller data sets, which in turn are randomly sampled to populate the training and test sets - see Figure 1.

In *Induction-based stratified sampling* (*IBSS*), we firstly analyse the predicting fields using an *Information Gain* algorithm [5] to assess the relative contribution of each predicting attribute to the classification decision. This analysis provides a numerical value for each predicting attribute, the higher the value the more predictive it is. We then create a partition of the entire data set based on the distribution of the top predicting attribute. The number of subsets in the partition varies with the data set but does not exceed 7 for the data sets used here. From this partition, we then sample, *completely randomly*, to create the training and test sets, thus ensuring that the distribution of the most predictive attribute in the entire data set is mapped into each of the training and test samples.

For *Cluster-based stratified sampling* (*CBSS*), a k-means clustering algorithm is applied to generate k clusters, where k is determined by the size of the data set, varying between 5 and 30 for the data sets used here. Each cluster contains instances which are 'similar' to one another based on the metric used, which in this case is the unweighted minimum distance to centroid. In this metric, all attributes have equal weighting. In other words, no knowledge of highly predictive variables are used to influence the clustering. From each cluster, an approximately equal number of instances are *randomly sampled* to generate the training and test sets. A similar approach was made in [9], in which a Kohonen SOM was used to cluster the data prior to the use of a neural net to predict carbon-13 NMR chemical shifts of alkanes.

For each data set and for each sampling technique used, the data set is firstly partitioned into approximately equal-sized training and test sets according to the sampling technique used, C5 [5] is applied to the training set to generate the model and then the performance of the model is tested on the test set. This is repeated 4 times and the accuracies presented in the following section are those for the test sets, averaged over the 5 runs. The standard deviations of those accuracies are also presented.

Finally, we wish to compare the results of our sampling techniques using a single classifier with the results using random sampling with a multiple classifier model. To effect this comparison, C5 is applied with and without boosting for random sampling. The software, *SPSS Clementine*, is used for all experiments. This uses C5 as the tree induction algorithm, and has a facility for implementing boosting.

4 Results

Tables 2 and 3 show respectively, for each data set and for each experiment, the average accuracy and standard deviation over 5 runs. The final row in each table shows, respectively, the average accuracy and the average standard deviation over all the data sets.

With reference to Table 2, we note that *IBSS* has improved the performance of C5 significantly for some data sets, compared with *SRS*, e.g. *Hepatitis* from 78.20% to 83.12%. For other data sets, e.g. *PID*, the improvement using *IBSS* is less impressive. Nevertheless, averaged over all data sets, C5 with *IBSS* has presented an improvement in accuracy of 1.93% over C5 with *SRS*. *CBSS* is showing a similar performance, with substantial gains in accuracy for some data sets, e.g. *Iris*, and with no, or little gain for others, e.g. *Ionosphere*. Averaged over all data sets, *CBSS* achieves an improvement in accuracy of 1.62% over *SRS*.

Comparing the results of *IBSS* and *CBSS* with *SRS+Boosting*, we note that, although the former achieve better accuracies on some individual data sets, such as *Credit-A* and *Hepatitis*, overall, *Boosting* is showing the biggest increase in

Table 2. Classification accuracies on test sets using three sampling techniques-SRS, IBSS and CBSS. For each data set and each method, the entries denote the average of classification accuracies over 5 runs. For comparison, we also present the results of SRS with Boosting.

	Sampling Technique			
Data Set	SRS	SRS+Boosting	IBSS	CBSS
Boston-H	82.53	83.63	83.00	84.02
Credit-A	84.52	85.45	87.08	86.46
Credit-G	71.64	74.40	72.56	73.96
Heart-C	77.37	79.74	79.58	77.52
Hepatitis	78.20	79.74	83.12	80.37
Ionosphere	89.09	93.30	89.41	89.09
Iris	91.93	93.07	96.00	96.51
LD-BUPA	64.86	67.17	67.17	66.65
PID	72.45	73.33	72.66	73.83
Sonar	73.46	76.73	76.73	75.28
WBC	94.63	96.69	94.62	94.84
average	80.06	82.11	81.99	81.68

Table 3. Standard deviations of accuracies on test sets using three sampling techniques. For each data set and each method, the entries denote the standard deviation of classification accuracies over 5 runs. For comparison, we also present the results of SRS with Boosting.

	Sampling Technique			
Data Set	SRS	SRS+Boosting	IBSS	CBSS
Boston-H	0.18	0.72	0.00	1.26
Credit-A	1.31	0.95	0.16	1.15
Credit-G	0.92	1.93	0.82	0.88
Heart-C	5.38	3.59	2.36	1.83
Hepatitis	3.14	3.78	2.43	1.61
Ionosphere	3.51	2.21	0.92	3.51
Iris	2.06	1.46	0.00	2.26
LD-BUPA	1.04	2.36	0.64	2.49
PID	1.35	1.23	0.00	2.87
Sonar	2.85	1.97	2.30	2.44
WBC	1.30	0.82	0.87	1.10
average	2.09	1.91	0.95	1.95

improvement. Nevertheless, the stratified sampling methods are able to 'boost' the performance of a single classifier significantly.

From the standard deviations shown in Table 3, we note that there is a significant drop in the **variation** of accuracies over the 5 runs when *IBSS* is employed, in some cases dropping to zero. Averaging the spread over all data sets, a value of 0.95 is achieved, compared to 2.09 for C5 with *SRS*. This indicates a more consistent performance of the single classifier with the use of *IBSS*. The reduction in variance using *CBSS*, however, is less impressive.

5 Conclusion

We have presented two forms of stratified sampling, both based on some weak knowledge gained in a pre-processing stage. The first, *Induction-based stratified sampling*, generates the training and test sets from a number of partitions of the original data set created using an *information gain* analysis of the predicting variables. The second form, *Cluster-based stratified sampling*, is based on a clustering of the entire data set into k clusters, using the k-means algorithm, from which the training and test sets are randomly sampled. No knowledge is used of the key predicting variable in this clustered sampling.

Both techniques have been shown to improve the overall accuracy of the classifier, in this case, C5, and to provide a more consistent performance. The significance is that a *single* classifier can be 'boosted' without the need for multiple applications, thus yielding a single, and hence more easily interpretable, decision tree.

References

1. Breiman, L.: Bias, variance, and arcing classifiers. Technical report 460, Department of Statistics, University of California at Berkeley (1996)
2. Breiman, L.: Bias, variance, and arcing classifiers. Machine Learning **26** (1998)
3. Breiman, L.: Bagging predictors. Machine Learning **24** (1996) 123–140
4. Freund, Y., Schapire, R.E.: Experiments with a new boosting algorithm. In: International Conference on Machine Learning. (1996) 148–156
5. Quinlan, J.R.: C4.5: Programs for Machine Learning. Morgan Kaufmann, San Mateo (1993)
6. Shannon, W.: Averaging classification tree models (1998) In Interface '98 Proceedings.
7. Quinlan, J.R.: Miniboosting decision trees. Journal of Artificial Intelligence Research (1998)
8. Murthy, S.K., Kasif, S., Salzberg, S.: A system for induction of oblique decision trees. Journal of Artificial Intelligence Research **2** (1994) 1–32
9. Svozil, D., Pospíchal, J., Kvasnicka, V.: Neural-network prediction of Carbon-13 NMR chemical shifts of alcanes. J. Chem. Inf. Comp. Sci. **35** (1995) 924–928

Learning to Classify Biomedical Terms Through Literature Mining and Genetic Algorithms

Irena Spasić[1], Goran Nenadić[2], and Sophia Ananiadou[3]

[1] Department of Chemistry
University of Manchester Institute of Science and Technology
I.Spasic@umist.ac.uk
[2] Department of Computation
University of Manchester Institute of Science and Technology
PO Box 88, Manchester, M60 1QD, UK
G.Nenadic@umist.ac.uk
School of Computing, Science and Engineering
University of Salford, M5 4WT, UK
S.Ananiadou@salford.ac.uk

Abstract. We present an approach to classification of biomedical terms based on the information acquired automatically from the corpus of relevant literature. The learning phase consists of two stages: acquisition of terminologically relevant contextual patterns (CPs) and selection of classes that apply to terms used with these patterns. CPs represent a generalisation of similar term contexts in the form of regular expressions containing lexical, syntactic and terminological information. The most probable classes for the training terms co-occurring with the statistically relevant CP are learned by a genetic algorithm. Term classification is based on the learnt results. First, each term is associated with the most frequently co-occurring CP. Classes attached to such CP are initially suggested as the term's potential classes. Then, the term is finally mapped to the most similar suggested class.

1 Introduction

The biomedical literature has been rapidly expanding due to the new discoveries reported almost on a daily basis [1]. The biomedical articles are swamped by newly coined terms denoting newly identified compounds, genes, drugs, reactions, etc. The knowledge repositories need to efficiently adapt to the advent of new terms by assorting them into appropriate classes in order to allow biomedical experts to easily acquire, analyse and visualise information of interest. Due to an enormous number of terms and the complex structure of the terminology[1], manual update approaches are inevitably inflicted by inefficiency and inconsistencies. Thus, reliable term recognition and classification methods are absolutely

---

[1] For example, UMLS (www.nlm.nih.gov/research/umls/) contains more than 2.8 million terms assorted into 135 classes.

essential as means of support for automatic maintenance of large knowledge repositories.

Still, term classification in the biomedical domain is by no means straightforward to implement, as the naming conventions do not necessarily systematically reflect terms' functional properties. Hence, the contexts in which terms are used need to be analysed. In most of the approaches exploiting contextual features, contexts have been typically represented using "bag-of-words" approach (e.g. [4]) or pre-defined sets of patterns (e.g. [6]). Contextual features can be used to classify terms by methods such as nearest neighbour, maximum entropy modelling, naive Bayes classification, decision trees, support vector machines, etc.

In our approach, important contextual features are learnt in the form of generalised regular expressions which describe the morpho-syntactic structure and lexico-semantic content of term contexts. The classes that are compatible with specific patterns are learnt by a genetic algorithm. The nearest neighbour algorithm (based on the similarity measure that compares lexical, syntactic and contextual features) is applied to these classes in order to perform classification.

The remainder of the paper is organised as follows. In Section 2 we describe the acquisition of contextual patterns, while Section 3 gives details on the genetic algorithm used to learn the most probable classes for terms used with these patterns. The procedure for classification of terms based on the acquired patterns and the corresponding classes is given in Section 4. Finally, in Section 5 we describe the evaluation strategy and provide the results, after which we conclude the paper.

2 Mining the Literature for Contextual Features

Our approach to the extraction of contextual features is based on automatic pattern mining, whose aim is to automatically identify, normalise and harvest the contextual patterns providing the most relevant information on the terms they surround. A contextual pattern (CP) is defined as a generalised regular expression describing the structure of a term's context. We considered two types of context constituents: morpho-syntactic (e.g. noun phrases, prepositions, etc.) and terminological (i.e. term occurrences). Term contexts are generalised by mapping the constituents to their categories. In addition, lemmatised lexical forms can be used to instantiate specific constituents in order to specify their semantic content, e.g.:

V	PREP	TERM	NP	PREP
V	PREP	TERM:*nuclear_receptor*	NP	PREP:*of*
V:*belong*	PREP:*to*	TERM:*nuclear_receptor*	NP:*superfamily*	PREP:*of*

The main challenge is to "optimise" CPs so as to provide a suitable balance between their generality and partiality towards specific classes of terms. With this in mind, the categories that are not particularly significant in providing useful contextual information (e.g. determiners, linking words, etc.) [6] can be safely removed from the CPs. On the other hand, categories with high information content (e.g. terms, verbs, etc.) need to be instantiated, because they provide good discriminatory features for term comparison. The generality of a CP is also affected by its length. While the decisions about the categories and instantiation are manually encoded based on the existing observations, the problem of variable pattern lengths is addressed automatically. The *CP-value* measure is used to determine the statistical relevance of CPs and indirectly the appropriate length of individual CPs[2].

First, for each term occurrence the maximal left context is extracted without crossing the sentence boundaries. The results of morpho-syntactic and terminological processing encoded in the XML-tagged corpus are used to automatically discard some categories, remove their lexical content or to keep the lemmatised lexical form (as discusses above). The remainder represents an initially selected left CP. Iterative removal of the left-most constituent until the minimal CP length[3] is reached results in a number of shorter left CPs.

If a CP does not occur nested inside other CPs, then its CP-value is proportional to its frequency and length. Otherwise, we take into account both the absolute frequency (positive impact) and the frequency of nested occurrences (small negative impact), thus measuring the frequency of its independent occurrences. Further, since a CP is more independent if it appears nested inside a larger number of different CPs, we reduce the negative impact by dividing it with the number of such CPs. Formally:

$$CP(p) = \begin{cases} \ln|p| \cdot f(p) & \text{, if } p \text{ is never nested} \\ \ln|p| \cdot \left(f(p) - \frac{1}{|T_p|}\sum_{q \in T_p} f(q)\right) & \text{, otherwise} \end{cases}$$

where $f(p)$ is the absolute frequency of the CP p, $|p|$ is its length, and T_p is a set of all CPs that contain p. CPs with high CP-values are usually general patterns, the ones with low CP-values typically are rare patterns, while the middle-ranked CPs represent relevant domain-specific patterns[4].

3 A Genetic Algorithm for Class Selection

Given a CP, we define a *class selection* (CS) as a set of classes applicable to the majority of terms (from the training set) used in contexts described by the CP. Generally, a CS represents a hypothesis about the classes of terms complementing the corresponding CP. With that respect, each CS can be quantified by its *precision* and *recall* calculated as $P = A/(A+B)$ and $R = A/(A+C)$, where A, B and C denote the numbers of *true positives*, *false positives* and *false negatives*

---

[2] We will describe the way of processing the left contexts. The right contexts are treated analogously.
[3] The minimal and maximal CP length have been empirically set to two and ten respectivelly.
[4] We used the CP-value to discard 20% of the top-ranked CPs and 30% of the bottom-ranked CPs.

respectively, which are calculated as follows based on the set of training terms $\{t_1,...,t_m\}$ co-occurring with the corresponding CP:

$$A = \sum_{i=1}^{m} |CS \cap C(t_i)| \quad B = \sum_{i=1}^{m} |CS \setminus C(t_i)| \quad C = \sum_{i=1}^{m} |C(t_i) \setminus CS|$$

In the above formulas $C(t_i)$ ($i = 1,...,m$) denotes the set of actual classes for the term t_i. In general, the recall of a CS increases with its size as the probability of some of its classes applying to individual terms is higher, while its precision is decreasing as many of the classes would not apply to individual terms. The goal, thus, is to find a CS of an optimal size and content so as to provide suitable recall and precision. In our approach, we opted to use a genetic algorithm (GA) to learn the CSs automatically, since GAs are particularly suited for the optimisation problems [3].

GAs are meta-heuristics incorporating the principles of natural evolution and the idea of "survival of the fittest" [3]. An *individual* encodes a solution as a sequence of genes. In the initial phase of a GA a number of solutions is generated, usually at random. Selection, crossover, mutation, and replacement are applied in this order aiming to gradually improve the quality of the solutions and the possibility of finding a sufficiently good solution. *Selection* is usually defined probabilistically: the better the solution, the higher the probability for that solution to be selected as a parent. Selected individuals are recombined by applying the *crossover* between pairs of individuals. The offspring is expected to combine the good characteristics of their parents, possibly giving way to better solutions. The *mutation* operator introduces diversity into a population by modifying a solution, possibly introducing previously unseen good characteristics into the population. *Fitness function* quantifies the quality of individuals. The ones with the best fitness values *replace* less fit individuals. Once a suitable solution has been found or the number of iterations exceeds some threshold, the iterations of the GA are stopped.

In our approach, each individual (i.e. CS) is represented as a sequence of genes, where each gene denotes whether the corresponding class is a member of the CS. The goal is to optimise a CS so as to enhance its recall $R(CS)$ and precision $P(CS)$. The fitness f of a CS is calculated as follows: $f(CS) = w_R \cdot R(CS) + w_P \cdot P(CS)$, where w_R and w_P are the weights modelling the preferences towards precision and recall[5]. The objective is to find a solution with a (near)maximal fitness value. The initial population is formed by generating random individuals. We used uniform crossover: genes at each fixed position are exchanged with 50% probability. Individuals are mutated with 1% probability by a randomly changing a randomly chosen gene.

4 Term Classification

Let $CP = \{cp_1,...,cp_n\}$ be a set of automatically extracted CPs. During the phase of learning the CSs, each cp_i ($i = 1,...,n$) is associated with a class se-

---

[5] In our experiments we used equal weights for precision and recall.

lection it may be complemented with, $CS_i = \{c_{i,1}, ..., c_{i,m_i}\}$. Each CS typically contains multiple classes. In order to link a term to a specific class, we score each class by a hybrid term similarity measure, called the *CLS measure*, which combines contextual, lexical and syntactic properties of terms [7]. This measure, however, applies to terms, while we need to compare *terms* to *classes*. We, therefore, set the similarity between a term t and a class $c_{i,j}$ ($j = 1, ..., m_i$) to be proportional to the average similarity between the term and the terms from the given class. More formally, if $e_1, ..., e_k$ are randomly chosen terms[6] from that class that occur in the corpus, then term-to-class similarity is calculated in the following way:

$$S(t, c_{i,j}) = \frac{\frac{1}{k}\sum_{i=1}^{k} CLS(t, e_i)}{\sqrt{\sum_{i=1}^{k} CLS^2(t, e_i)}}$$

Note that the described method implicitly incorporates the class probability factors. The more frequently a certain class complements the given CP, the more likely it will be present in the corresponding CS.

5 Experiments and Evaluation

We performed the classification experiments on a corpus of 2072 abstracts retrieved from MEDLINE (www.ncbi.nlm.nih.gov/PubMed/). The corpus was terminologically processed by using the C/NC-value method for term recognition [2]. Terms were tagged with the classification information obtained from the UMLS ontology. We focused on a subtree describing chemical substances (13 classes). Terms from this hierarchy were used as part of the training (1618 terms) and testing (138 terms) sets. A total of 1250 CPs have been automatically extracted from the corpus. We conducted experiments with 631 most relevant CPs (the ones most frequently co-occurring with terms). Based on the training set, CPs were associated with the CSs, e.g. the pattern V:*activate* PREP:*by* TERM was associated with the following CS: {*immunologic factor, receptor, enzyme, hormone, pharmacologic substance*}.

Each testing term was associated with the CP it most frequently co-occurred with. The CS learnt for that CP was used to classify the term in question. For example, the term *ciprofibrate*, most frequently occurring with the above CP, was correctly classified as a *pharmacologic substance*. Table 1 summarises the classification results achieved by our method and compares them to three baseline methods, which include random, majority and naive Bayes classification. The baseline methods map a term respectively to (1) a random class, (2) a class with the highest number of term occurrences in the corpus, and (3) the most probable class based on the words found in its context.

A comparison to other methods reported in the literature would require the results obtained on the same set. Most of these methods were either unavailable or designed for specific classes (e.g. [5]). Nonetheless, most of the results were

---

[6] We preselected ten terms for each class.

Table 1. Evaluation of the classification results[7]

Method	Precision	Recall	F-measure
CP/CS	61%	38%	47%
random	11%	8%	9%
majority	35%	25%	29%
naive Bayes	42%	18%	25%

reported for fewer number of classes, while the probability of missing a correct class increases with the higher number of classes available. It is then natural for the performance measures to provide "poorer" values when tested on broader classification schemes. For example, our method achieved 61% precision for 13 classes, while Hatzivassiloglou et al. [5] achieved 67% for three classes.

6 Conclusion

We presented a term classification method, which makes use of the structured contextual information acquired automatically through contextual pattern mining. The presented term classification approach revolves around these patterns. Namely, they are used to collect unclassified terms and to suggest their potential classes based on the classes automatically predicted by a genetic algorithm, which optimises precision and recall estimated on the set of training terms. The suggested classes are compared through their terms to the given term by a similarity measure, which takes into account lexical, syntactic and contextual information.

Note that terms can be compared directly to all classes in the classification scheme in order to perform the nearest neighbour classification directly. However, the class pruning approach has been adopted in order to enhance the computational efficiency of the classification process itself. In this approach, the contextual and classification information learned offline needs to be updated periodically in order to reflect the changes in the corpus of literature and the information available in the ontology.

The precision of our method could be improved by analysing and exploiting orthographic and lexical term features characteristic of specific classes (e.g. suffix *-ase* for the class of enzymes). On the other side, the recall could be improved by taking into account more context patterns and by using larger corpora.

References

1. Blaschke, C., Hirschman, L., Valencia, A.: Information Extraction in Molecular Biology. Briefings in Bioinformatics 3/2 (2002) 154-165

---

[7] F-measure is calculated according to the following formula: $F = 2 \cdot P \cdot R/(P+R)$, where precision P and recall R are calculated as before.

2. Frantzi, K., Ananiadou, S., Mima, H.: Automatic Recognition of Multi-Word Terms. Int. J. on Digital Libraries 3/2 (2000) 117-132
3. Goldberg, D.: Genetic Algorithms in Search, Optimization, and Machine Learning. Addison-Wesley (1989) 432
4. Grefenstette, G. Exploration in Automatic Thesaurus Discovery. Kluwer Academic Publishers (1994)
5. Hatzivassiloglou, V., Duboue, P., Rzhetsky, A.: Disambiguating Proteins, Genes, and RNA in Text: A Machine Learning Approach. Bioinformatics 1/1 (2001) 1-10
6. Maynard, D., Ananiadou, S.: Identifying Terms by Their Family and Friends. Proceedings of COLING 2000, Luxembourg (2000) 530-536
7. Nenadić, G., Spasić, I., Ananiadou, S.: Mining Term Similarities from Corpora. Terminology 10/1, (2004) 55-80

PRICES: An Efficient Algorithm for Mining Association Rules

Chuan Wang and Christos Tjortjis

Information Systems Group, Department of Computation
University of Manchester Institute of Science and Technology
P.O. Box 88, Manchester, M60 1QD, UK
C.Wang-2@postgrad.umist.ac.uk, christos@co.umist.ac.uk

Abstract. In this paper, we present PRICES, an efficient algorithm for mining association rules, which first identifies all large itemsets and then generates association rules. Our approach reduces large itemset generation time, known to be the most time-consuming step, by scanning the database only once and using logical operations in the process. Experimental results and comparisons with the state of the art algorithm *Apriori* shows that PRICES very efficient and in some cases up to ten times as fast as *Apriori*.

1 Introduction

Association rules, is a data mining technique which identifies relationships between items in databases. The process can be decomposed into two steps: large itemsets generation and association rules generation [1]. It is well established that, while association rules generation is rather straightforward, large itemset generation can be a bottleneck in the process. A number of algorithms have been proposed in order to increase the efficiency of the process [1-7]. We discuss and review the most prominent ones in section 2.

Here we present a new algorithm for mining association rules called PRICES. The algorithm uses the same two steps as in other algorithms; it is however faster as it scans the database only once, to store transactions information in the memory by a succinct form we call *Prices Table*. This table is then pruned by creating a pseudo transaction table called *Pruned Prices Table*, which contains all 1-size large itemsets after eliminating all 1-size small itemsets. Recursion is used to generate k-size (k>1) large itemsets from the Pruned Prices Table and (k-1)-size large itemsets. Finally, association rules are generated using the large itemsets. The innovation of the algorithm is that it uses logical operations, such as AND, OR, XOR and left-shift in the process of generating large itemsets and association rules, thus accelerating the process. Experimental results have shown that PRICES is efficient and outperforms *Apriori* in terms of speed.

A more detailed description of PRICES is given in Section 3. Section 4 presents experimental results and comparisons with *Apriori*. Conclusions and directions for further work are outlined in section 5.

2 Background

Since the introduction of mining association rules in [1], many algorithms that discover large itemsets have been proposed. The number of times an algorithm scans the entire database is a significant factor in terms of speed as it determines the number of time consuming I/O operations involved.

AIS generates all large itemsets by making multiple passes over the database [1]. After reading a transaction, large itemsets are extended by appending lexicographically larger items to generate candidate itemsets. If the *support* for candidate itemsets is above a minimum threshold, they are chosen as large itemsets, and the next pass commences, until there are no more large itemsets. A limitation of AIS is that it only produces one item in the consequent of rules.

Apriori is a well-known improvement over AIS, which utilizes the concept that any subset of a large itemset is a large itemset [2]. It improves candidate generation by joining large itemsets together. DHP is a hash-based Apriori-like algorithm, effective in generating large 2-itemsets [5]. However, both Apriori and DHP scan the database many times producing a substantial I/O overhead.

The Partition algorithm reduces the number of database scans to 2 [6]. It partitions the database into small segments. Local large itemsets of each segment are then united and a further entire database scan is needed to generate the global large itemsets. The Sampling algorithm improves on the Partition algorithm [7]. It reduces the number of database scans to one in the best case and two in the worst. A sample is drawn and large itemsets of it are generated and finally large itemsets are found. The sample is crucial because an unrepresentative one can cause a very big candidate set.

SETM is an algorithm designed for using SQL to generate large itemsets [4]. Large itemsets are in the form of <TID, itemset> where TID is a unique identifier for each transaction. One disadvantage of SETM is that it generates too many candidate itemsets, thus reducing efficiency.

All in all, the number of database scans needed by AIS, Apriori DHP and SETM, depends on the number of items while Partition and Sampling algorithms reduce this number to 2, despite their other limitations.

3 The Algorithm PRICES

PRICES is an algorithm which mines association rules in two steps by use of logical operations. First, large itemsets are identified, and then association rules are generated. Section 3.1 presents basic principles and underlying assumptions used by the algorithm. Large itemsets generation is described in section 3.2, and association rules generation is explained in section 3.3.

3.1 Basic Principles and Assumptions

Prices uses logical operations such as AND, OR, XOR and left-shift to generate large itemsets and association rules. In addition, every item in the transactions is given a unique *value*. Every transaction can be represented by a *price,* which is the sum of item values it consists of. Items values are assumed be such that that no value can be the sum of other values. Therefore, every price represents a unique itemset pattern.

For example, if there are 5 items, A, B, C, D and E in a database, let the value of item A be 2^4, the value of item B 2^3 and so on. The price of transaction {A, C, D} will be 10110 in binary mode. In this way, an itemset can also be represented as a price.

Under this assumption, we can apply logical operation AND to the price of one transaction and the price of one itemset to determine whether this transaction "contains" this itemset, by comparing the result with the itemset price. For example, transaction {A, C, D} (price P_T = 10110) contains itemset {A, C} (price P_{AC} = 10100) because the result of P_T AND P_{AC} is equal to P_{AC}. Therefore, our task is to identify all the itemsets prices from {00...01} to {11...11} occurring above a threshold in the prices of transactions.

For a better understanding of the algorithm we shall use the following example for the rest of the discussion: consider a database with transaction information as in Table 1 and assume that minimum support and confidence are both set to 50%.

Table 1. A database example.

TID	Items
T_1	ACD
T_2	BCE
T_3	ABCE
T_4	BE

Table 2. The Prices Table (PT).

TID	Items	Prices
T_1	ACD	10110
T_2	BCE	01101
T_3	ABCE	11101
T_4	BE	01001

3.2 Large Itemset Generation

The PRICES algorithm generates large itemsets in three steps. First, the *Pruned Prices Table (PPT)* is created, then all large 2-itemset are created and finally, all large itemsets are generated.

PRICES scans the database, calculates the prices of all transactions and stores these in memory using an array called *Prices Table (PT)*. Table 2 shows the PT for the example given in section 3.1.

It is known that any itemset which contains a small itemset will also be small [2]. Therefore, we can prune the PT by eliminating the column of small items. This is done in two steps: first generate the *Large Bit Mark* (LBM), which is the price of the itemset which contains all large 1-itemsets; then create the *Pruned Prices Table*. To generate the LBM we set the price of the first 1-size candidate to 1 and apply a left-shift operation to generate the second candidate price and so on. We calculate each candidate's support. If a candidate is large, the corresponding position in LBM is set to 1, otherwise to 0. In addition, the large 1-size itemsets, along with the support and size, are stored in L.

Given the LBM and PT, we can generate the Pruned Prices Table by eliminating the columns which have 0 in the corresponding position of LBM. One 0 in the LBM indicates that the corresponding item is small and thus any itemset containing this is also small. Therefore, removing these items shrinks the PT without affecting the generation of large itemsets.

By applying these steps to our example, we obtain the respective LBM as seen in Table 3. Table 4 shows how the pruned price of T_1 is generated from LBM and T_1.

Table 3. Generation of the LBM.

	A	B	C	D	E
Support	2	3	3	1	3
comp. with minsup	>=	>=	>=	<	>=
LBM	1	1	1	0	1

Table 4. Price and Pruned Price of T_1.

	A	B	C	D	E	
P_1	1	0	1	1	0	10110
LBM	1	1	1	0	1	11101
PP_1	1	0	1	-	0	1010

As every single item in the Pruned Prices Table is large, every 2-size itemset composed of different single item is a candidate. We calculate the support of every candidate and if it is large, we record it into L, along with its support and size. We also use the OR operation to compose two different item prices into one price. For example, the price of itemset {A, E} (10001) can be derived by applying OR to itemset {A} (10000) and {E} (00001).

k-size large itemsets can then be generated from (k-1)-size large itemsets and the PPT. We use the XOR operation as a difference indicator from which we can find how many different bits (items) there are between two (k-1)-size large itemsets. To generate a candidate c_k, two (k-1)-size large itemsets must have exactly two different bits. Hence, the fact that 2-size itemset composed by two different bits of two (k-1)-size large itemsets is included in large 2-itemsets (L_2) is a prerequisite of that the itemset composed by these two (k-1)-size large itemsets is a candidate. Furthermore, whether all the other (k-1)-size subsets of this potential c_k are included in L_{k-1} are checked. Finally, the candidate support is calculated and recorded it if large. This is recursively repeated until less than k large (k-1)-size itemsets are found.

Finally, in order to get the large itemsets from L, we restore the prices in L from pruned prices and map those into itemsets. According to the definition of LBM, a 0 is inserted into pruned prices at corresponding positions to restore prices. Once the prices are restored, we can map these into itemsets based on the previous definition of the relationship between price and itemset.

3.3 Association Rules Generation

In this section, we present the way to generate association rules from the final set of large itemsets. We know that an association rule $X \rightarrow Y$ holds if: (1) $X \cap Y = \phi$; (2) $X, Y, X \cup Y \in L$; (3) $\dfrac{s(X \cup Y)}{s(X)} \geq$ minconf.

Therefore, for every two large itemset l_i and $l_j \in L$, if l_i AND $l_j = 0$ (1), $l_i \cup l_j \in L$ (2) and $\dfrac{s(l_i \cup l_j)}{s(l_i)} \geq$ minconf (3) are all met, then the rule $l_i \rightarrow l_j$ holds.

4 Experimental Results

In order to evaluate the performance of PRICES, we developed a prototype and carried out experiments. We created several synthetic datasets by using Quest dataset generator [9]. The average transaction length is 10 and the average size of potentially maximal large itemsets is 4. Table 5 shows the datasets we generated.

Table 5. Synthetic datasets.

#	No. of transactions	No. of items	Name
1	1,000	100	T1K.I100
2	10,000	100	T10K.I100
3	100,000	100	T100K.I100
4	1,000,000	100	T1M.I100

For comparison purposes we used an implementation of the state of the art *Apriori* algorithm obtained from Weka Data Mining System [8]. All the experiments were executed on a Personal Computer at 1800MHz, with 256MB of main memory, running Windows XP Professional. In order to get more accurate results, we executed each experiment three times. Average execution times are shown in Fig. 1.

Results show that PRICES is faster to Apriori as it only scans the database once and uses logical operations performed in the main memory. The pruning technique used in PRICES also contributes to the high performance. The most important finding of the result analysis is that the larger the database grows in terms of transactions number, the faster PRICES gets compared to Apriori. So for example for a dataset with a million transactions PRICES is more than ten times faster than Apriori.

5 Conclusions and Further Work

In this paper, we proposed PRICES, a new efficient algorithm for mining association rules. Its major advantage is that it only scans the database once and any consecutive processing takes places in memory using logical operations. Extensive experiments using different synthetic datasets were conducted to assess the performance of the algorithm. Results have been positive and PRICES outperformed *Apriori* in terms of speed.

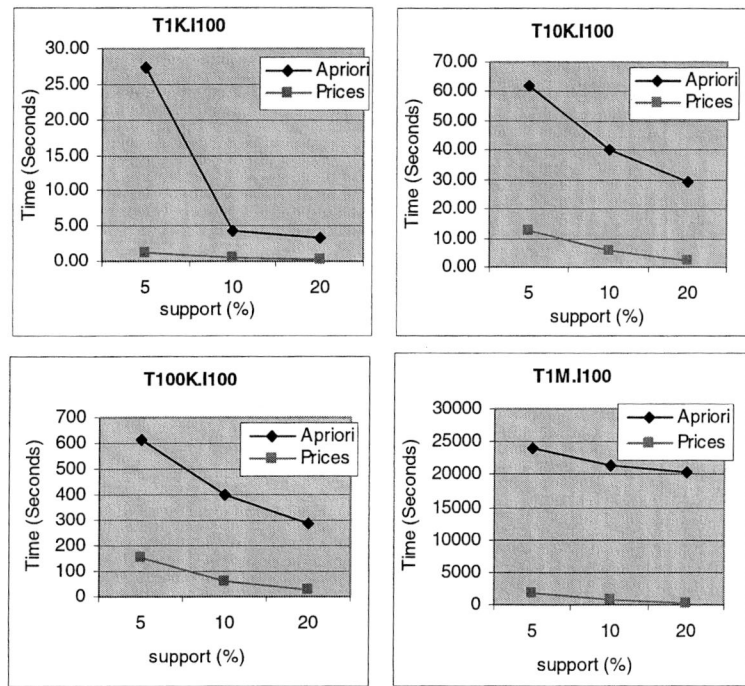

Fig. 1. Experimental results.

We are currently experimenting with memory requirements and various techniques to address performance deterioration due to I/O overhead when data do not fit in memory due to the possibly very large size of datasets. Plans for further work include devising an extension of the algorithm to match the needs of different applications, such as document retrieval, information recovery and text mining.

References

1. R. Agrawal, T. Imielinski, and A.N. Swami. Mining Association Rules between Sets of Items in Large Databases. *Proceedings of the 1993 ACM SIGMOD Int'l Conf. Management of Data*, pp. 207-216, Washington, D.C., May 1993.
2. R. Agrawal, R. Srikant. Fast Algorithms for Mining Association Rules in Large Databases. *Proc. 20th Int'l Conf. Very Large Data Bases*, September 1994.
3. L. Dong and C. Tjortjis. Experiences of Using a Quantitative Approach for Mining Association Rules, *Proc.4th Int'l Conf. Intelligent Data Engineering Automated Learning* (IDEAL 03) in Lecture Notes in Computer Science Series Vol. 2690, pp. 693-700
4. M. Houtsma and A. Swami. Set-Oriented Mining for Association Rules in Relational Databases, *Proc. 11th IEEE Int'l Conf. Data Engineering*, pp. 25-34,Taipei,Taiwan,March, 1995.
5. J.S. Park, M.S. Chen and P.S. Yu. Using a Hash-Based Method with Transaction Trimming For Mining Association Rules. *IEEE Transactions on Knowledge and Data Engineering*, September/October 1997.

6. A. Savasere, E. Omiecinski, and S.B. Navathe. An Efficient Algorithm for Mining Association Rules in Large Databases, *Proc. ACM SIGMOD Int'l Conf. Management of Data*, SIGMOD 1998, June 2-4, 1998, Seattle, Washington, USA.
7. H. Toivonen. Sampling Large Databases for Association Rules, *Proc. 22nd Int'l Conf. Very Large Databases*, pp. 134-145, Mumbai, India, 1996.
8. www.cs.waikato.ac.nz/~ml/weka. Weka Experiment Environment, Weka Data Mining System. (Last accessed in March, 2004).
9. http://www.almaden.ibm.com/software/quest/. Intelligent Information Systems, IBM Almaden Research Center. (Last accessed in January, 2004).

Combination of SVM Knowledge for Microcalcification Detection in Digital Mammograms

Ying Li[1,2] and Jianmin Jiang[1]

[1] University of Bradford, Bradford, UK
{l.ying2,J.Jiang1}@bradford.ac.uk
[2] Math Dept., Sun Yat-Sen University, Guangzhou, China, 510275
stsljh@zsu.edu.cn

Abstract. In this paper, we propose a novel combinational SVM algorithm via a set of decision rules to achieve better performances in microcalcification detection inside digital mammograms towards computer aided breast cancer diagnosis. Based on the discovery that the polynomial SVM is sensitive to MC (microcalcification) pixels and the linear SVM is sensitive to non-MC pixels, we designed an adaptive threshold mechanism via establishment of their correspondences to exploit the complementary nature between the polynomial SVM and the linear SVM. Experiments show that the proposed algorithm successfully reduced false positive detection rate while keeping the true positive detection rate competitive.

1 Introduction

At present, breast cancer remains to be the most frequent form of cancers in women, especially in the western countries. It is also the leading cause of mortality in women in the past decades. Primary prevention seems impossible since the cause of this disease still remains unknown. Therefore, early detection of breast cancer plays leading roles in improving breast cancer prognosis. In the recognised earlier diagnosis process, MC (microcalcification) clusters are one of the early indicators of breast cancer and they appear in 30-50% of mammographically diagnosed cases.

There exist many methods for MC detection (a thorough review of various methods can be found in Nishikawa [1]), in which representative approaches include Bayesian modeling [2], multi-resolution analysis via wavelet transforms [3], fuzzy logic [4], TMNN (two-stage multilayer neural network) [5] and others.

Support Vector Machine (SVM) is a learning tool originated in modern statistical learning theory [6]. In recent years, SVM learning has found a wide range of real-world applications. The formulation of SVM learning is based on the principle of structural risk minimization. Instead of minimizing an objective function based on the training samples, such as mean square error (MSE), the SVM attempts to minimize the upper-bound on the generalization error. As a result, an SVM tends to perform well when applied to data outside the training set.

Recently, two papers were published to report how the SVM can be applied to detect MC clusters. In the first paper, Bazzani et al. [7] proposed a method for MC detection based on multi-resolution filtering analysis and statistical testing, in which a SVM classifier was used to reduce the false detection rate. The described method uses the extracted image feature to formulate the basis of detection. In the other paper, Issam El-Naqa et al. [8] directly uses a finite image window as the input to the SVM classifier. To suppress the image background, the author proposed to apply a sharp high-pass filter to each mammogram. The author also proposed a so-called SEL scheme [8] to make use of all those samples with MC absent.

In this paper, we describe a combinational SVM algorithm with multiple SVMs to detect microcalcifications inside digital mammograms. The description is structured into three sections. In addition to the introductory section, the rest of the paper contains section-2, where the proposed method is discussed, and section-3 to report the experimental results and concluding remarks.

2 The Proposed Algorithm Design

As mentioned by Issam El-Naqa et al [8], MC detection is actually a two-class pattern classification problem. At each location in a mammogram (pixel-by-pixel), we apply SVM to determine whether an MC is present or not. We refer to these two classes throughout the paper as "MC present" (labelled +1) and "MC absent" (label -1). We define the input pattern to the SVM classifier to be a small window with 9x9 pixels centred at the location of interest. It is in fact an 81 dimension grey level or intensity vector. Further details about the principle of SVM are referred to reference [8].

In general, all SVMs can be classified into two types: linear SVM and non-linear SVM. For non-linear SVM, a kernel function is required, which plays a central role in implicitly mapping the input vectors into a high-dimensional feature space. In our work, two most commonly used kernels are considered. The polynomial kernel:

$$K(x, y) = (x^T y + 1)^p, p > 0 \qquad (1)$$

and the Gaussian RBF kernel:

$$K(x, y) = \exp(-\frac{\|x-y\|^2}{2\sigma^2}), \sigma > 0 \qquad (2)$$

To train the SVMs, we manually selected 624 MC pixels and 51248 Non-MC pixels from 26 mammograms as our SVM training data set. Since we have three SVM models (linear SVM, polynomial SVM and GBF SVM), we need to select the best two SVMs and their associated parameters in order to ensure that the proposed combination of SVMs achieves the best possible performances in MC detections. To this end, we carried out an extensive empirical studies in evaluating the three SVMs in terms of MC detections[10]. Following the spirit of the reference [8], we applied a 10-fold cross validation to the 624 MC pixels and 1248 Non-MC pixels. The evaluation results are presented in terms of generalization errors, which are illustrated in Table 1. The so-called generalization error is defined as the total number of incorrectly classified samples divided by the total number of samples classified, representing the proportion of errors made in the detection process. As a matter of fact, there is an important parameter C in SVMs, which controls the trade-off between empirical risk and the model complexity [8]. Hence, the generalization error is dependent on this parameter C. As a result, the generalization error for each SVM can be described as the function of C:

Generalization error of Linear SVM = $f(C)$
Generalization error of Polynomial SVM = $g(p,C)$
Generalization error of RBF SVM = $h(\sigma,C)$

where f, g, h are functions.

In Table-1, only the generalization error level is presented indicating the general trend across a certain range of C values. As an example, $O(0.0336)$ for linear SVM in Table 1 means that when C varies from 0.1 to 10^6, the Generalization Error of linear SVM varies from 0.0336-0.001 to 0.0336+0.001 (within the vicinity of 0.0336). We mathematically denote this variance with similar order as $O(0.0336)$.

Table 1. Generalization error level for linear SVM, polynomial SVM and RBF SVM.

		Generalization Error Level
Linear SVM		$O(0.0336)$
Polynomial SVM	$p=1$	$O(0.0326)$
	$p=2$	$O(0.0291)$
	$p=3$	$O(0.0216)$
	$p=4$	$O(0.0207)$
	$p=5$	$O(0.3364)$
RBF SVM	$\sigma=10^{-1}$	$O(0.3384)$
	$\sigma=10^1$	$O(0.3330)$
	$\sigma=10^3$	$O(0.3324)$
	$\sigma=10^5$	$O(0.3330)$

From these results, it can be seen that the polynomial SVM ($p=4$) and the linear SVM provides the best possible potential for our proposed combination. Therefore, we choose these two SVMs as the candidates for our proposed combination algorithm design. As theoretical analysis of various SVMs proves difficult, we adopted such empirical studies and evaluations as an alternative to determine the candidates for our proposed algorithm.

The combinational SVM design is essentially a decision making process, where the nature of the two different SVMs, as observed from the above empirical studies, should be fully exploited. In other words, while the sensitivity of linear SVM to non-MC pixels could help to reduce the false positive detection (normal pixel being detected as MC pixel), the sensitivity of non-linear SVM to MC pixels will certainly help to increase the true-positive detection. Therefore, a decision-making process in consideration of their complementary nature is needed in order to improve their existing performances. As a matter of fact, such a decision making process is modelled by the decision function $f(x)$ in a single SVM, where x is an 81 dimensional intensity vector (i.e. with 81 elements produced by the input window with 9x9 pixels). This is because that the SVM training produces a hyper-plane that separates all the input samples into two-classes. As a result, given an unknown pixel in an unknown ROI (region of interest), a decision can be made based on the value of $f(x)$, which is defined as follows [8]:

$$\text{SVMresult} = \begin{cases} 1, \text{if } f(x) > 0 \\ -1, \text{if } f(x) <= 0 \end{cases} \quad (3)$$

To make a coordinated decision between the two SVMs adopted, we need to establish some knowledge-based rules to balance the two SVMs. Given an unknown ROI and an unknown pixel x, we have two SVMs to classify all the input pixels into two classes, MC or non-MC. For the convenience of discussion, we denote the classification results by the non-linear SVM and the linear SVM as $d^{(1)}$ and $d^{(2)}$, where $\{d^{(1)} = f_1(x), d^{(2)} = f_2(x)\} \in R$, and their corresponding decision values as S1 and S2 respectively, (note the values of S1 and S2 are either -1 or +1), To combine the two SVMs, we define the decision rules as follows:

- If S1 is equal to S2, the CombinedSVM = S1 (S1=1 means a MC pixel; and S1 = -1 means a Non-MC pixel);
- If S1 is not equal to S2, which represents the focus of the problem to be addressed here, the decision value for the combined SVM needs to be determined by a well-balanced comparison between $d^{(1)}$ and $d^{(2)}$. Since SVM essentially relies on its training to classify all the inputs into two classes, its output, the value of $f(x)$, represents a kind of distance from the boundary of the classification. Therefore, it can be assumed that the larger the distance, the more reliable the classification result. To this end, a simple decision rule seems to be reasonable such as: CombinedSVM=S1, if $d^{(1)} > d^{(2)}$. However, this simple rule is equivalent to using $d^{(2)}$ as the threshold. Since the linear SVM is sensitive to non-MC, such rule will lead to the final decision to be exactly the same as the polynomial SVM whenever S1 = +1. Consequently, we ended up with a final decision that does not have any balance between the two SVMs. To increase the balance towards S2 when S1=+1, for example, the threshold needs to be increased. One simple solution is to add a weighting value to change the rule as: CombinedSVM=S1, if $d^{(1)} > Cd^{(2)}$. The problem here is that the weight value, C, must be adaptive to the content of the mammogram regions being classified. To achieve such an adaptability, we propose to establish a correspondence between the two SVM results. In other words, for each point of $d^{(1)}$, we determine a corresponding point in the domain of $d^{(2)}$, which can be represented by $\Psi(d^{(2)})$, and we then take this value as the threshold to formulate the final decision rule.

To examine the relationship between the two SVMs, we can visualise the SVM results by transforming them into images, i.e. mapping the values of $f(x)$ into grey level intensities. Similarly, the decision values can also be visualized by binary images (+1 corresponding to white pixels and -1 to black pixels). Figure 1 illustrates one example of such visualizations, in which part-(a) for polynomial SVM and part-(b) for linear SVM. In each part, the top sample shows the result image and the bottom sample

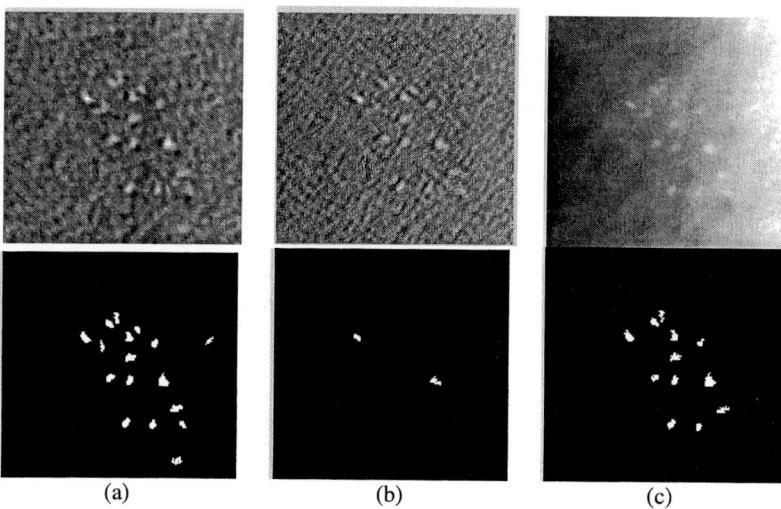

Fig. 1. Part-(a), result image and the decision value image for polynomial SVM; Part-(b), result image and the decision value image for linear SVM; Part-(c) original image (ROI); combined decision value image.

shows the decision value image. As a result, given two SVM result images and the two decision value images, all those white pixel regions inside both decision value images can be examined in order to establish their correspondences. Specifically, for the largest MC region in the polynomial SVM result image that contains N MC pixels, we extract their locations inside the result image as: $(i_1, j_1), \ldots, (i_N, j_N)$ and their decision values as $d_1^{(1)}, \ldots, d_N^{(1)}$. In the linear SVM images, the same locations and their decision values can also be extracted, which are represented as $d_1^{(2)}, \ldots, d_N^{(2)}$. For these two sets of points and their decision values, a correspondence can be established by fitting these two data sets, $\{d_1^{(1)}, \ldots, d_N^{(1)}\}$ and $\{d_1^{(2)}, \ldots, d_N^{(2)}\}$ into a straight line by using the mean square error method. Therefore, for each decision value $d^{(2)}$, an adaptive threshold can be determined by such straight line fitting, which can be represented as: $d = \Psi(d^{(2)})$. Figure 2 illustrates one example of such line fitting to establish the correspondence between the two SVMs. The final decision rule can be designed as follows:

$$\text{CombinedSVM} = \begin{cases} s1 & \text{if } d^{(1)} > \Psi(d^{(2)}) \\ s2 & \text{else} \end{cases} \quad (4)$$

3 Experimental Results and Concluding Remarks

Our experimental data set is obtained from the Digital Database of Screening Mammography (DDSM) [9]. In line with medical imaging specifications, all the mammograms selected are of a pixel depth of 12 bits. Our training set, as mentioned before, is 26 mammograms, among which, we manually selected 624 Mc pixels and 51248 Non-MC pixels as the training samples for both SVMs. Our test data set includes 399 sub-images, which are cut from 214 different mammograms, in which 299 of them are MC-present images and the remaining 100 are normal ones (MC-absent).

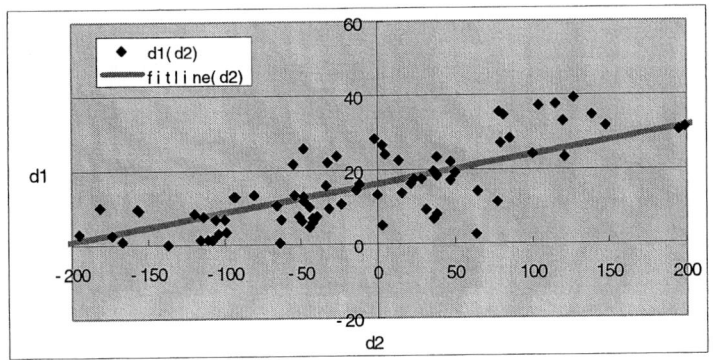

Fig. 2. Fit a data set in $d^{(1)} - d^{(2)}$ space with a straight line, d1, d2 stands for $d^{(1)}$ and $d^{(2)}$.

Table 2 summarises the final experimental results, which illustrates that, compared with individual SVMs, the proposed combination achieves significant reduction of false positive detection while the true positive detection rate is still preserved.

Table 2. Summary of experimental results.

	FP	TP
Polynomial SVM	42%	96.7%
Linear SVM	4%	68.3%
Combined Method	30%	96.32%

In this paper, we proposed a set of decision rules for a combinational SVM detection of microcalcifiations inside digital mammograms. The proposed algorithm exploits the complementary nature of the two SVMs and thus provides the potential to be further developed into useful tools for computer aided breast cancer diagnosis systems. Finally the authors wish to acknowledge the financial support from Yorkshire Cancer Research for the work reported.

References

1. R. M. Nishikawa: Detection of microcalcifications. in Image-Processing Techniques for Tumor Detection, R. N. Strickland, Ed. New York: Marcel Decker, 2002.
2. N. Karssemeijer: A stochastic model for automated detection calcifications in digital mammograms. in Proc. 12th Int. Conf. Information Medical Imaging, Wye, U.K.(1991) 227–238, 1991.
3. R. N. Strickland and H. L. Hahn: Wavelet transforms for detecting microcalcifications in mammograms. IEEE Trans. Med. Imag., 15, 218–229, 1996.

4. H. Cheng, Y. M. Liu, and R. I. Freimanis: A novel approach to microcalcifications detection using fuzzy logic techniques. IEEE Trans. Med. Imag., 17, 442–450, 1998.
5. S. Yu and L. Guan: A CAD system for the automatic detection of clustered microcalcifications in digitized mammogram films. IEEE Trans. Med. Imag., 19, 115–126, 2000.
6. V. Vapnik, Statistical Learning Theory. New York: Wiley, 1998.
7. A. Bazzani, A. Bevilacqua, D. Bollini, R. Brancaccio, R. Campanini, N.Lanconelli, A. iccardi, and D. Romani: An SVM classifier to separate false signals from microcalcifications in digital mammograms. Phys.Med. Biol., 46, 1651–1663, 2001.
8. El-Naqa, I., Yongyi Yang, M.N. Wernick, N.P. Galatsanos, and R.M. Nishikawa: A support vector machine approach for detection of microcalcifications. IEEE Transactions on Medical Imaging, 21, 1552-1563, 2002.
9. M. Heath, KW Bowyer and D. Kopans et al: Current status of the Digital Database for Screening Mammography. Digital Mammography, Kluwer Academic Publishers, 457-460, 1998.
10. Y. Li, J. Jiang and R. Qahwaji empirical study of SVM classification of pixels into ROIs in digital mammograms, To be presented at IWDM04: International Workshop on Digital Mammography, North Carolina, USA, June 18-21, 2004.

Char: An Automatic Way to Describe Characteristics of Data

Yu-Chin Liu[1,2] and Ping-Yu Hsu[3]

[1] Department of Business Administration, National Central University
Chung-Li, Taiwan 320, R.O.C.
[2] Department of Information Management, TungNan Institute of Technology
Taipei, Taiwan 222, R.O.C.
92441002@cc.ncu.edu.tw
[3] Department of Business Administration, National Central University
Chung-Li, Taiwan 320, R.O.C.
pyhsu@mgt.ncu.edu.tw

Abstract. As e-business software prevails worldwide, large amount of data are accumulated automatically in databases of most sizable companies. Managers in organizations now face the problems of making sense out of the data. In this paper, an algorithm to automatically produce characteristic rules to describe the major characteristics of data in a table is proposed. In contrast to traditional Attribute Oriented Induction methods, the algorithm, named as *Char Algorithm*, does not need a concept tree and only requires setting a desired coverage threshold to generate a minimal set of characteristic rules to describe the given dataset. Our simulation results show that the characteristic rules found by *Char* are fairly consistent even when the number of records and attributes increase.

1 Introduction

Data mining is a process of extraction of implicit, previously unknown and potentially useful information from data [1]. Data mining is application-dependent, namely, different applications may require different mining techniques to cope with [2]. The major techniques include mining association rules, finding classification rules, data clustering and data generalization [2].

Mining association rules in relational databases has attracted many researchers in recent years. It is to acquire strong association rules in the form of "If one buys x, then he/she buys y" [3]. Data classification is to classify a set of data set based on their values of certain attributes into different classes [4]. Data clustering groups a set of data such that objects in the same cluster are similar to each other and are dissimilar to objects in different clusters. Lastly but not least, data generalization is to summarize a large set of data from a relatively lower concept level to higher ones [5].

With the proliferation of databases, organizations can now easily collect customer data for market segmentations. The technique commonly used to summarize customers' characteristics is data generalization and the Attribute Oriented Induction method is the most famous one. It generalizes data along the concept hierarchy pre-assigned to attributes. When the process completes, data in generalized attributes are replaced with items in higher positions in the concept hierarchy and the number of different entries in each attribute as well as the entire data set are reduced to be less than pre-defined thresholds.

The traditional data generalization method based on users can supply comprehensive and simple enough concept trees. However, setting up a reasonable concept tree for each attribute is the most difficult part since it requires domain knowledge which may not be possessed by practitioners. Hence, traditional data generalization can be viewed as semi-automatic data summary technique which requires human intervention in defining concept trees.

In this paper, a novel approach is proposed to find characteristic rules of tabular data without the hassle of defining concept hierarchies. It identifies the combinations of attributes and values that can describe significant portions of the data. These combinations are termed as the characteristic rules. With the method, users can get summary that are able to describe a pre-defined percentage of data.

Table 1. The training set of 20 customers.

Customer_ID	Mstatus	Age	Elevel
001	M	1	Y
002	M	1	Y
003	S	1	Y
004	S	2	N
005	M	1	Y
006	S	1	Y
007	M	1	Y
008	S	2	N
009	M	2	N
010	S	2	Y
011	M	1	Y
012	S	2	Y
013	M	1	Y
014	M	2	N
015	M	1	Y
016	S	2	N
017	M	1	Y
018	S	2	N
019	S	1	Y
020	S	1	Y

An example in Table 1 shows a list of customers buying Plasma TVs. The table contains four attributes including **Customer_ID**, **Age** with "1" for age under 45 and "2" for age above 45, **Mstatus** with "M" for Married and "S" for Single, as well as **Elevel** recorded whether the customer has a bachelor degree or not.

Three characteristic rules with quantitative measures are observed from Table 1,

Customers with {Elevel=Y, Age=1, Mstatus=M} are likely to buy a Plasma TV. (40%)

Customers with {Elevel=N, Age=2, Mstatus=S} are likely to buy a Plasma TV. (20%)

Customers with {Elevel=Y, Age=1, Mstatus=S} are likely to buy a Plasma TV. (20%)

Since there are three attributes and each has two possible values, the total numbers of possible combinations of attributes and values are 2*2*2=8, which are termed as basic potential characteristics. The disjunctive combinations of basic possible characteristics form the set of potential characteristic rules. The basic potential characteristics are listed in Table 2 with the first field recording the identification of the combination and the corresponding counts in the right-most field.

Table 2. The Eight Basic Potential Characteristics in Table 1.

Combination_ID	Mstatus	Age	Elevel	Count
C1	M	1	Y	8
C2	M	1	N	0
C3	M	2	Y	0
C4	M	2	N	2
C5	S	1	Y	4
C6	S	1	N	0
C7	S	2	Y	2
C8	S	2	N	4

Readers can observe that C1, C5 and C8 have significantly higher numbers of occurrences than others. These three characteristics may be the characteristic rules for Table 1. Although the rest of basic potential characteristics don't have high frequency counts, the disjunctive combinations of them may still qualify for characteristic rules. In fact, to find all the possible characteristic rules is a potentially huge problem.

In this example, the number of possible characteristic rules is equal to (2+1)*(2+1)*(2+1)=27, where each "2" stands for the number of distinct values in the attribute and the extra "1" stands for the omission of the attribute. In the running example, three characteristic rules describe 80% of the data and the remaining 24 characteristic rules describe only 20% of the data.

To the best of our knowledge, no other published work exists to summarize the characteristic rules without pre-defined concept hierarchies. The new algorithm automatically performs such summary with only one threshold supplied by users to specify the desired coverage threshold over the entire dataset. In this paper, an algorithm, *Char*, is designed to generate characteristic rules with quantitative measure from the given database. A characteristic rule is an assertion which characterizes a concept satisfied by a large number of records in the target table. In *Char*, entropies are used to select attributes and values which can best describe the data. A depth-first *Char Tree* is built in the process with attributes labeled on nodes and values labeled on edges. The attribute that can reduce the most entropy on the dataset is selected as the root of the tree. Attributes or values that can't reduce any entropy are purged from the tree. When the tree construction is completed, all characteristic rules are discovered. *Char* then returns the set of characteristic rules which can describe large enough portion of the data with the minimal number of characteristic rules.

The remaining of the paper is organized as follows. In Section 2, a brief literature review of finding characteristic rules is given. Section 3 introduces the *Char Algorithm* in details. The experiment results in Section 4 show that, if the values in attributes of the given dataset distributed with normal distribution, *Char* can find characteristic rules effectively and efficiently, regardless of the number of possible characteristic rules or records in the dataset. Finally, the conclusion is drawn in Section 5.

2 Related Work

Mining characteristic rules has been studied for years. In the field of data mining, this topic is further categorized into data generalization and induction. As described in [2], the methods for generalization of datasets can be further classified into two approaches: (1) data cube approach [6][7] and (2) Attribute-Oriented Induction approach [13][14]. The main concept of the data cube approach is to use drill up and down operations to analyze data in a cube. Drill up summarizes measures by grouping data with dimensional attributes selected by users and drill down split the summary according to user specified attributes. The data cube approach requires human intervention in performing data analysis.

The Attribute-Oriented Induction method performs attribute by attribute using attribute removal and concept ascension. It takes advantage of having concept trees for each relevant attributes by domain experts in advance. But in reality, the concept trees may not exist and different expert may have quite different view of the same data. Furthermore, this approach needs to set many thresholds to avoid over-generalization, but users may not be able to know these appropriate threshold values.

Classification algorithms, such as ID3 [8], are known for their ability to discriminate data between positive and negative classes. During the learning process, positive data are used to generalize rules and negative data to specialize the rules. These algorithms can't be applied to discover characteristic rules of the database table since with the closed world assumption, most databases do not record negative records.

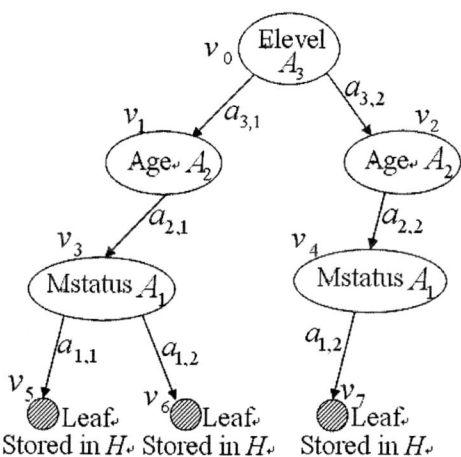

Fig. 1. The *Char Tree* of Table 1.

3 The Proposed Methodology

The methodology is composed of three steps. In first step, the relevant attributes for generating characteristic rules are collected. In the Second step, a *Char Tree* is built to explore the characteristic rules of the given database. In the third step, characteristics rules are established by listing all paths from the root to *leaf* nodes in the *Char Tree* built in the previous step. Here, we focus on the second step.

3.1 Preliminaries and Definitions

Assuming the training dataset is stored in file D, and $|D|$ denotes the total number of records. The set of all attributes in D is represented by A and $|A|$ is the number of attributes in A. Please note that values of attributes are discrete or transformed to band values. For every attribute A_j, $DV(A_j)$ stands for the possible distinct values of A_j and $|DV(A_j)|$ denotes the number of distinct values of A_j in database D. The elements of $DV(A_j)$ are listed as $a_{j,1}, a_{j,2}, \ldots a_{j,|DV(A_j)|}$. For each $A_j \in A$, the union set of $DV(A_j)$ in D is denoted by DV. For example, $DV(A_1) = \{M, S\} = \{a_{1,1}, a_{1,2}\}$ in Table 1.

Now, we are ready to define the *Char Tree*.

Definition 1. A *Char Tree* of a database D is defined as $T(V, E, A, DV, L)$, where V is the set of nodes, E is the set of edges connecting nodes, A is the set of attributes in the data set D, DV is the set of distinct values in the dataset D, and L is the label on nodes and edges. The tree has following characteristics:

1. If a node, v, in V has no incident edge, then v is the root of the tree.
2. Other than the root, every node has exactly one incident edge.
3. L is polymorphism in that $L : V \rightarrow A$ and $L : E \rightarrow DV$, given an edge e in E, emitting from v_1, then $L(e)$ is an element of $DV(L(v_1))$.

Each node on the *Char Tree* denotes one attribute picked to be in the condition of possible characteristic rules and each edge is marked with a distinct value of the selected attribute. A sample of *Char Tree* of data in Table 1 is shown in Figure 1.

Definition 2. Given a node, v, on a *Char Tree* $T(V, E, A, DV, L)$, the attributes selected along the path originated from the root is denoted by $S_A(v)$.

$S_A(v) = \bigcup \{L(v_p)\}$, where $v_p \in V$ and v_p is an ancestor of v.

Definition 3. Let v be a node in a *Char Tree* $T(V, E, A, DV, L)$, the negation set of attributes of $S_A(v)$ is defined as $\overline{S_A}(v) = A - S_A(v)$.

Namely, $\overline{S_A}(v)$ represents the unselected attributes which can be chosen at node v.

Definition 4. Given a node, v, in a *Char Tree* $T(V, E, A, DV, L)$, the selected value of v is defined as $S_v(v) = \bigcup \{L(e)\}$, where e represents the edges of the directed path from the root to the node v.

For each edge e of the tree, $L(e)$ represents the restriction of attributes and values from the parent node to its corresponding child node. In Figure 1, $S_v(v_3) = \{a_{2,1}, a_{3,1}\}$

Definition 5. Given a dataset, D, let A_s be a set of attributes and $A_s \neq \emptyset$, the set of all distinct values of the attribute set A_s is defined as follow:

$DV(A_s) = DV(A_j)$, if A_s is a singleton,

$DV(A_s) = \underset{A_j \in A_s}{\textstyle\bigtimes} DV(A_j)$, for others

The result of the **X** operator defined above is a set instead of a vector. Following, the definition of the number of tuples in a dataset on node v of *Char Tree* is described.

Definition 6. Given a dataset, D, a *Char Tree*, T, of D, and a node v in T, the number of records in D which satisfy $S_v(v)$ and also have the value a_s is denoted by $F(D,T,v,a_s)$, where for each subset, A_s, of $\overline{S_A}(v)$:

$$F(D,T,v) = \sum_{a_s \in DV(A_S)} F(D,T,v,a_s)$$

If the occurrence probability of each element in $DV(A_s)$ is uniformly distributed, then attribute A_s can't provide any benefit in summarizing the data. On the other hand, if there is a value, a_s, in $DV(A_s)$ occurs much more frequently than others, then a_s may be a selected value of one characteristic rule in D.

Definition 7. Given a dataset, D, a *Char Tree T of D*, a node v in T as well as an attribute set A_S of D, the *conditional entropy* of attribute set A_S on node v is denoted as: [12]

$$H(A_S|S_v(v)) = -\sum_{a_s \in DV(A_S)} p(a_s|S_v(v)) \log p(a_s|S_v(v)), \text{ where } p(a_s|S_v(v)) = \frac{F(D,T,v,a_s)}{F(D,T,v)}$$

An attribute has the maximal entropy when all distinct values of A_S are uniformly distributed in the database, which is denoted by $H_{max}(A_S) = -\log(1/|DV(A_S)|)$.

Definition 8. Given a dataset, D, a *Char Tree*, T, of D, a node v in T and an attribute set, A_S, of D, the deviation of the value distribution of attribute set A_S from uniform distribution is measured by *Redundancy*, which is denoted as : [12]

$$Redundancy(A_S|S_v(v)) = 1 - \frac{H(A_S|S_v(v))}{H_{max}(A_S|S_v(v))}$$

Redundancy measures the difference between the value distribution of attribute set A_S and uniform distribution. If the *Redundancy of A_S* is close to 1, then some value combinations of attribute set A_S occur much more frequently than others. These value combinations should be chosen as characteristic rules.

$\overline{S_A}(v)$ represents the set of the attributes which can be further used to discern the characteristic rules. However, if occurrence probabilities of all value combinations of $\overline{S_A}(v)$ are uniformly distributed, the remaining unselected attributes can't provide any information to distinguish the characteristic rules.

Definition 9. Given a dataset, D, a *Char Tree*, T, of D, and a node in T, v, the "*Information Loss*" of a node v is denoted as

$$IL(v) = Redundancy(\overline{S_A}(v)|S_v(v)) = 1 - \frac{H(\overline{S_A}(v)|S_v(v))}{H_{max}(\overline{S_A}(v)|S_v(v))}$$

$IL(v)=0$ when the elements of $\overline{S_A}(v)$ are uniformly distributed given $S_v(v)$ in D. In such a case, $\overline{S_A}(v)$ can't provide any valuable information. On the contrary, if $IL(v)>0$, $\overline{S_A}(v)$ can be used to further discriminate the characteristic rules of D.

3.2 The Char Algorithm of Constructing Char Tree

Given a dataset, many characteristic rules may be found. Each of the rules covers certain percentage of the records in the dataset. The proposed *Char Algorithm* allows users to specify the minimum aggregate coverage rate that must be covered by the returned set of characteristic rules. The minimum aggregate percentage is denoted by *Char_threshold*. Hence, if the *Char_threshold* is set to 80%, the characteristic rules found by this algorithm should represent at least 80% characteristics of these records.

When more than one set of characteristic rules satisfy the *Char_threshold* requirement, the set with the minimal number of characteristic rules yet has the largest aggregate coverage rate are returned. To do so, in *Char*, the set of characteristic rules are stored in a sorted list with the descending order of $F(D,T,v)$s. When a new characteristic rule is discovered, the coverage rate of this element is examined against *Char_minC*, the minimum coverage rate a characteristic rule must have to be considered in the returned set. *Char_minC* is set to zero until the first such set of characteristic rules is found. After the set is discovered, *Char_minC* is set to least coverage rate which is the last element in the set. If a newly discovered characteristic rule has larger coverage rate than *Char_minC*, it is inserted into the list; otherwise, the new element is discarded. After the insertion, the algorithm then delete characteristic rules, whose coverage rate are no longer required to fulfill the *Char_threshold*, from the sorted list.

The tree is constructed with depth-first strategy. The root node is created first. For each node, v, that has at least one attribute in $\overline{S_A}(v)$ and $F(D,T,v) > Char\_minC$, the *Redundancy* of every attribute in $\overline{S_A}(v)$ is evaluated and the attribute, A_k with the maximum *Redundancy* is selected as $L(v)$. If $Redundancy(A_k)=0$, $IL(v)$ will be calculated. Under such circumstances, if $IL(v)>0$, choose arbitrary attribute in $\overline{S_A}(v)$ as A_k. For the node v with $Redundancy(A_k)>0$ or $IL(v)>0$, an edge emitted from v is created for each $a \in DV(A_k)$ with $F(D,T,v,a) > Char\_minC$. From left to right, the labels assigned to the new edges are arranged in the descending order of the $F(D,T,v,a)$s. A node will be labeled as "*leaf*", if it meets any of the *leaf* conditions which are (1) $\overline{S_A}(v)=\emptyset$, and (2) $IL(v)=0$. And then, the algorithm checks if the paths leading from the root to the *leaf* node can generate characteristic rules that have enough coverage of underlying data and delete the paths that cannot meet the criteria.

The major steps of the algorithm are listed as follows:

Step 1. Step 1. Create the root node, Set the root node as v, and Set *Char_minC*=0.

Step 2. Step 2. Among the attributes in $\overline{S_A}(v)$, pick A_k with the highest $Redundancy_{(A_k|S_v(v))} > 0$ then label A_k to v. However, if $Redundancy_{(A_k|S_v(v))} = 0$ then goto Step 5.

Step 3. Step 3. For each $a \in DV(A_k)$ with $F(D,T,a,v) > Char\_minC$, create a child node and link an edge from v to the child node as well as mark the label of the edge with $A_k = a$ by the descending order of the $F(D,T,a,v)$s from left to right.

Step 4. Step 4. Choose the next node v in the depth-first traversal order. If all possible nodes have been checked, exit the program.
Step 5. Step 5. If $\overline{S_A}(v)=\emptyset$, label this node as *leaf*, goto Step 7.

  ElseIf $Redundancy_{(A_k|S_v(v))}=0$ then calculate $IL(v)$.

  If $IL(v)=0$, label the node as *leaf* and goto Step 7. Else goto Step 6.
Else goto step 2
Step 6. Step 6. Choose an arbitrary attribute $A_k \in \overline{S_A}(v)$, designated A_k as the node v, goto Step 3.
Step 7. Put the v into a sorted list, H, in the descending order of $F(D,T,v)$.
Step 8. If $\sum_{S_v(v) \in H} F(D,T,v) \geq |D| * Char\_threshold$, then

  Find the node v' in H such that
  $$\sum_{\substack{v > v' \\ H}} F(D,T,v) < |D|*Char\_threshold \quad \text{and} \quad \sum_{\substack{v \geq v' \\ H}} F(D,T,v') \geq |D| * Char\_threshold$$
  adjust Char_minC to $F(D,T,v')$
EndIf
goto Step 4.

Table 3. Description of Attributes.

Attr.	Description	# of Values	Distribution
A1	Age	3	Normal
A2	Gender	2	Normal
A3	Age	3	Uniform
A4	Hobby	5	Uniform
A5	Occupation	5	Normal
A6	Marital status	3	Normal
A7	Education level	3	Normal
A8	Make of the car	3	Normal
A9	Values of the house	3	Normal

4 Experimental Results

In this section, firstly, through 45 experiments on 15 datasets with some attributes values normally distributed, we would like to demonstrate the numbers of characteristic rules discovered are fairly few compared to the possible characteristic rules, and the numbers of characteristic rules found are stable when the numbers of tuples and attributes increase.

The datasets used in the section are derived from the modification of well-known synthetic data proposed in [9][10][11]. Nine potential attributes are generated with two have uniformly distributed values and seven have normally distributed values. The attribute definitions are in Table 3.

Table 4. The numbers of characteristic rules found.

Schema1 (possible characteristic rules 1728)				Schema2 (possible characteristic rules 27648)				Schema3 (possible characteristic rules 663552)			
size	70%	75%	80%	size	70%	75%	80%	size	70%	75%	80%
2k	15	21	28	15k	15	22	56	200k	139	181	470
4k	5	5	8	25k	15	18	22	400k	139	174	221
6k	5	5	6	30k	15	18	22	600k	139	174	220
8k	5	5	6	50k	15	18	22	800k	138	173	219
10k	5	5	6	100k	15	18	22	1kk	138	173	219

Three schemas are used to generate fifteen datasets. The schemas are composed of five, seven and nine attributes, respectively. Each schema is materialized with five datasets. Each dataset is evaluated by *Char* three times, with *Char_threshold* set at 70%, 75% and 80% respectively. The experimental results are listed in Table 4.

From Table 4, readers can observe that the number of characteristic rules generated for each data set is fairly stable and does not grow with the number of records. Therefore, it is clear that if combinations of attributes and values of the given datasets are not uniformly distributed, *Char* can discover them consistently. Three found rules with quantitative measures in Schema1 are listed as follows:

Rule 1: Customers with $\{a_{21}, a_{13}, a_{53}\}$ are likely to buy Plasma TV. (26.25%)
Rule 2: Customers with $\{a_{21}, a_{13}, a_{52}\}$ are likely to buy Plasma TV. (16.2%)
Rule 3: Customers with $\{a_{21}, a_{12}, a_{53}\}$ are likely to buy Plasma TV. (11.6%)

Table 5. The percentage of characteristic rules found in DataSets.

	Schema1	Schema2	Schema3
Possible characteristic rules	1,728	27,648	663,552
Char threshold=70%	0.2894%	0.0543%	0.0208%
Char threshold=75%	0.2894%	0.0651%	0.0261%
Char threshold=80%	0.3472%	0.0796%	0.033%

The significance of *Char* is further elaborated with the result of Schema2 in Table 4. The number of possible characteristic rules for Schema2 is 27,648(=(3+1)*(2+1)*(3+1)*(5+1)*(5+1)*(3+1)*(3+1)), *Char* discovers 15, 18 and 22 characteristic rules when *Char_threshold* =70%, 75% and 80%, respectively. In the case of *Char_threshold* = 75%, 18 rules (only 0.0651% of possible rules) can describe 75% customers' characteristics. The other 99.9349% rules descr-ibe only 25% of tuples in the dataset. The percentages of characteristic rules discove-red by *Char* are listed in Table 5.

From Table 5, readers can find that as the number of attributes increases, the number of possible characteristic rules increases dramatically, but the number of characteristic rules found by *Char* increases much slowly. Meanwhile, it also shows that the percentage of characteristic rules decreases when the number of attributes increases. Hence the characteristics rules of the given data set are discovered effectively by *Char*.

In addition to performing experiments on synthetic data, three experiments on the member table of a real mid-size chain supermarket are also performed. The table has 12 attributes, including *CardNumber*, *CustomerName*, *Sex*, *BirthDate*, *Address*, *No_Family_Member*, *Occupation*, *EducationLevel*, *MaritalStatus*, *DistantToStore*, *AgeLevel*, and *ApplyDate*. To find the demographic description of the members, five irrelevant attributes, namely, attributes, *CardNumber*, *CustomerName*, *BirthDate*, *Address* and *ApplyDate*, are excluded. The table has 158,392 records with possible rule space of 117,600. The three experiments set *Char_threshold* to 70%, 75% and 80%, respectively and the percentage of discovered characteristic rules take only 0.33%, 0.43% and 0.56% of the space. This means that 0.33% of the rules in the rule space can describe 70% of the members.

Finally, 10 independent datasets, each with five attributes and 500,000 records, are also generated. The attributes of the datasets are randomly picked from the nine attributes listed in the Table 3 of the paper. The datasets are fed to *Char* with *Char_threshold* = 80%, and the percentages of rule found by *Char* are 0.87%, 0.69%, 0.75%, 0.26%, 0.75%, 0.87%, 1.13%, 1.04%, 0.87% and 0.52%.

5 Conclusions

In this paper, we investigate a new approach for generating characteristic rules for knowledge discovery in databases. Our approach bases on the concept of the *Redundancy* and constructs the *Char Tree* to generate the characteristic rules. The proposed algorithm provides an easy and effective way to perform the specialization task on the whole possible characteristics.

The *Char Algorithm* needs only one threshold (*Char_threshold*) which can be set intuitively by any user. It is used effectively to distinguish the most important characteristics from thousands or millions or even more possible rules. As described in Section 1, this method has many applications in practice. Furthermore, it can be used to generate discrimination rules between different databases. We may also apply this new method to discover the data evolution regularities.

This algorithm is by no means perfect and still has rooms for extension. For example, in each node of *Char Tree*, the *Char* examines the *Redundancy* of single attributes. In the future, *Char* can be extended to consider a set of attributes in each node. The extension can help to discover characteristic rules with the highest redundancy. However, to grip the benefit without paying too much performance cost, the *Char* will need to be further refined.

Acknowledgement

This study is supported by the MOE Program for Promoting Academic Excellence of Universities: Electronic Commerce Environment, Technology Development, and Application (Project Number: 91-H-FA08-1-4).

References

1. G. Piatetsky-Shapiro and W. J. Fayyad, and P. Smith, From data mining to knowledge discovery: An overview. In U.M. Fayyad, F. Piatetsky-Shapiro, P. Smyth, and R. Uthurusamy, editors, Advances in knowledge Discovery and Data Mining, page 1-35. 1996, AAAI/MIT Press.
2. M.-S. Chen, J. Han and P. S. Yu, Data Mining: An Overview from a Database Perspective. IEEE Transactions on Knowledge and Data Engineering, 8(6): 866-883, 1996.
3. R. Agrawal, I. Imielinski, and A. Swami, Mining association rules between sets of items in large databases. In Proc. of 1993 ACM-SIGMOD Int. Conf. Management of Data (SIGMOD'93), pages 207-216, May 1993, Washington, DC.
4. R. S. Michalski, J. G. Carbonell, and T. M. Mitchell, Machine Learning: An Artificial Intelligence Approach, Vol. 1. San Mateo, CA: Morgan Kaufmann, 1983.
5. J. Han, M. Kamber, Data Mining: Concepts and Techniques, San Francisco, CA: Morgan Kaufmann, 2001.
6. A. Gupta, V. Harinarayan, and D. Quass. Aggregate-Query processing in data warehousing environment. In Proc. 21st Int. Conf. Very Large Data Bases. Pages 358-369, Zurich, Switzerland, Sept. 1995.
7. V. Harinarayan, J.D. Ullman, and A. Rajaraman. Implementing data cubes efficiently. In proc. 1996 Int'l Conf. on Data Mining and Knowledge Discovery (KDD'96) Portland, Oregon, August 1996.
8. J. R. Quinlan. Induction of decision trees. Machine Learning, 1:81-106, 1986.
9. R. Agrawal, T. Imielinski, & A. Swami, Database mining: a performance perspective. IEEE Transactions on knowledge and Data Engineering, 5(6), 1993, 914-925
10. J. C. Shafer, R. Agrawal, & M. Mehta, SPRINT: A scalable parallel classifier for data mining. Proceedings of the 22nd International Conference on Very Large Databaes (pp.514-555). 1996, Mumbai(Bombay), India.
11. M. Wang, B. Iyer, & J.S. Vitter, Scalable mining for classification rules in relation databases. Proceedings of International Database Engineering and Applications Symposium(pp. 58-67). 1998, Cardiff, Wales, UK
12. David J.C. MaCay, Information Theory, Inference, Learning Algorithms. The 6th edition, Cambridge University Press, September 2003.
13. J. Han and Y. Fu. Dynamic generation and refinement of concept hierarchies for knowledge discovery in databases. In Proc. AAAI'94 Workshop on Knowledge Discovery in Databases (KDD'94), pages 158-168, Seattle, WA, July 1994.
14. J. Han and Y. Fu. Exploration of the power of attribute-oriented induction in data mining, In U.M. Fayyad, G. Piatetsky-Shapiro, P. Smyth, and R. Uthurusamy, editors, Advances in Knowledge Discovery and Data Ming, pages 399-421. AAAI/MIT Press, 1996.

Two Methods for Automatic 3D Reconstruction from Long Un-calibrated Sequences

Yoon-Yong Jeong, Bo-Ra Seok, Yong-Ho Hwang, and Hyun-Ki Hong

Dept. of Image Eng., Graduate School of Advanced Imaging Science, Multimedia and Film
Chung-Ang Univ., 221 Huksuk-dong, Dongjak-ku, Seoul, 156-756, Korea
{kburngae,hwangyongho}@hotmail.com, qalito@yahoo.co.kr,
honghk@cau.ac.kr

Abstract. This paper presents two methods for automatic 3D reconstruction: the one is a quantitative measure for frame grouping over long un-calibrated sequences, and the other is 3D reconstruction algorithm based on projective invariance. The first method evaluates the duration of corresponding points over sequence, the homography error, and the distribution of correspondences in the image. By making efficient bundles, we can overcome the limitation of the factorization, which is the assumption that all correspondences must remain in all views. In addition, we use collinearity among invariant properties in projective space to refine the projective matrix. That means any points located on the 2D imaged line must lie on the reconstructed projective line. Therefore, we regard the points unsatisfying collinearity as outliers, which are caused by a false feature tracking. After fitting a new 3D line from projective points, we iteratively obtain more precise projective matrix by using the points that are the orthogonal projection of outliers onto the line. Experimental results showed our methods can recover efficiently 3D structure from un-calibrated sequences.

1 Introduction

3D reconstruction and camera recovery from un-calibrated image sequences have long been one of the central topics in computer vision. Building 3D models of outdoor scenes, which are widely used in virtual environment and augmented reality, has always been a difficult problem [1~3]. This paper aims at automated 3D reconstruction for multi-view pose and geometry estimation over long sequences.

Obtaining a projective reconstruction of a scene is the first step towards affine or metric reconstruction, and it is classified into the merging-based method and the factorization [3]. In general, merging algorithms are reliant on a good initial estimate of structure, and are also susceptible to drift over long sequences. Since factorization methods calculate all camera projection matrices and structure at the same time, they suffer less from drift and error accumulation. However, the factorization is hard to analyze precisely long sequences because it is based on the assumption that all correspondences must remain in all views from the first frame to the last [4,5].

In order to overcome the limitation of the factorization, we present a quantitative measure based on the number of matching points between frames, the homography error, and the distribution of matching points in the image. The full sequence is segmented efficiently into sub-sequences that is suitable for projective reconstruction. All of projective reconstructions in sub-sequences are registered into the same coordinate frame, and we reject the projective matrix with large errors among the obtained matrices based on LMedS (Least median of square). Finally, we can obtain a precise absolute quadric, and reconstruct the scene structure [6].

As features are tracked over images, they may be lost due to poor localization by the tracking algorithm, or because they move beyond the frame boundary. The unavoidable outliers inherent in the given correspondence matches may severely disturb projective estimation. Although many approaches to automatic 3D reconstruction were proposed, no studies have ever tried to remove the outliers and estimate more precise projective matrix by using geometric invariance in the projective space. This paper presents a novel 3D reconstruction based on projective invariance from uncalibrated sequences.

In order to cope with the effects by the outliers, we regard the points unsatisfying collinearity as erroneous outliers, which are caused by a false feature tracking. Obtaining points on the projective space from images is followed by refinement of the projective matrix. In this process, we select any points satisfying collinearity in the projective space to refine the projective matrix. This work is targeted on architectural scenes with a polyhedral shape.

2 Previous Studies on 3D Reconstruction

One of classical methods for 3D analysis of scenes is a stereoscopic system based on camera calibration [7]. However, the method has difficult in dealing with a large number of images because strong calibration process for many cameras, which is complex and difficult process, is needed. Recently auto-calibration algorithms have been actively researched to avoid calibrating the camera and the object in the scene, because pre-procedures for calibration have a couple of limitations. Automatic methods can estimate camera parameters and 3D positions by using self-calibration. Table 1 summarizes classification of previous methods for camera and scene recovery.

Table 1. Previous methods for camera and scene recovery.

Images	Previous methods	Camera Calibration	User Input
Stereo images	T.Kanade & M.Okutomi [9]	Strong	Auto
Image sequence	P.Debevec & J.Malik [10]	No (User Input)	Interactive design
	S.Gibson [11]	Auto-calibration	Semi-automatic (User input for modeling VE)
	T.Sato [12]	Weak (prior intrinsic parameters)	Auto (multiple baseline stereo)
	A.Zisserman [1], S.Gibson [3], A. Heyden [13]	Auto-calibration	Auto

3 Proposed Methods for Automatic 3D Reconstruction

3.1 Projective Reconstruction

Factorization methods recover 3D structure and camera motion from m un-calibrated images of a scene containing 3D points of n. Let X_p ($p = 1, \ldots, n$) be the unknown homogeneous 3D point vectors, P_i ($i = 1, \ldots, m$) the unknown 3×4 image projections, and x_{ip} the measured homogeneous image point vectors, respectively. Modulo some scale factors λ_{ip}, called projective depths, the image points are projected from the world points as:

$$\lambda_{ij} x_{ij} = P_i X_j \qquad (1)$$

Using the point projections derives a single $3m \times n$ matrix equation. The Singular Value Decomposition (SVD) can factorize the rescaled measure matrix and estimate camera and structure information. For application of the factorization method over long sequences, we derive a new quantitative measure to break the full sequence into sub-sequences. The goal of our measure is to determine frame groups that are suitable for multi-view pose and geometry estimation based on the factorization.

3.2 Quantitative Measure for Frame Grouping

Correspondences between the first frame and the successive frames gradually diminish as the frame number grows over video sequence. The number of corresponding points on both the first and the second frame in the sequence, N_f is used for frame grouping. At the first, we examine how many corresponding points on the first pair remain on the successive frames as:

$$N_r = \left(1 - \frac{N_m}{N_f}\right), \qquad (2)$$

where N_m is the number of correspondences between neighboring frames.

In general, the motion between frames has to be fairly small so that a precise correspondence can be established by using automatic matching, while significant parallax and large baseline is desirable for 3D analysis [3]. The homography error (H_{err}) is used to evaluate the baseline length between two views. In addition, it means how many feature points are distributed on a planar surface. If corresponding points are distributed on many surfaces, it is difficult to establish one-to-one correspondences due to self-occlusion, so the homography error increases. In other words, the greater homography error is, the more precise 3D reconstruction is achieved. In Eq. (3) for the homography error, x_i and $x_i{'}$ are corresponding points on two views, N and H are the total number of corresponding points and the homography, respectively.

$$H_{err} = \frac{1}{N}\sum_{i=1}^{N} d(x_i, H'_{x_i}). \qquad (3)$$

If corresponding points are evenly distributed on the image, we can obtain a more precise fundamental matrix [14]. Since the fundamental matrix contains all available information of the camera motion, the use of evenly distributed points improves motion and camera estimation results. To evaluate the degree of the point distribution in the image, we divide the entire image uniformly into sub-regions based on the number of corresponding points, and then calculate the point density of sub-region and that of the image. Standard deviation of the point density to represent the distribution of correspondences:

$$\sigma_p = \sqrt{\frac{1}{N}\sum_{i=1}^{N}\left(\frac{N_{S_i}}{A_s} - \frac{N}{A}\right)^2}, \qquad (4)$$

where N and N_{S_i} are the total number of corresponding points, and that in the ith region. A and A_s are the area of the image and that of each sub-region, respectively.

We define a new quantitative measure based on the above considerations:

$$S = \omega_1 N_r + \omega_2 \left(\frac{1}{H_{err}}\right) + \omega_3 \sigma_p, \qquad (5)$$

where S and ω_n are the score for grouping frames and the relative weights for each term, respectively. If S is above the threshold value, a new sub-sequence is generated. The full sequence is divided into several sub-sequences, and then we register the projective matrix of each sub-sequence.

Since there is a homography between camera projective matrices of two groups, they can be merged in a projective space [1]. In order to proceed from projective matrix to a complete description of the scene, we need to register all projective relations into the same coordinate frame. In auto-calibration, absolute dual quadric (ADQ) is estimated from projective reconstruction to recover metric structure of the views. We iterate LMedS based sampling and compute residuals, then find ADQ with minimum median residual for rejection of the key-frames causing ADQ estimation to fail. After ADQ is re-estimated from the camera matrix set, we recover camera matrices of the rejected frames by using the camera resection, and reconstruct finally the scene structure [6].

3.3 3D Reconstruction Based on Projective Invariance

This paper presents a novel 3D reconstruction based on collinearity among invariant properties in projective space. Since collinearity is preserved in projective space, any points located on the 3D line must lie on the projected 2D line. Obtaining points in the projective space from images is followed by refinement of the projective matrix. In this process, only the points satisfying collinearity are selected instead of the reconstructed point in the projective space. This work is targeted on architectural scenes with a polyhedral shape. Because many man-made objects are constructed by using predefined rules, they often have many line segments.

At the first, we apply Canny edge operator for detection of the 2D line, and then select the feature points on the line. After these points are reconstructed in the projective space, we make 3D line fitting from the projective points. More specifically, any points located on the 2D line should be on the reconstructed projective line. In order to remove outliers that occurred in a false feature tracking, we determine whether the points satisfy collinearity in the projective space. Our algorithm obtains the points that are the orthogonal projection of outliers onto the line, and then we compute iteratively the projective matrix by using the points.

4 Experimental Results

The proposed algorithm is compared with the merging method on the real images. The number of frames and the image size are 20 and 800×600. Fig. 1 shows five frames among the Bear images and the 3D model, respectively. Our method divides the sequence into two groups and registers projective relations directly. Fig. 2 presents comparison of accumulation errors of camera parameters. The sequential merging algorithm is dependent on an initial estimate of structure, and the error is propagated more and more over time. Comparison results show that the proposed method can estimate more precisely camera parameters, and thence reconstruct more robust 3D model as the frame number increases. The merging method estimates projective matrices from all of the views in order, while the proposed algorithm achieves projective reconstruction at a time on each group. Our reconstruction times are less than 20 seconds, and those of the previous 43 seconds. Therefore, our method has more computational efficiency than the merging method. Fig. 3 represents that the proposed algorithm based on collinearity achieves a more precise 3D reconstruction model than the merging method.

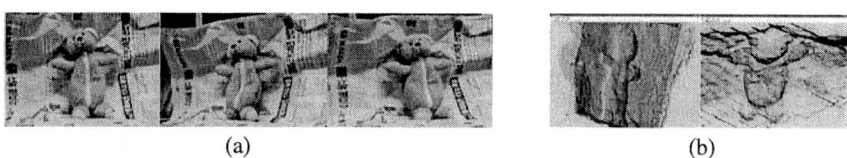

(a)   (b)

Fig. 1. (a) Bear images (1, 9, and 17 frame) (b) reconstructed 3D model.

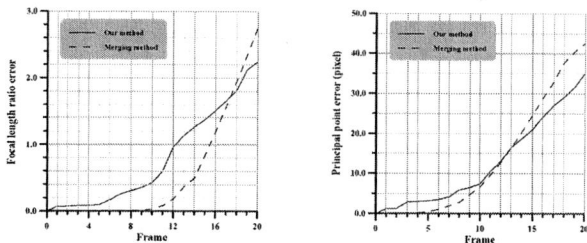

Fig. 2. Comparison of accumulation error of camera parameters.

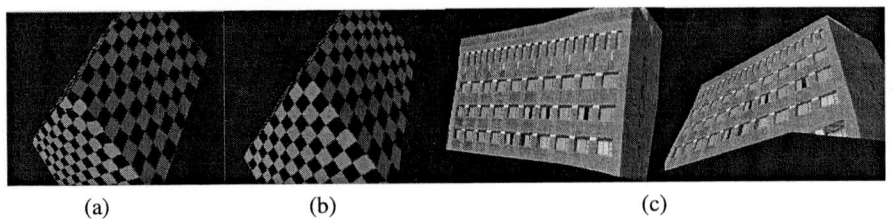

Fig. 3. 3D reconstruction model by (a) merging method (b) and (c) the proposed algorithm.

5 Conclusion

This paper proposes a novel frame grouping measure over long un-calibrated sequences to overcome the limitation of the factorization. Furthermore, we use collinearity among invariant properties in projective space to refine the projective matrix. Experimental results demonstrated that our algorithms can recover more precise 3D structure than previous methods. Further study will include another geometric invariance in projective space.

Acknowledgment

This research was supported by the Ministry of Education, Korea, and under the BK21 project, and the Ministry of Science and Technology, Korea, under the NRL(2000-N-NL-01-C-285) project.

References

1. A.W. Fitzgibbon and A. Zisserman, "Automatic camera recovery for closed or open image sequences," *In proc. of 6th European Conference on Computer Vision*, June 3 (1998) 311-326
2. K. Cornelis, M. Pollefeys, M. Vergauwen, and L. V. Gool, "Augmented reality from un-calibrated video sequences," *In proc. SMILE 2000, Lecture Notes in Computer Science*, 2018, (2001) 144-160
3. S. Gibson, J. Cook, T. Howard, R. Hubbold, and D. Oram, "Accurate camera calibration for off-line, video-based augmented reality," *In proc. IEEE and ACM ISMAR*, Darmstadt, Germany, Sep. (2002)
4. A. Chiuso, P. Favaro, H. Jin, and S. Soatto, "Motion and structure causally integrated over time," *IEEE Trans. on Pattern Matching and Machine Intelligence*, 24(4), (2002) 523-535
5. P. Sturm and B. Triggs, "A factorization based algorithm for multi-image projective structure and motion," *In proc. of 4th European Conference on Computer Vision*. Cambridge, England, April, (1996) 709-720
6. R. Hartley and A. Zisserman, *Mutiple View Geometry in Computer Vision*, Cambrige Univ. Press. (2000)

7. Z. Zhang, "Computing rectifying homographies for stereo vision," *In proc. of IEEE CVPR*, Fort Collins Colorado, June (1999) 125-131
8. S. S. Intille and A. F. Bobick, "Disparity-space images and large occlusion stereo," *2nd European Conference on Computer Vision*, Stockholm Sweden (1994) 179-186
9. D. Kanade and M. Okutomi, "A stereo matching algorithm with an adaptive window: theory and experiment," *IEEE Transactions of Pattern Anal. Machine Intell.*, 16(9), (1994) 920-932
10. P. Debecec, C. Taylor, and J. Malik, "Modeling and rendering architecture from photos: a hybrid geometry and image-base approach," *In proc. of SIGGRAPH 96*, (1996) 11-20
11. S. Gibson, R. J. Hubbold, J. Cook, and T. Howard, "Interactive reconstruction of virtual environments from video sequences," *Computer Graphics*, 27, (2003) 293-301
12. T. Sato, M. Kanbara, N. Yokoya, and H. Takemura, "Dense 3-D reconstruction of outdoor scene by hundreds-baseline stereo using a hand-held video camera," *In proc. of IEEE Workshop on Stereo and Multi-baseline vision*, (2001)
13. A. Heyden, R. Berthilsson, and G. Sparr, "An iterative factorization method for projective structure and motion from image sequences," *Image and Vision Computing* (1999) 981-991
14. R. Hartley, "In Defence of the 8-Point algorithm," *In proc. IEEE ICCV*, (1995) 1064-1070

Wrapper for Ranking Feature Selection*

Roberto Ruiz, Jesús S. Aguilar-Ruiz, and José C. Riquelme

Departamento de Lenguajes y Sistemas, Universidad de Sevilla
Avda. Reina Mercedes /N. 41012 Sevilla, España
{rruiz,aguilar,riquelme}@lsi.us.es

Abstract. We propose a new feature selection criterion not based on calculated measures between attributes, or complex and costly distance calculations. Applying a wrapper to the output of a new attribute ranking method, we obtain a minimum subset with the same error rate as the original data. The experiments were compared to two other algorithms with the same results, but with a very short computation time.

1 Introduction

Feature selection methods can be grouped into two categories from the point of view of a method's output. One category is about ranking feature according to same evaluation criterion; the other is about choosing a minimum set of features that satisfies an evaluation criterion. There are several taxonomies of these evaluation measures in previous work, depending on different criterions: Langley [1] group evaluation functions into two categories: filter and wrapper. Blum y Langley [2] provide a classification of evaluation functions into four groups, depending on the relation between the selection and the induction process: embedded, filter, wrapper, weight. Another different classification, Doak [3] and Dash [4] provide a classification of evaluation measure based on their general characteristics more than in the relation with the induction process. The classification realized by Dash, shows five different types of measures: distance, information, dependence, consistency y accuracy.

In this paper, we propose a new feature selection criterion not based on calculated measures between attributes, or complex and costly distance calculations. This criterion is based on a unique value called NLC. It relates each attribute with the label used for classification. This value is calculated by projecting data set elements onto the respective axis of the attribute (ordering the examples by this attribute), then crossing the axis from the beginning to the greatest attribute value, and counting the Number of Label Changes (NLC) produced.

All filter methods use heuristics based on general characteristics to evaluate the merit of a feature or a features' subsets. However, the wrappers include the learning algorithm as a part of their evaluation function. Wrappers usually provide better accuracy but are computationally more expensive than the Filter

---

* This work has been supported by the Spanish Research Agency CICYT under grant TIC2001-1143-C03-02.

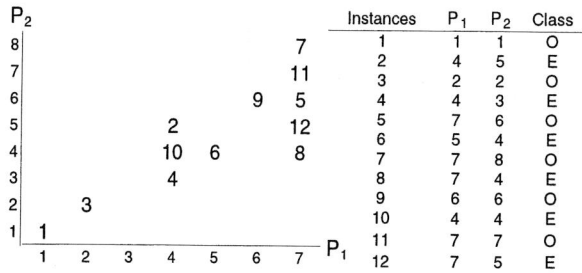

Fig. 1. Data set with twelve elements and two classes (Even,Odd)

schemes. In our algorithm, we want to take advantage of the two methods. The ranked list of features sorted according to each NLC is produced. The Starting point is the empty set, and we add features from the list sequentially in the same order. The features are added depending on whether or not they increase the performance of the learner.

2 Number of Label Changes (NLC)

2.1 Definitions

To describe the definitions below, let us consider the situation depicted in Figure 1, with twelve elements numbered and two labels (O-odd numbers and E-even numbers).

Definition 1. *Let the attribute P_j be a continuous or discrete variable that takes values in $A_j = [a_j, b_j] \subseteq \mathbb{R}$ if it is a continuous attribute, and if it is a discrete attribute, let A_j be a set of possible values. Let Ω be a set of m attributes.*

In Figure 1, P_1 and P_2 are continuous attributes, $A_1 = [1,7]$, $A_2 = [1,8]$ and $\Omega = \{P_1, P_2\}$.

Definition 2. *Let Λ be a set of discrete labels.*

In Figure 1, $\Lambda = \{E, O\}$ depending on the instance number.

Definition 3. *An example e is a tuple of values $(p_1, p_2, \ldots, p_m, l) \in A_1 \times \cdots \times A_m \times \Lambda$ where p_j is the value of the attribute P_j. If P_j is continuous $p_j \in [a_j, b_j]$. If P_j is discrete $p_j \in A_j$. $l \in \Lambda$ is the label of e. Let E be the set of all examples in the training set. Therefore, $E \subseteq A_1 \times \cdots \times A_m \times \Lambda$. Let n be the cardinal of E.*

In Figure 1, E is the table on the right, and $e_5 = (7, 6, O)$.

Definition 4. *We define the functions π_j, $\forall j : 1..m$ and lab.*

$$\pi_j : E \to A_j \quad \pi_j(e) = p_j \quad \wedge \tag{1}$$
$$lab : E \to \Lambda \quad lab(e) = l \tag{2}$$

In Figure 1,

$$\pi_1(e_1) = 1 \quad \forall i : 1..12 \; \pi_1(e_i) = \{1, 4, 2, 4, 7, 5, 7, 7, 6, 4, 7, 7\}$$
$$lab(e_1) = O \; \forall i : 1..12 \; lab(e_i) = \{O, E, O, E, O, E, O, E, O, E, O, E\}$$

Definition 5. *Let $\sigma_j(E) = < e_1, \ldots, e_n >$ be an ordered sequence of E by the attribute j, then we say that there is a multiple ordered subsequence (m.o.s.) and we denote S if*

$$\exists \, i, k > 0 \; / \; e_{i-1} <_j e_i =_j \cdots =_j e_{i+k} <_j e_{i+k+1} \tag{3}$$

being the m.o.s. $S = < e_i, \ldots, e_{i+k} >$ (if $i = 1$ the first condition is removed) A majority label of an m.o.s., $ml(S)$, is the mode of de set $\{lab(e_j)\}_{j=i+1}^{k}$.

m.o.s. in Figure 1 are:
$S = < e_4, e_{10}, e_2 >$ is an m.o.s. by the attribute P_1, because the examples e_4, e_{10} and e_2 have the same value (4) for P_1. $ml(S) = E$ because all the examples are even numbers.

Definition 6. *Let $\sigma_j(E) = < e_1, \ldots, e_n >$ be an ordered sequence of E by the attribute j, then we say that there is a simple ordered subsequence (s.o.s.) and we denote S if*

$$\exists \, i, k > 0 \; / \; e_{i-1} =_j e_i <_j e_{i+1} <_j \cdots <_j e_{i+k-1} <_j e_{i+k} =_j e_{i+k+1} \tag{4}$$

being the s.o.s. $S = < e_{i+1}, e_{i+2}, \ldots, e_{i+k-1} >$ (if $i = 1$ the first condition is removed) The instance e_{i+1} is called first example, $fe(S)$, and e_{i+k-1} last example $le(S)$.

s.o.s. in Figure 1 are:
$S = < e_1, e_3 >$ is an s.o.s. by the attribute P_1, because the examples e_1 and e_3 have different values (1 and 2) for P_1. $fe(S) = e_1$ and $le(S) = e_3$.

Theorem 1. *Given an ordered sequence of examples $\sigma_j(E)$ by an attribute j, it can be divided into subsequences where there is an s.o.s., or a m.o.s., or a sequence of the subsequences of one after the other. We take into account that one m.o.s. always comes after an s.o.s., but after an m.o.s. an s.o.s. or an m.o.s. can come In general, $\sigma_j(E) = S_1, S_2, \ldots, S_r$ where if S_i is an s.o.s. then S_{i+1} is m.o.s., and if S_i is an m.o.s., then S_{i+1} can be an s.o.s. or m.o.s.*

Definition 7. *Given an ordered sequence S of k examples $S = < e_1, e_2, \ldots, e_k >$ we define the function $ch : S - \{e_k\} \rightarrow \{0, 1\}$*

$$ch(e_i) = \begin{cases} 1 \; si & lab(e_i) \neq lab(e_{i+1}) \\ 0 \; si & lab(e_i) = lab(e_{i+1}) \end{cases} \quad \forall i : 1 \ldots (k{-}1) \tag{5}$$

In Figure 1, for P_2, in the s.o.s. $S = < e_1, e_3, e_4 >$:

$$ch(e_1) = 0 \quad \text{because } lab(e_1) = lab(e_3)$$
$$ch(e_3) = 1 \quad \text{because } lab(e_3) \neq lab(e_4)$$

Table 1. Main Algorithm

```
Input: E training (n examples, m attributes)
Output: E reduced (n examples, k attributes)
   for each attribute P_j ∈ Ω
      QuickSort(E,j)
      NLC(j)
   Attribute Ranking
   S ← "first-f (first ranked att.)"
   F ← "initial set of n features - first-f"
   Calculate ER (Error Rate) with S
   repeat until F = "empty set"
      if ER with S ⋃ first-f > √ ER with S
         S ← S ⋃ first-f
      F ← F - first-f
```

Definition 8. *Given a set E of examples, $\sigma_j(E)$ the ordered sequence by the attribute j and $S_1 \ldots S_r$, we define the function $NLC : \Omega \to \mathbb{N}$*

$$NLC(j) = \sum_{i=1}^{r} nch(S_i) \qquad (6)$$

In Figure 1, $\sigma_1(E) = S_1, S_2, S_3, S_4$, where $S_1 = <e_1, e_3>$, $S_2 = <e_4, e_{10}, e_2>$, $S_3 = <e_6, e_9>$, $S_4 = <e_8, e_{12}, e_5, e_{11}, e_7>$ with $nch(S_1) = 1$, $nch(S_2) = 0$, $nch(S_3) = 1$, $nch(S_4) = 4 \Rightarrow NLC(P_1) = 6$. We also obtain $NLC(P_2) = 2$.

3 Algorithm

The algorithm is very simple and fast (Table 1). It has the capacity to operate with continuous and discrete variables as well as with databases which have two classes or multiple classes.

There are two phases in the algorithm: Firstly, the attributes are ranked. For each attribute, the training-set is ordered and we count the NLC throughout the ordered projected sequence. In the second place, we deal with the list of attributes one time. We obtain the Naive Bayes [5] error rate with the first attribute in the list and it is marked as selected. We obtain the Naive Bayes [5] error rate again with the first and the second attributes. The second will be marked as selected depending on the accuracy obtained is significatively better ($> \sqrt{}$). Next step is classify again with the marked attributes and the next attribute on the list, and it will be marked depending on the accuracy obtained. Repeat the process until the last attribute on the ranked list is reached.

4 Experiments

In this section we compare the quality of selected attributes by the NCL measure with the selected attributes by the other two methods: Information Gain (IG)

Table 2. Accuracy of attribute selection with C4.5, 1NN and naive Bayes

DATA SET	C4.5			1NN			NAIVE		
	NLC	RLF	IG	NLC	RLF	IG	NLC	RLF	IG
ANNEAL	87.99 × ×	93.65	94.31	88.09 × ×	94.54	94.88	86.86 × ×	91.64	92.87
BALANCE	78.39	78.39	78.39	86.88	86.88	86.88	88.81	88.81	88.81
G_CREDIT	70.30	71.20	71.70	63.60 ×	69.70	70.60	69.80 ×	71.20	72.40
DIABET.	74.87	75.65	75.65	69.80	68.76	68.76	76.03	76.55	76.55
GLASS	58.07	63.51	61.75	55.63	60.80	57.08	51.06	49.16	47.25
GLASS2	78.49 √	64.85	77.83	76.54	67.32	74.89	73.60 √	62.50	73.64
HEART-S	74.44	76.67	72.22	71.48	73.70	69.26	73.33	75.93	71.48
IONOSPH	87.16	90.02	89.73	87.45	88.02	87.44	87.73	89.15	88.88
IRIS	92.00	93.33	93.33	92.67	94.67	91.33	92.67	94.67	92.67
KR-VS	94.27	94.27	94.27	94.27	94.27	94.27	94.27	94.27	94.27
LYMPH	74.95	71.62	74.95	74.29	70.95	74.95	74.95	72.29	74.95
SEGMENT	96.75 √	95.89	96.54	96.71	97.01	96.84	88.61 √	85.71	89.48
SONAR	70.67	68.83	72.10	62.45	65.83	65.31	72.05	72.17	72.52
SPLICE-2	93.92	93.70	93.95	87.99	88.12	87.59	94.14	94.08	93.89
VEHICLE	64.87	59.57	63.23	60.27	54.84	56.62	47.53 √	50.83	45.52
VOWEL	77.37	74.85	78.38	94.04 √	87.58	94.75	63.23 √	60.30	63.64
WAVE	77.78 √	76.38	77.52	78.26 √	75.74	78.14	81.84 √	80.62	81.96
ZOO	85.18	87.09	88.18	85.18	87.09	88.18	84.18	86.18	84.18

and the ReliefF method [6]. The quality of each selected attribute was tested by means of three classifiers: the Naive Bayes [5], C4.5 [7] and 1-NN [8].

The implementation of the induction algorithms and the others selectors was done using the Weka library [9] and the comparison was performed with eighteen databases of the University from California Irvine [10]. The measures were estimated taking the mean of a ten-fold cross validation, and the same folds were used for each algorithm training-sets. To asses the obtained results, two paired t statistical tests with a confidence level of 95% were realized.

In order to establish the number of attributes in each case, we deal with the list of attributes once. We obtain the Naive Bayes error rate with the first attribute in the list and it is marked as selected. We obtain the Naive Bayes error rate again with the first and the second attributes. The second will be marked as selected depending on whether the accuracy obtained is significantly better. The next step is to classify again, with the marked attributes, and the next attribute on the list. Then it will be marked depending on the accuracy obtained. Repeat the process until the last attribute on the ranked list is reached.

Table 2 shows a summary of the results of the classification using C4.5, 1NN and NB. The table shows how often each method performs significantly better (denoted by √) or worse (denoted by ×) than ReliefF (RLF) and Information Gain (IG). In ten of the one hundred and eight cases, the set of attributes selected by the NLC measure yields better accuracy than the two other methods. In ninety they are equal, and in eight they are worse than the other. Only in AN-NEAL and GERMAN_CREDIT the accuracy is lower than the other methods, but the number of attributes selected is significantly better in both cases.

Algorithms reach a similar percentage of the original features retained (24% NLC, 22% RLF and 25%IG).

5 Conclusions

In this paper we present a deterministic attribute selection algorithm. It is a very efficient and simple method used in the preprocessing phase. A considerable reduction of the number of attributes is produced. It does not need distance nor statistical calculations, which could be very costly in time (correlation, gain of information, etc.). The computational cost to obtain the ranked list is lower than other methods $O(m \times n \times \log n)$. NLC takes 0.792 seconds in reducing 18 data sets whereas ReliefF takes 566 seconds and IG 2.19 seconds.

We conclude that by applying NLC, the knowledge attained in the original training file is conserved into the reduced training file, and the dimensionality of data is reduced significantly. We obtain similar results with the three methods, but needing much less time with NLC.

References

1. Langley, P.: Selection of relevant features in machine learning. In: Procs. Of the AAAI Fall Symposium on Relevance. (1994) 140–144
2. Blum, A., Langley, P.: Selection of relevant features and examples in machine learning. In: Artificial Intelligence. (1997) 245–271
3. Doak, J.: An evaluation of search algorithms for feature selection. Technical report, Los Alamos National Laboratory (1994)
4. Dash, M., Liu, H.: Feature selection for classification. Intelligent Data Analisys **1** (1997)
5. Duda, R., P.Hart: Pattern Classification and Scene Analysis. John Willey and Sons (1973)
6. Kononenko, I.: Estimating attributes: Analysis and estensions of relief. In: European Conference on Machine Learning. (1994) 171–182
7. Quinlan, J.: Induction of decision trees. Machine Learning **1** (1986) 81–106
8. Aha, D., Kibler, D., Albert, M.: Instance-based learning algorithms. Machine Learning **6** (1991) 37–66
9. Witten, I.H., Frank, E.: Data Mining: Practical machine learning tools with Java implementations. Morgan Kaufmann (1999)
10. Blake, C., Merz, E.K.: Uci repository of machine learning databases (1998)

Simultaneous Feature Selection and Weighting for Nearest Neighbor Using Tabu Search

Muhammad Atif Tahir, Ahmed Bouridane, and Fatih Kurugollu

Queens University of Belfast
BT71NN, Northern Ireland
a.tahir@qub.ac.uk

Abstract. Both feature selection and feature weighting techniques are useful for improving the classification accuracy of K-nearest-neighbor (KNN) rule. The term feature selection refers to algorithms that select the best subset of the input feature set. In feature weighting, each feature is multiplied by a weight value proportional to the ability of the feature to distinguish among pattern classes. In this paper, a tabu search based heuristic is proposed for simultaneous feature selection and feature weighting of KNN rule. The proposed heuristic in combination with KNN classifier is compared with several classifiers on various available datasets. Results have indicated a significant improvement of the performance in terms of maximizing classification accuracy.

1 Introduction

Both feature selection and feature weighting techniques are useful for improving the classification accuracy of K-nearest-neighbor (KNN) rule [1-3]. The term feature selection refers to algorithms that select the best subset of the input feature set. Feature selection leads to savings in measuring features (since some of the features are discarded) and the selected features retain their original physical interpretation [4]. The feature selection is NP-hard problem. Feature weighting is a more general method in which the original set of features is multiplied by a weight value proportional to the ability of the feature to distinguish among pattern classes [1,2]. A good review of Feature Weighting algorithms was done by Wettschereck et al. [3]. They are mainly divided into two groups. One method attempts to find a sets of weight through iterative algorithm and uses the performance of classifier as a feedback to select a new set of weights [1]. Another one obtains the weights using pre-existing model's bias e.g. conditional probabilities, class projection, and mutual information [2].

Feature selection algorithms [3-5] perform best when the features used to describe instances are either highly correlated with the class label or completely irrelevant while Feature Weighting is more appropriate for tasks where features vary in their relevance. Recently, Raymer et al. have used genetic algorithms to perform feature selection and feature weighting simultaneously [1]. Results indicated an increased classification accuracy over other classifiers. Tabu search (TS) has been applied to the problem of feature selection by Zhang and Sun [5].

In their work, the tabu search performs feature selection in combination with Mahalanobis distance as a objective function. This objective function is used to evaluate the classification performance of each subset of features selected by the TS. Feature selection vector in TS is represented by a 0/1 bit string where 0 shows feature is not included in the solution while 1 shows feature is included. The experimental results on *synthetic data* have shown that the tabu search not only has a high possibility to obtain the optimal or near-optimal solution, but also requires less computational time than the other suboptimal and genetic algorithm methods.

A modified tabu search algorithm is proposed in this paper to perform both feature selection and feature weighting simultaneously with the objective of improving the classification accuracy. This approach uses both feature weight vector and feature binary vector on the encoding solution of tabu search. Feature weight vector consists of real values while feature binary vector consists of either 0 or 1. KNN classifier is used to evaluate each weight set evolved by TS. Neighbors are calculated using Euclidean distance. Classification accuracy obtained from TS/KNN classifier is then compared with published results for several commonly-employed pattern classification algorithms.

This paper is organized as follows. Section 2 gives an overview about tabu search followed by the proposed implementation of tabu search for feature selection and weighting. Section 4 discusses the results obtained from the experiments. Section 5 concludes the paper.

2 Overview of Tabu Search

Tabu Search (TS) was introduced by Fred Glover [6] as a general iterative metaheuristic for solving combinatorial optimization problems. Tabu Search is conceptually simple and elegant. It is a form of local neighborhood search. Each solution $S \in \Omega$ has an associated set of neighbors $N(S) \subseteq \Omega$ where Ω is the set of feasible solutions. A solution $S' \in N(S)$ can be reached from S by an operation called a *move to S'*. TS moves from a solution to its best admissible neighbor, even if this causes the objective function to deteriorate. To avoid cycling, solutions that were recently explored are declared forbidden or tabu for a number of iterations. The tabu status of a solution is overridden when certain criteria (aspiration criteria) are satisfied.

3 Proposed Tabu Search Technique for Simultaneous Feature Selection and Extraction

Encoding Solution: The structure of the TS encoding solution is illustrated in Figure 1. This structure is already used as a chromosome in genetic algorithms [1]. It is adopted for our proposed tabu search method. This is split into two parts. The first part, $W_1 W_2 ...... W_n$ consists of a real-valued weight for each of the n features. An initial investigation was carried out to assess the contribution

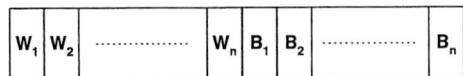

Fig. 1. The Structure of Encoding Scheme used in TS.

of weights. In this implementation, weights ranging from 1.0 to 500.0 have been used. The second part, $B_1 B_2 ...... B_n$, consists of 0/1 bit string for each of the n features.

Objective Function: The objective function is to minimize equation 1.

$$Cost = \alpha * \sum_{i=1}^{n} C_i * M_i + \beta * F \qquad (1)$$

where n is the number of classes, C_i is the misclassification cost for each sample in class i [1], and M_i is the total number of misclassified samples for class i. F is the number of features selected. α and β are constants set as 25.0 and 1.0 respectively. Thus, tabu search places maximum emphasis upon achieving high classification accuracy while reducing the overall feature set is secondary goal.

Initial Solution: All features are included in the initial solution.

Neighborhood Solutions: For tabu search, it is important that there should be a move from one solution to different neighbors. In our approach, neighbors are generated from both parts of the encoding solution. $R * N$ different neighbors are generated from the first part by assigning R random weights to N different features. Also, M different neighbors are generated by randomly adding or deleting a feature from the second part. Thus, the total number of neighborhood solutions (V^*) in an iteration is $R * N + M$. Fig 2 shows an example showing different neighbors from the initial solution. Each neighbor solution is a single move from the initial/previous solution. Among the neighbors, the one with the best cost (i.e. the solution which results in the minimum value of Equation 1) is selected and considered as the new current solution for the next iteration.

Tabu Moves: A tabu list is maintained to prevent returning to previously visited solutions. This list contains information that, to some extent, forbids the search from returning to a previously visited solution. In our implementation, if a feature is added/deleted or weighted at iteration i, then this feature is added in the tabu list along with the information that whether it is added/deleted or weighted.

Aspiration Criterion: Aspiration criterion is a method used to override the tabu status of moves whenever appropriate. It temporarily overrides the tabu status if the move is sufficiently good. In our approach, a feature which is in the tabu list is allowed to be added/deleted or weighted, if it results in a better cost.

Termination Rule: Termination condition is a predefined number of iterations.

---

[1] In some datasets, classification-cost penalties are available.

W_1	W_2	....	W_n	B_1	B_2	....	B_n
10.1	1	....	1	1	1	....	1
4.1	1	....	1	1	1	....	1
1	1.8	....	1	1	1	....	1
1	5.8	....	1	1	1	....	1
1	1	....	1	0	1	....	1
1	1	....	1	1	0	....	1
1	1	....	1	1	1	....	0

Fig. 2. An example showing different possible neighbors from the initial solution. $V^*=7$, $M=3$, $N=2$ and $R=2$.

4 Experiments

We have performed a number of experiments and comparisons on several benchmarks from the Statlog project [7] and UCI [9] in order to demonstrate the performance of the proposed classification system. A short description is given below:

- Statlog Australian Credit Approval (*Australian*): 690 prototypes, 14 features, 2 classes. Divided into 10 sets for cross-validation.
- Statlog Heart (*Heart*): 270 prototypes, 13 features, 2 classes (Absent or present). Divided into 9 sets for cross-validation. Cost Matrix is available for this dataset [7].
- Statlog Diabetes (*Diabetes*): 768 prototypes, 8 features, 2 classes. Divided into 12 sets for cross validation.
- UCI Balance (*Balance*): 625 prototypes, 4 features, 3 classes. Divided into 10 sets for cross validation.
- Statlog Vehicle (*Vehicle*): 846 prototypes, 18 features, 4 classes. Divided into 9 sets for cross validation.

Classification results have been obtained by using N-Fold Cross Validation [8] in order to have uniform comparison as these datasets are previously tested by using N-fold Cross Validation in the literature [7, 8, 2]. Each dataset is divided into *N* blocks using *N-1* blocks as a training set and the remaining block as a test set. Therefore, each block is used exactly once as a test set. For datasets with more than two classes, Fuzzy KNN classifier is used to avoid ties [10].

Table 1 shows the comparison of classification error rate (in %) between TS and other classifiers [8, 2] for different datasets. The combination of feature selection and feature weighting technique using the proposed tabu search has achieved higher accuracy to all datasets except Balance and Vehicle. Even for Balance and Vehicle datasets, TS/KNN is better than many well-known classifiers.

Table 1. Results of various classifiers as reported in [8, 2] in comparison with TS feature selection and feature weighting. * means without considering cost matrix.

	Australian	Heart	Diabetes	Vehicle	Balance
Alloc80	20.1	40.7	30.1	17.3	-
CART	14.5	45.2	25.5	23.5	-
C4.5	15.5	78.1	26.2	26.6	23.4
Discrim	14.1	39.3	22.5	21.6	-
NBayes	15.1	**37.4**	26.2	55.8	9.6
QDisc	20.7	42.2	26.2	**15.0**	-
LogDisc	14.1	39.6	22.3	19.2	-
Cal5	13.1	44.4	25.0	27.9	-
Radial	14.5	78.1	24.3	30.7	-
CDW [2]	15.2	19.4*	24.8	28.15	**9.17**
NewId	18.1	84.4.6	28.9	29.8	-
KNN	18.1	47.8	32.4	27.5	12.0
TS/KNN	**11.9**	**37.4, 12.9***	**22.1**	23.0	10.2

Table 2. Comparison of TS with feature selection, TS with feature weighting and TS with feature selection and feature weighting. FS = Feature Selection, FW = Feature Weighting.

	Australian	Heart	Diabetes	Vehicle	Balance
FS	12.8	47.0	23.5	25.3	12.0
FW	11.9	45.9	**22.1**	23.6	10.2
FS/FW	**11.9**	**37.4**	**22.1**	23.0	10.2

Table 3. Feature weights obtained by TS for various datasets.

Australian (K=5)	0, 1, 0, 0, 51.4, 0, 0, 459.3, 0, 1, 0, 490.1, 1, 1
Heart (K=5)	271.1, 0, 279.5, 0, 0, 0, 0, 0, 162.8, 0, 0, 400.8, 331.5
Diabetes (K=5)	222.9, 85.9, 0, 0, 0, 385.8, 0, 74.7
Vehicle (K=4)	1, 0, 1, 0, 1, 0, 1, 1, 0, 1, 1, 1, 0, 0, 0, 0, 1, 1.35
Balance (K=13)	172.0, 107.3, 79.6, 80.3

Table 2 shows a comparison of TS with feature selection, TS with feature weighting, and TS with both feature selection and feature weighting. Thus, a key advantage of using proposed technique is that it combines various benefits of feature selection and weighting into a single method. The relationship between the original features and the transformed features is easy to analyze and identify.

Table 3 shows the feature weights obtained by TS for various datasets. Thus, the TS with simultaneous feature selection and weighting not only have the ability to find weights for KNN classifier that result in higher classification accuracy but also have the ability to reduce the size of feature vector. Table 4 shows the tabu run time parameters chosen after preliminary experimentation was completed. The number of iterations is 500 for all datasets.

Table 4. Tabu Run Time Parameters. V^* = Number of neighborhood solutions, T = Tabu List Size, R*N = neighbors for first part of encoding scheme, M = neighbors for second part of encoding scheme (Section 3).

	Australian	Heart	Diabetes	Vehicle	Balance
$V^*(R*N+M)$	10*2+5=25	10*2+5=25	10*2+3=23	10*2+5=25	10*2+2= 22
T	4	4	3	4	1

5 Conclusion

In this paper, a tabu search method is proposed for simultaneous feature selection and feature weighting using KNN rule. The simultaneous feature selection and feature extraction using tabu search has proved effective for maximizing classification accuracy. The proposed technique is compared with different classifiers on various available datasets. Results have indicated that simultaneous feature selection and extraction not only have the ability to find weights for KNN classifier that result in higher classification accuracy but also have the ability to reduce the size of feature vector.

References

1. M. L. Raymer et al. Dimensionality Reduction using Genetic Algorithms. IEEE Trans. on Evolutionary Computation, **4(2)**, (2000), 164–171.
2. R. Paredes and E. Vidal. A Class-Dependent Weighted Dissimilarity Measure for Nearest Neighbor Classification Problems. Pattern Recognition Letters, **21(12)**, (2000), 1027–1036.
3. D. Wettschereck, D. W. Aha, and T. Mohri. A Review and Empirical Evaluation of Feature Weighting Methods for a Class of Lazy Learning Algorithms. Artificial Intelligence Review. **11(1-5)**, (1997), 273-314.
4. A. K. Jain, R. P. W. Duin, and J. Mao. Satistical Pattern Recognition: A Review. IEEE Trans. on Pattern Analysis and Machine Intelligence, **22(1)**, (2000), 4–37.
5. H. Zhang and G. Sun. Feature selection using tabu search method. Pattern Recognition, **35**, (2002), 701–711.
6. F. Glover. Tabu search I. ORSA Journal on Computing, **1(3)**, (1989), 190–206.
7. Statlog Corpora. Dept. Statistics and Modelling Science (Stams). Stratchclyde University, http://www.liacc.up.pt/ML/statlog/.
8. D. Michie, D. J. Spiegelhalter and C. C. Taylor. Machine Learning, Neural and Statistical Classification. Ellis Horwood, (1994).
9. C. Blake, E. Keogh, and C. J. Merz. UCI Repository of machine learning databases, University of California, Irvine.
10. J. M. Keller, M. R. Gray, and J. A. Givens. A Fuzzy K-Nearest Neighbor Algorithm. IEEE Trans. on Systems, Man, and Cybernetics, **15(4)**, (1985), 580–585.

Fast Filtering of Structural Similarity Search Using Discovery of Topological Patterns*

Sung-Hee Park and Keun Ho Ryu

Database Laboratory, Chungbuk National University, Cheongju, 361-763, Korea
{shpark,khryu}@dblab.chungbuk.ac.kr

Abstract. Similarity search for protein 3D structure databases is much more complex and computationally expensive. It is essential to improve performance on the existing comparison systems such as DALI and VAST. In our approach, the structural similarity search composes of a filter step to generate small candidate set and a refinement step to compute structural alignment. This paper describes fast filtering of similarity search using discovery of topological patterns of secondary structure elements based on spatial relations. Our system is fully implemented by using Oracle 8i spatial. Experimental results show that our method is approximately three times faster than DaliLite.

1 Introduction

The prediction of protein functions has become the hot topic and major concern in bioinformatics. One of approaches for predicting protein structures is to compare a new protein with those proteins whose functions have been known. To compare protein structures, structural similarity search is more useful technique in case of attempting to identify structurally similar proteins even though their sequences are not similar at the level of amino acids.

The diversity of the techniques that involve molecular atomic distance [1, 2] and topology[3] demonstrates that the comparison problem is more complex and computationally expensive. Many methods perform a single step of similarity search at the atomic coordinate level by running a whole scan of entire structure databases. The existing comparison systems such as DALI[1] and VAST[4] do not provide search result on time.

The objective of our work is to develop a fast filtering method for similarity search in a 3D protein structure database. Therefore, we adopt two-phase query processing composed of a filter step and a refinement step. Our method is based on the fact that topological properties are invariant even if geometric features such as length and angle are easily changed. In this paper, we describe the comparison of similarity of a query protein with that of proteins in 3D structure database using topological patterns. The multi-levels of the geometry of proteins are represented by spatial data types. The spatial topological patterns of SSEs are discovered by spatial operators based on 9IM topological relations[5]. An algorithm of fast similarity search compares patterns of a

---

* This work was supported by KRF 2003-908-D00041, KISTEP and the RRC of MOST and KOSEF in Korea.

query protein with those of proteins in the structure database. The search results can be aligned by publicly available alignment tools such as DALI, SSAP, and LOCK.

2 The Representation of Geometry and Topology

The geometry of proteins means the shape of 3D structures in proteins. The most common secondary structures are the helices and sheets, consisting of strands. A SSE(Secondary Structure Element) includes two ending Cα atoms and the list of Cα atoms between them. A SSE is approximated to a vector between two ending position of the SSE. Therefore, SSEs are modeled as line segments of 10 – 20 connected points.

A biological meaning of topology refers to the spatial relations of 3D folds. The topology describes how the spatial arrangement of SSEs is connected. According to representation of the geometry by spatial types, the spatial arrangement of SSEs is considered as topology of spatial geometry. Among many topological properties of proteins, we focus on topological relations between binary SSEs.

We apply 9IM(Intersection Matrix)[5] defined by Clementini. The 9-Intersection Matrix is defined as the location of each interior and boundary with respect to other objects exterior. Therefore, the binary topological relation R between two lines, A and B, in R2 is based upon the comparison of A's interior($A°$), boundary(∂A), and exterior($A-$) with B's interior($B°$), boundary(∂B), and exterior($B-$). These six objects can be combined such that they form nine fundamental descriptions of a topological relation between two lines and be concisely represented by a 3×3 matrix, called the 9-intersection.

$$R(A, B) = \begin{bmatrix} A° \cap B° & A° \cap \partial B & A° \cap B^- \\ \partial A \cap B° & \partial A \cap \partial B & \partial A \cap B^- \\ A^- \cap B° & A^- \cap \partial B & A^- \cap B^- \end{bmatrix}$$

Eight different types of topological relations can be induced two lines in R^2 as shown in Fig. 1. The relations are 2D topological operators computed by the join operation of two Rtree indexes.

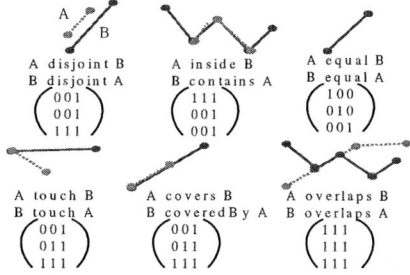

Fig. 1. Spatial topological relations.

Table 1. Topology String.

Topological Relation ($\odot$)	SSE types		
	Helix $\odot$ Helix	Helix $\odot$ Strand	Strand $\odot$ Strand
Overlap	A	D	G
Equal	B	E	H
Touch	C	F	I

3 The Discovery of Topology Patterns

Fig. 2 shows the overall architecture of a similarity search system based on the proposed methods. In the preprocessing step, spatial types of SSEs are stored into a database by forming spatial object indexed by Rtree. Building a structure database is based on a spatial database.

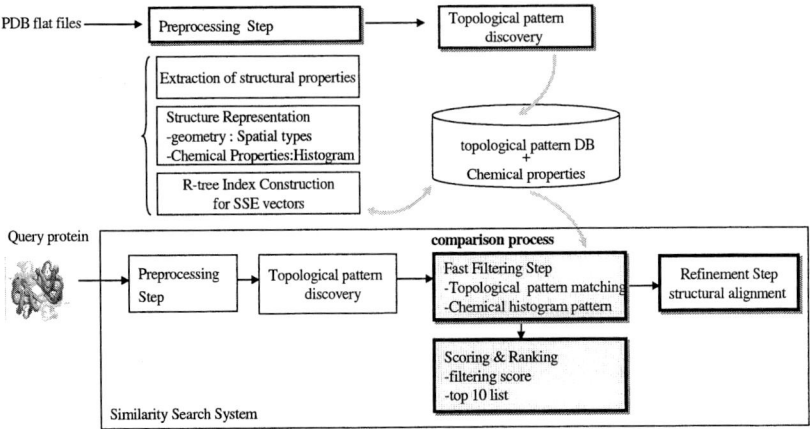

Fig. 2. Overall architecture of a similarity search system.

We define a binary relation and a n-ry topological relation which represent sequences of binary topological relations among consecutive SSEs. Topological pattern lists denote different topology patterns in a protein structure.

We restrict the types of SSEs to α-helix and β-strand and consider three major topological relations in Table 1 because *overlap* includes *inside, contains, cover, coveredBy*. There are nine patterns possible considering combination of SSE types with three topological relation. Given a protein P={ S_1, ... S_k}, S_i and S_j are SSEs, the types of a SSE are S^T = {H, S}, a set of topological relations R={overlap, touch, equal}, where $0 < i, j < k$, k is number of SSEs in Protein P, H = Helix and S= Strand. The following definition denotes the construction of the topological relations and topological pattern lists.

Definition 1 (binary topological relation) Let R^2 = { $S_i \odot S_j$} be a binary topological relation, where $S_i \neq S_j$, |R|=2 (number of SSE), $\odot \in R$ and S_i^T, $S_j^T \in$ {H, S}.

Definition 2 (n-ary topological relation) Let R^n = {($S_1 \odot S_2$), ($S_2 \odot S_3$), ...,($S_i \odot S_q$), ($S_q \odot S_j$),...,($S_{n-1} \odot S_n$)} be n-ary topological relation, where if $0 < i < q < j \leq n$ and the order of all SSEs is sequence, binary topological relations R^2 must be sequence between consecutive SSEs, |R| = n, $\odot \in R$ and S_i^T, $S_j^T \in$ {H, S}.

Definition 3 (topological pattern list) Let $T = \langle(S_1 \odot S_2), ((S_i \odot S_q), (S_q \odot S_j)), \ldots, (S_{n-1} \odot S_n)\rangle$ be topological pattern list, where $L= \{R^2, R^3, \ldots, R^n\}$, $n \in k$ and $|L|$ is number of all the topological relations appearing in protein P.

The n-ary topological relations reveal consecutive contact patterns of SSEs, and topological pattern lists present combination of the binary and n-ary topological relations. To compare topological pattern lists, all the binary topological relations are mapped to characters in Table 1 and the n-ary topological relation is mapped to a string, so it is called a topology string. The topological pattern list is translated into a set of topology strings. At the end, problem of similarity search is infered to find similar lists of topology strings in the topological pattern database.

4 Similarity Search

When a query structure is submitted, all the topological relations in the query structure are explored. The list of topology strings are built in the same way as shown in Table 1. Then we compare the list of topology strings with those of the database. Problem of similarity search is translated into the comparison of lists of strings between query protein and proteins in the database. Candidate proteins are ranked by frequencies of matched strings among database objects against the query protein.

Searching Database: To find similar protein structures, the match of topology strings is computed under constraints with length difference of SSEs joined in topological relations. We evaluate the following predicates.

Given topology strings sets for query protein $Q=\{a_1, \{a_2, a_3\}, \ldots, \{a_{n-1}, a_n\}\}$ and a protein in the database $P=\{b_1, b_2, \ldots, b_m\}$, the two topology strings a_1 and b_1 are regarded as the match if and only if:

$(0.5 < (SSELen(a_i)/SSELen(b_j)) < 2) \cap (D(H(a_i), H(b_j)) < 3)$, where $a_i = b_j$, $Sq_i^T = Sp_{i+1}^T$, and $Sq_j^T = Sp_{j+1}^T$, if $a_i \equiv (Sq_i \odot Sq_{i+1})$ and $b_j \equiv (Sp_j \odot Sp_{j+1})$.

The rates of length of SSEs in a pair of the matched strings satisfy at most $\delta (0.5 < \delta < 2)$. Maximum frequencies denote the number of elements in intersection set between P and Q. The similarity score S is calculated as (the total number of SSEs in the pairs of the matched strings /(number of SSEs in a query protein + number of SSEs in a protein in a database).

Scoring and Ranking: The results are ranked according to similarity score S and then reported. We calculate the scores of all the proteins in the database simultaneously and report the top 10 scores and top 100 scores.

5 Experimental Results

The 3D structure database was built from 586 proteins released in PDB #101 that were representative proteins from different SCOP Classes. We used the same query proteins for performance evaluation, which Singh and Brutlag[6] used for evaluation of the existing structure comparison programs.

Table 2. Query Proteins.

PDB id	Name	# Residue	SCOP Class	SCOP fold
1mbd	Sperm whale myglobin	153	All-α	Globin-like
1tph-2	Triose phosphate isomerase, chain 2	245	α and β(α/β)	β/α (TIM) barrel
8fab-A	Immunoglobulin, chain A	106-208	All-y	Immunoglobulin-like y sandwich

In the second experiment for accuracy test, we used N-termial Zn bining domain of HIV integrates family that was included in DNA/RNA-binding 3-helical bundle fold and all alpha class in the SCOP. Our similarity search algorithms were run on a Compaq ProliantML330e server with a 800 MHz CPUs and 512bytes memory. We used the spatial types and topological operators in ORACLE 8i DBMS.

5.1 Experiment 1: Performance

Execution time for similarity search to three sample proteins is shown in Fig. 3. The results showed that our method is approximately up to three times faster than Dali-Lite[7].

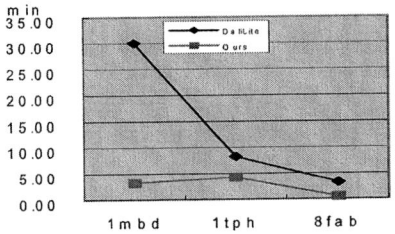

Fig. 3. Comparison of execution time for similarity search.

Table 3. Accuracy evaluation.

Query protein	Num. of TP	Num. of FP	PPV
1k6y	40	19	67.8%
1wja	7	1	83.3.%
1wjc	7	1	75.0 %
1wjd	7	1	92.9%
1wje	7	1	85.7.%
1e0e	6	2	75.0 %

5.2 Experiment 2: Accuracy

We compared our results with SCOP classification hierarchy. If our result proteins belong to the same SCOP family as the query protein is included, it is counted as a true positive. We calculated the positive predictive value(PPV) for evaluating the accuracy of the comparison follows.

PPV = (number of True Positives/ True Positive(TP) +False Positive(FP)) * 100

It is observed that the matched proteins have almost the same as those of the SCOP family as shown Table 3. However, the cases that PDB flat files lack SSEs or have missing values for SSEs do not denote exact results because our comparison method is based on similarity of a SSE level. The accuracy of comparison of structures is reasonable to be accepted as the filtering step for structure similarity search.

Our method has disadvantages despite of very fast search response. That is, it took 1 hour and 23 minutes to build the topology pattern list on around 586 proteins in our experiments. Most of time consumption is in the parsing step for extracting SSEs.

6 Conclusions

To improve performance of existing structural comparison for protein 3D structure databases, we proposed new filtering of fast similarity search based on topological pattern discovery. Topological patterns of proteins were discovered by spatial relation 9IM. The experimental results showed that similarity of topological patterns rapidly generated small candidate set to be used in more accurate alignment methods. Compared with the existing methods, this method uses spatial characteristics of protein structures, which are purely represented by using the existing spatial databases. This approach also has an advantage of speed in performance. It indicates that topological properties of protein structures are proper to be taken in a filter step of fast structural similarity search from the fact that topology of protein structures is invariant even though the geometry of proteins is sensitive to its changes.

References

1. L. Holm, C. Sander: Proein structure comparison by alignment of distance matrices, J. of Mol. Biol., 233, 123-138, 1993.
2. C. A. Orengo, W.R. Taylor: SSAP: sequential structure alignment program for protein structure comparison. J. of *Methods in Enzym.*, 266, 617-635, 1996.
3. D. Gilbert, D.R. Westhead, N. Nagano, J. M. Thornton: Motif-based searching in TOPS protein topology databases.,J. of *Bioinformatics*, 15, 317-326, 1999.
4. J-F. Gibrat, T. Madej, H. Bryant: Surprising similarities in structure comparison, *Current Opinion in Structural Biology*, 6, 377-385, 1996.
5. E. Clementini, P. Felice, P. van Oostrom: A small set of formal topological relationships suitable for end-user interaction. In: Proc. of Spatial Databases Symp., Singapore, 277-295, 1993.
6. Amit P. Singh, Douglas L. Brutlag: Protein Structure Alignment: A Comparison of Methods, Dept. of Biochemistry, Stanford Univ, 2000.
7. L. Holm, J. Park: DaliLite workbench for protein structure comparison, *Bioinformatics*, 1, 566-567, 2000.
8. S. H. Park, K. H. Ryu, H. S. Son: Modeling Protein Structures with Spatial Model for Structure Comparison, *LNCS*, 2690, 490-497, 2003.

Detecting Worm Propagation Using Traffic Concentration Analysis and Inductive Learning*

Sanguk Noh[1], Cheolho Lee[2], Keywon Ryu[3], Kyunghee Choi[3], and Gihyun Jung[4]

[1] School of Computer Science and Information Engineering
The Catholic University of Korea, Korea
sunoh@catholic.ac.kr
[2] National Security Research Institute, Korea
chlee@etri.re.kr
[3] Graduate School of Information and Communication
Ajou University, Korea
{ryujeen,khchoi}@ajou.ac.kr
[4] Division of Electronics Engineering
Ajou University, Korea
khchung@ajou.ac.kr

Abstract. As a vast number of services have been flooding into the Internet, it is more likely for the Internet resources to be exposed to various hacking activities such as Code Red and SQL Slammer worm. Since various worms quickly spread over the Internet using self-propagation mechanism, it is crucial to detect worm propagation and protect them for secure network infrastructure. In this paper, we propose a mechanism to detect worm propagation using the computation of entropy of network traffic and the compilation of network traffic. In experiments, we tested our framework in simulated network settings and could successfully detect worm propagation.

1 Introduction

As a vast number of services have been flooding into the Internet, it is more likely for the Internet resources to be exposed to various hacking activities such as Code Red in 2001 and SQL Slammer worm in 2003, respectively [3, 7, 8, 10]. Since various worms quickly spread over the Internet using self-propagation mechanism, it is crucial to detect worm propagation and protect them for secure network infrastructure. In our previous work, we have suggested our method to detect distributed denial-of-service (DDoS) attacks through the analysis of network traffic, and reported its resulting performance in [11]. We, in this paper, extend our efforts to detect worm propagation using the computation of entropy of network traffic and the compilation of network traffic.

---

* This work has been supported by the Korea Research Foundation under grant KRF-2003-041-D20465, and by the KISTEP under National Research Laboratory program.

For self-propagation, most worms scan target ports, identify a specific port, connect a host using the port chosen, for example, tcp/80 port in case of Code Red, and infect the host [3, 10]. The infected host, further, tries to copy its worm to others. From this phenomenon, we could observe that the egress network traffic on the specific port of the infected host abruptly increases. Our intuition to this observation leads to the analysis of network traffic using the computation of entropy representing the volatility of network traffic. To detect the worm propagation, then, we compile a pair of network traffic and worm infection into a set of reactive rules using various learning algorithms.

There has been lots of related work to analyze worm pattern and detect worm propagation [1, 14, 15]. Most approaches model the collateral effects of self-propagation while our approach focuses on the worm propagation itself. In other words, since our framework models the pattern of network traffic on infected hosts, we could apply our framework to general worm propagation situations, regardless of the various behavior patterns of unknown worms.

In the next section, we will address the question of how to detect worm propagation. Towards this end, this paper proposes traffic concentration analysis and network traffic compilation method. In section 3, we describe experimental setting and experimental results. We summarize our conclusions and further research issues in section 4.

2 Detecting Worm Propagation

To identify worm propagation on the Internet, we need to keep track of session information, as consisting of ports and IP addresses for source and destination hosts. A worm randomly generates a pool of IP addresses for destinations, scans their exploiting ports, for example, port tcp/80 in case of Code Red, and exploits vulnerabilities of the open ports. In this section, we will introduce a framework of traffic concentration analysis to represent any changes of the session information in the presence/absence of a worm. Further, using inductive learning algorithms, we compile a tuple of session information and worm infection into rules to detect self-propagating worms.

2.1 Traffic Concentration Analysis

Based upon the observation of the features of a fast spreading worm, as mentioned in section 1, it is notable that the randomness (or volatility) of IP addresses increases in order to infect vulnerable hosts as many as possible, and the randomness of ports decreases, since the exploiting ports for propagation are limited. To present the randomness of network traffic, we use the computation of entropy, which is originally reported in [4], as follows:

$$E(s) = -\sum_{i=1}^{n} p_i \log_2(p_i), \qquad (1)$$

where

S = {srcAddr, srcPort, dstAddr, dstPort};
$E(s)$ is the entropy of the class $s \in S$;
p_i is the probability of the i-th member in a class s.

In equation 1, S can be one of session information, and p_i can be the ratio of the number of the member i of a class, say, srcAddr, in S to the total number of the members of the class. The entropies of session information provide the randomness of network traffic. The lower entropy of target addresses and ports describes a network status that the less number of target addresses and ports are shown given a set of sessions.

2.2 Detecting Worms Using Inductive Learning Algorithms

We propose a network monitoring agent architecture, as consisting of a packet collecting agent and an adaptive reasoning agent - an alarming agent - that analyze network traffic, detect the spread of worms upon the network traffic concentration, and finally issue an alarm in case of the worms. To inspire adaptability into our alarming agents, we use various machine learning algorithms and, using learning techniques, compile the models of network traffic into a set of rules.

Bayes rule examines whether or not a property observed as evidence belongs to a specific hypothesis (or class), given a set of data distribution. Bayes theorem [6] can be defined as follows:

$$P(h_j | x_i) = \frac{P(x_i | h_j)P(h_j)}{\sum_{j=1}^{m} P(x_i | h_j)P(h_j)}, \quad (2)$$

where

A set of observable attributes, $X = \{x_1, x_2, \ldots, x_n\}$;
A set of hypotheses in a domain, $H = \{h_1, h_2, \ldots, h_m\}$;
$P(h_j|x_i)$ is the posterior probability of the hypothesis h_j, $h_j \in H$,
given that x_i, $x_i \in X$, is an observable event.

In our framework, the set of observable attributes, X, consists of the entropies of session information, i.e., ports and addresses for source and destination hosts, and the hypotheses are either no worm infection or worm infection. Given the set of data as evidence Bayes rule allows us to assign probabilities of hypotheses, $P(h_j|x_i)$. Our alarming agents compute $P(h_j|x_i)$ during on-line, and set an alarm when the probability of worm infection given input is greater than that of no infection.

The decision tree approach such as C4.5 [12] and CN2 [2] is to divide the domain space into classified regions, which are given by a set of classes $C = \{c_1, c_2, \ldots, c_m\}$. The basic idea of the decision tree-based induction algorithms finds out a set of ordered attributes, $X = \{x_1, x_2, \ldots, x_n\}$, which split the datasets into a correct classification with the highest information gain first. A decision tree has internal nodes labeled with attributes $x_i \in X$, arcs associated with the parent attributes, and leaf nodes corresponding to classes $c_j \in C$.

The decision tree-based induction algorithms, thus, generate a tree representing a model of network traffic in the simulated network setting. Once the tree is built using training data, the optimal rules from the tree can be obtained and are applied to the new network traffic to determine whether or not a host is infected by a worm.

Let S be the set of traffic states that the adaptive reasoning agent can discriminate among. Let L be the set of compilation methods (learning algorithms) that the agent employs. Given a learning method $l \in L$, a compilation procedure of an adaptive reasoning agent implements a function $\rho_l: S \rightarrow \{worm\ infection,\ no\ worm\ infection\}$, representing whether or not a worm spreads in the state $s \in S$. Thus, various machine learning algorithms compile the models of network traffic into different functions ρ_l. We generate the training examples for these learning algorithms from TCP-based network environments.

3 Experiments

We have implemented a simulated network environment using SPECweb99 [13], Code Red [3], and libpcap [9]. In the simulated, Web-based setting, the SPECweb99 located in Web clients generates web traffic, the Code Red on Web server simulates worm's self-propagating activities, and the libpcap used by a packet collecting agent captures the stream of network traffic. While the Web clients request the Web server that they should be serviced, the Code Red performs network scanning for its self-propagation.

We construct the simulated network environment on LINUX machines, which consist of Web server using Apache, Web clients using SPECweb99, Code Red using newly created data set, based on the worm propagation pattern in [3], a network monitoring device including a packet collecting agent and an alarming agent (700 MHz Pentium III, 256 MB memory), and the network bandwidth of 100 Mbps. In the simulated network architecture, our agents working on the network monitoring device capture the egress network traffic from the infected Web server, and set an alarm if they detect a worm.

We tested our framework in the simulated network environment and measured traffic concentration degrees of network traffic from the Web server. The network traffic models were generated in two settings: the normal Web server without worm's activity and the Web server infected by Code Red. For each network traffic setting, we changed two factors, Simultaneous Connections (SC) and Requests per Connection (R/C), to get various Web traffic patterns. The SC indicates the number of HTTP connections at a given time, which approximates the number of users. The R/C represents the number of requests to be issued in a HTTP connection. In the experiment, we used 5, 10, 25, 50, 75 and 100 for SC and 1, 2, 5, and 10 for R/C. The sampling time to compute traffic concentration degrees was 1 second.

3.1 The Analysis of Network Traffic

Using our Traffic Concentration Analysis (TCA) mechanism, we measured the degree of network traffic concentration on the egress network traffic from the web server, in absence of worm propagation and in presence of worm propagation, respectively. The experimental results of normal Web traffic are illustrated in figure 1 (a). Even if SC ranges from 5 to 100, the results are almost identical.

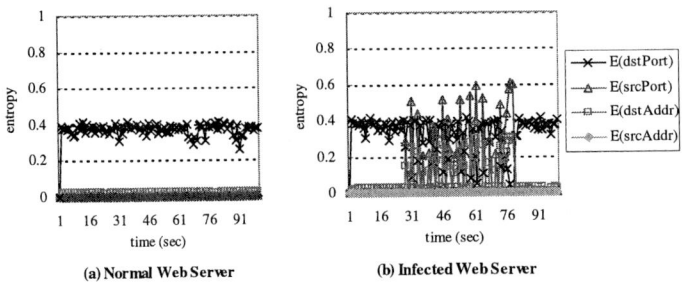

Fig. 1. Entropy distributions in the normal Web server and the infected one. Entropy changed when infected by Code Red. The self-propagation activities were performed from 25 to 75 seconds in (b).

In figure 1 (a), since there was only one server, both of $E(srcAddr)$ and $E(srcPort)$ were clearly 0 while $E(dstPort)$ was, on the average, 0.3483, and $E(dstAddr)$ was almost 0. This result indicated that a specific web server using a tcp/80 port made connections with various destination ports for a unique session between the web server and many web clients. On the other hand, figure 1 (b) presents the distinctive pattern of network traffic when the Code Red spread. During the worm propagation ranging from 25 to 75 seconds, the average of $E(srcPort)$ was 0.3212, and the average of $E(dstAddr)$ was 0.1175. The entropy of destination port, $E(dstPort)$, varied from 0 to 0.4, due to the fact that the worm process on the infected hosts used a specific port, i.e., tcp/80 in our experiment, on the destination.

3.2 Worm Detection Performance

To construct compiled rules for our alarming agents, we used three machine learning algorithms: C4.5 [12], CN2 [2], and naïve Bayesian classifier [5]. C4.5 represents its output as a decision tree, and the output of CN2 is an ordered set of if-then rules. For the Bayesian classifier, the results are represented as rules specifying the probability of occurrence of each attribute value given a class [2], in our case "attacks" and "no attacks."

Using the three learning algorithms [6] and the training examples as inputs, we could get the compiled rules. To evaluate the quality of various rule sets generated by different learning algorithms the performance obtained was expressed in terms of the ratio of {total number of alarms – (number of false alarms + number of missed alarms)} to the total number of alarms. The false alarm is defined as the alert turns on when the worm propagation attack does not occur, and the missed alarm is defined as the alert does not turn on when the worm propagation does occur.

To find a meaningful size of the training set which could guarantee the soundness of the learning hypothesis, we generated several sets of training examples whose size was 400 through 2400 by interval 200, respectively. The resulting performances (accuracy) and the sizes of training examples are shown in figure 2.

For benchmark, we measured the detection performance using Valdes' work [15], which considers only source addresses and destination ports of all the ingress packets through routers into the network infrastructure. In figure 2, the size of training examples was 2600 tuples for both mechanisms. As far as using TCA mechanism, the naïve Bayesian classifier showed the best performance of 90%, on the other hand, using Valdes' mechanism, the best performance achieved by the naïve Bayesian classifier was 82%. It turned out that our mechanism slightly outperformed the Valdes' work in the simulated, small scaled network setting.

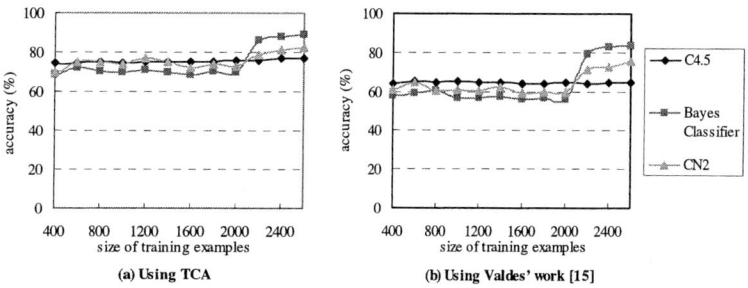

Fig. 2. Worm detection performance using the compiled rules in TCA and Valdes' work.

We analyzed the performance results using the standard analysis of variance (ANOVA) method. Since naïve Bayesian classifier showed best performances, as depicted in figure 2, in both schemes, its ten best performances were used for ANOVA test. The average performance of worm monitoring through TCA was 87.61 ± 1.49 while that of worm monitoring through Valdes' work was 81.74 ± 2.12, and then, the resulting f value of ANOVA method was 17.09. Since the computed value of $f=17.09$ in ANOVA exceeds 8.28 $(=f_{.01,1,18})$, we know that the two mechanisms were not all equally effective at the 0.01 level of significance, i.e., the differences in their performance were not due to chance with probability of 0.99. We, thus, conclude that our alarming agent's performance using the TCA mechanism was better than that of Valdes' worm detection mechanism.

4 Conclusions

In this paper, we have presented the network traffic concentration in terms of entropy, when a worm quickly spreads across Web servers, and compiled a pair of network traffic concentration and the presence/absence of worm into a set of state-action rules using the inductive learning algorithms. We applied the resulting compiled rules to a simulated Code Red, and tested the detection performance of our framework. The experimental results showed that our scheme slightly outperformed a benchmarked one by about 10%. We believe that our framework is applicable when a randomness of network traffic becomes prohibitive, and is valuable to detect self-propagating worms on the Internet. For future work, we will extend our framework to various kinds of worm propagation in scaled-up network settings. We are analyzing the features of non autonomous propagation worms, for example, email attachment worms using SMTP protocol.

References

1. Berk, V.H. et al.: Using Sensor Networks and Data Fusion for Early Detection of Active Worms. SPIE AeroSense, 2003.
2. Clark, P. and Niblett, T.: The CN2 Induction Algorithm. *Machine Learning Journal* 3, 261-283, 1989.
3. Danyliw, R. and Householder, A.: CERT Advisory CA-2001-19 "Code Red" Worm Exploiting Buffer Overflow in IIS Indexing Service DLL. CERT Coordination Center, 2001.
4. Gray, R.M.: Entropy and Information Theory. Springer-Verlag, 39-40, 1990.
5. Hanson, R., Stutz, J., and Cheeseman, P.: Bayesian Classification Theory. Technical Report FIA-90-12-7-01, NASA Ames Research Center, AI Branch, 1991.
6. Holder, L.: ML v2.0: Machine Learning Program Evaluator. available on-line: http://www-cse.uta.edu/~holder/ftp/ml2.0.tar.gz.
7. Houle, J.K., and Weaver, M.G.: Trends in Denial of Service Attack Technology. CERT Coordination Center, 2001.
8. Lan, K. et al.: Effect of Malicious Traffic on the Network. PAM, 2003.
9. Lawrence Berkeley National Labs Network Research Group.: libpcap. available on-line: http://ftp.ee.lbl.gov.
10. Moore, D. et al.: The Spread of the Sapphire/Slammer Worm. available on-line: http://www.cs.berkeley.edu/~nweaver/sapphire/, 2003.
11. Noh, S. et al.: Detecting Distributed Denial of Service (DDoS) Attacks through Inductive Learning. Lecture Notes in Computer Science, Vol. 2690, Springer-Verlag, 286-295, 2003.
12. Quinlan, J.R.: C4.5: Programs for Machine Learning. Morgan Kaufmann Publishers (1993.
13. Standard Performance Evaluation Corporation: SPECweb99 Benchmark. available on-line: http://www.spec.org/osg/web99.
14. Toth, T. and Kruegel, C.: Connection-history based Anomaly Detection. The 2002 IEEE Workshop on Information Assurance and Security, 2002.
15. Valdes, A.: Entropy Characteristics of Propagating Internet Phenomena. The Workshop on Statistical and Machine Learning Techniques in Computer Intrusion Detection, 2003.

Comparing Study for Detecting Microcalcifications in Digital Mammogram Using Wavelets

Ju Cheng Yang, Jin Wook Shin, and Dong Sun Park

Dept. of Infor.& Comm.Eng. and CAIIT, Chonbuk National University[*]
Jeonju, Jeonbuk, 561-756, Korea
yangjucheng@hotmail.com

Abstract. A comparing study for detection microcalcifications in digital mammogram using wavelets is proposed. Microcalcifications are early sign of breast cancer appeared as isolated bright spots in mammograms, however, they are difficult to detect due to their small size (0.05 to 1 mm of diameter). From a signal processing point of view, microcalcifications are high frequency components in mammograms. To enhance the detection performance of the microcalcifications in the mammograms we use the wavelet transform. Due to the multi-resolution decomposition capacity of the wavelet transform, we can decompose the image into different resolution levels which are sensitive to different frequency bands. By choosing an appropriate wavelet with a right resolution level, we can effectively detect the microcalcifications in digital mammogram. In this paper, several normal wavelet family functions are studied comparably, and for each wavelet function, different resolution levels are explored for detecting the microcalcifications. Experimental results show that the Daubechies wavelet with 4th level decomposition achieves the best detecting result of 95% TP rate with FP rate of 0.3 clusters per image.

1 Introduction

Breast cancer is still one of main mortality causes in women, but the early detection can increase the chance of cure [1]. Microcalcifications are small-sized structures, which may indicate the presence of cancer since they are often associated to the most different types of breast tumors. However, they have very small size and the X-ray systems limitations lead to constraints to the adequate visualization of such structures. These limitations may cause false identification of microcalcifications in mammogram with visual examination. In addition, the human eyes are not able to distinguish minimal tonality differences [2], which can be another constraint when mammogram image presents poor contrast between microcalcifications and the tissues around them. Computer-aided diagnosis (CAD) schemes are being developed in order to increase the probabilities of early detection [3-5].

---

[*] This work was supported by grant No.R05-2002-000-01335-0 from the Basic Research Program of the Korea Science & Engineering Foundation.

There have been several methods for detecting microcalcifications using multi-resolution approaches based on wavelet transform [13-15]. A wavelet transform can decompose an image into sub-images using sub-band decomposing filters- banks. In [14], a low-high (LH), high-low (HL) and high-high (HH) sub-bands at full size are obtained, which correspond to horizontal, vertical and diagonal details. Sum of the sub-bands (LH+HL+HH) gives an image containing small elements (microcalcifications) detected in each direction. But this assembly showed a problem of locating small details objects that have a small size in only one direction [12]. This would lead to a false detection. In [15], since the microcalcifications correspond to high-frequency components of the image spectrum, detection of microcalcifications is achieved by decomposing the mammograms into different frequency sub-bands, suppressing the low-frequency sub-band, and, finally, reconstructing the mammogram from the sub-bands containing only high frequencies. In this approach, the authors used the Daubechies family wavelet function with two decomposing levels and these selections may not be sufficient to detect sophisticated malignant microcalcifications.

In this work, we adopt the same idea as in [15] for detecting microcalcifications in digital mammogram. In addition to the basic approach, we attempt to improve the performance of detecting microcalcifications by using four representative wavelet mother functions with four decomposing levels and then choosing the best results among them. Then an adaptive threshold method is applied to label the microcalcifications in the reconstructed image for better observation, so that the result is a binary image containing only microcalcifications.

This paper is organized as fellows: In section 2, we introduce wavelet detect method. In section 3, comparing study by using different wavelet family functions will be discussed. Experimental results will be shown in section 4 and conclusion is in section 5.

2   Wavelet Transform

The wavelet transform is defined as in Eq. (1) [10],

$$WTf(x) = \frac{1}{\sqrt{a}} \int f(x) \psi(\frac{x-b}{a}) dx \qquad (1)$$

This transform can be seen as a mathematical microscope whose position zooms on location b with a magnification $1/a$, and whose optical characteristics is described by the mother wavelet $\psi(x)$. It has been shown that the dilations and translations,

$$\psi_{jt}(x) = 2^{-j/2} \psi(2^{-j} x - k), (j,k) \in Z^2 \qquad (2)$$

of a mother wavelet [10, 11] can be used as an orthonormal basis for the multi-resolution decomposition of signals into octave sub-bands (by means of dilation) with an excellent spatial location property (by means of translation). The translation index

k is measured in terms of the wavelet's support width. In multi-resolution analysis, Mallat [10] also defines the dilations and translations of the lowpass filtering or scaling function as in Eq. (3)

$$\phi_{jk}(x) = 2^{-j/2} \phi(2^{-j}x - k), (j,k) \in Z^2 \qquad (3)$$

The wavelet transform of a given signal $f(x)$ may be interpreted as the decomposition of the signal into a set of time frequency functions by the use of translated and dilated basis functions of a mother wavelet, i.e.,

$$f(x) = \sum_{j=1}^{J} \sum_{k} d_{jk} \psi_{jk}(x) + \sum_{k} S_{jk} \phi_{jk}(x) \qquad (4)$$

where J is the maximum level of decomposition.

A bi-dimensional wavelet can be understood as a unidimensianl one first along with axes x and then along with axis y. In this way, by applying convolution of low and high pass filters on the original data, the signal can be decomposed into specific sets of coefficients at each level of decomposition: Low frequency coefficients ($A_{2^j}^d f$); Vertical high frequency coefficients ($D_{2^j}^1 f$); Horizontal frequency coefficients ($D_{2^j}^2 f$), and High frequency coefficients in both directions ($D_{2^j}^3 f$), the $A_{2^j}^d f$ coefficients in turn represent the entry of the next level of decomposition. The decomposition process proposed by Mallat [6] is used in our work to represent the pyramidal algorithm for bi-dimensional wavelet transform. Fig. 1 shows a diagram of the decomposition process.

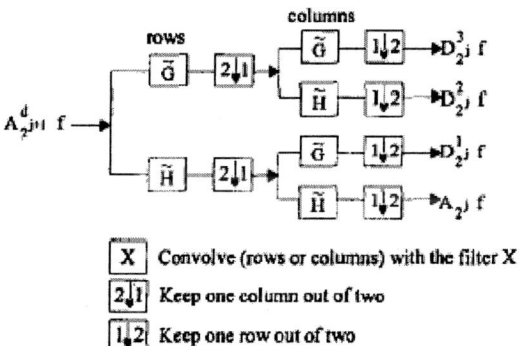

Fig. 1. Decomposition processes for computing a wavelet transform.

After obtaining the four set of coefficients, suppressing the low-frequency sub-band is required, and, finally, reconstructing the mammogram from the sub-bands containing only high frequencies is performed. Fig. 2 shows the detection flow by this method.

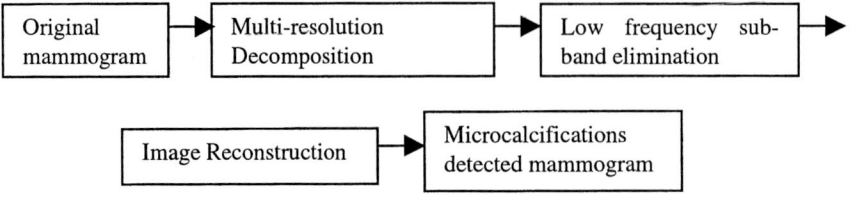

Fig. 2. The detection flow by this method.

Table 1. The properties of normal family wavelets.

Family	Haar	Daubechies	Biorthogonal	Coiflets	Symlets	Morlet	Mexican hat	Meyer
Abbreviation	haar	db	bior	coif	sym	morl	mexh	meyr
Orthogonal	yes	yes	no	yes	yes	no	no	yes
Biorthogonal	yes	yes	yes	yes	yes	no	no	no
Compact support	yes	yes	yes	yes	yes	no	no	no
CWT	yes	yes	yes	yes	yes	yes	yes	yes
DWT	yes	yes	yes	yes	yes	**NO**	**NO**	yes
Support width	1	2N-1		6N-1	2N-1	finite	finite	finite
Filters length	2	2N		6N	2N	[-4,4]	[-5,5]	[-8,8]
Symmetry	yes	near	**NO**	near	near	yes	yes	yes

3 Wavelet Comparing

Table 1 shows the general properties of representative normal wavelet family functions [11]. We exclude the Morlet and Mexican hat wavelets from the experiments since they cannot be decomposed by DWT (Discrete Wavelet Transforms). And the Haar wavelet is a type of the Daubechies wavelet(Haar is db1), so that in this experiment, we use four wavelet family functions for detecting microcalcifications excluding the Haar, that is, Daubechies (db4), Biothgonal (bior3.7), Coieflets (coif3) and Symlets (sym2) wavelets, are chosen for this study. Among them, Biothgonal wavelet is bi-orthogonal, but it is not orthogonal and not symmetric. On the other hand, other three wavelets are orthogonal, bi-orthogonal as well as near symmetric. These different characteristics will affect their detecting results.

4 Experiments

The digital mammogram database used in this work is the MIAS (Mammographic Image Analysis Society [7]) database. The images in this database were scanned with a Joyce-Loebl microdensitometer SCANDIG-3, which has a linear response in the optical density range 0-3.2. Each pixel is 8-bits deep and at a resolution of 50um x 50um. And regions of microcalcifications have marked by the veteran diagnostician. Twenty five images (twelve with benign and thirteen with malignant microcalcifications) are selected for this experiment.

For comparing study wavelet transform method, four typical family wavelets and four decomposing levels are considered. We first decompose the mammogram by using db4, bior3.7, coif3 and sym2 wavelet mother functions, and for each family wavelet, the image is decomposed into 4 levels (the first level is the original image). For each level(from the 2nd level), the detection of microcalcifications is accomplished by setting the wavelet coefficients of upper-left sub-band to zero in order to suppress the image background information before reconstructing image. Then a reconstructed image can be assembled by combining all high-frequency components. So for each family wavelet we will obtain three reconstructed images. The final images are obtained using an adaptive threshold method to label the microcalcifications in the resulting mammograms. The results are shown below as Fig.4-7. From Fig.4-7 we can see that the reconstructed images with the 4th level decomposition are better than those from lower-level decomposition.

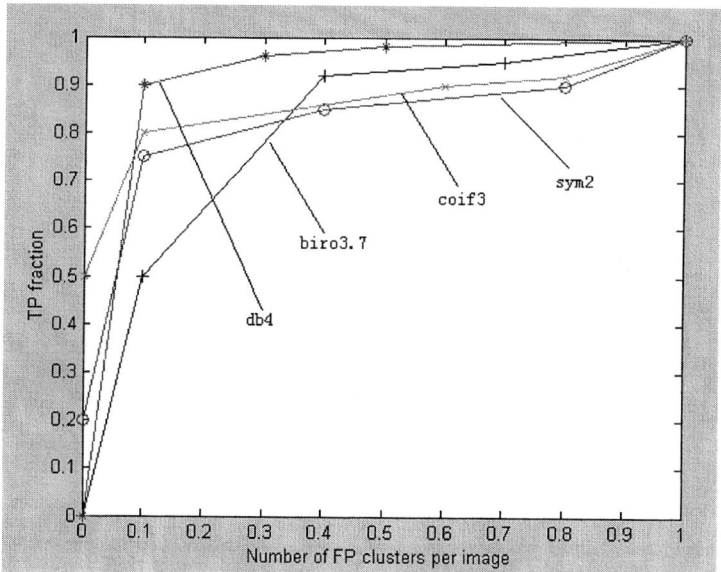

Fig. 3. Comparison of pooled ROC curves of the proposed algorithm using db4, biro3.7, coif3, sym2 wavelet respectively with the 4th level decomposition.

The performance of the proposed algorithm is evaluated by a free-response receiver operating characteristic (FROC) in terms of true-positive (TP) fraction for a given number of false-positive (FP) clusters per image as shown in Fig.3. Fig.3 shows us that the db4 wavelet with the 4th level decomposition achieves the best detecting result of 95% TP rate with FP rate of 0.3 clusters per image and the worst one is using biro3.7 wavelet of 76% TP rate with FP rate of 0.3 clusters per image. Also the result show that using coif3 and sym2 can achieve 82%, 79% TP rate with FP rate of 0.3 clusters per image respectively.

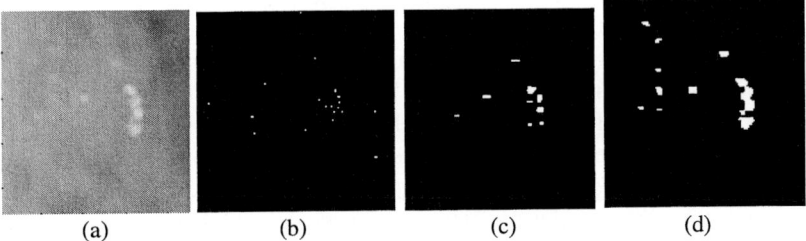

Fig. 4. (a) The ROI of mdb219ll. (b), (c), (d): reconstructed image from level 2nd, level 3rd, level 4th respectively by using db4 wavelet.

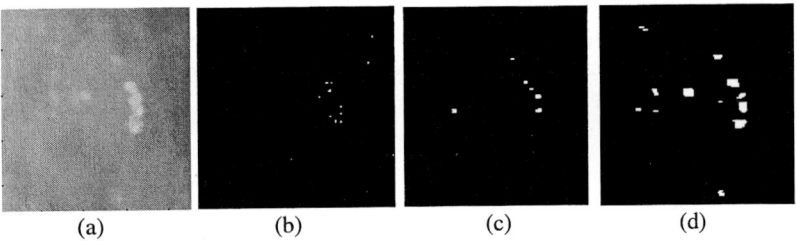

Fig. 5. (a) The ROI of mdb219ll. (b), (c), (d): reconstructed image from level 2nd, level 3rd, level 4th respectively by using biro3.7 wavelet.

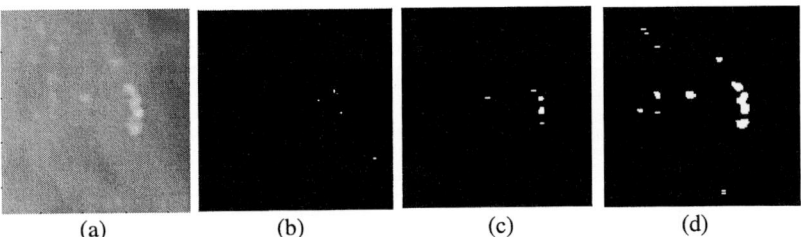

Fig. 6. (a) The ROI of mdb219ll. (b), (c), (d): reconstructed image from level 2nd, level 3rd, level 4th respectively by using coif3 wavelet.

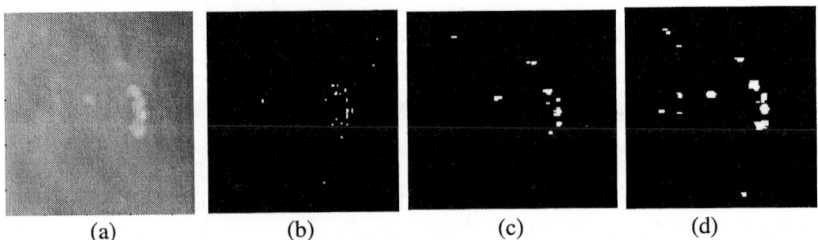

Fig. 7. (a) The ROI of mdb219ll. (b), (c), (d): reconstructed image from level 2nd, level 3rd, level 4th respectively by using sym2 wavelet.

5 Conclusion

In this work, we comparably study the detection of microcalcifications by using wavelets. Several normal wavelet family functions are studied, and for each wavelet function, four resolution levels are explored for detecting the microcalcifications. Experimental results show that the proposed detection method generates accurate positions of microcalcifications in digital mammogram and the best detecting result is that using the Daubechies wavelet with 4th level decomposition can achieve a 95% TP rate with FP rate of 0.3 clusters per image. Further experiments have proceeded to obtain more objective results.

References

1. J.Dengler et al.Segmentation of microcalcifications in mammograms, IEEE, Med. Trans. on Imag., 12, 634-64, 1993.
2. R.C.Gonzalez, R.C.$P.Wintz, Digital Image Processing, Addioson -Wesley Publishing Company,USA,1987.
3. R.M.Nishikawa et al., Computer-aided detection and diagnosis of masses and clustered microcalcifications from digital mammograms, state of the Art in Digital Mammographic, Image Analysis World Scientific Publishing Co., 1993.
4. H-P.Chan et al., Image Feature analysis and computer-aided diagnosis in digital radiography. I.Automated detection of microcalcifications in mammography, Medical Physics, 14, 538-548, 1987.
5. L.Shen at al., Detection and classification of mammographic calcifications, Intern. Journal of Pattern Recognition and Artif. Intellig., 7,1403-1416,1993.
6. S.G.. Mallat, A theory for Multiresolution Signal Decomposition: The Wavelet Representation, IEEE Transactions on Pattern Analysis and Machine Intelligence,11,674-693, 1989.
7. http://www.wiau.man.ac.uk/services/MIAS.
8. R.M. Haralick, S.R.Sternberg, and X,Zhuang, Image analysis using mathematical morphology, IEEE Trans.Pattern Anal.Mach,Intell., 9,532-550, 1987.
9. L.W. Bassett, Mammographic analysis of calcifications, Radiol. Clin. No. Amer. l30, 93-105,1992.
10. S.Mallat, A theory for multiresolution signal decomposition: The Wavelet Representation, IEEE Trans. Pattern. Annal.Machine Intell., 11, 674-693, Jul.1989.
11. I. Daubechies, Orthonormal Bases of Compactly Supported Wavelet, Comm.on Pure and Applied Mathematics, 41, 906-966,1988.
12. R.Mata, E.Nava, F. Sendra, Microcalcifications detection using multiresolution methods, Pattern Recognition, 2000, Proceedings, 15th International Conference. 4, 344 –347, 2000.
13. H.Yoshida, K.Doi, and R.M. Nishikawa, Automated detection of clustered microcalcifications in digital mammograms using wavelet transform techniques, in proc. SPIE, 2167, 868-886, 1994.
14. R.N.Strickland and H.I. Hahn, Wavelet transform for detecting microcalcifications in mammograms, IEEE Trans. Med. Imag., 15, 218-229, 1996.
15. T.C.Wang, N.B. Karayiannis, Detection of microcalcifications in digital mammograms using wavelets, Medical Imaging, IEEE Transactions, 17 , 498 -509, 1998.

A Hybrid Multi-layered Speaker Independent Arabic Phoneme Identification System

Mian M. Awais, Shahid Masud, Shafay Shamail, and J. Akhtar

Department of Computer Science, Lahore University of Management Sciences
Sector-U, D.H.A., Lahore 54792, Pakistan
{awais,smasud,sshamail,jakhtar}@lums.edu.pk

Abstract. A phoneme identification system for Arabic language has been developed. It is based on a hybrid approach that incorporates two levels of phoneme identification. In the first layer power spectral information, efficiently condensed through the use of singular value decomposition, is utilized to train separate self-organizing maps for identifying each Arabic phoneme. This is followed by a second layer of identification, based on similarity metric, that compares the standard pitch contours of phonemes with the pitch contours of the input sound. The second layer performs the identification in case the first layer generates multiple classifications of the same input sound. The system has been developed using utterances of twenty-eight Arabic phonemes from over a hundred speakers. The identification accuracy based on the first layer alone was recorded at 71%, which increased to 91% with the addition of the second identification layer. The introduction of singular values for training instead of power spectral densities directly has resulted in reduction of training and recognition times for self-organizing maps by 80% and 89% respectively. The research concludes that power spectral densities along with the pitch information result in an acceptable and robust identification system for the Arabic phonemes.

1 Introduction

This paper presents an application of Self-Organizing Maps (SOM), arranged in a concurrent architecture [1,2], to solve the Arabic phoneme identification problem. The identification of phonemes is achieved through the training of SOM on a hybrid feature set that comprises of dimensionally reduced power spectral information and pitch contours of the sample sound waves. SOM have a wide range of applicability to complex real world problems, including speech recognition [1,3], mainly because SOM can be conveniently characterized by a vector space that comprises different patterns existing in the input data space. These vector spaces are developed based on the excitatory and inhibitory behavior of the output neurons in SOM [4,5]. One neuron or a group of neurons in the output layer contribute to a distinct input in time and space that results in classification and statistical data extraction.

A number of speech identification studies conducted in the past have used Neural Networks [5,6,7], Hidden Markov Models (HMM) [8], pitch contours [9,10], knowledge-base [11] and speech models [12]. However, the hybrid feature set used in the present paper for training the concurrently arranged SOM for identification of Arabic phonemes has not been previously reported in the literature.

The rest of the paper is organized as follows: Section 2 discusses the extraction methodology adopted for hybrid feature set. It briefly describes the basic working of SOM, concurrent arrangement of SOM and the multi-level recognition methodology that has been implemented. Section 3 explains the recognition algorithm developed whereas the results obtained from the experiments conducted using the hybrid algorithm are given in Section 4, followed by conclusions.

2 Proposed Recognition Methodology

There are two methods by which SOM can be applied to the extracted feature set of the sound waves. Firstly, a Single SOM (SSOM) can be trained for all the phonemes under consideration. In this arrangement the number of output neurons for the SOM is same as the number of phonemes to be recognized. It was observed that the weight optimization in this approach is computationally complex and longer training times are required. In the second method, Concurrent SOM (CSOM) can be realized in which separate SOM are developed and trained to recognize distinct phonemes [1]. Thus for 28 different phonemes there are 28 separate SOM that have to be developed, each trained on positive as well as negative examples. The latter approach has been adopted in this paper in the development of a novel hybrid multi-layered Arabic phoneme identification system. Though the weight optimization problem reduces in this approach, the overall development time for the whole system increases.

In order to reduce this development time, a new data reduction approach that minimizes the training data without compromising the effectiveness and the accuracy of the recognition system, is suggested. The overall feature set used in this system consists of power spectral densities and pitch contours of the recorded sound waves. The power spectral density feature is used for the first level and the pitch contour information is applied for the second level identification. Some explanation of the feature set, data minimization method and the need for the identification levels is discussed below.

2.1 Extraction of Hybrid Feature Set

As mentioned above, the hybrid feature set used in this work is extracted using Power Spectral Densities (PSD) [13] and pitch contours. PSD facilitate in the recognition of consonants present in the speech sample. Consonants are generally difficult to identify in time-domain because of the variation in their noise levels and speaker dependent properties. Time windowing approach is commonly used in order to extract the dominant frequencies through PSD calculation. In the present work PSD have been calculated using a commonly available package [14] through the implementation of Gaussian windowing approach.

These PSD for each phoneme utterance are represented by an $m \times n$ matrix that can be directly processed through the recognition module. However, this matrix is of a high order. Therefore the recognition module requires a longer training time especially when CSOM are used. In order to reduce this training time Singular Value Decomposition (SVD) has been performed on PSD matrix. The SVD decomposes the given matrix into three simpler matrices, including a diagonal matrix that has unique singular values on the diagonal, arranged in descending order, for every input matrix. The results presented in this paper suggest that the first 10 dominant singular values that are unique for every PSD matrix for a phoneme can be used for training the SOM without affecting the recognition accuracy.

2.2 First Recognition Layer of SOM

Once the singular values have been calculated, the SOM in a concurrent architecture are then employed to extract clusters of different phonemes for recognition. We have made use of SOM proposed by Kohonen [15] that is based on the principal of 'winner takes all'. This algorithm keeps certain biological similarity with the cortical maps [4]. If the input vector is x, and weights between the input layer and the maps are w, the winning neuron k is given as:

$$k = \min_{i,\, j \in \dim x,\, \dim y} \left\| x - w_{ij} \right\| \qquad (1)$$

This neuron excites the neurons in its close neighborhood according to the mexican hat function given in equation (2).

$$C(k_i, k_j, t) = \exp\left(\frac{-\left\| k_i - k_j \right\|^2}{(\alpha(t) S_o)^2} \right) \qquad (2)$$

where S_0 is the number of neurons per dimension, k_i is the winner neuron, k_j is its neighboring neuron and $\alpha(t)$ is the learning rate. The Hebb's law was used for training the Self Organizing Maps. The weight updating equations for winning and losing neurons are given by equations (3) and (4) respectively.

$$\frac{\partial w_{ij}}{\partial t} = \alpha(t)(x_{ij} - w_{ij}) \qquad (3)$$

$$\frac{\partial w_{ij}}{\partial t} = 0 \qquad (4)$$

2.3 Second Layer of Recognition Using Pitch Contours

The first layer of recognition results in some misclassifications i.e., more than one SOM is activated for the same input sound, resulting in a conflict and thus reducing the overall accuracy of system. In order to improve the efficiency, a second layer of identification has been implemented. It has been observed that unique clusters of pitch values for different phonemes can be obtained when pitch values are plotted against the frame number for different speakers [9]. The second level recognition is thus based on identifying the pitch cluster to which the input sounds belong. This second level pitch based clustering does not work for all the misclassifications, and some overlapping clusters are also formed. Thus one may conclude that only certain misclassifications, obtained in the first level identification, can be resolved through the identification of pitch clusters at the second level. The details are discussed in the following sections.

2.4 Recognition Algorithm

This section describes the complete algorithm for the developed system as shown in Figure 1. The operation starts by randomly acquiring the sound utterances of different phonemes by the speakers. After performing manual segmentation of phonemes, the PSD of the phoneme samples are calculated and are subjected to SVD. The first 10 dominant singular values are then obtained and provided to the trained CSOM. If only one CSOM is activated the recognition system outputs the recognized phoneme. However, in case multiple CSOM are activated, the conflict in phoneme recognition is resolved through invoking the second layer of recognition, which is based on pitch contours. If the second layer of recognition system successfully resolves the conflict, the recognized phoneme becomes the output; otherwise a misclassification error is generated. The complete algorithm is shown in Figure 1.

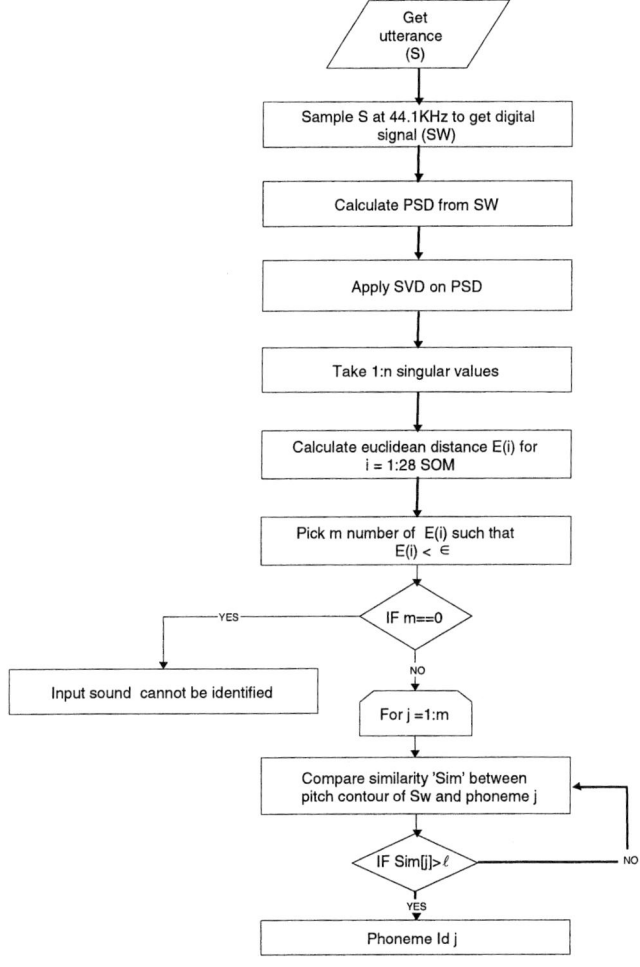

Fig. 1. Recognition Algorithm.

3 Implementation and Results

The system has been trained for 28 basic Arabic phonemes. Sound samples of one hundred different speakers were recorded at sampling rate of 44.1 KHz. Two subsets were developed from the recorded data, the training subset and the validation subset. The training dataset for the development of the recognition system comprised 70% of the total recorded sounds For PSD calculations, maximum sampling frequency of 8KHz and frequency step of 20Hz with Gaussian window shapes was used. The PSD matrix thus obtained was decomposed using singular value decomposition technique. The first 10 dominant singular values were then used to train the SOM. The accuracy was tested against the entire phonetic sound set in the validation phase.

3.1 Validation Results

The validation tests for CSOM architecture were conducted in three ways. The details of these tests are as follows:

1) *Individual SOM Testing*: SOM were tested individually for a specific phoneme for which they were developed, e.g., SOM for /a:/ was tested for /a:/ phonetic sounds and so forth. Figure 2 shows the results of this validation test (marked as individual). It can be noted that every SOM performed very well with accuracy greater than 80% with the exception of 25th phoneme. The overall accuracy for this test was recorded at 92%.
2) *CSOM Testing*: In this type of validation test the SOM were arranged in concurrent form and each SOM was cross validated for every type of phonetic sound, e.g., phonetic sound for /a:/ was presented to every SOM and the performance accuracy was recorded. Due to wrong classifications of several phonemes the overall accuracy of the identification system reduced to 72% (Figure 2, marked as All). As an example phoneme /a:/ had an accuracy of recognition of 100% in individual SOM testing which reduced to 57% when tested in concurrent form. This happened because of wrong classification of /a:/ as /H/. Similarly some other phonemes were wrongly identified. Thus need for introducing a second level of identification arose to enhance the classification accuracy. A second layer of identification for concurrent arrangement was implemented which was based on matching the pitch contours of the recorded sounds with the standard pitch contours of the phonemes to be recognized.
3) *Testing with Pitch Post Processor*: As explained above the overall accuracy of the concurrent system reduced drastically due to several misclassifications. In order to increase the accuracy, especially for the concurrent form of arrangement in the recognition system, a post processor based on pitch contour comparison was introduced, after the preliminary identification tests through the CSOM were conducted. The pitch based post-processing layer compared the standard pitch contours with pitch contours of the input sounds. Extensive experimentations, as discussed in section 2.3, showed that distinct pitch patterns were present for most of the sounds recorded for standard phoneme utterances. These distinct patterns helped in resolving some of the misclassifications observed during the application of CSOM arrangement. For example, in case of /a:/ versus /H/, unique pitch contours made it possible to distinctly identify the two phonemes, thus resulting in an

increased identification rate. Figure 3 represents the distinct pitch patterns obtained for more than 18 speakers for phonemes /a:/ and /H/ utterances. This observation provided a way to eliminate the misclassification generated because of the concurrent arrangement of SOM between the two phonemes. Similarly misclassifications of several other phonemes were resolved through analyzing the pitch variation at different frame numbers. Some of the examples include conflicts between /d/ and /X/, /a:/ and /H/, and /b/ and /z/. By introducing the pitch based layer of identification after CSOM arrangement, the overall accuracy of the recognition system increased to 91% from 72%. The effect can be observed in Figure 2 (marked as With Pitch).

The recognition accuracy achieved in our system can be well compared with the accuracies of some previously reported systems. Díaz et al [6] reported an overall accuracy of 66.10% when they used CSOM for the recognition of English digits from 1 to 9. Samouelian [16] showed overall accuracy of 62%-73.6% for English consonant recognition. Wooters and Stolcke [17] used Multi Level Perceptrons and claimed an average recognition accuracy of around 74.13%. Our system based on Arabic language clearly showed a higher degree of recognition accuracy as compared to existing recognition systems.

3.2 Training and Validation Time

The training and recognition times of the SVD based recognition system were recorded and compared with the non-SVD based recognition system (the SOM directly trained on the PSD). The experimental results showed immense CPU timesavings of up to 80% and 89% in training and recognition respectively. The results during the validation phase have shown that the reduced dataset used for training did not affect the overall accuracy of the recognition process. So if enough singular values are used, which in our case were 10, the performance of the system does not deteriorate.

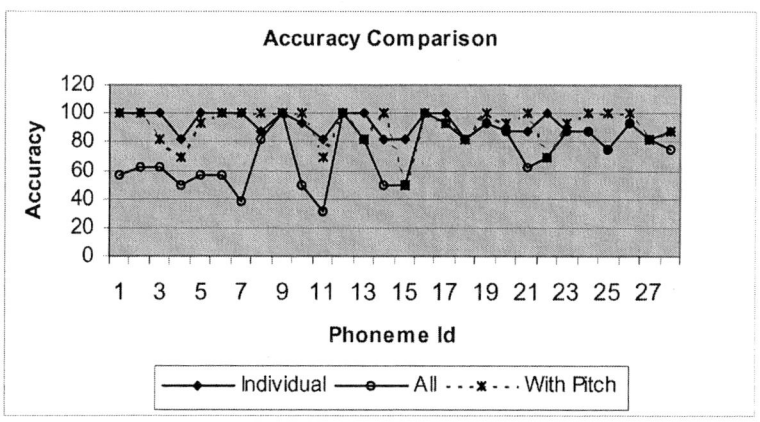

Fig. 2. Comparative Accuracy Profiles.

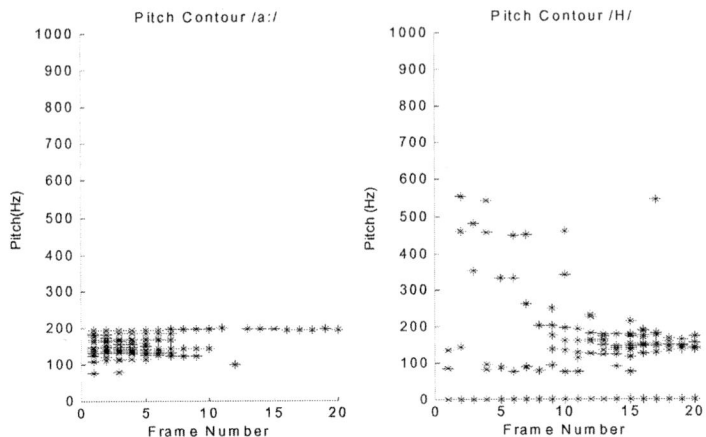

Fig. 3. Pitch Contours of /a:/ and /H/ for 18 Persons.

4 Conclusion

This paper presents a hybrid Arabic phoneme recognition system based on PSD, singular values, self-organizing maps and pitch contours of phonemes. The development time of CSOM has been dramatically reduced due to the introduction of SVD. The recognition accuracy of CSOM enhanced manifold when pitch analyzer was introduced as a post processor. This shows the utility of pitch feature in phoneme recognition for various phonetic sounds. An overall recognition accuracy of 91% has been achieved with reduction in training and recognition times by a factor of 80% and 89% respectively. The recognition accuracy displayed by our system can be well compared with other systems proposed in the literature.

Acknowledgement

We acknowledge Lahore University of Management Sciences (LUMS) for funding this research work.

References

1. Neagoe, V.E., Ropot, A.D.: Concurrent Self-Organizing Maps for Pattern Classification. IEEE International Conference on Cognitive Informatics (2002) 304-312
2. Song, H.H., Lee, S.W.: A Self-Organizing Neural Tree for Large-Set Pattern Classification. IEEE Trans. Neural Network. Vol. 9. no. 3 (1998) 369-379
3. Giurgiu, M.: Self-Organizing Feature Maps and Acoustic Segmentation Applied for Automatic Speech Recognition. In Proceedings of International Workshop on Speech and Computer. SPECOM '96. St. Petersburg (1996)

4. Kohonen, T.: Physiological Interpretation of the Self- Organizing Map Algorithm. Neural Networks. Vol. 6. (1993) 895-905
5. Somervuo, P.: Self-Organizing Maps for Signal and Symbol Sequences. PhD Thesis Helsinki University of Technology. Neural Networks Research Centre (2000)
6. Díaz, F., Ferrández, J. M., Gómez, P., Rodellar, V., Nieto, V.: Spoken-Digit Recognition using Self-organizing Maps with Perceptual Pre-processing. International Work-Conference on Artificial and Natural Neural Networks. IWANN'97. Lanzarote. Spain (1997) 1203-1212
7. Yuk, D.S., Flanagan, J.: Telephone Speech Recognition using Neural Networks and Hidden Markov Models. In Proceedings of International Conference on Acoustic Speech and Signal Processing. ICASSP '99 (1999) 157-160
8. Renals, S., Morgan, N.: Connectionist probability estimation in HMM speech recognition. Tech. Rep. TR-92-081. International Computer Science Institute. Berkeley CA. USA (1992)
9. Rabiner, L., Juang, B.H. Fundamentals of Speech Recognition. Prentice Hall Inc. Englewood Cliffs. New Jersey (1993)
10. Wong, Y. W., Chang, E.: The Effect of Pitch and Lexical Tone on Different Mandarin Speech Recognition Tasks. In proceedings of Eurospeech 2001. Vol. 4. Aalborg. Denmark (2001) 2741-2744
11. Zue, V.W., Lamel, L.F.: An Expert Spectrogram Reader: A Knowledge-Based Approach to Speech Recognition. In Proceedings of IEEE International Conference on Acoustic Speech Signal Processing. Tokyo. Japan (1986) 1197-1200
12. Kirchhoff, K.: Novel Speech Recognition Models for Arabic. Johns-Hopkins University. Technical Report (2002)
13. Kitaoka, N., Yamada, D., Nakagawa, S.: Speaker Independent speech recognition using features based on glottal sound source. In Proceedings of International Conference on Spoken Language Processing. ICSLP'02 (2002) 2125-2128
14. Praat web page: www.praat.org
15. Kohonen, T.: New Developments and Applications of Self-Organizing Maps. In Proceedings of the 1996 International Workshop on Neural Networks for Identification, Control, Robotics, and Signal/Image Processing. NICROSP '96 (1996) 164-172
16. Samouelian, A.: Knowledge Based Approach to Consonant Recognition. In Proceedings of International Conference on Acoustic Speech and Signal Processing ICASSP '94 (1994) 77-80
17. Wooters, C.C., Stolcke, A.: Multiple-pronunciation Lexical Modeling in a Speaker-independent Speech Understanding System. In Proceedings of Intl. Conf. on Spoken Language Processing. ICSLP '94 (1994) 453-456

Feature Selection for Natural Disaster Texts Classification Using Testors

Jesús A. Carrasco-Ochoa and José Fco. Martínez-Trinidad

Computer Science Department
National Institute of Astrophysics, Optics and Electronics
Luis Enrique Erro No. 1 Sta María Tonanzintla, Puebla, CP: 72840, Mexico
{ariel,fmartine}@inaoep.mx

Abstract. In this paper, the feature selection for classification of natural disaster texts through testors, is presented. Testors are features subsets such that no class confusion is introduced. Typical testors are irreducible testors. Then they can be used in order to select which words are relevant to separate the classes, and so, be useful to get better classification rates. Some experiments were done with KNN and Naive Bayes Classifiers, results were compared against frequency threshold and information gain methods.

1 Introduction

In the last years the online information has growth rapidly so it is necessary to classify and to get interesting knowledge from texts. Text classification is an area that has become very important for handling and organizing text data. The goal of text classification is the classification of documents into a fixed number of predefined classes. One document can be in multiple, exactly one or no class at all. This is a supervised problem of Pattern Recognition.

The first step in text categorization [1] consists in transforming documents, which are strings of characters, into a representation suitable for the feature selection algorithm and the classification task. Then words are used to represent documents and each distinct word corresponds to a feature. In this way, there are two representations. The first one is the Boolean representation where a feature takes value zero (if the word does not appear in the document) or one (if the word appears in the document) and numeric representations where the value of the attribute is the number of times that a word occurs in the document, i.e., the frequency of apparition.

These representations produce very high-dimensional feature spaces with 10000 features or more [2]. In this circumstance the traditional methods for feature selection can not be applied to solve the problem.

In this paper, the problem of feature selection is faced using Testor Theory [3]. The algorithms for computing testors are limited to problems with few features because computing testors is of exponential complexity. Therefore, in this work we present how the problem was solved using genetic algorithms [4,5] to compute testors in a reasonable time for very high-dimensional feature spaces as occurs in the text classification problems. The proposed method was applied on a problem of natural disaster texts classification. For this problem, all testors that were found are of a very small cardinality and they have high classification rates.

In the section 2, some basic definitions about testor theory are given; in the section 3, the genetic algorithms to search testors and typical testors are described; in the section 4, some experiments with natural disasters texts are shown; finally in section 5, we expose our conclusions and future work.

2 Testor Theory

Into the framework of the Logical Combinatorial Pattern Recognition, feature selection is solved using Testor Theory [3]. A testor is defined as follows:

Definition 1. A subset of features T is a testor if and only if when all features are eliminated, except those from T, there is not any pair of equal subdescriptions in different classes.

The definition 1 says us that a testor is a subset of features, which allows complete differentiation of objects from different classes. Within the set of all testors, there are some testors, which are irreducible. These testors are called typical testors. Typical testors are defined as follows:

Definition 2. A subset of features T is a typical testor if and only if T is a testor and there is not any other testor T' such that $T' \subset T$.

The definition 2 says us that a typical testor is a testor where every feature is essential, this is, if any of them is eliminated the resultant set is not a testor.

Given these definitions, it is easy to verify if a feature subset is or not a testor and also if it is or not typical. But the calculation of all typical testors is important because they are all subsets of features that can completely differentiate objects from different classes and they are not redundant. However, if the definition 2 is used to calculate all typical testors, all 2^n different subsets of features must be verified. For each one, you have to decide if it is a testor, then you must decide if it is typical.

Since this process is of exponential complexity with regard to the number of features, many different algorithms to calculate all typical testors have been developed, but all of them are of exponential complexity for the worst case.

3 Genetic Algorithms for Testor Calculation

In this section, based in the method proposed in [6], where a genetic algorithm for typical testor computation is introduced, we propose some modifications to get algorithms suitable for problems with very high-dimensional feature spaces as those that appear in text classification.

The individuals handled by the genetic algorithms will be different sets of features. These sets are represented as n-uples formed by the values 0 and 1 (genes), these values represent the absence or presence of a feature, and n represents the total number of features.

The individuals are denoted as I_i $i=1,...,p$, where p is the number of individuals in the population.

As it was mentioned, it is easy to decide if a feature subset is or not a testor and also if it is or not typical, so we can use a *fitness function* which returns the following values: 0 for individuals representing non testors, 1 for those individuals which are testors and 2 for individuals that are typical testors. In this way if an individual I_i (a selection) is a typical testor then it will be a more capable individual.

In order to apply the crossover operator the population is ordered in descending form regarding individuals' fitness. The individuals with fitness 2 are transformed for the new population exchanging the 0's by 1's and vice versa. The rest individuals are crossed taking the first individual I_f with the highest fitness and the last one I_l (that has the smallest fitness), using as crossing point $n/2$ (the half of the individual). After, the second individual is crossed with the penultimate one; this operation is repeated until finishing with the population. In this process, a mask randomly built with 0's and 1's of length n, and another one with its complement, are used. Then crossover operator applies the AND operator between the first half of I_f and the first half of the mask, and between second half of I_f and the second half of the complement mask. Meanwhile the AND operator between the first half of I_l and the first half of the complement mask, and second half of I_l and the second half of the mask, is applied. In this way, two new individuals are built.

The mutation operator is guided by the individuals' fitness. If the fitness is 2 then randomly we choose two genes with different value and change the 0 by 1 and the 1 by 0. In this way we force to search in other direction. If the fitness is 1 then randomly we choose a 1 in the individual and it is changed by 0. Therefore, a testor is in the way to a typical testor. Finally, if the fitness is 0 then we randomly choose a 0 in the individual and it is changed by 1.

The use of these operators (crossover and mutation) in the genetic algorithm for very large individuals does not produce typical testors; therefore as first modification we change the fitness function to eliminate the typical testor condition in order to find only testors. The structure of the algorithm is maintained and when an individual is a testor, it is stored if previously it was not stored.

The structure of the genetic algorithm is as follows:

Genetic Algorithm (TFS-GA)
Input: *size:* size of population; *Num_iter:* Number of iterations
1. *Generate_initial_population(population, size)*
2. *Evaluate_population(population)*
3. *Repeat for i=1 until i=Num_iter*
4.   Store testors of population
5.   *Crossover(population, population2)*
6.   *Evaluate_population(population2)*
7.   *Mutation(population2)*
8.   *Evaluate_population(population2)*
9.   *population=population2*
10. END.

In order to produce typical testors, a second modification was done using the original fitness function and changing the crossover operator as follows: the population is ordered in descending form regarding individuals' fitness. The first individual (that has the highest fitness) and the last one (that has the smallest fitness) are taken and crossed (using 1-point crossing with crossing point $n/2$, the half of the individual). After, the second individual is crossed with the penultimate one; this process is repeated until finishing with the population. The same mutation operator was used. In Addition, the structure of the genetic algorithm was modified as below.

Genetic Algorithm (TTFS-GA)
Input: *size:* size of population;   *Num_iter:* Number of iterations
1. Generate_initial_population(population, size)
2. Evaluate_population(population)
3. Repeat for i=1 until i=Num_iter
4.   Store typical testors of population
5.   Crossover2(population, population2)
6.   Evaluate_population(population2)
7.   Mutation(population, population3)
8.   Evaluate_population(population3)
9.   Pick_out_next_population
10. END.

The function *Pick_out_next_population* chooses from *population2* and *population3* to the most capable individuals (those with highest fitness) that will form a new population for the next iteration. The original population is discarded.

Table 1. Classification rates with KNN and Naïve Bayes classifiers using testors and typical testors as feature selection for the Boolean representation.

	Testor	Size	KNN	Naïve Bayes
Typical (TTFS-GA)	1	14	88.0000	88.0000
	2	15	87.2000	89.0667
	3	15	87.4667	89.3333
	4	16	85.3333	90.4000
	5	16	87.2000	89.8667
	6	19	89.3333	89.8667
	7	19	89.8667	90.4000
	8	19	90.1333	90.9333
	9	19	90.1333	91.4667
	10	19	90.9333	90.6667
Non Typical (TFS-GA)	1	29	90.1333	88.2667
	2	29	90.9333	91.2000
	3	31	89.3333	90.1333
	4	31	89.8667	93.3333
	5	31	91.2000	92.2667
	6	36	91.2000	93.8667
	7	58	92.0000	92.0000
	8	71	92.5333	93.3330
	9	89	91.7333	93.0667
	10	102	92.5333	94.1333

4   Experimental Results

In this section, some experiments of feature selection for text classification are presented. A comparison, of the classification rate obtained with testors as feature selection against selection by frequency threshold and information gain methods, is made. The texts collection used for our experiments was a set of 375 documents in Spanish about natural disasters in Mexico, divided into four classes: hurricane, inundation, drought, and irrelevant. Databases for experimentations were the same used in [7].

This problem has 14,562 terms which are used to describe the documents, so the initial data was contained in two matrixes of 14,562×375 (one for Boolean representation and other one for numeric representation). Due to this size, traditional feature selection methods including testor theory methods are inapplicable, so the testor search methods described in section 3 were used.

For the Boolean case, using TTFS-GA we found 10 typical testors from 14 to 19 terms and also using TFS-GA we found 10 testors which are non-typical but with sizes from 29 to 102, in about ten minutes. Classification rates using KNN (K-nearest neighbors with K=1) and Naïve Bayes classifiers with each testor (both typical and non typical) as feature selection, are shown in Table 1.

Table 2. Classification rates with KNN and Naïve Bayes classifiers using testors and typical testors as feature selection for the numeric representation.

	Testor	Size	KNN	Naïve Bayes
Typical (TTFS-GA)	1	11	84.5333	84.2667
	2	12	81.3333	84.5333
	3	12	82.6667	84.0000
	4	15	84.5333	83.7333
	5	15	85.0667	84.5333
	6	15	85.3333	82.9333
	7	16	84.2667	82.1333
	8	16	86.1333	82.9333
	9	16	87.2000	80.8000
	10	16	88.0000	80.5333
Non Typical (TFS-GA)	1	29	89.8667	91.4667
	2	32	92.2667	93.6000
	3	47	88.5333	92.2667
	4	52	91.4670	93.6000
	5	52	92.0000	92.0000
	6	60	91.4667	93.6000
	7	85	91.7333	92.5333
	8	88	92.8000	94.9333
	9	93	90.9333	93.0667
	10	104	92.5333	96.0000

For the frequency case, using TTFS-GA we found 10 typical testors form 11 to 16 terms and also using TFS-GA we found 10 which are non-typical but with sizes from 29 to 104. Classification rates using KNN (K-nearest neighbors with K=1) and Naïve Bayes classifiers with each testor (both typical and non typical) as feature selection, are shown in table 2.

We have used 10-fold cross-validation for performing all the experiments, that is, the data was randomly divided into ten equally sized subsets, and then in each experiment one subset was used for testing and the other nine for training.

The results were compared against those reported in [7], where two methods for feature selection were used. The first method consists in fixing a threshold to the frequency of each term into the complete collection and selecting only such terms with frequency higher than the fixed threshold. The second methods selects all terms with non-zero information gain. The comparison is shown in table 3.

5 Conclusions

Feature selection for text classification is a difficult task due to the large number of terms used to describe the documents. Because of this high dimensionality, traditional techniques for feature selection based on typical testors can not be applied. Testor theory is a useful tool for feature selection but the algorithms developed into this theory are of very high complexity. Therefore, in this paper two strategies to allow

Table 3. Classification rates with KNN and Naïve Bayes classifiers using the best testors and typical testors as feature selection for Boolean and numeric representations, compared against results given in [7].

		Sizes KNN / NaïveBayes	KNN	Naïve Bayes
Boolean	Typical Testors (TTFS-GA)	19 / 19	90.9333	91.4667
	Non Typical Testors (TFS-GA)	71 / 36	92.5333	93.8667
	Frequency > 10	2550 / 2550	90.9300	93.3000
	Information gain > 0	214 / 214	92.8000	97.0600
Frequency	Typical Testors (TTFS-GA)	16 / 12	88.0000	84.5333
	Non Typical Testors (TFS-GA)	88 / 104	92.8000	96.0000

feature selection through testors, were proposed. These new strategies allow finding testors and typical testors of a very small cardinality in a short time.

From experimentation, we can conclude that it is possible to get a very small subset of terms with only a marginal reduction of the classification quality. This is very important when a very large collection of documents must be classified, like in internet searches.

As future work, we are going to test some supervised classification methods developed into the framework of the logical combinatorial pattern recognition [8] in order to find better classification rates. Also we are going to find a conceptual interpretation of the selection done by testor for the problem of natural disaster texts classification, for trying to find a linguistic explanation of why these few terms are enough to separate the classes.

Acknowledgement

This work was financially supported by CONACyT (Mexico) through project J38707-A.

References

1. Salton, M. J. McGill. An Introduction to Modern Information Retrieval. McGraw-Hill, 1983.
2. Joachims. Text Categorization with Support Vector Machines: Learning with many relevant features. Proc. 10th European Conference on Machine Learning (ECML), Springer Verlag, 137-142, 1998.
3. Lazo-Cortes M., Ruiz-Shulcloper J. and Alba-Cabrera E. An overview of the evolution of the concept of testor, Pattern Recognition, 34, 753-762, 2001.
4. Mitchel M. An introduction to genetic algorithms. MIT Press, 1996.
5. Goldberg D. Genetic algorithms in search, optimization and machine learning. Addison Wesley, 1989.
6. Sánchez, G., Lazo, M., Fuentes, O., Genetic algorithm to calculate typical testors of minimal cost, Proc. IV Iberoamerican Simposium on Pattern Recognition (SIARP' 99), La Havana, Cuba, 207-213, 1999 (In Spanish).
7. Alberto Téllez-Valero, Manuel Montes-y-Gómez, Olac Fuentes-Chavez, Luis Villaseñor-Pineda, Automatic classification of texts about natural disasters in Mexico, to appear in Proc, International Congress on Computer Science Research, Oaxtepec, México, 2003 (In Spanish).
8. Martínez-Trinidad J. F. and Guzmán-Arenas A. The logical combinatorial approach to pattern recognition an overview through selected works, Pattern Recognition, 34, 741-751, 2001.

Mining Large Engineering Data Sets on the Grid Using AURA

Bojian Liang[1] and Jim Austin[1]

Department of Computer Science
University of York, Heslington, York, YO10 5DD
{austin,bojian}@cs.york.ac.uk

Abstract. AURA (Advanced Uncertain Reasoning Architecture) is a parallel pattern matching technology intended for high-speed approximate search and match operations on large unstructured datasets. This paper represents how the AURA technology is extended and used to search the engine data within a major UK eScience Grid project (DAME) for maintenance of Rolls-Royce aero-engines and how it may be applied in other areas. Examples of its use will be presented.

1 Introduction

DAME (Distributed Aircraft Maintenance Environment) is a major UK eScience Grid project aiming to build a **Grid test-bed for Distributed Diagnostics**. The application demonstrator of DAME is a distributed aircraft maintenance environment for Rolls–Royce aero–engines. Distributed diagnostics is a generic problem that is fundamental in many fields such as medical, transportation and manufacturing. Intelligent feature extraction and data mining are the two main tasks closely related to the early processing of the engine fault detection and novelty detection. Each engine on a civil airliner is capable of generating around 1GBs of vibration and performance data per flight. At present, these data are searched locally for the presence of features known to be associated with fault condition and for deviations from a model of known operation (novelty detection). There is no mechanism for searching a globally distributed database of past experience to find any similar novelties. Neither is there a mechanism for collecting any relevant collateral information to provide the owner of the data with decision support.

Time series signal is a series of values of a variable at successive times. Analysis of time series can be within the time domain or frequency domain [1][2][3]. Both the engine vibration and performance data are the time series signal. The healthy of an operating engine can be featured by some kind of patterns and values of the signals. Monitoring of time series, fast searching for similar pattern through the time series from database have attracted more and more attentions.

AURA (Advanced Uncertain Reasoning Architecture) is a parallel pattern matching technology developed as a set of general–purpose methods for searching large unstructured datasets. The DAME system is able to take data from a fleet of aircraft and store this data in distributed data stores for later searching and matching. DAME has combined AURA based search technology with CBR (Case–Based Reasoning) and advanced pattern-matching methods to provide an integrated high performance engineering maintenance system. The system is designed to deal with up to 1TBs of data arriving daily to be stored for later searching. A signal data exploration tool has been implemented as the front end of the AURA technology allowing a user search for signal data similar to one that an operator may be interested in. The tool may be used for any time series based data.

2 The Binary CMM and the AURA Implementation

The AURA technology is based on a high–performance neural network called Correlation Matrix Memory (CMM) [4][5]. AURA defines a set of pre– and post–processing methods for different data as well as a neural network based data storage system. Recently, the methods have been extended to deal with vibration based time series data and being developed for distributed Grid enabled datasets within the DAME project. The latest development of AURA include the new AURA C++ library, the new hardware prototype (PRESENCE-II) and a Grid enabled AURA pattern match service. Many applications for AURA are being developed. These include a postal address matching, high-speed rule-matching systems [6], fraudulent benefit claims detection system (FEDAURA), structure–matching (e.g 3D molecular structures) [7], human face recognition and trademark–database searching [8].

2.1 Correlation Matrix Memories

Correlation Matrix Memory (CMM) is a type of binary associative neural network. A CMM with m columns and n rows can be represented by a $n \times m$ matrix with binary weights, $\mathbf{M}$. Given a n-dimension binary input pattern $\mathbf{I}_k$ and a m-dimension binary associated output pattern $\mathbf{O}_k$, the training of a CMM can be written as:

$$\mathbf{M}_k = \mathbf{M}_{k-1} \cup \mathbf{I}_k^T \mathbf{O}_k. \qquad (1)$$

Where, $\mathbf{M}_{k-1}$ and $\mathbf{M}_k$ are the CMM pattern before and after the kth learning operation. $\cup$ denotes a logical OR operation. A CMM recall , $\mathbf{S}_i$, referring to input pattern $\mathbf{I}_i$ is given by:

$$\mathbf{S}_i = \mathbf{I}_i \mathbf{M}. \qquad (2)$$

The recall $\mathbf{S}_i$ is usually not a binary vector. It can be thresholded to from a binary pattern, $\mathbf{O}_i$, which indicates the possible matches, or used as integer vector which represents a measure of the match. The integer value of the elements of the recall vector $\mathbf{S}_i$ is called **the score** of the CMM matching.

2.2 The AURA Implementation

The current AURA implementations include the software and hardware prototypes. The software AURA implementation is a C++ library which provides API in AURA applications for pattern storage, pattern retrieval and translating between external and internal representations from a wide range of data types. Within project DAME, a distributed Grid enabled DAME pattern match service based on the AURA technology has been developed. The Grid services include the Data extractor, AURA data store, AURA encoder, AURA-G pattern match service and a set of post–processing packages.

The binary neural network based architecture used in AURA can be efficiently implemented in hardware. PRESENCE II (**PaRallEl StructureEd Neural Computing Engine**) is the latest generation of AURA hardware implementation. At the heart of the card is a large Field Programmable Gate Array. The FPGA interfaces to a fast Digital Signal Processor, up to 4GBs of SDRAM memory, two independent fast Zero-Bus-Turnaround memories, dual high-speed data channels, Sundance digital I/O header and a mezzanine expansion card connector. With each on-board resource given an independent interface to the FPGA, the designer is able to implement bus structures of choice, rather than the board itself imposing a fixed wiring scheme. Additional host system resources (system memory, I/O devices etc) are accessible via the PCI bus as bus master.

3 Implementation of the DAME Pattern Search Engine

A crucial part of engine health monitoring is the search and detection of abnormal patterns and values within the vibration and performance data which are represented as time series data. The difficulties of such pattern search lie in the fact that the search over terabytes of data and the limited knowledge of patterns of fault conditions that are to be found. The AURA technology provides solutions for high speed pattern match from huge volume of data. A set of methods for pre– and post–processing makes it possible to handle the imprecisely defined fault patterns.

3.1 The Similarity Measures

Matching two time series with the same length is main approach in time series pattern matching. This can be extended to the *subsequence matching* which assumes that the length of the main series is longer than that of the query. In the subsequence matching, the query is used to scan the whole length of the main series. The best match and the offset of the subsequence are reported. For example, the engine data record of one flight may be as long as several hours while the query pattern which represents the fault condition a few seconds. The search engine is required to find all the similar patterns with the query from thousands of engine data records and locate the time instances of the best match over the records.

Definition of measures is crucial for pattern matching. Depending the application, different measures can be applied to the search engine to obtain the required output. Although AURA supports several similarity measures, correlation and Euclidean distance are the two main measures used in the engine data time series pattern match.

Given the length, n, of two sequences $Q = q_1, q_2, ..., q_n$ and $S = s_1, s_2, ..., s_n$ the Euclidean distance is defined as:

$$D(Q, S) = \sqrt{\sum_{i=1}^{n}(q_i - s_i)^2}. \tag{3}$$

Euclidean distance provides similarity measure for time series patterns with both similar amplitude and shape. However, the performance of a search engine using the Euclidean distance measure becomes poor for matching signals with similar shape but different amplitude. Normalised correlation measure is invariant of amplitude scaling. It is one of the most widely used similarity measures for "shape" matching. Correlation of two time series Q and S is defined as:

$$M(Q, S) = \frac{\sum_{i=1}^{n} s_i q_i}{\sqrt{\sum_{i=1}^{n} q_i^2 \sum_{i=1}^{n} s_i^2}}. \tag{4}$$

Using the same components of the correlation, Euclidean distance measure can be re-written as:

$$D(Q, S) = \sqrt{\sum_{i=1}^{n} q_i^2 + \sum_{i=1}^{n} s_i^2 - 2 \sum_{i=1}^{n} s_i q_i} \tag{5}$$

The DAME search engine firstly applies correlation measure to retrieve a set of subsequences with the similar shape. Then, the K nearest neighbour algorithm may be applied to obtain required subsequences.

3.2 Architecture of the Search Engine

The DAME pattern search engine is an application for time series signal pattern match based on the AURA technology. The efficient AURA indexing technology significantly reduces the overall computation of the matching. A special CMM architecture is designed to compute the Euclidean distance and the correlation similarity measure in one fly with very little additional computation. Fig.1 shows the CMM structures of the search engine. Data in the main data store is loaded to the main CMM (CMM-2). The intermediate results store in CMM-3. Operation on CMM-3 generates the final results in CMM-4. For subsequence matching, the non-maximum measurements on CMM-4 can be depressed and only one best subsequence for each record is reported.

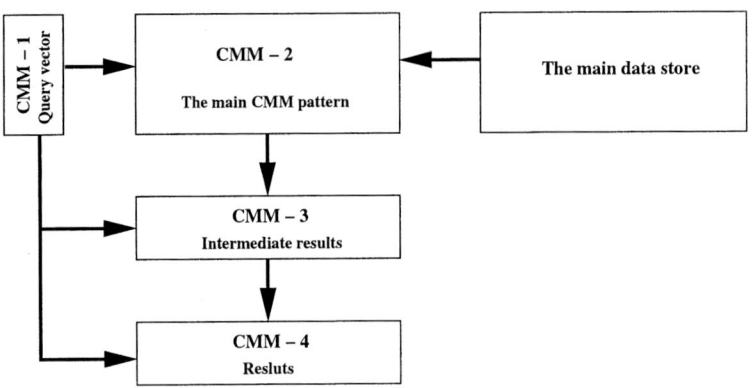

Fig. 1. Architecture of the search engine.

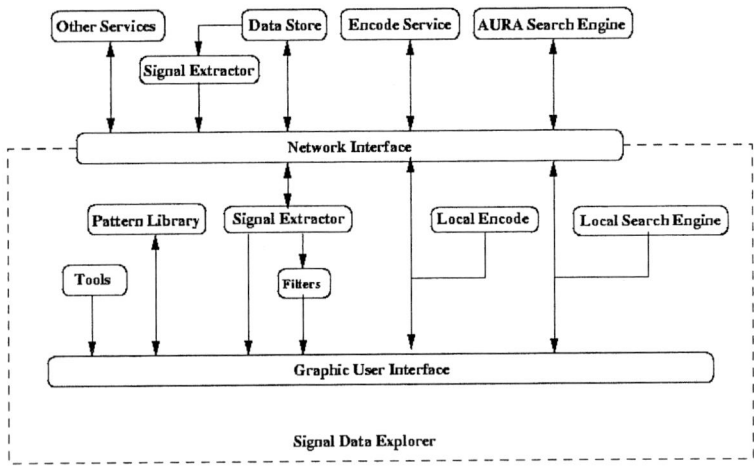

Fig. 2. Architecture of the DAME signal data explorer.

4 The DAME Signal Data Explorer

The DAME system provides a collection of diagnostic tools, which can be used in an automatic sequence, usually by a Maintenance Engineer, or interactively by a Domain Expert. The DAME Signal Data Explorer (SDE) is a tool vital to the work of the Domain Expert for engine diagnosis. Using the SDE a Domain Expert can view raw engine data, extract and view features from the raw data, select a pattern or Region Of Interest (ROI) and search for similar patterns in the terabytes of data stored from previous and recent flights over the Grid. It is a important tool within the DAME system. Fig.2 shows the architecture of the SDE. The graphic user interface and the build-in tools allow the user to play the time series data, select the ROI from the view, probe for particular parameters instance hidden in the data record and invoke the searching over the

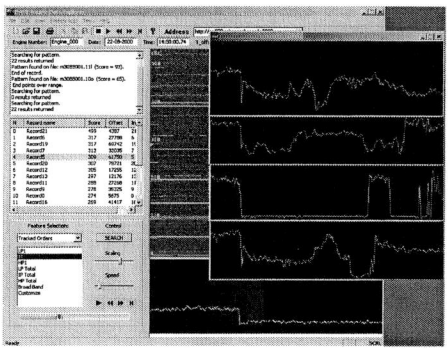 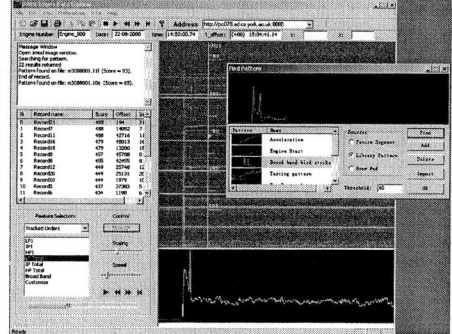

(a) Pattern displayed as a result of search (b) Pattern found from the current feature set matching a template.

Fig. 3. Application examples.

Grid. A pattern finder provides means to find the next similar pattern from the current engine data set – an equivalent of finding a word from text file. A library of fault pattern is contained within the SDE. User can manage the library by add, delete and edit the patterns stored in the library. Patterns in the library can be chosen to form a group of patterns which represents a particular fault. The AURA search engine allows these patterns to be searched in parallel. In the future, the search engine and searching task can be configured in time using a task planner equipped with the SDE. A build-in search engine makes it possible to use the SDE separately from the Grid.

5 Application Examples

The following screen-shots (Fig.3) show particular examples of the operation of the SDE. The first example (Fig.3-a) is an application of searching for similar pattern with the input template from large volume of history data store. The ROI is highlighted as the searching template. Search results are listed in the results window. The first four best matches are displayed. The second example (Fig.3-b) is to find similar pattern with the template from the current test data record: A query pattern is imported from the pattern library view. The next similar pattern is displayed on the bottom window.

Acknowledgements

This project was supported by a UK eScience Pilot grant from EPSRC (GR/R67668/01), as well as support from our industrial collaborators Rolls-Royce, Data Systems and Solutions and Cybula Ltd.

References

1. Priestley, M. B. : Spectral Analysis and Time Series, Vols. 1 and 2, Academic Press, New York. (1981).
2. Box, G. E. P., Jenkins, G. M., and Reinsel, G. C. : Time Series Analysis, Forecasting and Control. 3rd ed. Prentice Hall, Englewood Clifs, NJ. (1994).
3. Brockwell, Peter J., and Davis, Richard A. : Time Series: Theory and Methods. Springer-Verlang (1987).
4. Austin, J.: Distributed associative memories for high speed symbolic reasoning. In, IJCAI Working Notes of workshop on connectionist-Symbolic Integration, ¿From Unified to Hybrid Approaches.(1995) 87-93.
5. Austin, J., Kennedy, J., and Lees, K. : The advanced uncertain reasoning architecture. In Weightless Neural Network Workshop, 1995.
6. Austin, J., Kennedy, J., and Lees, K. : A neural architecture for fast rule matching. In Artificial Neural Networks and Expert Systems Conference (ANNES 95), Dunedin, New Zealand, December 1995.
7. Turner, A., and Austin, J. : Performance evaluation of a fast chemical structure matching method using distributed neural relaxation. In fourth International Conference on Knowledge-based Intelligent Engineering Systems, August 2000.
8. Alwis, S.,and Austin, J. : A novel architecture for trade-mark image retrieval systems. In Electronic Workshops in Computing. Springer, 1998.

Self-tuning Based Fuzzy PID Controllers: Application to Control of Nonlinear HVAC Systems

Behzad Moshiri and Farzan Rashidi

Center of Excellence for Control and Intelligent Processing
Department of Electrical and Computer Engineering, Tehran University, Tehran, Iran
moshiri@ut.ac.ir, f.rashidi@ece.ut.ac.ir

Abstract. Heating, Ventilating and Air Conditioning (HVAC) plant is a multivariable, nonlinear and non minimum phase system, which its control is very difficult. For this reason, in the design of HVAC controller the idea of self tuning controllers is being used. In this paper a robust and adaptive self tuning based fuzzy PID controller for control of nonlinear HVAC systems is presented. To illustrate the effectiveness of the proposed method some simulations are given. Obtained results show that the proposed method not only is robust, but also it gives good dynamic response compared with traditional controllers. Also the response time is also very fast despite the fact that the control strategy is based on bounded rationality. To evaluate the usefulness of the proposed method, we compare the response of this method with PID controller. The obtained results show that our method has the better control performance than PID controller.

Nomenclature

h_w	Enthalpy of liquid water	W_o	Humidity ratio of outdoor air
h_{fg}	Enthalpy of water vapor	V_{he}	Volume of heat exchanger
W_s	Humidity ratio of supply air	W_3	Humidity ratio of thermal space
C_p	Specific heat of air	T_o	Temperature of outdoor air
M_o	Moisture load	Q_o	Sensible heat load
T_2	Temperature of supply air	T_3	Temperature of thermal space
V_s	Volume of thermal space	ρ	Air mass density
f	Volumetric flow rate of air	gpm	Flow rate of chilled water

1 Introduction

The consumption of energy by heating, ventilating, and air conditioning (HVAC) equipment in commercial and industrial buildings constitutes fifty percent of the world energy consumption [1]. In spite of the advancements made in computer technology and its impact on the development of new control methodologies for HVAC systems aiming at improving their energy efficiencies, the process of operating HVAC equipment in commercial and industrial buildings is still an low-efficient and high-energy consumption process [2]. Classical HVAC control techniques such as ON/OFF controllers and PID controllers are still very popular because of their low cost. However, in the long run, these controllers are expensive because they operate at very low energy efficiency and fail to consider the complex nonlinear characteristics of the MIMO HVAC systems and the strong coupling actions between them. The problem of HVAC control can be posed from two different points of view. In the first, one aims at reaching an optimum consumption of energy. In the second, that is more common in HVAC control, the goal is keeping moisture, temperature, pressure and other air conditions in an acceptable range. Several different control and intelligent strategies have been developed in recent years to achieve the stated goals fully or partially [3]. Although several intelligent and classical control strategies have been designed for HVAC system, but due to its non-minimum phase, multivariable, nonlinear and nonlinearizable with constraints on its supply air temperature, none of them provide all goals such as adaptive set point tracking or disturbance rejection. The purpose of this paper is to suggest another control approach, based on robust self tuning fuzzy PID controller to achieve faster response with disturbance rejection and reduced overshoot and rise time. In the subsequent sections, we discuss the HVAC system, our proposed controller, and its application in the closed loop control system, simulation and some concluding.

2 HVAC Model

In this part, we give some explanations about the HVAC model that we have used. Fig. 1 shows the structure of the HVAC system. For simulation of HVAC systems, some different models have been proposed and considered. In this paper, we used the model developed in [4], since it aims at controlling the temperature and humidity of the Variable Air Volume (VAV) HAVC system. The state space equations governing the model are as follows:

$$\dot{x}_1 = 60u_1\alpha_1(x_3 - x_1) - 60u_1\alpha_2(W_s - x_2) + \alpha_3(Q_o - h_{fg}M_o) \quad (1)$$

$$\dot{x}_2 = 60u_1\alpha_2(W_s - x_2) + \alpha_4 M_o \quad (2)$$

$$\dot{x}_3 = 60u_1\beta_1(x_1 - x_3) - 60u_1\beta_3(0.25W_o + 0.75x_2 - W_s) - 6000u_2\beta_2 + 15u_1\beta_1(T_o - x_1) \quad (3)$$

$$y_1 = x_1, y_2 = x_2 \quad (4)$$

In which the parameters are:

$$u_1 = f, u_2 = gpm, x_1 = T_3, x_2 = W_3, x_3 = T_2 \quad (5)$$

$$\alpha_1 = 1/V_s, \alpha_2 = h_{fg}/C_pV_s, \alpha_3 = 1/\rho C_pV_s, \alpha_4 = 1/\rho V_s, \beta_1 = 1/V_{he} \quad (6)$$

$$\beta_2 = 1/\rho C_p V_{he}, \beta_3 = h_w/C_p V_{he} \quad (7)$$

And the numerical values are given in table 1. The system has delayed behavior which is represented via linearized, first order and time delay system. Furthermore, the model represents a MIMO system in which one of the I/O channels has a right half plane zero, meaning that it is non-minimum-phase.

Table 1. Numerical Values for system parameters.

$\rho = .074\ lb/ft^3$	$C_p = .24\ Btu/lb.°F$	$V_s = 58464\ ft^3$	$T_o = 85°F$	$M_o = 166.06\ lb/hr$
$V_{he} = 60.75\ ft^3$	$W_s = .007\ lb/lb$	$W_o = .0018\ lb/lb$	$Q_o = 289897$	$\tau = .008\ hr, k = 5$

3 Fuzzy PID Controller

In recent years, fuzzy logic controllers, especially PID type fuzzy controllers have been widely used in industrial processes owing to their heuristic nature associated with simplicity and effectiveness for both linear and nonlinear systems. In fact, for multi-input multi-output (MIMO) systems, most of fuzzy logic controllers are essentially of PD type, PI type or PID type with nonlinear gains. Because of the nonlinearity of the control gains, fuzzy PID controllers possess the potential to achieve better system performance over conventional PID controllers provide the nonlinearity can be suitably utilized [5]. On the other hand, due to the existence of nonlinearity, it is usually difficult to conduct theoretical analyses to explain why fuzzy PID controllers can achieve better performance. Consequently it is important, from both theoretical and practical points of view, to explore the essential nonlinear control properties of fuzzy PID controllers, and find out appropriate design methods which will assist control engineers to confidently utilize the nonlinearity of fuzzy PID controllers so as to improve the closed-loop performance. Fig. 2 shows the structure of proposed fuzzy PID controller [6]. As can be seen the fuzzy PID controller is made of multiple rule bases where the result of one rule base inference is passed on to the next as fact. In this manner higher dimensions of inference can be grouped into smaller sets and combined using rules. In the proposed method, the result of the PD rule base is passed on to the PID rule base to combine with the integral feedback. In the PID rule base, the system applies integral feedback only when the result of the PD rule base is nearly zero, indicating that the system dynamics have settled. This structure is quite similar to the hierarchical structure of behavior-based controllers. In terms of behavior-based control, the integral term is the base function and typically controls the system. The higher-level PD function assumes control when command or disturbance dynamics are present. Control returns to the base function when the dynamics have settled. When applied as a fuzzy logic controller, this approach results in a smooth blending of the integral feedback.

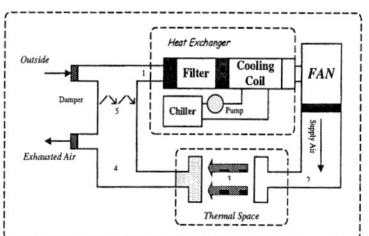

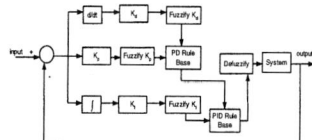

Fig. 1. Model of the HVAC system.   Fig. 2. The structure of fuzzy PID controller.

A look at the rule bases shows how the integral feedback is intelligently applied. The two rule bases are shown in Tables 2 and 3. The PID rule base only applies integral feedback when the result of the PD rule base is Zero (ZE). Otherwise it passes the values from the PD rule base. The PD rule base is slightly modified from a typical linear rule base to remove all the ZE values except at the center of the rule base. In this manner, the PD rule base will only pass on a ZE value when both the error and the change in error terms are ZE indicating the system has settled. The other fuzzy values used in this paper are Negative Big (NB), Negative Small (NS), Positive Small (PS), and Positive Big (PB).

Table 2. PID Rule Base.

		\multicolumn{5}{c}{PD value}				
		NB	NS	ZE	PS	PB
δe	NB	NB	NS	NB	PS	PB
	NS	NB	NS	NS	PS	PB
	ZE	NB	NS	ZE	PS	PB
	PS	NB	NS	PS	PS	PB
	PB	NB	NS	PB	PS	PB

Table 3. PD Rule Base.

		\multicolumn{5}{c}{de}				
		NB	NS	ZE	PS	PB
e	NB	NB	NB	NB	NS	NS
	NS	NB	NS	NS	NS	PS
	ZE	NB	NS	ZE	PS	PB
	PS	NS	PS	PS	PB	PB
	PB	PS	PS	PB	PB	PB

4 Simulation Results

In this section, we describe the circuits we have used for controlling the HVAC plant. The structure of the control circuit we implemented in our study is illustrated in figure 3. The actual plant model involves four inputs and three output processes, of which two inputs can be manipulated for achieving desired performance levels. Figures 4-7 show the membership function sets for the inputs and outputs.

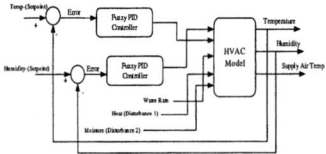

Fig. 3. Control circuit with two controllers.

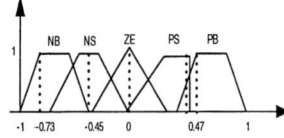

Fig. 4. Error input fuzzy sets.

We wish to track temperature and humidity to their respecting set point levels of 73°F and 0.009, while maintaining the supply air temperature within the range of 40°F to 100°F. The performance levels achieved via the two alternative approaches are outlined in table 4. As can be seen, although both control approaches perform well, but the performance of FPID controller is better than PID controller in terms of rise-time, settling-time and overshoot.

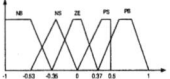 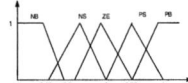 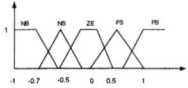

Fig. 5. Rate error input fuzzy sets. Fig. 6. Integral error fuzzy sets. Fig. 7. Output fuzzy sets.

We examined the robustness of these controllers with respect to external disturbances. To do that, we fed the plant with time-variable heat and moisture disturbance signals in the form given in figure 8.

Table 4. Performance characteristics of HVAC system with two Fuzzy PID and PID controllers.

	S-SError (Temp-Humi)	Rise-Time (Temp-Humi)	POS (Temp-Humi)
FPID	0.01%-0.00%	0.001-0.0002	02.28- 0.00
PID	0.00%-0.00%	0.009-0.002	49.96-43.33

As observed in the figure 8, there is some deterioration from the nominal amounts of the two external disturbances. The responses of both control approaches are given in the figures 9. As can be seen, the fuzzy PID controller shows the better control performance than PID controller in terms of settling time, overshot and rise time.

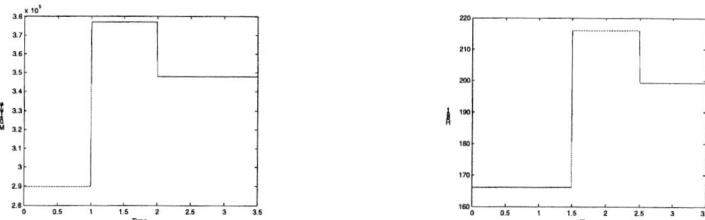

Fig. 8. The heat and moisture disturbance signals for robustness consideration.

The outputs of the system, with the presence of disturbance variations, show that the fuzzy PID controller can track the inputs suitably. But the performance of PID controller is too poor.

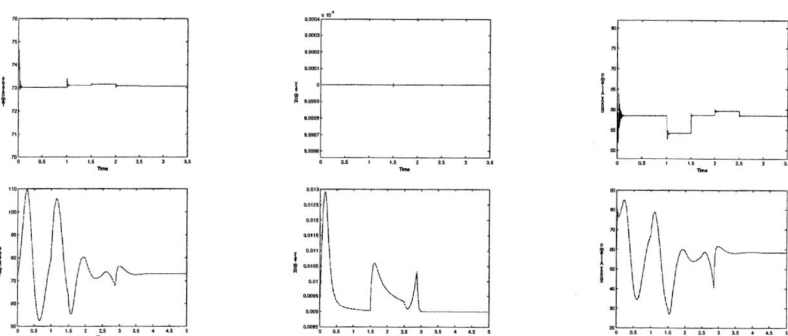

Fig. 9. HVAC system responses of the two controllers with the presence of disturbance variations (Up: Fuzzy PID, Down: PID).

5 Conclusion

In this paper, we showed the applicability of the self tuning based fuzzy PID controller to the fulfillment of complex tasks of adaptive set point tracking and disturbance rejection of HVAC systems. The control of the non-minimum phase, multivariable, nonlinear and nonlinearizable plant with constraints on its supply air temperature is indeed a demanding task from control theoretic viewpoint. The controller presented in this paper possessed excellent tracking speed and robustness properties. The flexibility of the controller also means that it is possible to pursue further objectives e.g. trading off response speed with smoothness of control effort, as well as steady state and transient characteristics of the responses.

References

1. Newman, H. M., "Direct Digital Controls for Building Systems" John Wiley, 1994
2. Hartman, T. B., "Direct Digital Controls for HVAC Systems" MC Graw-Hill, 1993
3. Rashidi, F., Moshiri, B., "Design of a Robust Sliding Mode Fuzzy Controller for Nonlinear HVAC Systems", Lecture notes in artificial intelligence, 2004
4. Serrano, B. A., Velez-Reyes, M., "Nonlinear Control of A Heating, Ventilation and Air Conditioning Systems with Thermal Load Estimation" IEEE Transaction on Control Systems Technology, Volume 7, 1999
5. Petrov, M., I.Ganchev and I.Dragotinov. "Design Aspects Of Fuzzy PID Controllers", 5th International Conference on Soft Computing Mendel'99, pp.277-283, 1999
6. James M. Adams and Kuldip S. Rattan, "Intelligent Control of a Direct-Drive Robot using Multi-Stage Fuzzy Logic", 44 IEEE Midwest Symposium on Circuits and Systems, 2001

Ontology-Based Web Navigation Assistant

Hyunsub Jung[1], Jaeyoung Yang[2], and Joongmin Choi[3]

[1] KT Corp., Korea
flyhigh@kt.co.kr
[2] Openbase Inc., Korea
jyyang@openbase.co.kr
[3] Department of Computer Science and Engineering
Hanyang University, Ansan, Korea
jmchoi@cse.hanyang.ac.kr

Abstract. This paper proposes a navigation assistant that provides more personalized Web navigation by exploiting domain-specific ontologies. In general, an ontology is regarded as the specification of conceptualization that enables formal definitions about things and states by using terms and relationships between them. In our approach, Web pages are converted into concepts by referring to domain-specific ontologies which employ a hierarchical concept structure. This concept mapping makes it easy to handle Web pages and also provides higher-level classification information. The proposed navigation assistant eventually recommends the Web documents that are intimately associated with the concept nodes in the upper-levels of the hierarchy by analyzing the current Web page and its outwardly-linked pages.

1 Introduction

With the rapid growth of the Internet, people are facing the information overload that makes the users spend more time and put more efforts to find the information they need. To resolve this problem, the idea of *Web personalization* has been suggested by using the mining technology[8]. The mining methodologies that help the navigation by personalized information can be classified into Web content mining, Web usage mining, and ontology-based mining.

Webwatcher[5], Syskill&Webert[9], Letizia[7], and Webmate[3] use the Web content mining technique. WebPersonalizer[8] combines the Web usage mining with the Web content mining in order to make more sophisticated recommendation. Another research on the personalization by using Web usage mining can be found in [10]. OBIWAN[2] uses ontologies to help navigation. This system is based on a personal ontology, and each site has an agent that communicates with regional agents which provide and characterize web pages in a local site.

Despite numerous studies have been done, previous researches about the Web personalization reveal many problems. First, most personalization methods only adopt lexical analysis by using term frequencies to measure the impact of words, without considering their semantic relations to other terms in the document. Second, they assume that the user's information needs are fixed, only fail to cope

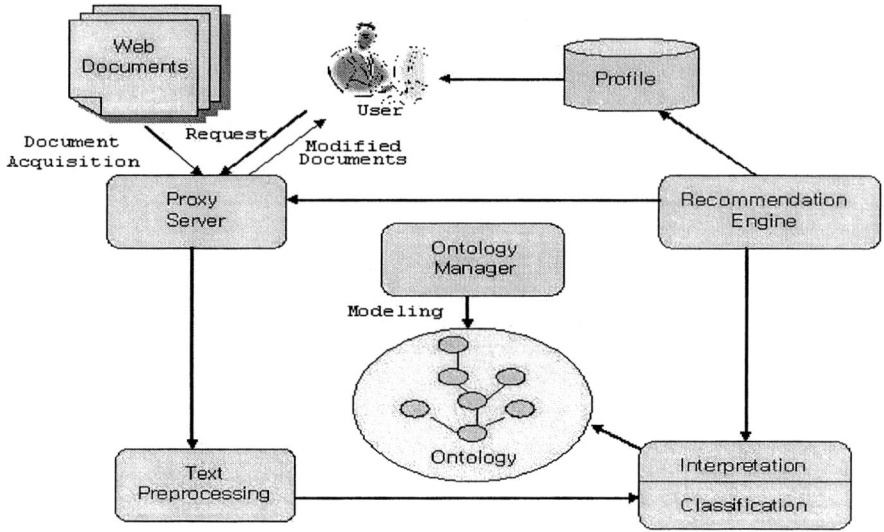

Fig. 1. Architecture for our personalized Web navigation system

with the frequent changes in user interests. Third, most systems require explicit inputs from the user about whether he or she has interests in the topic. This could be a burden to the user who would not want to interact with the system, and also the results may be subjective. Consequently, the performance of a system adopting this strategy may not get better without explicit inputs. Finally, for the systems using the Web mining techniques, extracting useful information is itself a hard work and the performance is not promising for frequently-changed Web pages.

We try to solve these problems by using an ontology-based recommendation agent. We propose a Web navigation agent that facilitates effective browsing by providing personalized information for the domain of Web news sites in which the semantic structures of Web documents are clearly defined and the changes in contents occur frequently. By this agent, Web pages are classified according to the ontology that describes the semantic structures of pages. This classification leads the agent to identify semantic contents and relations contained in the pages, and grasp users' specific intentions while browsing. For recommendation, Web pages are fetched by a look-ahead search and those matched with the user need are selected as locally optimal pages. We use the selected pages to construct a user profile in order to provide more personalized and high-level news articles that satisfy user's interests. The general architecture of our personalized Web navigation system is depicted in Fig. 1.

2 Ontology as a Knowledge Base

In this paper, we use an ontology as a knowledge base[4]. The knowledge base is treated as a vocabulary that consists of logical terms and axioms. Our assistant

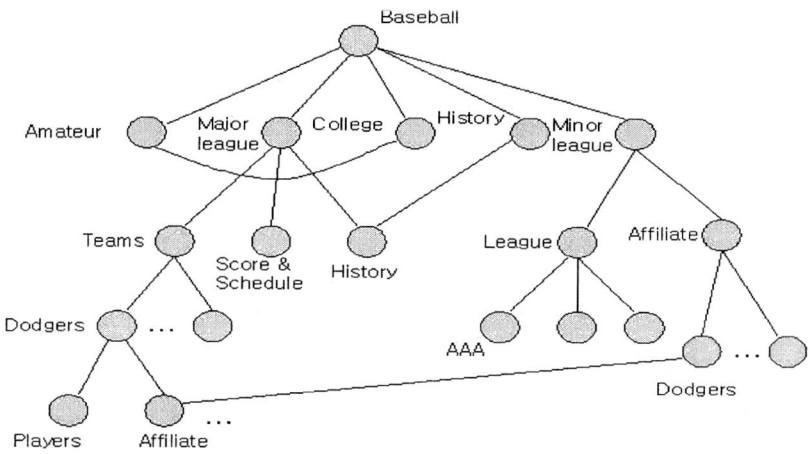

Fig. 2. Ontology for the *baseball* domain

agent is able to convert the contents in a page into a corresponding set of concepts. An advantage of this concept mapping is that the agent can provide the information about a Web page not by a sequence of frequently-occurring terms but by a hierarchy of concepts so that the agents can recognize what is contained in a page.

We focus on constructing the ontology for the classification of Web documents[6]. In order to facilitate the description and the classification of the hierarchical conceptual structure of Web pages, the ontology is represented by a hierarchy of nodes where each node denotes a *concept*, a *feature*, a *relation*, or a *constraint*. A concept is a name to represent a node. A feature consists of words and phrases (a sequence of words) to describe a concept. A relation describes the interrelationship between concepts by using OOP-like relationships such as *isA*, *partOf*, and *hasPart*. The *isA* relation defines a generalization or specialization connection, and *partOf* and *hasPart* relations define inclusion connections. A constraint has two conditions: *isRelatedTo* and *followedBy*. Closely related features or conditions are used to solve ambiguity in word-based document analysis to improve the accuracy.

Figure 2 shows an example ontology for the *baseball* domain. Here, *history* is defined as a child concept of *baseball* which is the topmost concept, and at the same time, another *history* is defined in the path of *baseball-major league-history*. This feature is realized in the XML representation by using the nested concept definitions and the constraint descriptions.

3   Navigation Assistant as a Classifier

The classification of Web pages is a task of mapping a document to a suitable node in the concept hierarchy. Documents are mapped to the most relevant node by navigating the concept hierarchy from the root node, and only those children nodes whose parent node is satisfied with the similarity measure are considered. Otherwise the last traversed node will be the proper node for the document. Clearly, a document is not necessarily mapped to a leaf node in the hierarchy. As a result, we are able to represent a concept hierarchy using a small number of nodes, and do more sophisticated recommendation using hierarchical classification. Our navigation assistant can also provide high-level Web document recommendation using this concept hierarchy.

Equation (1) is the similarity measure function for the classification. A node with the highest score will be the relevant concept that is regarded as the class for a document.

$$Sim(Node, d) = \frac{\sum_{i=0}^{N} freq_{i,d}/Max_{l,d}}{N} \cdot \frac{V_d}{V} \qquad (1)$$

In this equation, d is the current document, $Node$ is a node in the concept hierarchy, N is the total number of features, $freq_{i,d}$ is the frequency weight of the feature i in d, $Max_{l,d}$ is the maximum of all values of $freq_{i,d}$, V is the total number of constraints, and V_d is the number of satisfied constraints in d. Relations are also used in the course of classifying document in a way that, if a node is related with other nodes in terms of partOf or hasPart relationship, the navigation assistant measures the similarity including these relationships. Then, the assistant records the last mapped node along with the path from the root to this mapped node in the user profile.

To recommend personalized Web documents, we use a user profile that reflects the user's interests and preferences. In the user profile, each interest is represented by a pair of information <P, R>, where P is the path for a mapped node from the root in the hierarchy after the classification, and R is the number of requests to the corresponding document for the same interest. In this way, the user profile can be regarded as a weighted ontology with the concept hierarchy in which a weight is represented by a number that reflects the degree of fitness to user interests.

Candidate documents are fetched by using the look-ahead search starting from the user-specified document. Recommendations are done based on a measure called the *recommendation score(RS)* that is calculated and assigned to each candidate document. Equation (2) shows how to measure the recommendation score for a page. This equation considers two factors: the one is the frequency-based factor that normalizes the number of visits to the node(or the path to the node) which is associated with the page. The other is the location-based factor that considers the node position in the concept hierarchy.

$$RS(p) = \frac{freq_i}{Max\ freq_l} \cdot \frac{1}{Wdist(p)} \cdot \frac{1}{Cdist(p)} \qquad (2)$$

In this equation, $Wdist(p)$ is a Web distance that denotes the number of hyperlinks from the current page to p in the Web space, and $Cdist(p)$ is a concept distance that is the distance between p and a node reflecting user's interest in the concept hierarchy. We assume that the nearest document from the currently visiting node in the concept hierarchy is the most relevant page, so we assign a high RS score to this node. Weights are assigned differently by traversing the path from the current node to the root node. An advantage of using this strategy is that the navigation assistant is able to recommend a concept in the upper level of the hierarchy. As the final step, the user gets the Web page that is regarded as relevant by the agent based on RS scores, and this recommended page is augmented with the links to other relevant documents.

4 Experimental Results

To evaluate the performance of our classification procedure using ontology, we test the system with the wired news about the baseball. The ontology about the baseball is already shown in Fig. 2. We collect documents in the *recreation*, *sports*, and *baseball* categories of the Yahoo search engine. We select those documents that belong to this category in Yahoo and also to a concept in the ontology at the same time. We feed these documents to the classification module to examine whether they are classified into the same category as in Yahoo. We have tested the total of 421 document pages about *baseball*, 56 of which belong to the *history* category, 79 to *amateur*, 122 to *college*, 108 to *minor league*, and 56 to *major league*.

For the purpose of precision comparison, we test two different methods: the one is constructing the ontology solely by a human and the other is constructing it automatically by using the TF-IDF technique[1]. The procedure of automatic construction of the ontology is as follows. As we already have the ontology frame, we calculate term weights by using TF-IDF for the documents in each category of Yahoo so as to generate the features used in leaf nodes of the ontology. We select 10 low ranked terms as the features and assign these features to each leaf node. Then, we go up one level to a parent node and filter out 10 low ranked features from the child nodes.

Figure 3 shows the precision measures about whether the documents are classified into the *baseball* class, which is the topmost class in the hierarchy. In this experiment, we compare the manual ontology construction method with the automatic one. The average precision for the manually-built ontology is 82.7% and that of automatically-built ontology is 84.2%. From this result, we can notice that the constructing method using TF-IDF shows a little bit better performance than the manual method. It is mainly caused by the TF-IDF characteristics that prefer terms occurred in several documents uniformly.

5 Conclusion

In this paper, we propose a personalized assistant that helps a user with the navigation on the Web by using ontology. The navigation assistant represents the semantic relationship between Web documents by a concept structure, and classifies them using the ontology that consists of the concepts. The navigation

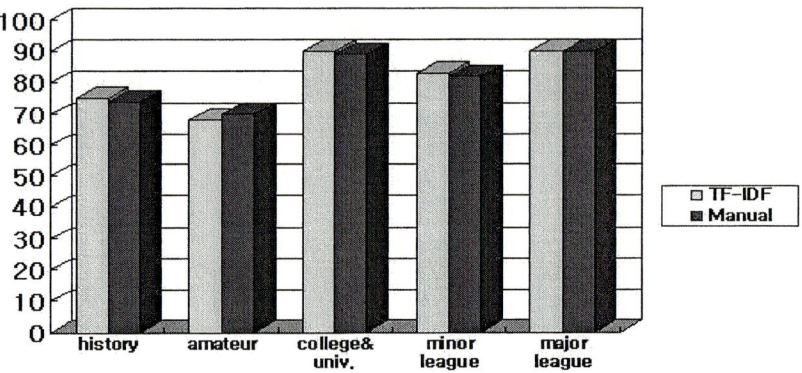

Fig. 3. Percentage of being classified into the *baseball* class

assistant based on the ontology identifies user's information need more efficiently and correctly. The agent is able to provide personalized information based on the user profile when the user is browsing the Web. We are currently developing an interface for extracting semantic concepts and relationships to facilitate the automatic or semi-automatic construction. In the future, since the look-ahead search takes a fair amount time, a new method that reduces the time to fetch documents in the next hyperlink level should be studied.

References

1. R. Baeza-Yates and B. Ribeiro. *Modern Information Retrieval*, Addision Wesley, 1998.
2. J. Chaffee and S. Gauch. Personal Ontologies for Web Navigation. In *Proc. 9th Intl. Conf. on Information and Knowledge Management (CIKM'00)*, pp.227-234, 2000.
3. L. Chen and K. Sycara. Webmate: A Personal Agent for Browsing and Searching. In *Proc. 2nd Intl. Conf. on Autonomous Agents*, pp. 132-139, 1998.
4. T. Gruber. Toward Principles for the Design of Ontologies Used for Knowledge Sharing. *International Journal on Human and Computer Studies*, 43(5/6): 907-929, 1995.
5. T. Joachims, D. Freitag, and T. Mitchell. Webwatcher: A Tour Guide for The World Wide Web. In *IJCAI'97*, pp.770-777, 1997.
6. W. Koh and L. Mui. An Information Theoretic Approach to Ontology-based Interest Matching. In *IJCAI'01 Workshop on Ontology Learning,*, 2001.
7. H. Lieberman. Letizia: An Agent that Assists Web Browsing. In *IJCAI'95*, pp.475-480, 1995.
8. B. Mobasher, R. Cooley, and J. Srivastava. Automatic Personalization Based on Web Usage Mining. *Communications of ACM*, 43(8): 144-151, 2000.
9. M. Pazzani, J. Muramatsu, and D. Billsus. Syskill&Webert: Identifying Interesting Web Sites. In *AAAI'96*, pp.54-61, 1996.
10. M. Spiliopoulou. Web Usage Mining for Web Site Evaluation. *Communications of ACM*, 43(8): 127-134, 2000.

A Hybrid Fuzzy-Neuro Model for Preference-Based Decision Analysis

Vincent C.S. Lee[*] and Alex T.H. Sim

School of Business Systems, Faculty of Information Technology
Monash University, 63 Wellington Road, Vic 3800, Australia
vincent.lee@infotech.monash.edu.au

Abstract. A hybrid fuzzy-neuro model that combines frame-based fuzzy logic system and neural network learning paradigm, hereinafter called FRN, is proposed to support innovative decision analysis (selection and assessment) process. The FRN model exploits the merits of reasoning from a frame-based fuzzy expert system in combination with preference-based learning derived from a supervised neural network. The FRN has proven to be useful and practical in filtering out all possible decision analyses. A salient feature of FRN is its ability to adapt to user's sudden change of preference in the midst of model implementation. A case study on the decision analysis (assessment and selection) of preference-based product is included to illustrate the implementation of FRN model.

Keywords: Hybrid AI model, frame-based fuzzy systems, neural network, preference, and premium goods.

1 Introduction

Premium goods are subject to high variability in terms of personal taste and individual perceived value for money and prestige. To model the selection and assessment process of premium goods would therefore involve some kind of preference-based criteria, which often express in linguistic variables/values [1]. Rule-based fuzzy logic [2] is a proven AI tool for solving problem using linguistic and imprecise terms. It has, however, limited power to adapt to sudden change of human judgment and preference. Thus to improve its adaptability to sudden change of linguistic variables, integration with other intelligent techniques has been proposed [3]. Sudden change in human preference may be caused by emotional and economic considerations. In the selection of product and service, incomplete or poor quality information is normally due to uncertainty found in individual preference. A judgment or feeling of satisfaction is hard to be precisely defined. Confronting with such episode, hybridising two or more AI techniques is of great help to decision maker in making an effective choice amongst alternatives.

---

[*] Corresponding author.

This paper proposes a hybrid fuzzy-neuro model that combines frame-based fuzzy logic system and neural network learning paradigm, hereinafter called FRN to support innovative decision analysis (selection and assessment) process. The FRN model exploits the merits of reasoning from a frame-based fuzzy expert system in combination with preference-based learning derived from a supervised neural network. The FRN has proven to be useful and practical in filtering out all possible decision analyses. A salient feature of FRN is its ability to adapt to user's sudden change of preference in the midst of model implementation. A prototype has been built based on FRN for test of its capability on selecting and assessing either new or used premium family car, an example of premium goods. Also, the system caters for customer visual selection of a product, and self-evaluation of own choices to accommodate a sudden change of user selection. By utilizing data from a survey carried out around Monash Caulfield, the prototype is able to give recommendation out of many possible choices to many prospective users. The system works gracefully in our example of niche market car seller. The FRN model has proven to be useful and practical in filtering out tremendous possible combinations of choices. It adapts to instantaneous interruption of user's sudden change of preference in the midst of model implementation.

2 The Proposed Design of FRN Hybrid Model

Figure 1 shows a ten steps FRN model development methodology with a selective loop at the end of it. For user, the methodology is an interactive process with selective feedback whereby for the developer, the program is a one time effort.

Step 1 starts with definition of the problem and seek for the target of objects within the problem domain.

Step 2 is for the developer to identify possible explicit and implicit attributes associated with the objects. For example, if we want to employ sales representative to a company, the object is applicants. The explicit attributes are gender, communication skill level, personal traits, etc. The implicit attributes are an applicant's qualification, education level, and so forth.

Step 3 of the FRN model development methodology is to construct a frame-based fuzzy system using only the explicit attributes, defined earlier, as its variables. This will effectively filter out much unwanted data.

Step 4 is the construction of a rule based fuzzy system follows, to evaluate the remaining implicit attributes.

Step 5 is carried out a preference-based questionnaire survey , in the midst of both software developments. The survey aims to obtain various neurons weights to construct a recommendation model on the topic.

Step 6 is the construction of neural network model.

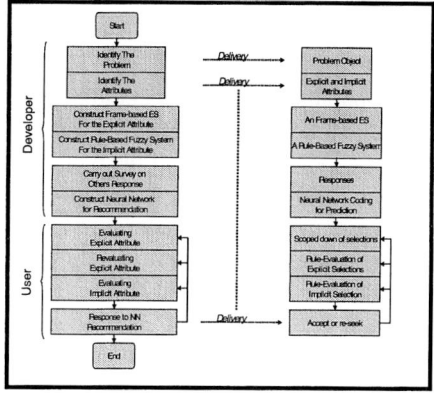
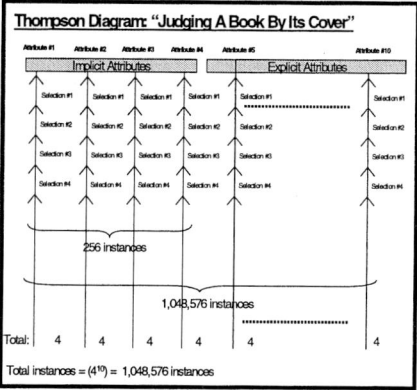

Fig. 1. Development Methodology for a FRN model.

Fig. 2. Data Scope Down Effect.

Step 7 a user will first interact with the frame-based fuzzy system. Since an object has numerous of attribute by putting up explicit attribute up front, FRN effectively scoped down tremendous amount of selection. For example, an object of 10 attributes with 4 selections per attribute would need around a million data records in its fuzzy associative memory. This confuses user and is not efficient. By using only 4 explicit attributes, user interactions can be reduced to only 256 choices. On rule evaluation, FRN model uses a modified fuzzy logic method proposed by Lovrich et. al. [6]. The advantage of this modified method is that it bypasses the need to have a huge rule database. Thus also save much construction time in relating antecedences to consequences. It is a matrix of fuzzy attributes versus its membership.

Step 8 a user is to selectively fill-in the perceived degree of membership. Most importantly, each user is let to evaluate only on their preferred choice from a vast combination of all the possible instances. This reduces both the user and developer time in relating many unrelated rules with assumed degree of memberships.

Step 9 Evaluate implicit attributes. In previous example of 10 attributes with 4 selections per attribute, one could have 1,048,576 rules. However, we have built a frame based system with only 256 instances to allow user to select their choices. User would normally conclude with less than 10 instances or preferences from the frame based system. As with rule base fuzzy system in a modified spreadsheet, users will gives their degrees of membership on the 10 preferences, without the need to predefine its antecedent-consequent relationship by system developer. As a result, users would normally have their list of evaluation result, such as:

Preference #1: 92% (auto calculate by the system)
Preference #2: 93% (auto calculate by the system)
.
.
Preference #10: 96% (auto calculate by the system)

User can choose to conclude with the highest evaluation or to evaluate their preference by giving a variety of degree of membership to any of the preference selected.

Step 10 Neural Network recommends to users for popular choices that could be made by others within the same demographic area through prediction based on survey data. At the end of the methodology users are given a choice to either restart the methodology run (start from frame based fuzzy system), branch into the midst of methodology (revise their evaluation on selected preference in rule based fuzzy system) or simply to get more inputs from prediction (by using Neural Network). This final step of the FRN model development methodology ensures that user is at least satisfied with their so-far effort in choosing a preference.

In this prototype FRN model, it uses explicit attributes in the frame-based for expert knowledge representation. In this project, it is possible to scope down from a need of 2 millions selection records to only 525 cars selection in the database. It is also discovered that the database can be further trimmed down because some combinations are invalid. For example, there is no combination for size of family with convertible body type and etc. The database has been further scoped down to have only 314 selections. An adaptive filter is used to filter out 99.98% of the possible combinations. A user is let to judge only within 314 selections by their feeling, preference based on pictures. This will be a much easier task for user, in compare to browse all the related 2 million records within a fuzzy associative memory.

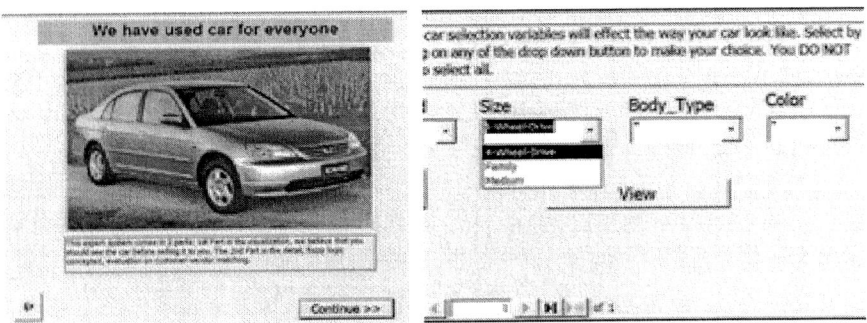

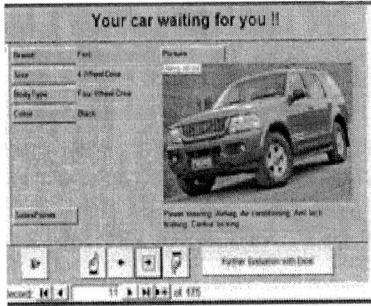

Fig. 3. Frame Based Fuzzy System with Its Example on Selections.

Lovrich et. al. [6] method of rule evaluation is applied within a customized spreadsheet to facilitate easier interaction between user and the rule based system interface. The spreadsheet as shown in Figure 4 has incorporated market niche focus of a car seller.

The coloured columns, which are hidden from customer denotes the seller's limitation in getting the type of car. These columns can be used to rank niche car seller with their preference of sales. Customer is presented with the screen given in Figure 5.

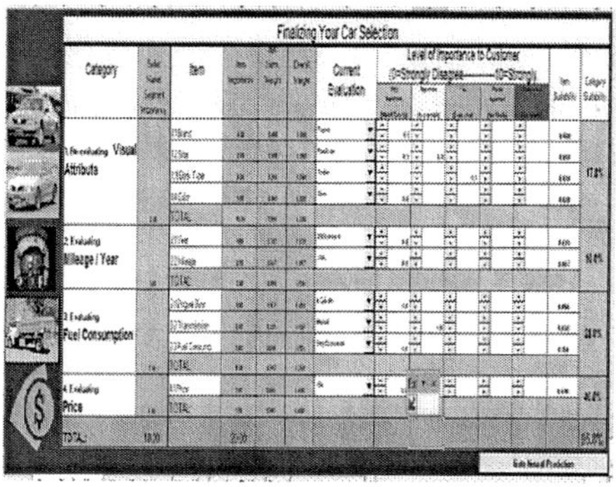

Fig. 4. Seller Screen of Preference [7]. 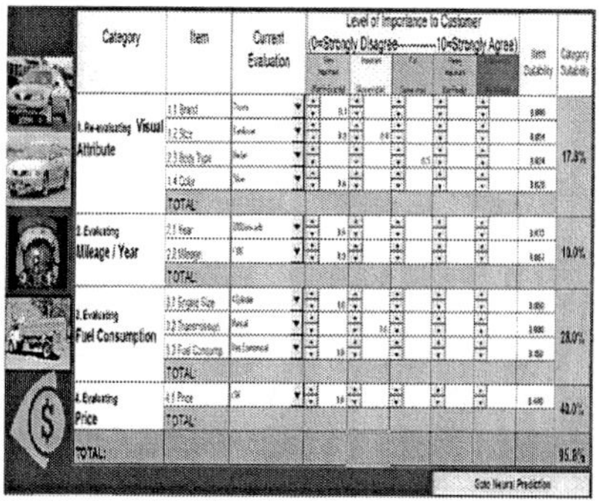   **Fig. 5.** Customer Screen of Preference.

On the 1st category of rule-based evaluation, an user will re-evaluate a few visual attributes selected through frame based system, earlier on. From experience, it normally consists of less then 10 selections. This is followed by the evaluation of 3 categories of implicit attributes. Users can click and select another type of preference from the "Current Evaluation". A high percentage of suitability indicates that there is a match between customer satisfaction and a seller's product. At any time users can turn to neural network to predict for insights from others selection.

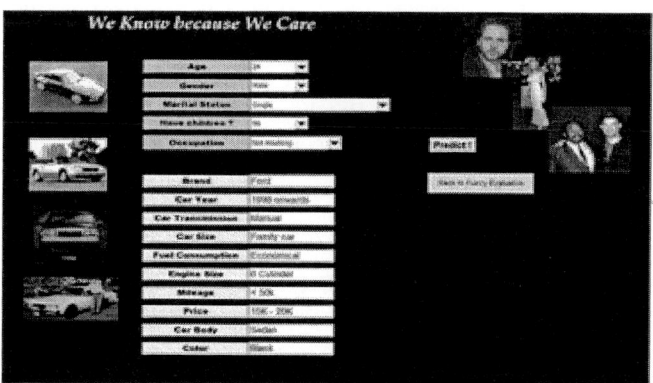

Fig. 6. Neural Network Recommendation Model [8].

3 Case Study Results and Discussions

The 10 steps FRN model development methodology has been fully followed in this proto-type project. The results obtained are fascinating. Tremendous amount of record selections were scoped down in its frame-based evaluation. A high percentage of 99.98% of choices has been sifted. The frame-based knowledge representation guides users to their preferred choices and allow users' instances intuitive preference selection. FRN based software also attracts user to continue using it for its simplicity and graphical presentation. A modified rule-based system in FRN model has bypassed the need to spend a long time in fine-tuning and building a rule based fuzzy logic system. It gives user the convenience to evaluate product in more detail only on preferred product. This saves time for both software developer and to user. The back propagation trained neural network employed in this project on the other hand, utilised survey demographic profile and is to predict customers choice preference based on the similar and historical demographic profile. A user selects his/her profile such as age, income, marital status, etc. The system will recommend the popular choice of from many alternatives. Most importantly, a system constructed based on the FRN model allows consistent users' iterations and feedbacks in the midst of evaluation. Examples are:

i) After sometimes, user suddenly change their mind and would want to totally revised their selection of product visual attribute;
ii) After looking at popular choice of many provided by neural network, user wanted to revise or simulate another product selection;
iii) User might have not enough information and confused but want to simulate and learn his or her validity of product choices;

Questionnaire survey of user preference has been carried out via field interviews by second author. Sample of questionnaires can be made available to interested readers. The questionnaire consists of two sections, general questions and the factors that customers would consider while buying a car. First section of the survey questionnaires asks personal and demographic data. The second section surveys the factors that affect customer choice in selecting a car. Each data is treated as a linguistic variable and descriptive adjectives are assigned. During this linguistic translation, a "dictionary" of descriptive adjectives is created. We assumed five suitability levels - Very important (VI); Important (I); Fair (F); Rarely important (RI); Unimportant (UI). The scales of a candidate's suitability and their corresponding linguistic values are shown in Table 1.

Table 1. A Fuzzy Dictionary.

Linguistic Value	Degree of suitability
Very Important	0.80-1.00 (80%-100%)
Important	0.60-1.00 (60%-100%)
Fair	0.40-0.80 (40%-80%)
Rarely Important	0.20-0.60 (20%-60%)
Unimportant	0.00-0.40 (0- 40%)

The neural input variables, extracted from demographic profile of the prospective customers, comprise age, gender (male/female), marital_status (single/married), married with children (Yes/No) and occupation (Not Working, Part-Time/Casual, Full-Time). The recommendations, i.e.output variables are Brand (or Model), Age (in years), Transmission, Dimension, Fuel Consumption, Engine Size, Odometer Reading, Price, Body Type and Body Colour. Since, only numerical data is acceptable to the system, most categorical inputs/outputs have to be transformed. Among the available techniques, 1-out-of-N encoding technique is chosen due to its simplicity to use. For example, Occupation is symbolised using 3 variables 00, 01, 11 for its status of "No Occupation", "Occupation 1" and "Occupation 2". This method of encoding transformation is also needed for categorical output variables such as Brand, Transmission, Dimension, Fuel Consumption, Engine Size, Body Type and Colour of Car.

In the case study all categorical output variables had been used for classification purposes and all numerical output variables are meant for prediction. Here, neural network is to memorize rather than generalize a recommendation. 10% of data has been used for testing and 90% as training set. In building neural recommendation model, we have used three-layer MFNN with back propagation to build and train the neural network model. This project has used 9-11 hidden neurons with learning rate between 0.3-0.5, momentum 0.2-0.3, initial weights 0.3, number of epochs ranging from 3,000 – 12,000. "best training set" option has been selected. The parameters chosen are based on Smith's recommendation [9].

As a result, out of forty questionnaires answered, the average age of survey responders is twenty-five years old; mostly male, single, and have no permanent income. The employed Neural network by knowing a customer's demographic profile has tried to predict customer preference, based on similarity in its historical demographic profile. The project embraced three artificial intelligence techniques in the FRN model that has greatly proven its usage in market niche car seller business.

4 Conclusion

The proposed FRN model has shown its strength in catering for human changeable and instantaneous style of decision-making. A software prototype based on the FRN model development methodology has been built and it shows a strong ability to help subjective decision making in product assessment and selection. FRN based software is effective, as software developing is just a one-time effort but user can repetitively simulate, learn and iteratively evaluate their various choice of product selection. It is also efficient as in our case study 99.98% unwanted data is filtered to save time and kept users' interest in using the system. Finally, the project can be extended to incorporate all the programs into a single platform such as using Microsoft VB.net to realize undivided integration between multiple systems. More training data for neural network can further increase its generalisation ability.

Acknowledgement

Alex T.H. Sim acknowledges the funding support from Universiti Teknologi Malaysia (UTM), Malaysia for doing this research project at the School of Business Systems, Monash University, Australia.

Reference

1. Turban, E., *Decision Support Systems and Expert Systems*. 1995: Englewood Cliffs, NJ., Prentice-Hall.
2. Negnevitsky, M., *Artificial Intelligence: A Guide to Intelligent Systems*. 2002: Pearson Education Limited, England
3. Goonatilake, S. Intelligent hybrid systems for financial decision making. in Proceedings of the 1995 ACM symposium on Applied computing 1995, Nashville, Tennessee, United States. Feb 1995.
4. Wolpert, D.H. and Macready, W. G., No Free Lunch Theorems for Optimisation, in IEEE Transactions on Evolutionary Computtation, vol. 1, no. 1, pp. 67-82.
5. Mason, D.G., et al., *Self-Learning Fuzzy Logic Control of Anaesthetic Drug Infusions*. IEE, Savoy Place, London; UK, 1998.
6. Lovrich, M., S. PetroLazarevic, and B. Brown, *A Fuzzy Approach To Personnel Selection*. Working Paper, Monash University, Melbourne; Australia., November 1999. 44/99: p. 12.
7. *Pictures (CarSales)*. Oct 2002, CarSales.com.au limited.
8. *Pictures (f2)*. Oct 2002, f2 Limited.
9. Smith, K.A., *Introduction to Neural Networks and Data Mining for Business Applications*. 1999: Eruditions Publishing, Melbourne, Australia.

Combining Rules for Text Categorization Using Dempster's Rule of Combination

Yaxin Bi[1,2], Terry Anderson[3], and Sally McClean[3]

[1] School of Computer Science
Queen's University of Belfast, Belfast, BT7 1NN, UK
[2] School of Biomedical Science
University of Ulster, Coleraine, Londonderry, BT52 1SA, UK
y.bi@ulster.ac.uk
[3] Faculty of Engineering
University of Ulster, Newtownabbey, Co. Antrim, BT37 0QB, UK
{tj.anderson,si.mcclean}@ulster.ac.uk

Abstract. In this paper, we present an investigation into the combination of rules for text categorization using Dempster's rule of combination. We first propose a boosting-like technique for generating multiple sets of rules based on rough set theory, and then describe how to use Dempster's rule of combination to combine the classification decisions produced by multiple sets of rules. We apply these methods to 10 out of the 20-newsgroups – a benchmark data collection, individually and in combination. Our experimental results show that the performance of the best combination of the multiple sets of rules on the 10 groups of the benchmark data can achieve 80.47% classification accuracy, which is 3.24% better than that of the best single set of rules.

1 Introduction

For the general problem of automatic classification, different machine learning methods obtain different degree of success, but none of them is totally perfect, or at least not as good as expected in practice [1]. Therefore it is desirable to create an effective methodology for taking advantage from different methods and combining the decisions made by different methods, so that more precise decisions could be achieved. In this research, we investigate an approach for combining multiple decisions derived from multiple sets of rules based on Demspter's rule of combination. Each set of rules is generated by a single rough sets-based inductive learning method, and is referred to as a classifier as in the boosting method [2]. The advantage of our approach is its ability to combine multiple sets of rules into a highly accurate classification rule by modelling the accumulation of evidence.

Boosting learning techniques have been developed by Freund and Schapire [2]. They work by repeatedly running a given weak learning algorithm on various distributions over training data, and then combining the classifiers produced by a weak leaner in a single composite classifier. Several derivatives based on the boosting techniques have been developed in recent years. For example, Friedman et al. have developed a method for decomposing a decision tree of larger size into a number of very small trees in terms of truncated tree induction (TTI) [3]. The work shows that a single decision tree is often dramatically outperformed by voting based on multiple smaller decision trees.

In our work we describe a rough sets-based inductive learning method for generating multiple sets of weighted rules, instead of using boosting techniques. The main idea of the rough set-based induction algorithm is to evaluate dependency among the attributes of a training data set. The dependency of different combinations of attributes will be analysed, and the subsets of attributes with the same dependency as that of the whole set of attributes will be generated. In this way, each of the subsets has an ability to discriminate instances in the data set with the same role as the whole set of attributes does. The subsets of attributes generated in this way are called reducts, and in turn are used to construct multiple sets of rules, referred to as classifiers.

To combine decisions from multiple sets of rules, we propose to use Dempster's rule of combination. In this situation, we regard each classification decision from classifiers as a piece of evidence, and the rule strength associated with a decision as the degree of belief indicating how likely it is that a new document belongs to the class. Therefore Demspter's rule of combination provides an effective solution to combine these decisions.

2 Rough Sets for Rule Generation

To describe an inductive learning method based on rough set theory. We introduce the definitions of several essential concepts below [4].

A decision system can be defined as $S = \langle U, A, V, f \rangle$, where $U = \{u_1, \ldots, u_{|U|}\}$ is a collection of objects, $A = \{a_1, \ldots, a_{|A|}\}$ is a set of attributes, $V = \{V_{a_1}, \ldots, V_{a_{|A|}}\}$ is a set of attribute values, in which $V_{a_i} = \{V_{a_{i1}}, \ldots, V_{a_{ik}}\}$ is the domain of attribute a_i; and $V_{a_{ij}}$ is a categorical value. We define f as a function over U, A, and V. Attribute A is further divided into two parts – the condition attribute C and decision attributes D such that $A = C \cup D$ and $C \cap D = \phi$.

Definition 1 With an attribute $a \in A$, two instances $u, v \in U$ are defined as an *equivalence relation* over U if and only if $f(u, a) = f(v, a)$, denoted by τ.

Definition 2 With an *equivalence relation* τ associated with the set of attributes D, a partition operation on a decision system under τ_A is defined as U/τ_A (U/A for short), where $U/A = \{X_1, \ldots, X_m\}$, and each X_i is called an *equivalence class*, and for any two instances u and v, if $u, v \in X_i$ and $a \in A$, then $f(u, a) = f(v, a)$.

Definition 3 Given a subset of attributes $B \subseteq A$, if there is $Q \subseteq B$, $U/\tau_B = U/\tau_Q$ and Q is minimal among all subsets of B, then Q is defined as a *reduct* of B. The component attributes of a reduct are significant so that none of them can be omitted. Notice that more than one reduct may exist.

Definition 4 Suppose the decision attribute D is a singleton, i.e. $D = \{d\}$, and $U/\tau_d = \{X_1, \ldots, X_k\}$ be a partition over U with respect to d, for each subset $X \subseteq U/\tau_d$ and a subset of condition attributes $B \subseteq C$, we associate two subsets with X as follows:

$$\underline{B}X = \cup \{Y \in U/B \mid Y \subseteq X\} \quad (1)$$
$$\overline{B}X = \cup \{Y \in U/B \mid Y \cap X \neq \phi\} \quad (2)$$

where $\underline{B}X$ and $\overline{B}X$ are called the *lower* and *upper approximations*, respectively. To express the quantitative relationship between a subset of condition attributes $B \subseteq C$ and a decision attribute d, we define a measure, the *dependency degree*, denoted by $\gamma_B(X)$ below:

$$\gamma_B(D) = \sum_{X \in U/D} \frac{|\underline{B}X|}{|U|} \quad (3)$$

A rough set-based approach to inductive learning consists of a two-step process. The first step is to find multiple single covering solutions for all training instances held in a decision table. Specifically, given a set of condition attributes A and a subset $B \subseteq A$, a covering attribute set is found directly by computing its dependency degree $\gamma_B(D)$. The direct solution involves adding an attribute at a time, removing the attribute covered by the attribute set, and then the process is repeated until $\gamma_B(D)$ is equal to $\gamma_A(D)$. At the end of the induction of conjunctive attributes, more than one covering set – reduct – will be found.

The second step is to transform rules from multiple sets of reducts and weight each rule based on counting the identical attribute values. As a result, a number of rule sets will be produced, denoted by $\Re = \{R_1, R_2, ..., R_{|\Re|}\}$, where $R_i = \{r_{i1}, r_{i2}, ..., r_{|Ri|}\}$, $1 \leq i \leq |\Re|$. Each set of rules is called *intrinsic* rules, referred to as a classifier. It plays an independent role in classifying unseen instances. The relation between two sets of intrinsic rules is in disjunction normal form (DNF) as are the rules within R_i. To examine effectiveness of using multiple classifiers to classify unseen cases, our approach does not involve rule any optimzation between multiple sets of rules. More details about these algorithms can be found in [5].

A general DNF model does not require mutual exclusivity of rules within a set of intrinsic rules and/ or between different sets of intrinsic rules. The DNF used in this context differs from the conventional way in which only one of the rules is satisfied with a new instance. Instead, all the rules will be evaluated for a new instance. Rules for either the same classes or different classes can potentially be satisfied simultaneously. In the case of different classes, conflicting conclusions occur. One solution for this is to rank rules for each class according to a class priority as established in some way, such as information gain, the latest class is taken as the final class [6, 7]. The other solution is based on the majority voting principle, in which the conflicting conclusions are resolved by identifying the most satisfied rules [8]. In contrast, our approach makes use of as much rule-based evidence as possible to cope with conflicting conclusions through Dempster's rule of combination.

3 Demspter Shafer Theory of Evidence

The Demsper-Shafer theory of evidence allows us to combine pieces of evidence from subsets of the frame of discernment that consists of a number of exhaustive and mutually exclusive propositions h_i, i = 1, .., n. These propositions form a universal set Θ. For any subset $H_i = \{h_{i1}, ..., h_{ik}\} \subseteq \Theta$, h_{ir} (0< r ≤ k) represents a proposition, called *focal element*. When H_i is a one element subset, i.e. $H_i = \{h_i\}$, it is called a *singleton*. All the subsets of Θ constitute powerset 2^Θ, i.e. $H \subseteq \Theta$, if and only if $H \in 2^\Theta$. The D-S theory uses a numeric value in the range [0, 1] to represent the strength of some evidence supporting a subset $H \subseteq \Theta$ based on a given piece of evidence, denoted by $m(H)$, called the *mass function*, and uses a sum of the strengths for all subsets of H to indicate the strength of belief about proposition H on the basis of the same evidence, denoted by $bel(H)$, often called the *belief function*. Notice that $bel(H)$ is equal to $m(H)$ if the subset H is a singleton. More details can be found in [9].

4 Modelling Text Categorization

In this section, we start by discussing the general form that a text classifier based on Rough Sets may have. Let $D = \{d_1, d_2, ..., d_{|D|}\}$ be a collection of documents, where $d_i = \{w_{i1}, ..., w_{in}\}$, and $C = \{c_1, c_2, ..., c_{|C|}\}$ be a set of predefined categories, then rules for assigning documents into the predefined categories can be regarded as a mapping function $R: D \rightarrow C \times [0,1]$, where numeric values between 0 and 1, expressed by *stg*, indicate how likely a given document d belongs to category c, which can be represented by IF $R(d)$ THEN category = c with *stg*.

5 The Combination Method

Let $\Theta = \{c_1, c_2, ..., c_{|\Theta|}\}$ be a frame of discernment, and let $R_i = \{r_{i1}, r_{i2}, ..., r_{i|R_i|}\}$ be a set of intrinsic rules as above. Given a test document d, if k rules activated, i.e. r_{ij+1}, $r_{ij+2}, ..., r_{ij+q}$ where $1 \le j, q \le |R_i|$, then q decisions are inferred from R_i. Formally, this inference process can be expressed by $r_{ij+1}(d) \rightarrow h_1|stg_{j+1}$, $r_{ij+2}(d) \rightarrow h_2|stg_{j+2}$, ..., $r_{ij+q}(e) \rightarrow h_q|stg_{j+q}$, where $h_s \in 2^\Theta$, $s \le q$, and stg_{j+s} are rule strengths expressing the extent to which documents belong to the respective categories in terms of degrees of confidence. At the end of the inference process, a set of decisions will be obtained, and denoted by $H' = \{h_1, ..., h_q\}$, where $H' \subseteq 2^\Theta$.

Suppose we are given multiple classifiers $\Re = \{R_1, R_2, ..., R_{|\Re|}\}$ and a set of categories $\Theta = \{c_1, c_2, ..., c_{|\Theta|}\}$, for a new document d, the category predictions of multiple classifiers $R_1, R_2, ..., R_{|\Re|}$ will be applied to the document, resulting in $R_i(d) = H_i$. If only one of the classifiers is activated, such as $R_1(d) = H_1$, then H_1 will be ranked in decreasing order. If the top choice of H_1 is a singleton, it will be assigned to the new document, otherwise lower ranked decisions will be considered for the further selection. When K classifiers are activated, the multiple sets of classification decisions H_1, $H_2, ..., H_K$ are obtained, where $H_i = \{h_{i1}, h_{i2}, ..., h_{|H_i|}\}$, $H_i \subseteq 2^C$, and the corresponding rule strengths are $\varpi(H_i) = \{\varpi_i(h_{i1}), \varpi_i(h_{i2}), ..., \varpi_i(h_{|H_i|})\}$. After normalizing $\varpi(H_i)$ by using the method introduced in Section 4.1, we can obtain K mass functions, denoted $m_1, m_2, ..., m_K$. With all of these outcomes along with the mass functions, we can gradually combine them to decide the final decisions as follows:

$$[...[m_1 \oplus m_2] \oplus ... \oplus m_K] \quad (4)$$

6 Experiment and Evaluation

For our experiments, we have chosen a benchmark dataset, often referred to as 20-newsgroup. It consists of 20 categories, and each category has 1,000 documents (Usenet articles), so the dataset contains 20, 000 documents in total. Except for a small fraction of the articles (4%), each article belongs to exactly one category [10]. We have used 10 categories of documents, 10, 000 documents in total, to reduce the computational requirements. The documents within each category are further randomly split into two groups, one consisting of 800 documents for training, and the other including 200 documents, but only 100 of the 200 documents are selected for testing. A measure called micro-averaged F_1 is used as an evaluation criterion in this experiment [11].

6.1 The Experiment Results

For our experiments, ten reducts have been computed, and ten corresponding sets of intrinsic rules in turn have been constructed, denoted by $R_0, ..., R_9$. In the following, we will not distinguish between the concepts of rules and reducts if no confusion occurs. Prior to evaluating the effectiveness of different combinations of reducts, we first carry out the experiments on individual reducts. Figure 1 presents the performance of each set of intrinsic rules. It can be seen that the best performing reduct is R_4.

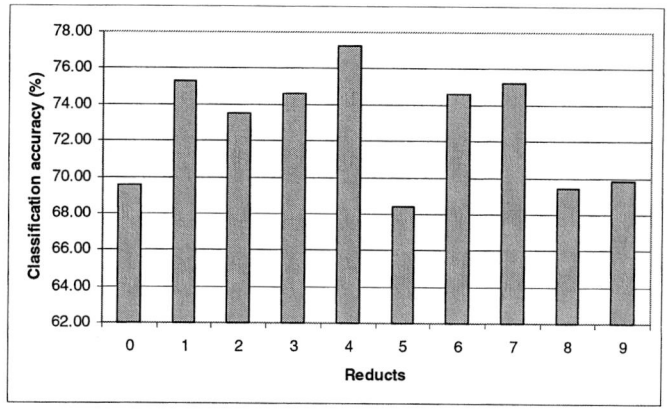

Fig. 1. The performance of different sets of intrinsic rules.

To examine of the effectiveness of combined reducts in classification, we first rank these reducts in decreasing order based on their classification accuracy, and then take R_4 with the best performance, and then combine it with R_1, R_2, R_3, R_6, R_7. The combined results are denoted by $R_{41}, R_{42}, R_{43}, R_{46}, R_{47}$ and they will be ranked. The best performing combination R_{46} is chosen, and in turn is combined with R_1, R_2, R_3, R_7, resulting in ranked combinations of $R_{461}, R_{462}, R_{463}, R_{467}$.

As illustrated in Figure 2, in comparison with R_{46}, their classification accuracy performance has dropped. To examine the change in performance with the addition of more reducts, R_{461} and R_{463} are taken for further combinations, it is surprising that the performance increases. However, the performance degrades again with more reducts being combined. Therefore, it can be concluded that the combination of the best individual reduct with a reduct having a fairly modest performance is the best combination in achieving the highest predictive performance. The graphs in Figures 2 illustrate the trends discussed above. It shows that the best combinations are the combinations of two results, and the performance of the best combination is 3.24% better than the best individual in the first group.

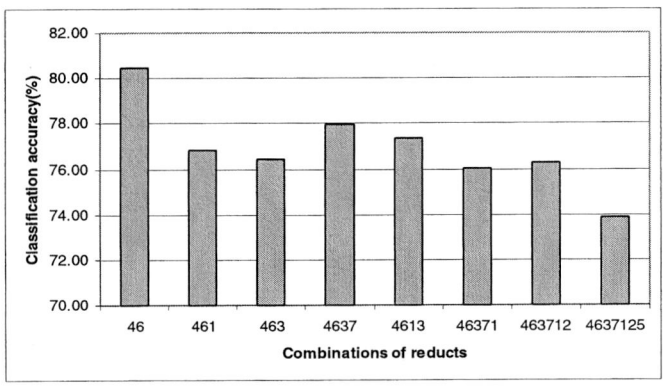

Fig. 2. The performance of the combined reducts.

7 Conclusion

In this work, we have presented a boosting-like method for generating multiple sets of rules which is built on Rough Set theory, and a novel combination function for combining classification decisions derived from multiple sets of rule classifiers based on the Dempster's combination rule. Preliminary experiments have been carried out on 10 of 20-newsgroups benchmark data, individually and in combination. We found that the combination which can achieves the highest predictive performance is a combination of two reduts of which one is the best, and the other should have reasonable predictive performance.

Acknowledgements

This work was partly funded by the Centre for Software Process Technologies at the University of Ulster which is supported by the EU Programme for Peace and Reconciliation in Northern Ireland and The Border Region of Ireland (PEACE II).

Reference

1. Xu, L., Krzyzak, A., and Suen, C. (1994). Associative Switch for Combining Multiple Classifiers. Journal of Artificial Neural Networks. Vol 1(1), pp77-100.
2. Freund, Y and Schapire, R.(1996). Experiments with a new boosting algorithm. In Machine Learning: Proceedings of the Thirteenth International Conference, pp148-156.
3. Friedman, J., Hastie, T., & Tibshirani, R. (1998). Additive logistic regression: A statistical view of boosting (Technical Report). Stanford University Statistics Department. www.stat-stanford.edu/~tibs.
4. Pawlak Z. Rough Set: Theoretical aspects of reasoning about data. Kluwer Academic, 1991
5. Bi, Y. (2004). Combining Multiple Pieces of Evidence for Text Categorization using Dempster's rule of combination. Internal report.
6. Quinlan, J. R. (10093). C4.5: Programs for Machine Learning. San Matero: Morgan Kaufmann.
7. Apte, C., Damerau, F., Weiss, S. (1994). Automated Learning of Decision Text Categorization. ACM Transactions on Information Systems, Vol. 12 (3), pp 233-251.
8. Weiss, S. M. and Indurkhya, N. (2000). Lightweight Rule Induction. Proceedings of the International Conference on Machine Learning (ICML).
9. Shafer, G.(1976). A Mathematical Theory of Evidence, Princeton University Press, Princeton, New Jersey.
10. Joachims, T. (1998). Text categorization With Support Vector Machines: Learning With Many Relevant Features. In Proceedings 10th European Conference on Machine Learning (ECML), Springer Verlag, 1998.
11. van Rijsbergen, C. J. (1979). Information Retrieval (second edition). Butterworths.

Genetic Program Based Data Mining for Fuzzy Decision Trees

James F. Smith III

Naval Research Laboratory, Code 5741
Washington, D.C., 20375-5000
Telephone: 202.767.5358
jfsmith@drsews.nrl.navy.mil

Abstract. A data mining procedure for automatic determination of fuzzy decision tree structure using a genetic program is discussed. A genetic program is an algorithm that evolves other algorithms or mathematical expressions. Methods of accelerating convergence of the data mining procedure including a new innovation based on computer algebra are examined. Experimental results related to using computer algebra are given. A comparison between a tree obtained using a genetic program and one constructed solely by interviewing experts is made. A genetic program evolved tree is shown to be superior to one created by hand using expertise alone. Finally, additional methods that have been used to validate the data mining algorithm are discussed.

1 Introduction

A fuzzy logic resource manager (RM) has been developed that automatically allocates resources in real-time. It uses standard sensor output as input and runs on very general platforms. This paper describes an automated procedure for extracting from a data base the necessary rules for the RM in the form of fuzzy decision trees.

Section 2 briefly introduces the ideas of fuzzy logic and discusses the RM's four major decision trees. Section 3 introduces genetic programs, examines a significant fuzzy decision subtree evolved by a genetic program and introduces the concept of self-morphing fuzzy decision trees. Section 4 discusses three methods of validating the fuzzy decision trees mined using the genetic program. Finally, section 5 provides a summary.

2 A Brief Introduction to Fuzzy Logic and the Resource Manager

The particular approach to fuzzy logic used by the RM is the fuzzy decision tree [1,2]. The fuzzy decision tree is an extension of the classical artificial intelligence concept of decision trees. The nodes of the tree of degree one, the leaf nodes, are labeled with what are referred to as root concepts. Nodes of degree greater than unity are labeled with composite concepts, i.e., concepts constructed from the root concepts [3,4] using "AND," "OR," and "NOT." Each root concept has a fuzzy membership function assigned to it. The membership functions for composite concepts are constructed from those assigned to the root concepts using fuzzy logic connectives and modifiers. Each root concept membership function has parameters that are determined by genetic algorithm based optimization [4,5].

The resource manager is made up of four decision trees, the isolated platform decision tree (IPDT), the multi-platform decision tree (MPDT), the fuzzy parameter selection tree and the fuzzy strategy tree. The IPDT provides a fuzzy decision tree that allows an individual agent to respond to a threat [4]. The other decision trees are discussed in the literature.

The structure of each of these trees, i.e., how edges are connected must be determined. This is equivalent up to free parameters to determining the rules that characterize the control process. These rules were originally determined by interviewing experts. Finally, section 3 will describe a method based on the theory of evolution of automatically data mining these rules from a data base of scenarios.

To be consistent with terminology used in artificial intelligence and complexity theory [6], the term "agent" will sometimes be used to mean platform, also a group of allied platforms will be referred to as a "meta-agent." Finally, the terms "blue" and "red" will refer to "agents" or "meta-agents" on opposite sides of a conflict, i.e., the blue side and the red side.

3 Discovering the IPTD Fuzzy Decision Tree's Structure Using a Genetic Program

The IPDT allows a blue agent that is alone or isolated to determine the intent of a detected agent. It does this by processing data measured by the sensors. Even when an incoming agent's ID is very uncertain, the IPDT can still establish intent based on kinematics. When faced with multiple incoming agents the IPDT can establish a queue of which agents to attack first. Various subtrees of the IPDT have been discussed extensively in the past [4].

Data mining is the efficient extraction of valuable non-obvious information embedded in a large quantity of data [7]. Data mining consists of three steps: the construction of a database that represents truth; the calling of the data mining function to extract the valuable information, e.g., a clustering algorithm, neural net, genetic algorithm, genetic program, etc; and finally determining the value of the information extracted in the second step, this generally involves visualization.

In a previous paper a genetic algorithm (GA) was used as a data mining function to determine parameters for fuzzy membership functions [4]. Here, a different data mining function, a genetic program [8] (GP) is used. A genetic program is a problem independent method for automatically evolving computer programs or mathematical expressions.

The GP data mines fuzzy decision tree structure, i.e., how vertices and edges are connected and labeled in a fuzzy decision tree. The GP mines the information from a database consisting of military scenarios. Whereas, the GA based data mining procedures determine the parameters of and hence the form of fuzzy membership functions, the GP based procedure actually data mines fuzzy if-then rules. GP based data mining will be applied to the construction of the IPDT.

To use the genetic program it is necessary to construct terminal and function sets relevant to the problem. The terminal set used for construction of subtrees of the IPDT is given below.

$$T=\{\text{close, heading\_in, elevation, ranging, banking, elevating, interaction, friend, lethal, uncertain, marginal-ID}\}. \quad (1)$$

The elements of this terminal set are fuzzy root concepts that are explained in the literature [4].

The function set, F, consists of the logical operations of "AND" and "OR" as well as the logical modifier "NOT," i.e.,

$$F=\{\text{AND}(1), \text{OR}(1), \text{AND}(2), \text{OR}(2), \ldots, \text{NOT}\}. \quad (2)$$

More than one form of AND and OR appear in (2), i.e., AND(1), AND(2), OR(1), OR(2), etc., because fuzzy logic allows more than one mathematical form for AND and OR.

The fitness function for data mining the IPDT subtree is

$$fitness(i) \equiv g(i, n_{db}, n_{time}, \tau) - a\, l(i) - CPU(i) \quad (3)$$

with

$$g(i, n_{db}, n_{time}, \tau) \equiv \frac{1}{n_{time} \cdot n_{db}} \sum_{j=1}^{n_{db}} \sum_{k=1}^{n_{time}} \chi(\tau - |\mu_{gp}(i, t_k, e_j) - \mu_{expert}(t_k, e_j)|) \quad (4)$$

where the function g is the basic fitness; e_j is the jth element of the database; t_k is the kth time step; n_{db} is the number of elements in the database; n_{time} is the number of time steps; τ is the tolerance; $\mu_{gp}(i, t_k, e_j)$ is the output of the fuzzy decision tree created by the GP for the ith element of the population for time step t_k and database element e_j; $\mu_{expert}(t_k, e_j)$ is an expert's estimate as to what the fuzzy decision tree should yield as output for time step t_k and database element e_j; α is the parsimony coefficient; $l(i)$ is the length of the ith element of the population, i.e., the number of nodes in the fuzzy decision tree corresponding to the ith element; $CPU(i)$ is the CPU penalty for the ith element of the population; $\chi(t)$ is the Heaviside step function which is unity for $t \geq 0$ and zero otherwise.

Observe, that the form of (3,4) reflects that the expert's estimate, $\mu_{expert}(t_k, e_j)$ is uncertain, and need only be reproduced within a tolerance, τ. Also, to increase the robustness of the GP created tree, the fitness of the fuzzy decision tree used by the GP is found by averaging over time and the database.

The parsimony pressure, $\alpha \bullet l(i)$, appearing on the right-hand-side of (3) provides a penalty that reduces the ith population element's fitness if it is longer than needed. Thus given two trees that are both effective, the smaller tree will have the higher fitness. This provides a computational implementation of Occam's razor [9].

The CPU penalty function provides a penalty for a tree being too CPU-intensive. If two trees have the same basic fitness, g, and length, but one requires more CPU time, the more CPU-intensive tree will have a lower overall fitness. Analogous extensions penalizing a tree for being too memory intensive are possible.

It is observed when using GPs that candidate solutions increase significantly in length during the evolutionary process. It is an empirically observed rule [10] that for every 50 generations, trees will grow by a factor of three in length. Many adhoc procedures have been developed to control this aspect [10-11], e.g., parsimony pressure described above, Koza depth limits, tournaments, etc. These procedures have the problem that they can prune away parts of a decision tree useful during low probability events.

When mathematical expressions are constructed by a GP that reproduce the entries in a database within some tolerance, the process is referred to as symbolic regression [10]. It is found in symbolic regression that candidate solutions are frequently not in algebraic simplest form and this is the major source of their excess length. When candidate solutions are too long this is referred to as bloat.

A simple method of reducing length of candidate solutions that are mathematical expressions is to introduce computer algebra for automated simplification. This results in not only simpler solutions, but also the GP converges more rapidly and its CPU time requirements are reduced. It is found for simple cases, databases obtained from polynomials or the reciprocal of polynomials with the addition of noise that algebraic simplification improves convergence by more than a factor of three.

The genetic program terminates after one of the following occurs: the number of generations reaches a preset maximum, the fitness has not changed by a preset amount in a certain number of generations or the fitness is within an acceptable tolerance of the maximum value.

Figure 1 depicts the IPDT subtree evolved by using GP based data mining. This subtree was originally drawn based on experts' intuition [11]. The fact that the GP was able to evolve a tree already known based on interviewing experts is a form of validation for the GP based procedure.

In Figure 1, a line on a vertex denotes the logical connective "AND," a vertex without a line indicates the logical connective "OR," and a circle on an edge denotes the logical modifier "NOT." The concepts, labeling each box, have been developed in the literature [4,11].

This subtree of the IPDT has been rediscovered by data mining a database of military scenarios using a GP. Other more sophisticated trees have been discovered by GP based data mining, but this simple tree is considered here to illustrate the process. The GP in many different runs was successful in constructing this subtree as expected, however, it did not always construct the same tree. The concept on the right-hand-side of the tree labeled "status" is a placeholder. In some trees constructed by the GP, its value was "not a friend" in others "status" took the value "lethal." The value "lethal" was originally proposed by experts, but has proven to be less effective than the GP suggested value of "not a friend."

In Figure 1, the concepts are assigned one of three priority levels. A box with a pure white background represents a highest priority concept. Intermediate priority concepts have lines in the background of their box. Lowest priority concepts have boxes with a dotted background. When there is a significant amount of time available all concepts are evaluated. When there is less time the lowest priority concepts are not evaluated, i.e., only the highest and middle priority concepts are evaluated. During the most time-critical periods only the highest priority concepts are evaluated. Finally, the number of priority levels need not be fixed at three, there can be more or less. A similar priority scheme is applied to the different mathematical forms of "AND" and "OR."

Based on input indicating the time-criticality of situations the RM can opt to evaluate or not evaluate certain concepts and also use simpler or more complicated mathematical forms for logical connectives. Deleting certain concepts effectively changes the shape of the fuzzy decision tree, i.e., the tree "morph's." Since the RM can elect to do this itself based on input, this ability is referred to as the *self-morphing property*.

Even though fuzzy logic is fast, compact and reliable if many agents within a decision support algorithm have their own fuzzy decision trees, then eventually the decision support algorithm becomes computationally intensive if each tree has its most complicated form. The self-morphing property allows the fuzzy decision trees to return high quality decisions even when operating in a complicated environment.

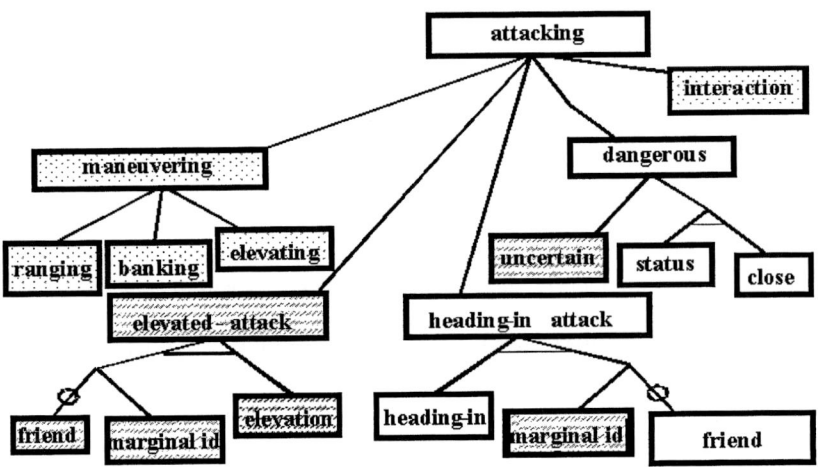

Fig. 1. A significant subtree of the IPDT that was evolved by the genetic program.

4 Evaluation of the Data Mined Decision Trees

Three different approaches for the validation of the data mined decision trees are discussed in this section. These approaches are the evaluation of the RM within a digital game environment [4,11]; testing the RM using a hardware simulator; and comparing the decision trees obtained through data mining to similar ones created solely through interviewing experts.

The scenario generator (SG) game simulation is described in detail elsewhere [4,11]. So only a quick summary will be given here. The SG allows the creation of a very general digital simulation environment that may have a map with desert, forest, jungle, urban areas, and water. Very general blue agents, i.e., the defending platforms each one of which runs its own copy of the RM can be placed within the environment. The agents can be ships, planes, helicopters, soldiers, decoys, etc. The SG allows the agents to be equipped with very general sensors, weapons, etc. Likewise, the SG allows very general red agents to be created and well equipped. The SG has two modes of operation, computer vs. computer (CVC) mode, and human vs. computer mode (HVC). In both modes each blue agent has its own copy of the RM. The blue agent's RM exercises all control functions over that agent and only that agent. In CVC mode each red agent is controlled by its own computerized logic different from the RM. In HVC mode, a human expert controls one red agent per time step through a GUI. The human player can select a different red agent each time step to control: those red agents not under human control run under computer logic as in CVC mode. Many different conflicts can be simulated using the SG, the results are stored in a database and also a computer movie. Human experts have evaluated many of the computer movies and agreed on the excellent decisions made by the decision tree of Figure 1.

Evaluation using a hardware simulator (HS) is similar to the work done with the SG, but in this case the digitally simulated radars, communication systems, and sensor displays of the SG are replaced with real hardware systems. In this application the RM is used as a controller on the HS, allowing evaluation of the RM. As in the previous approach to validation, experts concluded that the decision tree of Figure 1 made excellent decisions during the HS test.

The final contribution to the validation effort consists of comparing decision trees created through data mining to those designed solely using rules obtained by interviewing experts. As discussed in previous sections the GP is able to recreate the IPDT found through consulting with experts to acquire "if-then" rules. However as stated above, the GP does not always reproduce the known tree. In the case of the IPDT, the second tree created through data mining is arguably superior to the one arising from "if-then" rules provided by experts. It is useful to be able to recreate known decision trees, this establishes confidence in the data mining process. The most important ability of the GP based data mining procedure is to be able to construct decision trees for situations for which human expertise is not available.

Finally, even though the RM has been very successful when subjected to the test described above, field test are planned. Experiments in the field will expose the RM to conditions difficult to simulate digitally or in hardware.

5 Summary

A fuzzy logic based algorithm for optimal allocation of resources distributed over many agents is under development. A method for automatically determining fuzzy decision tree structure, and hence the related fuzzy if-then rules from databases is discussed. This method uses a genetic program, an algorithm that automatically evolves other computer programs or mathematical expressions. The use of parsimony pressure to limit the length of the fuzzy decision tree, while maintaining the tree's effectiveness is discussed. A procedure for reducing excessive length in intermediate solutions using computer algebra is introduced. The procedure is found to reduce the length of many intermediate trees accelerating convergence in some cases by a factor of more than three. An explicit fitness function including parsimony pressure and a CPU penalty is examined. The advantages of a tree evolved through this process, differing from a related one obtained from human expertise, are considered. The self-morphing property, the ability of a fuzzy decision tree to change its computational requirements in real-time is introduced. These concepts are discussed in terms of a significant fuzzy decision tree evolved by a genetic program. Finally, extensive efforts to validate the resource manager are discussed.

References

1. Blackman, S., Popoli, R.: Design and Analysis of Modern Tracking Systems. Artech House, Boston, (1999) Chapter 11.
2. Tsoukalas, L.H., Uhrig, R.E.: Fuzzy and Neural Approaches in Engineering. John Wiley and Sons, New York, (1997) Chapter 5.
3. Zimmerman, H. J.: Fuzzy Set Theory and its Applications. Kluwer Academic Publishers Group, Boston, (1991) Chapter 1.
4. Smith, III, J.F., Rhyne, II, R.: A Resource Manager for Distributed Resources: Fuzzy Decision Trees and Genetic Optimization. In: Arabnia, H. (ed.): Proceeding of the International Conference on Artificial Intelligence, IC-AI'99, Vol. II. CSREA Press, Las Vegas, (1999) 669-675.
5. Goldberg, D.E.: Genetic Algorithms in Search, Optimization and Machine Learning. Addison-Wesley, Reading, (1989).
6. Holland, J. H.: Hidden Order How Adaptation Builds Complexity. Perseus Books, Reading, (1995) 1-15.
7. Bigus, J.P.: Data Mining with Neural Nets. McGraw-Hill, New York, (1996) Chapter 1.
8. Koza, J.R., Bennett III, F.H., Andre, D., Keane, M.A.: Genetic Programming III: Darwinian Invention and Problem Solving. Morgan Kaufmann Publishers, San Francisco, (1999) Chapter 2.
9. Gribbin, J.: Companion to the Cosmos. The Orion Publishing Group Ltd, London, (1996) 299.
10. Luke, S., Panait, L.: Fighting Bloat With Nonparametric Parsimony Pressure. In: Guervos, J.J.M (ed.): Parallel Problem Solving from Nature - PPSN VII, 7th International Conference. Proceedings. LNCS Vol.2439. Springer-Verlag Berlin, (2002) 411-421.
11. Smith, III, .J.F., Rhyne II, R. D.: Fuzzy logic resource manager: tree structure and optimization. In: Kadar, I. (ed.): Signal Processing, Sensor Fusion, and Target Recognition X, Vol. 4380. SPIE Proceedings, Orlando, (2001) 312-323.

Automating Co-evolutionary Data Mining

James F. Smith III

Naval Research Laboratory, Code 5741
Washington, D.C., 20375-5000
Telephone: 202.767.5358

Abstract. An approach is being explored that involves embedding a fuzzy logic based resource manager in an electronic game environment. Game agents can function under their own autonomous logic or human control. This approach automates the data mining problem. The game automatically creates a cleansed database reflecting the domain expert's knowledge, it calls a data mining function, a genetic algorithm, for data mining of the data base as required and allows easy evaluation of the information extracted. Co-evolutionary fitness functions are discussed. The strategy tree concept and its relationship to co-evolutionary data mining are examined as well as the associated phase space representation of fuzzy concepts. Co-evolutionary data mining alters the geometric properties of the overlap region known as the combined admissible region of phase space significantly enhancing the performance of the resource manager. Significant experimental results are provided.

1 Introduction

A resource manager (RM) based on fuzzy logic has been developed that automatically allocates resources in real-time over a group of dissimilar platforms linked by communication. The particular approach to fuzzy logic that is used is the fuzzy decision tree, a generalization of the standard artificial intelligence technique of decision trees [1].

The RM must be able to make decisions based on rules provided by experts. The fuzzy logic approach allows the direct codification of expertise forming a fuzzy linguistic description [2], i.e., a formal representation of the system in terms of fuzzy if-then rules. This has proven to be a flexible structure that can be extended or otherwise altered as doctrine sets, i.e., the expert rule sets change.

The fuzzy linguistic description builds composite concepts from simple logical building blocks known as root concepts through various logical connectives: "and", "or", etc. Optimization is used to determine the parameters that control the shape of the fuzzy root concept membership functions.

The optimization procedures employed here are a type of data mining. Data mining is defined as the efficient discovery of valuable, non-obvious information embedded in a large collection of data [3]. The genetic optimization techniques used here are efficient, the relationship between parameters extracted and the fuzzy rules are certainly not a priori obvious, and the information obtained is valuable for decision-theoretic processes. Also, the algorithm is designed so that when the scenario databases change as a function of time, then the algorithm can automatically re-optimize allowing it to discover new relationships in the data. The RM can be embedded in a computer game that experts can play. The software records the result of the RM and the expert's interaction, automatically assembling a database of scenarios. After the end of the game, it makes a determination of whether or not to re-optimize the RM using the newly extended database.

To be consistent with terminology used in artificial intelligence and complexity theory [4], the term "agent" will sometimes be used to mean platform, also a group of allied platforms will be referred to as a "meta-agent". Finally, the terms "blue" and "red" will refer to "agents" or "meta-agents" on opposite sides of a conflict, i.e., the blue side and the red side.

Section 2 briefly introduces fuzzy decision trees. Section 3 discusses optimization with a focus on genetic algorithms and co-evolutionary data mining. Section 4 advances a theory that allows automatic construction of co-evolutionary fitness functions. Section 5 references validation efforts. Finally, section 6 discusses results for co-evolutionary data mining experiments and related conclusions.

2 Fuzzy Decision Trees

The particular approach to fuzzy logic used here is the fuzzy decision tree. The fuzzy decision tree is an extension of the classical artificial intelligence concept of decision trees. The nodes of the tree of degree one, the leaf nodes, are labeled with what are referred to as root concepts. Nodes of degree greater than unity are labeled with composite concepts, i.e., concepts constructed from the root concepts [5,6] using "and", "or", and "not". Each root concept has a fuzzy membership function assigned to it. The membership functions for composite concepts are constructed from those assigned to the root concepts using fuzzy logic connectives and modifiers. Each root concept membership function has parameters that are determined by optimization as described in section 3. The fuzzy concepts are discussed in the literature [6,7,8].

3 Genetic Algorithm Based Optimization and Data Mining

The parameters of the root concept membership function are obtained by optimizing the RM over a database of scenarios using a genetic algorithm (GA) [6,9]. Once the root concept membership functions are known, those for the composite concepts [6] follow immediately. At this point the necessary fuzzy if-then rules for the RM have been fully determined. A detailed discussion of the GA for data mining as well as the construction of the chromosomes and fitness functions are given in the literature [6].

The application of the genetic algorithm is actually part of the second step in a three-step data mining process. The first step is the collection of data and its subsequent filtering by a domain expert, to produce a scenario database of good quality. The second step involves the use of various data mining functions such as clustering and association, etc. During this step, genetic algorithm based optimization is used to mine parameters from the database. These parameters allow the fuzzy decision tree to form optimal conclusions about resource allocation. In the third and final step of the data mining operation, the RM's decisions are analyzed by a domain expert to determine their validity.

The game software records the events of the game. The record contributes to a database for re-optimization, allowing the RM to learn from human or computerized opponents.

3.1 Co-evolution

In nature a system never evolves separately from the environment in which it is contained. Rather, both the biological system and its environment simultaneously evolve. This is referred to as co-evolution [10]. In a similar manner, the fuzzy resource manager should not evolve separately from its environment, i.e., enemy strategies should be allowed to simultaneously evolve. Certainly, in real world situations if the enemy sees the resource manager employ a certain range of techniques, they will evolve a collection of counter techniques to compete more effectively with the resource manager.

In a previous paper [6] an approach to co-evolution involving averaging over a database of military scenarios was reported. The current approach involves both blue and computerized red meta-agents each having fuzzy decision trees and strategy trees. Both types of tree will be subject to adaptation during optimization. A strategy tree differs from a decision tree in that it is one meta-agent's model of another meta-agent's decision tree.

3.2 Strategy Tree Approach to Co-evolutionary Data Mining

The RM has many concepts that overlap conceptually in phase space reducing the likelihood that red can win against blue [7,8]. Each concept gives rise to an admissible region in a two-dimensional phase subspace. In a particular phase subspace, the overlap of various fuzzy concepts gives rise to an overall admissible region for the RM that is an intersection of the individual regions related to each fuzzy concept. This overall admissible region is referred to as the combined admissible region. In this way, by having many overlapping fuzzy concepts, the area of phase space that red can occupy without alerting blue is made smaller. Since sensors have finite resolution and time is considered discrete a smaller phase space area implies a smaller number of trajectories or patterns of behavior that red can execute safely, resulting in a more effective RM.

The fuzzy concepts "close" and "ranging" overlap in the range-rate versus range phase subspace. The combined admissible region for "close" and "ranging" for a given maximum radar range has an area much less than that of the admissible region of "close" alone [7].

4 Automatic Construction of a Fitness Function for Co-evolution

When re-optimizing, it is necessary to incorporate knowledge of an agent's history, specifically those events that led to re-optimization. A method of doing this is to construct fitness functions that contain a history of the agent and upon maximization result in agents that will not reproduce past mistakes.

This subsection develops an algorithm for the automatic construction of such functions. Let $\mu_{attacking}$ refer to the output of blue's isolated platform decision tree (IPDT) or red's strategy tree that attempts to reproduce the decisions made by blue's IPDT [7]. In the development below Heaviside step functions are approximated by sigmoidal functions as described in the literature [8]. A logarithm is taken to produce a smoother fitness function. Replacing the Heaviside step function with the sigmoid produces a smoother approximation to the original fitness function. The sigmoid based fitness function carries approximately the same data base information as the one based on Heaviside step functions. Since it falls off more slowly, a chromosome with many good traits that would have had a zero probability of surviving in the population under the fitness function based on Heaviside step function now has a non-zero probability of survival. Taking the logarithm of the product of the sigmoidal functions also helps to accelerate convergence in some cases. For the fitness function considered below the zero order fitness function has not been included as a simplifying approximation.

4.1 Red Fitness

Let N_G be the number of co-evolutionary generations; and T, be a vector of length L_T containing the time-steps that will be used in the fitness calculation, up to and including the last time-step in each co-evolutionary generation. In practice, this vector contains the time-steps at which a blue platform detected a red platform on radar. Let $\mu_{t,g}$ be red's estimate of the value of blue's fuzzy grade of membership for "attacking", i.e., $\mu_{attacking}$ at time t in co-evolutionary generation g, and let τ be the threshold value for $\mu_{attacking}$. The quantities β_1 and β_2 are constants that determine the weights of the next to last L_T -1 time-steps and the last time-step, respectively. The parameter, lb, is introduced to establish a lower bound and C is a constant which ensures that the fitness is positive.

Different formulas are used depending on whether the position data being employed to evaluate the fitness comes from a game in which red won or one in which blue won. If blue won, then $\mu_{attacking}$ must have been above threshold at the last time-step, but below threshold at previous time-steps. In this case, the red fitness is given by:

$$fit = \sum_{g=1}^{N_G} \left\{ max\left[lb, log\left(\frac{1}{1+exp\left[\beta_2\left(\tau - \mu_{T(L_T),g}\right)\right]} \right) \right] \right\} +$$

$$\sum_{g=1}^{N_G} \left\{ \sum_{t=1}^{L_T-1} max\left[lb, log\left(\frac{1}{1+exp\left[\beta_1\left(\mu_{T(t),g} - \tau\right)\right]} \right) \right] \right\} + C.$$

(1)

If red won, then $\mu_{attacking}$ was never above threshold, and the red fitness is given by:

$$fit = \sum_{g=1}^{N_G} \sum_{t=1}^{L_T} max\left[lb, log\left(\frac{1}{1+exp[\beta_1(\mu_{T(t),g} - \tau)]}\right)\right] + C. \quad (2)$$

If there are multiple blue platforms, a red platform's fitness is the sum of its fitness scores for each blue platform. If there are multiple red platforms, the red meta-agent fitness is the sum of all individual fitness values. Finally, for all forms of the red fitness function the β_1 and β_2 values currently being used are $\beta_1 = 10^3$ and $\beta_2 = 10^6$.

4.2 Fitness with Multiple Red Strategies

Let there be N red strategies. For each strategy, a game is played and an extension of the database is made. Let $F_j(i)$ be the fitness of the ith individual in the GA's population as calculated by the above functions using a database subset taken from a game in which the jth red strategy was used. The fitness of the ith individual over all N red strategies is given by:

$$fit(i) = \frac{1}{N} \sum_{j=1}^{N} \frac{F_j(i)}{max(F_j)}. \quad (3)$$

Up to now, only red fitness functions have been constructed. Blue fitness functions can be created in a similar fashion. The blue fitness functions will not be considered due to space limitations.

4.3 Red Strategies

In order to prevent blue from executing an action against red, red must behave in such a way that none of the blue membership functions exceed threshold. Three red strategies, i.e., red paths through the combined admissible region of phase space are used. The blue membership functions partition phase space into two disjoint regions made up of a combined admissible region, the region where the grade of membership is below threshold and no action is taken, and an inadmissible region, where the grade of membership is above threshold and a blue action is executed.

For this example, red uses three different trajectories to remain within the combined admissible region. In all three trajectories, the heading angle assumes a value of π as red approaches the goal distance, d. Red can do this without initiating a blue action since blue's radar rotates and as such is not always looking at red.

There are many possible strategies that red can pursue in phase space. A more detailed analysis of potential strategies will be considered in a future publication.

5 Validation

The third step of the data mining problem involves validation, i.e., determination of the value of the information data mined. This is intrinsically coupled to the validation of the resource manager itself. Both data mined information and the RM have been subjected to significant evaluations using the scenario generator [7,8]. Through this process the data mined information has been shown to be extremely valuable and the decisions made by the RM of the highest quality.

6 Experimental Results and Conclusions

The following simple experiment uses the fuzzy concepts "close" and "ranging" to illustrate the co-evolutionary approach. Red starts 28.28 nautical miles from blue. For this simple experiment the three red strategies of subsection 4.3 are used against blue. Blue is considered stationary throughout the experiment; and the neutral travels a curved trajectory, but never gets closer to blue than 26 nautical miles. Also, the neutral's heading is never directly toward blue: it is always off by at least three degrees.

In this data mining process there were 30 co-evolutionary generations. Of these 30, blue won 24 and red won six. Within the first 14 co-evolutionary generations blue's and red's α's converge to the same value. This implies that red learned blue's parameter. Also, it can be shown mathematically that the values of the final parameters of "close" selected for blue result in a RM that red can not beat when there is one blue agent, one red agent and one neutral agent. This mathematical procedure will be described in greater detail in a future publication.

Both red and blue have similar parameters at the end of the co-evolutionary data mining process. Although blue's parameters are not equal to those of red in general, they agree within an acceptable tolerance.

References

1. Blackman, S., Popoli, R.: Design and Analysis of Modern Tracking Systems. Artech House, Boston, (1999) Chapter 11
2. Tsoukalas, L.H., Uhrig, R.E.: Fuzzy and Neural Approaches in Engineering. John Wiley and Sons, New York, (1997) Chapter 5
3. Bigus, J.P.: Data Mining with Neural Nets. McGraw-Hill, New York, (1996) Chapter 1
4. Holland, J. H.: Hidden Order How Adaptation Builds Complexity. Perseus Books, Reading, (1995) 1-15
5. Zimmerman, H. J.: Fuzzy Set Theory and its Applications. Kluwer Academic Publishers Group, Boston, (1991) Chapter 1
6. Smith, III, J.F., Rhyne, II, R.: A Resource Manager for Distributed Resources: Fuzzy Decision Trees and Genetic Optimization. In: Arabnia, H. (ed.): Proceeding of the International Conference on Artificial Intelligence, IC-AI'99. CSREA Press, Las Vegas, (1999) 669-675

7. Smith, III, J.F., Rhyne, II, R.: Fuzzy Logic Resource Management and Coevolutionary Game-Based Optimization. NRL/FR/5741--01-10001, Naval Research Laboratory, Washington D.C. 20375-5000, September 2001
8. Smith, III, J.F., Rhyne, II, R.: Methods of Automated Rule Discovery in a Multi-agent Adversarial Distributed Environment. In: Smari, W. (ed.): Proceeding of the International Symposium on Information Systems and Engineering, ISE'2001. CSREA Press, (2001) 25-31
9. Goldberg, D.E.: Genetic Algorithms in Search, Optimization and Machine Learning. Addison-Wesley, Reading, (1989)
10. Cliff, D, Miller, G. F.: Co-evolution of Pursuit and Evasion II: Simulation Methods and Results. In: Maes, P., Mataric, M., Meyer, J.-A., Pollack, J., Wilson, S.W. (eds.): Proceedings of the Fourth International Conference on Simulation of Adaptive Behavior (SAB96). MIT Press Bradford Books, Cambridge, (1996) 1-10

Topological Tree for Web Organisation, Discovery and Exploration

Richard T. Freeman and Hujun Yin

Department of Electrical & Electronics Engineering
University of Manchester Institute of Science and Technology
Manchester, M60 1QD, UK
rics@swift.ee.umist.ac.uk, h.yin@umist.ac.uk
http://www.rfreeman.net

Abstract. In this paper we focus on the organisation of web contents, which allows efficient browsing, searching and discovery. We propose a method that dynamically creates such a structure called *Topological Tree*. The tree is generated using an algorithm called Automated Topological Tree Organiser, which uses a set of hierarchically organised self-organising growing chains. Each chain fully adapts to a specific topic, where its number of subtopics is determined using entropy-based validation and cluster tendency schemes. The Topological Tree adapts to the natural underlying structure at each level in the hierarchy. The topology in the chains also relates close topics together, thus can be exploited to reduce the time needed for search and navigation. This method can be used to generate a web portal or directory where browsing and user comprehension are improved.

1 Introduction

With the increasing demand to improve knowledge transfer, competitiveness and efficiency more information technology services and consultancies are offering enterprise portals, data mining and business intelligence solutions. These technologies are related to content and knowledge management, which are particularly valuable with the drastic and increasing amount of content available on the Internet and corporate Intranets. This may contain valuable employee best practices, knowledge and experiences, which are significant assets to a company especially with increased mobility of employees. There is a demand for efficient searching, exploring and knowledge discovery. The main underlying technologies used for textual content are *text mining* (e.g. [6]), *document classification* (e.g. [13]) and *document clustering* (e.g. [11]). Document clustering does not rely on human labelling, thus can provide an objective, automated hierarchy of topics for organisation, searching and browsing purposes. This is the focus of the paper.

Agglomerative [11] or divisive hierarchical methods (e.g. [14]) are commonly used document clustering algorithms that both typically generate a dendrogram. These can be useful for searching and retrieval [15] but are less useful for exploring and browsing a large number of topics. Other methods such as the self-organising maps (SOMs) have also been used for this purpose. For example, the

WEBSOM generates a fixed size 2-dimensional map where the topic clusters can be visualised and where the topology preservation properties ensure that similar topics are located close to one another [8]. Other SOM variants include the growing hierarchical SOM (GH-SOM) [10] or tree growing cell structures (TreeGCS) [7]. In the GH-SOM a set of 2-dimensional maps are grown dynamically until a fixed threshold is reached, then documents clustered to particular nodes are further clustered in child maps. In the TreeGCS growing cells structures are used to organise the documents. The deletion of nodes then allows the formation of sub-structures, in which the clustered patterns are placed in a dendrogram.

2 Topological Tree Generation

The proposed Automated Topological Tree Organiser (ATTO) uses self-organising chains as building blocks and dynamic hierarchy as structure. The preliminary idea of a 1-dimensional, tree type growing SOM was first explored by the authors for document organisation in [4] and later enhanced using contextual indexing terms [3]. The process of the tree type SOM is to let each chain grow until some terminating measure is reached. However this has to be decided before the training. If the criterion is set too high then the chain becomes too indiscriminative, or too low the chain becomes a flat partition. The early method uses the Euclidean distance, while the cosine correlation metric is arguably more appropriate in a sparse document space [11]. An enhancement was made using the correlation metric and the turning point in the average similarity to find the chain size [5]. Once a chain is trained each node is tested to determine if documents clustered to it should be further clustered in a child chain. This process is similar to divisive clustering except that the number of clusters is not limited or pre-defined.

In the proposed ATTO, the size of each chain is independently determined through a validation process using an entropy-based criterion. Once the size is determined, documents clustered to a node are tested using a cluster tendency method, to determine if they should form a leaf node or to be further expanded into a child chain. The successive addition of child chains effectively forms a taxonomy of topics possessing topology at each level. In addition, methods are used to deal with fast dot-product of sparse vectors, winner search method, and weight update function. Furthermore adaptive node insertion for each chain is performed using both interpolation and extrapolation. The nodes in the tree are also given insightful representative labels using a method taking into account of term frequencies and the node weights. Important relations between terms in the same cluster are also extracted using association rule mining. A general diagram showing the overall system and its features is shown in Fig. 1.

2.1 Document Parsing and Feature Selection

In the pre-processing stage the document files in the dataset are crawled, text enclosed in the title tags are recorded and the html parsed into plain text. The

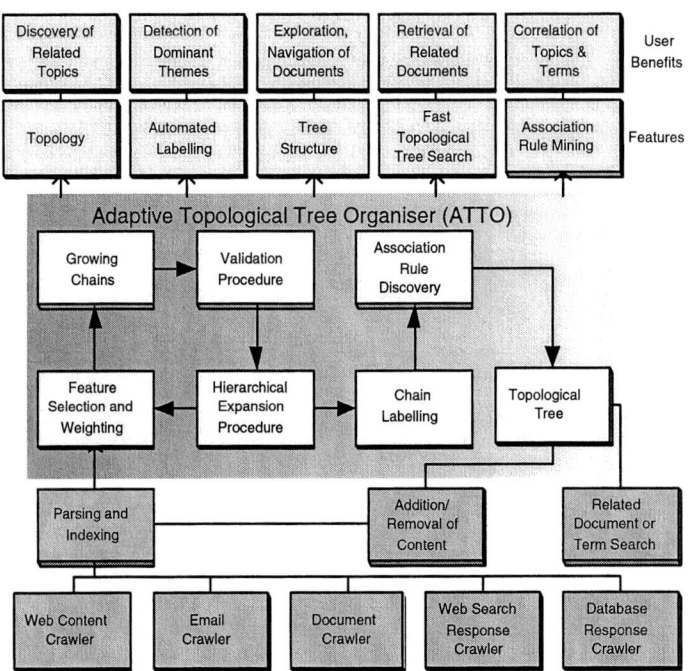

Fig. 1. The overall Topological Tree generation

title and body text are then indexed using a sliding window of sizes p (e.g. $p = 4$, up to 4 successive words are used for each term) over sentences, ignoring common words in a stop-list. Since the number of terms can grow significantly, the least discriminative terms are discarded: those occurring in less than a few documents and those occurring in more than a large percentage of the total documents. In the vector space model [11] a document is stored as $[f_1, f_2, ..., f_N]$, where f_i is the frequency of term i and N is the total number of unique terms. Since a document vector is sparse, its term frequencies can be stored in a compressed representation as a hash table for efficient retrieval,

$$\mathbf{x} = [\{\gamma_1, \rho_1\}, \{\gamma_2, \rho_2\}, ..., \{\gamma_r, \rho_r\}], \gamma_k \in \{V | f_{\gamma_k} \neq 0\}, k = 1, 2, ...r \quad (1)$$

where $\mathbf{x}$ is a document vector stored as term γ and weighted frequency ρ pairs, γ_k refers to the γ_k-th term in the vocabulary V, r is the total number of terms in the document. Term weighting ρ and feature selection are detailed in [5].

2.2 Growing Chains

The ATTO uses a set of chains adaptively developed by a growing chains (GC) algorithm. Each chain begins with two nodes and grows until the termination process stops it. In the root chain the weights of the nodes are initialised to small random values, while child chains are initialised through interpolating its parent nodes. There are two important steps in the GC training: the search for the best matching unit and the update of the weights of the winner and its neighbourhood. At time t, an input document vector $\mathbf{x}(t)$ is mapped to a chain consisting of n nodes, where each node j has a weight vector $\mathbf{w}_j = [w_{j1}, w_{j2}, ..., w_{jN}]^T$ of N dimensions. The similarity metric can be calculated efficiently by exploiting the sparseness of $\mathbf{x}(t)$,

$$S_{dot}(\mathbf{x}(t), \mathbf{w}_j) = \sum_{k=1}^{r(t)} \rho_k \cdot w_{j\gamma_k}, \forall \{\gamma_k, \rho_k\} \in \mathbf{x}(t) \quad (2)$$

The best matching unit $c(\mathbf{x})$ is the node with maximum S_{dot} amongst all nodes n with respect to a document vector $\mathbf{x}(t)$,

$$c(\mathbf{x}) = \arg\max_{j} \{S_{dot}(\mathbf{x}(t), \mathbf{w}_j)\}, j = 1, 2, ..., n \quad (3)$$

The weights of the winner node and of its neighbourhood are updated using,

$$\mathbf{w}_j(t+1) = \frac{\mathbf{w}_j(t) + \alpha(t) h_{j,c(x)}(t) \mathbf{x}(t)}{\|\mathbf{w}_j(t) + \alpha(t) h_{j,c(x)}(t) \mathbf{x}(t)\|} \quad (4)$$

where α is the learning rate. To monitor the activity of each node a counter is used to record its winning times, which is set to zero at the creation of the chain and reinitialised after a new node is added. A new node is inserted once the training has converged, indicated by the stabilisation of a measure measure termed average similarity ($AvgSim$),

$$AvgSim = \frac{1}{n} \sum_{j=1}^{n} \frac{1}{m_j} \sum_{\forall \mathbf{x} \in C_j} (S_{dot}(\mathbf{x}, \mathbf{w}_j)), m_j \neq 0 \quad (5)$$

where m_j is the number of documents clustered in a particular node C_j by Eq. 3. Just before a new node is inserted an entropy-based validation measure is recorded. This measure is chosen over a weight-based measure, since this is already given by $AvgSim$ and optimised by the GCs. To discourage the tree from becoming a flat partition, the validation measure penalises larger number of clusters, as in the Schwarz's Bayesian information criterion [12]. The validation is also applied locally to a particular chain, taking into account its particular reduced and specialised vocabulary.

$$\Theta(n) = \frac{1}{m} \sum_{j=1}^{n} m_j \cdot \left(-\sum_{i} p(t_i|C_j) \log p(t_i|C_j) \right) + \frac{1}{2} n \log m \quad (6)$$

where $p(t_i|C_j)$ is the probability that a term t_i belongs to cluster C_j and m the total number of documents.

Once the validation measure is recorded, the new node is inserted in the proximity of the node with the largest activity, to its left or right, depending on which leads to a higher *AvgSim*. The new node's weight is initialised through interpolating or extrapolating the neighbouring nodes.

Once the map has reached a size of n_{max} the training is terminated and the optimum chain size τ is determined using,

$$\tau = \arg\min_{n} \{\Theta(n)\}, n = 2, 3, .., n_{\max} \quad (7)$$

2.3 Creating the Topological Tree

After the root chain has been trained and optimum number of nodes τ identified, each node is tested to see whether documents clustered to it need a further sub-level division. One heuristic approach is to allow a minimum number of documents in each child chain. Another test then checks the number of terms in the chain vocabulary. If the chain only contains few terms this indicates that the parent node is sufficiently specialised and the documents may already be very similar. The final test is to use a cluster tendency method called *term density test*, which relates number of average frequency of terms to number of terms in dictionary, to determine if it is worth while further clustering the set [2]. If any of these tests fail then the parent node becomes a leaf node.

If a node spans a child chain, then all documents mapped to the node form a new subset of documents with reduced vocabulary. The weights of these nodes are initialised using the weights of the parent nodes to speed up the convergence.

2.4 Node Labelling and Descriptors

The browsing experience of the Topological Trees is enhanced through an automated selection of suitable labels for each node. They can be found by calculating the dot-product ts_i and frequency of occurrence f_i of each term i for all documents in a cluster. Simultaneously ranking f_i and ts_i (as primary key) provided understandable and high quality cluster labels.

Further details of a particular cluster can be displayed as well as the term associations for its documents. These are found using techniques from association rule mining, similar to those used in clustering frequent term sets [1]. When a node is selected, a ranked list of unidirectional co-occurring relations between two terms or more is displayed.

3 Experiments and Comparisons

The bisecting k-means method [14] was used as a basis for empirical comparison with the ATTO. A moderate dataset of 1097 randomly selected documents from the Addison Wesley website[1] was chosen to allow human verification of clustering results. To reduce excessive depth of the bisecting k-means dendrogram all excessive connections without a divisive split were removed.

---

[1] http://www.aw.com

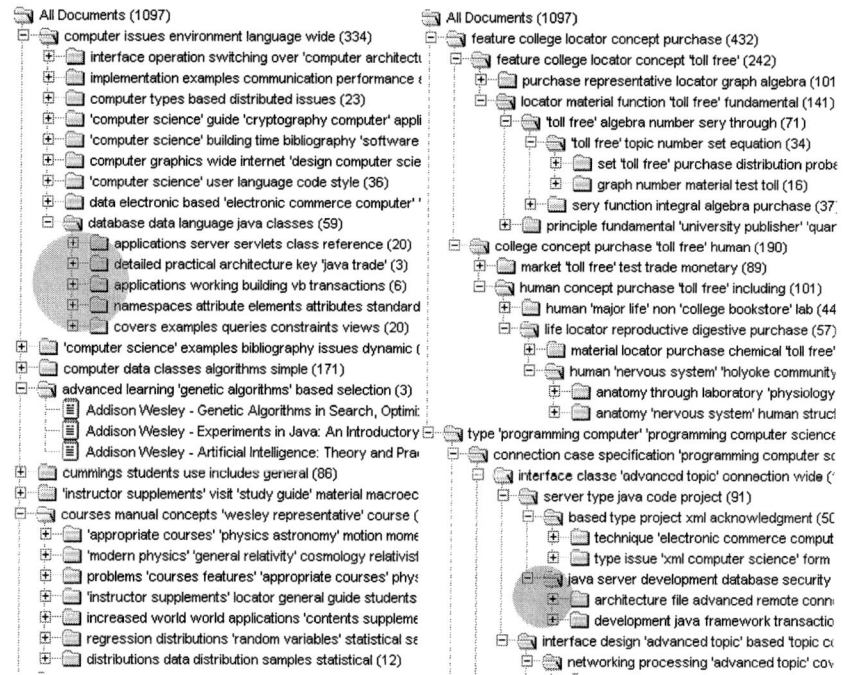

Fig. 2. ATTO Topological Tree (left) and bisecting k-means binary tree (right)

The left of Fig. 2 shows the Topological Tree generated by the ATTO. From top to bottom the following themes can be observed: computer languages, computer development, computer algorithms, life sciences, economics and mathematics. The right of Fig. 2 shows the binary tree generated by the bisecting k-means. The upper levels deals with mathematics/life sciences and lower section with computer science. The two highlighted regions compare both approaches on the topic of databases and it can be observed that the Topological Tree spreads the topic further at a shallower stage than the bisecting k-means. The Topological Tree is clearly less complex, so avoiding deeper divisions aiding visualisation, exploration and understanding. The topology also ensures that similar topics can easily be found in neighbouring nodes. This further allows quick retrieval of documents given a query by allowing expansion of the retrieved documents or search for related topics.

4 Discussions and Conclusions

We have presented a self-organising method for generating a Topological Tree, where the size of each level is determined through validation. Compared to the existing SOM-based methods the proposed Topological Tree is adaptive, dynamically validated and is natural for visualisation and exploring as in many file managers. The topology provides a unique feature that can be used for finding related topics during browsing and extending the search space, a clear distinctive advantage over other clustering algorithms. The topology is obtained without any further processing like reordering the leaf nodes [9] or making use of more advanced representations like graph structures. Topological trees can be defined as a hybrid graph-tree, where the hierarchical relations are represented between clusters.

References

1. F. Beil, M. Ester, and X. Xu. Frequent term-based text clustering. In *Proc. SIGKDD'02*, pages 436–442, Edmonton, Canada, 2002.
2. A. El-Hamdouchi and P. Willett. Techniques for the measurement of clustering tendency in document retrieval systems. *Journal of Information Science*, 13(6):361–365, 1987.
3. R. Freeman and H. Yin. Self-organising maps for hierarchical tree view document clustering using contextual information. In H. Yin, N. Allinson, R. Freeman, J. Keane, and S. Hubbard, editors, *LNCS 2412, Intelligent Data Engineering and Automated Learning*, pages 123–128, Manchester, UK, 2002.
4. R. Freeman, H. Yin, and N. M. Allinson. Self-organising maps for tree view based hierarchical document clustering. In *Proc. IJCNN'02*, volume 2, pages 1906–1911, Honolulu, Hawaii, 2002. IEEE.
5. R. T. Freeman and H. Yin. Tree view self-organisation of web content. *Neurocomputing*, in press 2004.
6. M. A. Hearst. Untangling text data mining. In *Proc. ACL'99*, 1999.
7. V. J. Hodge and J. Austin. Hierarchical growing cell structures: Treegcs. *IEEE Trans. Knowledge & Data Engineering*, 13(2):207–18, 2001.
8. T. Kohonen, S. Kaski, K. Lagus, J. Salojarvi, J. Honkela, V. Paatero, and A. Saarela. Self organization of a massive document collection. *IEEE Trans. Neural Networks*, 11(3):574–85, 2000.
9. S. A. Morris, B. Asnake, and G. G. Yen. Dendrogram seriation using simulated annealing. *Information Visualization*, 2(2):95–104, 2003.
10. A. Rauber, D. Merkl, and M. Dittenbach. The growing hierarchical self-organizing map: exploratory analysis of high-dimensional data. *IEEE Trans. Neural Networks*, 13(6):1331–1341, 2002.
11. G. Salton. *Automatic text processing - the transformation, analysis, and retrieval of information by computer*. Addison-Wesley, 1989.
12. G. Schwarz. Estimating the dimension of a model. *The Annals of Statistics*, 6(2):461–464, 1978.
13. F. Sebastiani. Machine learning in automated text categorization. *ACM Computing Surveys*, 34(1):1–47, 2002.
14. M. Steinbach, G. Karypis, and V. Kumar. A comparison of document clustering techniques. In *Proc. KDD'2000, Boston, USA*, 2000.
15. C. J. Van Rijsbergen. *Information Retrieval*. Butterworth, 2 edition, 1979.

New Medical Diagnostic Method for Oriental Medicine Using BYY Harmony Learning

JeongYon Shim

Division of General Studies, Computer Science, Kangnam University
San 6-2, Kugal-ri, Kihung-up,YongIn Si, KyeongKi Do, Korea
mariashim@kangnam.ac.kr

Abstract. In help of BYY harmony learning for binary independent factor analysis, an automatic oriental medical diagnostic approach is proposed. A preliminary experiment has shown a promising result on the diagnostic problem of 'Flaming-up liver fire' with medical data from oriental medical diagnosis.

1 Introduction

As efficacy of oriental medicine is improved, it becomes ever interested recently. In the oriental medicine, health and illness are not viewed being static and isolated from other aspects of a person's life. Rather they are regarded as dynamic states that uniquely reflects an individual as a whole, including body, mind and spirit, etc. An oriental medical doctor is trained to believe that any illness in one part of the body is related to a vulnerability or weakness in another part. Oriental medicine views illness as a fundamental imbalance or disharmony between Yin and Yang energy. Because oriental medicine is essentially holistic in nature, it encompasses many different healing methods. The multidisciplinary approach to health and illness is very different from the conventional western medicine. In oriental medicine, doctor tries to find the hidden causal factors from the observed symptoms of patient and discover the fundamental disharmony among the hidden causal factors. The key approach of healing method in oriental medicine is to recover body's harmony by compensating insufficient hidden causal factors with herbal medicine.

In western medical area, various medical diagnostic systems using computer technologies have been developed for many years. Starting from MYCIN which stands for If-Then production rule based system, many medical expert systems have been successfully applied to medical diagnostic area with advantages of easy implementation, easy transformation of rules from the expert knowledge, etc. However, it may caused the redundant rules extracted. Another method is using conventional neural network model with a good generalization and fault tolerance, but it has the deficiency of explanation.

In oriental medical area, it is not easy to apply these technologies efficiently due to the complexity and peculiarity of an oriental medical diagnostic process. Oriental doctors regard hidden causal factors of disease as being of most importance in diagnosis. Efforts are put on finding these factors from the observed symptoms and making harmony via an oriental healing process. Thus, a new new method suitable for developing oriental medical diagnostic system is strongly desired.

Bayesian Ying Yang (BYY) harmony learning on independent factor model has provided a useful tool for extracting the independent factors from the observed mixed data. Its ability of adaptive learning and of determining number of independent factors makes it a more appropriate method than the production rule based model for oriental medical domain. In this paper, we develop an oriental medical diagnostic system based on the BYY binary independent model that was implemented in a three layer structure.

2 BYY Harmony Learning

2.1 BYY Harmony Learning and Model Selection

The Bayesian Ying-Yang (BYY) learning was proposed as a unified statistical learning framework by L. Xu firstly in 1995 [5] and systematically developed in past years. The details are referred to a recent summary in [3]. The key idea of Bayesian Ying Yang system is to consider the joint distribution of x, y via two types of Bayesian decomposition of the joint density $q(x|y)q(y) = q(x,y), p(x,y) = p(y|x)p(x)$. Without any constraints, the two decompositions should be theoretically identical. However, the four components in the two decompositions are usually subject to certain structural constraints.

Usually, $p(x)$ is given by a nonparametric estimate from samples of x. Here, we simply consider

$$p_0(x) = \frac{1}{N} \sum_{t=1}^{N} \delta(x - x_t). \tag{1}$$

A combination of the structures for the rest three components $q(y)$, $q(x|y)$, and $p(y|x)$ is referred as a system architecture. Among three typical structures, we consider a specific backward architecture. That is, we consider $q(y) = q(y|\psi)$ and $q(x|y) = q(x|y, \theta)$ in parametric models, letting $p(y|x)$ to be free to be determined via BYY harmony learning, by which the *fundamental learning principle* is to make p, q be best harmony in a twofold sense:
- The difference between p, q should be minimized.
- p, q should be of the least complexity.

Mathematically, a functional $H(p\|q)$ is used to measure the degree of harmony between p and q as follows.

$$H(p\|q) = \frac{1}{N} \sum_{t=1}^{N} \sum_{y} p(y|x) \ln [q(x|y, \phi)q(y|\psi)], \\ - \ln z_q. \tag{2}$$

where z_q is a term that has three typical representations. The simplest case is $z_q = 1$ and correspondingly the learning is called empirical learning. This paper considers this simple case only. The other two cases are referred to [3]. In mathematical implementation, BYY harmony learning is made via

$$\max_{\theta, k} H(p\|q), \tag{3}$$

which can be implemented either in a parallel way such that model selection is made automatically during parameter learning or in a sequential way such that model selection is made after parameter learning [3].

Specifically, setting $z_q = 1$ and maximizing $H(p\|q)$ with respect to a free $p(y|x)$ lead to

$$p(y|x) = \delta(y - \hat{y}),$$
$$\hat{y} = arg \max_y[q(x|y, \phi)q(y|\psi)],$$
$$H(p\|q) = \frac{1}{N} \sum_{t=1}^{N} \ln [q(x|\hat{y}_t, \phi)q(\hat{y}_t|\psi)]. \quad (4)$$

Furthermore, maximizing $H(p\|q)$ with respect to ϕ, ψ leads to the following adaptive updating rules

$$q_j = \frac{1}{1 + e^{-\xi_j}},$$
$$\xi_j^{new} = \xi_j^{old} + \eta(y^{(j)} - q_j),$$
$$e = x - A^{old}\hat{y}, \ A^{new} = A^{old} + \eta e \hat{y}^T,$$
$$\Sigma^{new} = (1 - \eta)\Sigma^{old} + \eta e e^T, \quad (5)$$

where $\eta >$ is a learning step size. An adaptive learning is thus made by repeatedly getting $\hat{y}$ by eq.(4) and making the updating by eq.(8), which is firstly given in [4] and then further refined with new features in [2].

Model selection, i.e., to deciding the number of k hidden independent factors, is an important issue in building an appropriate independent binary factor model. As shown in [2,3], one advantage of the BYY harmony learning is that k can be determined automatically during parameter learning. To realize this point, what needs to do is set k large enough and implement parameter learning by

$$\max_\theta H(\theta), H(\theta) = H(\theta, k), \quad (6)$$

during which θ tends to a value θ^* such that the resulted BYY system is equivalent to having an appropriate scale $k^* < k$.

We can also make parameter learning and model selection sequentially in two steps. With k prefixed, we enumerate k from a small value incrementally, and at each specific k we perform parameter learning by repeating getting $\hat{y}$ by eq.(4) and then making updating by eq.(8), resulting in the best parameter value θ^*. Then, we select a best k^* by

$$\min_k J(k), J(k) = -H(\theta^*, k), \quad (7)$$

If there are more than one values of k such that $J(k)$ gets the same minimum, we take the smallest. Specifically, for an independent binary factor model we have [2]

$$\max_k J(k) = -0.5 d \log \sigma^2 + \sum_{j=1}^{m}[q_j \log q_j +$$
$$(1 - q_j) \log(1 - q_j)]. \quad (8)$$

3 Oriental Medical Diagnosis Using BYY Harmony Learning

In help of BYY binary independent factor analysis, an automatic oriental medical diagnostic system can be obtained in a three layer structure performed by a two step algorithm.

At Step I, the factor model $x = Ay + e$ from a training set of symptoms of past patients is learned. Also, the best k^* is selected by model selection during the parameter learning.

Given $q(x|y,\phi) = G(x|Ay, \sigma^2 I)$ and binary factors $y = [y^{(1)}, ..., y^{(k)}]^T$ with each $y^{(j)}$ taking either '1' denoting that this factor affects an observed symptom or '0' denoting that this factor is irrelevant to the symptom. Adopting this binary independent factor model in an oriental diagnostic system is justified because it is quite nature to believe that hidden factors should be of the least redundancy among each other and a compound factor can be further decomposed into simpler factors. Also, it is reasonable to believe an observed symptom resulted from one or more particular hidden factors occurs, with '1' denoting the occurrence of such a factor and '0' denoting not. Each $y^{(j)}$ is distributed by their associative relations inside that pattern.

This step I can be adaptively implemented by iterating eq.(4) and eq.(8), which are summarized as follows:

As each x_t comes, we implement three steps iteratively until it converges.

STEP I

(1) Get $y_t = arg\,max_y[q(x_t|y)q(y)]$ or
$y_t = argmin_y\{0.5(\frac{\|x - Ay\|}{\sigma})^2 - \sum_{j=1}^{k}[y^{(j)}lnq_j + (1-y^{(j)})ln(1-q_j)]\}$.

(2) Get $e_t = x_t - A^{old}y_t$,
update $A^{new} = A^{old} + \eta e_t y_t^T$,
$\sigma^{2\,new} = (1-\eta)\sigma^{2\,old} + \eta\|e_t\|^2$.

(3) Let $q_j = 1/[1 + exp(-c_j)]$,
update $c_j^{new} = c_j^{old} + \eta(y_t^{(j)} - q_j)$;

where $\eta > 0$ is a small step size.

At Step II, we set up another mapping by

$$p(z|y, B, b) = \prod_{j=1}^{m} p_j^{z^{(j)}}(1 - p_j)^{1-z^{(j)}},$$
$$p_j = 1/(1 + e^{-u_j}),$$
$$u = [u_1, \cdots, u_m]^T, \quad By + b = u. \tag{9}$$

It can be made by getting a set of training pair y, z with y obtained from Step I by the mapping $x \to z$ and with z obtained from the corresponding records of diagnostic decision by an oriental medical expert.

The B, b can be learned via the maximum likelihood learning adaptively, which is summarized below:

STEP II

(1) Get $u = [u_1, \cdots, u_m]^T$, $B\hat{y} + b = u$,
$p_j = 1/(1 + e^{-u_j})$,
$f = [f_1, .., f_m]^T$, $f_j = z_j - p_j$
(2) update $B^{new} = B^{old} + \eta f \hat{y}^T$,
$b^{new} = b^{old} + \eta f$.

We implement two steps iteratively with the gained $\hat{y}$ from Step I and the corresponding teaching signal z, until it converges.

4 Experiments

We applied this system to the problem of diagnosing the disease 'Flaming-up liver fire' which is a name of oriental medicine, including the western disease names of chronic cholecystitis, chronic hepatitis, neurosis, hypertension, otitis, and infectious disease. As shown in Fig.1, the oriental medical diagnostic system has a three layered structure. This system receives six observed symptom data from 200 patients, extracts hidden causal factors, and produces the diagnostic results. The six symptom data consists of headache, dizziness, pink eye, rapid pulse, bitter tastes and fever.

We obtained the estimated matrices A and B as follows. Fig.2 represents the error curve of Step I and Fig.3 shows the error curve of step II. The best $k^* = 5$ was selected by model selection. We tested this system with 200 sample data of the patients and compared its diagnostic output data to the diagnostic results of a human doctor. We get the accuracy of 93% though the oriental medical diagnostic process is highly heuristic.

This system can provide a further explanation in the help of oriental medical doctor. The role of the medical expert is to discriminate the separated hidden factors by analyzing the relationship between the observed symptoms and separated factors after learning. In this experiment, medical expert discriminated the five factors to fire, heat, dampness,cold and wind. Then this system provides not only diagnosing the disease name but also explaining the causes of disease and suggesting the healing method with oriental herbal medicine.

A
0.9293 0.2953 0.3213 0.2460 0.5692
0.4376 0.9703 0.2918 0.3590 0.4839
0.5144 0.3509 1.0386 0.4017 0.6298
0.2806 0.3989 0.4403 0.8965 0.4731
0.3935 0.3720 0.3225 0.5627 0.9788
0.4828 0.3704 0.4027 0.4742 0.3672

B
-2.16226 -1.859138 -0.513366 -2.031206 -2.056148

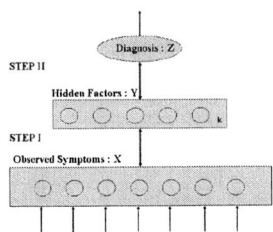 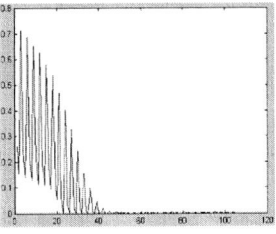 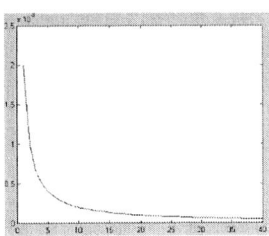

Fig. 1. Fig.1 Oriental Medical diagnostic system

Fig. 2. Fig.2 Error curve of StepI

Fig. 3. Fig.3 Error curve of StepII

5 Conclusion

A new medical diagnostic method for oriental medicine has been adopted from BYY harmony learning was proposed. The model can not only recover the hidden factors from the visible observed symptoms but also produce the reasonable diagnostic results. An preliminary experiment is demonstrated with success.

Acknowledgements

This work was supported by a Kangnam University Research Grant in(2004)

References

1. Spearman,C., " General intelligence objectively determined and measured", *Am. J. Psycol. 15, 201-293,1904*.
2. Xu, L, "BYY Learning, Regularized Implementation, and Model Selection on Modular Networks with One Hidden Layer of Binary Units", *Neurocomputing*, Vol.51, p227-301.
3. Xu, L., "Best Harmony, Unified RPCL and Automated Model Selection for Unsupervised and Supervised Learning on Gaussian Mixtures, Three-Layer Nets and ME-RBF-SVM Models", *International Journal of Neural Systems, Vol. 11*, No. 1, pp43-69, 2001.
4. Xu, L., "Bayesian Kullback Ying-Yang Dependence Reduction Theory", *Neurocomputing 22*, No.1-3, 81-112, 1998.
5. Xu, L.(1995&96), "A unified learning scheme: Bayesian-Kullback YING-YANG machine", *Advances in NIPS 8*, eds., D. S. Touretzky, et al, MIT Press, 1996, 444-450. Preliminarily on *Proc. ICONIP'95*, 1995, 977-988.

An Intelligent Topic-Specific Crawler Using Degree of Relevance*

Sanguk Noh[1], Youngsoo Choi[2], Haesung Seo[2], Kyunghee Choi[2], and Gihyun Jung[3]

[1] School of Computer Science and Information Engineering
The Catholic University of Korea, Bucheon, Korea
sunoh@catholic.ac.kr
[2] Graduate School of Information and Communication
Ajou University, Suwon, Korea
{drabble,retry,khchoi}@ajou.ac.kr
[3] Division of Electronics Engineering
Ajou University, Suwon, Korea
khchung@ajou.ac.kr

Abstract. It is indispensable that the users surfing on the Internet could have web pages classified into a given topic as correct as possible. Toward this ends, this paper presents a topic-specific crawler computing the degree of relevance and refining the preliminary set of related web pages using term frequency/document frequency, entropy, and compiled rules. In the experiments, we test our topic-specific crawler in terms of the accuracy of its classification, the crawling efficiency, and the crawling consistency. In case of using 51 representative terms, it turned out that the resulting accuracy of the classification was 97.8%.

1 Introduction

The Internet, the world's end-to-end communications network, is now ubiquitous in everyday's life. It would be necessary for users surfing on the Internet to access a pool of web pages that could be relevant to their interesting topics. It is crucial that the users could have not only the web pages probably related to a specific topic as many as possible, but also the web pages classified into the given topic as correct as possible. This paper, therefore, presents (1) a topic-specific crawler which collects a tapestry of web pages through the calculation of degree of relevance, and (2) a web page classification mechanism to refine the preliminary set of web pages using term frequency/document frequency, the computation of entropy, and the compiled rules.

To crawl any web pages related to a specific topic [1, 3, 5], we use the degree of relevance, which represents how much a web page could be relevant to the topic. For the computation of the degree of relevance, we exploit the relationship between any

---

* This work has been supported by the Korea Research Foundation under grant KRF-2003-041-D20465, and by the KISTEP under National Research Laboratory program.

web page and web pages linked within the web page, and the number of keywords shown in the web page, compared with the predefined set of key phrases. To identify the contents of web pages [9, 12], we propose a combined mechanism which computes the product of term frequency and document frequency [6, 8] and prioritizes the terms based on the calculation of entropies [10]. Based on a selected set of terms, we assign any web page into a topic (or category). Our approach to identifying associations between a web page and a predefined category is to use term-classification rules compiled by machine learning algorithms, which provide a high degree of relationship between them, if any. We wish our topic-specific crawler could be used to collect any web pages probably related to a certain topic, and refine them into the category to improve the correctness of the classification.

In the following section of this paper, we will describe the details of our framework for computing the degree of relevance to a specific topic and the weights of terms representing a specific web page. Section 3 describes experimental results to evaluate our topic-specific crawler using benchmark dataset as a case study. In conclusions we summary our work and mention further research issues.

2 An Intelligent Topic-Specific Crawler

2.1 Crawling Strategy

To crawl any web pages related to a specific topic, we need to decide the degree of relevance, which represents how much a web page could be relevant to the topic. For the computation of the degree of relevance, in this paper, we consider the relationship between any web page and web pages linked within the web page, and the number of keywords shown in the web page, given the predefined set of key phrases. The degree of relevance, R_i, of the web page i, can be defined as follows:

$$R_i = (1-\rho) \lambda_i / |K| + \rho R_j , \qquad (1)$$

where

- R_j denotes the degree of relevance for the web page j, containing the URL of web page i, which is already crawled;
- ρ is a constant reflecting how much R_i could be affected by R_j ($0 < \rho < 1$);
- λ_i is the number of keywords shown in a given web page i;
- K is the pre-defined set of key phrases. $|K|$ is the cardinality of K.

Our topic-specific crawler provides a priority queue with two operations, i.e., enqueue and dequeue, to handle URLs probably related to a certain topic. Let's suppose that there is an URL which might be representative for a given topic. As starting with the URL in the priority queue, the crawler dequeues it from the queue and fetches its contents. Our crawler computes the degree of relevance R_i for the hyperlinks in the web page i. In case that the hostname of the newly found hyperlink is the same of the web page *i*, the hyperlink cannot be enqueued into the queue and is simply disregarded. According to R_i, then, the hyperlinks whose hostnames are different from that of web page *i* can be prioritized into the queue. To crawl further web pages, the crawler dequeues the hyperlinks from the priority queue given their degree of relevance. The above crawling process will be continued until the queue is empty.

2.2 Classifying Web Pages

To refine the set of possibly related web pages, which are collected by our topic-specific crawler, we propose an online web page classification mechanism [6]. Let *I* be the set of terms in a specific web page, i.e., {1, 2, ..., m}, and let *J* be the set of web pages which are classified into a specific class, i.e., {1, 2, ..., n}. From the perspective of information retrieval [8], Term Frequency (TF) and Document Frequency (DF) are combined as follows:

$$W_{i,j} = \frac{TF_{i,j}}{\max_{k \in I} TF_{k,j}} \times \frac{DF_i}{n}, \qquad (2)$$

where

- $W_{i,j}$ is the weight of the term $i \in I$ in the web page $j \in J$;
- $TF_{i,j}$ is the frequency of the term $i \in I$ in the web page $j \in J$;
- DF_i is the number of web pages which the term *i* occurs;
- *n* is the total number of web pages for a specific class.

The above equation 2 indicates that, if a specific term more frequently occurs than other terms within a web page, and if the term can be found among most web pages, the weight of the term will be greater than those of the other terms. By computing the weights of terms, the terms relevant to a topic can be prioritized. The highly representative terms could be used to denote a class in a hierarchy of concepts.

Having the terms related to classes, we classify any web page into one of the classes, which are the components of taxonomy. For the classification of a web page, we compute the entropies of the terms, originally reported in [10]. The entropy of a word (or a term) provides the expected amount of information for correct classification. The lower entropy needs the less information to classify an example web page. For the efficient classification, therefore, our approach uses the attributes which have lower entropies. The computation of entropy can be achieved using the following formula [10]:

$$E_S = -\sum_{i=1}^{n} p_i \ln p_i , \qquad (3)$$

where

- S is the set of web pages in our framework, which can be classified into a number of classes n whose probabilities are $p_1, \ldots, p_n$, respectively;
- E_S is the entropy of the set S, representing the expected amount of information to classify the web pages in the set S into a specific class.

For example, when a set consists of two classes of positive and negative, we assume that the ratio of the number of positive examples to the total number of examples in the set is the class probability, say, p1, and, similarly, the other ratio is p2. The entropy of the set S, then, can be computed by $-(p1 \ln p1 + p2 \ln p2)$.

Given entropy, we compute information gain, $Gain(\alpha)$, which represents the classifying possibility of an attribute α, as follows:

$$Gain(\alpha) = E_S - \sum_{j=1}^{m}\left(\frac{|S_{\alpha_j}|}{|S|} \times E_{S_{\alpha_j}}\right), \quad (4)$$

where
- S_{α_j}, $S_{\alpha_j} \subseteq S$, is the set of web pages containing the attribute α whose value is $j \in \{1, \ldots, m\}$. $|S_{\alpha_j}|$ is the total number of web pages in S_{α_j}.

In our framework, attributes present terms within a class. The computed values of gain factors of attributes rank the terms as the possibility of the classification. We choose the representative terms based upon their information gain.

To classify a web page, we need to assemble attributes into a tuple. Let A be a set of attributes. The selection of attributes can be achieved using the following heuristic rule:

$$H_\mu = \{\alpha \mid \alpha \in A, Gain(\alpha) \geq \mu \}. \quad (5)$$

The threshold μ is to filter out insignificant terms within each class. The resulting H_μ is a set of attributes which are highly related to the class, based on information gain.

For the automated classification of web pages, firstly, the attributes are prioritized using the computation of TF-DF and information gain. Secondly, we compile the tuples obtained into a set of terms-classification rules using several machine learning algorithms [4]. The compiled rules enable us to classify any web page into a topic.

3 Evaluation

We tested our topic-specific crawler in terms of (1) the accuracy of its classification, (2) the crawling efficiency, and (3) the crawling consistency. In the experiments, we used the benchmark dataset provided by Sinka et al. [11], which consists of Banking and Finance, Programming Language, Science, and Sport. In particular, one subclass of each theme was chosen, i.e., 'Commercial Banks,' 'Java,' 'Astronomy,' and 'Soccer,' respectively.

Regarding the classification accuracy of our crawler, we needed to determine the proper number of terms through the computation of term-frequency/document-frequency and entropy, and measured the classification accuracy using the terms selected and the rules compiled by machine learning algorithms. First, we randomly chose 100 web pages from each category, thus, 400 web pages total. Given the 100 web pages of each category, the equations 2 and 4 were applied to them to identify the representative and discriminative terms. There were about 241 terms, on the average, per web page and the weights of the terms were computed using TF-DF and entropy.

To determine the terms as inputs of inductive learning algorithms, we applied the equation 5 to the terms, and selected the representative terms whose gain factors were greater than the threshold μ. In the experiment, we changed the thresholds ranging from 0.01 to 0.31, and then, measured the accuracy of terms-classification rules using 3600 web pages which were not used for training purposes. We compiled a set of training tuples into terms-classification rules using C4.5 [7], CN2 [2], and back-propagation [13] learning algorithms. The performances of three machine learning algorithms were measured in terms of classification accuracy, as depicted in figure 1.

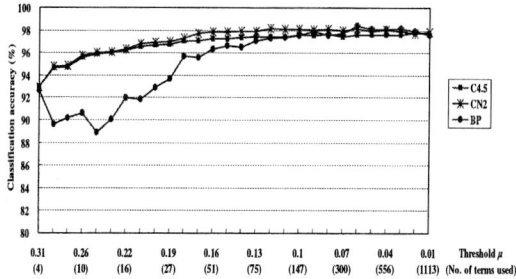

Fig. 1. Classification accuracies of three learning algorithms according to the changes of threshold μ. In horizontal axis, the number of terms as inputs of three learning algorithms was also given below the threshold μ ranging from 0.01 to 0.31.

As the threshold μ decreased, the number of representative terms increased, and the accuracy of classification approximately went up. In figure 1, we could observe the tradeoff between the number of significant terms and the quality of classification. As a result, for the classification accuracy of, say, 97.8%, we could choose 51 terms, as representative ones, out of about twenty five thousand unique terms, and construct the hierarchy of concepts with these terms. The computation of entropies, thus, enables us to reduce the dimension of resulting terms.

We define the crawling efficiency as a ratio of (the number of URLs related to a specific topic/the total number of URLs crawled). The crawling efficiency enables us to determine the best ρ affecting the degree of relevance, R_i, as described in equation 1. For our topic-specific crawler, we selected 20 terms as the elements of the pre-defined set of key phrases K, given the resulting classification accuracy of figure 1, and randomly chose ten starting URLs as the seeds of crawling process for each category. Since it turned out that CN2 [2] provide the best classification accuracy from figure 1, we used the terms-classification rules compiled by CN2. Using the compiled rules, we measured the crawling efficiency with ρ varying from 0.1 to 0.9 by the interval 0.2, as depicted in figure 2, when the total number of URLs crawled was 10,000.

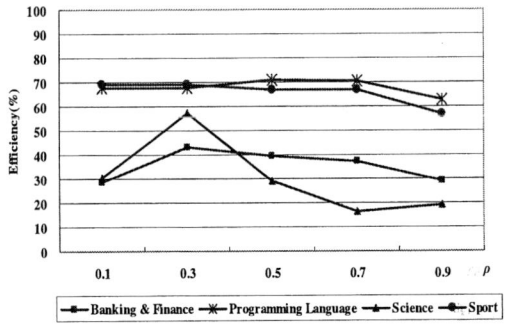

Fig. 2. The efficiency of our topic-specific crawler for four categories, when ρ ranges from 0.1 to 0.9, respectively.

When ρ was 0.1 and 0.9, respectively, the crawling efficiency of our crawler was not good in almost all of four categories. Since the fact that ρ was 0.1 indicated that the degree of relevance for the web page i was little affected by that of the web page j, the web page i belonging to the topic could not be fetched earlier than others. In case that ρ was 0.9, since the degree of relevance for the web page i definitely depended on the degree of relevance for the web page j, the web page i not being related to the topic could be fetched earlier than others. In the experiment, it turned out that the optimal ρ was 0.3 for Banking & Finance and its efficiency 43% was the best, as shown in figure 2. We could also decide the optimal ρ's for Programming Language, Science, and Sport, namely, 0.5, 0.3, and 0.3, and those crawling efficiencies were 71%, 57%, and 69%, respectively.

In the third experiment, the consistency of our topic-specific crawler was measured in terms of the number of the resulting URLs overlapped [1]. Using our topic-specific crawler with different starting URLs, two sets of URLs crawled were compared to calculate the percentage of URLs overlapped. Our topic-specific crawler, of course, was equipped with classification rules compiled by CN2, as was shown in figure 1, and the optimal ρ's, as was shown in figure 2. The consistency of our topic-specific crawler, thus, could be summarized into figure 3.

For all of four categories, the percentage of the URLs overlapped was above 70%, up to 85%. The experimental results imply that our topic-specific crawler is fairly consistent, regardless of the starting URLs randomly chosen. We wish our topic-specific crawler could be consistent for any other topic.

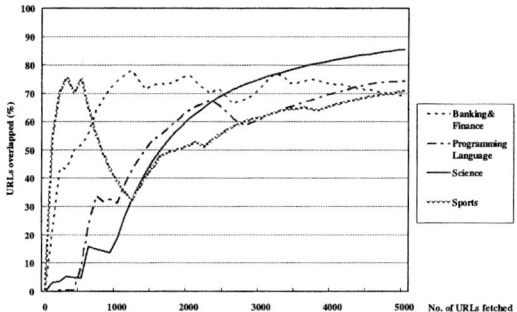

Fig. 3. The crawling consistency of our topic-specific crawler in four categories, when it fetched 5000 URLs total for each category.

4 Conclusions

To collect any web pages probably related to a certain topic, we exploited the degree of relevance considering the relationship between any web page and web pages linked within the web page, and the number of keywords found in the web page. To refine the set of possibly related web pages, which were collected by our topic-specific crawler, further, we calculated term frequency/document frequency and entropy for representative terms. Using inductive learning algorithms and a neural network algorithm, we compiled the tuples obtained into a set of terms-classification rules. In the experiments, the best classification performance for our topic-specific crawler was achieved when CN2 was used for compilation, and its classification accuracy using the compiled rules was 97.8% with 51 representative terms. We also measured the crawling efficiency, which enables us to determine the best ρ affecting the degree of relevance. Lastly, to benchmark our topic-specific crawler within our framework, its consistency was tested with different starting URLs. It turned out that the topic-specific crawler was fairly consistent, given the resulting URLs overlapped. For future research, we will expand our crawler to collect related web pages as broadly as possible, and to provide its best performances given a specific topic. We will continuously apply our crawler to various topics and test it in a real network infrastructure on the Internet.

References

1. Chakrabarti, S. et al.: Focused crawling: a new approach to topic-specific Web resource discovery. In Proceedings of 8th International World Wide Web Conference (1999).
2. Clark, P. and Niblett, T.: The CN2 Induction algorithm. *Machine Learning Journal*, Vol. 3, No.4 (1989) 261-283.
3. Diligenti, M. et al: Focused crawling using context graphs. In Proceedings of VLDB (2000) 527-534.

4. Holder, L.: ML v2.0, available on-line: http://www-cse.uta.edu/~holder/ftp/ml2.0.tar.gz.
5. Menczer, F. et al.: Topic-driven crawlers: Machine learning issues. ACM TOIT (2002).
6. Noh, S. et al.: Classifying Web Pages Using Adaptive Ontology. In Proceedings of IEEE International Conference on Systems, Men & Cybernetics (2003) 2144-2149.
7. Quinlan, J. R.: C4.5: Programs for Machine Learning. Morgan Kaufmann. (1993).
8. Salton, G. and Buckley, C.: Term weighting approaches in automatic text retrieval. *Information Processing and Management*, Vol 24, No. 5 (1988) 513-523.
9. Sebastiani, F.: Machine learning in automated text categorization. *ACM Computing Surveys*, Vol 34, No. 1 (2002) 1-47.
10. Shannon, C. E.: A mathematical theory of communication. *Bell System Technical Journal*, Vol 27, (1984) pp. 379-423 and 623-656.
11. Sinka, M. P. and Corne, D. W.: A large benchmark dataset for web document clustering, *Soft Computing Systems: Design, Management and Applications*, Vol 87, IOS Press (2002) 881-890.
12. Sun, A., Lim, E. and Ng, W.: Web classification using support vector machine, In Proceedings of WIDM (2002).
13. Tveter, D. R.: Backprop Package, http://www.dontveter.com/nnsoft/bp042796.zip (1996).

Development of a Global and Integral Model of Business Management Using an Unsupervised Model

Emilio Corchado[1,2], Colin Fyfe[2], Lourdes Sáiz[1], and Ana Lara[1]

[1] Department of Civil Engineering, University of Burgos, Spain
[2] Applied Computational Intelligence Research Unit, University of Paisley, Scotland
{escorchado,lsaiz,amlara}@ubu.es, Colin.Fyfe@paisley.ac.uk

Abstract. In this paper, we use a recent artificial neural architecture called Co-operative Maximum Likelihood Hebbian Learning (CMLHL) in order to categorize the necessities for the Acquisition, Transfer and Updating of Knowledge of the different departments of a firm. We apply Maximum Likelihood Hebbian learning to an extension of a negative feedback network characterised by the use of lateral connections on the output layer. These lateral connections have been derived from the Rectified Gaussian distribution. This technique is used as a tool to develop a part of a Global and Integral Model of business Management, which brings about a global improvement in the firm, adding value, flexibility and competitiveness. From this perspective, the model tries to generalise the hypothesis of organizational survival and competitiveness, so that the organisation that is able to identify, strengthen, and use key knowledge will reach a pole position.

1 Introduction

We apply a novel method which is closely related to factor analysis (FA) and exploratory projection pursuit (EPP). It is a neural model based on the Negative Feedback artificial neural network, which has been extended by the combination of two different techniques. Initially by the selection of a proper cost function from a family of them, to identify the right distribution related to the data problem. This method is called Maximum-Likelihood Hebbian learning (MLHL) [5]. Then, lateral connections derived from the Rectified Gaussian Distribution [10] [11] were added to the MLHL architecture [5]. These enforced a greater sparsity in the weight vectors. In this study we have focus our attention, specifically, on the problem of knowledge management from a pragmatic and managerial point of view that contemplates the possibility that knowledge can be classified and organised in order to achieve a better understanding. This issue is based, above all, on understanding the distinctions between transformations in forms of knowledge, starting from an inferior level – data and information – and advancing towards other higher levels, such as knowledge itself and its management, individual, and even organizational responsibilities.

2 A Family of Learning Rules

The model used in this study is based on the Negative Feedback Network [7]. Consider an N-dimensional input vector, $\mathbf{x}$, and a M-dimensional output vector, $\mathbf{y}$, with W_{ij} being the weight linking input j to output i and let η be the learning rate. We can express this as:

$$y_i = \sum_{j=1}^{N} W_{ij} x_j, \forall i \quad (1)$$

The activation is fed back through the same weights and subtracted from the inputs

$$e_j = x_j - \sum_{i=1}^{M} W_{ij} y_i, \forall j, \quad (2)$$

After that simple Hebbian learning is performed between input and outputs:

$$\Delta W_{ij} = \eta e_j y_i \quad (3)$$

This network is capable of finding the principal components of the input data [7] in a manner that is equivalent to Oja's Subspace algorithm [9], and so the weights will not find the actual Principal Components (PCA) but a basis of the subspace spanned by these components. Factor Analysis is a technique similar to PCA in that it attempts to explain the data set in terms of a smaller number of underlying factors. However FA begins with a specific model and then attempts to explain the data by finding parameters which best fit this model to the data.

Let the residual [8] after feedback have probability density function

$$p(\mathbf{e}) = \frac{1}{Z} \exp(-|\mathbf{e}|^p) \quad (4)$$

A general cost function associated with this network is

$$J = -\log p(\mathbf{e}) = |\mathbf{e}|^p + K \quad (5)$$

where K is a constant. Therefore performing gradient descent on J we have

$$\Delta W \propto -\frac{\partial J}{\partial W} = -\frac{\partial J}{\partial \mathbf{e}} \frac{\partial \mathbf{e}}{\partial W} \approx y(p|\mathbf{e}|^{p-1} sign(\mathbf{e}))^T \quad (6)$$

where T denotes the transpose of a vector.

Therefore the network operation is as before (feedforward (Eq.1), feedback (Eq.2)), but now the weight change is as follows:

weight change: $\quad \Delta W_{ij} = \eta . y_i . sign(e_j) | e_j |^{p-1} \quad (7)$

This method has been linked to the standard statistical method of EPP [6, 5].

3 Lateral Connections

The Rectified Gaussian Distribution (RGD) [11] is a modification of the standard Gaussian distribution in which the variables are constrained to be non-negative, enabling the use of non-convex energy functions.

The multivariate normal distribution can be defined in terms of an energy or cost function in that, if realised samples are taken far from the distribution's mean, they will be deemed to have high energy and this will be equated to low probability. More formally, the standard Gaussian distribution may be defined by:

$$p(\mathbf{y}) = Z^{-1} e^{-\beta E(\mathbf{y})}, \qquad (8)$$

$$E(\mathbf{y}) = \frac{1}{2} \mathbf{y}^T \mathbf{A} \mathbf{y} - \mathbf{b}^T \mathbf{y} \qquad (9)$$

The quadratic energy function $E(\mathbf{y})$ is defined by the vector $\mathbf{b}$ and the symmetric matrix $\mathbf{A}$. The parameter $\beta = 1/T$ is an inverse temperature. Lowering the temperature concentrates the distribution at the minimum of the energy function.

An example of the RGD is the cooperative distribution. The modes of the cooperative distribution are closely spaced along a non-linear continuous manifold.

Neither distribution can be accurately approximated by a single standard Gaussian. Using the RGD, it is possible to represent both discrete and continuous variability in a way that a standard Gaussian cannot.

The sorts of energy function that can be used are only those where the matrix A has the property:

$$\mathbf{y}^T \mathbf{A} \mathbf{y} > 0 \text{ for all } \mathbf{y} : y_i > 0, i = 1...N \qquad (10)$$

where N is the dimensionality of $\mathbf{y}$. This property blocks the directions in which the energy diverges to negative infinity.

The cooperative distribution in the case of N variables is defined by:

$$A_{ij} = \delta_{ij} + \frac{1}{N} - \frac{4}{N} \cos\left(\frac{2\pi}{N}(i-j)\right) \text{ and} \qquad (11)$$

$$b_i = 1 \qquad (12)$$

where δ_{ij} is the Kronecker delta and i and j represent the identifiers of output neuron.

To speed learning up, the matrix A can be simplified [2] to:

$$A_{ij} = \left(\delta_{ij} - \cos(2\pi(i-j)/N)\right) \qquad (13)$$

The matrix A is used to modify the response to the data based on the relation between the distances between the outputs.

We use the projected gradient method, consisting of a gradient step followed by a rectification:

$$y_i(t+1) = [y_i(t) + \tau(\mathbf{b} - \mathbf{A}\mathbf{y})]^+ \qquad (14)$$

where the rectification $[\ ]^+$ is necessary to ensure that the y-values keep to the positive quadrant. If the step size τ is chosen correctly, this algorithm can provably be shown to converge to a stationary point of the energy function [1]. In practice, this stationary point is generally a local minimum.

The mode of the distribution can be approached by gradient descent on the derivative of the energy function with respect to $\mathbf{y}$. This is:

$$\Delta \mathbf{y} \propto -\frac{\partial E}{\partial \mathbf{y}} = -(\mathbf{Ay} - \mathbf{b}) = \mathbf{b} - \mathbf{Ay} \quad (15)$$

which is used as in Eq.14.

Now the rectification in Eq.14 is identical to the rectification which Corchado [3] used in the Maximum-Likelihood Network. Thus we will use this movement towards the mode in the FA version [2] of the Maximum-Likelihood Network before training the weights as previously. The net result will be shown to be a network which can find the independent factors of a data set but do so in a way which captures some type of global ordering in the data set.

We use the standard Maximum-Likelihood Network but now with a lateral connection (which acts after the feed forward but before the feedback). Thus we have:

Feedforward:
$$y_i = \sum_{j=1}^{N} W_{ij} x_j, \forall i \quad (16)$$

Lateral Activation Passing: $\quad y_i(t+1) = [y_i(t) + \tau(b - Ay)]^+ \quad (17)$

Feedback:
$$e_j = x_j - \sum_{i=1}^{M} W_{ij} y_i, \quad (18)$$

Weight change: $\quad \Delta W_{ij} = \eta \cdot y_i \cdot sign(e_j) |e_j|^{p-1} \quad (19)$

Where the parameter τ represents the strength of the lateral connections.

4 Real Data Set and Results

In this study we have analysed a multinational group, leader in the design and production of a great variety of components for the automotive industry. The justification of this choice lies in the fact that the characteristics of its management represent a favourable environment and opportune moment for the introduction of Knowledge Management. It is an undergoing organizational change and faces great growth and expansion, which requires a rapid adaptation to the demands of the sector, with greater resources, imminent transfers and accurate forecasting of knowledge, together with the immediate demand to capitalise on them, to share and use them within the firm.

The design of the preliminary theoretical model of Knowledge Management is based on three components: the Organisation -Strategy and People-, Processes - Acquisition, Transfer and Updating of Knowledge- and Technology –Technological Aids-, from which the propositions of the model are defined. The population sample used came to 277 registries (individuals) that correspond with the "necessities of knowledge" showed by the head of eleven departments of the company studied. This knowledge gathers different stages (knowledge levels) that depict the current situation of each department for the tasks or activities assigned to each department to be successfully accomplished. Also, it has been possible to obtain valuable data on the degree of importance for the company of the gathered knowledge. This way, it is possible to identify the lack of the knowledge that it is necessary to perform the activity, so as to make the right decision on its acquisition in terms of how it is acquired, or what is the cost or time needed. In the same way, it is possible to specify the knowledge possessedwhich is not comprehensively employed, either because the person does not use it in its entirety, or because it has additional value and potential use, also, for other departments. Furthermore, it is possible to include the analysis corresponding to the necessary evolution of the present knowledge to detect new knowledge, to eliminate the obsolete knowledge and to validate new needs, among others.

The results obtained from the application to this date set is shown in Fig. 1a. Fig. 1b explains the result shows by Fig.1. The following explanation is based on Fig. 1.

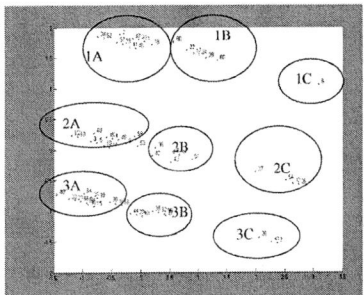

Fig. 1a: CMLHL on the real data.

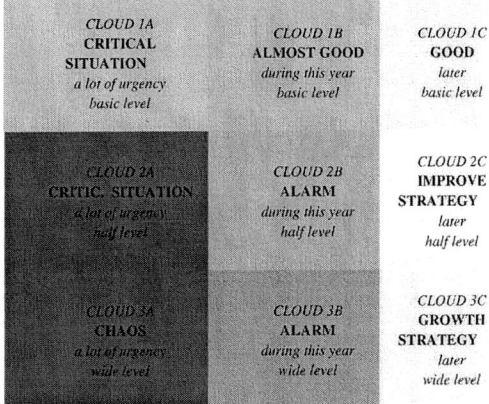

Fig. 1b: Results Representation.

Fig. 1. Fig.1a shows the result of CMLHL on the data. The projection identifies separated clusters (clouds), each of then has been labeled. We have identified mainly 9 cluster or clouds. Fig. 1.b is a graphical explanation of Fig.1a.

In terms of firm type, the positions of cloud 1C are related with a GOOD SITUATION. The firm is located in this place because the level of knowledge required is low and therefore the acquisition of knowledge is not a priority and also it would be at a very basic level. Also the fact that only one point (point 6 in Fig. 1a.) appears underlines the fact that the company only has to acquire knowledge only in one specific area.

In the contrasting case, in the area occupied by the clouds labelled as 3A, there is a lot of urgency to acquire knowledge at a wide level. This area is called "CHAOS". In a similar way, in the area occupied by the clouds 1A and 2A there is a need to acquire knowledge urgently at a half and a basic level. It could be that in these cases there is a holding of knowledge that can put the company in a CRITICAL SITUATION, since it may depend on the concession of new projects, the incorporation of new clients and all those parameters that somehow help to generates activity within the firm.

The area occupied by the points of the cloud 2C outlines the possibility to acquire knowledge at a later stage but at a half level. This could mean an IMPROVE STRATEGY in the firm, where it needs to improve in what it already possesses.

However, cloud 3C, represents the situation on that the firm has to acquire the knowledge later but at a wide level. This means that the company should think about the idea of enlarging and growing, both in terms of new processes and in new products. This is: GROWTH ESTRATEGY.

The points corresponding to area 1B, are related to an ALMOST GOOD area, because the knowledge is needed urgently and at a basic level. Cloud 2B and 3B identify an ALARM area, because there is no urgency and the level needed is half.

5 Conclusions

We have presented and applied a recent model called CMLHL as a novel and robust tool to identify critical situations that allow firms to take decisions about acquisition, transfer and updating processes about knowledge management.

We have applied some other methods such as PCA or MLHL. CMLHL provides more sparse projections than the others [10] and captures some type of global ordering in the data set.

Future work will be based on the study of different distributions and learning rules to improve the whole architecture.

References

1. D.P. Bertsekas, Nonlinear Programming. Athena Scientific, Belmont, MA, (1995)
2. D. Charles, Unsupervised Artificial Neural Networks for the Identification of Multiple Causes in Data. PhD thesis, University of Paisley. (1999)
3. E. Corchado and C. Fyfe, Orientation Selection Using Maximum Likelihood Hebbian Learning, International Journal of Knowledge-Based Intelligent Engineering Systems Volume 7 Number 2, ISSN: 1327-2314. Brighton, United Kingdom. April (2003).
4. E. Corchado, Y. Han, C. Fyfe. Structuring global responses of local filters using lateral connections. J. Exp. Theor. Artif. Intell. 15(4): 473-487 (2003)
5. E. Corchado, D. MacDonald, and C. Fyfe, Maximum and Minimum Likelihood Hebbian Learning for Exploratory Projection Pursuit, Data mining and Knowledge Discovery, Kluwer Academic Publishing. May 2004, vol. 8, no. 3, pp. 203-225. (2004)
6. J. Friedman and J. Tukey. A Projection Pursuit Algorithm for Exploratory Data Analysis. IEEE Transaction on Computers, (23): 881-890. (1974)
7. C. Fyfe A Neural Network for PCA and Beyond, Neural Processing Letters, 6:33-41. 1996.
8. C. Fyfe, and E. Corchado, Maximum Likelihood Hebbian Rules. European Symposium on Artificial Neural Networks. (2002)
9. E. Oja, Neural Networks, Principal Components and Subspaces, International Journal of Neural Systems, 1:61-68. (1989)
10. E. Corchado, C. Fyfe: Connectionist Techniques for the Identification and Suppression of Interfering Underlying Factors. International Journal of Pattern Recognition and Artificial Intelligence. Vol. 17, No 8, 1447-1466. (2003)
11. H.S. Seung, N.D. Socci, and D. Lee, The Rectified Gaussian Distribution, Advances in Neural Information Processing Systems, 10. 350 (1998)

Spam Mail Detection Using Artificial Neural Network and Bayesian Filter

Levent Özgür, Tunga Güngör, and Fikret Gürgen

Boğaziçi University, Computer Engineering Department, Bebek
34342 İstanbul, Turkey
{Ozgurlev,Gungort,Gurgen}@boun.edu.tr

Abstract. We propose dynamic anti-spam filtering methods for agglutinative languages in general and for Turkish in particular, based on Artificial Neural Networks (ANN) and Bayesian filters. The algorithms are adaptive and have two components. The first one deals with the morphology and the second one classifies the e-mails by using the roots. Two ANN structures, single layer perceptron and multi layer perceptron, are considered and the inputs to the networks are determined using binary and probabilistic models. For Bayesian classification, three approaches are employed: binary, probabilistic, and advance probabilistic models. In the experiments, a total of 750 e-mails (410 spam and 340 normal) were used and a success rate of about 90% was achieved.

1 Introduction

The electronic mail (e-mail) concept makes it possible to communicate with many people in an easy and cheap way. But, many *spam mails* are received by users without their desire. As time goes on, a higher percentage of the e-mails is treated as spam. Some studies were performed to determine the proportion of the spam mails within all e-mails [1,2] and they indicated that more than 10% of the e-mails were spam.

Many methods have been proposed to alleviate this problem. We can group them into two categories: static methods and dynamic methods. Static methods base their spam mail identification on a predefined address list. Dynamic methods, on the other hand, take the contents of the e-mails into consideration and adapt their spam filtering decisions with respect to this content. Naive Bayesian algorithms were used on manually categorized normal and spam mails [3]. Rule based systems were also used and some rule learning methods (ripper, tf-idf) were discussed [4,5]. Lewis proposed a model of feature selection and extraction [6,7] and found that the optimal feature set size was 10-15. Dagan proposed a model based on mistake driven learning [8].

The aim of this paper is to propose dynamic anti-spam filtering methods that are based on Artificial Neural Network (ANN) and Bayesian filtering. We develop several algorithms and compare their success rates. The research is directed towards agglutinative languages in general and Turkish in particular. Dynamic methods are currently being applied to languages like English successfully. However, there are no studies on Turkish, which has a complex morphology. Here we take the special features of Turkish into account, propose solutions, and develop filtering algorithms.

To classify e-mails, first a data set containing examples of spam and normal mails is compiled. The content of each e-mail is analyzed, some features of the text are identified, and these features are mapped to a vector space. The features that will be used for the classification may be some selected words, as in this research. In the classification process for agglutinative languages, the features cannot be the surface forms of the words; the root words must be identified before processing an e-mail.

2 Morphology Module and Data Set

The anti-spam filtering system described in this paper is composed of two modules: Morphology Module (MM) and Learning Module (LM). A Turkish morphological analysis program was prepared based on [9]. Turkish is an agglutinative language in the sense that a single word in Turkish may correspond to a phrase made up of several words in a non-agglutinative language. This makes the morphological analysis in this language more complex than the analysis in languages like English.

Besides the morphological complexity, another important issue that must be dealt with is the use of special Turkish characters ('ç','ğ','ı','ö','ş','ü'). People frequently use "English-versions" of them ('c','g','i','o','s','u', respectively) instead of their correct forms. In this study, all possible variations in a given word are examined until an acceptable Turkish word is found. The success rate of the MM is over 90% and the time complexity is about one second for an average length e-mail.

410 spam and 340 normal mail examples were collected under different e-mail addresses. From these e-mails, two files were created, one containing all the spam mails and the other containing all the normal mails. The mails were then parsed by the MM and the root forms of the words were identified. The module outputed two files to be processed by the LM, one containing the roots of all the words in the spam mails and the other containing the roots of all the words in the normal mails.

3 Artificial Neural Network Classification

In this study, two ANN algorithms were applied to the data obtained as the output of the morphology module: Single Layer Perceptron (SLP) and Multi Layer Perceptron (MLP) [10].

In order to determine the root words that will serve as the features in the classification process, the concept of *mutual information* was used [3]. The feature vector can be defined as a group of critical words that are used in classification. First the candidate words (in this study, all the words in the training data) are identified. A mutual information score for each candidate word W was obtained as follows:

$$\text{MI}(W) = \sum_{w \in \{0,1\}, c \in \{\text{spam,normal}\}} P(W=w, C=c) * \log \frac{P(W=w, C=c)}{P(W=w)P(C=c)} \quad (1)$$

where C denotes the class (spam or normal), P(W=w,C=c) is the probability that the word W occurs (W=1) or not (W=0) in spam (C=spam) or normal (C=normal) mails, P(W=w) is the probability that the word W occurs (W=1) or not (W=0) in all e-mails, and P(C=c) is the probability that an e-mail is spam (C=spam) or normal (C=normal). The probabilities were obtained from the examples in the training set.

A number of words with the highest mutual information scores were selected. We refer to this number as the *feature vector size*. The highest valued words are most probably the words occurring frequently in one class of e-mails and not so much in the other. The algorithms were executed with different feature vector sizes.

After the feature vector size and the root words that form the feature vector are identified, it is necessary to determine the range of values that each element of the vector can take. Each vector element corresponds to an input node in the ANN and the value of that element corresponds to the value of the node.

A message was represented by a vector $X=(x_1,x_2,...,x_n)$, where n is the feature vector size and x_i, $1 \leq i \leq n$, denotes the value of the ith word in the feature vector. There are two main approaches for value assignments: *binary model* and *probabilistic model*. In the binary model, the problem is whether the word occurs in the text or not:

$$x_i = \begin{cases} 1, & \text{if } i^{th} \text{ word of the feature vector occurs in the e - mail} \\ 0, & \text{otherwise} \end{cases} \quad (2)$$

This formula does not take the length of the text and the number of occurrences of the word into consideration. Thus, when the text is very short or long, or when a word occurs several times in an e-mail, the results may not reflect the real situation. The probabilistic model takes these into consideration and uses the following estimation:

$$x_i = \frac{\text{number of occurrences of } i^{th} \text{ word of the feature vector in the e - mail}}{\text{number of all words in the e - mail}} \quad (3)$$

4 Bayesian Classification

Bayesian classifier (filter) is a fundamental statistical approach in machine learning [11]. In our study, the Bayesian approach was used as an alternative to the ANN approach to compare their performances for classification in agglutinative languages.

Given an e-mail, the feature vector $X=(x_1,x_2,...,x_n)$ corresponding to the e-mail was formed in the same way as ANN. Let C_1 denote the class of spam mails and C_2 the class of normal mails. The conditional probability that the message belongs to class C_i, i=1,2, can be calculated by the following formula after some transformations [12]:

$$P(C_i | X) \approx \sum_{j=1}^{n} \log(P(x_j | C_i)) \quad (4)$$

where $P(x_j|C_i)$ is the probability that j^{th} word occurs given the class C_i. This operation does not compute a probability, but rather a score: Given the feature vector X, we decide that the e-mail is spam if $P(C_1|X)>P(C_2|X)$ and normal if $P(C_2|X)>P(C_1|X)$.

Equation 4 is the general form for a Bayesian classifier. In this study, we used three different models of Bayesian classification: *binary model*, *probabilistic model*, and *advance probabilistic model*. The binary model is based on whether a word occurs or not in an e-mail. Thus, the score for an e-mail with a feature vector X belonging to class C_i, i=1,2, was calculated by the formula:

$$P(C_i \mid X) = \sum_{j=1}^{n} \begin{cases} cP_{ij}, & \text{if } j^{th} \text{ word of feature vector occurs in e-mail} \\ -P_{ij}, & \text{otherwise} \end{cases} \quad (5)$$

P_{ij} was obtained by dividing the number of e-mails in class C_i containing the jth word by the total number of e-mails in class C_i. In e-mails, occurrence of an input word usually indicates a stronger idea than a non-occurrence. c is the *coefficient level* which indicates the level of this strength. c was taken between 1 and 41 in different runs.

In the probabilistic model, the number of word occurrences is taken into account:

$$P(C_i \mid X) = \sum_{j=1}^{n} \begin{cases} c(P_{ij}H_j), & \text{if } j^{th} \text{ word of feature vector occurs in e-mail} \\ -P_{ij}, & \text{otherwise} \end{cases} \quad (6)$$

P_{ij} is the total number of occurrences of jth word in all e-mails in class C_i over the total number of e-mails in C_i. H_j is the number of occurrences of the jth word in this e-mail.

In the advance probabilistic model, the length of the e-mail is also considered:

$$P(C_i \mid X) = \sum_{j=1}^{n} \begin{cases} c(P_{ij}H_j)/Counter, & \text{if } j^{th} \text{ word of feature vector occurs in e-mail} \\ -P_{ij}/Counter, & \text{otherwise} \end{cases} \quad (7)$$

P_{ij}, c, and H_j are the same as in the previous model. *Counter* is the total number of words in that e-mail, indicating that the length of the e-mail was also considered.

5 Experiments and Results

We performed several experiments by using the methods discussed. In an experiment, we first determined the method (ANN or Bayesian filter) and the parameters of the method. In the case of ANN, the program was executed with three different feature vector sizes (10, 40, and 70) and the success rate was obtained as a function of vector size. For each vector size, six runs were performed. In each run, 5/6 of the e-mails was used for training and the rest for testing. The average of the results in the six runs was then taken as the final result for that vector size and network.

If Bayesian filter was used in the experiment, the program was executed with a feature vector size of 70 only and with five different coefficient levels: 1, 11, 21, 31, and 41. The other vector sizes were not used since the ANN algorithms gave the best results with 70 inputs. The success rate was obtained as a function of coefficient level. The overall results of the algorithms are summarized in Table 1. All the algorithms were implemented on an Intel Pentium PC running at 1.6 GHz with 256 MB RAM.

First the success of ANN was measured. For SLP, binary model and probabilistic model were used. The probabilistic model seemed to achieve more successful results; so with MLP, only the probabilistic model was considered. In addition, MLP was implemented with different numbers of hidden layer nodes. The inputs were selected as the words occurring frequently in spam mails and seldom in normal mails by using a special form of Equation 1. The words with the highest mutual information scores were selected. In this way, the words that are used frequently in spam mails were biased. The intuition here is that such words are good candidates for filtering. Also,

Table 1. Success rates and time complexities of algorithms.

Algorithm	Success rate	Average time (s)
SLP (binary model + Turkish words + spam words as candidate)	79	1.5
SLP (probabilistic model + Turkish words + spam words as candidate)	81	4
MLP (probabilistic model + 150 hidden nodes + Turkish words + spam words as candidate)	83	19
MLP (probabilistic model + 250 hidden nodes + Turkish words + spam words as candidate)	83	>100
SLP (probabilistic model + all words (Turkish and non-Turkish) + spam words as candidate)	85	45
SLP (probabilistic model + all words (Turkish and non-Turkish) + all words as candidate (spam and normal))	83	46
SLP (probabilistic model + all words (Turkish and non-Turkish) + all words as candidate (spam and normal, spam more weighted))	86	46
Bayesian (binary model)	89	46
Bayesian (probabilistic model)	86	46
Bayesian (advance probabilistic model)	84	46

only Turkish words were sent to the LM. That is, when the root form of a word could not be found by the MM, the word was not included in the learning process.

We noted that optimal number of inputs is between 40 and 70. The probabilistic model achieves slightly better performance (81%) than the binary model (79%). When compared with SLP, MLP algorithms give better results only with large hidden layer node numbers. This time complexity yields inefficient results for such a filtering application. Thus, SLP with probabilistic model was selected to be the most efficient.

We developed some more models to work with SLP. The first of these used the non-Turkish words in addition to Turkish words. The surface form of a word was used when a root form of the word could not be found by the MM. With this modification, the success rate has reached to 85%. The reason of the improvement on success may be the fact that some non-Turkish words (*http*, *www*, *com*, etc.) are frequently used in Turkish spam mails while not so much used in normal mails. Thus, they can be said to be better classifiers than most of the Turkish words in the e-mails.

In addition to the words occurring frequently in spam mails, we also included those that occur frequently in normal mails. In the analysis of spam mails, this approach showed better results than the previous one; but, a decline of success was observed with normal mails. The average success rate was 83%. In another model, the probabilities of spam words were multiplied empirically by 3/2. This model has shown the best performance (86%) among all of ANN models.

In another experiment, the performance of the Bayesian classification method was analyzed. The binary Bayesian approach seems more successful than ANN (89%). But, there is a decline of success in probabilistic and advance probabilistic models.

6 Conclusions

In this paper, we proposed several methods for anti-spam filtering in agglutinative languages. We implemented and compared success rates of the algorithms. We dealt with two phases. In the first, a morphological analysis program was prepared, which extracted the root forms in 750 e-mails with 90% success and 3000 words/min. In the second, the roots were used by LM. ANN and Bayesian filter were employed, which gave about 90% success. The experiments have shown that some non-Turkish words that occur frequently in spam mails were better classifiers than most Turkish words.

In future studies, we plan to improve the algorithms by taking the attachments of the e-mails (pictures, text files, etc.) into account. The existence and the type of such attachments seem to give important information for detecting spam mails.

References

1. Spam–off the Menu? In: NISCC Quarterly Review, January-March. London (2003) 14-17
2. http://www.turk.internet.com/haber/yazigoster.php3?yaziid=8859
3. Androutsopoulos, I., Koutsias, J.: An Evaluation of Naive Bayesian Networks. In: Potamias, G., Moustakis, V., van Someren, M. (eds.): Machine Learning in the New Information Age. Barcelona Spain (2000) 9-17
4. Apte, C., Damerau, F., Weiss, S.M.: Automated Learning of Decision Rules for Text Categorization. ACM Transactions on Information Systems. 12-3 (1994) 233-251
5. Cohen, W.: Learning Rules That Classify E-Mail. In: Hearst, M.A., Hirsh, H. (eds.): AAAI Spring Symposium on Machine Learning in Information Access. AAAI Press, Stanford California (1996) 18-25
6. Lewis, D.: Feature Selection and Feature Extraction for Text Categorization. In: DARPA Workshop on Speech and Natural Language. Morgan Kaufmann, Harriman New York (1992) 212-217
7. Lewis, D., Croft, W.B.: Term Clustering of Syntactic Phrases. In: Vidick, J.L. (ed.): ACM SIGIR International Conference on Research and Development in Information Retrieval. Brussels Belgium (1990) 385-404
8. Dagan, I., Karov, Y., Roth, D.: Mistake-Driven Learning in Text Categorization. In: Cardie, C., Weischedel, R. (eds.): Conference on Empirical Methods in Natural Language Processing. ACM, Providence Rhode Island (1997) 55-63
9. Güngör, T.: Computer Processing of Turkish: Morphological and Lexical Investigation. PhD Thesis. Boğaziçi University, İstanbul (1995)
10. Bishop, C.: Neural Networks for Pattern Recognition. Oxford University (1995)
11. Mitchell, T.M.: Machine Learning. McGraw-Hill, New York (1997)
12. Gama, J.: A Linear-Bayes Classifier. In: Monard, M.C., Sichman, J.S. (eds.): Lecture Notes in Computer Science, Vol.1952. Springer-Verlag, Heidelberg (2000) 269-279

An Integrated Approach to Automatic Indoor Outdoor Scene Classification in Digital Images

Matthew Traherne and Sameer Singh

ATR Lab, Department of Computer Science
University of Exeter, Exeter EX4 4QF, UK
{M.Traherne,S.Singh}@ex.ac.uk

Abstract. This paper describes a method for automatic indoor/outdoor scene classification in digital images. Digital images of the inside of buildings will contain a higher proportion of objects with sharp edges. We used an edge detection algorithm on these images and used a method to collect and measure the straightness of the lines in the image. This paper highlights a novel integrated method of measuring these straight lines, and training a neural network to detect the difference between a set of indoor and outdoor images.

1 Introduction

This paper describes a method for automatic indoor/outdoor scene classification in digital images. This image analysis challenge is an important stage in computer vision, and as such there has been extensive research in this field. Despite this, the issue remains open to further research.

Human vision allows us to instantly identify image contents. It can be argued that backgrounds are identified by reasoned knowledge of the proper placement of objects within the image. For example humans know that trees and grass are invariably found outdoors, so any image containing these can be assumed to be outdoors. Previous experiments have focused on trying to find these objects and therefore identify the scene of the image. [1], [2], [3], [4], [5].

Classification of objects in images has been achieved using colour and texture properties [1], [3], [5], [7], [13], [14] and also edge and shape detection [3], [4] and classification from semantic content [8], [9]. Also some work has focused on the semantic analysis of text found with images [1], and other research has focused on the overall colour and texture of the image. [2], [6], [7]. Finally one piece of previous work has taken features from edge direction histogram [13].

The problem with most of these classifiers is that a vast knowledge of objects, and their normal placement, colours and textures is required. If an unrecognised object is found, then this will have no effect on the images' classification. A possible reason for difficulty of this problem is due to the diversity of potential background scenes. For the purpose of this paper the number of potential classifications has been reduced to just indoor and outdoor.

This aim of this document is to show a simple technique that requires very little training, and can match the accuracy of the more advanced methods.

This document outlines the general method that is used, and then describes the technical implementation of this method. The results will provide evidence that using line straightness is an accurate way of classifying indoor and outdoor images.

2 Method

It should be observed that images that are taken inside a building are going to contain a lot of man-made objects. The background itself is going to be man-made.

A general feature of man-made objects is that they are all very linear. For example, images taken inside a building will contain a higher proportion of straight edges, whereas images taken outdoors will have a higher proportion of natural objects with very few straight lines.

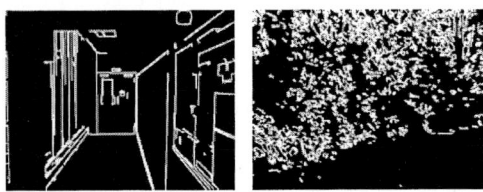

Fig. 1. Edges in indoor and outdoor images.

We can quickly see this when we look at two indoors and outdoors images, after Canny edge detection [15] (Fig. 1.). The task of this paper is to highlight an integrated method of using a measure of straightness on these lines to analyse any digital image and classify its location.

This assumption can quickly break down when we consider outdoor images containing many man made objects, one example is city and landscape classification. [12]. The aim of this paper is to show that there are still significant disproportions of straight lines in images that are taken outside buildings to those taken of the inside of buildings. This imbalance will allow any classifier to distinguish between the two.

For both training and testing purposes we used image data that had been carefully labelled, and checked for correctness. For the use of this paper, an image benchmark has been created. The benchmark has 150 images in three classes, indoors, outdoors and mixed. The indoor class contains only images of the inside of buildings. The outdoor class contains only images of outdoor scenery. The mixed class contains images with outdoor scenery but with man man-made objects within the image, for example buildings.

The benchmark is available for download online at:
http://www.dcs.exeter.ac.uk/people/mtrahern/lines/

Images showing the results from the canny edge detection algorithm used are also available for download on this site.

The first stage of the process is to find the edges in the image. The Canny edge detection formula is well known and is regularly used in image analysis. The Canny method finds areas in the image where the intensity suddenly changes; these pixels are then marked as an edge. After all the edges have been found they are stored as unique lines in a matrix, as opposed to creating an image.

The Canny thresholds should be specified at the start of the project and kept constant throughout the experiments. The two threshold values are used to give the user some control over the density of edges detected. Initially a Gaussian derivative filter is used on the image, and then edge pixels are found using non-maximum suppression so that edges will only be one pixel in width. All pixels above the higher threshold and neighbour pixels above the lower threshold are kept, and these form the final image. The optimal values of 100 and 300 (0.1 and 0.3) were found through experimentation.

It is essential to remove any excess noise from the stored line matrix, as unwanted or insignificant lines can inadvertently affect the final result. From the results of 100 images, it was found that any line shorter than 100 pixels could be considered noise. By simply cropping any line that is shorter than 100 pixels all noise is removed.

Each line is given a value for straightness calculated by:

$$D = \frac{Log(r)}{Log(L)} \quad (1)$$

Where D is the measure of line straightness, L is the length of the line in pixels, r is the length of the straight line between first point and last point. This formula provides a ratio between the length of the line and the distance between the first and last node.

This formula gives a value of straightness of 1 when the line is perfectly straight and the value of the measurement of straightness tends towards zero as the line becomes less straight.

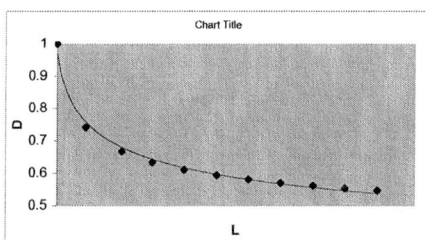

Fig. 2. A graph showing the measurement of straightness of a line decreasing as the length of the line increases. The distance between the start point and the end point are kept constant.

An average of the line straightness for each image is created. The values listed in Fig. 3 were selected after experimentation as the best representation of average line straightness.

The value for highest line straightness was not used as, though experimentation, it was found that the most images contained at least one perfectly straight line.

The expected results are listed in Fig. 3. The left column shows the predicted results for indoor images, the right shows outdoor images. In general we should expect to see more straight long lines in the indoor images and many more short un-straight lines in the outdoor images.

The final stage is to train a KNN to classify the images.

	I	O
Average Line Length	⇑	⇓
Average Line Straightness	⇑	⇓
Lowest Line Straightness	⇑	⇓
Variance of Line Straightness	⇓	⇑
Number of Lines	⇓	⇑

Fig. 3. Expected results.

3 Results

Initially a linear discriminate analysis algorithm gave 91% accuracy, and 94% with PCA reduced data. To validate the results, "leave one out" K nearest neighbour cross validation was used.

K	Results
1	91%
3	95%
5	95%
7	94%

Fig. 4. KNN results.

This test clearly shows that line straightness is a reliable method for classifying indoor and outdoor images. To prove that the method had the ability to identify images taken indoors and images that are outdoors but contain man made objects, a new class, "Mixed", was added. In this class images were deliberately chosen that contained both buildings and organic outdoor material.

To check that a new class was being added that would lie somewhere between indoor and outdoor images but closer to outdoor, an initial test was carried out on the mixed images using the network trained using only indoor and outdoor images. The results were encouraging as 64% of the images fell towards the outdoor and 36% towards the indoor.

This initial result showed that there was a separate cluster of results between the original two. I retrained the network using 2 classes, using the original training set for indoor and outdoor and adding the mixed set as outdoor.

The results are promising, however with an increased classification ideally a larger dataset should be used.

K	Results
1	82%
3	88%
5	86%
7	88%
9	87.33%

Fig. 5. KNN results.

Using the same K nearest neighbour "leave one out" network, the results shown in Fig. 5 were achieved.

This test shows that the system can recognise outdoor images, even when man made objects appear within the image.

4 Conclusion

This paper describes an integrated approach to automatic scene detection using measurements of line straightness. It shows the potential of this system by creating two classes, indoors and outdoors, with 50 images in each class. The proposed method correctly classifies 95% of the images.

Furthermore, a new set of images was added to the dataset. This dataset was added because it contained images of man-made objects, such as buildings, but it should still be classifies as outdoors.

The results showed that 95% of the test images were correctly classified as outdoor, with an overall 88% correct classification.

This proves that even with these simplified experiments line straightness is a very valid method to be used for automatic classification. However, there is a large scope for future development in this area.

Fig. 6 shows a room with stacked books creating a very natural appearance when the edges are found. Although there are some very straight lines, these do not compare to the number of short un-straight lines.

Fig. 6. Inconsistent result.

Using a superior method of measuring straight lines, images such as that in figure 3 would receive a greater probability of being indoors.

Enhancing the measure of line straightness should improve the accuracy of any classifier. For example, each straight section on a long line should be treated as separate lines, meaning that this line would have a better straightness value.

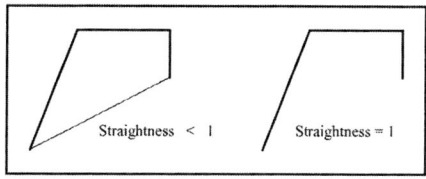

Fig. 7. Enhanced line detection.

This updated method of measurement would increase the number of very straight lines in an indoor image, and increases the separation of indoor and outdoor images making it easier for a network to detect the difference.

This method shows that using edge detection on an image is a new and novel approach to detecting the differences between indoor and outdoor images. However, it should be used as one in many methods to classify images. In [7], [11] Fitzpatric uses combination classifiers to increase the accuracy of classification.

References

1. S. Paek et al., Integration of visual and text-based approaches for the content labelling and classification of photographs, *ACM SIGIR'99 Workshop on Multimedia Indexing and Retrieval*, Berkeley, CA, August 1999.
2. Oliva et al., Global semantic classification of scenes using power spectrum templates, *CIR-99: The Challenge of Image Retrieval*, Newcastle upon Tyne, UK, February 1999.
3. T. Hermes et al., Image retrieval for information systems, in: W. R. Niblack, R. C. Jain (Eds.), *Storage and Retrieval for Image and Video Databases III*, Proc SPIE 2420,1995, pages. 394-405
4. C. Hampton et al., Survey of Image Segmentation, 1998
5. J. Luo, A. Savakis, Indoor vs Outdoor Classification of Consumer Photographs Using Low-Level and Semantic Features, *IEEE Internation Conference on Image Processing Vol 2*, Thessaloniki, Greece, Pages 745-748, July 2001
6. M. Szummer, R. Picard, Indoor-outdoor image classification, *IEEE International Workshop on Content-based Access of Image and Video Databases (CAIVD98)*, Bombay, India, 1998, pp. 42-51
7. P. Fitzpatrick, Indoor/Outdoor scene classification project, *Pattern Recognition and Analysis*
8. Vailaya, A. K. Jain, Incremental learning for Bayesian classification of images, *IEEE International Conference on Image Processing (ICIP '99)*, Kobe, Japan, October 1999.
9. J. P. Eakins, Towards intelligent image retrieval, *Pattern Recognition Volume 35, Number 1*, Pages 3-14, January 2002
10. Vailaya, A. Jain, Reject Option for VQ-based Bayesian Classification, *IEEE International Conference on Pattern Recognition*, Barcelona, Spain, Page 2048, September 2000
11. James, S. Chang, Integrated Multiple Classifiers In Visual Object Detectors Learned From User Input, *IEEE International Conference on Image Processing (ICIP 2002)*, Rochester, NY, September 2002.
12. Vailaya, A. Jain, and H. J. Zhang, On Image Classification: City vs. Landscape, *IEEE Workshop on Content-Based Access of Image and Video Libraries*, Santa Barbara, CA, USA, June 1998.
13. L. Zhang et al., Boosting Image Orientation Detection with Indoor vs. Outdoor Classification, *IEEE Workshop on Applications of Computer Vision*, Orlando, Florida, USA, page 95, December 2002.
14. N. Serrano et al., A Computationally Efficient Approach to Indoor/Outdoor Scene Classification, *IEEE International Conference on Pattern Recognition*, Quebec City, QC, Canada, page 40146 August 2002.
15. J. Canny, A computational approach to edge detection, *IEEE Transactions Pattern Analysis and Machine Intelligence* (IEEE PAMI), 8(6), pp. 679-698, 1986.

Using Fuzzy Sets in Contextual Word Similarity

Masrah Azmi-Murad and Trevor P. Martin

Department of Engineering Mathematics, University of Bristol, Bristol BS8 1TR, UK
{masrah.azmi-murad,trevor.martin}@bris.ac.uk

Abstract. We propose a novel algorithm for computing asymmetric word similarity (AWS) using mass assignment based on fuzzy sets of words. Words in documents are considered similar if they appear in similar contexts. However, these similar words do not have to be synonyms, or belong to the same lexical category. We apply AWS in measuring document similarity. We evaluate the effectiveness of our method against a typical symmetric similarity measure, TF.IDF. The system has been evaluated on real world documents, and the results show that this method performs well.

1 Introduction

The purpose of an information retrieval system is to retrieve all possible relevant documents, and at the same time retrieving as possible few of the irrelevant documents. A successful information retrieval system enables the user to determine quickly and accurately whether the contents of the documents are satisfactory. Information retrieval plays a significant role in web searching, which allows people access to various sources of information from anywhere and at anytime. Only relevant documents should be returned based on a user's query. In order to better represent the documents, those with similar topics or contents are grouped together. There have been several different kinds of document grouping in the literature, among them a vector space model [2] using TF.IDF [2] technique.

The TF.IDF allows searching using natural language. This method proved to be better than Boolean model in grouping similar documents together by using a keyword matching. Documents and queries are represented as vectors in term space. The algorithm for calculating weight is given by

$$w_{ik} = tf_{ik} * \log(N/df_k) . \tag{1}$$

where tf_{ik} is the frequency of k_{th} term in document i, df_k is the number of documents in which a word occurs and N is the total number of documents in the collection. Cosine measure [2] is used to measure the angle between two vectors, i.e., a document d_j and a user query, q. Two vectors are considered identical if the angle is $\phi = 0$. The degree of similarity of the document d_j with regard to the query q is given by the cosine of the angle between these two vectors, i.e.

$$sim(d_j, q) = \frac{\vec{d_j} \bullet \vec{q}}{|\vec{d_j}| \times |\vec{q}|} = \frac{\sum_{i=1}^{t} w_{i,j} \times w_{i,q}}{\sqrt{\sum_{i=1}^{t} w^2_{i,j}} \times \sqrt{\sum_{j=1}^{t} w^2_{i,q}}} . \tag{2}$$

Many document retrieval systems use the vector model with TF.IDF technique because it is simple and fast. However, there are a few problems of using the TF.IDF. For example, TF.IDF cannot reflect similarity of words and only counts the number of overlapping words and it ignores synonymy and syntactic information. TF.IDF uses keywords to find documents that contain words that match the query, which could lead to many irrelevant documents returned, as the search will find words in any location and in any document. There could also be some relevant documents missing, as they use different words to express the same interests. Every insertion and deletion on the document collection will force the IDF [2] value to change and will need to be updated.

In this paper, we demonstrate how finding an asymmetric similarity relation of words performs better document similarity measure, an approach that differs from conventional implementation of similarity measures. Our experiments show that the use of fuzzy sets in computing word similarity can produce higher similarity values between documents in the corpus.

2 Mass Assignment Theory and Fuzzy Sets

A fuzzy set [1] is an extension to a classical set theory, which has a problem of defining the border of the set and non-set. For example, consider a height of a person with labels such as *tall, medium, short*. These labels are fuzzy because not everyone will agree with the same subset of the value domain as satisfying a given label. If they did, we could write precise definitions of *tall, medium* and *short* in this context.

A *mass assignment (MA)* theory [4] has been developed to provide a formal framework for manipulating both probabilistic and fuzzy uncertainties. For example, the voting model, suppose we have a set of people labeled 1 to 10 who are asked to accept or reject a dice value of x as *small*. Suppose everyone accepts 1 as *small*, 80% accept 2 as *small* and 20% accept 3 as *small*. Therefore, the fuzzy set for *small* is defined as

$$small = 1 / 1 + 2 / 0.8 + 3 / 0.2 . \qquad (3)$$

where the membership value for a given element is the proportion of people who accept this element as satisfying the fuzzy set. The probability mass on the sets is calculated by subtracting one membership from the next, giving MA_{small} as

$$MA_{small} = \{1\} : 0.2, \{1, 2\} : 0.6, \{1, 2, 3\} : 0.2 . \qquad (4)$$

The mass assignments above correspond to families of distribution. In order to get a single distribution, the masses are distributed evenly between elements in a set. This distribution is known as *least prejudiced distribution (LPD)* [4] since it is unbiased towards any of the elements. Thus, in the example above, the mass of 0.6 is distributed equally among 1 and 2 and the mass 0.2 is distributed equally among 1, 2 and 3. Therefore, the *least prejudiced distribution* for *small* is:

$$LPD_{small} = 1 : 0.2+0.3+0.0667=0.5667, \ 2 : 0.3+0.0667=0.3667, \ 3 : 0.0667 . \qquad (5)$$

2.1 Semantic Unification

Semantic unification [4] is the process of calculating conditional probabilities of fuzzy sets. A mass assignment with the *LPD* can be used to determine the point semantic unification. For example, suppose the fuzzy set for *medium* in the voting model is

$$medium = 2/0.2 + 3/1 + 4/1 + 5/0.2 . \quad (6)$$

and the mass assignment would be

$$MA_{medium} = \{3, 4\} : 0.8, \{2, 3, 4, 5\} : 0.2 . \quad (7)$$

Thus, the least prejudiced distribution is

$$LPD_{medium} = 2 : 0.05, 3 : 0.45, 4 : 0.45, 5 : 0.05 . \quad (8)$$

Suppose we want to determine the *Pr(about_3|medium)*, and the fuzzy set is

$$about\_3 = 2/0.4 + 3/1 + 4/0.4 . \quad (9)$$

with mass assignment as

$$MA_{about\_3} = \{3\} : 0.6, \{2, 3, 4\} : 0.4 . \quad (10)$$

The point semantic unification can be calculated using the following tableau.

Table 1. Tabular Form of the Pr(about_3|medium).

	0.8 : {3,4}	0.2 : {2,3,4,5}
0.6 : {3}	1/2 x 0.8 x 0.6	1/4 x 0.2 x 0.6
0.4 : {2,3,4}	0.8 x 0.4	3/4 x 0.2 x 0.4

The entries in the cells are the supports from the individual terms of the mass assignments. Each entry has an associated probability. Thus, the *Pr(about_3|medium)* is 0.65. The computation of the probability above can be shown using the following formula. Consider two fuzzy sets *f1* and *f2* defined on a discrete universe X. Let:

$\mu_{f1}(x)$ be the membership of element x in the fuzzy set *f1*.

$MA_{f1}(S)$ be the mass associated with set S.

$LPD_{f1}(x)$ be the probability associated with element x in the *LPD*.

Then

$$Pr(f1|f2) = \sum_{S1 \subseteq X, S2 \subseteq X, S1 \cap S2 \, \varphi} \frac{MA_{f1}(S1) \times MA_{f2}(S2)}{|S2|}$$
$$= \sum_{x \in X} \mu_{f1}(x) \times LPD_{f2}(x) . \quad (11)$$

3 Experiment

In this chapter, we present an algorithm for finding word relations and algorithm for computing document similarities. The purpose of measuring pairwise document similarity is to allow documents with similar values grouped together. We use a Reuters text collection (www.research.att.com/~lewis/reuters21578.html) to retrieve relevant documents in response to a query. As mentioned in Harris [5], words that occur in documents in similar contexts tend to have similar meanings. Consider the following example, taken from [6]

> A bottle of *tezgüno* is on the table.
> Everyone likes *tezgüno*.
> *Tezgüno* makes you drunk.
> We make *tezgüno* out of corn.

From the sentences above, we could infer that *tezgüno* may be a kind of an alcoholic beverage. This is because other alcoholic beverage tends to occur in the same contexts as *tezgüno*. This assumption is based on a principle known as the Distributional Hypothesis [5].

We use this idea to produce a set of related words, which can be used as the basis for taxonomy, or to cluster documents. In this experiment, we use Fril [3] to compute asymmetric similarity such that the similarity between *<term1>* and *<term2>* is not necessarily the same as between *<term2>* and *<term1>*. Thus, *ws(<term1>,<term2>) ≠ ws(<term2>, <term1>)*. This is because to compute similarity between two fuzzy sets, i.e. *ws(<term1>,< term2>)*, we will multiply the elements of fuzzy sets of *<term1>* with the corresponding elements in frequency distributions of *<term2>*. In order to calculate *ws(<term2>, <term1>)*, we will multiply the elements of fuzzy sets of *<term2>* with the corresponding elements in frequency distributions of *<term1>*. In most cases, the number of elements for two fuzzy sets is different; therefore, the similarity measures will be different. Our method is based on finding the frequencies of *n-tuples* of context words in a set of documents. Consider the sentences below

> *The quick brown fox jumps over the lazy dog.*
> *The quick brown cat jumps onto the active dog.*
> *The slow brown fox jumps onto the quick brown cat.*
> *The quick brown cat leaps over the quick brown fox.*

For each word x, we incrementally build up a set *context-of-x* containing pairs of words that surround x, with a corresponding frequency, e.g. for *brown* we have *(quick, cat)* occurs three times, *(quick, fox)* occurs two times and *(slow, fox)* occurs once. We use mass assignment theory to convert these frequencies to fuzzy sets, and obtain the membership as *{ (quick, cat):1, (quick, fox):0.833, (slow, fox):0.5 }*. For any two words *<term1>* and *<term2>*, Pr (*<term1>|<term2>*) measures the degree to which *<term1>* could replace *<term2>*, and can be calculated by semantic unification of the two fuzzy sets characterising their contexts. For example, suppose the fuzzy context set of *grey* is *{(quick, cat):1, (slow, fox):0.75}*. We calculate

$$\Pr(\text{brown}|\text{grey}) = 0.8125, \quad \Pr(\text{grey}|\text{brown}) = 0.625$$

This gives an asymmetric word similarity matrix $M^{(w)}$, whose rows and columns are labeled by all the words encountered in the document collection. Each cell $M^{(w)}$ (i, j) holds a value between 0 and 1, indicating to which extend a word i is contextually similar to word j. For any word we can extract a fuzzy set of similar words from a row of the matrix. Many of the elements are zero. We also note that there are important efficiency considerations in making this a totally incremental process, i.e. words (and documents) can be added or subtracted without having to recalculate the whole matrix of values. As would be expected, this process gives both sense and nonsense.

Related words appear in the same context (as with *grey* and *brown* in the illustration above), however, unrelated words may also appear, e.g. the phrase *slow fat fox* would lead to a non-zero similarity between *fat* and *brown*.

We use the word similarity matrix in computing document similarity for the purpose of grouping similar documents together. This would help the user to navigate easily through similar documents. The similarity measure is defined as

$$sim(d_a, d_b) = \sum_{a \in doc1} \sum_{b \in doc2} ws(w_i, w_j) \times w_{ia} \times w_{jb} .$$ (12)

where $ws(w_i, w_j)$ is the word similarity of two fuzzy sets, and w_{ia} and w_{jb} are the normalized weight of word i and j in document a and b respectively. In Chapter 4, we present the results of average similarity of each document by dividing the pairwise similarity measures with the total number of documents in the collection.

4 Results

To evaluate our method, we compare our system with TF.IDF. We use Reuters collection in testing our system, in which 4535 documents are used as a training set and about 4521 documents are used as a test set. Like many other document retrieval techniques, we applied the process of Porter stemming and discarding common words using a stop list. Several short queries were used to ensure that our system produces expected results all through out the testing, and these are reported elsewhere. However, in this paper we will only present the preliminary results, using Query 1: *"bomb attack in Madrid"* and Query 2: *"digital library"*. Based on Query 1, the training set has thirty-eight relevant documents retrieved while test set has fifty-four. Based on Query 2, training set has twenty-two documents and test set has thirty documents. Both TF.IDF and AWS produce the same sets of documents in this case.

Table 2. The Fuzzy Approach as a Measure of Contextual Word Similarity

Training				Test			
word i	word j	$ws(w_i, w_j)$	$ws(w_j, w_i)$	word i	word j	$ws(w_i, w_j)$	$ws(w_j, w_i)$
injured	wound	0.148	0.857	police	shepherd	0.303	0.091
said	quote	0.488	0.024	said	confirm	0.109	0.013
grain	currency	0.2	0.5	military	Pentagon	0.385	0.045
surplus	unwanted	1	1	slump	fell	0.333	0.5

Table 2 shows some selection of asymmetric similarity between words taken from an example Query 1. Most word pairs are plausible although some, for example, *grain* and *currency* may be dissimilar. As mentioned earlier in Chapter 3, the asymmetric word similarity is purely due to similar contexts, and may not lead to similar meaning. As shown in Figure 1, document-document similarity measures using AWS is consistently about 10% higher than using TF.IDF, taken over both document sets, with much less computation required for the AWS calculations.

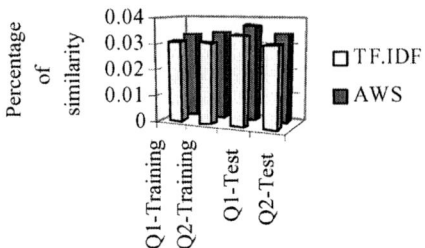

Fig. 1. Average document similarity taken from both training and test set using queries 1 and 2.

5 Conclusions and Future Work

In this paper, we presented the asymmetry in similarity between words using fuzzy sets for the benefit of document groupings. We have shown that implementing asymmetric fuzzy sets of words in measuring pairwise document similarity produces higher document values. Our method shows a satisfactory result when compared with a conventional similarity measure. We are currently continuing testing our system with a large document collection and longer queries to ensure that it will produce a consistently satisfactory result.

We plan to summarize individual documents in each group, using a short paragraph or a few keywords that describe the content of the document. This is to help user better understand the information contained in each document, hence, user may save time and choose an accurate document to his interests.

References

1. L. A. Zadeh. Fuzzy Sets. Information and Control. 1965. Vol. 8. pp. 338-353
2. R. Baeza-Yates and B. Ribeiro-Neto. Modern Information Retrieval. ACM Press. 1999
3. J. F. Baldwin, T. P. Martin and B. W. Pilsworth. Fril-Fuzzy and Evidential Reasoning in Artificial Intelligence. Research Studies Press, England. 1995
4. J. F. Baldwin, J. Lawry and T. P. Martin. A Mass Assignment Theory of the Probability of Fuzzy Events. Fuzzy Sets and Systems. 1996 (83) pp. 353-367
5. Z. Harris. Distributional Structure. In: Katz, J. J. (ed.) The Philosophy of Linguistics. New York: Oxford University Press. pp. 26-47
6. P. Pantel and D. Lin. Discovering Word Senses from Text. In Conference on Knowledge Discovery and Data Mining. 2002. Alberta, Canada

Summarizing Time Series: Learning Patterns in 'Volatile' Series

Saif Ahmad, Tugba Taskaya-Temizel, and Khurshid Ahmad

Department of Computing, University of Surrey, Guildford, GU2 7XH
Surrey, UK
{s.ahmad,t.taskaya,k.ahmad}@surrey.ac.uk
http://www.computing.surrey.ac.uk

Abstract. Most financial time series processes are nonstationary and their frequency characteristics are time-dependant. In this paper we present a time series summarization and prediction framework to analyse nonstationary, volatile and high-frequency time series data. Multiscale wavelet analysis is used to separate out the trend, cyclical fluctuations and autocorrelational effects. The framework can generate verbal signals to describe each effect. The summary output is used to reason about the future behaviour of the time series and to give a prediction. Experiments on the intra-day European currency spot exchange rates are described. The results are compared with a neural network prediction framework.

1 Introduction

Understanding and interpreting time varying phenomena are amongst the key challenges in various branches of science and technology. Autoregressive analysis of time series has been carried out over the last 50 years [2] with encouraging results. However, such techniques do not quite explain nonstationary phenomena [6], which may be characterised by long-range dependencies [22].

Techniques for time series analysis have ranged from machine learning approaches, which use artificial neural networks for prediction of stock time series [23], to genetic algorithms that learn to predict [10]. Data mining concepts with the aim to discover hidden patterns, similarity searches, and incremental mining have also been applied to time serial databases [11], [12] and [20]. Agrawal et al. introduce the concept of a shape definition language (SDL), which allows a variety of queries about the shapes, found in historical time sequences [1]. Natural language generation (NLG) based systems produce English language summaries of time varying phenomena by performing tasks such as microplanning and syntactic realisation on the analysed data [3] and [19].

Financial time series exhibit quite complicated patterns (for example, trends, abrupt changes, and volatility clustering), which appear, disappear, and re-appear over time [8]. Such series are often referred to as nonstationary, whereby a variable has no clear tendency to return to a fixed value or linear trend. Most of the time series analysis techniques discussed above, fail to address the transient nature of such time series. In short, 'sharp variations' [14] in a time series are excluded, and these variations are of interest to theoreticians and practitioners.

Wavelet analysis is a relatively new field in signal processing. Wavelets are mathematical functions that 'cut' up data into different frequency components, and then study each component with a resolution matched to its scale – a scale refers to a time horizon [7]. Wavelet filtering is particularly relevant to volatile and time-varying characteristics of real world time series and is not restrained by the assumption of stationarity [16]. The wavelet transform decomposes a process into different scales [15], which makes it useful in differentiating seasonalities, revealing structural breaks and volatility clusters, and identifying local and global dynamic properties of a process at these timescales [9]. Wavelet analysis has been shown to be especially productive in analysing, modeling, and predicting the behaviour of financial instruments as diverse as shares and exchange rates [4], [17] and [18].

In this paper, we propose an automatic time series analysis approach based on providing a summary of the data with respect to the 'chief features' of the data, which may be predictive of future events and behaviour. We extract important occurrences (for example turning points) from the data and look for their possible reappearance in the future. Our time series summarization framework adapts concepts from multiscale wavelet analysis to deal with nonstationary, nonperiodic, and volatile financial time series data. More specifically, our framework uses the discrete wavelet transform (DWT) and multiscale volatility analysis to summarize features like trend, cycle (seasonality), turning points and variance change in the original data and facilitates a prediction based on these features. We present our framework and report results on Intraday tick data for the British Pound (£) – US Dollar ($) exchange rate series and compare our results with a neural network prediction framework: the fit to the data is quite good (mean square error = 0.0000381) and compares well with predictions based on the use of neural networks where the mean square error is around 20 times higher.

2 Motivation

With the advent of the Internet and online data vendors, more and more financial time series data is being recorded, supplied and stored online. In financial markets, traders both 'bid', price at which they are prepared to buy and 'ask', price at which they will sell. This system of bid / ask pricing ensures the sell / purchase of instruments without any delay. A day's trading (comprising almost 24 hours) for such data could generate 25,000 to 30,000 *ticks* per day per instrument.

The engineering of this high-frequency data, that is acquiring, preprocessing, and analysing the data is made more complex by nonstationarities in the data. The tick data arrives at irregular intervals and in order to use time series analysis techniques on such unordered data, some pre-processing is required. Data *compression* is one such pre-processing technique that aggregates the movement in the dataset over a certain period of time. The *compression* acts as a surrogate for the original: the maxima (High) and minima (Low) of the data over a fixed interval (typically, one minute) and the value at the start (Open) and the end (Close) of the minute acts as the surrogate for other data during the minute. Data *compression* essentially yields four new time series: Open, High, Low, and Close data values. For instance, the Intraday trading of an exchange rate instrument (£/$) comprising over 25,000 data points can be compressed into 1-minute slices resulting in 1440 data points per day.

In order to identify key patterns of behaviour in a non-linear time series x_t, particularly in its return value, $r_t = \log(x_t/x_{t-1})$, or its volatility, $v_t = |r_t|$, it is important to understand that there may be purely local changes in time domain, global changes in frequency domain, and there may be changes in the variance parameters. The discrete wavelet transformation (DWT) is one such technique for parameterizing this dynamic behaviour.

Neural network literature suggests that they can learn the behaviour of a time series and produce results that compare well with other nonlinear approaches to time series analysis – for example, nonlinear autoregressive (AR) analysis. Instead of statistically computing AR coefficients, a neural network learns the behaviour of the time series by a change in the weights of the interconnected neurons comprising the network. Once trained, the network can predict the future behaviour of the time series [5] and [21].

In this paper, we will compare the two parameterizing techniques, namely, wavelet analysis and neural networks.

3 Wavelet Analysis of Time Series: Annotation and Prediction

3.1 A Brief Note on the DWT

The Discrete Wavelet Transform represents a signal as a sum of approximations (As) and details (Ds) that are localized in time and frequency. The DWT is a discrete convolution process that can be expressed by the following formula:

$$w * x_t = \sum_{i=-\infty}^{\infty} w_i x_{t-i} \qquad (1)$$

Here x_t is the original signal while w is the low- or high-pass filter corresponding to the *prototype* wavelet. In practice, the DWT is implemented via a pyramidal algorithm [13]. By achieving good time-frequency resolution the DWT is able to tame nonstationarities and volatilities to discover interesting local and global patterns in a signal. In Eq (1), w_i are a set of parameters that encapsulate the behavior of a nonlinear time series and as such wavelet analysis can be used to learn various behavioral patterns in a time series. The details (D_i) at various levels (i = 1 to L) of decomposition help capture local fluctuations over the whole period of a time series. The key frequency components at each decomposition level helps in summarizing the behavior of a time series up until the immediate past as also the future behavior. The highest-level approximation (A_L) captures the overall movement (trend) of the time series.

The decomposition of a series into the details and approximations will help, as we will show, in the annotation of the series: wavelet analysis can be used to identify variance change in addition to trend and seasonal components. Once identified, a set of pre-stored phrases can be attached to the series as a whole or to discrete points in the series – the annotation of volatilities, trends and seasonal variations can then be produced automatically. The details and approximations can be used to forecast the future seasonal variations and trends [17].

3.2 Algorithms for Summarizing and Predicating Patterns

We have developed two algorithms that can automatically summarize and predict a locally volatile time series (tick data) in terms of the 'chief features' of the series including turning points, trend, cycle, and variance change.

I. Compress the tick data to get Open (O), High (H), Low (L) and Close (C) value for a given compression period (for example, one minute or five minutes).

II. Calculate the level L of the DWT needed based on number of samples N in **C** of Step I,
$L = \text{floor} [\log(N)/\log(2)]$.

III. Perform a level-L DWT on **C** based on results of Step I and Step II to get,
$D_i, i = 1, \ldots, L$, and A_L.

III-1. Compute **trend** by performing linear regression on A_L.

III-2. Extract **cycle** (seasonality) by performing a Fourier power spectrum analysis on each D_i and choosing the D_i with maximum power as D_S,
$$\tilde{D}_i(k) = (1/N) \sum_{t=0}^{N-1} D_i(t).e^{-j2\pi f k t}, k = 0,1,\ldots,N-1$$

III-3. Extract **turning points** by choosing extremas of each D_i.

IV. Locate a **single variance** change in the series by using the NCSS index on **C**,
$$\tilde{P}_k = \frac{\sum_{t=Lj-1}^{k} \tilde{w}_{j,t}^2}{\sum_{t=Lj-1}^{N-1} \tilde{w}_{j,t}^2}, k = Lj-1,\ldots,N-2$$
where, w_j is the *level-j* DWT of the volatility series v_t of **C**.

V. Generate a graphical and verbal **summary** for results of Steps III-1 to III-3 and IV.

Fig. 1. Time series summarization algorithm.

In Fig. 1., we present the first algorithm – the *time series summarization algorithm*. It uses the DWT to process the raw time series and its first difference expressed through its volatility to extract numerical values corresponding to the 'chief features'. The system then generates a graphical and a verbal summary, describing the market dynamics at different scales (time horizons). The separation of a time series into its time scale components using the DWT facilitates forecasting by applying the appropriate procedure to each component – the aggregate forecast can then be obtained by recombining the component series.

The second algorithm, *time series prediction algorithm*, is presented in Fig. 2. After the time series has been summarized and separated into 'key' components, the trend and seasonal components are projected separately and then recombined to give an aggregate forecast. The seasonal component is symmetrically extended based on its distinct amplitude and period. The trend, which is linear in the level-L DWT approximation, is modeled by a first order polynomial function. The time series prediction algorithm does not predict the exact future values of a time series; it rather gives the overall market movement and major fluctuations for the forecast period specified. If we are able to extend all the wavelet components (A_L and every D_j) and recombine the individual extensions, we can get an exact forecast for the specified period. However, the dynamics of other wavelet components, for example the irregular fluctuations, are more complicated and need more study before they can be modeled or extended with a fair degree of confidence.

I. Summarize the tick data using the time series summarization algorithm of Fig. 1.
II. For a N-step ahead **forecast**, extend the **seasonal** component D_S *symmetrically* N points to the right to get $D_{S,\ forecast}$.
III. For a N-step ahead **forecast**, extend the **trend** component A_N *linearly* N points to the right to get $A_{N,\ forecast}$.
IV. Add the results of Steps II and III to get an **aggregate** N-step ahead **forecast**,
$Forecast = D_{S,\ forecast} + A_{N,\ forecast}$

Fig. 2. Time series prediction algorithm.

4 A Prototype System for Annotating and Predicting Time Series

We have developed a prototype system in Matlab®, a commercial mathematical package developed by *The MathWorks, Inc.* The system can automatically annotate and predict a time series. The prototype has sub-systems for compressing tick data, performing the DWT analysis, and the fast Fourier transform analysis on the compressed data. The compressed data is decomposed into trend and seasonal components for annotation purposes; annotation being performed by using a set of phrases that are selected by looking, for example, at the derivative of the seasonal and trend components. The prediction module of the prototype can project these components separately and recombine them to give an aggregate forecast.

4.1 An Experiment on the £/$ Tick Data

Consider the five minutes compressed tick data for the £/$ exchange rate on March 18, 2004 (Fig. 3). We use our summarization algorithm (Fig. 1) and prediction algorithm (Fig. 2) to process this data. The results are compared with a neural network prediction framework employing multi-layer perceptrons (MLPs); the DWT results look more promising than the MLP.

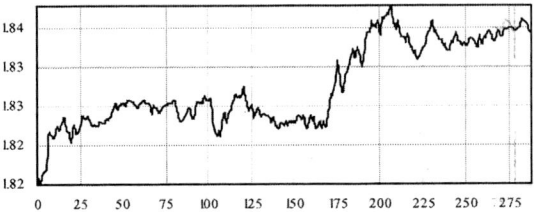

Fig. 3. Analyzed signal – the £/$ exchange rate on March 18, 2004 compressed to 5 minutes.

4.2 Annotation

The graphical summary produced by the system using the time series summarization algorithm is shown in Fig. 4.

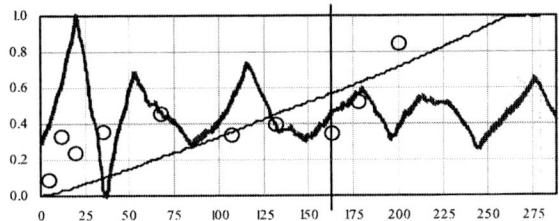

Fig. 4. Graphical summary of series of Fig. 3 showing trend, seasonality, turning points and variance change.

The open circles show turning points, the vertical line shows the variance change location, the thick fluctuating line shows the seasonal component and the thin slanting line shows the trend. The values of all components in Fig. 4 have been scaled between zero and one for display purposes.

The verbal summary of the extracted features produced by the system is shown in Table 1, which can be used to annotate a time series. The trend information suggests a long-term upward movement. However, a major inflexion point at t = 260 where the slope drops drastically by 94 percent suggests a downtrend. The cyclical component peaks with a period of 30 to 60, suggesting that this seasonal behaviour will continue in the near future.

After summarizing the time series and separating it into its time scale components using the DWT, we are now ready to project these components separately and recombine the projections to get an aggregate forecast for the next day.

Table 1. Verbal summary of series of Fig. 3.

Feature	Phrases	Details
Trend	1st Phase	$x_1^{Trend} = 6.36e - 5t + 1.81, t < 260$
	2nd Phase	$x_2^{Trend} = 3.65e - 6t + 1.83, 261 < t < 288$
Turning Points	Downturns	108, 132, 164, and 178
	Upturns	5, 12, 20 36, 68, and 201
Variance Change	Location	164
Cycle	Period	42
	Peaks at	21, 54, 117, 181, 215, and 278

4.3 Prediction

For prediction, we use the 'chief features' of the previous day (March 18, 2004), the trend and information about the dominant cycle (Table 1), to reproduce the elements of the series for the following day (March 19, 2004). The prediction results are shown in Fig. 5. The prediction (bottom curve) is in agreement with the actual time series (top curve), which shows a downturn. The cyclical fluctuations in the prediction curve do not seem to match too well and there is an observable divergence after observation number 125. However, as the market seems to pick up after observation number 250, the prediction curve also starts to pick up. The correlation between the predicted and actual time series is 62.4 % and the mean square error is 0.0000381.

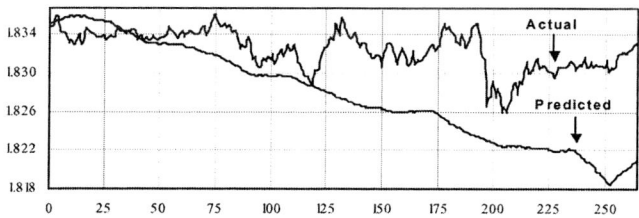

Fig. 5. Next day (March 19, 2004) forecast (bottom curve) of series of Fig. 3 along with the actual series (top curve) for the next day.

4.4 Predicting with Neural Networks: A Comparison

For evaluating our results, we use a multi layer perceptron (MLP) to perform nonlinear AR prediction on the five minutes compressed tick data for the £/$ exchange rate on March 18, 2004 (Fig. 3). This MLP has the following configuration: 11 input layers, 8 hidden layers and 1 output layer. The number of tapped delays in the input layer is 10. Backpropagation is used for training to predict the next value. Fig. 6 shows the results of the analysis.

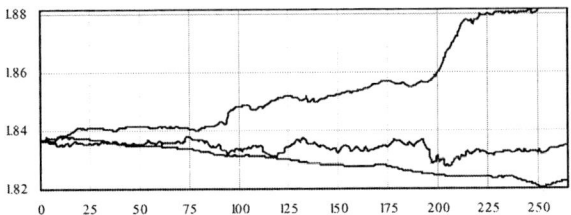

Fig. 6. Forecast comparison: from top, the first curve is the MLP prediction, second is the actual (test) data and the third is the DWT prediction.

There is clearly a greater divergence from the original for the MLP prediction, the root mean square error being about 17 times that of the DWT prediction (0.000673 vs. 0.0000381). The basic assumption in the MLP prediction approach is that of short-range dependency, where it is assumed the next value of a time series is dependant only on the previous value. However for many financial time series data, for example foreign exchange rates, the correlations between variables do not decay at a sufficiently fast rate and observations separated by great periods of time would still exhibit significant correlation. Such time series are said to be generated by long-memory or long-range dependent processes and require different approaches to modeling than the so-called short-memory processes (for example AR models). The wavelet analysis has been shown to approximately decorrelate time series with long memory structure [22]. This provides a sound technique for testing and modeling nonstationary features without knowing the exact nature of the correlation structure of a given time series. This could perhaps be the reason for a better fit to the data obtained using the DWT as compared to the MLP (Fig. 6).

Table 2 shows a comparison of the mean square error and correlation statistics for the two methods. The mean square error for the MLP prediction is 17 times higher than the DWT prediction. Moreover, the correlation between the actual and predicted for the DWT is very good (+ 62.4 %) as compared to a negative correlation (- 61.8 %) for the MLP.

Table 2. Comparison between DWT and MLP.

	Prediction	Mean Square Error	Correlation
DWT	Trend + Seasonality	0.0000381	+ 62.4 %
MLP	All Values	0.000673	- 61.8 %

5 Conclusions

In this paper we have presented a time series summarization, annotation, and prediction framework based on the multiscale wavelet analysis to deal with nonstationary, volatile and high frequency financial data. We have shown that the multiscale analysis can effectively deconstruct the total series into its constituent time scales: specific forecasting techniques can be applied to each timescale series to gain efficiency in forecast. The results of experiments performed on Intraday exchange data show promise and clearly point towards the advantages of the wavelet analysis over neural networks for summarizing and predicting highly volatile time series. However, continuously evolving and randomly shocked economic systems demand for a more rigorous and extended analysis, which is being planned.

The next and perhaps theoretically and empirically more challenging step is to consider and understand the dynamics of other time scale components generated by the wavelet analysis, for example the irregular fluctuations and the decorrelated white noise. Successful analysis of agents operating on several scales simultaneously and of modeling these components could result in more exact forecasts.

References

1. Agrawal, R., Psaila, G., Wimmers, E. L., and Zait, M., "Querying Shapes of Histories," *Proceedings of the International Conference on Very Large Data Bases (VLDB)*, pp. 502-514, 1995.
2. Box, G. E. P, and Jenkins, G. M., "Time Series Analysis: Forecasting and Control," *Time Series and Digital Processing*, Second Edition, Holden Day, San Francisco, 1976.
3. Boyd, S., "TREND: A System for Generating Intelligent Description of Time-Series Data", *Proceedings of the IEEE ICIPS*, 1998.
4. Brock, W. A., "Whither Nonlinear?," *Journal of Economic Dynamics and Control*, vol. 24, pp. 663-678, 2000.
5. Campolucci P., Piazza F., "On-Line Learning Algorithms for Locally Recurrent Neural Networks," *IEEE Transactions on Neural Networks*, vol. 10, no. 2, pp. 253-271, 1999.
6. Chatfield, C., "The Analysis of Time Series: An Introduction," Fifth Edition, Chapman and Hall/CRC, 1996.
7. Daubechies, I., "Ten Lectures on Wavelets," SIAM, Philadelphia, 1992.
8. Gençay, R., Selçuk, F., Whitcher, B., "An Introduction to Wavelets and Other Filtering Methods in Finance and Economics," Academic Press, 2002.
9. Gençay, R., Selcuk, F., Whitcher, B., "Differentiating Intraday Seasonalities Through Wavelet Multi-scaling," *Physica A*, vol. 289, pp. 543-556, 2001.
10. Kaboudan, M. A., "Genetic Programming Prediction of Stock Prices," *Computational Economics*, vol. 16, pp. 207-236, 2000.
11. Keogh, E., and Pazzani, M., "An Indexing Scheme for Fast Similarity Search in Large Time Series Databases," *Proceedings of 11th Int'l Conference on Scientific and Statistical Database Management*, 1999.

12. Keogh, E., Chakrabarti, K., Pazzani, M., and Mehrotra, S., "Locally Adaptive Dimensionality Reduction for Indexing Large Time Series Databases," *SIGMOD Record* (ACM Special Interest Group on Management of Data), pp. 151-162, 2001.
13. Mallat, S., "A Theory for Multiresolution Signal Decomposition: The Wavelet Representation," *IEEE Transactions on Pattern Analysis and Machine Intelligence*, vol. 11, pp. 674-693, 1989.
14. Mallat, S., and Zhong, S., "Characterization of Signals from Multiscale Edges," *IEEE Transactions on Pattern Analysis and Machine Intelligence*, vol. 14, no. 7, pp. 710- 732, 1992.
15. Meyer, Y., "Wavelets: Algorithms and Applications," *Society for Industrial and Applied Mathematics*, Philadelphia, 1993.
16. Qian, S., and Chen, D., "Understanding the Nature of Signals whose Power Spectra Change with Time," *IEEE Signal Processing Magazine*, 1999.
17. Ramsey, J. B., and Zhang, Z., "The Analysis of Foreign Exchange Data Using Waveform Dictionaries," *Journal of Empirical Finance*, vol. 4, pp. 341-372, 1997.
18. Renaud, O., Starck, J., L., and Murtagh, F., "Prediction Based on a Multiscale Decomposition," *International Journal of Wavelets, Multiresolution and Information Processing*, Vol. 1, No. 2, pp. 217-232, 2003.
19. Sripada, S. G., Reiter, E., Hunter, J., and Yu, J., "Generating English Summaries of Time Series Data Using the Gricean Maxims", *SIGKDD*, USA, 2003.
20. Walid, G. A., Mohamed, G. E., and Ahmed, K. E., "Incremental, Online, and Merge Mining of Partial Periodic Patterns in Time Series Databases," *IEEE Transactions on Knowledge and Data Engineering*, vol. 16, no. 3, pp. 332-342, 2004.
21. Wan E., "Time Series Prediction Using a Neural Network with Embedded Tapped Delay-Lines in Predicting the Future and Understanding the Past," *SFI Studies in the Science of Complexity*, Addison-Wesley, Eds. A. Weigend , N. Gershenfeld, 1993.
22. Whitcher, B., Percival, D. B. and Guttorp, P., "Multiscale Detection and Location of Multiple Variance Changes in the Presence of Long Memory," *Journal of Statistical Computation and Simulation*, Vol. 68, pp. 65-88, 2000.
23. Zemke, S., "Bagging Imperfect Predictors," *Proceedings of Artificial Neural Networks in Engineering*, St. Louis, Missouri, pp. 1067-1072, 1999.

Cosine Transform Priors for Enhanced Decoding of Compressed Images

Amos Storkey and Michael Allan

School of Informatics
University of Edinburgh
5 Forrest Hill, Edinburgh, EH1 2QL

Abstract. Image compression methods such as JPEG use quantisation of discrete cosine transform (DCT) coefficients of image blocks to produce lossy compression. During decoding, an inverse DCT of the quantised values is used to obtain the lossy image. These methods suffer from blocky effects from the region boundaries, and can produce poor representations of regions containing sharp edges. Such problems can be obvious artefacts in compressed images but also cause significant problems for many super-resolution algorithms. Prior information about the DCT coefficients of an image and the continuity between image blocks can be used to improve the decoding using the same compressed image information. This paper analyses empirical priors for DCT coefficients, and shows how they can be combined with block edge contiguity information to produce decoding methods which reduce the blockiness of images. We show that the use of DCT priors is generic can be useful in many other circumstances.

1 Introduction

A number of image compression methods, most notably including baseline JPEG (joint photographic experts group), use quantisation of the discrete cosine transform (DCT) coefficients in order to obtain a lossy compressed representation of an image. Put simply, baseline JPEG splits each image into 8x8 blocks and then performs a DCT on each image block. These are then quantised according to a preset quantisation schema which depends on the compression rate required. The quantised coefficients are then losslessly compressed and encoded to a bitstream, usually using Huffman codes. To decode the jpeg, the quantised coefficients are the obtained from the bitstream using the relevant lossless decompression. The quantised coefficients are then used directly in the inverse DCT to recreate the image.

The deficits of this scheme are that it can produce blocky artefacts [1] as each 8x8 block is treated independently, and that it can produce poor representation of regions with significant high frequency information.

In this paper we recognise the fact that the quantised DCT coefficients provide upper and lower bounds for the true coefficients. It is also possible to obtain empirical prior DCT coefficient distributions from the examination of many other 8x8 patches from a database of uncompressed images. Furthermore we can examine the pixel differences across block boundaries in the uncompressed image database and use that information as a prior measure for the blockiness effects of compressed images.

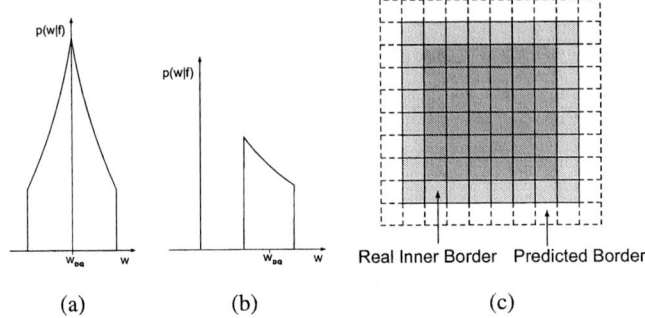

Fig. 1. Prior distribution of DCT coefficients given known quantised coefficients **f**. (a) Zero-quantised coefficient. (b) Non-zero quantised coefficient. (c) Predicted border-pixels are given by inner border-pixels.

2 The Probabilistic Model

Consider first a single 8x8 image patch, and the set of pixels bordering each edge of that 8x8 patch. Let **w** denote the vector of DCT coefficients, **v** denote the set of quantised coefficients (and implicitly the constraints they give to the real coefficients). Let **y** denote the border-pixel intensities. Suppose we have some prior distribution over DCT coefficients $P(\mathbf{w})$ and are given the true border-pixel intensities **y**, and quantised DCT coefficients. Then we wish to calculate the posterior distribution

$$P(\mathbf{w}|\mathbf{y}, \mathbf{v}) \propto P(\mathbf{y}|\mathbf{w})P(\mathbf{w}|\mathbf{v}) \qquad (1)$$

Here $P(\mathbf{w}|\mathbf{v})$ is the prior distribution $P(\mathbf{w})$ constrained to the region implied by the quantised coefficients **v**, and renormalised. This is illustrated in Figure 1. $P(\mathbf{y}|\mathbf{w})$ is given by the model $P(\mathbf{y}|\mathbf{x})$ of the observed border pixels given the predicted border pixels **x** produced by the extrapolating the DCT basis functions 1 pixel over the boundary of the 8x8 region. This is simple to calculate using the basis function symmetry, and amounts to using the inner border pixels as the predicted border pixels (see figure 1).

3 Prior Distributions

To use the above model two prior distributions are needed. First a prior distribution $P(\mathbf{w})$ for the DCT coefficients is required. Second we need the distribution of the true border pixels $P(\mathbf{y}|\mathbf{x})$ given the predicted values. Forms for both of these can be obtained empirically from a set of training images.

The source images used in this report can be found at http://www.hlab.phys.rug.nl/archive.html. The images were taken with a Kodak DCS420 digital camera. For details and a description of the calibration see the Methods section of [7]. The images contain many similar scenes of urban areas, landscapes and woodland areas. The linear intensity images have been used rather than the de-blurred set in order to reduce the possibility of artefact introduction. The camera used to capture the images does not deliver the two

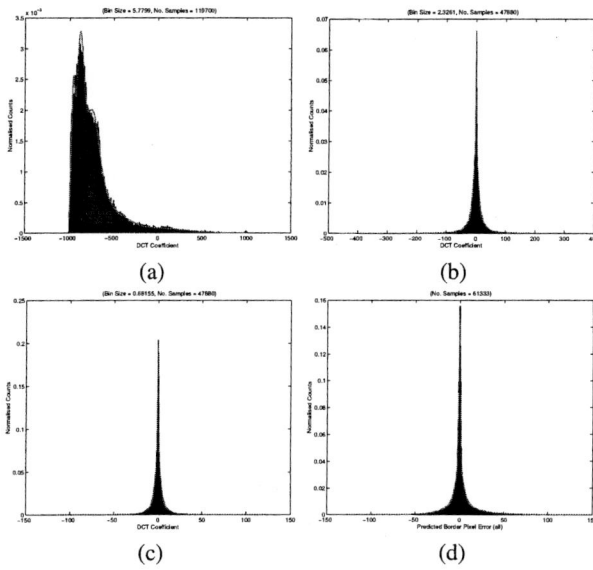

Fig. 2. Distribution of DCT coefficients: (a) The DC coefficient, (b) The (2,2) coefficient, (c) the (4,6) coefficient. (d) Distribution of differences between the predicted and true border pixels.

outermost pixels along the edges and so it was necessary to remove them. To maintain an image that contains a whole number of 8x8 blocks, the eight outermost pixels along the edges were cropped. Also to reduce processing time the images were reduced in size by a factor of two along both the width and height using pixel averaging. The 12-bit images were intensity-scaled linearly to between 0 and 255 to comply with the JPEG standard. The first twenty images in the set were used as training images. The prior over discrete cosine transform coefficients was modelled as a factorised distribution $P(\mathbf{w}) = \prod_i P(w_i)$ where w_i is the ith DCT coefficient. Then the prior for each coefficient was set using empirical values the training images. Histograms of the priors are given in Figure 2. Note that the lowest frequency coefficient (commonly called the DC coefficient) has a different structure from the other (AC) coefficients. The AC coefficients appear to have the same form, but have different distribution widths, where the higher frequency components are more tightly distributed around zero. The prior over the border pixels was also factorised into independent distributions for each pixel. The distribution of the difference between the predicted pixel value and the true pixel value was used as the model for $P(\mathbf{y}|\mathbf{w})$. The distribution obtained is illustrated in Figure 2d. More general forms for $P(\mathbf{y}|\mathbf{w})$ were tried, but they had little effect on the final outcome. Gaussian mixture models were fit to these histograms to provide a working functional representation of the distribution.

4 Intermediate Results

Although the form of model described is not the final model, as the true border pixel information is not available, it is instructive to see how it performs. Conjugate gradient

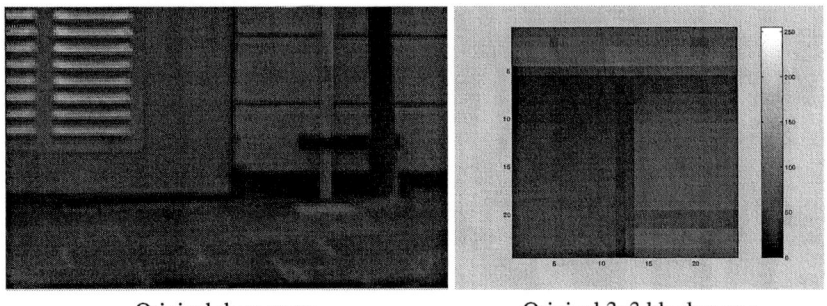

Original door scene   Original 3x3 block scene

Fig. 3. Two original scenes.

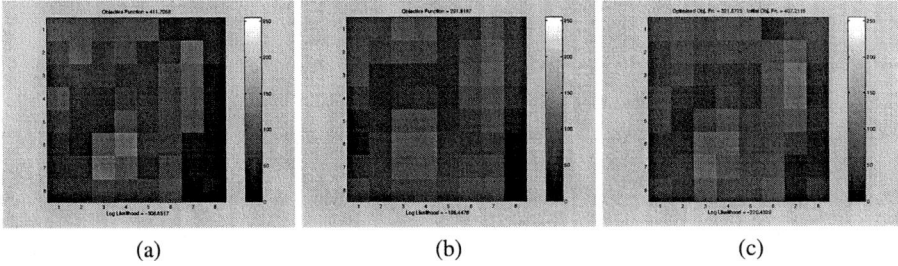

(a)   (b)   (c)

Fig. 4. Results of optimisation. (a) Original patch (b) Patch reconstructed from quantised DCT, (c) reconstructed from optimised DCT.

optimisation was used to calculate the maximum a posteriori (MAP) DCT coefficients given the border pixel data and the quantised DCT coefficients. To test how well the original values can be recovered if a nearby local minima is found, the coefficients were initialised at the original values. For the image patch illustrated in figure 3b, and with a standard lossy decoding given by Figure 4a, we obtain Figure 4b using this approach. A representation of the true, quantised and optimised DCT coefficients are given in Figure 5. We can also initialise the values at the quantised coefficients. Figure 6 shows the use of this approach on a test image.

Quantifiable assessment of image quality is notoriously hard and generally an unreliable measure of performance. However it is possible to use a perceptual error measure such as those of [4, 8, 5]. For example, with the image illustrated the perceptual error measure of [8] improves from 8.46 to 8.39. In general we find that for regions with fewer patches containing clear edges or linear features, most error measures (mean square error, signal to noise ratio, peak signal to noise ratio, perceptual error measure) improve, whereas there is loss in systems where edges occur. This is due to the fact that the current factorised prior does not contain edges and features as part of its model. For fuller comparisons with other techniques see [2].

5 Full Model

As the true pixel data is not available for the border pixels, the model just described is not directly useful. However it can be incorporated into a Markov Random Field model

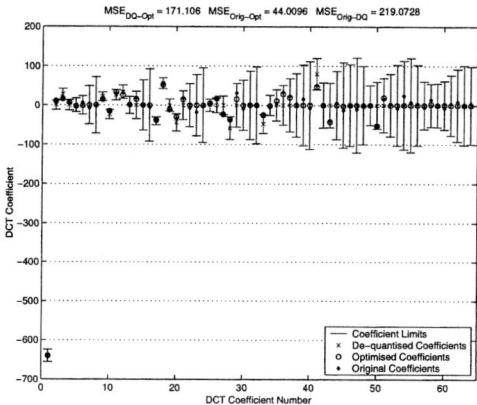

Fig. 5. Comparison of the different DCT coefficients.

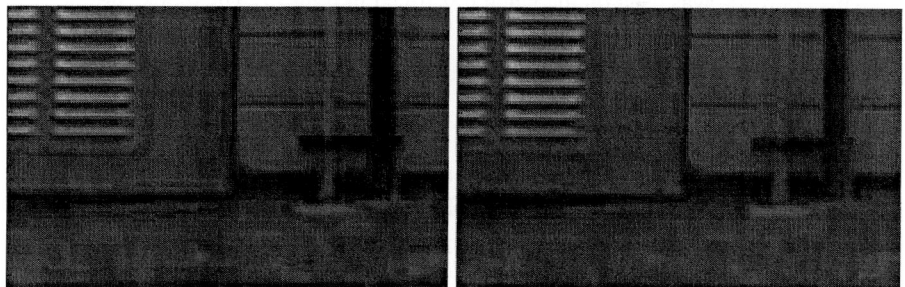

Reconstructed using quantised coefficients   Reconstructed using optimised coefficients

Fig. 6. Results on door scene from 3.

which can then be optimised using an iterative checkerboard approach. The simplest model is to use a model of the form

$$P(X) \propto \prod_i P(X_i) \prod_{(i,j) \in A, k} P(X_i^k - X_j^k) \qquad (2)$$

where X_i are the pixel values of the ith image patch and X_i^s is the kth border pixel of the ith patch, and A is the set of indices (a, b) of adjacent image patches. Note that $P(X_i)$ and $P(X_i^k - X_j^k)$ are now clique potentials and not probability distributions. This model can be optimised using an iterative checkerboard scheme. First the coefficients of the 'black' coloured patches are fixed and $\prod_i P(X_i) \prod_{i \in W, j \in A(i), k} P(X_i^k - X_j^k)$ is optimised, for W denoting the indices of the 'white' patches and $A(i)$ the adjacent patches to patch i. Then the white patches are fixed to their optimised values and the corresponding equation for the black patches is optimised. This process is repeated until a suitable convergence criterion is satisfied. Due to the symmetry of the $P(X_i^k - X_j^k)$, each step is guaranteed to increase the global $P(X)$. Note each $P(X_i)$ is implicitly given by the

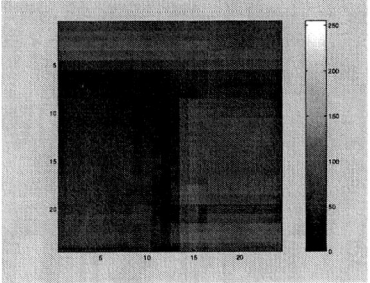 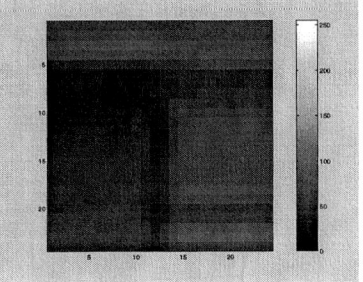

Reconstructed using quantised coefficients. Reconstructed using optimised coefficients.

Fig. 7. Results of checkerboard iteration on 3x3 block scene.

prior over DCT coefficients and the quantised coefficients. Again the optimisation was initialised at the known quantised values.

This approach was used on the patch illustrated in figure 7. The blocky artefacts of the quantised coefficients are significantly reduced.

6 Continued Work

Blockiness artefacts are only one of the problems of compressed images. More significant issues arise from within block edges. However the process of allowing freedom to choose the coefficients from within the range of values given by the quantised coefficients can be used in conjunction with any other information about the image patches. This might include more general patch priors than those given by factorised coefficients. We are currently working on a fuller quantitative analysis of these techniques.

One area of interest is that the artefacts of jpeg are often serious problems in super-resolution. [3] provides a good example of this. As this work places jpeg modelling within a probabilistic framework, we are working on ways to combine it directly with a number of super-resolution methods such as [6].

Acknowledgements

Amos Storkey thanks Microsoft Research, Cambridge for his fellowship.

References

1. Albert J. Ahumada and Rensheng Horng. De-blocking dct compressed images. In *Human Vision, Visual Proc. and Digital Disp. V, SPIE Proc.*, volume 2179, pages 109–116, 1994.
2. M. Allan. Probabilistic methods for improving image decoding. Master's thesis, Division of Informatics, University of Edinburgh, 5 Forrest Hill, Edinburgh, EH1 2QL, UK, 2003.
3. W. T. Freeman, T. R. Jones, and E. C. Pasztor. Example-based super-resolution. *IEEE Computer Graphics and Applications*, 2002.
4. John Lazzaro and John Wawrzynek. Jpeg quality transcoding using neural networks trained with a perceptual error measure. In *Neural Computation*, volume 11, pages 267–296, 1999.

5. M. Miyahara, K. Kotani, and V.R. Algazi. Objective picture quality scale (pqs) for image coding. In *International Conference on Image Processing*, volume 3, 1995.
6. A. J. Storkey. Dynamic structure super-resolution. In S. Thrun S. Becker and K. Obermayer, editors, *Advances in Neural Information Processing Systems 15 (NIPS2002)*, pages 1295–1302. MIT Press, 2003.
7. J.H. van Hateren and A. van der Schaaf. Independent component filters of natural images compared with simple cells in primary visual cortex. In *R.Soc.Lon.B*, pages 359–366, 1998.
8. Andrew B. Watson. Dctune: A technique for visual optimisation of dct quantisation matrices for individual images. In *Society for Information Display Digest of Technical Papers*, volume XXIV, pages 946–949, 1993.

Partial Discharge Classification Through Wavelet Packets of Their Modulated Ultrasonic Emission

Mazen Abdel-Salam[1], Yassin M.Y. Hasan[1],
Mohammed Sayed[2], and Salah Abdel-Sattar[1]

[1] Electrical Engineering Dept., Assiut University, Assiut, Egypt
{mazen,ymyhasan}@aun.edu.eg
[2] Upper Egypt Electricity Production Company, Assiut, Egypt

Abstract. Locating and classifying partial discharge due to sharp-edges, polluted insulators and loose-contacts in power systems significantly reduce the outage time, impending failure, equipment damage and supply interruption. In this paper, based on wavelet packets features of their modulated ultrasound emissions, an efficient novel scheme for neural network recognition of partial discharges is proposed. The employed preprocessing, wavelet features and near-optimally sized network led to successful classification up to 100%, particularly when longer duration signals are processed.

1 Introduction

Partial discharge as weak points in electrical power networks include sharp-edges, polluted insulators and loose-contacts [1]. In general, the basic weak points (sharp-edges, baby-arcs and loose-contacts) generate audio noise, radio interference complaints and/or ultrasonic noise emissions. Hence, there are more than one sensor type to detect and locate them [2-4].

The ability to locate and identify the weak points guides the maintenance staff to take a proper action such as hot washing of lines and insulators, short-circuiting the gaps by better bonding or tightening the connections, and by smoothening the coronating points to suppress corona activity. Thus, major reduction in the outage time, impending failure, equipment damage and supply interruption can be attained.

Several techniques for partial discharge identification [4,5] using artificial neural network (ANN) have been proposed based on various feature extraction methods such a segmented time domain data compression [6] and short duration Fourier transform [7]. Alternatively, the wavelet transform (WT) [8], a mathematical tool developed in the 1980s, has been recently applied to many problems in power systems, such as analysis and visualization of electrical transients [9].

This paper uses the wavelet packets for feature extraction of modulated versions of the different ultrasound emissions from the basic weak points. The rest of the paper is organized as follows: Section 2 presents background on WT and ANN. Section 3 introduces the proposed methodology. Then, Section 4 gives details on the experimental set-up and design of the ANN used. Next, Section 5 presents results and discussion. Finally, Section 6 gives the conclusion.

2 Background

The WT represents an efficient technique for feature extraction of non-stationary signals due to its crucial properties, such as good time-frequency localization, computational efficiency, multi-resolution analysis and energy compaction as well as decorrelation capabilities [8]. In wavelet analysis, the signal $f(t)$ looks like as a signal passing through 2 perfect reconstruction quadrature mirror filters followed by down sampling by a factor of 2 [8]. Multiple levels of the WT involves successively decomposing the low pass band only at each level. Alternatively, decomposing both the low and high bands of the transformed signal at all levels of the wavelet tree, results in the wavelet packets (WP) [8,11] which allows higher resolution at high frequencies.

Inspired by biological nervous systems, ANNs are composed of interconnected simple processing elements (neurons). A weighted sum of the neuron's inputs subjected to a linear or nonlinear (typically sigmoid-shaped) activation function constitutes an artificial neuron. ANNs are trained to perform pattern recognition tasks by adjusting the (synaptic) weights of the connections[10] using a representative training set of input feature vectors and their corresponding target vectors. The generalization capability of a neural network is evaluated by its ability to recognize patterns which were not encountered during the training stage. The multilayer perceptron (MLP) is a feed-forward ANN (FFANN) with one input layer, one or more hidden layers and one output layer. The power of MLP comes from the theory that states: 2-layer FFANN with sufficiently many neurons in the single hidden layer is sufficient to classify linearly non-separable sets [10,12,13].

3 Proposed Methodology

An ANN pattern recognition scheme is developed to identify the basic weak points based on WP features. So, the proposed methodology consists of three main stages: Sensing of weak points and preprocessing, feature extraction using WP and weak point discrimination using ANN.

The set used for sensing weak points in power systems is the ultraprobe2000 set, which detects ultrasonic frequencies between 20kHz and 100kHz. The optimum frequency corresponds to the maximum reading is 32kHz [14].

To provide more reliable and robust features to the classification stage, the sections of the detected signal are preprocessed. Each 16384-sample windowed section x of the sensed signals is preprocessed as follows:

a Elimination of any DC distortion in the processed section x, to get a zero-mean signal x_1.
b Low pass filtering followed by down sampling x_1 using a half-band low pass filter to obtain a smoothed signal x_2.
c Power normalization of x_2 to get a unity power signal $x_n = x_2 / m_2(x_2)^{1/2}$, where $m_2(x_2)$ denotes the estimated 2nd order central moment of x_2, mainly to avoid the undesirable effects of parameters such as the applied voltage value, distance, sensitivity of the Ultraprobe set, relative position/orientation,….etc. which may badly affect the classification decision.

Three-level WP decomposition with a Daubechies' mother function, has been applied to x_n. This chosen size of the wavelet tree was experimentally sufficient to result in discriminating features as illustrated later. The following features are used to constitute a 17×1 feature vector:

- The mean of the absolute value of x_n, i.e. $m_1(|x_n|)$. This feature mainly emphasizes the time diversity of weak point waveforms.
- The 2nd order central moments of the leaves' wavelets coefficients of the wavelet tree, providing information on the power distribution among the leaves of the tree.
- The 3rd order central moments of the wavelet coefficients of the leaves of the wavelet tree which are added to improve the classification as mentioned later.

Extracted features are initially used to train a 2-layer MLP using error back-propagation (BP) algorithm [10]. Then the trained ANN is used in weak points recognition.

4 Experimental Set-Up and Neural Network Design

The expected weak points in the high voltage power network including sharp-edges, polluted insulators and loose-contacts were simulated and stressed in the laboratory by AC voltage, Fig. 1. Precautions have been made to avoid the occurrence of partial discharge on high voltage connections. This is why all circuit connections were made from thick straight conductors with copper spheres at ends. In case of sharp-edge weak point, different sharp-edges with different edge diameters (for example 0.5mm, 1mm and 1.8mm) were used to make sure that the obtained neural network is more general irrespective of the sharpness of weak point. Different applied voltage values were attempted starting from 10kV until 105kV.

A total of 5100 data sections of each weak point type have been recorded (during a long period, over 10 months, and at various weather conditions: atmospheric temperature and humidity percentage) and preprocessed as discussed in Section 3. Then, their 5100 17x1 feature vectors are computed as explained in Section 3.

To design a 2-layer FFANN having a 17-M-3 structure, i.e., 17 inputs, M hidden neurons and 3 output neurons, we first set the desired output (Target) corresponding to the various weak point types to be {+1 -1 -1}, {-1 +1 -1} and {-1 -1 +1} for sharp-edge, baby-arc, loose-contact weak points, respectively.

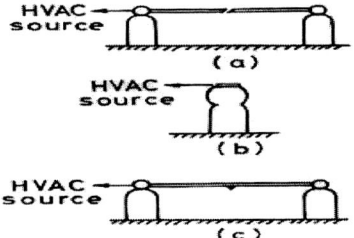

Fig. 1. Laboratory simulation of different weak points.
(a) Loose contact (b) Polluted insulator. (c) Sharp edge.

Then, to properly size the hidden layer, we adopted a network growth procedure guided by both the network's training and validation performance (as a good estimate of it generalization capabilities). The procedure finds the experimentally optimum number of hidden neurons as follows: Disjoint training and validation sets constituting 50% and 20% of the overall data set, respectively, have been uniformly randomly selected. Then, starting with a small number (4 neurons), the number of hidden neurons has been successively incremented and each new network structure has been trained using error BP algorithm. To conditionally stop the training procedure, a training performance goal 0f 0.01 (mean square error) and 350 maximum number of epochs have been chosen. The rates of correctly classified validation patterns have been computed for the trained ANN. When the average rate of correct validation classification manifested no further improvement or even started going down, we stopped enlarging the size of the hidden layer. The procedure has been repeated 12 times. On the average, it has been experimentally found that learned networks with a number of hidden neurons > 15, did not significantly improve the rate of the correctly classified validation patterns. Consequently, 15 hidden neurons are used.

After optimally choosing the ANN structure (17-15-3), 66% of the data sections (10098 sections, 3366 for each weak point type and 16384 samples each) were uniformly randomly selected and used to train the selected structure.

5 Results and Discussion

Table 1 summarizes the average (over 10 random experiments) testing results (±standard deviation) of successfully trained ANNs using a total of 5202 sections; 1734 representing sharp-edge weak points, 1734 representing baby-arc weak points and 1734 representing loose-contact weak points. Fig. 2 depicts the simulation results when concatenating the feature vectors of the three weak points and sequentially applying the 5202 17×1 feature vectors to the trained ANN. To get robust and more reliable network decisions, we considered the outputs laying in between -0.3 and 0.3 as zero, meaning that the ANN "cannot identify" the weak point type. In case of sharp-edge weak point, 97.23 % identification rate was obtained, indicating that 1686 out of 1734 were recognized correctly. In case of baby-arc weak point, 96.19 % identification rate was obtained, indicating that 1668 out of 1734 were recognized correctly. In case of loose-contact weak point, 96.42 % identification rate was obtained, indicating that 1672 out of 1734 were recognized correctly.

It should be mentioned that when the 3rd order central moments were excluded from the feature vector (i.e., using only 9×1 vectors) the generalization capabilities markedly degraded with a ~15% drop in the average correct classification rate. On the other hand, consistent identification rate improvement and noticeable reduction in the training time have been observed when using $|x_n|-m_1(|x_n|)$, i.e., a zero-mean version of the rectified normalized signal $|x_n|$ instead of x_n as an input to the wavelet packets analysis stage. Specifically, the identification rate has been increased to 98.56 % for sharp-edge weak points, 99.08 % for baby-arc weak points, and 99.08 % for loose-contact weak points. In general, it has been experimentally verified that increasing the acquisition time into ≥ 30sec. (i.e. ≥ 14 consecutive sections), individually processing each section and then classifying the weak point based on majority voting over the ANN's responses of all sections, consistently resulted in 100% correct classifications.

Table 1. The details of weak points data used for ANN training/testing and results.

Weak point type		Sharp-edge	Baby-Arcs	Loose-contact
Total Data	Sections	5100	5100	5100
Data Used For Training	Sections	3366	3366	3366
	%	66	66	66
Data Used For Testing	Sections	1734	1734	1734
	%	34	34	34
Recognized Data	Sections	1686 ± 9.037	1668 ± 9.39	1672 ± 10.05
	%	97.23 ± 0.52	96.19 ± 0.54	96.42 ± 0.6
Error	%	0.39	2.51	2.87
Cannot be Identified	%	2.35	1.25	0.66

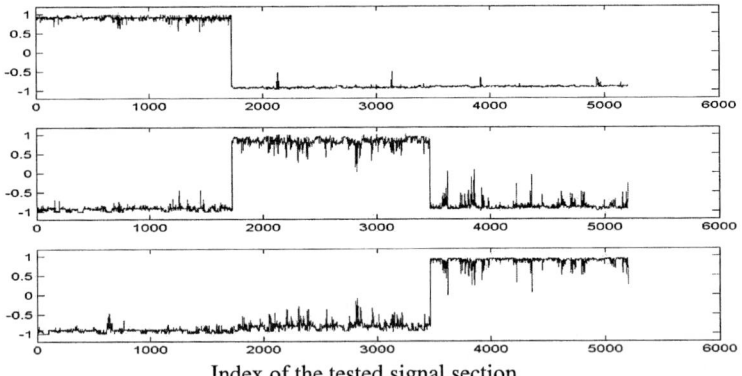

Index of the tested signal section

Fig. 2. ANN response for Sharp-edge, Baby-arcs and Loose-contact. Sharp-edge: 1 → 1734, Baby-arc: 1735 → 3468, Loose-contact: 469 → 5202 From top to bottom, responses of the 1st, 2nd and 3rd output neurons.

6 Conclusion

The proposed ANN recognition of weak points in power systems based on wavelet packets features is experimentally proved to be effective with very high average identification rates. These rates are further improved and the training time is reduced when the wavelet analysis is done for full-wave rectified normalized version of the detected signals. So, we have been currently investigating the recognition of additional weak points such as multiple sharp-edges and combined baby-arcs and sharp-edges. Preliminary results are encouraging.

References

1. Naidu, S., Kamaraju, V.: High Voltage Engineering. McGraw-Hill, New York (1995)
2. Popeck, A., Knapp, R.F.: Measurement and Analysis of Audible Noise from Operating 765 kV Transmission Lines. IEEE Trans. on Power Apparatus and Systems, Vol.100, No.4 (1981) 2138-2148
3. Golinski, J., Malewski, R., Train, D.: Measurements of RIV on Large EHV Apparatus in High Voltage Laboratory. IEEE Trans. on power Apparatus and Systems, Vol.98, No.3 (1979) 817-822
4. Abedel-salam, M., et. al.: Early Detection of Weak Points in MEEC Electrical Power Network. 17^{Th} Int. CIRED Conf. on Electricity Dist., Barcelona (2003)
5. Ghirelli, L.: Acoustical Method for Partial Discharge Detection in High Voltage Capacitors. Int. conference of partial discharges, Canterbury, UK (1993) 92-93
6. Werle, P., Akbari, A., Borsi, H., Gockenbach, E.: Partial Discharge Localization on Power Transformers Using Neural Networks Combined with Sectional Winding Transfer Functions as Knowledge Base. IEEE Proc. Int. Conf. on Properties and Application of Dielectric Materials, Nagoya/Japan (2003) 1154 – 1157
7. Tian, Y., Lewin, P.L., Davies, A.E., Sutton, S.J., Swingler, S.G.: Application of Acoustic Emission Techniques and Artificial Neural Networks to Partial Discharge Classification IEEE Int. Symp. on Electrical Insulation, Boston, MA, USA (2002)
8. Burrus, C.S., Gopinath, R.A., Guo, H.: Introduction to Wavelets and Wavelet Transforms. Prentice Hall, New Jersey (1998)
9. Cornforth, D., Middleton, R.H., Tusek, D.J: Visualisation of Electrical Transients Using The Wavelet Transform. The Int. Conf. on Advances in Intelligent Systems: Theory and Applications, Canberra, Australia (2000)
10. Looney, C.G.: Pattern Recognition Using Neural Networks. Oxford, (1997)
11. Coifman, R.R., Wickerhauser, M.V.: Entropy-Based Algorithms for Best Basis Selection. IEEE Trans. On Information Theory, Vol.38, No.2 (1992) 713-718
12. Musavi, M.T., Chan, K.H., Hummels, D.M., Kalanti, K.: "On The Generalization Ability of Neural Network Classifier. IEEE Trans. Pattern Analysis and Machine Intelligence, Vol.16, No.6 (1994) 659-663
13. Gori, M., Scarselli, F.: Are Multilayer Perceptrons Adequate for Pattern Recognition and Verification. IEEE Trans. Pattern Anal. Mach. Intel.., Vol.20, No.11 (1998) 1121-1132
14. Ultraprobe-2000.: A product manufactured by UE Systems. USA (Available Online: http://www.uesystems.com)

A Hybrid Optimization Method of Multi-objective Genetic Algorithm (MOGA) and K-Nearest Neighbor (KNN) Classifier for Hydrological Model Calibration

Yang Liu, Soon-Thiam Khu, and Dragon Savic

Department of Engineering, Exeter University, Exeter, EX4 4QF, UK
{Yang.Liu,S.T.Khu,D.Savic}@exeter.ac.uk

Abstract. The MOGA is used as automatic calibration method for a wide range of water and environmental simulation models. The task of estimating the entire Pareto set requires a large number of fitness evaluations in a standard MOGA optimization process. However, it's very time consuming to obtain a value of objective functions in many real engineering problems. We propose a unique hybrid method of MOGA and KNN classifier to reduce the number of actual fitness evaluations. The test results for multi-objective calibration show that the proposed method only requires about 30% of actual fitness evaluations of the MOGA.

1 Introduction

Calibration is the process of modifying the input parameters to a numerical model until the output from the model matches an observed set of data [1]. More recently, the emphasis is on the inclusion of two or more model performance measures for automatic calibration i.e. multi-objective calibration [2]. Genetic algorithm has proved to be successful in calibrating hydrologic models [3], [4], [5]. The limitation of using GA is its expensive computational requirement [4], [5]. The MOGA optimization process needs to evaluate the fitness function thousands of times before converging towards the Pareto set. It is immediately apparent to users of automatic calibration that if one can reduce the number of function calls, the time required for calibration will be reduced.

A new approach using an innovative hybridisation of MOGA and KNN classifier is proposed for automatic calibration of numerical models. Training data are produced from early generations of the MOGA, and the KNN classifier is used to predict rank or level for each solution. The proposed method is used to calibrate a popular rain-runoff model, MIKE11/NAM, applied to a Danish catchment.

2 NAM Model and Objection Functions

The model used in this study is the NAM rainfall-runoff model that forms of the rainfall-runoff module of the MIKE 11 river modelling system [1]. The calibration parameters used are the same as those from [1]. This catchment has an area of 130km², an average rainfall of 710 mm/year and an average discharge of 240 mm/year. The catchment is dominated by clayey soils, implying a relatively flashy flow regime. For the calibration, a 5-year period (1 Jan. 1984–31 Dec. 1988) was used where daily data of precipitation, potential evapotranspiration, mean temperature, and catchment runoff are available. Two of objective functions are used in this study and are given as follows:

Average Root Mean Squared-Error (RMSE) of low flow Events:

$$F_1(\theta) = \frac{1}{M_l} \sum_{j=1}^{M_l} \left[\frac{1}{n_j} \sum_{i=1}^{n_j} [Q_{obs,i} - Q_{sim,i}(\theta)]^2 \right]^{1/2} \qquad (1)$$

Average Root Mean Squared-Error (RMSE) of peak flow Events:

$$F_2(\theta) = \frac{1}{M_p} \sum_{j=1}^{M_p} \left[\frac{1}{n_j} \sum_{i=1}^{n_j} [Q_{obs,i} - Q_{sim,i}(\theta)]^2 \right]^{1/2} \qquad (2)$$

In Eqs. (1)–(2), $Q_{obs,i}$ is the observed discharge at time i, $Q_{sim,i}$ is the simulated discharge, M_p is the number of peak flow events, M_l is the number of low flow events, n_j is the number of time steps in peak/low event no. j, and θ is the set of model parameters to be calibrated. Peak flow events were defined as periods with flow above a threshold value of 4.0 m³/s, and low flow events were defined as periods with flow below 0.5 m³/s.

3 Model Calibration

Calibration is the process of modifying the input parameters to a numerical model until the output from the model matches an observed set of data. The parameters of such model cannot, in general, be obtained directly from measurable quantities of catchment characteristics, and hence model calibration is needed [1], [2].

4 Multi-objective Genetic Algorithm (MOGA)

The previous study demonstrates that MOGA method is an effective and efficient search algorithm [2], [6]. Contrary to single-objective problems, multi-objective problems have a set of alternative solutions. It is not possible to determine objectively among such solutions which one is the best, and such solutions are called Pareto, non-dominated, non-inferior, or efficient solutions [2], [7]. We have implemented a fast and elitist multi-objective genetic algorithm called the Non-Dominated Sorting Genetic Algorithm II (NSGA-II) [7]. The NSGA-II algorithm may be stated as follows:

1. Create a random parent population of size N;
2. Sort the population based on the nondomination;
3. Assign each solution a fitness (or rank) equal to its nondomination level (minimization of fitness is assumed);
4. Use the usual binary tournament selection, recombination, and mutation operators to create a offspring population of size N;

5. Combine the offspring and parent population to form extended population of size 2N;
6. Sort the extended population based on nodomination;
7. Fill new population of size N with the individuals from the sorting fronts starting from the best;
8. Invoke the crowded-comparison operator to ensure diversity if a front can only partially fill the next generation (This strategy is called "niching") ;
9. Repeat the steps (2) to (8) until the stopping criterion is met.

5 K-Nearest Neighbor Classifier

There are many nonlinear classification methods such as artificial neural networks (ANN), support vector machine (SVM) and KNN classifier. Unlike other common classifiers, a KNN classifier stores all of the training samples and does not build a classifier ahead of time until a new sample needs to be classified, and it is extremely simple to implement [8],[9]. When given a new sample, a KNN classifier searches the training space for the k training samples that are closest to the new sample. The new sample is assigned the most common class among the k nearest neighbors [8]. In this experiment, the new sample is assigned the same rank of the training sample that is closest to it in training space. Euclidean distance is used to measure the distance from one class sample to another [9].

6 A Hybrid Optimization Method of NSGA and KNN Classifier

We propose a dynamic learning approach to update KNN and correct the NSGA's converging route. The hybrid algorithm (NSGA-KNN) is presented below and illustrated in Figure1:

1. Run the NSGA-II for g number of generations of population size, p; Compute the initial training samples size $s = p \times g$;
2. If the current generation $c > g$, sort these s points according to nondomination;
3. Assign a prediction rank to each solution using KNN classifier instead of running simulation model and then sort the new population based on prediction ranks in descending order (Minimization of fitness is assumed);
4. Select n best solutions in the new population and evaluate the true fitness values using simulation model;
5. Sort these $s = s + n$ points according to nondominatin and record ranks for these n points;
6. Replace these previous n prediction ranks (step (3)) with true ranks (step (5));
7. Use $s = s + n$ points as new training samples to update KNN for next generation;
8. Perform NSGA operations (selection, crossover, mutation and elitist strategy) without "niching" ;
9. Repeat the steps (2) to (8) until the stopping criterion is met.

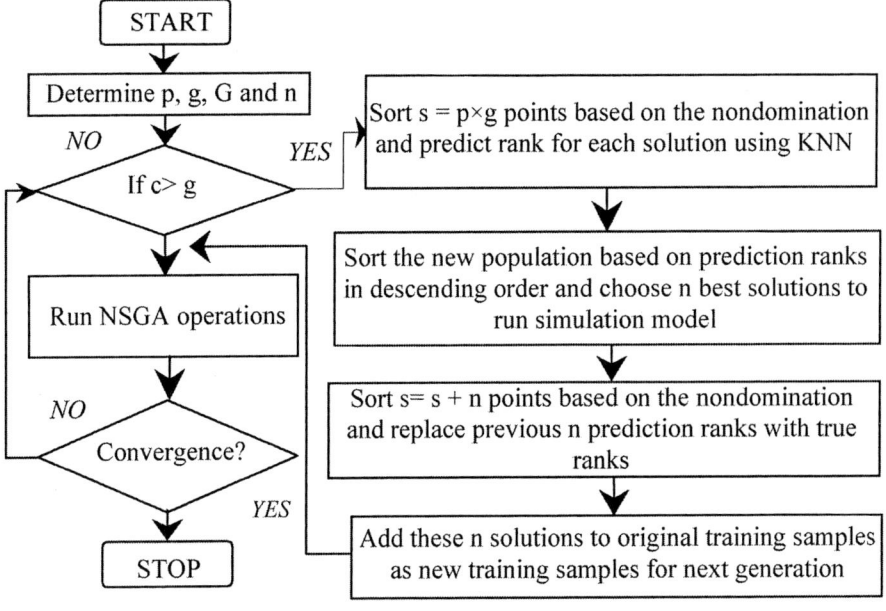

Fig. 1. Flowchart of NSGA-KNN method.

7 Experimental Results

The relevant experiment parameters using the NSGA-KNN and NSGA for NAM model calibration are suggested in Table 1. Preliminary optimization runs showed that entire population converged towards the optimal Pareto set after about 10,000 evaluations. Thus, for each test, a maximum number of model evaluations equal to 10,000 were employed as a stopping criterion and a population of p=100 was used. Hence, the number of simulation runs for the test function using the hybrid method can be calculated by:

$$p \times g + n \times (G - g)$$
$$= 100 \times 10 + 20 \times (100 - 10) = 2800$$
(3)

where G is the total number of generations.

Table 1. Experiment parameters of the NSGA-KNN and NSGA calibration.

Parameter	p	g	G	n	k
Recommended value	100	10	100	20	1

Fig. 2 showed that the NSGA-KNN gave us close Pareto front as the NSGA's after 100 generations and it only required about 30% simulation runs of the NSGA. The KNN can provide more prediction accuracy when dynamically update it. The parame-

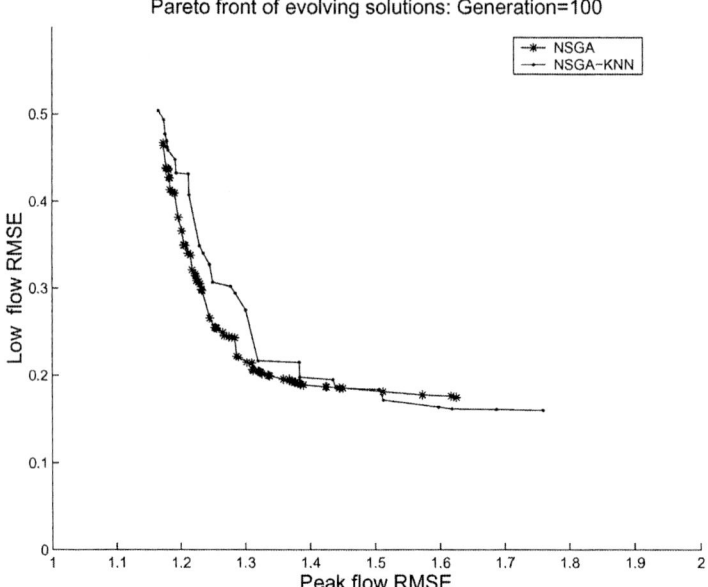

Fig. 2. Pareto fronts using NSGA-KNN and NSGA for NAM model calibration.

ter of k=1 was found to provide best result in previous sensitivity analysis. The more simulation runs will be called to converge towards the optimal Pareto set using the NSGA-KNN whatever we increase (n>20) or decrease (n<20) the parameter value of n. The limitation of using the NSGA-KNN is that the Pareto front is smaller than the NSGA's because the NSGA-KNN is an approximation optimization model.

8 Conclusion

The hybrid optimization method has been proposed in this paper. By combing KNN, the NSGA saved about 70% of the time consuming fitness evaluations required to solve a test case while still achieving accurate solutions, and this hybrid optimization method probably can be extended to 2-D and 3-D hydrological model calibration problems.

Acknowledgements

The Authors would like to thank ABP Marine Environmental Research Ltd, UK for funding the work as well as DHI water & Environment, Demark for their software support.

References

1. Madsen H.: Automatic calibration of a conceptual rainfall-runoff model using multiple objectives. Journal of Hydrology, Vol. 235, (2000) 276-288
2. Yapo P.O., Gupta H.V., Sorooshian S.: Multi-objective global optimization for hydrologic models. Journal of Hydrology, Vol. 181, (1998) 23-48
3. Wang Q.J.: The genetic algorithm and its application to calibrating conceptual rainfall-runoff models. Journal of Water Resource Research, Vol. 27, (1991) 2467-2471
4. Khu S.T., Liu Y., Madsen H., Savic D.A.: A fast evolutionary-based meta-modeling approach for the calibration of a rainfall-runoff model. The International Environmental Modeling and Software Society Conference (2004)
5. Khu S.T., Liu Y., Madsen H., Savic D.A.: A fast calibration technique using a hybrid Genetic algorithm – neural network approach: application to rainfall - runoff models, the Sixth International Conference of Hydroinformatics (2004)
6. Khu S.T., Madsen H.: A new approach to multi-criteria calibration of rainfall-runoff model. International Conference on Water and Environment: Watershed Hydrology (2003)
7. Deb K., Agrawal S., Pratap A., Meyarivan T.: A fast elitist non-dominated sorting genetic algorithm for multi-objective optimization: NSGA-II. IEEE Transactions on Evolutionary Computation, Vol. 6. No. 2, (2002)182-197
8. Dasarathy B.V.: Nearest-Neighbor Classification Techniques. IEEE Computer Society Press, CA (1991)
9. Beale R., Jackson R.: Neural Computing: An Introduction, Institute of Physics Publishing, London (2001)

Cluster-Based Visualisation of Marketing Data

Paulo J.G. Lisboa[1] and Shail Patel[2]

[1] School of Computing and Mathematical Sciences, John Moores University
Liverpool L3 3BX, England
P.J.G.Lisboa@livjm.ac.uk
http://www.cms.livjm.ac.uk/research/snc/neural.htm
[2] Corporate Research, Unilever R & D, Colworth House, Sharnbrook
Bedford MK44 1LQ, England
Shail.Patel@Unilever.com

Abstract. Marketing data analysis typically aims to gain insights for targeted promotions or, increasingly, to implement collaborative filtering. Ideally, data would be visualised directly. There is a scarcity of methods to visualise the position of individual data points in clusters, mainly because dimensionality reduction is necessary for analysis of high-dimensional data and projective methods tend to merge clusters together. This paper proposes a cluster-based projective method to represent cluster membership, which shows good cluster separation and retains linear relationships in the data. This method is practical for the analysis of large, high-dimensional, databases, with generic applicability beyond marketing studies. Theoretical properties of this non-orthogonal projection are derived and its practical value is demonstrated on real-world data from a web-based retailer, benchmarking with the visualisation of clusters using Sammon and Kohonen maps.

1 Introduction

Market analysis is among a plethora of important applications for visualisation and retrieval in large databases. Increasingly, Marketing data are typically very high dimensional, comprising for instance product categories in shopping-basket analysis, requiring projection to lower-dimensions for their analysis typically using singular-value decomposition [1].

Ideally, the data would be directly visualised but this is possible only for unrealistically small dimensions. Given that marketing data are typically segmented, or clustered, as part of routine analysis, it is worth pursuing visualisation methods which use cluster-based information to visualise individual data points in the context of cluster membership, for instance to see whether a customer is positioned near the core of a segment or at a particular boundary between segments. The validity of this approach will have to be tested against direct mapping of data in sub-spaces of true data space, spanned by covariates for which the data segments. Clearly, if the segments separate in a sub-space then they necessarily separate also in the full-dimensional data space.

The role of clustering is relevant also with regard to current developments in collaborative filtering, for which a prior segmentation can improve accuracy and speed of personalised recommendations by enabling current methods to be applied within appropriate customer segments, rather than to the whole population [2],[3].

Visualisation of high-dimensional data has come a long way since bi-plots, but the new methods have, for various reasons, not found widespread acceptance among marketing practitioners. Two examples of more recent methodologies are Sammon mapping [4] and unsupervised neural networks, in particular Kohonen's Self-Organised Maps (SOM) [5] and Generic Topographic Mapping (GTM) [6],[7]. Shortage of space prevents a detailed discussion of these methods here. Sammon maps and Kohonen's SOM are arguably the most widely used among these algorithms, so they will serve as benchmarks in this study.

This paper defines a non-orthogonal linear map that uses cluster membership to compress high-dimensional databases into a practical low-dimensional projection.

2 Description of the Data

The primary data used in this study comprises shopping-based spending of 37,500 consumers from Swiss web-retailer *Le Shop* aggregated into 16 typical super-market product categories. Cumulative spending profiles were acquired for the period 31st March 1998 to 31st August 2002 and represented as proportional spending across the full 16-dimensional vector. There are 3,324,505 recorded transactions over this period but a significant proportion are from first-time users, i.e. consumers who are new to this retailer. Since we are interested in segmenting persistent patterns of behaviour, these first-time consumers were removed from the data, reducing the data base to the profiles of 20,000 consumers.

3 The Adaptive Resonance Theory Algorithm in Brief

Segmentation was carried out by two methods, k-means clustering and Adaptive Resonance Theory (ART) models [8]. The ART-2 algorithm applies to Euclidean normalised data positive definite continuous data. This is ideally suitable for shopping basket analysis as there is no loss of information during normalisation of proportion of spending, which is simply mapped the outer surface of a hyper-pyramid onto the hyper-sphere fitted to its vertices.

In normalised data of dimensionality d, there is a trivial correspondence between Euclidean distance and projective angle, since

$$\left|\left(\hat{x}-\hat{p}\right)\right|^2 = 2.\left(1-\hat{x}.\hat{p}\right) = 2.(1-\cos(\theta)) \qquad (1)$$

where is the θ angle between the normalised vectors. In addition to controlling for this angle using the so-called vigilance parameter, the ART algorithm as a further test, namely

$$\hat{x}.\hat{p} \geq \alpha.\sum_{i=1}^{d}\hat{x}_i \quad \text{i.e.} \quad \hat{x}.\hat{p} \geq \alpha.\sqrt{d}.\left(\hat{x}.\hat{1}_d\right) \qquad (2)$$

which when $\alpha = 1/\sqrt{d}$ only permits vectors to associated with prototypes that are nearer than the vector of ones which marks main diagonals in a unit hypercube. This feature of the algorithm forces it to act as a bi-sector, with the very useful consequence that prototypes are preferentially located near the main axis, that is to say, producing clusters, or segments, with profiles that are easier to interpret because they have low entropy, comprising a few very high attributes in a background that is clutter free.

4 Method for Cluster-Based Visualisation

Consider data points $\underline{x}_i$ with i=1:n segmented into groups with prototype $\underline{p}_j$ with j=1:n. For the purpose of this paper there is no need to dwell on the difference between clustering and segmentation, as it is immaterial whether or not there is a significant gap between the segments, as would normally be expected to be the case between identifiable clusters. Segments may comprise a partition of a continuous manifold, and indeed this is the case for these data, so long as the segments do not overlap.

A generic approach to visualise membership of one from n clusters, while preserving local neighbourhood relationships in the data structure is by means of the following linear projection

$$\rho(\underline{x}_i) = \sum_{j=1}^{n_c} \left(\underline{x}_i \cdot \underline{p}_j \right) \underline{b}_j \qquad (3)$$

where $\underline{b}_j$ is a suitable low-dimensional representation of the prototype for segment j, taken in this paper to be the eigenvectors of the first three principal components of the sub-space spanned by the data prototypes. In this example, the data and hence the six cluster prototypes are 16-D. Projecting the data onto the prototypes generates a 6-D subspace of which the three eigenvectors with the largest eigenvalues describe 79% of the variance.

5 Mathematical Features of Visualisation Through Cluster-Based Projections

Let the $\underline{x}, \underline{p}$ represent a data point and the nearest cluster prototype to it in data space, and let $\underline{a}, \underline{b}$ denote their corresponding 3-D projections using eq. (3). By definition, we have

$$\frac{\underset{\sim}{a}.\underset{\sim}{b}_k}{\left|\underset{\sim}{a}\right|\left|\underset{\sim}{b}_k\right|} = \frac{\sum_{j=1}^{n_c}\left(\underset{\sim}{x}.\underset{\sim}{p}_j\right)\underset{\sim j}{b}.\underset{\sim k}{b}}{\sqrt{\sum_{\{i,j\}=1}^{n_c}\left(\underset{\sim}{x}.\underset{\sim}{p}_i\right)\left(\underset{\sim}{x}.\underset{\sim}{p}_j\right)\underset{\sim i}{b}.\underset{\sim j}{b}\left|\underset{\sim}{b}_k\right|}} \quad (4)$$

$$\approx 1 - \frac{1}{2}\cdot\frac{\sum_{\{i,j\}\neq k}^{n_c}\left(\underset{\sim}{x}.\underset{\sim}{p}_i\right)\left(\underset{\sim}{x}.\underset{\sim}{p}_j\right)\underset{\sim i}{b}.\underset{\sim j}{b}}{\left(\underset{\sim}{x}.\underset{\sim}{p}_k\right)^2\left|\underset{\sim}{b}_k\right|^2} \; up\;to\;O \sim \left(\frac{\sum_{j\neq k}^{n_c}\left(\underset{\sim}{x}.\underset{\sim}{p}_j\right)\underset{\sim j}{b}.\underset{\sim k}{b}}{\left(\underset{\sim}{x}.\underset{\sim}{p}_k\right)\left|\underset{\sim}{b}_k\right|^2}\right)^m$$

where $m \geq 2$. Eq. (4) suggests that the if the data points tend to align with the prototypes for their assigned clusters in data-space, then this alignment should be present also in the 3-D projective space. This can be determined empirically with the results shown in Figs. 1 and 2.

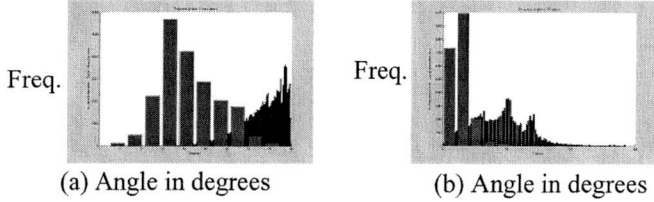

(a) Angle in degrees   (b) Angle in degrees

Fig. 1. Projection angles within- *(broad bars)* and out-of-class *(thin bars)* for ART clusters *(a)* in data space and *(b)* in the 3D projective space generated by the cluster prototypes. Note that in each projection approximately 90% of the data project closer to the corresponding cluster prototype than to the other cluster prototypes, within 60^0 in *(a)* and $20°$ in *(b)*.

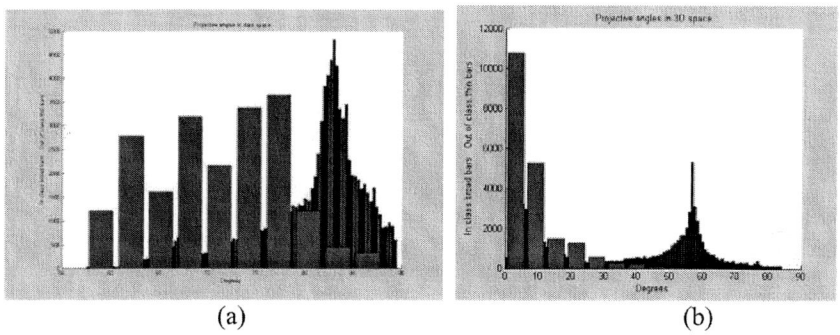

(a)   (b)

Fig. 2. Projection statistics as above, for k-means clustering. The separation between histograms is not as good as for the ART clusters, in particular generating a strongly bi-modal distribution in 3D projective space.

This map is clearly not an orthogonal expansion as the bases vectors $\underset{\sim}{b_j}$ are not constrained by orthogonality. However, the linearity of the map has the consequence that co-linear points in the full-dimensional data space remain co-linear after this projection, i.e.

$$\rho\left(\varepsilon.x_a +(1-\varepsilon).x_b\right)=\varepsilon.\rho\left(x_a\right)+(1-\varepsilon).\rho\left(x_b\right). \tag{5}$$

Therefore, a path joining two points in data-space in a straight line as $0 \leq \varepsilon \leq 1$ will map onto a straight line in the projective space, thus preserving some of the original structure of the data. It clearly does not follow that nearby points in the projective space are near in the data, though the converse necessarily applies.

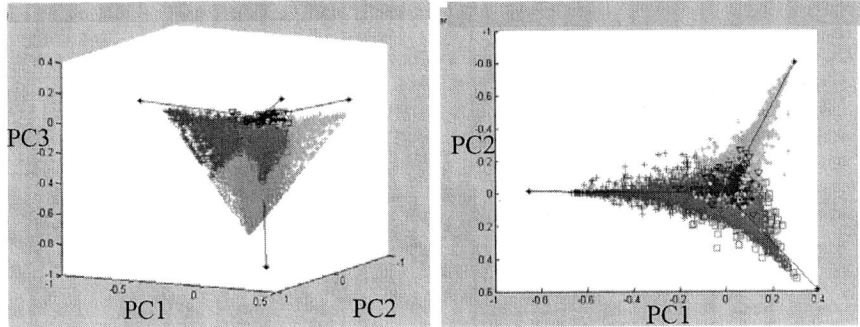

Fig. 3. Two views of 20k shopping baskets from a web-based supermarket segmented using ART-2 with cluster-based visualization, showing the basis vectors as lines linked to stars.

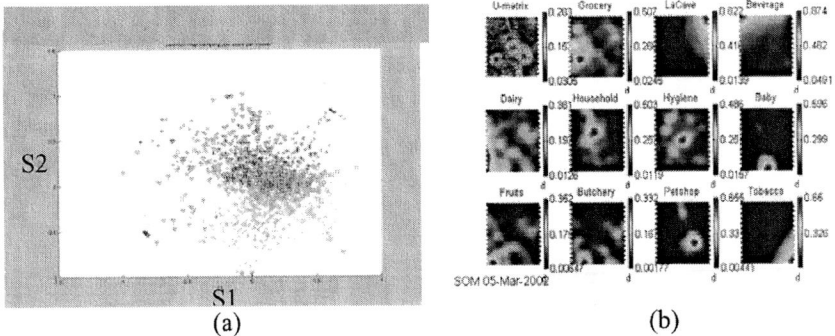

Fig. 4. Projection onto the first two principal components of the same data, with the same labels as in Fig. 1, using *(a)* Sammon mapping and *(b)* and attribute map for a Kohonen-SOM.

6 Empirical Comparison of Clustering Methods

The direct mapping of proximal data onto nearby points in the cluster-based projection defined by equation (3) implies that within-segment distances in full-dimensional space will, in the projective space, remain closer than between-segment distances.

This opens-up the possibility of identification of the data by reference to the relative position of segment prototypes, but the issue remains of whether the segment identity will be apparent at a sufficiently low dimension to allow direct visualisation. Results from segmentation with ART are shown in Fig. 3. Three more usual visualisation methods are principal component projections, Sammon maps and Kohonen's SOM, shown in Fig. 4. Neither of these representations hark back to the true structure of the data, as shown in Fig. 5.

7 Conclusions

A cluster-based linear projection was proposed for direct visualisation of high-dimensional data by reference to segment prototypes. The resulting map is not significantly affected by the addition or removal of a small number of points, as is the case for instance with Sammon mapping, but it is sensitive the segmentation structure imposed on the data.

While the proposed method defines a non-orthogonal projection, it nevertheless preserves the linear structure of the data, while permitting a straightforward identification of segment-based consumer profiles from which strategic insights and algorithms for automated recommendations can be derived.

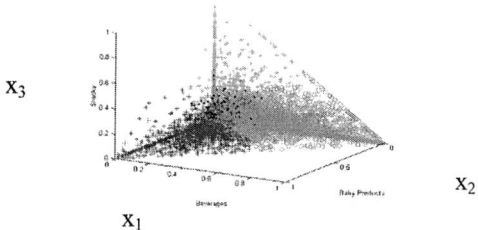

Fig. 5. Direct visualisation of LeShop data using 3 co-ordinates identified from the ART cluster profiles. The out-of-cluster data are represented by filled circles. This map can be compared with the generic cluster projective map in Fig. 3.

Acknowledgments

The authors are grateful to www.LeShop.ch for permission to use their data in this study and to Unilever Corporate Research for clearance to publish these results.

References

1. Gabriel, K. R. (1971). The biplot graphical display of matrices with applications to principal component analysis. *Biometrika*, 58:453–467.
2. Herlocker, J.L., Konstan, J.A., Borchers, A. And Riedl, J. (1999). An algorithmic framework for performing collaborative filtering, Proc. 1999 Conf. of Research and Development in Information Retreival, Berkeley, CA.

3. Sarwar, B., Karypis, G, Konstan, J. and Riedl, J. (2000). Analysis of recommendation algorithms for e-commerce, EC'00 int. conf. of the ACM, October 17-20, Minneapolis, Minnesota.
4. Sammon, J.W. Jr. (1969). A nonlinear mapping for data structure analysis, IEEE Trans. Comput. 18,:401-409.
5. Kohonen, T. (1982). Self-organized formation of topologically correct feature maps. Biological Cybernetics, 43:59 – 69.
6. Bishop, C.M., Svensén, M. and Williams, C.K.I. (1998). GTM: the Generative Topographic Mapping, *Neural Computation,* 10, 1: 215-234.
7. Vellido, A., Lisboa, P.J.G. and El- Deredy, W. (2003) Selective smoothing of the Generative Topographic Mapping, IEEE Transactions on Neural Networks, 14, 4:847-852.
8. Carpenter, G.A. and Grossberg, S. (1991). ART-2: Self-organization of stable category recognition codes for analogue input patterns, *in* Carpenter, G.A. and Grossberg, S. 'Pattern recognition by self-organizing neural networks' MIT Press.

Dynamic Symbolization of Streaming Time Series

Xiaoming Jin, Jianmin Wang, and Jiaguang Sun

School of Software, Tsinghua University
Beijing, 100084, China
xmjin@mail.tsinghua.edu.cn

Abstract. Symbolization of time series is an important preprocessing subroutine for many data mining tasks. However, it is usually difficult, if not impossible, to apply the traditional static symbolization approach on streaming time series, because of either the low efficiency of re-computing the typical sub-series, or the low capability of representing the up-to-date series characters. This paper presents a novel symbolization method, in which the typical sub-series are dynamically adjusted to fit the up-to-date characters of streaming time series. It works in an incremental form without scanning the whole date set. Experiments on data set from stock market justify the superiority of the proposed method over the traditional ones.

Keywords: Data mining, symbolization, stream, time series

1 Introduction

Recently, data mining applications on streaming time series, where new data item is frequently append in the end, have received growing interest in both research and industrial fields [1,2]. Examples of such data include stock price, telecommunication data, weather data, astronomical data, medical data, audio data, and sensor data.

Symbolization of time series is an important preprocessing subroutine for many data mining tasks [3,4], such as rule discovery, classification, prediction, and query by content, etc. Briefly, the problem is to map the time series to a symbol sequence, in which each symbol represents the series movements at a certain time point. For example, the time series of daily stock price can be simply represented by a symbol sequence in which each symbol indicates the daily price movement, then the symbol sequence can be examined for discovering rules such as "the price of stock *A* goes up and falls the next day, then it goes up the third day." Researches on this topic are mainly motivated by two issues: First, analysts are usually interested in high level representation of the time series rather than the primitive quantitative values. Second, the problem of knowledge discovery in symbolic (event) sequences has been studied extensively, whereupon vast algorithms, methods, and data structures had been proposed. Symbolization could enable the applications of these approaches in mining time series data.

Generally, symbolization can be viewed as an explaining process that classifies (or approximates) each individual "atomic" sub-series to the movements of a typical sub-series, e.g. "go up", "oscillate", which is retrieved or defined beforehand. A common approach for generating the typical sub-series is to choose it manually based on the domain experts' analysis and explanation. However, it is usually too expensive to find and explore all sub-series candidates except simple or trivial ones. A more applicable methodology is to generate the typical sub-series automatically based on the data [5]. We only focus on the later in this paper.

Consider the problem of symbolizing streaming time series, the potential series movements are obviously time varying, whereupon the typical sub-series should also be adjusted to be time varying correspondingly. On this occasion, it is usually difficult, if not impossible, to apply the traditional static approach from a practical point of view, because the typical sub-series are based on a snapshot of the time series, and therefore may fail to give a good representation of the new data. Alternatively, the typical sub-series can be re-generated concurrently with the updating process. However, without an incremental method, such re-generation will need all the data scanned, whereupon the time complexity might be extremely poor.

To our knowledge, this problem has not been well considered in the KDD field. In this paper, we present a novel symbolization method, in which the typical sub-series are dynamically adjusted to fit the up-to-date characters of time series. Our approach consists of off-line initialization phase and on-line updating phase. In the first phase, a traditional cluster based method is applied on the initial time series, and the initial typical sub-series are generated. In the second phase, whenever the time series is updated, the typical sub-series are updated concurrently by examining new coming sub-series, and then the symbolic sequence is updated based on the last version of typical sub-series.

The rest of this paper is organized as follows: Section 2 discusses some related work. Section 3 formally defines the problem. Section 4 describes our approach. Section 5 gives the empirical study on the proposed approach. Finally, Section 6 offers some concluding remarks.

2 Related Work

The most intuitive way for symbolizing time series is based on the subjective explanation. A shape definition language was proposed in [6]. In [5], the time series was symbolized using cluster based method for discovering rules with the format "if event A occurs, then event B occurs within time T." This method was then used as a preprocessing subroutine in many works that focus on mining time series [3,4]. Our approach can be viewed as an expansion of this method to facilitate the data mining processes on streaming time series. [7] claimed that the method in [6] was meaningless if the step of sliding window was set to be 1. Actually, this problem could be solved by increasing the step of the sliding windows. Another kind of related work is in the context of dimension reduction [8] where the representation is a combination of transform coefficients instead of symbols.

3 Problem Descriptions

A time series $X=x_1,\ldots,x_N$ is a sequence of real numbers, each number represents a value at a time point. The sub-series $X_s=x_m,\ldots,x_n$ is denoted by $X[m,n]$. And $|X_s|=n-m+1$ denotes the length of X_s.

As we introduced in section 1, the purpose of symbolization is to represent the series behaviors at each individual time point. Then it is intuitive that we first divide the time series to extract the sub-series within each time interval, and then symbolize each sub-series individually by comparing the sub-series with a group of typical sub-series. A *typical sub-series* is a prevalent sub-series that represents a typical form of sub-series movement. Here we use a simple, but prevalent model that is sliding window approach: Given time series X, a sliding window of width w and step k, window sub-series are the contiguous sub-series $W_n=X[nk-k+1, nk-k+w-1]$ extracted sequentially by sliding the window through the time series. Given a time series X and all its window sub-series W_n, symbolization is to convert X to a temporal sequence $S=s_1, s_2, \ldots, s_M$, which is a ordered list of symbols where each symbol S_n comes from a predefined alphabet Σ, and represents the series behavior of the n-th window sub-series W_n.

The motivation of this paper is to facilitate the data mining process on streaming time series, where new data items are generated and appended to the time series frequently. On this occasion, the incremental symbolizing process can be formalized as follows: Whenever a time series X is updated to XY ($XY=x_1,\ldots,x_N,y_1,\ldots,y_K$ is the direct connection of $X=x_1,\ldots,x_N$ and $Y=y_1,\ldots, y_K$), update the representing symbol sequence from S_X to S_XS_Y, where S_X, S_Y correspond to original time series X and the update Y respectively.

There are three sub-problems have to be considered to solve this problem: 1) dynamic update of the typical sub-series, 2) dynamic update of the symbol mapping model corresponded with emerging typical sub-series or vanished ones, and 3) incremental symbolization based on the up-to-date typical sub-series synchronized by 1) and 2).

4 Dynamic Symbolizing Approach

Our dynamic symbolizing approach, which handles streaming time series, is an expansion of the *cluster based approach* [6] that was originally developed for static time series. The key idea is that instead of using the static cluster as the typical sub-series, we dynamically maintain the cluster information. Our approach consists of off-line initializing phase and on-line updating phase. In the first phase, the traditional cluster based method is applied on the initial time series, and the resulting cluster centers are saved as the initial typical sub-series. In the second phase, whenever the time series is updated, both the typical sub-series and the mapping alphabet are updated concurrently by examining only the updated window sub-series, then the symbolic sequence of the updated sub-series is generated based on the up-to-date version of typical sub-series.

For precise representation of the movements, each sub-series W_n was first normalized to $W_n'=(W_n-E(W_n))/D(W_n)$ where $E(W_n)$ and $D(W_n)$ are the mean and the standard deviation of W_n respectively (W_n is defined in section 3).

In the off-line initialization phase, a cluster based method are applied, which can be summarized as follows: first all W_n are normalized to W_n', and then all W_n' are clustered into sets $C_1, \ldots, C_H$. For each cluster C_h, a symbol a_h from alphabet Σ is inducted. Then the symbolic sequence S is obtained by looking for each sub-series W_n' the cluster $C_{j(n)}$ such that $W_n' \in C_{j(n)}$, and using the corresponding symbol $a_{j(n)}$ to represent the sub-series W_n, i.e. $S = a_{j(1)}, a_{j(2)}, \ldots, a_{j(M)}, M = \lfloor N/k \rfloor$.

Here a greedy cluster method is applied as the cluster subroutine. For each W_n', this cluster method first finds the cluster center q that is nearest to W_n'. If the distance is less than a predefined threshold d_{max}, W_n' is added to the cluster whose center is q and the center of q is regenerated as the average of all the sub-series in it, otherwise a new cluster with center W_n' is created. In the above process, Euclidian distance is used as the distance measurement, which is defined as $D(X,Y) = (\sum_n (x_n - y_n)^2)^{1/2}$.

In the on-line updating phase, the cluster information is updated by introducing the new window sub-series and removing the window sub-series which is "old" enough. This process is illustrated in Fig. 1. Here it is assumed that the typical sub-series evolve with the update of time series, whereupon the sub-series that are generated too long ago have minor impact on the current typical sub-series. Hence a threshold *maximal time range*, T_{max}, is introduced in the updating process to constrain the considered sub-series to be relatively "new".

Given original time series X, appended sub-series Y, and maximal time range T_{max}, the detailed updating method is illustrated as follows:

1) Extract all sub-series W_n'' that are contained in clusters, and with the generation time t such that $t < T_{now} - T_{max}$ where T_{now} denotes the current time.
2) Remove each W_n'' from the corresponding clusters $C_{j(n)}$, and the cluster center $q_{j(n)}$ is recomputed as the point-wise average of all the sub-series remained in $C_{j(n)}$. If $C_{j(n)}$ becomes empty after the deletion, remove it.
3) Extract and normalize all window sub-series contained in Y, let the resulting sub-series be W_m'.
4) For each W_m', added it to cluster $C_{j(m)}$ and generate a symbol $a_{j(m)}$ for it. The adding method used in this step is same as that in the off-line phase.

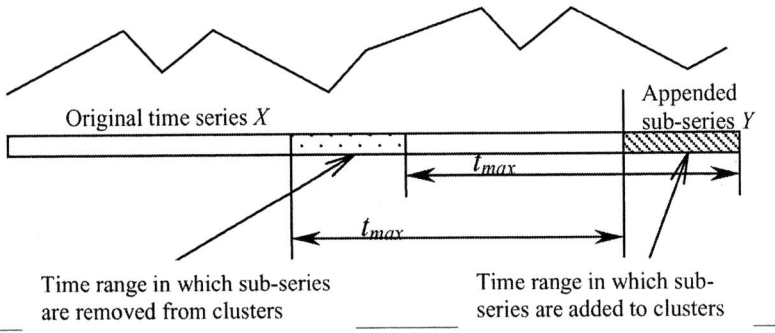

Fig. 1. On-line symbolization process.

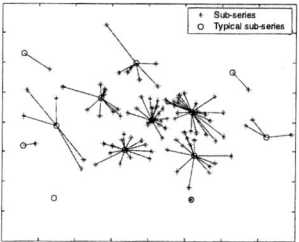 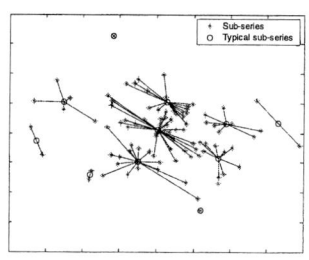

Fig. 2. Symbolization results generated by static approach.

Fig. 3. Symbolization results generated by re-computation approach

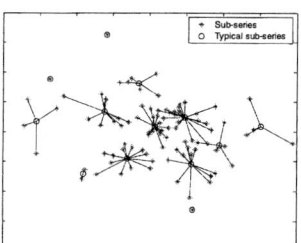 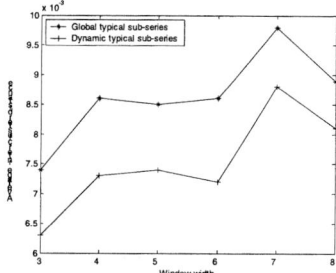

Fig. 4. Symbolization results generated by dynamic symbolization approach.

Fig. 5. Comparisons of the meaningfulness of the symbolization results

5 Experimental Evaluations

The experimental data were time series that consists of daily closing prices extracted from stock market. The performance of symbolization approach is evaluated by the average distance of the original sub-series and the corresponding typical sub-series. That is: the similar the representation is to the original sub-series, the better.

Due to space limitation, we present only part of our experimental results in detail. Fig. 2 shows the symbolization results generated by the traditional static approach that considers the global typical sub-series. Lines in the figure represent that a window sub-series W_n' in one end is grouped into the cluster $C_{j(n)}$ in the other end, whereupon the sub-series will be represented by the symbol corresponding to that cluster. Fig. 3 shows the symbolization results generated by the re-computation approach where typical sub-series were generated by examining only the most recent data. Experimental results generated by our dynamic symbolization approach are shown in Fig. 4. During all these experiments, the window width and window step were both set to be 3. Noted that, there are only 2 independent values in each normalize sub-series. Therefore, results can be shown in a 2D figure without losing information.

By visual analysis, we could find that our approach performed similarly with the re-computation approach in terms of the meaningfulness of the results. However, the re-computation approach need the clusters wholly regenerated whenever the data are updated, which might result in extremely poor time complexity for mining streaming time series, whereas our approach only need the updated sub-series to be examined.

In addition, our approach outperforms the traditional static approach that grouped many sub-series into relatively incompact clusters. We also experimented with various window widths. The results, which are shown in Fig. 5, also justify the superiority of our approach over the static one.

6 Conclusion

In this paper, we present a novel symbolization method for streaming time series. In our approach, the typical sub-series are dynamically adjusted to fit the up-to-date characters of time series. Experimental results show that our approach can generate symbolic sequences that are as meaningful as that generated by the re-computation approach which is effective but very expensive in time expense. On the other hand, our approach outperforms the traditional static approach in terms of meaningfulness of the results. In future, we intend to generalize our symbolization approach by introducing more sophisticated cluster models and window models.

Acknowledgements

The work was partly supported by the NSFC 60373011 and the National Basic Research Program of China (973 Program) 2002CB312000.

References

1. Y. Zhu, D. Shasha. Fast approaches to simple problems in financial time series streams, Workshop on management and processing of data streams. 2003.
2. Z. Yao, L. Gao, X. S. Wang: Using triangle inequality to efficiently process continuous queries on high-dimensional streaming time series. In proc. of SSDBM 2003. 2003.
3. X. Jin, Y. Lu, C. Shi. Distribution discovery: local analysis of temporal rules. In proc. of the 6th Pacific-Asia Conf. on knowledge discovery and data mining (PAKDD'02). 2002.
4. N. Radhakrishnan, J. Wilson, P. Loizou. An alternate partitioning technique to quantify the regularity of complex time series. International Journal of Bifurcation and Chaos, Vol. 10, No. 7, 1773-1779. 2000.
5. G. Das, K. Lin, H. Mannila, G. Renganathan, P. Smyth. Rule discovery from time series. In proc. of the 4th International Conference on Knowledge Discovery and Data Mining (KDD'98). 1998.
6. R. Agrawal, G. Psaila, E. Wimmers, M. Zaot. Querying shapes of histories. In proc. of the 21st international conference on very large database (VLDB'95). 1995.
7. E. Keogh, J. Lin, W. Truppel. Clustering of time series subsequences is meaningless. In proc. of ICDM 2003. 2003.
8. Rakesh A, Christos F, Efficient similarity search in sequence databases. In proc. of FODO 1993, 1993.

A Clustering Model for Mining Evolving Web User Patterns in Data Stream Environment

Edmond H. Wu[1], Michael K. Ng[1], Andy M. Yip[2], and Tony F. Chan[2]

[1] Department of Mathematics, The University of Hong Kong
Pokfulam Road, Hong Kong
hcwu@hkusua.hku.hk, mng@maths.hku.hk
[2] Department of Mathematics, University of California
405 Hilgard Avenue, Los Angeles, CA 90095-1555, USA
{mhyip,chan}@math.ucla.edu

Abstract. With the fast growing of the Internet and its Web users all over the world, how to manage and discover useful patterns from tremendous and evolving Web information sources become new challenges to our data engineering researchers. Also, there is a great demand on designing scalable and flexible data mining algorithms for various time-critical and data-intensive Web applications. In this paper, we purpose a new clustering model for generating and maintaining clusters efficiently which represent the changing Web user patterns in Websites. With effective pruning process, the clusters can be fast discovered and updated to reflect the current or changing user patterns to Website administrators. This model can also be employed in different Web applications such as personalization and recommendation systems.

1 Introduction

With the fast growing of our capabilities in data acquisition and storage technologies, tremendous amount of datasets are generated and stored in databases, data warehouses, or other kinds of data repositories such as the World-Wide Web. Nowadays, many current and emerging Web applications require realtime monitoring and analyzing user patterns in the Web. However, most of the existing Web usage analysis and data mining techniques focused on finding patterns (e.g., association rules or clusters) from related static or historical databases, which greatly limits their wide adoption in online environments. Hence, some recent research in Web mining focuses on how to manage and discover useful patterns from various types of Web data stored in different databases for particular tasks, such as system performance monitoring and user patterns discovery [1,2,4,5]. However, little work was done to adopt methods for clustering the patterns discovered. Therefore, this paper is also an extension of previous work.

The rest of the paper is organized as follows: In section 2, we will introduce the concept of dense regions discovery. Then, in section 3, we purpose the clustering model for evolving dense clusters discovery. After that, we give the experimental results on real Web data in section 4. Finally, we will address the potential Web applications and give some conclusion in sections 5 and 6.

2 An Algorithm for Mining Association Patterns

We first give our definition of dense region: Given a data matrix X, a submatrix $X(R,C)$ of X is called a maximal dense region with respect to v, if $X(R,C)$ is a constant matrix whose entries are v and any proper superset of $X(R,C)$ is non-constant. In many practical applications (e.g., basket analysis from customer transaction databases), a data mining goal is to find association patterns from multidimensional data. For example, we may want to find the groups of customers who will buy the same products. The problem transfers into finding association patterns among all the customers and products. For instance, Yang et al [3] suggested an algorithm for finding error-tolerant frequent itemsets from high-dimensional data, such as binary matrices.

In this research, we use Dense Regions (DRs) to represent association patterns (i.e., subset of a matrix with the same value). In practice, the matrices for dense regions discovery are large and sparse. Hence, efficient algortihms are needed for mining dense regions. In [5], we present an algorithm for mining dense regions in large data matrices. Due to the limited length of this paper, we employ the algorithm in the experiments to find dense regions and we omit the detailed introduction of it.

Example 1. Let X be a 5 × 5 data matrix given by the first matrix below. Using our algorithm for mining dense regions, we first filter out unqualified rows and columns (see the second matrix). Then, the dense regions of X with value 1 are returned by the algorithm shown in the four matrices in the brace.

$$\begin{pmatrix} 1 & 1 & 1 & 0 & 0 \\ 1 & 1 & 0 & 1 & 0 \\ 0 & 1 & 1 & 0 & 1 \\ 0 & 1 & 1 & 1 & 0 \\ 0 & 0 & 0 & 1 & 0 \end{pmatrix} \rightarrow \begin{pmatrix} 1 & 1 & 1 & 0 \\ 1 & 1 & 0 & 1 \\ 0 & 1 & 1 & 0 \\ 0 & 1 & 1 & 1 \end{pmatrix} \rightarrow \left\{ \begin{pmatrix} 1 & 1 & * & * \\ 1 & 1 & * & * \\ * & * & * & * \\ * & * & * & * \end{pmatrix}, \begin{pmatrix} * & 1 & 1 & * \\ * & * & * & * \\ * & 1 & 1 & * \\ * & 1 & 1 & * \end{pmatrix}, \begin{pmatrix} * & * & * & * \\ * & 1 & * & 1 \\ * & * & * & * \\ * & 1 & * & 1 \end{pmatrix}, \begin{pmatrix} * & 1 & * & * \\ * & 1 & * & * \\ * & 1 & * & * \\ * & 1 & * & * \end{pmatrix} \right\}.$$

3 The Clustering Model for Streaming Data

In this section, we first present a clustering method for mining clusters of dense regions (association patterns) from matrices (multidimensional data) and then purpose some strategies to maintain the evolving clusters in streaming data. Here, we use $|D|$ to represent the total number of entries in a dense region D.

3.1 Definition of Dense Clusters

Definition 1 (Dense Region Pairwise Overlap Rate). *Given two dense regions D_i and D_j, the Dense Region Pairwise Overlap Rate (DPOR) of D_i is defined as the ratio:*

$$DPOR(D_i, D_j) = \frac{|D_i \cap D_j|}{|D_i|} \quad (1)$$

Definition 2 (Dense Region Union Overlap Rate). *Given a set of dense regions* $\mathcal{D} = \{D_1, ..., D_n\}$, *the Dense Region Union Overlap Rate (DUOR) is defined as the ratio:*

$$DUOR(\mathcal{D}) = \frac{|\bigcap_{i=1}^{n} D_i|}{|\bigcup_{i=1}^{n} D_i|} \quad (2)$$

Here, we use $DPOR$ and $DUOR$ to measure the extent of association (overlap) among different dense regions. Based on them, we give the definition of dense clusters as follows:

Definition 3 (Dense Clusters). *Given a set of dense regions* $\mathcal{D} = \{D_1, ..., D_n\}$, *a Dense Cluster* $\mathcal{DC} = \bigcup_{i=1}^{k} D_i$ *is defined as a subset of* $\mathcal{D}$ *with k DRs such that:*

- *For any* $D_i \in \mathcal{DC}$, $DPOR(D_i, \mathcal{DC}) \geq MinDPOR$ *and for any* $D_j \notin \mathcal{DC}$ *but* $D_j \in \mathcal{D}$, $DPOR(D_j, \mathcal{DC}) < MinDPOR$, *where MinDPOR is the minimal threshold of DPOR.*
- *For* $\mathcal{DC}$, $DUOR(\mathcal{D_C}) \geq MinDUOR$, *where MinDUOR is the minimal threshold of DUOR.*

Example 2. In Example 1, the 2nd and 4th dense regions D_2 and D_4 have common entries. In this case, $DPOR(D_2, D_4) = 3/6 = 50\%$, $DPOR(D_4, D_2) = 3/4 = 75\%$, $DUOR(D_2 \cup D_4) = 3/7 = 43\%$. If we set $MinDPOR = 50\%$ and $MinDUOR = 40\%$, then $D_2 \cup D_4$ is a dense cluster (DC) in matrix X.

3.2 Dense Cluster Generation and Maintenance

With the definition and data structure of dense cluster, we propose an algorithm for mining dense clusters from evolving data patterns. Because dense clusters denote a set of overlapping dense regions, in the inital stage, we use the algorithm in [5] to find dense regions in the given data matrices.

We propose a data model for mining dynamic dense regions and dense clusters in data stream environment. The main attributes of a dense region DR include: Dense Region ID, Timestamps(starting time T_s and ending time T_e of the DR), Dense Region Indexes(row and column indexes of D in matrix X). The main attributes of a dense cluster DC contain: Dense Cluster ID, Timestamps(T_s and T_e of the DC), Dense Cluster Indexes ($DPOR$, $DUOR$ and IDs of its DRs).

Using the indexing scheme for DRs and DCs above, we can employ greedy methods to find all the dense clusters satisfying the preset conditions. Besides MinDPOR and MinDUOR, we also set a threshold MinDC (the minimal size of a dense cluster) to restrain the size of the dense clusters found by the algorithm. It means that for any DC, the total number of entries $|DC| = |\bigcup_{i=1}^{n} D_i| \geq MinDC$. The benefit of setting MinDC is that we can filter out trivial clusters which are not so useful to analyze data patterns. What's more, we can do some pruning on the dense regions to improve the effciency of the algorithm.

Lemma 1 (Pruning). *Given a set of dense regions* $\mathcal{D} = \{D_1, ..., D_n\}$, *for any two dense region* $D_i, D_j \in \mathcal{D}$, *if* $DPOR(D_i, D_j) < MinDUOR$, *then* $(D_i \cup D_j)$ *and any of its superset containing* D_i *and* D_j *cannot be a Dense Cluster.*

Proof. From the definition of $DPOR(D_i, D_j) = \frac{|D_i \cap D_j|}{|D_i|}$, we have:

$$DUOR(\mathcal{D}) = \frac{|\bigcap_{i=1}^{n} D_i|}{|\bigcup_{i=1}^{n} D_i|} \leq \frac{|D_i \cap D_j|}{|D_i \cup D_j|} \leq DPOR(D_i, D_j) < MinDUOP$$

Hence, $\mathcal{D}$ cannot be a dense cluster by the definition of DC. □

Lemma 2 (Pruning). *Given a set of dense regions $\mathcal{D} = \{D_1..., D_n\}$, for any two dense region $D_i, D_j \in \mathcal{D}$, if $|D_i| < MinDUOR \times |D_j|$, then $(D_i \cup D_j)$ and any of its superset cannot be a Dense Cluster.*

Proof. From the definition of DUOR and Dense Cluster, we have:

$$DUOR(\mathcal{D}) \leq DUOR(D_i \cup D_j) = \frac{|D_i \cap D_j|}{|D_i \cup D_j|} \leq \frac{|D_i|}{|D_j|} < MinDUOR$$

Hence, $\mathcal{D}$ cannot be a dense cluster by the definition of DC. □

Lemma 3 (Pruning). *Given a set of dense regions $\mathcal{D} = \{D_1..., D_n\}$, for any dense region $D_i \in \mathcal{D}$, if $|D_i| < MinDC \times MinDUOR$, then any superset of D_i cannot be a Dense Cluster.*

Proof. From the definition of DUOR and Dense Cluster, we have:

$$DUOR(\mathcal{D}) = \frac{|\bigcap_{i=1}^{n} D_i|}{|\bigcup_{i=1}^{n} D_i|} \leq \frac{|D_i|}{MinDC} < MinDUOR$$

Hence, D cannot be a dense cluster by the definition of DC. □

Therefore, given a set of candidate dense regions $\mathcal{D} = \{D_1, D_2..., D_n\}$, we can use Lemmas 1, 2 and 3 to eliminate unqualified dense regions and finally find the qualifying dense clusters. The benefit of adopting pruning process is that it can greatly improve the efficiency of the algorithm so that the clustering model can be applied in online clustering of evolving association patterns (dense regions). We summarize the dynamic clustering algorithm as follows:

Begin
1. Use DRIFT algorithm (refer to [5]) to mine dense regions from streaming data
2. Set the clustering model thresholds (e.g.,MinDPOR, MinDUOR, MinDC)
3. Prune out unqualified dense regions (DRs)
4. For each qualifying DR, search the set of DRs to form a DC in a greedy manner
5. Indexing and storing all the dense clusters (DCs) found
6. If a new DR generates, test whether this DR can be merged in any existing DC
7. If a old DR eliminates, test whether any DC needs to be eliminated or updated
8. Maintain and update the Dense Clusters by the changing Dense Regions
9. Output the clustering results at certain time point if any query arrives
End

Table 1. Real Web Datasets and the corresponding Dense Regions found

Dataset	No.Accesses	No.Sessions	No.Visitors	No.Pages	No. DRs	Average Size	Maximal Size
ES1	583,386	54,300	2,000	790	104	13 × 15	47 × 32
ES2	2,534,282	198,230	42,473	1,320	350	15 × 14	29 × 46
ES3	6,260,840	517,360	50,374	1,450	978	16 × 21	23 × 42
ES4	78,236	5,000	120	236	56	12 × 14	34 × 25
ES5	7,691,105	669,110	51,158	1,609	1,231	17 × 13	39 × 51

4 Experiments

We used the Web usage data from ESPNSTAR.com.cn, a sports Website to test and evaluate the performance and effectiveness of our clustering model proposed. Table 1 shows the statistics of the Website pages accessed by Web users during two months in 2003. The three right-most columns denote the dense regions found from these datasets by using our dense regions discovery algorithm. (In the data matrices, rows represent Website visitors, columns denote Web pages, here, we set the minimal size of the dense regions to be is 10 × 10.)

We propose several clustering experiments below to evaluate the performance of the clustering algorithm using different model thresholds.

Example 1: We use all the DRs from these datasets for dense cluster discovery. The result in Fig 1 showed that when MinDPOR is increasing, the running time will be decreased. It can be explained that many DRs are unqualified and then eliminated during the pruning process. (Here, MinDUOR=0.5, MinDC=200)

Example 2: The result in Fig 2 reveals a linear relationship when varying MinDUOR. (Here, MinDPOR=0.6, MinDC=200)

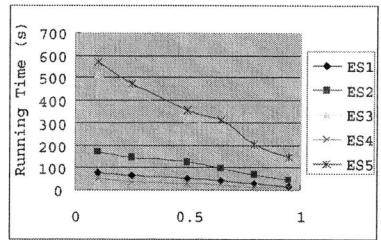
Fig. 1. Varying MinDPOR

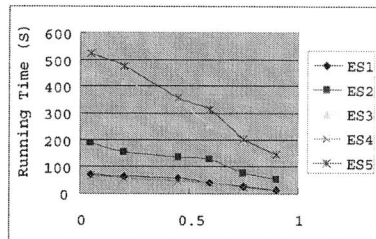
Fig. 2. Varying MinDUOR

Example 3: We also test the sensitiveness of the clustering algorithm by varying preset minimal size of dense cluster. The results in Fig 3 show that the setting of MinDC will effect the total clustering time. In practice, larger size of dense clusters is more interesting. (Here, MinDPOR=0.6 and MinDUOR=0.5)

Example 4: We further test the scalability of the clustering algorithm. The results in Fig 4 show that when the number of DRs is increased, the running time is also increased linearly. It showed that it is feasible to apply this algorithm for online clustering of DRs (Here, we use ES3 and ES5 for testing, MinDPOR=0.6, MinDUOR=0.5, MinMinDC=200).

Above experimental results evaluate the effectiveness of pruning process and the feasibility of the clustering model for practical data mining tasks.

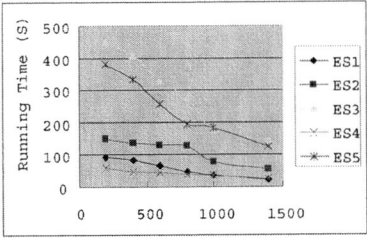

Fig. 3. Varying MinDC   **Fig. 4.** Varying MinDRs

5   Web Applications

In this section, we will address how to apply the clustering model in practical Web mining applications. In our previous work [1,2,5], we proposed some novel methods to discover potential users patterns from multidimensional Web datasets for effective Web mining, such as associatin rules [2], dense regions [5].

Web administrators can use the clustering model for evolving analysis of Web usage. For example, in the experiments, we use the sports Website's datasets which contain the Web accesses information during some periods. The clustering model can help us identify groups of users with common interest which are in the same cluster, or separate different Web users to promote different Web services(e.g., invite football fans to subscribe new football member service).

What's more, we can reorganize the Web pages and content so that it can meet the need of more customers. For instance, if some Web user clusters or Web page clusters are growing, it means these Web users are more interested in the Website or the Web pages are getting more popular among the visitors at a particular time. Acquiring such information, the Website administrators can fast response to such pattern changes and then optimize their Web services provided. In practice, the clustering model can be used for online monitoring Web usage, Web personalization, recommendation, and system performance analysis etc.

6   Conclusions

In this paper, we demonstrate the use of dense regions to capture characteristics of streaming data and propose a clustering model for their discovery. The experiments show that it is effective and efficient, no matter for offline or online clustering applications. It can be employed in different Web mining applications, such as Web user patterns discovery and evolving anlaysis. In the future, we will extend the clustering model for other data mining applications.

References

1. E. H. Wu, M. K. Ng, and J. Z. Huang, *On improving website connectivity by using web-log data streams*, Proc. of the 9th International Conference on Database Systems for Advanced Applications (DASFAA 2004), Jeju, Korea, 2004.
2. E. H. Wu, M. K. Ng, *A graph-based optimization algorithm for Website topology using interesting association rules*, Proc. of the Seventh Pacific-Asia Conference on Knowledge Discovery and Data Mining (PAKDD 2003), Seoul, Korea, 2003.
3. C. Yang, U. Fayyad, and P. S. Bradley, *Efficient discovery of error-tolerant frequent itemsets in high dimensions*, Proceedings of the Seventh ACM SIGKDD Conference, San Francisco, California, pp. 194–203, 2001.
4. Q. Yang, J. Z. Huang and M. K. Ng, *A data cube model for prediction-based Web prefetching*, Journal of Intelligent Information Systems, 20:11-30, 2003.
5. Andy M. Yip, Edmond H.Wu, Michael K.Ng, Tony F. Chan, *An efficient algorithm for dense regions discovery from large-scale data stream*, Proc. of the 8th Pacific-Asia Conference on Knowledge Discovery and Data Mining (PAKDD2004), 2004.

An Improved Constructive Neural Network Ensemble Approach to Medical Diagnoses

Zhenyu Wang, Xin Yao, and Yong Xu

CERCIA, School of Computer Science, The University of Birmingham
Birmingham B15 2TT, UK
{msc44zxw,x.yao,y.xu}@cs.bham.ac.uk

Abstract. Neural networks have played an important role in intelligent medical diagnoses. This paper presents an Improved Constructive Neural Network Ensemble (ICNNE) approach to three medical diagnosis problems. New initial structure of the ensemble, new freezing criterion, and a different error function are presented. Experiment results show that our ICNNE approach performed better for most problems.

1 Introduction

Recently, using artificial neural network (NN) for medical purposes has been shown to be an interesting topic. Most of the work has been focused on achieving better classification performance. A NN ensemble (NNE) consisting of several individual NNs seemed to be quite suitable for this purpose [1]. But the generalization abilities of both NN and NNE are highly influenced by their architectures. On the other hand, there is no rule to design a best NN architecture. So in most applications, NN design is a tedious trial-and-error process. It requires a designer to have a lot of prior knowledge about the problem. Constructive Algorithm for training a NN is one of the solutions to constructing ideal NN architectures which starts with a small network and dynamically grows its size to a near optimal one. But applying this technology to the ensemble design was only recently considered, called *Constructive Neural Network Ensemble* (CNNE) [2]. CNNE uses incremental training, in association with evolutionary algorithms and negative correlation learning, to determine a set of satisfactory architectures [2]. Different from many other training algorithms, CNNE adjusts both the connection weights and the structure of the ensemble. Therefore, it can automatically design and train a satisfactory NNE.

However, some details in CNNE can also be further improved, e.g., initial structure, freezing criterion, and error function for classification problems. In this paper, we will modify these details and present an improved CNNE (ICNNE) to three medical diagnosis problems, i.e., breast cancer, diabetes, and heart disease. The results are compared with previous intelligent medical diagnosis studies.

2 Negative Correlation Learning

In NNE training, most of the previous methods followed two stages: first train individual NNs, and then combine them to form an ensemble [3]. Usually, all individual NNs were trained sequentially and independent of each other. In this way, one NN in the ensemble may be quite simular to others. In order to uncouple individual NNs in the ensemble, a more attractive new technology, called *Negative Correlation Learning* (NCL), was presented by Liu and Yao [1]. Different from the previous methods, NCL trained all the individual networks in the ensemble simultaneously and each network interacted with others through a correlation penalty function [1][3]. These interactions reflecting negative correlation learning emphasised on diversity among different NNs [3]. The major steps of NCL are summarized as follows:

Let M be the number of individual NNs in the ensemble, given a training data set of size N, where $T=[(x_1,t_1),(x_2,t_2),...,(x_N,t_N)]$.

Step 1: Compute the output of the each individual $F_i(n)$ in the ensemble. Calculate the output of ensemble $F(n)$ according to:

$$F(n) = \frac{1}{M}\sum_{i=1}^{M} F_i(n). \quad (1)$$

Step 2: Use individual outputs and ensemble output to define the penalty function p_i by the following equation:

$$p_i(n) = (F_i(n) - F(n))\sum_{j\neq i}(F_j(n) - F(n)). \quad (2)$$

Step 3: Add penalty term to error function, the new error function for each individual NN in ensemble is given by:

$$E_i = \frac{1}{N}\sum_{n=1}^{N}(-t(n)lnF_i(n) - (1-t(n))ln(1-F_i(n)) + \lambda p_i(n)), \quad (3)$$

where the λ is used to adjust the strength of penalty.

Step 4: Use backpropagation algorithm with the new error function to adjust the weights.

3 The ICNNE Algorithm

In this section, we will describe our ICNNE algorithm in detail. We divide all the sample patterns into three parts, 1/2 for training the NNE, 1/4 for the validation set, the rest for testing. The major steps of this algorithm are summarized as follows:

Step 1: Get a minimal NN architecture

The algorithm starts with a minimal NNE architecture, i.e., an individual NN with three layers, and only one node in the hidden layer. The number of the input nodes is the same as the number of elements in one training pattern. The number of output nodes is depended on how many different classes the problem has. Randomly initialize all connection weight in a certain small range. Label this NN with Q.

Step 2: Train NNE via NCL
Train the NNE by using the NCL algorithm.
Step 3: Compute the error on the validation set
Use current ensemble to compute the error of the ensemble on the validation set. The ensemble error is defined as the following cross-entropy:

$$E = \frac{1}{N}\sum_{n=1}^{N}(\frac{1}{M}\sum_{i=1}^{M}(-t(n)lnF_i(n) - (1-t(n))ln(1-F_i(n)))). \qquad (4)$$

If the ensemble error E is acceptable, less than a pre-defined small value, stop training. Otherwise, the NNE is not trained sufficiently or the ensemble architecture is insufficient [2], the ensemble architecture should be modified, in other words, the architecture should grow.

The error of every unlabeled individual NNs were compared with the E_i of previous epochs, if the error constantly descends, save weight matrices of current ensemble. Otherwise, if the error constantly increases, which means the NN is over-fitting, get back to the previous weight matrix and freeze this NN.

So in this step, the validation set will be used to calculate both the individual NN error E_i and ensemble error E. E_i is used for determined whether this individual NN should be frozen or trained further. E is used to determine whether the NNE error is acceptable or not.

Step 4: Add a hidden node to the labeled NN
First, add a hidden node to the labeled NN if the criteria for nodes addition is reached, and for halting network construction is not reached, then go to Step 2, get ready for further training.

Step 5: Add a new minimal NN architecture
When the criteria for halting network construction is reached, the labeled NN has reached the maximum number of hidden nodes. So we need add a new minimal NN in the ensemble. Label new NN with Q. Go to Step 2, get ready for further training.

There are three major differences between our ICNNE algorithm and original CNNE. First, original CNNE started with two minimal individual NNs. But the best structure is problem-dependent. Sometimes, a single NN can solve the problem very well and we do not need to add another one in order to achieve an ensmble. Second, in orginal CNNE, the previous trained NNs were immediately frozen when a new NN was added. But these previous NNs may not be trained sufficiently. Third, orginal CNNE used the most common error function, sum-of-squares error function, for all the problems. In our ICNNE algorithm we use the cross-entropy error function since it is better for our medical diagnosis problems.

To sum up, the algorithm tries to minimize the ensemble error first by training, then by adding a hidden node to an existing NN, and lastly by adding a new NN [2]. After training, a near minimal ensemble architecture with an acceptable error is found. More details of the training algorithm are described as follows.

3.1 Conditions for Nodes Addition and Network Addition

We use simple criteria to decide when to add hidden nodes to a Q-labeled NN and when to halt the modification of the NN and to add a new network to the ensemble. The contribution of an individual NN is defined by:

$$C_i = \frac{1}{E} - \frac{1}{E^i}, \qquad (5)$$

where C_i is the contribution of an individual NN i, E is the ensemble error including NN i, E_i is the ensemble error excluding NN i.

3.2 Hidden Nodes Addition

Add a new node the labeled NN when it can not improve the contribution to the ensemble by a threshold, ϵ, after a certain number of training epochs, indicated by r. The number of training epoch r is specified by a user. The criterion is tested for every r and can be described as

$$C_i(t+r) - C_i(t) < \epsilon, t = r, 2r, 3r, ... \qquad (6)$$

A mutation operator will be applied for hidden nodes addition process. Two nodes are created by splitting an existing node [2], the weight of the new nodes are mutated as:

$$W_{ij}^1 = (1+\beta)W_{ij}; W_{ij}^2 = -\beta W_{ij}, \qquad (7)$$

where W represents the weight vector of the existing node, and W^1 is the weight from input to hidden layer, W^2 is the weight from hidden to output layer, β is the mutation parameter. The value of β can be either a user specified fixed number or a random one, but it should be within a certain small range. One significant advantage of applying evolutionary algorithm to nodes addition process is that the new NN can maintain a better behavioral link with its predecessor, thus we don't need to adjust the weights of the connection to the new node [2].

3.3 Network Addition

Following the criteria of contribution, we will add a new network when the labeled NN fails to improve contribution after the addition of a certain number of hidden nodes, m_h. In other words, add a new NN when the following is true,

$$C_i(m+m_h) \leq C_i(m), m = 1, 2, 3, ... \qquad (8)$$

When there is only one NN in the ensemble, we add new nodes and another NN after fixed numbers of epoch.

4 Experiment Resluts

The classification performance of our ICNNE algorithm is tested on three medical diagnoses problems. The medical databases used in this paper were obtained from the UCI Machine Learning Repository (ftp://ice.uci.edu) [4]. The characteristics of dataset are summarized in Table 1.

Table 1. Characteristics of datasets

Data set	Train set	Validation set	Test set	Input attributes	Output classes
Breast Cancer	332	175	175	9	2
Diabetes	384	192	192	8	2
Heart Disease	134	68	68	13	2

4.1 Experiment Setup

The input attributes are rescaled to between 0 and 1. One bias node with a fixed input of 1 was used for the hidden and output layers, and the activation function for hidden and output layers were both logistic sigmoid function. The connection weights were randomly initialized in between -0.5 and +0.5. The mutation parameter was set to 0.2, the strength of penalty was to 0.5. m_h was choosen to 4, r to 30, ϵ to 0.35. The output of ensemble was the simple averaging. We repeated our simulations 30 times in each test.

4.2 Results and Comparison

Figure 1 shows three samples of training processes. We find from Figure 1 that when a new NN with one hidden node and random initial weights was added to the ensemble, there is a sharpe increase in the validation error. But eventually, with the increase of the number of both NNs and training epoches, the validation errors gradually reduced to a satisfactory level. This shows the NNE generally outperforms a single NN. Because the initial error of heart disease problem is quite small, at the first few training epochs, when adding untrained nodes, the validation error may be increased (right figure).

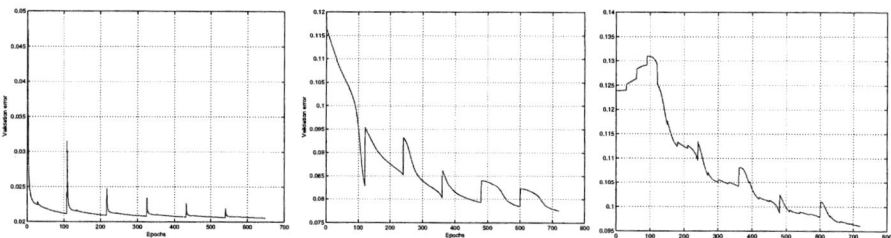

Fig. 1. Three samples of training processes, breast cancer(left), diabetes (middle), heart disease (right). Each peak in this Figure represents the moment when a new NN was added to the ensemble. X-axis: the number of epochs, Y-axis: validation error

The ICNNE method is compared with some other approaches on three medical diagnosis databases in Table 2. The other data were obtained from [2].

The results show that ICNNE can generally achieve better performance for most of the problems. ICNNE performs the best for diabetes and heart disease problems. But for breast cancer problem, CNNE is the best. Since the breast

Table 2. Compare the testing error of ICNNE with previous works, based 30 runs

	Breast Cancer	Diabetes	Heart disease
ICNNE Mean	0.021	0.094	0.113
SD	0.008	0.006	0.015
CNNE[2] Mean	0.013	0.198	0.134
SD	0.007	0.001	0.015
EPNet[2]	0.014	0.224	0.167
Bagging[2]	0.034	0.228	0.170
Arc-boosting[2]	0.038	0.244	0.207

cancer problem is a relative easy one, it is difficult for ICNNE to further improve the result [2].

5 Conclusions

We have proposed an improved constructive algorithm to automatically design a near minimal NNE in this paper. In this approach, users only needed to specify two most important parameters (m_h and r). Comparing with some previous work [2], less prior knowledge was requested from users, and a relative better performance was obtained.

References

1. Liu, Y., Yao, X.: Ensemble learning via Negative Correlation. Neural Networks, **12** (1999) 1399-1404
2. Monirual Islam, Md., Yao, X., Murase, K.: A Constructive Algorithm for Training Cooperative Neural Network Ensembles. IEEE Transactions on Neural Network, **4** (2003) 820-834
3. Liu, Y., Yao, X., Higuchi, T.: Evolutionary Ensembles with Negative Correlation Learning. IEEE Transactions on Evolutionary Computation, **4** (2000) 380-387
4. Blake, C.L., Merz, C.J.: UCI Repository of Machine Learning Databases [http://www.ics.uci.edu/ mlearn/MLRepository.html], Irvine, CA:University of California,Department of Information and Computer Science (1998)

Spam Classification Using Nearest Neighbour Techniques

Dave C. Trudgian

Department of Computer Science, University of Exeter, Exeter, EX4 4QF, UK

Abstract. Spam mail classification and filtering is a commonly investigated problem, yet there has been little research into the application of nearest neighbour classifiers in this field. This paper examines the possibility of using a nearest neighbour algorithm for simple, word based spam mail classification. This approach is compared to a neural network, and decision-tree along with results published in another conference paper on the subject.

1 Introduction

Although it is a popular topic in machine learning, little attention has been paid to the possibility of using instance-based nearest neighbour techniques for spam (unsolicited email) filtering. This paper will examine the performance of a nearest neighbour classifier and compare it to other, more common, methods in use today.

A simple feature extraction process will be explained first that will provide the neccessary numerical data for the classifier which will then be described in more detail.

2 Feature Extraction

The feature extraction engine is sometimes considered to be more important than the classification algorithm in the problem of spam filtering. Various techniques to extract features from mail have been proposed and implemented, in combination [1] as well as singularly. These techniques include examining headers, testing rules against the message body and identifying the occurrences of common words in the mail.

Unfortunately investigation into the different methods of feature extraction is outside the scope of this paper. We wish to compare the performance of classification algorithms rather than experiment with the various sophisticated feature extraction methods involving linguistics online learning etc.

To this effect our feature extraction will consist of creating a word list comprised of the 150 most common words in spam mail, along with the 50 most common words in ham mail. The occurrences of each word will then be counted to give a feature vector in 200 dimensions for each mail.

2.1 Pre-processing

Due to the prevalence of html and binary attachments in modern email a degree of pre-processing is required on messages to allow effective feature extraction. Valid words must be identified with reasonable accuracy, but without great computational expense. Here the following steps are used:

- All message headers are stripped as only message content is required.
- The message body is trimmed to 12000 characters so that large encoded binary attachments are not processed.
- The message is converted to upper case.
- All new-lines are converted to spaces.
- The message is tokenised using the space character as a delimiter.
- Any tokens with non-alphabetical, or non-hyphen characters are ignored.
- Remaining tokens of between 3 and 20 characters are considered to be valid words.

Although undoubtedly crude this pre-processing is relatively inexpensive and appears to work well.

2.2 Word List Creation

The creation of the word list involves a pseudo-probabilistic method. Taking n as the number of messages, o_i as the number of occurrences of a word in message i, every word is allocated a score, s, where:

$$s = \sum_{i=1}^{n} \frac{o_i}{n} \qquad (1)$$

This method is used to create separate lists of scores for words in the ham and spam training sets. There will be overlap between these two sets due to the fact that many commonly used words will appear frequently in all mail, be it spam or ham. Common words are not important for classification and will be eliminated by now considering the difference in scores between the spam and ham lists. So, for the spam case:

$$S_{spam} = (\sum_{i=1}^{n_{spam}} \frac{o_{spam,i}}{n_{spam}}) - (\sum_{i=1}^{n_{ham}} \frac{o_{ham,i}}{n_{ham}}) \qquad (2)$$

Finally, the score lists are sorted with the 150 highest scoring spam words and 50 highest ham words selected for the final word list. Feature vectors can then be produced based on the occurrences of each of these words.

The asymmetric distribution of spam and ham words was adopted due to informal testing which achieved best performance with a 150/50 split. Classification using 200 spam words was more effective (94.3% accuracy) than when using 200 ham words (88.7% accuracy), indicating that a word list consisting mostly or entirely of common words in spam would be preferable.

Adding a minority of words drawn from ham email significantly reduces the risk of false positives. Using equal numbers of ham and spam words results in lower performance. It seems that the most common set of words in spam mail is more diverse than that of ham mail.

3 Nearest Neighbour Classification

A nearest neighbour classifier is a 'lazy learner' that does not process patterns during training. When a request to classify a query vector is made the closest training vector(s), according to a distance metric are located. The classes of these training vectors are used to assign a class to the query vector.

Due to the nature of the feature vectors, with features as positive integer values, the Euclidean distance metric will be used for both methods. This is in contrast to the Hamming distance metric used in [1] which uses a binary feature vector.

3.1 kd-Tree Method

This paper uses the kd-tree nearest neighbour algorithm implemented in the Mount's ANN library for C++ [2]. It has been modified slightly to compile cleanly on modern Linux systems.

The kd-tree method is one method with which the training data feature space can be decomposed and represented as a highly searchable tree structure. The algorithm that builds the tree will continuously partition the feature space into smaller boxes until a tree is formed in which each leaf node contains fewer points than a defined *bucket size*.

Partitioning is carried out according to a *splitting rule*, here Mount and Arya's suggested *sliding midpoint* rule is used [3]. A bucket size of 1 will also be used by default.

3.2 Approximate Nearest Neighbour Searching

Although most implementations of nearest neighbour classifiers locate the absolute nearest neighbours this may not always be required. Where there is a large data set and well defined clusters that separate classes it may be enough to simply identify the approximate nearest neighbours, saving on processing time.

The ANN library implements approximate nearest neighbour searching using a specified error bound. When an error bound ϵ is specified the distance to the neighbour returned may exceed the distance to the real neighbour by a factor of $(1+\epsilon)$.

3.3 Classification Rule

The classification rule governs how the nearest neighbours vote on the classification of a query point. In this paper a distance weighted approach with a threshold will be used. A mail will be classified as spam if

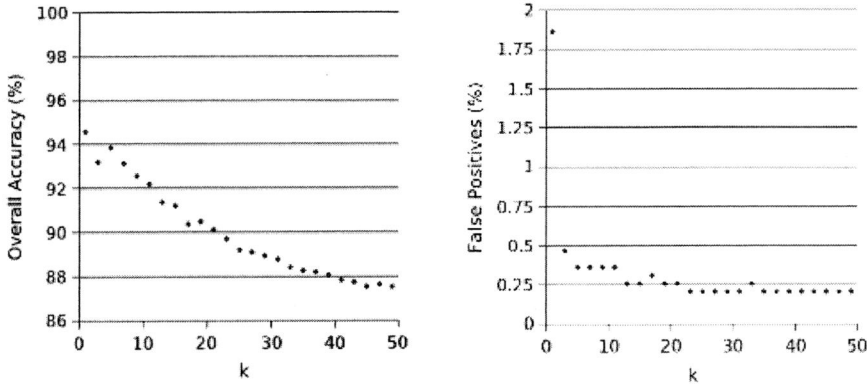

Fig. 1. Effects of varying k

$$\frac{1}{D}\sum_{k=1}^{K}\frac{1}{d_k} \geq t \qquad (3)$$

Where K is the number of nearest neighbours, D is the total distance between the query points and all neighbours, d_k is the distance between the query point and the kth neighbours. t is a fixed threshold value ($0 < t \leq 1$) that is a measure of the confidence required that a mail is spam in order to classify it as such.

3.4 Parameter Tuning

The classifier has four parameters that may be varied. By examining the relationship that each parameter has with accuracy and speed of classification sensible defaults were established:

$k = 5$ No. of nearest neighbours
$p = 4000$ Maximum training points
$t = 0.8$ Classification threshold
$\epsilon = 5$ Approximation error bound

As expected, increasing k resulted in lower false positive rates, the benefits of which are offset by lower overall accuracy. $k = 5$ was selected as a good compromise with reference to the graphs in Figure 1.

Increasing the number of training points, p gave rise to increased accuracy and lower speed, up to the point at which over-fitting began to occur (9000 points in this case). A default of a maximum of $p = 4000$ was chosen as a good compromise between speed and accuracy.

Altering the threshold simply adjusted the balance between false positive and false negative rates. A threshold of 0.8 was chosen to favour false negative classifications since false positives are more inconvenient.

Classification times appear to be inversely proportional to the error bound ϵ whilst accuracy decreases with a roughly linear path as per the graphs in Figure

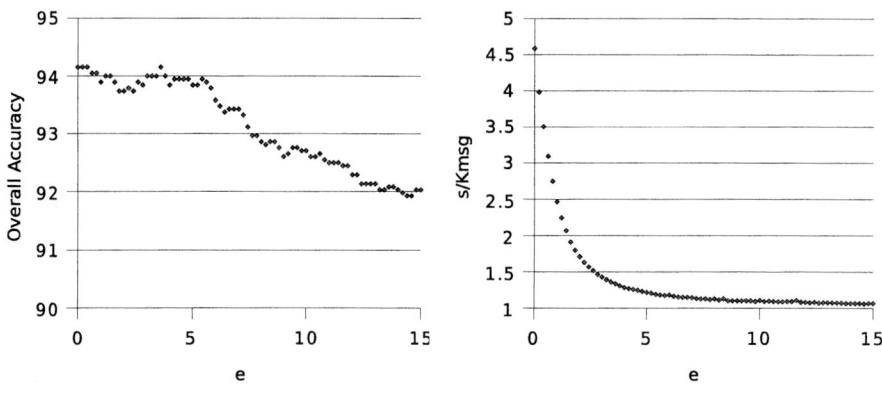

Fig. 2. Effects of varying e

2. Taking $\epsilon = 5$ seems to be a good choice. This offers classification times around a quarter of those where no approximation is used. Overall accuracy decreases by only 0.31%

4 Results

4.1 Test Conditions

Tests were run on all three corpora with two thirds of the available messages used for training, one third as unseen testing data. All tests were run on an AMD Athlon 1800XP system running Debian GNU/Linux. The C++ code is compiled with g++ and optimised for the Athlon cpu.

Throughout the tables of results *acc* is the overall accuracy as a percentage and *fp* is the false positive rate as a percentage of *all* messages. s/Kmsg lists the time taken to *classify* 1,000 patterns, feature extraction having been run previously.

4.2 Corpora

At the heart of any study into email classification there must be a robust, large corpus of mail that is publically available so that comparisons can be made. In this paper three corpora have been used to allow comparisons to be made with other published work and ensure that performance is tested across a varied range of email.

The SpamAssasin public corpus [4] is used to optimise the open source SpamAssassin filter. Constructed from the maintainers' personal email it is probably the most representative corpus of a typical user's mail that is available publically. This study uses the *easy_ham* & *easy_ham_2* collections to give a total of 3900 ham messages. 1899 spam messages will be used from the *spam* & *spam_2* collections. This gives a total of 5799 messages of which 32.7% are spam.

The Lingspam corpus [5] was made available by Ion Androutsopoulos and has been used in a considerable number of publications. Lingspam is composed of

2412 ham messages, with 481 spam messages. This gives a total of 2893 messages of which 16.6% are spam. All messages were taken from a linguist mailing list.

The PSAM synthetic corpus [6] was constructed by combining 7500 ham messages from the X-Free project's *Xpert* mailing list with 7500 spam messages from the Annexia spam archives [7]. The 50% spam factor is likely much more representative than the low 16.6% of Lingspam.

4.3 Performance at Sensible Defaults

When the default values for parameters identified previously were adopted, the results shown in Table 1 were obtained.

Table 1. Performance at Selected Defaults

Corpus	k	p	t	ϵ	acc	fp	s/Kmsg
SpamAssassin	5	3866	0.80	5	93.84	0.36	1.32
Lingspam	5	1928	0.80	5	94.61	0.00	1.06
Synthetic	5	4000	0.80	5	92.31	1.68	0.67

The results are extremely promising given the rudimentary feature extraction and the fact that the parameters have not been optimised to the test sets. False positive rates are low signifying that this classifier would not frequently mark legitimate email as spam. Overall accuracy is good, with over 90% of email classified correctly for each corpus.

The speed of the classifier is extremely impressive. Despite the high dimensionality of the data and the fact that in all cases thousands of training points are used each message is classified in less than 0.0015s. It is clear that the kd-tree representation and approximate neighbour searching allow high throughput without greatly compromising accuracy. Massey et al

4.4 Minimising False Positive Rates

An exhaustive search of parameter combinations was also carried out to identify the lowest false positive rates that could be obtained for each corpus. Users of spam filter systems generally prioritise the safe delivery of ham mail above the blocking of spam. It is reasonable to expect that a user would train a system with this is mind. An intelligent optimisation technique could be used to tune the classifier parameters to a users mail and requirements.

Table 2 shows that it is possible to achieve near zero false positives if the classifier is well tuned to the data. Overall accuracy has reduced for the SpamAssassin and Synthetic corpora as expected. Since the Lingspam corpus had 0 false positives with the default settings the exhaustive search has identified the best overall accuracy without any false positives.

The speed of classification has increased dramatically for the synthetic corpus due to the large p and absence of approximate searching ($\epsilon = 0$). This illustrates

Table 2. Lowest False Positive Rates

Corpus	k	p	t	ε	acc	fp	s/Kmsg
SpamAssassin	9	2400	0.90	8	89.91	0.00	0.66
Lingspam	17	1100	0.55	0	98.13	0.00	1.50
Synthetic	19	18500	0.95	0	91.31	0.08	12.26

that parameter optimisation should be carried out with regard to a cost function expressing the relative importance of accuracy and speed.

4.5 Comparisons

To compare the results of the ANN based classifier with other techniques the feature data was also classified with a back propagation neural network of 200 input, 5 hidden and 1 output neurons. Quinlan's C4.5 decision tree algorithm [8] was also used. The results can be seen in Table 3.

Massey et al [1] is a useful resource for comparing classification performance since it deals with six classification algorithms as well as five feature extraction methods. The 'PSAM' results shown in Table 3 are those for the Lingspam corpus and gain based classifier. The 'Hamming' result was the PSAM nearest neighbour

Table 3. Comparison of Results

Classifier	acc	fp
ANN	94.61	0.00
C4.5	98.25	1.97
Neural Net	95.61	0.46
PSAM Hamming	94.76	0.87
PSAM NBayes	94.76	0.87
PSAM Graham	97.38	1.25
PSAM Neuron	96.25	1.87
PSAM ID3	93.88	2.12
PSAM Neural Net	96.14	0.87

The ANN classifier performs relatively well, being the only classifier to achieve zero false positives. However, It falls behind all of the remaining classifiers in terms of overall accuracy with the exception of PSAM's ID3 decision tree. The C4.5 tree performs much more strongly than PSAM's ID3 implementation but both have high false positive rates reflecting the poor suitability of a decision tree to the highly dimensional numerical feature data.

5 Conclusions

It has been shown that by using a kd-tree and approximate searching a nearest neighbour classifier can operate quickly without great sacrifices in accuracy.

Comparison of the ANN classifier with C4.5, neural network and the PSAM paper techniques shows that the most promising methods of classification are nearest neighbour, neural network and Bayesian based. Amongst these classifiers there is relatively little difference in accuracy. Implementation issues are likely to be far more important when choosing a technique to adopt for a filtering application.

The ANN classifier has the advantage of a small number of parameters which could be optimised quickly using intelligent techniques due to the 'lazy learning' zero learning time of the system. When parameters are optimised for the email that is to be classified results can improve considerably.

The feature extraction methods used here are relatively crude, as is the gain based approach used in the PSAM paper. It is encouraging that simple word selection yields good accuracy since there is scope for improvement by refining feature extraction.

Acknowledgements

The authors wish to thank Bart Massey & Mick Thomure of Portland State University for their PSAM data and answers to emails; David Mount, for his ANN library.

Availability

The corpora used within this paper will be made available for download in standard UNIX formats at the address below, subject to the permissions of their creators.

http://www.trudgian.net/content/spamkann/

References

1. Massey, B., Thomure, M., Budrevich, R., Long, S.: Learning spam: Simple techniques for freely-available software. Usenix 2003, Freenix Track (2003)
2. Mount, D., Arya, S.: Ann: A library for approximate nearest neighbor searching (1997)
3. Arya, S., Mount, D.M., Netanyahu, N.S., Silverman, R., Wu, A.Y.: An optimal algorithm for approximate nearest neighbor searching in fixed dimensions. Journal of the ACM **45** (1998) 891–923
4. Justin, M.: Spamassassin public corpus (2003) Accessed 27/02/04.
5. Sakkis, G., Androutsopoulos, I., Paliouras, G., Karkaletsis, V., Spyropoulos, C., Stamatopoulos, P.: Ling-spam - from a memory-based approach to anti-spam filtering for mailing lists. Information Retrieval **6** (2003) 49–73
6. Group, P.: The portland spam automatic mail-filtering project (2003) Accessed 02/03/04.
7. Jones, R.W.M.: Annexia great spam archive (2003) Accessed 27/02/04.
8. Quinlan, J.R.: C4.5, Programs For Machine Learning. Morgan Kaufmann, California (1993)

Kernel Density Construction Using Orthogonal Forward Regression

Sheng Chen[1], Xia Hong[2], and Chris J. Harris[1]

[1] School of Electronics and Computer Science
University of Southampton, Southampton SO17 1BJ, UK
[2] Department of Cybernetics
University of Reading, Reading, RG6 6AY, UK

Abstract. An automatic algorithm is derived for constructing kernel density estimates based on a regression approach that directly optimizes generalization capability. Computational efficiency of the density construction is ensured using an orthogonal forward regression, and the algorithm incrementally minimizes the leave-one-out test score. Local regularization is incorporated into the density construction process to further enforce sparsity. Examples are included to demonstrate the ability of the proposed algorithm to effectively construct a very sparse kernel density estimate with comparable accuracy to that of the full sample Parzen window density estimate.

1 Introduction

Estimation of probability density functions is a recurrent theme in machine learning and many fields of engineering. A well-known non-parametric density estimation technique is the classical Parzen window estimate [1], which is remarkably simple and accurate. The particular problem associated with the Parzen window estimate however is the computational cost for testing which scales directly with the sample size, as the Parzen window estimate employs the full data sample set in defining density estimate for subsequent observation. Recently, the support vector machine (SVM) has been proposed as a promising tool for sparse kernel density estimation [2],[3].

Motivated by our previous work on sparse data modeling [4],[5], we propose an efficient algorithm for sparse kernel density estimation using an orthogonal forward regression (OFR) based on leave-one-out (LOO) test score and local regularization. This construction algorithm is fully automatic and the user does not require to specify any criterion to terminate the density construction procedure. We will refer to this algorithm as the sparse density construction (SDC) algorithm. Some examples are used to illustrate the ability of this SDC algorithm to construct efficiently a sparse density estimate with comparable accuracy to that of the Parzen window estimate.

2 Kernel Density Estimation as Regression

Given $\mathcal{D} = \{\mathbf{x}_k\}_{k=1}^N$ drawn from an unknown density $p(\mathbf{x})$, where the data samples $\mathbf{x}_k = [x_{1,k} \; x_{2,k} \cdots x_{m,k}]^T \in \mathcal{R}^m$ are assumed to be independently identically distributed, the task is to estimate $p(\mathbf{x})$ using the kernel density estimate of the form

$$\hat{p}(\mathbf{x}) = \sum_{k=1}^{N} \beta_k K(\mathbf{x}, \mathbf{x}_k) \tag{1}$$

with the constraints

$$\beta_k \geq 0, \quad k = 1, 2, \cdots, N, \quad \text{and} \quad \sum_{k=1}^{N} \beta_k = 1 \tag{2}$$

In this study, the kernel function is assumed to be the Gaussian function of the form

$$K(\mathbf{x}, \mathbf{x}_k) = \frac{1}{(2\pi\rho^2)^{m/2}} \exp\left(-\frac{\|\mathbf{x} - \mathbf{x}_k\|^2}{2\rho^2}\right) \tag{3}$$

where ρ is a common kernel width. The well-known Parzen window estimate [1] is obtained by setting $\beta_k = \frac{1}{N}$ for all k. Our aim is to seek a spare representation for $\hat{p}(\mathbf{x})$, i.e. with most of β_k being zero and yet maintaining a comparable test performance or generalization capability to that of the full sample optimized Parzen window estimate.

Following the approach [2],[3], the kernel density estimation problem is posed as the following regression modeling problem

$$f(\mathbf{x}; N) = \sum_{k=1}^{N} \beta_k q(\mathbf{x}, \mathbf{x}_k) + \epsilon(k) \tag{4}$$

subject to (2), where the empirical distribution function $f(\mathbf{x}; N)$ is defined by

$$f(\mathbf{x}; N) = \frac{1}{N} \sum_{k=1}^{N} \prod_{j=1}^{m} \theta(x_j - x_{j,k}) \tag{5}$$

with $\theta(x) = 1$ if $x > 0$ and $\theta(x) = 0$ if $x \leq 0$, the "regressor" $q(\mathbf{x}, \mathbf{x}_k)$ is given by

$$q(\mathbf{x}, \mathbf{x}_k) = \int_{-\infty}^{\mathbf{x}} K(\mathbf{u}, \mathbf{x}_k) \, d\mathbf{u} = \prod_{j=1}^{m} \left(1 - Q\left(\frac{x_j - x_{j,k}}{\rho}\right)\right) \tag{6}$$

with the usual Gaussian Q-function, and $\epsilon(k)$ denotes the modeling error. Let $\boldsymbol{\beta} = [\beta_1 \, \beta_2 \cdots \beta_N]^T$, $f_k = f(\mathbf{x}_k; N)$ and $\boldsymbol{\phi}(k) = [q_{k,1} \, q_{k,2} \cdots q_{k,N}]^T$ with $q_{k,i} = q(\mathbf{x}_k, \mathbf{x}_i)$. Then the regression model (4) for the data point $\mathbf{x}_k \in \mathcal{D}$ can be expressed as

$$f_k = \hat{f}_k + \epsilon(k) = \boldsymbol{\phi}^T(k)\boldsymbol{\beta} + \epsilon(k) \tag{7}$$

Furthermore, the regression model (4) over the training data set $\mathcal{D}$ can be written together in the matrix form

$$\mathbf{f} = \boldsymbol{\Phi}\boldsymbol{\beta} + \boldsymbol{\epsilon} \tag{8}$$

with the following additional notations $\boldsymbol{\Phi} = [q_{i,k}] \in \mathcal{R}^{N \times N}$, with $1 \leq i, k \leq N$, $\boldsymbol{\epsilon} = [\epsilon(1) \, \epsilon(2) \cdots \epsilon(N)]^T$, and $\mathbf{f} = [f_1 \, f_2 \cdots f_N]^T$. For convenience, we will denote the regression matrix $\boldsymbol{\Phi} = [\boldsymbol{\phi}_1\ \boldsymbol{\phi}_2\cdots\boldsymbol{\phi}_N]$ with $\boldsymbol{\phi}_k = [q_{1,k}\ q_{2,k}\cdots q_{N,k}]^T$. Note that $\boldsymbol{\phi}_k$ denotes the kth column of $\boldsymbol{\Phi}$ while $\boldsymbol{\phi}(k)$ the kth row of $\boldsymbol{\Phi}$.

Let an orthogonal decomposition of the regression matrix $\boldsymbol{\Phi}$ be

$$\boldsymbol{\Phi} = \mathbf{WA} \tag{9}$$

where $\mathbf{A}$ is an $N \times N$ upper triangular matrix with the unity diagonal elements, and $\mathbf{W} = [\mathbf{w}_1\ \mathbf{w}_2\cdots\mathbf{w}_N]$ with columns satisfying $\mathbf{w}_i^T \mathbf{w}_j = 0$, if $i \neq j$. The regression model (8) can alternatively be expressed as

$$\mathbf{f} = \mathbf{Wg} + \boldsymbol{\epsilon} \tag{10}$$

where the orthogonal weight vector $\mathbf{g} = [g_1\ g_2\cdots g_N]^T$ satisfies the triangular system $\mathbf{A}\boldsymbol{\beta} = \mathbf{g}$. The model $\hat{f}_k$ is equivalently expressed by $\hat{f}_k = \mathbf{w}^T(k)\mathbf{g}$, where $\mathbf{w}(k) = [w_{k,1}\ w_{k,2}\cdots w_{k,N}]^T$ is the kth row of $\mathbf{W}$.

3 The Sparse Density Construction

Let $\boldsymbol{\lambda} = [\lambda_1\ \lambda_2\cdots\lambda_N]^T$ be the regularization parameter vector associated with $\mathbf{g}$. If an n-term model is selected from the full model (10), the LOO test error [6]–[9], denoted as $\epsilon_{n,-k}(k)$, for the selected n-term model can be shown to be [9],[5]

$$\epsilon_{n,-k}(k) = \frac{\epsilon_n(k)}{\eta_n(k)} \tag{11}$$

where $\epsilon_n(k)$ is the n-term modeling error and $\eta_n(k)$ is the associated LOO error weighting given by

$$\eta_n(k) = 1 - \sum_{i=1}^{n} \frac{w_{k,i}^2}{\mathbf{w}_i^T \mathbf{w}_i + \lambda_i} \tag{12}$$

The mean square LOO error for the model with a size n is defined by

$$J_n = E\left[\epsilon_{n,-k}^2(k)\right] = \frac{1}{N}\sum_{k=1}^{N} \frac{\epsilon_n^2(k)}{\eta_n^2(k)} \tag{13}$$

This LOO test score can be computed efficiently due to the fact that the n-term model error $\epsilon_n(k)$ and the associated LOO error weighting can be calculated recursively according to

$$\epsilon_n(k) = f_k - \sum_{i=1}^{n} w_{k,i} g_i = \epsilon_{n-1}(k) - w_{k,n} g_n \tag{14}$$

$$\eta_n(k) = 1 - \sum_{i=1}^{n} \frac{w_{k,i}^2}{\mathbf{w}_i^T \mathbf{w}_i + \lambda_i} = \eta_{n-1}(k) - \frac{w_{k,n}^2}{\mathbf{w}_n^T \mathbf{w}_n + \lambda_n} \tag{15}$$

The model selection procedure is carried as follows: at the nth stage of selection, a model term is selected among the remaining n to N candidates if the resulting

n-term model produces the smallest LOO test score J_n. It has been shown in [9] that there exists an "optimal" model size n_s such that for $n \leq n_s$ J_n decreases as n increases while for $n \geq n_s + 1$ J_n increases as n increases. This property enables the selection procedure to be automatically terminated with an n_s-term model when $J_{n_s+1} > J_{n_s}$, without the need for the user to specify a separate termination criterion. The iterative SDC procedure based on this OFR with LOO test score and local regularization is summarized:

Initialization. Set λ_i, $1 \leq i \leq N$, to the same small positive value (e.g. 0.001). Set iteration $I = 1$.

Step 1. Given the current $\boldsymbol{\lambda}$ and with the following initial conditions

$$\epsilon_0(k) = f_k \text{ and } \eta_0(k) = 1, k = 1, 2, \cdots, N, \quad J_0 = \mathbf{f}^T\mathbf{f}/N$$

use the procedure as described in [4],[5] to select a subset model with n_I terms.

Step 2. Update $\boldsymbol{\lambda}$ using the evidence formula as described in [4],[5]. If $\boldsymbol{\lambda}$ remains sufficiently unchanged in two successive iterations or a pre-set maximum iteration number (e.g. 10) is reached, stop; otherwise set $I+=1$ and go to *Step 1*.

The computational complexity of the above algorithm is dominated by the 1st iteration. After the 1st iteration, the model set contains only $n_1 (\ll N)$ terms, and the complexity of the subsequent iteration decreases dramatically. As a probability density, the constraint (2) must be met. The non-negative condition is ensured during the selection with the following simple measure. Let $\boldsymbol{\beta}_n$ denote the weight vector at the nth stage. A candidate that causes $\boldsymbol{\beta}_n$ to have negative elements, if included, will not be considered at all. The unit length condition is easily met by normalizing the final n_s-term model weights.

4 Numerical Examples

In order to remove the influence of different ρ values to the quality of the resulting density estimate, the optimal value for ρ, found empirically by cross validation, was used. In each case, a data set of N randomly drawn samples was used to construct kernel density estimates, and a separate test data set of $N_{test} = 10,000$ samples was used to calculate the L_2 test error for the resulting estimate according to

$$L_2 = \frac{1}{N_{test}} \sum_{k=1}^{N_{test}} (p(\mathbf{x}_k) - \hat{p}(\mathbf{x}_k))^2 \tag{16}$$

The experiment was repeated by 100 different random runs for each example.

Example 1. This was a 1-D example with the density to be estimated given by

$$p(x) = \frac{1}{2\sqrt{0.5\pi}} \exp\left(-\frac{(x+4)^2}{0.5}\right) + \frac{1}{2\sqrt{2\pi}} \exp\left(-\frac{x^2}{2}\right). \tag{17}$$

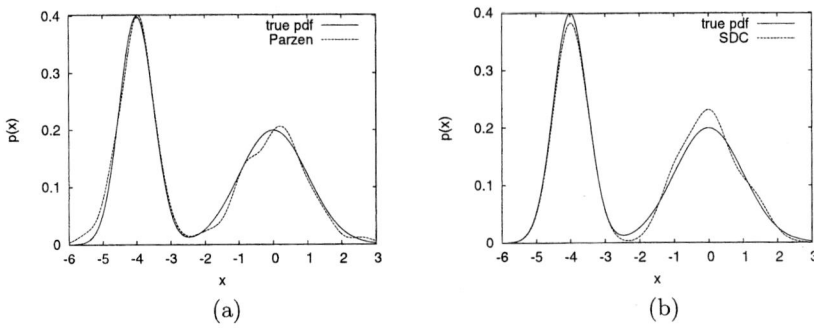

Fig. 1. (a) true density (solid) and a Parzen window estimate (dashed), and (b) true density (solid) and a sparse density construction estimate (dashed), for the one-dimensional example.

Table 1. Performance of the Parzen window estimate and the proposed sparse density construction algorithm for the one-dimensional example. STD: standard deviation.

method	L_2 test error (mean ± STD)	kernel number (mean ± STD)
Parzen	$(1.2663 \pm 0.8243) \times 10^{-3}$	200 ± 0
SDC	$(1.4301 \pm 1.2456) \times 10^{-3}$	6.1 ± 1.3

The number of data points for density estimation was $N = 200$. The optimal kernel widths were found to be $\rho = 0.3$ and $\rho = 0.5$ empirically for the Parzen window estimate and the SDC estimate, respectively. Table 1 compares the performance of the two kernel density construction methods, in terms of the L_2 test error and the number of kernels required. Fig. 1 (a) depicts the Parzen window estimated obtained in a run while Fig. 1 (b) shows the density obtained by the SDC algorithm in a run, in comparison with the true distribution. It is seen that the accuracy of the SDC algorithm was comparable to that of the Parzen window estimate, and the algorithm realized very sparse estimates with an average kernel number less than 4% of the data samples.

Example 2. In this 6-D example, the underlying density to be estimated was given by

$$p(\mathbf{x}) = \frac{1}{3(2\pi)^{6/2}} \left\{ \frac{1}{\det |\boldsymbol{\Gamma}_1|} \exp\left(-\frac{1}{2}(\mathbf{x} - \boldsymbol{\mu}_1)^T \boldsymbol{\Gamma}_1^{-1}(\mathbf{x} - \boldsymbol{\mu}_1)\right) + \right.$$

$$\frac{1}{\det |\boldsymbol{\Gamma}_2|} \exp\left(-\frac{1}{2}(\mathbf{x} - \boldsymbol{\mu}_2)^T \boldsymbol{\Gamma}_2^{-1}(\mathbf{x} - \boldsymbol{\mu}_2)\right) +$$

$$\left. \frac{1}{\det |\boldsymbol{\Gamma}_3|} \exp\left(-\frac{1}{2}(\mathbf{x} - \boldsymbol{\mu}_3)^T \boldsymbol{\Gamma}_3^{-1}(\mathbf{x} - \boldsymbol{\mu}_3)\right) \right\} \quad (18)$$

with

Table 2. Performance of the Parzen window estimate and the proposed sparse density construction algorithm for the six-dimensional example. STD: standard deviation.

method	L_2 test error (mean ± STD)	kernel number (mean ± STD)
Parzen	$(3.38 \pm 0.42) \times 10^{-9}$	600 ± 0
SDC	$(5.47 \pm 2.76) \times 10^{-9}$	14.9 ± 2.1

$$\boldsymbol{\mu}_1 = [1.0\ 1.0\ 1.0\ 1.0\ 1.0\ 1.0]^T, \quad \boldsymbol{\Gamma}_1 = \text{diag}\{1.0, 2.0, 1.0, 2.0, 1.0, 2.0\} \quad (19)$$

$$\boldsymbol{\mu}_2 = [-1.0\ -1.0\ -1.0\ -1.0\ -1.0\ -1.0]^T, \quad \boldsymbol{\Gamma}_2 = \text{diag}\{2.0, 1.0, 2.0, 1.0, 2.0, 1.0\} \quad (20)$$

$$\boldsymbol{\mu}_3 = [0.0\ 0.0\ 0.0\ 0.0\ 0.0\ 0.0]^T, \quad \boldsymbol{\Gamma}_3 = \text{diag}\{2.0, 1.0, 2.0, 1.0, 2.0, 1.0\} \quad (21)$$

The estimation data set contained $N = 600$ samples. The optimal kernel width was found to be $\rho = 0.6$ for the Parzen window estimate and $\rho = 1.1$ for the SDC estimate, respectively. The results obtained by the two density construction algorithms are summarized in Table 2. It can be seen that the SDC algorithm achieved a similar accuracy to that of the Parzen window estimate with a much sparser representation. The average number of required kernels for the SDC method was less than 3% of the data samples.

5 Conclusions

An efficient algorithm has been proposed for obtaining sparse kernel density estimates based on an OFR procedure that incrementally minimizes the LOO test score, coupled with local regularization. The proposed method is simple to implement and computationally efficient, and except for the kernel width the algorithm contains no other free parameters that require tuning. The ability of the proposed algorithm to construct a very sparse kernel density estimate with a comparable accuracy to that of the full sample Parzen window estimate has been demonstrated using two examples. The results obtained have shown that the proposed method provides a viable alternative for sparse kernel density estimation in practical applications.

References

1. E. Parzen, "On estimation of a probability density function and mode," *The Annals of Mathematical Statistics*, Vol.33, pp.1066–1076, 1962.
2. J. Weston, A. Gammerman. M.O. Stitson, V. Vapnik, V. Vovk and C. Watkins, "Support vector density estimation," in: B. Schölkopf, C. Burges and A.J. Smola, eds., *Advances in Kernel Methods – Support Vector Learning*, MIT Press, Cambridge MA, 1999, pp.293-306.
3. S. Mukherjee and V. Vapnik, "Support vector method for multivariate density estimation," *Technical Report*, A.I. Memo No. 1653, MIT AI Lab, 1999.
4. S. Chen, X. Hong and C.J. Harris, "Sparse kernel regression modeling using combined locally regularized orthogonal least squares and D-optimality experimental design," *IEEE Trans. Automatic Control*, Vol.48, No.6, pp.1029–1036, 2003.

5. S. Chen, X. Hong, C.J. Harris and P.M. Sharkey, "Sparse modeling using orthogonal forward regression with PRESS statistic and regularization," *IEEE Trans. Systems, Man and Cybernetics, Part B*, Vol.34, No.2, pp.898–911, 2004.
6. R.H. Myers, *Classical and Modern Regression with Applications.* 2nd Edition, Boston: PWS-KENT, 1990.
7. L.K. Hansen and J. Larsen, "Linear unlearning for cross-validation," *Advances in Computational Mathematics*, Vol.5, pp.269–280, 1996.
8. G. Monari and G. Dreyfus, "Local overfitting control via leverages," *Neural Computation*, Vol.14, pp.1481–1506, 2002.
9. X. Hong, P.M. Sharkey and K. Warwick, "Automatic nonlinear predictive model construction algorithm using forward regression and the PRESS statistic," *IEE Proc. Control Theory and Applications*, Vol.150, No.3, pp.245–254, 2003.

Orthogonal Least Square with Boosting for Regression

Sheng Chen[1], Xunxian Wang[2], and David J. Brown[2]

[1] School of Electronics and Computer Science
University of Southampton, Southampton SO17 1BJ, UK
[2] Department of Electronic and Computer Engineering
University of Portsmouth, Portsmouth PO1 3DJ, UK

Abstract. A novel technique is presented to construct sparse regression models based on the orthogonal least square method with boosting. This technique tunes the mean vector and diagonal covariance matrix of individual regressor by incrementally minimizing the training mean square error. A weighted optimization method is developed based on boosting to append regressors one by one in an orthogonal forward selection procedure. Experimental results obtained using this technique demonstrate that it offers a viable alternative to the existing state-of-art kernel modeling methods for constructing parsimonious regression models.

1 Introduction

The orthogonal least square (OLS) algorithm [1]–[4] is popular for nonlinear data modeling practitioners, for the reason that the algorithm is simple and efficient, and is capable of producing parsimonious linear-in-the-weights nonlinear models. Recently, the state-of-art sparse kernel modeling techniques, such as the support vector machine and relevant vector machine [5]–[8], have widely been adopted in data modeling applications. In most of these sparse regression techniques, a fixed common variance is used for all the regressor kernels and the kernel centers are placed at the training input data.

We present a flexible construction method that can tune the mean vector and diagonal covariance matrix of individual regressor by incrementally minimizing the training mean square error in an orthogonal forward selection procedure. To incrementally append regressor one by one, a weighted optimization search algorithm is developed, which is based on the idea from boosting [9]–[11]. Because kernel means are not restricted to the training input data and each regressor has an individually tuned diagonal covariance matrix, our method can produce very sparse models that generalize well.

2 Orthogonal Least Square Regression Modeling

Consider the modeling problem of approximating the N pairs of training data $\{\mathbf{x}_l, y_l\}_{l=1}^{N}$ with the regression model

$$y(\mathbf{x}) = \hat{y}(\mathbf{x}) + e(\mathbf{x}) = \sum_{i=1}^{M} w_i g_i(\mathbf{x}) + e(\mathbf{x}) \tag{1}$$

where $\mathbf{x}$ is the m-dimensional input variable, $y(\mathbf{x})$ is the desired output, $\hat{y}(\mathbf{x})$ is the model output, and $e(\mathbf{x})$ the modeling error at $\mathbf{x}$; w_i, $1 \leq i \leq M$, denote the model weights, M is the number of regressors, and $g_i(\bullet)$, $1 \leq i \leq M$, denote the regressors. The regressor is chosen to be the general Gaussian function $g_i(\mathbf{x}) = G(\mathbf{x}; \boldsymbol{\mu}_i, \boldsymbol{\Sigma}_i)$ with

$$G(\mathbf{x}; \boldsymbol{\mu}_i, \boldsymbol{\Sigma}_i) = \exp\left(-\frac{1}{2}(\mathbf{x}-\boldsymbol{\mu}_i)^T \boldsymbol{\Sigma}_i^{-1}(\mathbf{x}-\boldsymbol{\mu}_i)\right) \tag{2}$$

where the diagonal covariance matrix has the form of $\boldsymbol{\Sigma}_i = \text{diag}\{\sigma_{i,1}^2, \cdots, \sigma_{i,m}^2\}$. We will adopt an orthogonal forward selection to build up the regression model (1) by appending regressors one by one. By defining $\mathbf{y} = [y_1 \ y_2 \cdots y_N]^T$,

$$\mathbf{G} = [\mathbf{g}_1 \ \mathbf{g}_2 \cdots \mathbf{g}_M] \quad \text{with} \quad \mathbf{g}_k = [g_k(\mathbf{x}_1) \ g_k(\mathbf{x}_2) \cdots g_k(\mathbf{x}_N)]^T \tag{3}$$

$\mathbf{w} = [w_1 \ w_2 \cdots w_M]^T$ and $\mathbf{e} = [e(\mathbf{x}_1) \ e(\mathbf{x}_2) \cdots e(\mathbf{x}_N)]^T$, the regression model (1) over the training data set can be written in the matrix form

$$\mathbf{y} = \mathbf{Gw} + \mathbf{e} \tag{4}$$

Let an orthogonal decomposition of the regression matrix $\mathbf{G}$ be $\mathbf{G} = \mathbf{PA}$, where $\mathbf{A} = [\alpha_{i,j}]$ with $\alpha_{i,i} = 1$ and $\alpha_{i,j} = 0$ if $i > j$, and $\mathbf{P} = [\mathbf{p}_1 \ \mathbf{p}_2 \cdots \mathbf{p}_M]$ with orthogonal columns that satisfy $\mathbf{p}_i^T \mathbf{p}_j = 0$, if $i \neq j$. The regression model (4) can alternatively be expressed as

$$\mathbf{y} = \mathbf{P}\boldsymbol{\theta} + \mathbf{e} \tag{5}$$

where the orthogonal weight vector $\boldsymbol{\theta} = [\theta_1 \ \theta_2 \cdots \theta_M]^T$ satisfies the triangular system $\mathbf{Aw} = \boldsymbol{\theta}$. For the orthogonal regression model (5), the least square cost $J = \mathbf{e}^T\mathbf{e}/N$ can be expressed as

$$J = \frac{1}{N}\mathbf{e}^T\mathbf{e} = \frac{1}{N}\mathbf{y}^T\mathbf{y} - \frac{1}{N}\sum_{i=1}^{M}\mathbf{p}_i^T\mathbf{p}_i\theta_i^2 \tag{6}$$

Thus the least square cost for the k-term subset model can be expressed recursively as

$$J_k = J_{k-1} - \frac{1}{N}\mathbf{p}_k^T\mathbf{p}_k\theta_k^2 \tag{7}$$

where $J_0 = \mathbf{y}^T\mathbf{y}/N$. At the kth stage of regression, the kth term is selected to maximize the error reduction criterion $\text{ER}_k = \mathbf{p}_k^T\mathbf{p}_k\theta_k^2/N$, and the maximization is with respect to the weight θ_k, the mean vector $\boldsymbol{\mu}_k$ and the diagonal covariance matrix $\boldsymbol{\Sigma}_k$ of the kth regressor. The forward selection procedure is terminated at the kth stage if $J_k < \xi$ is satisfied, where the small positive scalar ξ is a chosen tolerance. This produces a parsimonious model containing k significant regressors.

3 Orthogonal Least Square with Boosting

At the kth stage of regression, the task is to maximize $f(\mathbf{u}) = \mathrm{ER}_k(\mathbf{u})$ over $\mathbf{u} \in U$, where the vector $\mathbf{u}$ contains the regressor mean vector $\boldsymbol{\mu}$ and diagonal covariance matrix $\boldsymbol{\Sigma}$. We use the following weighted search method to perform this optimization. Given s points of $\mathbf{u}$, $\mathbf{u}_1, \mathbf{u}_2, \cdots, \mathbf{u}_s$, let $\mathbf{u}_{best} = \arg\max\{f(\mathbf{u}_i), 1 \le i \le s\}$ and $\mathbf{u}_{worst} = \arg\min\{f(\mathbf{u}_i), 1 \le i \le s\}$. A $(s+1)$th value is generated by a weighted combination of $\mathbf{u}_i$, $1 \le i \le s$. A $(s+2)$th value is then generated as the mirror image of $\mathbf{u}_{s+1}$, with respect to $\mathbf{u}_{best}$, along the direction defined by $\mathbf{u}_{best} - \mathbf{u}_{s+1}$. The best of $\mathbf{u}_{s+1}$ and $\mathbf{u}_{s+2}$ then replaces $\mathbf{u}_{worst}$. The process is repeated until it converges. With the weightings updated by boosting [9]–[11], this leads to the following **OLSwB** algorithm.

Initialization: Give J_{k-1}, and the s randomly chosen initial values for $\mathbf{u}$, $\mathbf{u}_1, \mathbf{u}_2, \cdots, \mathbf{u}_s$. Set iteration index $t = 0$ and $\delta_i^{(t)} = \frac{1}{s}$ for $1 \le i \le s$.

1. For $1 \le i \le s$, generate $\mathbf{g}_k^{(i)}$ from $\mathbf{u}_i$, the s candidates for the kth model column, and orthogonalize them

$$\alpha_{j,k}^{(i)} = \frac{\mathbf{p}_j^T \mathbf{g}_k^{(i)}}{\mathbf{p}_j^T \mathbf{p}_j}, \quad 1 \le j < k, \quad \mathbf{p}_k^{(i)} = \mathbf{g}_k^{(i)} - \sum_{j=1}^{k-1} \alpha_{j,k}^{(i)} \mathbf{p}_j$$

2. For $1 \le i \le s$, calculate the loss of each point, namely

$$\theta_k^{(i)} = \frac{\left(\mathbf{p}_k^{(i)}\right)^T \mathbf{y}}{\left(\mathbf{p}_k^{(i)}\right)^T \mathbf{p}_k^{(i)}}, \quad J_k^{(i)} = J_{k-1} - \frac{1}{N}\left(\mathbf{p}_k^{(i)}\right)^T \mathbf{p}_k^{(i)} \left(\theta_k^{(i)}\right)^2$$

Step 1: Boosting

1. Find $\mathbf{u}_{best} = \arg\min\{J_k^{(i)}, 1 \le i \le s\}$ and $\mathbf{u}_{worst} = \arg\max\{J_k^{(i)}, 1 \le i \le s\}$.
2. Normalize the loss

$$\bar{J}_k^{(i)} = \frac{J_k^{(i)}}{\sum_{l=1}^{s} J_k^{(l)}}, \quad 1 \le i \le s$$

3. Compute a weighting factor β_t according to

$$\epsilon_t = \sum_{i=1}^{s} \delta_i^{(t)} \bar{J}_k^{(i)}, \quad \beta_t = \frac{\epsilon_t}{1 - \epsilon_t}$$

4. Update the weighting vector

$$\delta_i^{(t+1)} = \begin{cases} \delta_i^{(t)} \beta_t^{\bar{J}_k^{(i)}} & \text{for } \beta_t \le 1, \\ \delta_i^{(t)} \beta_t^{1-\bar{J}_k^{(i)}} & \text{for } \beta_t > 1, \end{cases} \quad 1 \le i \le s$$

5. Normalize the weighting vector

$$\delta_i^{(t+1)} = \frac{\delta_i^{(t+1)}}{\sum_{l=1}^{s} \delta_l^{(t+1)}}, \quad 1 \leq i \leq s$$

Step 2: Parameter updating
1. Construct the $(s+1)$th point using the formula

$$\mathbf{u}_{s+1} = \sum_{i=1}^{s} \delta_i^{(t+1)} \mathbf{u}_i$$

2. Construct the $(s+2)$th point using the formula

$$\mathbf{u}_{s+2} = \mathbf{u}_{best} + (\mathbf{u}_{best} - \mathbf{u}_{s+1})$$

3. Orthogonalize these two candidate model columns and compute their losses.
4. Choose a better point from $\mathbf{u}_{s+1}$ and $\mathbf{u}_{s+2}$ to replace $\mathbf{u}_{worst}$.

Repeat from *Step 1* until the $(s+1)$th value changes very little compared with the last round, or a preset maximum number of iterations has been reached.

From the converged population of s points, find $i_k = \arg\min\{J_k^{(i)}, 1 \leq i \leq s\}$ and select $\alpha_{j,k} = \alpha_{j,k}^{(i_k)}, 1 \leq j < k$,

$$\mathbf{p}_k = \mathbf{p}_k^{(i_k)} = \mathbf{g}_k^{(i_k)} - \sum_{j=1}^{k-1} \alpha_{j,k} \mathbf{p}_j$$

with $J_k = J_k^{(i_k)}$, and $\theta_k = \theta_k^{(i_k)}$. This determines the kth regressor.

4 Experimental Results

Example 1. The 500 points of training data were generated from

$$y(x) = 0.1x + \frac{\sin x}{x} + \sin 0.5x + \epsilon \tag{8}$$

with $x \in [-10, 10]$, where ϵ was a Gaussian white noise with zero mean and variance 0.01. The population size used in **OLSwB** was $s = 7$. With the modeling accuracy set to $\xi = 0.012$, the model construction procedure produced 6 Gaussian regressors, as summarized in Table 1. Fig. 1 (a) depicts the model output $\hat{y}(x)$ generated from the constructed 6-term model, in comparison with the noisy training data $y(x)$, and Fig. 1 (b) shows the corresponding modeling error $e(x) = y(x) - \hat{y}(x)$.

Example 2. This example constructed a model representing the relationship between the fuel rack position (input $u(t)$) and the engine speed (output $y(t)$)

Table 1. OLSwB modeling procedure for the simple function example.

regression step k	mean μ_k	variance σ_k^2	weight w_k	MSE J_k
0	–	–	–	0.8431
1	2.6911	4.2480	2.3527	0.3703
2	-4.0652	2.1710	-2.5197	0.0339
3	3.0314	2.0059	-1.0609	0.0172
4	-4.1771	1.0909	0.8982	0.0151
5	-1.9783	64.0000	0.1190	0.0129
6	6.6853	0.3894	0.1548	0.0118

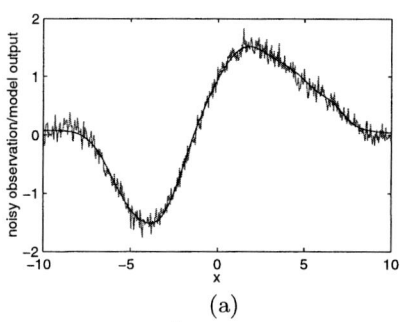
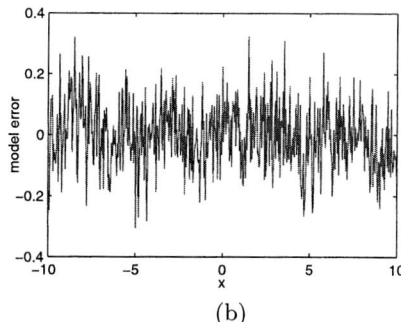

(a)   (b)

Fig. 1. The simple function approximation: (a) noisy training data $y(x)$ (rough light curve) and model output $\hat{y}(x)$ (smooth dark curve), and (b) modeling error $e(x) = y(x) - \hat{y}(x)$.

for a Leyland TL11 turbocharged, direct injection diesel engine operated at low engine speed. Detailed system description and experimental setup can be found in [12]. The input-output data set contained 410 samples. The first 210 data points were used in training and the last 200 points in model validation. The previous study [4] has shown that this data set can be modeled adequately as $y_i = f_s(\mathbf{x}_i) + \epsilon_i$, with $y_i = y(i)$, $\mathbf{x}_i = [y(i-1) \ u(i-1) \ u(i-2)]^T$, where $f_s(\bullet)$ describes the unknown underlying system to be identified and $\epsilon_i = \epsilon(i)$ denotes the system noise.

With a population size $s = 37$ and a preset modeling accuracy of $\xi = 0.00055$, the **OLSwB** modeling procedure produced 6 Gaussian regressors, as listed in Table 2. The MSE value of the constructed 6-term model over the testing set was 0.000573. Fig. 2 (a) depicts the model prediction $\hat{y}(t)$ superimposed on the system output $y(t)$ and Fig. 2 (b) shows the model prediction error $e(t) = y(t) - \hat{y}(t)$ for this 6-term model. It is worth pointing out that to achieve a same modeling accuracy for this data set the existing state-of-art kernel regression techniques required at least 22 regressors [4],[13].

5 Conclusions

A novel construction algorithm has been proposed for parsimonious regression modeling based on the OLS algorithm with boosting. The proposed algorithm

Table 2. OLSwB modeling procedure for the engine data set.

step k	mean vector $\boldsymbol{\mu}_k$	diagonal covariance $\boldsymbol{\Sigma}_k$	weight w_k	MSE $J_k \times 100$
0	–	–	–	1558.9
1	5.2219 5.5839 5.6416	7.3532 21.0894 22.4661	6.0396	0.3866
2	4.2542 5.2741 4.1028	1.8680 10.0863 49.8826	-1.2845	0.1311
3	3.8826 5.1707 6.3200	0.1600 0.1600 64.0000	-0.1539	0.0996
4	2.3154 3.2544 5.4897	0.9447 0.3329 11.7564	-0.1433	0.0913
5	4.0673 4.4276 3.5963	0.1608 18.3731 0.2207	0.1945	0.0740
6	2.3663 3.2377 5.1376	0.1754 0.9317 0.1600	0.9658	0.0547

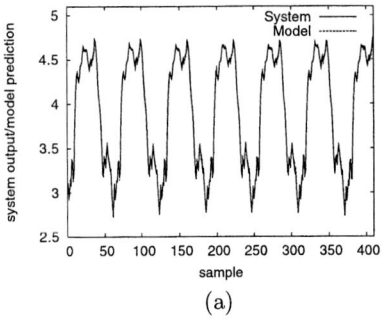
(a)

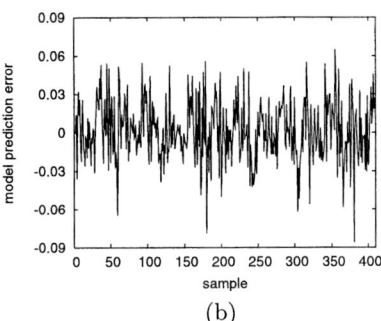
(b)

Fig. 2. The engine data set: (a) model prediction $\hat{y}(t)$ (dashed) superimposed on system output $y(t)$ (solid), and (b) model prediction error $e(t) = y(t) - \hat{y}(t)$.

has the ability to tune the mean vector and diagonal covariance matrix of individual regressor to incrementally minimize the training mean square error. A weighted optimization search method has been developed based on boosting to append regressors one by one in an orthogonal forward regression procedure. Experimental results presented have demonstrated the effectiveness of the proposed technique.

References

1. S. Chen, S.A. Billings and W. Luo, "Orthogonal least squares methods and their application to non-linear system identification," *Int. J. Control*, Vol.50, No.5, pp.1873–1896, 1989.
2. S. Chen, C.F.N. Cowan and P.M. Grant, "Orthogonal least squares learning algorithm for radial basis function networks," *IEEE Trans. Neural Networks*, Vol.2, No.2, pp.302–309, 1991.
3. S. Chen, Y. Wu and B.L. Luk, "Combined genetic algorithm optimisation and regularised orthogonal least squares learning for radial basis function networks," *IEEE Trans. Neural Networks*, Vol.10, No.5, pp.1239–1243, 1999.
4. S. Chen, X. Hong and C.J. Harris, "Sparse kernel regression modelling using combined locally regularized orthogonal least squares and D-optimality experimental design," *IEEE Trans. Automatic Control*, Vol.48, No.6, pp.1029–1036, 2003.

5. V. Vapnik, *The Nature of Statistical Learning Theory*. New York: Springer-Verlag, 1995.
6. V. Vapnik, S. Golowich and A. Smola, "Support vector method for function approximation, regression estimation, and signal processing," in: M.C. Mozer, M.I. Jordan and T. Petsche, Eds., *Advances in Neural Information Processing Systems 9*. Cambridge, MA: MIT Press, 1997, pp.281–287.
7. B. Schölkopf and A.J. Smola, *Learning with Kernels: Support Vector Machines, Regularization, Optimization, and Beyond*. Cambridge, MA: MIT Press, 2002.
8. M.E. Tipping, "Sparse Bayesian learning and the relevance vector machine," *J. Machine Learning Research*, Vol.1, pp.211–244, 2001.
9. Y. Freund and R.E. Schapire, "A decision-theoretic generalization of on-line learning and an application to boosting," *J. Computer and System Sciences*, Vol.55, No.1, pp.119–139, 1997.
10. R.E. Schapire, "The strength of weak learnability," *Machine Learning*, Vol.5, No.2, pp.197–227, 1990.
11. R. Meir and G. Rätsch, "An introduction to boosting and leveraging," in: S. Mendelson and A. Smola, eds., *Advanced Lectures in Machine Learning*. Springer Verlag, 2003, pp.119–184.
12. S.A. Billings, S. Chen and R.J. Backhouse, "The identification of linear and nonlinear models of a turbocharged automotive diesel engine," *Mechanical Systems and Signal Processing*, Vol.3, No.2, pp.123–142, 1989.
13. S. Chen, X. Hong, C.J. Harris and P.M. Sharkey, "Sparse modelling using orthogonal forward regression with PRESS statistic and regularization," *IEEE Trans. Systems, Man and Cybernetics, Part B*, Vol.34, No.2, pp.898–911, 2004.

New Applications for Object Recognition and Affine Motion Estimation by Independent Component Analysis*

Liming Zhang and Xuming Huang

Dept. E.E, Fudan University, Shanghai 200433, China
{lmzhang,022021035}@fudan.edu.cn

Abstract. This paper proposes a new scheme based on independent component analysis(ICA) for object recognition with affine transformation and for affine motion estimation between video frames. For different skewed shapes of recognized object, an invariant descriptor can be extracted by ICA, and it can solve some skewed object recognition problems. This method also can be used to estimate the affine motion between two frames, which is important in high compression rate coding such as MPEG4 or MPEG7 standard. Simulation results show that the proposed method has a better performance than other traditional methods in pattern recognition and affine motion estimation.

1 Introduction

Skewed objects recognition based on affine transform is a typical problem of rigid object recognition, and has important applications in computer vision. The fundamental difficulty in recognizing an object from 3-D space is that the appearance of shape depends on the observing angle. In general, affine transform can be considered as a depiction obtained from different angles for the same object. The ability to quickly recognize the same object under any affine transform and estimate the affine matrix is very important for the practical applications in military, industrial automation and video process, etc.

Recently, some methods have been proposed for the object recognition under affine transform. Affine moment methods[1] can be applied to gray-scale or binary images, but they are sensitive to variations in background shading or object illumination. Methods based on affine curves, such as affine arc length curve, enclosed area curve, curvature scale space[2,3]and Fourier descriptors are sensitive to the starting point. Oirrak et al proposed a new affine invariant descriptor using Fourier[4,5]. Applying it to the object recognition, one can accurately recognize the complicated objects under low optical distortion and estimate the coefficients of affine motion between two frames. Unfortunately, the recognition correct rate and the precision of motion estimation will decreases greatly when the distortion is large.

In this paper, we propose a new affine-invariant descriptor based on ICA. Suppose that the object contour is sampled N points for both original and affine-transformed

---

* This research is supported by the National Science Foundation (NSF 60171036), China.

images, X and X'. Their coordinates, $X(l) = [x(l)\ y(l)]^T$ and $X'(l) = [x'(l)\ y'(l)]^T$, can be considered as a linear combination of the same independent component $S(l) = [s_x(l)\ s_y(l)]^T$ with different combination parameters matrix A and A' respectively. The new try is to get an affine invariant object contour composed by $S(l)$ from X and X' using ICA, if X and X' represent the same object. The object recognition can be performed by using $S(l)$. Since ICA can estimate both $S(l)$ and combination component A, the affine invariant contour and affine motion parameters can be obtained simultaneously. It is robust to noise because the ICA method uses statistical information. The fast algorithm for ICA proposed by Hyvärinen[6,7] is adopted in this paper.

2   Object Recognition and Affine Matrix Computation Using ICA

Let X' be a linear affine transform from X with affine matrix Z and translation vector B, that can be written as

$$X'(l) = ZX(l - l_0) + B, \qquad (1)$$

Here, l_0 is the difference of starting point between contour X' and X. The translation vector B can be obtained by calculating the centroid of X' and X easily, so in the following, we take $B = 0$ for analytic convenience. Consider that X' and X are the linear combination of the same source S with A' and A, then $X'(l) = A'S'(l)$, $X(l - l_0) = AS(l - l_0)$. By using ICA, we can adapt matrix W' and W to obtain $S'(l)$ and $S(l - l_0)$, and A' and A, that satisfy

$$\begin{aligned} W'X'(l) &= W'A'S'(l) \approx S'(l), A' \approx W'^{-1}, \\ WX(l - l_0) &= WAS(l - l_0) \approx S(l - l_0), A \approx W^{-1}. \end{aligned} \qquad (2)$$

According to property of ICA by [6], the independent components satisfy

$$E\{S(l)S(l)^T\} = I. \qquad (3)$$

If $l_0 = 0$ in eq.(2), S and S' is almost the same, only the order of their elements is difference. A matrix M is considered as the relation between S and S'. It has

$$S'(l) = MS(l). \qquad (4)$$

Here, $M = \begin{vmatrix} \pm 1 & 0 \\ 0 & \pm 1 \end{vmatrix}$ is for same order, and $M = \begin{vmatrix} 0 & \pm 1 \\ \pm 1 & 0 \end{vmatrix}$ for antithesis order. As mentioned above, the independent component S and S' can be sampled N points $[S'] = [S'(1)\ S'(2)\ ...\ S'(N)]$ and $[S] = [S(1)\ S(2)\ ...\ S(N)]$. From eq.(3) we have $[S][S]^T = NI$. A cost function J_τ is considered to determine the shift l_0, that is

$$J_\tau = abs\left(\left|[S'][S_\tau]^T\right|\right) = abs\left(M\left[S_{l_0}\right][S_\tau]^T\right) = abs(R_s(\tau - l_0)) \qquad (5)$$

where $[S_i]$ denotes the $[S]$ with ring shifting i, then we obtain the shift l_0, i.e.

$$l_0 = \arg_\tau(\max J_\tau) \tag{6}$$

From eqs (3-6) we have

$$M = S'S_{l_0}^T / N. \tag{7}$$

Therefore, the object can be recognized by comparing $S'(l)$ with $MS(l-l_0)$. The affine matrix Z also can be estimated from formula (1), (2) and (4), that is

$$Z = W^{r-1} MW. \tag{8}$$

3 Simulation and Applications

In this section, some simulation results confirm our method proposed in section 2, and some applications show that the proposed method is better than Fourier transform method that is well known as an effective method recently.

Example 1: Fig.1 (a) is an airplane's contour, which is extracted by any image processing method, and its affine transform shape is shown in Fig.1 (b). Here the affine matrix $Z = \begin{bmatrix} 1 & 0.5 \\ 0.2 & -1 \end{bmatrix}$, $B = \begin{bmatrix} 40 \\ 140 \end{bmatrix}$, the difference of start sampled index for the two contours is 200. Start sample points are signed by asterisks in Fig.1 (a) and (b), respectively. Fig.2 shows the independent variables for Fig.1 (a) and (b) on x and y axis by using the proposed method.

From Fig.2, we can see that the random variables of the object and its skew shape using proposed method are the same. The affine invariant descriptor composed of two random variables of S is shown in Fig.3. For any kinds of affine transform for object in Fig.1 (a), the affine invariant descriptor is the same by using our method.

Example 2: To test the discrimination ability of our proposed method, we use real airplane images. Fig.4 (a) shows ten known airplane models that represent ten different objects. From different view angle, we will get different affine contour images. One kind of the affine models corresponding to 10 distorted images, with 40° skewed on horizontal and 10° on vertical direction are shown in Fig.4 (b) and we take these as test images. Table 1 shows the maximal similarity and recognition results (shown in the brackets) by using our method and the Fourier method. This result shows that our method can successfully discriminate objects in the case of high skew, and is better performance than the Fourier method. For slighter distortion our method also could recognize accurately.

Example 3: In this example we use the proposed method and Fourier method respectively to estimate the affine motion between shapes with noise and start index delay. The original shape is in Fig.1(a), the result is shown in Table 2. Here, we set start index delay, $l_0 = 200$, and the random noise's magnitude is 3 pixels.

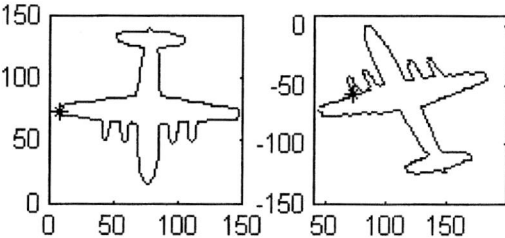

Fig. 1. (a) Airplane counter ; (b) skewed shape of (a).

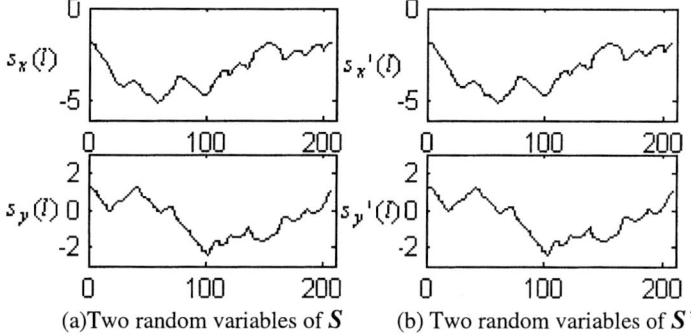

Fig. 2. The results, S and S' by using the proposed method for X and X'.

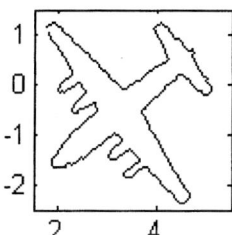

Fig. 3. The invariant descriptor of Fig.1.

Table 2 shows that the results obtained by proposed method are very close to simulated actual motion. It means that the proposed method works very well. It also shows that it has better performance than the Fourier method in motion estimation with noise and start index delay.

To test the robustness of the proposed method, we get the error data of ICA and Fourier method for different magnitude noise, Fig.5 gives the average result of 1000 times. It shows that the proposed method can still work well under strong noise, and it has better performance than the Fourier method.

Example 4: Two real key images taken from different angles are shown in Fig.6 (a) and (b). In Fig.6(c) and (d) the real line's contour is taken from Fig.6 (a) and (b). The dotted contour in Fig.(c) and (d) are the result of motion estimation from Fig.6(a) and (b) by using proposed method and Fourier method, respectively. It is obvious that the

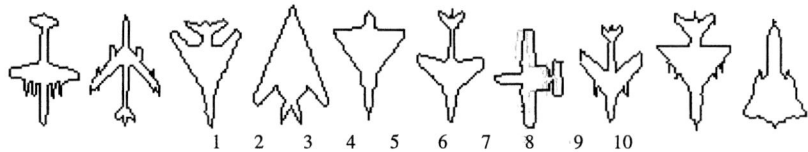

Fig. 4a. Ten known airplane models.

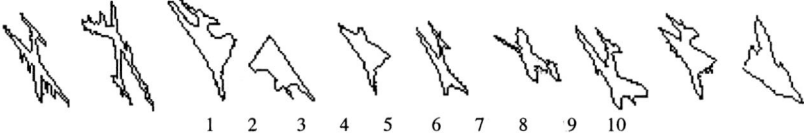

Fig. 4b. The skewed images correspond to the model images in Fig.4 (a) respectively.

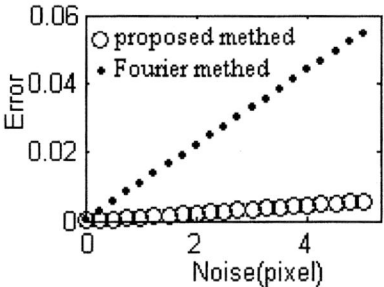

Fig. 5. The comparative result of proposed method and Fourier method.

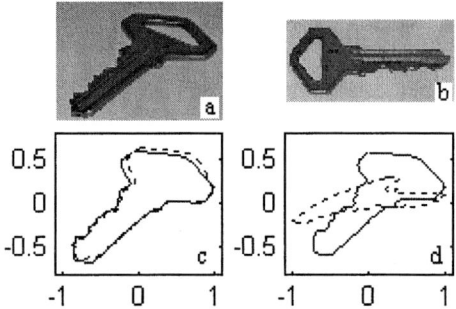

Fig. 6. Affine parameters estimation (a) and (b): The real key image taken from different angles; (c) The result by our method. (d) The result by Fourier method.

proposed method can estimate the affine parameters more precisely than Fourier method. The reason is that, in real application, the images taken from different angles do not satisfy affine transform relation strictly, and they are affected by illumination and noise, so the affine invariant descriptor deduced in the frequency domain or other transform domain does not work well, and our proposed method works in the spatial domain and the linear transform matrix W can be adaptive for different cases.

Example 5: To test our method's feasibility of real application, we get 1000 groups random shape with different number of contour points, and test the computational time of affine motion estimation using our method. The result is shown in Table 3.

From Table 3 we can see that the estimation of the start sample point by using ring shift algorithm will spend more time, but it still satisfy requirement of real world processing. For example, an affine motion object with 128 sample points on the contour in different starting sample point, it could estimate 35 frames per second, 1/0.02844=35.16 frames/second. In real image compression standard, such as MPEG4 and MPEG7, contour information is known in advance, and object movement between two frames is slight, alternate left and right ring shift can match the starting point quickly, so it will reduce the process time and can be applied to a real-time system.

Table 1. The recognized results for each test image in Fig.4 (b) using our method and the Fourier method respectively.

Test image	1	2	3	4	5
Our Method	0.9969(1)	0.9741(2)	0.9628(3)	0.9739(4)	0.9782(5)
Fourier method	0.9955(1)	0.9281(2)	0.9280(3)	0.9746(4)	0.8922(4)
Test image	6	7	8	9	10
Our Method	0.9872(6)	0.9980(7)	0.9768(8)	0.9798(9)	0.9863(10)
Fourier method	0.9784(6)	0.9447(4)	0.9571(8)	0.9115(4)	0.9261(6)

Table 2. The parameters of motion estimation by proposed method and Fourier method.

Affine Parameter	l_0	z_{11}	z_{12}	z_{21}	z_{22}
Actual Motion	200	0.6800	1.4300	-0.4700	0.9900
Proposed Method	200	0.6825	1.4270	-0.4698	0.9909
Fourier Method	200	0.6742	1.4367	-0.4835	1.0056

Table 3. Motion estimation time for different number of contour points.

Contour points / Start sample point	64(sec)	128(sec)	256(sec)
Same	0.00234	0.00250	0.00344
Differ	0.01484	0.02844	0.06590

4 Conclusion

A new scheme for affine invariant descriptor and affine motion estimation by ICA is proposed, in which we assume some random series, sampled from contour of an object and its any skewed shapes, can be considered as a linear combination of affine invariant independent components. Based on this we propose an objects recognition scheme for different affine transform which is implemented by computing the alternate matrix M and cost function J_τ. This method can also be used in affine motion estimation. Experimental results show that the performance of the proposed method is better than other traditional invariant methods, especially, in real world applications.

References

1. Zhao, A., Chen, J.: Affine curve moment invariants for shape recognition. Pattern Recognition, vol 30. no.6 (1997) 895-901
2. Arbter, K., Snyder, W. E., Burkhardt, H., Hirzinger, G.: Application of Affine-Invariant Fourier Descriptors to Recogniton of 3-D Objects. IEEE Trans. PAMI, vol 12. no.7 (1990) 640-647
3. Abbasi, S., Mokhtarian, F.: Affine-Similar Shape Retrieval: Application to Multiview 3-D Object Recognition. IEEE Trans. IP, vol 10, no.1 (2001) 131-139
4. Oirrak, A. E., Daoudi, M., Aboutajdine, D.: Estimation of general 2D affine motion using Fourier descriptors. Pattern Recognition, 35, (2002) 223-228
5. Oirrak, A. E., Daoudi, M., Aboutajdine, D.: Affine invariant descriptors using Fourier series. Pattern Recognition Letters, 23, (2002) 1109-1118
6. Hyvärinen, A.: Fast and robust fixed-point algorithms for independent component analysis. IEEE Trans. NN, vol 10, no.3 (1999) 626-634
7. Hyvärinen, A., Oja, E.: A fast fixed-point algorithm for independent component analysis. Neural Computation, 9, (1997) 1483-1492

Personalized News Reading via Hybrid Learning

Ke Chen[1] and Sunny Yeung[2]

[1] School of Informatics, The University of Manchester, Manchester M60 1QD, UK
[2] School of Computer Science, Birmingham University, Birmingham B15 2TT, UK

Abstract. In this paper, we present a personalized news reading prototype where latest news articles published by various on-line news providers are automatically collected, categorized and ranked in light of a user's habits or interests. Moreover, our system can adapt itself towards a better performance. In order to develop such an adaptive system, we proposed a hybrid learning strategy; supervised learning is used to create an initial system configuration based on user's feedbacks during registration, while an unsupervised learning scheme gradually updates the configuration by tracing the user's behaviors as the system is being used. Simulation results demonstrate satisfactory performance.

1 Introduction

The astonishing growth of the Internet makes huge amount of information on-line available and therefore is changing our economy and society [1]. In order to acquire useful information efficiently, a user demands powerful and easy-to-use Internet tools. On the other hand, different users have distinct habits or interests but most of web sites are designed for general purpose without considering individual's needs. Therefore, it would be a potential solution to develop personalized software in the client side to meet a user's requirements.

News reading has become an indispensable component of daily life for most of people. Traditionally news has been provided as a ready-made package that journalists produce according to the production rhythm of their media. Thanks to the Internet and the Web technology, on-line news has been offered by news providers, e.g. BBC, Internet portals, e.g. Yahoo, and most of traditional paper-based newspaper companies, which expedites news update and dissemination. Thus the production pace is also increased as more and more news organizations produce news 24-hour a day and seven days a week. As a consequence, on-line news articles have been one of the most important Web resources and nowadays more and more people enjoy reading news with the Web surfing.

Machine learning provides a promising way for a system to adapt itself towards better performance. Two major paradigms in machine learning are supervised and unsupervised learning. Supervised learning takes advantage of known examples to encode underlying regularities, while unsupervised learning uncovers intrinsic structures autonomously from data. In general, the supervised learning methodology is applied as sensible examples in the form of input/output pair can be collected, which often leads to better performance due to the availability of sufficient information. In contrast, the unsupervised learning methodology is adopted when there are only a set of data available without teacher's information.

For development of a personalized news reading system, supervised learning can be used for categorizing and ranking of news articles to suit a user down to the ground only if a set of news articles have been correctly labeled by a specific user. Although a user's cooperation is, to some extent, available, it is unrealistic to urge a user to label a significant number of news articles manually before he/she can benefit from doing so. On the other hand, a user's behaviors in access of Web news are always able to record, which turns out to be an important information source for personalization. Exploitation of such information offers an autonomous way for updating a personalized news reading system. In this paper, we present a hybrid learning strategy by combining supervised and unsupervised learning paradigms to create a personalized on-line news reading system. A small number of news articles are elaborately selected to be presented to a user in a questionnaire form, and feedbacks from a user become a set of examples to build up an initial naive Bayesian classifier for categorization and ranking. Furthermore, a user's behaviors in recorded log files are exploited by a self-learning scheme to update the system configuration. We have developed a prototype based on our hybrid learning strategy. Simulation results demonstrate its effectiveness in personalized on-line news reading.

The rest of the paper is organized as follows. Sect. 2 presents the system overview and our hybrid learning strategy. Sect. 3 reports simulation results, and the last section draws conclusions.

2 System Description

2.1 System Overview

As illustrated in Fig. 1, our personalized on-line news reading prototype is composed of three modules: *management*, *news processing* and *news query*.

In the management module, there are two schemes; i.e., download manager and categorization manager. The former is responsible for managing the automatic news collection, and the latter is used to control news categorization, ranking and user profile update. This module also provides an interface for a system administrator to maintain the system.

The news processing module consists of three schemes. The *news collection* scheme based on a crawling technique is used to automatically download news articles from a list of on-line news web sites. The scheme is controled by the download manager in the management module where a system administrator edits the list of URLs of on-line news web sites and specifies an update period. With such parameters, latest web news articles are collected periodically. Once the collection of news articles is performed, the *news preprocessing* scheme is activated to filter out HTML tags and to extract text contents of an news article.

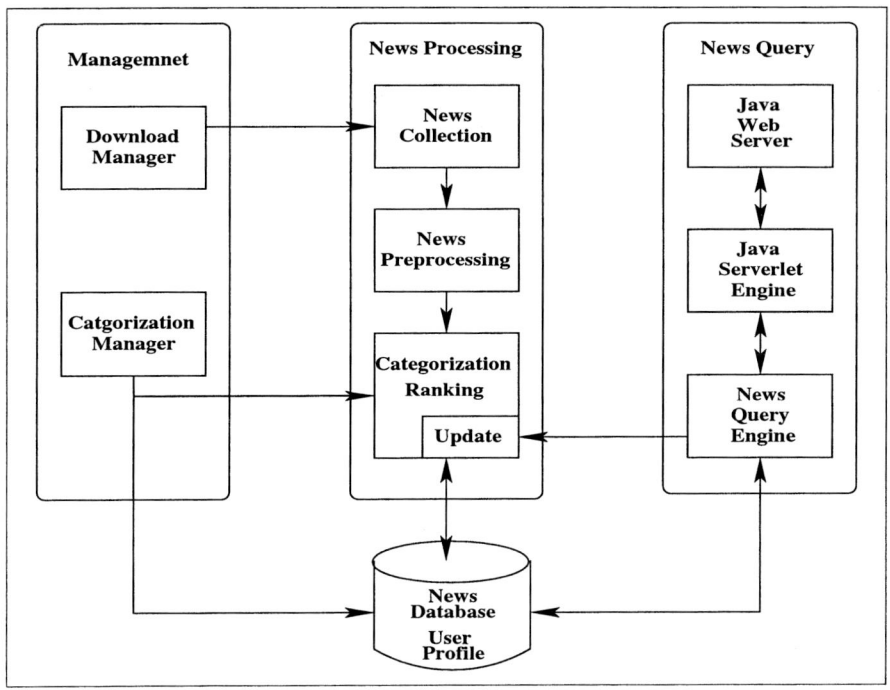

Fig. 1. The personalized news reading system architecture.

The *categorization/ranking* scheme works on the pure text to categorize news articles into a pre-specified news category where each news article is assigned to a single category by a naive Bayesian classifier described in Sect. 2.2. Based on the likelihood score of each article produced by the naive Bayesian classifier, the scheme ranks all the articles fallen into the same category such that articles can be presented in order. Note that personalization demands one classifier for each user. Therefore, each user has his/her own profile to produce personalized categorized results and ranking. Then both user profiles and URLs of categorized articles in order are stored into a database as depicted in Fig. 1.

The news query module provides a set of functions for a user to read or browse the personalized news articles based on his/her profile in the news database. Java development tools are applied to implement those functions. As a consequence, a user can read latest personalized news stored on the local server or retrieve earlier processed news with stored URLs in the news database for his/her personal interests. It is worth mentioning that unlike a conventional query engine we add a mechanism to capture a user's behaviors during accessing news articles. Once the user quits from the system, the processed information is sent to an update scheme in the news processing module, as depicted in Fig. 1, where the corresponding naive Bayesian classifier will be updated autonomously by an update scheme presented in Sect. 2.2.

2.2 Hybrid Learning Strategy

The core enabling technique in our system is a hybrid learning strategy by combining the improved naive Bayesian classifier [3] and a proposed unsupervised update scheme.

Given a set of categories $C = \{c_1, \cdots, c_I\}$ and a news article of J words, $w_1, \cdots, w_J$. Assume that words in the news article are independent of each other, we summarize the naive Bayesian classifier as follows:

$$P(c_i|w_1, \cdots, w_J) \simeq P(c_i) \prod_{j=1}^{J} P(w_j|c_i), \qquad (1)$$

and

$$c_{i^*} = \arg \max_{1 \leq i \leq I} P(c_i|w_1, \cdots, w_J). \qquad (2)$$

c_{i^*} is the category to which the news article is assigned. If there are more than one article in the same category, ranking will be performed based on the score of $P(c_i|w_1, \cdots, w_J)$ in (1). To create such a classifier, we need to estimate word and category probabilities, $P(c_i)$ and $P(w_j|c_i)$, for all categories, which can be done by simple event counting [3]. Due to the existence of infrequently encountered words, we further use a smoothing method to modify the probabilities [2,3], which results in an improved naive Bayesian classifier of robust results.

When personalized news articles are presented to a user, we assume that he/she is interested in only correctly categorized articles. Therefore, all the articles visited will be tagged as the new data to update his/her naive Bayesian classifier. This idea has been successfully applied in decision-making for speaker verification in our previous work [4]. For update, we need to know only the total number of articles, N_{doc} and the number of words in each category c_i, $n(c_i)$, used previously for estimating probabilities. Assume that in a session the user visited M_{doc} articles among $M(c_i)$ articles in category c_i. Furthermore, there are the number of words, $m(w_j; c_i)$, in category c_i. Thus, we update the corresponding naive Bayesian classifier as follows:

$$P(w_j|c_i) = \frac{n(c_i)P(w_j|c_i) + m(w_j; c_i)}{n(c_i) + \sum_{j=1}^{J} m(w_j; c_i)}, \qquad (3)$$

and

$$P(c_i) = \frac{N_{doc}P(c_i) + M(c_i)}{N_{doc} + M_{doc}}. \qquad (4)$$

The derivation of (2) and (3) is similar to the one in the appendix of [4]. Note that the smoothing technique [2,3] is further applied to (3) and (4) during the update prior to their use in (1) and (2) for decision making.

3 Simulations

We have implemented a prototype based on the architecture as illustrated in Fig. 1. The technical details on implementation and user interface can be found in [5]. Here we report only results achieved during simulations.

In our simulations, all news articles were downloaded automatically from three main news web sites, i.e., BBC, CNN and Yahoo, and updated on a hourly basis. We also limited the number of users so that the prototype accommodated ten users who could create their user profiles in the server (see Fig. 1). Eight categories were defined for all news articles, and total 160 deliberately selected articles were presented to users in a questionnaire form and users individually labelled all news articles in the questionnaire in light of their interests or habits. According to feedbacks, we created a naive Bayesian classifier for each user with his/her labeled articles.

Table 1. Precision and recall of test data without update as well as total relevant number, relevant retrieved number and retrieved number of each category for testing.

Category	Relevant	Relevant Retrieved	Retrieved	Recall	Precision
Politics	1238	738	946	59.9%	78.0%
Business/Finance	1047	689	938	65.8%	73.5%
Entertainment	948	627	799	66.1%	78.5%
Science	534	275	512	51.5%	53.7%
Technology	749	421	678	56.2%	62.1%
Health	583	424	498	72.7%	85.1%
Education	376	225	312	59.8%	72.1%
Sport	1042	637	766	61.1%	83.2%

Table 2. Precision and recall of test data with update as well as total relevant number, relevant retrieved number and retrieved number of each category for testing.

Category	Relevant	Relevant Retrieved	Retrieved	Recall	Precision
Politics	1238	1025	1174	82.8%	87.3%
Business/Finance	1047	923	972	88.2%	95.0%
Entertainment	948	803	887	84.7%	90.5%
Science	534	472	486	88.4%	97.1%
Technology	749	634	652	84.6%	97.2%
Health	583	506	519	86.8%	97.5%
Education	376	331	339	88.0%	97.6%
Sport	1042	955	979	91.7%	97.5%

In order to evaluate the performance of our prototype, we adopt the standard measure commonly used in information retrieval, *precision* and *recall*. For ten users, we report only averaging results here. For comparison, we have conducted two experiments; one is the use of only the initial naive Bayesian classifier and the other is the use of the naive Bayesian classifier with the update scheme presented in (3) and (4). As a result, Table 1 shows the results of initial naive Bayesian classifiers prior to update with users' behaviors. It is observed that the performance with only supervised learning is less acceptable by a user although it sounds reasonable for a naive Bayesian classifier. By introducing the update scheme presented in (3) and (4) into our prototype, we can make the system self-learn incrementally from users' behaviors. By using the same testing data, we show the performance of updated naive Bayesian classifiers in Table 2 for comparison.

From Tables 1 and 2, it is evident that the proposed update scheme significantly improves the performance of our prototype in both precision and recall. In particular, articles belonging to science or technology often have common words. Without unsupervised learning, the performance of a naive Bayesian classifier is unsatisfactory in categorizing such news. In contrast, the use of our update scheme leads to an acceptable performance. In addition, our ranking scheme simply based on likelihood scores works well; the target or click rate of top three articles in each category is at least 95.7% (for more simulation results, see [5]).

4 Conclusion

We have presented a personalized news reading prototype based on a hybrid learning strategy. Simulation results demonstrate the usefulness of our hybrid learning strategy. As a core enabling technique, our hybrid learning strategy combines the naive Bayesian supervised learning and a proposed autonomous update scheme. Unlike previous hybrid learning strategies, e.g. combination of supervised learning and semi-supervised learning paradigms [6], our hybrid learning strategy is simple yet effective. In particular, our update scheme exploits a user's preference information from his/her on-line behaviors autonomously and works in an incremental way, in particular, which is transparent to a user. Although users' behaviours might not always precisely reflect his/her preference, our simulation results indicate that the system actually works towards better performance. Based on the promising simulation results reported in this paper, we anticipate that our hybrid learning strategy can be extended to other learning systems that face a difficulty in collection of training data.

References

1. A. Y. Levy and D. S. Weld, "Intelligent Internet Systems," *Artificial Intelligence*, vol. 118, no. 1, pp. 1-14, 2000.
2. I. H. Witten and T. C. Bell, "The zero-frequency problem: Estimating the probabilities of novel events in adaptive text compression," *IEEE Transactions on Information Theory*, vol. 37, no. 4, pp. 545-558, 1991.
3. M. Craven et al., "Learning to construct knowledge bases from the WWW," *Artificial Intelligence*, vol. 118, no. 1, pp. 69-113, 2000.
4. K. Chen, "Towards better making a decision in speaker verification," *Pattern Recognition*, vol. 36, no. 2, pp. 329-346, 2003.
5. S. Yeung, *A Personalized New Reading System*, MSc Thesis, School for Computer Science, The University of Birmingham, U.K., 2002.
6. S. Chakrabarti, *Mining the Web: Discovering Knowledge from Hypertext Data*, Morgan Kaufmann, 2003.

Mercer Kernel, Fuzzy C-Means Algorithm, and Prototypes of Clusters

Shangming Zhou and John Q. Gan

Department of Computer Science
University of Essex
Colchester CO4 3SQ, UK
{szhoup,jqgan}@essex.ac.uk

Abstract. In this paper, an unsupervised Mercer kernel based fuzzy c-means (MKFCM) clustering algorithm is proposed, in which the implicit assumptions about the shapes of clusters in the FCM algorithm is removed so that the new algorithm possesses strong adaptability to cluster structures within data samples. A new method for calculating the prototypes of clusters in input space is also proposed, which is essential for data clustering applications. Experimental results have demonstrated the promising performance of the MKFCM algorithm in different scenarios.

1 Introduction

Since Vapnik introduced support vector machines (SVM) [1], the Mercer kernel based learning has received much attention in the machine learning community [2] [3] [4]. In [5], a fuzzy SVM was proposed, in which a certain membership degree is assigned to each input point of the SVM so that different points make different contributions to the learning of the decision surface. Chiang and Hao extended the support vector clustering (SVC) algorithm developed in [3] from one sphere scenario to multi-sphere scenarios and then constructed fuzzy membership functions of the clusters manually in terms of the spherical radius in feature space [6]. However, very few efforts were made to introduce the kernel treatment into fuzzy clustering.

The objective of this paper is to apply the kernel techniques to the fuzzy c-means (FCM) algorithm [7], which will improve the performance of the FCM algorithm and remove some of its constraints. The FCM algorithm has been applied in various areas, however, it makes implicit assumptions concerning the shape and size of the clusters, i.e., the clusters are hyper-spherical and of approximately the same size. Some efforts have been made to avoid these assumptions. The Mahalanobis distance is used in the Gustafson-Kessel (GK) fuzzy clustering algorithm [7] [8] instead of the Euclidean distance, in which the clusters are in fact assumed to be hyperelliptical. In order to detect non-hyperspherical structural subsets, Bezdek et al. [9] defined linear cluster structures of different dimensions in the fuzzy clustering process. In [10], Jerome et al. proposed a probabilistic relaxation fuzzy clustering algorithm based on the estimation of probability density function without assumptions about the size and shape of clusters. In this paper, a Mercer kernel based FCM (MKFCM) clustering algorithm is proposed to identify naturally occurring clusters while preserving the associated information about the relations between the clusters, which would remove the implicit assumption of hyper-spherical or ellipsoidal clusters within input data samples. However, one of the main problems in using kernel method for unsupervised clustering is that it is usually difficult to obtain the prototypes of clusters in both feature space and input space [11]. A new method for calculating cluster prototypes in input space is developed in this paper.

The organization of this paper is as follows. The next section describes the MKFCM clustering algorithm. The proposed algorithm is experimentally evaluated in section 3. Section 4 provides a conclusion.

2 MKFCM: An Unsupervised Fuzzy Clustering Algorithm

2.1 MKFCM Clustering Algorithm

Using the Euclidian distance, the FCM algorithm has the tendency to partition the data points into clusters of hyperspherical shape, with an equal number of data points in each cluster. By mapping the observed data points in input space $\Re^P$ into a high dimensional feature space Γ using a nonlinear function $\Phi(\cdot)$, the clustering process can be carried out in feature space rather than input space and the restrictions in input space about the cluster shapes may be avoided. The criterion function used in feature space is defined as

$$J_m(U,V^\Phi) = \sum_{k=1}^{c}\sum_{j=1}^{N}(u_{kj})^m D_{kj}^2 = \sum_{k=1}^{c}\sum_{j=1}^{N}(u_{kj})^m \|\Phi(x_j)-V_k^\Phi\|^2 \qquad (1)$$

where $U=(u_{kj})$ is a fuzzy c-partition of $\Phi(X)=\{\Phi(x_1),\cdots,\Phi(x_N)\}\in \Gamma$, which corresponds to the partition matrix of $X \in \Re^P$, and $V^\Phi = (V_1^\Phi,\cdots,V_c^\Phi)$ represent cluster prototypes in feature space, and $m \in [1,\infty)$ is a weighting exponent. As $m \to 1$, (1) becomes hard and converges in theory to a "generalized" kernel version of hard c-means solution as shown in [4], so m is generally assumed to belong to $(1,\infty)$ in (1). The optimal partition is obtained by minimizing (1) subject to the constraints $\sum_{k=1}^{c}u_{kj}=1, \forall j$.

Clearly the cluster prototypes V_k^Φ should lie in the span of $\Phi(x_1),\cdots,\Phi(x_N)$. Furthermore, by setting the partial derivatives of J_m w.r.t. V_k^Φ to zero, we obtain

$$V_k^\Phi = \sum_{j=1}^{N}\tilde{u}_{kj}\Phi(x_j) \qquad (2)$$

where $\tilde{u}_{kj} = (u_{kj})^m / N_k = (u_{kj})^m / \sum_{j=1}^{N}(u_{kj})^m$. Based on expression (2) for V_k^Φ, through some manipulations the criterion function (1) can be expressed as follows:

$$J_m(U) = \sum_{k=1}^{c}\sum_{j=1}^{N}(u_{kj})^m K_{jj} - \sum_{k=1}^{c}\frac{1}{N_k}\left(\sum_{j=1}^{N}\sum_{i=1}^{N}(u_{kj})^m(u_{ki})^m K_{ij}\right) \qquad (3)$$

where K_{ij} is a symmetric $N \times N$ kernel matrix defined by $K_{ij} = k(x_i, x_j) = \Phi(x_i) \cdot \Phi(x_j)$. From the above criterion function, it is clear that based on the kernel expression the clustering in feature space makes no implicit assumption concerning the shape of the clusters such as hyper-spherical or hyper-ellipsoidal structure in input space.

2.1.1 Optimal Partitioning Matrix

The first problem in developing the MKFCM algorithm is how to optimize the partitioning matrix U by minimizing (1) subject to the constraints $\sum_{k=1}^{c} u_{kj} = 1, \forall j$. Defining the following Lagrangian:

$$L(U, \beta) = J_m + \sum_{j=1}^{N}\beta_j(\sum_{k=1}^{c} u_{kj} - 1) \qquad (4)$$

and setting the Lagrangian's gradients to zero, by some manipulations we obtain

$$u_{kj} = \frac{(\rho_{kj})^{\frac{1}{1-m}}}{\sum_{k=1}^{c}(\rho_{kj})^{\frac{1}{1-m}}} \qquad (5)$$

where

$$\rho_{kj} =: K_{jj} - \frac{2}{N_k}\sum_{i=1}^{N}(u_{ki})^m K_{ij} + \frac{1}{N_k^2}\sum_{l=1}^{N}\sum_{i=1}^{N}(u_{kl})^m(u_{ki})^m K_{li} \qquad (6)$$

When $\rho_{kj} = 0$, i.e., the sample data x_j is located at the core center of the fuzzy set for the kth cluster, special care is needed. Firstly, the data classes can be divided into two groups I_j and $\tilde{I}_j$, where $I_j =: \{k \mid 1 \le k \le c; \rho_{kj} = 0\}$ and $\tilde{I}_j =: \{1, \cdots, c\} - I_j$ ($1 \le j \le N$). If $I_j \ne \phi$, then set $u_{kj} = 0$ for $k \in \tilde{I}_j$ and make $\sum_{k \in I_j} u_{kj} = 1$ for $k \in I_j$.

2.1.2 Cluster Prototypes in Input Space

Another problem in developing the MKFCM algorithm is how to obtain the cluster prototypes in input space. After an optimal partition U that minimizes criterion function (1) is obtained, the cluster prototypes V_k^Φ can be only expressed as expansions of mapped patterns. However, it is difficult to obtain explicit expressions for the mapped patterns, and even if explicit expressions are available it is not guaranteed that there exists a preimage pattern v_k in input space such that $\Phi(v_k) = V_k^\Phi$ since the mapping function Φ is nonlinear. The problem about cluster prototypes in kernel based clustering methods is far from being addressed in the literature [11]. This paper proposes a new method to calculate cluster prototypes in input space in terms of kernel function rather than mapping function. The basic idea is to approximate these prototypes in input space by minimizing the functional $W(v_k) = \|\Phi(v_k) - V_k^\Phi\|^2$. By replacing (2) for V_k^Φ, $W(v_k)$ can be expressed as follows:

$$W(v_k) = \sum_{l=1}^{N}\sum_{i=1}^{N} \tilde{u}_{kl}\tilde{u}_{ki} k(x_l, x_i) - 2\sum_{j=1}^{N} \tilde{u}_{kj} k(x_j, v_k) + k(v_k, v_k) \qquad (7)$$

As a matter of fact, the minimization of (7) corresponds to minimizing the distance between V_k^Φ and the orthogonal projection of V_k^Φ onto span $(\Phi(v_k))$, which is equivalent to maximizing the term: $(V_k^\Phi \cdot \Phi(v_k))^2 / (\Phi(v_k) \cdot \Phi(v_k))$. Scholkopf et al. approximated a preimage pattern in input space for a given mapped pattern in feature space in terms of this term [11]. This paper uses the minimization of (7) since it avoids complicated calculations of derivatives and the use of explicit expression of mapping function Φ.

In the following, Gaussian kernels $k(x, y) = \exp(-\|x - y\|^2 / \sigma^2)$ and polynomial kernels $k(x, y) = ((x \cdot y) + \theta)^d$ are discussed, where σ is the width of the Gaussian kernel, θ and d are the offset and exponential parameters of the polynomial kernel respectively. For Gaussian kernels, setting the gradient of (7) w.r.t. v_k to zero we obtain the approximated cluster prototypes in input space as follows:

$$v_k = \sum_{j=1}^{N}(u_{kj})^m k(x_j, v_k) x_j \bigg/ \left(\sum_{j=1}^{N}(u_{kj})^m k(x_j, v_k)\right) \qquad (8)$$

For polynomial kernels, by setting the gradient of (7) w.r.t. v_k to zero we have

$$v_k = \sum_{j=1}^{N}(u_{kj})^m ((x_j \cdot v_k) + \theta)^{d-1} x_j \bigg/ \left(N_k \cdot ((x_j \cdot v_k) + \theta)^{d-1}\right) \qquad (9)$$

2.2 Picard Iteration in the MKFCM Algorithm

It should be noted that the solutions given by (5), (8), and (9) are iterative. The Picard iteration is adopted in the MKFCM algorithm, which includes the following steps:

Step 1. Set the number of clusters c ($1 < c < N$), the weighting exponent $m \in (1, \infty)$, and the error threshold $\varepsilon_U \geq 0$. Choose a kernel function: Gaussian kernel or polynomial kernel. Initialize partition matrix $U^{(0)}$. Set $t=0$.

Step 2. Set $t:=t+1$. Update the fuzzy partition matrix $U^{(t)}$ in terms of (5) and (6).

Step 3. If $\|U^{(t)} - U^{(t-1)}\| < \varepsilon_U$, go to Step 4; otherwise go to Step 2.

Step 4. Calculate the cluster prototypes in input space:

Step 4.1 For optimal partition matrix $U^{(*)}$, set error threshold $\varepsilon_V \geq 0$. Initialize cluster prototypes $V^{(0)} = (v_1^{(0)}, \cdots, v_c^{(0)}) \in \Re^{Pc}$. Set $r=0$.

Step 4.2 Set r=:r+1. Update the cluster prototypes $V^{(r)}$ using (8) for Gaussian kernels or (9) for polynomial kernels.

Step 4.3 If $\|V^{(r)} - V^{(r-1)}\| < \varepsilon_V$, stop; otherwise go to Step 4.2.

3 Experimental Results

Two examples of unsupervised data clustering by the proposed MKFCM algorithm are given in this section. The first example uses the ringnorm dataset with 2 classes of vectors, each containing 20 attributes, which is available at DELVE repository (*http://www.cs.toronto.edu/~delve/data/ringnorm*). Breiman reported that the Bayes optimal misclassification rate on this data set is 1.3% [12], which can be considered as an expected target for the clustering methods to achieve. 300 data samples were used in our experiment, the same as in Breiman's. The labels in the ringnorm dataset were not used in the clustering process, but used for calculating the clustering error rate in order to evaluate the performance of the MKFCM algorithm. The error rate was calculated by converting the fuzzy partition to its closet hard partition via the maximum membership rule and then counting classification mistakes, as suggested in [7]. By using the MKFCM ($m=2$) with Gaussian kernel ($\sigma=6.5$) and polynomial kernel ($d=2$, $\theta=8$), the number of misclassifications was found to be 4 and 12 respectively, so the corresponding error rates were 1.33% and 4% separately. As a comparison, FCM ($m=2$) made 62 misclassifications with an error rate of 20.27%, meanwhile the decision trees CART achieved a misclassification rate of 21.4% [12] [13]. The advantage of the MKFCM algorithm is very obvious in this example.

The second example uses a 2-dimensional cross structure dataset to test the performance of the MKFCM in detecting non-hyperspherical clusters. The MKFCM algorithm with polynomial kernels is capable of obtaining parabola-shaped clusters, while the MKFCM algorithm with Gaussian kernels is able to find out two line-shaped clusters. However, the FCM algorithm has failed to detect the line-shape clusters due to its favor of hyperspherical or hyperelliptical clusters. Unfortunately, due to the limited space the clustering results in figures cannot be pasted here.

4 Conclusion

In this paper, a new fuzzy clustering algorithm is proposed by applying the Mercer kernel techniques to the FCM algorithm. The MKFCM algorithm makes no assumptions about the shape of clusters within data samples in input space, so it possesses strong adaptability to data cluster structures. In order to calculate the prototypes of clusters in input space in Mercer kernel based clustering methods, a method for approximating the prototypes of clusters in input space is developed. Experimental results have demonstrated the promising performance of the MKFCM algorithm.

References

1. Vapnik,V. N.: The Nature of Statistical Learning Theory. New York: Springer-Verlag (1995)
2. Schölkopf, B., Smola, A. J., Müller, K.-R.: Nonlinear Component Analysis as a Kernel Eigenvalue Problem. Neural Computation 10(1998)1299–1319
3. Ben-Hur, A., Horn, D., Siegelmann, H. T., Vapnik, V.: Support Vector Clustering. Journal of Machine Learning Research 2 (2001) 125-137
4. Girolami, M.: Mercer Kernel-based Clustering in Feature Space. IEEE Trans. on NN 13(2002)780-784
5. Lin, C.-F., Wang, S.-D.: Fuzzy Support Vector Machines. IEEE Trans. on NN 13(2002)464-471
6. Chiang, J-H., Hao, P.-Y: A New Kernel-based Fuzzy Clustering Approach: Support Vector Clustering with Cell Growing. IEEE Trans. on FS 11(2003)518-527
7. Bezdek, J. C.: Pattern Recognition with Fuzzy Objective Function Algorithms. Plenum Press, New York (1981)
8. Gustafson, D. E., Kessel, W.: Fuzzy Clustering with a Fuzzy Covariance Matrix. In: Fu, K. S. (ed): Proc. IEEE-CDC, Vol.2. IEEE Press, Piscataway, new Jersey (1979)761-766
9. Bezdek, J. C., Anderson, I.: An Application of the C-varieties Clustering Algorithm to Polygonal Curve Fitting. IEEE Trans. on SMC 15(1985)637-641
10. Jerome, C., Noel, B., Michel, H.: A New Fuzzy Clustering Technique based on PDF Estimation. Proceedings of Information Processing and Managing of Uncertainty (IPMU) (2002) 225-232
11. Schölkopf, B., Mika, S., Burges, C. J. C., Knirsch, P., Müller, K.-R., Ratsch, G., Smola, A. J.: Input Space versus Feature Space in Kernel based Methods. IEEE Trans. on NN 10(1999)1000–1017
12. Breiman, L.: Bias, Variance and Arcing Classifiers. Tech. Report 460, Statistics department, University of California, USA (1996)
13. Breiman, L., Friedman, J., Stone, C. J., Olshen, R. A.: Classification and Regression Trees. Chapman & Hall / CRC (1984)

DIVACE: Diverse and Accurate Ensemble Learning Algorithm

Arjun Chandra and Xin Yao

The Centre of Excellence for Research in Computational Intelligence and
Applications (CERCIA), School of Computer Science, The University of Birmingham
Edgbaston, Birmingham B15 2TT, UK

Abstract. In order for a neural network ensemble to generalise properly, two factors are considered vital. One is the diversity and the other is the accuracy of the networks that comprise the ensemble. There exists a tradeoff as to what should be the optimal measures of diversity and accuracy. The aim of this paper is to address this issue. We propose the DIVACE algorithm which tries to produce an ensemble as it searches for the optimum point on the diversity-accuracy curve. The DIVACE algorithm formulates the ensemble learning problem as a multi-objective problem explicitly.

1 Introduction

A key issue in neural computation is that of generalisation. Multi-layer perceptrons have been established as good neural computation models in addition to the fact that numerous techniques have been developed in order for such networks to be trained effectively resulting in better generalisation. A problem that perpetuates and haunts neural computation researchers and is akin to the problem of generalisation ability in neural networks is called the 'bias-variance' dilemma. Geman et al. [6] explained this dilemma very well.

One solution to tackling this dilemma is the use of a collection of predictors instead of one. Brown et al. [5] describe the notion of an ensemble of predictors, and show that such an architecture can be applied to any classification/regression problem. Ensembles have been shown to perform better than their members [7, 8].

Given that ensmebles work better when compared with a single predictor, there have been many inroads into improving the prediction ability of such aggregate systems in recent years. Liu and Yao [8] proposed the Negative Correlation Learning (NCL) algorithm wherein a penalty term is added to the error function which helps in making the individual predictors as different from each other as possible while encouraging the accuracy of individual predictors. This enables the mapping function learnt by the ensemble to generalise better when an unseen input is to be processed. As far as learning and ensemble creation are concerned there are techniques which invovle some manual interference/control as opposed to techniques which are inherently automatic [7]. An evolutionary approach to learning and creation of ensembles automatically was proposed in [7].

Abbass [4] proposed the Pareto-frontier Differential Evolution (PDE) method, which is an extension of the Differential Evolution (DE) algorithm proposed by Storn and Price [11]. In [1], an algorithm for ensemble learning called Memetic Pareto Artificial Neural Network (MPANN), which is a customised version of PDE for evolving neural networks, was proposed.

One very strong motivation for the use of evolutionary multi-criterion optimisation in the creation of an ensemble is that the presence of multiple conflicting objectives engenders a set of near optimal solutions. The presence of more than one optimal solution indicates that if one uses multiobjectivity while creating ensembles, one can actually generate an ensemble automatically where the member networks would inadvertently be near optimal.

Much of this paper deals with a formal description of our approach which is inspired by the MPANN and NCL algorithms but has a few differences. The idea was to evolve an ensemble such that the evolutionary process automatically takes care of the individual members being diverse and at the same time accurate enough in order that the final ensemble generalises well.

2 Diversity and Accuracy in Ensembles

This section gives a brief account of the notion of diversity and that of accuracy in the ensemble context. Then, certain aspects of MPANN and NCL algorithms, which are the main source of inspiration for our approach, are discussed.

Diversity. Brown et al. [5] gives a good account of why diversity is necessary in neural network ensembles and presents a taxonomy of methods that enforce it in practice. If two neural networks make different errors on the same data points/inputs, they are said to be diverse [5].

Accuracy. Accuracy could be defined as the degree of a network (ensemble member) performing better than random guessing on a new input [5].

The Trade-Off. If we train a network on the same dataset more than a certain number of times, its generalisation ability degrades. Since there is no proven equivalence between generalisation and training error, a network with minimum error on the training set may not have best generalisation [12]. Also, since a population is bound to have at least as much information as any single individual [12] it is always beneficial to make use of all these networks instead of just one. In addition, the more accurate the networks are, the more similar they are likely to be. We need ensembles for better generalisation and given the fact that similar members would preclude the need for ensembles, members have to be diverse. The more diverse the members are, the more well spread will their outputs be around the target value resulting in the expected/mean value of the member outputs being closer to this target value. The fact that the distribution of outputs should be around the target value necessitates accuracy. Hence, in order for an ensemble system to generalise well, the member networks, apart from being diverse, should also be accurate. More precisely, the member outputs should be *compactly well distributed around the desired value*. Herein lies the trade-off between diversity and accuracy under the ensemble setup. There has to be an optimum point on the diversity-accuracy curve where the networks are as diverse as they are accurate i.e. a point at which if the networks become more accurate, they would not be as diverse as they ought to be and vice-versa. The gist here is that since all networks in the ensemble try to provide a solution for the same task, so in order for them to work well, they should locally complement each other. The essence of our approach lies in the fact that it tries to figure out this near optimal trade-off in a multi-objective evolutionary setup.

2.1 Inspiration from MPANN and NCL

MPANN was proposed and successfully tested by Abbass [1] as a PDE approach to evolving neural networks. Our approach incorporates the evolutionary process from the MPANN algorithm in that the control structure of our approach remains similar to that of MPANN, but the way we formulate the problem at hand (the multi-objective problem) and the manner in which offspring are generated in this evolutionary process are different.

As far as NCL [8] is concerned, we use the notion of negative correlation in the formulation of our multi-objective problem. The penalty function used in NCL has an information theoritic aspect to it which we have tried to exploit in our approach by utilising this function for defining diversity.

Changes in MPANN for Our Approach. In MPANN [1] and in PDE [4], the use of a Gaussian distribution for crossover generates well-spread children around the main parent and along the directions of the supporting parents. With our approach, we tried to make the offspring generation process somewhat adaptive in the sense that, at the beginning of the evolutionary process, the children generated are more widely spread around the main parent. As the evolutionary process proceeds further, this spread is reduced such that in the end the offspring are generated in a manner similar to what happens with PDE i.e. using a Gaussian distribution with mean 0 and variance 1. In essence, we start with a Gaussian with mean 0 and large variance σ^2, where σ^2 was set as 2 and then we anneal this value such that initially the search mechanisim is explorative but with time as the variance decreases, the search process becomes more exploitative. Gaussian mutation is also incorporated in the search process. The other difference in our approach is in the formulation of the multi-objective problem which will be considered in the following section in greater detail and which proves a constructive confluence of NCL and MPANN.

3 DIVACE: Algorithm Formulation

Our approach, called DIVACE (DIVerse and ACcurate Ensemble learning), takes in ideas from MPANN and NCL algorithms. For the evolutionary process, we use

MPANN, and for diversity, we use the negative correlation penalty function of NCL as one of our objectives for the multi-objective problem. The two objectives on which to optimise the performance of the ensemble are accuracy and diversity.

Objective 1 – Accuracy. Given a training set T with N patterns. For each network k in the ensemble,

$$\text{(Minimise) Accuracy}_k = \frac{1}{N} \sum_{i=1}^{N} \left(f_k^i - o^i\right)^2, \quad (1)$$

where o^i is the desired output and f_k^i the posterior probability of the class (classification task) or the observed output (regression task) for one training sample i.

Objective 2 – Diversity. From NCL, the correlation penalty function is used as the second objective on which to optimise the ensemble performance. Let N be the number of training patterns and let there be M members in the ensemble, so for each member k, the following term gives an indication of how different it is from other members.

$$\text{(Minimise) Diversity}_k = \sum_{i=1}^{N} \left(f_k^i - f^i\right) \left[\sum_{j \neq k, j=1}^{M} \left(f_j^i - f^i\right)\right], \quad (2)$$

where f^i is the ensemble output for a training sample i. In the information theoritic sense, mutual information is a measure of the correlation between two random variables. A link between the diversity term used here (equation 2) and mutual information was shown in [9]. Minimisation of mutual information between variables extracted (outputs) by two neural networks can be regarded as a condition to ensure that they are different. It has been shown that negative correlation learning, due to the use of the penalty function, can minimise mutual information amongst ensemble members [9, 12]. Hence the use of this penalty function as the diversity term in DIVACE.

It should be noted here that DIVACE is in no way limited to the use of one particular term for diversity. Also, different accuracy measures and evolutionary processes could well be used. The idea is to address the diversity-accuracy trade-off in a multiobjective evolutionary setup.

DIVACE. Following is the DIVACE algorithm:

Step 1: Create a random initial population[1] (size M) of networks, the weights for each are uniformly distributed random values in $U(0, 1)$.
Step 2: Apply BP to all individuals in the population.
Step 3: Repeat until termination conditions (a certain number of generations in our case) are met.

---
[1] For training, we take all the networks in the population as our ensemble but for testing, we only use the final pareto set as the ensemble.

a) Evaluate the individuals in accordance with the two objective functions (Accuracy/quadratic error and diversity/penalty function of NCL[8]) and label the non-dominated set – Non-dominated sorting procedure by Srinivas and Deb [10] used here.
b) If the number of non-dominated individuals is less than 3 then a repair rule similar to that used in MPANN [3] is used.
c) All dominated solutions are deleted from the population.
d) Repeat until population size is M
   – Variance update: updating the variance value for the Gaussian distribution used in crossover. We do it according to

$$\sigma^2 = 2 - \left(\frac{1}{1 + e^{(\text{anneal\_time} - \text{generation})}} \right), \quad (3)$$

   where anneal_time is a parameter signifying exploration time/number of generations for which the search process is to be explorative. In our experiments, we use a value of 50 for the anneal_time parameter.
   – Select 3 parents at random from the population. Let α_1 be the main parent and α_2 and α_3 be the supporting parents.
   – Perform crossover: Produce a child which has an architecture which is similar to the parents but weights given by,

$$w_{hi} = w_{hi}^{\alpha_1} + N\left(0, \sigma^2\right)\left(w_{hi}^{\alpha_2} - w_{hi}^{\alpha_3}\right) \quad (4)$$

$$w_{oh} = w_{oh}^{\alpha_1} + N\left(0, \sigma^2\right)\left(w_{oh}^{\alpha_2} - w_{oh}^{\alpha_3}\right) \quad (5)$$

   – Perform mutation: Mutate the child with probability $1/|population|$ according to,

$$w_{hi} = w_{hi} + N\left(0, 0.1\right) \quad (6)$$

$$w_{oh} = w_{oh} + N\left(0, 0.1\right) \quad (7)$$

   – Apply BP to the child and add it to the population.

4 Results

This section presents some results obtained on testing DIVACE on 2 data sets (Australian credit card assessment dataset and Diabetes dataset), available by anonymous ftp from ice.uci.edu in /pub/machine-learning-databases. The experimental setup is similar to that in [2,3,7]. Table 1 shows the performance accuracy (accuracy rates/percentage accuracy) of the formed ensemble on the Australian credit card assessment dataset as well as the Diabetes dataset. During the course of the evolutionary process, it was expected that each member in the Pareto front (after every generation) would perform well on different parts of the training set. Since the results we get are quite comparable with previous results and as the multi-objective problem is formulated to enforce diversity, we can say that DIVACE performed verly well in finding an appropriate trade-off between accuracy and diversity among members.

Table 1. Performance (accuracy rates) of the ensemble formed using DIVACE on the Australian credit card assessment and Diabetes datasets.

	Australian credit card assessment dataset					
	Simple Averaging		Majority Voting		Winner-takes-all	
	Training	Testing	Training	Testing	Training	Testing
Mean	0.872	0.862	0.867	0.857	0.855	0.849
SD	0.007	0.049	0.007	0.049	0.007	0.053
Max	0.884	0.927	0.879	0.927	0.864	0.927
Min	0.859	0.753	0.856	0.768	0.842	0.753
	Diabetes dataset					
	Simple Averaging		Majority Voting		Winner-takes-all	
	Training	Testing	Training	Testing	Training	Testing
Mean	0.780	0.773	0.783	0.766	0.766	0.766
SD	0.006	0.050	0.005	0.057	0.017	0.049
Max	0.791	0.859	0.791	0.875	0.796	0.843
Min	0.768	0.687	0.772	0.671	0.730	0.671

Table 2. Comparison of DIVACE with the second formulation of MPANN in [2]. Shown in the table are the accuracy rates (on the test set) for both the datasets using simple average, majority vote and winner-takes-all strategies respectively.

Algorithm	Australian	Diabetes
DIVACE	0.862,0.857,0.849	0.773,0.766,0.766
MPANN [2]	0.844,0.844,0.824	0.744,0.744,0.746

5 Conclusion

In this paper, the problem of creating a diverse and accurate set of networks for an ensemble was discussed. The DIVACE algorithm performs very well on the training front, which is expected as we take into account the whole training set with consistent class distributions for each network. The noteworthy aspect here is that our algorithm produces competitive results (table 2) on the testing front as well when compared with the second formulation of the MPANN algorithm [2] which has a similar training setup. The whole idea behind this paper mainly was to present an ensemble learning technique which combines good ideas from both MPANN and NCL, as a result, addressing the trade-off between diversity and accuracy within an evolutionary multi-objective framework. The new algorithm, DIVACE, can produce accurate and diverse ensembles automatically using the multi-objective evolutionary approach.

References

1. H. A. Abbass. A memetic pareto evolutionary approach to artificial neural networks. In *Proceedings of the 14th Australian Joint Conference on Artificial Intelligence*, pages 1–12, Berlin, 2000. Springer-Verlag.

2. H. A. Abbass. Pareto neuro-evolution: Constructing ensemble of neural networks using multi-objective optimization. In *The IEEE 2003 Conference on Evolutionary Computation*, volume 3, pages 2074–2080. IEEE Press, 2003.
3. H. A. Abbass. Pareto neuro-ensemble. In *16th Australian Joint Conference on Artificial Intelligence*, pages 554–566, Perth, Australia, 2003a. Springer.
4. H. A. Abbass, R. Sarker, and C. Newton. PDE: A pareto-frontier differential evolution approach for multi-objective optimization problems. In *Proceedings of the IEEE Congress on Evolutionary Computation (CEC2001)*, volume 2, pages 971–978. IEEE Press, 2001.
5. Gavin Brown, Jeremy Wyatt, Rachel Harris, and Xin Yao. Diversity creation methods: A survey and categorisation. *Journal of Information Fusion (to appear)*, 2004.
6. S. Geman, E. Bienenstock, and R. Doursat. Neural networks and the bias/variance dilemma. *Neural Computation*, 4(1):1–58, 1992.
7. Y. Liu, X. Yao, and T. Higuchi. Evolutionary ensembles with negative correlation learning. *IEEE Transactions on Evolutionary Computation*, 4(4):380–387, November 2000.
8. Yong Liu and Xin Yao. Ensemble learning via negative correlation. *Neural Networks*, 12(10):1399–1404, 1999.
9. Yong Liu and Xin Yao. Learning and evolution by minimization of mutual information. In J. J. Merelo Guervós, P. Adamidis, H.-G. Beyer, J.-L. Fernández-Villacañas, and H.-P. Schwefel, editors, *Parallel Problem Solving from Nature VII (PPSN-2002)*, volume 2439 of *LNCS*, pages 495–504, Granada, Spain, 2002. Springer Verlag.
10. N. Srinivas and K. Deb. Multi-objective function optimization using non-dominated sorting genetic algorithms. *Evolutionary Computation*, 2(3):221–248, 1994.
11. R. Storn and K. Price. Differential evolution - a simple and efficient adaptive scheme for global optimization over continuous spaces. Technical Report TR-95-012, International Computer Science Institute, Berkeley, USA, 1995.
12. Xin Yao and Yong Liu. Evolving neural network ensembles by minimization of mutual information. *International Journal of Hybrid Intelligent Systems*, 1(1), January 2004.

Parallel Processing for Movement Detection in Neural Networks with Nonlinear Functions

Naohiro Ishii[1], Toshinori Deguchi[2], and Hiroshi Sasaki[3]

[1] Aichi Institute of Technology, Toyota, Japan
ishii@aitech.ac.jp
[2] Gifu National College of Technology, Gifu, Japan
deguchi@gifu-nct.ac.jp
[3] Fukui University of Technology, Fukui, Japan
h-sasaki@ccmails.fukui-ut.ac.jp

Abstract. In the neural networks, one of the prominent features, is parallel processing for the spatial information. It is not discussed theoretically to clarify the key features for the parallel processing in the neural network. In this paper, it is shown that asymmetric nonlinear functions, play an crucial role in the network parallel processing for the movement detection. The visual information is inputted first to the retinal neural networks, then is transmitted on the way and finally is processed in the visual network of the cortex and middle temporal area of the brain. In these networks, it is reported that some nonlinear functions will process the visual information effectively. We make clear that the parallel processing with the even and odd nonlinear functions, is effective in the movement detection.

1 Introduction

The visual information is processed firstly in the retina, thalamus on the way and finally in the cortex, which are on the visual pathway of the biological networks. It is expected that what kinds of functions are realized in the parallel structures of the networks. What are the relations between the parallel structures and the functions in the neural networks? In this paper, first we investigate relations between the functions and structures in the retina. Next, we will discuss the parallel processing for the movement detection in the visual area and the middle temporal area of the cortex.

Retinal ganglion cells produce two types of response: linear and nonlinear responses. The nonlinear responses are generated by the separate and independent nonlinear pathway on the visual one, which is different from the linear pathway[3, 9, 10]. The nonlinear pathway is composed of a sandwich model in filters concatenation. These nonlinear characteristics, are studied in the perception of the Fourier and non-Fourier motion movement in the visual processing, which shows the responses to the moving objects.[3, 7, 8, 13, 17]

Asymmetric neural networks are shown in the biological neural network as the catfish retina[9, 10]. Horizontal and bipolar cell responses are linearly related to the input modulation of light, while amacrine cells work linearly and nonlinearly in their responses[12]. As the movement detection mechanism, several models have been proposed in the biological system[1, 5, 11, 17]. To make clear the parallel processing mechanism for the movement detection in the neural network, the nonlinear analysis developed by N.Wiener[8], was applied to the network.

First, it is shown that an asymmetric neural network is closely related to the nonlinear characteristics of the networks. It is shown that the asymmetric networks with the odd order nonlinearity on one pathway and the even order nonlinearity on the other pathway, satisfy equations for the movement. Second, it is shown that the this relations hold in the parallel symmetric networks with half-wave rectification nonlinearity in the networks of visual cortex and the middle temporal area.

2 Asymmetric Neural Networks

A biological network of catfish retina is shown in Fig.1[5, 6, 9], which might process the spatial interactive information between bipolar cells B_1 and B_2. The bipolar B cell response is linearly related to the input modulation of light. The C cell shows an amacrine cell, which plays an important roll in the nonlinear function as squaring of the output of the bipolar cell B_2. Here, the impulse response functions of the cells B_1 and B_2, are assumed to be $h'_1(t)$ and $h''_1(t)$, respectively which are unknown parameters.

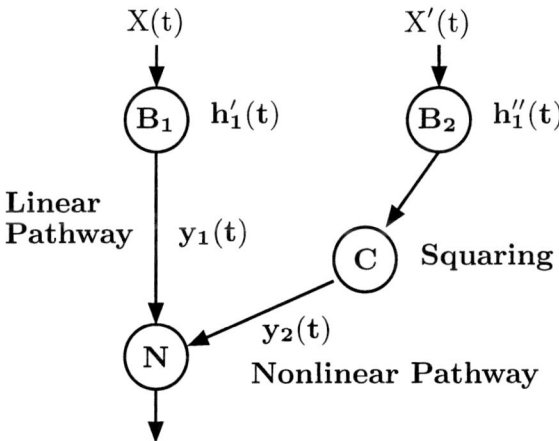

Fig. 1. Asymmetric neural network for spatial interaction

The **N** amacrine cell was clarified to be time-varying and differential with band-pass characteristics in the function. It is shown that N cell response is realized by a linear filter, which is composed of a differentiation filter followed by a low-pass filter[5, 6, 9]. Thus the asymmetric network in Fig.1 is composed of a linear pathway and a nonlinear pathway.

3 Asymmetric Neural Network with Quadratic Nonlinearity

Movement perception is carried out firstly in the retinal neural network. Fig.2 shows a schematic diagram of a motion problem in front of the asymmetric network in Fig.1. The dotted light is assumed to move from the left side to the right side, gradually. For the simplification of the analysis of the spatial interaction, we assume here the input functions $x(t)$ and $x''(t)$ to be Gaussian white noise, whose mean values are zero, but their deviations are different in their values. In Fig.2, moving stimulus shows that $x(t)$ merges into $x''(t)$, thus $x''(t)$ is mixed with $x(t)$. Then, we indicate the right stimulus by $x'(t)$. By introducing a mixed ratio, α, the input function of the right stimulus, is described in the following equation, where $0 < \alpha < 1$ and $\beta = 1 - \alpha$ hold.

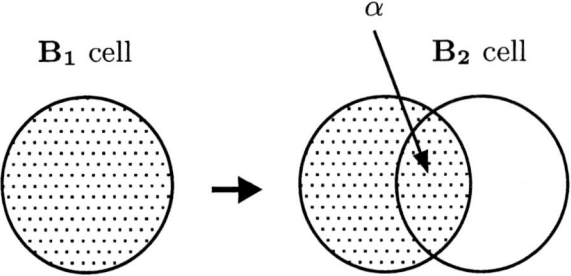

Fig. 2. Schematic diagram of the stimulus movement from the left to the right

Thus, the moving stimulus is described in the following equation.

$$x'(t) = \alpha x(t) + \beta x''(t) \qquad (1)$$

Let the power spectrums of $x(t)$ and $x''(t)$, be p and p', respectively and an equation $p = kp''$ holds for the coefficient k, because we assumed here that the deviations of the input functions are different in their values. Fig.2 shows that the dotted light is moving from the receptive field of $\mathbf{B_1}$ cell to the field of the $\mathbf{B_2}$ cell. The mixed ratio of the input $x(t)$, α is inputted in the receptive field of $\mathbf{B_2}$ cell.

First, on the linear pathway of the asymmetrical network in Fig.1, the input function is $x(t)$ and the output function is $y(t)$, where

$$y(t) = y_1(t) + y_2(t) \qquad (2)$$

We can compute the 0-th order Wiener kernel C_0, the 1-st order one $C_{11}(\lambda)$, and the 2-nd order one $C_{21}(\lambda_1, \lambda_2)$ on the linear pathway by the cross-correlations between $x(t)$ and $y(t)$. The suffix i, j of the kernel $C_{ij}(\bullet)$, shows that i is the order of the kernel and $j = 1$ means the linear pathway, while $j = 2$ means the nonlinear pathway. Then, the 0-th order kernel under the condition of the spatial interaction of cell's impulse response functions $h'_1(t)$ and $h''_1(t)$, becomes

$$C_0 = E[y(t)]$$
$$= p(\alpha^2 + k\beta^2) \int_0^\infty (h''_1(\tau_1))^2 d\tau_1 \qquad (3)$$

The 1-st order kernel is derived as follows,

$$C_{11}(\lambda) = \frac{1}{p} E[y(t)x(t-\lambda)] = h'_1(\lambda) \qquad (4)$$

since the last term of the second equation becomes zero. The 2-nd order kernel becomes,

$$C_{21}(\lambda_1, \lambda_2) = \frac{1}{2p^2} E[(y(t) - C_0)(x(t-\lambda_1)x(t-\lambda_2)]$$
$$= \alpha^2 h''_1(\lambda_1) h''_1(\lambda_2) \qquad (5)$$

From equations (1), (4) and (5), the ratio α, which is a mixed coefficient of $x(t)$ to $x'(t)$, is shown by α^2 as the amplitude of the second order Wiener kernel.

Second, on the nonlinear pathway, we can compute the 0-th order kernel C_0, the 1-st order kernel $C_{12}(\lambda)$ and the 2-nd order kernel $C_{22}(\lambda_1, \lambda_2)$ by the cross-correlations between $x(t)$ and $y(t)$ as shown in the following.

$$C_{12}(\lambda) = \frac{1}{p(\alpha^2 + k\beta^2)} E[y(t)x'(t-\lambda)]$$
$$= \frac{\alpha}{\alpha^2 + k(1-\alpha)^2} h'_1(\lambda) \qquad (6)$$

and

$$C_{22}(\lambda_1, \lambda_2) = h''_1(\lambda_1) h''_1(\lambda_2) \qquad (7)$$

The motion problem is how to detect the movement in the increase of the ratio α in Fig.2. This implies that for the motion of the light from the left side circle to the right one, the ratio α can be derived from the kernels described in the above, in which the second order kernels C_{21} and C_{22} are abbreviated in the representation of equations (5) and (7).

$$(C_{21}/C_{22}) = \alpha^2 \qquad (8)$$

holds. Then, from (8) the ratio α is shown as follows.

$$\alpha = \sqrt{\frac{C_{21}}{C_{22}}} \qquad (9)$$

The equation (9) is called here α - equation, which implies the movement stimulus on the network and shows the detection of the movement by the α.

Further, the following equation is derived similarly,

$$\frac{C_{12}}{C_{11}} = \frac{\sqrt{\dfrac{C_{21}}{C_{22}}}}{\dfrac{C_{21}}{C_{22}} + k\left(1 - \sqrt{\dfrac{C_{21}}{C_{22}}}\right)^2} \tag{10}$$

In the opposite direction from the right to left side stimulus, the schematic diagram of the stimulus movement, is shown in Fig.3.

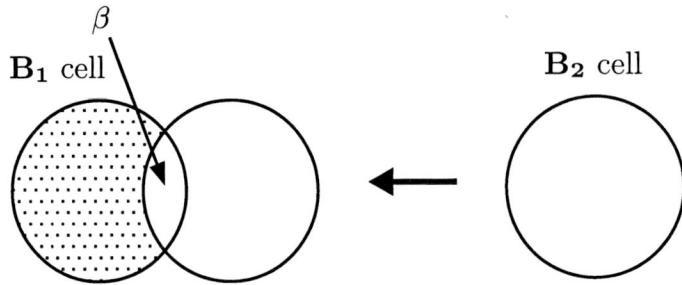

Fig. 3. Schematic diagram of the stimulus movement from the right to the left

Then, the following equations are derived on the linear pathway in Fig.1.

$$C_{11}(\lambda) = h'_1(\lambda) \tag{11}$$

$$C_{21}(\lambda_1, \lambda_2) = \frac{k^2 \beta^2}{(\alpha^2 + k\beta^2)^2} h''_1(\lambda_1) h''_1(\lambda_2) \tag{12}$$

Similarly, the following equations are derived on the nonlinear pathway,

$$C_{12}(\lambda) = \beta h'_1(\lambda) \tag{13}$$

$$C_{22}(\lambda_1, \lambda_2) = h''_1(\lambda_1) h''_1(\lambda_2) \tag{14}$$

From equations (11) and (13), the ratio β is derived, which is abbreviated in the notation

$$\beta = \frac{C_{12}}{C_{11}} \tag{15}$$

and the following equation is derived.

$$\frac{C_{11}}{C_{12}} = \frac{k\sqrt{\dfrac{C_{21}}{C_{22}}}}{\left(1 - \dfrac{C_{12}}{C_{11}}\right)^2 + k\left(\dfrac{C_{12}}{C_{11}}\right)^2} \tag{16}$$

Equations (10) and (16) are transformed to the following equations (17) and (18), respectively.

$$\alpha^3(k+1) - \alpha^2(3k+1) + \alpha(3k+1) - k = 0 \tag{17}$$

$$\alpha^3(k+1) - 2\alpha^2 k + 2k\alpha - k = 0 \tag{18}$$

To satisfy the equality between equations (17) and (18), the following equation must be satisfied.

$$\alpha^2(k+1) - \alpha k - \alpha = 0 \tag{19}$$

But, we have no α solutions in the equation (19) under the condition $0 < \alpha < 1$ and $k > 0$. This implies that equations (10) and (16), are different in their directional values for the stimulus movement. Thus, the equation (10) characterizes the preferred direction from the left to the right, while the equation (16) characterizes the null direction from the right to the left. Further, the differentiation of α - equations (9) and (15), shows the velocity of the moving stimulus. Thus, equations (9) and (10) (similarly (15) and (16)) show a representation of the optical flow of the moving stimulus. The asymmetric network characteristics are generalized as follows: the asymmetric network with the odd order nonlinearity on the one pathway and the even order nonlinearity on the other pathway, has both α - equation (9)(or (15)) and the directional equation (10)(or (16)).

4 Parallel Processing with Half-Wave Rectification Nonlinearity

In the cortical area V1 and the middle temporal area MT, the movement detection is carried out. These areas model is shown in Fig.4[15, 16]. We call here the parallel network with the half-wave rectification nonlinearity. In Fig.4, the half-wave rectification followed by the normalization, is approximated by the nonlinear function as a sigmoid function in the following,

$$f(x) = \frac{1}{1 + e^{-\eta(x-\theta)}} \tag{20}$$

By Taylor expansion of the equation (20) at $x = \theta$, the equation (21) is derived as follows,

$$f(x)_{x=\theta} = f(\theta) + f'(\theta)(x - \theta) + \frac{1}{2!}f''(\theta)(x - \theta)^2 + \cdots$$

$$= \frac{1}{2} + \frac{\eta}{4}(x - \theta) + \frac{1}{2!}\left(-\frac{\eta^2}{4} + \frac{\eta^2 e^{-\eta\theta}}{2}\right)(x - \theta)^2 \cdots \tag{21}$$

In the equation (21), the sigmoid function is approximated as the half-squaring nonlinearity, the parameter η becomes to be large as $\eta \geq 8$ and $\theta \simeq 0.5$ by max of $f(x) = 1$ in the equation (20). Thus, the first order $(x - \theta)$ term $\eta/4$ exists and the second order term $(x - \theta)^2$ also exists by the relation $\eta\theta \gg \log_e 2$.

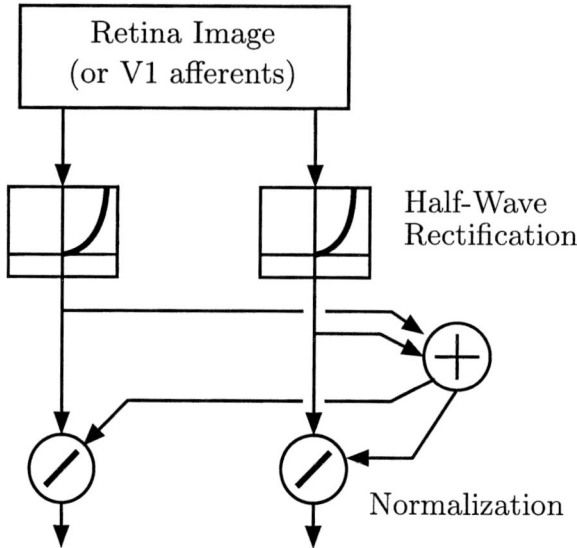

Fig. 4. Parallel network with half-rectification nonlinearity (Heeger and Simoncelli [15, 16])

The half-wave rectification, approximated by the sigmoid function, includes the 1-st, 2-nd $\cdots$ and the higher order nonlinearities. Then, the combination of the odd order nonlinearity on the left side pathway and the even order nonlinearity on the right side pathway, or vice versa, can detect the movement and the direction of the stimulus.

5 Conclusion

In this paper, the parallel processing mechanism of the neural networks are analyzed to make clear the relation between the structure and functions of the neural networks. First, the asymmetric network was analyzed functionally on the biological neural network. Next, the parallel network was analyzed on the visual cortex and middle temporal area. Then, it is shown that the asymmetric networks with nonlinear quadratic characteristic, satisfy both the moving detection equation (α -equation) and the movement direction equation. Further, this relation is generalized as follows: the asymmetric networks with the even – odd or the odd-even nonlinearities, satisfy both movement equations.

References

1. Hassenstein, B. and Reichard, W., "Systemtheoretische analyse der zeit-, reihenfolgen- and vorzeichenauswertung bei der bewegungsperzeption des russelkafers", Chlorophanus. Z. Naturf, 11b, pp.513–524, 1956.

2. Barlow, H.B. and Levick, R.W., "The mechanism of directional selectivity in the rabbit's retina", J. Physiol. 173: pp.377–407, 1965
3. Victor J.D. and Shapley K. M., "The nonlinear pathway of Y ganglion cells in the cat retina", J. Gen. Physiol., vol.74, pp.671–689, 1979
4. Ishii, N., "kernel correlations of movements in neural network", Proc. of Int. Conf. On Artificial Neural Networks, Vol. II, pp.110–113, 1994
5. Ishii, N., Sugiura, S., Nakamura, M., Yamauchi, K., "Sensory Perception, Learning and Integration in Neural Networks", Proc. IEEE Int. Conf. on Information Intelligence & Systems, pp.72–79 , 1999
6. Ishii, N. and Naka, K.-I., "Function of Biological Asymmetrical Neural Networks", Biological and Artificial Computation: From Neuroscience to Technology, LNCS vol.1240 Springer, pp.1115–1125, 1997
7. Korenberg, M.J., Sakai, H.M. and Naka, K.-I., "Dissection of the neuron network in the catfish inner retina", J. Neurophysiol. 61: pp.1110–1120, 1989
8. Marmarelis, P.Z. and Marmarelis, V.Z., Analysis of Physiological System: The White Noise Approach, New York: Plenum Press, 1978
9. Naka, K.-I., Sakai ,H.M. and Ishii, N., "Generation of transformation of second order nonlinearity in catfish retina", Annals of Biomedical Engineering, 16: pp.53–64, 1988
10. Shapley, R., "Visual cortex: pushing the envelope", Nature: neuroscience, vol.1, pp.95–96, 1998
11. Reichardt, W., Autocorrelation, a principle for the evaluation of sensory information by the central nervous system, Rosenblith Edition., Wiley, 1961
12. Sakuranaga, M. and Naka, K.-I., "Signal transmission in the catfish retina. III. Transmission to type-C cell", J. Neurophysiol. 58: pp.411–428, 1987
13. Tanb, E., Victor, J.D., and Conte,M.M., "Nonlinear preprocessing in short-range motion", Vision Research, 37: pp.1459–1477, 1997
14. Heeger, D.J., "Modeling simple-cell direction selectivity with normalized, half-squared, linear operators", J. Neurophysiol. 70 : pp.1885–1898, 1993
15. Heeger, D.J., Simoncelli,E.P., and Movshon,J.A., "Computational models of cortical visual processing", Proc. Natl. Acad. Sci, USA, vol. 93, pp.623–627, 1996
16. Simoncelli E.P., and Heeger, D.J., "A Model of Neuronal Responses in Visual Area MT", Vision Research, vol.38, pp.743–761, 1998
17. Lu , Z.L., and Sperling, G., "Three-systems theory of human visual motion perception: review and update", J. Opt. Soc. Am. A, Vol. 18, pp.2331–2370, 2001

Combining Multiple k-Nearest Neighbor Classifiers Using Different Distance Functions

Yongguang Bao[1], Naohiro Ishii[2], and Xiaoyong Du[3]

[1] Aichi Information System, Japan
baoyg@yahoo.com.cn
[2] Aichi Institute of Technology, Japan
ishii@aitech.ac.jp
[3] Renmin University of China, Beijing, China
Duyong@mail.ruc.edu.cn

Abstract. The k-nearest neighbor (KNN) classification is a simple and effective classification approach. However, improving performance of the classifier is still attractive. Combining multiple classifiers is an effective technique for improving accuracy. There are many general combining algorithms, such as Bagging, Boosting, or Error Correcting Output Coding that significantly improve the classifier such as decision trees, rule learners, or neural networks. Unfortunately, these combining methods do not improve the nearest neighbor classifiers. In this paper we present a new approach to combine multiple KNN classifiers based on different distance funtions, in which we apply multiple distance functions to improve the performance of the k-nearest neighbor classifier. The proposed algorithm seeks to increase generalization accuracy when compared to the basic k-nearest neighbor algorithm. Experiments have been conducted on some benchmark datasets from the UCI Machine Learning Repository. The results show that the proposed algorithm improves the performance of the k-nearest neighbor classification.

1 Introduction

The KNN[4] is one of the most common instance-based learning algorithms. To classify an unknown object, it ranks the object's neighbors among the training data and then uses the class labels of the k nearest neighbors to predict the class of the new object. Despite its simplicity, the KNN has many advantages over other methods. For example, it provides good generalization accuracy for a variety of real-world classification tasks and applications. However, improving accuracy and performance of classifiers are still attractive to many researchers.

Recently, researchers have begun paying attention to combining a set of individual classifiers, also known as a multiple model or ensemble approach, with the hope of improving the overall classification accuracy. Unfortunately, many combining methods such as Bagging, Boosting, or Error Correcting Output Coding, do not improve the kNN classifier at all. Alternatively, Bay [1] has proposed MFS, a method of combining kNN classifiers using multiple features subsets. Each individual classifier in MFS can access all the patterns in the original training set, but only to a random subset of features. MFS uses a simple voting from the output of each classifier to decide the final result. It has been confirmed that reconfiguring the original features into multiple subsets of features can be expected to reduce the bad influence of some ineffective features, especially for the kNN classifier, since it is also extremely sensitive to the features used. However, Bay has not described a certain way for selecting the features, in other words, MFS should be built by trial and error. To overcome this weakness, Itqon et al. [5] use the test features instead of the random features subsets to combine multiple kNN classifiers(TFKNN). The test features can be certainly obtained, and they except that introduction of the test features can improve the classification accuracy of the kNN classifier stably. The results in [5] showed combining multiple kNN classifiers by the test features improve the classification accuracy. However, the complexity of computing all test features is NP-hard, and the algorithm of computing test features in [5] is infeasible when the number of features is large, for example, to text classification problem.

In this paper, we present a new method of combining nearest neighbor classifiers with the goal of improving classification accaury. Our approach combines multiple kNN classifiers using different distance functions instead of the random feature subsets or the test features, to improve the porrformance of KNN.

The remainder of this paper is organized as follows: Section 2 introduces some distance functions, and describes the DKNN algorithm for combining multiple KNN classifiers. Section 3 describes experimental results. A short conclusion is given in the final section.

2 Classification from Multiple Distance Functions

2.1 Distance Functions

The choice of distance function influences the bias of the k-nearest neighbor (KNN) classification. There are many distance functions that have been proposed for the KNN classification [9]. Some functions work well for numerical attributes but do not appropriately handle nominal (i.e.,discrete, and perhaps unordered) attributes. Some work well for nominal attributes.

The most commonly used functions is the *Euclidean Distance function (Euclid)*, which is defined as:

$$D(x,y) = \sqrt{\sum_{i=1}^{m}(x_i - y_i)^2} \quad (1)$$

where x and y are two input vectors (one typically being from a stored instance, and the other an input vector to be classified) and m is the number of input variables (attributes) in the application.

One weakness of the basic Euclidean distance function is that if one of the input attributes has a relatively large range, then it can overpower the other attributes. Therefore, distances are often normalized by dividing the distance for each attribute by the range (i.e., maximum-minimum) of that attribute.

Euclidean distance function can not appropriately handle non-continuous input attributes. An attribute can be linear or nominal, and a linear attribute can be continuous or discrete. A *continuous* (or *continuously-valued*) attribute uses real values, such as the mass of a planet or the velocity of an object. A *linear discrete* (or *integer*) attribute can have only a discrete set of linear values, such as *number of children*.

One way to handle applications with both continuous and nominal attributes is to use a heterogeneous distance function that uses different attribute distance functions on different kinds of attributes. The *Heterogeneous Euclidean-Overlap Metric (HEOM)* uses the overlap metric for nominal attributes and normalized Euclidean distance for linear attributes. This function defines the distance between two values x and y of a given attribute a as:

$$HEOM(x,y) = \sqrt{\sum_{a=1}^{m} d_a(x_a, y_a)^2} \qquad (2)$$

Where

$$d_a(x,y) = \begin{cases} 1, & \text{if x or y is unknown, else} \\ overlap(x,y), & \text{if a is nominal, else} \\ \frac{|x-y|}{man_x - main_a}, & \end{cases} \qquad (3)$$

and function overlap is defined as:

$$overlap(x,y) = \begin{cases} 0, & x = y \\ 1, & other \end{cases} \qquad (4)$$

HEOM removes the effects of the arbitrary ordering of nominal values, but its overly simplistic approach to handling nominal attributes fails to make use of additional information provided by nominal attribute values that can aid in generalization.

The *Value Difference Metric (VDM)*, introduced by Stanfill and Waltz (1986), is an appropriate distance function for nominal attributes. A simplified version of the *VDM* (without the weighting schemes) defines the distance between two values x and y of an attribute a as:

$$vdm_a(x,y) = \sum_{c=1}^{C} |\frac{N_{a,x,c}}{N_{a,x}} - \frac{N_{a,y,c}}{N_{a,y}}|^q = \sum_{c=1}^{C} |P_{a,x,c} - P_{a,y,c}|^q \qquad (5)$$

where $N_{a,x}$ is the number of instances in the training set T that have value x for attribute a; $N_{a,x,c}$ is the number of instances in T that have value x for attribute a and output class c; C is the number of output classes in the problem domain; q is a constant, usually 1 or 2; and $P_{a,x,c}$ is the conditional probability that the output class is c given that attribute a has the value x, i.e., $P(c|x_a)$. As can be seen from (5), $P_{a,x,c}$ is defined as:

$$P_{a,x,c} = \frac{N_{a,x,c}}{N_{a,x}} \qquad (6)$$

where $N_{a,x}$ is the sum of $N_{a,x,c}$ over all classes, i.e.,

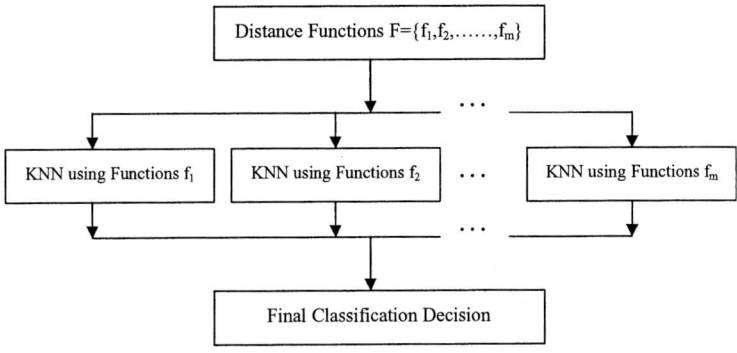

Fig. 1. Basic framework of KNN-DC

$$N_{a,x} = \sum_{c=1}^{C} N_{a,x,c} \qquad (7)$$

and the sum of $P_{a,x,c}$ over all C classes is 1 for a fixed value of a and x.

The weakness of *VDM* is that it is inappropriate to use the *VDM* directly on continuous attributes. One approach to the problem of using *VDM* on continuous attributes is discretization. Some models that have used the *VDM* or variants of it have discretized continuous attributes into a somewhat arbitrary number of discrete ranges, and then treated these values as nominal (discrete unordered) values. This method has the advantage of generating a large enough statistical sample for each nominal value that the P values have some significance. However, discretization loses much of the important information available in the continuous values. For example, two values in the same discretized range are considered equal even if they are on opposite ends of the range. Such effects can reduce generalization accuracy .

In [9], Wilson and Martinez proposed three new alternatives to overcome the weakness of *VDM*. The one is a *Heterogeneous Value Difference Metric(HVDM)* that uses Euclidean distance for linear attributes and *VDM* for nominal attributes. This method requires careful attention to the problem of normalization so that neither nominal nor linear attributes are regularly given too much weight. The other two distance functions are the *Interpolated Value Difference Metric (IVDM)* and the *Windowed Value Difference Metric (WVDM)*, which use discretization to collect statistics and determine values of $P_{a,x,c}$ for continuous values occurring in the training set instances, but then retain the continuous values for later use. During generalization, the value of $P_{a,y,c}$ for a continuous value y is interpolated between two other values of P, namely, $P_{a,x_1,c}$ and $P_{a,x_2,c}$, where $x_1 \leq y \leq x_2$. *IVDM* and *WVDM* are essentially different techniques for doing a nonparametric probability density estimation [8] to determine the values of P for each class. In [9], Wilson and Martinez also proposed a generic version of the *VDM* distance function, called the *discretized value difference metric (DVDM)*.

Table 1. Basic characteristics and generalization accuracy using one distance function

DataSet	Size	F_N	F_{Type}	C_N	Missing	EUCLID	HEOM	HVDM	DVDM	IVDM	WVDM
Breast	699	9	L9	2	16	96.28	96.71	96.28	**96.85**	**96.85**	**96.85**
Glass	214	9	C9	7		69.68	**70.56**	69.24	62.16	69.07	68.79
Iris	150	4	C4	3		94	94.67	94	91.33	96	96
Liver	345	6	C6	2		63.24	**63.5**	63.24	59.38	63.48	61.14
Pima	768	8	C8	2		73.56	73.56	73.56	73.96	72.66	**75.25**
Ionos	351	34	C34	2		83.75	85.17	83.75	91.44	90.57	**90.58**
Sonar	208	60	C60	2		84.14	83.19	84.14	77.36	81.76	**84.62**
Vehicle	846	18	C18	4		71.86	70.81	**72.1**	66.92	69.74	66.9
Vowel	528	10	C10	11		96.6	96.41	**96.79**	89.41	94.15	91.69
Wine	178	13	C13	3		94.44	95.56	94.44	96.63	**97.22**	**97.22**
Austra	690	14	C6N8			82.9	**85.22**	82.03	84.06	83.48	84.2
Credit	690	15	C6N9	2	67	81.01	84.64	84.35	85.07	83.91	**85.22**
Hepatit	155	19	C6N13	2	167	**83.12**	**83.12**	81.21	79.25	81.21	**83.12**
Flag	194	28	C3L7N18	8		45.42	52.53	**59.87**	56.29	57.32	56.26
Heart	270	13	C5L2N6	2		78.52	79.26	78.89	81.48	79.26	**81.85**
Bridges	106	11	C1L3N7	7	65	59.09	57.18	61.82	**62.82**	61.82	62.73
LED+17	1000	24	N24	10		46.2	47.8	66.7	66.2	66.2	**67.5**
LED	1000	7	N7	10		70.6	**71.3**	70	70.5	69.3	70.5
Promote	106	57	N57	2		82.18	84.82	**93.45**	**93.45**	**93.45**	**93.45**
Voting	435	16	N16	2	392	93.79	93.79	95.64	**95.64**	**95.64**	**95.64**
Zoo	90	16	N16	7		94.44	**95.56**	93.33	93.33	93.33	93.33
Avg						78.32	79.30	80.71	79.69	80.78	**81.09**

Table 2. Generalization accuracy using five/six distance functions

DataSet	EUHOHVDVIV	EUHOHVDVWV	EUHOHVIVWV	EUHODVIVWV	EUHVDVIVWV	HOHVDVIVWV	ALL
Breast	96.71	96.71	96.71	96.99	96.99	96.99	96.85
Glass	73.33	74.33	74.76	74.26	72.92	74.24	74.76
Iris	94.67	94.67	95.33	95.33	95.33	95.33	95.33
Liver	65.55	63.8	65.84	65.24	65.82	65.24	65.24
Pima	75.39	76.04	74.99	76.17	75.65	76.17	76.3
Ionos	90.29	90.58	90.01	91.14	91.14	91.14	90.58
Sonar	85.6	87.5	85.6	87.5	86.52	87.5	88
Vehicle	71.4	71.75	72.69	71.63	71.87	71.87	72.1
Vowel	97.36	96.98	96.98	97.17	97.17	97.17	97.74
Wine	96.67	96.67	96.67	96.67	96.67	96.67	96.67
Austral	85.36	85.36	85.22	85.51	85.07	85.51	85.36
Credit	86.09	85.65	85.65	86.09	85.07	85.36	86.38
Hepatit	82.58	82.58	82.54	81.25	82.5	82.5	83.25
Flag	60.92	60.37	60.92	60.89	59.34	59.82	60.37
Heart	82.59	82.22	82.22	82.59	84.44	83.33	82.59
Bridges	67.45	65.64	67.45	63.64	63.82	64.73	66.55
LED+17	66.1	66.2	66.2	66.1	67	67.3	66.4
LED	71.2	71.4	70.9	71.3	70.5	70.8	70.8
Promote	93.45	93.45	93.45	93.45	93.45	93.45	93.45
Voting	95.41	95.41	95.41	95.41	95.64	95.64	95.41
Zoo	94.44	95.56	94.44	95.56	93.33	93.33	95.56
Avg	82.50	82.52	82.57	82.57	82.39	82.58	82.84

2.2 The DKNN Algorithm

The algorithm for k-nearest neighbor classification from multiple different distance functions (DKNN-DC) is simple and can be stated as: Using simple voting, combining the outputs from multiple KNN classifiers, and each having access only to a distance function. We call this system k-nearest neighbor classification by distance functions combination(KNN-DC). First,the KNN-DC inputs several distance functions. Then, it uses each distance function to generates k nearest samples in training data. Then, it combines the all k nearest samples and determines the class of unknown object based on the simple voting. As can be seen

Table 3. Generalization accuracy using four distance functions

DataSet	EUHOHVDV	EUHOHVIV	EUHOHVWV	EUHODVIV	EUHODVWV	EUHOIVWV	EUHVDVIV
Breast	96.71	96.57	96.57	96.71	97	96.99	96.85
Glass	71.49	71.49	73.35	72.4	74.76	74.72	71.93
Iris	94.67	94.67	95.33	94.67	94.67	96	94.67
Liver	65.86	65.87	63.82	65.25	64.08	65.82	64.66
Pima	75.26	74.21	74.47	75.39	76.43	75.91	75.65
Ionos	87.74	86.3	88.02	90.29	90.87	90.58	90.87
Sonar	85.1	84.62	84.64	86.05	86.55	86.6	87.02
Vehicle	71.52	72.81	72.22	71.4	71.75	71.63	71.63
Vowel	96.79	97.17	96.6	97.17	96.79	97.36	97.17
Wine	96.11	96.67	95.56	96.67	96.67	96.67	97.22
Austral	85.07	85.51	85.22	84.93	85.22	85.22	83.77
Credit	85.36	85.07	84.93	85.65	85.07	85.07	85.07
Hepatit	81.21	81.88	81.25	83.17	82.46	81.21	82.54
Flag	59.84	61.45	59.87	59.87	59.32	60.89	60.89
Heart	81.11	80.37	80	80.74	81.11	82.59	82.96
Bridges	64.73	65.64	65.64	63.64	64.73	63.73	64.73
LED+17	65.8	65	65.3	65.1	65.6	65.5	67.5
LED	70.8	71.4	71.3	71.2	71.8	71.2	70.5
Promote	95.36	93.45	95.36	94.45	93.45	93.45	93.45
Voting	95.41	95.41	95.18	95.41	95.18	95.18	95.41
Zoo	95.56	95.56	95.56	95.56	95.56	95.56	93.33
Avg	81.98	81.96	81.91	82.18	82.34	82.47	82.28
EUHVDVWV	EUHVIVWV	EUDVIVWV	HOHVDVIV	HOHVDVWV	HOHVIVWV	HODVIVWV	HVDVIVWV
96.71	96.56	96.99	97.14	97	97.14	96.85	96.85
72.92	72.42	71.93	71.45	73.85	74.74	72.84	71.47
95.33	96	95.33	94.67	94.67	95.33	96	96
63.79	66.4	64.95	66.71	65.24	66.98	65.55	64.36
76.82	75.51	76.81	75.91	76.82	75.78	77.73	76.16
90.58	90.01	90.57	90.29	90.87	90.01	90	91.14
86.55	87.05	86.55	85.57	86.57	87.07	86.48	87.48
71.75	72.69	72.22	71.28	72.35	70.92	71.63	70.93
97.36	96.98	96.04	97.36	97.55	96.6	95.85	96.03
97.22	96.67	97.78	97.22	96.67	96.67	97.22	96.67
84.64	84.93	84.93	85.65	85.65	85.07	85.8	84.93
85.36	85.65	85.07	85.51	84.93	85.22	85.36	84.49
81.83	81.21	83.88	81.88	81.88	83.88	83.17	81.88
59.34	59.89	58.84	59.84	59.34	59.32	60.34	58.79
83.33	82.96	81.85	82.96	84.07	82.22	81.85	82.22
65.73	65.64	62.73	64.64	65.64	66.55	61.82	65.64
67.30	67.3	67.3	67.1	67.2	67.2	67.1	66.8
70.60	70.6	70.6	70.7	70.4	70.7	70.8	70.3
92.55	92.55	93.45	93.45	93.45	94.36	93.45	93.45
95.64	95.64	95.64	95.41	95.64	95.64	95.64	95.64
94.44	94.44	94.44	94.44	95.56	94.44	93.33	93.33
82.37	82.43	82.28	82.34	82.64	82.66	82.32	82.12

from the basic framework of KNN-DC, the KNN-DC has the same time complexity as the basic KNN. It is no problem to be applied in real-world application as the KNN. It overcomes the weakness of MFS and TFKNN.

3 Experimental Results

For evaluating the classification generalization accuracy of our algorithm, the DKNN algorithm was implemented and tested on 21 benchmark datasets from the UCI Machine Learning Repository [6]. The basic characteristics of the data sets contain the size of training data and test data, the number of the features (F_N) and feature type (F_{type}: L=Linear, N=Nominal, C=Continuous), the number of class (C_N) and the number of missing values (Missing), which was showed

Table 4. Generalization accuracy using three distance functions

DataSet	EUHOHV	EUHODV	EUHOIV	EUHOWV	EUHVDV	EUHVIV	EUHVWV	EUDVIV	EUDVWV	EUIVWV
Breast	96.28	96.71	96.71	96.71	96.57	96.57	96.57	96.99	96.99	96.99
Glass	69.70	73.35	72.86	74.29	71.93	71.97	72.90	70.04	71.04	73.38
Iris	94.67	94.67	94.67	95.33	94.67	94.67	95.33	94.67	95.33	96.00
Liver	62.95	64.97	67.87	64.39	63.52	67.30	62.94	66.13	62.61	64.97
Pima	73.56	75.52	75.38	75.38	75.26	74.60	74.99	76.30	77.21	74.99
Ionos	84.03	88.88	89.44	89.74	89.16	89.44	89.73	90.57	90.86	90.86
Sonar	83.67	85.60	84.17	86.07	86.55	85.10	86.55	85.55	87.00	86.07
Vehicle	72.10	70.93	71.87	71.63	71.39	72.57	72.22	70.80	71.63	71.51
Vowel	96.41	96.79	96.60	96.79	96.41	96.60	96.98	96.03	95.66	97.17
Wine	95.00	96.67	96.67	96.67	96.11	96.67	96.67	97.78	97.22	96.67
Austral	85.22	84.35	85.22	84.64	84.64	84.35	84.49	85.22	84.64	84.78
Credit	85.36	85.36	84.78	84.64	85.80	85.22	85.07	85.94	85.22	85.22
Hepatit	82.46	83.79	83.12	83.79	81.92	81.21	82.54	81.25	80.58	82.54
Flag	56.68	58.76	60.39	58.82	59.37	60.37	59.37	57.82	57.26	57.29
Heart	80.00	80.74	80.00	80.37	82.59	81.48	81.48	82.22	83.70	82.59
Bridges	62.91	63.82	64.64	63.73	67.55	66.55	65.55	64.73	62.82	62.82
LED+17	62.40	62.00	63.20	62.40	66.90	66.70	66.90	66.90	66.40	66.60
LED	71.50	71.10	71.60	71.40	71.20	70.70	70.40	71.00	70.70	70.90
Promote	94.45	94.45	94.45	94.45	94.45	94.45	94.45	94.45	94.45	94.45
Voting	95.41	95.41	95.41	95.41	95.41	95.41	95.41	95.41	95.41	95.41
Zoo	95.56	95.56	96.67	95.56	95.56	95.56	95.56	95.56	95.56	95.56
Avg	80.97	81.88	82.18	82.01	82.24	82.26	82.20	82.16	82.01	82.23

DataSet	HOHVDV	HOHVIV	HOHVWV	HODVIV	HODVWV	HOIVWV	HVDVIV	HVDVWV	HVIVWV	DVIVWV
Breast	96.71	96.71	96.71	96.99	96.99	96.99	96.99	96.99	96.99	96.85
Glass	73.83	74.24	73.81	72.79	73.81	74.26	71.00	71.04	74.78	67.71
Iris	94.67	94.67	95.33	94.67	95.33	96.00	94.67	95.33	96.00	96.00
Liver	64.97	67.87	64.39	66.12	63.49	65.83	66.13	62.61	64.97	64.97
Pima	75.52	75.38	75.38	77.34	77.99	75.78	76.30	77.21	74.99	77.08
Ionos	88.88	89.44	89.74	90.29	90.57	90.57	90.57	90.86	90.86	90.86
Sonar	85.60	84.17	86.07	85.52	84.60	86.07	85.55	87.00	86.07	84.12
Vehicle	70.93	71.51	71.52	70.57	71.28	69.74	70.92	71.40	71.75	70.10
Vowel	96.98	96.79	96.98	96.04	95.85	97.35	96.22	96.03	96.98	93.77
Wine	96.67	96.67	96.67	97.78	97.78	96.67	97.78	97.22	96.67	97.78
Austral	84.49	84.49	84.93	85.51	85.07	85.65	83.91	84.93	84.35	85.07
Credit	85.65	85.80	85.36	86.09	85.07	85.80	84.93	84.93	84.78	85.07
Hepatit	81.92	81.21	82.54	81.25	80.58	82.54	81.21	82.50	81.88	82.50
Flag	58.82	60.92	59.89	59.34	60.32	59.34	58.84	59.37	59.42	57.84
Heart	82.59	81.48	81.85	82.22	83.33	82.22	82.59	83.70	82.59	82.22
Bridges	64.73	68.36	66.45	64.64	63.64	64.45	67.45	65.64	67.45	63.64
LED+17	66.60	66.50	66.60	66.90	66.80	67.10	65.70	65.80	66.20	66.20
LED	70.40	71.00	71.10	70.80	70.10	71.10	70.40	70.30	70.40	70.40
Promote	93.45	93.45	93.45	93.45	93.45	93.45	93.45	93.45	93.45	93.45
Voting	95.41	95.41	95.41	95.41	95.41	95.41	95.64	95.64	95.64	95.64
Zoo	95.56	95.56	95.56	94.44	94.44	94.44	93.33	93.33	93.33	93.33
Avg	82.11	82.46	82.37	82.29	82.19	82.42	82.08	82.16	82.36	81.65

in Table 1. For each dataset, we used the 10-fold cross validation. That is, the whole dataset is partitioned into ten subsets. Nine of the subsets are used as training set, and the 10th is used as the test set, and this process is repeated ten times, once for each subset being the test set. Then, classification accuracy is taken as the average of these ten runs. In our experiment, set parameters $k = 3$ and use six functions in [9].

In order to see how the function number in KNN-DC affects generalization accuracy, results for from 3 to 6 function combination are tested for comparison with the basic nearest neighbor algorithm. The generalization accuracy using one function is shown in the Table 1, the highest accuracy achieved for each dataset is shown in bold type. As can be seen from Table 1, no function has the highest accuracy on all of the datasets.

The Tables 2 to 4 show the combining result by KNN-DC. The meaning of "EUHOHV" in Table 4 shows it using the EUCLID, HEOM and HVDM function, and the followings are similar. The average of generalization accuracy for each one is shown near the bottom of the table. As can be seen from Table 2 to 4, each combining case raises the average generalization accuracy on these datasets when compared with using one function. In the case of using six functions, it increases the average accuracy to 82.84%. The results presented above are theoretically limited to this set of applications, but the results indicate that KNN-DC is an efficient combing method and can be successfully applied to a variety of real-world applications.

4 Conclusions

In this paper, we introduced KNN-DC, an algorithm for combining multiple KNN classifiers using distinct distance functions combinations. The proposed algorithm seeks to increase generalization accuracy when compared to the basic k-nearest neighbor algorithm using one function. From the performance simulation on some benchmark datasets from the UCI Machine Learning Repository, we confirmed that KNN-DC improves the performance of the k-nearest neighbor classification and it is an efficient combing method.

References

1. S.D. Bay,"Combining Nearest Neighbor Classifiers Through Multiple Feature Subsets", Intelligent Data Analysis, 3(3), pp. 191-209, 1999.
2. Y.Bao,X.Du & N.Ishii,"Combining Feature Selection with Feature Weighting for k-NN Classifier", Proc.Third International Conference on Intelligent Data Engineering and Automated Learning(LNCS2412,Springer-Verlag),August.Manchester,UK,pp.461-468,2002.
3. Y.Bao & N.Ishii,"Combining multiple k-Nearest Neighbor Classifiers for Text Classification by Reducts", Proc.5th International Conference on Discovery Science(LNAI2534,Springer-Verlag),Germany,pp.361-368,November,2002.
4. T.M. Cover & P.E. Hart,"Nearest Neighbor Pattern classification", IEEE Transactions on Information Theory, Vol. 13, No.1, pp. 21-27, 1967.
5. Itqon, S. Kaneko & S. Igarashi," Combining Multiple k-Nearest Neighbor Classifiers Using Feature Combinations", Journal IECI, 2(3), pp. 23-319, 2000.
6. C.J. Merz & P. M. Murphy, 1998, UCI Repository of Machine Learning Databases, Irvine, CA: University of California Irvine, Department of Information and Computer Science, Internet: http://www.ics.uci.edu/ mlearn /MLRepository.html.
7. C. Stanfill & Waltz D.,"Toward memory-based reasoning", Communications of the ACM, Vol. 29, pp. 1213-1228, 1986.
8. Tapia, Richard A. & James R. Thompson, Nonparametric Probability Density Estimation. Baltimore, MD: The Johns Hopkins University Press, 1978.
9. Wilson, D. Randall, & Tony R. Martinez, "Improved Heterogeneous Distance Functions", Journal of Artificial Intelligence Research, Vol. 6, No. 1, pp. 1-34, 1997.
10. D.R.Wilson & T.R. Martinez,"An Integrated Instance-Based Learning Algorithm", Computational Intelligence, 16(1), pp. 1-28, 2000.
11. D.R.Wilson & T.R. Martinez,"Reduction Techniques for Instance-Based Learning Algorithms", Machine Learning, 38(3), pp. 257-28, 2000.

Finding Minimal Addition Chains Using Ant Colony

Nadia Nedjah and Luiza de Macedo Mourelle

Department of Systems Engineering and Computation
Faculty of Engineering, State University of Rio de Janeiro
Rua São Francisco Xavier, 524, Maracanã
Rio de Janeiro, RJ, Brazil
{nadia,ldmm}@eng.uerj.br
http://www.eng.uerj.br/ldmm/index.html

Abstract. Modular exponentiation is one of the most important operations in the almost all nowadays cryptosystems. It is performed using a series of modular multiplications. The latter operation is time consuming for large operands, which always the case in cryptography. Hence Accelerating public-key cryptography software or hardware needs either optimising the time consumed by a single modular multiplication and/or reducing the total number of modular multiplication required. This paper introduces a novel idea based on the principles of ant colony for finding a minimal addition chain that allows us to reduce the number of modular multiplication so that modular exponentiation can be implemented very efficently.

1 Introduction

The modular exponentiation is a common operation for scrambling and is used by several public-key cryptosystems, such as the RSA encryption scheme [1]. It consists of a repetition of modular multiplications: $C = T^E \mod M$, where T is the *plain text* such that $0 \leq T < M$ and C is the *cipher text* or vice-versa, E is either the *public* or the *private key* depending on whether T is the plain or the cipher text, and M is called the *modulus*. The decryption and encryption operations are performed using the same procedure, i.e. using the modular exponentiation.

A simple procedure to compute $C = T^E \mod M$ based on the paper-and-pencil method requires $E - 1$ modular multiplications. It computes all powers of $T : T \rightarrow T^2 \rightarrow T^3 \rightarrow \ldots \rightarrow T^{E-1} \rightarrow T^E$. This method computes more multiplications than necessary. The basic question is: what is the fewest number of multiplications to compute T^E, given that the only operation allowed is multiplying two already computed powers of T? Answering this question is *NP*-complete, but there are several efficient algorithms that can find a near optimal ones.

Ant systems [2] are distributed multi-agent systems [3] that simulate real ant colony. Each agent behaves as an ant within its colony. Despite the fact that ants have very bad vision, they always are capable to find the shortest path from their nest to wherever the food is. To do so, ants deposit a trail of a chemical substance called *pheromone* on the path they use to reach the food. On intersection points, ants tend to choose a path with high amount of pheromone. Clearly, the ants that travel through the shorter path are capable to return quicker and so the pheremone deposited on that path increases relatively faster than that deposited on much longer alternative paths. Consequently, all the ants of the colony end using the shorter way.

In this paper, we exploit the ant strategy to obtain an optimal solution to addition chain minimisation *NP*-complete problem. In order to clearly report the research work performed, we subdivide the rest of this paper into five important sections. First, in Section 2, we describe the addition chain-based methods and state the minimisation problem. Then, in Section 3, we present the proposed multi-threaded implementation of the ant system. Subsequently, in Section 4, we expose the results obtained by the ant system and compare them to those evolved using genetic algorithms as well as to those exploited by traditional methods such as *m*-ary and sliding window methods. Finally, we conclude the paper and comment the obtained results.

2 Addition Chain Minimisation

The addition chain-based methods use a sequence of positive integers such that the first number of the chain is 1 and the last is the exponent E, and in which each member is the sum of two previous members of the chain. For instance, the addition chain used by the paper-and-pencil method is $(1, 2, 3, ..., E-2, E-1, E)$. An *addition chain* of length l for an positive integer n is a sequence of positive integers $(a_1, a_2, \ldots, a_l)$ such that $a_1 = 1, a_l = n$ and $a_k = a_i + a_j, 1 \leq i \leq j < k \leq l$.

The algorithm used to compute the modular exponentiation $C = T^E \mod M$ based on a given non-redundant addition chain, is specified in Algorithm 1, wherein *PoT* stands for the array of *Powers of T*.

Algorithm 1. AdditionChainBasedMethod(T, M, E)
1:   Let $(a_1 = 1, a_2, \ldots, a_l = E)$ be the addition chain;
2:   $PoT[0] := T \mod M$;
3:   for $k := 1$ to l do
4:       Let $a_k := a_i + a_j | i < k$ and $j < k$;
5:       $PoT[k] := PoT[i] \times PoT[j] \mod M$;
6:   return $PoT[l]$;
end.

Finding a minimal addition chain for a given number is *NP*-hard [4]. Therefore, heuristics were devellopped to attempt to approach such a chain. The most used heuristic consists of scanning the digits of E from the less significant to the most significant digit and grouping them in partitions P_i. The size of the partitions can be constant or variable [4], [5], [6]. Modular exponentiation methods based on constant-size partitioning of the exponent are usually called *m-ary*, where m is a power of two and $\log_2 m$ is the size of a partition while methods based on variable-size windows are usually called *sliding window* [7].

3 Addition Chain Minimisation Using Ant System

In this section, we describe the model we used to simulate the ant colony based system. There are four main aspects: the shared memory SM through which the ants communicates; the ant local memory LM in which it stores the solution built so far; the solution evaluation and the state transition function.

3.1 The Ant System Shared Memory

The ant system shared memory is a two-dimension triangular array. The array has E rows. The number of columns depends on the row. It can be computed as in Eq. 1, wherein NC_i denotes the number of columns in row i.

$$NC_i = \begin{cases} 2^{i-1} - i + 1 & \text{if } 2^{i-1} \leq E \\ E - i + 1 & \text{otherwise} \end{cases} \quad (1)$$

An entry $SM_{i,j}$ of the shared memory holds the pheromone deposited by ants that used exponent $i + j$ as the i th. member in the built addition chain. Note that $1 \leq i \leq E$ and for row i, $0 \leq j \leq NC_i$. Fig. 1 gives an example of the shared memory for exponent 17. In this example, a table entry is set to show the exponent corresponding to it. The exponent $E_{i,j}$ corresponding to entry $SM_{i,j}$ should be obtainable from exponents from previous rows. Eq. 2 formalises such a requirement.

$$E_{i,j} = E_{k_1,l_1} + E_{k_2,l_2} \mid 1 \leq k_1, k_2 < i, 0 \leq l_1, l_2 \leq j, k_1 = k_2 \Longleftrightarrow l_1 = l_2 \quad (2)$$

Note that, in Fig. 1, the exponents in the shaded entries are not valid exponents as for instance exponent 7 of row 4 is not obtainable from the sum of two previous different stages, as described in Eq. 2. The computational process that allows us to avoid these exponents is of very high cost. In order to avoid using these few exponents, we will penalise those ants that use them and hopefully, the solutions built by the ants will be almost all valid addition chains.

3.2 The Ant Local Memory

Each ant is endowed a local memory that allows it to store the solution or the part of it that was built so far. This local memory is divided into two parts: the first part represents the (partial) addition chain found by the ant so far and consists of a one-dimension array of E entries; the second part holds the *characteristics* of the solution. The characteristics of a solution represents its fitness to the objective of the optimisation. The details of how to compute a possibly partial addition chain are given in the next section.

1											
2											
3	4										
4	5	6	7	8							
5	6	7	8	9	10	11	12	13	14	15	16
6	7	8	9	10	11	12	13	14	15	16	17
7	8	9	10	11	12	13	14	15	16	17	
8	9	10	11	12	13	14	15	16	17		
9	10	11	12	13	14	15	16	17			
10	11	12	13	14	15	16	17				
11	12	13	14	15	16	17					
12	13	14	15	16	17						
13	14	15	16	17							
14	15	16	17								
15	16	17									
16	17										
17											

Fig. 1. Example of the shared memory content for $E = 17$

3.3 Addition Chain Characteristics

The fitness evaluation of addition chain is done with respect to two aspects: *(i)* how much a given addition chain adheres to the Definition 1, i.e. how many members of the addition chain cannot be obtained summing up two previous members of the chain; *(ii)* how far the addition chain is reduced, i.e. what is the length of the addition chain. Eq. 3 shows how to compute the fitness of an addition chain.

For a valid complete addition chain, the fitness coincides with its length, which is the number of multiplications that are required to compute the exponentiation using the addition chain. For a valid but incomplete addition chain, the fitness is a the *relative* length of the chain. It takes into account the distance between exponent E and the last exponent in the partial addition chain. Note that valid incomplete addition chains may have the same fitness of some other valid and complete addition chain. For instance, addition chains (1, 2, 3, 6, 8) and (1, 2, 3, 6) for exponent 8 have the same fitness 4.

For an invalid addition chain, a penaly, larger than E, is introduced into the fitness value for each exponent for which one cannot find two (may be equal) members of the chain whose sum is equal to the exponent in question.

$$Fitness(E, (a_1, a_2, \ldots, a_n)) = \frac{E \times (n-1)}{a_n} + \sum_{\substack{k \mid 3 \leq k \leq n \\ \forall i,j,\ 1 \leq i,j < k, \\ a_k \neq a_i + a_j}} penalty \quad (3)$$

3.4 Pheromone Trail and State Transition Function

There are three situations wherein the pheromone trail is updated: *(a)* when an ant chooses to use exponent $F = i + j$ as the *i*th. member in its solution, the shared momory cell $SM_{i,j}$ is incremented with a constant value of pheromone $\Delta\phi$, as in Eq. 4; *(b)* when an ant halts because it reached a complete solution, say $A = (a_1, a_2, \ldots, a_n)$, all the shared memory cells $SM_{i,j}$ such that $i + j = a_i$ are incremented with pheromone value of $1/Fitness(A)$, as in Eq. 5. Note that the better is the reached solution, the higher is the amount of pheromone deposited in the shared memory cells that correspond to the addition chain members. *(c)* The pheromone deposited should evaporate. Priodically, the pheromone amount stored in $SM_{i,j}$ is decremented in an exponential manner [6] as in Eq. 6.

$$SM_{i,j} := SM_{i,j} + \Delta\phi, \quad \text{every time } a_i = i+j \text{ is chosen} \tag{4}$$

$$SM_{i,j} := SM_{i,j} + 1/Fitness((a_1, a_2, \ldots, a_n)), \quad \forall i,j \mid i+j = a_i \tag{5}$$

$$SM_{i,j} := (1-\rho)SM_{i,j} \mid \rho \in (0,1], \quad \text{periodically} \tag{6}$$

An ant, say A that has constructed partial addition chain $(a_1, a_2, \ldots, a_i, 0, \ldots, 0)$ for exponent E, is said to be in *step i*. In step $i+1$, it may choose exponent a_{i+1} as one of exponents $a_i + 1, a_i + 2, \ldots, 2a_i$, if $2a_i \leq E$. That is, the ant may choose one of the exponents that are associated with the shared memory cells $SM_{i+1,a_i-i}, SM_{i+1,a_i-i+1}, \ldots, SM_{i+1,2a_i-i-1}$. Otherwise (i.e. if $2a_i > E$), it may only select from exponents $a_i + 1, a_i + 2, \ldots, E$. In this case, ant A may choose one of the exponent associated with $SM_{i+1,a_i-i}, SM_{i+1,a_i-i+1}, \ldots, SM_{i+1,E-i-1}$. Furthermore, ant A chooses the new exponent a_{i+1} with the probability of $P_{i,j}$ of Eq. 7.

$$P_{i,j} = \begin{cases} \dfrac{SM_{i+1,j}}{\max_{k=a_i-i}^{2a_i-i-1} SM_{i+1,k}} & \text{if } 2a_i \leq E \text{ \& } j \in [a_i - i, 2a_i - i - 1] \\ \dfrac{SM_{i+1,j}}{\max_{k=a_i-i}^{E-i-1} SM_{i+1,k}} & \text{if } 2a_i > E \text{ \& } j \in [a_i - i, E - i - 1] \\ 0 & \text{otherwise} \end{cases} \tag{7}$$

4 Performance Comparison

The ant system described so far was implemented using Java as multi-threaded ant system. Each ant was simulated by a thread that implements the artificial ant computation of Algorithm 4. A Pentium IV-HT^{TM} of 1GH and 2GB was used to run the ant system and obtain the performance results.

We compared the performance of the *m*-ary methods to the genetic algorithm and ant system-based methods. The average lengths of the addition chains for different exponents obtained by using these methods are given in Table 1. The exponent size is that of its binary representation (i.e. number of bits). The ant system-based method always outperforms all the others, including the genetic algorithm-based method [7].

Table 1. Average length of addition chain for binary, quaternary and octal method vs. genetic algorithm and ant system-based methods

exponet size	Binary	Quaternary	Octal	Genetic Algorithms	Ant System
32	47	43	43	41	38
64	95	87	85	79	71
128	191	175	167	158	145

5 Conclusion

In this paper we applied the methodology of ant colony to the addition chain minimisation problem. We described how the shared and local memories are represented. We detailed the function that computes the solution fitness. We defined the amount of pheromone to be deposited with respect to the solution obtained by an ant. We showed how to compute the necessary probabilities and make the adequate decision towards a good addition chain for the considered exponent. We implemented the ant system described using muti-threading (each ant of the system was implemented by a thread). We compared the results obtained by the ant system to those of m-ary methods (binary, quaternary and octal methods). We also compared the obtained results to those obtained by the genetic algorithm. The ant system always finds a shorter addition chain.

References

1. Rivest, R., Shamir, A. and Adleman, L., A method for Obtaining Digital Signature and Public-Key Cryptosystems, Communications of the ACM, 21:120-126, 1978.
2. Dorigo, M. and Gambardella, L.M., Ant Colony: a Cooperative Learning Approach to the Travelling Salesman Problem, IEEE Transaction on Evolutionary Computation, Vol. 1, No. 1, pp. 53-66, 1997.
3. Feber, J., Multi-Agent Systems: an Introduction to Distributed Artificial Intelligence, Addison-Wesley, 1995.
4. Downing, P. Leong B. and Sthi, R., Computing Sequences with Addition Chains, SIAM Journal on Computing, vol. 10, No. 3, pp. 638-646, 1981.
5. Nedjah, N., Mourelle, L.M., Efficient Parallel Modular Exponentiation Algorithm, Second International Conference on Information systems, ADVIS'2002, Lecture Notes in Computer Science, Springer-Verlag, vol. 2457, pp. 405-414, 2002.
6. Stutzle, T. and Dorigo, M., ACO Algorithms for the Travelling Salesman Problems, Evolutionary Algorithms in Engineering and Computer Science, John-Wiley, 1999.
7. Nedjah, N. and Mourelle, L.M., Minimal addition chains using genetic algorithms, Proceedings of the Fifteenth International Conference on Industrial & Engineering Applications of Artificial Intelligence & Expert Systems, Lecture Notes in Computer Science, Springer-Verlag, vol. 2358, pp. 88-98, 2002.

Combining Local and Global Models to Capture Fast and Slow Dynamics in Time Series Data

Michael Small

Hong Kong Polytechnic University, Hong Kong
ensmall@polyu.edu.hk
http://small.eie.polyu.edu.hk

Abstract. Many time series exhibit dynamics over vastly different time scales. The standard way to capture this behavior is to assume that the slow dynamics are a "trend", to de-trend the data, and then to model the fast dynamics. However, for nonlinear dynamical systems this is generally insufficient. In this paper we describe a new method, utilizing two distinct nonlinear modeling architectures to capture both fast and slow dynamics. Slow dynamics are modeled with the method of analogues, and fast dynamics with a deterministic radial basis function network. When combined the resulting model out-performs either individual system.

1 Fast and Slow Dynamics

Scalar time series often exhibit deterministic dynamics on very different time scales (see Fig. 1). For example, sound waves can exhibit fast intra-cycle variation and slow inter-cycle fluctuations. It is difficult for a single model to describe both behaviors simultaneously. A standard method for treating such data is to first apply some statistical de-trending and to then model the residuals. In financial data analysis, one sees long term (cyclic) fluctuations and inter-or even intraday variability. Analysts will usually focus on either the long term trend or the rapid fluctuations, but not both.

In this paper we describe an alternative approach that is capable of capturing both fast and slow dynamics simultaneously. To model the slow dynamics we embed the scalar time series [7] and use the method of analogues [6]. The method of analogues essentially predicts the future by using the temporal successors of the preceding observations that are most like the current state. Such techniques have found wide application and have been seen to capture long term dynamics well [5]. The short term dynamics are now nothing more than the model prediction errors of the method of analogues prediction. We model the short time dynamics with a deterministic and parametric model structure. The choice of model structure is arbitrary, but we choose minimum description length radial basis function networks [2] because this is what we are familiar with [4, 1] .

We find that the result of this technique outperforms either of the standard methods for both experimental and artificial time series data. Moreover, this combined methodology allows us to produce realistic simulations of experimental time series data. In the next section, we describe the model structure. Following this, we present results for experimental and simulated time series data.

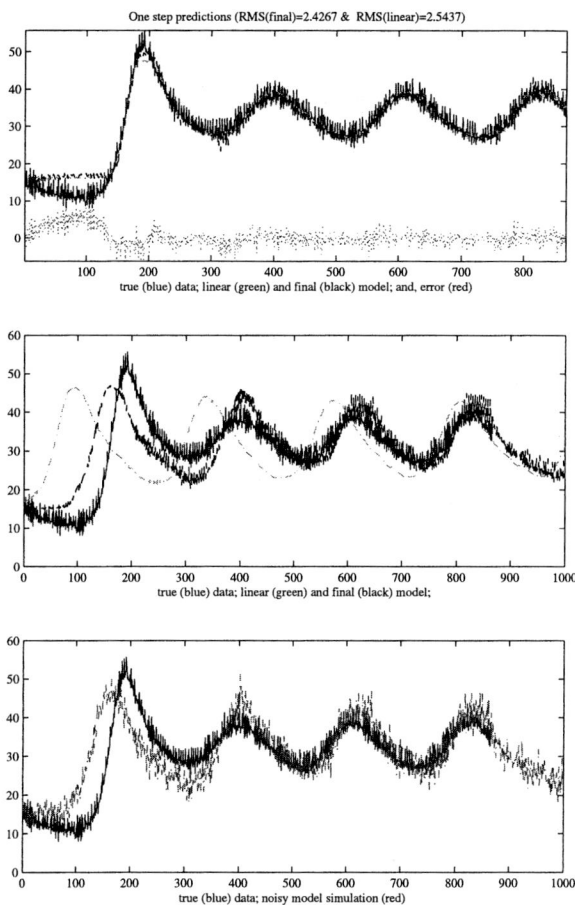

Fig. 1. Out-of-sample model predictions and simulations for the Lorenz+Ikeda system. The top panel shows the original data (solid line), out-of-sample one step model prediction (dot-dashed lines) and prediction errors (dotted). Both predictions via method of analogues (Eq. (1)) and the combined approach (Eq. (3)) are shown, but the difference is very slight (root-mean-square of 2.54 and 2.43 respectively). The middle panel shows simulations from both (1) (light dot-dashed lines) and (3) (dark dot-dashed lines). The new combined model approach performs qualitatively better. This is also apparent from the bottom panel showing a noisy simulation (iterated model predictions with Gaussian random variates added after each prediction time step) of (3) (dot-dashed) and the original data (solid). We used $v^{(A)} = (0, 1, 2, 3, 4, 5, 6, 7, 8, 66, 132)$ and $v^{(B)} = (0, 1, 2, 3)$.

2 The Model

Let x_t denote the observed state at time t. We build two predictive models $\mathcal{A}$ and $\mathcal{B}$ using the method of analogues and some parametric model structure (we choose to use radial basis functions). Let $v = (\ell_1, \ell_2, ..., \ell_n)$ denote an n dimensional embedding and $y_t = x_t - v = (x_{t-\ell_1}, x_{t-\ell_2}, \ldots, x_{t-\ell_n})$ the corresponding embedded point. According to various embedding theorems [7], the correct choice of v will ensure that the dynamic evolution of y_t will be equivalent to that of the underlying dynamical system that generated x_t. Of course, the "correct" choice of v is problematic, and has been the subject of considerable study [3]. In general one finds that there is no genuinely "correct" choice for systems with both fast and slow dynamics. Instead one must choose the v which captures the dynamics of interest best.

Let $v^{(A)}$ be an embedding suitable for modeling the long term dynamics (in general this means that the corresponding lags $\ell_i i$ will be large), and $v^{(B)}$ be an embedding suitable for modeling the short term dynamics (and probably containing relatively small lags). Let $y_t = x_{t-v^{(A)}}$ be the long term embedding and $z_t = x_{t-v^{(B)}}$ be the short term embedding.

Our implementation of the method of analogues is the following. For the current state x_t the prediction of the next state x_{t+1} is given by

$$\mathcal{A}(y_t) = \frac{1}{k} \sum_{i \in N_k} x_{i+1} \tag{1}$$

where $N_k = \{a_1, \ldots, a_k\}$ is the set of k nearest (Euclidean norm) neighbors of y_t among $\{y_1, \ldots, y_{t-1}\}$.

There are some computational issues which we will gloss over at this point. Primarily, one needs to choose k and often one takes a weighted mean instead of (1). Moreover, it is common practice to exclude the temporal neighbors from the sum of spatial neighbors (i.e. $|t - a_i|$ must exceed some threshold). For the current study we simply employ (1) and exclude all points a_i if $|t - a_i|$ is less than one half the pseudo-period of the time series.

Regardless, schemes such as Eq. (1) are excellent at capturing dynamics, but only on one time scale: usually related to the pseudo period of the time series.

Denote $\hat{x}_{t+1} = \mathcal{A}(y_t)$ and let $e_{t+1} = \hat{x}_{t+1} - x_{t+1}$ denote the model prediction error from the method of analogues. We now build a model $\mathcal{B}$ that predicts the model prediction error of model $\mathcal{A}$ from the prediction made by $\mathcal{A}$ and the current model state according to a second embedding $v^{(B)}$. That is,

$$\mathcal{B}(\hat{x}_{t+1}, z_t) = \sum_j^m \lambda_j \phi_j \left(\frac{\|(\hat{x}_{t+1}, z_t) - c_j\|}{r_j} \right) \tag{2}$$
$$= \hat{e}_{t+1}$$

where m is selected according to the minimum description length principle [2]; $\lambda_j, r_j \in \mathbf{R}$; and, ϕ_j are the radial basis functions (in our case, these are Gaussian). An obvious and useful extension of (2) is to incorporate linear and constant terms into the model, which is what we do. For m fixed by minimum description length, the remaining parameters are selected to minimize $\sum_t \|\hat{e}_{t+1} - e_{t+1}\|$.

Hence the final prediction of the next model state $\hat{x}_{t+1}$ from the current model state x_t is given by

$$\hat{x}_{t+1} = \mathcal{A}(x_{t-v^{(A)}}) + \mathcal{B}(\mathcal{A}(x_{t-v^{(A)}}), x_{t-v^{(B)}}). \tag{3}$$

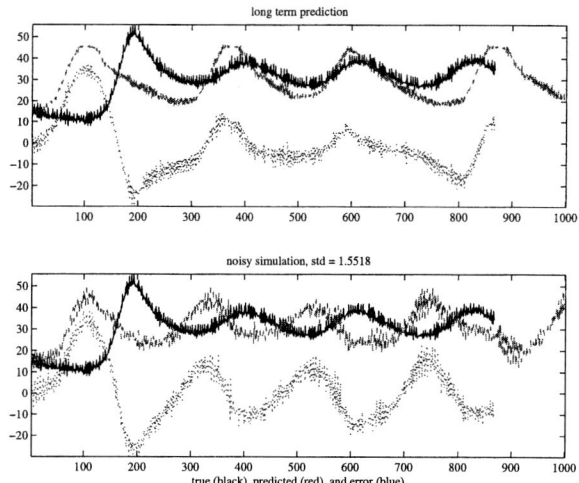

Fig. 2. Out-of-sample model prediction and simulation for the Lorenz+Ikeda system. The top plot is the model simulation using only the parametric modeling approach (2) (i.e. the method of analogues has $k = 0$). The bottom plot is noisy iterated simulations. Data is shown as a solid line, model simulations are dot-dashed and the model prediction error is dotted. The performance is inferior to that in Fig. 1. We used $v^{(B)} = (0, 1, 2, 3, 4, 5, 6, 7, 8, 66, 132)$.

3 Applications and Examples

We first apply the modeling procedure to an artificial system, the sum of a chaotic flow and a chaotic map. We integrate the Lorenz equations

$$\begin{pmatrix} \dot{x} \\ \dot{y} \\ \dot{z} \end{pmatrix} = \begin{pmatrix} s(y - x) \\ rx - y - xz \\ xy - bz \end{pmatrix} \quad (4)$$

($s = 10$, $r = 28$, and $b = 3$) with an integration time step of 0.003, and add the resultant time-series $z_n = z(0.003n)$ to the x component of iterates of the Ikeda map

$$\begin{aligned} u_{n+1} &= 1 + \mu(u_n \cos \theta_n - v_n \sin \theta_n) \\ u_{n+1} &= 1 + \mu(u_n \sin \theta_n + v_n \cos \theta_n) \\ \theta_n &= 0.4 - \frac{6}{1 + u_n^2 + v_n^2} \end{aligned} \quad (5)$$

where $\mu = 0.7$. Hence the time series under study $z_n + u_n$ exhibits both fast dynamics (thanks to the Ikeda map) and slow dynamics (from the Lorenz system). The data together with nonlinear model predictions using the scheme described in the previous section are shown in Fig. 1. For purposes of comparison, figure

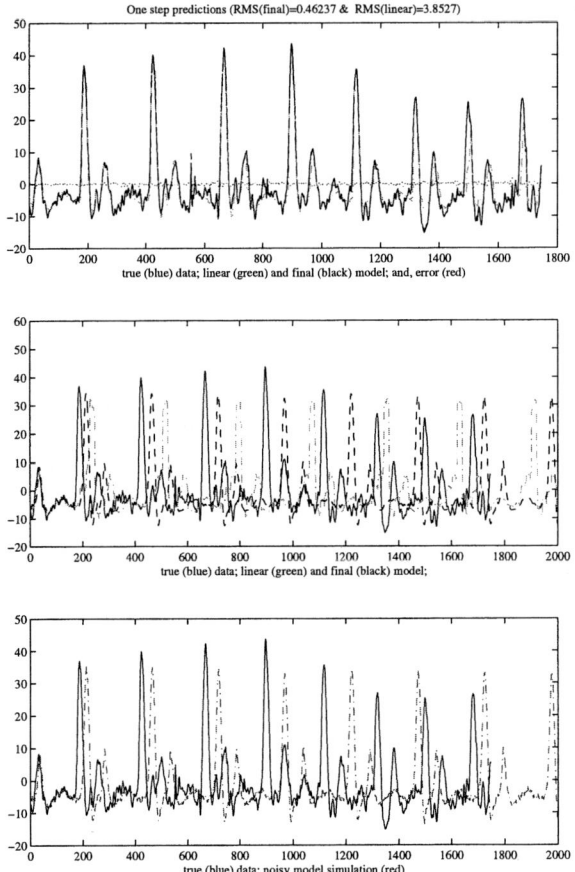

Fig. 3. Out-of-sample model prediction and simulation for pulse pressure waveform data (8000 data points sampled at 250 Hz). We adopt the same convention as in Fig. 1. Again, we see that the new technique performs best. We used $v^{(A)} = (0, 18, 36, ..., 252)$ and $v^{(B)} = (0, 1, 2, 3, 4, 9)$.

2 shows the results for the parametric modelling scheme alone (i.e. no method of analogues).

In Fig. 3 we illustrate results for time series data of finger tip pulse pressure wave of the author. This data represents the pulse pressure wave form measured at the finger tip and is therefore closely related both to ECG waveform data and the pulse measurements made in traditional Chinese medicine.

4 Conclusions

Provided the modeling algorithm to fit (2) is well designed, this new method will fit the data better than (1) alone. In our examples, we found that the long term behavior of the combined model (3) was also better. Moreover, we observed that applying only the nonlinear modeling routine (2), with the same range of embedding lags did not perform well. Primarily this is due to algorithmic problems in the nonlinear fitting procedure. There are more nonlinear parameters than can be practically selected. Nonetheless, this new method appears to avoid these problems and offers a new approach to modeling long term deterministic dynamics on various time scales.

In addition to the data presented in this paper we have repeated our analysis with human EEG time series and daily temperature records (over two decades). All experimental systems exhibited both quantitatively and qualitatively better results with the new modeling method.

Although we have used specific modeling procedures (1) and (2), there is nothing special about this choice. Quite probably the method of analogues could be used for both the fast and slow dynamics, thereby removing the dependence on parametric modeling. We will consider this problem in future work.

Acknowledgments

This work was supported by the Hong Kong University Grants Councils Competitive Earmarked Research Grant (No. PolyU 5235/03E) and the Hong Kong Polytechnic University Direct Allocation (No. A-PE46).

References

1. Judd, K., Small, M.: Towards long-term prediction. Physica D **136** (2000) 31–44
2. Judd, K., Mees, A.: On selecting models for nonlinear time series. Physica D **82**)(1995) 426–444
3. Small, M., Tse, C.K.: Optimal embedding parameters: A modelling paradigm. Physica D (to appear)
4. Small, M., et al.: Modeling continuous processes from data. Phys Rev E **65** (2002) 046704
5. Small, M., et al.: A surrogate test for pseudo-periodic time series data. Phys Rev Lett **87** (2001) 18810.
6. Sugihara, G., May, R.M.: Nonlinear forecasting as a way of distinguishing chaos from measurement error in time series. Nature **344** (1990) 734–741
7. Takens, F.: Detecting strange attractors in turbulence. Lecture Notes in Mathematics **898** (1981) 366–381.

A Variable Metric Probabilistic k-Nearest-Neighbours Classifier

Richard M. Everson and Jonathan E. Fieldsend

Department of Computer Science, University of Exeter, UK

Abstract. k-nearest neighbour (k-nn) model is a simple, popular classifier. Probabilistic k-nn is a more powerful variant in which the model is cast in a Bayesian framework using (reversible jump) Markov chain Monte Carlo methods to average out the uncertainty over the model parameters.
The k-nn classifier depends crucially on the metric used to determine distances between data points. However, scalings between features, and indeed whether some subset of features is redundant, are seldom known *a priori*. Here we introduce a variable metric extension to the probabilistic k-nn classifier, which permits averaging over all rotations and scalings of the data. In addition, the method permits automatic rejection of irrelevant features. Examples are provided on synthetic data, illustrating how the method can deform feature space and select salient features, and also on real-world data.

1 Introduction

One of the most popular methods of statistical classification is the k-nearest neighbour model (k-nn). Although the method has a ready statistical interpretation, and has been shown to have an asymptotic error rate no worse than twice the Bayes error rate [1], it appears in symbolic AI under the guise of case-based reasoning. The method is essentially geometrical, assigning the class of an unknown exemplar to the class of the majority of its k nearest neighbours in some training data. More precisely, in order to assign to a datum $\mathbf{x} \in \mathbb{R}^D$ a class y, given the known training data $\mathcal{D} = \{y_i, \mathbf{x}_i\}_{i=1}^{N}$, the k-nn method first calculates the distances $d_i = ||\mathbf{x} - \mathbf{x}_i||$. If there are Q classes, each of which is *a priori* equally likely, the probability that $\mathbf{x}$ belongs to the q-th class is then evaluated as $p(q \,|\, \mathbf{x}, k, \mathcal{D}) = k_q/k$, where k_q is the number of the k data points with the smallest d_i belonging to class q.

Classification thus crucially depends upon the metric used to determine the distances d_i. Usual practice is to normalise the data so that each of the D coordinates has, say, unit variance, after which Euclidean distance is used. However, as others have shown and we illustrate here, this may result in suboptimal classification rates. In this paper we use a variable metric of the form

$$d(\mathbf{x}_1, \mathbf{x}_2) = \{(\mathbf{x}_1 - \mathbf{x}_2)^T \mathbf{M} (\mathbf{x}_1 - \mathbf{x}_2)\}^{1/2} \qquad (1)$$

where **M** is a $D \times D$ symmetric matrix. Rather than seek a single, optimal metric we adopt the Bayesian point of view and average over all metrics each weighted by its posterior probability. Essential to this programme is Holmes & Adams' [2] recent recasting of the k-nn model in a Bayesian framework, which we briefly describe in the remainder of this section. In section 2 we describe how the k-nn model may be augmented with a variable metric. Illustrative results are presented in section 3 and the paper concludes with a brief discussion.

1.1 The Probabilistic k-nn Model

Holmes & Adams [2] have extended the traditional k-nn classifier by adding a parameter β which controls the 'strength of association' between neighbours. The likelihood of the data given parameters $\boldsymbol{\theta} = \{k, \beta\}$ is defined as

$$p(\mathcal{D}\,|\,\boldsymbol{\theta}) = \prod_{i=1}^{N} \frac{\exp[\beta \sum_{\mathbf{x}_j \sim \mathbf{x}_i}^{k} u(d(\mathbf{x}_i, \mathbf{x}_j))\delta_{y_i y_j}]}{\sum_{q=1}^{Q} \exp[\beta \sum_{j \sim i}^{k} u(d(\mathbf{x}_i, \mathbf{x}_j))\delta_{q y_j}]}. \qquad (2)$$

Here δ_{mn} is the Kronecker delta and $\sum_{\mathbf{x}_j \sim \mathbf{x}_i}^{k}$ means the sum over the k nearest neighbours of $\mathbf{x}_i$ (excluding $\mathbf{x}_i$ itself). If the non-increasing function of distance $u(\cdot) = 1/k$, then the term $\sum_{\mathbf{x}_j \sim \mathbf{x}_i}^{k} u(d(\mathbf{x}_i, \mathbf{x}_j))\delta_{y_i y_j}$ counts the fraction of nearest neighbours of k in the same class y_i as $\mathbf{x}_i$. In the work reported here we choose u to be the tricube kernel [3] which gives decreasing weight to distant neighbours.

Holmes & Adams implement an efficient reversible jump Markov chain Monte Carlo (RJMCMC) [4,5] scheme to draw T samples $\boldsymbol{\theta}^{(t)} = \{k^{(t)}, \beta^{(t)}\}$ from the posterior distribution of the parameters $p(\boldsymbol{\theta}\,|\,\mathcal{D})$. Uncertainty in k and β when classifying $\mathbf{x}$ can then be taken into account by averaging over all values of k and β:

$$p(y\,|\,\mathbf{x}, \mathcal{D}) = \int p(y\,|\,\mathbf{x}, \boldsymbol{\theta}, \mathcal{D}) p(\boldsymbol{\theta}\,|\,\mathcal{D})\, d\boldsymbol{\theta} \approx \frac{1}{T} \sum_{t=1}^{T} p(y\,|\,\mathbf{x}, \boldsymbol{\theta}^{(t)}, \mathcal{D}) \qquad (3)$$

where the predictive likelihood is

$$p(y\,|\,\mathbf{x}, \boldsymbol{\theta}, \mathcal{D}) = \frac{\exp[\beta \sum_{\mathbf{x}_j \sim \mathbf{x}}^{k} u(d(\mathbf{x}, \mathbf{x}_j))\delta_{y y_j}]}{\sum_{q=1}^{Q} \exp[\beta \sum_{\mathbf{x}_j \sim \mathbf{x}}^{k} u(d(\mathbf{x}, \mathbf{x}_j))\delta_{q y_j}]}. \qquad (4)$$

2 Variable Metric and Feature Selection

The relative scales on which features are measured are not usually clear *a priori* and the standard practice of normalisation to zero mean and unit variance may be detrimental to the overall classification rate. Many classifiers, such as linear discriminators or neural networks, discriminate on the basis of linear or nonlinear weighted combinations of the feature variables; these weights are adjusted during learning and may thus compensate for improper scaling of the data. The k-nn

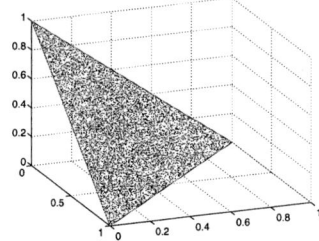 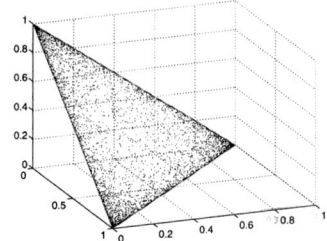

Fig. 1. Samples from 3-dimensional Dirichlet distribution. *Left:* Non-informative, $Dir(1,1,1)$. *Right:* Sparse distribution, $Dir(0.2, 0.2, 0.2)$.

classifier contains no such implicit scaling, making classifications on the basis of the exemplars within a spherical region of feature space. In order to compensate for this, we therefore adopt a metric of the form (1).

It is useful to write $\mathbf{M} = \mathbf{Q}\Lambda\mathbf{Q}^T$, where Λ is a diagonal matrix with non-negative entries λ_d on the diagonal, and $\mathbf{Q}$ is an orthogonal matrix. Then writing $\hat{\mathbf{x}} = \Lambda^{1/2}\mathbf{Q}\mathbf{x}$ shows that using metrics of this form is equivalent to rotating and scaling the data before using the standard Euclidean distance.

The $\mathbf{M} = \mathbf{Q}\Lambda\mathbf{Q}^T$ decomposition is convenient for setting priors as well as for computation. We augment the parameters θ of the probabilistic k-nn classifier with $\mathbf{Q}$ and $\boldsymbol{\lambda} = \text{diag}(\Lambda)$, and extend the Holmes & Adams RJMCMC sampler to draw samples from the joint posterior density $p(k, \beta, \boldsymbol{\lambda}, \mathbf{Q} \mid \mathcal{D})$. The likelihoods (2) and (4) are unchanged except that $d(\cdot, \cdot)$ depends upon $\boldsymbol{\lambda}$ and $\mathbf{Q}$.

Priors. As in the probabilistic k-nn model [2], we adopt a uniform prior $p(k) = 1/\min(k_{max}, N)$, with $k_{max} = 250$. The prior on β expresses a mild preference for small β: $p(\beta) = 2\mathcal{N}(0, 100)I(\beta > 0)$, where $I(\cdot)$ is the set indicator function.

Since we usually have no *a priori* preference for a particular rotation, a uniform prior over $\mathbf{Q}$ is appropriate. The prior for $\boldsymbol{\lambda}$ is a Dirichlet density:

$$p(\boldsymbol{\lambda}) = Dir(\boldsymbol{\lambda} \mid \alpha_1, \ldots, \alpha_D), \tag{5}$$

where all the hyper-parameters are equal: $\alpha_d = \alpha$ This prior ensures that $\lambda_d \geq 0$ so that $\mathbf{M}$ is non-negative definite; changes of sign in the scalings are irrelevant to the classification. In addition, only relative scales are important, which is enforced by fact that the weights λ_d are confined to a $(D-1)$-dimensional simplex: $\sum_{d=1}^{D} \lambda_d = 1$. The parameter α determines the shape of the prior distribution. As Figure 1 shows, when $\alpha = 1$ the prior is non-informative so that all scalings (points on the simplex) are equally likely. Setting $\alpha > 1$ encodes a belief that the scalings should be the same for each variable. Here it is more useful to set $\alpha < 1$ which reflects a belief that the scale factors are unequal, although as Figure 1 illustrates, no particular feature is favoured. If particular features or (with rotations by $\mathbf{Q}$) linear combinations of features are likely to be irrelevant, setting $\alpha < 1$ is tantamount to a sparse prior over the scalings, leading to the suppression of irrelevant feature combinations. Here we have used a mildly sparse prior, $\alpha = 0.8$.

Sampling. The Holmes & Adams RJMCMC sampler makes reversible proposals (k', β') from the current (k, β). To sample from the full parameter set we make additional proposals $\mathbf{Q}'$ and $\boldsymbol{\lambda}'$; the proposal $(k', \beta', \boldsymbol{\lambda}', \mathbf{Q}')$ being accepted with probability:

$$\min\left\{1, \frac{p(\mathcal{D} \mid k', \beta', \boldsymbol{\lambda}', \mathbf{Q}')}{p(\mathcal{D} \mid k, \beta, \boldsymbol{\lambda}, \mathbf{Q})} \frac{p(\boldsymbol{\lambda}')}{p(\boldsymbol{\lambda})} \frac{p(\beta')}{p(\beta)} \frac{p(\boldsymbol{\lambda} \mid \boldsymbol{\lambda}')}{p(\boldsymbol{\lambda}' \mid \boldsymbol{\lambda})}\right\}. \tag{6}$$

Proposals to change the scaling are made from a Dirichlet whose expected value is the current $\boldsymbol{\lambda}$; thus $\boldsymbol{\lambda}' \sim Dir(c\boldsymbol{\lambda})$ [6]. Proposals are thus centred on $\boldsymbol{\lambda}$ with their spread controlled by c, which is chosen during burn-in to achieve a satisfactory acceptance rate; in the work reported here $c = 400$. The proposal ratio for $\boldsymbol{\lambda}$ can be shown to be

$$\frac{p(\boldsymbol{\lambda} \mid \boldsymbol{\lambda}')}{p(\boldsymbol{\lambda}' \mid \boldsymbol{\lambda})} = \prod_{d=1}^{D} \frac{(\lambda_d')^{c\lambda_d - 1} \Gamma(c\lambda_d')}{(\lambda_d)^{c\lambda_d' - 1} \Gamma(c\lambda_d)}. \tag{7}$$

To ensure that $\mathbf{Q}$ is orthogonal, we use Cayley coordinates in which $\mathbf{Q}$ is represented as the matrix exponential $\mathbf{Q} = \exp(\mathbf{S})$ of a skew-symmetric matrix $\mathbf{S} = -\mathbf{S}^T$. Consequently $\mathbf{S}$ has $D(D-1)/2$ independent entries corresponding to the $D(D-1)/2$ degrees of freedom in a D-dimensional orthogonal matrix.

Proposals $\mathbf{Q}'$ are generated by perturbing $\mathbf{S}$ as follows: $\mathbf{S}' = \mathbf{S} + \mathbf{R} - \mathbf{R}^T$, where $R_{ij} \sim \mathcal{N}(0, \sigma^2)$. The variance of the perturbations to $\mathbf{S}$ is adjusted during burn-in to achieve a satisfactory acceptance rate. If the perturbations to $\mathbf{S}$ are symmetric, it is straightforward to show that $p(\mathbf{Q}' \mid \mathbf{Q}) = p(\mathbf{Q} \mid \mathbf{Q}')$, so there is no contribution to the acceptance probability (6) from the $\mathbf{Q}$ proposal ratio.

3 Illustration

We first illustrate the ability of the variable metric to deal with scaled, rotated and irrelevant data by applying it to synthetic data. We then apply it to well-known problems from the UCI machine learning repository [7].

The ability of the variable metric to adjust and compensate for improperly scaled data can be illustrated by the data shown in Figure 2. These two-dimensional, two-class data are separated by an elliptical boundary which is rotated with respect to the coordinate axes; there are 500 training and 284 testing examples. Although the variances of the data projected onto either of the features are equal, optimal classification is achieved if the data are rotated and scaled so that the class boundary is roughly circular.

As an initial illustration we consider the ellipse data, but with the axes of the ellipse aligned with the coordinate axes. As shown in Table 1, the probabilistic k-nn has a misclassification rate of 2.82%, whereas for the variable metric method the error is lowered to 1.76%. The mean posterior scaling factors are $\bar{\lambda}_1 = 0.37$ and $\bar{\lambda}_2 = 0.63$, which is close to the ratio $1:2$, the ratio of ellipse axes.

Simple scaling of the data is insufficient to render the class boundary circular when the class boundary ellipse is not aligned with the coordinate axes (see

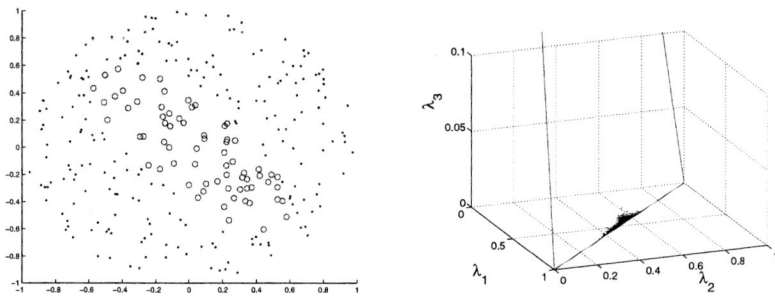

Fig. 2. *Left:* Synthetic data with rotated elliptical class boundaries. *Right:* Samples from posterior λ for synthetic rotated data, with an additional irrelevant feature.

Table 1. Mean classification error (%) for probabilistic and variable metric k-nn.

	Ellipse			UCI		
	Scaled	Rotated	Irrel.	Ion.	Pima	Wine
MAP $\beta = 1$ k-nn	2.82	2.82	6.69	7.94	26.04	4.49
probabilistic k-nn	2.82	2.82	4.23	5.30	22.92	3.37
variable metric k-nn	1.76	1.41	1.41	1.99	21.35	1.12

Figure 2); and the misclassification error is 3.16% for a variable metric method but with $\mathbf{Q} = \mathbf{I}$ fixed. However, permitting $\mathbf{Q}$ to vary recovers the lower error rate, and the mean posterior $\mathbf{Q}$ corresponds to rotations of $\pm 45°$.

As a final illustration on synthetic data, we add to the ellipse data a third variable x_3 which is irrelevant to classification. The right hand panel of Figure 2 shows samples from posterior distribution of λ_d. It can be seen that the irrelevant direction, corresponding here to λ_3, has been effectively suppressed so that the posterior $\boldsymbol{\lambda}$ lies very close to the two-dimensional simplex $\lambda_1 + \lambda_2 = 1$.

We also evaluate the performance of the variable metric k-nn classifier on three well-known data sets [7]. The Ionosphere dataset comprises 33 inputs, with 200 training and 151 test examples. The Pima indian diabetes data has 8 predictive variables. *A priori* choice of a metric here is difficult as these variables are measured in disparate units (e.g., kg/m^2, years, mm Hg). They were all normalised to zero mean and unit variance before classification. There were 576 training and 192 test samples. The Wine recognition data set has 13 continuous features on the basis of which an instance should be assigned to one of three classes. There is no standard training/test split for these data, so they were partitioned at random into training and test sets, each with 89 examples.

Following 10^5 burn-in MCMC steps, $T = 10^4$ samples (every 7th step) were collected for classification. Table 1 compares mean classification rates for the standard probabilistic k-nn method, the *maximum a posteriori* standard probabilistic k-nn classifier with β held at 1 and the variable metric model. The additional flexibility in the variable metric clearly permits better classification, achieving rates at least has high as those reported elsewhere, e.g., [8].

4 Conclusion

We have presented a straightforward scheme for learning a metric for the probabilistic k-nn classifier. Results on synthetic and real data show that the variable metric method yields improved mean classification rates and is able to reject irrelevant features. The variable metric methods presented here are particularly pertinent for k-nn classifiers, which otherwise have no mechanism for learning the data scaling, but the method can be applied to other classifiers. Although the variable metric method yields improved classification rates, it is computationally more expensive than fixed metric methods because distances must be recomputed for each $(\boldsymbol{\lambda}^{(t)}, \mathbf{Q}^{(t)})$ sample.

Here we have considered only linear scalings and rotations of the data. Current work involves expanding the class of metrics to include Minkowski metrics in the rotated space. Finally, we remark that it would be valuable to extend the considerable work (e.g., [9]) on *local* variable metrics to the Bayesian context.

Acknowledgements

We thank Trevor Bailey, Adolfo Hernandez, Wojtek Krzanowski, Derek Partridge, Vitaly Schetnin and Jufen Zhang for their helpful comments. JEF gratefully acknowledges support from the EPSRC, grant GR/R24357/01.

References

1. Cover, T., Hart, P.: Nearest neighbor pattern classification. IEEE Transactions on Information Theory **13** (1967) 21–27
2. Holmes, C., Adams, N.: A probabilistic nearest neighbour method for statistical pattern recognition. Journal Royal Statistical Society B **64** (2002) 1–12 See also code at http://www.stats.ma.ic.ac.uk/~ccholmes/Book_code/book_code.html.
3. Fan, J., Gijbels, I.: Local polynomial modelling and its applications. Chapman & Hall, London (1996)
4. Green, P.: Reversible jump Markov Chain Monte Carlo computation and Bayesian model determination. Biometrika **82** (1995)
5. Denison, D., Holmes, C., Mallick, B., Smith, A.: Bayesian Methods for Nonlinear Classification and Regression. Wiley (2002)
6. Larget, B., Simon, D.: Markov Chain Monte Carlo Algorithms for the Bayesian analysis of phylogenetic trees. Molecular Biology and Evolution **16** (1999) 750–759
7. Blake, C., Merz, C.: UCI repository of machine learning databases (1998) http://www.ics.uci.edu/~mlearn/MLRepository.html.
8. Sykacek, P.: On input selection with reversible jump Markov chain Monte Carlo sampling. In Solla, S., Leen, T., Müller, K.R., eds.: NIPS* 12. (2000) 638–644
9. Myles, J.P., Hand, D.J.: The multi-class metric problem in nearest neighbour discrimination rules. Pattern Recognition **23** (1990) 1291–1297

Feature Word Tracking in Time Series Documents

Atsuhiro Takasu[1] and Katsuaki Tanaka[2]

[1] National Institute of Informatics
2-1-2 Hitotsubashi, Chiyoda-ku, Tokyo 101-8430, Japan
takasu@nii.ac.jp
[2] AI Laboratory, RCAST, University of Tokyo
4-6-1 Komaba, Meguro-ku, Tokyo 101-8430, Japan

Abstract. Data mining from time series documents is a new challenge in text mining and, for this purpose, time dependent feature extraction is an important problem. This paper proposes a method to track feature terms in time series documents. When analyzing and mining time series data, the key is to handle time information. The proposed method applies non-linear principal component analysis to document vectors that consist of term frequencies and time information. This paper reports preliminary experimental results in which the proposed method is applied to a corpus of topic detection and tracking, and we show that the proposed method is effective in extracting time dependent terms.

1 Introduction

Documents are important sources for information extraction and many studies have considered retrieving, classifying and clustering documents. Most of these document processing methods handle documents as time independent information, where documents are usually represented with feature vectors consisting only of feature terms. However, documents are frequently time dependent. For example, news articles are typical time dependent documents that contain time related information, such as broadcast time and time of event occurrence described in the article. However, these forms of time information have not been used fully in the previous studies. For example, Reuters's news text is often used in the study of text categorization but the researchers have only used term frequency information.

For some applications, time is crucial information. Let us consider tracing the news related to a specific event. Then, we want to watch/read the news in chronological order and to know how some events affect later events. The information retrieval (IR) community has been handling time series documents as an information filtering task. In this task, documents are given one by one and a system selects the documents relevant to given topic. Recently, a new research project on topic detection and tracking (TDT) has been started[1]. In this project, several tasks are set for handling news articles, such as story segmentation, topic detection, and topic tracking.

Yang and her colleagues applied the k nearest neighbor (kNN) method to the topic tracking task, in which a set of documents are given one by one for each topic and the systems are required to find on-topic documents from these. In this study, they did not use time information. Ishikawa et al. [6] adopted a power law model of forgetfulness in a human memory and decreased the importance of a document using an exponential function of the elapsed time from its creation when calculating the term vectors of the documents. Franz et al. used a similar model for handling time information in news articles [5] and reported that the time information is useful for handling news articles. However, Branz et al. reported that time information was not useful in the topic tracking task in their experiments [3]. As far as we know, it is currently an open question as to whether time information is effective or not.

In this paper, we propose a feature term tracking method based on non-linear principal component analysis. This problem is the dual problem of topic tracking. In time series data, such as news articles, topics often drift. For example, consider a series of news articles about an earthquake. The news first focuses on the earthquake center and magnitude and then focuses on the human victims and property damage. With the topic drift, feature terms change. By tracking the feature term drift, we will be able to help users to comprehend a series of news articles.

2 Term Weight and Spectral Analysis

First we present an overview of the vector representation of documents and spectral analysis. In the following discussion, we use bold lower and upper case letters to represent a vector and a matrix, respectively. For a vector $\mathbf{v}$, $\mathbf{v}^i$ denotes the i-th component of $\mathbf{v}$. Similarly, for a matrix $\mathbf{M}$, $\mathbf{M}^{ij}$ denotes the component in the i-th row and j-th column of $\mathbf{M}$.

A document is usually represented with a document vector. Consider a set $W \equiv \{w_1, w_2, \cdots, w_m\}$ of feature terms, which are usually selected from words appearing in the documents depending on their effectiveness in differentiating documents from each other. For a document d, let f_i be the frequency of a feature term $w_i \in W$ in the document d; then, the document vector of d is represented with an m-dimensional vector whose i-th component is $tw(f_i)$ where tw is a weighting function. TF·IDF is a standard term weighting function [2] and many researchers have applied it to text retrieval, text categorization, text clustering, etc.

Spectral analysis such as Singular Value Decomposition (SVD) known as the Latent Semantic Index (LSI) [4] in the IR community, and Principal Component Analysis (PCA) are other ways of defining the document vector. When given a set of documents represented with document vectors, PCA derives the axes such that points projected on those axes have maximal variance or equivalently minimal information loss with respect to the square loss. It is well known that the axes coincide with the eigenvectors of the covariance matrix of document vectors. Eigenvectors are ordered into $\mathbf{e}_1, \mathbf{e}_2, \cdots, \mathbf{e}_m$ using the corresponding eigenvalues. For a document vector $\mathbf{d}$ and an eigenvector $\mathbf{e}_i$, their inner product

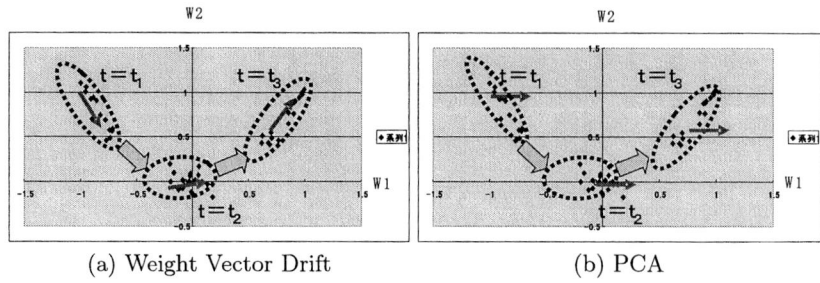

Fig. 1. Weight vector drift

$$p_i \equiv \mathbf{d} \cdot \mathbf{e}_i, \tag{1}$$

is called the i-th principal component of $\mathbf{d}$. In PCA, document vectors are usually reduced to a vector $(p_1, p_2, \cdots, p_k)$ consisting of $k(< m)$ principal components. As shown in Eq. (1), an eigenvector $\mathbf{e}_i$ can be seen as a weighting vector for the i-th principal component and its j-th component $\mathbf{e}_i^j$ represents the contribution of the feature term w_j to the i-th principal component. We use eigenvectors as feature term weight vectors and trace the feature term drift.

There is one problem when applying PCA to time series documents. Suppose the shape of a document cluster changes with time. Figure 1 (a) and (b) show a schematic example where documents are represented with two dimensional vector spaces in which feature terms w_1 and w_2 correspond to the horizontal and vertical axis, respectively. In these figures, each dot represents a document vector and dotted spheres represent document clusters at times t_1, t_2 and t_3. The arrows in figure 1 (a) show the weight vectors at each time t_1, t_2 and t_3. In this case, the contribution of term w_1 is dominant at time t_2, whereas both w_1 and w_2 contribute equally at times t_1 and t_3. When applying PCA to these document vectors, we obtain two eigenvectors corresponding to first and second principal components. Arrows in figure 1 (b) show the eigenvector corresponding to the first principal component. As shown in the figure, the eigenvector has the same direction for every cluster, independent of time. Therefore, we cannot extract time dependent contributions of feature terms by the usual PCA. To track the contribution of feature terms in the next section, we propose a non-linear spectral analysis method.

3 Term Weight Tracking by Kernel PCA

Kernel Principal Component Analysis (Kernel PCA) [7] is a non-linear method. In this section, we present an overview of Kernel PCA and then derive a term weight tracking method using it. In the kernel method, every data vector (document vector in this paper) $\mathbf{d}$ is mapped into a high dimensional feature space $\Phi(\mathbf{d})$ as shown in figure 2 (a). The feature space is implicitly defined by the kernel function that defines the inner product of document vectors $\mathbf{d}_1$ and $\mathbf{d}_2$ in

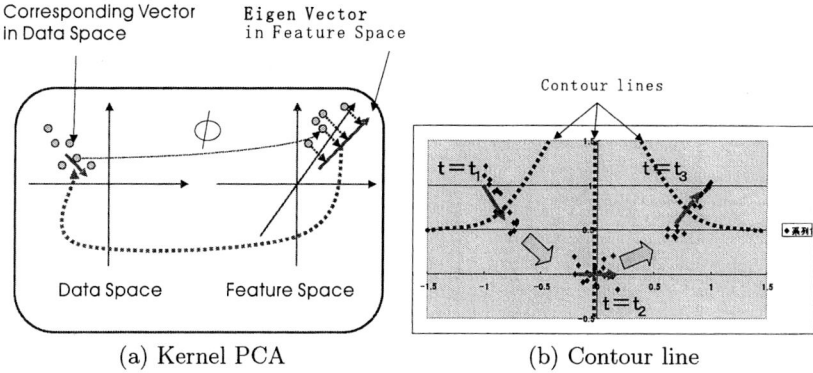

Fig. 2. Kernel PCA and Eigenvector in Data Space

the feature space as $\Phi(\mathbf{d})_1 \cdot \Phi(\mathbf{d})_2 \equiv K(\mathbf{d}_1, \mathbf{d}_2)$, and the mapping function Φ is not used explicitly.

Kernel PCA applies the principal component analysis to the document vectors in the feature space. Assume that we have a set $D \equiv \{\mathbf{d}_1, \mathbf{d}_2, \cdots, \mathbf{d}_n\}$ of documents and we wish to obtain the kernel PCA of D. Let $\mathbf{M}$ be a mean vector of D in the feature space, i.e., $\mathbf{M} \equiv \frac{1}{n} \sum_{i=1}^{n} \Phi(\mathbf{d}_i)$ and consider the set of document vectors in which each vector is centered on the mean vector, i.e., $\Phi'(\mathbf{d}) \equiv \Phi(\mathbf{d}) - \mathbf{M}$. Introduce the $n \times n$ matrix $\mathbf{S}$ whose ij-th component $\mathbf{S}^{ij}$ is $\Phi'(\mathbf{d}_i) \cdot \Phi'(\mathbf{d}_j)$ and consider its eigenvalue λ and eigenvector $\mathbf{e}$, i.e., $\lambda \mathbf{e} = \mathbf{S}\mathbf{e}$. For all eigenvalues of $\mathbf{S}$, align the eigenvectors in descending order of the corresponding eigenvalue. Using the k-th eigenvector $\mathbf{e}_k$ as coefficient, a vector $\mathbf{V}_k$ represents the axis for the k-th principal component in the feature space (an arrow in the feature space of figure 2 (a)) is given by the following equation [7]

$$\mathbf{V}_k = \sum_{i=1}^{n} \mathbf{e}_k^i \Phi'(\mathbf{d}_i) \ . \tag{2}$$

From Eq. (2), the k-th principal component of a document vector $\mathbf{d}$ is given by

$$\Phi'(\mathbf{x}) \cdot \mathbf{V}_k = \sum_{i=1}^{n} \mathbf{e}_k^i (\Phi'(\mathbf{d}_i) \cdot \Phi'(\mathbf{x}))$$
$$= \sum_{i=1}^{n} \mathbf{e}_k^i (\Phi(\mathbf{d}_i) - \mathbf{M}) \cdot (\Phi(\mathbf{x}) - \mathbf{M}) \tag{3}$$

To obtain the axis for k-th principal component in the data space, consider lines of constant principal component values (contour lines). Figure 2 (b) depicts three contour lines at the centers of three document clusters. Note that contour lines of kernel PCA are curves, whereas those of PCA are straight lines. Consider a vector orthogonal to the contour line as a weighting vector. Then, for any point $\mathbf{x} \equiv (x_1, x_2, \cdots, x_d)$ in the data space, the vector $\mathbf{w}_{x,k}$ for the k-th principal component axis (arrows in figure 2 (b)) is obtained by the following equation using Eq. (3)

$$\mathbf{w}_{x,k}^l \equiv \frac{\partial(\varPhi'(\mathbf{x}) \cdot \mathbf{V}_k)}{\partial x_l}$$
$$= \sum_{i=1}^n e_k^i \left(\frac{\partial K(\mathbf{d}_i, \mathbf{x})}{\partial x_l} - \frac{1}{n} \sum_{j=1}^n \frac{\partial K(\mathbf{d}_j, \mathbf{x})}{\partial x_l} \right). \quad (4)$$

Note that a vector $\mathbf{x}$ consists of weighted term frequencies $\mathbf{d} = (w_1, w_2, \cdots, w_m)$ and time t. Therefore, we can obtain the term weight at any feature space $\mathbf{d}$ and time t from Eq. (4). Assume that $\mathbf{x}_1, \mathbf{x}_2, \cdots, \mathbf{x}_t$ are cluster centers for each time $t_1, t_2, \cdots, t_t$; we can then track term weight changes by calculating $\mathbf{w}_{x_1,k}^l, \mathbf{w}_{x_2,k}^l, \cdots, \mathbf{w}_{x_t,k}^l$.

4 Preliminary Experiment

We applied the proposed term weight tracking method to the Topic Detection and Tracking - Phase 3 (TDT3) corpus. This corpus consists of news articles broadcasted by TV and radio programs. In this corpus, each article contains several segments called a "story", each of which is a news article on one of 60 topics. Although the corpus contains both English and Mandarin articles, we only used English articles in this experiment. Please refer to the Web site[1] for details.

We first removed stop words and then applied Porter's stemming algorithm [2] to the remaining words to obtain frequencies of each word in each story. Then, we selected 10,000 words on the basis of TF·IDF values and constructed a document vector for each story. We added broadcasted time of the news to the document vector as a component causing the dimension of the document vector to be 10,001.

In this experiment, we used the Radius Basis Function $e^{-\frac{||\mathbf{x}-\mathbf{y}||^2}{2\sigma^2}}$ as kernel. The partial differentiation of the kernel by a variable x_l is

$$\frac{\partial K(\mathbf{x}, \mathbf{y})}{\partial x_l} \equiv \frac{2(x_l - y_l)}{\sigma^2} K(\mathbf{x}, \mathbf{y}) \quad (5)$$

By substituting Eq. (5) into Eq. (4), we obtain the vector of the axis for the k-th principal component. For each topic, let $D \equiv \{\mathbf{d}_1, \mathbf{d}_2, \cdots, \mathbf{d}_n\}$ be the set of document vectors of the stories associated with the topic and a vector $\mathbf{w}_i$ be the axis at the point $\mathbf{d}_i$ obtained by Eq. (4). Then, we measure the weight drift of the term t_l as the sum of weight differences between consecutive documents in the time series, i.e.,

$$\sum_{i=1}^{n-1} |\mathbf{w}_i^l - \mathbf{w}_{i+1}^l|.$$

---

[1] http://www.ldc.upenn.edu/Project/TDT3/

The following terms are the top 10 ranked terms out of 10,000 terms according to the term weight drift for the topic "Cambodian Government Coalition".

Hun, Sen, opposition, government, party, Sam, Cambodia, Election, Friday, July.

On the other hand, the following terms are the top 10 for TF·IDF.

President, people, government, state, officials, police, party, political, minister, military.

Note that the term "Friday" has a high weight drift. This is because an important press conference was held on Friday and the date frequently appeared in the news articles. In this way, the proposed method tends to give high scores to time dependent terms. A similar tendency was observed for other topics.

5 Conclusion

In this paper, we propose a method for extracting term weight drift from time series documents. The key for time dependent document analysis is in handling the time information. The proposed method applies non-linear spectral analysis to document feature vectors consisting of term frequency and time information. Some previous researchers introduced time information into a TF·IDF scheme [6, 5], but there has not been any study on introducing time information into PCA, as far as the authors know. Preliminary experimental results indicate that the proposed method tends to extract terms that are important for the time aspect. Now, we plan to evaluate term weight drift extraction ability quantitatively and an on line calculation algorithm for kernel PCA is also planned for the future.

References

1. James Allan. *Topic Detection and Tracking: Event-based Infromation Organization.* Kluwer Academic Publishers, 2002.
2. R. Baeza-Yates and B. Ribeiro-Neto. *Modern Infromation Retrieval.* Addison Wesley, 1999.
3. Thorsten Brants, Francine Chen, and Ayman Farahat. A system for new event detection. In *Proceedings of the 23rd Annual International ACM SIGIR Conference on Research and Development in Information Retrieval*, pages 330–337, 2003.
4. S. Deerwester, S. T. Dumais, and R. Harshman. Indexing by latent semantic analysis. *Journal of American Society of Information Systems*, 41(2):391–407, 1990.
5. Martin Franz and J Scott McCarley. Unsupervised and supervised clustering for topic tracking. In *Proceedings of the 21th Annual International ACM SIGIR Conference on Research and Development in Information Retrieval*, pages 310–317, 2000.
6. Yoshiharu Ishikawa, Yibing Chen, and Hiroyuki Kitagawa. An on-line document clustering method based on forgetting factors. In *Proceedings of the 5th European Conference on Research and Advanced Technology for Digital Libraries*, pages 325–339, 2001.
7. Bernhard Scholkopf, Alexander Smola, and Klaus-Robert Muller. Nonlinear component analysis as a kernel eigenvalue problem. Technical Report 44, Max-Plank-Institute fur Biolgische Kybernetik, 1996.

Combining Gaussian Mixture Models

Hyoung-joo Lee and Sungzoon Cho

Department of Industrial Engineering, Seoul National University
San 56-1, Shillim-dong, Kwanak-gu, Seoul, 151-744 Korea
{impatton,zoon}@snu.ac.kr

Abstract. A Gaussian mixture model (GMM) estimates a probability density function using the expectation-maximization algorithm. However, it may lead to a poor performance or inconsistency. This paper analytically shows that performance of a GMM can be improved in terms of Kullback-Leibler divergence with a committee of GMMs with different initial parameters. Simulations on synthetic datasets demonstrate that a committee of as few as 10 models outperforms a single model.

1 Introduction

The goal of probability density estimation is, given a set of training samples, $\{\mathbf{x}_i\}_{i=1}^{N} \in R^d$, to develop a model, $\hat{p}(\mathbf{x})$, which approximates the true probability density function, $p(\mathbf{x}) \in R$, $0 \le p(\mathbf{x}) \le 1$, on an arbitrary input vector, $\mathbf{x} \in R^d$. Not only is probability density estimation important in itself, but it can be useful also for other problems such as clustering, classification, and novelty detection. One typical goodness-of-fit measure for probability density estimation is Kullback-Leibler divergence (KL) [6].

In this paper, a Gaussian mixture model (GMM) is considered which determines its parameters using the expectation-maximization (EM) algorithm [2, 3]. Recently, as neural networks are being extensively researched and utilized, many researchers have implemented GMMs based on self-organizing maps, a kind of neural network [4, 11]. A GMM developed by the EM algorithm, however, has several weaknesses due to the fact that it can be critically affected by initialization and noise. As a result, its goodness-of-fit may be poor and its results may become unstable.

This paper tries to overcome the weaknesses by applying the committee approach, which trains and combines several single models while using the same EM algorithm. In the past, the committee approach has been applied primarily to supervised learning problems such as classification and regression [1]. It has been proved that a committee can achieve a better performance than a single model [5, 8].

Taniguchi and Tresp have experimentally compared the performances of well-known committee methods [9]. Ormoneit and Tresp have experimentally investigated a committee of GMMs [7]. However, they have not mathematically analyzed the specific properties of the committee of GMMs. Instead, they used the prior research results of supervised learning to argue for the committee approach. In this paper, on

---

Given a sequence of N unlabeled examples, X={$x_1,x_2,...,x_N$}
For (j=1 to T)
{
Initialize the parameters of the jth Gaussian mixture model
Determine the parameters of the jth GMM, , based on dataset X
}

Fig. 1. The procedure to generate a committee of Gaussian mixture models.

the other hand, we show mathematically that a committee of GMMs outperforms an average single model in terms of KL and show experimentally that diversity in a committee leads to a better performance.

The next section outlines the method of constructing a committee of GMMs and then analyzes its performance. Section 3 shows the experimental results. Section 4 summarizes this paper and discusses the limitations and the research directions for the future.

2 Committee of Gaussian Mixture Models

The procedure to construct a committee of GMMs is straightforward. With a given set of training samples, $\{x_i\}_{i=1}^{N} \in R^d$, initialize a mixture model with K Gaussian components randomly, and then train the model on the training dataset. Repeat this process T times, and T GMMs, $\hat{p}_j, j = 1,2,\cdots,T$, are generated with different initial parameters. When a new input vector, $x \in R^d$ is given, a committee output, $\bar{p}(x)$ is averaged over the outputs of the single GMMs. This procedure is illustrated in Fig. 1 and (1).

$$\bar{p}(x) = \frac{1}{T}\sum_{j=1}^{T}\hat{p}_j(x) = \frac{1}{T}\sum_{j=1}^{T}\sum_{k=1}^{K}\{P_{j,k} \times \hat{p}_j(x|k)\} \qquad (1)$$

A committee consisting of T GMMs with different initial parameters provides a better goodness-of-fit than a single GMM does. Suppose that there exist two finite datasets, a training dataset, $X = \{x_i\}$, and a validation dataset, $V = \{x_m\}$. Further suppose that a population of models, $F = \{\hat{p}_j(x)\}$, has been generated, each of which approximates the true probability density function, $p(x)$. One would like to find the best approximation to $p(x)$ using F. One common choice is to use the naive model, $\hat{p}_{Naive}(x)$, which maximizes the log-likelihood on the validation dataset V. However, this is a problematic choice, especially when dealing with a finite real-world dataset.

First, by selecting only one model from the population, useful information in the other models is discarded. Second, since V is randomly sampled, it is possible that at least one other model has a higher log-likelihood on another previously unseen dataset, V', sampled from the same distribution. A more reliable estimate of goodness-of-fit is the average performance over the population.

Theorem 1. Suppose a committee that consists of T single GMMs. The KL value of the committee, $\mathrm{KL}(p(\mathbf{x}), \overline{p}(\mathbf{x}))$, is equal to or less than the average KL value of the T single GMMs, $\overline{\mathrm{KL}}$. That is,

$$\mathrm{KL}(p(\mathbf{x}), \overline{p}(\mathbf{x})) \leq \overline{\mathrm{KL}} = \frac{1}{T}\sum_{j=1}^{T} \mathrm{KL}(p(\mathbf{x}), \hat{p}(\mathbf{x})) \quad (2)$$

Proof. The KL of the committee and the average KL of the T single GMMs are, respectively,

$$\mathrm{KL}(p(\mathbf{x}), \overline{p}(\mathbf{x})) = \int p(\mathbf{x})\left[\log p(\mathbf{x}) - \log\left\{\frac{1}{T}\sum_{j=1}^{T} \hat{p}_j(\mathbf{x})\right\}\right]d\mathbf{x}. \quad (3)$$

$$\overline{\mathrm{KL}} = \frac{1}{T}\sum_{j=1}^{T}\mathrm{KL}(p(\mathbf{x}), \hat{p}_j(\mathbf{x})) = \int p(\mathbf{x})\left\{\log p(\mathbf{x}) - \frac{1}{T}\sum_{j=1}^{T}\log \hat{p}_j(\mathbf{x})\right\}d\mathbf{x}. \quad (4)$$

Then, from Eq. (3) and (4), the difference between the average KL of the T single GMMs and the KL of the committee becomes

$$\overline{\mathrm{KL}} - \mathrm{KL}(p(\mathbf{x}), \overline{p}(\mathbf{x})) = \int p(\mathbf{x})\left\{\log\left(\frac{1}{T}\sum_{j=1}^{T}\hat{p}_j(\mathbf{x})\right) - \frac{1}{T}\sum_{j=1}^{T}\log \hat{p}_j(\mathbf{x})\right\}d\mathbf{x}. \quad (5)$$

Since $\log(\cdot)$ is concave, the following holds:

$$\log\left\{\frac{1}{T}\sum_{j=1}^{T}\hat{p}_j(\mathbf{x})\right\} \geq \frac{1}{T}\sum_{j=1}^{T}\log \hat{p}_j(\mathbf{x}), \forall \mathbf{x}. \quad (6)$$

Therefore, we have

$$\overline{\mathrm{KL}} - \mathrm{KL}(p(\mathbf{x}), \overline{p}(\mathbf{x})) = \int p(\mathbf{x})\left\{\log\left(\frac{1}{T}\sum_{j=1}^{T}\hat{p}_j(\mathbf{x})\right) - \frac{1}{T}\sum_{j=1}^{T}\log \hat{p}_j(\mathbf{x})\right\}d\mathbf{x} \geq 0.$$

The equality holds when $\hat{p}_1(\mathbf{x}) = \cdots = \hat{p}_T(\mathbf{x}), \forall \mathbf{x}$. ∎

A committee of GMMs always has a KL value that is smaller than the average KL value of the single GMMs, unless all individual models are identical. Assume that the probability density of a single model contains an uncorrelated random noise, $\varepsilon_j(\mathbf{x})$ i.e., $\hat{p}_j(\mathbf{x}) = p(\mathbf{x}) + \varepsilon_j(\mathbf{x})$. Then averaging the single models is equivalent to averaging over the noise. In this sense, a committee can be considered as smoothing in the output space and thus can be regarded as a regularizer. The committee approach could be useful for the EM algorithm, since the algorithm tends to be sensitive to initialization and noisy data.

An additional benefit of the committee approach is that there is no restriction on how each of individual models should be built. The committee approach can be applied to other probability density estimators and it is possible to combine individual estimators developed by many different algorithms.

In Theorem 1, there is no improvement if all models from F are identical. It can be argued that the improvement of a diverse committee is larger than that of a uni-

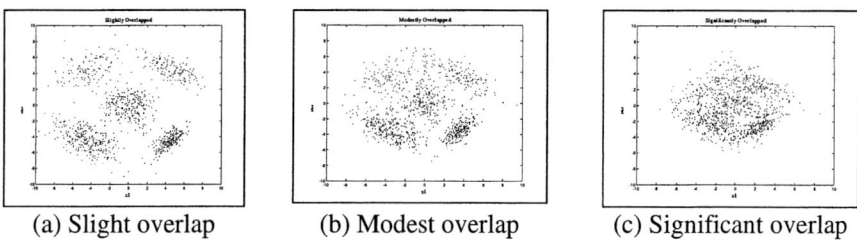

(a) Slight overlap   (b) Modest overlap   (c) Significant overlap

Fig. 2. 2D datasets with 3 different levels of overlapping.

form one. This argument is consistent with prior researches on supervised learning problems [5], although the proof is not included in this paper.

3 Experimental Results

For simplicity, experiments were conducted on 1D and 2D synthetic datasets, all of which were drawn from five Gaussian components. For 2D datasets, as in Xu's study [10], three datasets with different levels of overlapping were generated. The datasets are shown in Figs.2 and 3.

Heteroscedastic GMMs were trained using the traditional EM algorithm. The committee size, T, was fixed with 10 and the number of components in a GMM, $K=5$, is assumed to be known. For each dataset, 100 committees and 1000 single models were generated. Since all the true parameters are known, KL was used as a performance measure. The total diversity of a committee was calculated as in (7),

$$D = \int \left\{ \frac{1}{T} \sum_{j=1}^{T} \left(\overline{p}(\mathbf{x}) - \hat{p}_j(\mathbf{x}) \right)^2 \right\} d\mathbf{x}. \tag{7}$$

Statistical results are presented in Table 1, along with T-tests and F-tests. Since all hypotheses were resoundingly rejected, it is safe to say that a committee has a significantly lower KL value and a significantly smaller variance in its performance. In Fig. 3, a committee estimates the true probability density more closely than any single model.

A close relationship was found between diversity and performance of a committee. In Fig. 4, the horizontal and the vertical axes are the total diversity of a committee and the improvement over the average single GMM, respectively. A dot is plotted for each trial and the line is fitted by linear regression. For each dataset, diversity accounts for at least 65% of the variation of the improvement.

4 Conclusions and Discussion

In this paper, we apply the committee approach to improve performance and robustness of a single model. It has been analytically shown that a committee of GMMs strictly outperforms an average single GMM. In the simulations on synthetic datasets, a committee of only 10 GMMs has a significantly lower KL value than an average single model. It has been argued that larger diversity translates into a better performance. Although it has not been proven yet, simulation results were favorable to this argument. In addition, a committee resulted in less variability in its performance.

Table 1. Kullback-Lebiler divergences of committees and single GMMs.

Dataset		Model	Mean	Std	t (p-value)	F (p-value)
1D		Committee	0.0682	0.0082	-31.2694	0.1791
		Single GMM	0.1002	0.0193	(<0.0001)	(<0.0001)
2D	Slight Overlap	Committee	0.0322	0.0047	-8.1075	0.0197
		Single GMM	0.0415	0.0332	(<0.0001)	(<0.0001)
	Modest Overlap	Committee	0.0329	0.0028	-6.1476	0.0349
		Single GMM	0.0363	0.0149	(<0.0001)	(<0.0001)
	Significant Overlap	Committee	0.0217	0.0009	-6.5203	0.0129
		Single GMM	0.0235	0.0082	(<0.0001)	(<0.0001)

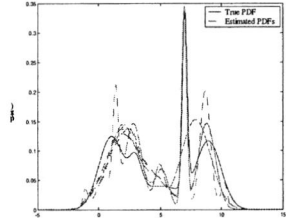
(a) Estimated by individuals

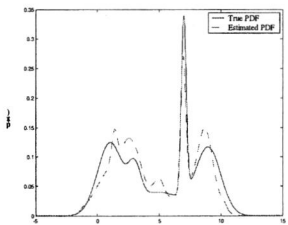
(b) Estimated by a committee

Fig. 3. True (solid) and estimated (dashed) 1D probability densities.

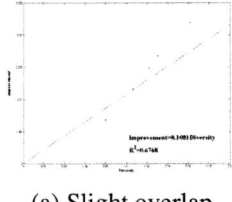
(a) Slight overlap

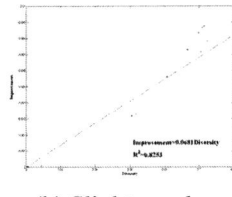
(b) Slight overlap

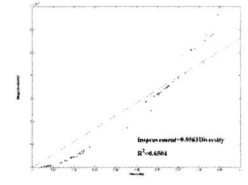
(c) Significant overlap

Fig. 4. Diversity and the improvement of performance for 2D datasets.

There are several limitations and a few directions for the future works. Needless to say, a committee is more complex than a single model. Theoretical and experimental analyses need to be done to shed light to how to determine the number of committee members and the number of components. The lower bound of KL of a committee needs to be analyzed as well. Since diversity is shown to be important in improving performance, we need to address how to achieve greater diversity. In addition, the committee approach needs to be tested on high dimensional and large-sized real-world data.

References

1. Bauer E, Kohavi R (1999) An empirical comparison of voting classification algorithms: bagging, boosting, and variants. Machine Learning 36: 105-139.
2. Bishop CM (1995) Neural Networks for Pattern Recognition. Oxford University Press, New York.
3. Dempster AP, Laird NM, Rubin DB (1977) Maximum likelihood from incomplete data via the EM algorithm. Journal of the Royal Statistical Society B39: 1-38.
4. Gray RM, Perlmutter KO, Olshen RA (1998) Quantization, classification, and density estimation for Kohonen's Gaussian mixture. In: Storer JA, Cohn M (eds) Proceedings of Data Compression Conference. IEEE Computer Society Press, California.
5. Krogh A, Vedelsby J (1995) Neural networks ensembles, cross validation, and active learning. In: Tesauro G, Touretzky D, Leen T (eds) Advances in Neural Information Processing Systems 7. MIT Press, Cambridge.
6. McLachlan G, Peel D (2000) Finite mixture models. John Wiley & Sons, New York.
7. Ormoneit D, Tresp V (1998) Averaging, maximum penalized likelihood and bayesian estimation for improving gaussian mixture probability density esimates. IEEE Transactions on Neural Networks 9(4): 639-650.
8. Perrone MP, Cooper LN (1993) When networks disagree : ensemble methods for neural networks. In: Mammone RJ (ed) Artificial Neural Networks for Speech and Vision. Chapman & Hall, New York.
9. Taniguchi M, Tresp V (1997) Averaging regularized estimators. Neural Computation 9(5): 1163-1178.
10. Xu L (1997) Bayesian Ying-Yang machine, clustering, and number of clusters. Pattern Recognition Letters 18: 1167-1178.
11. Yin H, Allinson NM (2001) Self-organizing mixture networks for probability density estimation. IEEE Transactions on Neural Networks 12(2): 405-411.

Global Convergence of Steepest Descent for Quadratic Functions

Zhigang Zeng[1,2], De-Shuang Huang[1], and Zengfu Wang[3]

[1] Intelligent Computing Lab, Institute of Intelligent Machines
Chinese Academy of Sciences, Hefei, Anhui, 230031, China
zhigangzeng@iim.ac.cn
[2] Department of Mathematics, Hubei Normal University
Huangshi, Hubei, 435002, China
[3] Department of Automation, University of Science and Technology of China
Hefei, Anhui, 230026, China

Abstract. This paper analyzes the effect of momentum on steepest descent training for quadratic performance functions. Some global convergence conditions of the steepest descent algorithm are obtained by directly analyzing the exact momentum equations for quadratic cost functions. Those conditions can be directly derived from the parameters (different from eigenvalues that are used in the existed ones.) of the Hessian matrix. The results presented in this paper are new.

1 Introduction

Back-propagation (BP) is one of the most widely used algorithms for training feedforward neural networks [1]. However, it is seen from simulations that it takes a long time to converge. Consequently, many variants of BP have been suggested. One of the most well-known variants is the back-propagation with momentum terms (BPM) [2], in which the weight change is a combination of the new steepest descent step and the previous weight change. The purpose of using momentum is to smooth the weight trajectory and speed the convergence of the algorithm [3]. It is also sometimes credited with avoiding local minima in the error surface. BP can be shown to be a straightforward gradient descent on the least squares error, and it has been shown recently that BP converges to a local minimum of the error. While it is observed that the BPM algorithm shows a much higher rate of convergence than the BP algorithm.

Although squared error functions are only quadratic for linear networks, they are approximately quadratic for any smooth error functions in the neighborhood of a local minimum. (This can be shown by performing a Taylor series expansion of the error function about the minimum point [3].) Phansalkar and Sastry [1] analyze the behavior of the BPM algorithm and show that all local minima of the least squares error are the only locally asymptotically stable poits of the algorithm. Hagiwara and Sato [5], [6] show that the momentum mechanism can be derived from a modified cost function, in which the squared errors are exponentially weighted in time. They also derive a qualitative relationship between the momentum term, the learning rate and the speed of convergence. Qian [7] demonstrates an analogy between the convergence of the momentum algorithm and the movement of Newtonian particles in a viscous medium. By utilizing a discrete approximation to this continuous system, Qian also derives the conditions for stability of the algorithm. Torii and Hagan [4] analyze the effect of momentum when minimizing quadratic error functions, and provide necessary and sufficient conditions for stability of the algorithm and present a theoretically optimal setting for the momentum parameter to produce fastest convergence.

In this paper, some global convergence conditions of the steepest descent algorithm are obtained by directly analyzing the exact momentum equations for quadratic cost functions. Those conditions can be directly derived from the parameters (different from eigenvalues that are used in [4]) of the Hessian matrix.

2 Problem Description

Our objective is to determine a set of network weights that minimize a quadratic error function. The quadratic function can be represented by

$$F(\mathbf{x}) = \frac{1}{2}\mathbf{x}^T \mathbf{H} \mathbf{x} + \mathbf{d}^T \mathbf{x} + c, \tag{1}$$

where $\mathbf{H}$ is a symmetric Hessian matrix with nonnegative eigenvalues (since the error function must be positive semidefinite). The standard steepest descent algorithm is

$$\Delta \mathbf{x}(k) = -\alpha \nabla F(\mathbf{x}(k)). \tag{2}$$

This algorithm is stable if α times the largest eigenvalue of the matrix $\mathbf{H}$ is less than 2 [1]. If we add momentum, the steepest descent algorithm becomes

$$\Delta \mathbf{x}(k) = \gamma \Delta \mathbf{x}(k-1) - (1-\gamma)\alpha \nabla F(\mathbf{x}(k)). \tag{3}$$

where the momentum parameter γ will be in the range $0 < \gamma < 1$.

The gradient of the quadratic function is

$$\nabla F(\mathbf{x}) = \mathbf{H}\mathbf{x} + \mathbf{d}, \tag{4}$$

where the matrix $\mathbf{H} = (h_{ij})_{n \times n}$.

3 Steepest Descent Without Momentum

Let
$$\bar{h}_{ij} = \begin{cases} \alpha h_{ii}, & i = j, \\ -\alpha |h_{ij}|, & i \neq j, \end{cases} \qquad \tilde{h}_{ij} = \begin{cases} 2 - \alpha h_{ii}, & i = j, \\ -\alpha |h_{ij}|, & i \neq j. \end{cases}$$

Denote matrices $\mathbf{H}_1 = (\bar{h}_{ij})_{n \times n}, \mathbf{H}_2 = (\tilde{h}_{ij})_{n \times n}$.

Theorem 1. If $\text{rank}(\mathbf{H}) = \text{rank}(\mathbf{H}, \mathbf{d})$, and when $\alpha h_{ii} \in (0, 1), i \in \{1, 2, \cdots, n\}$, $\mathbf{H}_1$ is a nonsingular M-matrix; when $\alpha h_{ii} \in [1, 2), i \in \{1, 2, \cdots, n\}$, $\mathbf{H}_2$ is a nonsingular M-matrix, then algorithm (2) is globally convergent.

Proof. Since rank($\mathbf{H}$) = rank($\mathbf{H}, \mathbf{d}$), there exist $\mathbf{x}^* \in \Re^n$ such that

$$\mathbf{H}\mathbf{x}^* = -\mathbf{d}.$$

Case I), when $\alpha h_{ii} \in (0,1), i \in \{1,2,\cdots,n\}$, $\mathbf{H}_1$ is a nonsingular M-matrix implies that there exist positive constants $\gamma_1, \gamma_2, \cdots, \gamma_n$ such that

$$\gamma_i \alpha h_{ii} - \sum_{j=1, j \neq i}^{n} \gamma_j \alpha |h_{ij}| > 0. \tag{5}$$

Let $\mathbf{y}(k) = (y_1(k), y_2(k), \cdots, y_n(k))^T$, where $y_i(k) = (x_i(k) - x_i^*)/\gamma_i$, then from (2),

$$\Delta y_i(k) = -\alpha \sum_{j=1}^{n} \gamma_j h_{ij} y_j(k)/\gamma_i. \tag{6}$$

Let $\eta_i(\lambda) = \gamma_i \lambda - \gamma_i(1 - \alpha h_{ii}) - \sum_{j=1, j\neq i}^{n} \gamma_j \alpha |h_{ij}|$, then $\eta_i(0) = -\gamma_i(1-\alpha h_{ii}) - \sum_{j=1, j\neq i}^{n} \gamma_j \alpha |h_{ij}| < 0$, $\eta_i(1) > 0$. Hence, there exists $\lambda_{0i} \in (0,1)$ such that $\eta_i(\lambda_{0i}) = 0$, and $\eta_i(\lambda) > 0$, $\lambda \in (\lambda_{0i}, 1)$.

In fact, we can choose $\lambda_{0i} = (1 - \alpha h_{ii}) + \sum_{j=1, j\neq i}^{n} \gamma_j \alpha |h_{ij}|/\gamma_i$. (5) implies $(1 - \alpha h_{ii}) + \sum_{j=1, j\neq i}^{n} \gamma_j \alpha |h_{ij}|/\gamma_i < 1$; $\alpha h_{ii} \in (0,1)$ implies $\lambda_{0i} > 0$.

Choose $\lambda_0 = \max_{1 \leq i \leq n}\{\lambda_{0i}\}$, then for $\forall j \in \{1, 2, \cdots, n\}$,

$$\eta_j(\lambda_0) \geq 0. \tag{7}$$

Let $\mathbf{y}_{\max}(0) = \max_{1 \leq i \leq n}\{|y_i(0)|\}$, then for $\forall i \in \{1, 2, \cdots, n\}$, $|y_i(t)| \leq \mathbf{y}_{\max}(0)\lambda_0^t$, where t is natural number. Otherwise, there exist $p \in \{1, 2, \cdots, n\}$ and natural number $q \geq 1$ such that one of the following two cases holds,

(i) $y_p(q) > \mathbf{y}_{\max}(0)\lambda_0^q$, and for all $j \neq p, j \in \{1, 2, \cdots, n\}$,

$$|y_j(s)| \leq \mathbf{y}_{\max}(0)\lambda_0^s, \quad -r \leq s \leq q; \quad |y_p(s)| \leq \mathbf{y}_{\max}(0)\lambda_0^s, \quad -r \leq s < q;$$

or (ii) $y_p(q) < -\mathbf{y}_{\max}(0)\lambda_0^q$, and for all $j \neq p, j \in \{1, 2, \cdots, n\}$,

$$|y_j(s)| \leq \mathbf{y}_{\max}(0)\lambda_0^s, \quad -r \leq s \leq q, \quad |y_p(s)| \leq \mathbf{y}_{\max}(0)\lambda_0^s, \quad -r \leq s < q.$$

Consider case (i), since $1 - \alpha h_{ii} > 0$,

$$\mathbf{y}_{\max}(0)\lambda_0^q < y_p(q) = (1 - \alpha h_{pp})y_p(q-1) - \alpha \sum_{j=1, j\neq p}^{n} \gamma_j h_{ij} y_j(q-1)/\gamma_p$$

$$\leq \mathbf{y}_{\max}(0)[(1 - \alpha h_{pp})\lambda_0^{(q-1)} + \alpha \sum_{j=1, j\neq p}^{n} \gamma_j |h_{ij}|\lambda_0^{(q-1)}/\gamma_p];$$

i.e., $\gamma_p \lambda_0 < \gamma_p(1 - \alpha h_{pp}) + \alpha \sum_{j=1, j\neq p}^{n} \gamma_j |h_{ij}|$, this contradicts (7). Hence, case (i) does not hold.

It is similar to the above proof that case (ii) does not hold. Hence $|y_i(t)| \leq \mathbf{y}_{\max}(0)\lambda_0^t$, $t \geq 1$.

Case II), when $\alpha h_{ii} \in [1, 2), i \in \{1, 2, \cdots, n\}$, since $\mathbf{H}_2$ is a nonsingular M-matrix, there exist $\rho_1, \rho_2, \cdots, \rho_n$ such that

$$\rho_i(2 - \alpha h_{ii}) - \sum_{j=1, j \neq i}^{n} \rho_j \alpha |h_{ij}| > 0. \tag{8}$$

Let $\mathbf{z}(k) = (z_1(k), z_2(k), \cdots, z_n(k))^T$, where $z_i(k) = (x_i(k) - x_i^*)/\rho_i$, then from (2),

$$\Delta z_i(k) = -\alpha \sum_{j=1}^{n} \rho_j h_{ij} z_j(k)/\rho_i. \tag{9}$$

Let $\bar{\eta}_i(\lambda) = \rho_i \lambda - \rho_i(\alpha h_{ii} - 1) - \sum_{j=1, j \neq i}^{n} \rho_j \alpha |h_{ij}|$, then $\bar{\eta}_i(0) = -\rho_i(\alpha h_{ii} - 1) - \sum_{j=1, j \neq i}^{n} \rho_j \alpha |h_{ij}| \leq 0$, $\bar{\eta}_i(1) > 0$. Hence, there exists $\lambda_{0i} \in [0, 1)$ such that $\bar{\eta}_i(\lambda_{0i}) = 0$, and $\bar{\eta}_i(\lambda) > 0$, $\lambda \in (\lambda_{0i}, 1)$.

In fact, we can choose $\lambda_{0i} = (\alpha h_{ii} - 1) + \sum_{j=1, j \neq i}^{n} \rho_j \alpha |h_{ij}|/\rho_i$. (8) implies $(\alpha h_{ii} - 1) + \sum_{j=1, j \neq i}^{n} \rho_j \alpha |h_{ij}|/\rho_i < 1$; $\alpha h_{ii} \in [1, 2)$ implies $\lambda_{0i} \geq 0$.

Choose $\lambda_0 = \max_{1 \leq i \leq n} \{\lambda_{0i}\}$, then for $\forall j \in \{1, 2, \cdots, n\}$, $\bar{\eta}_j(\lambda_0) \geq 0$. Let $\mathbf{z}_{\max}(0) = \max_{1 \leq i \leq n} \{|z_i(0)|\}$. It is similar to the proof of case (I) that $|z_i(t)| \leq \mathbf{z}_{\max}(0)\lambda_0^t, t \geq 1$.

By synthesizing the above proof, $\mathbf{x}(k) \to \mathbf{x}^*, k \to +\infty$; i.e., algorithm (2) is globally convergent.

Let $N_1 \bigcup N_2 = \{1, 2, \cdots, n\}$, $N_1 \bigcap N_2$ is empty.

Theorem 2. If rank($\mathbf{H}$) = rank($\mathbf{H}, \mathbf{d}$), and when $i \in N_1, \alpha h_{ii} \in (0, 1), \alpha h_{ii} - \sum_{j=1, j \neq i}^{n} \alpha |h_{ij}| > 0$; when $l \in N_2, \alpha h_{ll} \in [1, 2), (2 - \alpha h_{ll}) - \sum_{j=1, j \neq l}^{n} \alpha |h_{lj}| > 0$, then algorithm (2) is globally convergent.

Proof. When $i \in N_1$, it is similar to the proof of case I in Theorem 1 that $x_i(k) \to x_i^*, k \to +\infty$. When $l \in N_2$, it is similar to the proof of case II in Theorem 1 that $x_l(k) \to x_l^*, k \to +\infty$. Hence, algorithm (2) is globally convergent.

4 Steepest Descent with Momentum

Let

$$\hat{h}_{ij} = \begin{cases} (1 - \gamma)\alpha h_{ii} - 2\gamma, & i = j, \\ -(1 - \gamma)\alpha |h_{ij}|, & i \neq j, \end{cases} \quad \check{h}_{ij} = \begin{cases} 2 - (1 - \gamma)\alpha h_{ii} - 2\gamma, & i = j, \\ -(1 - \gamma)\alpha |h_{ij}|, & i \neq j. \end{cases}$$

Denote matrices $\mathbf{H}_3 = (\hat{h}_{ij})_{n \times n}, \mathbf{H}_4 = (\check{h}_{ij})_{n \times n}$.

Theorem 3. If rank($\mathbf{H}$) = rank($\mathbf{H}, \mathbf{d}$), and when $(1 - \gamma)\alpha h_{ii} - \gamma \in (0, 1), i \in \{1, 2, \cdots, n\}$, $\mathbf{H}_3$ is a nonsingular M-matrix; when $(1 - \gamma)\alpha h_{ii} - \gamma \in [1, 2), i \in \{1, 2, \cdots, n\}$, $\mathbf{H}_4$ is a nonsingular M-matrix, then algorithm (3) is globally convergent.

Proof. Since rank($\mathbf{H}$) = rank($\mathbf{H}, \mathbf{d}$), there exist $\mathbf{x}^* \in \Re^n$ such that

$$\mathbf{H}\mathbf{x}^* = -\mathbf{d}.$$

Case I), when $(1-\gamma)\alpha h_{ii} - \gamma \in (0,1), i \in \{1, 2, \cdots, n\}$, since $\mathbf{H}_3$ is a nonsingular M-matrix, there exist positive constants $\beta_1, \beta_2, \cdots, \beta_n$ such that

$$\beta_i((1-\gamma)\alpha h_{ii} - 2\gamma) - \sum_{j=1, j\neq i}^{n} \beta_j(1-\gamma)\alpha |h_{ij}| > 0. \tag{10}$$

Let $\mathbf{y}(k) = (y_1(k), y_2(k), \cdots, y_n(k))^T$, where $y_i(k) = (x_i(k) - x_i^*)/\beta_i$, then from (3),

$$\Delta y_i(k) = (\gamma - (1-\gamma)\alpha h_{ii}) y_i(k) - \gamma y_i(k-1) - (1-\gamma)\alpha \sum_{j=1, j\neq i}^{n} \beta_j h_{ij} y_j(k)/\beta_i. \tag{11}$$

Let $\eta_i(\lambda) = \lambda^2 - [1 + (\gamma - (1-\gamma)\alpha h_{ii}) + (1-\gamma)\alpha \sum_{j=1, j\neq i}^{n} \beta_j |h_{ij}|/\beta_i]\lambda - \gamma$, then $\eta_i(0) = -\gamma < 0$, $\eta_i(1) > 0$. Hence, there exists $\lambda_{0i} \in (0, 1)$ such that $\eta_i(\lambda_{0i}) = 0$, and $\eta_i(\lambda) > 0$, $\lambda \in (\lambda_{0i}, 1)$.

Choose $\lambda_0 = \max_{1 \leq i \leq n} \{\lambda_{0i}\}$, then for $\forall j \in \{1, 2, \cdots, n\}$,

$$\eta_j(\lambda_0) \geq 0. \tag{12}$$

Let $\mathbf{y}_{\max}(0) = \max_{1 \leq i \leq n}\{|y_i(0)|, |y_i(-1)|\}$, then $|y_i(t)| \leq \mathbf{y}_{\max}(0)\lambda_0^t, t \geq 1$. Otherwise, there exist $p \in \{1, 2, \cdots, n\}$ and natural number $q \geq 1$ such that one of the following two cases holds,

(i) $y_p(q) > \mathbf{y}_{\max}(0)\lambda_0^q$, and for all $j \neq p, j \in \{1, 2, \cdots, n\}$,

$$|y_j(s)| \leq \mathbf{y}_{\max}(0)\lambda_0^s, \quad -r \leq s \leq q, \quad |y_p(s)| \leq \mathbf{y}_{\max}(0)\lambda_0^s, \quad -r \leq s < q;$$

or (ii) $y_p(q) < -\mathbf{y}_{\max}(0)\lambda_0^q$, and for all $j \neq p, j \in \{1, 2, \cdots, n\}$,

$$|y_j(s)| \leq \mathbf{y}_{\max}(0)\lambda_0^s, \quad -r \leq s \leq q, \quad |y_p(s)| \leq \mathbf{y}_{\max}(0)\lambda_0^s, \quad -r \leq s < q.$$

Consider case (i), since $1 - ((1-\gamma)\alpha h_{ii} - \gamma) > 0$,

$$\mathbf{y}_{\max}(0)\lambda_0^q < y_p(q) = [1 + (\gamma - (1-\gamma)\alpha h_{pp})] y_p(q-1) - \gamma y_p(q-2)$$

$$-(1-\gamma)\alpha \sum_{j=1, j\neq p}^{n} \beta_j h_{pj} y_j(q-1)/\beta_p$$

$$\leq \mathbf{y}_{\max}(0)[(1 + (\gamma - (1-\gamma)\alpha h_{pp}))\lambda_0^{q-1} + \gamma \lambda_0^{q-2}$$

$$+ (1-\gamma)\alpha \sum_{j=1, j\neq p}^{n} \beta_j |h_{pj}| \lambda_0^{q-1}/\beta_p];$$

i.e., $\beta_p \lambda_0^2 < [(1 + (\gamma - (1-\gamma)\alpha h_{pp})) + (1-\gamma)\alpha \sum_{j=1, j\neq p}^{n} \beta_j |h_{pj}|/\beta_p]\lambda_0 + \gamma$, this contradicts (12). So case (i) does not hold.

It is similar to the above proof that case (ii) does not hold. Hence $|y_i(t)| \leq \mathbf{y}_{\max}(0)\lambda_0^t$, $t \geq 1$.

Case II), when $(1-\gamma)\alpha h_{ii} - \gamma \in [1, 2), i \in \{1, 2, \cdots, n\}$, since $\mathbf{H}_4$ is a nonsingular M-matrix, there exist $\rho_1, \rho_2, \cdots, \rho_n$ such that

$$\rho_i(2 - (1-\gamma)\alpha h_{ii} - 2\gamma) - \sum_{j=1, j\neq i}^{n} \rho_j(1-\gamma)\alpha |h_{ij}| > 0.$$

Let $\mathbf{z}(k) = (z_1(k), z_2(k), \cdots, z_n(k))^T$, where $z_i(k) = (x_i(k) - x_i^*)/\rho_i$, then from (3),

$$\Delta z_i(k) = (\gamma - (1-\gamma)\alpha h_{ii})z_i(k) - \gamma z_i(k-1) - (1-\gamma)\alpha \sum_{j=1, j\neq i}^{n} \rho_j h_{ij} z_j(k)/\rho_i.$$

Let $\bar{\eta}_i(\lambda) = \lambda^2 - [(1-\gamma)\alpha h_{ii} - \gamma - 1 + (1-\gamma)\alpha \sum_{j=1, j\neq i}^{n} \rho_j |h_{ij}|/\rho_i]\lambda - \gamma$, then $\bar{\eta}_i(0) = -\gamma < 0$, $\bar{\eta}_i(1) > 0$. Hence, there exists $\lambda_{0i} \in (0,1)$ such that $\bar{\eta}_i(\lambda_{0i}) = 0$, and $\bar{\eta}_i(\lambda) > 0$, $\lambda \in (\lambda_{0i}, 1)$.

Choose $\lambda_0 = \max_{1\leq i \leq n}\{\lambda_{0i}\}$, then for $\forall j \in \{1, 2, \cdots, n\}$, $\bar{\eta}_j(\lambda_0) \geq 0$.

Let $\mathbf{z}_{\max}(0) = \max_{1\leq i \leq n}\{|z_i(0)|, |z_i(-1)|\}$. It is similar to the proof of case (I) that $|z_i(t)| \leq \mathbf{z}_{\max}(0)\lambda_0^t, t \geq 1$.

By synthesizing the above proof, $\mathbf{x}(k) \to \mathbf{x}^*, k \to +\infty$; i.e., algorithm (3) is globally convergent.

5 Conclusion

In this paper, we analyze the effect of momentum on steepest descent training for quadratic performance functions, present some theoretical results on global convergence conditions of the steepest descent algorithm with momentum (and without momentum) by directly analyzing the exact momentum equations for quadratic cost functions. Those conditions can be directly derived from the parameters (different from eigenvalues that are used in the existed ones) of the Hessian matrix. The results presented in this paper are new.

References

1. Phansalkar, V. V., and Sastry, P. S.: Analysis of the Back-propagation Algorithm with Momentum. IEEE Trans. Neural Networks, **5** (1994) 505-506
2. Rumelhart, D. E., Hinton, G. E., and Williams, R. J.: Learning Representations by Back-propagating Errors. Nature, **323** (1986) 533-536
3. Hagan, M. T., Demuth, H. B., and Beale, M. H.: Neural Network Design. Boston, MA: PWS, (1996)
4. Torii, M., and Hagan, M. T.: Stability of Steepest Descent with Momentum for Quadratic Functions. IEEE Trans. Neural Networks, **13** (2002) 752-756
5. Hagiwara, M., and Sato, A.: Analysis of Momentum Term in Back-propagation. IEICE Trans. Inform. Syst., **8** (1995) 1-6
6. Sato, A.: Analytical Study of the Momentum Term in A Backpropagation Algorithm. Proc. ICANN91, (1991) 617-622
7. Qian, N.: On the Momentum Term in Gradient Descent Learning Algorithms. Neural Networks, **12** (1999) 145-151

Boosting Orthogonal Least Squares Regression

Xunxian Wang and David J. Brown

Computer Intelligence & Applications Research Group
Department of Creative Technologies
Buckingham Building, Lion Terrace
Portsmouth, PO1 3HE, UK
{xunxian.wang,david.j.brown)@port.ac.uk

Abstract. A comparison between the support vector machine regression (SVR) and the orthogonal least square (OLS) forward selection regression is given by an example. The disadvantage of SVR is shown and analyzed. A new algorithm by using OLS method to select regressors (support vectors) and boosting method to train the regressors' weight is proposed. This algorithm can give a small regression error when a very sparse system model is required. When a detailed model is required, the resulted train set error model and the test set error model may look very similar.

1 Introduction

Based on the empirical risk minimization principle (ERM), orthogonal least squares regression [1,2] has been successfully used for many years. In the recent years, SVR method [3,4], which is based on the structural risk minimization principle (SRM) has been proved to have some good advantages in machine learning tasks. One of the major requirements of a learning machine is its generalization ability, especially in the situation when the training set is not big enough. In this paper, a comparison of the SVR and the OLS forward selection (OLSFS) regression is given by an example with a small train set and a big test set. The disadvantage of SVR is shown and analyzed. A new algorithm using OLS method to select regressors (support vectors) and a boosting method [5,6] to train the regressor weights is proposed, which can give a good result when very sparse system model is required, and a good similarity result between the error models of train set and test set with a detailed system model.

2 Basic Algorithms of SVR and OLS

2.1 Support Vector Machine Regression

Given N pairs of training data $\{(x_k, y_k)\}_{k=1}^{l}$ where x is the m-dimensional input variable, the SVR problem can be stated as below [3,4]:

Maximize

$$W(\alpha,\alpha^*) = -\frac{1}{2}\sum_{i,j=1}^{l}(\alpha_i^* - \alpha_i)(\alpha_j^* - \alpha_j)K(x_i,x_j) - \varepsilon\sum_{i=1}^{l}(\alpha_i^* + \alpha_i) + \sum_{i=1}^{l}(\alpha_i^* - \alpha_i)y_i$$

$$\sum_{i=1}^{l}(\alpha_i^* - \alpha_i) = 0$$

Subject to $0 \leq \alpha_i^* \leq C, \quad i=1,\cdots,l$ (1)
$0 \leq \alpha_i \leq C, \quad i=1,\cdots,l$

Solving the above optimisation problem, the learning machine can be represented as

$$f(x) = \sum_{i=1}^{l}(\alpha_i^* - \alpha_i)K(x,x_i) + b \quad (2)$$

In this paper, Gaussian kernel is used in following format.

$$K(x,x_i) = G(x,x_i) = \exp(-\frac{(x-x_i)^2}{2\sigma^2})$$

2.2 Orthogonal Least Squares Forward Selection

In OLS method [1,2], we have

$$J_k(\theta,\lambda) = Y^TY - \sum_{i=1}^{k-1}\frac{(Y^Tp_i)^2}{\lambda + p_i^Tp_i} - \frac{(Y^Tp_k)^2}{(\lambda + p_k^Tp_k)} \quad (3)$$

The next appended regressor should be the one with the biggest value of the third item of equation (3). And

$$\theta = y^TP(\lambda I + P^TP)^{-1} \quad (4)$$

where Y denotes the output vector of the training set. $p_i, i=1,\cdots,k$ denote the orthogonalized regressors and P denotes the regressor matrix. λ denotes the regularization parameter and θ is the weight vector.

3 Experimental Comparison of OLS and SVMR

It is known that the least squares regression algorithm can be obtained when the white Gaussian system noise. To make the comparison fair, a uniform distribution noise is added in the following example. Furthermore, to evaluate the generalization ability efficiently, a small training set and a big test set are used generated by a 2-D sinc function with uniform noise as below

$$f(x,y) = \frac{5\sin\sqrt{(x-9.99)^2 + (y-9.99)^2}}{\sqrt{(x-9.99)^2 + (y-9.99)^2}} + e \quad (5)$$

where e has uniform (not normal) distribution in the interval [-025,0.25]. The input of the training set has size of 10×10 and is given by $\{x_i\}_{i=1}^{10} \times \{y_i\}_{i=1}^{10} = \{2i\}_{i=1}^{10} \times \{2i\}_{i=1}^{10}$; the test set is given by $\{x_i\}_{i=1}^{50} \times \{y_i\}_{i=1}^{50} = \{0.4i\}_{i=1}^{50} \times \{0.4i\}_{i=1}^{50}$ with the train set involved. In Fig.1 the train set, the noise test set (test set1, generated by equation (5)) and the pure test set (test set2, generated by equation (5) when $e=0$) are displayed. In kernel function, $\sigma^2 = 2$ is used in both of the methods. When set $C = 2, \varepsilon = 2$ in SVR, a 9-support vectors system model is generated shown in Fig. 2. In OLS with $\lambda = 0.03$, when 6 regressors (support vectors) are used, the results are in Fig 3. In both figures, the top left picture is the obtained train set model with the size of 10×10, the top right picture is the obtained test model of 50×50 size. The training error picture is depicted in the bottom left and in the bottom middle is the test error. To show the ability of noise depressing, the error between the pure 2-D sinc function and the test model is depicted in the bottom right of the relative figures. The statistical values of the three different error are written in the figure also, the first two columns are the error mean and error variance of the train set, the middle two columns are for the noisy test set (test set 1) and the lowest two columns are for the pure test set (test set 2). It is obvious that OLS can give a better regression result.

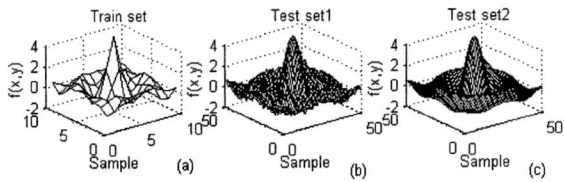

Fig. 1. The pictures of the system model: (a) train set, (b) noisy test set and (c) pure test set.

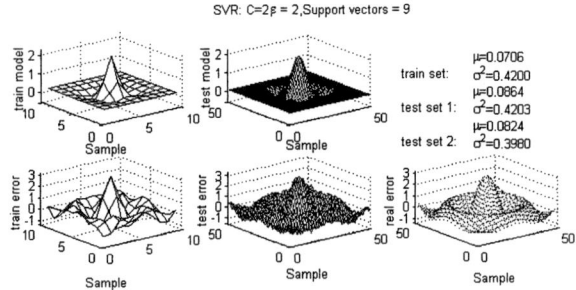

Fig. 2. SVR model with 9 support vectors. top-left: training model, top-right: test model, bottom left: training error, bottom middle: noisy test error, bottom right: pure test error.

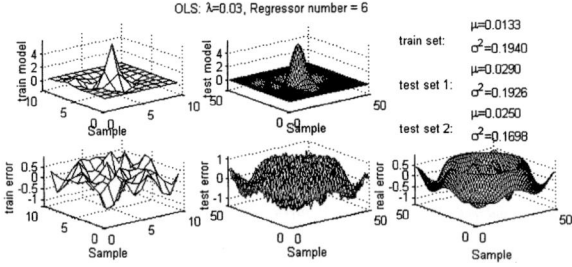

Fig. 3. OLS model with 6 regressors. top-left: training model, top-right: test model, bottom left: training error, bottom middle: noisy test error, bottom right: pure test error.

When set $C = 2, \varepsilon = 2 = 0.01$ in SVR, 97 support vectors are needed in the system modeling. When 39 regressors are used in the OLS. The similar results can be obtained in Fig.4(a), Fig.4(b).

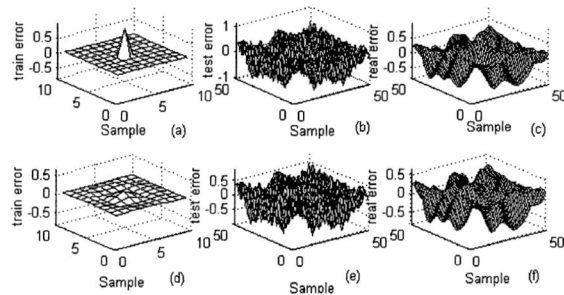

Fig. 4. The experiment results when 97 support vectors are used. The top row is with the SVR, the bottom is with OLS. (a), (d): train error. (b),(e): noisy test error. (c),(f): pure test error.

4 The Boosting Orthogonal Least Squares Vector Machine

It can be seen from the above results that the selection of the support vectors is not satisfied in the SVR when a very sparse system model is required. Actually, in SVR, a small change of each train data can result in different support vectors. In OLS, the criterion of selecting the regressors can guarantee that "good" regressors can be used first and this selection is based on all the data in the train set. In another side, a boosting algorithm – AdaBoost can force the regression surface going through the "middle" of all the train data, but the established system model is not sparse. If combining OLS with AdaBoost together, that is, use OLSFS to select support vectors and AdaBoost to force the regression line goes through the middle of the data, a sparse learning machine, which is similar to maximum margin regression concept can be established. it is named "boosting orthogonal least squares learning machine" (BOLS).

4.1 Basic Algorithm

AdaBoost algorithm [5]
Input: l training pairs $\{x_i, y_i\}_{i=1}^{l}$, distribution $d = [d(1) \cdots d(l)]^T$ over the training pairs, weak-learning algorithm WeakLearn, and integer T specifying number of iterations.
Initialize: The weighting vector $\delta^{(1)} = [\delta_1^{(1)} \cdots \delta_l^{(1)}]^T$ with $\delta_i^{(1)} = d(i)$ for $i = 1, \cdots, l$
Do for t=1,2,...T

$$\text{Set the distribution vector } p^{(t)} = [p_1^{(t)} \cdots p_l^{(t)}] \text{ to } p^{(t)} = \frac{\delta^{(t)}}{\sum_{i=1}^{l} \delta_i^{(t)}}$$

Call Weaklearn, provide it with the distribution $p^{(t)}$, and get back a hypothesis $h_t : X \rightarrow [0,1]$

Calculate the error of h_t:

$$\varepsilon_t = \sum_{i=1}^{l} p_i^{(t)} |h_t(x_i) - y_i|$$

Set $\beta_t = \dfrac{\varepsilon_t}{1-\varepsilon_t}$ and the new weight vector to

$$\delta_i^{(t+1)} = \delta_i^{(t)} \beta_t^{1-|h_t(x_i)-y_i|}, \ 1 \leq i \leq l$$

EndDo
Output the Hypothesis
Combining OLSFS with AdaBoost, the following algorithm is proposed.

BOLS vector machine algorithm

Initialise: Give l training pairs $\{x_i, y_i\}_{i=1}^{l}$ and set the initial distribution as $\delta = [\delta_1^0 \cdots \delta_l^0]^T = [1/l \cdots 1/l]^T$. Select k regressors denoted by $\{h_i\}_{i=1}^{k}$ by using OLSFS rule of equation (3), construct orthogonal matrix P. Set a small positive value ζ.

Do

Set $y^\delta = [\delta_1^t y_1, \cdots, \delta_l^t y_l]^T$

Calculate the weights of these k regressors by equation (4), that is

$\theta = y^{\delta T} P / (\lambda + 1)$

Construct system model by using equation (12) as $\hat{y}(x) = P\theta$

Calculate error by

$$\varepsilon_t = \sum_{i=1}^{l} \delta_i^{(t)} |\hat{y}(x_i) - y_i^\delta|$$

Set $\beta_t = \dfrac{\varepsilon_t}{1-\varepsilon_t}$ and the new weight vector to

$$\delta_i^{(t+1)} = \delta_i^{(t)} \beta_t^{1-|\hat{y}(x_i)-y_i^\delta|}, \ 1 \leq i \leq l$$

If $\max |\delta_i^{(t)} - \delta_i^{(t+1)}| \ i = 1, \cdots, l| < \zeta$, break the loop. Otherwise repeat the loop.

EndDo
Output: k final regressor weights

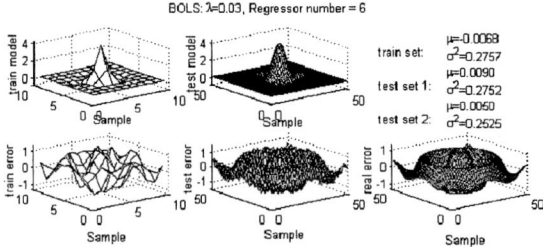

Fig. 5. OLSB model with 6 regressors. top-left: training model, top-right: test model, bottom left: training error, bottom middle: noisy test error, bottom right: pure test error.

4.2 Experiment Result

When 6 regressors are selected by OLS, the obtained results by using BOLS are shown in Fig. 5. Fig.6 shows the result when 97 regressors are used. It is very interesting that if we compare the similarity between the errors of train set and test set in Fig.6, they are very similar. From the shape of the error model established by train set, the error of the test model can be guessed with good accuracy. From this point of view, this new proposed method has better generalization ability.

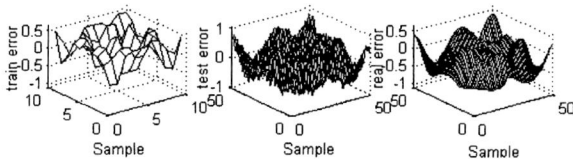

Fig. 6. OLSB model with 97 regressors. bottom left: training error, bottom middle: noisy test error, bottom right: pure test error.

5 Conclusions

A regression algorithm is proposed based on the support vector machine and orthogonal least squares forward selection method. When very sparse system model is required, this machine can give a better model than SVR. When a detailed system model is established, it can give a system model with good generalization ability.

References

1. Chen S., Wu Y. and Luk B.L., "Combined genetic algorithm optimization and regularized orthogonal least squares learning for radial basis function networks," *IEEE Trans. Neural Networks*, Vol.10, No.5, pp.1239–1243, 1999.
2. Chen S., Hong X. and Harris C.J., "Sparse kernel regression modeling using combined locally regularized orthogonal least squares and D-optimality experimental design," *IEEETrans. Automatic Control*, Vol.48, No.6, pp.1029–1036, 2003.
3. Vapnik, V. N, The nature of statistical learning theory; Springer, (2000).
4. Vapnik, V. N., Golowich S. and Smola A., Support vector method for function approximation, regression estimation, and signal processing. In M. C. Mozer, M. I. Jordan, and T. Petsche, editors, *Advances in Neural Information Processing Systems 9*, pages 281-287, Cambridge, MA, 1997. MIT Press.
5. Freund Y. and Schapire R.E., "A decision-theoretic generalization of on-line learning and an application to boosting," *J. Computer and System Sciences*, Vol.55, No.1, pp.119–139, 1997.
6. Meir R. and Ratsch G., "An introduction to boosting and leveraging," in: S. Mendelson and A. Smola, eds., *Advanced Lectures in Machine Learning*. Springer Verlag, 2003, pp.119–184.

Local Separation Property of the Two-Source ICA Problem with the One-Bit-Matching Condition[*]

Jinwen Ma[1,2], Zhiyong Liu[2], and Lei Xu[2]

[1] Department of Information Science, School of Mathematical Sciences and LMAM
Peking University, Beijing, 100871, China
jwma@math.pku.edu.cn
[2] Department of Computer Science & Engineering
The Chinese University of Hong Kong, Shatin, N. T., Hong Kong

Abstract. The one-bit-matching conjecture for independent component analysis (ICA) is basically stated as "all the sources can be separated as long as there is one-to-one same-sign-correspondence between the kurtosis signs of all source probability density functions (pdf's) and the kurtosis signs of all model pdf's", which has been widely believed in the ICA community, but not proved completely. Recently, it has been proved that under the assumption of zero skewness for the model pdf's, the global maximum of a cost function on the ICA problem with the one-bit-matching condition corresponds to a feasible solution of the ICA problem. In this paper, we further study the one-bit-matching conjecture along this direction and prove that all the possible local maximums of this cost function correspond to the feasible solutions of the ICA problem in the case of two sources under the same assumption. That is, the one-bit-matching condition is sufficient for solving the two-source ICA problem via any local ascent algorithm of the cost function.

1 Introduction

The independent component analysis (ICA) [1]-[2] tries to blindly separate the independent sources **s** from their linear mixture $\mathbf{x} = \mathbf{A}\mathbf{s}$ via

$$\mathbf{y} = \mathbf{W}\mathbf{x}, \quad \mathbf{x} \in \mathbb{R}^m, \quad \mathbf{y} \in \mathbb{R}^n, \quad \mathbf{W} \in \mathbb{R}^{m \times n}, \tag{1}$$

where **A** is a mixing matrix, and **W** is the unknown matrix to be estimated. Although the ICA problem has been studied from different perspectives [3]-[6], it can be typically solved by minimizing the following objective function:

$$D = -H(\mathbf{y}) - \sum_{i=1}^{n} \int p_{\mathbf{W}}(y_i; \mathbf{W}) \log p_i(y_i) dy_i, \tag{2}$$

---

[*] This work was supported by the Natural Science Foundation of China for Project 60071004 and also by the Hong Kong RGC Earmarked Grant CUHK 4184/03E.

where $H(\mathbf{y}) = -\int p(\mathbf{y})\log p(\mathbf{y})d\mathbf{y}$ is the entropy of $\mathbf{y}$, $p_i(y_i)$ is the pre-determined model probability density function (pdf), and $p_\mathbf{W}(y_i; \mathbf{W})$ is the probability distribution on $\mathbf{y} = \mathbf{Wx}$.

In literature, how to choose the model pdf's $p_i(y_i)$ remains a key issue for the Eq.(2) based ICA algorithms [7]-[8]. Actually, there has not existed any efficient method for the cases that sources of both super-gaussian and sub-gaussian coexist in a unknown manner. In order to solve this difficult problem, Xu, Cheung and Amari [8] summarized the one-bit-matching conjecture which states that "all the sources can be separated as long as there is a one-to-one same-sign-correspondence between the kurtosis signs of all source pdf's and the kurtosis signs of all model pdf's". This conjecture is far from trivial since, if it is true, the complicated task of learning the underlining distribution of each sources can be greatly simplified to the task of learning only its kurtosis sign. Although there have been many studies supporting the one-bit-matching conjecture, e.g., [9]-[12], there were little theoretical analysis [13] on the conjecture since its inception. Recently, Liu, Chiu & Xu [14] proved that under the assumption of zero skewness for the model pdf's, the one-bit-matching condition guarantees a successful separation solution of the ICA problem by globally maximizing a cost function derived from Eq.(2). However, since in practice the various ICA algorithms(e.g., [11]-[12]), which typically belong to gradient algorithm, cannot guarantee the global maximization, it is interesting to investigate the local maximums of the cost function.

In this paper, considering only the two-source case, we further prove that any local maximum of the cost function achieved in [14] correspond to a successful separation solution for the ICA. In Section 2 we introduce the cost function obtained in [14], and in Section 3 we present the main results, followed by a brief conclusion in Section 4.

2 The Cost Function

Under the zero skewness assumption for the model pdf's, the cost function derived from Eq.(2) is simply as follows [14]:

$$J(\mathbf{R}) = \sum_{i=1}^{n} \sum_{j=1}^{n} r_{ij}^4 \nu_j^s k_i^m, \tag{3}$$

where the orthonormal matrix $\mathbf{R} = (r_{ij})_{n \times n} = \mathbf{WA}$ is to be estimated instead of $\mathbf{W}$ since $\mathbf{A}$ is a constant matrix[1], ν_j^s is the kurtosis of the source s_j, and k_i^m is a constant with the same sign as the kurtosis ν_i^m of the model density $p_i(y_i)$ given by

$$k_i^m = \int g(y_i) \frac{H_4(y_i)}{24} \log(1 + \frac{\nu_i^m}{24} H_4(y_i))dy_i, \tag{4}$$

---

[1] Note that here we additionally assume that $\mathbf{A}$ is square and invertible.

where $g(y_i) = \frac{1}{\sqrt{2\pi}} \exp(-\frac{y_i^2}{2})$, and

$$H_4(y_i) = y_i^4 - 6y_i^2 + 3.$$

Under the one-bit-matching condition, with the help of certain permutation we can always get $k_1^m \geq \cdots \geq k_p^m > 0 > k_{p+1}^m \geq \cdots \geq k_n^m$ and $\nu_1^s \geq \cdots \geq \nu_p^s > 0 > \nu_{p+1}^s \geq \cdots \geq \nu_n^s$, which will be considered as the one-bit-matching condition in our study.

It has been proved in [14] that the global maximization of Eq.(3) can only be reachable by setting $\mathbf{R}$ an identity matrix up to certain permutation and sign indeterminacy. That is, the global maximization of Eq.(3) will recover the original sources up to sign and permutation indeterminacies. In the two-source case, below we further prove that the local maximums of $J(\mathbf{R})$ are also only reachable by the permutation matrices up to sign indeterminacy under the one-bit-matching condition.

3 The Main Theorem

We investigate the local maximums of the cost function $J(\mathbf{R})$ in the case of two sources, i.e., $n = 2$. For clarity, we define a $\mathbf{K}$ matrix by

$$\mathbf{K} = (k_{ij})_{n \times n}, \quad k_{ij} = \nu_j^s k_i^m.$$

Then, we have

$$J(\mathbf{R}) = \sum_{i=1}^n \sum_{j=1}^n r_{ij}^4 \nu_j^s k_i^m = \sum_{i=1}^n \sum_{j=1}^n r_{ij}^4 k_{ij}.$$

With the one-bit-matching condition, $\mathbf{K}$ as $n = 2$ can be considered in the two cases: (i) All $k_{ij} > 0$, in the situation that the two sources are both sub-gaussians or super-gaussians; (ii) $k_{11}, k_{22} > 0$, while $k_{12}, k_{21} < 0$, in the situation that there are one sub-gaussian source and one super-gaussian source with $\nu_1^s > 0 > \nu_2^s$ and $k_1^m > 0 > k_2^m$.

With above preparation, we have the main theorem concerning the local maximums of $J(\mathbf{R})$ in the two-source case under the one-bit-matching condition.

Theorem 1. *For the case of two sources under the one-bit-matching condition, the local maximums of $J(\mathbf{R})$ are only the permutation matrices up to sign indeterminacy.*

Proof: Since $\mathbf{R}$ is just a second-order orthonormal matrix in this case, according to the theory of topology, there are two disjoint fields of $\mathbf{R}$ that can be expressed by

$$\mathbf{R}_1 = \begin{pmatrix} \cos\theta & -\sin\theta \\ \sin\theta & \cos\theta \end{pmatrix},$$

and

$$\mathbf{R}_2 = \begin{pmatrix} \cos\theta & \sin\theta \\ \sin\theta & -\cos\theta \end{pmatrix},$$

respectively, with one variable $\theta \in [0, 2\pi)$. Actually, each $\mathbf{R}_1$ denotes a rotation transformation in $\mathbb{R}^2$ (i.e., the 2-dimensional real Euclidean space), while each $\mathbf{R}_2$ denotes a reflection transformation in $\mathbb{R}^2$.

Because $J(\mathbf{R}_1) = J(\mathbf{R}_2)$ and they have the same expression on $sin\theta$ and $cos\theta$, we need only to consider the form of $\mathbf{R}_1$ on solving the local maximums of the cost function. By derivation of $J(\mathbf{R}_1)$ with respect to θ, we have

$$\frac{dJ(\mathbf{R}_1)}{d\theta} = 4cos\theta sin\theta[-(k_{11} + k_{22})cos^2\theta + (k_{12} + k_{21})sin^2\theta], \tag{5}$$

$$\frac{d^2 J(\mathbf{R}_1)}{d^2\theta} = 4(k_{11} + k_{22})(3sin^2\theta cos^2\theta - cos^4\theta) + 4(k_{12} + k_{21})$$
$$\times (3sin^2\theta cos^2\theta - sin^4\theta). \tag{6}$$

Then, the extremum equation $\frac{dJ(\mathbf{R}_1)}{d\theta} = 0$ can be solved from the following two equalities, respectively.

$$sin\theta cos\theta = 0, \tag{7}$$

$$tan^2\theta = \frac{k_{11} + k_{22}}{k_{12} + k_{21}}. \tag{8}$$

We now solve the local maximums of $J(\mathbf{R}_1)$ from the two cases of $\mathbf{K}$ under the one-bit-matching condition, respectively.

(i). All $k_{ij} > 0$. That is, the two sources are both super-gaussian sources or sub-gaussian sources. According to Eq.(7), we only have the solutions $\theta = 0, \frac{\pi}{2}, \pi, \frac{3\pi}{2}$ that lead $\mathbf{R}_1$ to a permutation matrix up to sign indeterminacy. It can be easily found from Eq.(6) that the second order derivative of $J(\mathbf{R}_1)$ with respect to θ are all negative at these solutions. Thus, these solutions are all the local maximums of $J(\mathbf{R}_1)$.

As to Eq.(8), there are only two solutions for it. Suppose that $\hat{\theta}$ is such a solution. That is,

$$tan^2\hat{\theta} = \frac{k_{11} + k_{22}}{k_{12} + k_{21}}.$$

We then have

$$cos^2\hat{\theta} = \frac{k_{12} + k_{21}}{k_{11} + k_{22} + k_{12} + k_{21}}, \quad sin^2\hat{\theta} = \frac{k_{11} + k_{22}}{k_{11} + k_{22} + k_{12} + k_{21}}.$$

Substituting these expressions into Eq.(12), we have

$$\frac{d^2 J(\mathbf{R}_1)}{d^2\theta}\bigg|_{\theta=\hat{\theta}} = 4V^{-2}[3(k_{11} + k_{22})(k_{12} + k_{21})V - (k_{11} + k_{22})(k_{12} + k_{21})^2$$
$$-(k_{11} + k_{22})^2(k_{12} + k_{21})]$$
$$= \frac{8}{V}(k_{11} + k_{22})(k_{12} + k_{21})$$
$$> 0,$$

where $V = k_{11} + k_{22} + k_{12} + k_{21} > 0$. Thus, $\hat{\theta}$ is a local minimum of $J(\mathbf{R}_1)$. That is, the two solutions of Eq.(8) are local minimums of $J(\mathbf{R}_1)$.

Therefore, the local maximums of $J(\mathbf{R}_1)$ are only the permutation matrices up to sign indeterminacy in this case.

(ii). $k_{11}, k_{22} > 0$, while $k_{12}, k_{21} < 0$. That is, there are one super-gaussian source and one sub-gaussian source. In this case, the equality Eq.(8) cannot hold. Then, the solutions of $\frac{dJ(\mathbf{R}_1)}{d\theta} = 0$ are only those of Eq.(7), i.e., $\theta = 0, \frac{\pi}{2}, \pi$ and $\frac{3\pi}{2}$. It can be easily found from Eq.(6) that $\frac{d^2 J(\mathbf{R}_1)}{d^2\theta}$ are negative at $0, \pi$, but positive at $\frac{\pi}{2}, \frac{3\pi}{2}$, respectively. Therefore, 0 and π are local maximums of $J(\mathbf{R}_1)$, while $\frac{\pi}{2}$ and $\frac{3\pi}{2}$ are local minimums of $J(\mathbf{R}_1)$. Since these solutions are corresponding to the permutation matrices, the local maximums of $J(\mathbf{R}_1)$ are only the permutation matrices up to sign indeterminacy in this case, too.

Summing up the results in the two cases, we finally get that the local maximums of $J(\mathbf{R}_1)$ are only the permutation matrices up to sign indeterminacy. Because $J(\mathbf{R}_2)$ and $J(\mathbf{R}_1)$ have the same expression, we can have the same result for $J(\mathbf{R}_2)$. Therefore, in the case of two sources under the one-bit-matching condition, the local maximums of $J(\mathbf{R})$ are only the permutation matrices up to sign indeterminacy. The proof is completed. □

According to this theorem, when the skewness of each model probability density function is set to be zero, the two-source ICA problem can be successfully solved via any local descent algorithm of the typical objective function as long as the one-bit-matching condition is satisfied, i.e., the numbers of supper-gaussian and sub-gaussian model pdf's are equal to those of supper-gaussian and sub-gaussian sources, respectively.

4 Conclusion

Theoretically, we have proved the one-bit-matching conjecture in the case of two sources under the assumption of zero skewness for the model pdf's. That is, under the zero skewness assumption for the model pdf's, the two sources can be separated via any gradient algorithm if the one-bit-matching condition is satisfied when we select the model pdf's. This result has a strong significance on solving the ICA problem. Moreover, it also provides a good evidence for the one-bit-matching conjecture in the general case.

References

1. L. Tong, Y. Inouye, & R. Liu, "Waveform-preserving blind estimation of multiple independent sources," *IEEE Trans. on Signal Processing*, 41(7): 2461-2470, 1993.
2. P. Comon, "Independent component analysis–a new concept?," *Signal Processing*, 36: 287-314, 1994.
3. A. Bell & T. Sejnowski, "An information-maximization approach to blind separation and blind deconvolution," *Neural Computation*, 7: 1129-1159, 1995.
4. S. I. Amari, A. Cichocki, & H. Yang, "A new learning algorithm for blind separation of sources," *Advances in Neural Information Processing*, 8: 757-763, 1996.
5. E. Oja, "ICA learning rules: stationarity, stability, and sigmoids," in: C. Fyfe(Ed.), *Proc. of Int. ICSC Workshop on Independence and Artificial Neural Networks (I&ANN'98)*, 9-10 Febraury, Tenerife, Spain, ICSC Acadenic Press, New York, 1998, pp.97-103.

6. J. F. Cardoso, "Infomax and maximum likelihood for source separation," *IEEE Signal Processing Letters*, *4*: 112-114, 1999.
7. L. Xu, C. C. Cheung,& S. I. Amari, "Learned parametric mixture based ica algorithm," *Neurocomputing*, *22*: 69-80, 1998.
8. L. Xu, C. C. Cheung, & S. I. Amari, "Further results on nonlinearity and separation capability of a linear mixture ICA method and learned LPM," *Proceedings of the I&ANN'98, Editor: C. Fyfe*, 1998, pp: 39-45.
9. M. Girolami, "An alternative perspective on adaptive independent component analysis algorithms," *Neural Computation*, *10*: 2103-2114, 1998.
10. R. Everson & S. Roberts, "Independent component analysis: A flexible nonlinearity and decorrelating manifold approach," *Neural Computation*, *11*: 1957-1983, 1999.
11. T. W. Lee, M. Girolami, & T. J. Sejnowski, "Independent component analysis using an extended infomax algorithm for mixed subgaussian and supergaussian sources, *Neural Computation*, *11*: 417-441, 1999.
12. M. Welling & M. Weber, "A constrained EM algorithm for independent component analysis," *Neural Computation*, *13*: 677-689, 2001.
13. C. C. Cheung & L. Xu, "Some global and local convergence analysis on the information-theoretic independent component analysis approach," *Neurocomputing*, *30*: 79-102, 2000.
14. Z. Y. Liu, K. C. Chiu and L. Xu, "One-bit-matching conjecture for independent component analysis," *Neural Computation*, 16: 383-399, 2004.

Two Further Gradient BYY Learning Rules for Gaussian Mixture with Automated Model Selection[*]

Jinwen Ma, Bin Gao, Yang Wang, and Qiansheng Cheng

Department of Information Science, School of Mathematical
Sciences and LMAM, Peking University, Beijing, 100871, China
jwma@math.pku.edu.cn

Abstract. Under the Bayesian Ying-Yang (BYY) harmony learning theory, a harmony function has been developed for Gaussian mixture model with an important feature that, via its maximization through a gradient learning rule, model selection can be made automatically during parameter learning on a set of sample data from a Gaussian mixture. This paper proposes two further gradient learning rules, called conjugate and natural gradient learning rules, respectively, to efficiently implement the maximization of the harmony function on Gaussian mixture. It is demonstrated by simulation experiments that these two new gradient learning rules not only work well, but also converge more quickly than the general gradient ones.

1 Introduction

As a powerful statistical model, Gaussian mixture has been widely applied to data analysis and there have been several statistical methods for its modelling(e.g., the expectation-maximization(EM) algorithm [1] and k-means algorithm [2]). But it is usually assumed that the number of Gaussians in the mixture is pre-known. However, in many instances this key information is not available and the selection of an appropriate number of Gaussians must be made with the estimation of the parameters, which is rather difficult [3].

The traditional approach is to choose a best number k^* of Gaussians via some selection criterion. Actually, many heuristic criteria have been proposed in the statistical literature(e.g.,[4]-[5]). However, the process of evaluating a criterion incurs a large computational cost since we need to repeat the entire parameter estimating process at a number of different values of k.

Recently, a new approach has been developed from the Bayesian Ying-Yang (BYY) harmony learning theory [6] with the feature that model selection can be made automatically during the parameter learning. In fact, it was shown in [7] that this Gaussian mixture modelling problem is equivalent to the maximization of a harmony function on a specific architecture of the BYY system related

---

[*] This work was supported by the Natural Science Foundation of China for Project 60071004.

to Gaussian mixture model and a gradient learning rule for maximization of this harmony function was also established. The simulation experiments showed that an appropriate number of Gaussians can be automatically allocated for the sample data set, with the mixing proportions of the extra Gaussians attenuating to zero. Moreover, an adaptive gradient learning rule was further proposed and analyzed for the general finite mixture model, and demonstrated well on a sample data set from Gaussian mixture [8].

In this paper, we propose two further gradient learning rules to efficiently implement the maximization of the harmony function in a Gaussian mixture setting. The first learning rule is constructed from the conjugate gradient of the harmony function, while the second learning rule is derived from Amari and Nagaoka's natural gradient theory [9]. Moreover, it has been demonstrated by simulation experiments that the two new gradient learning rules not only make model selection automatically during the parameter learning, but also converge more quickly than the general gradient ones.

In the sequel, the conjugate and natural gradient learning rules are derived in Section 2. In Section 3, they are both demonstrated by simulation experiments, and finally a brief conclusion is made in Section 4.

2 Conjugate and Natural Gradient Learning Rules

In this section, we first introduce the harmony function on the Gaussian mixture model and then derive the conjugate and natural gradient learning rules from it.

2.1 The Harmony Function

Under the BYY harmony learning principle, we can get the following harmony function on a sample data set $D_x = \{x_t\}_{t=1}^N$ from a Gaussian mixture model (Refer to [6] or [7] for the derivation):

$$J(\Theta_k) = \frac{1}{N}\sum_{t=1}^{N}\sum_{j=1}^{k}\frac{\alpha_j q(x_t|m_j, \Sigma_j)}{\sum_{i=1}^{k}\alpha_i q(x_t|m_i, \Sigma_i)} ln[\alpha_j q(x_t|m_j, \Sigma_j)], \tag{1}$$

where $q(x|m_j, \Sigma_j)$ is a Gaussian density given by

$$q(x|m_j, \Sigma_j) = \frac{1}{(2\pi)^{\frac{n}{2}}|\Sigma_j|^{\frac{1}{2}}} e^{-\frac{1}{2}(x-m_j)^T \Sigma_j^{-1}(x-m_j)}, \tag{2}$$

where m_j is the mean vector and Σ_j is the covariance matrix which is assumed positive definite. α_j is the mixing proportion, $\Theta_k = \{\alpha_j, m_j, \Sigma_j\}_{j=1}^k$ and $q(x, \Theta_k) = \sum_{j=1}^{k} \alpha_j q(x|m_j, \Sigma_j)$ is just the Gaussian mixture density.

According to the best harmony learning principle of the BYY system [6] as well as the experimental results obtained in [7]-[8], the maximization of $J(\Theta_k)$ can realize the parameter learning with automated model selection on a sample data set from a Gaussian mixture. For convenience of analysis, we let $\alpha_j = e^{\beta_j}/\sum_{i=1}^k e^{\beta_i}$ and $\Sigma_j = B_j B_j^T$ for $j = 1, 2, \cdots, k$, where $-\infty < \beta_1, \cdots, \beta_k < +\infty$, and B_j is a nonsingular square matrix. By these transformations, the parameters in $J(\Theta_k)$ turn into $\{\beta_j, m_j, B_j\}_{j=1}^k$.

2.2 Conjugate Gradient Learning Rule

We begin to give the derivatives of $J(\Theta_k)$ with respect to β_j, m_j and B_j as follows. (Refer to [7] for the derivation.)

$$\frac{\partial J(\Theta_k)}{\partial \beta_j} = \frac{\alpha_j}{N} \sum_{i=1}^{k} \sum_{t=1}^{N} h(i|x_t) U(i|x_t)(\delta_{ij} - \alpha_i), \qquad (3)$$

$$\frac{\partial J(\Theta_k)}{\partial m_j} = \frac{\alpha_j}{N} \sum_{t=1}^{N} h(j|x_t) U(j|x_t) \Sigma_j^{-1} (x_t - m_j), \qquad (4)$$

$$\frac{\partial J(\Theta_k)}{\partial B_j} = \frac{\partial (B_j B_j^T)}{\partial B_j} \frac{\partial J(\Theta_k)}{\partial \Sigma_j}, \qquad (5)$$

where δ_{ij} is the Kronecker function, and

$$U(i|x_t) = \sum_{r=1}^{k} (\delta_{ri} - p(r|x_t)) \ln[\alpha_r q(x_t|m_r, \Sigma_r)] + 1,$$

$$h(i|x_t) = \frac{q(x_t|m_i, \Sigma_i)}{\sum_{r=1}^{k} \alpha_r q(x_t|m_r, \Sigma_r)}, \qquad p(i|x_t) = \alpha_i h(i|x_t),$$

$$\frac{\partial J(\Theta_k)}{\partial \Sigma_j} = \frac{\alpha_j}{N} \sum_{t=1}^{N} h(j|x_t) U(j|x_t) \Sigma_j^{-1} [(x_t - m_j)(x_t - m_j)^T - \Sigma_j] \Sigma_j^{-1}.$$

In Eq. (5), B_j and $\frac{\partial J(\Theta_k)}{\partial \Sigma_j}$ are considered as their vector forms, i.e., $vec[B_j]$ and $vec[\frac{J(\Theta_k)}{\partial \Sigma_j}]$, respectively. $\frac{\partial (B_j B_j^T)}{\partial B_j}$ is an n^2-order square matrix which can be easily computed.

Combining these β_j, m_j, and B_j into a vector θ_k, we have the conjugate gradient learning rule as follows:

$$\theta_k^{i+1} = \theta_k^i + \eta \widehat{s}_i, \qquad (6)$$

where η is the learning rate, and the searching direction $\widehat{s}_i$ is computed from the following iterations of conjugate vectors:

$$s_1 = -\nabla J(\theta_k^1), \quad \widehat{s}_1 = \frac{-\nabla J(\theta_k^1)}{\|\nabla J(\theta_k^1)\|}$$

$$s_i = -\nabla J(\theta_k^i) + v_{i-1} s_{i-1}, \quad \widehat{s}_i = \frac{s_i}{\|s_i\|}, \quad v_{i-1} = \frac{\|\nabla J(\theta_k^i)\|^2}{\|\nabla J(\theta_k^{i-1})\|^2},$$

where $\nabla J(\theta_k)$ is the general gradient vector of $J(\theta_k) = J(\Theta_k)$ and $\|\cdot\|$ is the Euclidean norm.

2.3 Natural Gradient Learning Rule

In order to get the natural gradient of $J(\Theta_k)$, we let $\theta_j = (m_j, B_j) = (m_j, \Sigma_j)$ so that $\Theta_k = \{\alpha_j, \theta_j\}_{j=1}^k$ which can be considered as a point in the Riemann space. Then, we can construct a $k(n^2 + n + 1)$-dimensional statistical model $S = \{q(x, \Theta_k) : \Theta_k \in \Xi\}$. The Fisher information matrix of S at a point Θ_k is $G(\Theta_k) = [g_{ij}(\Theta_k)]$, where $g_{ij}(\Theta_k)$ is given by

$$g_{ij}(\Theta_k) = \int \partial_i l(x, \Theta_k) \partial_j l(x, \Theta_k) q(x, \Theta_k) dx, \qquad (7)$$

where $\partial_i = \frac{\partial}{\partial \Theta_k^i}$ and $l(x, \Theta_k) = \ln q(x, \Theta_k)$. According to the following derivatives:

$$\frac{\partial q(x_t|\Theta_k)}{\partial \beta_j} = \alpha_j q(x_t|\theta_j) \sum_{i=1}^{k} (\delta_{ij} - \alpha_i), \qquad (8)$$

$$\frac{\partial q(x_t|\Theta_k)}{\partial m_j} = \alpha_j q(x_t|\theta_j) \Sigma_j^{-1}(x_t - m_j), \qquad (9)$$

$$\frac{\partial q(x_t|\Theta_k)}{\partial B_j} = \frac{\partial B_j^T B_j}{\partial B_j} \alpha_j q(x_t|\theta_j) \Sigma_j^{-1}[(x_t - m_j)(x_t - m_j)^T - \Sigma_j] \Sigma_j^{-1}, \qquad (10)$$

we can easily estimate $G(\Theta_k)$ on a sample data set through the law of large number. According to Amari and Nagaoka's natural gradient theory [9], we have the following natural gradient learning rule:

$$\Theta_k(m+1) = \Theta_k(m) - \eta G^{-1}(\Theta_k(m)) \frac{\partial J(\Theta_k(m))}{\partial \Theta_k}, \qquad (11)$$

where η is the learning rate.

3 Simulation Experiments

We conducted experiments on seven sets (a)-(g) of samples drawn from a mixture of four or three bivariate Gaussians densities (i.e., $n = 2$). As shown in Figure 1, each data set of samples consists three or four Gaussians with certain degree of overlap. Using k^* to denote the number of Gaussians in the original mixture, we implemented the conjugate and natural gradient learning rules on those seven sample data sets always with $k^* \leq k \leq 3k^*$ and $\eta = 0.1$. Moreover, the other parameters were initialized randomly within certain intervals. In all the experiments, the learning was stopped when $|J(\Theta_k^{new}) - J(\Theta_k^{old})| < 10^{-5}$.

The experimental results of the conjugate and natural gradient learning rules on the data sets (c) and (d) are given in Figures 2 & 3, respectively, with case $k = 8$ and $k^* = 4$. We can observe that four Gaussians are finally located accurately, while the mixing proportions of the other four Gaussians were reduced to below 0.01, i.e, these Gaussians are extra and can be discarded. That is, the correct number of the clusters have been detected on these data sets. Moreover, the

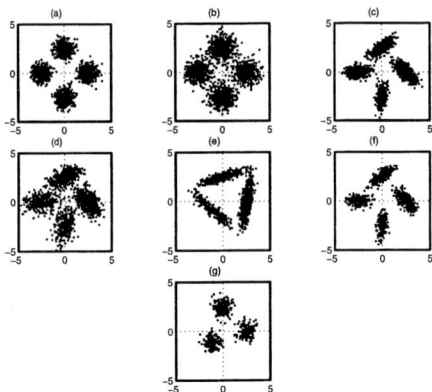

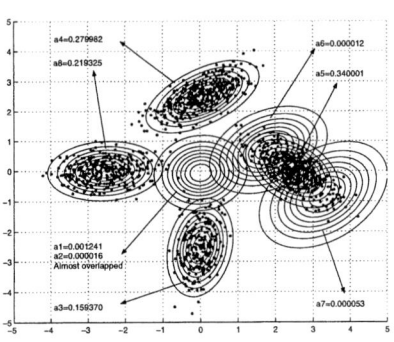

Fig. 1. Seven sets of sample data used in the experiments.

Fig. 2. The experimental result of the conjugate gradient learning rule on the data set (c) (stopped after 63 iterations).

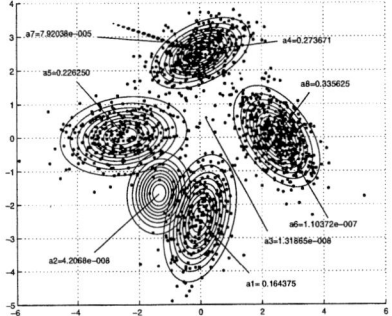

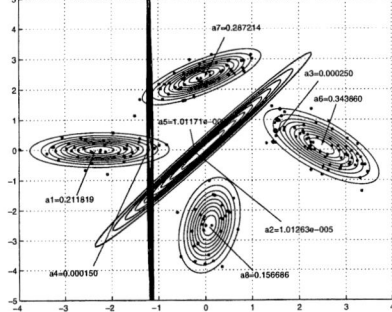

Fig. 3. The experimental result of the natural gradient learning rule on the data set (d) (stopped after 149 iterations).

Fig. 4. The experimental result of the natural gradient learning rule on the data set (f) (stopped after 173 iterations).

experiments of the two learning rules have been made on the other sample data sets in different cases and show the similar results on automated model selection. For example, the natural gradient learning rule was implemented on the data set (f) with $k = 8, k^* = 4$. As shown in Figure 4, even each cluster has a small number of samples, the correct number of clusters can still be detected, with the mixing proportions of other four extra Gaussians reduced below 0.01.

In addition to the correct number detection, we further compared the converged values of parameters (discarding the extra Gaussians) with those parameters in the mixture from which the samples come from. We checked the results in these experiments and found that the conjugate and natural gradient learning rules converge with a lower average error between the estimated parameters and the true parameters.

In comparison with the simulation results of the batch and adaptive gradient learning rules [7]-[8] on these seven sets of sample data, we have found that the conjugate and natural gradient learning rules converge more quickly than the two general gradient ones. Actually, for the most cases it had been demonstrated by simulation experiments that the number of iterations required by each of these two rules is only about one tenth to a quarter of the number of iterations required by either the batch or adaptive gradient learning rule.

As compared with each other, the conjugate gradient learning rule converges more quickly than the natural gradient learning rule, but the natural gradient learning rule obtains a more accurate solution on the parameter estimation.

4 Conclusion

We have proposed the conjugate and natural gradient learning rules for the BYY harmony learning on Gaussian mixture with automated model selection. They are derived from the conjugate gradient method and Amari and Nagaoka's natural gradient theory for the maximization of the harmony function defined on Gaussian mixture model. The simulation experiments have demonstrated that both the conjugate and natural learning rules lead to the correct selection of the number of actual Gaussians as well as a good estimate for the parameters of the original Gaussian mixture. Moreover, they converge more quickly than the general gradient ones.

References

1. R. A. Render and H. F. Walker, "Mixture densities, maximum likelihood and the EM algorithm," *SIAM Review*, vol.26, no.2, pp. 195-239, 1984.
2. A. K. Jain and R. C. Dubes, *Algorithm for Clustering Data,*, Englewood Cliffs, N. J.: Prentice Hall, 1988.
3. J. A. Hartigan, "Distribution problems in clustering," *Classification and clustering*, J. Van Ryzin Eds., pp. 45-72, New York: Academic press, 1977.
4. H. Akaike. "A New Look at the Statistical Model Identification," *IEEE Transactions on Automatic Control*, vol. AC-19, pp. 716-723, 1974.
5. G. W. Millgan and M. C. Copper, "An examination of procedures for determining the number of clusters in a data set," *Psychometrika*, vol.46, pp: 187-199, 1985.
6. L. Xu, "Best harmony, unified RPCL and automated model selection for unsupervised and supervised learning on Gaussian mixtures, three-layer nets and ME-RBF-SVM models," *International Journal of Neural Systems*, vol.11, no.1, pp. 43-69, February, 2001.
7. J. Ma, T. Wang and L. Xu, "A gradient BYY harmony learning rule on Gaussian mixture with automated model selection," *Neurocomputing*, vol.56, pp: 481-487, 2004.
8. J. Ma, T. Wang and L. Xu, "An adaptive BYY harmony learning algorithm and its relation to rewarding and penalizing competitive learning mechanism," *Proc. of ICSP'02*, 26-30 Aug. 2002, vol.2, pp: 1154 - 1158.
9. S. Amari and H. Nagaoka, *Methods of Information Geometry*, AMS, Oxford University Press, 2000.

Improving Support Vector Solutions by Selecting a Sequence of Training Subsets

Tom Downs and Jianxiong Wang

School of Information Technology and Electrical Engineering
The University of Queensland
{td,jxw}@itee.uq.edu.au

Abstract. In this paper we demonstrate that it is possible to gradually improve the performance of support vector machine (SVM) classifiers by using a genetic algorithm to select a sequence of training subsets from the available data. Performance improvement is possible because the SVM solution generally lies some distance away from the Bayes optimal in the space of learning parameters. We illustrate performance improvements on a number of benchmark data sets.

1 Introduction

The support vector machine (SVM) was introduced in [1] as a pattern classifier and, for a problem with two pattern classes, it seeks to determine a separating hyperplane that maximizes the margin of separation between the two. This is a relatively simple task if the patterns are linearly separable, but is also possible when they are not. This is because kernel functions exist that can implicitly map the patterns into a high-dimensional feature space where they *are* linearly separable.

For linearly separable training patterns there exists a continuum of separating hyperplanes. This means that we can choose from a continuum of values for the parameters of the equation of the separating hyperplane. This continuum of values defines a region in parameter space called *version space*. Thus, version space is that region of parameter space within which any point defines a hyperplane that classifies the training patterns correctly.

It is well-known that if the SVM finds a separating hyperplane, the parameter values of that hyperplane are located at the centre of the largest inscribable hypersphere in version space [2]. Let us call the centre of this hypersphere the *SVM Point*. It was shown in [3] that the point in version space that gives *optimum* generalization performance, the *Bayes Point*, need not be especially close to the SVM point, implying that the SVM will sometimes give quite inferior generalization performance. It was shown in [4] that for perceptron learning (which can be used for SVM learning [5]) the expected improvement in generalization performance obtained by using the Bayes Point rather than the SVM Point is 12% for a large set of training examples.

In this paper we use a genetic algorithm to select a sequence of training subsets from the available data. These subsets produce a sequence of SVM populations whose average generalization performance increases until overfitting on the validation set begins to occur. Although this is a brute force approach, it leads to a method that potentially provides the best possible classifier from a given set of data. It also provides some interesting possibilities for future investigation. Performance improvements gained are demonstrated on a variety of benchmark data sets.

2 The SVM Classifier

If the patterns $x_i \in \Re^n$ have labels $y_i \in \{\pm 1\}$ and are linearly separable in input space, the separating hyperplane $w \cdot x + b = 0$ must satisfy, for each training data sample (x_i, y_i), a set of constraints that are usually written in the form [1]:

$$y_i [w \cdot x_i + b] \geq 1 \qquad i = 1, 2, \ldots, m \qquad (1)$$

for a training set of m data points.

Equation (1) holds with equality for points of the two classes that are closest to the separating hyperplane. The distance between these two sets of points is easily shown to be $2 / \|w\|$. Thus, the margin of separation of the two classes in this linearly separable case can be maximized by minimizing $\frac{1}{2} \|w\|^2$ subject to the constraints (1). This minimization problem can be solved by forming a Lagrangian function in the usual way [1]. The solution then lies at the saddle point of the Lagrangian given by minimizing with respect to w and b, and maximizing with respect to the Lagrange multipliers. Conditions on w and b at the saddle point can be found by differentiating the Lagrangian and setting it to zero. These conditions on w and b allow them to be eliminated from the Lagrangian and all that remains then is to maximize with respect to the Lagrange multipliers. This step takes the form

$$\text{Maximize} \quad W(\alpha) = \sum_{i=1}^{m} \alpha_i - \frac{1}{2} \sum_{i=1}^{m} \sum_{j=1}^{m} \alpha_i \alpha_j y_i y_j (x_i \cdot x_j) \qquad (2)$$

subject to $\sum_{i=1}^{m} y_i \alpha_i = 0$, which is a condition obtained by minimizing with respect to w and b. The α_i are the Lagrange multipliers which are constrained to be non-negative.

Optimum values of w and b (ie those that define the hyperplane that provides the maximum margin of separation) can then be obtained by substituting the values of the α_i that maximize (2) into the conditions on w and b that hold at the saddle point.

In the case where data are not linearly separable, the SVM uses a nonlinear function $\phi(\cdot)$ to map the training vectors into a high-dimensional feature space where they *are* separable. When such a mapping function is employed, the procedure for determining the optimum hyperplane remains essentially unchanged except that the dot product in (2) becomes $\phi(x_i) \cdot \phi(x_j)$. The nature of the mapping $\phi(\cdot)$ is usually unimportant because there exist kernel functions K that can implement the dot product. That is, there exist kernel functions such that $K(x_i, x_j) = \phi(x_i) \cdot \phi(x_j)$ where the $\phi(\cdot)$ provide suitable mappings. Thus, when kernel functions are employed, (2) becomes:

$$\text{Maximize} \quad W(\alpha) = \sum_{i=1}^{m} \alpha_i - \frac{1}{2} \sum_{i=1}^{m} \sum_{j=1}^{m} \alpha_i \alpha_j y_i y_j K(x_i, x_j) \qquad (3)$$

Constraints on this maximization remain identical to those in the linearly separable case.

Kernel functions can be found to separate (in feature space) any two sets of patterns however much they may be intermingled. Separating highly intermingled patterns is generally not a good idea because it amounts to overfitting. To avoid this kind of overfitting a "soft" margin approach can be employed where some data points are allowed to violate the constraints in (1). This is achieved by the use of slack variables, as described in [1], and in the usual formulation, this requires no change to the optimization problem (3) other than the placement of an upper bound on the Lagrange multipliers.

3 The Bayes Point

A test pattern x is classified by the SVM according to the sign of

$$f(x) = w \cdot \phi(x) + b \qquad (4)$$

where w, $\phi(\cdot)$ and b are as defined earlier.

If a pattern classifier learns to classify a training set S without error, the optimal Bayes decision on a test example (in the absence of noise) is to classify according to the majority decision of all classifiers available within version space $V(S)$. For a classifier in the linear form (4), the Bayes decision function can be written:

$$f_{Bayes} = \int_{w \in V(S)} (w \cdot \phi(x)) dP(w \mid S) \qquad (5)$$

where $P(w \mid S)$ is a prior over version space which, in the absence of additional information, is taken as uniform. Given a uniform prior, the Bayes decision is simply the decision occupying the larger volume in $V(S)$. No analytic method exists for computing the volume integrals required by (5) and numerical methods cannot generally be used because feature spaces induced by kernels usually have a very high, sometimes infinite, dimension.

An alternative approach is to seek the Bayes Point, which is the point in version space that defines the classifier that makes the Bayes optimal decision. It was shown in [4] and [6] that as the dimension of version space increases, the Bayes Point rapidly converges on the centroid of version space, so that for high-dimensional feature spaces, the Bayes Point can be assumed to lie at the centroid.

This allows us to illustrate how the SVM Point and the Bayes Point differ depending on the shape of version space. Fig. 1 illustrates a case where the two differ substantially. In this figure, the SVM Point is indicated by the cross and the Bayes Point by the dot. Clearly, it is only when version space is reasonably spherical, or has certain kinds of symmetry, that we can expect the two to be close.

The above discussion indicates that we can determine the parameters of the Bayes optimum linear classifier by computing the centroid of version space. Unfortunately, exact determination of the centroid of a high-dimensional polygon is computationally intractable and some form of approximation is necessary. The best known methods are originally due to Rujan [3] and Watkin [6]. Rujan's method involves computing the trajectory of a billiard ball bouncing around in version space, and using the trajectory to estimate the centroid. This method was presented in [3] for the version space of a simple perceptron, but extended to kernel feature space in [2] and [7]. Watkin's approach [6] involved training a simple perceptron until it classified all training data

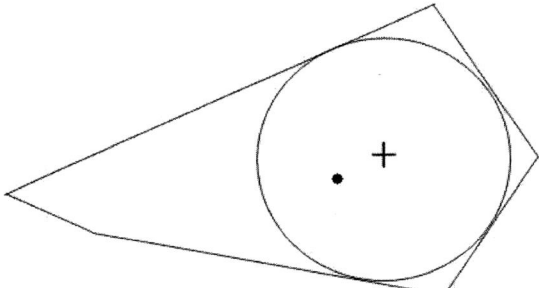

Fig. 1. Version Space.

correctly, so that its weight vector provided a point in version space. This was repeated from a number of random starting positions, so that a variety of points in version space were obtained. The centroid was then estimated by a simple averaging process. This method was extended to kernel feature space in [8].

The fact that version space only exists when the learning system makes no errors on the training set may seem strongly restrictive, but Bayes Point algorithms can be quite easily modified to allow for training errors – see [8].

Results published in [2] and [8] indicate that, as expected, the Bayes Point approach generally provides improved generalization performance over that achieved by the support vector approach.

4 Procedure and Results

Our method commences with the implementation of a standard SVM algorithm to determine the set **SV** of support vectors from the training data. The remainder of the training vectors are then stored as a separate set **NSV**, (non-SVs).

Suppose the set **SV** contains N support vectors. A population of P binary strings, each of length N, is then randomly generated and used to select a random subset of the support vectors from **SV**. Each entry in a binary string corresponds to one of the SVs and if entry i in the string is equal to unity, then SV i is added to the subset selected by that string. The SVs selected by the string are added to the set **NSV** to provide a new training set. This procedure is carried out for each binary string to give us P new training sets. Each of the new training sets is then employed to train a SVM and the performance of each of these SVMs on a validation set is used as a fitness function for a genetic algorithm (GA). The GA is applied to the population of binary strings to produce a new population whose average fitness is greater than that of the initial population. The process repeats and leads to a sequence of SVM sets whose average performance on the validation set monotonically increases. This does, of course, lead to overfitting, so a separate test set is required to indicate a suitable stopping point.

Table 1 contains results for six data sets, the first five being 2-class problems from the UCI database and the other coming from an object recognition problem in robotics that we have investigated at the University of Queensland [9]. Our algorithm leads to performance improvements on 5 of the 6 data sets.

Table 1. SVM classification performance before and after use of our algorithm.

Data set	#Training	#Validation	#Test	SVM_{Before}	SVM_{After}
Chess	1066	1066	1064	90.41%	93.14%
Letter (A&B)	519	519	517	93.42%	95.94%
Letter (O&G)	509	508	509	93.71%	95.09%
Breast	228	227	228	97.37%	97.37%
Pima	256	256	256	73.05%	75.39%
Robot	509	509	508	86.61%	89.40%

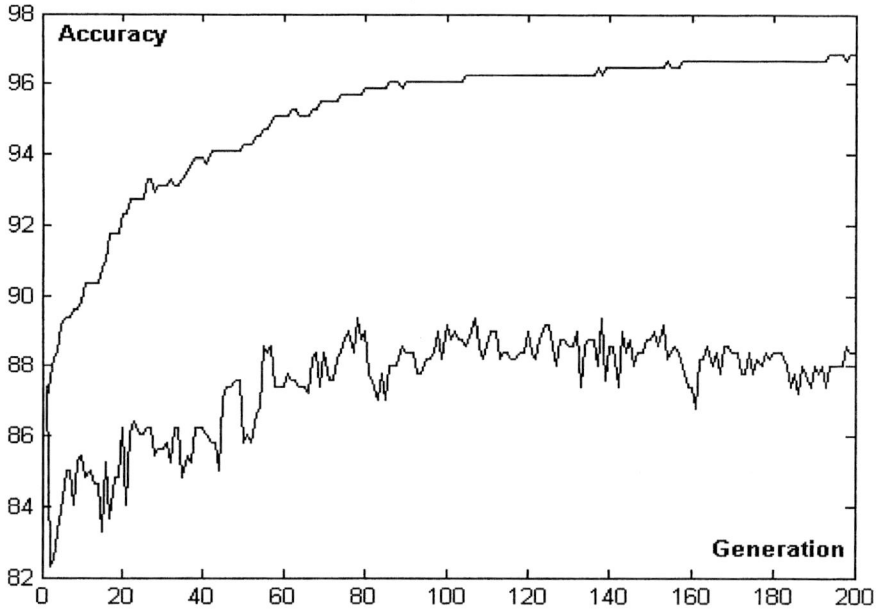

Fig. 2. Evolving performance on validation and test sets for robot data.

Figure 2 is a plot, for the robot data set, of classification accuracy on both the validation and test sets as the number of GA generations increases. The upper curve is for the validation set and performance on this set increases almost monotonically. The lower curve is for the test set for which performance initially drops substantially and then follows an increasing trend up to about 80 generations. After this, it begins to decline due to overfitting on the validation set.

5 Concluding Remarks

We have demonstrated how a GA can be applied successfully to produce a sequence of SVMs whose generalization performance gradually improves. This has been achieved by using performance as the fitness function for the GA which continually changes the mix of data used for training. Although it is a brute force approach it can, at least potentially, provide the best possible classifier from a given set of data.

In future work it would be interesting to track the behaviour of version space, the SVM Point and the Bayes Point during this kind of process, and it may be possible to do this for simple cases. Another possibility for future study concerns the characteristics of the training vectors that the GA selects for removal. It may be that they will be found to have something in common (perhaps something measurable like a norm) so that a more direct procedure for producing improved SVM solutions can be found.

References

1. B E Boser, I M Guyon and V N Vapnik, A training algorithm for optimal margin classifiers, *Proc. 5th Annual ACM Conference on Computational Learning Theory*, 144-152, 1992.
2. R Herbrich, T Graepel and C Campbell, Bayes Point machines: estimating the Bayes Point in kernel space, *Proc. IJCAI Workshop on Support Vector Machines*, 23-27, 1999.
3. P Rujan, Playing billiards in version space, *Neural Computation*, **9**, 99-122, 1997.
4. M Opper and D Haussler, Generalization performance of Bayes optimal classification algorithm for learning a perceptron, *Physical Review Letters*, **66**, 2677-2680, 1991.
5. T-T Friess, N Cristianini and C Campbell, The kernel adatron algorithm: a fast and simple learning procedure for support vector machines, *Proc 15th International Conference on Machine Learning*, 188-196, 1998.
6. T Watkin, Optimal learning with a neural network, *Europhysics Letters*, **21**, 871-877, 1993.
7. P Rujan and M Marchand, Computing the Bayes kernel classifier, in A J Smola et al (Eds.), *Advances in Large Margin Classifiers*, MIT Press, 2000, 329-347.
8. R Herbrich, T Graepel and C Campbell, Bayes Point machines, *Journal of Machine Learning Research*, **1**, 245-279, 2001.
9. J Wang and T Downs, Tuning pattern classifier parameters using a genetic algorithm with an application in mobile robotics, *Proc 2003 Congress on Evolutionary Computation*, 581-586, Canberra, 2003.

Machine Learning for Matching Astronomy Catalogues

David Rohde[1,2], Michael Drinkwater[1], Marcus Gallagher[2], Tom Downs[2], and Marianne Doyle[1]

[1] School of Physical Sciences
University of Queensland 4072, Australia
{djr,mjd,mtdoyle}@physics.uq.edu.au

[2] School of Information Technology and Electrical Engineering
University of Queensland 4072, Australia
{marcusg,td}@itee.uq.edu.au

Abstract. An emerging issue in the field of astronomy is the integration, management and utilization of databases from around the world to facilitate scientific discovery. In this paper, we investigate application of the machine learning techniques of support vector machines and neural networks to the problem of amalgamating catalogues of galaxies as objects from two disparate data sources: radio and optical. Formulating this as a classification problem presents several challenges, including dealing with a highly unbalanced data set. Unlike the conventional approach to the problem (which is based on a likelihood ratio) machine learning does not require density estimation and is shown here to provide a significant improvement in performance. We also report some experiments that explore the importance of the radio and optical data features for the matching problem.

1 Introduction

A data explosion is occurring in astronomy. New telescopes are producing high quality data of the sky in many wavelengths. New tools required for the management of these efforts are being developed by the International Virtual Observatory Alliance and its member organizations [1].

A major feature of the Virtual Observatory will be the amalgamation of different catalogues of objects. When precise positions are available in these catalogues the task is quite straightforward, but often there are significant positional uncertainties so that there may be multiple candidate matches.

The traditional method for this task is the likelihood ratio for source identification which measures the probability of finding a given object in an infinitesimal box relative to finding a background object in that box [2]. This approach, while having a good statistical grounding, is applicable to data from a single catalogue only and, because it requires distributions of variables, is restricted in the number of parameters it can incorporate. Machine Learning has previously been used in astrophysics for problems such as star-galaxy classification, morphology classification and other applications [3], but has not, to our knowledge, been applied to the matching of catalogues.

2 Astronomy Catalogues and the Problem Domain

The work described in this paper employs data obtained from both optical and radio telescope sources. The optical data used is the SuperCosmos Sky Survey [4]. This is a survey of the entire southern sky. The survey consists of digital scans of photographic plates in Blue (B), Red (R) and Infrared (I) colour bands, taken from the Schmidt telescopes. SuperCosmos provides a catalogue of objects (stars, galaxies and other objects) identified from these scans using image processing software. It is important to note that the optical data contains very accurate two dimensional positions of objects.

The radio survey used is the HI Parkes All Sky Survey (HIPASS), which is a survey for a single line of Hydrogen (HI)[1] (also over the entire southern sky) [5]. Signal processing techniques have been used to reduce this survey to a catalogue of 4329 objects or radio galaxies (sources of HI radiation). Each object in the catalogue is represented by 139 measured or derived quantities. Among these the fundamental variables are the *velocity* (a measure of how far the Doppler effect has shifted the line of HI; *width* (the spread of velocities within the galaxy); peak flux and integrated flux (area under the flux curve)[6]. It is important to note that this is a three dimensional catalogue which gives a relatively inaccurate position, but a precise velocity (and this assists the matching process, by use of velocity information in optical catalogues).

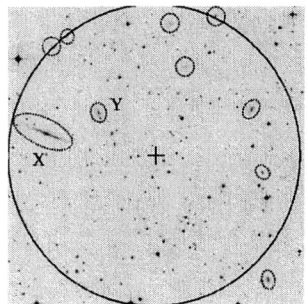 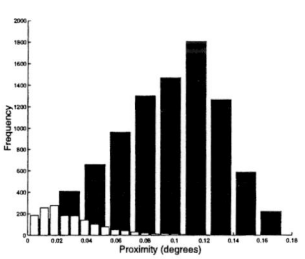

Fig. 1. (a) An optical image showing all the optical candidates within the region of uncertainty of a radio source. The candidates are marked by ellipses. External information shows that object X is the match, even though Y is closer to the radio source (marked with a +) (b) The distribution of matching (white) and non-matching (black) objects as a function of proximity to the radio source.

---

[1] HI is radio emission at a wavelength of 21cm from neutral hydrogen atoms, found in large quantities around some galaxies.

The HIPASS Catalogue is known to contain positional uncertainties of up to 5 arcminutes, where 1 arcminute = $\frac{1}{60}°$ ($\sigma = 1.05$ arcminutes). This is large enough that often there are multiple optical galaxies in the region of uncertainty. An example of a SuperCosmos image centered around a HIPASS radio source is shown in Fig 1 (a). The circle defines the region of uncertainty for the HI Source. Obviously there are many possible optical counterparts.

For approximately half of the HIPASS catalogue there is sufficient data from the NASA Extragalactic Database (NED) and the Six Degree Field Survey (6dF) to choose the correct galaxy [7] . Fig 1 (b) shows the distributions of the proximity to the radio source of the matching objects (white) and the distribution of all the non-matching candidate objects (black). Proximity is a parameter which describes the difference in position of the two candidate matches (one radio and one optical) in degrees. This histogram clearly demonstrates that proximity alone is insufficient to find the matching object.

3 Data Acquisition and Pre-processing

To produce positive training examples for matching galaxies, it was necessary to manually identify a matching galaxy for every radio object (HIPASS catalogue entry). This identification was done using external information from either the NED or 6dF databases.

Generating negative examples for classification is less straightforward. It is clear from Fig.1 that there are many optical objects within the 5 arcminute precision range of each radio source. In the main training set (T_{Main}), we assume there is exactly one matching optical object for every radio source.

As most small objects were non-matching (either because they were stars or very distant galaxies) all objects with area smaller than 140 pixels were deleted.

The data set T_{Main} has some interesting properties. The magnitude of separation between the optical and radio source will obviously be a dominating determinant of the probability that the objects match. And in spite of the deletion of smaller objects, the data is still unbalanced. There are on average 5.5 negative examples for every positive example and because we are attempting to match them to the same radio source, each one has identical radio information. This means that discrimination among candidates for a particular radio source must be largely done in terms of optical information but, as will become clear, the radio information is usually also helpful.

The majority of negative examples in T_{Main} are stars. This could led to the learning problem being biased towards performing star-galaxy classification rather than radio-optical galaxy matching. In order to investigate whether our system has been biased in this way, a second training set was created, with negative examples consisting of galaxies only. From the 6dF catalogue 648 galaxy-only negative examples were identified giving a training set that will be referred to as T_{Galaxy}. Basically, we used this data set to test that our system is able to identify galaxies that are not matches.

A third dataset was also considered. This data set contains positive examples from T_{Main} and negative examples each of whose data is made up of the radio data from one source and the optical data from an entirely different source. As we explain below, this data set was used to show that the radio data contributes to the matching process (even though it is the same for each candidate for a given radio source). We refer to this data set as $T_{Mismatch}$. Because this data set contains galaxies only, the star/galaxy class feature was removed. We also removed the proximity feature in order to observe the degree of matching possible using the remaining variables.

The features employed in our data consist of (i) four radio parameters - Velocity, Velocity range, log peak flux, log integrated flux; (ii) eight optical parameters - blue flux, the log of the ratio of blue flux to red flux, the log of the ratio of blue flux to infrared flux, log area (of object), semi-major and semi minor axis of the ellipse fitted to the object (iii) proximity of radio source and optical candidate (iv) a prediction of star-galaxy classification.

The star-galaxy feature is a prediction of whether an object is a star or galaxy, based on machine learning and a separate training set. An explanation of the process for obtaining this feature is provided in the following section.

For the $T_{Mismatch}$ data set, the proximity feature was not used because the optical data for the negative examples in this case comes from objects that are far removed from the radio source.

All feature values were standardized to the range [-1 1].

4 Experimental Methodology and Results

The matching performance of several models, including the likelihood ratio, was investigated.

The likelihood ratio method[2] estimates the probability that an object is a match relative to the probability that it is a background object. For optical candidates of magnitude m and type c (where type is usually star or galaxy) the likelihood L is given by:

$$L = \frac{q(m,c)f(r)}{n(m,c)} \quad (1)$$

where q is the probability density of m and c, f is the density of positional errors and n is a density for the existence of objects with parameters m and c.

The parameter c (star or galaxy) was estimated, for a given object, using a support vector machine (SVM) that had been trained on 1000 stars and 1000 galaxies. Following inspection of the training data the density q, for each value of c (galaxy, star), was approximated by a Gaussian approximation and the density n was approximated by an exponential.

Besides the likelihood ratio, various SVM and neural network models were also employed to assess matching performance on the data set T_{Main}. The training set consisted of 1597 positive matches and 8839 negative examples.

The SVM models we employed used polynomial kernels up to degree 3 and an RBF kernel with a variance of unity; the neural networks were the perceptron and feedforward nets with up to 6 hidden units. The cross-validation results obtained for several of these models are listed in Table 1. Also included is a

Table 1. Training Set 1: Performance of different algorithms with different parameters, kernels, soft margins.

Kernel or Algorithm	Positive Data % error	Negative Data % error	Overall % error
Linear	3.82	0.40	0.92
Poly d=2	2.50	0.34	0.67
Poly d=3	2.76	0.33	0.70
RBF	3.51	0.41	0.88
Perceptron	5.88	1.01	1.75
NN, 5HUs	2.63	0.40	0.74
Likelihood Ratio	5.51	1.01	1.70

Table 2. Input Importance on T_{Main}.

Proximity	Radio	True Pos % error (σ)	True Neg % error (σ)
Yes	Yes	2.50 (1.28)	0.34 (0.20)
Yes	No	3.38 (1.65)	0.41 (0.23)
No	No	5.76 (2.22)	0.69 (0.27)

result obtained using the likelihood ratio method which was obtained using a holdout test data set rather than cross-validation.

Table 1 shows that a polynomial degree 2 kernel gives the best performance but most of the other methods are also competitive. The reasonably good performance of the perceptron indicates that the dataset must be close to linearly separable. The relatively weak performance of the likelihood ratio method indicates that there are useful relations among the parameters that are ignored by the likelihood method but picked up by machine learning methods.

It was pointed out that all optical candidates for a particular radio source necessarily have the same radio data. So the question arises as to whether the radio data is at all helpful in the matching process (beyond pointing to a set of optical candidates). In an attempt to answer this question, the best performing model (SVM with degree 2 polynomial kernel) was applied to the matching problem with the data modified to exclude the radio features. The change in performance is shown in the second data line of Table 2. The third data line in Table 2 shows performance when both the radio and proximity data are removed from the training vectors. The fact that the SVM is still able to achieve an error rate of only a little under 6% indicates that the optical data is providing significant information regarding HI emissions.

Another concern expressed earlier was that models trained on these datasets would be biased by learning only to distinguish between stars and galaxies. The data set T_{Galaxy} is a galaxy-only set that we employed to establish our system's ability to identify galaxies that are not matches. The model was able to correctly identify 71.89% of the galaxies in this data set that are not matches, which shows that the system does indeed do more than simply distinguish between stars and galaxies.

In a further attempt to assess the significance of the radio data in assisting with the matching process, we constructed the data set $T_{Mismatch}$ described earlier in Section 3. On this data set, our system achieved a classification accuracy of 72.07%. When the radio features were removed from the data vectors, this accuracy dropped to 46.85% thus demonstrating the importance of the radio data.

5 Discussion

In this study we have shown that machine learning methods are able to outperform the likelihood ratio approach to identifying radio sources among optical candidates. This indicates that the assumptions underlying the likelihood ratio method lead to useful information being ignored.

We were also able to show (in Table 2) that optical features alone provide good performance on the matching task, demonstrating that optical data alone can be used to identify sources of HI radiation among candidates and can do so with remarkably good accuracy.

Table 2 also shows that when the proximity data is added to the optical data (in which case the machine learning system receives the same data as the likelihood method), performance increases significantly, and is slightly superior to that of the likelihood method.

Table 2 additionally shows that adding the radio data to the optical and proximity data leads to a further improvement in performance, demonstrating the importance of the radio data to the matching task, even though all candidates have the same radio data. The experiment with the mismatched data set provided additional evidence that radio data is a significant contributor to matching performance.

References

1. www.ivoa.net
2. W Sutherland and W Saunders. On the likelihood ratio for source identification. *Monthly Notices of the Royal Astronomical Society*, pages 413-420, 25 November 1992.
3. R Tagliaferri et al. Neural networks for analysis of complex scientific data: astronomy and geosciences, *Neural Networks* 16:297-319, 2003
4. M J Irwin N C Hambly and H T MacGillivray. The SuperCOSMOS Sky Survey - II image detection, parametrization, classification and photometry. *Monthly Notices of the Royal Astronomical Society*, pages 1295-1314, May 2001.
5. M J Meyer et al. The HIPASS CAtalogue: I - data presentation. *Monthly Notices of the Royal Astronomical Society*, pages 1195-1209, June, 2004.
6. D Barnes et al. The HI Parkes All Sky Survey: Souther observations, calibration and robust imaging. *Monthly Notices of the Royal Astronomical Society*, pages 486-498, 2001
7. M Doyle et al. HIPASS III optical counterparts. *Monthly Notices of the Royal Astronomical Society*, 2004 (in preparation)

Boosting the Tree Augmented Naïve Bayes Classifier

Tom Downs and Adelina Tang

The School of Information Technology & Electrical Engineering
The University of Queensland Brisbane Qld 4072 Australia
{td,atanglt}@itee.uq.edu.au

Abstract. The Tree Augmented Naïve Bayes (TAN) classifier relaxes the sweeping independence assumptions of the Naïve Bayes approach by taking account of conditional probabilities. It does this in a limited sense, by incorporating the conditional probability of each attribute given the class and (at most) one other attribute. The method of boosting has previously proven very effective in improving the performance of Naïve Bayes classifiers and in this paper, we investigate its effectiveness on application to the TAN classifier.

1 Introduction

It is well known that the training of a full Bayes network is NP-hard [1], because it requires consideration of the dependencies between each and every node in the network. The Naive Bayes (NB) method is essentially a maximally simplified version of the Bayes network since it assumes independence of all attributes for a given class. In some applications, the NB method has performed remarkably well, but in others, not so well.

A number of proposals have been made to relax the independence assumption of the NB approach. Among these is the Tree Augmented Naïve Bayes Network (TAN)[2] which includes an estimate of the conditional probability of each attribute given the class and (at most) one other attribute. In [2] the TAN was shown to outperform the NB method on most datasets in a substantial benchmark set. In [3] it was shown that the performance of the NB classifier could be improved significantly by application of the method of boosting [4]. In this paper, we investigate the performance achievements that can be achieved by applying boosting to the TAN.

2 The Naïve Bayes Classifier

Suppose we have a pattern classification problem in which each example is a vector of features F_i, $i = 1,2,\ldots,k$ and let a previously unseen example x have feature values x_1 through to x_k. If we have a multiclass problem, with classes C_1, C_2, ..., then the optimal estimate of class membership for x is the class C_i for which the probability

$$\Pr(C_i \mid F_1 = x_1 \text{ AND } F_2 = x_2 \text{ AND } \cdots \text{ AND } F_k = x_k).$$

has the largest value. By using Bayes' rule, this can be converted into the *discriminant function*:

$$f_i(x) = \Pr(C_i)\Pr(F_1 = x_1 \text{ AND } F_2 = x_2 \text{ AND } \cdots \text{ AND } F_k = x_k | C_i) .$$

and the pattern x is assigned to the class for which this function takes on the largest value.

If we now make the NB assumption that for each class C_i, the features F_j are statistically independent, the discriminant function becomes:

$$f_i(x) = \Pr(C_i) \prod_{j=1}^{k} \Pr(F_j = x_j | C_i) . \qquad (1)$$

and, importantly, the probabilities in this expression can be estimated from training data in a very simple way. All that is required is a count of the number of times each class occurs and the number of times each feature occurs for a particular class. The probability $\Pr(C_i)$ is simply the proportion of times class C_i occurs in the training data and the factors under the product sign are estimated using the formula:

$$\hat{\Pr}(F_j = x_j | \text{Class} = C_i) = \frac{\#(F_j = x_j \text{ AND Class} = C_i)}{\#(\text{Class} = C_i)} \qquad (2)$$

where $\#(\cdot)$ is a count of the number of occurrences of the term in brackets.

The computational simplicity of (1) and (2), coupled with surprisingly good classification performance, have meant that the NB classifier has been widely used for decades. And in recent times, the method of boosting has been applied to the NB classifier to improve its performance further.

3 The Tree Augmented Naïve Bayes Network (TAN)

The TAN was described in [2] as an extension of the dependency tree method developed by Chow and Liu [5] for approximating discrete probability distributions. Given a multivariate distribution $\Pr(x)$, Chow and Liu sought an optimal product approximation for which, in the 6-variable case, a typical example has the form

$$\Pr(x) \approx \Pr(x_1)\Pr(x_2|x_1)\Pr(x_3|x_2)\Pr(x_4|x_2)\Pr(x_5|x_2)\Pr(x_6|x_5) . \qquad (3)$$

The product on the right-hand side of (3) can be represented by a tree, as shown in Figure 1. Such trees are called dependence trees. Obviously, many product expansions of the form (3) exist for the 6-variable case, and Chow and Liu's method finds the one that gives the optimum approximation to the multivariate probability $\Pr(x)$. The method is based upon the concept of *mutual information* which, for variables x_i and x_j, is defined by:

$$I(x_i, x_j) = \sum_{x_i, x_j} \Pr(x_i, x_j) \ln \frac{\Pr(x_i, x_j)}{\Pr(x_i)\Pr(x_j)} . \qquad (4)$$

To each branch of a dependence tree, Chow and Liu assigned a weight equal to the mutual information between the variables at its nodes and showed that the dependence tree with the maximum total weight gives the optimum approximation to Pr(x).

The tree augmented naïve Bayes network is constructed in a similar way to dependence trees but is based upon *conditional mutual information* (CMI) which, for class C and variables x_i and x_j is defined by

$$I(x_i, x_j \mid C) = \sum_{x_i, x_j, C} \Pr(x_i, x_j, C) \ln \frac{\Pr(x_i, x_j \mid C)}{\Pr(x_i \mid C) \Pr(x_j \mid C)}. \tag{5}$$

The probabilities in (5) are estimated by frequency counts in a similar fashion to those in equation (2). To estimate Pr(x_i, x_j, C), the equivalent form Pr(x_i, $x_j \mid C$)Pr(C) is employed.

Calculating the CMI values for each i, j and ordering them according to magnitude allows construction of the maximum weighted spanning tree which is the tree with maximum likelihood given the data. This is done for each class.

For each completed tree, a *root variable* is arbitrarily chosen, and each branch is assigned a direction away from the root. The TAN is then obtained by adding a vertex representing the class C to the tree and inserting a branch directed from C to the node of each variable. The final form of the TAN is illustrated for a 2-class problem in Figure 2. Note that the structure of the tree given by the CMI calculation is generally different for each class.

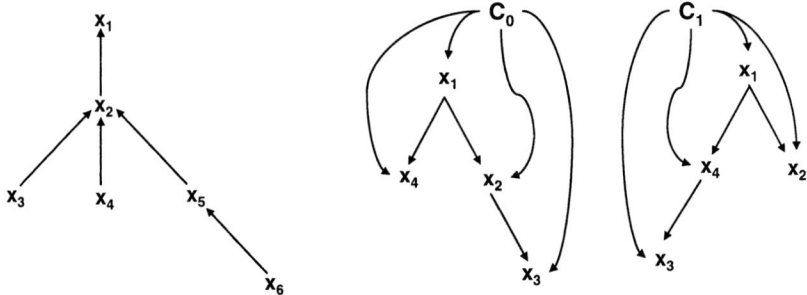

Fig. 1. Example of a dependence tree.   **Fig. 2.** TAN structure for a 2-class problem.

The TAN defines a likelihood function which, when multiplied by the class probability, gives us a discriminant function similar to (1), but now containing more dependencies among attributes. Thus, for instance, the discriminant functions defined by the TANs for classes C_0 and C_1 in Figure 2 are

$$f_0 = \Pr(C_0)\Pr(x_1 \mid C_0)\Pr(x_4 \mid x_1, C_0)\Pr(x_2 \mid x_1, C_0)\Pr(x_3 \mid x_2, C_0)$$

$$f_1 = \Pr(C_1)\Pr(x_1 \mid C_1)\Pr(x_4 \mid x_1, C_1)\Pr(x_2 \mid x_1, C_1)\Pr(x_3 \mid x_4, C_1)$$

An unknown test example x is classified by the TAN by having its variable values x_i substituted into these two discriminant functions and the one with the larger value gives the class.

4 Boosting the TAN

Boosting is an ensemble method that can be applied to both classification and regression. For classification, a sequence of classifiers is generated in such a way that the training of later classifiers in the sequence places greater emphasis on those training examples that earlier classifiers tended to misclassify. In our implementation, we train an ensemble of learning systems by selecting the training examples differently for each system. The training set for the first learning system is obtained by random selection (with replacement) from the full set of training data. Then, for the second learning system, the selection process is modified so that those examples that the first learning system classified incorrectly are more likely to be selected for use in training the second learning system. Data for additional learning systems are selected similarly, ensuring that examples that are proving more difficult to classify are given increasing emphasis in the training of each succeeding learning system. The algorithm can be stated (for data vectors x_i and their class labels y_i) as below. Some additional explanation of the procedure is given after the statement of the algorithm.

Input: Sequence of N examples $(x_1, y_1) \ldots (x_N, y_N)$.
Initialize: $D_1(i) = 1/N$ for all i.
   Do for $t = 1, 2, \ldots, T$:
1. Draw a sample S_t using distribution $D_t(i)$ and use it to train the TAN.
2. Calculate the error made by the TAN from the training examples:
$$\varepsilon_t = \sum_{i : h_t(x_i) \neq y_i} D_t(i) .$$
where $h_t(x_i)$ is the TAN's classification decision for training vector x_i on boosting round t.
3. Set $\beta_t = \varepsilon_t/(1-\varepsilon_t)$, so β_t varies between 0 and 1, having larger values for larger ε_t. (It is assumed that $\varepsilon_t < 0.5$ – if this was not true, the TAN would have learnt nothing.).
4. Update distribution D_i:
$$D_{t+1}(i) = \frac{D_t(i)}{Z_t} \times \begin{cases} \beta_t \text{ if } h_t(x_i) = y_i \\ 1 \text{ otherwise} \end{cases} .$$
where Z_t is a constant chosen to ensure that D_{t+1} is a distribution.

Output the final decision. This is a weighted vote with the weight on h_t being $\log(1/\beta_t)$ so that greater weight is given to functions that have lower error on the training set.

The initial training set is selected using the uniform distribution, so that all data examples are equally likely to be selected for training the first learning system. Then, in steps 2, 3 and 4, the distribution is changed to give more emphasis to examples that are classified incorrectly by the first system. In step 2, the error ε_t is calculated by summing the probabilities associated with each data point that the first system classifies incorrectly. Thus, if the first system gets half the examples wrong, ε_t will be equal to 0.5. But we assume that the first system does at least a little better than this so that $\varepsilon_t < 0.5$. β_t then varies between 0 and 1, having larger values for larger ε_t. So, in step 4, the values of selection probabilities for data that the first learner classifies correctly (ie those for which $h_t(x_i) = y_i$) are reduced, by being multiplied by β_t. The selection probabilities for data incorrectly classified are not reduced. The term Z_t is there to make all the probabilities add to unity. As a result of this procedure, the second learning system will place a little more emphasis on those examples that the first system found difficult to classify correctly. The process continues in the same way for additional learning systems.

Note that boosting can also be implemented by using the full set of data to train each system without any form of sampling. This is carried out by using a cost function that assigns a weight to each example. For the first system in the ensemble, all weights are equal, but for later systems a higher cost is assigned to those examples that are proving difficult to classify. The overall effect of this approach is much the same as that of weighted sampling but we were obliged to employ the weighted sampling method in this case because there is no obvious cost function for Bayesian network learning.

5 Results and Discussion

Results were obtained for datasets drawn from the UCI repository. Preprocessing was carried out as in [2], including the removal of instances with missing values and the discretization of continuous attributes using the methods of [6].

For the smaller data sets, generalization performance was estimated using five-fold cross validation. For the larger datasets, for which cross validation is too time-consuming, the data were split into training and test sets with the numbers in each set as shown in Table 1. The fact that the TAN takes account of some of the dependencies between variables means that some probability estimates are based upon very few instances. To improve the reliability of such estimates, a smoothing operation was introduced in [2] and this was also employed here.

The results listed in Table 1 for TAN[S] (TAN with smoothed estimates) are those quoted in [2]. The Table also contains results for our boosted version of TAN[S]. Results are averaged over ten runs. They show that in most cases the application of boosting led to small improvements in generalization performance on the average. But only in one case, data set 20, did it lead to a significant improvement. In a few cases, the boosting results show a slight deterioration in performance, but this is only due to statistical effects.

The fact that most performance improvements were only marginal is most likely due to the TAN being too "strong" a learner. Boosting performs best when applied to systems with relatively weak learning ability. It works well for Naïve-Bayes, but the pairwise dependence information included in the training of the TAN appears to be sufficient to reduce the effectiveness of boosting.

Table 1. Results.(CV-5 indicates five-fold cross validation).

No.	Dataset	Attributes / Classes	Training / Testing	TAN^S	BoostTAN
1	australian	14 / 2	690 / CV-5	84.20 ± 1.24	84.81 ± 3.54
2	breast	10 / 2	683 / CV-5	96.92 ± 0.67	97.59 ± 1.29
3	chess	36 / 2	2130 / 1066	92.31 ± 0.82	92.03 ± 1.77
4	cleve	13 / 2	296 / CV-5	81.76 ± 0.33	82.88 ± 3.33
5	crx	15 / 2	653 / CV-5	85.76 ± 1.16	86.00 ± 2.75
6	flare	10 / 3	1066 / CV-5	82.27 ± 1.86	82.44 ± 3.50
7	german	20 / 2	1000 / CV-5	73.10 ± 1.54	75.85 ± 3.27
8	glass	9 / 7	214 / CV-5	67.78 ± 3.43	69.53 ± 5.19
9	glass2	9 / 3	163 / CV-5	77.92 ± 1.11	77.58 ± 5.92
10	heart	13 / 2	270 / CV-5	83.33 ± 2.48	85.93 ± 3.72
11	hepatitis	19 / 2	80 / CV-5	91.25 ± 2.50	91.25 ± 6.72
12	iris	4 / 3	150 / CV-5	94.00 ± 1.25	94.67 ± 4.50
13	letter	16 / 26	15000 / 5000	85.86 ± 0.49	86.02 ± 2.75
14	lymphography	18 / 4	148 / CV-5	85.03 ± 3.09	86.67 ± 4.97
15	pima	8 / 2	768 / CV-5	75.52 ± 1.27	77.27 ± 3.90
16	satimage	36 / 6	4435 / 2000	87.20 ± 0.75	87.12 ± 0.73
17	segment	19 / 7	1540 / 770	95.58 ± 0.74	95.13 ± 2.17
18	shuttle-small	9 / 7	3866 / 1934	99.53 ± 0.15	99.47 ± 0.14
19	soybean-large	35 / 19	562 / CV-5	92.17 ± 1.02	92.41 ± 2.07
20	vehicle	18 / 4	846 / CV-5	69.63 ± 2.11	74.63 ± 1.89
21	vote	16 / 2	435 / CV-5	93.56 ± 0.28	94.37 ± 2.13
22	waveform	21 / 3	300 / 4700	78.38 ± 0.60	78.52 ± 0.63

References

1. Cooper, G.F.: The Computational-Complexity of Probabilistic Inference Using Bayesian Belief Networks. *Artificial Intelligence* **42**, 393-405, 1990.
2. Friedman, N., Geiger, D., Goldszmidt, M.: Bayesian network classifiers. *Machine Learning* **29**, 131-163, 1997.
3. Elkan, C.: Boosting and Naive Bayesian Learning, Dept. of Computer Science and Engineering, University of California San Diego, 1997.
4. Freund, Y., Schapire, R.E.: A decision-theoretic generalization of on-line learning and an application to boosting, *Journal of Computer and System Sciences*, **55**, 119-139, 1997.
5. Chow, C.K., Liu, C.N.: Approximating Discrete Probability Distributions with Dependence Trees, *IEEE Transactions on Information Theory*, **IT-14**, 462-467, 1968.
6. Dougherty, J., Kohavi, R., Sahami, M.: Supervised and Unsupervised Discretization of Continuous Attributes. *Proc 12th Int. Conf. on Machine Learning*, 194-202, 1995.

Clustering Model Selection for Reduced Support Vector Machines

Lih-Ren Jen and Yuh-Jye Lee

Department of Computer Science and Information Engineering
National Taiwan University of Science and Technology
Taipei, 106 Taiwan
lrjen@niu.edu.tw, yuh-jye@mail.ntust.edu.tw

Abstract. The reduced support vector machine was proposed for the practical objective that overcomes the computational difficulties as well as reduces the model complexity by generating a nonlinear separating surface for a massive dataset. It has been successfully applied to other kernel-based learning algorithms. Also, there are experimental studies on RSVM that showed the efficiency of RSVM. In this paper we propose a robust method to build the model of RSVM via RBF (Gaussian) kernel construction. Applying clustering algorithm to each class, we can generate cluster centroids of each class and use them to form the reduced set which is used in RSVM. We also estimate the approximate density for each cluster to get the parameter used in Gaussian kernel. Under the compatible classification performance on the test set, our method selects a smaller reduced set than the one via random selection scheme. Moreover, it determines the kernel parameter automatically and individually for each point in the reduced set while the RSVM used a common kernel parameter which is determined by a tuning procedure.

Keywords: Support Vector Machine, Reduced Set, Gaussian Kernel, Radial Basis Function Network, Model Selection, k-means Clustering Algorithm.

1 Introduction

In recent years support vector machines (SVMs) with linear or nonlinear kernels [1, 3, 10] have become one of the most promising learning algorithms. For the binary classification problems, SVMs are able to construct a nonlinear separating surface (if it is necessary), which is implicitly defined by a kernel function [10]. However, there are some major computational difficulties such as huge memory usage and long CPU time, in generating a nonlinear SVM classifier for a massive dataset. To overcome these difficulties the reduced support vector machine (RSVM) [4] was proposed.

In this paper, we apply the k-means clustering algorithm to each class to generate cluster centroids of each class and then use them to form the reduced set that is randomly selected in RSVM [4]. One of the most important ideas of

SVM is kernel technique that uses a kernel function to represent the inner product of two data points in the feature space after a nonlinear mapping. We will use the Gaussian kernel through this paper. The value of the Gaussian kernel can be interpreted as a measure of similarity between data points. In this case, the reduced kernel matrix records the similarity between the reduced set and the entire training dataset. This observation inspires us to select the most representative points of the entire training dataset to form the reduced set. Using the cluster centroids should be an intuitive heuristic. In order to catch the characteristic of each class we run the clustering algorithm on each class separately. This idea originally comes from [6]. The Gaussian kernel function contains a tuning parameter σ, which determines the shape of the kernel function. Choosing this tuning parameter is called the model selection which is a very important issue in nonlinear support vector machine. A bigger value of this parameter will give a better discriminate ability on training examples while may cause the overfitting risk, fitting the training data too well but losing the prediction ability on unseen data. In practice, the conventional SVM as well as RSVM determine this tuning parameter which is commonly used in kernel function via a tuning procedure [2]. While, in our approach the kernel parameter is determined automatically and individually for each point in the reduced set. This can be achieved by estimating the approximate density of each resulting cluster [9]. Once we have the reduced kernel matrix, we apply smooth support vector machine [4] to generate the final classifier. We apply our method on four benchmark datasets from the UCI Machine Learning Repository [8] and the face detection dataset[1]. Under the compatible classification performance on the test set, our method selects a smaller reduced set than the one via random selection scheme. Moreover, it determines the kernel parameter automatically and individually for each point in the reduced set while the RSVM used a common kernel parameter which is determined by a tuning procedure.

We briefly outline the contents of the paper and a word about our notation is given below. Section 2 provides the main idea and formulation for RSVM. In Section 3, we explain why we could use the former research results of RBFN, and describe our algorithm. The experiment results of our method are presented in Section 4. In Section 5, we conclude this paper. All notations used in the paper are listed as follows. All vectors will be column vectors unless otherwise specified or transposed to a row vector by a prime superscript $'$. The plus function x_+ is defined as $(x)_+ = \max\{0, x\}$. The scalar (inner) product of two vectors x and z in the n-dimensional real space R^n will be denoted by $x'z$ and the p-norm of x will be denoted by $\|x\|_p$. For a matrix $A \in R^{m \times n}$, A_i is the ith row of A which is *a row vector* in R^n. A column vector of ones of arbitrary dimension will be denoted by e. For $A \in R^{m \times n}$ and $B \in R^{n \times l}$, the kernel $K(A, B)$ maps $R^{m \times n} \times R^{n \times l}$ into $R^{m \times l}$. In particular, $K(x', z)$ is a real number, $K(x', A')$ is a *row* vector in R^m, $K(A, x)$ is a *column* vector in R^m and $K(A, A')$ is an $m \times m$ matrix. The base of the natural logarithm will be denoted by ε.

---

[1] Available at http://www.ai.mit.edu/projects/cbcl/

2 Reduced Support Vector Machines

We now briefly describe the RSVM formulation, which is derived from the generalized support vector machine (GSVM) [7] and the smooth support vector machine (SSVM) [5]. We are given a training data set $\{(x^i, y_i)\}_{i=1}^{m}$, where $x^i \in R^n$ is an input data point and $y_i \in \{-1, 1\}$ is class label, indicating one of two classes, A_- and A_+, to which the input point belongs. We represent these data points by an $m \times n$ matrix A, where the ith row of the matrix A, A_i, corresponds to the ith data point. We denote alternately A_i (a row vector) and x^i (a column vector) for the same ith data point. We use an $m \times m$ diagonal matrix D defined by $D_{ii} = y_i$ to specify the membership of each input point. The main goal of the classification problem is to find a classifier that can predict the label of new unseen data points correctly. This can be achieved by constructing a linear or nonlinear separating surface, $f(x) = 0$, which is implicitly defined by a kernel function. We classify a test point x belong to A_+ if $f(x) \geq 0$, otherwise x belong to A_-. We will focus on the nonlinear case that is implicitly defined by a Gaussian kernel function. The RSVM solves the following unconstrained minimization problem

$$\min_{(\bar{v},\gamma) \in R^{\bar{m}+1}} \frac{\nu}{2} \| p(e - D(K_\sigma(A, \bar{A}')\bar{v} - e\gamma), \alpha) \|_2^2 + \frac{1}{2}(\bar{v}'\bar{v} + \gamma^2), \tag{1}$$

where the function $p(x, \alpha)$ is a very accurate smooth approximation to $(x)_+$ [5], which is applied to each component of the vector $e - D(K_\sigma(A, \bar{A}')\bar{D}\bar{v} - e\gamma)$ and is defined componentwise by

$$p(x, \alpha) = x + \frac{1}{\alpha} \log(1 + \varepsilon^{-\alpha x}), \alpha > 0. \tag{2}$$

The function $p(x, \alpha)$ converges to $(x)_+$ as α goes to infinity. The reduced kernel matrix $K_\sigma(A, \bar{A}) \in R^{m \times \bar{m}}$ in (1) is defined by

$$K_\sigma(A, \bar{A}')_{ij} = \varepsilon^{-\frac{\|A_i - \bar{A}_j\|_2^2}{\sigma^2}}, \tag{3}$$

where $\bar{A}$ is the reduced set that is randomly selected from A in RSVM [5]. The positive tuning parameter ν here controls the tradeoff between the classification error and the suppression of $(\bar{v}, \gamma)$. Since RSVM has reduced the model complexity via using a much smaller rectangular kernel matrix we will suggest using a larger tuning parameter ν here. A solution of this minimization problem (1) for $\bar{v}$ and γ leads to the nonlinear separating surface

$$f(x) = \bar{v}' K_\sigma(\bar{A}, x) - \gamma = \sum_{i=1}^{\bar{m}} \bar{v}_i K_\sigma(\bar{A}_i, x) - \gamma = 0. \tag{4}$$

The minimization problem (1) can be solved via the Newton-Armijo method [5] directly and the existence and uniqueness of the optimal solution of this problem are also guaranteed. We note that this nonlinear separating surface (4) is a linear combination of a set of kernel functions $\{1, K_\sigma(\bar{A}_1, \cdot), K_\sigma(\bar{A}_2, \cdot), \cdots, K_\sigma(\bar{A}_{\bar{m}}, \cdot)\}$, where σ is the kernel parameter of each kernel function. In next section, we will apply k-means algorithm to each class to generate cluster centroids and then use these centroids to form the reduced set. Moreover we also give a formula to determine the kernel parameter σ for each point in the reduced set automatically.

3 Clustering Reduced Support Vector Machine

We proposed our new algorithm, Clustering RSVM (CRSVM), that combines the RSVM [4] and RBF networks algorithm together. The most popular RBF networks can be describe as

$$f(x) = w_0 + \sum_{h=1}^{\bar{m}} w_h \varepsilon^{-\frac{||x-c^h||_2^2}{2\sigma_h^2}}, \qquad (5)$$

where $c^h = (c_1, c_2, ..., c_n)$ is also a vector in the n-dimensional vector space and $||x - c^h||_2$ is the distance between training (test) vectors x and c^h. We can use the same decision rule in previous section for binary classification. That is, we classify a test point x belong to A_+ if $f(x) \geq 0$, otherwise x belong to A_-. By RBFN approaches, we have to choose three parameters (c^h, σ_h, w_h) in equation (5) based on the training dataset. For the first two parameters, many RBFN approaches were proposed that apply variant clustering algorithms such as k-means to training set to generate the cluster centroids as c^h. The parameter σ_h is estimated upon the distribution of clusters. Based on uniform distribution assumption, [9] estimates σ_h as

$$\sigma_h = \frac{\overline{R}(c^h) \cdot \delta \cdot \sqrt{\pi}}{\sqrt[n]{(r+1)\Gamma(\frac{n}{2}+1)}} \quad \text{where } \delta \cdot \sqrt{\pi} = 1.6210 \qquad (6)$$

and $\overline{R}(c^h)$ is defined as

$$\overline{R}(c^h) = \frac{n+1}{n}(\frac{1}{r}\sum_{q=1}^{r}||\hat{x}_q - c^h||_2), \qquad (7)$$

where $\hat{x}_1, \ldots, \hat{x}_r$ are the r nearest samples to the cluster centroid c^h. If the cluster size is smaller than r, we use the all examples in this cluster to compute $\bar{R}(c^h)$.

When the first two type-variables are selected, RBFN is trained to get the w_h and the estimation of σ_h as kernel parameter to generate the reduced kernel matrix [9]. We proposed a variant RSVM method that uses clustering centroids as reduced set. The Clustering Reduced Support Vector Machine (CRSVM) algorithm is described in below.

Algorithm 3.1 Clustering Reduced Support Vector Machine:

Let k be the number of cluster centroids for each class and r be a positive integer.
STEP 1. For each class, runs k-means algorithm to find the cluster centroids c^h. Use the clustering results to form the reduced set $\bar{A} = [c^1 c^2 ... c^{2k}]'$.
STEP 2. For each centroid c^h, computes the corresponding kernel parameter σ_h using the formula (6, 7).
STEP 3. Let A_i denotes the ith training point, use the resulting parameters from STEP 1 and 2 to construct the rectangular kernel matrix $K_\sigma(A, \bar{A}')_{ih} = \varepsilon^{-\frac{\|A_i - c^h\|_2^2}{2\sigma_h^2}}$, where $K \in R^{m \times 2k}$, for $i = 1, 2, ..., m$ and $j = 1, 2, ..., 2k$.
STEP 4. Apply the Newton-Armijo Algorithm [4] to solve the problem (1), where $K_\sigma(A, \bar{A}')$ is the reduced kernel matrix obtained in Step 3.
STEP 5. The separating surface is given as formula (4), where $(\bar{v}^*, \gamma^*) \in R^{\bar{m}+1}$ is the unique solution of problem (1) that got from step 4.
STEP 6. A new unseen data point $x \in R^n$ is classified as class +1 if $\bar{v}^{*\prime} K_\sigma(\bar{A}, x) - \gamma^* \geq 0$, otherwise x is classified as class -1.

The conventional SVMs as well as RSVM determine parameter used in kernel function via a tuning procedure [2]. While, in our approach the kernel parameter is determined automatically and individually for each point in the reduced set. This can be achieved by estimating the approximate density of each resulting cluster [9]. The numerical results are showed in Section 4.

4 Numerical Results

We normalized the dataset such that each attribute has 0-mean and 1-deviation, so that we can assume that each attribute has the similar contribution to the Gaussian kernel. In our experiment, the normalization procedure is very crucial.

The numerical results on four benchmark datasets and a real one are shown in Table 1. SSVM stands nonlinear smooth support vector machine with full Gaussian kernel. RSVM1 and RSVM2 stand for RSVM [4] with different size of reduced set. CRSVM used the same size of reduced set with RSVM1 which is smaller than the one used in RSVM2. We note that CRSVM only used a smaller reduced set than random selection scheme with compatible classification performance.

5 Conclusion

In this paper we propose a robust method to build the model of RSVM via RBF (Gaussian) kernel construction. Applying clustering algorithm to each class, we can generate cluster centroids of each class and use them to form the reduced set which is used in RSVM. We also estimate the approximate density for each cluster to get the kernel parameter that is used in Gaussian kernel. Under the compatible classification performance on the test set, our method selects a smaller reduced set than the one via random selection scheme. Moreover, it determines the kernel parameter automatically and individually for each point in the reduced

Table 1. Results of benchmarks (Test set correctness of ten-fold cross validation).

Classifier Dataset	CRSVM correctness(%) $\bar{m}$, time(sec.)	RSVM1 correctness(%) $\bar{m}$, time(sec.)	RSVM2 correctness(%) $\bar{m}$, time(sec.)	SSVM correctness(%) m, time(sec.)
Ionosphere 351 × 34	95.7 14, 2.98	94.4 14, 2.52	95.19 35, 3.64	94.35 351, 40.16
BUPA 345 × 6	73.4 14, 2.51	70.4 14, 1.31	74.86 35, 4.31	73.62 345, 34.25
Pima 768 × 8	77.6 30, 12.3	77.8 30, 6.31	78.64 50, 7.47	76.59 768, 234.8
Cleveland 297 × 13	85.7 12, 1.93	84.1 12, 1.01	86.47 30, 3.47	85.92 297, 27.14
Face Detection 6977 × 361	98.2 16, 280.97	95.2 16, 125.3	96.7 24, 205.4	96.7 6977, out of memory

set while the RSVM used a common kernel parameter which is determined by a tuning procedure.

References

1. C. J. C. Burges. A tutorial on support vector machines for pattern recognition. *Data Mining and Knowledge Discovery*, 2(2):121–167, 1998.
2. O. Chapelle, V. Vapnik, O. Bousquet, and S. Mukherjee. Choosing multiple parameters for support vector machines. *Machine Learning*, 46(1):131–159, 2002.
3. N. Cristianini and J. Shawe-Taylor. *An Introduction to Support Vector Machines*. Cambridge University Press, Cambridge, 2000.
4. Y.-J. Lee and O. L. Mangasarian. RSVM: Reduced support vector machines. Technical Report 00-07, Data Mining Institute, Computer Sciences Department, University of Wisconsin, Madison, Wisconsin, July 2000. Proceedings of the First SIAM International Conference on Data Mining, Chicago, April 5-7, 2001, CD-ROM Proceedings. ftp://ftp.cs.wisc.edu/pub/dmi/tech-reports/00-07.ps.
5. Yuh-Jye Lee and O. L. Mangasarian. SSVM: A smooth support vector machine. *Computational Optimization and Applications*, 20:5–22, 2001. Data Mining Institute, University of Wisconsin, Technical Report 99-03. ftp://ftp.cs.wisc.edu/pub/dmi/tech-reports/99-03.ps.
6. Abdelouahid Lyhyaoui, Manel Martinez, Inma Mora, Maryan Vazquez, Jose-Luis Sancho, and Anibal R. Figueiras-Vidal. Sample selection via clustering to construct support vector-like classifier. *IEEE Transactions on Neural Networks*, 10:1474–1481, 1999.
7. O. L. Mangasarian. Generalized support vector machines. In A. Smola, P. Bartlett, B. Schölkopf, and D. Schuurmans, editors, *Advances in Large Margin Classifiers*, pages 135–146, Cambridge, MA, 2000. MIT Press. ftp://ftp.cs.wisc.edu/math-prog/tech-reports/98-14.ps.
8. P. M. Murphy and D. W. Aha. UCI machine learning repository, 1992. www.ics.uci.edu/~mlearn/MLRepository.html.
9. Yen-Jen Oyang, Shien-Ching Hwang, Yu-Yen Ou, Chien-Yu Chen, and Zhi-Wei Chen. An novel learning algorithm for data classification with radial basis function networks. In *Proceeding of 9th International Conference on Neural Information Processing*, pages 18–22, Singapore, Nov. 2001.
10. V. N. Vapnik. *The Nature of Statistical Learning Theory*. Springer, New York, 1995.

Generating the Reduced Set by Systematic Sampling

Chien-Chung Chang and Yuh-Jye Lee

Department of Computer Science and Information Engineering
National Taiwan University of Science and Technology
Taipei, 106 Taiwan
{D9115009,yuh-jye}@mail.ntust.edu.tw

Abstract. The computational difficulties occurred when we use a conventional support vector machine with nonlinear kernels to deal with massive datasets. The reduced support vector machine (RSVM) replaces the fully dense square kernel matrix with a small rectangular kernel matrix which is used in the nonlinear SVM formulation to avoid the computational difficulties. In this paper, we propose a new algorithm, Systematic Sampling RSVM (SSRSVM) that selects the informative data points to form the reduced set while the RSVM used random selection scheme. This algorithm is inspired by the key idea of SVM, the SVM classifier can be represented by support vectors and the misclassified points are a part of support vectors. SSRSVM starts with an extremely small initial reduced set and adds a portion of misclassified points into the reduced set iteratively based on the current classifier until the validation set correctness is large enough. In our experiments, we tested SSRSVM on six public available datasets. It turns out that SSRSVM might automatically generate a smaller size of reduced set than the one by random sampling. Moreover, SSRSVM is faster than RSVM and much faster than conventional SVM under the same level of the test set correctness.

Keywords: Support vector machine, reduced support vector machine, reduced set, kernel function, systematic sampling.

1 Introduction

For the binary classification problems, SVMs are able to construct nonlinear separating surface (if it is necessary) which is implicitly defined by a kernel function [1, 9]. Nevertheless, there are some major computational difficulties such as large memory usage and long CPU time in generating a nonlinear SVM classifier for a massive dataset. To overcome these difficulties, the reduced support vector machine (RSVM) [5] was proposed. The RSVM replaces the fully dense square kernel matrix with a small rectangular kernel matrix which is used in the nonlinear SVM formulation to avoid the computational difficulties. This reduced kernel technique has been successfully applied to other kernel-based learning algorithms [3, 4].

In this paper, we use a systematic sampling mechanism to select a reduced set which is the most important ingredient of RSVM and name it as Systematic

Sampling RSVM (SSRSVM). This algorithm is inspired by the key idea of SVM that the SVM classifier can be represented by support vectors and the misclassified points are a part of support vectors. The SSRSVM randomly selects an extremely small subset as an initial reduced set. Then, a portion of misclassified points are added into the reduced set iteratively based on the current classifier until the validation set correctness is large enough. We tested SSRSVM on six public available datasets [2, 8]. The SSRSVM can generate a smaller reduced set than RSVM without scarifying the test set correctness.

A word about our notations is given below. All vectors will be column vectors unless otherwise specified or transposed to a row vector by a prime superscript '. For a vector $x \in R^n$, the plus function x_+ is defined as $(x)_+ = \max\{0, x\}$. The inner product of two vectors $x, z \in R^n$ will be denoted by $x'z$ and the p-norm of x will be denoted by $\|x\|_p$. For a matrix $A \in R^{m \times n}$, A_i is the ith row of A which is *a row vector* in R^n. A column vector of ones of arbitrary dimension will be denoted by e. For $A \in R^{m \times n}$ and $B \in R^{n \times l}$, the kernel $K(A, B)$ maps $R^{m \times n} \times R^{n \times l}$ into $R^{m \times l}$. In particular, $K(x', z)$ is a real number, $K(x', A')$ is a *row* vector in R^m, $K(A, x)$ is a *column* vector in R^m and $K(A, A')$ is an $m \times m$ matrix. The base of the natural logarithm will be denoted by ε.

This paper is organized as follows. Section 2 gives a brief overview of the reduced support vector machines and discusses some related work. In section 3, we describe how to select the reduced set systematically from the entire dataset. The experimental results are given in section 4 to show the performance of our method. Section 5 concludes the paper.

2 An Overview of the Reduced Support Vector Machines

We now briefly describe the RSVM formulation, which is derived from the generalized support vector machine (GSVM) [7] and the smooth support vector machine (SSVM) [6]. We are given a training data set $\{(x^i, y_i)\}_{i=1}^m$, where $x^i \in R^n$ is an input data point and $y_i \in \{-1, 1\}$ is class label, indicating one of two classes, A_- and A_+, to which the input point belongs. We represent these data points by an $m \times n$ matrix A, where the ith row of the matrix A, A_i, corresponds to the ith data point. We denote alternately A_i (a row vector) and x^i (a column vector) for the same ith data point. We use an $m \times m$ diagonal matrix D, $D_{ii} = y_i$ to specify the membership of each input point. The main goal of the classification problem is to find a classifier that can predict the label of new unseen data points correctly. This can be achieved by constructing a linear or nonlinear separating surface, $f(x) = 0$, which is implicitly defined by a kernel function. We classify a test point x belong to A_+ if $f(x) \geq 0$, otherwise x belong to A_-. We will focus on the nonlinear case which is implicitly defined by a Gaussian kernel function. The RSVM solves the following unconstrained minimization problem

$$\min_{(\bar{v}, \gamma) \in R^{\bar{m}+1}} \frac{\nu}{2} \|p(e - D(K(A, \bar{A}')\bar{v} - e\gamma), \alpha)\|_2^2 + \frac{1}{2}(\bar{v}'\bar{v} + \gamma^2), \qquad (1)$$

where the function $p(x, \alpha)$ is a very accurate smooth approximation to $(x)_+$ [6], which is applied to each component of the vector $e - D(K(A, \bar{A}')\bar{D}\bar{v} - e\gamma)$ and is defined componentwise by

$$p(x, \alpha) = x + \frac{1}{\alpha} \log(1 + \varepsilon^{-\alpha x}), \alpha > 0. \tag{2}$$

The function $p(x, \alpha)$ converges to $(x)_+$ as α goes to infinity. The reduced kernel matrix $K(A, \bar{A}) \in R^{m \times \bar{m}}$ in (1) is defined by

$$K(A, \bar{A}')_{ij} = \varepsilon^{-\mu \|A_i - \bar{A}_j\|_2^2}, \; 1 \leq i \leq m, \; 1 \leq j \leq \bar{m}, \tag{3}$$

where $\bar{A}$ is the reduced set that is randomly selected from A in RSVM [5]. The positive tuning parameter ν here controls the tradeoff between the classification error and the suppression of $(\bar{v}, \gamma)$. Since RSVM has reduced the model complexity via using a much smaller rectangular kernel matrix we will suggest using a larger tuning parameter ν here. A solution of this minimization problem (1) for $\bar{v}$ and γ leads to the nonlinear separating surface

$$f(x) = \bar{v}' K(\bar{A}, x) - \gamma = \sum_{i=1}^{\bar{m}} \bar{v}_i K(\bar{A}_i, x) - \gamma = 0. \tag{4}$$

The minimization problem (1) can be solved via the Newton-Armijo method [6] directly and the existence and uniqueness of the optimal solution of this problem are also guaranteed. We note that the computational complexity of solving problem (1) is depended on the size of the reduced set which is user prespecified in RSVM [5]. Moreover, the value of $K(A, \bar{A}')_{ij}$ in (3) can be interpreted as the *similarity* between examples A_i and $\bar{A}_j$. Hence the rectangular kernel matrix which is generated by a reduced set records the *similarity* between the entire training set and the reduced set. It seems indicate that if we had a more *representative* reduced set we should have a better classifier. In the next section, we describe how to generate a representative reduced set and apply it to RSVM.

3 Systematic Sampling for RSVM

We now propose a new algorithm to generate the reduced set which is consisting of the *informative* data points. This algorithm is inspired by the key idea of SVM, the SVM classifier can be represented by support vectors and the misclassified points are a part of support vectors. Instead of random sampling the reduced set in RSVM, we start with an extremely small initial reduced set and add a portion of misclassified points into the reduced set iteratively based on the current classifier. We note that there are two types of misclassified points and we select them respectively. We showed this idea in Fig. 1. The new reduced kernel matrix can be updated from the previous iteration. We only need to augment the columns which are generated by the new points in the reduced set. We stop this procedure until the validation set correctness is large enough.

Algorithm 3.1 Systematic Sampling RSVM Algorithm

(1) Randomly select an extremely small portion data points, such as $\bar{m} = 5$, from the entire training data matrix $A \in R^{m \times n}$ as an initial reduced set which is represented by $\bar{A}_0 \in R^{\bar{m} \times n}$.

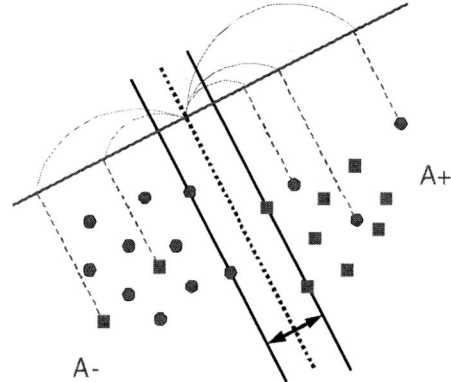

Fig. 1. The main idea of Systematic Sampling RSVM Algorithm

(2) Generate the reduced kernel matrix $K(A, \bar{A}'_0)$ and perform RSVM algorithm [5] to generate a tentative separating surface represented by $f(x) = 0$.

(3) Use the separating surface to classify the point which is in the training set but not in the current reduced set. Let $\bar{I}_+$ be the index set of misclassified points of positive example. That is, $\bar{I}_+ = \{i | f(A_i) \leq 0, A_i \in A_+\}$. Similarly, $\bar{I}_- = \{i | f(A_i) > 0, A_i \in A_-\}$.

(4) Sort the set $\bar{I}_+$ by the absolute value of $f(A_{\bar{I}_+})$ and the set $\bar{I}_-$ by $f(A_{\bar{I}_-})$ respectively. We named the resulting sorted sets $\bar{S}_+$ and $\bar{S}_-$.

(5) Partition $\bar{S}_+$ and $\bar{S}_-$ into several subsets respectively such that each subset has nearly equal number of elements. That is, let $\phi \neq \bar{sp}_i \subset \bar{S}_+, \forall i, 1 \leq i \leq k$ where k is the number of subsets. $\bar{S}_+ = \bar{sp}_1 \cup \bar{sp}_2 \cup \ldots \cup \bar{sp}_k$ and $\bar{sp}_i \cap \bar{sp}_j = \phi, \forall i \neq j, 1 \leq i, j \leq k$. Similarly, $\bar{S}_- = \bar{sn}_1 \cup \bar{sn}_2 \cup \ldots \cup \bar{sn}_k$ and $\bar{sn}_i \cap \bar{sn}_j = \phi, \forall i \neq j, 1 \leq i, j \leq k$. Then, choose one point from each subset and add these points into $\bar{A}_0$ to generate a new reduced set in place of $\bar{A}_0$.

(6) Repeat *Step* (2) $\sim$ (5) until the validation set correctness has arrived at the threshold which is user pre-specified.

(7) Output the final classifier, $f(x) = 0$.

We showed the numerical results to demonstrate the efficiency of our algorithm in the next section.

4 Experimental Results

All our experiments were performed on a personal computer, which utilizes a 1.47 GHz AMD Athlon(tm)XP 1700 PLUS processor and 256 megabytes of RAM. This computer runs on Windows XP operating system, with MATLAB 6 installed. We implemented the SSRSVM algorithm using standard native MATLAB codes. We used the Gaussian kernel in all our experiments. We test SSRSVM on six public available datasets which five from UC Irvine repository

Table 1. Tenfold cross-validation correctness results on six public datasets illustrate that the SSRSVM not only keep as good test set correctness as SSVM, RSVM and LIBSVM but less size of reduced set than RSVM. The bold type showed, when processing massive datasets, SSRSVM is faster than the other three methods. The computer ran out of memory while generating the full nonlinear kernel for the Mushroom and Face datasets. $\bar{m}$ denotes the average size of reduced set by running the SSRSVM algorithm. N/A denotes "not available" results because the kernel $K(A, A')$ was too large to store

Dataset Size	Tenfold Test Set Correctness % Tenfold Computational Time, *Seconds*							
	Methods							
	SSRSVM			RSVM			SSVM	LIBSVM
$m \times n$	Correctness Time *sec.*		$\bar{m}$	Correctness Time *sec.*		$\bar{m}$	Correctness Time *sec.*	Correctness Time *sec.*
Ionosphere 351 × 34	97.43 0.5620		20	96.87 0.6410		35	96.61 14.2190	95.16 0.1720
Cleveland Heart 297 × 13	86.20 0.5620		20.6	85.94 0.3750		30	86.61 7.2500	85.86 3.5460
BUPA Liver 345 × 6	74.80 0.4680		17.8	74.87 0.5000		35	74.47 10.1560	73.64 0.4620
Pima Indians 768 × 8	78.00 **0.9690**		17.4	77.86 1.5160		50	77.34 68.1560	75.52 26.8440
Mushroom 8124 × 22	89.23 **74.6870**		79	89.39 171.2500		215	N/A N/A	89.19 171.4840
Face 6977 × 361	98.51 **73.8120**		42.2	98.39 115.2660		70	N/A N/A	98.15 318.9400

[8] and one from MIT CBCL [2]. In order to give a more objective comparison, we run tenfold cross-validation on each dataset. All parameters in our experiments were chosen for optimal performance on a tuning set, a surrogate for a test set.

The experimental results demonstrated that SSRSVM not only keeps as good test set correctness as SSVM, RSVM and LIBSVM but has less size of reduced set than RSVM. In addition, the results showed, when processing massive datasets, SSRSVM is faster than the other three methods. Table 1 summarizes the numerical results and comparisons of our experiments. It shows a comparison on the testing correctness and time cost among SSRSVM, RSVM, SSVM and LIBSVM algorithms. Observing this table, to run SSRSVM algorithm, the testing correctness is as good as RSVM.

5 Conclusions

In this paper, we propose a Systematic Sampling RSVM (SSRSVM) algorithm that selects the informative data points to form the reduced set while the RSVM used random selection scheme. This algorithm is inspired by the key idea of SVM, the SVM classifier can be represented by support vectors and the misclassified points are a part of support vectors. SSRSVM starts with an extremely small initial reduced set and adds a portion of misclassified points into the reduced set iteratively based on the current classifier until the validation set correctness is large enough. In our experiments, we tested SSRSVM on six public available datasets. It turns out that SSRSVM might automatically generate a smaller size of reduced set than the one by random sampling. Moreover, SSRSVM is faster than RSVM and much faster than conventional SVM under the same level of the test set correctness.

References

1. C. J. C. Burges. A tutorial on support vector machines for pattern recognition. *Data Mining and Knowledge Discovery*, 2(2):121–167, 1998.
2. MIT Center for Biological and Computation Learning. Cbcl face database (1), 2000. http://www.ai.mit.edu/projects/cbcl.
3. G. Fung and O. L. Mangasarian. Proximal support vector machine classifiers. In F. Provost and R. Srikant, editors, *Proceedings KDD-2001: Knowledge Discovery and Data Mining, August 26-29, 2001, San Francisco, CA*, pages 77–86, New York, 2001. Asscociation for Computing Machinery. ftp://ftp.cs.wisc.edu/pub/dmi/tech-reports/01-02.ps.
4. Yuh-Jye Lee and Wen-Feng Hsieh. ϵ-ssvr: A smooth support vector machine for ϵ-insensitive regression. *IEEE Transactions on Knowledge and Data Engineering*, submitted 2003.
5. Yuh-Jye Lee and O. L. Mangasarian. RSVM: Reduced support vector machines. Technical Report 00-07, Data Mining Institute, Computer Sciences Department, University of Wisconsin, Madison, Wisconsin, July 2000. Proceedings of the First SIAM International Conference on Data Mining, Chicago, April 5-7, 2001, CD-ROM Proceedings. ftp://ftp.cs.wisc.edu/pub/dmi/tech-reports/00-07.ps.
6. Yuh-Jye Lee and O. L. Mangasarian. SSVM: A smooth support vector machine. *Computational Optimization and Applications*, 20:5–22, 2001. Data Mining Institute, University of Wisconsin, Technical Report 99-03. ftp://ftp.cs.wisc.edu/pub/dmi/tech-reports/99-03.ps.
7. O. L. Mangasarian. Generalized support vector machines. In A. Smola, P. Bartlett, B. Schölkopf, and D. Schuurmans, editors, *Advances in Large Margin Classifiers*, pages 135–146, Cambridge, MA, 2000. MIT Press. ftp://ftp.cs.wisc.edu/math-prog/tech-reports/98-14.ps.
8. P. M. Murphy and D. W. Aha. UCI machine learning repository, 1992. www.ics.uci.edu/~mlearn/MLRepository.html.
9. V. N. Vapnik. *The Nature of Statistical Learning Theory*. Springer, New York, 1995.

Experimental Comparison of Classification Uncertainty for Randomised and Bayesian Decision Tree Ensembles

Vitaly Schetinin, Derek Partridge, Wojtek J. Krzanowski, Richard M. Everson, Jonathan E. Fieldsend, Trevor C. Bailey, and Adolfo Hernandez

School of Engineering, Computer Science and Mathematics, University of Exeter, UK
{V.Schetinin,D.Partridge,W.J.Krzanowski,R.M.Everson,
J.E.Fieldsend,T.C.Bailey,A.Hernandez}@exeter.ac.uk

Abstract. In this paper we experimentally compare the classification uncertainty of the randomised Decision Tree (DT) ensemble technique and the Bayesian DT technique with a restarting strategy on a synthetic dataset as well as on some datasets commonly used in the machine learning community. For quantitative evaluation of classification uncertainty, we use an Uncertainty Envelope dealing with the class posterior distribution and a given confidence probability. Counting the classifier outcomes, this technique produces feasible evaluations of the classification uncertainty. Using this technique in our experiments, we found that the Bayesian DT technique is superior to the randomised DT ensemble technique.

1 Introduction

The uncertainty of classifiers used for safety-critical applications is of crucial importance. In general, uncertainty is a triple trade-off between the amount of data available for training, the classifier diversity and the classification accuracy [1 - 4]. The interpretability of classifiers can also produce useful information for experts responsible for making reliable classification, making Decisions Trees (DTs) an attractive scheme. The required diversity of classifiers can be achieved on the basis of two approaches: a DT ensemble technique [2] and an averaging technique based on Bayesian Markov Chain Monte Carlo (MCMC) methodology [3, 4]. Both DT techniques match the above requirements well and have revealed promising results when applied to some real-world problems [2 - 4].

By definition, DTs consist of splitting nodes and terminal nodes, which are also known as tree leaves. DTs are said to be binary if the splitting nodes ask a specific question and then divide the data points into two disjoint subsets called the left and the right branch. The terminal node assigns all data points falling in that node to the class whose points are prevalent. Within a Bayesian framework, the class posterior distribution having observed some data is calculated for each terminal node [3, 4].

The Bayesian generalization of tree models required to evaluate the posterior distribution of the trees has been given by Chipman *et al.* [3]. Denison *et al.* [4] have suggested MCMC techniques for evaluating the posterior distribution of decision trees. This technique performs a stochastic sampling of the posterior distribution.

In this paper we experimentally compare the classification uncertainty of the randomised DT ensemble technique and the Bayesian DT technique with a restarting strategy on a synthetic dataset and some domain problems from UCI Machine Learning Repository [5]. To provide quantitative evaluations of classification uncertainty, we use an Uncertainty Envelope dealing with the class posterior distribution and a given confidence probability [6]. Counting the classifier outcomes, this technique produces the feasible evaluations of the classification uncertainty.

Below in sections 2 and 3 we briefly describe the randomised and Bayesian DT techniques which are used in our experiments. Then in section 4 we briefly describe the Uncertainty Envelope technique used to quantitatively evaluate the uncertainty of the two classification techniques. The experimental results are presented in section 5, and section 6 concludes the paper.

2 The Randomised Decision Tree Ensemble Technique

Performance of a single DT can be improved by averaging the outputs of DTs involved in an ensemble [2]. The improvement is achieved if most of the DTs can correctly classify the data points misclassified by a single DT. Clearly, the required diversity of the classifier outcomes can be achieved if the DTs involved in an ensemble are independently induced from data. To achieve the required independence, Dietterich has suggested randomising the DT splits [2]. In this technique the best, in terms of information gain, 20 partitions for any node are calculated and one of these is randomly selected with uniform probability. The class posterior probabilities are calculated for all the DTs involved in an ensemble and then averaged.

A pruning factor, specified as the fewest number of data points falling in the terminal nodes, can affect the ensemble performance. However, within the randomised DT technique, this effect is insignificant when pruning does not exceed 10% of the number of the training examples [2]. More strongly the pruning factor affects the average size of the DTs, and consequently it has to be set reasonably.

The number of the randomised DTs in the ensemble is dependent on the classification problem and assigned by a user in an *ad hoc* manner. This technique permits the user to evaluate the diversity of the ensemble by comparing the performances of the ensemble and that of the best DT on a predefined validation data subset. The required diversity is achieved if the DT ensemble outperforms the best single DTs involved in the ensemble. Therefore this ensemble technique requires the use of n-fold cross-validation. In our experiments described in section 5 we used the above randomised DT ensemble technique. For all the domain problems the ensembles consist of 200 DTs. To keep the size of the DT acceptable, the pruning factor is set to be dependent on the number of the training examples. In particular, its value is set to 30 for problems with many training examples; otherwise it is 5. The performance of the randomised DT ensembles is evaluated on 5 folds for each problem.

3 The Bayesian Decision Tree Technique

In general, the predictive distribution we are interested in is written as the integral over parameters θ of the classification model

$$p(y\,|\,\mathbf{x},\mathbf{D}) = \int p(y\,|\,\mathbf{x},\theta,\mathbf{D})p(\theta\,|\,\mathbf{D})d\theta, \tag{1}$$

where y is the predicted class (1, ..., C), $\mathbf{x} = (x_1, ..., x_m)$ is the m-dimensional input vector, and $\mathbf{D}$ is the data.

The integral (1) can be analytically calculated only in simple cases. Moreover, part of the integrand in (1), the posterior density of θ conditioned on the data $\mathbf{D}$, $p(\theta\,|\,\mathbf{D})$, cannot be evaluated except in very simple cases. However, if we can draw values $\theta^{(1)},...,\theta^{(N)}$ from the posterior distribution of $p(\theta\,|\,\mathbf{D})$, then we can write

$$p(y\,|\,\mathbf{x},\mathbf{D}) \approx \sum_{i=1}^{N} p(y\,|\,\mathbf{x},\theta^{(i)},\mathbf{D})p(\theta^{(i)}\,|\,\mathbf{D}) = \frac{1}{N}\sum_{i=1}^{N} p(y\,|\,\mathbf{x},\theta^{(i)},\mathbf{D}). \tag{2}$$

This is the basis of the MCMC technique for approximating integrals [3, 4]. To perform the approximation, we need to generate random samples from $p(\theta\,|\,\mathbf{D})$ by running a Markov Chain until it has converged to the stationary distribution. After this we can draw samples from the Markov Chain and calculate the predictive posterior density (2). For integration over models in which the dimension of θ varies, MCMC methods permit Reversible Jumps as described in [4].

Because DTs are hierarchical structures, changes at the nodes located at the upper levels (close to their roots) can cause drastic changes to the location of data points at the lower levels. For this reason there is a very small probability of changing and then accepting a DT located near a root node. Therefore RJMCMC algorithms tend to explore the DTs in which only the splitting nodes located far from the root node are changed. These nodes typically contain small numbers of data points. Consequently, the value of the likelihood is not changed much, and such moves are always accepted. As a result, RJMCMC algorithms cannot explore a full posterior distribution.

The space which is explored can be extended by using a *restarting strategy* as Chipman *et al.* have suggested in [3]. The idea behind the restarting strategy is based on multiple runs of the RJMCMC algorithm with short intervals of burn-in and post burn-in. For each run, the algorithm creates an initial DT with the random parameters and then starts exploring the tree model space. Running short intervals prevents the DTs from getting stuck at a particular DT structure. More important, however, is that the multiple runs allow the exploring of the DT model space starting with very different DTs. So, averaging the DTs over all such run can improve the performance of the RJMCMC algorithm. The disadvantage, of course, is that the multiple short chains with short burn-in runs, will seldom reach a stationary distribution. The restarting strategy, as we see, does not limit the DT sizes explicitly, as would be done by a restricting strategy [4]. For this reason the restarting strategy seems to be the more practical. In section 4 we use this strategy in our comparative experiments. The quantitative comparison of the classification uncertainty is done within the Uncertainty Envelope technique described next.

4 The Uncertainty Envelope Technique

Let us consider a simple example of a classifier system consisting of $N = 1000$ classifiers in which 2 classifiers give a conflicting classification. Then for a given datum x the posterior probability $P_i = 1 - 2/1000 = 0.998$. In this case we can conclude that the multiple classifier system was trained well and/or the datum x lies far from the class boundaries. For this datum, and for each new data point appearing in some neighbourhood of the datum x, the classification uncertainty as the probability of misclassification is expected to be $1 - P_i = 0.002$. For other data points, the values of P differ and range between P_{min} and 1. It is easy to see that $P_{min} = 1/C$.

When the value of P_i is close to P_{min}, the classification uncertainty is highest and a datum x can be misclassified with a probability $1 - P_i = 1 - 1/C$. So we can assume some value of probability P_0 for which the classifier outcome is expected to be confident, that is the probability with which a given datum x could be misclassified is small enough to be acceptable. Given such a value of P_0, we can now specify the confidence or, *vice versa*, the uncertainty of classifier outcomes in statistical terms. The classification outcome is said to be *confidently correct*, when the probability of misclassification is acceptably small and $P_i \geq P_0$.

Additionally to the confidently correct output, we can specify a *confidently incorrect* output referring to a case when almost all the classifiers assign a datum x to a wrong class j, i.e., $P_j \geq P_0$. By definition this evaluation tells us that most of the classifiers fail in the same manner to classify a datum x. This can happen for different reasons, for example, the datum x could be mislabelled or corrupted, or the classifiers within a predefined scheme cannot properly distinguish such data points.

The remaining cases, for which $P_i < P_0$, are regarded as *uncertain classifications*. In such cases the classifier outcomes cannot be accepted with a given confidence probability P_0. The multiple classifier system labels such outcomes as uncertain.

The above three characteristics, confidently correct, confidently incorrect, and uncertain outcomes, seem to provide a good way of evaluating different types of multiple classifier systems on the same data. Comparing the values of these characteristics, we can quantitatively evaluate the classification uncertainty of these systems. Depending on the costs of types of misclassifications in real applications, we have to specify the value of the confidence probability P_0, say $P_0 = 0.99$.

5 Experiments and Results

First we conduct experiments on synthetic dataset and then on 7 domain problems taken from the UCI Repository. A two dimensional synthetic dataset was generated as a mixture of five Gaussians. The data points drawn from the first three Gaussians belong to class 1 and the data points from the remaining two Gaussians to class 2.

The mixing weights ρ_{ij} and kernel centres μ_{ij} of these Gaussians for class 1 are $\rho_{11} = 0.16$, $\mu_{11} = (1.0, 1.0)$, $\rho_{12} = 0.17$, $\mu_{12} = (0.7, 0.3)$, $\rho_{13} = 0.17$, $\mu_{13} = (0.3, 0.3)$ and for class 2 they are $\rho_{21} = 0.25$, $\mu_{21} = (-0.3, 0.7)$, $\rho_{22} = 0.25$, $\mu_{22} = (0.4, 0.7)$. The kernels all have isotropic covariance: $\Sigma_i = 0.03\mathbf{I}$. This mixture is an extended version of the Ripley data [7]. Because the classes overlap, the Bayes error on these data is 9.3%. 250 data points drawn from the above mixture form the training dataset. Another 1000 data points drawn from the mixture form the testing data.

Both the randomised DT ensemble and the Bayesian techniques were run on the above synthetic data. The pruning factor was set equal to 5. On the synthetic data, the ensemble output quickly converges and stabilizes after averaging 100 DTs. The mean size of DTs and the standard deviation over all 5 folds were 32.9 and 3.3, respectively. The averaged classification performance was 87.12%. Within the Uncertainty Envelope, the rates of confidently correct, uncertain, and confidently incorrect outcomes were 78.9%, 9.8%, and 11.3%, respectively. The widths of 2σ intervals for these outcomes were 34.9%, 43.7%, and 8.9%, respectively. We can see that the values of the intervals calculated for the confidently correct and the uncertain outcomes are very large. This happens because the randomised DT ensemble technique produces mostly uncertain outcomes on some of the 5 folds.

Using the restarting strategy, the Bayesian DTs were run 50 times; each time 2000 samples were taken for burn-in and 2000 for post burn-in. The probabilities of birth, death, change variable, and change rule were 0.1, 0.1, 0.1, and 0.7, respectively. Uniform priors on the number of inputs and nodes were used [4]. The resultant average classification performance was 87.20%, and the mean size and the standard deviation of the DTs were 12.4 and 2.5, respectively. The rates of confidently correct, uncertain and confidently incorrect outcomes were 63.30%, 34.40% and 2.30%, respectively. So we can see, first, that on the synthetic data the Bayesian DTs are much shorter than those of the randomised ensemble. Second, the randomised DT ensemble technique cannot provide reliable classifier outcomes. Of course, the 5 fold data partition used in the randomised DT technique makes an additional contribution to the classification uncertainty. However, practically this effect disappears for domain problems including more than 300 data points.

Table 1 lists the characteristics of the 7 domain problems used in our experiments; here *C*, *m*, *train*, and *test* are the numbers of classes, input variables, training and testing examples, respectively. This table also provides the performances of the Bayesian DT technique on these data.

Table 1. Performances of the Bayesian DTs with restarting strategy.

Data	Data characteristics				DT size	Perform, %	Uncertainty Envelope, %		
	C	m	train	test			Correct	Uncertain	Incorrect
Ionosphere	2	33	200	151	11.99±2.2	**95.35**	11.92	88.08	**0.00**
Winconsin	2	9	455	228	11.81±2.4	**99.12**	82.89	17.11	**0.00**
Image	7	19	210	2100	15.71±2.3	94.29	22.38	77.62	**0.00**
Votes	2	16	391	44	10.25±2.5	**95.45**	56.82	43.18	**0.00**
Sonar	2	60	138	70	9.94±1.8	**81.43**	0.00	100.00	**0.00**
Vehicle	4	18	564	282	47.78±4.6	69.86	3.90	96.10	**0.00**
Pima	2	8	512	256	11.99±22	79.69	34.77	60.55	**4.69**

The performances of the randomised technique are shown in Table 2. This table shows also the classification performance of the best single DTs selected on the validation subsets averaged over all the 5 folds. From Table 2, we can see that the randomised DT ensemble technique always outperforms the best single DTs.

Comparing the randomised and Bayesian DT ensembles, we can conclude that on all the datasets the Bayesian DTs are shorter by 2 to 3 times those of the randomised ensembles. Both ensembles have the same performance on the Image, Votes, Vehicle, and Pima datasets. However, on the remaining datasets, the Bayesian technique slightly outperforms the randomised ensemble technique.

It is interesting to note the Bayesian ensemble method always makes a smaller proportion of confidently correct classifications (although, variances from the randomised ensemble are very high). Likewise, the proportion of confidently incorrect classifications is always higher for the randomised ensemble. Indeed, on the synthetic data, the randomised ensemble classifiers on average make more confidently incorrect classifications (11.3%) than the Bayes error rate (9.3%), whereas the Bayesian ensemble makes only 2.3% confidently incorrect classifications.

In fact, as Table 1 shows, the Bayesian DTs seldom make confident, but incorrect classifications, though they make more uncertain classifications. Although it may be unrealistic to expect the confidently incorrect rate to approach the Bayes error rate with small datasets, these results suggest that the randomised ensemble tends to produce over-confident ensembles, while the Bayesian ensembles make few confident but incorrect classifications.

On the other hand, as exemplified by the Ionosphere and Sonar datasets, the Bayesian ensemble may yield accurate classifications, but the majority of them may be uncertain. The Sonar and Ionosphere data have 60 and 33 features respectively and relatively few data points, so it is unsurprising that the sparsity of data points in these high-dimensional datasets leads to uncertain classifications.

Table 2. Performances of the randomised DT ensembles.

Data	Single DT perform, %	DT size	Perform, %	Uncertainty Envelope, %		
				Correct	Uncertain	Incorrect
Ionosphere	88.8±8.0	21.2±1.3	94.4±0.7	**76.5±35.8**	7.0±44.4	16.5±18.4
Winconsin	96.1±1.7	32.7±1.5	97.7±1.2	96.7±7.90	1.4±9.2	1.9±1.8
Image	87.4±4.4	27.9±1.3	94.2±0.9	86.1±33.0	6.5±37.9	7.4±7.9
Votes	93.9±3.1	27.1±3.6	95.2±1.4	94.3±5.80	1.1±7.2	4.5±2.1
Sonar	70.7±7.8	17.8±0.8	78.3±5.5	**54.9±40.6**	9.6±60.5	35.6±31.8
Vehicle	69.0±4.5	115.8±3.2	71.9±2.2	**63.8±31.0**	8.8±50.2	27.4±20.1
Pima	77.3±1.2	33.6±4.0	80.2±2.4	66.7±47.0	14.6±65.3	18.7±19.6

6 Conclusion

We have experimentally compared the classification uncertainty of the randomised DT ensemble technique with the ensembles sampled from the Bayesian posterior using RJMCMC with a restarting strategy. The ensemble techniques both outperform the best single DT, having similar average classification rates. Far fewer confidently incorrect classifications are made by the Bayesian ensemble. This is clearly a very desirable property for classifiers in safety-critical applications in which confidently made, but incorrect, classifications may be fatal.

Acknowledgments

This research was supported by the EPSRC, grant GR/R24357/01.

References

1. Brieman L., Friedman J., Olshen R., Stone C.: Classification and Regression Trees. Belmont, CA: Wadsworth (1984)
2. Dietterich T.: Ensemble Methods in Machine Learning. In Kittler J., Roli, F. (eds), First International Workshop on Multiple Classifier Systems, Lecture Notes in Computer Science New York: Springer Verlag (2000) 1-15
3. Chipman H., George E., McCullock R.: Bayesian CART model search. J. American Statistics 93 (1998) 935-960
4. Denison D., Holmes C., Malick B., Smith A.: Bayesian Methods for Nonlinear Classification and Regression. Willey (2002)
5. Blake C.L., Merz C.J.: UCI Repository of machine learning databases http://www.ics.uci.edu/~mlearn/MLRepository.html. Irvine, CA: University of California, Department of Information and Computer Science (1998)
6. Fieldsend J., Bailey T.C., Everson R.M., Krzanowski W.J., Partridge D., Schetinin V.: Bayesian Inductively Learned Modules for Safety Critical Systems. Computing Science and Statistics, 35th Symposium on the Interface, Salt Lake City (2003)
7. Ripley B.: Neural networks and related methods for classification. J. Royal Statistical Society B 56:3 (1994) 409-456

Policy Gradient Method for Team Markov Games

Ville Könönen

Neural Networks Research Centre
Helsinki University of Technology
P.O. Box 5400, FI-02015 HUT, Finland
ville.kononen@hut.fi

Abstract. The main aim of this paper is to extend the single-agent policy gradient method for multiagent domains where all agents share the same utility function. We formulate these team problems as Markov games endowed with the asymmetric equilibrium concept and based on this formulation, we provide a direct policy gradient learning method. In addition, we test the proposed method with a small example problem.

1 Introduction

Applying multiagent reinforcement learning to large, realworld applications requires the use of function approximators such as neural networks. The recently proposed numeric methods for multiagent reinforcement learning deal mostly with value function approximation. In this paper, we propose an alternative approach by extending the direct policy gradient method proposed by Sutton et al. in [6] for multiagent domains.

The focus in this work is on team problems, i.e. problems in which all agents share the same utility function. We model the interaction between the agents as a Markov game endowed with the asymmetric equilibrium concept. Due to the sequential nature of the decision making and the shared utility function, the multiagent learning problem reduces to a form that is very close to the single-agent reinforcement learning. We provide a convergent learning rule that solves this learning problem and based on this rule, we formulate a direct policy gradient method. In addition, we test the proposed method with a small example problem.

2 Multiagent Reinforcement Learning

This section is mainly concerned with the basic problem settings and definitions of multiagent reinforcement learning based on Markov games. We start with some preliminary information about Markov games and then proceed to their solution concepts which are essential for the rest of the paper.

2.1 Markov Games

With multiple agents in the environment, the fundamental problem of using single-agent Markov decision processes is that the approach treats the other agents as a part of the environment and thus ignores the fact that the decisions of these agents may influence the state of the environment.

One possible solution to this problem is to use *competitive Markov decision processes, Markov games*. In a Markov game, the process changes its state according to the action choices of all agents and it can thus be seen as a multicontroller Markov decision process. Formally, we define a Markov game as follows:

Definition 1. *A* Markov game *(stochastic game) is defined as a tuple* $(S, A^1, \ldots, A^N, p, r^1, \ldots, r^N)$, *where N is the number of agents, S is the set of all states, A^i is the set of all actions for each agent $i \in \{1, N\}$, $p : S \times A^1 \times \ldots \times A^N \to \Delta(S)$ is the state transition function, $r^i : S \times A^1 \times \ldots \times A^N \to \mathbb{R}$ is the reward function for the agent i. $\Delta(S)$ is the set of probability distributions over the set S.*

As in the case of single-agent Markov decision processes, we need a *policy* π^i, i.e. a rule stating what to do, given the knowledge of the current state of the environment, for each agent i:

$$\pi^i : S \to A^i, \forall i \in \{1, N\}. \tag{1}$$

In Eq. (1), the policy π^i is assumed to be stationary, i.e. there are no time dependents in the policy. The value for each state-actions tuple is

$$Q^i_{\pi^1,\ldots,\pi^N}(s, a^1, \ldots, a^N) = r^i(s, a^1, \ldots, a^N) \\ + \gamma \sum_{s'} p(s'|s, a^1, \ldots, a^N) V^i_{\pi^1,\ldots,\pi^N}(s'), \tag{2}$$

where $r^i(s, a^1, \ldots, a^N)$ is the immediate reward for the agent i when actions $a^1, \ldots, a^N$ are selected in the state s and $V^i_{\pi^1,\ldots,\pi^N}(s)$ is the value of the state for the agent i.

2.2 Equilibria in Markov Games

In multiagent reinforcement learning, it is not sufficient to maximize the expected utilities of individual agents. Instead, our goal is to find an equilibrium policy π^i_* for each agent i. A Nash equilibrium policy is defined as follows:

Definition 2. *If N is the number of agents and Π^i is the policy space for the agent i, the policies $\pi^1_*, \ldots, \pi^N_*$ constitute a Nash equilibrium solution of the game if in every state s the following inequality holds for all $\pi^i \in \Pi^i$ and for all i:*

$$V^i_{\pi^1_*,\ldots,\pi^i,\ldots,\pi^N_*}(s) \leq V^i_{\pi^1_*,\ldots,\pi^N_*}(s).$$

The first reinforcement learning method utilizing the Nash equilibrium directly was proposed by Hu and Wellman in [1] and [2]. The Nash equilibrium is an appropriate solution concept if the roles of the learning agents are symmetric. If the roles are not symmetric, i.e. some agents decide their actions prior the other agents, the action decision process becomes sequential and the Stackelberg equilibrium should be used instead of Nash equilibrium. In this paper, we study sequential decision problems of two agents in which agent 1 makes its decision prior to agent 2. In this case, the policy function of agent 2 is also the function of the action enforcement of agent 1. Formally, the policy function of agent 2 takes the following form:

$$\pi^2 : S \times A^1 \to A^2. \tag{3}$$

The update rules for agents 1 and 2 are as follows [3]:

$$Q^1_{t+1}(s_t, a^1_t, a^2_t) = (1 - \alpha_t)Q^1_t(s_t, a^1_t, a^2_t) \\ + \alpha_t[r^1_{t+1} + \gamma \max_{b \in A^1} Q^1_t(s_{t+1}, b, Tb)] \tag{4}$$

$$Q^2_{t+1}(s_t, a^1_t, a^2_t) = (1 - \alpha_t)Q^2_t(s_t, a^1_t, a^2_t) \\ + \alpha_t[r^2_{t+1} + \gamma \max_{b \in A^2} Q^2_t(s_{t+1}, g(s_{t+1}), b)], \tag{5}$$

where T is an operator conducting the response of agent 2 (assumed to be unique) and $g(s_t)$ is the action enforcement of agent 1 in the state s_t. In team games, the rewards are the same for both agents and therefore one Q-function is sufficient for describing the whole system. In this case, the Stackelberg solution reduces to the MaxMax-solution and the corresponding update rule (the same for both agents) is as follows:

$$Q_{t+1}(s_t, a^1_t, a^2_t) = (1 - \alpha_t)Q_t(s_t, a^1_t, a^2_t) \\ + \alpha_t[r_{t+1} + \gamma \max_{b \in A^1} \max_{c \in A^2} Q_t(s_{t+1}, b, c)]. \tag{6}$$

The application of the asymmetric learning model to team games also gives a new justification for the use of the MaxMax-operator. However, if there exists an ordering among the agents and both agents know and agree on it, the use of Stackelberg solution solves the possible equilibrium selection problem. A thorough discussion on asymmetric multiagent reinforcement learning can be found in [3].

3   Policy Gradient Methods for Multiagent Domains

In this section, we extend the policy gradient method proposed by Sutton et al. in [6] for multiagent domains. We restrict our attention only to the start state formulation of the problem in which the goal of the agent is to maximize his expected discounted utility starting from the specific state. We start the section by introducing the concept of *joint policy function*. For brevity, all mathematics is presented for the case of two agents.

3.1 Joint Policy Function

We extend the stochastic parametrized policy function to multiagent domains by setting the variables of the function to consist of the state and the joint actions performed by the agents. Formally, this can be expressed as follows:

$$\pi(s, a^1, a^2; \boldsymbol{\theta}) = P(a^1, a^2 | s; \boldsymbol{\theta}), \tag{7}$$

where $\boldsymbol{\theta}$ is an arbitrary parameter vector. The distribution defines the probability of selecting the joint action (a^1, a^2) in the state $s \in S$.

3.2 Policy Gradient

The object function of the policy gradient method is the expected utility in the start state s_0:

$$\rho(s_0, \pi) = V_\pi(s_0) = \sum_{b \in A^1} \sum_{c \in A^2} \pi(s_0, b, c; \boldsymbol{\theta}) Q_\pi(s_0, b, c). \tag{8}$$

By differentiating Eq. (8) with respect to an arbitrary parameter θ we get the following equation (derivation of this equation follows the derivation of the single-agent case in [6]):

$$\frac{\partial \rho}{\partial \theta} = \sum_{s \in S} d_\pi(s) \sum_{b \in A^1} \sum_{c \in A^2} \frac{\partial \pi(s, b, c; \boldsymbol{\theta})}{\partial \theta} Q_\pi(s, b, c), \tag{9}$$

where $d_\pi(s)$ is the discounted weight (probability) of reaching state s starting from the initial state s_0 and following π. It is a real number and therefore we can exclude it from (9) and still get an unbiased estimate of the gradient if the state transitions are sampled by following π.

Now the only remaining step is to find a suitable approximator for the normally unknown Q_π function. Let the function $f(s, a^1, a^2; \boldsymbol{\omega})$ be our approximation for Q_π that is parametrized with the vector $\boldsymbol{\omega}$. Moreover, if we set an additional restriction that the function f fulfills the compatibility property [6]:

$$\frac{\partial f(s, a^1, a^2; \boldsymbol{\omega})}{\partial \omega} = \frac{\partial \ln \pi(s, a^1, a^2; \boldsymbol{\theta})}{\partial \theta} \tag{10}$$

it can be shown that the error due to the use of the function f in place of Q is orthogonal to the gradient of the policy function π. Hence we can replace the function Q with the function f in Eq. (9).

3.3 Value Function Approximation

A natural way to update the parameters $\boldsymbol{\omega}$ is to minimize the following error function at each time step t:

$$E_t = \frac{1}{2}[r_{t+1} + \gamma \max_{b \in A^1} \max_{c \in A^2} f(s_{t+1}, b, c; \boldsymbol{\omega}) - f(s_t, a_t^1, a_t^2; \boldsymbol{\omega})]^2. \tag{11}$$

In this paper, we use the Gibbs distribution as a policy function, i.e.:

$$\pi(s, a^1, a^2, \boldsymbol{\theta}) = \frac{e^{\boldsymbol{\theta}^T \phi(s, a^1, a^2)}}{\sum_{b \in A^1} \sum_{c \in A^2} e^{\boldsymbol{\theta}^T \phi(s, b, c)}}, \tag{12}$$

where $\phi(s, a^1, a^2)$ is a unit vector with the element corresponding to state-actions tuple (s, a^1, a^2) set to one. Correspondingly, the compatible function approximator f takes the linear form:

$$f(s, a^1, a^2, \boldsymbol{\omega}) = \boldsymbol{\omega}^T [\phi(s, a^1, a^2) - \sum_{b \in A^1} \sum_{c \in A^2} \phi(s, b, c) \pi(s, b, c)]. \tag{13}$$

In the above equation, the second term containing two sums is, in fact, the value of the state s and does not depend on the action choices a^1 and a^2. Therefore this term does not change the direction of the policy gradient in Eq. (9) and it is possible to learn the parameters $\boldsymbol{\omega}$ by using the standard learning rule presented in Eq. (6).

3.4 Extensions to General-Sum Problems

There are two ways to extend the above policy gradient method to general-sum problems:

1. Agents update the policy distribution π separately. In this case the goal is to find a policy that maximizes the total (summed) utility of the agents.
2. Agents use the conditional distributions, conditioned with the opponent's action
choice, to update π. A sketch of the method can be found in [4].

In both cases, the problem is that there is no convergent learning rule for teaching the parameters of the compatible function approximator f and therefore we restrict our attention to team games only.

4 Empirical Tests

In this section, we test the proposed policy gradient method with a simple soccer game that was originally proposed in [5]. In this game, there are three players (agents): one fixed-strategy opponent and two learning agents that constitute a team. The game is played on a 5 × 6 field illustrated in Fig. 1 (left). In this figure, the cell marked with **G1** is the goal for the learning agents and the cell **G2** for the fixed-strategy agent. The agents are capable of moving to four cardinal directions or staying in the current cell. There can be only one agent in a cell simultaneously. The agent having the ball loses it when colliding with another agent. In addition, each learning agent is capable to pass the ball to its team mate located within 2 cells.

A state consists of the agents' positions and the ball possession information. Initially the fixed strategy agent is located in the left half of the field and the learning agents in the right half of the field. The ball possession is selected randomly. The game ends when the agent possessing the ball reaches a goal cell. The cell **G1** produces the payoff of 1 and **G2** the payoff of -1. When the agent with the ball reaches the goal, players are returned back to random initial positions. After the agents select their actions using the Stackelberg equilibrium concept, the actions are carried out in random order. This induces stochastic state transitions to the Markov game. The fixed strategy player always moves toward the agent possessing the ball and when it gets the ball, it moves directly toward its goal cell.

We taught the model with 50000 games. The learning rate was decayed linearly with time in both value-function and policy function estimation. The discount factor $\gamma = 0.9$ and the maximum length of the game was restricted to 50 moves. During the learning, action selections were sampled from the joint policy function π. Additionally, the model was tested with 1000 games. In Fig. 1 (right), the average number of wins (averaged from 20 test runs) is plotted against the number of training rounds. From this figure, it can be seen that the number of wins increases along the number of training rounds. However, the system learns very fast in the beginning of the learning process, after that the learning continues but is not so dramatic.

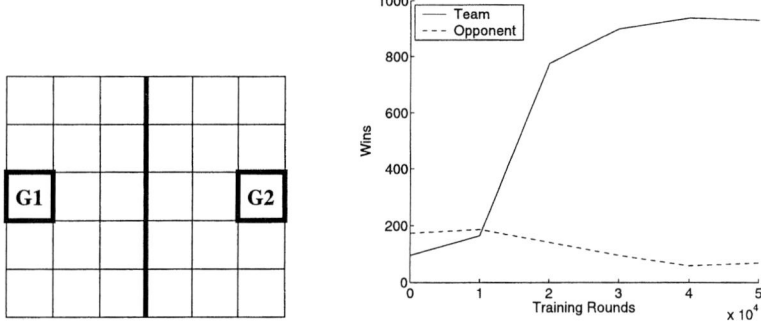

Fig. 1. Left: the game field in the soccer example. The cell **G1** is the goal for the learning agents and the cell **G2** for the fixed strategy opponent. Right: The number of wins plotted against the number of the training rounds.

5 Conclusions

We justified the use of the global maximum value of the state in the value function estimation by using the asymmetric learning model and based on this estimate, we provided the direct policy gradient method. Additionally we tested the policy gradient method with a simple example problem. Although the state-actions space was relatively large, the method learned very fast.

In future research, we will continue the development of the policy gradient method for general-sum games. Additionally, the method will be tested with larger problem instances.

References

1. J. Hu and M. P. Wellman. Multiagent reinforcement learning: Theoretical framework and an algorithm. In *Proceedings of the Fifteenth International Conference on Machine Learning (ICML'98)*, Madison, WI, 1998. Morgan Kaufmann Publishers.
2. J. Hu and M. P. Wellman. Nash Q-learning for general-sum stochastic games. *Journal of Machine Learning Research*, 4, 2003.
3. V. J. Könönen. Asymmetric multiagent reinforcement learning. In *Proceedings of the 2003 WIC International Conference on Intelligent Agent Technology (IAT-2003)*, Halifax, Canada, 2003. IEEE Press.
4. V. J. Könönen. Policy gradient method for multiagent reinforcement learning. In *Proceedings of the 2nd International Conference on Computational Intelligence, Robotics and Autonomous Systems (CIRAS 2003)*, Singapore, 2003.
5. L. Peshkin, K.-E. Kim, N. Meuleau, and L. P. Kaelbling. Learning to cooperate via policy-search. In *Proceedings of the Sixteenth Conference on Uncertainty in Artifical Intelligence (UAI-2002)*, Stanford, CA, 2000. Morgan Kaufmann Publishers.
6. R. S. Sutton, D. McAllester, S. Singh, and Y. Mansour. Policy gradient methods for reinforcement learning with function approximation. In *Advances in Neural Information Processing Systems*, volume 12, Cambridge, MA, 2000. MIT Press.

An Information Theoretic Optimal Classifier for Semi-supervised Learning

Ke Yin and Ian Davidson

University at Albany, Department of Computer Science
1400 Washington Ave. Albany, NY 12222
{ke,davidson}@cs.albany.edu

Abstract. Model uncertainty refers to the risk associated with basing prediction on only one model. In semi-supervised learning, this uncertainty is greater than in supervised learning (for the same total number of instances) given that many data points are unlabelled. An optimal Bayes classifier (OBC) reduces model uncertainty by averaging predictions across the entire model space weighted by the models' posterior probabilities. For a given model space and prior distribution OBC produces the lowest risk. We propose an information theoretic method to construct an OBC for probabilistic semi-supervised learning using Markov chain Monte Carlo sampling. This contrasts with typical semi-supervised learning that attempts to find the single most probable model using EM. Empirical results verify that OBC yields more accurate predictions than the best single model.

1 Introduction

Semi-supervised learning refers to building a model from a limited amount of labeled and plentiful unlabeled data. The situation arises usually because the process of obtaining abundant labeled data is expensive, if not impossible. As the limited amount of labeled data is not sufficient to build an effective model through standard supervised learning, the learner utilizes the information encompassed in the unlabeled data to improve performance.

An optimal Bayes classifier (OBC) averages the predictions over all models in the model space weighted by their posterior probabilities. For a given model space and prior distribution no classifier can obtain a lower risk (Mitchell, 1997). When the model space is "correct" and the data is sufficient, the posterior distribution is usually well enough peaked that the most probable model's prediction can approximate the OBC prediction. That is, though model uncertainty $(1 - p(\theta^* | D))$ exists, where $p(\theta^* | D)$ is the posterior probability of the most probable model, is not significant. The most probable model is typically found using EM or other greedy search techniques.

However, in semi-supervised learning the posterior distribution may be diffused given the limited labeled data. Therefore, an OBC for semi-supervised learning would be highly desirable. But implementing the OBC requires integration over the entire model space which is difficult for albeit trivial problems. This prevents its application in semi-supervised learning problems, where it potentially yields many benefits.

In this paper, we propose a method of constructing such an optimal Bayes classifier for semi-supervised learning based on an information theoretic approach. The work makes several novel contributions. Firstly, we formulate the message length for probabilistic semi-supervised learning models. Prior work in the minimum message length (MML) principle (Wallace & Freeman, 1987; Oliver & Baxter, 1994) and minimum description length (MDL) principle (Rissanen, 1987; Hansen & Yu, 2001) has shown its usefulness for applications in unsupervised learning (Oliver, Baxter & Wallace, 1996; Agusta & Dowe, 2003) and supervised learning (Quinlan & Rivest, 1989; Wallace & Patrick, 1993). Therefore, it is a natural progression to derive the message length formulation for the semi-supervised learning problem. Secondly, we show how such a message length calculation can be used in constructing an optimal Bayes classifier for semi-supervised learning problems. Finally, our empirical work verifies that OBC does indeed help semi-supervised learning by exceeding the performance of predictions made from the single most probable model.

2 Message Length Principle

In information theory, learning can be viewed as lossless compression of the data with aid of some model. More precisely, we would like to find some model, θ so that the total message length encoding of θ the data D given θ is as short as possible. The difference in message length to encode the data without the model and with the model indicates the generalization capability of the model. That is, models that result in shorter encodings perform better and the best single model results in the shortest total encoding.

As the length of the message rather than the content of the message indicate the quality of the model, we need only calculate the message length using the Shannon's code without constructing the actual message content. For any probability distribution $f(X)$, the message length of a prefix code to encode an event $X = x$ is $-\ln f(x)$ nits (1 nit equals to $\log_2 e$ bits). We encode the model using the model's prior distribution $p(\theta)$ and encode the data using conditional distribution $p(D|\theta)$. Wallace and Freeman (1987) showed the total message to encode data $X = \{x_1, x_2, ..., x_n\}$ with a model of d degree of freedom $\theta_1, \theta_2, ..., \theta_d$ is given by

$$-\ln h(\theta_1, \theta_2, ..., \theta_d) + \frac{1}{2}\ln |F(\theta_1, \theta_2, ..., \theta_d)| + \frac{d}{2} + \frac{1}{2}\ln(\kappa_d) - \ln f(X|\theta_1, \theta_2, ..., \theta_d) \quad (1)$$

Here, $h(\theta_1, \theta_2, ..., \theta_d)$ is the prior for the model parameters, $|F(\theta_1, \theta_2, ..., \theta_d)|$ stands for the determinant of the Fisher information matrix of the parameters, $\ln f(x_i|\theta_1, \theta_2, ..., \theta_d)$ is the log likelihood, and κ_d is the lattice constant (Conway & Sloane, 1988). The first four terms in equation (1) are the message length to encode the model and the last term is the message length cost to encode the data given the model.

We now propose the message length formulation for probabilistic models in semi-supervised learning. Let $D_l = \{(x_1, y_1), (x_2, y_2), ..., (x_n, y_n)\}$ be the labeled data, $D_u = \{x_{n+1}, x_{n+2}, ..., x_{n+m}\}$ be the unlabeled data. To formulate the message length calculations for a probabilistic model in semi-supervised learning problem we need to do the following:

1. Draw the graphical representation of the probabilistic model.
2. Encode the model following the links in the graphical representation from root nodes to leaf nodes, until the observed data are encoded. For labeled data, we encode both independent attributes *x* and class label *y*. For unlabeled data, we only encode independent attributes *x*.
3. Ignore/drop the constant terms in the message length distribution that does not vary in the chosen model space.

We would like to demonstrate this approach with an example semi-supervised learning problem that has been used frequently, a mixture Gaussian model. The model assumes that there are total k generating mechanisms of the data, we refer to each as a component. We use latent variable z to indicate the component index for the instances. For each component, it generates *x* according to some Gaussian distributions with parameters characteristic to this component. Similarly, each component generates class label *y* using multinomial distribution with parameters characteristic to this component. For labeled data, we can observe both *x* and *y* while for unlabeled data we only observe *x*. To predict the class label for a new instance x_{new}, we first find its component index (latent variable z_{new}) using the link between *x* and *z* and then predict its class label (y_{new}) using the link between *z* and *y*. A graphical representation of a mixture Gaussian model is given in Figure 1, where the arrows indicate stochastic dependencies and transparent rectangle indicates an array of objects.

The message length calculation is similar to that of Oliver and Baxter (2000), but extended to encode the given class labels as well. The total message length is

$$MsgLen(k,\mu,\sigma,\pi) = -\ln(k-1) + \frac{1}{2}\ln\frac{n^{k-1}}{\prod_{i=1}^{k}\omega_i} - \sum_{i=1}^{m+n}\ln\omega_{z(i)} + \frac{k-1}{2} + \frac{1}{2}\ln(\kappa_{k-1})$$

$$-\ln k! - k\ln\frac{1}{\sigma_*^2} + \frac{1}{2}\sum_{i=1}^{k}\ln\frac{2n_i^2}{\sigma_i^4} + k + \frac{1}{2}k\ln(\kappa_2) + \sum_{i=1}^{n+m}\left(\ln\left(\sqrt{2\pi}\sigma_{z(i)}\right) + \frac{(x_i - \mu_{z(i)})^2}{2\sigma_{z(i)}^2}\right) \quad (2)$$

$$-k\ln(c-1) + \frac{1}{2}\sum_{i=1}^{k}\ln\frac{m_i^{c-1}}{\prod_{j=1}^{c}\pi_{i,j}} + \frac{c-1}{2}k + \frac{1}{2}k\ln(\kappa_{c-1}) - \sum_{i=n+1}^{n+m}\ln\pi_{z(i),y(i)}$$

3 Constructing Optimal Bayes Classifier with Message Length Distribution

Although Bayesian model averaging improves the predictive accuracies, the calculation and maximization of the Bayesian integral is not easy. The main difficulty lies in the integration over the posterior distribution $p(\theta | D_l, D_u)$ that contains latent variables. We can approximate this integral by randomly generating models from the posterior distribution and summing the probability for each class from each model. As more probable models are drawn more often, this approach asymptotically approximate the Bayesian integral (Gilks, Richardson & Spiegelhalter, 1996).

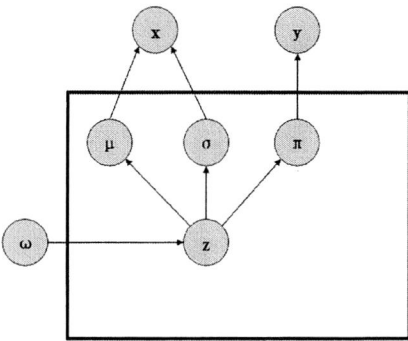

Fig. 1. Graphical Mixture Gaussian Model.

The message length calculation can be easily converted into the MML defined posterior probability distribution of the model

$$p(\theta | D_l, D_u) = \frac{e^{-MsgLen(\theta)}}{\sum_{\theta \in \Theta} e^{-MsgLen(\theta)}} \qquad (3)$$

Such a distribution is an approximation of the algorithmic probabilistic distribution, which is also known as the optimal predictive distribution, first proposed by Solomonoff (1964).

Notice that the distribution defined by equation (3) is invariant if all the message lengths are changed by a constant. That is, as message length itself might depend on a particular coding scheme, the posterior distribution does not. This is the reason why constant terms can be dropped in message length calculation.

Given the message length distribution, we would create a Markov process that generates the models according to the posterior distribution. This typically is achieved by using Gibbs algorithm or Metropolis-Hasting algorithm. Details on how to construct these samplers is generally given in our previous work (Yin & Davidson, 2004).

4 Empirical Results

In this section, we briefly compare the predictive performance between an optimal Bayes classifier as constructed above and the maximum likelihood classifier usually found by the EM algorithm. We abbreviate the semi-supervised optimal Bayes classifier as SS-OBC, and abbreviate the semi-supervised maximum likelihood classifier as SS-EM.

We use standard data sets from the UCI machine learning repository. For each dataset, we use 10% of the data as labeled data, 10% as the unlabeled data and 80% as the testing data. We choose small training set size mainly to test the classifiers' performance when data is scarce. Each dataset is randomly divided 100 times according to the above ratio with the mean and the standard deviation of the predictive errors reported below. We also include the p-value for a paired student T-test between the errors to indicate whether the error reduction is statistically significant. A p-value less than 0.05 indicate a statistically significant result at the 95% confidence level. We summarize our results in Table 1.

Table 1. Mean Predictive Error (Standard Deviation) For SS-OBC and SS-EM.

Data	SS-EM	SS-OBC	P value
Iris	17.5 (9.9)	10.9(6.9)	6.0E-08
Diabetes	21.2 (7.8)	20.6(6.8)	0.15
Wine	18.1(13.0)	12.4(7.9)	5.2E-05
Glass	56.3 (5.1)	53.7(7.8)	0.0006
Shuttle	21.6 (4.5)	18.6(5.0)	6.5E-08

We see that for all but one data set that SS-OBC performs significantly better than its SS-EM rival. Furthermore this improvement in accuracy is often accompanied by a reduction of the standard deviation of the performance. The reason that SS-OBC showed a non-statistical significant improvement on the Diabetes dataset is probably that the posterior distribution is already well peaked for the problem even with limited amount of data, thus an SS-EM can approximate SS-OBC fairly well as the Bayesian integral is dominated by the shortest model.

5 Conclusions and Future Work

Information theoretic methods provide message length as the measurement of model complexity from which we can calculate the posterior probability of the model. In this paper, we present procedures to construct optimal Bayes classifiers for probabilistic models in semi-supervised learning using a three step proceedure. The form of the message length calculation can be derived from the graphical representation of the probabilistic model by encoding the model parameters and the data in a top-down manner from root to leaf. This message length is then converted into the posterior distribution, which constitutes the "weights" used in the optimal Bayes classifier. We verify empirically that optimal Bayes classifier makes better predictions in semi-supervised learning compared to the maximum likelihood classifier found by EM. It also shows great robustness when amounts of labeled and unlabeled data are both restricted. These characteristic properties make optimal Bayes classifier a very useful predictor in semi-supervised learning.

As message length is a universal measurement of complexity, the methods described in this paper should also apply to non-probabilistic models in semi-supervised learning. The complexity of encoding probabilistic model has been well studied and showed deep relationships with other fundamental complexity knowledge such as entropy and Kolmogorov complexity. Meanwhile, encoding non-probabilistic model is far less well studied as the probabilistic counter part, and prone to be subjective. The encoding schemes for non-probabilistic models require careful crafting in order to maintain the conciseness of the code and need to be solved individually. In the future, we will investigate constructing optimal Bayes classifiers for some non-probabilistic models with existing encoding schemes such as C4.5 decision tree. Also, it would be interesting to investigate if the message length distribution among different models can produce normalized posterior distributions if we consider joint model spaces.

References

1. Agusta, Y. & Dowe, D. L. (2003). *Unsupervised Learning of Correlated Multivariate Gaussian Mixture Models Using MML.* Australian Conference on Artificial Intelligence.
2. Baxter, R. A., Oliver, J. J. (2000). *Finding Overlapping Components with MML.* Statistics and Computing 10, 5-16.
3. Conway, J. H., Sloane, N. J. A. (1988). *Sphere Packings, Lattices and Groups.* Springer-Verlag, London.
4. Gilks, W., Richardson, S. & Spiegelhalter, D. (1996). *Markov Chain Monte Carlo in Practice.* Interdisciplinary Statistics.Chapman and Hall.
5. Hansen, M. H. & Yu, B. (2001) *Model selection and the principle of minimum description length.* J. American Statistical Association, vol. 96, pp. 746-774.
6. Mitchell, T. (1997). *Machine Learning,* McGraw-Hill.
7. Oliver, J. J. & Baxter, R. A. (1994). *MML and Bayesianism: similarities and differences,* Dept. of Computer Science, Monash University, Clayton, Victoria 3168, Australia, Technical Report TR 206
8. Oliver, J. J., Baxter, R. A. & Wallace, C. S. (1996) *Unsupervised Learning Using MML,* Machine Learning, Proceedings of the Thirteenth International Conference.
9. Quinlan, R., Rivest, R. L. (1989). *Inferring Decision Trees Using the Minimum Description Length Principle.* Information and Computation. 80(3): 227-248 .
10. Rissanen, J. (1987). *Stochastic complexity.* J. Royal Statistical Society, Series B, vol. 49, no. 3, pp. 223-239.
11. Solomonoff, R. J. (1964). *A Formal Theory of Induction Inference.* Information and Control, Part I, (7), No.1, 1-22.
12. Stephens, M. (2000). Dealing with label-switching in mixture models. *Journal of the Royal Statistical Society, Series B,* **62**, 795--809
13. Wallace, C. S. & Boulton, D. M. (1968). *An Information Measure for Classification.* Computer Journal, 11:185-195.
14. Wallace, C. S. & Dowe, D. L. (1999), *Minimum Message Length and Kolmogorov Complexity.* The computer Journal 42(4) 270-283.
15. Wallace, C. S. & Freeman, P. R. (1987). *Estimation and inference by compact encoding* (with discussion). Journal of the Royal Statistical Society series B, 49:240-265.
16. Wallace, C. S. & Patrick, J. D. (1993). *Coding Decision Trees.* Machine Learning 11: 7-22.
17. Yin, K. & Davidson, I. (2004). *Bayesian Model Averaging Across Model Spaces via Compact Encoding.* Eighth International Symposium on Artificial Intelligence and Mathematics.

Improving Evolutionary Algorithms by a New Smoothing Technique[*]

Yuping Wang[1,2]

[1] Faculty of Science, Xidian University, Xi'an, 710071, China
[2] Department of Computer Science, Hong Kong Baptist University
Kowloon Tong, Hong Kong, China

Abstract. In this paper, a novel smoothing technique, which can be integrated into different optimization methods to improve their performance, is presented. At first, a new smoothing technique using a properly truncated Fourier series as the smoothing function is proposed. This smoothing function can eliminate many local minima and preserve the global minima. Thus it make the search of optimal solution more easier and faster. At second, this technique is integrated into a simple genetic algorithm to improve and demonstrate the efficiency of this technique. The simulation results also indicate the new smoothing technique can improve the simple genetic algorithm greatly.

1 Introduction

If a function $f(x)$ has many local minimum points, looking for its global minimum point by evolutionary algorithms is a very difficult task ([1], [2]). In the past ten years, a new type of approach to the multiple minima problem called smoothing technique has emerged, which is based on some principles on physics science such as deformation of the original energy (hyper-) surface so that local minima get smoothed out to some degree, making the problem of finding the global minimum less difficult. A large variety of so called smoothing techniques have been proposed. For examples, Convolution methods ([3]), Quantum methods ([4]), Statistical mechanics methods ([5]) and Variational methods ([6]), etc.

In this paper, a completely different smoothing technique is proposed. We make use of the properly truncated Fourier series to be as the smoothing function which can be easily calculated, and can maintain the overall or basic shape of the primary function but eliminate its many local minimum points. Moreover, this technique can be integrated into any other evolutionary algorithm to improve its efficiency.

Fourier series of a function is the sum of a series of trigonometric functions $Asin(\mu x)$ and $Acos(\mu x)$ with different frequencies μ from lower (smaller) to higher (larger) and different amplitudes A from larger to smaller. In mild conditions this series can converge to function $f(x)$ ([7]). Thus the sum of its first

---

[*] This work was supported in part by the National Natural Science Foundation of China (60374063), the Natural Science Foundation of Shaanxi Province (2001SL06), the SRF for ROCS, SEM.

finite terms (i.e. the truncated Fourier series) can be seen as an approximation to $f(x)$. The contribution of each sine and/or cosine term to the overall shape of the function is obviously dependent on its amplitude. Note that the amplitude of the k-th term in Fourier series approach to zero and the frequency of it approaches to infinite when k approaches to infinite. Thus this approximation throws away the terms with higher frequencies and smaller amplitudes but maintains the terms with lower frequencies and larger amplitudes. From the intuitive point of view, the higher frequency terms are with the smaller amplitudes and help to make up the finer details of the function, whereas the lower ones are with larger amplitude and contribute more to the overall or basic shape of the function. Thus this approximation can maintain the overall shape or basic shape of the objective function but eliminate its many local minimum points. We can see this approximation as a smoothing function to the original function.

The main idea of the proposed algorithm is as follows: The algorithm consists of two phases. In the first phase, we propose an efficient algorithm to calculate the truncated Fourier series. In the second phase, we use the truncated Fourier series as the smoothing function and integrate it into evolutionary algorithm to enhance the efficiency of the evolutionary algorithm.

2 Smoothing Function Using Truncated Fourier Series

A. *Fourier series of multidimensional functions defined on a hyperrectangle.*
We consider a global optimization problem of the following form:

$$\min\{f(x) \mid x \in [a_k, b_k]^n\}, \tag{1}$$

where the domain of $f(x)$ is set $V = [a_k, b_k]^n$. Then the Fourier series of $f(x)$ is

$$f(x) \sim \sum_m Z_m \exp(2\pi i m \cdot \frac{x}{c}), \tag{2}$$

where the sum is taken for all $m = (m_1, ..., m_n)$ with integer entries([7]), $Z_m = \frac{1}{c_1 c_2 \cdots c_n} \int_V f(x) \exp(-2\pi i m \cdot \frac{x}{c}) dx$ with $\frac{x}{c} = (\frac{x_1}{c_1}, ..., \frac{x_n}{c_n})$ and $c_k = b_k - a_k$ for $k = 1, 2, ..., n$.

B. *Compute smoothing function efficiently.*
Note that the Fourier coefficients in formula (2) are multiple integrals which generally can not be calculated directly, we calculate them by some numerical methods such as Monte Carlo method ([8]) in the following way. If we take N independent samples $x^1, x^2, ..., x^N$ of x, an unbiased estimator for Z_m is

$$\bar{Z}_m = \frac{1}{N} \sum_{k=1}^{N} f(x^k) \exp(-2\pi i m \cdot \frac{x^k}{c}), \tag{3}$$

where $x^k = (x_1^k, x_2^k, ..., x_n^k)$ for $k = 1, 2, ..., N$ and $\frac{x^k}{c} = (\frac{x_1^k}{c_1}, ..., \frac{x_n^k}{c_n})$. To compute smoothing function efficiently, we denote $b_0(x) = \bar{Z}_0 \exp(2\pi i 0 \cdot \frac{x}{c})$, $b_m(x) =$

$\bar{Z}_m \exp(2\pi i m \cdot \frac{x}{c}) + \bar{Z}_{-m} \exp(2\pi i(-m) \cdot \frac{x}{c})$ for $m = (m_1, ..., m_n)$ with $0 < \max\{m_k\} = \max\{m_k | m_k \geq 0, 1 \leq k \leq n\} \leq \lambda$ for an integer $\lambda > 0$, then $b_m(x)$ is a real number for any integer vector $m \geq 0$ and can be written as

$$b_0(x) = \frac{1}{N} \sum_{k=1}^{N} f(x^k), \quad b_m(x) = \frac{1}{N} \sum_{k=1}^{N} 2f(x^k) \cos(2\pi m \cdot \frac{x-x^k}{c}) \quad (4)$$

for any $0 \leq m \neq 0$. Then the smoothing function can be defined by

$$f_t(x) = \sum_{0 \leq \max\{m_k\} \leq \lambda} b_m(x). \quad (5)$$

Case 1: For small n. With the progress of the algorithm, some additional points, say $x^{N+1}, ..., x^M$, will be generated, it is not necessary to re-compute all terms $b_m(x)$'s in $f_t(x)$. In stead, we only need to modify the existing $b_m(x)$ and compute the new $b_m(x)$ by the following way.

$$\begin{cases} b_m(x) := \frac{1}{M} \sum_{k=1}^{M} 2f(x^k) \cos(2\pi m \cdot \frac{x-x^k}{c}), & \text{if} \max\{m_k\} > \lambda \\ b_m(x) := \frac{1}{M}[N \cdot b_m(x) + \sum_{k=N+1}^{M} 2f(x^k) \cos(2\pi m \cdot \frac{x-x^k}{c})], & \text{else} \end{cases} \quad (6)$$

Case 2: For large n. In order to save the computation, we take $\lambda = 1$. We can prove the following result.

Theorem 1. *Let $e_j^n = (0, .., 0, 1, 0, ..., 0) \in R^n$ with 1 being j-th component of vector e_j^n, $E_j = (1, ..., 1) \in R^j$, $g_k = 2\pi \frac{x-x^k}{c}$ and $\frac{g_k}{2} \cdot e_j^n$ represent the dot product of vectors $\frac{g_k}{2}$ and e_j^n. If $\lambda = 1$, then*

$$f_t(x) = \frac{2^{n+1}}{N} \sum_{k=1}^{N} f(x^k) [\prod_{j=1}^{n} \cos(\frac{g_k}{2} \cdot e_j^n)] \cos(\frac{g_k}{2} \cdot E_n) - \frac{1}{N} \sum_{k=1}^{N} f(x^k). \quad (7)$$

Using formulas (5) to (7) to compute $f_t(x)$ can save a lot of computation.

3 Improving the Evolutionary Algorithms by Smoothing Technique

The smoothing function method can be integrated into any evolutionary algorithm to improve it. As an example, we improve simple genetic algorithm (denoted as SGA) by smoothing function method to demonstrate the efficiency of the proposed algorithm. The improved algorithm is called Smoothed Simple Genetic Algorithm, briefly denoted as SSGA.

First we briefly introduce a simple genetic algorithm as follows.

Algorithm 1 (A simple genetic algorithm – SGA)

1. (initialization). Randomly generate initial population $P(0) = \{x^1, x^2, ..., x^{pop}\}$, let $t = 0$. Given probabilities of crossover and mutation p_c and p_m, respectively.

2. (Crossover). Select parents from the current population $P(t)$ by the crossover probability p_c. For each pair of chosen parents use one-point crossover operator to generate a pair of temporary offspring.
3. (mutation). Do the mutation and use mutation offspring to replace temporary offspring.
4. (Selection). Use a selection scheme to select the next generation population $P(t+1)$.
5. (Termination). If termination condition is satisfied, stop; otherwise, let $t = t+1$, go to step 2.

In algorithm 1, the real code representation is used, i.e., each chromosome is same as its original form x in the variable space of the problem. The mutation operator is performed in the following way: each offspring of crossover is selected with probability p_m to undergo mutation, and a randomly designated component (e.g., i-th component) of each chosen offspring randomly change its value in $[a_i, b_i]$. The selection scheme is performed based on the Roullete Wheel Selection scheme.

Algorithm 2 (Smoothed Simple genetic algorithm – SSGA)

First phase

1. Generate a population of uniformly distributed initial points in $[a_k, b_k]^n$ by the uniform distribution on $[a_k, b_k]^n$ or uniform design methods in ([8]), and calculate the initial smoothing function $f_t(x)$ by formulas (5)$\sim$ (7).
2. Optimize the current smoothing function $f_t(x)$ by the simple genetic algorithm through evolving the current population until the best solution found can not be improved further.
3. Modify the smoothing function by using the new points generated to get a new smoothing function, go to step 2.
4. If the several successive best solutions got in step 2 can not be improved, stop; otherwise, go to the second phase.

Second phase

5. Optimize the original function by the simple genetic algorithm using the final population got in step 2 as the initial population until the best solution can not be improved further.

4 Simulation Results

Test problems

$$F1(x) = -\sum_{i=1}^{n} \sin(x_i) \sin^{20}\left(\frac{i \times x_i^2}{\pi}\right),$$

where $n = 100$, $x_i \in [0, \pi]$, $i = 1 \sim 100$, $F1_{min} = -99.51$.

$$F2(x) = \frac{1}{n}\sum_{i=1}^{n}(x_i^4 - 16x_i^2 + 5x_i),$$

where $n = 100$, $x_i \in [-5, 5]$, $F2_{min} = -78.33$.

$$F3(x) = 1 + \sum_{i=1}^{n} \frac{x_i^2}{4000} - \prod_{i=1}^{n} \cos(\frac{x_i}{\sqrt{i}}),$$

where $n = 30$, $x_i \in [-600, 600]$, $i = 1 \sim 30$, $F3_{min} = 0$.

$$F4(x) = -20 \exp\left(-0.2\sqrt{\frac{1}{n}\sum_{i=1}^{n} x_i^2}\right) - \exp\left(\frac{1}{n}\sum_{i=1}^{n} \cos 2\pi x_i\right) + 20 + e,$$

where $n = 30$, $x_i \in [-32, 32]$, $i = 1 \sim 30$, $F4_{min} = 0$.

These test functions are all multimodal functions, where the number of local minima increases exponentially with the problem dimension ([2]). Thus they are challenging enough for performance evaluation. For example, test function $F1$ has 100! local minima and test function $F2$ has 2^{100} local minima. In Simulations we take population size $pop = 100$, $p_c = 0.1$ and $p_m = 0.08$. Algorithms stop when the best solution found so far can not be further improved in successive 30 generations after 3500 generations. we performed 100 independent runs for both SSGA and SGA on each test function and recorded: The best function value found in 100 runs, denoted as F_{min}. The mean of the function values found in 100 runs, denoted as F_{mean}. The worst function value found in 100 runs, denoted as F_{max}. The standard deviation of function values found in 100 runs, denoted as std. The mean CPU time (minutes) used for each function in 100 runs. The results are in the Tables 1 and 2.

Table 1. Comparison of mean solution, standard deviation and mean CPU time for SSGA and SGA

	F_{mean}		std		CPU_{mean}	
	SSGA	SGA	SSGA	SGA	SSGA	SGA
$F1$	-99.4673	-68.6778	1.77×10^{-3}	2.4070	46.4000	49.5670
$F2$	-78.3325	-69.2541	8.42×10^{-10}	0.9245	41.2680	45.5360
$F3$	6.53×10^{-9}	3.3428	1.93×10^{-9}	0.6717	26.6770	22.9590
$F4$	2.32×10^{-4}	7.3111	1.98×10^{-5}	0.7890	66.6050	22.9720

We can see from Table 1 that the mean solutions found by SSGA for all test functions are equal or very close to the optimal ones, while most of the mean solutions found by SGA are not close to the optimal ones. Moreover, For each test function, it can be seen from table 2 that both the best and worst solutions found by SSGA in 100 runs are very close to the optimal one and the standard deviations are very small, while the difference between the best and the worst solutions found by SGA is big and the standard deviations are relatively large. This illustrates that even for a non efficiency and unstable algorithm, SGA, its improved algorithm, SSGA, is efficient and very stable. Although SSGA

Table 2. Comparison of the best and worst solutions found by SSGA and SGA in 100 runs

	F_{min}		F_{max}	
	SSGA	SGA	SSGA	SGA
$F1$	-99.4764	-75.1053	-99.4667	-62.7859
$F2$	-78.3327	-71.4283	-78.3323	-67.0055
$F3$	3.0345×10^{-9}	2.1123	1.1774×10^{-8}	5.5760
$F4$	1.7797×10^{-4}	5.2180	2.7672×10^{-4}	9.0612

uses more CPU time than SGA for $F3$ and $F4$, SSGA is unnecessary to use so much time because it has found the optimal solutions in much fewer than 3500 generations.

References

1. R. Farmani, J. A. Wright.: Self-Adaptive Fitness Formulation for Constrained Optimization. IEEE Trans. Evolutionary Computation. **7** (2003) 445-455.
2. Y. W. Leung, Y. P. Wang.: An Orthogonal Genetic Algorithm with Quantization for Global Numerical Optimization. IEEE Trans. Evolutionary Computation. **75** (2001) 41-53.
3. I. Andricioaei, J.E. Straub.: Finding the Needle in the Haystack: Algorithms for Global Optimization. Computation in Physics. **10** (1996) 449-456.
4. P. Amara, D. Hsu, J.E. Straub.: Global Energy Minimum Searches Using An Approximate Solution of the Imaginary Time Schrödinger Equation. Computation in Physics. **97** (1993) 6715.
5. J. Pillardy, L. Piela.: Smoothing Techniques of Global Optimization: Distance Scaling Method in Searches for Most Stable Lennard-Jones Atomic Clusters. J. Comp. Chem. **19** (1998) 245-248.
6. H. Verschelde, S. Schelstraete, et al.: An Effective Potential for Calculating Free Energies. 1. General Concepts And Approximations. J. Chem. Phys. **106** (1997) 1556-1564.
7. Mark Cartwright. *Fourier methods for mathematicians, scientists and engineers.* Chichester, England, Ellis Horwood Limited, 1990.
8. F.T.Fang, Y.Wang. *Number-theoretic methods in statistics.* London, UK, Chapman & Hall, 1994.

In-Situ Learning in Multi-net Systems

Matthew Casey and Khurshid Ahmad

Department of Computing, School of Electronics and Physical Sciences
University of Surrey, Guildford, Surrey, GU2 7XH, UK
{m.casey,k.ahmad}@surrey.ac.uk

Abstract. Multiple classifier systems based on neural networks can give improved generalisation performance as compared with single classifier systems. We examine collaboration in multi-net systems through *in-situ learning*, exploring how generalisation can be improved through the simultaneous learning in networks and their combination. We present two in-situ trained systems; first, one based upon the simple ensemble, combining supervised networks in parallel, and second, a combination of unsupervised and supervised networks in sequence. Results for these are compared with existing approaches, demonstrating that in-situ trained systems perform better than similar pre-trained systems.

1 Introduction

The task of classifying data has been tackled by a number of different techniques. One such approach is the use of mixture models, which uses a combination of models to summarise a data set comprising a number of modes. Such mixture models are 'parsimonious in the sense that they typically combine distributions that are simple and relatively well-understood' [5] (p.267), of which the *mixture-of-experts* (ME) model is a good example. Mixture models are based on the assumption that each constituent of the mixture can classify one segment of the input, and that the combination is able to classify most, if not all, of the input. Such combinations appear intuitive, and have been used on a number of pattern recognition tasks, such as identity [6] and handwriting recognition [16]. The disadvantage with mixture models is the increase in processing time caused by multiple components, however they have a degree of elegance in that they combine a number of 'simple' classifiers.

The constituent classifier neural networks of a multiple classifier combination are further distinguished as either *ensemble* or *modular*; the former refers to a set of redundant networks, whilst the later has no redundancy (of which ME is an example). Such *multi-net systems* (see papers in [12]) typically combine networks in parallel, but the sequential combination of networks has also had some success [10]. Whether in parallel or in sequence, each constituent network of a multi-net system is combined using prior knowledge of how the combination is affected, exemplified by the pre-training of networks before combination. The question here is whether techniques such as ME, which can *learn* how to combine networks, offers any improvement over individually trained systems? In the context of multiple classifier systems, it is important to look at this *in-situ learning*, defined as the simultaneous training of the constituent networks, which 'provides an opportunity for the individual networks to interact' [9] (p.222). In this paper we evaluate the use of in-situ learning in the parallel and sequential combination of networks to help assess this as a general approach to learning in multi-net systems.

2 In-Situ Learning in Multi-net Systems

In this paper we consider two multi-net systems that exploit in-situ learning [3]. The first is a simple ensemble (SE) trained in conjunction with early stopping techniques: the *simple learning ensemble* (SLE). The second is a novel system consisting of a group of unsupervised networks and a single supervised network that are trained in sequence: *sequential learning modules* (SLM).

Simple Learning Ensemble: There have been two contrasting examples of in-situ learning in ensembles. Liu and Yao [8] defined the *negative correlation learning* algorithm for ensembles that trains networks in-situ using a modified learning rule with a penalty term, whereas Wanas, Hodge and Kamel's [14] multi-net system combines partially pre-trained networks before continuing training in-situ. Whilst we agree with Liu and Yao that in-situ learning is important, our work differs from theirs and Wanas et al's in two respects: first we use the same data set to train all of the networks, rather than using data sampling, and second we use early stopping to promote generalisation through assessing the *combined performance* of the ensemble, instead of introducing a penalty term to the error function, exploiting the interaction between networks [9]. Our approach is based upon the SE, but with each network trained in-situ. We use the generalisation loss [11] early stopping metric to control the amount of training based upon the measured generalisation performance.

Sequential Learning Modules: Sequential in-situ learning is a difficult area to develop for supervised classification because it depends upon having an appropriate error to propagate back through each network in sequence. This issue is apparent in the development of multi-layer, single network systems, where an algorithm such as backpropagation is required to assign error to hidden neurons. Bottou and Gallinari [2] discussed how error can be assigned to sequential networks in multi-net systems, but assumed that each such network used supervised learning. Our approach is to use unsupervised networks in sequence coupled with in-situ learning so that no such error is required, only an appropriate input to each network. We employ networks that use unsupervised learning in all but the last network to give an overall supervised system, but which does not propagate back error. This approach also allows unsupervised techniques to be used to give a definite classification through the assignment of a class by the last network.

3 Evaluating In-Situ Learning with Classification

The classification of an arbitrary set of objects is regarded as an important exemplar of learnt behaviour. We use well-known data sets [1], which have been used extensively in benchmarking the performance of classification systems, observing the behaviour of the proposed systems. We use the artificial MONK's problems [13] to test generalisation capability, whilst the Wisconsin Breast Cancer Database (WBCD) [15] is used to test pattern separation capability using real-life data (Table 1).

Table 1. Details of data sets used for experiments. For the MONK's problems, the validation data set includes the training data, which is also used for testing.

Data Set	Input	Output	Training	Validation	Testing	Examples/Class %	Notes
MONK 1	6	1	124	432	-	50:50	
MONK 2	6	1	169	432	-	67:33	
MONK 3	6	1	122	432	-	47:53	5% misclassified
WBCD	9	2	349	175	175	66:34	16 missing values

SLE systems consisting of from 2 to 20 multi-layer perceptrons (MLPs) trained using backpropagation were constructed to determine the effect of ensemble complexity on generalisation performance. Each network within the ensemble had the same network topology, but to generate diversity in the networks, each was initialised with different random real number weights selected using a normal probability distribution with mean 0, standard deviation 1. The backpropagation with momentum algorithm was used with the Logistic Sigmoid activation function, using a constant learning rate of 0.1 and momentum of 0.9.

For the SLM systems, we restrict ourselves to combining a self-organising map (SOM) [7] and a single layer network employing the delta learning rule. Neither of these is capable of solving a non-linearly separable classification problem; our hypothesis is that an in-situ trained combination of these can solve these more complex problems. The basic SOM algorithm was used on a rectangular map of neurons, with a Gaussian neighbourhood and exponential learning rate. To ensure that the output of the SOM can be combined with the single layer network, the output is converted into a vector by concatenating the winning values from each of the neurons, with '1' associated with the winning neuron and '0' for all other neurons. The single layer network using the delta learning rule had a constant learning rate of 0.1, and a binary threshold activation function.

Table 2. The number of input, hidden and output nodes per data set for each of the constituent networks used for the single network and ensemble systems (hidden nodes selected as in [13]).

System	MONK 1	MONK 2	MONK 3	WBCD
MLP				
MLP (ES)	6-3-1	6-2-1	6-4-1	9-5-2
SE (ES)				
SLE (ES)				

In order to understand the generalisation performance of the SLE and SLM systems, we compare the percentage test responses against those generated for single MLPs trained with and without early stopping, as well as simple ensembles formed from 2 to 20 MLPs pre-trained with early stopping. The architecture used for the various systems is shown in Table 2 and Table 3. Each of the systems underwent 100 trials to estimate the mean performance, training either for a fixed 1000 epochs, or with early stopping (ES) for a maximum of 1000 epochs.

Table 3. The different architectures used for the SLM system, shown as the topology of the SOM and the single layer network. For the SOM this is the number of inputs and nodes in the map. For the single layer network this is the number of input and output nodes.

System	MONK 1	MONK 2	MONK 3	WBCD
	6-5x5: 25-1	6-5x5: 25-1	6-5x5: 25-1	9-5x5: 25-2
SLM	6-10x10: 100-1	6-10x10: 100-1	6-10x10: 100-1	9-10x10: 100-2
	6-20x20: 400-1	6-20x20: 400-1	6-20x20: 400-1	9-20x20 400-2

3.1 Experimental Results

For each of the benchmark data sets, Table 4 shows the percentage mean number of correct test responses for the MLP, SE, SLE and SLM systems. Only the configuration of each system giving the highest mean test percentage is shown.

Table 4. Results for systems with the highest mean test response, with the number of networks / SOM configuration and mean test response, with standard deviation.

System	MONK 1		MONK 2		MONK 3		WBCD	
	Nets	Test %	Nets	Test %	Nets	Test %	Nets	Test %
MLP	1	84.44 ±12.15	1	66.29 ±35.21	1	83.39 ±47.57	1	95.90 ±3.93
MLP (ES)	1	57.13 ± 8.74	1	65.21 ± 2.68	1	63.10 ± 6.83	1	82.34 ±9.61
SE (ES)	3	55.75 ± 7.70	18	66.25 ± 0.81	18	66.03 ±23.10	20	91.94 ±1.69
SLE (ES)	20	**90.21 ± 6.16**	20	69.49 ± 1.24	19	78.57 ± 4.69	20	92.95 ±1.06
SLM	10x10	75.63 ± 4.78	20x20	**75.09 ±26.06**	10x10	**84.10 ± 1.76**	20x20	**97.63 ±0.83**

First we note that for the MONK 1 and 2, the SLE system gives a comparatively better generalisation performance when a relatively large number of networks are combined, with the performance of the SE decreasing with successively more networks. Here a more complex in-situ trained system gives better generalisation, in contrast to the far less complex pre-trained system. For MONK 3 and WBCD, the SLE improves upon the early stopping MLP and SE systems, but not the fixed MLP trained for 1000 epochs. The improvement in generalisation performance can be attributed to the increased training times experienced by the SLE algorithm with increasing numbers of networks as compared with the MLP with early stopping systems. For example, for MONK 1 with 2 networks, the maximum number of epochs is 27 (excluding outliers), which increases to 521 epochs for 20 networks. However, all these are less than the fixed 1000 epochs for the MLP systems, yet give a similar level of performance.

For the SLM system, we note that the sequential combination of networks successfully learns to solve each non-linearly separable task. This is perhaps surprising given that neither is individually capable, and despite the somewhat complex nature of the SLM systems with relatively high numbers of neurons. For MONK 2, 3 and WBCD, the SLM system out-performs the other single network and multi-net systems. For MONK 1 the results are better than both the SE and MLP with early stopping, but do not improve upon the SLE or fixed MLP.

The results for the SLM also show how the number of neurons within the SOM affects the overall performance of the system, perhaps in a similar way to the number of hidden neurons in an MLP. Here, increasing the map size tends to give both improved training and generalisation performance, reaching a peak commensurate with overfitting. For MONK 1 the response for the 10x10 map is better than for the 20x20 map, despite giving a 100% training response, as compared with the 10x10 response of 89.65%. Furthermore, increasing the map size also produces more reliable solutions in that the standard deviation decreases, whilst still maintaining a similar level of generalisation performance.

3.2 Discussion

These preliminary results are encouraging, and demonstrate that in-situ learning in parallel and sequential combinations of networks can give improved generalisation performance, as demonstrated by the results for SLE, and especially the SLM systems. Putting these into context with other reported results shows that they compare well, but it is recognised that some further investigation is required.

For the MONK's problems, optimal generalisation results have been reported with 100%, 100% and 97.2% for MONK 1, 2 and 3 respectively [13]. For the SLE systems the maximum values are 98.4%, 74.5% and 83.1%, and for the SLM systems 84.7%, 81.0% and 87.5%, showing that, whilst there is a small spread of values, further tuning is required to improve the maximum. Here, of interest is the way in which the results demonstrate the use of unsupervised learning in a modular system, giving a significant improvement in generalisation as compared with existing supervised techniques (MONK 2 and 3). For the WBCD data set, the SLM system with a mean of 97.63% again out-performs the SE, and is comparable to other multi-net systems such as AdaBoost with 97.6% [4]. Further work is required to assess the properties of these techniques with other data sets, and especially how the combination of unsupervised and supervised learning can be further exploited for classification tasks.

4 Conclusion

In this paper we have explored whether the use of simultaneous, in-situ learning in multi-net systems can provide improved generalisation in classification tasks. In particular, we have presented results for in-situ learning in an ensemble of redundant networks, and the in-situ learning in a sequential system, the latter of which builds upon the principle that 'simple' networks combined in a modular system are parsimonious, through the combination of supervised and unsupervised techniques.

Acknowledgements

The authors would like to thank Antony Browne and the two anonymous reviewers for their helpful comments.

References

1. Blake,C.L. & Merz,C.J. *UCI Repository of Machine Learning Databases.* http://www.ics.uci.edu/~mlearn/MLRepository.html. Irvine, CA.: University of California, Irvine, Department of Information and Computer Sciences, 1998.
2. Bottou, L. & Gallinari, P. A Framework for the Cooperation of Learning Algorithms. In Lippmann, R.P., Moody, J.E. & Touretzky, D.S. (Ed), *Advances in Neural Information Processing Systems*, vol. 3, pp. 781-788, 1991.
3. Casey, M.C. *Integrated Learning in Multi-net Systems.* Unpublished doctoral thesis. Guildford, UK: University of Surrey, 2004.
4. Drucker, H. Boosting Using Neural Networks. In Sharkey, A. J. C. (Ed), *Combining Artificial Neural Nets: Ensemble and Modular Multi-Net Systems*, pp. 51-78. London: Springer-Verlag, 1999.
5. Jacobs, R.A. & Tanner, M. Mixtures of X. In Sharkey, A. J. C. (Ed), *Combining Artificial Neural Nets: Ensemble and Modular Multi-Net Systems*, pp. 267-295. Berlin, Heidelberg, New York: Springer-Verlag, 1999.
6. Kittler, J., Hatef, M., Duin, R.P.W. & Matas, J. On Combining Classifiers. *IEEE Transactions on Pattern Analysis and Machine Intelligence*, vol. 20(3), pp. 226-239, 1998.
7. Kohonen, T. Self-Organized Formation of Topologically Correct Feature Maps. *Biological Cybernetics*, vol. 43, pp. 59-69, 1982.
8. Liu, Y. & Yao, X. Ensemble Learning via Negative Correlation. *Neural Networks*, vol. 12(10), pp. 1399-1404, 1999.
9. Liu, Y., Yao, X., Zhao, Q. & Higuchi, T. An Experimental Comparison of Neural Network Ensemble Learning Methods on Decision Boundaries. *Proceedings of the 2002 International Joint Conference on Neural Networks (IJCNN'02)*, vol. 1, pp. 221-226. Los Alamitos, CA: IEEE Computer Society Press, 2002.
10. Partridge, D. & Griffith, N. Multiple Classifier Systems: Software Engineered, Automatically Modular Leading to a Taxonomic Overview. *Pattern Analysis and Applications*, vol. 5(2), pp. 180-188, 2002.
11. Prechelt, L. Early Stopping - But When? In Orr, G. B. & Müller, K-R. (Ed), *Neural Networks: Tricks of the Trade, 1524*, pp. 55-69. Berlin, Heidelberg, New York: Springer-Verlag, 1996.
12. Sharkey, A.J.C. Multi-Net Systems. In Sharkey, A. J. C. (Ed), *Combining Artificial Neural Nets: Ensemble and Modular Multi-Net Systems*, pp. 1-30. London: Springer-Verlag, 1999.
13. Thrun, S.B., Bala, J., Bloedorn, E., Bratko, I., Cestnik, B., Cheng, J., De Jong, K., Dzeroski, S., Fahlman, S.E., Fisher, D., Hamann, R., Kaufman, K., Keller, S., Kononenko, I., Kreuziger, J., Michalski, R.S., Mitchell, T., Pachowicz, P., Reich, Y., Vafaie, H., van de Welde, W., Wenzel, W., Wnek, J. & Zhang, J. *The MONK's Problems: A Performance Comparison of Different Learning Algorithms.* Technical Report CMU-CS-91-197. Pittsburgh, PA.: Carnegie-Mellon University, Computer Science Department, 1991.
14. Wanas, N.M., Hodge, L. & Kamel, M.S. Adaptive Training Algorithm for an Ensemble of Networks. *Proceedings of the 2001 International Joint Conference on Neural Networks (IJCNN'01)*, vol. 4, pp. 2590-2595. Los Alamitos, CA.: IEEE Computer Society Press, 2001.
15. Wolberg, W.H. & Mangasarian, O.L. Multisurface Method of Pattern Separation for Medical Diagnosis Applied to Breast Cytology. *Proceedings of the National Academy of Sciences, USA*, vol. 87(23), pp. 9193-9196, 1990.
16. Xu, L., Krzyzak, A. & Suen, C.Y. Several Methods for Combining Multiple Classifiers and Their Applications in Handwritten Character Recognition. *IEEE Transactions on Systems, Man, and Cybernetics*, vol. 22(3), pp. 418-435, 1992.

Multi-objective Genetic Algorithm Based Method for Mining Optimized Fuzzy Association Rules

Mehmet Kaya[1] and Reda Alhajj[2]

[1] Department of Computer Engineering
Firat University, 23119 Elazig, Turkey
kaya@firat.edu.tr
[2] ADSA Lab & Department of Computer Science
University of Calgary, Calgary, Alberta, Canada
alhajj@cpsc.ucalgary.ca

Abstract. This paper introduces optimized fuzzy association rules mining. We propose a multi-objective Genetic Algorithm (GA) based approach for mining fuzzy association rules containing instantiated and uninstantiated attributes. According to our method, fuzzy association rules can contain an arbitrary number of uninstantiated attributes. The method uses three bjectives for the rule mining process: support, confidence and number of fuzzy sets. Experimental results conducted on a real data set demonstrate the effectiveness and applicability of the proposed approach.

1 Introduction

Mining association rules is one of the important research problems in data mining. We argue that equally important to the process of mining association rules is to mine optimized association rules. This has already been realized by some other researchers. The problem of finding optimized association rules was introduced by Fukoda et al [9]. They extended the results to the case where the rules contain two uninstantiated quantitative attributes on the left hand side [10]. Recently, Rastogi and Shim [11, 12] improved the optimized association rules problem in a way that allows association rules to contain a number of uninstantiated attributes.

The work presented in this paper reports the most recent results of our ongoing research on association rules mining. In this paper, we propose a novel method based on a multi-objective GA for determining the most appropriate fuzzy sets in fuzzy association rule mining in such a way that the optimized support and confidence satisfying rules will be obtained. Experimental results obtained using the Letter Recognition Database from the UCI Machine Learning Repository demonstrate that our approach performs well and gives good results even for a larger number of uninstantiated attributes.

The rest of the paper is organized as follows. Section 2 includes a brief overview of fuzzy association rules and introduces the multi-objective optimization problem. Section 3 gives our multi-objective GA based approach to mining optimized fuzzy association rules. The experimental results are reported in Section 4. Section 5 includes a summary and the conclusions.

2 Fuzzy Association Rules and Multi-objective Optimization

Given a database of transactions T, its set of attributes I, it is possible to define some fuzzy sets for attribute i_k with a membership function per fuzzy set such that each value of attribute i_k qualifies to be in one or more of the fuzzy sets specified for i_k. The degree of membership of each value of i_k in any of the fuzzy sets specified for i_k is directly based on the evaluation of the membership function of the particular fuzzy set with the specified value of i_k as input. We use the following form for fuzzy association rules.

Definition 1: A fuzzy association rule is expressed as: If Q={u_1, u_2, ..., u_p} is F_1={f_1, f_2, ..., f_p} then R={v_1, v_2, ..., v_q} is F_2={g_1, g_2, ..., g_q}, where Q and R are disjoint sets of attributes called itemsets, i.e., $Q \subset I$, $R \subset I$ and $Q \cap R = \phi$; F_1 and F_2 contain the fuzzy sets associated with corresponding attributes in Q and R, respectively, i.e., f_i is the fuzzy set related to attribute u_i and g_j is the fuzzy set related to attribute v_j.

A multi-objective optimization problem can be formalized as follows:

Definition 2: A multi-objective optimization problem includes, a set of *a* parameters (decision variables), a set of *b* objective functions, and a set of *c* constraints; objective functions and constraints are functions of the decision variables. The optimization goal is expressed as:

min/max $\quad y = f(x) = (f_1(x), f_2(x),...,f_b(x))$
contraints $\quad e(x) = (e_1(x), e_2(x),...,e_c(x)) \leq 0$
where $\quad x = (x_1, x_2,...,x_a) \in X$
$\quad\quad\quad\; y = (y_1, y_2,...,y_b) \in Y$

where x is decision vector, y is the objective vector, X denotes decision space, and Y is called objective space; constraints $e(x) \leq 0$ determine the set of feasible solutions.

In this paper, we considered the values of support and confidence utilized in the association rules mining process and number of fuzzy sets as objective functions. In this regard, a solution defined by the corresponding decision vector can be better than, worse, or equal to, but also indifferent from another solution with respect to the objective values. Better means a solution is not worse in any objective and better with respect to at least one objective than another. Using this concept, an optimal solution can be defined as: a solution which is not dominated by any other solution in the search space. Such a solution is called Pareto optimal, and the entire set of optimal trade-offs is called the Pareto-optimal set. In the next section, we describe how this multi-objective optimization method has been utilized to handle the mining of optimized fuzzy association rules.

3 The Proposed Multi-objective GA Based Approach

In this study, we use the support, confidence and number of fuzzy sets as objectives of the multi-objective GA. Our aim in using such an approach is to determine optimized fuzzy association rules. Therefore, by using this approach, the values of support and confidence of a rule are maximized in large number of fuzzy sets. According to our intuition, stronger rules can be mined with larger number of fuzzy sets because more appropriate fuzzy rules can be found as the number of fuzzy sets is increased.

Throughout this study, we proposed two different encoding schemes. The first handles the rules with instantiated attributes. In such a case, each individual represents the base values of membership functions of a quantitative attribute in the database. In the experiments, we used membership functions in triangular shape.

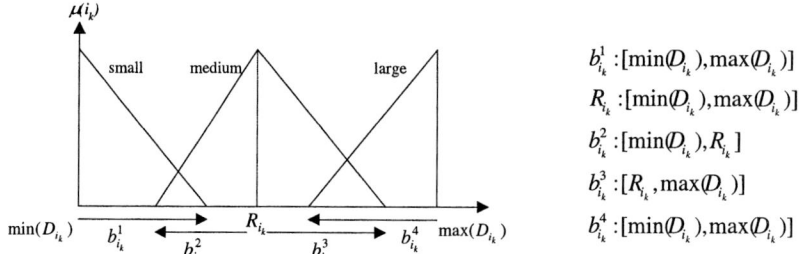

Fig. 1. Membership functions and base variables of attribute i_k.

To illustrate the encoding scheme utilized in this study, membership functions for a quantitative attribute i_k having 3 fuzzy sets and their base variables are shown in Figure 2. Each base variable takes finite values. For instance, the search space of the base value $b_{i_k}^1$ lies between the minimum and maximum values of attribute i_k, denoted $\min(D_{i_k})$ and $\max(D_{i_k})$, respectively. Enumerated next to Figure 2 are the search intervals of all the base values and the intersection point R_{i_k} of attribute i_k.

So, based on the assumption of having 3 fuzzy sets per attribute, as it is the case with attribute i_k, a chromosome consisting of the base lengths and the intersection point is represented in the following form: $b_{i_1}^1 b_{i_1}^2 R_{i_1} b_{i_1}^3 b_{i_1}^4 b_{i_2}^1 b_{i_2}^2 R_{i_2} b_{i_2}^3 b_{i_2}^4 ... b_{i_m}^1 b_{i_m}^2 R_{i_m} b_{i_m}^3 b_{i_m}^4$

To illustrate the process, consider 5 quantitative attributes and assumed that each attribute can have at most 5 fuzzy sets. So, a chromosome consisting of the base lengths and the intersecting points is represented in the following form:

$$w_{i_1} b_{i_1}^1 b_{i_1}^{12} R_{i_1}^1 b_{i_1}^2 b_{i_1}^3 R_{i_1}^2 b_{i_1}^4 b_{i_1}^5 R_{i_1}^3 b_{i_1}^6 b_{i_1}^7 R_{i_1}^4 b_{i_1}^8 b_{i_1}^9 R_{i_1}^5 b_{i_1}^{10} b_{i_1}^{11} ... w_{i_5} b_{i_5}^1 b_{i_5}^{12} ... R_{i_5}^5 b_{i_5}^{10} b_{i_5}^{11}$$

where, gene w_{i_j} denotes the number of fuzzy sets for attributes i_j. If the number of fuzzy set equals 2, then while decoding the individual, the first two base variables are considered and the others are omitted. However, if w_{i_j} is raised to 3, then the next three variables are taken into account as well. So, as the number of fuzzy set increases, the number of variables to be taken into account is enhanced too.

In the case of uninstantiated rule, we associate two extra bits with each attribute. If these two bits are 00 then, the attribute appears in the antecedent part. However, if it is 11 then the attribute appears in the consequent part. Other combinations denote the absence of the attribute in either of those parts. So, we have 2m extra bits in each chromosome, where m is the number of attributes in the database. The difference of this second approach from the first one is that it finds the relevant rules along with their number of fuzzy sets and the base values.

In the experiments, we used binary coding method. While the value of a variable (gene) is reflected under its own search interval, the following formula is employed:

$$b_{i_j}^k = \min(b_{i_j}^k) + \frac{d}{2^L - 1}(\max(b_{i_j}^k) - \min(b_{i_j}^k))$$

where d is the decimal value of the variable in search, L is the number of bits used to represent a variable in the encoding scheme, $\min(b_{i_j}^k)$ and $\max(b_{i_j}^k)$ are, respectively, the minimum and the maximum values of the reflected area.

As mentioned earlier, in multi-objective problems, both fitness assignment and selection must allow for several objectives. One of the methods used for fitness assignments is to make direct use of the concepts of Pareto dominance. In this concept, fitness value is computed using their ranks, which are calculated from the non-dominance property of the chromosomes. The ranking step tries to obtain the non-dominated solutions. According to this step, if c_i chromosomes dominate an individual then its rank is assigned as c_i+1. This process continues until all the individuals are ranked. After each individual has fitness value, the individuals with the smallest rank constitutes the highest fitness. Finally, selection (we have adopted elitism policy in our experiments), replacement, crossover and mutation operators are applied to form a new population as in standard GA. Finally, the whole multi-objective GA process employed in this study can be summarized as:

Algorithm 1 (Mining optimized fuzzy association rules)

Input: Population size: N; Maximum number of generations: G; Crossover probability: p_c; Mutation rate: p_m
Output: Nondominated set: S

1. Set $P_0 = \phi$ and $t = 0$,
   For h=1 to N do: Choose $i \in I$, where i is an individual and I is the individual space, according to some probability distribution, and set $P_0 = P_0 + \{i\}$
2. For each individual $i \in P_t$: Determine the encoded decision vector and objective vector and alculate the scalar fitness value $F(i)$ with respect to the approach mentioned above.
3. Set $P' = \phi$
   For h=1 to N do: Select one individual $i \in P_t$ with respect to its fitness value $F(i)$ and set $P' = P' + \{i\}$
4. Set $P'' = \phi$
   For h=1 to N/2 do: Choose two individuals $i, j \in P'$ and remove them from P' and recombine i and j; the resulting offspring are $k, l \in I$; then insert k, l into P'' with probability p_c, otherwise insert i, j into P''
5. Set $P''' = \phi$
   For each individual $i \in P''$ do: Mutate i with mutation rate p_m. The resulting individual is $j \in I$, and set $P''' = P''' + \{j\}$.
6. Set $P_{t+1} = P'''$ and $t = t + 1$.
   If $t \geq G$ or another termination criterion is satisfied then return $S = p(P_t)$, where $p(P_t)$ gives the set of nondominated decision vectors in P_t. In other words, the set $p(P_t)$ is the nondominated set regarding P_t. Otherwise go to Step 2, i.e., execute steps 2 to 6.

4 Experimental Results

We apply the proposed multi-objective GA based approach to the Letter Recognition Database from the UCI Machine Learning Repository. The database consists of 20K samples and 16 quantitative attributes. We concentrated our analysis on only 5 quantitative attributes. In all the experiments in this study, the GA process starts with a population of 50 individuals for both approaches, with instantiated and uninstantiated rules. Further, crossover and mutation probabilities are taken, respectively, as 0.8 and 0.01, and 4-point crossover operator is utilized.

Table 1. Objective values for the optimized fuzzy instantiated rules.

Number of Fuzzy Sets / Support (%) / Confidence (%)
2
36.86
69.43
30.61
72.66
25.48
78.11
3
27.14
63.24
25.20
76.16
21.45
84.17
4
23.26
54.75
20.34
82.15
19.21
87.05
5
8.52
41.63
7.21
67.37
6.18
80.12

Table 2. Objective values for the optimized instantiated rules by using discrete method.

Number of Discrete Intervals / Support (%) / Confidence (%)
2
21.66
57.21
20.48
59.40
19.23
66.11
3
13.07
47.15
11.12
53.27
10.17
68.23
4
8.42
38.46
8.20
46.12
7.78
68.17
5
6.21
51.13
6.02
67.12
5.88
71.76

The first experiment is dedicated to find the non-dominated set of the proposed method for an instantiated rule at 20K. The results are reported in Table 1, where the values of support and confidence for some non-dominated solutions are given for four different numbers of fuzzy sets. From Table 1, it can be easily seen that as the number of fuzzy sets increases, the support value of the instantiated rules decreases. This is true because a large number of sets will make quantities of an item in different transactions easily scatter in different sets. However, for each number of fuzzy sets, as the support value decreases, the confidence value increases because more specific rules are generated.

Table 3. Number of rules generated vs. number of generations.

Number of Generations	Number of Rules
250	136
500	182
750	204
1000	217
1250	223
1500	225
1750	225

The second experiment is dedicated for the case where the first experiment is repeated with discrete method instead of fuzzy sets. The results are reported in Table 2. An important point here is that the values of support and confidence are smaller than those of the fuzzy approach. This demonstrates an important feature of using fuzzy sets; they are more flexible than their discrete counterparts. As a result, stronger rules and larger number of rules can be obtained using fuzzy sets.

The final experiment is conducted to find the number of uninstantiated rules generated for different numbers of generations. We used stability of the rules as the termination criteria. The average results of 5 runs are reported in Table 3, from which it can be easily observed that the GA convergences after 1250 generations. In other words, it almost does not produce more rules. It is also observed that most of the rules include 2 quantitative attributes. Only 6 rules were obtained that contain all the attributes. In fact, most of the rules contain 2 attributes because a small number of attributes means the corresponding rule has a larger value of support, i.e., as the number of attributes in the rule increases, the support value of the rule decreases almost exponentially.

5 Summary and Conclusions

In this paper, we contributed to the ongoing research on association rules mining by proposing a multi-objective GA based method for mining optimized fuzzy association rules. Our approach uses three measures as the objectives of the method: support, confidence and number of fuzzy sets. The proposed method can be applied to two different cases: dealing with rules containing instantiated attributes and those with uninstantiated attributes. The former case finds only optimized sets of fuzzy rules, and the latter case obtains the most appropriate fuzzy sets along with uninstantiated attributes. The results obtained from the conducted experiments demonstrate the effectiveness and applicability of the optimized fuzzy rules over the discrete based rules with respect to the values of support and confidence. Currently, we are investigating the optimization of all fuzzy sets of the attributes in a single rule.

References

1. M. Delgado, N. Marin, D. Sanchez and M. A. Vila, "Fuzzy Association Rules: General Model and Applications", *IEEE TFS*, Vol.11, No.2, pp. 214-225, 2003.
2. M. Kaya, R. Alhajj, F. Polat and A. Arslan, "Efficient Automated Mining of Fuzzy Association Rules," *Proc. of DEXA*, 2002.
3. M. Kaya and R. Alhajj, "A Clustering Algorithm with Genetically Optimized Membership Functions for Fuzzy Association Rules Mining", *Proc. of Fuzz-IEEE*, St Louis, MO, 2003
4. M. Kaya and R. Alhajj, "Facilitating Fuzzy Association Rules Mining by Using Multi-Objective Genetic Algorithms for Automated Clustering", *Proc. of IEEE ICDM*, Melbourne, FL, 2003.
5. T. Fukuda, et al, "Mining Optimized Association Rules for Numeric Attributes", *Proc. of ACM SIGACT-SIGMOD-SIGART PODS*, 1996.
6. T. Fukuda, Y. Morimoto, S. Morishita and T. Tokuyama, "Data Mining Using Two Dimensional Optimized Association Rules: Scheme, Algorithms, and Visualization", *Proc. of ACM SIGMOD*, 1996.
7. R. Rastogi and K. Shim, "Mining Optimized Support Rules for Numeric Attributes", *Information Systems*, Vol.26, pp.425-444, 2001
8. R. Rastogi and K. Shim, "Mining Optimized Association Rules with Categorical and Numeric Attributes", *IEEE TKDE*, Vol.14, No.1, pp.29-50, 2002.

Co-training from an Incremental EM Perspective

Minoo Aminian

Computer Science Dept.
SUNY Albany, Albany, NY, USA, 12222
minoo@cs.albany.edu

Abstract. We study classification when the majority of data is unlabeled, and only a small fraction is labeled: the so-called semi-supervised learning situation. Blum and Mitchell's co-training is a popular semi-supervised algorithm [1] to use when we have multiple independent views of the entities to classify. An example of a multi-view situation is classifying web pages: one view may describe the pages by the words that occur on them, another view describes the pages by the words in the hyperlinks that point to them. In co-training two learners each form a model from the labeled data and then incrementally label small subsets of the unlabeled data for each other. The learners then re-estimate their model from the labeled data and the psuedo-labels provided by the learners. Though some analysis of the algorithm's performance exists [1] the computation performed is still not well understood. We propose that each view in co-training is effectively performing incremental EM as postulated by Neal and Hinton [3], combined with a Bayesian classifier. This analysis suggests improvements over the core co-training algorithm. We introduce variations, which result in faster convergence to the maximum possible accuracy of classification than the core co-training algorithm, and therefore increase the learning efficiency. We empirically verify our claim for a number of data sets in the context of belief network learning.

1 Introduction and Motivation

The learning from unlabeled and labeled data problem is an example of the next generation of learning. In this situation, also known as semi-supervised learning, the learner has a relatively small collection of labeled data points $D_l = \{(x_1, y_1) \ldots (x_n, y_n)\}$ and a large amount of unlabeled data $D_u = \{x_{n+1}, \ldots, x_{n+m}\}$. It is assumed that both labeled and unlabeled data are drawn from the same population, but it is too costly or difficult to label every single instance so only a small subset are given labels. The aim is to learn a function to predict the dependent variable y from the independent variables x. Interestingly it is possible to obtain a better (more accurate) classifier by using the unlabeled and labeled data than by just using the labeled data [6]. Many problems, particularly those in security, lend themselves to algorithms that can learn from carefully labeled data and large amounts of unlabeled data. There have been many success stories of semi-supervised learning for applications such as text processing [1] using basic classifiers such as naïve Bayes.

Co-training as first introduced by Blum and Mitchell [1], is a semi-supervised algorithm applicable to problems with two different views under conditions that the views are compatible and independent. By compatibility we mean all examples are classified identically in each view, and feature set independence requires that for any example $x = (x_1, x_2)$ belonging to the class c, x_1 and x_2 are conditionally independent given c. From the small set of labeled examples each learner creates an initial weak classifier (better than random guessing) and then applies this weak classifier to unlabeled data. Next, the **most-confident** examples (with associated pseudo-labels) from each view/learner are added to the initial training set and the learners rebuild their models. This process is repeated for a number of times until the learner's performance stabilizes or all the unlabeled data are labeled. Co-training can be viewed as a method of filling in the missing labels for the data much like EM. The EM algorithm is a general method of finding the maximum-likelihood estimate of the parameters of an underlying distribution from a given data set when the data is incomplete or has missing values [7]. However, unlike EM which performs quite poorly when the number of missing values is much larger, co-training performs quite well in this situation provided that its special assumptions of conditional independency, and compatibility hold.

Throughout this paper we will use graphical models of learning. Perhaps the simplest classification model is the Naïve Bayes classifier. In the multi-view situation we can define the instance space as $X = X_1 \times X_2$ where X_1 and X_2 are two different views or disjoint subsets of features. For an instance X with class c, out of a total of C classes, Bayesian inference assigns a label according to the maximum a posteriori class. Formally:

$$y = \arg\max_c p(c \mid X) \quad (1)$$

This paper makes two primary contributions. First, we illustrate that co-training can be viewed as using an EM-type algorithm. Second, we postulate variations of standard co-training motivated by our prior analysis that we empirically verify outperforms standard co-training. We begin this paper by showing that co-training can be viewed as combining incremental EM, which was first postulated by Neal and Hinton [3], with a classifier. In section 2 we briefly describe traditional EM with a single view. We then describe the Neal and Hinton's new view of EM with a single view and show that the extension to two views gives rise to another variant of co-training which can result in higher accuracy under certain conditions. Section 3 illustrates our variations of co-training which we empirically illustrate out-performs standard co-training. Section 4 compares the setting of these algorithms and gives an error analysis. Section 5 discusses relevant work and we summarize our contributions and conclude in section 6.

2 Semi-supervised Learning with EM

In a variety of settings we show the two steps (expectation and maximization) used in EM in the semi-supervised learning context.

2.1 Traditional and New View of EM with One View

Consider a data set that contains both observed data x and unobserved (or missing) data y. The goal of EM, is to find a model that maximizes the *complete* log likelihood of the data (both observed and missing): $L(\theta|x,y) = \log p(x,y | \theta)$. Since the value of y is unknown, EM maximizes the *expectation* of this quantity with respect to the distribution $Q(y) = p(y | x, \theta)$ by repeatedly applying the following:

E-step:
$$\text{Compute the distribution } \tilde{p}^i = p(y | x, \theta^{i-1}) \text{ over the range of } y$$

M-step:
$$\theta^i \leftarrow \arg\max_\theta E_{\tilde{p}^i}[\log p(x, y | \theta)]$$

In EM, we are basically maximizing a likelihood score function when some of the data are missing, and since in semi-supervised learning we can treat the unlabeled data as data with missing labels, it is possible to combine both labeled and unlabeled data to improve the parameter estimates. Therefore, in the context of semi-supervised learning, it is possible to use the traditional view EM to assign labels to *all* the unlabeled data probabilistically. Then train a new classifier using the labels for all the data, and iterate to convergence. For further details regarding EM, we refer readers to [7] and [3].

2.2 A New Incremental View of EM

Neal and Hinton [3] propose a new perspective of the EM procedure, that in each iteration updates the model parameters based on *part* of the training set instead of all of it. This is equivalent to *partially* labeling the training set. They discuss incrementally labeling one instance (filling in the missing value) or labeling a set of instances to save computation time. We now describe their approach formally for one view and will show how co-training is an extension to two views.

As incremental EM does not use all of the data we must divide the data into independent subsets according to those used at a particular time and then process them incrementally in the computation. Let the data x be broken into independent subsets $\{\vec{x}_k\}$, $k = 1, \ldots, K$. Let $\vec{x}_k$ have the probability $p(x_k | \theta)$, the unobserved variables be $y = \{\vec{y}_k\}$, $k = 1, \ldots, K$, and S_k be a sufficient statistic associated with $\vec{x}_k$. By sufficient statistics we mean a function of data from which we can estimate the parameters of the model distribution rather than using the data. For example the joint density of independent and identically distributed observations from a normal distribution for a typical data set $x = \{x_i\}_{i=1,\ldots,n}$ has the sample parameters $\{\sum_1^n x_i, \sum_1^n x_i^2\}$ as sufficient statistics, since from these we can estimate the mean and variance of the population. Then Neal and Hinton's incremental interpretation of EM can be viewed as follows:

Initialization: let $S(x, y) = \sum_i S_i(x_i, y_i)$ be the vector of sufficient statistics, starting with an initial guess for each subset, $S_i^{(0)}$, (e.g. set each S_i to zero) proceed with the following iterations:

E-step:

    Select some subset of data to label: $\vec{x}_k$.

    Compute $S_k^{j+1} = E_{\tilde{p}_k^{j+1}}[S_k(\vec{x}_k, y_k)]$, Note, this is the expectation of the sufficient statistic where the expectation is taken over:

$$\tilde{p}_k^{j+1}(y_k) = p(y_k \mid \vec{x}_k, \theta^j)$$

    Compute the summation of the sufficient statistics $S^{j+1} = \sum_i S_i^j$

M-step:

    Set θ^{j+1} that maximizes $E[S(x, y) \mid \theta] = S^{j+1}$.

Notice that selection of the subset of data or, $\vec{x}_k$, can be very flexible, for example, we can process the E-step on a single instance or on multiple instances and selection can be done sequentially or randomly. Incremental EM gives no indication how to select the instances, only that we should calculate the expectation over the sufficient statistic. As mentioned before, we can use traditional EM in the context of semi-supervised learning to assign labels to *all* the unlabeled instances in each iteration, regardless of the confidence assigned to each instance. An example of incremental version of EM, in each iteration selects the unlabeled instances that are classified most-confidently by the current model, and assigns labels only to them then adds these newly labeled instances to the labeled set. Then this new augmented labeled set is used to estimate model parameters again, and this process is repeated until all the unlabeled data is labeled.

Incremental EM has a sound theoretical foundation and stable convergence to stationary points can be guaranteed even when the likelihood does not increase monotonically [8].

We conclude this section by comparing the E and M steps of the traditional and incremental EM. While M-step is the same in both algorithms their difference lies in how they compute the sufficient statistics in the E-step. Given the current model parameters, traditional EM computes the expected sufficient statistics on all of the data while incremental EM computes the expected sufficient statistics on a selected subset of the data, S_k, and then computes complete expected sufficient statistics incrementally by keeping the past sufficient statistics of S_i with i other than k, and adding these values to S_k.

2.3 Co-training and Incremental EM

Our claim is that, in co-training each learning algorithm is effectively performing incremental EM, not that the two views together are performing incremental EM. In co-training each view/learner uses the initial labeled set to train a generative classifier, and then this classifier is applied to the unlabeled data. In each iteration, an equal number of most-confidently labeled instances from each view is combined as a hybrid set R = {R_1, R_2} to augment the pool of labeled data for the next time training of each classifier. This hybrid constitutes $\vec{x}_k$ in the incremental EM notation.

For our claim that a learner in co-training is performing incremental EM to hold, we need to show that the co-training labeling process is calculating (approximately) the expectation of the model's sufficient statistic (the E step) and that given this sufficient statistic the model maximizes the likelihood (the M step). Learners such as naïve Bayes and belief networks (with no missing **independent** variable values) choose the model that maximizes the likelihood (or MAP) estimate which is well known.

We are then left to show our approach calculates the expectation (over the conditional probabilities of each possible label) of the sufficient statistics. The sufficient statistics for graphical generative models with no missing independent variable values is simply the counts of each combination of events occurring. For R_1 (which are say instances labeled by learner A) the distribution over the conditional probabilities will be asymmetrical (because these are the most confidently labeled instances by this learner) that the expected value of the sufficient statistic will be approximately same as the product of the sufficient statistic and the highest conditional probability. For R_2 (which are instances labeled by the other learner) the distribution over the conditional probabilities will be typically uniform (because these are instances typically not confidently labeled by this view). Then if this learner were to calculate the sufficient statistics over an expectation with each class being equally probable this computation does not effect the model as the instance is "equally distributed" amongst all classes. Instead the expectation of the sufficient statistics for instances in R_2 is replaced by labeling according to another skewed distribution (this time created by the other learner). If this distribution is "correct" then the learner will converge more quickly by using these instances than if they were to be labeled by itself. In co-training the labeling from the other view plays a critical role. Since if it is coming from a *helpful* distribution, it can allow the view to correct its path to have faster convergence by providing it with more random examples. So given the conditional independence assumption, if each view can learn the target concept from random classification noise in the standard PAC learning model, then it can benefit from additional random examples provided by the other view especially during the time that it is a weak classifier. We will explore this analysis further in future works.

3 Variations to Co-training

The above analysis lends itself to creating variations that should improve the performance of co-training. We now discuss two of these that can be used together. Generalized co-training is a combined view variant to incremental EM where the learners label instances *together* and Co-MAX, which is consistent with the original co-training, except for instead of choosing a random pool U' from the unlabeled data, first find a set which is the best representative of the input distribution. Here, we should mention the setting under which these algorithms improve the co-training. Co-MAX will improve co-training whether the views are independent or not. Generalized co-training is a combined view EM, thus while it still has good performance even when the views are independent, it will perform better than co-training when there is a correlation between the views. Therefore, to improve co-training, when the views are independent we can use Co-MAX, and when the two views are correlated we can use generalized co-training.

3.1 Generalized Co-training

In Generalized co-training, we consider the most-confident instances based on the product of the conditional probabilities of each view to augment the training set, which means we do incremental EM using both views or in the E-step, we compute $p(c \mid X_1, X_2, \theta_1, \theta_2)$ and label the instances based on:

$$y = \underset{c}{\operatorname{argmax}}\, p(c \mid X_1, X_2, \theta_1, \theta_2)$$

Notice that in this approach, we are using a combined view EM based on $p(c \mid X_1, X_2, \theta_1, \theta_2)$ which if the views are conditionally independent will be:

$$p(c \mid x_1, x_2, \theta_1, \theta_2) \propto p(c \mid x_1, \theta_1) p(c \mid x_2, \theta_2) \qquad (6)$$

In co-training, independence of the two views plays an important role. Since when they are not tightly correlated, if they are helpful distributions, they can provide useful random examples for each other to boost up each other's performance especially when predictions are weak. Using combined view EM, if the two views are strongly independent, by multiplying the class probabilities from each view in equation (6), we are lowering down this effect especially where there is a disagreement between the two views, therefore the performance, though still high, will not be as good as regular co-training, while if there is a correlation between the two views, it will out perform regular co-training.

3.2 Co-MAX

As mentioned before to make best use of unlabeled data in semi-supervised learning, we can encode the prior knowledge or some aspect of input distribution. Co-training implements this idea by assuming compatibility of the target concept with the input distribution, and this is what we use to enhance the performance of co-training. Blum & Mitchell [1] state that in their earlier implementation of co-training, they allowed the two views to select examples directly from all of the unlabeled data, but have obtained better results using a smaller random pool. We believe that when learners are allowed to select their instances to label when they are weak classifiers may lead to an unrepresentative set of instances. Our second variation to co-training attempts to overcome this problem. If from unlabeled data, instead of picking a random pool we pick a set which is the best representative of input distribution, then the concept learnt from that set combined with the labeled set, is the most compatible with the input distribution, and therefore will speed up the process of learning. Implementing this idea, would provide co-training the best representative sample of unlabeled data, which combined with the labeled sample, makes the training set to learn from, and therefore conceives the target concept faster. We use the Bayesian Central Limit theorem, in order to find a set A, which is the best representative of input distribution in unlabeled data [2], and use that set instead of random pool U'.

3.3 An Algorithm to Implement Generalized Co-training and Co-MAX Together

In this section we describe an algorithm to implement the two previously mentioned extensions.

Table 1. Generalized Co-MAX.

> Given:
> - a target concept θ to learn and two views X_1 and X_2
> - a set of labeled data D_l
> - a set of unlabeled data D_u
>
> Generalized CO-MAX :
>   Choose m random samples of size r
>   Learn the network parameters for each dataset
>   Find the expected parameters over all models learnt
>   Pick a set A containing k top models closest to the average parameters
>   Run **co-training**(θ, D_l, A, X_1, X_2), but label each instance using equation (6)

4 Related Work

Co-EM [4] is another semi-supervised multi-view algorithm which is a hybrid of co-training and EM. However, in this algorithm each view labels iteratively **all** the unlabeled examples and uses the result to train the other view. Both co-training and Co-EM are highly sensitive to correlation of features in the domain. The basic difference between the two algorithms is that Co-EM uses *all* the unlabeled data in each iteration for training while co-training incrementally uses the unlabeled data by just adding the high-confidence predictions to the training set. The algorithm referred to as Co-Testing [3] is a multi–view active learning algorithm and starts with a few labeled examples and a pool of unlabeled data. Co-Testing searches for the most informative examples in the pool of unlabeled data and asks an oracle to label them. Finally Co-EMT [3] is based upon running Co-EM on both labeled and unlabeled examples first and asks an Oracle to label the examples where each view predicts a different label with high-confidence and adds the newly labeled contention points to the training set and repeats the process. Our extensions are different to these approaches as like co-training it incrementally labels the instances and does not require an oracle.

5 Empirical Results

In order to test our algorithm, we pick the Insurance and Alarm datasets from the Bayesian Network Repository. We implemented co-training in belief network by choosing two subnets that independent from each other cause the accident. Each of these nodes would represent one of the views, and we ran the core co-training algorithm on labeled data of size 100 to get the initial weak classifiers. Next we recorded the accuracy of these classifiers on a random pool of 1000 from 100,000 unlabeled data. For each classifier the 10 most-confident instances were picked and added to the training set and the two classifiers were trained again. The whole process repeats for a number of iterations until the learners error stabilizes. Next, we tried CO-MAX by running co-training algorithm, but this time instead of picking a random pool from unlabeled data based on the conditional probability of accident, we picked a pool of 10 training set of size 100, such that the conditional probability of the label in those models, based on the Kullback Leibler distance, were closest to the mean value and used that set as the pool of the unlabeled data to be added to the training set in the co-training algorithm. We used five different labeled training set and recorded the average accuracy. As the result in figure 1 and 2 show, our variations lead to convergence to the higher accuracy is less time than regular co-training.

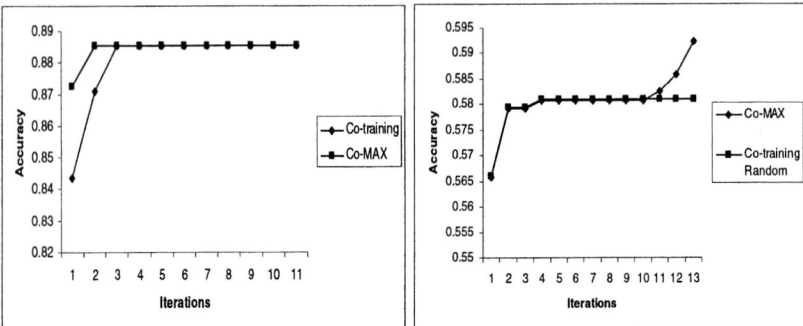

Fig. 1. The average comparative performance of co-training and co-max for two belief network data sets Alarm (Left) and Insurance (Right).

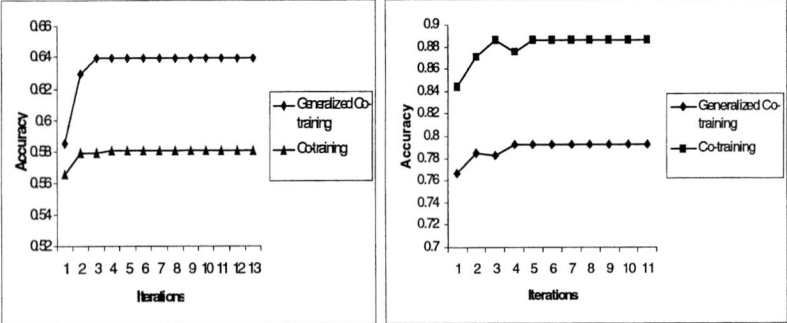

Fig. 2. For two data sets the performance of Generalized co-training and regular co-training. The views in the right figure (Alarm) are strongly independent, so the regular co-training has a better performance, while in the left figure (Insurance), the independence between the views is less, so Generalized co-training performs better.

6 Conclusion

We have focused on multi-view problems of learning a classification concept where majority of data is not labeled. This work is based on co-training, a well known multi-view algorithm. We show how to interpret co-training as incremental EM which motivates two efficient variations to co-training, CO-MAX, and Generalized co-training. We empirically verify that these improvements improve the accuracy of learning and reduces the time to reach convergence. Finally, we find that one variation of ours, generalized co-training out-performs co-training when the views are not completely independent.

References

1. A. Blum and T. Mitchell. Combining Labeled and Unlabeled Data with Co- training, COLT, 1998.
2. I. Davidson and M. Aminian. Using the Central Limit Theorem for Belief Network Learning. In Proceedings of the 8th Int. Symposium on A.I. and Math 2004
3. M. Neal and G. Hinton. A New View of the EM Algorithm that Justifies Incremental and Other Variants. In Biometrika, 1993.
4. Ion Muslea, Steven Minton, and Craig Knoblock. Active + Semi-Supervised Learning = Robust Multi-View Learning. In Proceedings of the 19th International Conference on Machine Learning, pages 435-442, 2002.
5. K. Nigam, R. Ghani. Understanding the Behavior of Co-training. In Proceedings of the Workshop on Text Mining at the Sixth ACM SIGKDD International Conference on Knowledge Discovery and Data Mining, KDD, 2000.
6. M. Seeger. Learning with Labeled and Unlabeled Data. Technical Report, 2000.
7. J. A. Bilmes. A Gentle Tutorial of the EM Algorithm, TR-97-021, April 1998
8. W. Byrne and A. Gunawardana. Comments on "Efficient Training Algorithm for HMM's Using Incremental Estimation", IEEE Transactions on Speech and Audio Processing, Vol. 8, No. 6, November 2000

Locally Tuned General Regression for Learning Mixture Models Using Small Incomplete Data Sets with Outliers and Overlapping Classes

Ahmed Rafat

Department of Computer Science, University of Exeter, Exeter EX4 4QF, UK
A.R.A.M.Salem@ex.ac.uk

Abstract. Finite mixture models are commonly used in pattern recognition. Parameters of these models are usually estimated via the Expectation Maximization algorithm. This algorithm is modified earlier to handle incomplete data. However, the modified algorithm is sensitive to the occurrence of outliers in the data and to the overlap among data classes in the data space. Meanwhile, it requires the number of missing values to be small in order to produce good estimations of the model parameters. Therefore, a new algorithm is proposed in this paper to overcome these problems. A comparison study shows the preference of the proposed algorithm to other algorithms commonly used in the literature including the modified Expectation Maximization algorithm.

1 Introduction

Finite mixture models (FMM) is a semi-parametric method that has the advantage of the analytic simplicity of the parametric methods and the advantage of the flexibility to model complex data distributions of the nonparametric methods [1]. It is shown in [2, 3] that FMM can model any arbitrary data distribution. In cluster analysis, FMM is used as a probabilistic algorithm for partitioning a given data (see for examples, [2, 4, 5]).

Parameters of the FMM are usually determined by the Expectation Maximization (EM) algorithm [6]. It is shown in [7] that the EM algorithm can be used in determining parameters of a multivariate normal distribution using a data set with missing values. The EM algorithm is modified in [8] to determine parameters of a mixture of multivariate normal distributions using an incomplete data (we refer to this algorithm as the MEM algorithm in the rest of this paper). However, the outcome of this algorithm is influenced by a lot of specific modelling assumptions such as the number of components and the probability distribution function of each component [9, 10]. In addition, this algorithm has a poor performance when the data size is small [9]. It is shown in [9] that better results can be obtained by imputing missing values using the distribution of the input feature vectors rather than using a priori probability distribution function used in the FMM.

In this paper, a new algorithm is proposed to overcome these problems. The proposed algorithm is less sensitive to the modelling assumptions than the modified EM algorithm [8] in estimating missing values. In addition, it is less sensitive to the learning problems of the EM algorithm in cases such as the occurrence of outliers in the data set and the overlapping among data classes.

2 The Proposed Algorithm for Learning FMM Parameters

The proposed algorithm uses the General Regression Neural Network (GRNN) [11], which is a kernel-based regression algorithm, in the E-step of the EM algorithm to obtain multiple imputations for each missing value in the data set. Each imputation is obtained via a non-linear multivariate regression using a group of fully observed feature vectors belonging to one of the FMM components. These groups are obtained using Bayes decision rule such that each fully observed feature vector $\mathbf{x}$ is assigned to a certain component i if $P(i|\mathbf{x}) > P(j|\mathbf{x})$ for all $j \neq i$, where $P(i|\mathbf{x})$ is the probability that $\mathbf{x}$ is generated from the component i. Then, some statistical moments necessary for the M-step are computed for each component. In the M-step of the EM algorithm, the maximum likelihood estimates of the FMM parameters are computed. The algorithm iterates until the convergence condition is achieved. The proposed algorithm is referred to as the Locally-tuned General Regression with the Expectation Maximization algorithm (LGREM).

Due to the use of the GRNN in estimating the missing values the LGREM algorithm learns a non-linear regression surface given the parameters of each component in the FMM. This allows the LGREM algorithm to have more flexibility in fitting the data distribution than the MEM algorithm, which estimates the missing values using linear multivariate regression given the parameters of each component in the FMM. Also, this allows the LGREM algorithm to impute the missing values in the data set with higher accuracy than the MEM algorithm. This is because the imputation of the missing values in the LGREM algorithm is less dependent on the estimation of the FMM parameters than in the MEM algorithm. This in turn makes the LGREM algorithm more robust than the MEM algorithm to the outliers and to the other breakdown processes in the model assumptions.

Description of the LGREM Algorithm. Suppose that the data set $\mathcal{R} = \{\mathbf{x}_1, \mathbf{x}_2, ..., \mathbf{x}_N\}$ consists of N feature vectors each of which is a vector in d-feature space such that each feature vector $\mathbf{x}_i = [x_{i1}, x_{i2}, ..., x_{id}]^T = (\mathbf{x}_i^o, \mathbf{x}_i^m)$, where o and m superscripts denote the observed and the missing values in this feature vector. This data set is assumed to be generated from a FMM of K multivariate normal distributions with unknown mixing coefficients $P(c)$, where $\sum_{c=1}^{K} P(c) = 1$, and $0 \leq P(c) \leq 1$. Let the probability density function of the feature vector $\mathbf{x}_i$, which is fully observed, given the kth component in the FMM be $p(\mathbf{x}_i | \boldsymbol{\theta}_k) = N(\mathbf{x}_i; \boldsymbol{\mu}_k, \boldsymbol{\Sigma}_k)$, where $\boldsymbol{\mu}_k$ and $\boldsymbol{\Sigma}_k$ are the mean and the covariance matrix of this component. The total density function of $\mathbf{x}_i$ from the FMM is then computed as $p(\mathbf{x}_i) = \sum_{c=1}^{K} P(c) p(\mathbf{x}_i | \boldsymbol{\theta}_c)$. The LGREM is then described as follows.

Step 0: Normalise the values on each data feature to be in the interval [0,1].

Step 1: Determine the optimum smoothing parameters σ_q, used in the estimation of the missing values in **Step 3**, for all incomplete data features using the leave-one-out method as shown in [11]. In computing the smoothing parameter for a certain incomplete data feature, the Euclidean distances used in the leave-one-out method are measured over the subspace that consists of the fully observed data features and the incomplete data features that have lower missing rates than the current one.

Step 2: Initialise the EM algorithm randomly.

Step 3: In the E-step, compute the following quantities for each model component c in the FMM.

- The posterior probabilities vector $\mathbf{z}_i$ for all feature vectors in the input data set $\mathcal{R}$ as follows,

$$\hat{z}_{ic} = \hat{P}(c) p(\mathbf{x}_i^o \mid \boldsymbol{\theta}_c) / \sum_{j=1}^{K} \hat{P}(j) p(\mathbf{x}_i^o \mid \boldsymbol{\theta}_j) \qquad (1)$$

- The estimates of the missing values in $\mathcal{R}$ starting with those values in the feature that has the minimum missing rate as follows,

$$E(\hat{x}_{iq}^c \mid \mathbf{x}_i^o, \mathbf{R}) = \sum_{k=1}^{n_o} x_{kq} \exp(-D_k^2 / 2\sigma_q^2) r_{kc} / \sum_{k=1}^{n_o} \exp(-D_k^2 / 2\sigma_q^2) r_{kc} \qquad (2)$$

where $\mathbf{R} = \{r_{kc}\}$ is the matrix of memberships for each feature vector $\mathbf{x}_k$ to each component c in the FMM such that r_{kc} is either one, if $\hat{z}_{kc} > \hat{z}_{kt}$ for all $t \neq c$, or zero otherwise, n_o is the number of feature vectors that are observed on both of the observed subspace for the feature vector $\mathbf{x}_i$ and the qth feature, and D_k^2 is the squared Euclidean distance between feature vectors $\mathbf{x}_k$ and $\mathbf{x}_i$ on the observed subspace of the feature vector $\mathbf{x}_i$.

After estimating its missing values, the qth feature is added to the group of fully observed features and this new group is then used in estimating missing values in the next feature that has the minimum missing rate.

- The necessary statistics for the M-step as follows,

$$E(z_{ic} x_{iq} \mid \mathbf{x}_i^o, \mathbf{R}) = \begin{cases} \hat{z}_{ic} x_{iq} & x_{iq} \in \mathbf{x}_i^o \\ \hat{z}_{ic} E(x_{iq}^c \mid \mathbf{x}_i^o, \mathbf{R}) & x_{iq} \in \mathbf{x}_i^m \end{cases} \qquad (3)$$

$$E(z_{ic} x_{iq} x_{iq'} \mid \mathbf{x}_i^o, \mathbf{R}) = \begin{cases} \hat{z}_{ic} x_{iq} x_{iq'} & x_{iq}, x_{iq'} \in \mathbf{x}_i^o \\ \hat{z}_{ic} x_{iq} E(x_{iq'}^c \mid \mathbf{x}_i^o, \mathbf{R}) & x_{iq'} \in \mathbf{x}_i^m \\ \hat{z}_{ic} E(x_{iq}^c \mid \mathbf{x}_i^o, \mathbf{R}) x_{iq'} & x_{iq} \in \mathbf{x}_i^m \\ \hat{z}_{ic} E(x_{iq}^c \mid \mathbf{x}_i^o, \mathbf{R}) E(x_{iq'}^c \mid \mathbf{x}_i^o, \mathbf{R}) & x_{iq}, x_{iq'} \in \mathbf{x}_i^m \end{cases} \qquad (4)$$

where $i, q, q' = 1, 2, \ldots, d$, E is the expectation operator.

Step 4: In the M-step, compute parameters of each component c in the FMM.

$$\hat{P}(c) = \frac{1}{N}\sum_{j=1}^{N}\hat{z}_{jc}, \quad \hat{\mu}_c = \frac{1}{N\hat{P}(c)}E(\sum_{j=1}^{N}z_{jc}\mathbf{x}_j \mid \mathbf{x}_j^o, \mathbf{R}) \quad (5)$$

$$\hat{\Sigma}_c = \frac{1}{N\hat{P}(c)}E(\sum_{j=1}^{N}z_{jc}\mathbf{x}_j\mathbf{x}_j^T \mid \mathbf{x}_j^o, \mathbf{R}) - \hat{\mu}_c\hat{\mu}_c^T \quad (6)$$

Step 5: After convergence, save the resulting FMM with the total data log-likelihood. The convergence of the EM algorithm in our experiments is achieved when the difference in the log-likelihood function between iterations (t) and (t-10) is less than or equal 10^{-10}.

Step 6: Repeat Steps 2-5 twenty times and then select the best FMM that corresponds to the maximum data log-likelihood.

Step 7: Use the best FMM in clustering feature vectors in the input data set according to Bayes decision rule.

Step 8: Estimate missing values in the data set as explained in Step 3.

3 Experiments

The LGREM algorithm is investigated against a number of commonly used algorithms in unsupervised learning of FMM parameters using a data set with missing values. These algorithms are the MEM algorithm and the EM algorithm after estimating the missing values in the input data set using different methods such as the GRNN (referred to as GREM), and the unconditional mean imputation method (referred to as MENEM). In the MENEM algorithm, the missing values in each feature are replaced with the mean of the observed values in that feature. Two data sets are used in this comparison study. The missing values are put with different missing rates in the third and in the fourth features of each data set. The mechanism of the occurrence of the missing values is missing completely at random [7]. Each one of the FMMs learnt by all algorithms consists of three Gaussian components that have non-restricted covariance matrices. These data sets are described as follows.

The First Data Set. The first data set is an artificial data set. It contains 151 feature vectors each of which is a vector in four-dimensional space. This data set contains a single outlier feature vector that is equal to $[\max(\mathbf{d1})/2, \max(\mathbf{d2})/2, \max(\mathbf{d3}), \max(\mathbf{d4})]^T$, where $\mathbf{d}_i$, i=1:4 are the features of the data set. The remaining feature vectors are generated equally from three 4D-Gaussian distributions. The mean vectors of these distributions are $\mu_1 = [2\ 2\ 2\ 2]^T, \mu_2 = [2\ 2\ 6\ 2]^T$, and $\mu_3 = [2\ 2\ 2\ 6]^T$. The covariance matrices of these distributions are identical and equal to $\Sigma = 0.5\mathbf{I}_4$, where $\mathbf{I}_4$ is the identity matrix of order four. The purpose of using this data set is to compare the algorithms in the presence of weak correlations between different pairs of the data features and the occurrence of an outlier in the data set.

The Second Data Set. The second data set is the Iris data set [12]. This data set contains 150 feature vectors each of which is a vector in four-feature space. These feature vectors represent three classes of equal size. Two of these classes are overlapping in the data space. Correlations between different pairs of features of this data set are moderate.

The evaluation criterion used in this study to compare the different algorithms is the Mis-Classification Error (MCE). It is computed by comparing the clustering results, obtained using Bayes decision rule, of the learned FMM with the true classification of the data feature vectors, assuming each class is represented by a component in the FMM. Components of the FMM are allocated to different data classes such that the total number of misclassified feature vectors in the data set is minimum. Let the number of feature vectors belonging to class i be N_i, from which N_i^m feature vectors are not clustered into the component that represents this class in the FMM. Then the MCE for class i is computed as $MCE(class_i) = N_i^m / N_i$. The total MCE is the average of all the class-MCEs and it is computed as $MCE(total) = \sum_{i=1}^{K} MCE(class_i) / K$.

Tables 1 and 2 show comparisons of different pairs of the algorithms using the Student's paired t-test with each one of the data sets. This test examines the statistical significance of the difference in performance of a certain pair of algorithms using their pairs of the total MCEs obtained from ten different experiments. In each experiment, a different group of feature vectors is randomly selected to contain missing values. The results of this test are shown for each pair of percentages of missing values in the third and in the fourth features respectively of each one of the data sets. Each P-value in the tables represents the probability that Student's t statistic (T-value) calculated on paired data is higher than observed, i.e. the significance level. The shaded cells in each table represent the cases in which the difference in performance of certain pairs of algorithms are statistically significant according to the 5% significance level.

Table 1. Comparing different pairs of algorithms using the first data set.

Missing %	T(LGREM,GREM)		T(LGREM,MEM)		T(LGREM,MENEM)	
	P	T	P	T	P	T
(5%,10%)	0.00	-8.86	0.22	-1.31	0.00	-8.49
(10%,20%)	0.00	-16.15	0.13	-1.68	0.00	-6.66
(15%,30%)	0.00	-9.67	0.00	-3.84	0.00	-16.52
(20%,40%)	0.00	-6.62	0.00	-5.23	0.00	-8.57
(25%,50%)	0.01	-3.04	0.00	-4.25	0.00	-4.99

Table 2. Comparing different pairs of algorithms using the Iris data set.

Missing %	T(LGREM,GREM)		T(LGREM,MEM)		T(LGREM,MENEM)	
	P	T	P	T	P	T
(5%,10%)	0.89	-0.14	0.00	-4.71	0.02	-2.81
(10%,20%)	0.04	-2.43	0.00	-6.46	0.00	-9.80
(15%,30%)	0.34	-1.02	0.01	-3.63	0.00	-5.12
(20%,40%)	0.21	-1.34	0.00	-4.72	0.00	-6.21
(25%,50%)	0.00	-4.05	0.00	-4.39	0.00	-5.65

4 Discussion of the Results

Tables 1 and 2 show that the LGREM algorithm produces the minimum total MCE among all algorithms (T-statistic is always negative). Both tables show the preference of the LGREM algorithm to other algorithms in the case of weak correlations between data features, the occurrence of some outliers in the data set, or the overlapping among data classes in the data space. In these cases, local tuning of the general regression used in the LGREM algorithm is less dependent on the overall correlations than the general regression used in the GREM algorithm. Therefore the LGREM algorithm outperforms the GREM algorithm when features of the data are weakly correlated. In addition, estimating the missing values from the observed feature vectors belonging to each cluster used in the LGREM algorithm is less dependent on the FMM parameters than the maximum likelihood estimation used in the MEM algorithm. Therefore, the LGREM algorithm outperforms the MEM algorithm in cases such as the occurrence of some outliers in the data set or the overlapping among data classes in the data space.

5 Conclusion

In this paper, the LGREM algorithm is proposed to estimate FMM parameters using small incomplete data sets with outliers, and overlapping among classes. A comparison study shows the preference of the proposed algorithm to the MEM algorithm and to other algorithms commonly used in the literature.

References

1. Tråvén, H.G.C.: A Neural Network Approach to Statistical Pattern Classification by "Semiparametric" Estimation of Probability Density Functions. IEEE Trans. on Neural Networks, 2(3) (1991) 366-377
2. Bishop, C. (ed.): Neural Networks for Pattern Recognition. Oxford University Press (1995)
3. Gokcay, E., Principe, J.C.: Information Theoretic Clustering. IEEE Trans. on Pattern Analysis and Machine Intelligence, 24(2) (2002) 158-171
4. Banfield, J., Raftery, A.: Model-Based Gaussian and Non-Gaussian Clustering. Biometrics, 49 (1993) 803-821
5. Webb, A. (ed.): Statistical Pattern Recognition. Arnold (1999)
6. Dempster, A.P., Laird, N.M., Rubin, D.B.: Maximum Likelihood From Incomplete Data Via The EM Algorithm (with discussion). J. of Royal Statistical Society, B39 (1977) 1-38
7. Little, R.J.A., Rubin, D.B. (eds.): Statistical Analysis with Missing Data. John Wiley & Sons, New York (1987).
8. Ghahramani, Z., Jordan, M.I.: Supervised learning from incomplete data via an EM approach. In: Cowan, J.D., Tesauro, G., Alspector, J. (eds.): Advances in Neural Information Processing Systems, Vol. 6. Morgan Kaufmann Publishers, San Francisco, CA, USA (1994) 120-127
9. Yoon, S.Y., Lee, S.Y.: Training Algorithm with Incomplete Data for Feed-Forward Neural Networks. J. of Neural Processing Letters, 10 (1999) 171-179
10. Troyanskaya, O., Cantor, M., Sherlock, G., Brown, P., Hastie, T., Tibshirani, R., Botstein, D., Altman, R.B.: Missing Value Estimation Methods for DNA Microarrays. Bioinformatics, 17(6) (2001) 520-525
11. Specht, D.F.: A General Regression Neural Network. IEEE Trans. on Neural Networks, 2(6) (1991) 568-576
12. Fisher, R.A.: The use of multiple measurements in taxonomic problems. Annals of Eugenics, 7 (1936) 179-188

Credit Risks of Interest Rate Swaps: A Comparative Study of CIR and Monte Carlo Simulation Approach

Victor Fang[1] and Vincent C.S. Lee[2,*]

[1] Department of Accounting and Finance, Faculty of Business and Economics
Monash University
victor.fang@buseco.monash.edu.au

[2] School of Business Systems, Faculty of Information Technology, Monash University
vincent.lee@infotech.monash.edu.au
http://www.bsys.Monash.edu.au

Abstract. This paper compares the credit risk profile for two types of model, the Monte Carlo model used in the existing literature, and the Cox, Ingersoll and Ross (CIR) model. Each of the profiles has a concave or hump-backed shape, reflecting the amortisation and diffusion effects. However, the CIR model generates significantly different results. In addition, we consider the sensitivity of these models of credit risk to initial interest rates, volatility, maturity, kappa and delta. The results show that the sensitivities vary across the models, and we explore the meaning of that variation.

Keywords: Credit risk profile, Interest Rate Models, Monte Carlo Method.

1 Introduction

"The CIR approach has two principal advantages over Monte-Carlo simulation: it makes it easier and quicker to evaluate an instrument's riskiness, its contractual terms and the behaviour of the underlying variable."

Bond, Murphy and Robinson (1994, p. 5)

The possibility of substantial credit exposure motivated the Basle supervisors committee (1994) to establish more stringent guidelines relating to the management of credit risk. Credit risk measurement and its volatility has become a central consideration, and following their use in Basle Capital Accord, it is widely accepted that Monte Carlo simulation methods are an effective mechanism for estimating this risk. Sample paths of interest rates are simulated, and the credit exposure evaluated in a distributional sense (see Hull (1989, 1993). The expected replacement cost can then be determined as the expected maximum credit risk. Monte Carlo methods have derived their currency from a perception that they are versatile and permit the incorporation of financial theory (see Ferran and Handjinicolaou (1987)).

---

* Corresponding author.

Simulation methods do, however, have a downside. The sensitivity of credit risk measurement to underlying attributes and parameters, such as the volatility of short-term rates, term structure changes, and the coupon and maturity of the debt, can only be extracted through extensive simulation (see Bond, Murphy and Robinson (1994)). A response surface analysis then provides an estimate of the sensitivities (as an example of response surface analysis, see Bicksler and Chen (1986)). These sensitivities can be used to adjust estimates of credit risk, or at least to provide extreme bounds to the estimates of credit risk. Because of the simplicity of this approach, and its atheoretical nature, there is some uncertainty as to its robustness. It is also the case that simulation methods have tended to assume a flat yield curve, a limitation noted by (Bond, Murphy and Robinson (1994)).

The present paper considers an alternative to the Monte Carlo methodology which embeds the measurement of credit risk in an option setting, by using existing models of the term structure. In particular, we consider the measurement of the credit risk by using the mean-reverting model of Cox, Ingersoll and Ross (1985) denoted by CIR. CIR is a theoretically sound equilibrium based on the whole term structure of interest rate (see Hull, 2001). There are other interest rate models such as Vasicek, Heath, Jarrow and Morton, Hull and White, etc (see Hull, 2001).

This paper is structured as follows: Section 2 briefly sets out the expectations model and develops a testable implication. Section 3 discusses the data used and Section 4 reports the empirical results. Conclusions of the paper are given in Section 5.

2 Monte Carlo and CIR Models

Two widely approaches for estimating credit risk are considered seriatim.

2.1 Monte Carlo Simulation

This approach entails calculating the replacement cost of swaps from randomly generated interest rate paths. The nature of the interest rate paths will depend on the properties of the probability distribution function. We invoke similar assumptions to that of Federal Reserve/Bank of England (1987) and Simons (1993) studies where interest rates are assumed to follow geometric Brownian motion. The interest rate paths can be described by:

$$I_j = I_{j-1} * e^x$$

where I_j is the interest rate at time j, x is a normally distributed random number with mean zero and a standard deviation equalling the historical volatility of interest rates. Under this data generating process, changes in interest rates are serially uncorrelated, and exhibit no trend. Interest rates are then determined over the life of the swap, from an initial level I_0 to the maturity of the swap.

In common with other studies, we use a matched pair technique to neutralise the effect of market risk. One swap is assumed to pay the fixed rate, and its reverse swap is assumed to receive the fixed rate. We have obtained interest rate setting base on 2 June 2000. The interest rates setting are given as follows.

Swap Yield Curve

Period (years)	Swap Yield (%)
0.5	6.33
1.0	6.36
2.0	6.47
3.0	6.55

A thee-year matched pair swaps is used with an initial rate of 6.55%. These interest rate settings are varied in the sensitivity analysis below. The settlement date for the swap is each 6 months. In each simulation run, the replacement cost is calculated at each time interval. This replacement cost is determined by comparing the original fixed rate and the current fixed rate of comparable remaining maturity. The current fixed rate is generated from the Monte Carlo simulation. The difference between these two rates which in turn discount to the present value is the replacement cost. This procedure is repeated for 1000 number of interest rate scenarios so as to generate a probability distribution for the replacement cost at each time interval over the life of the swap.

In the sensitivity analysis, this measure of potential credit exposure is assessed by varying the following parameters and contractual terms:

i) initial level of interest rates
ii) the volatility of the interest rates
iii) maturity of the swap

The *ceteris paribus* effects of each factors is assessed. As foreshadowed above, one of the limitations of the Monte Carlo methodology is its atheoretical nature, which implies some uncertainty in extrapolating the results of the sensitivity analysis to adjustment in the credit risk. From previous studies, such as Hull (1990) and Bond, Murphy and Robinson (1994), we can anticipate that our results will show that the potential credit risk of a swap will be positively related to the initial level of interest rates, the volatility of the interest rates and the maturity of the swap.

2.2 The Cox, Ingersoll and Ross Model (CIR)

The term structure model of Cox, Ingersoll and Ross (1985) is based on the assumption that the short term rate follows a mean reverting stochastic process as

$$dr_t = k(\theta - r_t)dt + \sigma\sqrt{r_t}\,dW_t \qquad (2.1)$$

where r_t is the instantaneous interest rate, k is the speed at which r_t is being pulled towards the long-term mean rate θ and σ is the volatility of the instantaneous interest rate. W_t is a standard Wiener process where $dW_t \sim N(0, dt)$.

Cox, Ingersoll and Ross show that the value (at time t) of a pure discount bond that pays \$1 at time T, given the current short rate, is given as:

$$P(t,T) = \alpha(T-t)e^{-\beta(T-t)r_t} \qquad (2.2)$$

where the functions $\alpha(T-t)$ and $\beta(T-t)$ are as defined as follows:

$$\alpha(T-t) = \left[\frac{2\gamma \cdot e^{(k+\gamma+\lambda)(T-t)/2}}{2\gamma+(\gamma+k+\lambda)(e^{\gamma(T-t)}-1)}\right]^{2k\theta/\sigma^2}$$

$$\beta(T-t) = \frac{2(e^{\gamma(T-t)}-1)}{2\gamma+(\gamma+k+\lambda)(e^{\gamma(T-t)}-1)}$$

$$\gamma = [(k+\lambda)^2 + 2\sigma^2]^{1/2}$$

From the above equations, thus the continuously compounded yield to maturity, $y(t,T)$, of a pure discount bond is given by:

$$y(t,T) = \frac{r_t \beta(T-t) - \log \alpha(T-t)}{T-t} \qquad (2.3)$$

The above equation defines the term structure of interest rate in a CIR environment.

In our study, we replaced the standard Wiener process dW_t in CIR model with the Milstein approximation, a higher order approximation. The Milstein approximation (Kloeden et al (1991)) is given by:

$$Y_{t+1} = Y_t + a(Y_t)\delta t + b(Y_t)\delta W_t + b(Y_t)b'(Y_t)\int_{\tau_t}^{\tau_{t+1}}\int_{\tau_t}^{s_1} dW_{s_2} dW_{s_1} \qquad (2.4)$$

where dW_{s_1} and dW_{s_2} are different independent components of the Wiener process.

From Ito calculus it can be shown that the multiple stochastic integral is:

$$\int_{\tau_t}^{\tau_{t+1}}\int_{\tau_n}^{s_1} dW_{s_2} dW_{s_1} = 1/2\{(\delta W_t)^2 - \delta t\} \qquad (2.5)$$

Therefore, the Milstein approximation is quite simple in form and has a stronger order of convergence in sample paths. By substituting the Milstein approximation into CIR model, a modified CIR equation is derived:

$$dr_t = k(\theta - r_t)dt + \sigma\sqrt{r_t}\,dW_t + \frac{\sigma^2}{2}r_t(dW_t^2 - dt) \qquad (2.6)$$

From the above equation, we are able to calculate the instantaneous rate (r_{t+dt}) at time ($t+dt$). From this instantaneous rate, we are able to derive a term structure of interest rates at time ($t+dt$). The potential credit exposure is determined by comparing the original fixed rate of the interest rate swap and the current rate of comparable remaining maturity calculated from the CIR model. The difference between these two rates is then discount to the present value. This procedure is repeated 1000 times so as to obtain an average replacement cost at each time interval over the life of the swap.

If $\theta >$ or $< r_t$, and $k \neq 0$, then the yield curve will have an upward or downward slope. We expect the potential credit risk of swap will increase. However, the magnitude of the increase will depend on k, the speed of the mean reversion.

3 Comparative Empirical Results and Sensitivity Analysis

The following graphs show the potential credit risk over the life of a matched pair interest rate swaps under different models of evaluations.

Figure 3.1 shows the expected credit exposure over the life of the swap calculated using the Monte Carlo model for a 3-year, 6.55% half-yearly coupon, matched pair par swap. The volatility of the interest rate is 12.23%. The average expected credit exposure is 0.67% of the notional principal of the swap. This simulation assumes that the default always occurs, but the timing of default is assumed to be random, with an equal likelihood of default occurring at any point during the life of the swap.

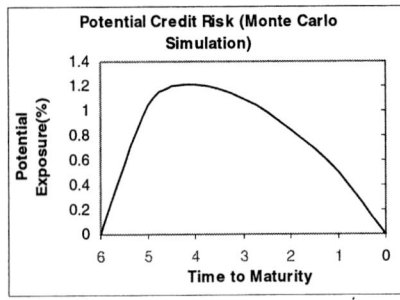
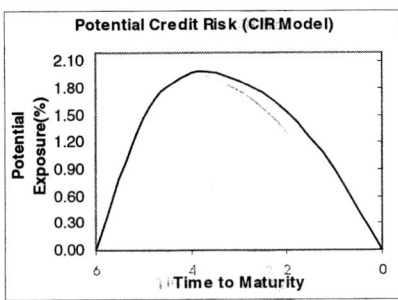

Fig. 3.1. Potential Credit Risk (Monte Carlo Simulation).

Fig. 3.2. Potential Credit Risk (CIR Model).

To estimate the parameters k, θ and σ, we follow the technique used in Gupta and Subrahmanyam (2001). The sample consists of weekly observations of 90 days bank bill yield from January 1995 to December 1999.

Figure 3.2 shows the expected credit exposure over the life of the swap calculated using the Cox, Ingersoll and Ross model for a 3-year, 6.55% half-yearly coupon, matched pair par swap. The long term equilibrium rate and growth rate are 10.82% and 22.85% respectively. The volatility of the interest rate is 12.23%. The average expected credit exposure under this model is 1.11% of the notional principal of the swap.

As discussed above, we expect the credit risk to exhibit a concave or humped-back profile over the life of the swap, reflecting the amortisation and offsetting diffusion effect. This characteristic of gradually increasing, and then declining exposure holds for all par swaps regardless of maturity and the level of initial interest rate. We can observe that the graphs in Figures 3.1 and 3.2 all exhibit this characteristic, as required by the theoretical expectations. From the results presented using one scenario, we note that there is a marked difference in the credit exposures for the CIR model relative to the Monte Carlo model. This is amplified in the sensitivity analysis below.

4 Comparative Sensitivity Analysis

4.1 The Effect of Initial Level of Interest Rates on Swap Exposure

Figure 4.1 displays the effect of initial level of interest rates on swap exposure using the Monte Carlo approach and CIR approach. It is clear that the expected credit exposure using CIR approach is significantly higher than that of the Monte Carlo approach.

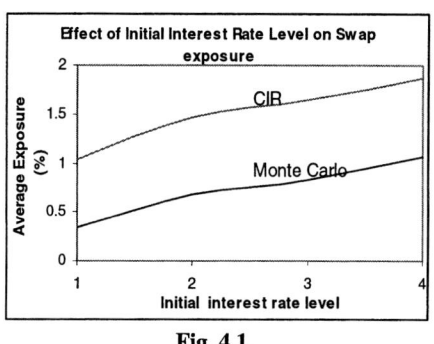
Fig. 4.1.

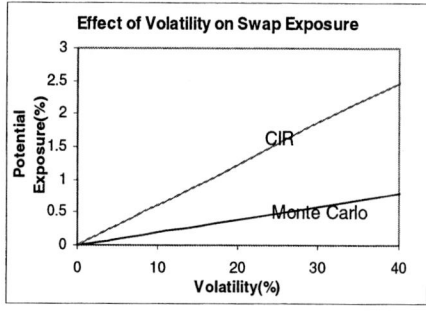
Fig. 4.2.

4.2 The Effect of Volatility on Swap Exposure

Figure 4.2 shows that the average exposure increases linearly with volatility in each model. This again is consistent with expectations. However, the slope of the average exposure using CIR model is steeper as volatility increases, compared to Monte Carlo model.

4.3 The Effect of Maturity on Swap Exposure

Figure 4.3 indicates that the average credit exposure increases as the maturity increases under both models. However, the rate of increase of the credit risk under Monte Carlo dominates that of the CIR model.

4.4 The Effect of Kappa (k) on Swap Exposure

Figure 4.4 shows that k has significant effect on swap exposure and the effect varies according to the shape of the yield curves. When $k=0$, the average swap exposures under the 3 different yield curves do not differ significantly. However, as k increases and when the yield curve is flat, the average swap exposure decreases gradually. When the yield curve is upward or downward sloping, the average swap exposure decreases much gently as k increases until k reaches 1.25, then the average swap exposure begins to rise.

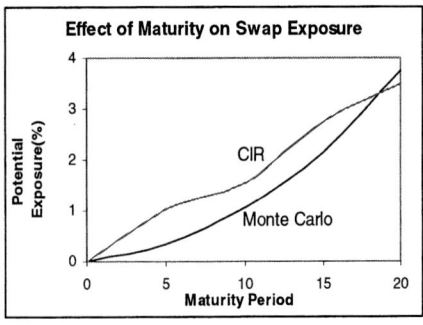
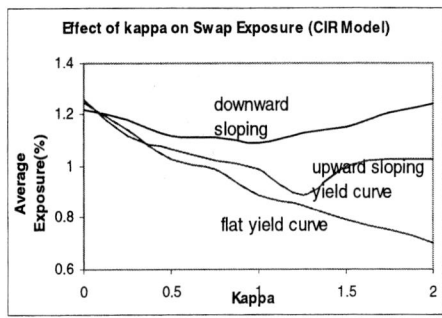

Fig. 4.3.   Fig. 4.4.

5 Conclusions

Two approaches: traditional Monte Carlo approach and second-order simulation approach based on the mean reverting model of Cox, Ingersoll and Ross had been used to estimate the potential credit risk of a 3-year matched pair par interest rate swap. The profiles of potential credit risk generated by these two models exhibit the anticipated 'hump-backed' shape, but the credit risks associated with the CIR model appear uniformly and significantly larger. Our results also indicate that initial level of interest rates and the volatility of interest rates generally have a positive relationship with the swap exposure. The exposure is also positively related to the maturity of the swap. These results are consistent with previous empirical evidence. In addition, our results show that generally the effect of kappa (k) in CIR model on swap exposure varies according to the shape of the yield curve, reaffirming the non-triviality of the flat yield curve assumption. It has the advantage of a theoretical basis, exhibits the appropriate behaviour empirically, and is not attenuated by the uncertainty of the Monte Carlo method. In future research, the methods will be estimated and tested with real data.

References

1. Basle Committee on Banking Supervision (1994), 'Basle Capital Accord: the capital treatment of the Credit Risk associated with certain Off-balance sheet items', BIS, July 1994.

2. Bicksler and Chen (1986) ' An Economic Analysis of Interest Rate Swaps' Journal of Finance 41, 645-655
3. Bond, G Murphy and G Robinson 1994 'Potential Credit Exposure on Interest Rate Swaps' Working Paper, Bank of England 1994
4. Cox, Ingersoll, and Ross (1985) ' A Theory of the Term Structure of Interest Rates' Econometrica Vol 53, No 2 March 1985
5. Federal Reserve Board and Bank of England (1987) 'Potential Credit Exposure on Interest Rate and Foreign exchange Rate related Instruments' Unpublished staff paper.
6. Ferran and Handjinicolaou (1987) ' Understanding Swaps Credit Risk: The Simulation Approach' Journal of International Securities markets' 1987, 135-148
7. Gupta,A., and Subrahmanyam, M.G., (2000) "An empirical Examination of
8. the Convexity Bias in the pricing of interest rate swaps", Journal of Financial Economics, Vol 55, pp.239-279.
9. Hull J. (1989) ' Assessing Credit Risk in a Financial Institution's Off-balance Sheet Commitments' Journal of Financial and Quantitative Analysis 24, 489-501
10. Hull, J. (2001) 'Options, Futures, and Other Derivative Securities' Prentice-Hall International, 2001.
11. Kloeden, P.E, Platen, and Schurz, H.(1991) ' The numerical solution of Non-Linear Stochastic Dynamical Systems: A Brief Introduction' International Journal of Bifurcation and Chaos, Vol 1 1991
12. Simons, K. (1993) 'Interest Rate Structure and the Credit risk of Swaps' New England Economic Review August 1993.

Cardinality Constrained Portfolio Optimisation

Jonathan E. Fieldsend[1], John Matatko[2], and Ming Peng[2]

[1] Department of Computer Science, University of Exeter, UK
[2] Department of Accounting and Finance, University of Exeter, UK

Abstract. The traditional quadratic programming approach to portfolio optimisation is difficult to implement when there are cardinality constraints. Recent approaches to resolving this have used heuristic algorithms to search for points on the cardinality constrained frontier. However, these can be computationally expensive when the practitioner does not know *a priori* exactly how many assets they may desire in a portfolio, or what level of return/risk they wish to be exposed to without recourse to analysing the actual trade-off frontier.
This study introduces a parallel solution to this problem. By extending techniques developed in the multi-objective evolutionary optimisation domain, a set of portfolios representing estimates of all possible cardinality constrained frontiers can be found in a single search process, for a range of portfolio sizes and constraints. Empirical results are provided on emerging markets and US asset data, and compared to unconstrained frontiers found by quadratic programming.

1 Introduction

Given constraints on the number of stocks to hold in a portfolio, due to the costs of monitoring and portfolio re-weighting, the question arises as to how to choose the 'best' portfolio given particular risk/return preferences and these cardinality constraints. The number of stocks needed to achieve a particular diversification gain depends on the correlation among stock returns; the lower the correlation, the more stocks are needed. Campbell *et al.* [1] show that although overall market volatility has not increased in recent years, individual stock returns have become less correlated with each other. Consequently, more stocks are thought to be needed in a portfolio than in the period studied by [2] (1926-1965).

Markowitz [3] defined the set of optimal portfolios that are on the efficient frontier, based on estimated moments of the sampled distribution. Ignoring the uncertainty inherent in the underlying probability model, the portfolio that maximizes expected return, through to the one which minimises risk, is in this set. This approach reduces the task of choosing an optimal portfolio to choosing a portfolio from this efficient frontier.

When there are no cardinality constraints, quadratic programming (QP) can be effectively used to determine an optimal portfolio's weights, given 'a' different assets. With μ_i being the expected return of the ith asset, and $V_{i,j}$ the covariance between assets i and j, this takes the general form: $\min\{\sigma_P\}$, where

$\sigma_P = \sqrt{\Sigma_{i=1}^a \Sigma_{i=1}^a w_i w_j V_{i,j}}$, subject to $\Sigma_j^a w_i \mu_i = r_P^*$ and $\Sigma_i^a w_i = 1$, where w_i is the portfolio weight of the ith asset, and r_P^* is the desired expected return of the portfolio. In more formal notation, expected return of a portfolio (r_P) equals $\boldsymbol{\mu}^T \mathbf{w}$ and risk (σ_P) equals $\mathbf{w}^T V \mathbf{w}$. Commonly there is also a no short selling constraint $0 \leq w_i \leq 1$. However, when realistic cardinality constraints are imposed QP cannot be applied to find optimal subsets.

We introduce a heuristic model to search for all the cardinality constrained (CC) efficient portfolio frontiers available for any set of assets. We illustrate the differences that arise in the shape of this efficient frontier when such constraints are present, and test for significant difference between these frontiers and the unconstrained efficient (UC) frontier found using quadratic programming.

2 Heuristic Search Methods

Heuristic search approaches addressing the portfolio search problem when cardinality constraints are imposed have recently been developed [4,5]. These have taken the form of optimising a composite weighting of σ_P and r_P, typically $\max\{\lambda r_P - (1-\lambda)\sigma_P\}$, where $0 \leq \lambda \leq 1$. Problematic however is that the cardinality to be searched needs to be defined *a priori*, and a separate run is needed for each portfolio to be optimised. If a range of cardinalities need to be compared then obviously this increases the computational cost further.

Multi-objective evolutionary algorithms (MOEAs) represent a popular approach to confronting these types of problem by using evolutionary search techniques [6]. Here we investigate the use of a modified MOEA to optimise CC portfolio frontiers in parallel (optimising all plausible values of k in a single process). Novel search processes are incorporated in this algorithm to enable it to maintain these disparate frontier sets and efficiently compare new portfolios during the search process. Prior to this however the concepts of Pareto optimality (central to modern MOEAs) and non-dominance will be briefly described.

2.1 Pareto Optimality

The multi-objective optimisation problem seeks to simultaneously extremise D objectives: $y_i = f_i(\mathbf{w})$, where $i = 1, \ldots, D$ and where each objective depends upon a vector $\mathbf{w}$ of n parameters or decision variables. The parameters may also be subject to the m constraints: $e_j(\mathbf{w}) \geq 0$ where $j = 1, \ldots, m$. In the context of portfolio optimisation, these may be constraints on the maximum/minimum proportion of a portfolio that can be derived from a particular market or sector, or a minimum/maximum weight an asset can have in a portfolio.

Without loss of generality it is assumed that these objectives are to be minimised (minimising $-1 \times r_P$ is analogous to maximising r_P), as such the problem can be stated as: minimise $\mathbf{y} = \mathbf{f}(\mathbf{w}) = (f_1(\mathbf{w}), f_2(\mathbf{w}), \ldots, f_D(\mathbf{w}))$, subject to $\mathbf{e}(\mathbf{w}) = (e_1(\mathbf{w}), e_2(\mathbf{w}), \ldots, e_m(\mathbf{w}))$. A decision vector $\mathbf{u}$ is said to *strictly dominate* another $\mathbf{v}$ (denoted $\mathbf{u} \prec \mathbf{v}$) if $f_i(\mathbf{u}) \leq f_i(\mathbf{v}) \; \forall i = 1, \ldots, D$ and $f_i(\mathbf{u}) < f_i(\mathbf{v})$ for some i. A set of M decision vectors is said to be a *non-dominated set*

Algorithm 1 Algorithmic description of the multi-objective optimiser.

g, *maximum number of algorithm iterations*
$\mathcal{H}$, *Set of sets of portfolios defining the c different estimated frontiers*
1: $t := 0$, $\mathcal{H}_k^t = \emptyset$ $\forall k = 1, \ldots, a$
2: $\mathcal{H}_{k,1}^t := random\_portfolio(k)$ $\forall k = 1, \ldots, a$
3: while $(t < g)$
4:     $k = U(1, a)$
5:     $\mathbf{w} := select(\mathcal{H}^t, k)$
6:     $\mathbf{w} := adjust(\mathbf{w})$
7:     $\mathbf{y} := evaluate(\mathbf{w})$
8:     $\mathcal{H}^{t+1} = check\_insert\_remove(\mathcal{H}^t, \mathbf{w}, \mathbf{y})$
9:     $t := t + 1$
10: end

(an estimated Pareto front) if no member of the set is dominated by any other member. The *true* Pareto front is the non-dominated set of solutions which are not dominated by any feasible solution. In the context of portfolio optimisation, the efficient frontier can be seen as an example of a Pareto optimal set.

2.2 The Proposed Model

If we are not concerned with constraints other than cardinality, then cardinality can be incorporated as a third objective to be minimised, therefore aiming to find the 3-dimensional surface defining the trade-off between risk, return and cardinality minimisation. We can then extract the 2-dimensional cardinality constrained frontier for any particular k. According to finance theory for higher cardinality levels (more assets) the CC front extracted will be short, as identical risk/return levels may be available at a lower cardinality for high r_P and σ_P. With no other constraints this is not a problem as the lower cardinality portfolios are equivalent to higher cardinality portfolios with some weights equal to zero. If however there are other constraints (as mentioned in Section 2.1), this transformation may no longer be possible. As such CC portfolio optimisation with MOEAs is interesting, as we need to maintain a separate estimated Pareto set for each cardinality, k. (NB, in the empirical results shown here there are no additional constraints, so the cardinality constraint is effectively a maximum one).

One solution would be to run separate 2-objective MOEAs for each k, (extending the approach used previously in [7] for UC optimisation). However, although more computationally efficient than the existing heuristic methods used in the application domain, this may still be computationally expensive for a large number of k. Instead here we search for each k constrained front in parallel, and constructively use information from each of these fronts to improve the search process of the others. The decision vector $\mathbf{w}$ here consists of the weights of the a different available assets. A description of the MOEA used, based on a simple (1+1)-evolution strategy [8] is provided in Algorithm 1.

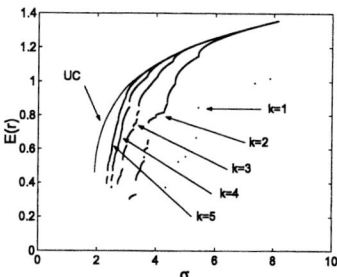
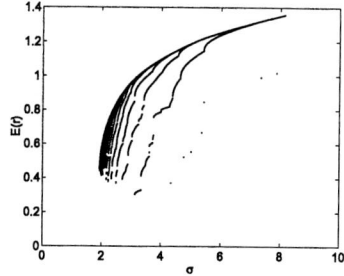

Fig. 1. *Left*: EM UC frontier found exactly using QP and the first 5 optimised CC fronts. *Right*: All 40 optimised EM CC fronts and the UC frontier.

The algorithm maintains a set of sets $\mathcal{H}$ of the a different CC efficient frontiers. Each of these $\mathcal{H}_k$ cardinality sets is initialised with a random portfolio (line 2), with random non-negative w_is, where $\Sigma_{i=1}^{a} w_i = 1$ and the number of non-zero w_i equals k. The algorithm proceeds at each iteration by first randomly selecting an archive with cardinality k at that generation t, $\mathcal{H}_k^t$, and copying a portfolio from it (using partitioned quasi-random selection [8]). This copied portfolio $\mathbf{w}$ is then adjusted (line 6); this takes the form of weight adjustment 50% of the time, otherwise a weight adjustment plus dimensionality change. When only weights are adjusted $\mathbf{w} :\sim Dir(b\mathbf{w})$, where Dir denotes the Dirichlet distribution. By sampling a Dirichlet with parameters equal to the current weights, and a large enough multiplying constant b (set at 400 here), the new weights will be close to the original values [9]. In addition, sampling from a Dirichlet ensures $\Sigma_{i=1}^{a} w_i = 1$, $w_i \geq 0$, and any w_i that were previously zero will remain zero. When dimensionality change is also implemented either a non-zero value in $\mathbf{w}$ set to zero (asset removal) or a zero valued w_i is assigned a value drawn from $U(0, 1/k)$ (where U denotes the Uniform distribution and k is the number of active assets in the *new* portfolio). In both cases new weights are then drawn from $Dir(b\mathbf{w})$. The new portfolio $\mathbf{w}$ is evaluated on line 7, r_P and σ_P are then assigned to $\mathbf{y}$. Using $\mathbf{y}$ the new portfolio can be compared to the relevant $\mathcal{H}_k^t$ (line 8), to see if it is non-dominated, and if so, any dominated portfolios are removed when it is inserted into $\mathcal{H}_k^{t+1}$.

3   Empirical Results

Empirical evaluation of this new method is provided here on weekly stock data from the US S&P 100 index and emerging markets (EM) stock. Both sets were obtained from Datastream and were those stocks within the index that persisted from January 1992 to December 2003. Using the first 500 points of the returns data, Algorithm 1 was run for 10^7 portfolio evaluations.

Figure 1 shows the CC frontiers found by the MOEA on the EM asset set, the CC frontiers rapidly approaching the UC frontier (also shown) as k is increased. Using the methodology described in [10], coupled with methods developed in the

Table 1. Cardinality for which the CC is not significantly better than the UC segment.

Partition (low risk to high risk)	1	2	3	4	5	6	7	8	9	10
EM opt. CC level when no sig difference to UC	-	8	5	4	4	3	3	2	2	2
S&P opt. CC level when no sig difference to UC	-	9	6	5	4	3	3	3	2	2

Table 2. *Ex ante* performance of minimum variance CC portfolios ($k = 10$).

	EM					S&P				
t (weeks)	4	12	26	52	104	4	12	26	52	104
σ_P of opt. CC portfolio	0.93	3.26	2.58	2.42	2.20	0.55	2.86	2.35	2.98	3.34
Mean of bootstrap CCs σ_P	2.13	3.39	3.05	2.77	2.55	1.44	2.98	2.63	3.08	3.33
Rank of opt CC (/1001)	279	414	120	134	96	45	481	307	579	623

MOEA community, we can test if the optimised CC frontiers are significantly different from the UC frontier. We do this by sampling means and covariances from the posterior distribution of the S&P and EM data, and evaluating the optimised portfolios with respect to these. The UC frontier is sliced into 10 evenly spaced segments (with respect to σ_P). The portfolios lying in each segment, and those on the CC frontier defined by the σ_P bounds of the relevant UC segment are then re-evaluated with new covariances and means sampled from the posterior distribution of the stocks. The resultant sets of points are then compared by calculating the proportion of points **y** in each set which are strictly dominated by those in the other set [8]. This is performed for 1000 different samples from the posterior, and the difference in the respective proportions assessed as to whether they are statistically different from 0. Table 1 shows that for both asset sets, apart from the lowest risk levels, the optimised UC portfolios are not significantly different from the CC frontier except for a relatively small k.

The previous analysis has shown that it is possible to replicate closely the mean and variance of an efficient portfolio with a portfolio composed of a relatively small number of stocks. The analysis is however *ex post* and might be of little help to portfolio managers concerned with choosing investment positions *ex ante*. Thus while we have shown that optimising a (CC) portfolio could take us close to the UC frontier, it might be that the benefits that we know exist *ex post* are impossible to realise *ex ante*. In the preliminary proof of concept study here, we solely concentrate on the *global minimum variance portfolio*. This frees us from the difficulty of having to estimate expected returns on the portfolio [10]. To actually evaluate the performance of our historically optimal CC portfolio we use a bootstrapping technique. We draw without replacement k random integers, all between 1 and a. The global MV portfolio formed from stocks in our dataset corresponding to the k integers is then calculated using QP. The standard deviation of the weekly returns for the portfolio is derived, beginning with week 501 for a period of t weeks, $t = 4, 12, 26, 52, 104$. This is repeated 1000 times. Descriptive statistics are reported in Table 2 for $k = 10$.

In both asset sets the largest reduction in volatility, compared to the mean bootstrapped CC portfolio, is in the shortest period ($t=4$) after portfolio formation. After this, performance is mixed with the US data showing only a small or no improvement for longer horizons, while the EM *ex ante* optimal portfolio does offer 14.7% risk reduction at the 104 week horizon. The short term result does appear consistent with ARCH type modelling of volatility movements.

4 Discussion

A new approach to discovering cardinality constrained portfolios has been described here, using MOEAs to search for and maintain a number of different CC frontiers. Empirical results show that *ex post* with a relatively small cardinality level one can attain performance that is not significantly different than the unconstrained frontier and *ex ante* there is some level of persistence in the portfolio weights found. The authors are currently applying the methodology to both within and across markets, with additional constraints recommended by fund managers. In addition the authors are investigating non-Markovitz formulations of risk, and the use of higher moments within the general framework.

Acknowledgements

We thank Richard Everson for his helpful comments. JEF is supported by the EPSRC, grant GR/R24357/01. MP is supported by a university scholarship.

References

1. Campbell, J., Lettau, M., Malkiel, B., Xu, Y.: Have individual stocks become more volatile? An empirical exploration of idiosyncratic risk. J. Finance **56** (2001) 1–43
2. Fisher, L., Lorie, J.: Some studies of variability of returns on investments in common stocks. J. Bus. **43** (1970) 99–134
3. Markowitz, H.: Portfolio Selection: Efficient Diversification of Investments. John Wiley & Sons (1959)
4. Chang, T.J., Meade, N., Beasley, J., Sharaiha, Y.: Heuristics for cardinality constrained portfolio optimisation. Comp. & Operations Res. **27** (2000) 1271–1302
5. Doerner, K., Gutjahr, W., Hartl, R., Strauss, C., Stummer, C.: Ant colony optimization in multiobjective portfolio selection. In: Proceedings of the 4th Metaheuristics Intl. Conf., MIC'2001, July 16–20, Porto, Portugal. (2001) 243–248
6. Deb, K.: Multi-objective optimization using evolutionary algorithms. Wiley (2001)
7. Lin, D., Wang, S., Yan, H.: A multiobjective genetic algorithm for portfolio selection. In: Proceedings of ICOTA 2001, December 15-17, Hong Kong,. (2001)
8. Fieldsend, J., Everson, R., Singh, S.: Using Unconstrained Elite Archives for Multi-Objective Optimisation. IEEE Trans. on Evol. Comp. **7** (2003) 305–323
9. Larget, B., Simon, D.: Markov chain Monte Carlo algorithms for the Bayesian analysis of phylogenetic trees. Mol. Bio. & Evol. **16** (1999) 750–759
10. Li, K., Sarkar, A., Wang, Z.: Diversification benefits of emerging markets subject to portfolio constraints. J. Empirical Finance **10** (2003) 57–80

Stock Trading by Modelling Price Trend with Dynamic Bayesian Networks

Jangmin O[1], Jae Won Lee[2], Sung-Bae Park[1], and Byoung-Tak Zhang[1]

[1] School of Computer Science and Engineering, Seoul National University
San 56-1, Shillim-dong, Kwanak-gu, Seoul, Korea 151-744
{jmoh,sbpark,btzhang}@bi.snu.ac.kr
[2] School of Computer Science and Engineering, Sungshin Women's University,
Dongsun-dong, Sungbuk-gu, Seoul, Korea 136-742
jwlee@cs.sungshin.ac.kr

Abstract. We study a stock trading method based on dynamic bayesian networks to model the dynamics of the trend of stock prices. We design a three level hierarchical hidden Markov model (HHMM). There are five states describing the trend in first level. Second and third levels are abstract and concrete hidden Markov models to produce the observed patterns. To train the HHMM, we adapt a semi-supervised learning so that the trend states of first layer is manually labelled. The inferred probability distribution of first level are used as an indicator for the trading signal, which is more natural and reasonable than technical indicators. Experimental results on representative 20 companies of Korean stock market show that the proposed HHMM outperforms a technical indicator in trading performances.

1 Introduction

Stock market is a core of capitalism where people invest some of their asset in stocks and companies might raise their business funds from stock market. Since the number of investors is increasing everyday in this century, the intelligent decision support systems aiding them to trade are keenly needed. But attempts on modelling or predicting the stock market have not been successful in *consistently* beating the market. This is the famous Efficient Market Hypothesis (EMH) saying that the future prices are unpredictable since all the information available is already reflected on the history of past prices [4]. However, if we step back from *consistently*, we can find several empirical results saying that the market might be somewhat predictable [1].

Many of technical indicators such as moving averages have been developed by researchers in economic area [3]. There are some weak points in technical indicators. For example, if we use RSI, we must specify its parameters. The curves of RSI are heavily influenced by the parameters. Also, there are some vagueness in their interpretations, which might be varied according to the subjectiveness of the interpreters.

In this paper, we propose a trend predictor of stock prices that can produce the probability distribution of trend states under the dynamics of trend and price of a stock. To model the dynamics, we design a hierarchical hidden Markov model, a variant of dynamic bayesian networks (DBN). Given observed series of prices, a DBN can probabilistically inference hidden states from past to current. Also we can sample or predict the future from learned dynamics. To use an indicator of bid and ask signals, it is more natural to use our HHMM model than technical indicators.

The resulting trading performance is compared with the performances of a technical indicator through a simulated trading on Korean stock market.

2 HHMM for Mining Trend Patterns

The hierarchical hidden Markov model is an extension of the hidden Markov model (HMM) that is designed to model domains with hierarchical structure and dependencies at multiple length scales [2]. In HHMM, there are production states emitting single observations and abstraction states emitting sequences. An abstract state calls sub-HHMM which is responsible for emitting single observations or calls recursively other sub-HHMMs. HHMM can be converted to HMM, but its inference and learning are prohibited since the conversion leas to severely increased node sizes and multi fan-ins. Given a sequence of length T, the original inference algorithm for HHMM was $O(T^3)$ which is prohibitive when long sequences. Fortunately, there is efficient techniques to convert HHMM to DBN allowing $O(T)$ inference time as usual DBN [2, 6]. Figure 1 is an HHMM for mining trend patterns of stock prices which is designed in this paper.

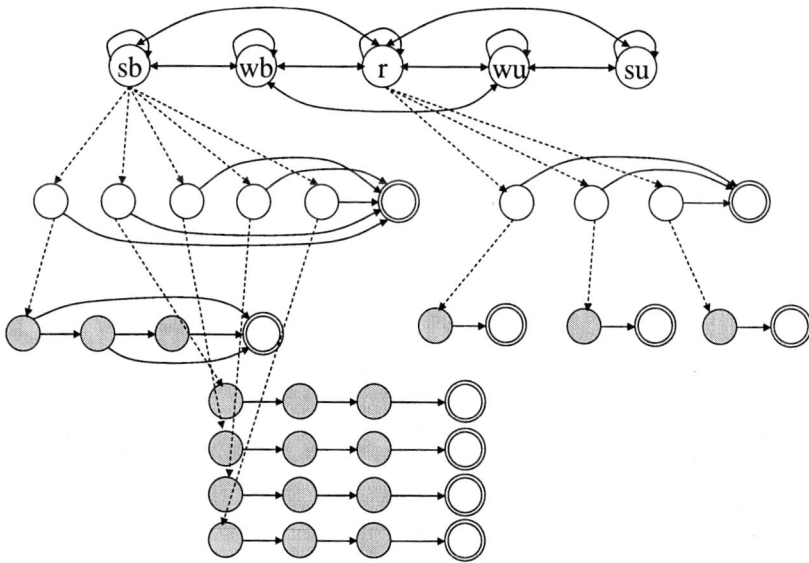

Fig. 1. State transition diagram for HHMM modelling the trend patterns of stock prices. Gray nodes are observation nodes, double circles are end states, and white circles are hidden states.

2.1 Fist Level

First level of HHMM is about the states of the trend. We divide the trend into five classes such as *strong bear* (sb), *weak bear* (wb), *random walk* (r), *weak bull* (wu), and *strong bull* (su) in Fig. 1. The sequence of price is the realization of the sub-HHMMs at the lower level called from this abstract states.

2.2 Second Level

In second level, there are five abstract states called from first level except the state r. These abstract states call their sub-HMMs of third level. In this paper, we choose observation at time t as relative closing price (RC) and is defined as

$$\text{RC}(t) = \frac{\text{close}(t) - \text{close}(t-1)}{\text{close}(t-1)}$$

where close(t) means closing price at day t.

As sub-HMM for the random walk, the simple mixture of Gaussian is introduced as shown the right-center in Fig. 1. The number of mixture components is set to three. And the hidden states of second level for random walk correspond to the mixture components. Each component has its own emission node at third level, which produces a Gaussian random variable.

After the k-means clustering on the pool of RC from the training data set, the gaussian emission node of each component is initialized with mean and covariance of clustered data. The transition probabilities from r to three abstract states of second level are initialized as the priors of clustered data.

2.3 Third Level

Bottom level HMMs are responsible for emission of outputs. We assume that there are five backbones which are Markov chains of length three. Each backbone is connected to one of abstract state in second level. To construct backbones, we use k-means clustering. From training data set, every RC sequence of length three is produced into a pool. Five clusters are produced from this pool by k-means clustering algorithm. Figure 2 shows the results of clustering and Fig. 3 shows the prior probabilities of the center of each cluster. Four clusters except '4' are used to initialize four Markov chains as shown bottom in Fig. 1.

While cluster '4' takes about 35% of sequences, the center of the cluster is nearly deviated from zero. Therefore to compromise the information loss from k-means clustering, we design a flexible HMM for this cluster which is capable of escaping its backbone at anytime as shown left-center in Fig. 1.

The means and covariances of Gaussians in backbones are initialized as the results of clustering. The transition probabilities from first level except r to second level is initialized as priors of Fig. 3.

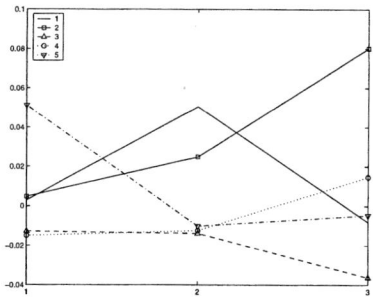
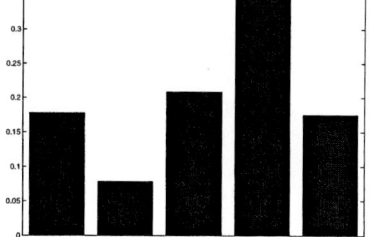

Fig. 2. Centers of five clusters.   **Fig. 3.** Priors of five clusters.

2.4 Training the Model

To train our HHMM model, we adapt a semi-supervised learning techniques. Rather than learning HHMM from only observed RC sequences, we manually labelled the hidden states in the first level. We consider in this paper the trend as the interval to which the gradient of moving average of future price including current price belongs. Moving average (MA) is defined as

$$MA(i)^W = \sum_{t=0}^{W-1} \text{close}(i+t)$$

where i is the i-th day and W is the length of window to be considered. The trend of i-day is labelled to one of five hidden states according to the gradient of the moving average line. Using the labelled data, the HHMM is trained by EM algorithm for dynamic Bayesian Networks.

3 Experiment

In Korean stock market, there are about 2,000 companies. Among those, we target the 20 candidates included in Korea Leading Company Index (KLCI) announced by Daewoo Securites Co., Ltd. The company names are listed in the first column of Table 1. The training data set is constructed from January 1998 to June 2003. From July 2003 to January 2004 is used as test set.

To construct, inference, and learn HHMM, we use *Bayes Net Toolbox* and slightly modify it [5]. Among several inference algorithms, jtree_2TBN_inf_engine, one of online smoothing algorithms is used.

Table 1 summarizes the trading results on the test period. Baseline 1 is the imaginary profit as if we would hold a stock during entire test period. Baseline 2 is the cumulative profit when we use TRIX, a technical indicator, of which gold cross is used as bid signal and dead cross is used as ask signal. HHMM is the cumulative profit of proposed method. We take a bid signal if the sum of probabilities of su and wu gets greater than 0.5 and a ask signal if the sum for sb and wb gets lower than 0.5.

Table 1. Comparison of the trading performances.

Company	Baseline 1	Baseline 2	HHMM
Samsung Electronics	47.38	14.67	29.78
SK Telecom	-1.39	-4.68	6.33
POSCO	25.87	2.08	18.66
KEPCO	10.96	1.07	4.91
KT	-8.80	-5.91	3.28
Hyundai Motors	52.21	27.61	32.14
LG Electronics	30.00	17.70	19.66
Samsung SDI	75.00	14.95	30.22
Hyundai MOBIS	52.55	49.78	53.83
Shinsegae	44.53	10.02	18.76
KT&G	32.58	16.08	17.12
LG Chemical	19.56	22.80	25.01
DSME	30.85	-2.20	33.12
KOGAS	0.74	-1.24	-0.50
Hankook Tire	74.49	29.35	24.53
NC Soft	13.49	3.76	15.77
Hanlla Climate Control	55.65	16.94	27.01
Cheil Industries	5.71	17.87	9.66
Daum Communication	-32.75	-11.42	-0.71
Handsome	2.91	4.07	21.09

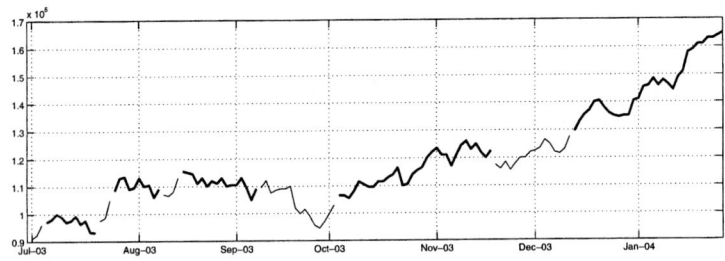

Fig. 4. Simulated trading on Samsung SDI.

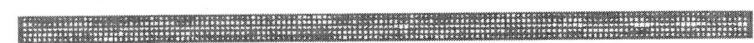

Fig. 5. Hinton diagram.

For the test period, Korean stock market is in its bull market. So in several cases, Baseline 1, simple buy-and-wait strategy, wins other two methods. But HHMM outperforms Baseline 2 in most cases. Furthermore, HHMM minimizes the loss when the stock is declined in the whole period such as Daum Communication.

Figure 4 shows the simulated trading of Samsung SDI with HHMM in detail. The thick lines represent holding periods of stock. Figure 5 shows a Hinton diagram for filtered distribution of the trend states, that is $P(s_t|y_{t-19:t})$. Each row means sb, wb, r, wu, and su respectively from top to bottom. The larger white box is, the higher the probability is.

4 Conclusion

In this paper, a hierarchical hidden Markov model is designed to model the dynamics of trend of stock prices. The learned HHMM captures some characteristics of dynamics and the trend predicted by the model can be used as an effective indicator for trading signal.

There are some rooms to expand our HHMM model. The trading volume is generally assumed more chaotic than price series but it might be a key factor of the price trend through more complicated relations. We are trying to find a way to incorporate the information of trading volume.

Acknowledgement

This research was supported in part by the Ministry of Education and Human Resources Development under the BK21-IT Program. The RIACT at Seoul National University provides research facilities for this study.

References

1. Fama, E. F. and K. R. French. Dividend Yields and Expected Stock Returns. *Journal of Financial Economics*, 22, pp. 3-26, 1988.
2. Fine, S., Y. Singer, and N. Tishby, The Hierarchical Hidden markov Model Analysis and Applications, *Machine Learning*, 32, pp. 41-62, 1998.
3. Kendall, S. M. and K. Ord. *Time Series*. Oxford, New York, 1997.
4. Malkiel, B. G. *A Random Walk Down Wall Street*. Norton, New York, 1996.
5. Murphy, K. P. *Bayes Net Toolbox for Matlab*.
   http://www.ai.mit.edu/~murphyk/Software/BNT/bnt.html, 2004.
6. Murphy, K. P. and M. Paskin. Linear Time Inference in Hierarchical HMMs. *In Proceedings of Neural Information Processing Systems*, 2001.

Detecting Credit Card Fraud by Using Questionnaire-Responded Transaction Model Based on Support Vector Machines

Rong-Chang Chen[1], Ming-Li Chiu[2], Ya-Li Huang[2], and Lin-Ti Chen[2]

[1] Department of Logistics Engineering and Management
rcchens@ntit.edu.tw
[2] Department of Information Management
National Taichung Institute of Technology
No. 129, Sec. 3, Sanmin Rd., Taichung, Taiwan 404, R.O.C.

Abstract. This work proposes a new method to solve the credit card fraud problem. Traditionally, systems based on previous transaction data were set up to predict a new transaction. This approach provides a good solution in some situations. However, there are still many problems waiting to be solved, such as skewed data distribution, too many overlapped data, fickle-minded consumer behavior, and so on. To improve the above problems, we propose to develop a personalized system, which can prevent fraud from the initial use of credit cards. First, the questionnaire-responded transaction (QRT) data of users are collected by using an online questionnaire based on consumer behavior surveys. The data are then trained by using the support vector machines (SVMs) whereby the QRT models are developed. The QRT models are used to predict a new transaction. Results from this study show that the proposed method can effectively detect the credit card fraud.

1 Introduction

Fraudulent transactions cost cardholders and issuing banks hundreds of millions of dollars each year. It is thus very important to present an effective method to prevent credit card fraud. In dealing with the credit card fraud problem, conventionally, actual transaction data are used to build up a system for predicting a new case [1–5]. This approach indeed provides a good solution in some situations. However, there are still some problems for using this approach [1–3]:

- The system should be able to handle skewed distributions, since only a very small percentage of all credit card transactions is fraudulent.
- There are too many overlapping data. Many genuine transactions may resemble fraudulent transactions. The opposite also happens, when a fraudulent transaction appears to be normal.
- The systems should be able to adapt themselves to new consumer behavior.
- There are no or few transaction data for new users.

To improve the problems mentioned above, a personalized system is proposed in this study. We first collect personal transaction data of users by a self-completion online questionnaire. The questionnaire-responded transaction (QRT) data, including both the normal (normal QRT) and the abnormal parts (abnormal QRT), are regarded as the transaction records and are used to construct a personalized (QRT) model, which is in turn used to predict and decide whether a new, actual transaction to be processed is a fraud or not. Since the consumer behavior of an unauthorized use is usually different from that of the legal cardholder, this kind of fraud can be avoided. This method is particularly suitable to new users since there are no or few transaction data for them. Thus, even if a thief uses a credit card applied with the personal information of others or a card is illegally intercepted, the fraud can be prevented. In addition, the collected abnormal QRT data can be used to improve the skewed distribution, which has a very small percentage of abnormal data.

The rest of this paper is organized as follows. Section 2 gives a brief overview of SVMs. The proposed approach is described in Section 3. Section 4 presents the experimental results. Finally, conclusions are presented in Section 5.

2 Support Vector Machines (SVMs)

Some artificial intelligence techniques and data mining tools have been successfully applied to fraud detection, such as, case-based reasoning (CBR), neural network, learning machines, and more. Amongst them, the support vector machines (SVMs) are an emerging powerful machine learning technique to classify and do regression. Support Vector Machines (SVMs) were developed by V.N. Vapnik [6] and have been presented with sound theoretical justifications to provide a good generalization performance compared to other algorithms [7]. The SVM has already been successfully used for a wide variety of problems, like pattern recognition, bio-informatics, natural language learning text mining, and more [8,9]. The SVM has some desirable properties that make it a very powerful technique to use: only a small subset of the total training set is needed to split the different classes of the problem, computational complexity is reduced by use of the kernel trick, over-fitting is avoided by classifying with a maximum margin hyper-surface, and so on.

SVMs are a method for creating a classification or a general regression functions from a set of training data. For classification, SVMs can find a hyper-surface in the space of possible inputs. This hyper-surface will split the negative examples from the positive examples. The split will be chosen so that it has the largest distance from the hyper-surface to the nearest of the positive and negative examples. This makes the classification correct for testing data that is near, but not identical to the training data.

In this study, we will use SVMs to classify the transactions.

3 Approach

The proposed method is illustrated in Fig. 1. First, the transaction data of users are collected by using an online, self-completion questionnaire system. Then, the

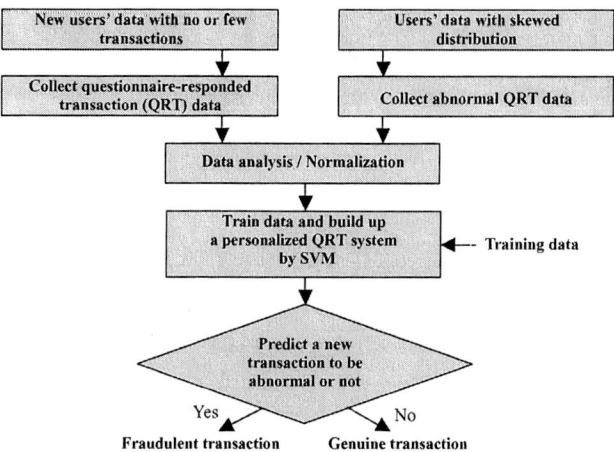

Fig. 1. The procedure for predicting fraud.

data are trained by SVMs whereby QRT models will be set up. Finally, these QRT models are used to classify a new transaction as a fraudulent or a genuine transaction.

Data-Collection Method. There are many methods to collect data. Amongst them, interviews and questionnaires are two of the most common survey methods. The biggest advantages of self-completion questionnaires over structural interviews are that they can save money and take less time, as well as allow larger samples to be acquired. In particular, if we allow the questionnaires to be delivered on Internet, the benefits of self-completion questionnaires would be considerably increased.

Online Questionnaire System. A successful questionnaire must fulfill three requirements [10]: (1) The questions must be clear and unambiguous. (2) The presentation of questions must be standardized. (3) An efficient, reliable and preferably, cost-effective way of translating the data for subsequent analysis must be used. Following the above suggestions, an online questionnaire system is developed. The design platform of online questionnaire system is Windows 2000, IIS 5.0. The program used is ASP. The database is SQL 2000. The pilot work has been executed to ensure that a good final questionnaire is developed. Questions are designed based on an individual's consuming preference [11,12]. Participants can access a batch of 15-20 questions each time and can decide to answer more batches by clicking on the button for continue.

Consumer behavior varies considerably with each individual. It is, therefore, reasonable to classify their behavior according to several main properties. The gathered personal QRT data are mainly composed of several parts: gender, age, transaction time, transaction amount, and transaction items.

Personalized Model vs. Group-Based Model. In general, a consumer group has similar consumer behavior. Thus, it is reasonable to use a group-based model to predict an individual's behavior. However, when dealing with the transaction item, like a coin having two sides, one will do it, the other not. Under this situation, if we put each user's data into the same model, the accuracy would not be so high. Therefore, we propose to develop personalized models to improve on the prediction-accuracy.

Detailed Database (Ddb) vs. Broader Database (Bdb). The questions in the online questionnaire are based on two different databases, broader database (Bdb) and detailed database (Ddb). The major difference between them is the definition of the transaction items. For instance, in the Bdb, we will classify keyboard, mouse and so on as computer accessories. By contrast, in the Ddb, they will be classified as an individual transaction item, respectively.

4 Results and Discussion

In this paper, we used mySVM [8], which was run on a Pentium III 667 PC with 256K of RAM, and Windows 2000 Professional operating system, to train all QRT data.

More than 100 junior college students were invited to answer the questionnaire. They are in their early twenties. Most students did not have any credit card; a few had one card, only. Most participants were willing to answer approximately 105-120 questions which took about 15 minutes to answer. Totally, about 12,000 QRT data were collected. One interesting finding is that the QRT data are not very skewed. The ratio of positive (normal) samples to total samples has a range from 0.35 to 0.67.

For convenience, let Ntrain be the number of the training data, Ntest be the number of test data, and R be the ratio of positive (+, normal) samples to negative (-, abnormal) samples. The prediction accuracy is denoted as P. P(+/+) represents the accuracy of normal samples predicted to be normal, P(+/-) represents the percentage of normal samples predicted to be abnormal, and so on. Finally, let P_- represent the personalized model and Q_- represent the group-based model.

The effect of testing data distribution is shown in Fig. 2(a). The ratios of $N_{test}/(N_{test}+N_{train})$ are 0.33, 0.42, 0.5, and 0.75, respectively. R=1. The SVMs are not very sensitive to the testing distribution, as indicated in Fig. 2(a).

Figure 2(b) shows the effect of N_{test} on the P(-/-). N_{test} is varied from 20 to 70. N_{test} is set to be 50% of N_{train} and $R = 1$. The database used is the Ddb. A personalized QRT model (P_Ddb) is set up for a middle-age man, who provided 3-year real transaction data of his credit card. Note that all his real data are normal. Therefore, to correctly predict a fraudulent behavior, abnormal data must be generated. This is a limit case of skewed distribution. To solve this problem, we collect the abnormal QRT data, which can be considered as fraudulent transaction data, to set up a P_Ddb model. The testing data are also substituted into youth-group model (youth G_Ddb) based on over 100 youths.

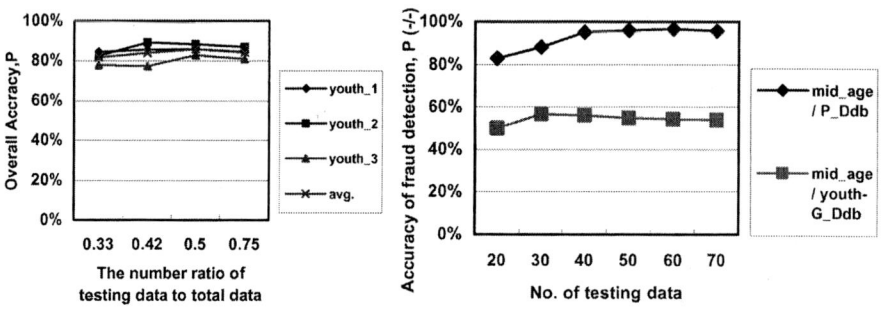

(a) The effect of testing data distribution.

(b) The variation of P(-/-) with N_{test}.

Fig. 2. The effect of testing data and the variation of P(-/-).

Figure 2(b) shows that the P_Ddb model can predict correctly the abnormal data even with a low N_{test}. To obtain a high P(-/-), $N_{test} = 40$, where the total number of data is 120, is enough. This is important information since people are usually not willing to spend too much time to answer questions. As mentioned above, most participants were willing to answer about 105-120 questions. As one might expect, the P_Ddb result is much better than that in youth G_Ddb, indicating that different consumer group has different behavior. Thus, stratification or discrimination is needed to predict accurately the consuming behavior.

The comparison of accuracy of the personalized models and the group-based model is illustrated in Table 1. $R = 1$. The results show that the overall P of P_Ddb is a little higher than that of G_Ddb.

Table 1. Summary of overall P.

	P_Ddb	P_Bdb	G_Ddb	avg.
youth_1	83%	81%	87%	83%
youth_2	88%	90%	83%	87%
youth_3	83%	76%	73%	77%
avg.	84%	82%	81%	82%

For fraud detection, the P(-/-) is the most concerned, since a high P(-/-) allows only a small percentage of fraudulent behavior. Therefore, multiple models are employed to improve P(-/-). The testing data are tested in three different models, i.e., (P_Ddb), (P_Bdb), and (G_Ddb). There are three different rules: the "1-" rule stands for a situation that if there are 1 or more than 1 abnormal prediction, the predicted result is considered as abnormal. Similarly, the "2-" rule represents that if there are 2 or more than 2 abnormal predictions, the behavior is regarded as abnormal. Figure 3 shows that the "1-" rule can enhance

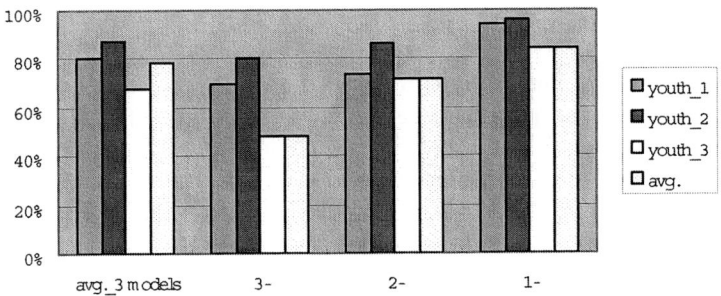

Fig. 3. The change of fraud detection accuracy P(-/-) with different rules.

Table 2. Summary of costs and ΔP.

Actual	Predicted behavior	
transaction	Genuine	Fraudulent
Genuine	0 $\Delta P(+/+)$	Reconfirmation, Cr $\Delta P(+/-)$
Fraudulent	Fraudulent, Cf $\Delta P(-/+)$	Reconfirmation, Cr $\Delta P(-/-)$

Table 3. Summary of accuracy difference ΔP. The difference is defined as the accuracy of "-1" rule minus the accuracy of P_Ddb, P_Bdb, and G_Ddb, respectively.

	P_Ddb			P_Bdb		
	$\Delta P(+/-)$	$\Delta P(-/+)$	$\Delta P(-/-)$	$\Delta P(+/-)$	$\Delta P(-/+)$	$\Delta P(-/-)$
youth_1	18%	-18%	18%	14%	-16%	16%
youth_2	8%	-8%	8%	18%	-10%	10%
youth_3	14%	-22%	22%	8%	-28%	28%
avg.	13%	-16%	16%	13%	-18%	18%
	G_Ddb			Average Δp		
	$\Delta P(+/-)$	$\Delta P(-/+)$	$\Delta P(-/-)$	$\Delta P(+/-)$	$\Delta P(-/+)$	$\Delta P(-/-)$
youth_1	6%	-8%	8%	13%	-14%	14%
youth_2	-8%	-2%	2%	6%	-7%	7%
youth_3	-4%	-28%	28%	6%	-26%	26%
avg.	-2%	-13%	13%	8%	-16%	16%

P(-/-) considerably, as compared to the average P(-/-) from three models (avg._3 models) without using any rules.

Tables 2 and 3 show the summary of ΔP and costs. There are mainly two kinds of costs: fraud loss cost Cf and reconfirmation cost Cr. In general, Cf>>Cr. Thus, if we can improve P(-/-), we can save lots of cost. Employing the "-1" rule, the average ΔP of 3 youths is about 16%. Multiplying this percentage by the fraud amount, the benefit of improving detection accuracy is considerable.

5 Conclusions

We have presented a new method to solve the credit card fraud problem. Our method is to collect the questionnaire-responded transaction (QRT) data of users by using an online questionnaire and then employ the SVMs to train data and to develop the QRT models, which are then used to decide whether a new transaction to be processed is a fraud or otherwise.

The results from this study show that the proposed method can effectively detect fraud. Even without actual transaction data or with little transaction data, a fraud can be detected with high accuracy by the QRT model, especially by using a personalized model.

References

1. S. Maes, K. Tuyls, B. Vanschoenwinkel, and B. Manderick, "Credit Card Fraud Detection Using Bayesian and Neural Networks," Proc. NEURO Fuzzy, Havana, Cuba (2002).
2. P.K. Chan, W. Fan, A. L. Prodromidis, and S.J. Stolfo, "Distributed Data Mining in Credit Card Fraud Detection," IEEE Intel. Sys., Nov.-Dec. (1999) 67-74.
3. R. Brause, T. Langsdorf, and M. Hepp, "Neural Data Mining for Credit Card Fraud Detection," IEEE Int. Conf. Tools with Artif. Intel. (1999).
4. P. Chan and S. Stolfo, "Toward Scalable Learning with Nonuniform Class and Cost Distributions: A Case Study in Credit Card Fraud Detection," Proc. 4th Int. Conf. Knowl. Disco. and D. Min., Menlo Park, Calif. (1997) 164-168.
5. R. Wheeler and S. Aitken, "Multiple Algorithm for Fraud Detection," Knowl. Based Sys., (13) (2000) 93-99.
6. V.N. Vapnik, "The Nature of Statistical Learning Theory," Springer (1995).
7. C.J.C. Burges, "A Tutorial on Support Vector Machines for Pattern Recognition," Da. Min. and Knowl. Disco., Vol. 2, No.2 (1998) 955-974.
8. S. Ruping, "mySVM-Manual," Computer Science Department, AI Unit University of Dortmund, Oct. 30 (2000).
9. M. Berry and G. Linoff, "MData Mining Techniques for Marketing, Sales, and Customer Support," Wiley Computer Pub. (1997).
10. R. Sapsford, "Survey Research," SAGE Pub. (1999).
11. http://www.104pool.com/.
12. http://survey.yam.com/life2000.

Volatility Forecasts in Financial Time Series with HMM-GARCH Models

Xiong-Fei Zhuang and Lai-Wan Chan

Computer Science and Engineering Department
The Chinese University of Hong Kong, Shatin, Hong Kong
{xfzhuang,lwchan}@cse.cuhk.edu.hk

Abstract. Nowadays many researchers use GARCH models to generate volatility forecasts. However, it is well known that volatility persistence, as indicated by the sum of the two parameters G_1 and A_1[1], in GARCH models is usually too high. Since volatility forecasts in GARCH models are based on these two parameters, this may lead to poor volatility forecasts. It has long been argued that this high persistence is due to the structure changes(e.g. shift of volatility levels) in the volatility processes, which GARCH models cannot capture. To solve this problem, we introduce our GARCH model based on Hidden Markov Models(HMMs), called HMM-GARCH model. By using the concept of hidden states, HMMs allow for periods with different volatility levels characterized by the hidden states. Within each state, local GARCH models can be applied to model conditional volatility. Empirical analysis demonstrates that our model takes care of the structure changes and hence yields better volatility forecasts.

1 Introduction

Volatility analysis of financial time series is an important aspect of many financial decisions. For example, fund managers, option traders and etc., are all interested in volatility forecasts in order to either construct less risky portfolios or obtain higher profits. Hence, there is always a need for good analysis and forecasting of volatility.

In the last few decades, many volatility models have been put forward. The most popular and successful models among these are the autoregressive conditional heteroskedasticity (ARCH) models by Engle [2] and extended to generalized ARCH (GARCH) by Bollerslev [3]. Their success stems from their ability to capture some stylized facts of financial time series, such as time-varying volatility and volatility clustering. Other volatility models include the stochastic volatility (SV) models and etc..

Although standard GARCH models improve the in-sample fit a lot compared with constant variance models, numerous studies find that GARCH models give unsatifactory forecasting performances, see [4]. Andersen and Bollserslev [5] pointed our that GARCH models give good volatility forecasting by increasing the data sampling frequecy, such as intra-day data. Increasing the sampling frequency may also lessen the effect of the structure changes. Our research work, however, focus on the commonly used inter-day data. Hence the effect of structure changes is unavoidable.

In our paper we argue that the usually overstated volatility persistence in GARCH models may be the cause of poor forecasting performances. And many researchers show that this well-known high persistence may originate from the structure changes in the volatility processes, which GARCH models cannot capture. For example, Lamoureux [1] demonstrated that any shift in the structure of financial time series(e.g. the shift of unconditional variance) is likely to lead to misestimation of the GARCH parameters in such a way that they imply too high a volatility persistence.

One approach for modelling volatility structure changes is to use a Hamilton type regime switching (RS) model [6]. The earlier RS applications [7] tend to be rigid, where conditional variance is a constant within each regime. Recent extensions by Cai [8] apply an ARCH specification into the RS model to allow conditional variance to be time dependent.

Our goal is to solve the problem of excessive persistence in original GARCH models by introducing Hidden Markov Models to allow for different volatility states (periods with different volatility levels) in time series. And also, within each state, we allow GARCH models to model the conditional variance. As a result, our model is more parsimonious than Cai [8] because they use an ARCH class specification in each regime. The resulting HMM-GARCH model indeed yields better volatility forecast compared to original GARCH models for both artificial data and real financial data, in-sample as well as out-of-sample.

The overview of this paper is as follows. In section 2, we will formally define our HMM-GARCH model. In section 3, we will give a detailed description of the data, methodology and the empirical results of our volatility forecasting experiments. Finally, our conclusion is in section 4.

2 HMM-GARCH Model

2.1 GARCH Models

First, let us consider a time series Y, and observation y_t ($t = 1, 2, \ldots, T$) is the value of Y at time step t. Here we consider the GARCH(1,1) models, which are adequate for modelling volatilities in most financial time series (see [9]). The GARCH(1,1) model is as follows:

$$y_t = C + \epsilon_t \tag{1}$$

$$\sigma_t^2 = K + G_1 \sigma_{t-1}^2 + A_1 \epsilon_{t-1}^2 \tag{2}$$

In the conditional mean model Eq.(1), each observation y_t consists of a conditional mean C, plus an uncorrelated, white noise innovation ϵ_t. In the conditional variance model Eq.(2), the conditional variance σ_t^2 consists of a constant K, plus a weighted average of last period's forecast, σ_{t-1}^2, and the last period's squared innovation ϵ_{t-1}^2. Also we need $K > 0$, $G_1 > 0$ and $A_1 > 0$ to ensure a positive conditional variance σ_t^2. A convenient way to express the innovation is $\epsilon_t = Z_t \sigma_t$, where Z_t is an i.i.d. process with zero mean and unit variance. For the parameter estimates of the GARCH(1,1) model, the likelikhood functions have been maximized by using the BFGS optimization algorithm in the MATLAB optimization routines.

2.2 Hidden Markov Models

The basic concept of a Hidden Markov model is a doubly embedded stochastic process with an underlying stochastic process (the state sequence) that is not observable or hidden. The state sequence is a Markov process and it is called hidden because it can only be observed through another stochastic process (observation sequence), where each observation is a probabilistic function of the corresponding state.

We now define the notation of an HMM [10] which will be used later. Given the time series Y, an HMM is characterized by the following: 1) N, the number of states in the model. In our model the states refer to different variance levels. We denote the state set as $S = \{S_1, S_2, \cdots, S_N\}$, and the state at time t as q_t, $q_t \in S$. 2) The state transition probability distribution $A = \{a_{ij}\}$ where $a_{ij} = P[q_t = S_j | q_{t-1} = S_i], 1 \leq i, j \leq N$. 3) The observation probability distribution B. 4) The initial state distribution π. For convenience, we used the compact notation $\lambda = (A, B, \pi)$ to indicate the complete parameter set of the model.

Given the form of the HMMs, the goal is to find the best model for a given time series through optimally adjusting model parameters ($\lambda = (A, B, \pi)$).

2.3 HMM-GARCH Model

Our model is a hybrid model of the original GARCH models and HMMs.

First, we use HMMs to divide the entire time series into regimes with different volatility levels. The return of the time series is assumed to be modelled by a mixture of probability densities and each density function corresponds to a hidden state with its mean and variance. Viterbi algorithm [10] in HMMs is used to find the state sequence in the time series. Then we get the subsets of original time series corresponding to different states (volatility levels).

Second, within each regimes, we allow GARCH models with different parameter sets to model the local conditional variance as:

$$y_t = C^i + \epsilon_t \qquad (3)$$

$$\sigma_t^2 = K^i + G_1^i \sigma_{t-1}^2 + A_1^i \epsilon_{t-1}^2 \qquad (4)$$

where i denotes the state of the time series at time t. K^i, G_1^i and A_1^i are the parameter sets of local GARCH models related to state i.

Third, for the volatility forecast σ_t^2 of the global model, we need to predict the state i of time series at time $t + 1$ (next state). To make the prediction of the next state, we define $\alpha_t(i) = P(y_1, y_2, ..., y_t, q_t = i|\lambda)$, we can then estimate the probability of next state in terms of the transition probabilities a_{ij} as:

$$P(q_{t+1} = j|y_1, y_2, \cdots, y_t, \lambda) = \frac{P(y_1, y_2, \cdots, y_t, q_{t+1} = j|\lambda)}{P(y_1, y_2, \cdots, y_t|\lambda)} \quad (5)$$

$$= \frac{\sum_{i=1}^{N} \alpha_t(i) a_{ij}}{\sum_{j=1}^{N} (\sum_{i=1}^{N} \alpha_t(i) a_{ij})} \quad (6)$$

where $\alpha_t(i)$ can be estimated from the forward-backward algorithm [10].

After the next state i at time $t+1$ has been determined as above, we can choose the corresponding local GARCH model with parameter sets K^i, G_1^i and A_1^i to make volatility forecast.

3 Volatility Forecast Evaluation and Comparison

3.1 Data and Methodology

We used both artificial data sets and real financial data sets in our volatility forecast experiments. We considered both the in-sample forecasting performances and the out-of-sample forecasting performances.

First, we used artificial data because we know the exact regime switching processes in the time series in order to testify if our model solve the problems of excessive persistence in original GARCH models. We generated an artificial data set of total length 550 that switches between two GARCH processes. The diagonal elements a_{ii} of the transition matrix A are $a_{11} = 0.98$ and $a_{22} = 0.96$.

Second, to test if our model is useful in practice, we used real financial data sets (stock return time series) in our experiments. All 5 stocks are chosen from the Hang Seng Index (HSI) components with stock ID: 1, 3, 11, 17, 179 (from 2001/02/01 to 2003/05/01), a total of 550 days.

For all data sets, we use the rolling window in the experiments, 500 observations (about 2 years) were employed for training and in-sample evaluation purposes. The next observation was used for out-of-sample evaluation purposes.

3.2 Empirical Results and Evaluation

Since the actual volatility at time t is not observable, we need some measures of volatility to evaluate the forecasting performance. In this paper we use the standard approach suggested by Pagan and Schwert [7]. A proxy for the actual volatility $\hat{\sigma}_t^2$ is given by

$$\hat{\sigma}_t^2 = (y_t - \bar{y})^2 \quad (7)$$

where $\bar{y}$ is the mean of the time series over the sample period.

Mean Squared Error (MSE), a commonly used method in the literature, is used in this paper:

$$MSE = T^{-1} \sum_{t=1}^{T} (\hat{\sigma}_t^2 - \sigma_t^2)^2 \quad (8)$$

Table 1 and 2 below show the evaluation results. We use a two-state HMM-GARCH model in our experiments. In both tables, t-v represents true value, HG stands for HMM-GARCH model and o-G stands for original GARCH model. s_1 and s_2 indicate the two states with low and high volatility levels, respectively. MSE_1 is the in-sample MSE while MSE_2 is the out-of-sample MSE. The asterisks (*) means the results is significant at the 10% level.

Table 1. MSE for the artificial data set and the true parameter sets compared with those obtained from HMM-GARCH model and original GARCH models.

models	C	K	G_1	A_1	G_1+A_1	MSE_1	MSE_2
t-v (s_1)	$1\cdot 10^{-3}$	$1\cdot 10^{-5}$	0.20	0.10	0.30	/	/
(s_2)	$1\cdot 10^{-3}$	$5\cdot 10^{-5}$	0.60	0.30	0.90		
HG (s_1)	$1\cdot 10^{-3}$	$1\cdot 10^{-5}$	0.35	0.16	0.51	$0.83 \cdot 10^{-5}$	$0.35 \cdot 10^{-7}$*
(s_2)	$1\cdot 10^{-3}$	$7\cdot 10^{-5}$	0.65	0.32	0.97		
o-G	$1\cdot 10^{-3}$	$2\cdot 10^{-5}$	0.58	0.41	0.99	$0.93 \cdot 10^{-5}$	$0.43 \cdot 10^{-7}$*

Table 2. MSE for the stock return data sets and the parameter sets obtained from HMM-GARCH model and original GARCH models. (We ignore C, K here because we only care about the volatility persistence for real financial data.)

stock	models	G_1	A_1	G_1+A_1	MSE_1	MSE_2
001	HG (s_1)	0.88	0.00	0.88		
	(s_2)	0.06	0.00	0.06	$0.13 \cdot 10^{-5}$	$0.03 \cdot 10^{-5}$*
	o-G	0.80	0.12	0.92	$0.14 \cdot 10^{-5}$	$0.04 \cdot 10^{-5}$*
003	HG (s_1)	0.55	0.11	0.66		
	(s_2)	0.47	0.00	0.47	$0.49 \cdot 10^{-7}$*	$0.16 \cdot 10^{-7}$*
	o-G	0.60	0.13	0.73	$0.51 \cdot 10^{-7}$*	$0.18 \cdot 10^{-7}$*
011	HG (s_1)	0.88	0.00	0.88		
	(s_2)	0.01	0.00	0.01	$0.11 \cdot 10^{-6}$	$0.01 \cdot 10^{-6}$*
	o-G	0.90	0.06	0.96	$0.13 \cdot 10^{-6}$	$0.03 \cdot 10^{-6}$*
017	HG (s_1)	0.93	0.02	0.95		
	(s_2)	0.03	0.00	0.03	$0.16 \cdot 10^{-4}$	$0.02 \cdot 10^{-4}$*
	o-G	0.67	0.29	0.96	$0.20 \cdot 10^{-4}$	$0.03 \cdot 10^{-4}$*
179	HG (s_1)	0.57	0.00	0.57		
	(s_2)	0.07	0.00	0.07	$0.74 \cdot 10^{-5}$*	$0.07 \cdot 10^{-5}$*
	o-G	0.95	0.02	0.97	$0.82 \cdot 10^{-5}$*	$0.12 \cdot 10^{-5}$*

The results above show that HMM-GARCH model recovers the switching processes between two different volatility regimes with different volatility persistence ($G_1 + A_1$). However, the original GARCH models can not capture such volatility structure changes and always show a very high volatility persistence. As a result, we can see that HMM-GARCH model gives better volatility forecasts because the MSE of HMM-GARCH model is significantly smaller than the original GARCH models for most of the time.

4 Conclusion

This paper is based on the well-known fact that the volatility persistence of widely-used GARCH models is usually too high so that original GARCH models give poor volatility forecasts. And one possible reason for this excessive persistence is the structure changes (e.g. shift of volatility levels) in the volatility processes, which GARCH models cannot capture.

Therefore, we developed our HMM-GARCH model to allow for both different volatility states in time series and state specific GARCH models within each state. Our model shares the basic regime-switching concept of other recent RS applications (see [8], and [11]), and is more parsimonious in each state by allowing GARCH type heteroskedasticity.

The empirical results for both artificial data and real financial data show that the excessive persistence problems disappear in our model. And as a result, the forecasting performance of our model outperforms original GARCH models for both in sample and out-of-sample evaluation. These results suggest that it is promising to study volatility persistence in more detail, including the hidden regime-switching mechanisms, to improve volatility forecasts in future research.

Acknowledgement

The authors would like to thank The Research Grants Council, HK for support.

References

1. Lamoureux, C., and etc., Persistence in Variance, Structural Change, and the GARCH Model. *J. Bus Econ. Statist.*, 8:2, 225-234, 1990.
2. Engle, Robert F., Autoregressive Conditional Heteroskedasticity with Estimates of the Variance of United Kingdom Inflation. *Econometrica*, 50:4, 987-1007, 1982.
3. Bollerslev, T. Generalized Autoregressive Conditional Heteroskedasticity. *J. Econometrics*, 31, 307-327, 1986.
4. Figlewski, S. Forecasting Volatility. *Financial Markets, Institutions and Instruments*, 6, 1-88, 1997.
5. Andersen, T.G. and T. Bollerslev Answering the Skeptics: Yes, Standard Volatility Models do Provide Accurate Forecasts. *Inter. Econ. Review*, 39, 885-905, 1998.
6. Hamilton, J.D. Time series analysis. Princeton University Press, 1994.
7. Pagan, A. R., G. W. Schwert, "Alternative Models for Conditional Stock Volatility. *J. Econometrics*, 45, 267-290, 1990.
8. Cai, J. A Markov Model of Unconditional Variance in ARCH. *J. Bus Econ. Statist.*, 12, 309-316, 1994.
9. Bollerslev, and etc., ARCH Modeling in Finance: A Review of the Theory and Empirical Evidence. *J. Econometrics*, 52, 5-59, 1992.
10. Rabiner, L.R, A tutorial on hidden Markov models and selected applications in speech recognition. *Proc. of the IEEE*, 77:2, 1989.
11. Ser-Huang Poon and Clive W.J. Granger Forecasting Volatility in Financial Markets: A Review. *J. Economic Literature*, XLI, 478-539, 2003.

User Adaptive Answers Generation for Conversational Agent Using Genetic Programming

Kyoung-Min Kim, Sung-Soo Lim, and Sung-Bae Cho

Dept. of Computer Science, Yonsei University
134 Shinchon-dong, Seodaemoon-ku, Seoul 120-749, Korea
{kminkim,lss}@sclab.yonsei.ac.kr, sbcho@cs.yonsei.ac.kr

Abstract. Recently, it seems to be interested in the conversational agent as an effective and familiar information provider. Most of conversational agents reply to user's queries based on static answers constructed in advance. Therefore, it cannot respond with flexible answers adjusted to the user, and the stiffness shrinks the usability of conversational agents. In this paper, we propose a method using genetic programming to generate answers adaptive to users. In order to construct answers, Korean grammar structures are defined by BNF (Backus Naur Form), and it generates various grammar structures utilizing genetic programming (GP). We have applied the proposed method to the agent introducing a fashion web site, and certified that it responds more flexibly to user's queries.

1 Introduction

As information intensive society appears, a great deal of information is provided through diverse channels. Users also require an effective information providing service. Accordingly, we have researched the conversational agent that exchanges information between users and agents using natural language dialogue [1]. The belief that humans will be able to interact with computers in conversational speech has long been a favorite subject in science fiction. This reflects the persistent belief that spoken dialogue would be one of the most natural and powerful user interfaces to the computer [2]. Most of conversational agents lack flexibility in diverse situations because of responding repeatedly to users with the fixed answers stored in the reply database in advance. In this paper, we propose the conversational agent responding with various sentences constructed through evolutionary process to improve the user's adaptability. By the following, it can generate various answers with matching essential keywords, which are in answer scripts, to sentence structures. Accordingly, it leads more adaptive interaction to users.

2 Related Works

2.1 Conversational Agent

A conversational agent provides users with proper information by using natural language [1]. It is a program that understands natural language and is capable of responding in an intelligent way to a user request [3,4]. The dialogue can be an effective user interface in a more complicated system, since the natural language dialogue is effective in the flexibility, succinctness, and expressive power [5].

ELIZA (http://wwwai.ijs.si.eliza), the first conversational agent, uses the simple pattern matching technique. ALICE (http://alicebot.org) utilizes the simple sequential pattern matching based on keywords. They have the shortcomings of not being able to take into accounts user's intentions. It also takes considerably much time and effort in constructing response database based on script technique.

2.2 Natural Language Generation (NLG)

The main goal of NLG is to investigate how computer programs can produce high-quality natural language text from computer-internal representations of information [6,7]. The stages of NLG for a given application are disciplined in the order of text planning, sentence generation, and speech synthesis. Generation techniques can be classified into four main types that are canned text systems, template systems, phrase-based systems, and feature-based systems.

The grammar testing system is the first generating program, which is designed by Yngve (1962) and Friedman (1969). The applied fields of NLG range from question-answering system, expert system, database system, CAD system, and CAI system to non-conversation applications that are automatic abstracting system, report generator, and so on.

3 Generating Answers by GP

3.1 Conversational Agent System

Figure 1 shows the overall procedure of the proposed conversational agent. The proposed method uses several preprocessing processes such as morpheme analysis, spacing words, and keyword extraction. In preprocessing process, keywords are extracted from the input query, and then matching is conducted by comparing them with keywords in answer-scripts. Since the proposed method analyzes queries in a specific domain, keywords are defined as words frequently appeared on that domain, and answer-scripts are constructed with those keywords. Words, which are not related with the target domain, are ignored, and only keywords are used for the matching. When the query does not have adequate keywords, the matching is failed and the agent replies with a sentence such as "I don't understand" or "Input another query."

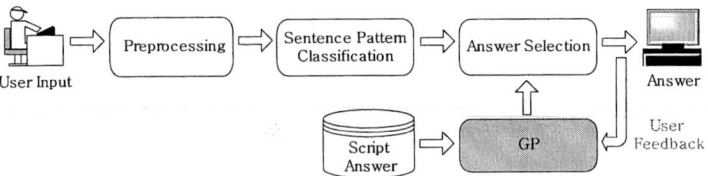

Fig. 1. The system architecture.

In sentence pattern categorization step, a query is classified into two general categories, question and statement, which are subcategorized into primary and secondary (Table 1). Automata that are constructed on keywords and their sequential information implement the sentence pattern classification module. An initial grammar structure is generated according to the sentence pattern. It constructs the first answer by matching the keywords extracted to the initial grammar structure generated. The following sentence structures for new answers are framed by the evolutionary process between the initial grammar tree generated and other trees. Therefore, it increases the flexibility of a dialogue because it can transfer answers of different types for the same query every time.

Table 1. The sentence pattern categorization.

Pattern	Keyword Type
Primary Question	Any, Can, Description, Fact, Location, Method, …
Secondary Question	Compare, Confirm, Cost, Directions, DoHave, …
Primary Statement	Any, Message, Act, Have, Is, Want, Fact, Other
Secondary Statement	Time, Conditional, Cause, Feeling
System Definition	RobotName, WhatUserMeant, …

3.2 Korean Grammar Rules

The early natural language generation was nothing but that prepared sentences send out changing little by little without sufficient information about grammar or lexical meaning. It might be short of the flexibility for various situations. A method of settlement is to use the grammar that can define finite rules being able to create infinite natural language [8].

In language processing fields, it generally analyzes a given sentence with a tree form. Each node of a tree represents a sentence component, which is categorized to NP, VP, and so forth according to function. The method, thus, applies grammar rules and generates various replies on a question. Grammars defined in this paper are as follows:

$$S \rightarrow VP + e$$
$$VP \rightarrow V \mid NP + c \mid Z + VP \mid NP + j + VP \mid V + e + VP$$
$$NP \rightarrow N \mid N + j + NP \mid Z + NP \mid VP + e + NP \mid N + NP$$

(S: a sentence; VP: a verb phrase; NP: a noun phrase; V: a verb; N: a noun; Z: an adverb; e: the ending of a word; c: a copula; j: an auxiliary word)

3.3 Answers Generation Using GP

It is difficult to generate an appropriate answer structure according to user's question pattern. Therefore, it can generate various grammar trees as evolving grammar structures according to each sentence pattern. The proposed method can create many answers by matching essential answer keywords, which are in answer scripts, to the parse tree generated. Figure 2 shows the procedure of generating answers. The proposed method is as follows:

- It analyzes a user's query pattern.
- It generates a random n tree whose depth is d based on defined grammar (3.2).
- It sets up the fitness of a chromosome as 0.5 (Fitness rate: 0~1).
- It selects a random chromosome tree among chromosome trees that have the fitness value more than average.
- It applies keywords extracted from answer scripts to the sentence structure of a s-elected tree. The script file form is same as Table 2. The <ANSWER> tag only has essential keywords of the answer for a user's query. Other constituents aptly utilize keywords or components of an input query.
- Then, the appropriate initial reply is output.
- After checking the displayed response, a user puts a score with five scales from -2 to +2. The next answer is adjusted to user's feedback.
- New sentence structures are generated continuously through evolving between the initial selected tree and random trees generated according to sentence patterns.

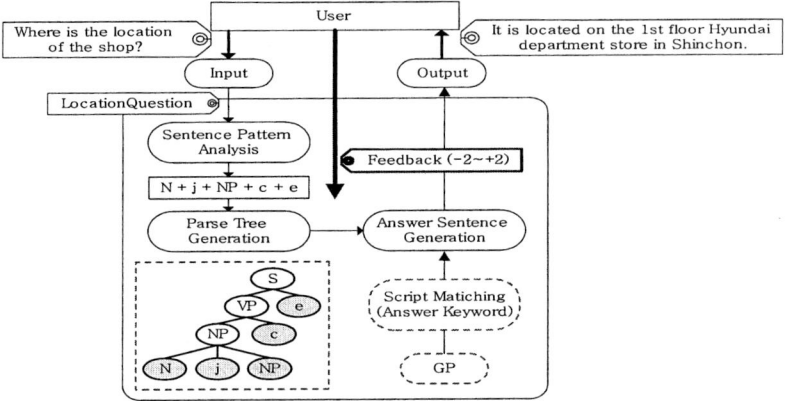

Fig. 2. The process of generating answer sentences.

Table 2. The example of scipt database.

<SCRIPT>
<TOPIC> a topic according to the subject </TOPIC>
<CLASS> a sentence pattern </CLASS>
<KEYWORD> a query based on keywords </KEYWORD>
<ANSWER> a answer based on essential keywords </ANSWER>
</SCRIPT>
<SCRIPT>
<TITLE> shop_location </TITLE>
<CLASS> ?LocationQuestion </CLASS>
<KEYWORD> shop location </KEYWORD>
<ANSWER><C> Shinchon Hyundai Department B1 </C></ANSWER>
</SCRIPT>

It selects 80% of high ranks after aligning with descending order based on the fitness of a chromosome. The chromosomes removed in selection process are generated by crossover operation of the two chromosomes survived. The fitness of a chromosome generated takes the average of two chromosomes crossed. It also carries out mutation operation at a fixed rate (5%).

Genetic algorithm that uses humans to provide fitness, rather than a programmed function to compute fitness, is called an interactive genetic algorithm [9]. In this paper, we can apply GP for generating answers by initializing the population of individuals encoded from sentence structure features, setting and evolving the fitness as 'whether the answer sentence generated is natural'. It is hard to set a clear standard because user's feedback is intervened individual subjectivity in a sizable portion. However, it is almost impossible to make suitable fitness function.

4 Experimental Results

We have conducted in two sides for verification of various replies. It sets the initial population size as 100 and tested 5 types (LocationQuestion, WhoQuestion, MethodQuestion, TimeQuestion, and DesciptionQuestion) among sentence patterns more than 30 types (Table 1) presented before.

4.1 Usability Test for Answer Sentences Generated

It inputs the questions according to sentence patterns of 5 types at random. While repeating dialogues on the same question by each 10 times, we get user's feedback scores. We confirm whether it is actually natural sentences generated or not. Then, it observes how much user's feedback affects the replies later.

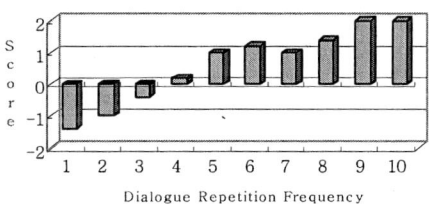

Fig. 3. The user evaluation for reply sentences.

Figure 3 shows the variation of average scores on dialogue iteration. Seen in the result, answers are improved gradually in the process of repeating dialogue, and more adaptive answers to the user are generated with the feedback.

4.2 Diversity Evaluation for Answers Generated

We have confirmed the various replies generated with new grammar structures against the same question through the examples of actual dialogue (Table 3 and Figure 4). In conversation 1, an incomplete sentence displayed with the first reply. The

Table 3. An example of conversation.

[Conversation 1]
YOU: Where is the location of the shop?
BOT: Shinchon Hyundai Department B1 (N+N+N)
    Feedback[-2~2]: >> -1
BOT: The shop is on the 1st floor Hyundai Department Store. (N+N+j+N+j+V+e)
    Feedback[-2~2]: >> 1
BOT: It is located on the 1st floor Hyundai Department Store in Shinchon. (N+j+N+N+V+e)
    Feedback[-2~2]: >> 2

[Conversation 2]
YOU: What kind of style is good?
BOT: Casual pants and the shirt are good. (N+N+j+N+j+V+e)
    Feedback[-2~2]: >> 1
BOT: The Striped skirt and the shirt matched. (N+N+j+N+N+j+V+e)
    Feedback[-2~2]: >> 2

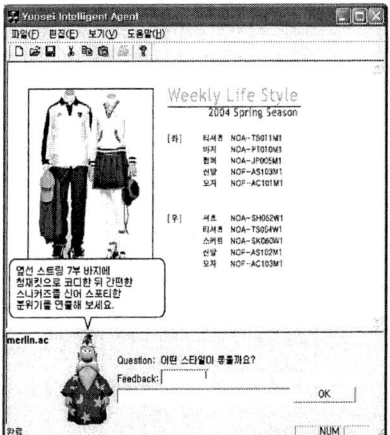

Fig. 4. An example of actual conversation with the system interface.

user gave '-1' as feedback value, and then a new reply of almost perfect grammar structure was displayed with the following reply. It can be also known that grammar structures were changed every time through tree structure representations in a parenthesized passage. The system saves it with optimal solution if a user gives to the '+2' point that is a peak on a generation reply. Afterward, the same reply is displayed on the same question according to priority. In addition, seen in conversation 2, it has an effect on various answers generation by replies generation of new contents because answer script part deals with several lines.

5 Conclusion and Future Works

As the conversational agents respond with fixed answers, they tend to lack of the flexibility and adaptability. In this paper, we have exploited such possibility on generating answers of various types with the same stimuli, instead of just generating different answers for each query. While conventional conversational agents have static answers, the proposed agent has dynamic answers adapted to query' sentence structures through the evolution. We have confirmed that the method increases the adaptability to users. However, it is difficult to define perfect grammars for Korean. It thus needs more studies on Korean grammar to analyze the structure of Korean sentences.

Acknowledgements

The work was supported by Korea Brain Science and Engineering Research Program sponsored by Korean Ministry of Science and Technology.

References

1. S. Macskassy and S. Stevenson, "A conversational agent," Master Essay, Rutgers University, 1996.
2. J. Allen, D. Byron, M. Dzikovska, G. Ferguson, L. Galescu and A. Stent, "Towards conversational human-computer interaction," AI Magazine, 22(4), pp. 27-38, Winter 2001.
3. A. Pollock and A. Hockley, "What's wrong with internet searching," D-Lib Magazine, http://www.dlib.org/dlib/march97/bt/03pollock.html.
4. Y. Yang, L. Chien and L. Lee, "Speaker intention modeling for large vocabulary mandarin spoken dialogues," Proc. of the Fourth Int. Conf. on Spoken Language, pp. 713-716, 1996.
5. P. Nugues, C. Godereaux, P.-O. El-Guedj and F. Revolta, "A conversational agent to navigate in virtual worlds," Proc. of the Eleventh Twente Workshop on Language Technology, pp. 23-33, S. LuperFoy, A. Nijholt and G. Zanten eds., Universiteit Twente, Enschede, June 1996.
6. W. Weiwei, L. Biqi, C. Fang and Y. Baozong, "A natural language generation system based on dynamic knowledge base," Proc. of the Third Int. Conf. on ICSP, pp. 765-768, 1996.
7. J. Allen, Natural Language Understanding, Benjamin Cummings, 1987.
8. M.M. Lankhorst, "Grammatical interface with a genetic algorithm," Technical Report, Dept. of CS. University of Groningen, Groningen, The Netherlands, 1994.
9. H. Takagi, "Interactive evolutionary computation: Fusion of the capabilities of EC optimization and human evaluation," Proc. of the IEEE, 89(9), pp. 1275-1296, 2001.

Comparing Measures of Agreement for Agent Attitudes

Mark McCartney and David H. Glass

School of Computing and Mathematics, University of Ulster
Newtownabbey, Co. Antrim, UK, BT37 0QB
{m.mccartney,dh.glass}@ulster.ac.uk

Abstract. A model for the interaction of three agents is presented in which each agent has three personality parameters; tolerance, volatility and stubbornness. A pair of agents interact and evolve their attitudes to each other as a function of how well they agree in their attitude towards the third agent in the group. The effects of using two different measures of agreement are compared and contrasted and it is found that although the measures used have quite different motivations and formulations, there are striking similarities between the overall results which they produce.

1 Introduction and Description of the Model

One of the many applications of agent engineering is sociodynamics. Sociodynamics is a relatively new field of interdisciplinary study which aims to provide quantitative models for how social groups evolve in a range of contexts. It combines expertise from disciplines such as physics and mathematics [1] and computer science [2], and finds applications in areas such as sociology [3] and evolutionary anthropology [4]. In this paper we present a model which describes a simple virtual society based on social agents. These agents have no purpose or goal (i.e. they have no teleology), instead they merely compare and update the attitudes they have to each other at each discrete time-step via certain rules. We construct a model which is easily generalized to deal with N agents [5], but in this paper we only investigate its behaviour for the minimal group size allowable by the model, namely N=3.

Consider a group of agents Let $a_{ij}(t) \in [0,1]$ be a measure of agent j's attitude to agent i at time t. If $a_{ij}(t)=1$ j considers i a close friend, and at the other extreme if $a_{ij}(t)=0$ j considers i a sworn enemy. At each time-step we allow each agent to update their attitude to the other agents in the group via a rule of the form

$$a_{ij}(t+1) = f_j\left(C\left(a_{ki}(t), a_{kj}(t)\right), a_{ij}(t)\right) \tag{1}$$

where $C\left(a_{ki}(t), a_{kj}(t)\right) \in [0,1]$ is a measure of the *agreement* or *coherence* of i and j's attitudes to the third member of the group k, and

$$f_j(C,a) = \begin{cases} \min(a+\Delta_j,1) & \forall C > \frac{1}{2}(1+\sigma_j) \\ a & \forall \frac{1}{2}(1-\sigma_j) \leq C \leq \frac{1}{2}(1+\sigma_j) \\ \max(a-\Delta_j,0) & \forall C < \frac{1}{2}(1-\sigma_j) \end{cases} \quad (2)$$

where $\Delta_j, \sigma_j \in [0,1]$. Thus, according to (1) and (2) agent j updates its attitude to i by increasing it by an amount Δ_j if the agreement between i and j's attitudes to k is greater than some threshold $\frac{1}{2}(1+\sigma_j)$, decreasing it by an amount Δ_j if the agreement between i and j's attitudes to k is less than $\frac{1}{2}(1-\sigma_j)$, and leaves the attitude unchanged otherwise. We can think of agent j as having two personality attributes; with σ_j being a measure of how stubborn j is (the larger the value of σ_j the greater the agreement/disagreement must be before j changes its attitude) and Δ_j being a measure of j's volatility (the larger the value of Δ_j the greater the potential change in attitude in a single time step).

2 Measures of Agreement

The measure of agreement or coherence of attitudes, $C(.)$, is clearly crucial to the dynamics of the above system. This raises the question as to how the agreement of attitudes should be represented and whether choosing different measures of agreement will result in substantially different dynamics. In this paper two measures will be investigated and the corresponding dynamics compared.

The first measure of agreement is based on a fuzzy NXOR operator and has been discussed in [5]. The fuzzy NXOR is defined as follows,

$$C_1^\alpha(x,y) = x \overline{\vee}^\alpha y = \begin{cases} \left(\frac{\alpha-1}{\alpha}\right)|x-y|+1 & \forall |x-y| < \alpha \\ \left(\frac{\alpha}{\alpha-1}\right)(|x-y|-1) & \forall |x-y| \geq \alpha \end{cases} \quad 0 < \alpha < 1 \quad (3)$$

where x and y are the attitudes of i and j to k.

The α above $\vee$ denotes that we have a family of fuzzy NXORs determined by the value of the parameter α. As α increases the NXOR relation becomes more tolerant of difference between x and y. Thus, for small values of α the NXOR initially decreases rapidly until $|x-y| = \alpha$ and then decreases more slowly to x NXOR $y = 0$, but for values of α close to one the NXOR decreases slowly until $|x-y| = \alpha$ and then decreases more rapidly to x NXOR $y = 0$. When $\alpha = 1/2$ equation (3) reduces to the single straight line relation

$$C_1^{\frac{1}{2}}(x,y) = x \overline{\vee}^{1/2} y = 1 - |x-y|. \quad (4)$$

Thus we say that *the parameter α denotes the level of tolerance of difference.* An extremely intolerant agent will have a very low value of α, whereas an extremely tolerant agent will have a value of α close to unity. In general each agent will have a different value for α, and thus each agent will have three personality attributes; tolerance, α, stubbornness, σ, and volatility Δ.

The second measure of agreement we consider is based on recent work on a probabilistic measure of coherence which has been discussed in [6,7]. The concept of coherence is extremely difficult to define, although it is generally accepted that there are degrees of coherence. Consider, for example, the coherence between the belief A that a die will come up 2, 3 or 4 and the belief B that it will come up 3, 4 or 5. In such a case it seems that the coherence of A and B should take on an intermediate value. Furthermore, it seems reasonable that the cases of logical contradiction and logical equivalence should yield extreme values of coherence (e.g. the values 0 and 1 respectively if coherence is taken as a measure on the interval [0,1]). A simple example of a measure that captures these intuitions in terms of the probability of the beliefs A and B is given by,

$$C(A,B) = \frac{P(A \wedge B)}{P(A \vee B)} \tag{5}$$

which yields a coherence of ½ in the die example.

This leaves the questions of how the coherence of two attitudes can be represented in the current context and how the tolerance can be represented in a way analogous to the fuzzy NXOR function discussed earlier. Suppose person i is updating their attitude to j by comparing attitudes to k and that person i has a tolerance of α. This can be represented by taking i's attitude to k to be an interval [x - α, x + α], or more correctly [max(x - α, 0), min(x + α,1)], rather than simply the value x. Similarly i would represent j's attitude to k by [max(y - α, 0), min(y + α,1)], rather than the value y. The coherence measure would then simply yield the value given by taking the overlap of the two intervals divided by the total range of the interval [0,1] covered by the two intervals, which we can express as

$$C_2^\alpha(x,y) = \frac{\|[\max(x-\alpha,0), \min((x+\alpha,1)] \cap [\max(y-\alpha,0), \min((y+\alpha,1)]\|}{\|[\max(x-\alpha,0), \min((x+\alpha,1)] \cup [\max(y-\alpha,0), \min((y+\alpha,1)]\|} \tag{6}$$

where $\|\cdot\|$ represents the total length of the enclosed interval(s).

In the case where neither of the intervals for the attitude of i and j to k reach the limiting values of 0 or 1, the agreement is given by

$$C_2^\alpha(x,y) = \begin{cases} \dfrac{2\alpha - |x-y|}{2\alpha + |x-y|} & \forall \, |x-y| < 2\alpha \\ \\ 0 & \forall \, |x-y| \geq 2\alpha \end{cases}. \tag{7}$$

Unlike the fuzzy NXOR function, this function has a continuous first derivative with respect to $|x-y|$ in the interval $[0,\max(2\alpha,1))$ given by

$$\frac{-4\alpha}{(|x-y|+2\alpha)^2} \qquad (8)$$

which tends to a value of $-1/\alpha$ in the limit as $|x-y|$ tends to 0. The fuzzy NXOR function has a derivative with respect to $|x-y|$ of $1-1/\alpha$ for $|x-y|<\alpha$ and so, for a given value of the tolerance α, the coherence function will fall off more sharply from 1 for small values of $|x-y|$ than the fuzzy NXOR function.

The above discussion needs to be modified since equation (7) will not be correct in cases where the intervals representing the attitudes are limited by the values 0 or 1. This restriction will give rise to a substantial difference between the fuzzy NXOR function C_1^α and the coherence function C_2^α, since for large values of α the latter will often be close to 1 (and will in many cases equal 1). For example, suppose x = 0.8, y = 0.2 and α = 0.8. In this case the coherence measure yields a value of 1 while the fuzzy NXOR measure yields a value of 0.85.

Figure 1 shows the distribution of C_1^α and C_2^α respectively for 10,000 random pairs of attitudes for values of tolerance ranging from 0 to 1. Both functions are strongly peaked at values close to 0 for low α and close to 1 for high α. However, in the case of the coherence measure the peak is for values of the coherence of *exactly* 0 for low α and *exactly* 1 for high α, while for fuzzy NXOR there is an approximately linear dependence on α for α close to 0 or close to 1. The reason the coherence measure takes on a value of 0 in so many cases is clear from equation (7), while the reason for it taking on values of 1 has been discussed in the previous paragraph.

3 Results

We restrict ourselves to the case where all three agents have exactly the same personality (i.e. the same values of α, σ and Δ) and randomly select an initial set of attitudes. We then allow the agents to interact for 300 time-steps and then evaluate the average change in attitudes,

$$A = \frac{1}{6}\sum_{i=1}^{3}\sum_{\substack{j=1 \\ j\neq i}}^{3}\left(a_{ij}(300) - a_{ij}(0)\right). \qquad (9)$$

Interaction for 300 time steps is enough to allow for equilibrium to be reached. This equilibrium will often, though not always, be static [8]. This process is repeated for 1000 different randomly chosen initial sets of attitudes, and an average of these is taken. We fix $\Delta=0.1$ and examine how the average change in attitude behaves as α and σ are varied.

Figures 2(a) and 2(b) show the average change as a function of tolerance α and stubbornness σ for the two measures C_1^α and C_2^α respectively. Many features of these results are very similar. For example, in both cases there is a clear pattern from an average decrease in attitudes for low values of α, through a region where there is little average change to a region where there is a large increase in the average change for high values of α. Furthermore, both approaches give rise to regions where the average change remains similar for a range of values of α and σ. They also agree that these regions have sharp boundaries where a small change in α and/or σ can result in a substantial difference in the average change.

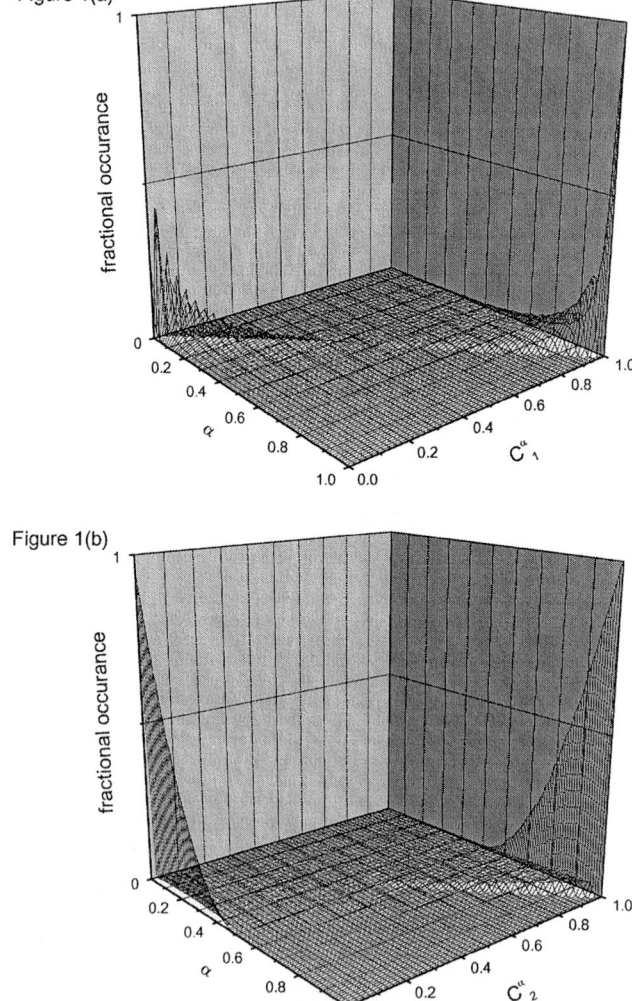

Fig. 1. Fractional occurance of agreement for a given tolerance α for samples of 10000 randomly chosen initial pairs of attitudes using (a) the fuzzy NXOR measure (3), (b) the coherence measure (6).

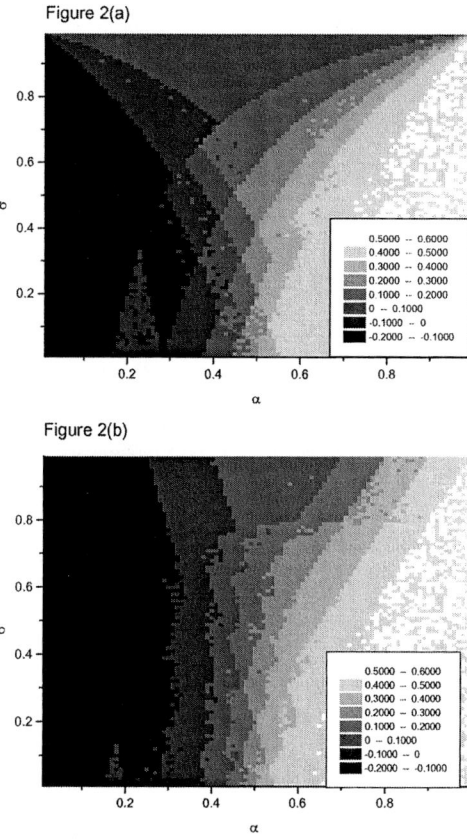

Fig. 2. Average change in group attitude as given by equation (9) averaged over 1000 randomly chosen initial sets of attitudes for (a) the fuzzy NXOR measure (3), (b) the coherence measure (6).

The agreement between the two approaches is most striking for low values of σ and for high values of α. In particular, both approaches find a linear boundary between the regions with a positive change of 0.4-0.5 and 0.5-0.6 which lies between the points (0.7,0.4) and (1.0,1.0) in the (α,σ)-plane. The most noticeable disagreement between the two approaches occurs for high values of σ. According to the fuzzy NXOR model, C_1^α, there is very little average change occurring in this region and this is particularly true for intermediate values of α. The coherence model, C_2^α, also has little average change for high σ and intermediate values of α, but it shows much more average change for low and high α. This is due to the feature of the coherence measure, discussed earlier, that for low and high α it has a large proportion of attitudes with a coherence of exactly 0 and 1 respectively and so overcomes the stubbornness σ even if it is extremely close to 1. However, at $\sigma = 1$, the change in the coherence measure does in fact go to zero.

The foregoing discussion explains why the dynamics based on the coherence model show much less sensitivity to stubbornness (as can be seen from figure 4) than the fuzzy NXOR model: the extreme values of coherence overcome even high values of stubbornness. This would suggest that the dynamics based on the fuzzy NXOR model gives a better representation of the relationship between tolerance and stubbornness. Nevertheless, the striking agreement between models using such different measures of agreement gives us confidence that the dynamics give a reasonable representation of the problem and are not totally dependent on the particularities of the measure of agreement chosen.

References

1. Helbing, D.: Quantitative Sociodynamics, Kluwer Academic Publishers (1995)
2. Davidsson, P.: Agent Based Simulation: A computer Science View. Journal of Artificial Societies and Social Simulation 5 (2002) http://www.soc.surrey.ac.uk/JASSS/5/1/7.html
3. Liebrand, W.B.G.: Nowak A and Hegselmann R (eds) Computer Modelling of Social Processes, Sage (1998)
4. Henrich, J. and Gil-White, F.J.: The evolution of prestige Freely conferred deference as a mechanism for enhancing the benefits of cultural transmission. Evolution and Human Behavior 22 (2001) 165-196
5. McCartney, M. and Pearson, D.: Social Agents and Commonality. *submitted to* IEEE Transactions on Systems, Man and Cybernetics (2004)
6. Olsson, E.J.: What is the problem of coherence and truth? The Journal of Philosophy. 99(5) (2002) 246-272
7. Glass, D.H.: Coherence, explanation and Bayesian networks. In 'Proceedings of the Irish conference in AI and Cognitive Science'. Lecture notes in AI, Vol. 2646, Springer-Verlag, New York, (2002) 177-182.
8. McCartney, M. and Pearson, D.: Social Agents in Dynamic Equilibrium. In 'Artificial Neural Nets and Genetic Algorithms' ed. Pearson, D.W., Steele, N. C. , Albrecht, R.F. , Springer Wien New York(2003) 256-259

Hierarchical Agglomerative Clustering for Agent-Based Dynamic Collaborative Filtering

Gulden Uchyigit and Keith Clark

Department of Computing, Imperial College
South Kensington Campus, London SW7 2AZ
{gu1,klc}@doc.ic.ac.uk

Abstract. *Collaborative Filtering* systems suggest items to a user because it is highly rated by some other user with similar tastes. Although these systems are achieving great success on web based applications, the tremendous growth in the number of people using these applications require performing many recommendations per second for millions of users. Technologies are needed that can rapidly produce high quality recommendations for large community of users.
In this paper we present an agent based approach to collaborative filtering where agents work on behalf of their users to form shared "interest groups", which is a process of pre-clustering users based on their interest profiles. These groups are *dynamically* updated to reflect the user's evolving interests over time.

1 Introduction

The huge amount of Information available in the currently evolving world-wide information infrastructure can easily overwhelm end-users, a situation that is likely to worsen in the future, unless the end user has the ability to filter information based on its relevance. *Content-based filtering* systems infer a user's profile from the contents of the items the user previously rated and recommends additional items of interest according to this profile. In contrast, *Collaborative filtering* systems [1], [6], [3], [5], work by collecting human judgements (known as ratings) for items in a given domain and correlating people who share the same information needs or tastes. These systems generally have the following problems. They rely on an overlap of user rated items (i.e if the user's did not rate any common items then their profiles can not be correlated). The enormous number of items available to rate in many domains makes the probability of finding user's with similar ratings significantly low. Since, recommender systems are used by a large number of users, correlation based algorithms need to search through a large neighbourhood of user's in real time.

An alternative approach and one that we use is *content based collaborative filtering* techniques. Such systems [10], [11], [12] combine both the content and collaborative information.

We utilise the content of the items the users have rated to infer their interest profile and we then use these profiles to *dynamically form* interest groups which

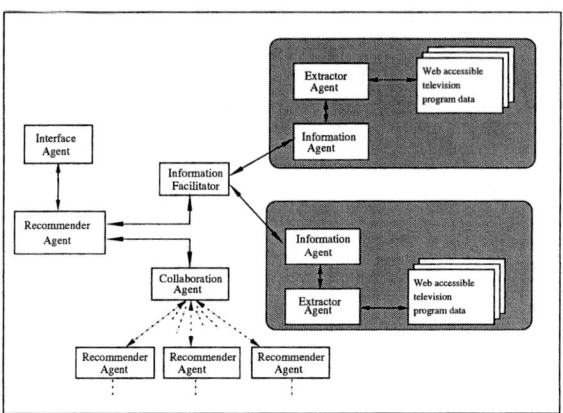

Fig. 1. Overview of the Agent Architecture

are continuously updated with changing user interests. These interest groups are smaller to analyse compared with the correlation based algorithms where a large neighbourhood of users need to be analysed every time a collaboration recommendation is to be given.

2   System Overview

The personalised TV recommender (for more details see [4]) provides the user with recommendations from online TV guides and other web accessible TV program information. It creates, learns and modifies the user profile automatically based on user feedback on the programs that they have already seen.

A network of agents work behind the scenes, completely hidden from the user to model and learn user preferences in order to provide the program recommendations. A pictorial overview of the agent architecture is given in Figure 1. For each user interacting with the system there is an associated *interface agent* and a *recommender agent*. The interface agent handles all user interactions with the system. It is also able to map user requests and actions into a form understandable by the recommender agent. The recommender agent, on the other hand, does not directly interact with the user but it is the only agent in the system that knows about the user's viewing preferences. Since the recommender agent has to accomplish numerous complex tasks related both to the user and the other agents, it needs to have a picture of the current state of affairs. In particular its knowledge component has a representation for:

- *the user's world*, the kind of viewing habits a user has, his current viewing interests and his past history with respect to the viewed programs. This information is represented in the form of a user profile.
- *the available agents* and their capabilities. It is able to coordinate a number of agents and knows what tasks they can accomplish, what resources they have and their availability.

For the collaborative recommendation component one *collaboration agent* exits. Recommender agents register their user's interest profile with this agent. It then uses these registered interest profiles to automatically and dynamically create and maintain interest groups within main categories of programs. For example, there is a set of interest groups for *situation comedies*, another set of interest groups for *documentaries* and so on. When one of the users reports that they have unexpectedly enjoyed a program (unexpectedly because the program was not recommended by their agent) their recommender agent will immediately inform the collaboration agent. This will then route this information to all the recommender agents in the same interest group. Each of these agents will recommend this new program to its user if the user hasn't yet seen it. They can then catch the program on a repeat or on its next episode, if it is a series or a serial. More generally, each time the user gives feedback on the programs they have watched the recommender agent updates the user's profile using descriptions of the viewed programs. This in turn causes the interest groups to be updated. It may be the case that an updated user profile is moved from one interest group to another by the collaboration agent, or it may be used to form the nucleus of a new grouping.

3 Building and Maintaining Interest Groups

The collaboration agent clusters user's into interest groups based on the similarity of their profiles for each interest category. Users are not clustered based on their entire profile contents since it may be the case that two users have similar tastes in *comedies* but quite different tastes with respect to *sports* programs.

For the process of clustering we adapted the Hierarchical Agglomerative Clustering (HAC) algorithm [7], [8], [9], to cluster user profiles. The HAC process repeatedly merges the two most similar clusters until only one cluster remains. This results in a *single* hierarchy or *dendrogram* to use the correct terminology.

Our adaption of this algorithm for clustering users based on their profiles is as follows. The first phase involves *initialisation* where each separate interest profile is represented as one element cluster. There then follows the process of merging the two most similar clusters until one of the *two* possible termination conditions are satisfied. Either, the similarity of any two clusters is less than 0.7 or only one cluster remains. For the similarity measure between clusters, we use vector similarity [2]. Figure 3 is the pseudo-code of our algorithm for clustering the user profiles in a given category.

Figure 3 shows the clusters formed for three different categories of interest. At present we keep the similarity levels fixed for every category. One of our future plans is to determine experimentally the *optimal* similarity levels for the different categories. For the formation of the *interest groups*, the collaboration agent generates the clusters that have an internal profile similarity greater than 0.7. In Figure 3 the Drama category has three clusters (clusters are determined by horizontal lines in the dendrogram). These are $\{d_1, d_2, d_3, d_4\}$, $\{d_5, d_6\}$, $\{d_7, d_8, d_9\}$ where, $d_1, d_2, d_3, d_4, d_5, d_6, d_7, d_8, d_9$ are the individual interest profiles for the drama category of nine people.

Input
P={$p_1, p_2, ..p_N$ }
Initialise
- start with clusters that contain a single user profile
  C={$c_1, c_2, ..c_N$ } a set of clusters
  c_i={p_i} for $1 \leq i \leq N$
  $S = 0$
- Repeat the following steps iteratively until there is only one cluster left or $S \leq 0.7$
  for $k = N - 1$ to 1 do
- identify the two clusters that are most similar

$$S = (c_j, c_m) = arg \max sim(c_j, c_m)$$

where, $sim(c_j, c_m)$ is the cosine similarity

$$\frac{c_j \bullet c_m}{|c_j| \times |c_m|}$$

- merge them to form a single cluster
  $c^* = \{c_j \cup c_m\}$
- update the clusters
  $C_k = C_{k-1} - \{c_{i,j}, c_{i,m}\} + c^*$

Fig. 2. Pseudo-code of our clustering algorithm

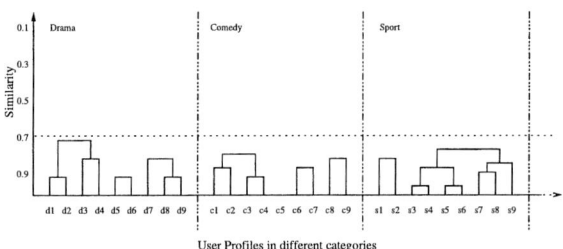

Fig. 3. Profile hierarchies for different categories

For maintaining the interest groups the agent re-clusters the profiles on a weekly basis. As a result of re-evaluating the clusters, the clusters are updated to reflect the user's changing interests. This may result in new clusters being formed or existing clusters being augmented.

4 Evaluations

4.1 Experimental Results

We conducted a number of simulation experiments to assess the validity of our architecture. One of which was to observe the performance with the changing user interests. To do this we observed what would happen to the performance

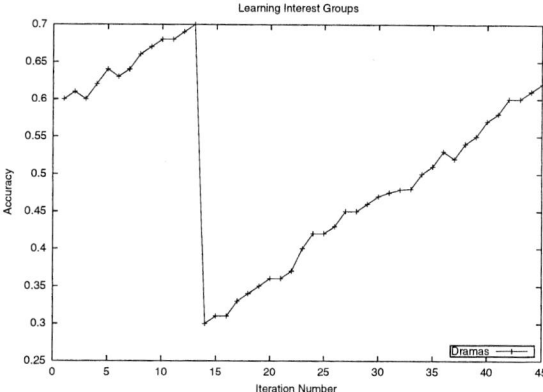

Fig. 4. Results of the simulation

when there is a sudden change in the user profiles. Figure 4 shows results of the simmulation experiments performed within the Drama category. We report the average accuracy of the predictions given to all the interest groups over 45 iterations. At each iteration the partial profiles are re-clustered (i.e the interest groups are updated). After iteration 13 we purposely got the simmulated user agents to report programs that are different to the partial profiles. This is like having user's discover new programs that were not recommended to them by their recommender agents. Only some of the simmulated user agents had their complete profiles updated with this new program information. At iteration 14 this rapid change within the simmulated user's profile is indicated as a sudden drop in the average accuracy of the predictions. But this is followed by a steady increase in the accuracy of the predictions with the other iterations indicating recovery of the interest groups as they are dynamically updated.

5 Summary and Future Work

In this paper we presented an agent-based collaborative filtering technique that gives users TV program recommendations. The system automatically learns a user profile for each user. The user interest profiles for each category are then clustered by the agents on behalf of their users in order to form interest groups of users with similar interests. When one user in the group then discovers an interesting program then every user in their interest group for the category of the program are informed. Our approach to collaborative filtering makes it possible for users evolving interests to be considered in the collaborative filtering process.

In our future work we intend to determine experimentally optimal similarity measures for the clusters of each category. We would also like to expand this idea to have the agents automatically determine these similarity measures. We also intend to evaluate our system with real users and compare its performance with that of other collaborative filtering methods and also measure its performance in different domains.

References

1. J. Konstan, B. Miller, D. Maltz, J. Herlocker,L. Gordon and J.Riedl.: GroupLens:Applying Collaborative Filtering to Usenet News. Communications of the ACM. March 1997.
2. G.Salton and M. Gill. Introduction to Modern Information Retrieval. McGraw-Hill, New York, 1983.
3. Shardanand, U., and Maes, P. Social information Filtering: Algorithm for Automating "Word of Mouth". In Proceedings of CHI'95 1995.
4. Uchyigit, G. and Clark, K. An Agent Based Electronic Program Guide. Workshop on Personalization in Future TV in conjunction with 2nd International Conference on Adaptive Hypermedia and Adaptive Web Based Systems , May 2002 Malaga Spain, (Springer-Verlag Lecture Notes in Computer Science).
5. Loren Terveen, Will Hill, Brian Amento, David McDonald and Josh Creter.:PHOAKS: A System for Sharing Recommendations. Communications of the ACM. March 1997.
6. Henry Kautz, Bart Selman and Mehul Shah.: Refferal Web: Combining Social Networks and Collaborative Filtering. Communications of the ACM. March 1997.
7. Everitt, B. "Cluster Analysis", Haslsted Press (John Wiley and Sons), New York, 1980.
8. Rasmussen, E. "Information Retrieval, Data Structure and Algorithms", Chapter 16: Clustering Algorithms, W. B. Frakes and R.Baeza-Yates, eds., Prentice Hall 1992.
9. Willett P. , "Recent trends in hierarchic document clustering: a critical review", in Information Processing and Management, 34:5, 1988.
10. Basu C, Hirsh H. and Cohen W. Recommendation as classification: Using Social and content-based information in recommendation. In proceedings of the Fifteenth National Conference on Artificial Intelligence, pages 714-720, 1998.
11. Claypool M, Gokhale A. and Miranda T. Combining content-based and collaborative filters in an online newspaper. In proceedings of the ACM SIGIR Workshop on Recommender Systems- Implementation and Evaluation, 1999.
12. Good N, Schafer J. B, Konstan J. A, Brochers A, Sarwar B. M, Herlocker J. L, and Riedl J. Combining collaborative filtering with personal agents for better recommendations. In proceedings of the Sixteenth National Conference on Artificial Intelligence, pages 439-446 1999.

Learning Users' Interests in a Market-Based Recommender System*

Yan Zheng Wei, Luc Moreau, and Nicholas R. Jennings

Intelligence, Agents, Multimedia Group
School of Electronics and Computer Science
University of Southampton, UK
{yzw01r,L.Moreau,nrj}@ecs.soton.ac.uk

Abstract. Recommender systems are widely used to cope with the problem of information overload and, consequently, many recommendation methods have been developed. However, no one technique is best for all users in all situations. To combat this, we have previously developed a market-based recommender system that allows multiple agents (each representing a different recommendation method or system) to compete with one another to present their best recommendations to the user. Our marketplace thus coordinates multiple recommender agents and ensures only the best recommendations are presented. To do this effectively, however, each agent needs to learn the users' interests and adapt its recommending behaviour accordingly. To this end, in this paper, we develop a reinforcement learning and Boltzmann exploration strategy that the recommender agents can use for these tasks. We then demonstrate that this strategy helps the agents to effectively obtain information about the users' interests which, in turn, speeds up the market convergence and enables the system to rapidly highlight the best recommendations.

1 Introduction

Recommender systems have been widely advocated to help make choices among recommendations from all kinds of sources [1]. Most of the existing recommender systems are primarily based on two main kinds of methods: content-based and collaborative. However, both kinds have their weaknesses: the former cannot easily recommend non-machine parsable items, whereas the later fail to accurately predict a user's preferences when there are an insufficient number of peers. Given this, it has been argued that there is no universally best method for all users in all situations [2].

In previous work, we have shown that an information marketplace can function effectively as an overarching coordinator for a multi-agent recommender system [3, 4]. In our system, the various recommendation methods, represented as agents, compete to advertise their recommendations to the user. Through this competition, only the best items are presented to the user. Essentially, our

---

* This research is funded by QinetiQ and the EPSRC Magnitude project (reference GR/N35816).

system uses a particular type of auction and a corresponding reward regime to incentivise the agents to bid in a manner that is maximally consistent with the user's preferences. Thus, good recommendations (as judged by the user) are encouraged by receiving rewards, whereas poor ones are deterred by paying to advertise but by receiving no rewards.

While our system works effectively most of the time, an open problem from the viewpoint of the individual recommenders remains: *given a set of recommendations with different rating levels, in what order should an agent advertise them so that it can learn the user's interests as quickly as possible, while still maximizing its revenue?* To combat this, we have developed a reinforcement learning strategy, that enables an agent to relate the user's feedback about recommendations to its internal belief about their qualities and then to put forward those that are maximally consistent with this.

Against this background, this paper advances the state of the art in the following ways. First, a novel reinforcement learning strategy is developed to enable the agents to effectively and quickly learn the user's interests while still making good recommendations. Second, from an individual agent's point of view, we show the strategy enables it to maximize its revenue. Third, we show that when all agents adopt this strategy, the market rapidly converges and makes good recommendations quickly and frequently.

2 A Market-Based Multi-agent Recommender System

Different recommendation methods use different metrics and different algorithms to evaluate the items they may recommend. Thus, the internal rating of the quality of a recommendation can vary dramatically from one method to another. Here, we term this internal evaluation the method's *internal quality* (INQ). However, a high INQ recommendation from one method does not necessarily mean the recommendation is any more likely to better satisfy a user than a low INQ item suggested by another. Ultimately, whether a recommendation satisfies a user can only be decided by that user. Therefore, we term the user's evaluation of a recommendation the *user's perceived quality* (UPQ).

With these concepts in place, we now briefly outline our market-based recommender (as per Fig. 1). Each time when the marketplace calls for a number (S) of recommendations, each agent submits S recommendations and bids a price for each of them. Consequently, the marketplace ranks all items in decreasing order of price and displays the top S items to the user and, meanwhile, each corresponding agent pays for each displayed item an amount of credit equal to its bid for that item. The user then visits a number of the displayed items and gives each a rating (i.e. UPQ) based on how it satisfies him. Finally, the market rewards the agents with positive UPQ recommendations an amount of credit that is proportional to their UPQs. Thus, the system completes one round of operation and proceeds with another, following the same basic procedure.

We have shown that, to make effective recommendations, an agent needs to classify its recommendations into a number (G) of INQ levels (segments) and be able to correlate these segments to the UPQs [4]. Indeed, an agent that has sufficient experience of the user's feedback can learn the user's interests by correlating its recommendations (and their corresponding INQ segments) to the rewards (that reflect their UPQs). This enables a self-interested agent to consciously make recommendations from those INQ segments that correspond to high UPQs so that it can best satisfy the user and, thus, gain maximal revenue. To effectively compute the agents' revenue, we define an agent's *immediate reward* (made from a specific recommendation in one auction round) as the reward it received minus the price it has paid for the advertisement. With this, the agent needs to learn how much immediate rewards, on average, it can expect for items in each INQ segment. We term this average immediate reward for each INQ segment an agent's *expected revenue*. Thus, an agent can maximize its revenue by frequently bidding those recommendations from the segments with high expected revenue.

However, when an agent starts bidding, it has no information about the expected revenue for each segment. Therefore, the agent needs to interact in the marketplace by taking actions over its G segments to learn this information. In this context, the agent's learning behaviour is on a

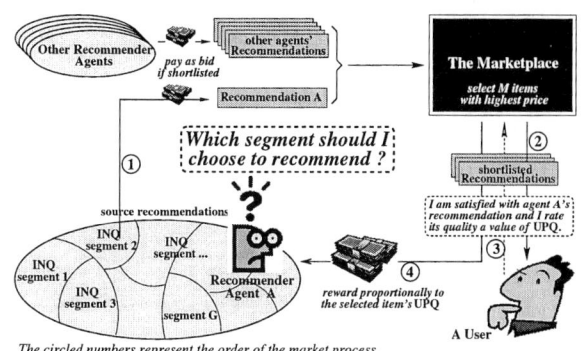

Fig. 1. An Agent's Learning Problem

"trial-and-error" basis, in which good recommendations gain rewards whereas bad ones attract a loss. This kind of trial-and-error learning behaviour is exactly what happens in Reinforcement Learning [5]. Thus, to be more concrete, an agent needs an algorithm to learn the expected revenue over each segment as quickly as possible and still maximizing revenue.

3 The Learning Strategy

This section aims to address the problem of producing the expected revenue profile over an agent's G segments. In detail, an agent needs to execute a set of *actions* (bidding on its G segments), $(a_1, a_2, \cdots, a_G)$, to learn the expected revenue of each segment ($R(a_i)$, $i \in [1..G]$). Specifically, an action a_i that results in its recommendation being displayed to the user must pay some amount of credit. Then, it may or may not receive an amount of reward. We record the tth immediate reward that a_i has received as $r_{i,t}$ ($t = 1, 2, \cdots$). From a statistical perspective, the expected revenue can be obtained from the mean value of the series of discrete immediate reward values, i.e. $r_{i,t}$. In this context, the Q-learning technique provides a well established way of estimating the optimality [6]. In particular, we use a standard Q-learning algorithm to estimate $R(a_i)$ by learning the mean value of the immediate rewards:

$$\hat{Q}_i := (1 - \frac{1}{t_0 + t}) \cdot \hat{Q}_i + \frac{1}{t_0 + t} \cdot r_{i,t}, \qquad (1)$$

where $\hat{Q}_i$ is the current estimate of $R(a_i)$ (before we start learning, all $\hat{Q}_i$s are initialized with a positive value) and $\frac{1}{t_0+t}$ is the learning rate that controls how much weight is given to the immediate reward as opposed to the old estimate (t_0 is positive and finite). As t increases, $\hat{Q}_i$ builds up an average of all experiences, and converge to $R(a_i)$ [5].

To assist the learning algorithm, an exploration strategy is needed to decide which specific action to perform at each specific t. In fact, it is hard to find the absolutely best strategy for most complex problems. In reinforcement learning practice, therefore, *specific* approaches tend to be developed for specific contexts. They solve the problems in question in a reasonable and computationally tractable manner, although they are often not the absolutely optimal choice [6]. In our context, knowing how much can be expected through each action, an agent can use a probabilistic approach to select actions based on the law of effect [7]: *choices that have led to good outcomes in the past are more likely to be repeated in the future*. To this end, a *Boltzmann exploration* strategy fits our context well; it ensures the agent exploits higher $\hat{Q}$ value actions with higher probability, whereas it explores lower $\hat{Q}$ value actions with lower probability [5]. The probability of taking action a_i is formally defined as:

$$P_{a_i} = \frac{e^{\hat{Q}_i/T}}{\sum_{j=1}^{G} e^{\hat{Q}_j/T}} \qquad (T > 0), \qquad (2)$$

where T is a system variable that controls the priority of action selection. In practice, as the agent's experience increases and all $\hat{Q}_i$s tend to converge, the agent's knowledge approaches optimality. Thus, T can be decreased such that the agent chooses fewer actions with small $\hat{Q}_i$ values (meaning trying not to lose credits) and chooses more actions with large $\hat{Q}_i$ values (meaning trying to gain credits).

4 Evaluation

This section reports on the experiments to evaluate the learning strategy. We previously showed that our marketplace is capable of effectively incentivising good methods to relate their INQs to the UPQs and this capability is independent of the specific form of the correlation between the two qualities [4]. Here, we simply assume that there are four good recommendation methods in our system and they have a linear correlation between their INQs and the UPQs. To correlate these two qualities, all agents divide their INQ range into $G = 20$ equal segments. Q_{init} is set to 250, $T = 200$ and $t_0 = 1$ for all agents. The market each time calls for $S = 10$ recommendations. With these settings, we are going to evaluate

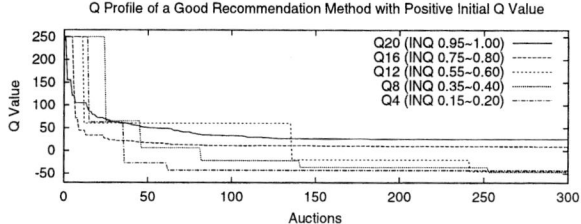

Fig. 2. Q-Learning Convergence

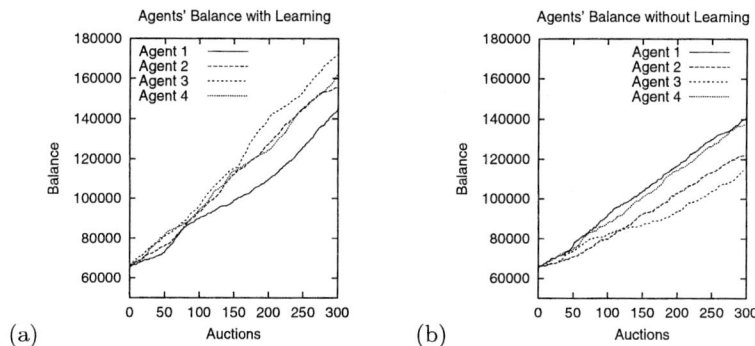

Fig. 3. Recommenders' Balance

the system according to the properties that we want the learning strategy to exhibit:

• **Q-Learning Convergence to Optimality:** $\hat{Q}$ values' convergences are important because, otherwise, an agent will have no incentive to bid. To evaluate this, we arranged 300 auctions. We find that an agent's $\hat{Q}$ values always converge (as per Fig. 2) such that high INQ segments' $\hat{Q}$s converge to high values and low INQ segments' $\hat{Q}$s converge to low values (because of the linear correlation between INQs and UPQs). This is because the recommendations from a segment corresponding to higher UPQs receive more immediate reward than those corresponding to lower UPQs.

• **Revenue Maximization:** All recommendation methods are self-interested agents that aim to maximise their revenue by advertising good recommendations and by receiving rewards. To demonstrate this property, we organized two set of experiments. One with four learning agents and the other with four non-learning agents (i.e. bidding randomly), with all other settings remaining the same. We find that the learning agents consciously raise good recommendations more frequently than non-learning ones. Thus, the former can make, on average, significantly greater amounts (about 43%) of credit than the latter (see Fig. 3(a) and (b)).

• **Quick Market Convergence:** Market convergence (prices of recommendations of different UPQ levels converge to different price levels) enables the agents

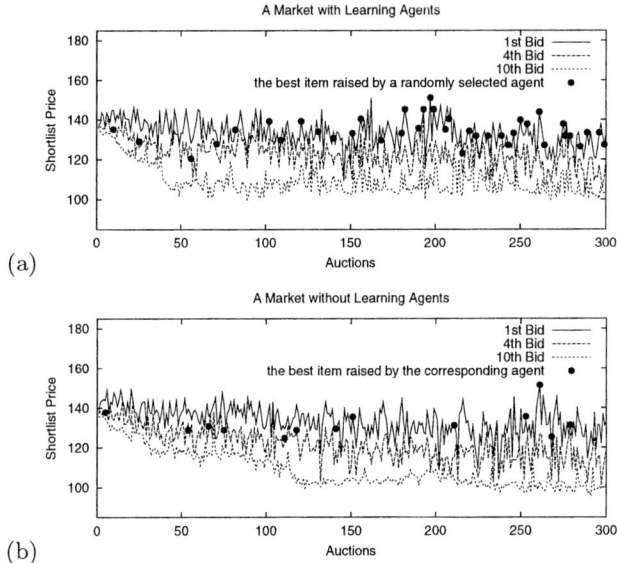

Fig. 4. Market Convergence

to know what prices to bid for recommendations with certain UPQs to gain maximal revenue [3, 4]. Thus, quick market convergence let agents reach this state quickly. To evaluate this, we contrast the learning market with the non-learning one using the same settings when assessing revenue maximization. We find that the former always converges quicker than the latter. Specifically, the former (Fig. 4(a)) converges after about 40 auctions, whereas the latter (Fig. 4(b)) does after about 120 auctions. Indeed, as the learning agents' $\hat{Q}$ profiles converge, more high quality recommendations are consistently suggested (since high $\hat{Q}$ values induce high probability to bid these items because of equation (2)) and this accelerates effective price iterations to chase the market convergence.

•**Best Recommendation's Identification:** To evaluate the learning strategy's ability to identify the best recommendation (with the top UPQ) quickly and bid it consistently, we use the same set of experiments that were used to assess the market convergence. We then trace the top UPQ item highlighted by a randomly selected learning agent and the corresponding one in the non-learning market in Fig. 4 (a) and (b) respectively (see the circle points). Fig. 4(a) shows that this item's bidding price keeps increasing till it converges to the first bid price of the displayed items. This means that as long as the agent chooses this particular item to bid in an auction (after the market converges), it is always displayed in the top position. However, in contrast, this phenomenon proceeds slowly in a non-learning market (see Fig. 4(b)). Additionally, a learning agent raises the best recommendation more frequently (39 times, see Fig. 4(a)), about three times as much, compared to a non-learning one (13 times, see Fig. 4(b)).

5 Discussion and Future Work

The learning strategy presented in this paper significantly improves our previously reported market-based recommender system [3, 4] by speeding up the market's ability to make good recommendations. In terms of learning users' interests, most existing recommender systems use techniques that are based on two kinds of features of recommendations: objective features (such as textual content in content-based recommenders) and subjective features (such as user ratings in collaborative recommenders). However, many researchers have shown that learning techniques based on either objective or subjective features of recommendations cannot successfully make high quality recommendations to users in all situations [8, 9, 2]. The fundamental reason for this is that these existing learning algorithms are built *inside* the recommenders and, thus, the recommendation features that they employ to predict the user's preferences are fixed and cannot be changed. Therefore, if a learning algorithm is computing its recommendations based on the features that are relevant to a user's context, the recommender is able to successfully predict the user's preferences (e.g. a customer wants to buy a "blue" cup online and the recommendation method's learning algorithm is just measuring the "colour" but not the "size" or the "price" of cups). Otherwise, if the user's context related features do not overlap any of those that the learning algorithm is computing on, the recommender will fail (e.g. the user considers "colour" and the learning algorithm measures "size"). To overcome this problem and successfully align the features that a learning technique measures with a user's context in all possible situations, we seek to integrate multiple recommendation methods (each with a different learning algorithm) into a single system and use an overarching marketplace to coordinate them. In so doing, our market-based system's learning technique encapsulates more learners and each learner computes its recommendations based on some specific features. Thus, our approach has a larger probability of relating its features to the user's context and so, correspondingly, has a larger opportunity to offer high quality recommendations.

To conclude, to be effective in a multi-agent recommender system (such as our market-based system), an individual agent needs to adapt its behaviour to reflect the user's interests. However, in general, the agent initially has no knowledge about these preferences and it needs to obtain such information. But, in so doing, it needs to ensure that it continues to maximize its revenue. To this end, we have developed a reinforcement learning strategy that achieves this balance. Essentially, our approach enables an agent to correlate its INQs to the UPQs and then direct the right INQ recommendations to the right users. Specifically, through empirical evaluation, we have shown that our strategy works effectively at this task. In particular, a good recommendation method equipped with our learning strategy is capable of rapidly producing a profile of the user's interests and maximizing its revenue. Moreover, a market in which all agents employ our learning strategy converges rapidly and identifies the best recommendations quickly and consistently. For the future, however, we need to carry out more extensive field trials with real users to determine whether the theoretical properties of the strategy do actually hold in practice.

References

1. Resnick, P., Varian, H.R.: Recommender Systems. Commun. of the ACM **40** (1997) 56–58
2. Herlocker, J., Konstan, J., Terveen, L., Riedl, J.: Evaluating collaborative filtering recommender systems. ACM Trans. Information Systems **22** (2004) 5–53
3. Wei, Y.Z., Moreau, L., Jennings, N.R.: Recommender systems: A market-based design. In: Proc. 2nd International Joint Conference on Autonomous Agents and Multi Agent Systems (AAMAS03), Melbourne (2003) 600–607
4. Wei, Y.Z., Moreau, L., Jennings, N.R.: Market-based recommendations: Design, simulation and evaluation. In: Proc. 5th International Workshop on Agent-Oriented Information Systems (AOIS-2003), Melbourne (2003) 22–29
5. Mitchell, T.: Machine Learning. McGraw Hill (1997)
6. Kaelbling, L.P., Littman, M.L., Moore, A.W.: Reinforcement learning: A survey. Journal of Artificial Intelligence Research **4** (1996) 237–285
7. Thorndike, E.L.: Animal intelligence: An experimental study of the associative processes in animals. Psychological Monographs **2** (1898)
8. Shardanand, U., Maes, P.: Social information filtering: algorithms for automating "word of mouth". In: Proc. Conf. on Human factors in computing systems. (1995) 210–217
9. Montaner, M., Lopez, B., Dela, J.L.: A taxonomy of recommender agents on the internet. Artificial Intelligence Review **19** (2003) 285–330

Visualisation of Multi-agent System Organisations Using a Self-organising Map of Pareto Solutions

Johnathan M.E. Gabbai[1], W. Andy Wright[2], and Nigel M. Allinson

[1] UMIST, Manchester M60 1QD, England
[2] BAE SYSTEMS, ATC PO Box 5, FPC 267, Bristol BS34 7QW, England

Abstract. The structure and performance of organisations – natural or manmade – are intricately linked, and these multifaceted interactions are increasingly being investigated using Multi Agent System concepts. This paper shows how a selection of generic structural metrics for organisations can be explored using a combination of Pareto Frontier exemplars; extensive simulations of simple goal-orientated Multi Agent Systems, and exposé of organisational types through Self-Organising Map clusters can provide insights into desirable structures for such objectives as robustness and efficiency.

1 Background and Motivation

The increasing trends for complexity in industry and the lack of explicit Multi Agent Systems (MAS) research into organisations outside of coordination techniques [1, 2] is the basis of our research programme. An organisation's behaviour/performance is primarily a function of its environment, the composition of its individual agents and how they interact. In turn, how agents are connected determines an organisation's structure [3]. Our underlying research questions include how to measure and visualise the relationships between structure and performance, and why organisational structures/attributes (e.g. centralised, hierarchical) are more suited specific performance requirements. To examine these research questions, an extendable simulation has been developed that can construct organisations of varying complexity and size to solve simple tasks. This is discussed in §3, proceeding an overview of our work to develop a method of graphing organisational structure and a set of generic metrics to quantify structural relationships.

2 Relating Organisational Structure to Performance

Much work has been carried out in the MAS and Distributed Artificial Intelligence (DAI) community to formalise individual utterances between agents [4]. These 'conversations' have been retrospectively examined using methods developed for Social Network and Dooley Graphs, where nodes represent identities of particular agents as well as the state of information transferred [5]. In our simulation, we chart the conversations between agents and the type of information conveyed. The graphs can be described in matrix form, which lends itself to deeper analysis of organisational structure. Using this organisational structure matrix, we can quantify the type of structure based on a set of metrics. Below is an overview of some of these metrics. For a full description of how the network graphs are constructed, matrices developed and details of all metrics see [6].

- Centrality of communication – The overall cohesion of a network graph, indicating the extent to which a graph is organised around its most central point [7]. This metric has been adapted to cope with multiple connections afferent or efferent between two or more points. A measure of '1' indicates a fully centralised network while '0' indicates no communication or fully decentralised network where all communication is equal between nodes.
- Degree hierarchy – Krackhardt [8] developed a measure of degree of hierarchy that indicates the extent to which relations among the nodes in a network are ordered and there is little, if any, reciprocity. A measure of '1' indicates a fully hierarchical network while '0' indicates a flat organisational structure.
- Specialisation – In heterogeneous organisations, capabilities and skills will be unevenly distributed. For each particular capability, we measure the volatility of distribution in agents over the entire organisation. A measure of '1' indicates a fully specialised skill, meaning only one agent has a particular skill. '0' indicates that all agents have the said skill with equal degree.
- Heterogeneity of capabilities – The heterogeneity of capabilities looks at how capabilities are distributed throughout an organisation while '0' indicates that the sum of each capability throughout the group is equal. The greater the difference, the more this measure will tend towards '1'.

Using these generic metrics, we can relate them to organisations and their specific performance metrics in an effort to understand how structure affects performance, and aid our understanding and design of organisations.

3 Organisational Metrics Concept Demonstrator

The Java based Organisational Metrics Concept Demonstrator (OMCD) simulation is based on a two-dimensional grid which has no boundary conditions and where the agents have a simple "find and remove" objective. The agents move around the grid using a random walk searching for one or more 'targets'. When a target appears within an agent's search range, the agent communicates that a potential target has been found by placing a communication 'signal' around the target. The signal is strongest at the source, and tails off to zero at the edges. Agents that can remove targets and are within the signal's region will travel up the signal gradient to the source. The communication is recorded in a relationship matrix outlined in §2. To summarise, an agent, j, will have one or more capabilities, i, defined as c_{ij} where

$j \in \square \wedge j \leq N_a$, $i = \{\text{search, remove, communicate}\}$ and N_a is the total number of agents in the organisation. c_{ij} describes the range of capability i; if no capability is present, c_{ij} is zero. Validation of the model and further details about the simulation are covered in [6].

3.1 Time Taken to Reach Termination Condition

The termination condition of the simulation is defined as the removal of all targets in the environment. The time taken, τ, to remove all targets is the average time taken from a set of simulations, or epochs ε, based on a single scenario configuration, but with random start positions. The average time taken has an error margin determined through standard statistical methods. The normalised time taken which also includes the 'cost of organisation' dimensional parameter is defined as:

$$\tilde{\tilde{\tau}} = \frac{\bar{\tau}}{D}\left(w_{N_a} \cdot \tilde{N}_a + \sum_{i=1}^{N_c} w_{c_i} \cdot \sum_{j=1}^{N_a} \tilde{c}_{ij} \right) \quad (1)$$

where D is the grid area and $\bar{\tau}$ is the average time taken. The number of agents and each agent capability is normalised over the entire data set so that $\tilde{N}_a$ and $\sum_{i=1}^{N_a} \tilde{c}_{ij}$ for $\forall j = \{0,1\}$. Weights can be assigned to the number of agents, w_{N_a} and the individual capabilities, w_{c_i} to signify relative financial cost or bias of capabilities.

There are drawbacks in using such a weighting system for bias allocation (a uniformly acceptable solution may lose out to a one with mainly good parameters and one or two unacceptable ones), but for this analysis such an approach is sufficient, as we are assigning costs rather preference to parameters.

3.2 Robustness to Failure

Resistance and adaptability to failure (or changes to environmental factors) ought to be a major design consideration in large organisations. This is increasingly the case in intricate organisations, where the need for "efficiency" has led to organisations and systems to be on the perpetual brink of collapse. Organisations have various modes of failure. They include single point failure of a member, agent or node through to full homogeneous failure where all members of a network with the same vulnerability fail (for example a virus affecting all unprotected computers running a specific operating system). In this discussion we explore the single point failure of the most influential agent.

We define influence as the degree centrality of an agent (communication afferent and efferent) combined with the contribution to global utility an agent provides via the removal of targets. For every scenario, agents are defined as belonging to an organisational set A such that $\forall j : a_j \in A$. To test the effect of failure, the most influential agent, a'_j, is removed. Formalised, we define this as:

$$a'_j : \max \left(w_d \tilde{c}_{D_j} + w_u \tilde{t}_j \right) \notin A \text{ for } \forall j \qquad (2)$$

where $\tilde{c}_{D_j}$ and $\tilde{t}_j$ are normalised measures of agent degree centrality and contribution to global utility. Weights w_d and w_u are also assigned respectively. Once the most influential agent is removed, the scenario is repeated with the reduced organisational set. The new normalised time taken, $\tilde{\tau}'$, as defined in (1) is then used to determine the robustness to failure, given by $\left(\tilde{\tau}' / \tilde{\tau} \right) - 1$.

4 Simulation Results and Analysis

To explore the relationship between structure and performance of predominantly heterogeneous organisations, we examine a single premise in detail; namely, the materiel cost of the organisation is kept constant with three agents and 37 arbitrary $unit^2$ of capabilities (the minimum required for a full range of capabilities distributed to three agents) that are distributed in every possible combination to the three agents (i.e. the bracketed term in (1) is constant although this changes for $\tilde{\tau}'$). w_{N_a} and $\forall i : w_{c_i}$ defined in (1) are set to '1'; w_d and w_u defined in (2) are set to '½'. Environmental conditions are kept constant; the unbounded environment size is 100 $unit^2$ and the number of targets is three. In all, over 6,000 scenarios were run. The resulting dataset is presented in Fig. 1.

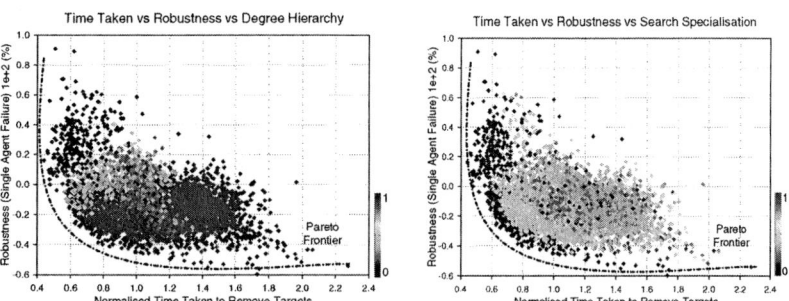

Fig. 1. Normalised time taken to remove all targets for a heterogeneous organization with fixed materiel, with the colour scale showing two different organisational structure metrics namely Degree Hierarchy on left and Search Specialisation on right.

The surface in the above figures labelled "Pareto Frontier" [9] around the axis represents the trade off between time taken and robustness. Depending on requirements, an optimal point along that curve can be determined. In fact, we have found that when normalised time taken is plotted against robustness to failure for any set of organisational configurations the output always forms a Pareto frontier. The left hand graph shows how the degree of hierarchy affects the performance; flat organisations tend to be more efficient in removing targets but are prone to significant failure whereas hierarchical organisations are less efficient, but more robust. The right hand graph explores the relationship of search specialisation. We see that a homogeneous distribution of the search skill provides the best performance. Interestingly this is followed by a second band indicating that when only one agent has the search skill the organisation performs well, and is less prone to failure. However, it is difficult to pick up organisational types unless they are in the extremities as discussed above.

The high-dimensional measurement space that results from the use of numerous metrics thus requires the application of powerful data visualisation tools. One such tool is the Self-Organising Map (SOM), which permits an ordered two-dimensional representation of much higher dimensional input spaces [10]. In essence, a SOM employs unsupervised clustering techniques that can reveal meaningful groupings of parameters that may form distinct classes of organisations. Using the SOMine software package, a SOM trained output map for the data generated from this scenario is shown in Fig. 2.

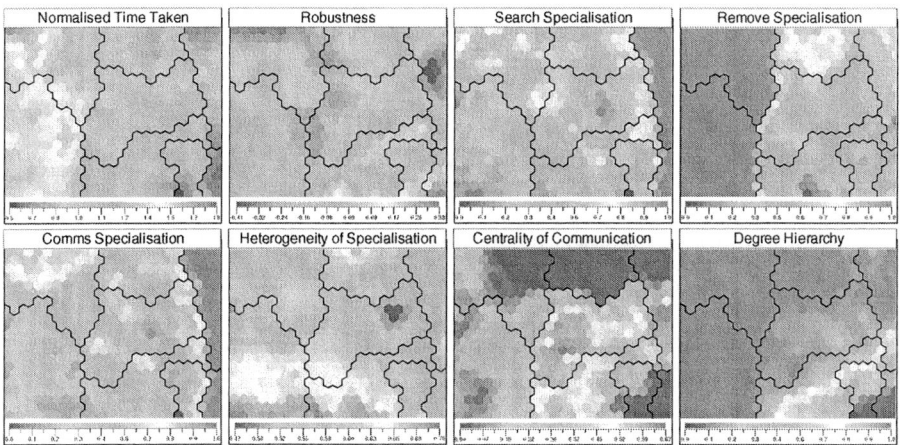

Fig. 2. SOM showing the two performance objectives (Time taken, and Robustness) and structural configurations that describe the organisations. Clusters are marked using boundaries.

Here we see how differing organisational structures are suited to subtly different performance requirements. A small cluster exists where uncoordinated search-heavy agents perform efficiently and are not too prone to failure (bottom left). Another region is where agents are far more specialised and rely a lot more on communication and coordination to be both efficient and robust (top right). We can also see that in general, organisations with a high degree of removal capability tend to perform better, but this performance is enhanced with regard to robustness agents communicate (middle right). Altering the cost weights in (1) will affect this observation. We can quantify these observations by highlighting regions in the SOM and extract statistical

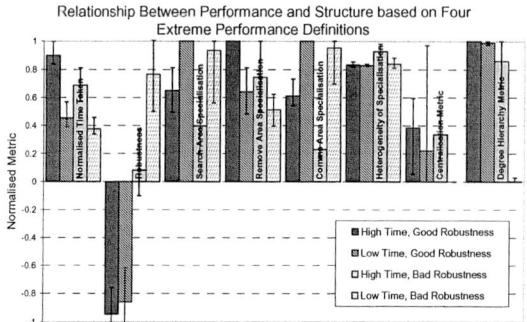

Fig. 3. SOM requirement extremities quantified.

data for all the parameters within the region. In this particular case, we are interested in the extremities of our organisational requirements.

Through visual inspection, four data sets for low/high time taken, good/bad robustness combinations were extracted and are shown in Fig. 3. Looking at the graph, we confirm that though organisations with no coordination perform marginally better in finding targets quickly, they are very poor at handling member failure. Organisations that have an element of centralisation and hierarchy, thus implying communication and coordination, tend to compensate for lack of brute force with communication.

5 Future Work

Our research program will be to extend the simulation and analysis framework so that corresponding organisational models can be incorporated into feedback learning systems.

Acknowledgements

This work is supported by an EPSRC studentship and BAE SYSTEMS, for an Engineering Doctorate (EngD) based at UMIST.

References

1. J. Odell, V. D. Parunak, and M. Fleischer, "The Role of Roles," *Journal of Object Technology*, vol. 2, pp. 39-51, 2003.
2. L. Gasser, "Perspectives on Organizations in Multi-agent Systems," in *LNAI: Multi-Agent Systems and Applications*, vol. 2086, *Lecture Notes in Artificial Intelligence*, M. Luck, V. Marik, O. Stepankova, and R. Trappl, Eds. Prague, Czech Republic: Springer Verlag, 2001, pp. 1-16.
3. E. Bonabeau, G. Theraulaz, D. J.L, S. Aron, and S. Camazine, "Self-organization in social insects," *Trends Ecol. Evoll.*, pp. 188-193, 1997.

4. P. Cohen and H. Levesque, "Communicative Actions for Artificial Agents.," presented at First International Conference on Multi-Agent Systems, 1995.
5. H. V. D. Parunak, "Visualizing agent conversations: Using Enhanced Dooley graphs for agent design and analysis.," presented at 2nd International Conference on Multiagent Systems, 1996.
6. J. M. E. Gabbai, W. A. Wright, and N. M. Allinson, "Measuring and Visualizing Organizations by Relating Structure to Performance," presented at IEEE International Conference on Industrial Informatics (INDIN 2003), Banff, Alberta, Canada, 2003.
7. L. C. Freeman, "Centrality in Social Networks I: Conceptual Clarification," *Social Networks*, vol. 1, pp. 215-239, 1979.
8. D. Krackhardt, J. Blythe, and C. McGrath, "KrackPlot 3.0: An improved network drawing program," *Connections*, vol. 2, pp. 53-55, 1994.
9. V. Pareto, *Manual of Political Economy*, English translation ed. New York: Macmillan, 1971.
10. T. Kohonen, *Self-Organising Maps*, vol. 1. Berlin: Springer, 1995.

Author Index

Abdel-Salam, Mazen 540
Abdel-Sattar, Salah 540
Aguilar-Ruiz, Jesús S. 31, 384
Ahmad, Khurshid 523, 752
Ahmad, Saif 523
Akhtar, J. 416
Al-Shahib, Ali 52
Alhajj, Reda 758
Allan, Michael 533
Allinson, Nigel M. 841
Aminian, Minoo 765
An, Jiyuan 272
Ananiadou, Sophia 345
Anderson, Terry 457
Angiulli, Fabrizio 203
Austin, Jim 266, 430
Awais, Mian M. 416
Azmi-Murad, Masrah 517
Azuaje, Francisco 31

Bae, Myung Jin 241
Bagnall, Anthony J. 339
Bailey, Trevor C. 726
Bao, Yongguang 634
Bellotti, Tony 46
Benito, Mónica 326
Berry, Ian 117
Bi, Yaxin 457
Bosin, Andrea 253
Bouridane, Ahmed 390
Brazier, Karl J. 333
Brown, David J. 593, 678

Carrasco-Ochoa, Jesús A. 424
Casey, Matthew 752
Chan, Lai-Wan 807
Chan, Tony F. 71, 565
Chandra, Arjun 619
Chang, Chien-Chung 720
Chang, Jeong-Ho 85
Chang, Yuan-chin Ivar 132
Chen, Ke 607
Chen, Lin-Ti 800
Chen, Ping 279
Chen, Rong-Chang 800
Chen, Sheng 586, 593

Chen, Yi-Ping Phoebe 272
Cheng, Qiansheng 690
Cheung, Yiu-ming 11
Ching, Wai-Ki 17
Chiu, Ming-Li 800
Cho, Sung-Bae 813
Cho, Sungzoon 666
Choi, Joongmin 443
Choi, Kyunghee 402, 491
Choi, Youngsoo 491
Clark, Keith 827
Corchado, Emilio 499
Culverhouse, Phil F. 65

Davidson, Ian 740
Deguchi, Toshinori 626
de Korvin, Andre 279
Dessì, Nicoletta 253
Diprose, Jon 117
Do, Tien Dung 306
Downs, Tom 696, 702, 708
Doyle, Marianne 702
Drinkwater, Michael 702
Du, Ji-Yan 314
Du, Xiaoyong 634

Eom, Jae-Hong 85
Esnouf, Robert 108, 117
Everson, Richard M. 654, 726

Fang, Victor 780
Fieldsend, Jonathan E. 654, 726, 788
Fong, Alvis C.M. 306
Freeman, Richard T. 478
Fukasawa, Takuya 320
Fung, Eric S. 17
Fyfe, Colin 499

Gabbai, Johnathan M.E. 841
Gallagher, Marcus 702
Gammerman, Alex 46
Gan, John Q. 191, 613
Gao, Bin 690
Gilbert, David 52
Gill, Abdul A. 339
Girolami, Mark 52

Author Index

Glass, David H. 820
Goh, Jen Ye 225
Güngör, Tunga 505
Gürgen, Fikret 505

Harris, Chris J. 586
Hasan, Yassin M.Y. 540
He, Chao 52
Hernandez, Adolfo 726
Hong, Hyun-Ki 377
Hong, Xia 586
Hsu, Ping-Yu 366
Hu, Chenyi 279
Huang, De-Shuang 11, 314, 672
Huang, Xin 11
Huang, Xuming 600
Huang, Ya-Li 800
Hui, Siu Cheung 306
Hwang, Yong-Ho 377

Ishii, Naohiro 626, 634

Jacques, Yannick 25
Javadi, Akbar 179
Jen, Lih-Ren 714
Jennings, Nicholas R. 833
Jeong, Yoon-Yong 377
Jiang, Jianmin 359
Jin, Xiaoming 559
Jung, Gihyun 402, 491
Jung, Hyunsub 443

Kaski, Samuel 92
Kawaguchi, Youhei 39
Kaya, Mehmet 758
Kelly, Tim P. 266
Khu, Soon-Thiam 546
Kim, Byoung-Hee 125
Kim, Eun Hee 259
Kim, Jong Kuk 241
Kim, Kyoung-Min 813
Kim, Yong-Gi 247
King, Ross D. 99
Könönen, Ville 733
Krzanowski, Wojtek J. 726
Kurd, Zeshan 266
Kurugollu, Fatih 390

Lara, Ana 499
Le, Jiajin 166
Lee, Cheolho 402

Lee, Hyoung-joo 666
Lee, Jae Won 794
Lee, Ki Young 241
Lee, Vincent C.S. 232, 449, 780
Lee, Young-il 247
Lee, Yuh-Jye 714, 720
Li, Ying 359
Liang, Bojian 430
Lim, Sung-Soo 813
Lin, Sung-Chiang 132
Lisboa, Paulo J.G. 552
Liu, Da-Xin 300
Liu, Jianwei 166
Liu, Yang 546
Liu, Yu-Chin 366
Liu, Zhiyong 684
Lu, Dongxin 211
Luo, Zhiyuan 46

Ma, Jinwen 684, 690
Martin, Trevor P. 517
Martínez-Trinidad, José Fco. 424
Masud, Shahid 416
Matatko, John 788
Mayo, Chris 117
McCartney, Mark 820
McClean, Sally 457
Mikolajczack, Jérôme 25
Miura, Takao 148
Miyazaki, Masatoshi 320
Möller-Levet, Carla S. 1
Moreau, Luc 833
Moshiri, Behzad 437
Mourelle, Luiza de Macedo 642

Nakagawa, Tadasuke 39
Nedjah, Nadia 642
Nenadić, Goran 345
Ng, Michael K. 17, 71, 565
Nikkilä, Janne 92
Noh, Sanguk 402, 491

O, Jangmin 794
Ohkawa, Takenao 39
Ouali, Mohammed 99
Özgür, Levent 505

Park, Dong Sun 409
Park, Seong-Bae 125
Park, Sung-Bae 794
Park, Sung-Hee 396

Partridge, Derek 726
Patel, Shail 552
Peng, Ming 788
Pes, Barbara 253
Peña, Daniel 326
Pizzuti, Clara 203
Porter, Matthew 185

Qiang, Zhang 152

Rafat, Ahmed 774
Rahayu, Wenny 293
Ramstein, Gérard 25
Rashidi, Farzan 437
Rayward-Smith, Vic J. 173
Ren, Wei 285
Reynolds, Alan P. 173
Richards, Graeme 173, 333
Riquelme, José C. 384
Rohde, David 702
Roos, Christophe 92
Ruffolo, Massimo 203
Ruiz, Roberto 384
Rusu, Laura Irina 293
Ryu, Keun Ho 259, 396
Ryu, Keywon 402

Sáiz, Lourdes 499
Sarvesvaran, Swapna 78
Sasaki, Hiroshi 626
Savic, Dragon 546
Sayed, Mohammed 540
Schetinin, Vitaly 726
Seo, Haesung 491
Seok, Bo-Ra 377
Shamail, Shafay 416
Shim, JeongYon 485
Shin, Jin Wook 409
Shin, Moon Sun 259
Shioya, Isamu 148
Shrestha, Nripendra Lal 39
Shuqin, Zhang 211
Sim, Alex T.H. 232, 449
Singh, Maneesha 179, 185
Singh, Sameer 179, 185, 218, 285, 511
Small, Michael 142, 648
Smith, George D. 339
Smith, James F., III 464, 471
Spasić, Irena 345
Storkey, Amos 533
Sun, Jiaguang 559

Tahir, Muhammad Atif 390
Takamitsu, Tomoya 148
Takasu, Atsuhiro 660
Takata, Toyoo 320
Tan, Aik Choon 52
Tanaka, Katsuaki 660
Tang, Adelina 708
Taniar, David 159, 225, 293
Taskaya-Temizel, Tugba 523
Thomson, Rebecca 108
Tjioe, Haorianto Cokrowijoyo 159
Tjortjis, Christos 352
Traherne, Matthew 511
Trudgian, Dave C. 578

Uchyigit, Gulden 827

Wang, Ben 191
Wang, Chuan 352
Wang, Hong-qiang 11
Wang, Hongbin 65
Wang, Jessica JunLin 218
Wang, Jiahong 320
Wang, Jianmin 559
Wang, Jianxiong 696
Wang, Li-Ming 314
Wang, Wenjia 58, 333
Wang, Xunxian 593, 678
Wang, Yang 690
Wang, Yuping 746
Wang, Zengfu 672
Wang, Zhenyu 572
Wei, Yan Zheng 833
Wilson, Julie 117
Wright, W. Andy 841
Wu, Edmond H. 71, 565

Xu, Lei 684
Xu, Qinying 272
Xu, Yong 572

Yang, Jaeyoung 443
Yang, Jie 197
Yang, Ju Cheng 409
Yang, Yongtian 211
Yang, Zhang 152
Yao, Xin 572, 619
Yeung, Sunny 607
Yin, Hujun 1, 78, 478
Yin, Ke 740

Yip, Andy M.   71, 565
Younsi, Reda   58
Yu, Shoujian   166
Yun, Jiang   152

Zeng, Zhigang   672
Zhang, Byoung-Tak   85, 125, 794
Zhang, Jian-Pei   300
Zhang, Liming   600
Zhang, Ming-Yi   314
Zhang, Wan-Song   300
Zhanhuai, Li   152
Zhao, Wen-Bo   314
Zhao, Xing-Ming   11
Zhao, Yi   142
Zheng, Yuanjie   197
Zhou, Shangming   613
Zhou, Yue   197
Zhuang, Xiong-Fei   807

Lecture Notes in Computer Science

For information about Vols. 1–3057

please contact your bookseller or Springer

Vol. 3177: Z.R. Yang, R. Everson, H. Yin (Eds.), Intelligent Data Engineering and Automated Learning – IDEAL 2004. XVIII, 852 pages. 2004.

Vol. 3172: M. Dorigo, M. Birattari, C. Blum, L. M.Gambardella, F. Mondada, T. Stützle (Eds.), Ant Colony, Optimization and Swarm Intelligence. XII, 434 pages. 2004.

Vol. 3158: I. Nikolaidis, M. Barbeau, E. Kranakis (Eds.), Ad-Hoc, Mobile, and Wireless Networks. IX, 344 pages. 2004.

Vol. 3157: C. Zhang, H. W. Guesgen, W.K. Yeap (Eds.), PRICAI 2004: Trends in Artificial Intelligence. XX, 1023 pages. 2004. (Subseries LNAI).

Vol. 3156: M. Joye, J.-J. Quisquater (Eds.), Cryptographic Hardware and Embedded Systems - CHES 2004. XIII, 455 pages. 2004.

Vol. 3153: J. Fiala, V. Koubek, J. Kratochvíl (Eds.), Mathematical Foundations of Computer Science 2004. XIV, 902 pages. 2004.

Vol. 3152: M. Franklin (Ed.), Advances in Cryptology – CRYPTO 2004. XI, 579 pages. 2004.

Vol. 3150: G.-Z. Yang, T. Jiang (Eds.), Medical Imaging and Virtual Reality. XII, 378 pages. 2004.

Vol. 3148: R. Giacobazzi (Ed.), Static Analysis. XI, 393 pages. 2004.

Vol. 3146: P. Érdi, A. Esposito, M. Marinaro, S. Scarpetta (Eds.), Computational Neuroscience: Cortical Dynamics. XI, 161 pages. 2004.

Vol. 3144: M. Papatriantafilou, P. Hunel (Eds.), Principles of Distributed Systems. XI, 246 pages. 2004.

Vol. 3143: W. Liu, Y. Shi, Q. Li (Eds.), Advances in Web-Based Learning – ICWL 2004. XIV, 459 pages. 2004.

Vol. 3142: J. Diaz, J. Karhumäki, A. Lepistö, D. Sannella (Eds.), Automata, Languages and Programming. XIX, 1253 pages. 2004.

Vol. 3140: N. Koch, P. Fraternali, M. Wirsing (Eds.), Web Engineering. XXI, 623 pages. 2004.

Vol. 3139: F. Iida, R. Pfeifer, L. Steels, Y. Kuniyoshi (Eds.), Embodied Artificial Intelligence. IX, 331 pages. 2004. (Subseries LNAI).

Vol. 3138: A. Fred, T. Caelli, R.P.W. Duin, A. Campilho, D.d. Ridder (Eds.), Structural, Syntactic, and Statistical Pattern Recognition. XXII, 1168 pages. 2004.

Vol. 3136: F. Meziane, E. Métais (Eds.), Natural Language Processing and Information Systems. XII, 436 pages. 2004.

Vol. 3134: C. Zannier, H. Erdogmus, L. Lindstrom (Eds.), Extreme Programming and Agile Methods - XP/Agile Universe 2004. XIV, 233 pages. 2004.

Vol. 3133: A.D. Pimentel, S. Vassiliadis (Eds.), Computer Systems: Architectures, Modeling, and Simulation. XIII, 562 pages. 2004.

Vol. 3131: V. Torra, Y. Narukawa (Eds.), Modeling Decisions for Artificial Intelligence. XI, 327 pages. 2004. (Subseries LNAI).

Vol. 3130: A. Syropoulos, K. Berry, Y. Haralambous, B. Hughes, S. Peter, J. Plaice (Eds.), TEX, XML, and Digital Typography. VIII, 265 pages. 2004.

Vol. 3129: Q. Li, G. Wang, L. Feng (Eds.), Advances in Web-Age Information Management. XVII, 753 pages. 2004.

Vol. 3128: D. Asonov (Ed.), Querying Databases Privately. IX, 115 pages. 2004.

Vol. 3127: K.E. Wolff, H.D. Pfeiffer, H.S. Delugach (Eds.), Conceptual Structures at Work. XI, 403 pages. 2004. (Subseries LNAI).

Vol. 3126: P. Dini, P. Lorenz, J.N.d. Souza (Eds.), Service Assurance with Partial and Intermittent Resources. XI, 312 pages. 2004.

Vol. 3125: D. Kozen (Ed.), Mathematics of Program Construction. X, 401 pages. 2004.

Vol. 3124: J.N. de Souza, P. Dini, P. Lorenz (Eds.), Telecommunications and Networking - ICT 2004. XXVI, 1390 pages. 2004.

Vol. 3123: A. Belz, R. Evans, P. Piwek (Eds.), Natural Language Generation. X, 219 pages. 2004. (Subseries LNAI).

Vol. 3121: S. Nikoletseas, J.D.P. Rolim (Eds.), Algorithmic Aspects of Wireless Sensor Networks. X, 201 pages. 2004.

Vol. 3120: J. Shawe-Taylor, Y. Singer (Eds.), Learning Theory. X, 648 pages. 2004. (Subseries LNAI).

Vol. 3118: K. Miesenberger, J. Klaus, W. Zagler, D. Burger (Eds.), Computer Helping People with Special Needs. XXIII, 1191 pages. 2004.

Vol. 3116: C. Rattray, S. Maharaj, C. Shankland (Eds.), Algebraic Methodology and Software Technology. XI, 569 pages. 2004.

Vol. 3114: R. Alur, D.A. Peled (Eds.), Computer Aided Verification. XII, 536 pages. 2004.

Vol. 3113: J. Karhumäki, H. Maurer, G. Paun, G. Rozenberg (Eds.), Theory Is Forever. X, 283 pages. 2004.

Vol. 3112: H. Williams, L. MacKinnon (Eds.), Key Technologies for Data Management. XII, 265 pages. 2004.

Vol. 3111: T. Hagerup, J. Katajainen (Eds.), Algorithm Theory - SWAT 2004. XI, 506 pages. 2004.

Vol. 3110: A. Juels (Ed.), Financial Cryptography. XI, 281 pages. 2004.

Vol. 3109: S.C. Sahinalp, S. Muthukrishnan, U. Dogrusoz (Eds.), Combinatorial Pattern Matching. XII, 486 pages. 2004.

Vol. 3108: H. Wang, J. Pieprzyk, V. Varadharajan (Eds.), Information Security and Privacy. XII, 494 pages. 2004.

Vol. 3107: J. Bosch, C. Krueger (Eds.), Software Reuse: Methods, Techniques and Tools. XI, 339 pages. 2004.

Vol. 3106: K.-Y. Chwa, J.I. Munro (Eds.), Computing and Combinatorics. XIII, 474 pages. 2004.

Vol. 3105: S. Göbel, U. Spierling, A. Hoffmann, I. Iurgel, O. Schneider, J. Dechau, A. Feix (Eds.), Technologies for Interactive Digital Storytelling and Entertainment. XVI, 304 pages. 2004.

Vol. 3104: R. Kralovic, O. Sykora (Eds.), Structural Information and Communication Complexity. X, 303 pages. 2004.

Vol. 3103: K. Deb, et. al. (Eds.), Genetic and Evolutionary Computation – GECCO 2004. XLIX, 1439 pages. 2004.

Vol. 3102: K. Deb, et. al. (Eds.), Genetic and Evolutionary Computation – GECCO 2004. L, 1445 pages. 2004.

Vol. 3101: M. Masoodian, S. Jones, B. Rogers (Eds.), Computer Human Interaction. XIV, 694 pages. 2004.

Vol. 3100: J.F. Peters, A. Skowron, J.W. Grzymała-Busse, B. Kostek, R.W. Świniarski, M.S. Szczuka (Eds.), Transactions on Rough Sets I. X, 405 pages. 2004.

Vol. 3099: J. Cortadella, W. Reisig (Eds.), Applications and Theory of Petri Nets 2004. XI, 505 pages. 2004.

Vol. 3098: J. Desel, W. Reisig, G. Rozenberg (Eds.), Lectures on Concurrency and Petri Nets. VIII, 849 pages. 2004.

Vol. 3097: D. Basin, M. Rusinowitch (Eds.), Automated Reasoning. XII, 493 pages. 2004. (Subseries LNAI).

Vol. 3096: G. Melnik, H. Holz (Eds.), Advances in Learning Software Organizations. X, 173 pages. 2004.

Vol. 3095: C. Bussler, D. Fensel, M.E. Orlowska, J. Yang (Eds.), Web Services, E-Business, and the Semantic Web. X, 147 pages. 2004.

Vol. 3094: A. Nürnberger, M. Detyniecki (Eds.), Adaptive Multimedia Retrieval. VIII, 229 pages. 2004.

Vol. 3093: S.K. Katsikas, S. Gritzalis, J. Lopez (Eds.), Public Key Infrastructure. XIII, 380 pages. 2004.

Vol. 3092: J. Eckstein, H. Baumeister (Eds.), Extreme Programming and Agile Processes in Software Engineering. XVI, 358 pages. 2004.

Vol. 3091: V. van Oostrom (Ed.), Rewriting Techniques and Applications. X, 313 pages. 2004.

Vol. 3089: M. Jakobsson, M. Yung, J. Zhou (Eds.), Applied Cryptography and Network Security. XIV, 510 pages. 2004.

Vol. 3087: D. Maltoni, A.K. Jain (Eds.), Biometric Authentication. XIII, 343 pages. 2004.

Vol. 3086: M. Odersky (Ed.), ECOOP 2004 – Object-Oriented Programming. XIII, 611 pages. 2004.

Vol. 3085: S. Berardi, M. Coppo, F. Damiani (Eds.), Types for Proofs and Programs. X, 409 pages. 2004.

Vol. 3084: A. Persson, J. Stirna (Eds.), Advanced Information Systems Engineering. XIV, 596 pages. 2004.

Vol. 3083: W. Emmerich, A.L. Wolf (Eds.), Component Deployment. X, 249 pages. 2004.

Vol. 3080: J. Desel, B. Pernici, M. Weske (Eds.), Business Process Management. X, 307 pages. 2004.

Vol. 3079: Z. Mammeri, P. Lorenz (Eds.), High Speed Networks and Multimedia Communications. XVIII, 1103 pages. 2004.

Vol. 3078: S. Cotin, D.N. Metaxas (Eds.), Medical Simulation. XVI, 296 pages. 2004.

Vol. 3077: F. Roli, J. Kittler, T. Windeatt (Eds.), Multiple Classifier Systems. XII, 386 pages. 2004.

Vol. 3076: D. Buell (Ed.), Algorithmic Number Theory. XI, 451 pages. 2004.

Vol. 3075: W. Lenski, Logic versus Approximation. VIII, 205 pages. 2004.

Vol. 3074: B. Kuijpers, P. Revesz (Eds.), Constraint Databases and Applications. XII, 181 pages. 2004.

Vol. 3073: H. Chen, R. Moore, D.D. Zeng, J. Leavitt (Eds.), Intelligence and Security Informatics. XV, 536 pages. 2004.

Vol. 3072: D. Zhang, A.K. Jain (Eds.), Biometric Authentication. XVII, 800 pages. 2004.

Vol. 3071: A. Omicini, P. Petta, J. Pitt (Eds.), Engineering Societies in the Agents World. XIII, 409 pages. 2004. (Subseries LNAI).

Vol. 3070: L. Rutkowski, J. Siekmann, R. Tadeusiewicz, L.A. Zadeh (Eds.), Artificial Intelligence and Soft Computing - ICAISC 2004. XXV, 1208 pages. 2004. (Subseries LNAI).

Vol. 3068: E. André, L. Dybkjær, W. Minker, P. Heisterkamp (Eds.), Affective Dialogue Systems. XII, 324 pages. 2004. (Subseries LNAI).

Vol. 3067: M. Dastani, J. Dix, A. El Fallah-Seghrouchni (Eds.), Programming Multi-Agent Systems. X, 221 pages. 2004. (Subseries LNAI).

Vol. 3066: S. Tsumoto, R. Słowiński, J. Komorowski, J.W. Grzymała-Busse (Eds.), Rough Sets and Current Trends in Computing. XX, 853 pages. 2004. (Subseries LNAI).

Vol. 3065: A. Lomuscio, D. Nute (Eds.), Deontic Logic in Computer Science. X, 275 pages. 2004. (Subseries LNAI).

Vol. 3064: D. Bienstock, G. Nemhauser (Eds.), Integer Programming and Combinatorial Optimization. XI, 445 pages. 2004.

Vol. 3063: A. Llamosí, A. Strohmeier (Eds.), Reliable Software Technologies - Ada-Europe 2004. XIII, 333 pages. 2004.

Vol. 3062: J.L. Pfaltz, M. Nagl, B. Böhlen (Eds.), Applications of Graph Transformations with Industrial Relevance. XV, 500 pages. 2004.

Vol. 3061: F.F. Ramos, H. Unger, V. Larios (Eds.), Advanced Distributed Systems. VIII, 285 pages. 2004.

Vol. 3060: A.Y. Tawfik, S.D. Goodwin (Eds.), Advances in Artificial Intelligence. XIII, 582 pages. 2004. (Subseries LNAI).

Vol. 3059: C.C. Ribeiro, S.L. Martins (Eds.), Experimental and Efficient Algorithms. X, 586 pages. 2004.

Vol. 3058: N. Sebe, M.S. Lew, T.S. Huang (Eds.), Computer Vision in Human-Computer Interaction. X, 233 pages. 2004.